OI™ Programmer's Guide

Second Edition

Here is what some of the leading object oriented developers in the industry are saying about *OI*™ *Programmers's Guide:*

"Once our programmers have used the OI library, they never want to go back to their C-based toolkits. I would recommend OI for any project trying to get the most out of object oriented programming and C++. The OI book does an excellent job of describing the many advanced features of the OI toolkit. It is successful both as a reference book and an advanced tutorial on OI programming concepts."

—Larry Podmolik, Andersen Consulting

"It's hard to imagine what might have been accomplished by now on the UNIX desktop if OI had only been available from the very beginning. Despite the very best intentions of the designers of Xt, anyone who's done any significant Xt or Motif or OPEN LOOK programming knows how futile trying to do true object oriented programming in C can be. OI represents all of that done over again, with the benefits of hindsight and C++, and done right this time."

—Jordan Hubbard, Lotus Development, Ireland

"Because OI is a truly object oriented toolkit, not just a C++ veneer over a functionally oriented toolkit, a truly object oriented product is very easy to create. Subclassing OI components and adding our product specific behavior to the subclasses allowed us to create an architecture that is easily maintainable, extensible, and comprehensible. The OI toolkit allowed us to not only create a great looking user interface, but a strong product architecture as well."

—Bob Rose, CenterLine Software, Inc.

OI™ Programmer's Guide

Second Edition

Amber Benson

Gary Aitken

P T R Prentice Hall
Englewood Cliffs, New Jersey 07632

Editorial/production supervision: *Dit Mosco*
Cover design: *Aren Graphics*
Manufacturing buyer: *Alexis Heydt*
Acquisitions editor: *Mike Meehan*

 ©1994 by ParcPlace Systems, Inc.
Published by P T R Prentice Hall
Prentice-Hall, Inc.
A Paramount Communications Company
Englewood Cliffs, New Jersey 07632

The publisher offers discounts on this book when ordered in bulk quantities. For more information, contact:

> Corporate Sales Department
> PTR Prentice Hall
> 113 Sylvan Avenue
> Englewood Cliffs, NJ 07632
>
> Phone: 201-592-2863
> Fax: 201-592-2249

Printed in the United States of America
10 9 8 7 6 5 4 3 2 1

ISBN 0-13-120248-0

Prentice-Hall International (UK) Limited, *London*
Prentice-Hall of Australia Pty. Limited, *Sydney*
Prentice-Hall Canada Inc., *Toronto*
Prentice-Hall Hispanoamericana, S.A., *Mexico*
Prentice-Hall of India Private Limited, *New Delhi*
Prentice-Hall of Japan, Inc., *Tokyo*
Simon & Schuster Asia Pte. Ltd., *Singapore*
Editora Prentice-Hall do Brasil, Ltda., *Rio de Janeiro*

13 OI_menu_cell

14 OI_button_menu and OI_trans_menu

15 OI_excl_menu, OI_excl_check_menu, OI_excl_rect_menu

16 OI_poly_menu, OI_poly_check_menu, OI_poly_rect_menu

17 OI_abbr_menu

18 OI_dialog_box

19 Convenience Dialog Boxes Derived from OI_ms_dialog_box

20 OI_prompt_dialog_box

21 OI_select_dialog_box

22 OI_file_dialog_box

23 OI_command_dialog_box

24 OI_paned_box

25 OI_glyph

26 OI_display_1d

27 OI_gauge

28 OI_ctlr_1d

29 OI_slider

30 OI_scroll_bar

31 OI_base_text and OI_multi_text

32 OI_scroll_text

33 OI_scroll_box

34 OI_scroll_menu

35 OI_menu_box

36 OI_panner

37 OI_separator

38 OI_connection

39 The OI Resource Mechanism

40 The OI Translation Mechanism

41 Deriving Your Own Classes

42 OI_class

43 OI_cb_inf

44 OI_layout_method and Its Subclasses

Appendices

Index

Notes to the Reader

Intended Audience

This book will teach you how to program using the Object Interface (OI) library; it will also serve as a useful reference guide. It is not meant to teach you how to use the X Window System or about C++ and object-oriented programming. Neither is it meant to be an in-depth look at the OPEN LOOK or Motif interaction and appearance models. We assume you are already familiar with UNIX and programming in C++, and that you either have experience in the X Window System and object-oriented programming, or that you have reference books on these subjects. If you want to read more about these subjects, see the Related Reading Section later in these notes. Although this book is meant for the programmer rather than the application user, we include runtime interaction descriptions for each class of OI objects.

The Structure of This Book

This book can serve as both a programmer's guide and a reference manual.

Using This Book as a Programmer's Guide

For an overview and introduction to OI, read Chapters 1 and 2. These chapters provide a quick tour of the major features of programming using OI, and include discussions on the structure and relationships involved.

Chapter 3 tells you how to compile and link an OI application; it also contains important information about executing an OI application.

If you are just learning OI, you should read Chapters 4, 5 and 6 next, because this information is the foundation upon which the rest of the book is based.

Chapters 7 through 37 discuss each class of objects which you can display on the screen. These chapters are presented in order from the simplest to the most complex rather than in an alphabetic order. You can read these chapters in any order, depending on your needs and interests, but keep in mind that each succeeding chapter may build on what was discussed in previous chapters. Within each chapter, we present the basic material first, then go on to more specific items. For a first pass through the book to get familiar with OI, you may want to read only the first few sections of these chapters, going back later for a more in-depth view of OI.

Chapter 38 discusses the OI connection to the X server.

Chapters 39 and 40 show you how to use the OI resource and translation mechanisms, and Chapters 41, 42 and 43 show you how to derive your own OI subclasses. You may want to wait until you are familiar with OI to read these chapters.

Using This Book as a Reference Manual

Once you are familiar with OI, you can use this book as an OI reference manual. At the beginning of each chapter is a table of contents for that chapter, listing page numbers for member function descriptions as well as section headings. Member function descriptions within the chapter are grouped according to functionality. The chapters that discuss an OI class also have an alphabetical function index after the chapter table of contents but before the chapter text. Free-standing functions that apply to the class (mostly object creation functions) and all member functions described in the chapter are included. Also in this index are all member functions of base classes. The purpose of the chapter index is to provide you with an alphabetical list of all member functions which you can use for objects of the class described in that chapter.

Resources, translations, and callbacks for each class of objects are listed in the last three sections of the class chapter.

Appendix A is a copy of the layout reference manual page, Appendix B is an alphabetical index of all callbacks available to the programmer, Appendix C is an alphabetical index of OI resources, and Appendix D is an alphabetical index of all OI functions and member functions.

There is a complete subject index at the back of the book.

Examples

The OI examples range from simple ones intended only to show how to get an object on the screen, to those that, if expanded, could be useful programs. For the most part, in the interest of brevity, we have attempted to confine each programming example to a single page. For this reason, much of the explanation of the code is contained in the text. Good programming practice, however, dictates that there be substantially more included in the way of comments.

These examples are included with the OI library distribution. They are usually in the directory *inst_path*/OI/demos/oibook, where *inst_path* is the installation path at your site.

Terminology and Font Conventions used in This Book

You always refers to you as an OI and C++ programmer, except in sections titled "Runtime Interaction." In these sections *you* refers to the person running an application using the object being described.

The user always refers to the person running an application and interacting with the object being described. Note that *client* refers to a particular type of program running in the X Window environment, not to a person.

Italics are used when a term is being defined and also for function arguments. **Boldface Helvetica** is used to refer to any OI item or C++ variable. `Courier` is used for C++ code examples.

Where functions are defined, the function name is in **Helvetica boldface**, followed by the usage in `Courier`, followed by *argument* descriptions and other discussion.

Implementation Notes

This book is intended to apply to any implementation of OI, regardless of hardware or supporting software. The OI library requires at least 2.1 of AT&T's C++ compiler. It has been ported to SunOS-sparc, Solaris, AIX-RS/6000, HP-UX-HP9000/700, IRIX-SGI, Ultrix-DEC, Linux-i386; it has been ported to a few other platforms as well. The OI library contains implementations of Motif, 2-D OPEN LOOK, and 3-D OPEN LOOK.

Historical Note

In early 1987, Solbourne Computer was in the same windowing system quandary as was most of the computer industry. As a workstation manufacturer, Solbourne needed to provide a windowing system for their hardware. At that time, Sun Microsystem's NeWs and the X Window System from MIT were both being touted as the up-and-coming answer. It was unclear which would prevail as the predominant windowing system. Solbourne chose to write new tools using the X Window system and C++ as the development environment. Fortunately for them, X has become a de facto industry standard. However, the original dilemma was soon replaced by a similar one: which particular user-interface would predominate in the X world? The two current candidates are OPEN LOOK and Motif. To compound Solbourne's problem, existing toolkits of which they were aware needed a C interface or were in a state of flux.

As a result, Solbourne decided to build its own toolkit, designed for application development that would be independent of whatever particular user-interface standard should emerge. The intent was that if an interface became obsolete, Solbourne could modify the toolkit, and all the applications would still work. As it turned out, they did better than they had initially hoped. Rather than modifying the toolkit to support a different interface, they were able to construct it such that it could support multiple user interfaces, deferring until execution time the choice of which interface to use. This toolkit is OI.

Application development proceeded simultaneously with the development of the toolkit, driving much of the development effort. Because of this, OI has capabilities responsive to the needs of real application programmers, not just a committee of toolkit designers. Concurrent applications ranged from simple demonstrations to desktop tools such as mail and news readers, a debugger (pdb), a window manager (swm), and a user interface builder (uib, later renamed to ObjectBuilder). These are now commercially available, state-of-the-art products. Many of their features are a direct result of the capabilities provided by the OI toolkit on which they are based.

OI, pdb and ObjectBuilder are now the property of ParcPlace Systems, Inc.

Thinking about programming using OI

The key to understanding OI probably lies in grasping these concepts:

- The OI class hierarchy—see Chapter 2. All the class trees in this book put the base classes toward the top, and derived classes below their base classes.
- The OI object tree—the instances of OI classes you create, that is, your OI objects, form an object tree. This tree structure is independent of the X windows hierarchy, and can be dynamic (you can reparent objects to change the object tree).
- Once you have created an application, compiled and linked it, it can be run in either OPEN LOOK or Motif.
- OI programs are not procedural; instead they are event driven. See Chapter 2.

- Most OI object attributes and behavior can be controlled using resources and translations—see Chapters 39 and 40.

Rules of Thumb

Here are a set of "rules" to keep in mind while learning to program using the OI toolkit. They are not hard-and-fast rules; they are ideas to consider as you learn and program.

- Try not to use global data. There are several ways to pass data along with an object. See `set_data` and any object member function which takes an `OI_*_fnp` or `OI_*_memfnp` as an argument.
- C++ is designed to make object-oriented programming easy. If you are dealing with structures, seriously consider making the structures classes with their own set of member functions. It takes more time up front, but will more than pay off in the long run. In general, do not allow access to any data values in classes; force all access through member functions.
- Consider subclassing from an existing OI class if you have data which always "belongs" to an object of that class. An example would be an entry field which corresponds to a database field.
- Avoid unnecessary casting, particularly for functions. Define all functions to be used as callbacks using the complete function prototype. To avoid warnings for unused arguments, specify their types only; don't give them a name. For example:

```
void button_click(OI_menu_cell*, void*, OI_number)
```

Acknowledgments

Our thanks go to everyone in the OI group, who provided support and suggestions, and who kindly reviewed the many drafts of the manuscript: Andy Gerber, Tom LaStrange, Kuntal Rahwal, Kelly Rise and Kate Wille, and especially Warner Losh, Steve Misek and Martin Newmark for extra reviews and comments. Many thanks to Diana Martin-Buck for editing, indexing, manuscript preparation and error checking.

Related Reading

X Window System by Robert W. Scheifler and James Gettys with Jim Flowers, Ron Newman, and David Rosenthal, Digital Press

The X Window System series, O'Reilly & Associates, Inc.

The C++ Programming Language by Bjarne Stroustrup, Addison-Wesley, Second Edition

The Annotated C++ Reference Manual by Margaret A. Ellis and Bjarne Stroustrup, Addison-Wesley

OSF/Motif Style Guide, Open Software Foundation, Prentice Hall

OSF/Motif User's Guide, Open Software Foundation, Prentice Hall

OPEN LOOK Graphical User Interface Functional Specification, Sun Microsystems, Inc., Addison-Wesley

<u>OPEN LOOK Graphical User Interface Application Style Guidelines</u>, Sun Microsystems, Inc., Addison-Wesley

Request for Comments

Please write to tell us about any errors or omissions you find in this book or how you think it could be improved, so that we can provide you with the best information possible.

Our U.S mail address and e-mail addresses are:

ParcPlace Boulder
4909 Pearl East Circle, Suite 200
Boulder, Colorado 80301

Internet:oi-support@boulder.parcplace.com

Chapter 1
A Tour of OI

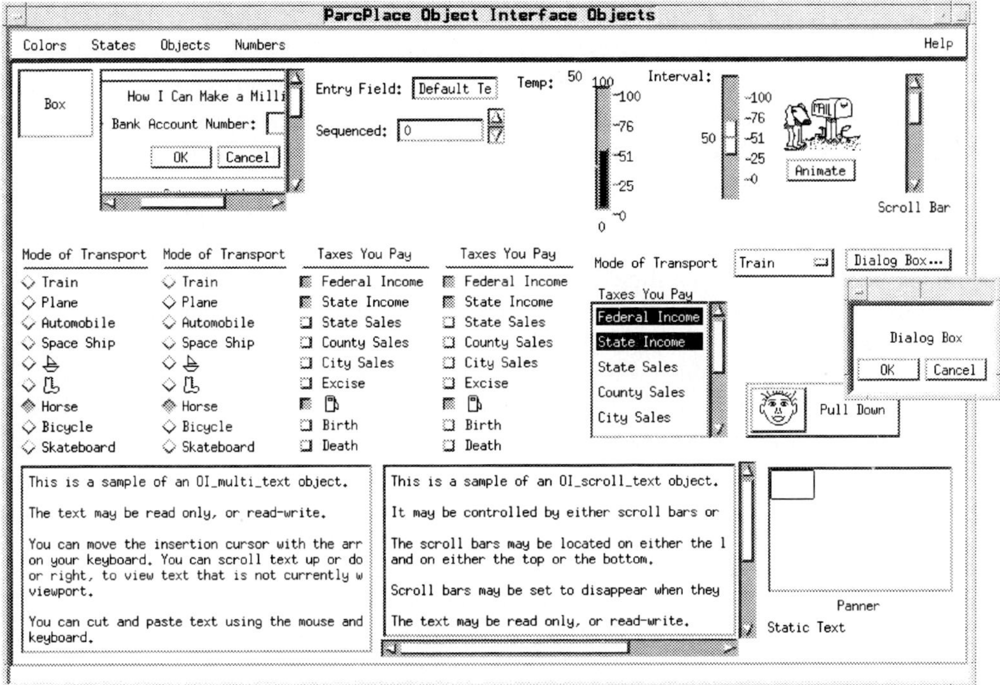

A Tour of OI

1.1   What Is the OI Library?

The Object Interface (OI) is a library of class definitions and procedures written in C++, an object-oriented language. Using OI you can build applications with a Graphical User Interface (GUI) in the X Window System environment. OI gives you an easy way to create and implement objects such as application windows, menus, dialog boxes, or entry fields. The OI header files assume that you are programming in C++, although you may also use C procedures in your program.

Like other toolkits, OI provides a basic set of objects used in constructing a user interface. Unlike other toolkits, these objects are generic in nature. The particular appearance and behavior of an object may be determined at execution time—a runtime command line argument to your program or an X resource determines which interaction and appearance model will be used. OI currently supports the Motif and the 2-D and 3-D OPEN LOOK models. Thus with only a single source and executable, your program can conform to more than one interaction and appearance model.

Other OI benefits are:

- Your source code is written in C++. C++ performs much better compile- and link-time type checking than C does, thus lowering your debugging time.
- OI users have true C++ support, allowing you to do full subclassing and use member functions for callbacks. If you are programming in C++, but using a C-based toolkit, these capabilities are missing, and many of the benefits and design goals of object-oriented programming are lost.
- OI's tree structure is dynamic. You can reuse objects in different contexts, thus saving resources.
- OI maintains an object tree structure that is independent of the X window tree structure. The usefulness of this independent structure becomes apparent when you consider that a child of an X window may only display within the boundaries of its parent, whereas you may wish to have a logical child window be larger than or overlap its parent in your application (for example, a pop-up dialog box). Having a logical object tree which reflects the application's needs, rather than the window system's constraints, means many fewer global variables and much cleaner, easier-to-debug code.
- OI provides a hypertext help object capable of displaying text, bitmaps, and trees of toolkit objects. You can write your program to provide dynamic, context-sensitive help.
- OI is international, that is, it supports multiple languages. The same application can be run in different languages using a runtime command line argument or X resource. You can even run different portions of the same application in different languages.
- There are a relatively small number of powerful objects in OI which can be used in many ways, rather than a large number of special-purpose objects. This arrangement makes it easier to find the object you need and easier to remember what each object does.
- OI provides a rich set of layout methods for managing geometry and object placement. This set includes both row and column based layout methods as well as layout methods to simplify single and multiple row alignment, column titles, and horizontal and vertical tree layout. These layout methods can be further subclassed by the user.
- OI supports drag and drop protocols for both OPEN LOOK and Motif, allowing OI clients to interact gracefully on the heterogeneous desktop so common in today's workplace.
- OI permits error message registration which can be further modified (for internationalization) through the resource manager.
- OI supports translations and accelerators on all objects.
- OI provides ICCCM (Inter-Client Communication Conventions Manual) support. This is a set of conventions in the X Window System specifying how clients should communicate with each other.
- OI provides support for window managers which provide a virtual root window larger than the actual root window.
- OI supports multiple connections to the X server and multiple screens.
- OI provides support for animation of bitmap graphics.
- You have direct access to Xlib functions if needed.
- OI has a "fastdraw" execution-time option which deliberately sacrifices some appearance factors in favor of increased drawing speed. This achieves much better performance when applications are run with an X terminal over RS232 lines.

- Command line arguments and X resources allow the user to specify attributes such as background color, foreground color, font, which language to use, or the interaction and appearance model (Motif or OPEN LOOK) at invocation time.
- OI has been ported to a wide range of standard unix environments, including Sparc and Sparc compatibles, HP, Dec, IBM, Silicon Graphics, and various pc platforms.

1.2   An Example: Hello World

Let's get started by writing a simple program using OI:

```
#include <OI/oi.H>                    /* HelloWorld.C */

int main(int argc, char **argv)
{
        OI_connection        *conp;        // connection to server
        OI_app_window        *wp;          // main application window pointer
        OI_static_text       *tp;          // text pointer

    if (conp = OI_init(&argc,argv,"HelloWorld")) {
        wp = oi_create_app_window("main",1,1,"Main");
        wp->set_layout(OI_layout_row);
        tp = oi_create_static_text("text","Hello World! ");
        tp->layout_associated_object(wp,1,1,OI_active);
        wp->set_associated_object(wp->root( ),OI_def_loc,OI_def_loc,OI_active);
        OI_begin_interaction( );
    }
}
```

Program 1-1   Hello World (HelloWorld.C)

Since OI is a library of routines to be used in your program, you must write a main program, just as you would in any other C++ application.

The variables **conp**, **wp**, and **tp** declare pointers to OI objects. Using OI, you will probably never declare OI objects, only pointers to OI objects. (Declaring a static or automatic OI object variable in a main program won't work, since **OI_init** must have been called to set up the OI context before a constructor for an OI object will work correctly.) An **OI_connection** is an object representing the particular X Window System display and screen on which a group of objects is being displayed. It is the "connection" to the X server. An **OI_app_window** is an object that is the outside wrapping for an application: the application window. An **OI_static_text** is an object that is a one-line, read-only text string.

OI_init performs internal initialization and establishes a connection to the X server. The call to **OI_init** establishes the application's class name, "HelloWorld", which is used when OI fetches X resources for the application. **OI_init** returns a pointer to the **OI_connection** object that it creates or NULL if it fails.

The next five lines of code create objects and build an object tree. The call to **oi_create_app_window** creates an application window, 1 by 1 pixels in size, with a name "main" and a title "Main", which is displayed in the window manager title bar. (You supply a name for each object you create in an OI program; as you will see later, the object name is quite useful for accessing different objects in different parts of your program.) This call creates the object, but does not display it. The object is not attached to any other objects—it is in the *orphanage* object. Every newly created object is initially a child of the orphanage. The variable wp points to the application window object.

The next line of code executes an OI_app_window member function, set_layout, which tells OI to prepare the application window "main" to have objects laid out in it. OI can do automatic layout for you. This saves you the trouble of counting pixels and placing objects on the screen, only to have the spacing be wrong when someone changes the font size for your application. The call to set_layout (OI_layout_row) configures "main" to have row-major layout format. Because OI's layout facility resizes objects within which other objects are laid out, the final size of the application window may not be (and in this case, will not be) the size you originally declared it to be. Instead, it will be automatically sized to fit its children.

The call to oi_create_static_text creates an OI_static_text object with the name "text" and containing the string "Hello World!". As noted previously, the newly created object will be in the orphanage.

In the next line of code, layout_associated_object attaches its object tp ("text") as the child of the object pointed to in the first argument wp ("main"). In other words, the static text is moved from the orphanage and "parented" to the application window. It is laid out inside the application window, at column 1, row 1, as indicated by the second and third arguments. The last argument tells OI that "text" is to be in the active state (displayed). Now we have an object tree consisting of an application window with one child, a static text. At this point, nothing has yet appeared on the screen, since we have associated nothing to the root window.

In the next line of code we use set_associated_object to make the application window wp a child of the root window. The second and third arguments indicate the location at which the object is to be displayed—in this case, wherever the window manager and user interaction cause it to be located. The function set_associated_object, like layout_associated_object, associates the object for which it is called to the object pointed to in the first argument. The difference is that set_associated_object "hard-codes" the location of the child to be the pixel x and y offsets you specify as arguments, and does not use OI's automatic layout facility.

Ordinarily, unless you are writing a window manager, you should use set_associated_object instead of layout_associated_object when you are parenting an object to the root window. This is because the behavior of such a parenting is not guaranteed—the window manager has ultimate control over object placement.

At this point the application becomes visible on the screen.

In the last line of code, the call to the function OI_begin_interaction starts up interaction with the user. This function loops indefinitely, waiting for any input from the user and processing input as it arrives. We'll discuss OI_begin_interaction and its counterparts, OI_end_interaction and OI_fini, in the next example, Section 1.3, "Hello World with Exit Button."

Because nothing in this program tells it to stop, it remains on the screen until you use a window manager function to terminate it, or kill it manually via an appropriate operating system command.

A note here about terminology: we use the terms "parent", "child", and "sibling" in the obvious manner. The OI_app_window object "main" is the *parent* of the OI_static_text object "text"; conversely, "text" is a *child* of "main". We also use two new verbs, "to parent" and "to unparent." After creating the static text, we *parented* it to "main". If we were to detach "text" from "main", making it a child of the orphanage, we would say we were *unparenting* it. If we had created a second OI_static_text "text2" and parented it to "main", "text" and "text2" would be *siblings*. Note that no object has more than one parent, but any object may have zero, one or more children.

An *object tree* diagram is a pictorial representation of the object tree created in an OI program, showing the relationships between objects, that is, which objects are children or descendants of others, and, conversely, which objects are parents or ancestors of others. The object tree for the Hello World program looks like this:

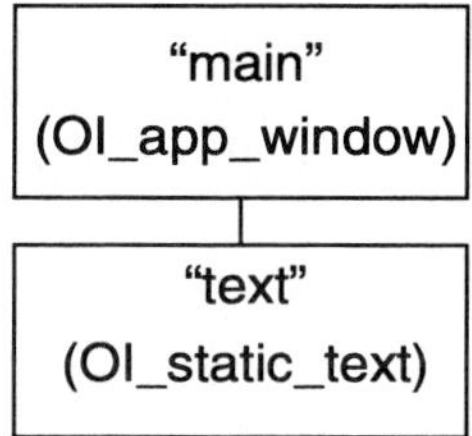

Figure 1-1   Object Tree for Hello World Program

Note that the object tree diagram in Figure 1-1 contains both the object name and the class of the object in each box. You should get into the habit of naming all your objects, because you will need them for finding your way around your object tree.

To run this program, enter the code into your machine, using **vi** or some other text editor, and compile and link it.

```
C++ HelloWorld.C -lOI -lXext -lX11 -o HelloWorld
```

(If this doesn't work, see Chapter 3, "Compiling, Linking, and Executing an OI Program.") If you name the executable **HelloWorld**, you may run it using Motif by typing

```
HelloWorld -motif
```

You can use OPEN LOOK in either a two-dimensional look or a three-dimensional look. To run it using 2-D OPEN LOOK, you type

```
HelloWorld -openlook2d
```

To run it using 3-D OPEN LOOK, you type

```
HelloWorld -openlook3d
```

This is what you see on your screen when you use the Motif model:

Figure 1-2   Hello World, Motif Model

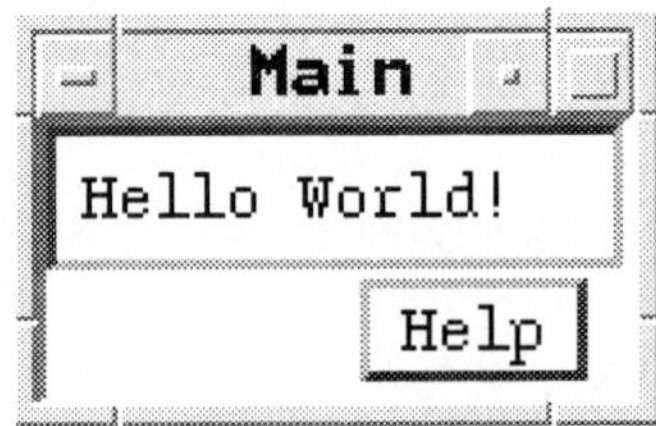

This is what you see when you use the 3-D OPEN LOOK model:

Figure 1-3   Hello World, OPEN LOOK Model

With such a simple example, the 2-D and 3-D OPEN LOOK models look nearly identical.

If you leave off the command line argument specifying the model, you get the default, Motif. However, the default model can be changed. (See Chapter 39, "The OI Resource Mechanism".)

The help button you see in each of these windows is part of the application window. Each OI application window normally has a title bar and some window decoration (both supplied by the window manager, not OI), and a help button. In these screen dump illustrations, and in all such illustrations throughout this book, applications run using the Motif model are shown using a Motif window manager, and those run using the OPEN LOOK model are shown using an OPEN LOOK 3-D window manager. (The window manager used in these illustrations is **swm**, which was developed using OI.)

1.3   Hello World with Exit Button

Since there is nothing you can do with the previous example except look at it and kill it, and since most of the fun of a GUI interface is pressing buttons and such, Program 1-2 shows a more complicated version of the "Hello World" program that allows the user to exit by clicking the mouse on an "exit" menu cell in the application. The highlighted lines in Program 1-2 indicate lines added to Program 1-1 to create the new program.

```
#include <OI/oi.H>                  /* HelloExit.C */

int main(int argc, char **argv)
{
        void                exit_program(OI_menu_cell*,void*,OI_number);

        OI_connection       *conp;
        OI_app_window       *wp;
        OI_static_text      *tp;
        OI_menu             *mp;

//                          Specify the "exit" button
    static OI_cell_spec     e_cell[] = {
    {"exit","Exit",exit_program},
    };

    if (conp = OI_init(&argc,argv,"HelloExit")) {
        wp = oi_create_app_window("main",1,1,"Main");
        wp->set_layout(OI_layout_row);

        tp = oi_create_static_text("text","Hello World!");
        tp->layout_associated_object(wp,1,1,OI_active);

//                          Create menu from static OI_cell_spec structure
        mp = oi_create_button_menu("menu",OI_count(e_cell),
                                        &e_cell[0],OI_horizontal);
        wp->set_main_menu(mp);
        wp->set_associated_object(wp->root( ),OI_def_loc,OI_def_loc,OI_active);

        OI_begin_interaction( );
        OI_fini( );
    }
}

void exit_program(OI_menu_cell*, void*, OI_number)
{
    OI_end_interaction( );
    return;
}
```

Program 1-2 Hello World with Exit Button (HelloExit.C)

Let's discuss the added lines:

exit_program is defined as a menu cell *action callback* function. It is the function that will be executed when the user moves the mouse pointer over the "exit" menu cell on the screen and clicks the SELECT mouse button.

mp is a menu pointer; it will point to the menu containing the exit button when the menu is created.

e_cell defines the values used to create the exit button itself. This line of code indicates that the menu cell should have a name "exit", a label "Exit", and that **exit_program** is the action function to execute when the user clicks on the menu cell. The OI_cell_spec does not create the menu cell; it merely defines values used to create it.

The menu (named "menu") and its single menu cell are created using the oi_create_button_menu call. The menu is parented to the application window, and specified to be the main menu for the application, using set_main_menu. This is what you would see on the screen if you were to run this program:

Figure 1-4   Hello World with Exit Button, Motif

Figure 1-5   Hello World with Exit Button, OPEN LOOK 3-D

In Figure 1-4 you can see that the help button has moved from the footer to the main menu. OI moves it to the main menu (if there is one), to be compliant with the Motif Style Guide.

Notice the empty space at the bottom of the application. This space only looks empty—it contains a help line and status line, where OI displays short error messages. (You can display messages there as well—see Chapter 8, "OI_app_window").

The call to OI_begin_interaction, as we said before, initiates interaction with the user. It loops indefinitely, waiting for user input, and never returns until you call OI_end_interaction in some function in your program. In this case, the only interaction possible is clicking on the "exit" button. When (and if!) the user does click on the "exit" button, this action activates the button and OI invokes the callback function exit_program. Notice that exit_program is executed, but OI_begin_interaction is still executing as well. (For more discussion on callback routines, see Section 2.5, "Callbacks and Event-Driven Programming," on page 2-16) In this simple example, the only action **exit_program** takes is to call **OI_end_interaction**, but in more complicated applications, such a callback function might close files, release memory, or perform other clean-up operations for your application. When you call **OI_end_interaction**, it tells **OI_begin_interaction** to return after all the currently executing callback functions have completed; no more interaction with the user can take place in the application unless you call **OI_begin_interaction** again.

The last line of the main program is a call to **OI_fini**; this function cleans up prior to exit and closes the connection to the X server. You should always call **OI_fini** before terminating your program.

Another note on terminology: when the user clicks the mouse button while the mouse pointer is on a menu cell (in this case, the "exit" button), we say the user *activates* the menu cell. A menu cell may be activated in several ways: the user may click on it, the user may use keyboard strokes, or you may activate it programmatically by using such member functions as **select** or **select_cell**.

The object tree for Program 1-2 looks like this:

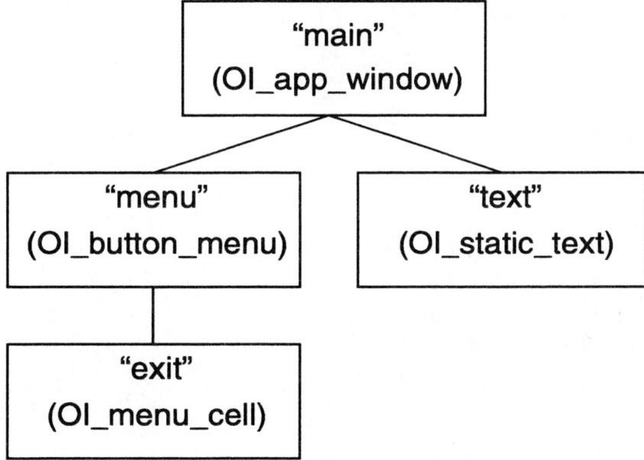

Figure 1-6 Object Tree for Hello World with Exit Button

1.4   Classes of Displayable OI Objects

To show you most of the possible displayable objects and controls OI contains, Figure 1-7 shows the Periodic Chart of OI in Motif format, and Figure 1-8 shows the Periodic Chart of OI in OPEN LOOK 3-D format. The objects not shown in the Periodic Chart are the specialized subclasses of **OI_dialog_box**, the **OI_menu_box**, and the **OI_paned_box** (See Chapters 19 through 23, Chapter 35, and Chapter 24).

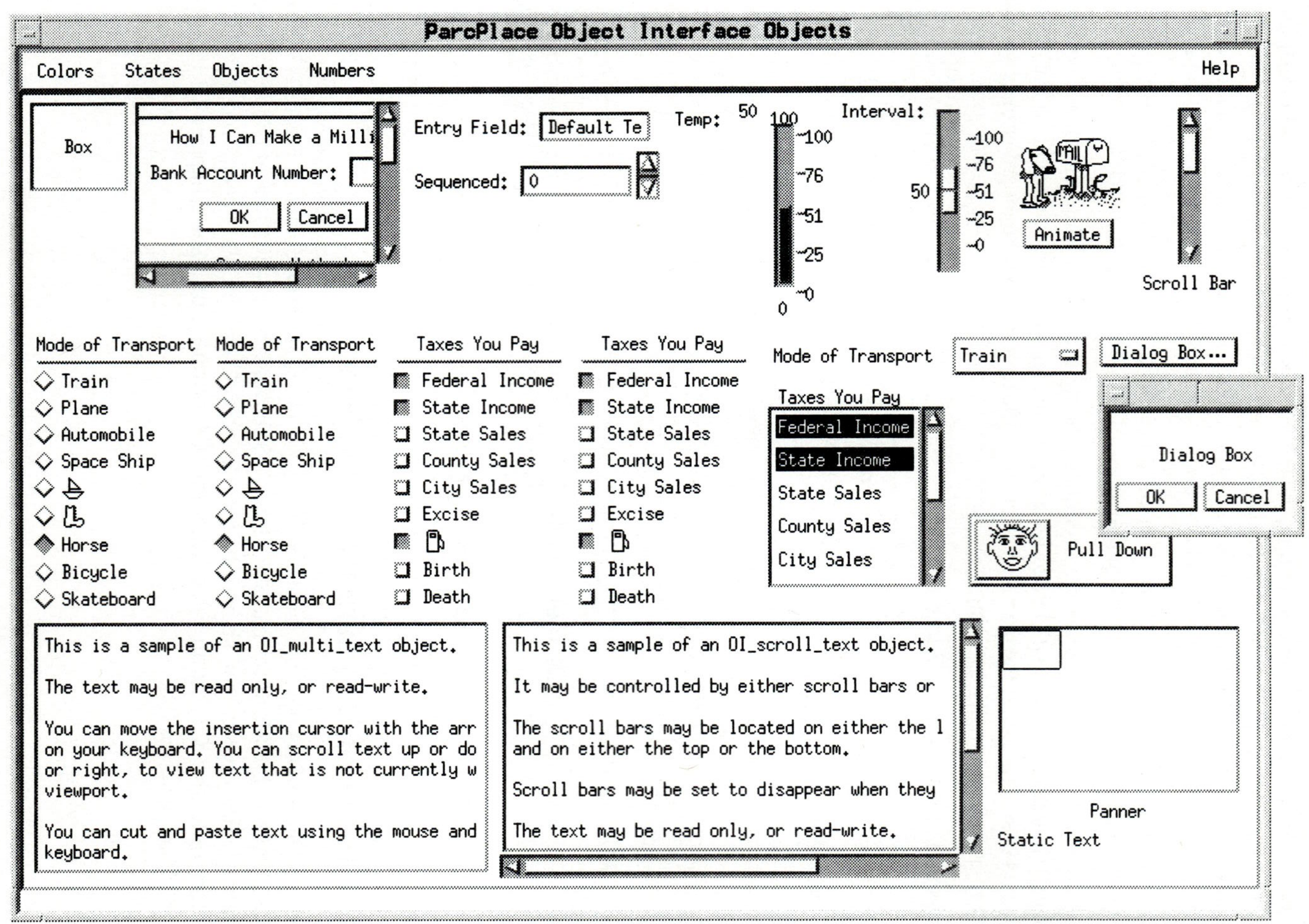

Figure 1-7   OI Periodic Chart, Motif Model

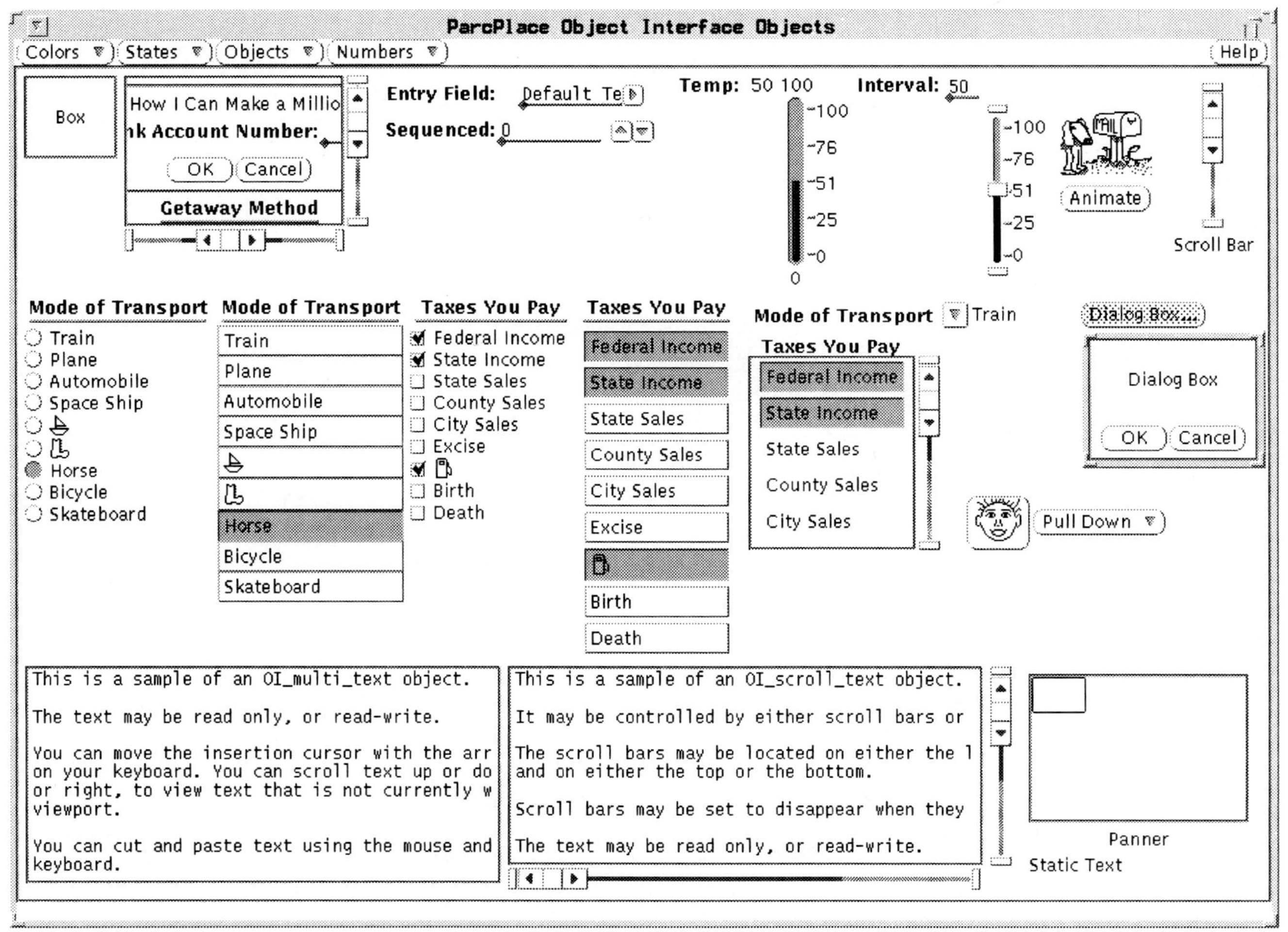

Figure 1-8   OI Periodic Chart, OPEN LOOK Model

The window containing the Periodic Chart is itself an OI object; it is an **OI_app_window**. This is a window surrounded by a border, title bar, help text area, and help button. The **OI_app_window** is generally used as the top-level object for a complete application. The actual appearance of the title bar on an **OI_app_window** is determined by the window manager you are running, not by the OI interaction model for the program.

For a full description of the capabilities of each of these displayable objects, see the chapter for that object. Here each object in the periodic chart is described briefly and shown in both Motif (left) and OPEN LOOK (right) models. The objects shown in the first row of the Periodic Chart left to right are:

OI_box—A box without decoration where you can put objects or other graphics.

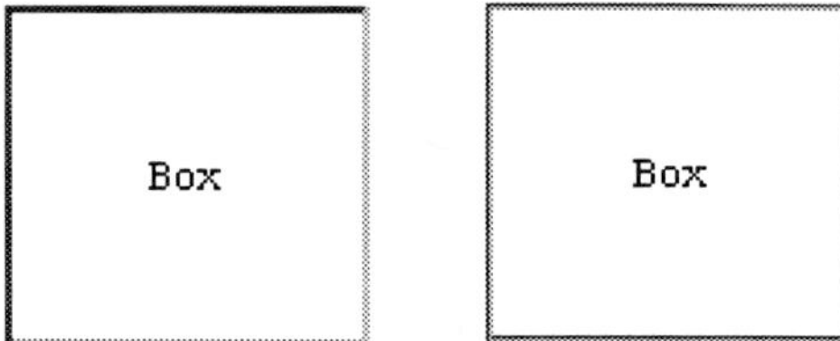

OI_scroll_box—A box with attached controllers for scrolling. The controllers are made from the **OI_scroll_bar** and **OI_panner** objects. The portion of the underlying box which is visible through the viewport is determined by the current position of the controllers. The box may contain arbitrary OI objects and object trees, or other graphics your program draws using **Xlib** functions.

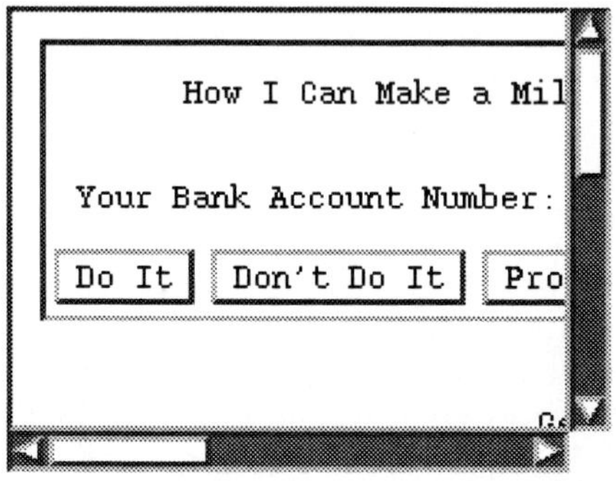

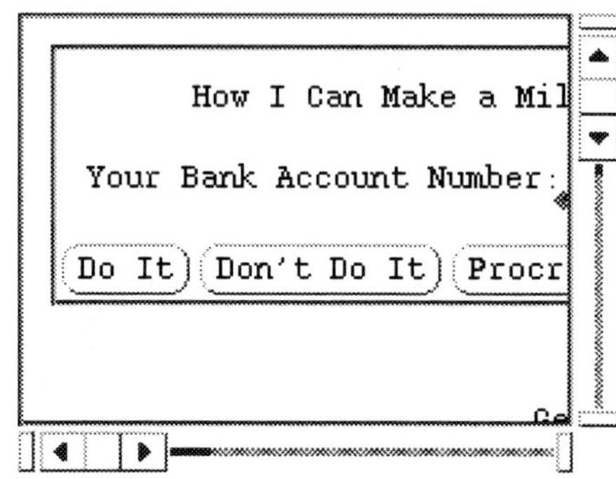

OI_entry_field—An optionally labeled area for keyboard data entry. If the length of the text area to be filled is specified to be longer than the length of the visible text area, the text area can be scrolled.

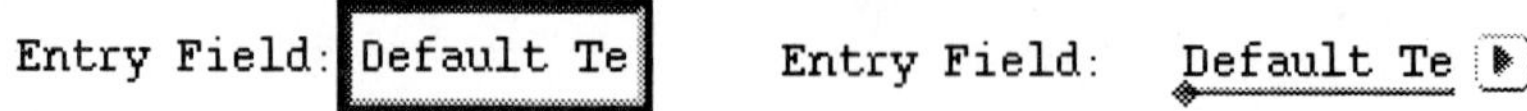

OI_seq_entry_field—An optionally labeled area for sequenced data entry. The value can be entered via the keyboard, and it can be incremented and decremented by clicking on the up and down arrow boxes. The values are not limited to numeric quantities; they may be any sequence, such as a list of database entries or any arbitrary text.

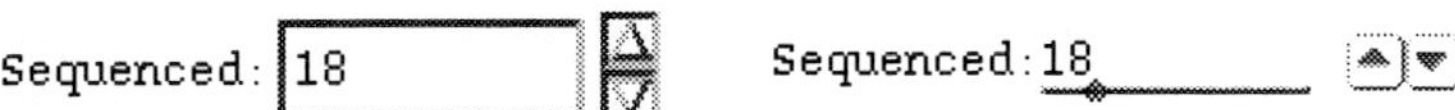

OI_gauge—A gauge that graphically displays a numerical value relative to a range of possible values. Gauges have optional labels, tic marks, and a current-value field.

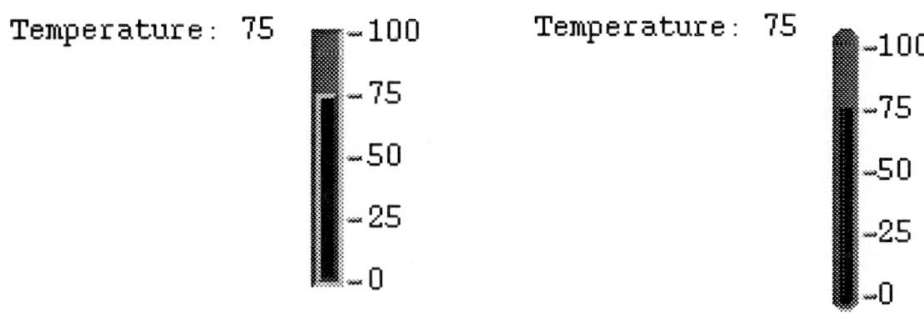

OI_slider—An object for displaying and modifying a value with a known range of values. As with gauges, the label, current value, and tic marks are optional.

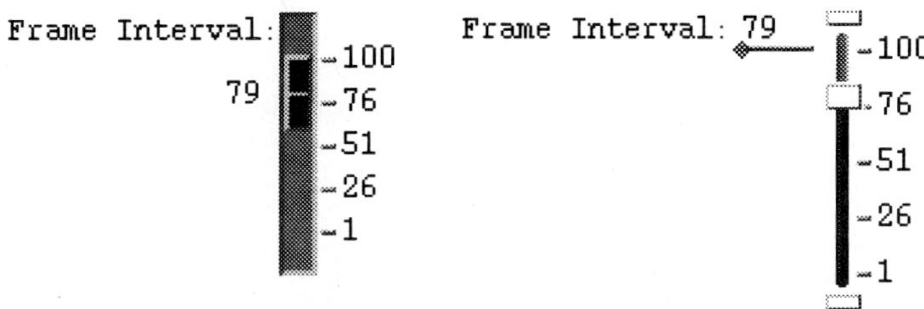

OI_glyph—A rectangular graphic object of any size that is generated from an X bitmap or pixmap file, data, or an X Pixmap. Glyphs can be animated; that is, you can specify a sequence of images to display in sequence over a period of time. The Motif and OPEN LOOK versions of this object look the same, except for the outside frame if frame width is not zero.

OI_button_menu—A button menu display (in this case a single-cell button menu; see the "Pull-down menu" example later in this section for a two-cell button menu). When the user clicks on a cell of the menu, the cell is *activated*, and a procedure is called.

OI_scroll_bar—A one-dimensional controller for another object. Moving the handle adjusts the part of the object which is visible in the viewport. You usually won't need to directly create an OI_scroll_bar, since scroll bars are built-in components of an OI_scroll_box, OI_scroll_menu, or OI_scroll_text object.

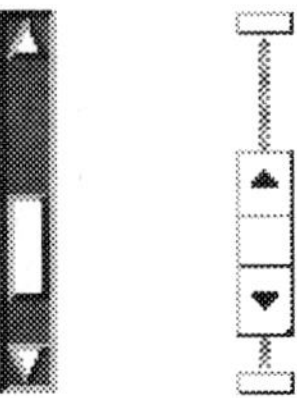

OI_excl_check_menu—A menu that remembers its state, but for which no more than one item may be selected at a time (exclusive selection). A procedure may inquire as to which cell, if any, is currently on. You may specify a procedure to be called when a cell is turned on or off. Each cell consists of a text or glyph label preceded by a glyph (shown in these examples as circles and diamonds) indicating whether the cell is selected or deselected. The menu may be oriented either horizontally or vertically.

OI_excl_rect_menu—Identical in behavior to an OI_excl_check_menu; only the appearance is different. The cells are text or glyph labels enclosed in a rectangle. The rectangle for the cell which is selected is heavily outlined. Since Motif has no menu of this form, an OI_excl_check_menu is used instead when the application is run in Motif mode.

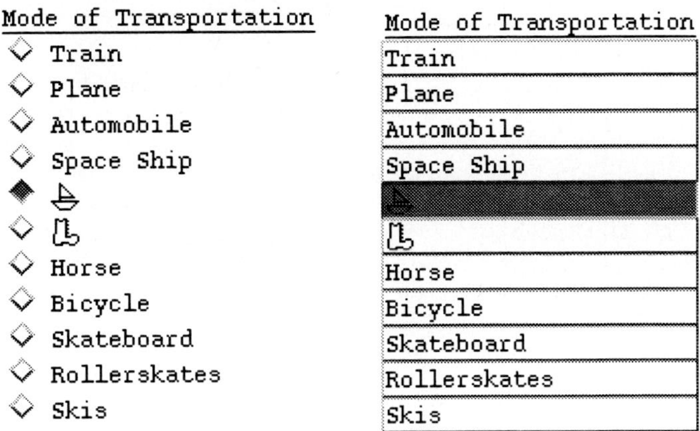

OI_poly_check_menu- A menu that remembers its state, and for which zero or more items may be selected at a time (non-exclusive selection). A procedure may inquire as to which cells, if any, are currently on. Other attributes are similar to an OI_excl_check_menu.

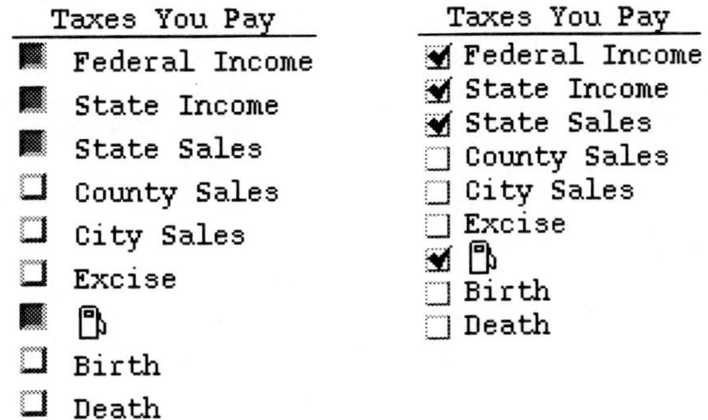

OI_poly_rect_menu—Identical in behavior to an OI_poly_check_menu; only the appearance is different. The cells are text or glyph labels enclosed in a rectangle. The rectangles for the cells which are selected are heavily outlined. Since Motif has no menu of this form, an OI_poly_check_menu is used instead when an application using an OI_poly_rect_menu is run in Motif mode.

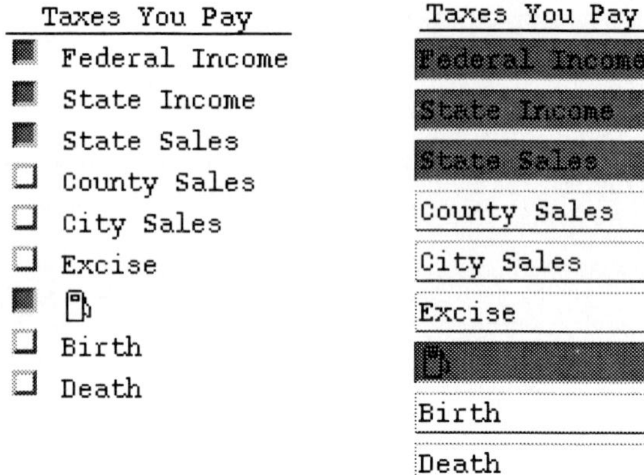

OI_abbr_menu—An abbreviated form of a normal button menu or exclusive selection menu. The default cell (for button menus) or the cell currently in the selected state (for exclusive menus) is the only cell displayed. The entire menu is available as a pop-up, and the default/current selection may be changed via user interaction as well.

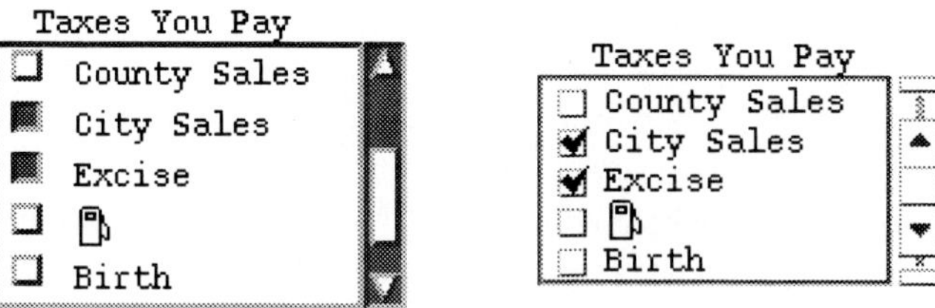

OI_scroll_menu—A menu in which not all of the items show at once. The menu may be scrolled using the attached scroll bar. Any of the basic menu types (OI_button_menu, OI_excl_*_menu, OI_poly_*_menu) may be scrolled. The menu may be vertical, scrolling up and down, or horizontal, scrolling left and right. Although Motif does not have rectangle exclusive or poly menus, it does have rectangle scroll menus, so if you request an OI_excl_rect_menu or an OI_poly_rect_menu for a Motif scroll menu, you will indeed get a rectangle menu. An OI_scroll_menu may be used as a pop-up or a pull-down as well as a normally visible menu.

OI_button_menu—For a description of OI_button_menu, see the "Animate" button example, described previously. This button menu has two cells. A button cell label may be either text or a glyph. The right cell has a pull-down menu attached.

A pull-down menu is not a separate OI object. "Pull-down menu" is the name given to any OI menu (OI_button_menu, OI_excl_*_menu, OI_poly_*_menu, OI_scroll_menu) that is activated by pressing the appropriate mouse button in its parent menu cell. Pull-down menus may be cascaded to form chains of "walking" menus. Pop-up menus are ones that pop up when the user pressed or clicks on the parent object, which is usually not a menu cell.

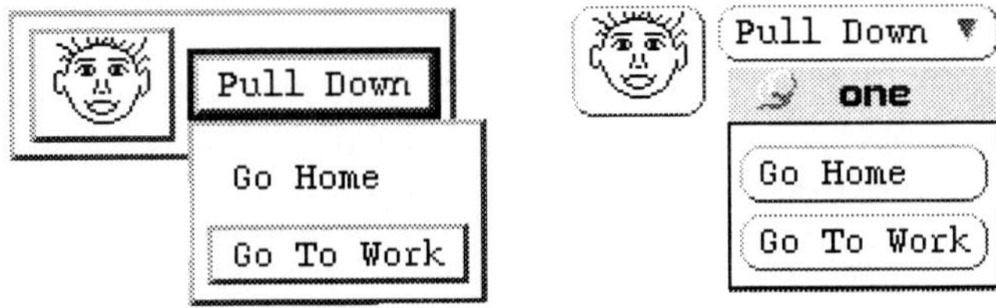

OI_dialog_box—An OI_box with an optional title and an OI_button_menu centered at the bottom. Although only one type of dialog box is shown here for each model, there are several different types of dialog boxes available.

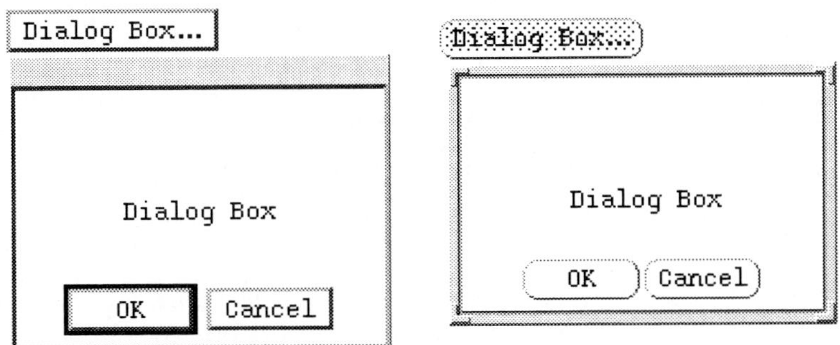

OI_multi_text—A text object of more than one line. The Motif and OPEN LOOK versions of this object look the same except for the insert cursor and the bevels.

```
This is a sample of an OI_multi_text object.

The text may be read only, or read-write.

You can move the insertion cursor with the arrow k
on your keyboard. You can scroll text up or down,
or right, to view text that is not currently withi
viewport.

You can cut and paste text using the mouse and the
```

OI_scroll_text—Similar to an **OI_scroll_box** except that the underlying object is required to be an **OI_multi_text**.

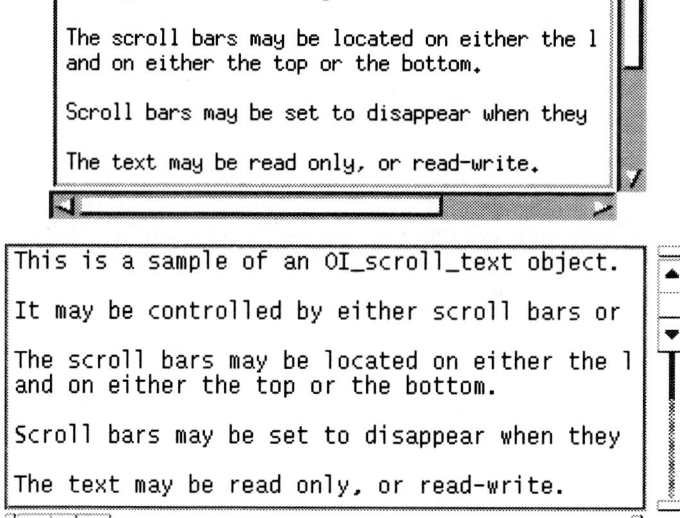

OI_panner—A two-dimensional controller consisting of an outer rectangle representing the object being manipulated and an inner rectangle representing a viewport to the object. Moving the inner rectangle adjusts the part of the object appearing in the viewport. The Motif and OPEN LOOK versions of this object look the same except for the outside box.

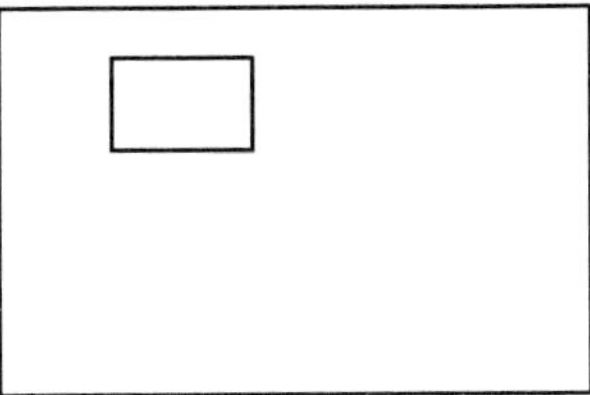

OI_static_text—A one-line text string. The Motif and OPEN LOOK versions of this object look the same.

Static Text

OI_help—Clicking on the help button in the OI_app_window or pressing the HELP key (see Chapter 8, "OI_app_window" for information about the HELP key) causes the help window to pop up. In it is help information that is controlled by both the user and the application.

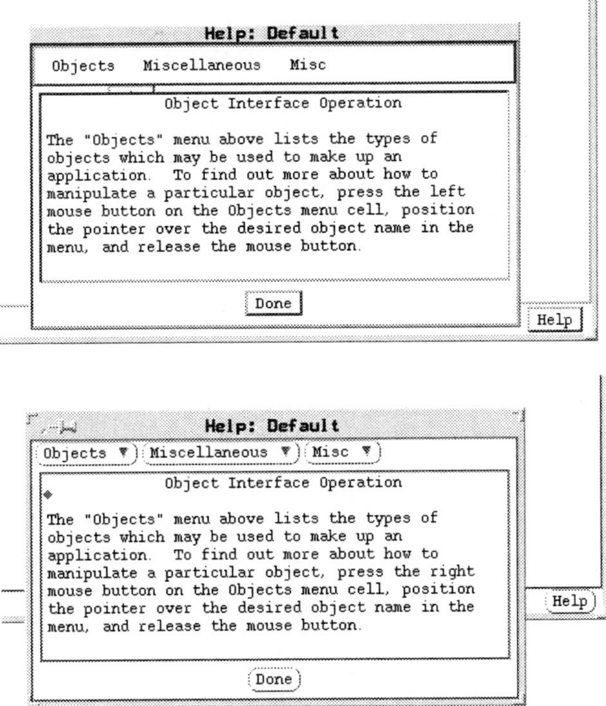

OI_separator—A line to visually separate other objects. This object is not in the periodic chart. A separator may be either horizontal or vertical.

Each of the objects described above is an OI object that you create and use in your program, and which can be displayed on the screen. However, not all OI objects can be seen, and you will need to know what these objects are and how to use them.

1.5   Other OI Classes

There are classes in OI whose objects cannot be displayed. There are also some which cannot be created directly, but which are made when you create some displayable object. These classes are briefly described below. Note that this is not an exhaustive list; there are several classes of objects that OI uses internally.

OI_connection—An object used to represent the particular X Window System display and screen upon which a group of objects is to be displayed. You need at least one of these, and you create it using the function OI_init.

OI_callback—The most distant base class of all displayable OI objects. If you define your own classes which are going to have member functions to be used as OI callback routines, your user-defined classes must be derived from OI_callback. If your classes are derived from an OI class (such as OI_box), they are automatically derived from OI_callback, since all OI classes are ultimately derived from OI_callback.

OI_base_text—The base class for all scrolling text classes such as OI_multi_text and OI_scroll_text. It has very little functionality itself, it merely vectors calls to the scrolling text object to do the real work.

OI_cb_inf—OI creates an OI_cb_inf object for each callback, such as the call to exit_program in the HelloExit example. An OI_class object is created when you register a subclass (See Chapter 43).

OI_class—OI creates an OI_class object for each class in the OI hierarchy; this object contains necessary information about that class. An OI_class object is created when you register a subclass (See Chapter 42).

OI_d_tech—Derived from OI_callback, OI_d_tech is the base class for all displayable objects in OI. As such, all displayable objects have access to OI_d_tech's member functions; these are the common function capabilities that all displayable objects have. You never directly create an OI_d_tech; you get one as part of any displayable OI object you create. For example, layout_associated_object is an OI_d_tech member function; you call it for any displayable OI object of any class that you want to automatically lay out.

OI_display_1d—An object of this class is used to display the value of a one-dimensional quantity. It has no visual attributes or user interaction attributes; it is merely the mathematical model for representing display values. It has values for resources such as number of tick marks and tick labels.

OI_ctlr_1d—The base class for scroll bars and sliders. It keeps track of the scaling information, labels, and values, but it does not implement any of the display attributes since the appearance and user interactions are handled by its derived classes.

OI_lang_server_input—The base class for text entry objects. It implements the language server interface for those languages which require one, such as Japanese.

OI_ms_dialog_box—The base class for message dialog boxes; you get one as part of any message dialog box you create.

OI_menu—The base class for all menu classes; you get one as part of any menu object you create. It provides a common set of functions for all menus.

OI_basic_menu—The base class for "basic" menus. The two more complex menus, **OI_abbr_menu** and **OI_scroll_menu**, are actually compound objects which include an **OI_basic_menu** as one of their components.

OI_excl_menu—The base class for **OI_excl_check_menu** and **OI_excl_rect_menu**. This class represents the interaction method for menus which remember their state and which allow at most one cell to be selected at any point in time.

OI_poly_menu—The base class for **OI_poly_check_menu** and **OI_poly_rect_menu**. It represents the interaction method for menus which remember their state and which allow any number of cells to be selected at any point in time.

OI_trans_menu—The base class for **OI_button_menu**. It represents the interaction method for menus that do not remember their state. When a cell in an **OI_trans_menu** is selected, it calls its action routine and is deselected as soon as the action routine returns.

OI_w_d_tech—Derived from **OI_d_tech**, **OI_w_d_tech** is the base class for all displayable objects in OI which have their own private X window. **OI_w_d_tech** has no public member functions; it is basically a class for internal OI use.

OI_wl_d_tech—Derived from **OI_d_tech**, **OI_wl_d_tech** is the base class for all displayable objects in OI which do not have their own private X window. **OI_wl_d_tech** has no public member functions; it is basically a class for internal OI use.

Chapter 2
OI—A Closer Look

OI—A Closer Look

2.1   Class Tree

Because you can use member functions from base classes of any OI objects, it is important to know the OI class hierarchy. The OI class tree is diagrammed in Figure 2-1. Classes of objects that you can create directly in your program are shown with black borders in this figure. Classes of objects that OI creates as a base class for one of the objects you create, or creates for internal purposes, are shown with gray borders.

For example, if you have an OI_seq_entry_field object, you may use member functions for any of the classes you encounter on the tree as you work your way toward the root (OI_callback). These include member functions for OI_entry_field, OI_lang_server_input, OI_w_d_tech, OI_d_tech, and OI_callback, as well as member functions defined for OI_seq_entry_field alone. (OI_lang_server_input and OI_w_d_tech have no public member functions needed when programming; so you may ignore them.) You can find descriptions of the member functions for each class in the chapter bearing the class name.

As a practical matter, you will need to learn what member functions are available for OI_d_tech (see Chapter 6, "OI_d_tech") first. You can use these member functions for any displayable OI object.

A word of warning to those of you who like to dig through the header files to look at the implementation and see what extra goodies lie there. There are member functions which are public, and therefore technically usable, but which are not documented in this book. They appear in sections appropriately marked in the header files. You should not use them. They are present for internal OI toolkit use only, and may be removed, modified, or renamed without warning at some time in the future.

2.2   Object Tree

If you are new to C++ programming, remember that an object is a single instance of a class. The OI class hierarchy shown in Figure 2-1 is the logical structure imposed by deriving classes from base classes. This has no relationship to the object tree you build in your program. In your program you explicitly create a hierarchy of objects by defining parent/child relationships between objects that you have created.

Take another look at Figure 1-6, "Object Tree for Hello World with Exit Button," on page 1-9. This object hierarchy is built, block by block, when you parent one object to another. Notice that the program's object tree is unrelated to the class tree shown in Figure 2-1.

It is also true that the OI object tree for your application is independent of the window tree for your application created by the X server. This is illustrated (as well as some other new concepts) by the next example. Program 2-1 displays a menu which allows the user to change the color appearing in a box by clicking on a menu cell.

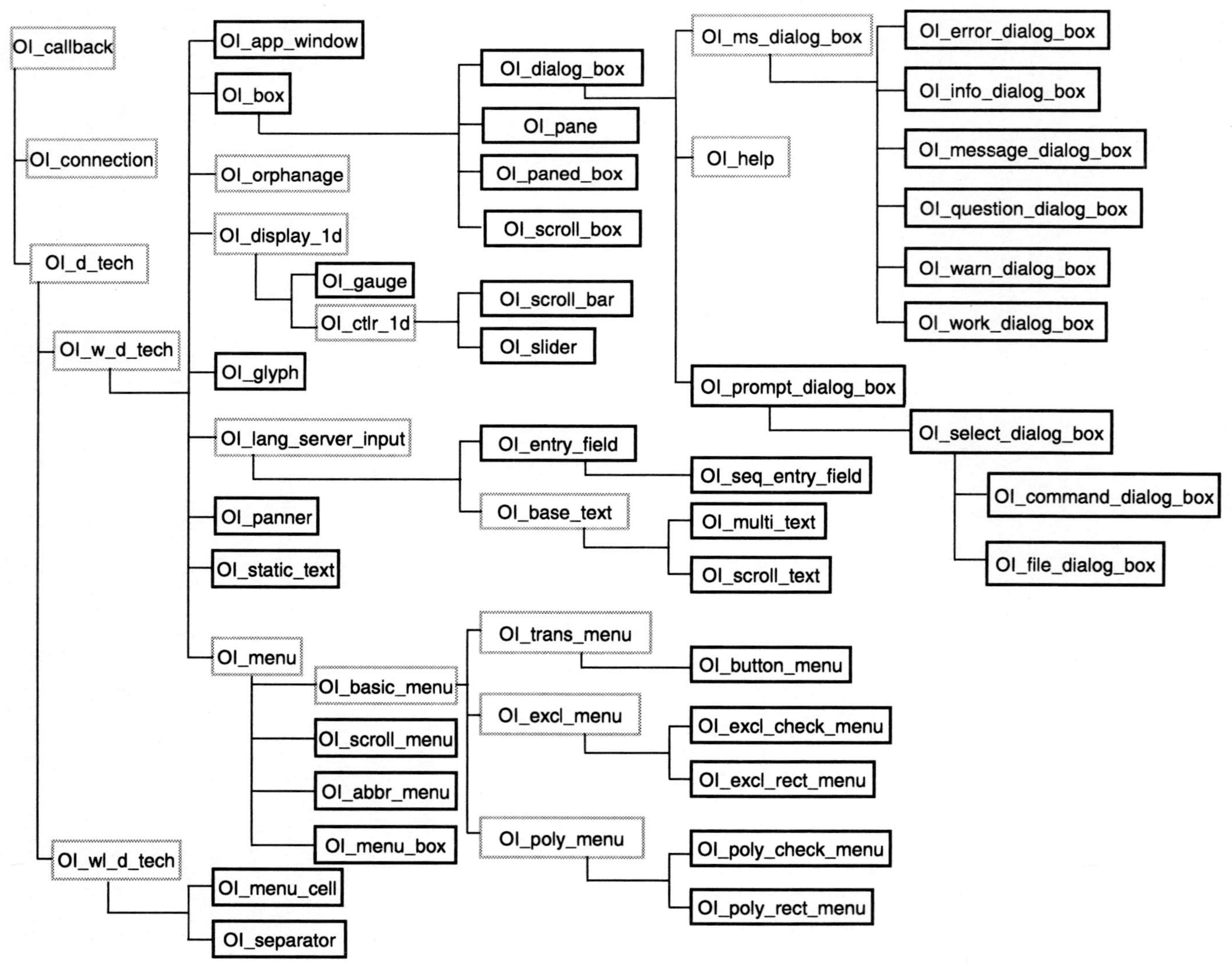

Figure 2-1   OI Class Hierarchy

```
#include <OI/oi.H>                              /* ColorsMenu.C */
int main(int argc,char **argv)
{
        void                    set_color(OI_menu_cell*,void*,OI_number);

        OI_connection           *conp;
        OI_app_window           *wp;
        OI_menu                 *mp;
        OI_box                  *bp;

static OI_cell_spec             colors[] = {
    {"red","Flaming Red",set_color},
    {"orange","Warm Orange",set_color},
    {"yellow","Sun Yellow",set_color},
    {"blue","Chilling Blue",set_color}
    };

    if (conp = OI_init(&argc,argv,"ColorsMenu")) {
        wp = oi_create_app_window("main",1,1,"Colors");
        wp->set_layout(OI_layout_row);

        mp = oi_create_button_menu(
            "color_menu",OI_count(colors),colors,OI_vertical,"Colors");
        mp->layout_associated_object(wp,10,10,OI_active );

        wp->set_associated_object(wp->root( ),OI_def_loc,OI_def_loc,OI_active );

        bp = oi_create_box("color_box",100,60);
        bp->set_associated_object(wp,110,20,OI_active );
        bp->disallow_clip( );
        OI_begin_interaction( );
        OI_fini( );
    }
}

void    set_color(OI_menu_cell *mcp,void*,OI_number)
{
        OI_box                  *bp;

    bp = (OI_box*)mcp->app_window( )->descendant("color_box");
    bp->set_bkg_color(mcp->name( )) ;
    return;
}
```

Program 2-1   Colors Menu (ColorsMenu.C)

In this program, we use the layout code for the menu, but call **set_associated_object** and **disallow_clip** for the box to specifically locate the box outside its parent's boundaries. If we had used the layout code for the box, the application window would expand to encompass the box within its boundaries.

colors defines the values for the menu cells but does not create the menu cells. The first cell will have a name "red" and a label "Flaming Red". **set_color** is the name of the routine that will be called when the user activates this cell by moving the mouse pointer over the cell and clicking a mouse button. The application window is created with name "main", size 1 by 1 pixel, and title "Colors". The button menu is then created from the **OI_cell_spec** structure **colors**, with name "color_menu", vertical orientation, and label "Colors". "color_menu" is parented to "main" and laid out in column 1, row 1. The use of the layout facility causes "main" to expand to the size necessary to contain "color_menu". At this point we parent "main" to the root window, and it becomes visible on the screen.

oi_create_box makes a box with name "color_box" and size 100 by 60 pixels. Using **set_associated_object**, we parent "color_box" to "main", at location 110 pixels in the x direction (right) and 20 pixels in the y direction (down) from the upper left hand corner of "main". This positions the box partially within "main" and partially outside "main". By default, any object positioned with any portion outside its parent is *clipped* to its parent's boundaries—that is, only the portion of the object that is within the parent's boundaries is visible. (So if you are not using the automatic layout facility, it is possible to position an object completely outside its parent, and it will never show up.) Because we want to see the entire box, we call **disallow_clip** for "color_box".

We now call **OI_begin_interaction** to allow the user to interact with the program. If you run this program, this is what you see:

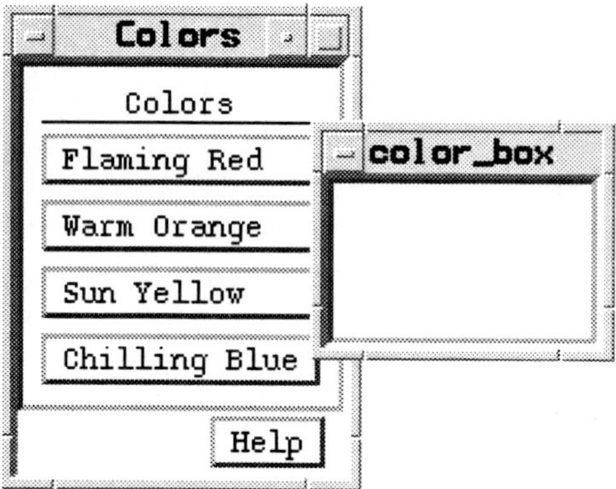

Figure 2-2   Colors Menu, Motif

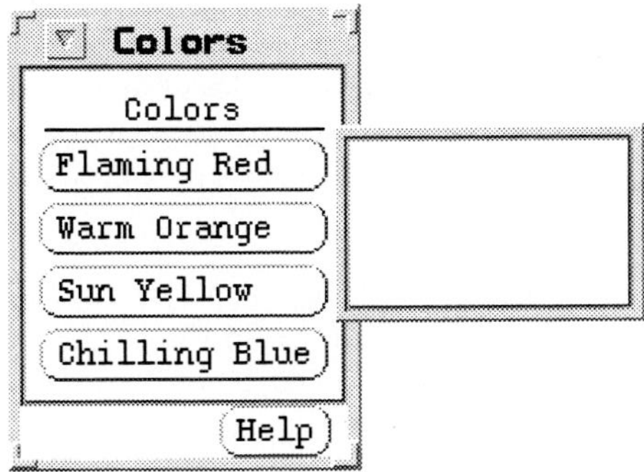

Figure 2-3   Colors Menu, OPEN LOOK 3-D

2.2.1   Finding Your Way Around The Object Tree

The object tree created by Program 2-1, "Colors Menu (ColorsMenu.C)," is as follows:

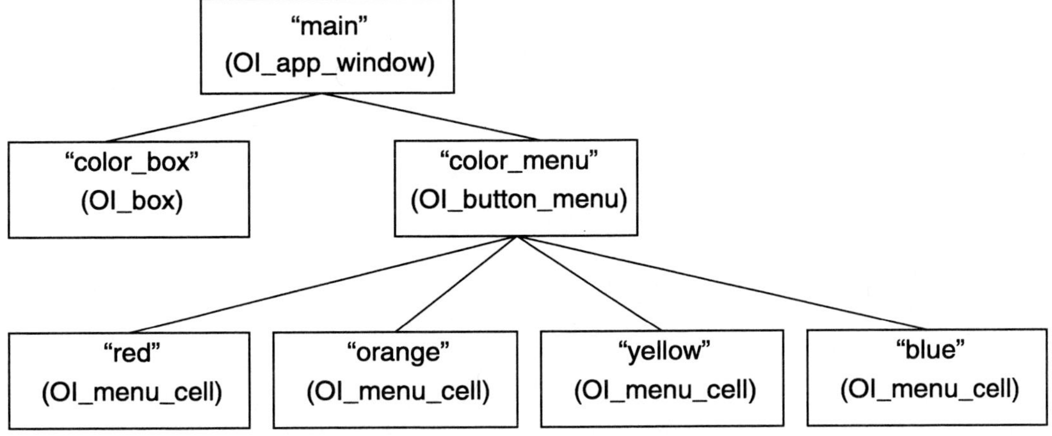

Figure 2-4   Object Tree for Colors Menu Program

In the "Colors Menu" program, each time the user activates a button (menu cell), the function set_color is executed. OI automatically passes in mcp as a pointer to the menu cell that was activated. bp is declared as a pointer to a box. The next line of code does the following things: finds the ancestor application window of the activated menu cell, finds the descendant of that application window which is named "color_box", and casts the resulting object pointer to be a pointer to an OI_box. The arguments to a menu cell action callback function are pre-defined by OI, and all you have to work with when the function is executed is a pointer to the activated menu cell. Since we want to set the background color of "color_box", we need a pointer to it, so we can call set_bkg_color for it. Performing operations like these are what we mean by "finding your way around the object tree." If you name your objects appropriately, you can find the correct object by traversing up and down the object tree in this fashion. In this manner you can avoid using global variables, thus improving the independence of the modules of your program and helping you achieve the goal of a loosely coupled system. (There are other ways of passing information to callback programs. See Section 2.5, "Callbacks and Event-Driven Programming," on page 2-16.)

The next line of code sets the background of the box to be the color which is used as the name of the activated menu cell. Notice that for this to work, the name of the cell must be a color in the color database for your X server; but the label on the face of the cell can be any appropriate text (or a glyph).

(Experienced C++ users may note that in this example it is not truly necessary to have a pointer to an OI_box in the callback routine set_color. A pointer to an OI_d_tech would do just as well. This is because the function descendant returns a pointer to an OI_d_tech and set_bkg_color is an OI_d_tech member function.)

2.2.2   OI Object Tree vs. X Window System Tree

The object tree created in this program is different than the X Window System tree. In the X Window System, any children of an X window appear only within the boundaries of the parent window. The box "color_box", which is logically the child of the main application window in the program, must be a top-level window in X's view of things. OI allows you to use an object tree structure identical to the logical structure of your program, rather than constraining your logical design to the limits of the windowing system.

2.2.3   Object Tree Creation Order

It is useful to know that the order in which you create and parent objects is unimportant, as far as the final object tree structure or the final appearance of the objects on the screen is concerned. In Program 2-1, "Colors Menu (ColorsMenu.C)," we could have created the box first, then the menu, then the application window.

However, the order in which you associate the top level object with the root and associate objects with their parents may affect the visual display at the time you are building your tree. For example, suppose you create a 1x1 application window and immediately associate it with the root, then create other objects and lay them out in the application window immediately after creating them, as shown in this code segment:

```
OI_app_window              *wp;
OI_box                     *bp;
OI_gauge                   *gp;
OI_entry_field             *efp;

wp = oi_create_app_window("main",1,1,"Main");
wp->set_layout(OI_layout_row);
wp->set_associated_object(wp->root( ),OI_def_loc,OI_def_loc,OI_active);
bp = oi_create_box("box",...);
bp->layout_associated_object(wp,1,1,OI_active);
gp = oi_create_gauge("gauge",...);
gp->layout_associated_object(wp,1,2,OI_active);
efp = oi_create_entry_field("entry_field",...);
efp->layout_associated_object(wp,2,1,OI_active);
OI_begin_interaction( );
```

Example 2-1   Object Tree Creation Order # 1

With this example, what appears on the screen first is a tiny application window. As each new object is laid out, the application window expands and the new object appears.

If you would prefer not to see all this growth occur, but would like to see the finished layout only, you would delay associating the application window with the root until just prior to calling **OI_begin_interaction**, as shown below. We also have rearranged the creation and parenting of the other objects to show that the final appearance on the screen is independent of this order. Notice that regardless of tree construction order, the row and column in which each object appears remains the same.

```
OI_app_window              *wp;
OI_box                     *bp;
OI_gauge                   *gp;
OI_entry_field             *efp;

wp = oi_create_app_window("main",1,1,"Main");
wp->set_layout(OI_layout_row);
efp = oi_create_entry_field("entry_field",...);
efp->layout_associated_object(wp,2,1,OI_active);
gp = oi_create_gauge("gauge",...);
gp->layout_associated_object(wp,1,2,OI_active);
bp = oi_create_box("box",...);
bp->layout_associated_object(wp,1,1,OI_active);
wp->set_associated_object(wp->root( ),OI_def_loc,OI_def_loc,OI_active);
OI_begin_interaction( );
```

Example 2-2   Object Tree Creation Order # 2

Whichever of the two code segments you were to use, this is what would be on the screen after OI_begin_interaction had been called:

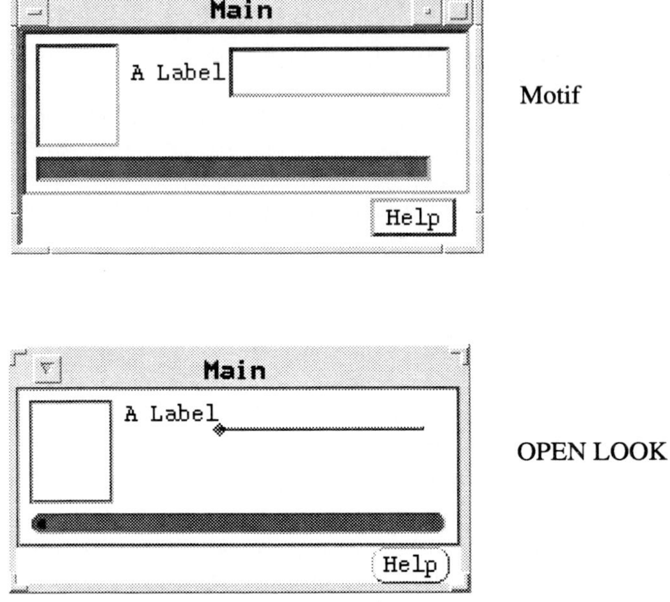

Figure 2-5   Object Tree Creation Order Program

2.2.4   Object Tree Summary

- When you create an object, it is independent of all other objects—it is in the **orphanage**.
- You must place top-level objects on the root; otherwise they are left in the **orphanage**, and nothing ever appears on the screen!
- The order in which you create and parent objects is not important. The order may, however, affect whether or not objects shuffle and resize visually on the screen during the process.
- You may unparent an object (which puts it in the **orphanage**) or reparent an object to a new parent.

2.3   General Capabilities Common to all Displayable Objects

Now that you have seen a few examples, you will need to learn some of the attributes of all OI objects.

- OI objects are as generic as possible. For this reason, there is a large number of member functions for the class OI_d_tech, the base class of all displayable objects. You never create an OI_d_tech object directly; one is automatically created for you each time you create a displayable OI object. You can use OI_d_tech's functions for every displayable object.

- Every object has a name; you use this name to traverse the object tree as discussed above.
- Every object has a *state* which is set when you call set_associated_object or layout_associated_object and which you can change using other function calls such as set_state. The state can be one of

OI_active	Possibly visible, responsive to user input.
OI_not_displayed	Not visible, not responsive to user input.
OI_inactive	Possibly visible, not responsive to user input.
OI_active_not_displayed	Not visible, but responsive to user input (pop-up or pull-down menus and dialog boxes).

  By *possibly visible* we mean that the object's X window is mapped and the object are visible if all of its ancestors are visible and if either some part of the object exists within the parent's boundaries or the object is set to be unclipped. If the object is *not visible*, the X window for the object is unmapped or not yet created.
- Every object has a single parent. This parent may be the root, the orphanage, or another object.
- Every object has a location relative to its parent. The location is the x and y offset from the upper left corner of the object to the upper left corner of the parent, in pixels, regardless of whether the object is clipped or not.
- Every object has zero or more children.
- You may attach *user-data* to an object. You may have specific data that you wish to associate with an object. For example, if you have created a gauge that is meant to represent the current value of a changing resource (CPU usage, perhaps), you might need to have a pointer to the resource data structure each time your callback for the gauge is executed. You can set the data to belong to the object, thus avoiding the use of global data; whenever you have a pointer to the object, you also have access to the user-data. You set and retrieve this data with the functions set_data and data respectively. If you derive your own sub-classes, you usually do not need to use the data pointer, since you define the class to contain any additional information needed by the object.
- All objects support resize, focus in/out, and delete callback functions. This means that you can perform additional tasks if necessary whenever the object is resized, gains or loses input focus, or is deleted.
- Each object can interface to the OI_app_window error (help) line. This means that in any object which is a descendant of an OI_app_window, if there is an error in user interaction or any other occurrence that necessitates displaying a message to the user for help, you can display a line of text in the ancestor application window using the OI_d_tech member functions set_help_str and push_help_str.

2.4   General Considerations

2.4.1   OI Configuration

There are several command-line arguments that set up and modify the visible attributes of your program as it executes. In the "Hello World" example, you saw how three of them control which interaction and appearance model OI uses. All of the command-line arguments are listed and explained in Chapter 3, "Compiling, Linking, and Executing an OI Program." OI attributes may also be specified via the **.Xdefaults** file or other X resource database files or methods. See Chapter 39, "The OI Resource Mechanism."

Almost all user interaction with OI objects through the keyboard and the mouse are defined through default translations. The default runtime interaction for each object is described in the chapter on that object. The default translations for each object are also defined there. See also Chapter 40, "The OI Translation Mechanism."

Do not include the "." or ":" characters in the name of your executable program. This is because the X resource manager cannot properly resolve command line arguments that change the default attributes for an executable whose name contains these characters.

2.4.2   Naming Objects

Every time you create an OI object, you give it a *name*. Do not confuse the name of the object with the class name; an object of class **OI_box** (class name) might have an instance name "my_box" (object name). Object names are important; you will need the names to find your way around the object tree and to make debugging easier.

You give an OI object a name when you create it; the first argument in all **oi_create_*** functions is the name of the object:

```
sp = oi_create_slider("my_slider",90,OI_vertical);
```

You can change the name of an object with the function **set_name**:

```
sp->set_name("chocolate_slider");
```

In Program 2-1, "Colors Menu (ColorsMenu.C), on page 2-3" we define the names of menu cells using the **OI_cell_spec** structure.

If you call **oi_create_*** with NULL as the first argument, OI automatically gives the object a name. It is not usually a good practice to do this. If you use automatic naming, users may be prevented from using the resource manager to change object attributes, since the name OI supplies may change in future OI releases.

Do not use the following characters in an object's name: @ , . : ? / * or blank, as they are special characters used by OI. In general, you should use only alphanumeric and the underscore characters in object names.

The full object path-name of an object starts with its most distant ancestor and includes all the intervening ancestor names separated by a slash ("/") character. You can get the name and the full name of an object using the **OI_d_tech** member functions **name** and **full_name**:

```
printf("Object name: %s, Full name: %s",bp->name( ),bp->full_name( ));
```

If inserted in Program 2-1, "Colors Menu (ColorsMenu.C)," the above line of code would display

```
Object name: color_box, Full name: main/color_box
```

The most important reason to name your objects is to be able to access descendants or ancestors from different modules of your program without having to resort to global variables and the inevitable ensuing rat's nest. The typical OI program has an object tree which is several layers deep, and finding objects in a fashion similar to that shown for finding "color_box" in Program 2-1, "Colors Menu (ColorsMenu.C)" keeps your code clean.

Another good reason to name your objects is that it makes debugging easier. OI creates a separate X window for each OI object except **OI_menu_cell** and **OI_separator** objects. If you use utilities to look at the properties of the X window in which the object is displayed, and you run an OI program with the resource **nameObjects** set to True, the name you have given the object shows up in the **WM_NAME** property.

2.4.3   Automatic Object Layout

In general, you should use the OI automatic layout facility to create your object tree whenever possible. Using the layout facility provides such benefits as:

- OI automatically resizes a parent object to encompass all its laid-out children when a new object is parented to it.
- You will have much less work to do in determining the positions of objects in the first place, and much less work to do down the road in resizing and repositioning objects when you make changes in the application.
- If the user uses the X resource mechanism to modify objects' properties which affect their size, such as font or frame width, your objects will all still be properly sized and positioned.

Using automatic layout, you can

- Specify the layout method a parent object uses. The supplied layout methods include many variants of row and column based layouts, and tree layouts.
- Specify the amount of white space surrounding the child objects that are laid out.
- Specify "gravity" of child objects so that they try to position themselves to a specified edge or the middle of the parent.
- Resize a child object and let the layout facility rearrange its siblings to fit and resize the parent to encompass the new arrangement.
- Align objects (such as entry fields) along the right edge of their labels.

The most common functions that you use for automatic layout are

```
set_layout
set_gravity
layout_associated_object
suspend_layout
resume_layout
```

See Chapter 6, "OI_d_tech," for an example and a detailed discussion of these functions.

2.4.4   Callbacks for Your Own Classes

OI_callback is the most distant base class of all displayable OI objects. If you define your own classes which are going to have member functions to be used as OI callback routines, your user-defined classes must be derived from **OI_callback**. If your classes are derived from an OI class (such as **OI_box**), they are automatically derived from **OI_callback**, since all OI classes are ultimately derived from **OI_callback**.

2.4.5   Focus Groups

OI uses focus groups to allow the user to use the keyboard to traverse between objects and groups of objects within an application. A *focus group* is a group of objects with a defined order of input-focus traversal, that is, the input focus can be moved from one object to another as a result of keyboard operations, without manipulating the mouse. There are two types of traversal: between objects of a given group, and between groups of objects.

2.4.5.1   Default Focus Traversal

If you do not explicitly set up traversal ordering, OI sets up a default Tab traversal order. To move from one object to the next using this default traversal, the user must press the Tab (or Ctrl/Tab) key to move the focus from one object to the next. Pressing Shift/Tab (or Ctrl/Shift/Tab) moves the focus to the previous object in the traversal.

If you use a layout method on the top-level parent object, the default traversal order follows the layout sequence, by rows if the layout method is derived from OI_layout_row, by columns if the layout method is derived from OI_layout_column, and in a left-most, depth first node ordering if the layout method is tree based. If you do not use a layout method, the default traversal order corresponds to the order in which you associate the objects to the top-level parent object.

2.4.5.2   Establishing Your Own Focus Traversal

You can establish your own focus groups and focus traversal order using the OI_d_tech member functions set_first_focus, set_next, and set_next_group. You can establish groups of objects with a traversal order between the groups so that the user can move from group to group using Tab to traverse forward and Shift/Tab to traverse backwards. Within each group, you can establish a traversal order so that the user can move from object to object within the group using the Return key or the Down Arrow Key to move to the next object, and the Up Arrow Key to move to the previous object in the group.

2.4.6   Casting

In your use of OI you will find that you must sometimes cast variables to be of the appropriate type. There are many OI functions which return a pointer to an OI_d_tech object, but what you often need is a pointer to another class of object derived from OI_d_tech. For example, suppose the procedure you are writing has a pointer bmp that already points to a button menu. You know that the menu appears in a dialog box; the dialog box is the parent of the menu. You need to have a pointer to the dialog box because you want to set the title of the dialog box to "My new title". Your code would look like this:

```
    OI_dialog_box           *dp;
    OI_button_menu          *bmp;
dp = (OI_dialog_box*)bmp->parent( );
dp->set_title("My new title");
```

Example 2-3   Casting A Variable to a Different Class

The procedure **parent** returns a pointer to the parent of the object on whose behalf it is called. Obviously the parent could be any one of several types of OI objects; therefore **parent** returns a pointer to an **OI_d_tech**, the general object type. **dp** must be declared to be a pointer to an **OI_dialog_box**, however, because the function **set_title** is a member function of **OI_dialog_box** and not of **OI_d_tech**. Therefore, you must cast the pointer returned from **parent** to be the class type corresponding to the actual object.

You should use casts only when necessary, and with care, since they effectively disable some of the type checking of the C++ compiler. In the above example, it is up to you to ensure that **bmp->parent( )** is really an **OI_dialog_box**. If it was only a plain **OI_box**, the compiler would not complain, but your program would not function correctly. Unfortunately, there is no practical way around this problem. You can, however, use the **OI_d_tech** member function **is_derived_from** to determine an object's class and **ancestor_derived_from** to find an ancestor of a particular class. These will not remove the need for the cast, but do allow you to insure that an object is of the proper type and that the type cast is therefore valid.

C++ gives you compile-time errors if you do not cast your variables appropriately. This will help you catch mistakes where you inadvertently use the wrong variable name, or try to do illegal operations. Note that it is legal to set a variable which is a base class pointer equal to a derived class pointer, but not vice-versa (remember that **OI_box** is derived from **OI_d_tech**):

```
OI_d_tech              *dtp;
OI_box                 *bp;
dtp = bp;              // legal
bp = dtp;              // illegal
bp = (OI_box*)dtp;     // legal
```

Example 2-4   Class Pointer Legality

2.4.7   Animation

Using OI you can animate images on the screen. The illusion of animated glyphs is produced by displaying in rapid sequence a series of bitmaps. There are two interfaces for producing animation.

In the simplest form, you supply OI with a vector of pixmaps, all the same size, and a time-interval. (One way to create your own bitmaps is by using the X program **bitmap**.) You can then play the pixmaps through either once or continuously, with each pixmap remaining on the screen for the specified time interval. This method works well for simple tasks like animating an icon, where all images are the same size and the base image location does not move. The functions you use to perform this type of animation are:

```
uniform_pixmap_series
animate
```

These functions are described in Chapter 25, "OI_glyph" and Chapter 38, "OI_connection."

For more complex situations, you can use a more general interface. In this case you register a function (which you write yourself) which OI calls when it needs information for the next frame. This function must return information sufficient to do fairly complex animation: a new location for the glyph, a new size for the glyph, a new pixmap for the glyph, and a new time interval until the next frame. The function you use to perform this type of animation is

```
animate_custom
```

This function is described in Chapter 25, "OI_glyph."

2.4.8   Help Facilities

There are two forms of help available in OI. There is a help line in the OI_app_window footer, in which a single line of text can be displayed. OI displays its own error or help messages here, and you can display help information specific to your application in this location as well. The functions you use to do this are:

```
push_help_str
pop_help_str
set_help_str
help_str_posted
help_str
help_stack_size
```

These functions are described in Section 6.12, "Interfaces to the Help Mechanism," on page 6-97.

The second form of help is a form of hypertext, which you would use to display more complex help information. This form of help is an OI_help object which is activated when the user activates the help menu button in the application window or presses the HELP key when the mouse pointer is over some part of the application. All applications automatically get an OI_help hypertext help object attached to each OI_app_window. If you do not provide your own help file, OI displays generic OI object help when the **OI_help** object is activated. Here is what the first frame of the default help looks like:

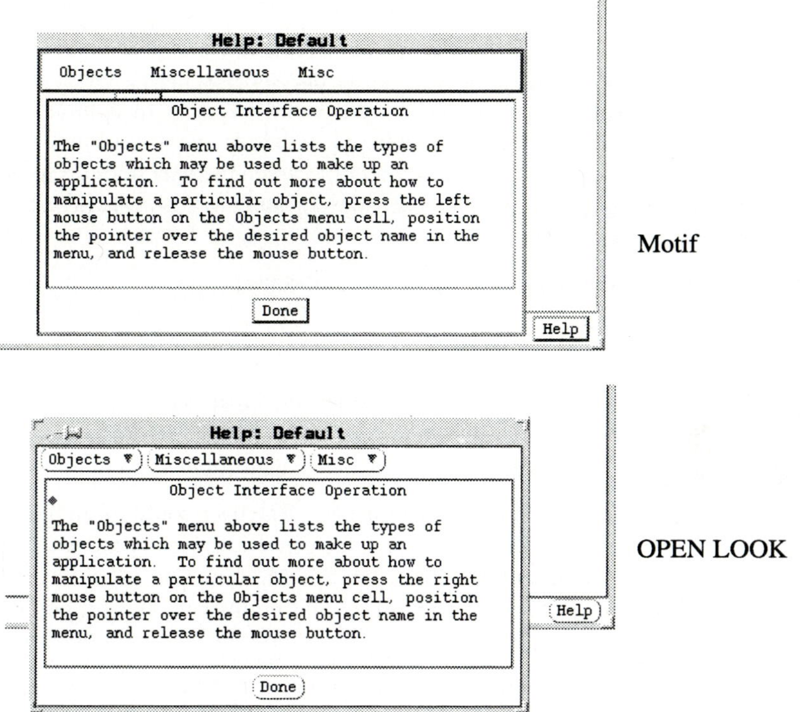

Figure 2-6   Default Help Object

The menu at the top of the help object allows the user to move throughout the help domain. The help domain is considered to be a set of files, each containing hypertext information. The text may also contain highlighted keywords which the user may click on to switch to a new topic.

You may fill the help object with any arbitrary text (following the hypertext file format rules)—a help object could be used for purposes other than providing help.

The functions you use in your program to use this type of help mechanism are:

```
help
set_help
push_help
pop_help
help_file
help_topic
set_key_help
```

The rules for writing hypertext help files as well as descriptions of these functions can be found in Section 8.6.3, "Hypertext Help Mechanism," on page 8-18.

2.5   Callbacks and Event-Driven Programming

Before we discuss the basic structure of an OI program, we need to discuss callback routines in more detail.

Programs written using OI are *event-driven*, meaning that outside *events* (such as user actions or time-outs) determine the order in which processing occurs. This is in contrast to a procedural interface, where the program determines the order in which processing occurs. An event-driven program sits around waiting for the user to do something; when the user does do something (press a key, click a mouse button), the program must react appropriately to this *event*. The event determines what happens next, not the program.

To illustrate this point, consider the following procedural statements:

    Get valid item number.
    Get item size.

The procedural interface in this example assumes that Get item size is only executed after Get valid item number has executed correctly. Therefore, the code for Get item size can assume that the item number is correct and can use the item number to determine valid item sizes.

In an event-driven environment, this may not be the case. The user could fill in the size first. If you presented both items in OI_entry_field type objects, the user could simply move to the size field and start typing. You can enforce order, but the techniques are different. One possible solution would be to display only the item number at first, then after a valid number is entered, pop up a dialog box which displays the size entry field (and any other fields or options related to the item).

The following program illustrates the philosophy of event-driven programming. This program displays an OI_static_text object, and allows the user to change the font of the text by clicking on a font menu cell, and to change the contents of the text by entering characters in an OI_entry_field.

```
#include <OI/oi.H>                      /* Callbacks.C */
int main(int argc,char **argv)
{
        void                    chng_font(OI_menu_cell*,void*,OI_number);
        OI_ef_entry_chk_status chng_text(OI_entry_field* ,void*,
                                              OI_ef_entry_chk_status);

        OI_app_window           *wp;
        OI_d_tech               *dtp;
        OI_entry_field          *efp;
static  OI_cell_spec            fonts[] = {
        {"5x8","5x8",chng_font},
        {"7x13B","7x13 Bold",chng_font},
        {"8x16","8x16",chng_font},
        {"16x26bold","16x26 Bold",chng_font},
        };

    if (OI_init(&argc,argv,"Callbacks")) {
        wp = oi_create_app_window("Main",1,1,"Callback Example");
        wp->set_layout(OI_layout_row);

        dtp = oi_create_static_text("LabelText","This is Static Text");
        dtp->layout_associated_object(wp,1,1,OI_active);

        efp = oi_create_entry_field("EditText",16,"Enter new text: ",NULL,256);
        efp->set_entry_check(chng_text);
        efp->layout_associated_object(wp,1,3,OI_active);

        dtp = oi_create_excl_check_menu(
            "FontMenu",OI_count(fonts),fonts,OI_vertical,"Font");
        dtp->layout_associated_object(wp,1,2,OI_active);

        wp->set_associated_object(wp->root( ),OI_def_loc,OI_def_loc,OI_active);
        OI_begin_interaction( );
        OI_fini( );
    }
}


void    chng_font(OI_menu_cell *cellp,void*,OI_number)
{
    if (cellp->selected( ))
        cellp->app_window( )->descendant("LabelText")->set_font(cellp->name( ));
    return;
}


OI_ef_entry_chk_status chng_text(OI_entry_field *efp,void*,OI_ef_entry_chk_status)
{
        OI_static_text          *stp;
    stp = (OI_static_text*)efp->ancestor("Main")->subobject("LabelText");
    stp->set_text(efp->part_text( ));
    return(OI_ef_entry_chk_ok);
}
```

Program 2-2   Callbacks to Change Text and Font (Callbacks.C)

Here is the object tree created in this program:

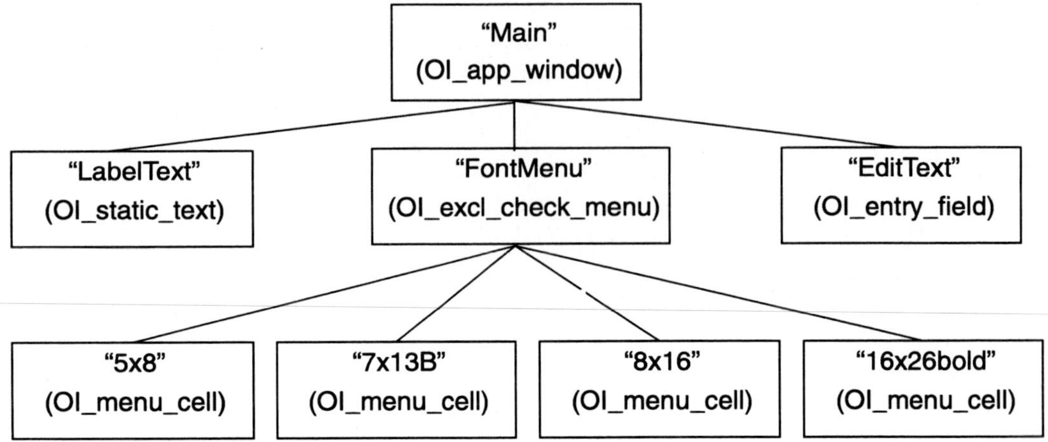

Figure 2-7   Object Tree for Callback Example Program

This program displays the following image on the screen when it is first started:

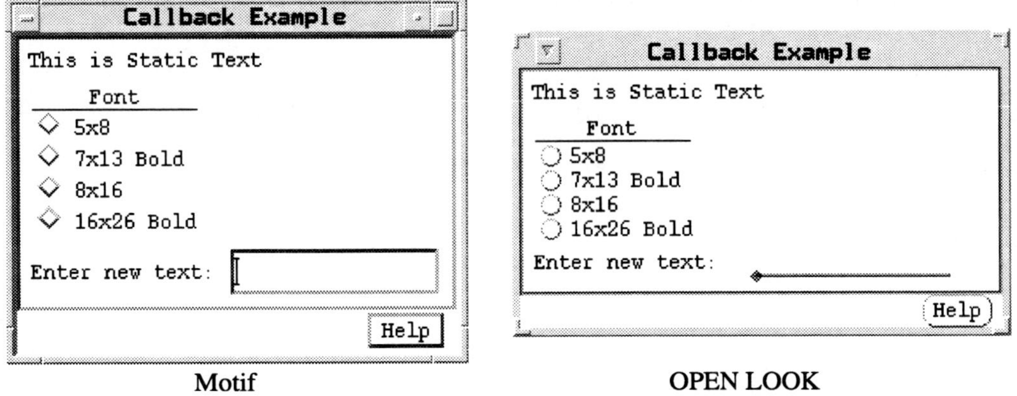

Figure 2-8   Callback Example, Start Up

In this example, you do not know whether the user will decide to enter something in the entry field first, or choose a font from the menu first, or if either event will occur at all; the program must be prepared to react to any events in the order in which they occur.

You prepare for handling these events when you set up the object tree. You tell OI which procedure to call when a menu cell is activated or when text is entered by registering *callback routines*, which are procedures to call when the appropriate event occurs. You *register* a callback routine—tell OI which callback routine to execute when a certain event occurs in an object—by calling a particular member function for the object.

In Program 2-2, the callback routine chng_font is registered for each menu cell when the menu is created using the function oi_create_excl_check_menu and the cell specifications in fonts. This callback registration causes the following to happen: during program execution, every time the user activates one of the font menu cells, the routine chng_font will be executed. chng_font traverses the object tree up to the application window, then back down the tree to the object named "LabelText". It then sets the font for "LabelText" to be the font which corresponds to the name of the menu cell. No casting is necessary since the three functions app_window, descendant and set_font all are member functions for OI_d_tech, and the first two return a pointer to an OI_d_tech object.

The callback routine chng_text is registered using the OI_entry_field member function set_entry_check. Because of this registration, every time the user enters characters in the entry field labeled "Enter new text:" and presses the Return key, the function chng_text will be executed. chng_text also traverses the object tree to find the object "LabelText". In this case we must cast the result of the call to subobject to be an OI_static_text, because in the next line we use set_text, which is not an OI_d_tech member function, but a member function of OI_static_text.

This is a picture of the program after the user has activated the last menu cell:

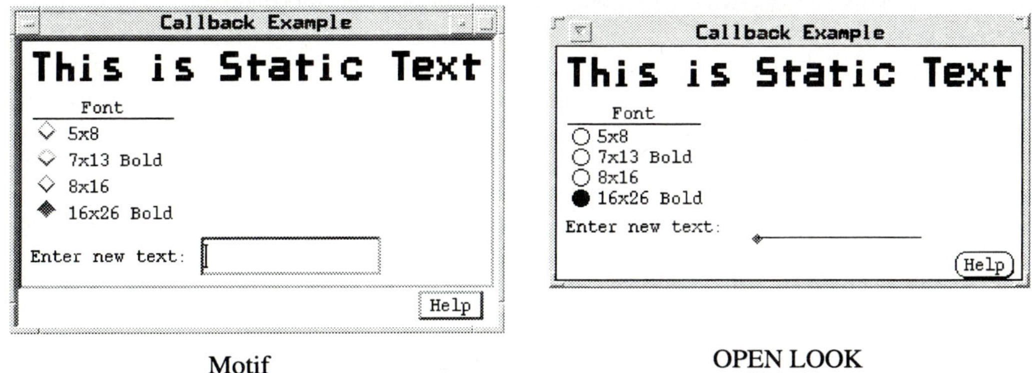

Motif   OPEN LOOK

Figure 2-9 Callback Example, Last Cell Selected

Here it is after the user has entered text and selected the first menu cell:

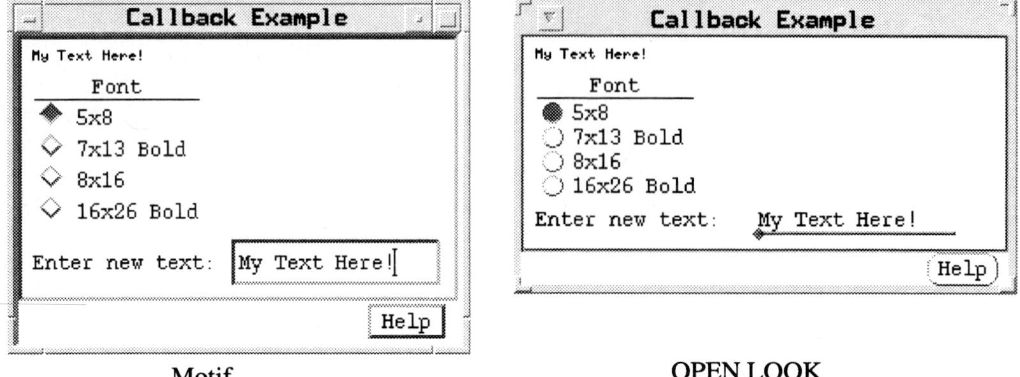

Motif   OPEN LOOK

Figure 2-10   Callback Example, Text Entered and First Cell Selected

Notice the following items in the code for this example:

- Since we used the automatic layout facility by calling layout_associated_object to build the object tree, the application window resizes itself each time the text or the font for the static text changes.
- We used an exclusive check menu for the fonts instead of a button menu as we did for the colors program. With the exclusive check menu, you can query the menu at any point in your program to see which cell is in the selected state, thus determining which font the user last chose. The user can also see what the current state is. With a button menu this is not possible; a button simply fires (is activated) and then returns to the deselected state.
- We used dtp, a pointer to an OI_d_tech object, to point to the static text and the menu when we created them, and when we added them to the layout. We did this to show that it was not strictly necessary to have pointers to OI_static_text and OI_menu when we created and parented these objects, since layout_associated_object is an OI_d_tech member function. However, to make it more meaningful it is probably better practice to use, for example,

```
OI_menu                 *mp;
```
and
```
OI_static_text          *stp;
```
- However, we did have to use a pointer to an OI_entry_field when we created the entry field, because set_entry_check is a member function for OI_entry_field and not OI_d_tech.
- In order to illustrate the possibilities, we used two different ways to traverse the object tree to find the static text in the two callback routines. chng_font uses app_window to find the closest application window to the object for which app_window is being called. It then calls descendant to find the descendant of the application window with name "LabelText". chng_text uses ancestor to find the closest ancestor object with the name "Main", then uses subobject to find the application window's direct child with name "LabelText". Either method is better than making a global variable that points to the static text and that can be

accessed in the callback routines. A third possibility, not illustrated here, would be to use the member function ancestor_derived_from.

- We used the cell name rather than the cell label to actually set the font in chng_font. This is so that the label can be more descriptive if necessary. Also, the user may change the text in the cell label via the resource mechanism; in this case, if the cell label were used to change the font the program wouldn't work. If, however, you wanted the user to be able to change the possible font choices via the resource mechanism, you could use the cell label instead of the cell name. (For this to work, the user must make labels that are valid font names.)
- The object names in this example are in a different style than those in the previous examples. Here we use capitals, whereas previously we used lowercase and underbars. Whatever object naming scheme you use, be consistent.
- It would be possible to write this program with the function chng_font renamed to be set_font. Notice that chng_font (potentially renamed set_font) calls an OI_static_text member function named set_font. Doing this would be perfectly legal and would work. While the C++ compiler would never confuse these two functions because one is a member function and one is a free-standing function, a human might confuse them. Because of this potential for confusion, we recommend that you do not follow this practice.

Other examples of callback routines you might write would be a procedure to call when a slider is moved, a routine to call when an object gains the input focus, or a procedure to call when the user dismisses a dialog box. Most non-OI calculations you may need to perform in your program, such as totalling the amount of an order, storing a record in a file, or searching a catalogue for a particular item, must be done either in callback functions, or in functions called from callback functions. Each of these actions will, of necessity, be triggered by some action the user takes or some other outside event.

2.5.1   Registering a Callback Routine

You usually register callback routines before you call OI_begin_interaction, but you may register them, or even change the registrations, during the course of interacting with the user. You essentially tell OI, "This is the procedure I want you to execute when this menu cell fires." The procedure does not get called until the user actually clicks on the menu button; it may never get called.

Remember that if you are registering a callback for an object of your own class, it must ultimately be derived from OI_callback, which is the most distant base class of all displayable OI objects. If you do not do this, your application will not behave correctly.

In many cases you will register a callback for an object when you create it. You can do this when you create menu cells, for example. You can also register a callback for an object at any time in your program after you have created the object, using an appropriate member function.

You can register more than one callback of a given type for an object; this is known as *multiple* callbacks. See Section 6.18, "Determining and Adding Callbacks; Multiple Callbacks," on page 6-117 for information on multiple callbacks.

A callback function may be a free-standing function, or it may be a member function for one of your own classes of objects. Because of this, there are always two forms for any OI function which registers a callback: one to register a free-standing function, and one to register a member function. These are overloaded functions (they have the same name and return value type, but a different set of arguments). For example, the two forms of **set_click** are:

```
void OI_box::set_click(
    OI_click_fnp        fnp,            // pointer to callback function
    void                *argp=NULL)     // arbitrary argument for fnp


void OI_box::set_click(
    OI_callback         *objp,          // memfnp's object
    OI_click_memfnp     memfnp,         // pointer to callback member function
    void                *argp=NULL)     // arbitrary argument for memfnp
```

The **set_click** functions register a callback function to be invoked whenever the user clicks a mouse button one or more times on the object. If your callback function is not a member function, you must use the first form. If your callback function is a member function, use the second form.

In the second form, *objp* points to a C++ object, and *memfnp* points to a member function for that object. When the member function is invoked, it will be called as if you had written *objp->memfnp*. As discussed in Chapter 41, "Deriving Your Own Classes," the class of your object *objp* must have **OI_callback** as its most distant base class.

Every function such as **set_click** which registers a callback has an argument *argp*. This argument is optional, and may be any valid expression that can be cast to a pointer. You can use it to pass additional information to the function *fnp* or *memfnp*.

Throughout this book, wherever a function is defined which registers a callback function, the form of the callback itself is also defined, so you will know what arguments the callback takes, and what it should return. Also, the type of the callback is mentioned, so that you can use it to find the callbacks for objects and to register multiple callbacks for objects. See Section 6.18, "Determining and Adding Callbacks; Multiple Callbacks," on page 6-117 for more information on multiple callbacks. Continuing with the **set_click** example: this callback is identified within OI as a **cbClick** callback function, and this is how the callback is defined:

Writing the Click Callback Function

If the **cbClick** callback function is not a member function, write it in this form:

```
void fn(
    OI_d_tech   *oi_objp,       // pointer to OI object clicked on
    void        *argp,          // arbitrary argument
    OI_number   n_clicks,       // number of clicks
    OI_number   btn,            // mouse button number clicked
    OI_number   mod,            // modifier bits on at click time
    OI_number   x,              // x position where click occurred
    OI_number   y)              // y position where click occurred
```

and if the **cbClick** callback function is a member function, write it in this form:

```
void obj_class::memfn(
        OI_d_tech  *oi_objp,          // pointer to OI object clicked on
        void       *argp,             // arbitrary argument
        OI_number  n_clicks,          // number of clicks
        OI_number  btn,               // mouse button number clicked
        OI_number  mod,               // modifier bits on at click time
        OI_number  x,                 // x position where click occurred
        OI_number  y)                 // y position where click occurred
```

where *obj_class* is the class of the object whose member function is *memfn*.

When your callback function is invoked, *argp* will be the argument specified in the **set_click** call. *oi_objp* will be a pointer to the OI object where the click occurred. This may well be a totally different object from the object on whose behalf the member function is being executed (the *objp* passed in the **set_click** call).The other arguments will have values as defined above.

Example 2-5 shows how to register the free-standing function **where** to be called when the user clicks on an **OI_box** object, and Example 2-6 shows the function **where** itself.

```
void where(OI_d_tech*,void*,OI_number,OI_number,OI_number,OI_number,OI_number);

OI_box  *bp;

bp = oi_create_box("my_box",200,300);
bp->set_click(where);
```
Example 2-5   Registering a Callback Function

```
void where(OI_d_tech *oi_objp,void*,OI_number,OI_number,OI_number,
                                OI_number xloc,OI_number yloc)
{
    printf("Click on %s at location %d, %d\n",oi_objp->name( ),xloc,yloc);
    return;
}
```
Example 2-6   Writing a Click Callback Function

Example 2-5 and Example 2-6 show the same example for the case in which the function **where** is a member function for an object of class **MyClass**.

```
class MyClass:public OI_callback {
public:
void where(OI_d_tech*,void*,OI_number,OI_number,OI_number,OI_number,OI_number);
};

OI_box  *bp;
MyClass *clsp;

clsp = new MyClass( );
bp = oi_create_box("my_box",100,100);
bp->set_click(clsp,(OI_click_memfnp)&MyClass::where);
```

Example 2-7   Registering a Callback Member Function

```
void MyClass::where(OI_d_tech *oi_objp,void*,OI_number,OI_number,OI_number,
                                     OI_number xloc,OI_number yloc)
{
    printf("Click on %s at location %d, %d\n",oi_objp->name( ),xloc,yloc);
    return;
}
```

Example 2-8   Writing a Click Callback Member Function

2.5.2   Callback Routine Arguments

The arguments for any callback routine are predefined, according to the type of callback. You can read about these argument definitions in each chapter under individual functions that register callback routines.The first argument usually points to the OI object which is making the callback. For example, when a menu cell is activated, the first argument to the cell callback is a pointer to the activated cell. The second argument (always called *argp* in the documentation) is one you may define at the time you register the callback, and which, like the callback itself, you may change at any time in your program. The remaining arguments, if any, depend on the particular type of callback.

An important place to look for information when you write your callback is in the pointer to the object for which the callback is being executed. Any information about that object that you can get through member functions is available to you. Also, by traversing the object tree forward or backward from this object, you can reach any other object in the tree (if you have named your objects appropriately).

The next program, Program 2-3, changes Program 2-2, "Callbacks to Change Text and Font (Callbacks.C)," to use argp to pass to the callback functions chng_font and chng_text a pointer to the OI_static_text object "LabelText". Lines of code that have changed from Program 2-2 are highlighted.

```c
#include <OI/oi.H>                              /* CallbackArgp.C */
int main(int argc,char **argv)
{
        void                    chng_font(OI_menu_cell*,void*,OI_number);
        OI_ef_entry_chk_status chng_text(OI_entry_field*,void*,
                                          OI_ef_entry_chk_status);

        OI_app_window           *wp;
        OI_d_tech               *dtp;
        OI_entry_field          *efp;
        int                     i;

static  OI_cell_spec            fonts[] = {
        {"5x8","5x8",chng_font},
        {"7x13B","7x13 Bold",chng_font},
        {"8x16","8x16",chng_font},
        {"16x26bold","16x26 Bold",chng_font},
        };
    if (OI_init(&argc,argv,"CallbackArgp")) {
        wp = oi_create_app_window("Main",1,1,"Callback Example");
        wp->set_layout(OI_layout_row);
        dtp = oi_create_static_text("LabelText","This is Static Text");
        dtp->layout_associated_object(wp,1,1,OI_active);
        efp = oi_create_entry_field("EditText",16,"Enter new text: ",NULL,256);
        efp->set_entry_check(chng_text,dtp);
        efp->layout_associated_object(wp,1,3,OI_active);
        for (i=0 ; i<OI_count(fonts) ; i++)
            fonts[i].argp = dtp;
        dtp = oi_create_excl_check_menu(
            "FontMenu",OI_count(fonts),fonts,OI_vertical,"Font");
        dtp->layout_associated_object(wp,1,2,OI_active);
        wp->set_associated_object(wp->root( ),OI_def_loc,OI_def_loc,OI_active);
        OI_begin_interaction( );
        OI_fini( );
    }
}
void    chng_font(OI_menu_cell *cellp,void *argp,OI_number)
{
        OI_d_tech               *dtp;
    dtp = (OI_d_tech*)argp;
    dtp->set_font(cellp->name( ));
    return;
}
OI_ef_entry_chk_status chng_text(OI_entry_field *efp,void *argp,
                                          OI_ef_entry_chk_status)
{
        OI_static_text          *stp;
    stp = (OI_static_text*)argp ;
    stp->set_text(efp->part_text( ));
    return(OI_ef_entry_chk_ok);
}
```

Program 2-3   Callbacks to Change Text and Font, Using argp (CallbackArgp.C)

This time when we register the callback function chng_text, we set the argument argp to be a pointer to the OI_static_text object "LabelText". When the user types text in the entry field and presses return, chng_text is executed and receives a pointer to "LabelText" in the second argument. Now we do not have to traverse the object tree to find a pointer to "LabelText". We do have to cast argp to an OI_static_text pointer, however, because it comes in as a void*.

(Experienced C++ programmers: You could define chng_text to take an OI_static_text* as its second argument, thus avoiding the need to cast argp. However, this would simply move the problem—you would have to cast the address of chng_text in set_entry_check to be of type OI_ef_entry_check_fnp:

```
efp->set_entry_check((OI_ef_entry_check_fnp)&chng_text,dtp);
```

We recommend you declare functions with the proper argument types if possible, and cast the argument argp, since it allows the C++ compiler and linker to check for proper calling sequences.)

In order to set the argument argp to point to "LabelText" for all the menu cells defined in fonts, we waited until we had created "LabelText" and had a pointer to it (dtp), and then set the argp element of each menu cell specification to be dtp. In chng_font we do not traverse the object tree to find "LabelText"; instead, the pointer comes in as argp. In this case, we need only cast argp to be an OI_d_tech pointer since set_font is an OI_d_tech member function. (Notice that you could, equally correctly, cast it to be an OI_static_text pointer, since OI_static_text is derived from OI_d_tech. You could not do without casting it at all, however, since you cannot call a member function for a void*.)

The object tree, the visual display, and the user interaction of Program 2-3 are identical to those of Program 2-2.

In this example, we used argp to pass a pointer to an OI object. However, you can use argp to pass whatever information you find necessary to your callback routine.

2.5.3 Passing More than One Value to a Callback Routine

Sometimes you may need to pass more than one value to a callback, but since you are constrained to a single argument argp, you may feel a sense of frustration. Fear not, it can be done! You can declare a structure with as many elements in it as values you need to pass. Fill the structure with the values, and make argp point to this structure.

If you find yourself making such a structure to pass information too many times (some people would claim that once is too many), you should consider deriving your own subclass, and declaring the object to be of that class. Then you can carry the information in the object itself, and access it through member functions for your class. See Chapter 41, "Deriving Your Own Classes."

2.5.4 Accessing Data for an Object Through the Object Data Pointer

All OI objects carry around an object data pointer. This is an arbitrary pointer which you can set to point to any data you choose, and is not used by OI in any manner. You attach data to an object with the OI_d_tech member function set_data and retrieve it with the OI_d_tech member function data. In general, you should not attach data to an object simply to make passing information to a particular callback easier (use *argp* in the callback for that purpose). Instead, the data should be intrinsically applicable to that object in all of its contexts; it should "belong" to that object. Any time you can access the object, you can access its data also.

For example, suppose you create a slider to control an external device such as a water valve. Moving the slider up opens the valve more and moving it down closes it more. You could use set_data to point to the valve data structure for the slider. Then wherever you have a pointer to the slider, you also have access to the valve data. Again, this is a good case for deriving your own subclass of OI_slider.

2.5.5   Passing Information to and from a Callback Routine—Summary

Since the arguments to a callback routine are constrained to be as defined by OI, these are the only ways you can pass information to and from your callback routines:

- Use the pointer to the object for which the callback is executed (this gives you information about the object through its member functions, as well as allowing you to traverse the object tree to other objects).
- Use data attached to the object with member functions set_data and data.
- Set argp to point to whatever value you need in your callback.
- Make a structure, fill it with data, and make argp point to it.
- Derive your own subclass—the object will carry the data with it.
- Store the information in global data structures. This is not a recommended practice.

2.5.6   Callback Event Processing Sequence

Figure 2-11 shows the order of processing that occurs when a user clicks a mouse button on an OI_button_menu cell.

Once the user has released the mouse button and your callback has been activated (called), OI does not process any other events or proceed with any other processing until your callback returns. In other words, no more user interaction can occur during the time your callback is executing. The only exception to this rule is if your callback calls one of the following control functions: OI_wait_done, the OI_dialog_box member function wait_button, or the OI_entry_field member function wait_done.

An important item to note: because OI may still manipulate the object after your callback finishes, you must be sure not to delete the object or any of its ancestors during a callback. (However, you can delay the delete until after OI is done with the object. See delete_delayed and delete_all_delayed in Chapter 6, "OI_d_tech.") In general, don't do anything that changes the context of the object in a callback unless you are aware of the consequences and are prepared to handle them. For example, don't change the slider handle location in a slider handle movement callback unless you take into account the recursive nature of this action.

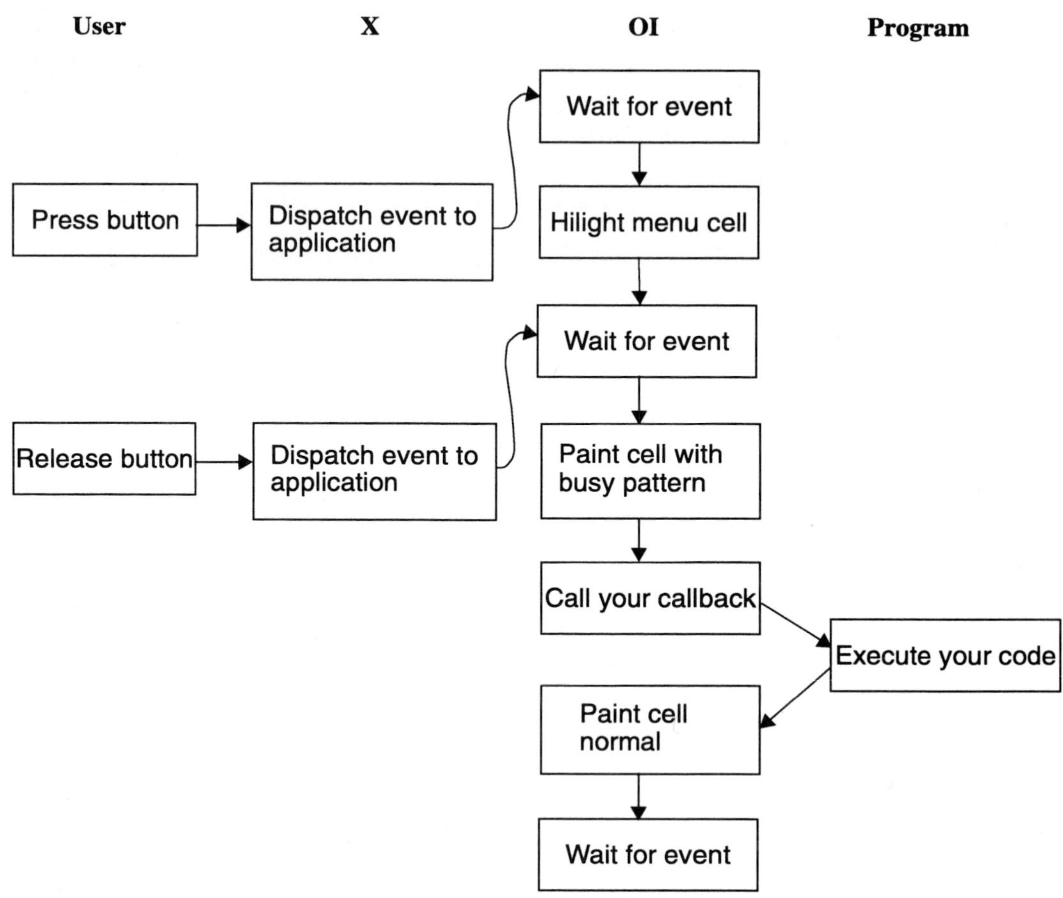

Figure 2-11   Callback Event Processing Sequence

2.6   Overall Structure and Flow of Control

As you have seen, objects in OI are arranged as one or more trees; the top-level objects are usually **OI_app_window** objects. Many applications will only have one top-level object. A complete program using OI consists at least of the following pieces:

- A "main program" with this structure:
    Initialize OI (OI_init)
    Create objects, build object tree/forest, set up callbacks
    Start interactions with user (OI_begin_interaction)
    Clean up (OI_fini)

- One or more callback routines which are not directly called from the main program. (Most of the real work of the program gets done in your callbacks or routines which they invoke.)

You always use this structure, with the addition that you may create objects at any time after you call OI_init. In particular, you can dynamically create objects, reparent them, and delete them during the time OI_begin_interaction is active (that is, in a callback routine).

Sometimes you register callback functions in the **oi_create_*** functions; there are also other member functions that you can use to register callback routines, after an object has been created. Different types of callbacks have different argument lists and different types of values to be returned, all specified by OI.

The basic structure of an OI program is shown in Figure 2-12.

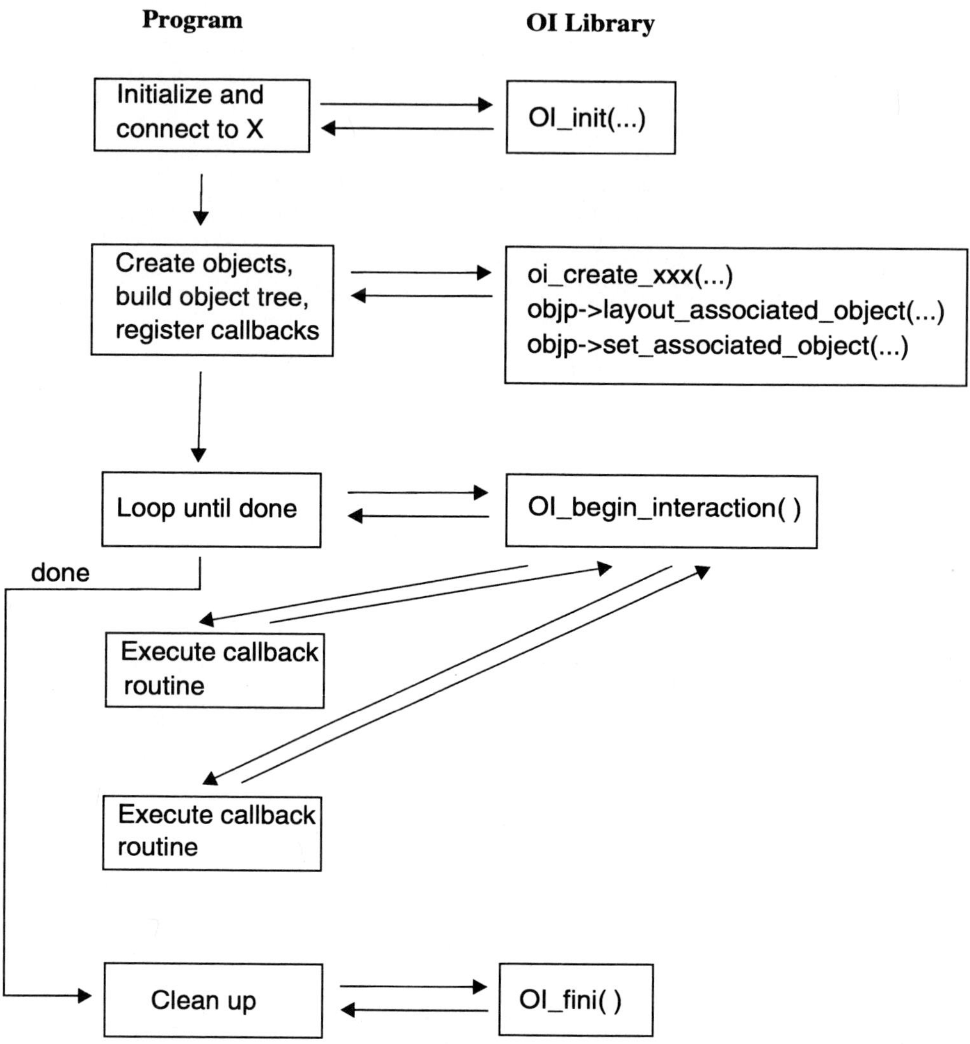

Figure 2-12   Basic OI Program Structure

The flow of control in Program 2-2, "Callbacks to Change Text and Font (Callbacks.C)," can be diagrammed this way:

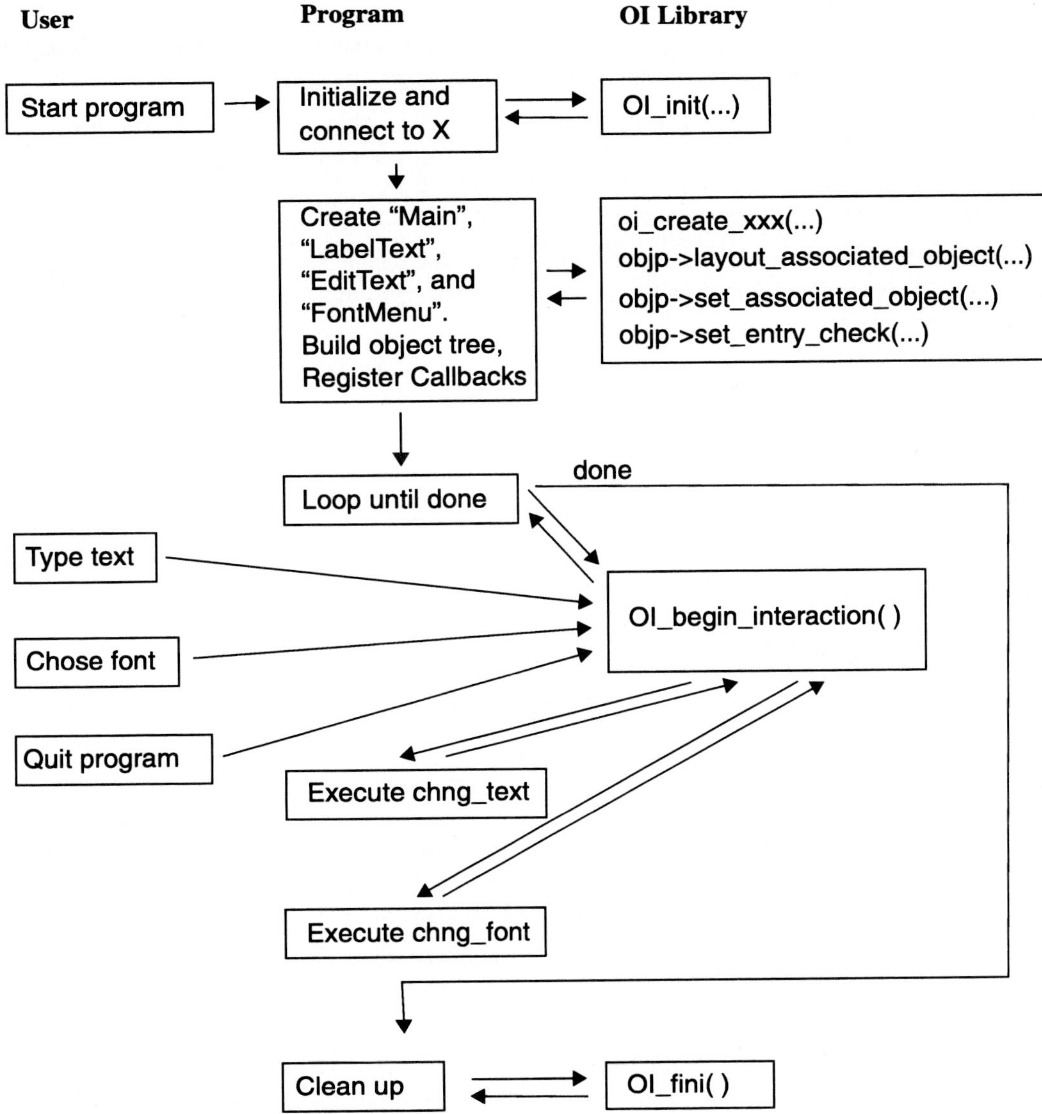

Figure 2-13 Flow of Control for "Callbacks to Change Text and Font" Program

Notice that the order of calling the callback routines and ending the program is totally dependent on the order of the user input events.

2.6.1   Procedure Control Statements

The act of associating an object with another object often makes new objects visible on the screen. However, just because an object is visible on the screen does not imply that the user can interact with it. The user can only interact with objects when OI is in some kind of loop where it is looking for events to process. In our previous examples, this happens when we call OI_begin_interaction.

In these examples, we build an object tree, associate the top level object (the OI_app_window) with the root, and then call OI_begin_interaction. The act of associating the OI_app_window with the root makes the application window and all its children visible on the display. However, until we call OI_begin_interaction, the user cannot interact with it.

For a more detailed look at the event-processing loop, see Chapter 5, "Initialization, Termination, and Other Independent Functions," and the discussion of OI_begin_interaction and OI_wait_done.

The OI functions which implement event loops so that user events can be processed are:

- OI_begin_interaction
- OI_wait_done
- OI_dialog_box member function wait_button
- OI_entry_field member function wait_done

OI_wait_done is the general mechanism used to process events; the other procedures use OI_wait_done to perform their functions.

2.7   Making Your Own OI and Non-OI Classes

As you first begin to use OI, you will probably use only objects from those classes that OI provides. However, you may find that at some point you will want to create your own classes of objects.

There is no easy way to identify the point at which you should decide to make your own class. Experienced object-oriented programmers may use their own classes for almost everything. Programmers new to C++ will seldom do so. Many tasks can be done without deriving your own classes. However, once you understand class derivations and object oriented programming better, you may find that deriving your own classes makes your programming task easier.

Any time you have additional data you would like to associate with an object, or you have functions to operate on an object, you have a situation in which you should at least consider deriving your own subclass.

For example, if you have an entry field which accepts only hexadecimal numbers as input, you could derive a subclass of OI_entry_field or OI_seq_entry_field which understands hexadecimal input.

As another example, if you have a gauge which is monitoring an external sensor, you could set a time-out to call a function every second and pass the function a pointer to the gauge. You could set the gauge's data pointer to indicate the information necessary to read the proper sensor. Alternately, you could derive your own subclass of gauge which contains the information necessary to identify the sensor, and has member functions for handling the time-out. The constructor for your gauge could set the time-out automatically.

The classes you define may be derived from OI classes, or they may be independent of them. However, if you intend to use member functions for a class as OI callback routines, then the class must use OI_callback as its first base class. Since all of the OI classes already have OI_callback as a base class, any subclass you derive from an OI class automatically has OI_callback as a base class.

When you subclass from an OI class, your subclass will maintain model-dependent aspects. If you follow the procedure described in Chapter 41, "Deriving Your Own Classes," Section 41.3, "Creating a Fully OI-Compliant Subclass," your class will be a "complete" OI class, indistinguishable from those supplied with the toolkit. Chapter 41 also shows examples of subclassing.

2.8   Resource Management

The *X Resource Manager* is a term loosely applied to a collection of Xlib procedures used to merge several ASCII files (one of which is .Xdefaults), a server property (RESOURCE_MANAGER), and values hardcoded by the application to produce a *resource database*, which determines a unique value for each resource of each object or application. The procedures resolve conflicts between multiple settings for the same resource according to their internal precedence rules.

Using the resource manager, you can set properties (resources) for the application at execution time. You can set such items as color, frame width, font, object size, and cursor shape. Almost every aspect of every OI object can be set using resources.

OI fetches resources for each OI object when you parent the object to another object whose top ancestor has already been parented to the root. If the top ancestor has not yet been parented to the root, the resources are fetched when the ancestor is parented to the root. If you reparent an object to a different parent, OI re-fetches resources for the object and its descendants.

Using member functions described in Chapter 6, "OI_d_tech" and Chapter 38, "OI_connection," you can control resource fetching for each object. In your application you can supply default resources which are different from those supplied by OI. You can also specify how resources are converted from the string specification in the resource database to actual data values. The chapters on individual classes describe the resources that each particular class supports.

If you create your own OI subclass, you can specify resources for that subclass which are different from the resources for the class from which it is derived.

For more information on resource control, see Chapter 39, "The OI Resource Mechanism."

2.9   Event Translation Mechanism

OI provides several member functions such as set_click which allow you to specify the behavior of a program when X events, or a sequence of X events, occur. These functions are a convenient interface for many of the most commonly occurring event sequences. The translation mechanism provides similar capabilities, but with a significant advantage—the user can modify the behavior at runtime by specifying additions or changes to the translations you provide as a programmer.

A *translation* consists of a list of X events (*event names*), and a list of procedures to call (*actions*) when those events occur on a particular object. Translations are object-specific. The translations are specified as text strings, and can be set via an X resource. The format is identical to that used by Xt-based toolkits, consisting of event names separated from the actions by a colon.

In OI version 4.0, all objects are driven by translations. This means that much of the interaction between the user and the object, such as the effects of mouse button clicks or press and releases, and many keystrokes are defined through translations and can be changed through the translation mechanism if desired.

For example, the line below specifies a simple translation which calls the procedure "print_file" when "control p" is pressed:

```
ctrl<Key>p:print_file( )
```

In order to use your own translations (ones that are not already known to OI) for a particular object, you must make them known to the translation manager using the OI_d_tech member function push_actions. You may then specify translations for an object by specifying them in a resource file (for example, .Xdefaults) or by using one or more of the following OI_d_tech member functions:

```
set_translations
augment_translations
override_translations
```

An *accelerator* is a translation which specifies a simple keystroke(s) to speed user interaction with an object, and is in effect regardless of whether the object is visible or has the input focus. Typically, accelerators are used to provide keyboard access to functionality otherwise available only in pop-up or pull-down menus. All OI objects allow accelerators. A *mnemonic* is similar to an accelerator except that it only has effect when the object to which it applies is visible.

Accelerators and mnemonics are specified via an X resource, and are handled automatically. Accelerators and mnemonics automatically show up on menu cell labels.

For more information and examples of translations, see Chapter 40, "The OI Translation Mechanism."

Chapter 3
Compiling, Linking, and Executing an OI Program

Compiling, Linking, and Executing an OI Program

3.1   Source File Naming Conventions

C++ compilers usually expect their source files to have one of two extensions: .c or .C. We suggest you use .C for your C++ source files, reserving .c for C source files. Similarly, we suggest you use the extension .H for C++ header files and reserve .h for C header files.

3.2   Compiling and Linking an OI Program

OI programs are compiled using your system's C++ compiler/translator. The procedure will vary depending on your particular type of system and how C++ is installed. The procedures shown below are the ones supplied in "standard" installations of AT&T's C++ on a UNIX system.

In all source files in which you use OI objects, a line of the form

```
#include <OI/oi.H>
```

will suffice to include declarations of OI objects and related member functions. oi.H and the files it references are normally located in /usr/include/OI.

If you are only using a few types of objects, your file will compile faster if you explicitly include only those headers for the classes you are using. The include file names do not correspond exactly to the class names in most cases, due to file name length restrictions on older unix systems. Table 3-1 shows the header files and corresponding class names.

Table 3-1   Class Header File Names

Class	Header File Name
OI_abbr_menu	abrmnu.H
OI_app_window	appwin.H
OI_box	box.H
OI_button_menu	btnmnu.H
OI_callback	callback.H
OI_command_dialog_box	cmddlg.H
OI_connection	connect.H
OI_ctlr_1d	ctlr_1d.H
OI_d_tech	d_tech.H
OI_dialog_box	dlgbox.H

Table 3-1 Class Header File Names

Class	Header File Name
OI_display_1d	dpy_1d.H
OI_entry_field	entfld.H
OI_error_dialog_box	errdlg.H
OI_excl_menu	exmnu.H
OI_excl_check_menu	exchkmnu.H
OI_excl_rect_menu	exrctmnu.H
OI_file_dialog_box	filedlg.H
OI_gauge	gauge.H
OI_glyph	glyph.H
OI_multi_text	mlttxt.H
OI_menu	mnu.H
OI_menu_box	mnubox.H
OI_message_dialog_box	msgdlg.H
OI_panner	panner.H
OI_prompt_dialog_box	pmptdlg.H
OI_paned_box	pnbox.H
OI_poly_menu	pymnu.H
OI_poly_check_menu	pychkmnu.H
OI_poly_rect_menu	pyrctmnu.H
OI_question_dialog_box	quesdlg.H
OI_scroll_bar	scrlbar.H
OI_scroll_box	scrlbox.H
OI_scroll_menu	scrlmnu.H
OI_scroll_text	scrltxt.H

Table 3-1 Class Header File Names

Class	Header File Name
OI_select_dialog_box	seldlg.H
OI_slider	slider.H
OI_seq_entry_field	sqentfld.H
OI_static_text	stattxt.H
OI_warn_dialog_box	warndlg.H
OI_work_dialog_box	workdlg.H

If you have only a few source files, you can compile and link all at once:

```
CC -g main.C sub.C -lOI -lXext -lX11 -o myprog
```

CC invokes the C++ compiler. Use the appropriate compiler command for your installation. **-g** is optional and is used if you are going to use some form of symbolic debugger (for example **dbx** or **pdb**); it causes symbols to be retained for debugging purposes. **-lOI**, **-lXext**, and **-lX11** link the OI and X libraries. The extension library, **Xext**, is used for shaped glyphs. **-o myprog** specifies that the output (executable) file will be named **myprog**. If you omit **-o myprog**, the executable will be named **a.out**. You should always specify a name for the executable rather than using the default, and that name should not include a "." character. The reason for this is that it is not possible to specify resources for any executable whose name contains this character.

The OI library is normally located in **/usr/lib/libOI.***, where * is "a" for a static library, and something different such as ".**so**",".**sa**" or".**sl**" for a dynamic library. These library files usually also have version numbers appended. In any case, "**-lOI -Xext -lX11**" should correctly link your program. Similarly, the X window system library is normally located in **/usr/lib/libX11.*** and **/usr/lib/libXext.***. Since the OI library makes calls to the X library, **-lOI** should always precede **-Xext -lX11**.

Here is a sample makefile which builds any program with the source code in a file *.C. It produces an executable with the same name as the source file, but with no extension:

```
#Makefile for arbitrary OI source in a single file
SUFFIXES: .C
.C: ;    C++ -g $< -lOI -lXext -lX11 -o $*
```

Example 3-1 Makefile for Arbitrary Source in a Single File

If you have a large number of source files, you may want to compile source files independently of the link. The following line compiles **sub.C** and produces an output file with the extension .o:

```
CC -c -g sub.C
```

This produces an object file sub.o, and no executable file. To link many .os into an executable file:

```
CC main.o sub.o -lOI -lXext -lX11 -o myprog
```

3.2.1　Shared Libraries and User-Derived Subclasses

On systems with shared libraries, a separate shared library, libOIreg, is provided in addition to libOI. libOIreg contains a separate copy of a module for the procedure OI_reg_derived_classes. The sole purpose of this extra library is to allow user-derived subclasses to be automatically linked into an application. To do this, you build a new libOIreg which contains a version of OI_reg_derived_classes which calls the class registration functions for the new classes. You must link your application with the dynamic libraries, and you must explicitly link libOIreg ahead of libOI (-lOIreg -lOI). In addition, the end user must have the library search path configured so that your new libOIreg is encountered before the default libOIreg. For example, on SunOS, use:

```
setenv LD_LIBRARY_PATH    /usr/me/lib
```

Your libOIreg must also contain the implementation of the new classes. (On some systems, such as Sun, this last requirement can be circumvented.) In summary, in order to provide your own subclassed objects with a shared library:

- Write the new classes.
- Write a new OI_reg_derived_classes to register the new classes.
- Build a new libOIreg shared library containing the new OI_reg_derived_classes and the new classes themselves.
- Explicitly link libOIreg ahead of libOI.
- Set the environment so the load path includes the new shared library.
- Run the program.

3.3　Running Your Program

Since this is a programmer's guide, not a user's guide, we are not going to explain every detail about how the user interacts with programs that use OI. Objects are manipulated differently depending on the interaction model used. However, there are some usage descriptions in the chapters that deal with displayable OI objects and controls.

Before running your program, you may want to check whether the environment variable OI_LIB is defined. If it is not specifically set, it defaults to /usr/lib/X11. By convention, OI_LIB contains subdirectories for OI applications which contain application-specific information such as help files. In particular, the default help files are located in $OI_LIB/OI.

3.3.1　Command-Line Arguments

There are several command-line arguments that set up and modify your program's attributes when it executes. In the "Hello World" example, you saw how three of them control which interaction and appearance model OI uses. The user may also specify OI attributes via the .Xdefaults file or other X resource database mechanism (see Chapter 39, "The OI Resource Mechanism" and the Resource section in the chapter for each OI class).

When you call OI_init in your program, it processes any command-line arguments that OI understands. OI_init removes these command-line values from argv, and decrements argc by the number of command-line arguments removed. If you need the original values for argc and argv, before any arguments are removed, use the functions OI_command_argc and OI_command_argv.

All programs using OI accept the command-line arguments shown in Table 3-2. You can specify your own command-line options for your application if necessary (see Chapter 39, "The OI Resource Mechanism," Section 39.3.4, "Defining Command Line Options" on page 39-30). You can shorten any of these command line arguments by truncation as long as the result is unambiguous. For example, to run a program named my_app with the X server in synchronous mode, either of the following two lines would work:

```
my_app -synchronous

my_app -sync
```

Table 3-2 Command-Line Arguments

Argument	Companion Argument	Description
-background	*color*	background color
-bd	*color*	border color
-bg	*color*	background color
-bordercolor	*color*	border color
-borderwidth	*number*	border width
-bw	*number*	border width
-config	*file_name*	merge *file_name* into the resource database
-debug		enable protocol error handler*
-display	*host:dpy.scn*	X server to connect to*
-fastdraw		sacrifice appearance for faster drawing*
-font	*font_name*	default text font
-fn	*font_name*	default text font
-foreground	*color*	foreground color
-fg	*color*	foreground colo

Table 3-2 Command-Line Arguments

Argument	Companion Argument	Description
-geometry	*widxht+x+y*	initial size and location*
-icongeometry	*x+y*	initial icon location
-iconic		start in iconic state
-iconX	*x*	initial icon x location*
-iconY	*y*	initial icon y location*
-motif		use the Motif interaction model
-name	*name_string*	name for this instance of program*
-ol		use the most appropriate OPEN LOOK model*
-ol2d		use the 2-D OPEN LOOK model
-ol3d		use the 3-D OPEN LOOK model
-openlook		use the most appropriate OPEN LOOK model*
-openlook_2d		use the 2-D OPEN LOOK model
-openlook_3d		use the 3-D OPEN LOOK model
-reverse		reverse foreground and background colors
-rv		reverse foreground and background colors
-synchronous		put X server in synchronous mode*
-title	*title_string*	title for main window*
-xrm	*'resource_string:value'*	arbitrary resource:value pair, quoted*

*Many of the command-line arguments are self-explanatory; those needing more description are explained below.

-config

> -config specifies a resource specification file to apply to the application. The file is merged into the resource database at the very end, after all other files have been read. (See Section 39.2 on page 39-9 for more information.)

-debug

If -**debug** is specified, any X protocol error or fatal OI error causes an error message to be printed on **stderr** followed by a core dump. Note that running an OI application with a command line of -**debug** is different than compiling with a flag of -**g**. If the command-line argument -**debug** is not specified, the error messages still print when these errors occur, but a core dump is not produced. In addition, specifying -**debug** causes the X server to be synchronized in some parts of the library. This synchronization causes commands to the server to go out to the server as they occur, whereas ordinarily commands are buffered. The synchronization allows you to run a debugger on the same X server to debug the OI program. If commands are buffered, the debugger could be blocked whenever the OI program grabs the pointer or the server.

-display

If -**display** *host:dpy.scn* is specified, the program's display is targeted for machine *host* on the network, on display and screen *dpy.scn*. If this argument is not specified, the display is taken from the environment variable **DISPLAY**, if it exists; otherwise, the display is targeted for the originating host, display and screen using **unix:0.0**.

-fastdraw

If -**fastdraw** is specified, the appearance of objects drawn on the screen will be compromised for faster drawing. This is useful if your program is displaying on an X terminal over an RS232 line or if you have a slow X server.

-geometry

-**geometry** specifies an initial size and location for the main application window. The units for the size and location coordinates specified for -**geometry** are in pixels, in logical root window coordinates. The first **OI_app_window** created is assumed to be the "main" window, and the options are applied to that window only.

This example starts **my_app** with an application window that is 300 pixels wide, 200 pixels tall, at location x=0 (the left side of the screen), and y=500 (500 pixels down from the top of the screen):

```
my_app -geometry 300x200+0+500
```

If no location is given, then the window is placed using the window manager's default placement mechanism:

```
my_app -geometry 300x200
```

This line specifies location only:

```
my_app -geometry +0+500
```

-icongeometry

-**icongeometry** specifies the initial application icon location in pixels, in logical root window coordinates. The format of the argument for -**icongeometry** is the same as for -**geometry**; however, the size components, if present, are ignored.

-iconX

> This argument specifies the x component of -icongeometry.

-iconY

> This argument specifies the y component of -icongeometry.

-name

> If -name *name_string* is specified, *name_string* will be the value of the instance portion of the WM_CLASS property for this instance of the execution of the program. If -title is not also specified, *name_string* will be the value of the WM_NAME property, and will be displayed in the title bar of the main application window (assuming the window manager uses WM_NAME). For more discussion of -name and -title, see OI_init in Chapter 5, "Initialization, Termination, and Other Independent Functions."

-openlook, -ol

> OI will use the OPEN LOOK model for the application. If the monitor is monochrome, the 2-D model is used; if the monitor is color, the 3-D model is used.

-synchronous

> This argument causes OI to force the X server connection into synchronous mode. This drastically slows response time, but makes debugging some aspects of an application much easier. In particular, if you are debugging code which does drawing using Xlib procedure calls, you will be able to see the effect of each call immediately when you step over it. It is also useful to ascertain whether a bug is timing-dependent or not. If the bug can be reproduced when running in synchronous mode, it is most likely not timing dependent.

-title

> If -title *title_string* is specified, the WM_NAME property of the program will have the value *title_string*. *title_string* will be displayed in the title bar of the main application window (assuming the window manager uses WM_NAME). For more discussion of -name and -title, see OI_init in Chapter 5, "Initialization, Termination, and Other Independent Functions."

-xrm

> If -xrm *'resource_string:value'* is specified, the value string is used to set the X resource resource_string in the X resource database.

> Note that you can retrieve X resource strings in your program using the OI_connection and OI_d_tech member functions.

3.3.2   Special Keys

Some OI objects take special notice of certain keys. These keys are used for editing, cursor control, and other such actions. These actions and their default key bindings are described at the end of each chapter in the "Translations" section.

It is possible to redefine the actions each key performs by including translation resources in the .Xdefaults file or other X Resource Database file. This facility is explained in Chapter 40, "The OI Translation Mechanism."

Throughout the book we reference key presses through their functional names, such as the PASTE key. Table 3-4 and Table 3-3 show the default key bindings for different keyboards and their functional names. If you have a different keyboard than these, you can change the default translations to better match your keyboard.

Table 3-3 Motif Default Key Bindings

Functional Name	Sun	HP	IBM	DEC	SGI
CUT	L10 (Cut)	Shift-Delete	Shift-Delete	Shift-Delete	Shift-Delete
COPY	L6 (Copy)	Ctrl-Insert	Ctrl-Insert	Ctrl-Insert	Ctrl-Insert
PASTE	L8 (Paste)	Shift-Insert	Shift-Insert	Shift-Insert	Shift-Insert
HELP	Help or F1 or Mod1 /	Help or F1 or Mod1 /	Help or F1 or Mod1 /	Help or F1 or Mod1 /	Help or F1 or Mod1 /
NEXTTABGROUP	Tab	Tab	Tab	Tab	Tab
PREVTABGROUP	Shift-Tab	Shift-Tab	Shift-Tab	Shift-Tab	Shift-Tab
HOME	R7		Home		Home
END	R13		End		End
PAGEUP	R9	Next	PageUp	Prev Screen	PageUp
PAGEDOWN	R15	Previous	PageDown	Next Screen	PageDown
INSERT	Keypad 0		Insert	InsertHere	Insert
MENUDEFAULT	Control	Control	Control	Control	Control
<Activate main menu>	F10	F10	F10	F10	F10
<Activate popup menu>	F4	F4	F4	F4	F4

Table 3-4 OPEN LOOK Default Key Bindings

Functional Name	Sun	HP	IBM	DEC	SGI
CUT	L10 (Cut)	Shift-Delete	Shift-Delete	Shift-Delete	Shift-Delete
COPY	L6 (Copy)	Ctrl-Insert	Ctrl-Insert	Ctrl-Insert	Ctrl-Insert
PASTE	L8 (Paste)	Shift-Insert	Shift-Insert	Shift-Insert	Shift-Insert
HELP	Help or F1 or Mod1 /	Help or F1 or Mod1 /	Help or F1 or Mod1 /	Help or F1 or Mod1 /	Help or F1 or Mod1 /
NEXTFIELD	Tab	Tab	Tab	Tab	Tab
PREVFIELD	Shift-Tab	Shift-Tab	Shift-Tab	Shift-Tab	Shift-Tab
MENUDEFAULT	Control	Control	Control	Control	Control

3.3.3 Mouse Buttons

The meaning of mouse buttons varies slightly depending on the interaction model you are using. The user can change the default mouse button assignment by using the program **xmodmap**.

Mouse button usage varies depending over which type of object the mouse pointer is positioned (described in the corresponding chapter). The default mouse button assignments are shown in the next two tables:

Table 3-5 Motif Default Mouse Button Assignments

Button	Name	Usage
Left	SELECT	Used to select (highlight) text (cut/copy) and establish the insertion point for entering the text. Also used to make menu selections from menus which are not pop-up menus. Also used to operate sliders, scrollbars, and other objects. Used to activate pull-down menus.
Middle	DRAG	Used to insert previously selected text (paste). Used as a "go to" pointer for scroll bars and sliders.
Right	MENU or CUSTOM	Used to activate and make selections from pop-up menus.

Table 3-6 OPEN LOOK Default Mouse Button Assignments

Button	Name	Usage
Left	SELECT	Used to select (highlight) text (cut/copy) and establish the insertion point for entering the text. Used to make menu selections from menus which are not pull-down or pop-up menus. Also used to operate sliders, scrollbars, and other objects.
Middle	ADJUST	Used to extend a text selection.
Right	MENU	Used to activate and make selections from pull-down and pop-up menus. Used as a "goto" pointer for scroll bars and sliders.

Chapter 4
OI Naming Conventions, Constants, and Types

OI Naming Conventions, Constants and Types

4.1 Naming Conventions

The external symbols used in the OI library all begin with either "OI_" or "oi_". The only exception is the symbol PIXEL. You are free to use all other symbol names, with the exception of symbol names already used by the X Window System (the OI header files include the X header files). Unfortunately, X has a large set of possible names covering all symbols beginning with an upper-case letter, so you must be careful to avoid the numerous potential conflicts.

A consequence of the OI external symbol naming convention is that OI independent functions (which are external symbols) all start with "oi_" or "OI_", whereas OI member functions start with other letters. Thus

```
sp = oi_create_slider(...);
```

is a call to an external function that creates a slider and returns a pointer to the slider, and

```
sp->set_span(100);
```

is a call to an **OI_slider** member function that sets the span of the slider.

You do not need to worry about conflicting with any of the member function names, unless you are deriving your own subclass. This is because any function, structure or variable that you create yourself will not be a member of the OI class, and thus there will be no name conflict.

If you create subclasses of OI objects, potential naming conflicts can occur. OI member function names are all lowercase letters. In addition, those which are made up of more than one word separate the words with an underscore (as in **set_span**, above). You can check your member functions against the OI header files for any possible name conflicts.

4.2 Class Type

The names of all OI classes start with "OI_", for example, **OI_app_window**, **OI_static_text**, **OI_box**. Because all OI functions that create new OI objects return a pointer to the object, you should define your OI objects by their pointers, as shown here:

```
OI_app_window           *wp;
OI_box                  *bp;
```

4.3 Function Typedefs

There are several references throughout this book to functions with names of the form **OI_*_fnp**. These are typedefs for a particular type of function with a particular argument list. Some examples are: **OI_action_fnp**, **OI_help_fnp**, **OI_event_fnp**. These are usually *callback* functions—functions that are to be called when a specified event occurs. They are also usually functions that you must write yourself.

For example, referring back to Program 2-2, "Callbacks to Change Text and Font (Callbacks.C)," on page 2-17, remember that we created an **OI_static_text** and an **OI_entry_field**, and set up the callback function **chng_text** for the entry field so that when the user typed text into the entry field and pressed the Return key, the text in the static text changed to be the entered text.

In this example, every time the user strikes the Return key in the entry field, the function **chng_text** is called. **chng_text** is an **OI_ef_entry_check_fnp**. All **OI_ef_entry_check_fnp**s must be defined to be of the form

```
OI_ef_entry_chk_status <function_name>(
        OI_entry_field              *efp,     // entry field where char was entered
        void                        *argp,    // arbitrary argument
        OI_ef_entry_chk_status stat)          // status from previous call
```

This is a function that you write yourself; in it you perform the actions necessary when the Return key is pressed. You never call this function directly; it is called by OI when the user strikes the Return key. This is why the argument list is so important in callback functions—they must be written to conform exactly to what OI is expecting.

Throughout this book, various callback functions named **OI_*_fnp** are referenced. In each case the expected argument list is specified. When you write your callback function, you must use this argument list.

For some objects, you can specify the name of a callback routine in the call to the create function. For example, here a callback **adj_temp** is specified as a callback for a slider:

```
void            adj_temp(OI_slider*,void*,OI_slider_event,long);
OI_slider       *sp;
OI_entry_field *efp;
efp = oi_create_entry_field("my_field",20,"MY Field");
sp = oi_create_slider("my_slider",150,OI_vertical,max,min,&adj_temp,efp);
```

In this example, if the user moves the position of the slider handle, OI calls the function **adj_temp**.

All callback functions receive an optional argument, *argp*, which you can specify to be whatever you like. In the above slider example, this argument is specified to be *efp*, a pointer to an **OI_entry_field** object.

In some cases you will want to register a member function rather than a free-standing function; this is discussed in the next section.

4.4 C++ Member Function Typedefs

For any function type of **OI_*_fnp**, there is a corresponding member function type **OI_*_memfnp**. These correspond to a particular type of C++ member function with a particular argument list. Some examples are: **OI_action_memfnp**, **OI_help_memfnp**, **OI_event_memfnp**. Just as with the independent functions discussed in the previous section, these are usually *callback* functions—functions that are to be called when a specified event occurs. You must usually write these functions yourself.

If the entry check callback function described in the previous section were a member function, it would be defined to be of the form:

```
OI_ef_entry_chk_status obj_class::<function_name>(
        OI_entry_field   *efp,        // entry field where char was entered
        void             *argp)       // arbitrary argument
```

All the discussion in the previous section applies to these member functions, with the following difference:

When you create an object (say, a slider) and wish to specify a member function rather than an independent function as a callback routine, you specify not only the name of the callback routine in the call to the create function, but also a pointer to the object on whose behalf the callback will be called:

```
void       my_object::adj_temp(OI_slider*,void*,OI_slider_event,long);
OI_slider  *sp;
my_object  *mp;
sp = oi_create_slider("my_slider",50,OI_vertical,
                                 max,min,mp,&my_object::adj_temp);
```

The functions used to specify member function callbacks and independent function callbacks are *overloaded* functions—the compiler determines which one to perform from the parameters used.

4.5   Types and Constants

There are many data structures, enumerated types and constants used throughout OI. You will find definitions of the ones you will need to deal with in the chapter for the class to which that structure, variable or constant applies. They are also listed in the book index by name. However, we list here some types and constants of global interest.

NULL

Defined as 0.

NULL_PMF

Gets around an AT&T C++ 2.00.04 bug when initializing struct fields to a NULL pointer to a member function.

OI_bool

A boolean value. Its value can be one of the constants

OI_yes   true
OI_no   false

OI_yes is non-zero; OI_no is zero.

OI_number

A signed number that fits in 16 bits.

OI_orient

The orientation of an OI object. It can have values

OI_horizontal	Horizontal orientation.
OI_vertical	Vertical orientation.

OI_stat

A status value resulting from a call to an OI function. Values >= 0 are successful; those < 0 are fatal. An OI_stat with a value of OI_ok is 0. For a listing of all possible status values, see Table 5-1 and Table 5-2 on page 5-14.

OI_state

The state of an OI object. You normally specify the state of an object when you parent it to another object. Its state may change during execution of the program. The state of an object can be one of the following:

OI_active	The object is potentially visible (although usually subject to clipping to the parent's boundaries) and can accept input if all of its ancestors are also set to an OI_active state. In order for an object to be visible on the screen, all of its ancestors must be visible (either OI_active or OI_inactive).
OI_inactive	The object is potentially visible but cannot accept input.
OI_not_displayed	The object is not visible and cannot accept input. This is the initial state of all objects.
OI_active_not_displayed	The object is not visible, but can accept input (e.g., a pop-up). Only menus and dialog boxes can have this state.

PIXEL

An unsigned long representing the pixel value corresponding to a particular color.

Chapter 5
Initialization, Termination, and Other Independent Functions

Initialization, Termination, and Other Independent Functions

Initialization, Termination, and Other Independent Functions

All the functions described in this chapter are *free-standing* functions; that is, they are not member functions of any object. It is worthwhile becoming familiar with these routines—some you will use frequently (such as OI_init, OI_begin_interaction, OI_fini), and some provide useful OI functionality dissimilar to any other OI functions (for example, OI_fork).

5.1   Initialization Routines

Before you can perform any other OI function, you must call OI_init.

OI_init   (Free-standing function)

```
OI_connection *OI_init(
    int                 *argcp=NULL,        // pointer to main program argc
    char                **argv=NULL,        // main program argv
    const char          *app_classp=NULL,  // class name for the application
    const char          *app_namp=NULL,    // instance name of application
    XrmOptionDescRec    *app_rmtblp=NULL,  // X resource option table
    int                 app_rmtbl_siz=0)   // number of entries in app_rmtblp
```

OI_init initializes OI and opens a connection to the X server. This must be the first OI function you call in your application. The display station which will be used for input and output is determined by the command-line argument -display if it was used in starting the program. Otherwise, if the environment variable DISPLAY is set, its value is used. If neither of these is specified, OI uses unix:0.0. Both the command-line argument -display and the environment variable DISPLAY are specified in the form name:dsp.scn, where name is "unix" for the workstation on which the process is running or the host name for some other system on the network, dsp is the display number, and scn is the screen number.

OI_init calls the procedure OI_reg_derived_classes to register any subclasses you have created (See Chapter 41, "Deriving Your Own Classes."), OI_reg_layout_methods to register any layout methods you have created, and OI_reg_messages to register application status messages.

OI_init returns a pointer to an OI_connection if it succeeds and NULL if it fails.

argcp points to the argc variable with which the main program was called. Note that this is the address of argc (&argc), not the actual value.

argv is the argv variable with which the main program was called. Any strings which are processed by OI_init are removed from *argcp* and *argv*. Therefore, upon return from OI_init, *argcp* will contain a count of the number of strings remaining in *argv*. For example, suppose your program is started with the following command line:

```
MyApp -display turtle:0.0 -foo
```

After the call to OI_init, *argc* will have been reduced to 2, and *argv* will contain pointers to the strings MyApp (argv[0]) and -foo (argv[1]).

app_classp is a pointer to the class name for this application. If *app_classp* is NULL, it will be replaced by the name with which the program was invoked (that is, argv[0]).

app_namp is a pointer to the name for this particular invocation of the application. It should normally be NULL, unless you want this invocation of the program to have a different name than the one it was started with. If *app_namp* is NULL and the -name command-line argument is present, the name specified by -name is used for *app_namp*. If *app_namp* is NULL and the -name command-line argument is not present, the class name (*app_classp* or argv[0]) is used.

app_classp and *app_namp* are used in setting resources for OI.

The next two arguments, *app_rmtblp* and *app_rmtbl_size*, are used to specify command line options unique to this particular application. The user will also be able to set these options through resources. They are explained more fully in Chapter 39, "The OI Resource Mechanism." If your application has no special command line options, or you do not want the options to be controllable via the X resource manager, you should omit *app_rmtblp* and *app_rmtbl_size*.

Whenever you start a program, it has an *instance name* and a *class name*. These are the name and class, respectively, that the application has for this particular time it is run—this *instance* of the application, or this *invocation* of the application. The instance name and class name are used when OI fetches resources for the application. They are also used, along with the "-title" command line argument, to set the values of the X properties WM_NAME and WM_CLASS. Normally the window manager uses WM_NAME for the text in the title bar of a main window. It may use WM_CLASS to determine the kind of decoration to put on the window.

In the simplest case, you do not supply *app_classp* or *app_namp* in OI_init, you do not set any resources for the application in the X resource database, and you start the program with no command line arguments. In this case, the instance name and the class name are both set to the name used to start the program (to *invoke* the program). For example, if your program is named MyApp, then both the instance name and the class name are set to MyApp. If you use utilities to look at the properties of the X window, WM_NAME will be the title of the application window (the fourth argument in oi_create_app_window), and WM_CLASS will be the instance name followed by the class name, in this case "MyApp MyApp".

The fourth argument in a call to oi_create_app_window is also used to set the default value for the WM_NAME property on an OI_app_window. Also, whenever argv[0] is used as the instance/class name, only the last component of the path name specified is used.

Unless you are writing a window manager, you will probably have little use for the property WM_CLASS. However, in case you need to use it, we include it in this example: the following table shows the value of WM_NAME and WM_CLASS for the main OI_app_window in an application MyApp for various combinations of command line arguments, assuming the program contains the following two lines of code:

```
OI_init(&argc,argv,"MyTest");
wp = oi_create_app_window("main",100,50,"My Title");
```

Application Invocation	Instance Name	Class Name	WM_NAME	WM_CLASS
MyApp	MyApp	MyTest	My Title	MyApp MyTest
MyApp -name foo	foo	MyTest	foo	foo MyTest
MyApp -title bar	MyApp	MyTest	bar	MyApp MyTest
MyApp -name foo -title bar	foo	MyTest	bar	foo MyTest

OI_command_argc

(Free-standing function)

```
int OI_command_argc( )
```

See **OI_command_argv**.

OI_command_argv

(Free-standing function)

```
char **OI_command_argv( )
```

OI_command_argc and **OI_command_argv** return the original values for **argv** and **argc** before any arguments were removed by **OI_init** processing. The zero-th argument (command name) is not included in the argv list. The strings returned by **OI_command_argv** are static, so you should copy them if you are going to modify them.

OI_common_argc

(Free-standing function)

```
int OI_common_argc( )
```

See **OI_common_argv**.

OI_common_argv

(Free-standing function)

```
char **OI_common_argv( )
```

OI_common_argc and **OI_common_argv** return those portions of the original command line which are understood by all OI clients (that is, the ones in the Table 3-2, "Command-Line Arguments" on page 3-5). The zero-th argument (command name) is not included in the argv list. The strings returned by **OI_common_argv** are read-only, so you should copy them if you are going to modify them. If you fork a subprocess, you can use these to pass the forking process's attributes to the new process.

OI_Xt_argc

(Free-standing function)

```
int OI_Xt_argc( )
```

See **OI_Xt_argv**.

OI_Xt_argv

(Free-standing function)

```
char **OI_Xt_argv( )
```

OI_Xt_argc and **OI_Xt_argv** return those portions of the original command line which are understood by all Xt-based clients. The zero-th argument (command name) of argv is not included. The strings returned by **OI_Xt_argv** are read-only, so you should copy them if you are going to modify them.

OI_begin_interaction   (Free-standing function)

```
void OI_begin_interaction( )
```

OI_begin_interaction begins interaction with the user. Before you call **OI_begin_interaction**, you should build the basic object tree for your OI program and parent the top-level objects (such as the main **OI_app_window**) to the root in state **OI_active**. You may use the **OI_d_tech** member function **set_associated_object**, specifying its state to be **OI_active**, or you may use a combination of **set_associated_object** in state **OI_not_displayed** followed at some later point by **set_state(OI_active)**. Your program will accept no input from the user until you call **OI_begin_interaction** (or another routine which allows user interaction such as **wait_button** or **wait_done**). You can call this routine more than once if necessary. (See Example 5-1 on page 5-32 for an example where **OI_begin_interaction** can be called more than once.)

OI_begin_interaction calls **OI_wait_done** to perform its tasks. For a discussion of the actual process, see **OI_wait_done** in Section 5.5.3, "Event Processing," on page 5-25. **OI_begin_interaction** never returns until your program calls **OI_end_interaction**, a fatal error occurs, or the user quits or exits the application using a window manager facility.

5.2   Termination Routines

OI_end_interaction   (Free-standing function)

```
void OI_end_interaction( )
```

OI_end_interaction terminates interaction with the user, causing **OI_begin_interaction** to return. You can call this routine more than once in your program if necessary.

OI_fini   (Free-standing function)

```
void OI_fini( )
```

OI_fini cleans up prior to exit. You should call **OI_fini** before terminating, as it is responsible for closing the connection to the X server.

5.3   Convenience Functions

These functions apply to only one connection and can be used only when your application has no more than one connection. They map to the corresponding member function for the single connection. See Chapter 38, "OI_connection," for additional discussion about single and multiple connections, and for descriptions of the **OI_connection** member functions which correspond to these.

OI_find_obj   (Free-standing function)

```
OI_d_tech *OI_find_obj(
    const XEvent        *ep,             // pointer to X event
    OI_number           n_obj_tree=0,    // number of object trees in obj_forest.
    OI_d_tech           **obj_forest=NULL) // forest of object trees
```

OI_find_obj returns a pointer to the lowest level object under the mouse pointer position defined in the X event *ep*. *Lowest level object* means the object farthest down the object tree which is visible under the mouse pointer.

ep is a pointer to an X event. Typically you receive *ep* as an argument in an OI_event_fnp or OI_event_memfnp callback function that you have set up using the free-standing function OI_dispatch_insert or the OI_connection member function dispatch_insert.

n_obj_tree is the number of object trees in *obj_forest*.

obj_forest is a forest of object trees. It is a vector of pointers to the top-level object in each of the trees in the forest. The object returned by OI_find_obj must be located in one of the object trees passed in *obj_forest*; otherwise OI_find_obj returns NULL.

OI_str_color   (Free-standing function)

```
OI_stat OI_str_color(
    const char          *str,            // color name string
    PIXEL               *pxlp)           // pointer to returned PIXEL value
```

Converts a string representation for a color value (for example, "green") to a PIXEL value.

OI_get_resource   (Free-standing function)

```
OI_bool OI_get_resource(
    const char          *strp,           // resource name
    const char          **typp,          // pointer to type of value returned
    const char          **valp,          // pointer to value returned
    OI_bool             nocase=OI_yes)    // force to lower case
```

OI_get_resource fetches the value of resource *strp* from the OI resource database for this connection. *typp* is backfilled with a string describing the type of value returned, and *valp* is backfilled with the actual value for the resource. If *nocase* is OI_yes, the return value is forced to lower case. OI_get_resource returns OI_yes if it is successful; otherwise it returns OI_no.

OI_call_action_proc   (Free-standing function)

```
OI_bool OI_call_action_proc(
    OI_d_tech              *objp,       // pointer to OI object in which fn_nam is to be invoked
    const char             *fn_nam,     // name of the action routine
    const XEvent           *event,      // contents of event argument passed to fn_nam
    const char *const      *params,     // contents of the params argument passed to fn_nam
    unsigned int           num_params)  // number of entries in params
```

OI_call_action_proc searches for the action routine name *fn_nam* in the translation tables for object *objp*. If it does not find it there, it then searches the action tables for the current default connection. If found, the function is invoked with the specified *objp*, *event* and *params* parameters. OI_call_action_proc returns OI_yes if the function was found and invoked; otherwise it returns OI_no.

OI_dispatch_insert   (Free-standing function)

```
void OI_dispatch_insert(
    Window              win,              // X Window ID
    int                 event_type,       // event type
    unsigned long       event_mask,       // event mask
    OI_event_fnp        fnp,              // pointer to callback function
    void                *argp=NULL,        // arbitrary argument for fnp
    OI_number           psn=-1)           // position in dispatch table


void OI_dispatch_insert(
    Window              win,              // X Window ID
    int                 event_type,       // event type
    unsigned long       event_mask,       // event mask
    OI_callback         *objp,             // memfnp's object
    OI_event_memfnp     memfnp,           // pointer to callback member function
    void                *argp=NULL,        // arbitrary argument for memfnp
    OI_number           psn=-1)           // position in dispatch table


void OI_dispatch_insert(
    Window              win,              // X Window ID
    unsigned long       event_mask,       // event mask
    OI_event_fnp        fnp,              // pointer to callback function
    void                *argp=NULL,        // arbitrary argument for fnp
    OI_number           psn=-1)           // position in dispatch table
```

```
void OI_dispatch_insert(
    Window              win,            // X Window ID
    unsigned long       event_mask,     // event mask
    OI_callback         *objp,          // memfnp's object
    OI_event_memfnp     memfnp,         // pointer to callback member function
    void                *argp=NULL,     // arbitrary argument for memfnp
    OI_number           psn=-1)         // position in dispatch table
```

The **OI_dispatch_insert** functions register a callback function to be invoked whenever the specified event occurs. They insert an entry into the dispatch table for the current default connection. *memfnp* points to a member function for the object pointed to by *objp*. If your click function is a member function, when it is invoked it will be called as if you had written *objp->memfnp*. See Section 2.5, "Callbacks and Event-Driven Programming," on page 2-16, for more explanation.

event_type and *event_mask* are the same arguments that you would use in an XSelectInput Xlib library call. *argp* is optional, and can be any valid expression that can be cast to a pointer. You can use it to pass additional information to the function *fnp* or *memfnp*. *psn* is the position in the dispatch table in which to insert the entry. The default, -1, causes OI to insert the entry in the first available open space. If *psn* specifies a position already occupied in the table, the other entries are moved down to make room for this one.

The first two forms of **OI_dispatch_insert** require the argument *event_type*; the last two do not use this argument. If you use a form with *event_type*, the callback is only be invoked when an event of type *event_type* occurs. If you use a form with no *event_type*, and an event comes in, if the actual type of the event is one which is selected by the event mask, a match is considered to have occurred and the callback is invoked.

Writing the Dispatch Event Callback Function

If the callback function is not a member function, write it in this form:

```
void fn(
        const XEvent    *ep,        // pointer to event
        void            *argp)      // arbitrary argument
```

and if the callback function is a member function, write it in this form:

```
void obj_class::memfn(
        const XEvent    *ep,        // pointer to event
        void            *argp)      // arbitrary argument
```

where *obj_class* is the class of the object whose member function is *memfn*. When your callback function is invoked, *argp* will be the argument specified in the **OI_dispatch_insert** call, and *ep* will be a pointer to the event which has occurred.

OI_dispatch_remove   (Free-standing function)

```
void OI_dispatch_remove(
    Window              win,            // X Window ID
    int                 event_type,     // event type
    unsigned long       event_mask,     // event mask
    OI_event_fnp        fnp,            // pointer to callback function
    void                *argp=NULL)     // arbitrary argument for fnp

void OI_dispatch_remove(
    Window              win,            // X Window ID
    int                 event_type,     // event type
    unsigned long       event_mask,     // event mask
    OI_callback         *objp,          // memfnp's object
    OI_event_memfnp     memfnp,         // pointer to callback member function
    void                *argp=NULL)     // arbitrary argument for memfnp

void OI_dispatch_remove(
    Window              win,            // X Window ID
    unsigned long       event_mask,     // event mask
    OI_event_fnp        fnp,            // pointer to callback function
    void                *argp=NULL)     // arbitrary argument for fnp

void OI_dispatch_remove(
    Window              win,            // X Window ID
    unsigned long       event_mask,     // event mask
    OI_callback         *objp,          // memfnp's object
    OI_event_memfnp     memfnp,         // pointer to callback member function
    void                *argp=NULL)     // arbitrary argument for memfnp
```

OI_dispatch_remove removes an entry from the dispatch table. Arguments are the same as for **OI_dispatch_insert**.

5.4 Error Message Routines

OI maintains an internal global error status called **OI_status**. **OI_status** is ordinarily **OI_ok**, meaning everything is progressing as expected. If an error occurs, OI sets **OI_status** to something other than **OI_ok** and calls **OI_print_error** which can display an error message on **stderr**. In general, if an error message has already been sent to stderr for a given value of **OI_status**, **OI_print_error** does not display it again. See Figure 5-1 on page 5-10 for details on the actions of **OI_print_error**. All OI output to **stderr** occurs through **OI_print_error**.

You can change this default error handling behavior in several ways:

- You can call **OI_print_error** to handle errors you detect. You can send **OI_print_error** a message to display (as one of the arguments) or you can have it print the message associated with the **OI_status** value.

- You can register error callback function(s) using OI_push_stderr to handle error messages in a different way than the default and, if you wish, keep any messages from going to stderr through the return value of the error callback. You can remove any error callback function using OI_pop_stderr.
- You can register your own OI_status values using OI_reg_status. The messages associated with these values will then be printed by OI_print_error when you call OI_print_error with NULL for the *msg* argument (if the error is not handled by your error callbacks). This is a good plan if your application might be used with a language other than the one in which you wrote it (such as English), because the error messages can then be customized by use of the resource ErrorMessage, discussed below.
- By setting the resource ErrorMessage and its sub-resources, you (or the user) can change the wording of OI's default error messages or error messages you register via OI_reg_status. See Section 5.4.1, "Changing Error Messages via Resources," on page 5-14.

OI_print_error   (Free-standing function)

```
void OI_print_error(
    const char      *namp,                  // identifying name
    const char      *msg=NULL,              // message to print
    OI_bool         ignore_sub=OI_yes)      // ignore subsequent errors of same type?
```

OI_print_error handles the display of error messages, according to the following rules:

OI_print_error maintains an internal state which is the global error status (OI_status) at the time of the last call to OI_print_error. A call to OI_print_error is ignored if the current value of OI_status matches the internal state. If *ignore_sub* is OI_yes, the current value of OI_status is saved as the internal state, causing OI to ignore subsequent calls with the same status. Otherwise, the state is forced to OI_ok.

If any error handlers have been registered via OI_push_stderr, they are called in reverse order from the order in which they were pushed (in other words, the most recent push is called first). If one of the pushed error handlers returns a non-zero (true) value, OI_print_error assumes the error handler has processed the error and no further error processing is necessary. None of the remaining pushed error handlers is called, and OI_print_error does not display any message.

If, after calling all error handlers, none has processed the error (they all returned zero), OI_print_error displays *msg* on stderr, identifying it with *namp*, which should identify the object or routine in which the error occurred. If *msg* is NULL, the message associated with the current value of OI_status is used. These rules are shown graphically in Figure 5-1.

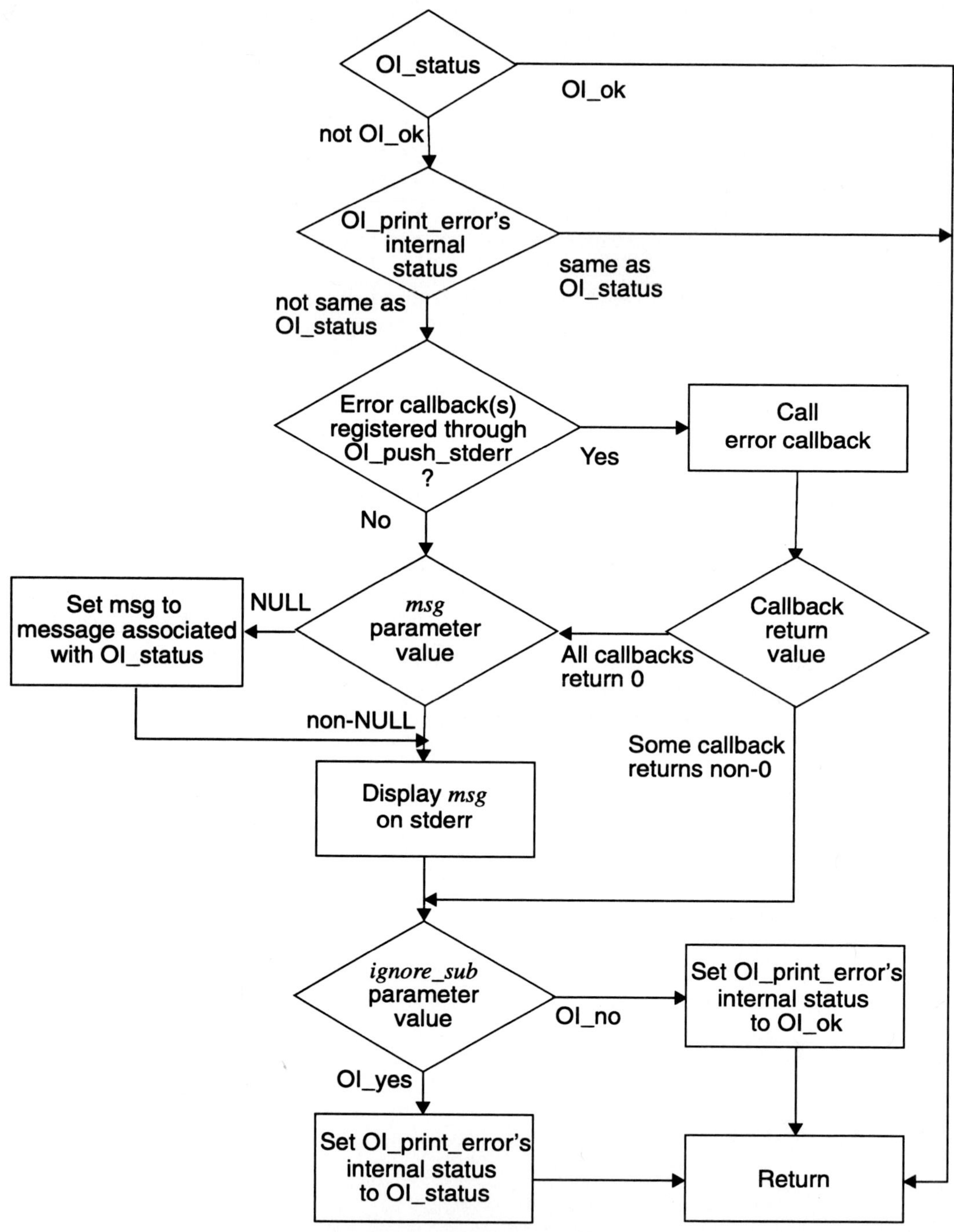

Figure 5-1   OI_print_error Procedure

OI_format_error   (Free-standing function)

```
char *OI_format_error(
   OI_stat              stat,            // OI_status value
   ...)
```

OI_format_error formats an error message corresponding to the error status value *stat*, and returns a pointer to the formatted message. It has a variable-length argument list. The first argument is always an **OI_stat** value. **OI_format** finds the error message corresponding to *stat*, then uses any remaining arguments to substitute for any conversion specifications (such as "%s" or "%d") found in the error message, using the same format conversion specifications as sprintf. Program 5-1 on page 5-12 contains an example of **OI_format_error** usage.

OI_reg_status   (Free-standing function)

```
OI_stat OI_reg_status(
   OI_severity     svr,            // severity level of the status
   const char      *def_msg,       // default message text
   const char      *res_nam)       // resource name for message
```

OI_reg_status registers a status and an error message with OI. *svr* is the severity level of the status and may be any of the following values:

OI_severity_warning	Warning only.
OI_severity_fatal	Fatal error. **OI_print_error** rings the bell if the message goes to **stderr**. If the application is run with the command-line argument -debug, the application aborts.

def_msg is the default message text for the status, which by convention is the same as the name of the variable used to store the returned value. *res_nam* is the resource name for the status. *def_msg* may be a sprintf-style format specification. Program 5-1 shows an example of registering and printing your own status and error messages.

OI_init automatically calls **OI_reg_messages**. You may write a module to replace the empty one supplied by the library, and register your messages there.

```
#include <OI/oi.H>              RegError.C

 main (int argc, char **argv)
 {
         OI_stat              my_stat;
         OI_stat              my_stat_with_args;

     if (OI_init(&argc,argv,"RegError")) {

       // Register error messages so text may be modified via a resource
       my_stat = OI_reg_status(OI_severity_fatal,"My fatal error message",
                       "MyMsg");
       my_stat_with_args = OI_reg_status(OI_severity_warning,
                       "This message has one arg: \"%s\"", "MyMsgWArgs");

       // Set status as if fatal error had occurred and invoke error mechanism
       OI_status = my_stat;
       OI_print_error("RegError");

       // Set status and invoke error mechanism with runtime argument value
       OI_status = my_stat_with_args;
       OI_print_error("RegError", OI_format_error(my_stat_with_args,
                                    "Variable Information"));
       OI_fini( );
     }
 }
```

Program 5-1   Registering Error Statuses and Messages (RegError.C)

When **RegError** is run, the bell rings and these messages appear in the terminal emulator from
which the program was run (if they have not been changed by the resource **ErrorMessage**—see
Section 5.4.1, "Changing Error Messages via Resources," on page 5-14):

```
*** RegError: Error, "My fatal error message"
*** RegError: Warning, This message has one arg: "Variable Information"
```

OI_push_stderr   (Free-standing function)

```
    void OI_push_stderr(
       OI_stderr_fnp          fnp,              // pointer to error callback function
       void                   *argp=NULL)       // arbitrary argument for fnp


    void OI_push_stderr(
       OI_callback            *objp,            // memfnp's object
       OI_stderr_memfnp       memfnp,           // pointer to callback member function
       void                   *argp=NULL)       // arbitrary argument for memfnp
```

The **OI_push_stderr** functions register a callback function to be invoked whenever a message
is ready to go out to **stderr**. The error function so registered is only called during execution of
OI_print_error. You can write the error function to augment or circumvent OI's default error
processing. If your error function is a member function, when it is invoked it will be called as

if you had written *objp->memfnp*. See Section 2.5, "Callbacks and Event-Driven Programming," on page 2-16, for more explanation.

argp is optional, and can be any valid expression that can be cast to a pointer. You can use it to pass additional information to the function *fnp* or *memfnp*.

Writing the Error Callback Function

If the callback function is not a member function, write it in this form:

```
int fn(
            const char          *msg,        // error message
            void                *argp,       // arbitrary argument
            OI_stat             stat)        // current OI_status value
```

and if the callback function is a member function, write it in this form:

```
int obj_class::memfn(
            const char          *msg,        // error message
            void                *argp,       // arbitrary argument
            OI_stat             stat)        // current OI_status value
```

where *obj_class* is the class of the object whose member function is *memfn*. When your callback function is invoked, *msg* will be the *msg* argument with which OI_print_error was called, unless it was NULL, in which case *msg* will be the error message associated with *stat*. *stat* will be the current OI_status value, and *argp* will be the argument specified in the OI_push_stderr call.

Write the callback function to return non-zero if you want OI_print_error to discontinue processing for this error (that is, not to call any other registered error callback function, and not to display any message to stderr). Return zero if you want OI_print_error to call any remaining error callback functions, and if none returns non-zero, to display the message on stderr.

OI_pop_stderr   (Free-standing function)

```
void OI_pop_stderr(
    OI_stderr_fnp           fnp,            // pointer to error callback function
    void                    *argp=NULL)     // arbitrary argument for fnp
```

```
void OI_pop_stderr(
    OI_callback             *objp,          // memfnp's object
    OI_stderr_memfnp        memfnp,         // pointer to member callback function
    void                    *argp=NULL)     // arbitrary argument for memfnp
```

OI_pop_stderr removes an error callback previously registered using OI_push_stderr. The arguments are the same as for OI_push_stderr. All of the arguments must match the corresponding arguments used in OI_push_stderr in order for an entry to be removed. This is not a "pop" in the true sense of the word, since even though error callbacks are pushed on a stack, and are called in the order of that stack, you can remove any error callback via OI_pop_stderr, leaving all other callbacks on the error stack without disturbing their order.

5.4.1   Changing Error Messages via Resources

As mentioned above, you can change the default error messages using the resource **ErrorMessage** and the error status resource name. The third argument to **OI_reg_status** is the resource name to use for the error message. OI uses **OI_reg_status** to register error statuses and default messages, so you can use resources to change both OI's default error messages and any you register yourself using **OI_reg_status**. If you change an error message which contains sprintf format specifications (%s or %d), your message must contain the same number and type of format specifications. They must be in the same order as the original message, or you may change the order if you use the **sprintf**-style argument number specifications designed for this purpose.

For example, if you wanted to change the message for **OI_no_file** (see Table 5-2, below) for the application **MyApp**, you could put the following line in your **.Xdefaults** file or in the application defaults file, or in a language override file for the application:

```
MyApp*ErrorMessage.OI_no_file:      "Put the file \"%s\" in your home directory"
```

If you put the following line in your **.Xdefaults** file:

```
*ErrorMessage.MyMsg:                "New Error Message"
```

and then run Program 5-1 (on page 5-12), you get the following output

```
*** RegError: Error, "New Error Message"
*** RegError: Warning, This message has one arg: "Variable Information"
```

5.4.2   Error Status Values and Messages

The error values shown in Table 5-1 and Table 5-2 are possible values of **OI_status** and also of any function that returns an **OI_stat** value. If a function returns an **OI_stat**, **OI_status** usually has the same value. However, any OI routine can change the value of **OI_status**, regardless of its return type or value.

Table 5-1 OI_severity_warning Error Statuses

Error status value	Corresponding message
OI_bad_ef_def_size	Default entry_field string longer than field size
OI_bad_ef_max_size	Entry_field maximum size less than display size
OI_bad_font	Unable to load font: \"%s\"
OI_bad_layout	Invalid layout method
OI_bad_pix_data	Pixmap data bad
OI_bad_pix_file	Pixmap file bad
OI_conflicting_callback	Callback %s of type %s (%s) conflicts with existing callback of type %s (%s)

Table 5-1 OI_severity_warning Error Statuses

Error status value	Corresponding message
OI_convert_failed	Failed to convert \"%s\", of type \"%s\"
OI_file_not_found	file \"%s\" not found
OI_help_bad_link	Hypertext help link invalid: \"%s\"
OI_help_no_file	Help file \"%s\" not found or unreadable
OI_help_no_topic	Help topic \"%s\" not found in file \"%s\"
OI_help_too_long	Hypertext help line too long: \"%s\"
OI_invalid_resource_value	Resource \"%s\" for object %s has invalid value \"%s\"
OI_layout_bad_state	state OI_active_not_displayed invalid in layout_associated_object
OI_lm_already_defined	Layout method %s already defined
OI_lm_base_not_layout	Layout method %s, base class %s not a layout method
OI_lm_base_undefined	Layout method %s, base class %s not registered
OI_no_color	Can't allocate color
OI_no_converter	No converter for \"%s\" to \"%s\"
OI_no_layout_set	No layout set on parent
OI_obsolete_resource	Resource \"%s\", has been obsoleted
OI_unknown_object	Unable to create an object of type %s named %s

Table 5-2 OI_severity_fatal Error Statuses

Error status value	Corresponding message
OI_bad_association	invalid association
OI_bad_base_class	base class \"%s\" is not registered
OI_bad_callback	invalid callback type, can't be decoded
OI_bad_cell	cell information is invalid
OI_bad_class	unregistered class for variable \"%s\"

Table 5-2 OI_severity_fatal Error Statuses

Error status value	Corresponding message
OI_bad_class_init	unable to initialize class
OI_bad_create	cannot create X window for object
OI_bad_location	specified location is invalid
OI_bad_menu	invalid / inappropriate menu type
OI_bad_model	invalid interaction model
OI_bad_object	invalid or unknown object
OI_bad_op	invalid operation for object of this type
OI_bad_resource	resource not found
OI_bad_scroll_comb	invalid combination of scroll_bars, panners, and objects to scroll
OI_bad_size	invalid size
OI_bad_state	invalid state
OI_bad_subobject	desired subobject does not exist
OI_bad_sys_time	your eval period has expired
OI_bad_trigger	invalid button number for menu trigger
OI_bad_value	invalid value for object
OI_cell_firing	cannot fire cell when another cell in same menu already firing
OI_constructor_failure	constructor for object failed
OI_expired	your evaluation period has expired
OI_fork_failed	fork failed - OI_fork_stat contains wait(3) status
OI_no_app_window	no enclosing application window exists
OI_no_char	character does not exist
OI_no_child_close_x	child process cannot disinherit X connection
OI_no_connect	cannot connect to X server
OI_no_file	file \"%s\" not found

Table 5-2 OI_severity_fatal Error Statuses

Error status value	Corresponding message
OI_no_line	line does not exist
OI_no_mem	insufficient dynamic memory
OI_no_move	move not allowed for object
OI_no_resize	resize not allowed
OI_no_unsel	menu does not allow deselection
OI_not_same_root	object and intended parent are not on same root window
OI_obj_inactive	object is inactive, can't be activated
OI_objsetup_failure	Unable to build object (%s) of type (%s)
OI_wl_bad_op	invalid operation for windowless object

5.5 Other Independent Routines

5.5.1 Timing Routines

There are certain classes of programs which need to perform some action at periodic intervals, even if the user is not actively doing anything with the program. For example, a clock needs to update its display periodically; a mail reader may need to check for newly-arrived mail. Use the timing routines described below for this purpose. In particular, you should use them in preference to system signals (interrupts), since a signal can occur at any time, and the OI toolkit is likely to be in an indeterminate state when a signal occurs. If you make calls to the OI library from within a signal handler, it is quite likely that the program state would become hopelessly garbled and eventually corrupt data or crash. Using the timing routines insures that the state of the OI toolkit continues to be consistent.

An idle timeout function (one registered by OI_add_timeout) is executed when OI has been idle for *ms* milliseconds. A wall timeout function (one registered by OI_add_wall_timeout) is executed every *ms* milliseconds, unless OI is in an unstable state. The timeout will then be delayed until OI is in a stable state.

Both wall timeouts and idle timeouts are repeating. You may mix idle and wall timeouts. A fast wall timeout will not prevent slower idle timeouts from occurring. The presence of wall timeouts may cause some idle timeouts to happen faster and with more regularity than they would without the wall timeout because they are then reached whenever any type of timeout callback happens, rather than just when an idle timeout is called. For example, if you have only set a five-second idle timeout, it will be triggered only after OI has been idle for five consecutive seconds. If you have set a one-second wall timeout as well, the idle timeout will be triggered after five one-second idle periods.

You can also register another type of callback function—one which gets executed as soon as, and whenever, OI has nothing else to do. This is an idle callback (not to be confused with an idle timeout callback) and is registered by OI_add_idle.

OI_add_timeout   (Free-standing function)

```
void OI_add_timeout(
    long                    ms,             // time out period in milliseconds
    OI_timeout_fnp          fnp,            // pointer to timeout callback function
    void                    *argp=NULL)     // arbitrary argument for fnp


void OI_add_timeout(
    long                    ms,             // time out period in milliseconds
    OI_callback             *objp,          // memfnp's object
    OI_timeout_memfnp       memfnp,         // pointer to callback member function
    void                    *argp=NULL)     // arbitrary argument for memfnp
```

The **OI_add_timeout** functions register a callback function to be invoked whenever no OI activity has occurred for *ms* milliseconds. The timeout will repeat each time OI is idle for *ms* milliseconds until you delete the timeout using OI_delete_timeout. If your timeout function is a member function, when it is invoked it will be called as if you had written *objp->memfnp*. See Section 2.5, "Callbacks and Event-Driven Programming," on page 2-16, for more explanation.

ms is the period of time in milliseconds. If no activity has occurred after *ms* milliseconds, the callback function is performed. *argp* is optional, and can be any valid expression that can be cast to a pointer. You can use it to pass additional information to the function *fnp* or *memfnp*.

Writing the Timeout Callback Function

If the callback function is not a member function, write it in this form:

```
void fn(
        void                    *argp)          // arbitrary argument
```

and if the callback function is a member function, write it in this form:

```
void obj_class::memfn(
        void                    *argp)          // arbitrary argument
```

where *obj_class* is the class of the object whose member function is *memfn*. When your callback function is invoked, *argp* will be the argument specified in the OI_add_timeout call.

The callback will be executed each time there is no activity for *ms* milliseconds; you must use OI_delete_timeout to remove it. You may add as many timeouts with different time intervals as you need. Note, however, that timeouts have a granularity of the shortest interval. For example, suppose you register a timeout for 4 seconds and another for 10 seconds. Because the shortest interval of the two timeouts is 4 seconds, each timeout will occur at multiples of 4 seconds. In other words, the 10-second timeout will be called after 12 seconds (4 seconds*3) have elapsed, not 10 seconds.

For the purposes of this timeout callback function, inactivity means a period during which no X events are processed, and no file I/O is waiting to be processed due to **OI_io_dispatch_insert** callback function registrations (see below). In other words, the program has been blocked due to no activity.

Program 5-2 shows a call to **OI_add_timeout** which registers the callback **nothing_happened** to be called if no activity has occurred for 600 milliseconds. The entry field exists in this program only to allow the user to provide some activity. If you run this program and do nothing, every 600 milliseconds the message "Nothing has happened" will appear on the terminal emulator from which you ran the program. If any activity at all occurs in the application, the message will not appear. *Activity* here means typing any key while the mouse is in the entry field, clicking any button of the mouse while it is in the entry field, moving the mouse into and out of the entry field or the application window, or covering and uncovering the application, causing it to repaint.

```
#include <OI/oi.H>                          /* TimeOut.C */

int main(int argc, char **argv)
{
        void                    nothing_happened(void*);

        OI_connection           *conp;
        OI_app_window           *wp;
        OI_entry_field          *efp;

    if (conp = OI_init(&argc,argv,"This is app_classp","This is app_namp")) {
        wp = oi_create_app_window("main",1,1,"TimeOut Demo");
        wp->set_layout(OI_layout_row);

        efp = oi_create_entry_field("entry_field",15,"Enter Text Here!");
        efp->layout_associated_object(wp,2,1,OI_active);

        OI_add_timeout(600,nothing_happened);
        wp->set_associated_object(wp->root( ),OI_def_loc,OI_def_loc,OI_active);
        OI_begin_interaction( );
        OI_fini( );
    }
}

void    nothing_happened(void*)
{
    printf("Nothing has happened\n");
    return;
}
```

Program 5-2 Timeout Example (TimeOut.C)

OI_delete_timeout   (Free-standing function)

```
void OI_delete_timeout(
    OI_timeout_fnp          fnp,            // pointer to callback function
    void                    *argp=NULL)     // arbitrary argument for fnp


void OI_delete_timeout(
    OI_callback             *objp,          // memfnp's object
    OI_timeout_memfnp       memfnp,         // pointer to member callback function
    void                    *argp=NULL)     // arbitrary argument for memfnp
```

OI_delete_timeout removes a timeout previously added using **OI_add_timeout**. The arguments are the same as for **OI_add_timeout**. All of the arguments must match the corresponding arguments used in **OI_add_timeout** in order for an entry to be removed.

OI_add_wall_timeout   (Free-standing function)

```
void OI_add_wall_timeout(
    long                    ms,             // time out period in milliseconds
    OI_timeout_fnp          fnp,            // pointer to timeout callback function
    void                    *argp=NULL)     // arbitrary argument for fnp


void OI_add_timeout(
    long                    ms,             // time out period in milliseconds
    OI_callback             *objp,          // memfnp's object
    OI_timeout_memfnp       memfnp,         // pointer to callback member function
    void                    *argp=NULL)     // arbitrary argument for memfnp
```

The **OI_add_wall_timeout** functions register a callback function to be invoked every *ms* milliseconds, unless OI is in an unstable state. The timeout will then be delayed until OI is in a stable state. In other words, OI calls a wall timeout registered for *ms* milliseconds as soon as both *ms* milliseconds have passed and OI is in a stable state. The timeout will repeat each *ms* milliseconds until you delete the timeout using **OI_delete_wall_timeout**.

If OI is executing a long callback you have written or is waiting in an **OI_fork** call, a wall timeout may be delayed.

Wall timeouts are implemented in the event loop of OI and do not use signals. Their granularity is as fine as your system can return in **gettimeofday**. This is typically 10-20ms. Using wall timeouts will cause more system calls to be made in OI's main event loop. Too many wall timeouts may make the interactive response time of the application feel sluggish.

All arguments and the writing of the timeout callback function are identical to those for **OI_add_timeout**.

OI_delete_wall_timeout   (Free-standing function)

```
void OI_delete_wall_timeout(
    OI_timeout_fnp fnp,                 // pointer to callback function
    void *argp=NULL)                    // arbitrary argument for fnp


void OI_delete_wall_timeout(
    OI_callback          *objp,         // memfnp's object
    OI_timeout_memfnp    memfnp,        // pointer to member callback function
    void                 *argp=NULL)    // arbitrary argument for memfnp
```

OI_delete_wall_timeout removes a timeout previously added using **OI_add_wall_timeout**. The arguments are the same as for **OI_add_wall_timeout**. All of the arguments must match the corresponding arguments used in **OI_add_wall_timeout** in order for an entry to be removed.

OI_add_idle   (Free-standing function)

```
void OI_add_idle(
    OI_timeout_fnp       fnp,           // pointer to idle callback function
    void                 *argp=NULL)    // arbitrary argument for fnp


void OI_add_idle(
    OI_callback          *objp,         // memfnp's object
    OI_timeout_memfnp    memfnp,        // pointer to callback member function
    void                 *argp=NULL)    // arbitrary argument for memfnp
```

The **OI_add_idle** functions register a callback function to be invoked whenever OI has nothing else to do. It is called once, and not called again until OI becomes non-idle, then becomes idle again. In this context, OI is considered *non-idle* only when an I/O callback occurs, that is, one which you have registered via **OI_io_dispatch_insert**. In addition, deleting the idle callback and reinserting it will reset the interval state so the idle callback will fire the next time OI has nothing to do. The arguments and the writing of the idle callback function are identical to those for **OI_add_timeout**. *fnp* or *memfnp* will replace any previously registered idle callback.

OI_delete_idle   (Free-standing function)

```
void OI_delete_idle( )
```

OI_delete_idle removes a timeout previously added using **OI_add_idle**.

5.5.2   Communicating with the Outside World

Event-driven X programs pose some difficulties when you need to process input and output asynchronously as well as the X events. If your program is blocked due to no X activity, it would never wake up to process the outside (non-X) I/O. Similarly, if it is blocked due to no outside I/O (for example, a device **read** procedure call), the user would not be able to interact with the program until the read procedure returned. To solve this problem, you inform OI of the file descriptors you are interested in, and it arranges to make callbacks to you so you can read/write the files when necessary. In this manner, OI can monitor all I/O events, including X events, to ensure that blocking on one channel does not prevent processing on another.

OI_io_dispatch_insert   (Free-standing function)

```
OI_stat OI_io_dispatch_insert(
    int             fd,              // file descriptor
    int             mask,            // I/O type
    OI_io_fnp       fnp,             // pointer to callback function
    void            *argp=NULL)      // arbitrary argument for fnp


OI_stat OI_io_dispatch_insert(
    int             fd,              // file descriptor
    int             mask,            // I/O type
    OI_callback     *objp,           // memfnp's object
    OI_io_memfnp    memfnp,          // pointer to callback member function
    void            *argp=NULL)      // arbitrary argument for memfnp
```

The **OI_io_dispatch_insert** functions register a callback function to be invoked whenever I/O is ready on a file descriptor *fd*. If your I/O callback function is a member function, when it is invoked it will be called as if you had written *objp->memfnp* See Section 2.5, "Callbacks and Event-Driven Programming," on page 2-16, for more explanation.

fd is the file descriptor in whose I/O events you are interested. *mask* is a boolean combination of the constants **OI_user_input**, **OI_user_output**, and **OI_user_except** which indicates the type of I/O you are interested in—input, output or exceptions. *argp* is optional, and can be any valid expression that can be cast to a pointer. You can use it to pass additional information to the function *fnp* or *memfnp*.

Writing the I/O Callback Function

If the callback function is not a member function, write it in this form:

```
int fn(
        int fd,                      // fd of interest
        void *argp)                  // arbitrary argument
```

and if the callback function is a member function, write it in this form:

```
int obj_class::memfn(
        int fd,                      // fd of interest
        void *argp)                  // arbitrary argument
```

where *obj_class* is the class of the object whose member function is *memfn*. When your callback function is invoked, *argp* will be the argument specified in the **OI_io_dispatch_insert** call.

The return value of the function is currently not used. We recommend always returning a value of 1 for compatibility with possible future enhancements.

You may register separate callback routines for each of the three types of I/O on a single file descriptor, or you may register a single callback routine for a combination of types.

Program 5-3 shows a simple use for OI_io_dispatch_insert. This program makes an application window with an entry field. The user types a file name in the entry field. The callback for the entry field opens the file and registers an I/O callback, input_ready. input_ready reads a record from the file and prints it. If an end-of-file is detected, input_ready removes the I/O dispatch table entry and closes the file.

```
#include <OI/oi.H>                              /* IODispatch.C */
int main(int argc, char **argv)
{
        OI_ef_entry_chk_status open_file(OI_entry_field*,void*,
                                                OI_ef_entry_chk_status);
        OI_connection           *conp;
        OI_app_window           *wp;
        OI_entry_field          *efp;
    if (conp = OI_init(&argc,argv,"IODispatch")) {
        wp = oi_create_app_window("main",200,100,"I/O Callbacks");
        wp->set_layout(OI_layout_row);
        efp = oi_create_entry_field("file_name",16,"Enter File Name: ",NULL,200);
        efp->set_entry_check(open_file);
        efp->layout_associated_object(wp,1,1,OI_active);
        wp->set_associated_object(wp->root( ),OI_def_loc,OI_def_loc,OI_active);
        OI_begin_interaction( );
        OI_fini( );
    }
}


int input_ready(int fd, void *argp)
{
        FILE                    *filep;
        char                    buf[513];
    filep = (FILE*) argp;
    if(fgets(buf,sizeof(buf),filep))
        printf("Record read: %s\n",buf);
    else {
        OI_io_dispatch_remove(fd,OI_user_input);
        fclose(filep);
    }
    return(1);
}
OI_ef_entry_chk_status
open_file(OI_entry_field *efp,void*, OI_ef_entry_chk_status stat)
{
        int                     input_ready(int,void*);
        FILE                    *filep;
        int                     fd;
        OI_ef_entry_chk_status ret_val;
    ret_val = OI_ef_entry_chk_bad;
    if (stat == OI_ef_entry_chk_ok) {
    filep = fopen(efp->part_text( ),"r");
        if (filep) {
            fd = fileno(filep);
            OI_io_dispatch_insert(fd,OI_user_input,&input_ready,(void*)filep);
            ret_val = OI_ef_entry_chk_ok;
        }
    }
    return(ret_val);
}
```

Program 5-3 I/O Dispatch Example (IODispatch.C)

OI_io_dispatch_remove   (Free-standing function)

```
void OI_io_dispatch_remove(
    int               fd,              // file descriptor
    int               mask)            // I/O type
```

OI_io_dispatch_remove removes an entry inserted using **OI_io_dispatch_insert**. *fd* and *mask* must match the arguments used to insert the entry.

OI_fork   (Free-standing function)

```
void OI_fork(
    const char        *argp)           // command string
```

OI_fork (and **OI_fork_nowait**, see below) forks a new process and executes a user command from within an OI application. **OI_fork** waits until the process terminates before returning. *argp* is the command string that specifies the process to be started by **OI_fork**.

For a way to build a UNIX command that can be forked, see Section 6.17, "Forming a UNIX Command," on page 6-112.

Two member functions, **fork** and **fork_nowait**, are specific to an **OI_dialog_box**, and are meant to fork a command based on the contents of the dialog box (See Chapter 18, "OI_dialog_box").

OI_fork_nowait   (Free-standing function)

```
int OI_fork_nowait(
    const char        *argp)           // command string
```

OI_fork_nowait is identical to **OI_fork** (above), except that it returns immediately without waiting until the process terminates. **OI_fork_nowait** returns the process ID of the forked process.

5.5.3   Event Processing

You will rarely use the control functions discussed below except in special circumstances. Mostly they are used internally by OI itself; for example, **OI_wait_done** is used to implement **OI_begin_interaction** and the **OI_dialog_box** member function **wait_button**.

OI_wait_done   (Free-standing function)

```
void OI_wait_done(
    OI_bool           *flagp)          // control flag
```

OI_wait_done allows processing to occur until *flagp* is **OI_no**, a fatal error occurs, or you call **OI_end_interaction**. *flagp* is a pointer to a boolean flag. It is set to **OI_yes** immediately after entry into **OI_wait_done**, after which the flag is never modified by OI. Consequently, a call to **OI_wait_done** will never return unless your program specifically sets the flag to **OI_no** at some point, a fatal error occurs, or you call **OI_end_interaction**.

OI_wait_done processes input in the following order:

OI_wait_done issues a **select** system call to find out which file descriptors are ready for I/O to be processed. If any X Window System I/O is waiting, it is processed. If you have registered an interest in any other file descriptors (*fds*) (using OI_io_dispatch_insert) and those *fds* are ready for I/O, your procedure is called to process the I/O. Finally, if no I/O or X events were processed and if any time-out has expired, it is processed. This procedure is diagrammed in Figure 5-2.

```
While still interacting and flag is true:
    If X Event to process:
        Process it (this may mean calling one of your callbacks).
    Else:
        For each I/O stream:
            If I/O event to process:
                Process it (this includes calling one of your callbacks).
                Reset idle pending.
        For each time-out added via OI_add_timeout:
            If time-out expired:
                Process it (this may include calling one of your callbacks).
        If no I/O or XEvents processed:
            If idle time-out exists and idle pending:
                Process it (this may include calling one of your callbacks).
                Reset idle pending.
        Else:
            For each wall clock time-out:
                If time-out expired
                    Process it (this may include calling one of your callbacks).
```

Figure 5-2 OI_wait_done Procedure Description

Note that if any of the callbacks in Figure 5-2 takes a long time to complete (say, 10 minutes), no other user interaction can occur during your callback execution, unless your callback recursively calls OI_wait_done.

OI_flush   (Free-standing function)

```
void OI_flush( )
```

OI_flush flushes the output buffer to the X server and processes all pending events to update the display. For example, if you set a multi-text object to display the contents of a file, then proceed with intensive processing, you might want to call this routine at some point to ensure that the display is updated.

OI_handle_event   (Free-standing function)

```
void OI_handle_event(
    const XEvent        *ep)              // pointer to X event
```

OI_handle_event matches an X event with its dispatch table entries and calls the procedures registered for it. For each procedure, the event is passed as the first argument, and an optional user argument is passed as the second argument. See **OI_dispatch_insert** for information on setting up dispatch table entries.

OI maintains a dispatch table describing X windows and the procedures that are to be called when events of various types occur for the windows. When using OI, all X events are normally fielded (received) by an OI function such as **OI_wait_done**. These functions use **OI_handle_event** to cause the events to be processed.

You will not normally need to use **OI_handle_event** unless you are writing your own custom version of **OI_wait_done**.

OI_next_event   (Free-standing function)

```
OI_bool OI_next_event(
    XEvent                  *ep)          // pointer to X event
```

OI_next_event backfills *ep* with pointer to the next X event. The "next event" is the X event at the head of the event queue. You should use **OI_next_event** instead of XNextEvent so I/O and timer dispatching will occur when no X events are available. **OI_next_event** returns an **OI_bool** indicating whether or not a valid X event has been backfilled into *ep*.

OI_event_loop   (Free-standing function)

```
void OI_event_loop(
    OI_bool                 *flagp)       // control flag
```

OI_event_loop is the actual while-loop used by **OI_wait_done** (and consequently, **OI_begin_interaction**) to process X events, I/O events, and time-out events. It calls the procedure **OI_next_event** to get the next X event or process the next I/O or time-out event. **OI_event_loop** is provided in a separate object file so that you can override it if necessary. For example, you may need to query some conditions between each event processing step, modify I/O queues, etc. *flagp* is the argument passed to **OI_wait_done**. The actual loop looks like this:

```
#include <OI/defs.H>
#include <OI/globals.H>
#include <OI/functs.H>
#include <OI/private.H>
#include <OI/evlpstk.H>

void OI_event_loop (
    OI_bool                      *flagp)              // process as long as flag is true

        XEvent                   event;

    OI_event_loop_stkp->push(flagp);
    while (OI_dialog_active && OI_max_fd) {
        // Loop through all outstanding wait flags
        // If any have cleared, force ours clear and terminate
        if (OI_event_loop_stkp->validate()) {
            if (OI_next_event(&event))
                            OI_handle_event(&event);
        }
        else
            break ;
    }
    OI_event_loop_stkp->pop();
    return;
}
```

5.5.4   Action Functions and Translation Tables

You will only need these functions if you are registering your own action functions to be used in
translations or if you are registering your own translations for an object. Several of the functions
listed here use a pointer to an array of **OI_actions_rec** structures. An **OI_actions_rec** structure
looks like this:

```
struct OI_actions_rec {
    char                      *string;    // function name
    OI_translation_fnp        proc;       // free-standing function
    OI_callback               *objp;      // pointer to object if memfnp is used
    OI_translation_memfnp     memfnp;     // member function
};
```

See Chapter 40, "The OI Translation Mechanism" for more information, and an explanation of
the use of these functions.

OI_add_actions   (Free-standing function)

```
void OI_add_actions(
    OI_actions_rec     *act_fns,      // list of action function names and addresses
    unsigned int       count)         // number of action functions in act_fns
```

OI_add_actions informs OI that the *count* action functions specified in the structure pointed
to by *act_fns* are available for use in translations for any object on the default connection. You

should use OI_add_actions only if your application has only one connection, otherwise you should use the OI_connection function add_actions (below).

OI_compile_action_table   (Free-standing function)

```
OI_compiled_action_table OI_compile_action_table(
    OI_actions_rec      *act_fns,        // list of action function names and addresses
    unsigned int        count)           // number of action functions in act_fns
```

OI_compile_action_table "compiles" the *count* items in the action table specified by *act_fns* to an OI internal form. It does not register them; you must use OI_add_actions or an OI_d_tech or OI_connection member function to do this.

OI_parse_translation_table   (Free-standing function)

```
OI_translation_table *OI_parse_translation_table(
    const char          *trns)          // character representation of the translation table
```

OI_parse_translation_table changes the translation table *trns* from character form to OI's internal form. See Example 41-3 on page 41-14 for an example using OI_parse_translation_table.

5.5.5   Registering Your Own Layout Methods, Status Messages, Subclasses

These routines are empty procedures by default. You can override them with your own version which will be called when OI is initialized (when you call OI_init). They provide a central place for you to register your own classes, layout methods, and error messages.

OI_reg_layout_methods   (Free-standing function)

```
void OI_reg_layout_methods( )
```

OI_init automatically calls OI_reg_layout_methods. You may write a module to replace the empty one supplied by the library, and register your layout methods there.

OI_reg_messages   (Free-standing function)

```
void OI_reg_messages( )
```

OI_init automatically calls OI_reg_messages. You may write a module to replace the empty one supplied by the library, and register your messages there.

OI_reg_derived_classes   (Free-standing function)

```
void OI_reg_derived_classes( )
```

OI_init automatically calls OI_reg_derived_classes. You may write a module to replace the empty one supplied by the library, and register your layout methods there. See Chapter 41, "Deriving Your Own Classes."

5.5.6　Miscellaneous Functions

OI_count   (Free-standing function)

```
int OI_count(
    array pointer      arrp)          // pointer to array whose elements are to
                                      be counted
```

OI_count is a macro which returns the number of elements within an array at compile time. *arrp* can be a pointer to any type of array. The value returned is equivalent to (sizeof(*arrp*)/sizeof(*arrp*[0])).

OI_translate_filename   (Free-standing function)

```
char *OI_translate_filename(
    const char         *filename)     // file name to translate
```

OI_translate_filename translates *filename* into an equivalent full pathname. This means that any environment variable or '~' which appears at the beginning of *filename* will be replaced with a full pathname. The returned value is a pointer to an internal static buffer which is overwritten with each call to **OI_translate_filename**. Since OI itself uses **OI_translate_filename**, you should copy the returned value if you are planning to save it for later use. For example, if **/usrs/william** is the home directory for user **amber**, the following line would print "/usrs/william":

```
printf("%s\n",OI_translate_filename("~william"));
```

OI_search_path   (Free-standing function)

```
char *OI_search_path(
    const char             *filename,     // file to search for
    const char * const     *filepaths)    // vector of paths to search
```

OI_search_path searches for a file *filename* in the directories listed in *filepaths*, which must be a NULL-terminated list of strings. The search ends when the first file *filename* is found. If *filename* is found, **OI_search_path** returns the complete pathname. Otherwise, **OI_search_path** returns *filename*.

OI_default_connection   (Free-standing function)

```
OI_connection *OI_default_connection( )
```

OI_default_connection returns a pointer to the current default connection.

OI_class_tree   (Free-standing function)

```
OI_class *OI_class_tree( )
```

OI_class_tree returns a pointer to the top of the OI class hierarchy for this application; that is, it returns a pointer to the root of the data structure describing all the classes registered for the application.

OI_refresh   (Free-standing function)

```
void OI_refresh(
    OI_d_tech          *objp)          // object to repaint
```

OI_refresh re-paints the object *objp*.

OI_delete_delayed_queue_length   (Free-standing function)

```
OI_number OI_delete_delayed_queue_length()
```

OI_delete_delayed_queue_length returns the length of the delete-delayed queue. This is the maximum number of objects the queue can hold, not the current number of objects in the queue.

OI_set_delete_delayed_queue_length   (Free-standing function)

```
void OI_set_delete_delayed_queue_length(
    OI_number          q_len)          // length of delete-delayed queue
```

OI keeps a queue of objects for which you have called **delete_delayed** or **delete_all_delayed**. When the queue is full and you call **delete_delayed** or **delete_all_delayed** for another object, one or more objects in the queue are actually deleted in a first-in first-out manner. **OI_set_delete_delayed_queue_length** sets the delete-delayed queue length to *q_len*; if this shortens the queue, some objects may get deleted. The default length of the queue is one. (See Section 6.3.7, "Deleting and Unparenting Objects," on page 6-37.)

5.5.7   Processing Signals

You must take special care when you deal with system signals. Since a signal may occur at any point in time, there is a good chance that it will occur when OI is in some indeterminate state. When writing a signal handler, you should never perform any activity which deals with OI objects (such as adding or deleting objects). This is because if OI is in an indeterminate state, your OI operations may fail, and/or the whole program may fail. To get around this problem, the following procedure is recommended:

A signal handler should set a flag indicating the type of signal which has occurred, and then call **OI_end_interaction** to gracefully exit the OI event-handling mechanism. The program should then check the flag, do the appropriate thing, and restart interactions by calling **OI_begin_interaction** again. For example:

```
        int                sig_type;
    do {
        sig_type = 0;
        signal(SIGALARM,catchalarm);
        alarm(TIME);
        OI_begin_interaction( ) :
        if (sig_type) {
            do appropriate signal processing
        }
    } while (sig_type);

void catchalarm( )
{
    sig_type = SIGALARM;
    OI_end_interaction( );
}
```

Example 5-1   Signal Processing

5.6   Resources

For more information on resource management, see Chapter 39, "The OI Resource Mechanism."

Table 5-3   Resources

Resource	Description	Possible Values	Default Value
ErrorMessage	Specifies the error message to use with the named error status. See Section 5.4.1, "Changing Error Messages via Resources," on page 5-14.	Any sprintf-style string that matches the original error message in format specification.	(No default)

5.7   Callback Functions

Table 5-4 lists the callbacks available for all OI applications and the page number of the corresponding explanatory material. See Section 6.18, "Determining and Adding Callbacks; Multiple Callbacks," on page 6-117 for additional information about manipulating callbacks.

Table 5-4   Callbacks

Callback Typedef	Description	Page Number
OI_event_fnp/memfnp	Dispatch callback function	5-6
OI_stderr_fnp/memfnp	Error callback function	5-12
OI_timeout_fnp/memfnp	Timeout callback function	5-18, 5-20
OI_io_fnp/memfnp	I/O callback function	5-22
OI_translation_fnp/memfnp	Translation action callback function	5-28

Chapter 6
OI_d_tech

OI_d_tech Member Functions

OI_d_tech

6.1　Description

OI_d_tech, short for *OI display technique*, is the base class for all displayable OI objects. You do not explicitly create an OI_d_tech; you get it as part of the process of creating another OI object. Because you can use the OI_d_tech member functions for any OI object, you should become familiar with them—you will use them in every OI program.

6.2　Class Tree

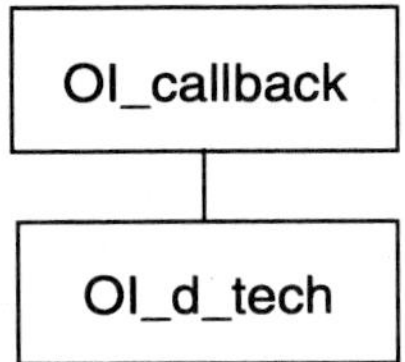

6.3　Building and Changing the Object Tree

You will use the functions described here in constructing your object tree and positioning your objects on the screen. An object always has exactly one parent; the initial parent of all objects is an non-displayed holding area called the *orphanage*. Every time you create a new OI object (usually using the oi_create_* functions described for each object), you normally associate the object with its parent via either layout_associated_object or set_associated_object. This inserts the object into the object tree (specifies its new parent) and specifies its positioning and visibility within its new parent.

In general, you create the main application window first. You then create other objects and parent them to the main application window or one of its descendants using set_associated_object or layout_associated_object. Finally, you parent the main application window to the root window using set_associated_object. You can have more than one top-level object; not all top-level objects need be application windows.

6.3.1　Naming Objects

You specify a *name* for each OI object when you create it (see the oi_create_* functions for each object). If you specify NULL as the object name, OI assigns a name to the object. You can also explicitly rename an existing object using the member function set_name.

> Do not include these characters in an object's name:
>
> @　,　.　:　/ ? \　*　or blank.

You cannot include these characters in an object's name because they are interpreted as special characters by OI and/or the X resource manager. In general, we recommend you use only alphanumeric characters and the underscore in object names.

Naming your objects carefully is important for two reasons. First, names provide a means for you to traverse the object tree when necessary. Second, users can, if they desire, modify individual object attributes using the X resource manager if the objects are named.

Some of the **OI_d_tech** functions use an object name as an argument. This name is used in finding children (descendants) or parents (ancestors) of any given object.

The complete path-name to an object starts with its most distant ancestor and includes all intervening ancestor names separated by a slash ("/") character. Unnamed segments of the path are left empty. For example:

```
wp = oi_create_app_window("my_window",...) ;
wp->set_layout(...)
bp = oi_create_box("my_box",...) ;
bp->set_layout(...)
bp->layout_associated_object(wp,...) ;
tp = oi_create_static_text("my_text",...) ;
tp->layout_associated_object(bp,...) ;
```

The name of the static text in this example is "my_text", and its full name is "my_window/my_box/my_text".

Some OI objects are compound objects—that is, they are constructed as a collection of more primitive objects—and OI gives standard internal names to these more primitive components. These names all begin with the character "@"; you should never use this character in constructing your own object names. For example, an **OI_dialog_box** has a row of buttons across the bottom. This **OI_button_menu** object is the "more primitive object." When you create the dialog box, you give the dialog box a name, but the button menu is given a name by OI. Currently this menu is named "@buttons", but you should never use this name directly, because it is not guaranteed to remain the same across new releases of OI. All OI objects which are constructed of more primitive components (*internal objects*) have member functions which allow you to access their components. In the case of the button menu in the dialog box, this member function is **buttons**.

name   (Member function)

```
const char *OI_d_tech::name( )
```

name returns the name of the object.

full_name   (Member function)

```
char *OI_d_tech::full_name( )
```

full_name returns the complete path-name of the object.

set_name   (Member function)

```
void OI_d_tech::set_name(
    const char *namp)                    // points to the new name
```

set_name sets the name of the object. This function sets only the object name; the prefix portion of its object path-name is unaffected. Do not include these characters in an object's name: @ / . , : * ? \ or blank. It is best to use only alphanumeric characters and the underscore in object names.

6.3.2   Using Automatic Layout

One of the more painful tasks in setting up a graphically oriented interface is positioning objects relative to each other. This becomes even harder when you consider that the size of an object cannot, in general, be known until execution time, since the user can change the final object size by modifying resources (such as font). To simplify this task, OI provides an automatic layout facility. Using this facility, you specify the relative location of objects to each other, rather than absolute locations within the parent. OI then automatically positions the objects, and adjusts their relative positions whenever the size of one of the objects changes. If the layout methods OI supplies are not sufficient, you can define your own layout method (see Section 44.4, "Designing Your Own Layout Method," on page 44-22).

You are not constrained to use the layout facility, since you can set objects into their parents using pixel locations (see 6.3.3, "Using Manual Layout" on page 6-25). However, you will find that using automatic layout will simplify your programming tasks and, later, your maintenance tasks.

If, after reading this section, you need more information regarding automatic layout or need to use OI_layout_method member functions (or member functions of classes derived from OI_layout_method), see Chapter 44, "OI_layout_method and Its Subclasses."

To use the layout facility, first call the member function **set_layout** to specify the *layout method* for the parent object. There are several possible OI-supplied layout methods as shown in Table 6-1.

The terms used in this book which refer to an object that was associated to its parent using the automatic layout facility are: "the object has been *laid out* in its parent" or "the object was added to the *layout*." To refer to an object for which **set_layout** has been called, we say "the parent is *laid out*."

Table 6-1   OI Layout Methods

Layout Method	Description
OI_layout_none	No layout specified—this is the default
OI_layout_row	Children are laid out horizontally, in rows. Within a row, objects are arranged in columns, independently of the column positions of objects in other rows. Row and column numbers need not be consecutive.

Table 6-1   OI Layout Methods

Layout Method	Description
OI_layout_row_aligned	Children are laid out as for OI_layout_row, with the addition that the children in the first column of each row have their "active portions" aligned vertically. The *first column* is the left-most occupied column in each row; the actual column numbers need not be the same. This means the label portion of OI_entry_field, OI_seq_entry_field, OI_gauge, OI_slider, and horizontal OI_menu objects in the first column are to the left of an alignment point, and the remainder of these object are to the right of the alignment point. All other objects in the first column are to the right of the alignment point.
OI_layout_column	Children are laid out vertically, in columns. Within a column, objects are arranged in rows independently of the row position of objects in other columns. Row and column numbers need not be consecutive.
OI_layout_row_column	Children are laid out in a grid. Objects are arranged in rows dependent upon the column position of objects in other rows. Each object may be thought of as being contained in an invisible box. All boxes in a given row will be of equal height, and all boxes in a given column will be of equal width. Row and column numbers need not be consecutive. Objects are positioned according to their gravity and space parameters within their invisible bounding box.
OI_layout_titled_row_column	Children are laid out in a grid as specified in OI_layout_row_column. Children with row numbers less than zero are laid out using the OI_layout_row method.
OI_layout_row_column_aligned	Children are laid out in a grid as specified in OI_layout_row_column. Within each column, objects are aligned at the alignment point as explained for OI_layout_row_aligned.
OI_layout_wrapped_row	Children are laid out as specified in OI_layout_row. In addition, you may specify the maximum number of objects (columns) in a given row. When this maximum is reached in any given row, subsequent objects added to the row are wrapped into a "sub-row." The sub-row's appearance is the same as any other row, but its row number is the same as the original row.

Table 6-1 OI Layout Methods

Layout Method	Description
OI_layout_wrapped_column	Children are laid out as specified in OI_layout_column. In addition, you may specify the maximum number of objects (rows) in a given column. When this maximum is reached in any given column, subsequent objects added to the column are wrapped into a "sub-column."
OI_layout_horz_tree	Children are laid out in a horizontal tree, connected with lines, with parent-nodes to the left and children-nodes to the right.
OI_layout_vert_tree	Children are laid out in a vertical tree, connected with lines, with parent-nodes above and children-nodes below.

When you call **set_layout**, you can also specify the default spacing to use between objects.

Once you establish the layout method for the parent object via **set_layout**, you can attach child objects to the parent using one of the member functions **layout_associated_object**, **add_to_layout** or **abs_layout_associated_object**. It is here that you specify placement values (row and column numbers for row and column layouts, parent-node and sibling-node for tree layouts) for the child object, referred to as the *geometry* of the laid-out object. At the time you call one of these functions, the object is displayed on the screen if its state and its ancestors' states allow it to be visible. Remember, however, that it cannot accept input from the user until you call one of OI's control functions (**OI_begin_interaction**, **OI_wait_done**, the **OI_dialog_box** member function **wait_button**, or the **OI_entry_field** member function **wait_done**).

Example 6-1 shows a minimal set of calls to use the automatic layout code, laying out two child objects within a parent object. Most examples and programs throughout this book use the automatic layout mechanism.

```
wp = oi_create_app_window("main",1,1);  //"main" is the parent object
wp->set_layout(OI_layout_row);          //establish layout method for the parent
ep = oi_create_entry_field("my_fld",...);
ep->layout_associated_object(wp,2,3,OI_active);  //"my_fld" is a child of "main"
gp = oi_create_gauge("my_gg",...);
gp->layout_associated_object(wp,11,3,OI_active); //"my_gg" is a child of "main"
wp->set_associated_object(wp->root( ),OI_def_loc,OI_def_loc,OI_active);
```

Example 6-1 Building an Object Tree Using Automatic Layout

In Example 6-1, note that we specified 1 by 1 pixels for the size of "main". This is because OI resizes a parent object whenever child objects are laid out in it, so the original size specification is immaterial.

When a child object which has been laid out in its parent is removed from the parent (using **unparent**, one of the **del** or **delete** member functions, **remove_from_layout**, the C++ **delete** operator, or another **set_associated_object** or **layout_associated_object** for the object), the original parent re-adjusts its size and the organization of its children to fit the remaining children.

The layout code is designed to position objects precisely in relation to one another. Consequently, you should not call **disallow_clip** for objects you are laying out, since doing so would put the positioning of the objects under the control of two potentially competing processes—OI and the window manager.

6.3.2.1 Sizing and Spacing in a Layout

The exact spacing between objects which are packed together is determined by the objects' total space. Laid out objects have spacing attributes that non-laid out objects do not have; these values are returned by the member functions **top_space**, **bottom_space**, **left_space**, and **right_space**. The member function **all_space_x** returns the total horizontal space occupied by an object, which is the sum of the values returned by **left_space**, **space_x**, and **right_space**. Similarly, the member function **all_space_y** returns the vertical space, which is the sum of the values returned by **top_space**, **space_y**, and **bottom_space**. You normally need not deal with these attributes, since setting the default spacing using **set_layout** is usually more convenient. However, you can explicitly set the spacing attributes for any object by using the functions **set_space** and **set_*_space**.

The spacing between two objects packed together is the sum of their complementary spacing components. The default spacing you specify in **set_layout** is the total space between two objects. The layout mechanism modifies the space attributes of objects using default spacing to achieve the desired results. The top and left space components of all objects with default spacing are set to the default values; the bottom and right space are set to zero except for objects in the last row, last column, or bottom right of a tree. Note that an object's total space requirements are not constant if it uses the default spacing; its bottom and right space components can change as a result of other sibling objects being added or removed from the layout.

6.3.2.2 Removing and Adding Objects in a Layout

The layout mechanism does not consider the state of an object when determining sizing and spacing. A child object which has state **OI_not_displayed** will not be visible when laid out in its parent, but it will still take up space. This allows you to use an invisible object such as a box with zero frame width to get the desired spacing, and allows you to make an object appear and disappear by changing its state using **set_state**. In this case, other objects in the layout remain in their respective positions.

add_to_layout and **remove_from_layout** are useful if you want to make an object invisible for a time, and need to be able to make it visible at a later time, but you want the vacated space closed up. For example, to remove a box pointed to by **bp** from the layout in parent object **prntp**, first you have to find the geometry of the box in its parent's layout, using the **OI_layout_method** member function **geometry**:

```
prntp->layout_method( )->geometry(bp,&geom_1,&free_1,&geom_2,&free_2);
bp->set_state(OI_not_displayed);
bp->remove_from_layout( );
```

and to add it again later:

```
bp->add_to_layout(geom_1,geom_2);
bp->set_state(OI_active);
if (free_1)
    delete (OI_layout_geometry_spec*)geom_1;
if (free_2)
    delete (OI_layout_geometry_spec*)geom_2;
```

suspend_layout and **resume_layout** are two more **OI_d_tech** member functions which you use to prevent movement on the screen from occurring as you change an object's layout. For the next example, we assume an object tree has already been created, and the main application window has been associated with the root and **OI_begin_interaction** has been called. Thus the application is visible on the screen. We also assume that in some callback we decide to delete an object and create and add a new object to the layout. We use **suspend_layout** for the parent object before we change its layout; this prevents the window from shrinking and growing each time we remove or add an object to its layout. We use **resume_layout** for the parent after we have finished deleting and adding children, so that it will reflect the new layout:

```
...get pointers wp to the main application window and ep to entry field "my_fld"
wp->suspend_layout( );
ep->del( );                                      // remove "my_fld" from layout
bp = oi_create_box("my_box",...);
bp->layout_associated_object(wp,11,4,OI_active); // "my_box" new child of "main"
wp->resume_layout( );
```

These calls not only save time in recomputing children's positioning, but they also prevent the screen from "flashing," which many users find annoying.

6.3.2.3   Ordering Objects Within a Row, Column, or Grid Layout

You do not have to space column and row numbers evenly when you are specifying child object locations in a row, column, or row-column layout. You can use any sequence of integers for column and row numbers; it is only the relationship between two numbers which determines relative positioning. In addition, the order of insertion is not important (unless row numbers collide, or column numbers collide, as discussed below).

In a row-major layout (OI_layout_row, OI_layout_row_aligned or OI_layout_wrapped_row), all child objects with the same row number appear in the same row. Within that row, objects are ordered left to right in ascending sequence by column number. If you insert a child object in the same row as another child object, and both objects have the same column number, OI places the new object ahead of the existing one—that is, the new object retains the column number, and the existing object's column number is incremented. If the existing object's new column number conflicts with its neighbor, OI increments the neighbor's column number; the column numbers are adjusted in this manner until the conflict is resolved. Objects in different rows, but with the same column number, may not be aligned vertically—row-major layout is not a grid.

Column-major (OI_layout_column or OI_layout_wrapped_column) insertions are handled in a similar manner.

If you specify a grid layout (OI_layout_row_column, OI_row_column_aligned, or OI_layout_titled_row_column), the objects are laid out in a matrix-like fashion. The row and column numbers need not be consecutive, but all objects with the same row number are in the same horizontal row and all objects with the same column number are in the same vertical column. If there are collisions in the row or column numbers of objects, they are handled in the same fashion as described above for row-major layout.

Within each major component (row in row-major layout, column in column-major, or within the "invisible" box in grid layout), the position of each object is further influenced by its *gravity*. Gravity determines the direction OI moves the object if there is any extra space in the layout. Gravity is expressed in compass directions; as you might expect, north is at the top of the screen, south is bottom, east is right and west is left. The default gravity for every object is northwest (OI_grav_northwest). You can set the gravity of an object using the member function **set_gravity**.

See Section 44.3.1, "Intricacies of Layout Spacing," on page 44-2 for a more detailed discussion of spacing in these types of layouts.

6.3.2.4   Aligning Objects on the Right Side of Labels

If you are using a row-major or grid layout method, you have a choice of aligning objects on their left edges (OI_layout_row, OI_layout_wrapped_row, OI_layout_row_column, OI_titled_row_column) or aligning objects on the right edge of their labels or titles (OI_layout_row_aligned or OI_layout_row_column_aligned). Figure 6-1 shows an application run using the Motif model with OI_layout_row, and Figure 6-2 shows the same application using OI_layout_row_aligned.

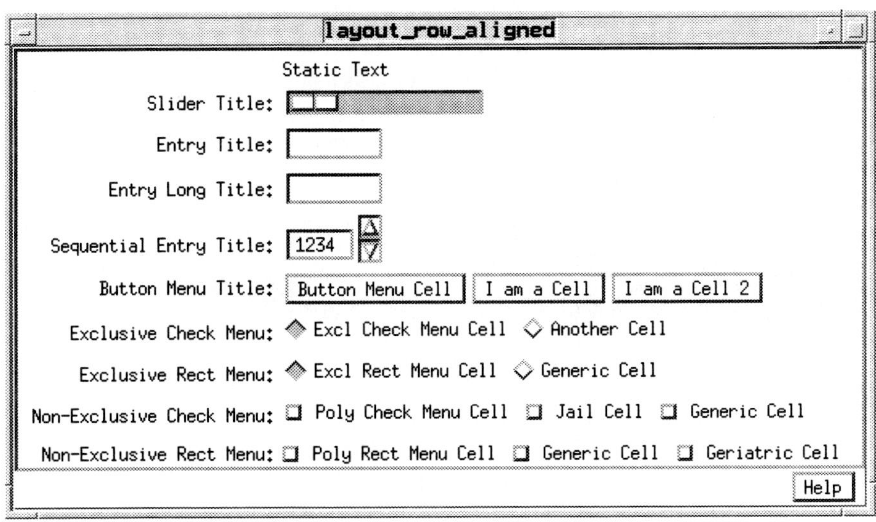

Figure 6-1   Objects Laid Out Using OI_layout_row

Figure 6-2   Objects Laid Out Using OI_layout_row_aligned

6.3.2.5   Using Titled Column Layout

Titled layout (OI_layout_titled_row_column) allows you to put one or more titles at the top of the layout. To do this, give the title object a row number less than zero and a gravity of OI_grav_center. Figure 6-3 shows an example of a static text object used this way; its row number is -1 and column number is 1. You can have several objects with row numbers less than zero to create more complex titles.

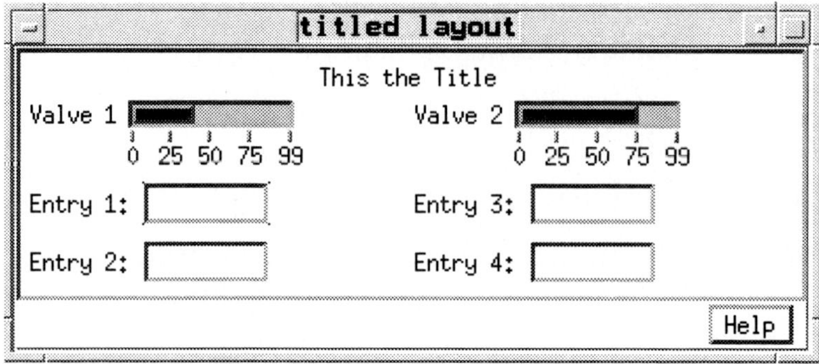

Figure 6-3　Titled Grid Layout

6.3.2.6　Using Wrapped Layout

If you specify a wrapped layout (OI_layout_wrapped_row, OI_layout_wrapped_column), the layout behaves identically to the non-wrapped layout (OI_layout_row or OI_layout_column), except that when you have added the maximum number of objects to the row (or column), the next object added to that row (column) appears as though it were added to a new row. However, the newly added object still has its original row number—it is merely in a "sub-row." To set the maximum number of objects in a row or column, use the OI_lm_wrapped_row or OI_lm_wrapped_column member function **set_wrap** (see page 44-21). Figure 6-4 shows an OI_layout_wrapped_row layout. The children objects are boxes containing static text; the text shows the row number and column number of its box in the layout.

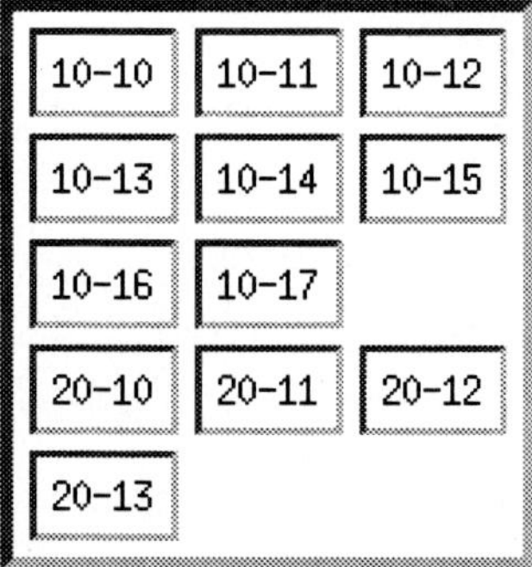

Figure 6-4　Wrapped Row Layout

6.3.2.7   Using Tree Layout

If you specify a vertical tree layout (OI_layout_vert_tree), you specify objects that should be the *parent-node* (the node above) and the *sibling-node* (the node to the right) of the child object. For example, consider the existing tree consisting of objects A, B and C:

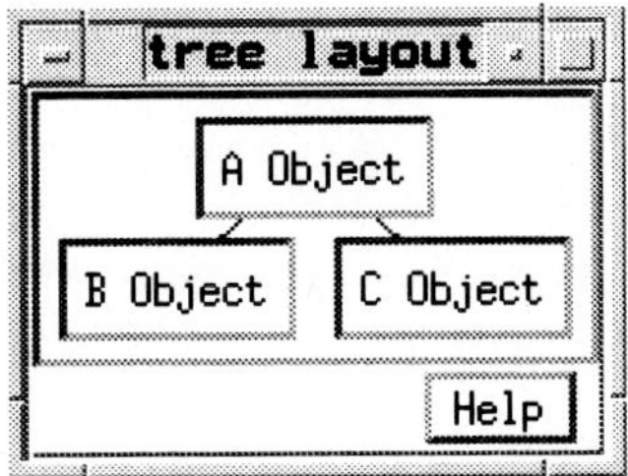

Figure 6-5   Tree Layout

To insert an object D into the tree, between B and C, you specify A as the node above and C as the node to the right:

```
OI_app_window          *wp;
OI_d_tech              *obj_a, *ojb_b, *obj_c, *obj_d;

wp->set_layout(OI_layout_vert_tree);
obj_d->layout_associated_object(wp,obj_a,obj_c,OI_active);
```

resulting in the following tree:

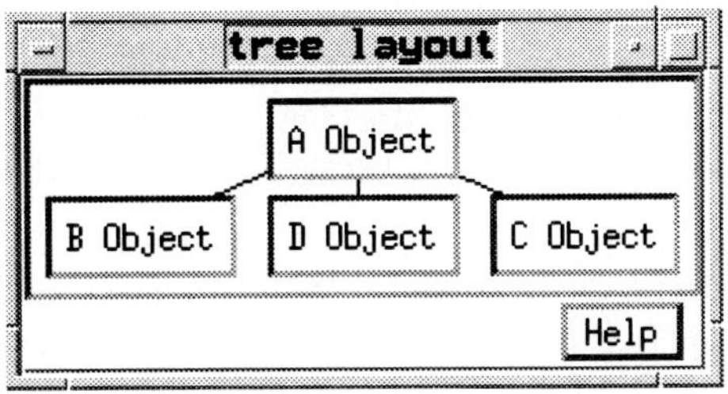

Figure 6-6   Tree Layout with Added Object

Similarly, if you specify a horizontal tree layout (OI_layout_horz_tree), you specify the parent-node and the sibling-node, but in this case these are the objects that should be the node to the left of and the node below the child object.

Specifying NULL for the parent-node causes the child to become the root of the tree layout. Specifying NULL for the sibling-node causes the child to become the right-most (vertical trees) or bottom-most (horizontal trees) node for the parent-node.

6.3.2.8   Parenting Using Automatic Layout

set_layout   (Member function)

```
void OI_d_tech::set_layout(
    OI_layout          layout_type,     // layout specification
    OI_number          vert=-1,         // default vertical spacing in pixels
    OI_number          horz=-1)         // default horizontal spacing in pixels
```

set_layout specifies the layout method OI is to use in positioning child objects within this object when it is used as a parent object. The only types of objects that you should call set_layout for are containers: objects of class OI_app_window, OI_box, OI_pane, or any of the dialog boxes. *layout_type* can have one of the following values (see Table 6-1 on page 6-3 for descriptions):

OI_layout_none
OI_layout_row
OI_layout_row_aligned
OI_layout_column
OI_layout_row_column
OI_layout_titled_row_column
OI_layout_row_column_aligned
OI_layout_wrapped_row
OI_layout_wrapped_column
OI_layout_horz_tree
OI_layout_vert_tree

vert and *horz* are the default spacing between child objects. The default value for *vert* of -1 means use the standard default (5 pixels). The default value for *horz* of -1 means use the same value as for *vert*. Because of the dynamic nature of the OI library, you may change the layout method at any time. If an exact conversion from one layout to another is not possible, an approximation is made. For example, converting within the row-column based methods is exact, but row-column to tree is not.

If you call this function for an OI_app_window object, it is vectored to the interior object. If you call it for an OI_scroll_box object, it is vectored to the object-box.

Examples:

To set the layout row-major, with the default vertical and horizontal spacing of 5 pixels:
```
wp->set_layout(OI_layout_row);
```

To set the layout with vertical and horizontal spacing of 10 pixels:
```
wp->set_layout(OI_layout_row,10);
```

To set the layout with vertical spacing of 10 pixels and horizontal spacing of 15 pixels:
```
wp->set_layout(OI_layout_row,10,15);
```

layout   (Member function)

```
OI_layout OI_d_tech::layout( )
```

layout returns the layout type for this object when it is used as a parent object. This will be one of the layout methods listed for **set_layout** or **OI_layout_none** (meaning that **set_layout** has not been called for the object). If you call this function for an **OI_app_window** object, it is vectored to the interior object. If you call it for an **OI_scroll_box** object, it is vectored to the object-box.

layout_method   (Member function)

```
OI_layout_method *OI_d_tech::layout_method( )
```

If this object has an interior object (**OI_app_window**, **OI_scroll_box**), **layout_method** returns a pointer to the **OI_layout_method** object used for the layout for the interior object of this object. If this object has no interior object, **layout_method** returns a pointer to the **OI_layout_method** object used for this entire object. See Chapter 44, "OI_layout_method and Its Subclasses," for more information.

abs_layout_method   (Member function)

```
OI_layout_method *OI_d_tech::abs_layout_method( )
```

abs_layout_method returns a pointer to the **OI_layout_method** object used for the layout for this entire object. If this object has no interior object, **abs_layout_method** behaves identically to **layout_method**. See Chapter 44, "OI_layout_method and Its Subclasses," for more information.

set_gravity   (Member function)

```
void OI_d_tech::set_gravity(
    OI_gravity          grav)            // gravity for object
```

set_gravity sets the gravity for this object when it is used as a child object. This call only makes sense if you are going to make the object a child of another object using the automatic layout facility, and are not using a tree layout method. The gravity is the direction the object moves when extra empty space is available in the parent's layout. Default gravity for the object is **OI_grav_northwest**. *grav* can have the following values:

```
OI_grav_north
OI_grav_south
OI_grav_east
OI_grav_west
OI_grav_northwest
OI_grav_northeast
OI_grav_southwest
OI_grav_southeast
OI_grav_center
```

gravity   (Member function)

```
OI_gravity OI_d_tech::gravity( )
```

gravity returns the gravity of this object. If **set_gravity** has not been called for the object, the gravity is **OI_grav_northwest**.

user_layout_ok   (Member function)

```
OI_bool OI_d_tech::user_layout_ok( )
```

user_layout_ok returns **OI_yes** if it is valid to lay out other objects in this object—that is, to call **set_layout** for this object; otherwise it returns **OI_no**. The only types of objects that you should call **set_layout** for are containers: objects of class **OI_app_window**, **OI_box**, **OI_pane**, or any of the dialog boxes.

layout_associated_object   (Member function)

```
OI_stat OI_d_tech::layout_associated_object(
    OI_d_tech           *prntp,          // pointer to new parent object
    void                *geom_1,         // geometry parameter 1
    void                *geom_2,         // geometry parameter 2
    OI_state            state=OI_same)   // new state of child object


OI_stat OI_d_tech::layout_associated_object(
    OI_d_tech           *prntp,          // pointer to new parent object
    OI_number           colno,           // column location of child object
    OI_number           rowno,           // row location of child object
    OI_state            state=OI_same)   // new state of child object
```

layout_associated_object lays out the object as the child of object *prntp* with state *state*. You **must** set the layout method for the parent, by calling **set_layout**, before you call **layout_associated_object** for the child object. If you have specified a row-column layout for the parent object, *colno* is the column number and *rowno* is the row number. If you have specified vertical tree layout for the parent object, *geom_1* is a pointer to the object in the tree above this object (the parent-node), and *geom_2* is a pointer to the object in the tree to the right of this object (the sibling-node). If you have specified horizontal tree layout for the parent object, *geom_1* is a pointer to the parent-node to the left of this object, and *geom_2* is a pointer to the sibling-node below this object. If you use zero for both the row and column, you must cast at least the first of these two arguments to **OI_number**, as shown here:

```
objp->layout_associated_object(parent, (OI_number)0, 0, OI_active);
```

If you have specified your own layout method for the parent object, and the geometry co-ordinates are neither **OI_number** nor a pointer, you must cast them to **void***. All of the OI-supplied layout methods use either **OI_number** or pointer geometry co-ordinates.

Note that the order of arguments in the second form is (*colno, rowno*), **not** (*rowno, colno*) as you might expect. The order of these arguments is horizontal location, vertical location—think (x,y), not (row,col). *state* controls the visibility of the object and whether it can accept input. It can have the following values:

OI_active
: The object is potentially visible (although usually subject to clipping to the parent's boundaries) and can accept input if all of its ancestors are also set to an OI_active state. In order for an object to be visible on the screen, all of its ancestors must be visible (either OI_active or OI_inactive), and its top ancestor must be parented to the root.

OI_inactive
: The object is visible (subject to the same visibility constraints as OI_active), but it can not accept input. Some objects in this state appear stippled.

OI_not_displayed
: The object is not visible and cannot accept input. The object still takes up space in the layout even though it is not visible. This is the initial state of all objects.

If you omit *state*, the current state of the child object is used. If you invoke layout_associated_object more than once for the same child object, the child is removed from its original parent before it is associated with its new parent. If the new parent is the same as the old, the object is moved to the new geometry in the same parent.

If you call this function for an OI_app_window object, it is vectored to the interior object. If you call it for an OI_scroll_box object, it is vectored to the object-box.

abs_layout_associated_object   (Member function)

```
OI_stat OI_d_tech::abs_layout_associated_object(
    OI_d_tech          *prntp,                  // pointer to new parent object
    void               *geom_1,                 // geometry parameter 1
    void               *geom_2,                 // geometry parameter 2
    OI_state           state=OI_same)           // new state of child object


OI_stat OI_d_tech::abs_layout_associated_object(
    OI_d_tech          *prntp,                  // pointer to new parent object
    OI_number          colno,                   // column location of child object
    OI_number          rowno,                   // row location of child object
    OI_state           state=OI_same)           // new state of child object
```

You will probably only need this function if you derive your own subclass and want to insert a new piece into one of the "outside" regions of an OI_app_window, OI_scroll_text, OI_scroll_box, or OI_scroll_menu.

abs_layout_associated_object lays out the object as the child of object *prntp* with layout geometry *geom_1* and *geom_2* or *colno* and *rowno* and with state *state*. See the discussion above under layout_associated_object for use of *geom_1* and *geom_2* or *colno* and *rowno*.

abs_layout_associated_object is identical to layout_associated_object except that abs_layout_associated_object does not place objects into the "most likely" interior object as does layout_associated_object. In other words, it allows you to add objects to an

OI_app_window object in places other than the interior box, and it allows you to add objects to an OI_scroll_box in places other than the object box. All OI compound objects use some layout method based on OI_lm_row_col. You can find out where the component objects (such as the help text object in an OI_app_window object) are placed by doing the following: Use a member function to get a pointer objp to the component object. Then execute something like:

```
OI_layout_method        *lmp;
OI_d_tech               *objp;
```

```
if (objp->is_laid_out_child) {
    lmp = objp->abs_parent( )->abs_layout_method( );
    if (lmp->is_derived_from("OI_layout_row_col")) {
        row - ((OI_lm_row_col*)lmp)->row_position(objp);
        col = ((OI_lm_row_col*)lmp)->column_position(objp);
    }
}
```

Armed with this information, you can determine the values for *colno* and *rowno* to place your object appropriately.

is_laid_out_child   (Member function)

```
OI_bool OI_d_tech::is_laid_out_child( )
```

is_laid_out_child returns OI_yes if the object is laid out in its parent; otherwise it returns OI_no.

freeze   (Member function)

```
void OI_d_tech::freeze( )
```

freeze freezes the display of the object and all its clipped children. This prevents the user from seeing object movement until the work is complete.

unfreeze   (Member function)

```
void OI_d_tech::unfreeze( )
```

unfreeze resumes normal display of an object and all its clipped children.

suspend_layout   (Member function)

```
void OI_d_tech::suspend_layout( )
```

suspend_layout disables the repositioning of children of this parent object. This permits you to lay out many objects without having the screen reshuffle each time a new object is added or deleted. It also improves efficiency, particularly when there are many children being added, since the layout computations are done only once when you call resume_layout. You should use resume_layout to force re-layout of the object.

If you call this function for an OI_app_window object, it is vectored to the interior object. If you call it for an OI_scroll_box object, it is vectored to the object-box.

resume_layout   (Member function)

```
void OI_d_tech::resume_layout(
    OI_bool              resize=OI_yes)      // resize object
```

resume_layout re-enables repositioning of children for this parent object. All laid out children are positioned properly and the parent rc-sizcd accordingly as a result of this call. If *resize* is **OI_yes** (the default), the size of the object is recomputed to fit its children. If *resize* is **OI_no**, the children are forced to some geometry using the current size of the object.

If you call this function for an **OI_app_window** object, it is vectored to the interior object. If you call it for an **OI_scroll_box** object, it is vectored to the object-box.

add_to_layout   (Member function)

```
OI_stat OI_d_tech::add_to_layout(
    void                 *geom_1,           // geometry 1 parameter
    void                 *geom_2)           // geometry 2 parameter


OI_stat OI_d_tech::add_to_layout(
    OI_number            colno,             // column number
    OI_number            rowno)             // row number
```

add_to_layout moves this child object within its parent's layout. **add_to_layout** effectively does a **layout_associated_object** on the object to *geom_1* and *geom_2*, or *colno* and *rowno*, with its current state and within its current parent. You can use **add_to_layout** to modify the geometry of an already laid out child object, as well as converting a non-laid out child object to a laid out child object. **add_to_layout** always returns **OI_ok**. If you set both the column and row to 0, you must cast at least the first one to **OI_number**.

If you call this function for an **OI_app_window** object, it is vectored to the interior object. If you call it for an **OI_scroll_box** object, it is vectored to the object-box.

remove_from_layout   (Member function)

```
OI_stat OI_d_tech::remove_from_layout(
    long                 x=OI_def_loc,      // new x location, in pixels
    long                 y=OI_def_loc)      // new y location, in pixels
```

remove_from_layout removes this child object from its parent's layout and inserts the object as a non-laid out child of its existing parent. It effectively calls **set_associated_object** for the object with its current state and parent at location *x* and *y*. If *x* and *y* are not provided, they default to the object's current location. The end result is that the object is no longer laid out, but it retains the same parent and the same state. The parent is re-laid out; other laid out children may shuffle to take up the space formerly occupied by the object which was removed. **remove_from_layout** always returns **OI_ok**.

If you call this function for an **OI_app_window** object, it is vectored to the interior object. If you call it for an **OI_scroll_box** object, it is vectored to the object-box.

6.3.2.9   Modifying Automatically Laid-Out Object Spacing

The only control you have over the positioning of objects that are automatically laid out is through

- their geometry
- their object gravity
- their size tracking
- the amount of white space you allow around each object

You can set the spacing for all objects laid out within a parent by specifying the second and third arguments when you call **set_layout** for the parent. Use **is_default_horz_space_set**, **default_horz_space**, **is_default_vert_space_set**, and **default_vert_space** to find out their current values.

Use **set_space** or **set_*_space** to set the spacing for child objects individually. Use **is_*_space_set** or __*_space__ to inquire about the current settings for any child object.

is_default_horz_space_set   (Member function)

```
OI_bool OI_d_tech::is_default_horz_space_set( )
```

is_default_horz_space_set returns **OI_yes** if the default horizontal white space has been explicitly set through a call to **set_layout** for this parent object; otherwise it returns **OI_no**.

default_horz_space   (Member function)

```
OI_number OI_d_tech::default_horz_space( )
```

default_horz_space returns the horizontal white space to be used in laying out objects in this parent object, in pixels.

is_default_vert_space_set   (Member function)

```
OI_bool OI_d_tech::is_default_vert_space_set( )
```

is_default_vert_space_set returns **OI_yes** if the default vertical white space has been explicitly set through a call to **set_layout** for this parent object; otherwise it returns **OI_no**.

default_vert_space   (Member function)

```
OI_number OI_d_tech::default_vert_space( )
```

default_vert_space returns the vertical white space to be used in laying out objects in this parent object, in pixels.

set_space   (Member function)

```
void OI_d_tech::set_space(
    OI_number          space)                // white space in pixels
```

set_space sets the left, right, top, and bottom white space for this child object to *space* pixels. This spacing becomes effective immediately. You normally need not use this function, since it is usually sufficient to set default spacings in the parent's **set_layout** call. Remember that the total space between two laid out objects is the sum of their complimentary space values (for example, if A and B are laid out next to each other with A to the left of B, the space between them is the sum of A's right-space and B's left-space).

set_horz_space   (Member function)

```
void OI_d_tech::set_horz_space(
    OI_number          space)          // white space in pixels
```

set_horz_space sets the white space required for this child object to be *space* on each side. This spacing takes effect immediately.

set_vert_space   (Member function)

```
void OI_d_tech::set_vert_space(
    OI_number          space)          // white space in pixels
```

set_vert_space sets the white space required for this child object to be *space* on the top and on the bottom. This spacing takes effect immediately.

is_top_space_set   (Member function)

```
OI_bool OI_d_tech::is_top_space_set( )
```

is_top_space_set returns OI_yes if you have called set_top_space, set_vert_space, or set_space, for this child object; otherwise it returns OI_no.

set_top_space   (Member function)

```
void OI_d_tech::set_top_space(
    OI_number          space)          // white space in pixels
```

set_top_space sets the top white space required for this child object. This spacing takes effect immediately.

top_space   (Member function)

```
OI_number OI_d_tech::top_space( )
```

top_space returns the top white space to be used if this object is laid out in its parent.

is_bottom_space_set   (Member function)

```
OI_bool OI_d_tech::is_bottom_space_set( )
```

is_bottom_space_set returns OI_yes if you have called set_bottom_space, set_vert_space, or set_space, for this child object; otherwise it returns OI_no.

set_bottom_space   (Member function)

```
void OI_d_tech::set_bottom_space(
    OI_number          space)          // white space in pixels
```

set_bottom_space sets the bottom white space required for this child object. This spacing takes effect immediately.

bottom_space   (Member function)

```
OI_number OI_d_tech::bottom_space( )
```

bottom_space returns the bottom white space to be used if this object is laid out in its parent.

is_left_space_set   (Member function)

```
OI_bool OI_d_tech::is_left_space_set( )
```

is_left_space_set returns **OI_yes** if you have called **set_left_space**, **set_horz_space**, or **set_space**, for this child object; otherwise it returns **OI_no**.

set_left_space   (Member function)

```
void OI_d_tech::set_left_space(
   OI_number            space)            // white space in pixels
```

set_left_space sets the left white space required for this child object. This spacing takes effect immediately.

left_space   (Member function)

```
OI_number OI_d_tech::left_space( )
```

left_space returns the left white space to be used if this object is laid out in its parent.

is_right_space_set   (Member function)

```
OI_bool OI_d_tech::is_right_space_set( )
```

is_right_space_set returns **OI_yes** if you have called **set_right_space**, **set_horz_space**, or **set_space**, for this child object; otherwise it returns **OI_no**.

set_right_space   (Member function)

```
void OI_d_tech::set_right_space(
   OI_number            space)            // white space in pixels
```

set_right_space sets the right white space required for this child object. This spacing takes effect immediately.

right_space   (Member function)

```
OI_number OI_d_tech::right_space( )
```

right_space returns the right white space to be used if this object is laid out in its parent.

all_space_x   (Member function)

```
OI_number OI_d_tech::all_space_x( )
```

If this object is laid out in its parent or has had its left and right white space set, then **all_space_x** returns the total space occupied by the object in the x direction (**space_x**) plus the object's left and right white space. Otherwise the return value is undefined.

all_space_y   (Member function)

```
OI_number OI_d_tech::all_space_y( )
```

If the object is laid out in its parent or has had its top and bottom white space set, then all_space_y returns the total space occupied by the object in the y direction (space_y) plus the object's top and bottom white space. Otherwise the return value is undefined.

6.3.2.10 Determining Automatically Laid-Out Object Positions

You can determine the positions of automatically laid-out objects by determining the type of layout being used and then calling the appropriate layout member functions. See Chapter 44, "OI_layout_method and Its Subclasses," for more information.

6.3.2.11 Size Tracking For Automatically Laid-Out Objects

So far, we have always discussed the layout mechanism in situations where the parent object grows and shrinks to fit its children. However, there are often situations where you would like at least some of the children to grow and shrink to fit the parent. You do this by marking a child object as a *size-tracker*. Row-major, column-major and grid layouts understand size-tracking children; tree layouts ignore size-tracking. If an object has a row, column or grid layout method set for it (you have called set_layout for it) and its size is changed (via the window manager, a call to set_size, or due to a modification of its laid out children), OI recomputes the location of its laid out children. If the parent object is larger than necessary, or some of its rows/columns are larger than others, there is some excess space. Normally, the excess space is interspersed between the child objects. (See Section 6.3.2.1, "Sizing and Spacing in a Layout" on page 6-6) However, if one or more of the children is a size-tracker, the space is used to expand the designated children instead. The discussion below assumes row-major layout; analogous situations exists for other layout methods.

Consider the objects in Table 6-2.

Table 6-2 Objects For Size Tracking Example

Object	Column Position	Row Position	Gravity	Width	Height
A	5	10	NW	10	10
B	10	10	NW	10	10
C	15	10	NE	10	10
D	2	20	SW	10	10
E	4	20	C	10	10
F	6	20	NE	10	10
G	10	40	NW	100	10

After initial row-major layout, the objects in Table 6-2 appear this way:

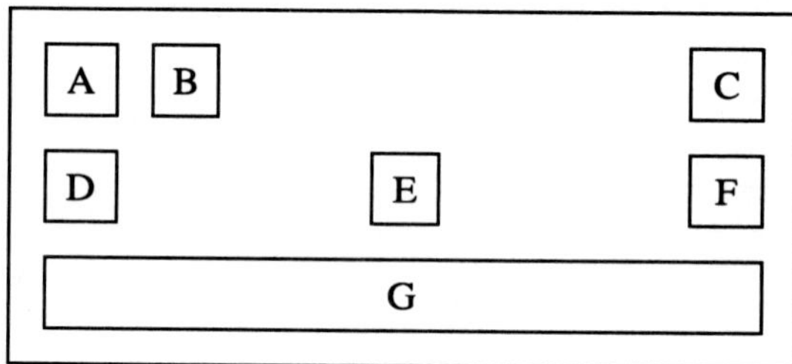

Figure 6-7 Layout for Table 6-2

Notice the places where the extra space has been inserted. In row 10, A and B form a cluster which has an affinity for the west; C has an affinity for the east. The extra space is placed in the hole between the two clusters. Similarly, in row 20, D has an affinity for the west, and F for the east. E has no east-west affinity, and forms a separate floating cluster. There are two distinct holes in this row, and the free space is divided up evenly between them. However, if A is made a horizontal size-tracker, the result would be as shown in Figure 6-8:

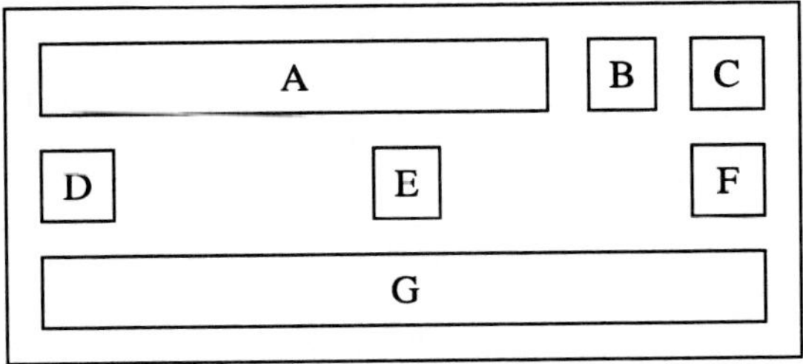

Figure 6-8   Layout for Table 6-2, A a Horizontal Size-Tracker

Since row 10 has a horizontal size-tracker, the extra space is given to the size-tracker object instead of being inserted between the clusters of objects. If E and F were also horizontal size-trackers, the result would be this:

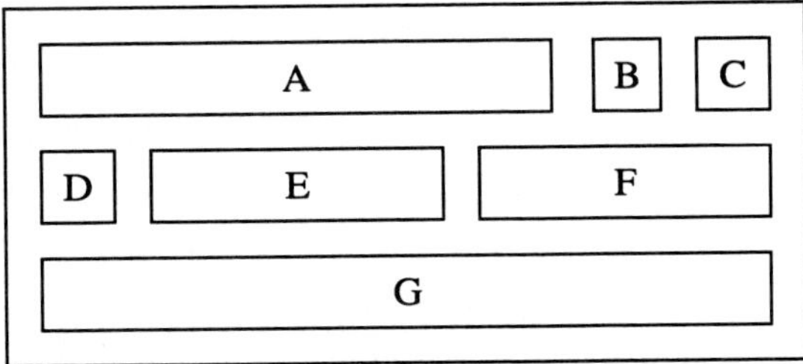

Figure 6-9   Layout for Table 6-2, A, E and F Horizontal Size-Trackers

Whenever the parent object changes size, the extra space is recomputed and redistributed to any size-trackers. Note that if the parent is made sufficiently small, the size-trackers may be forced to be a size smaller than their original size.

If B, E, and G were made to be full (horizontal and vertical) size-trackers, and the parent object were made taller, the result would be:

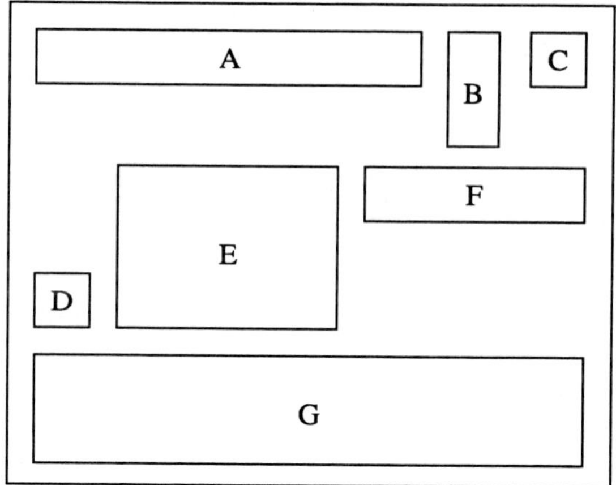

Figure 6-10   Layout for Table 6-2, Made Taller, B, E, and G Size-Trackers

set_size_track

(Member function)

```
void OI_d_tech::set_size_track(
   OI_size_track      trk)              // tracking direction and relation
```

set_size_track marks the object as one whose size should "track" that of its parent. Size-tracking only applies if the parent is laid out using a row, column or grid layout. Thus, when the parent grows or shrinks, the object grows and shrinks in a corresponding manner. *trk* specifies the directions in which the object should track these size changes. The possible values for *trk* are expressed as a bit field and can be any of the following values, either alone or combined with a boolean **or** in any combination.

OI_size_track_none
> The object does not track its parent in any direction. This is the default.

OI_size_track_horizontal
> The object tracks its parent in the horizontal direction when either the parent is resized explicitly or a sibling (another child of the parent) is added or removed.

OI_size_track_vertical
> The object tracks its parent in the vertical direction when either the parent is resized explicitly or a sibling (another child of the parent) is added or removed.

OI_size_track_full
> The object tracks its parent in both the horizontal and the vertical direction when either the parent is resized explicitly or a sibling (another child of the parent) is added or removed.

size_track   (Member function)

```
OI_size_track OI_d_tech::size_track( )
```

size_track returns the type of size tracking the object does when its laid-out parent is resized. This value will be a combination of those listed for the argument *trk* for **set_size_track**. If the object's parent is not laid-out, the return value is undefined.

6.3.3   Using Manual Layout

The automatic layout mechanism discussed in the previous section is by far the most convenient means of positioning objects for most situations. However, there are situations when it should not, or cannot, be used. Among them are the following:

- When you parent a top-level object (usually an **OI_app_window**) to the root.
- When you parent an object (usually a dialog box) whose visibility is not constrained to be within its parent's borders (see **allow_clip** and **disallow_clip**) to another object.
- When you parent a pop-up object (usually a menu or a dialog box in state **OI_active_not_displayed**) to another object.
- When you are using custom geometries which do not fit any of the default layout methods and you have decided not to create your own layout method.

In these cases, you must use the manual layout mechanism. You do this by calling **set_associated_object** instead of **layout_associated_object**.

When you parent an object using **set_associated_object**, you specify the location of the object relative to its parent. Note that an object is *clipped* to its parent (only the portion of the child that exists within the boundaries of the parent appears on the display) unless you call the **OI_d_tech** member function **disallow_clip** for the child object to prevent clipping.

As with **layout_associated_object**, at the time you call **set_associated_object**, the object is displayed on the screen if its state and its ancestors' states allow it to be visible. Remember, however, that it cannot accept input from the user until you call one of the control functions (**OI_begin_interaction**, **OI_wait_done**, the **OI_dialog_box** member function **wait_button**, or the **OI_entry_field** member function **wait_done**).

The example below shows two objects parented to a main window using the manual layout mechanism.

```
wp = oi_create_app_window("main",200,300);      //"main" is the parent object
wp->set_associated_object(wp->root( ),OI_def_loc,OI_def_loc,OI_not_displayed);
ep = oi_create_entry_field("my_fld",...);
ep->set_associated_object(wp,20,30,OI_active); // "my_fld" is a child of "main"
gp = oi_create_gauge("my_gg",...);
gp->set_associated_object(wp,20,wp->avail_loc_y( )+10,OI_active);
                                        // "my_gg" is a child of "main"
wp->set_size(wp->avail_loc_x( )+10,wp->avail_loc_y( )+10);
wp->set_state(OI_active);
```

Example 6-2   Building an Object Tree Using Manual Layout

There are several items of interest illustrated in Example 6-2:

- The OI_app_window object "main" is specified to be 200 by 300 pixels originally, and is resized to enclose all its children after all the children are inserted.
- The OI_box member functions avail_loc_x and avail_loc_y are used to find the next reasonable location for "my_gg" and to determine the appropriate size for the parent application window "main".
- "main" is parented to the root before any children are parented to it. The reason for this is that resources for a child object are only fetched if the parent (or one of its ancestors) is already associated with the root. If the resources should change the size of the child object (by, for example, changing the font to be used in the entry field), the result of the call to avail_loc_y would be different than if the parent were not already associated with the root and resources had not been fetched.
- "main" is parented to the root in state OI_not_displayed and then its state is changed to OI_active after it is resized. This is done so that nothing appears on the screen until the entire object tree is built.

When you choose to use manual layout, you are responsible for all aspects of the layout. The parent object is not sized to fit its children. Children can overlap; you are responsible for placing them so they do not overlap, and re-adjusting their locations and sizes as necessary. The OI_box member functions avail_loc_* will help when you are initially placing objects in objects of class OI_app_window, OI_box, OI_pane, or OI_dialog_box.

6.3.3.1 Parenting Using Manual Layout

set_associated_object   (Member function)

```
OI_stat OI_d_tech::set_associated_object(
    OI_d_tech           *prntp,              // pointer to new parent object
    long                loc_x=OI_def_loc,    // x location of child object
    long                loc_y=OI_def_loc,    // y location of child object
    OI_state            state=OI_same)       // new state of child object
```

set_associated_object attaches the object as the child of object *prntp* at location *loc_x*, *loc_y* with state *state*. In some situations, you can use the constant OI_def_loc instead of a number for *loc_x* and/or *loc_y*. You may use OI_def_loc (and usually should use it) in the following situations:

- When you are parenting a top-level object (usually the main OI_app_window) to the root.
- When you are parenting a pop-up menu to another object. This causes the pop-up to appear at its default location (usually the pointer location) based on the interaction model.

- When you are parenting a pull-down/pull-right menu or a pop-up dialog box to a menu cell. This causes the object to appear, when it is activated, at its default location based on the interaction model.

state controls the visibility of the object and whether it can accept input. It can have the values:

OI_active	The object is potentially visible (although usually subject to clipping to the parent's boundaries) and can accept input if all of its ancestors are also set to an OI_active state. In order for an object to be visible on the screen, all of its ancestors must be visible (either OI_active or OI_inactive), and its top ancestor must be parented to the root.
OI_inactive	The object is visible (subject to the same visibility constraints as OI_active), but it cannot accept input.
OI_not_displayed	The object is not visible and cannot accept input. This is the initial state of all objects. Some objects in this state appear stippled.
OI_active_not_displayed	The object is not visible, but can accept input (for example, a pop-up menu). Only menus and dialog boxes can have this state.

If you omit *state*, it defaults to OI_same, indicating that the current state of the child object is used. If you invoke set_associated_object more than once for the same child object, the child is removed from its original parent before it is associated with its new parent.

6.3.3.2 Positioning Manually Laid-Out Objects

The functions defined below allow you to change the position of an object. Note that an object is initially positioned when you associate it with its parent using layout_associated_object or set_associated_object; you will usually not need to reposition objects further. (See Section 6.7.1, "Determining Object Location," on page 6-43 for some related functions.) Do not call these functions for an object which is laid out using OI's automatic layout mechanism.

A top-level object or any object whose visibility is not constrained to be within its parent's borders (see allow_clip and disallow_clip) can be moved about the display using the window manager's move facilities. Whenever an object is moved, its children normally follow it and the relative positions of the children to the parent are preserved. Note that this applies to any child object, independently of whether its visibility is constrained to be within its parent's borders. This is called *location tracking*. Most objects may also be moved (repositioned) from within your program. Examples of objects which cannot be moved are interior objects (components) of the more complex objects, such as a scroll bar within a scroll box object. You can mark your objects as movable or not, and inquire into their move permissions. Attempts to move an object marked as unmovable from within your program will fail. Note, however, that you cannot prevent a top-level object or an object whose visibility is not constrained by its parent's borders from being moved via the window manager.

When you call the **OI_d_tech** member function **disallow_clip** for an object, location tracking is enabled by default; this means the location of this unclipped object is **not** independent of its parent's location. If you call **allow_independent_loc** for the object (or specify **OI_yes** as the parameter in **disallow_clip**), location tracking is disabled and the object's location is independent of its parent's location. However, note that an object's location is always relative to its parent's location, even if it is independent of it.

set_loc   (Member function)

```
OI_stat OI_d_tech::set_loc(
    long                    x,              // x coordinate
    long                    y)              // y coordinate
```

set_loc sets the location of the upper-left outside corner of the object, relative to the upper-left inside corner of its parent, to be (x, y). This call effectively moves the object to x, y. Note that this function works for any object, independently of whether its visibility is constrained by its parent's borders (see **allow_clip** and **disallow_clip**).

set_loc_outside_rel   (Member function)

```
OI_stat OI_d_tech::set_loc_outside_rel(
    long                    x,              // x coordinate
    long                    y)              // y coordinate
```

set_loc_outside_rel is the same as **set_loc**, except that x and y are relative to the outside, not the inside, of the parent object. You normally only use this function to position objects for which you have called **disallow_clip** so they line up exactly with their top-level parent.

set_root_loc   (Member function)

```
OI_stat OI_d_tech::set_root_loc(
    long                    x,              // x coordinate
    long                    y)              // y coordinate
```

set_root_loc sets the location of the upper-left outside corner of the object relative to the upper-left corner of the physical display. This call not only positions the object, it also prevents clipping by its parent. The object's parent remains unchanged. An object for which you have called **set_root_loc** does not follow its parent when the parent is moved, but remains in the same place on the screen. See also **disallow_clip**.

is_independent_loc   (Member function)

```
OI_bool OI_d_tech::is_independent_loc( )
```

You should only call **is_independent_loc** for an object if you have disabled clipping for it (you have called **disallow_clip** for it). If location tracking is enabled for the object, **is_independent_loc** returns **OI_no**. If location tracking is disabled for the object, **is_independent_loc** returns **OI_yes**. If the object can be clipped by its parent, the value returned is undefined.

allow_independent_loc   (Member function)

```
void OI_d_tech::allow_independent_loc( )
```

allow_independent_loc disables the location tracking for the object. This prevents an object whose visibility is not constrained by its parent's borders (see **allow_clip** and **disallow_clip**) from following its parent when the parent is moved (usually via the window manager). Note that you can effectively enable **allow_independent_loc** by specifying **OI_yes** as the first argument to **disallow_clip**. Remember that an object's location is relative to its parent's location, even if the location is independent of its parent's location—that is, if you call the **OI_d_tech** member function **loc**, **loc_x** or **loc_y** for an object, the value returned is always relative to the parent's location.

disallow_independent_loc   (Member function)

```
void OI_d_tech::disallow_independent_loc( )
```

disallow_independent_loc re-enables the location tracking of the unclipped object.

force_within_abs_root   (Member function)

```
void OI_d_tech::force_within_abs_root(
    long                x,              // x coordinate
    long                y,              // y coordinate
    OI_d_tech           *prnt_obj=NULL)  // pointer to pseudo parent object
```

force_within_abs_root places the object at location (x, y) relative to *prnt_obj*, as for **set_loc**, with the exception that x and y are modified as necessary to ensure that the entire object appears on the display. *prnt_obj* is a pointer to another object which is this object's logical parent for this operation. If *prnt_obj* is NULL, the object's actual parent is also its logical parent. In other words, if *prnt_obj* points to an object other than the actual parent, **force_within_abs_root** places the object as if it were parented to *prnt_obj*.

is_horz_move   (Member function)

```
OI_bool OI_d_tech::is_horz_move( )
```

is_horz_move returns **OI_yes** if the object is allowed to be moved horizontally; otherwise it returns **OI_no**.

allow_horz_move   (Member function)

```
void OI_d_tech::allow_horz_move( )
```

allow_horz_move configures the object so that it can be moved horizontally. This is the default.

disallow_horz_move   (Member function)

```
void OI_d_tech::disallow_horz_move( )
```

disallow_horz_move configures the object so that it cannot be moved horizontally.

is_vert_move (Member function)

```
OI_bool OI_d_tech::is_vert_move( )
```

is_vert_move returns OI_yes if the object is allowed to be moved vertically; otherwise it returns OI_no.

allow_vert_move (Member function)

```
void OI_d_tech::allow_vert_move( )
```

allow_vert_move configures the object so that it can be moved vertically. This is the default.

disallow_vert_move (Member function)

```
void OI_d_tech::disallow_vert_move( )
```

disallow_vert_move configures the object so that it cannot be moved vertically.

is_move (Member function)

```
OI_bool OI_d_tech::is_move( )
```

is_move returns OI_yes if the object is allowed to be moved, horizontally, vertically, or both; otherwise it returns OI_no.

allow_move (Member function)

```
void OI_d_tech::allow_move( )
```

allow_move configures the object so that it can be moved both horizontally and vertically.

disallow_move (Member function)

```
void OI_d_tech::disallow_move( )
```

disallow_move configures the object so that it cannot be moved either horizontally or vertically.

6.3.4   Clipping

By default, every object is *clipped* by its parent. This means that any portion of the object that is located outside the parent is not visible on the display. If you want the object to appear (when its state allows) regardless of the parent's boundaries, you must specifically prevent clipping for that object. The following functions affect the clipping of an object; set_root_loc also affects clipping.

When you call disallow_clip for an object, by default the location of this unclipped object is **not** independent of its parent's location. When the parent moves, this object moves to maintain its location relative to its parent. This mirrors the behavior the object would have if it were still clipped by its parent. If you specify OI_yes as the parameter in disallow_clip (or call allow_independent_loc for the object), the object's location is independent of its parent's location; moving the parent object does not cause the object to move.

is_clip   (Member function)

```
OI_bool OI_d_tech::is_clip( )
```

is_clip returns **OI_yes** if clipping for the object is currently enabled (the default condition). If you have called **disallow_clip** for the object, **is_clip** returns **OI_no**.

allow_clip   (Member function)

```
void OI_d_tech::allow_clip( )
```

allow_clip restores an object for which **set_root_loc** or **disallow_clip** was called to a normal state: it is clipped by its parent and follows its parent (preserving the relative location to its parent) when the parent is moved about the display.

disallow_clip   (Member function)

```
void OI_d_tech::disallow_clip(
    OI_bool              ind_loc=OI_no)     // is object independent of parent?
```

disallow_clip prevents the object from being clipped by any of its ancestors. If *ind_loc* is **OI_no** (the default), the object follows its parent if the parent moves. If *ind_loc* is **OI_yes**, the object's location is independent of its parent's movement. Setting *ind_loc* to **OI_yes** is equivalent to calling **allow_independent_loc** for the object after calling **disallow_clip**.

You normally use **disallow_clip** for an **OI_dialog_box** object. You parent the dialog box to another object such as an **OI_app_window**, and call **disallow_clip** to prevent the dialog box from being clipped to the **OI_app_window** boundaries. Do not call **disallow_clip** for objects to be laid out using OI's automatic layout facility; it generally does not make sense.

Parenting a dialog box to an **OI_menu_cell** object automatically invokes **disallow_clip** on behalf of the dialog box; as does parenting a sub-menu to an **OI_menu_cell** object.

6.3.5   Descendants

These functions help you find children and more distant descendants of any given OI object. *Child* and *descendant* refer to objects further down the object tree than is the object for which you have called the member function. The motivation for using these functions is often to avoid using global variables in your OI programs. For example, suppose you have a dialog box with an entry field named "entry_1" in it. Although the current routine you are in may only have a pointer *dbp* to the dialog box and none to the entry field, you can find the entry field, and then set its default text to "my new text" this way:

```
    OI_dialog_box          *dbp ;
    OI_entry_field         *efp ;
efp = (OI_entry_field*)dbp->subobject("entry_1");
efp->set_default_text("my new text");
```

Example 6-3   Finding a Subobject of an Object

The function **subobject** searches for an immediate descendant by name. Notice that since **subobject** returns a pointer to an **OI_d_tech**, and since **set_default_text** is a member function of an **OI_entry_field** but not **OI_d_tech**, the result of the call to **subobject** must be cast to be an **OI_entry_field***.

You can use two other member functions, **num_props** and **numbered_child**, to traverse all children of a given object and get a pointer to an arbitrary child object. **num_props** returns the number of children an object has. The number returned does not count internal OI objects. For example, in a dialog box, **num_props** does not count the button menu at the bottom of the box. In effect, **num_props** returns the number of children you have added to the object. Similarly, **numbered_child** returns a pointer to the nth child, again ignoring internal OI objects.

Example 6-4 shows a function which recursively clears all **OI_entry_field** objects that are descendants of the original argument object.

```
#include <OI/oi.H>
void    clear_kids(OI_d_tech *parent_objp)
{
        OI_d_tech               *child_objp;
        int                     i;

    for (i=0 ; i<parent_objp->num_props( ) ; i++){
        child_objp = parent_objp->numbered_child(i);
        if (child_objp->is_derived_from("OI_entry_field"))
            ((OI_entry_field*)child_objp)->set_text("",OI_no);
        else
            clear_kids(child_objp);
    }
    return;
}
```

Example 6-4   Clearing All Entry Field Descendants of an Object

subobject   (Member function)

```
OI_d_tech *OI_d_tech::subobject(
    const char          *namp)              // name of subobject to find


OI_d_tech *OI_d_tech::subobject(
    XrmQuark            qrk)                // name of subobject as XrmQuark
```

subobject returns a pointer to the direct descendant object (child) whose name is specified in *namp* or *qrk*. In the case where the desired object is not an immediate descendant, you can specify a path in *namp* (or *qrk*) to the descendant. You can convert a string to an XrmQuark using the Xlib function **XrmStringToQuark**.

For example, if you have a pointer *wp* to a main application window, which has a child dialog box named "water_system", one of whose children is a slider named "irrig_gate", you can get a pointer to the slider this way:

```
    sp = (OI_slider*)wp->subobject("water_system/irrig_gate");
```

descendant   (Member function)

```
OI_d_tech *OI_d_tech::descendant(
    const char            *namp)          // name of descendant to find
```

descendant returns a pointer to the first descendant whose name is specified by *namp*. This function potentially takes a relatively long time, as it recursively descends all possible children of the current object in its search for the object *namp*. It returns NULL if it finds no descendant of this name.

The order of searching is undefined; you should normally only use this function when you know that your object names are unique, or when similarly-named objects are functionally equivalent for the intended purpose.

Here is an example of finding the object "water_system/irrig_gate" in a different way than shown under **subobject** above:

```
sp = (OI_slider*)wp->descendant("irrig_gate");
```

This is only guaranteed to find the same object as the example above if *wp* has only one descendant named "irrig_gate".

descendant_by_window   (Member function)

```
OI_d_tech *OI_d_tech::descendant_by_window(
    Window                win)            // window owned by descendant to find
```

Each displayable OI object whose class is derived from **OI_w_d_tech** is associated with a separate X window. Each X window has a unique Window id. **descendant_by_window** returns a pointer to the first descendant object which uses window *win*. If *win* belongs to the current object, the current object is returned. If no descendant uses window *win*, NULL is returned. For windowless objects, **descendant_by_window** searches for a windowed descendant which matches *win*. You may need to use this function if you are handling XEvents.

next_child   (Member function)

```
OI_d_tech *OI_d_tech::next_child(
    OI_d_tech             *this_child)    // child whose next sibling you want
```

next_child returns a pointer to the next direct descendant (child) of the object, assuming the current child is *this_child*. No ordering of children is guaranteed. You can use this call to traverse all the children of an object. To get a pointer to the first child of an object, set *this_child* to NULL. When all children of the object have been found, **next_child** returns NULL. Children which are internal OI objects are ignored. For example, **next_child** never returns a pointer to the button menu at the bottom of a dialog box. This function is not as fast as the **OI_d_tech** member function **numbered_child**.

The traversal sequence is by rows if the layout method is

> **OI_layout_row**
> **OI_layout_row_aligned**
> **OI_layout_row_column**
> **OI_layout_titled_row_column**

```
OI_layout_row_column_aligned
OI_layout_wrapped_row.
```

The sequence is by columns if the layout method is

```
OI_layout_column
OI_layout_wrapped_column.          .
```

If the layout is **OI_layout_vert_tree**, the default traversal order is from top to bottom, traversing the left-most nodes first, then the next to left-most, recursively, until finally the right-most nodes are visited. If the layout is OI_layout_horz_tree, the same method of traversal is used, except the order is from left to right, traversing the top-most nodes first.

If you have used manual layout, the default traversal order corresponds to the order in which you associated the objects to the top-level parent object.

Here is an example of finding all the direct descendants of a dialog box **dbp**:

```
OI_d_tech               *dtp;
OI_box                  *dbp;
dtp = NULL;
while (dtp = dbp->next_child(dtp)) {
    ...                         // do processing here for the child found
}
```

prev_child   (Member function)

```
OI_d_tech *OI_d_tech::prev_child(
    OI_d_tech            *this_child)        // child whose previous sibling you want
```

prev_child returns a pointer to the previous direct descendant (child) of the object, assuming the current child is *this_child*. No ordering of children is guaranteed. You can use this call to traverse all the children of an object in a similar manner to **next_child**. The previous child and next child are related in the expected manner—for example, if **dtp** points to a child of **objp**, and the following lines of code are executed,

```
dtp1 = objp->next_child(dtp);
dtp2 = objp->prev_child(dtp1);
```

then **dtp2** will point to the same object as **dtp**.

numbered_child   (Member function)

```
OI_d_tech *OI_d_tech::numbered_child(
    OI_number            chld_num)           // number of child to find
```

numbered_child returns a pointer to the *child_num*th direct descendant (child) of the object. Although the children are numbered in this call, no ordering of children is guaranteed. You use this call to traverse all the children of an object. If *child_num* is less than zero or greater than or equal to the number of the object's children, **numbered_child** returns NULL. Children which are internal OI objects are ignored. For example, **numbered_child** never returns a pointer to the button menu at the bottom of a dialog box. This function is faster than **next_child**. For example, to find all the direct descendants of a dialog box **dbp**:

```
    int                 i;
    OI_d_tech           *dtp;
    OI_box              *dbp;
for (i=0 ; i<dbp->num_props( ) ; i++){
    dtp = dbp->numbered_child(i);
    ...                         // do processing here for the ith child
}
```

num_props   (Member function)

```
OI_number OI_d_tech::num_props( )
```

num_props returns the number of direct descendants (children) of the object. The number returned does not include a count of internal OI objects. For example, the button menu at the bottom of a dialog box is not included in this count. In effect, num_props returns the number of children you have parented to the object.

is_descendant   (Member function)

```
OI_bool OI_d_tech::is_descendant(
    OI_d_tech           *objp)          // pointer to OI object
```

is_descendant returns OI_yes if *objp* is a descendant of the current object; otherwise it returns OI_no.

6.3.6   Ancestors

These functions help you find parents and more distant ancestors of any given OI object. The motivation for using these functions is to avoid using global variables. For example, suppose you have a dialog box containing many entry fields; together these fields represent one record of an employee file. If the user types a number into the field named "emp_num," you want its callback routine to find the appropriate employee record and fill in the field named "emp_name." The callback routine will have a pointer to the entry field "emp_num," but none to the parent dialog box, or to the entry field "emp_name." Suppose the string you want to display in the "emp_name" entry field is contained in the variable *enam.* You accomplish the task by finding the parent of "emp_num", then finding its child named "emp_name" this way:

```
    OI_entry_field          *enump ;
    OI_entry_field          *enamep ;
enamep = (OI_entry_field*)enump->parent( )->subobject("emp_name") ;
enamep->set_default_text(enam) ;
```

ancestor   (Member function)

```
OI_d_tech *OI_d_tech::ancestor(
    const char          *namp)          // name of ancestor object
```

```
OI_d_tech *OI_d_tech::ancestor(
    XrmQuark            qrk)             // name of ancestor object as XrmQuark
```

ancestor returns a pointer to the closest ancestor of the current object with name *namp* or *qrk*. It traverses up the object tree, starting at the current object's parent, and stops when it finds an object whose name matches *namp* (or *qrk*). ancestor returns NULL if no such object is found. You can convert a string to an XrmQuark using the Xlib function XrmStringToQuark.

ancestor_derived_from   (Member function)

```
OI_d_tech *OI_d_tech::ancestor_derived_from(
    const char          *cls,              // class name as string
    OI_bool             intrnl=OI_no)      // consider internal objects?


OI_d_tech *OI_d_tech::ancestor_derived_from(
    XrmQuark            qrk,               // class name converted to XrmQuark
    OI_bool             intrnl=OI_no)      // consider internal objects?


OI_d_tech *OI_d_tech::ancestor_derived_from(
    OI_class            *cls_obj,          // pointer to class object
    OI_bool             intrnl=OI_no)      // consider internal objects?
```

ancestor_derived_from returns a pointer to the nearest ancestor derived from the specified class of object. *cls* is the OI class of the object, delimited by quotes (for example, "OI_app_window" or "OI_menu_cell"). If *intrnl*=OI_yes, objects that OI creates for internal use are considered; otherwise they are ignored. ancestor_derived_from returns NULL if no such object is found.

qrk is an XrmQuark representation of the OI class name. You can convert a string to an XrmQuark using the Xlib function XrmStringToQuark.

cls_obj is a pointer to the class object for the desired class. Using this form is the most efficient. Use *class_type*::clsp for this pointer. For example, to find an object derived from an OI_poly_menu, set *cls_obj* to OI_poly_menu::clsp. For backward compatibility with early OI releases, many OI classes (but not all) also have a synonym for *class_type*::clsp; it is *class_type*, all capitalized. For example, the obsolete form is OI_POLY_MENU for *cls_obj* instead of OI_poly_menu::clsp if you prefer.

app_window   (Member function)

```
OI_app_window *OI_d_tech::app_window( )
```

app_window returns a pointer to the nearest ancestor that is an application window. It returns NULL if none exists.

parent   (Member function)

```
OI_d_tech *OI_d_tech::parent( )
```

parent returns a pointer to the parent of the object. parent only finds objects you have created, never any internal OI objects (such as the viewport in a scroll box). parent returns the closest ancestor to the object that is not an internal OI object. The parent of a top-level object is *connection*->root( ) and that of a newly created object is the orphanage.

abs_parent   (Member function)

```
OI_d_tech *OI_d_tech::abs_parent( )
```

abs_parent returns a pointer to the *absolute* parent of the object. The absolute parent of an object is its immediate parent. In many cases this is the same as its logical parent. However, some objects parent their children not to themselves directly, but to some interior object. For example, objects parented to an app_window are actually parented to the interior box. For these children, **parent** is the app_window, and **abs_parent** is the interior of the interior box (3D models use a two level box).

root_ancestor   (Member function)

```
OI_d_tech *OI_d_tech::root_ancestor( )
```

root_ancestor returns a pointer to the most distant ancestor which is not a root object (that is, the object just below the root). If the object is in the orphanage or is a descendant of an object in the orphanage, **root_ancestor** returns a pointer to the orphanage. Otherwise, it returns a pointer to the top-level ancestor whose parent is the *root* object.

top_ancestor   (Member function)

```
OI_d_tech *OI_d_tech::top_ancestor( )
```

top_ancestor returns a pointer to the most-distant ancestor that is not the orphanage. If the object is a direct descendant of the orphanage, **top_ancestor** returns a pointer to the object itself. If the object is a descendant of an object in the orphanage, **top_ancestor** returns a pointer to the object in the orphanage. Otherwise, it returns a pointer to the top-level ancestor whose parent is the *root* object.

top_X_ancestor   (Member function)

```
OI_d_tech *OI_d_tech::top_X_ancestor( )
```

top_X_ancestor returns a pointer to the most-distant ancestor in the X Window hierarchy that is not the orphanage. If the object is a direct descendant of the orphanage, **top_X_ancestor** returns a pointer to the object itself.

6.3.7   Deleting and Unparenting Objects

The functions discussed here allow you to delete objects. There are may reasons to delete an object. One might be the following: suppose you create a menu at execution time with labels taken from names in the /etc/passwd file on a user-specified system on the network. If the user specifies a new system, you need to delete the old menu and create a new menu from the /etc/passwd file on the new system.

You can either delete objects immediately (using the C++ **delete** operator, or the member functions **del** or **delete_all**), or in a delayed mode (using **delete_delayed** or **delete_all_delayed**). Be sure the objects are no longer in use before you delete them. You cannot use **del** or **delete_all** for an object (or any ancestor of the object) in a callback for that object. For example, suppose you are writing a callback function for a menu cell, and in this callback you would like to delete the parent menu (perhaps to replace it with a different menu). You cannot delete the menu immediately because it is still in use (the callback for the menu cell is still executing). In this case you must use delete_delayed or delete_all_delayed; these functions unparent the object but wait until some time later before performing the delete.

OI keeps a *delete-delayed* queue, which is a first-in, first-out queue of objects for which you have called delete_delayed or delete_all_delayed that have not yet been deleted. When you call delete_delayed or delete_all_delayed again, the object at the top of the queue is deleted and the object for which you just called one of these functions is entered at the bottom of the queue. The delete-delayed queue's default length is one. You can change the queue's length using the function OI_set_delete_delayed_queue_length (see page 5-31).

Note that you should not use delete_delayed or delete_all_delayed instead of the immediate delete functions unnecessarily. Because of the queue implementation for delete_delayed and delete_all_delayed when you call delete_delayed or delete_all_delayed, there is a potential for failure. For example, suppose you have not changed the default delete-delayed queue length of 1, and suppose you have two menus, "A" and "B". Suppose further you have a callback registered for a cell in menu "A". In this callback you first call delete_delayed for menu "A", then immediately call delete_delayed for menu "B". "A" is pushed onto the delete_delayed queue first. When "B" is pushed onto the queue, "A" is pushed out the end of the queue and deleted. Since you are still in the callback for the cell of menu "A", you get a core dump.

del   (Member function)

```
void OI_d_tech::del( )
```

del immediately deletes the object. del is a synonym for the C++ **delete** operator. Any of the object's children which are not internal to OI (which you specifically parented to the object) are reparented to the orphanage. If the object is still in use, you should use delete_delayed instead of del. Note that if you call del many times for objects that have children and do not reuse the children or delete them, these children tie up resources unnecessarily, until the program terminates.

delete_delayed   (Member function)

```
void OI_d_tech::delete_delayed( )
```

delete_delayed immediately unparents the object from its current parent (thus removing it from the display) and reparents it to the orphanage. The object is not actually deleted until some time later. This deletion delay exists specifically so that OI can properly finish up already-started operations on an object. Use this function or delete_all_delayed when you want to delete an object that is currently in use (that is, the delete is being performed from a callback function for the object or one of its descendants).

delete_all   (Member function)

```
void OI_d_tech::delete_all( )
```

delete_all deletes the object and all of its descendants. If the object is still in use, you should use delete_all_delayed instead of delete_all.

delete_all_delayed   (Member function)

```
void OI_d_tech::delete_all_delayed( )
```

delete_all_delayed immediately unparents the object from its current parent (thus removing it from the display) and reparents it to the orphanage. The object and all of its descendants are not actually deleted until some time later. This deletion delay exists specifically so that OI can finish up already-started operations on an object. Use this function or **delete_delayed** when you want to delete an object that is currently in use (that is, the delete is being performed from a callback function for the object or one of its descendants).

unparent   (Member function)

```
void OI_d_tech::unparent( )
```

unparent disassociates the object from its parent. The object is reparented to the orphanage; you can subsequently associate it with a new parent.

set_destroy   (Member function)

```
void OI_d_tech::set_destroy(
    OI_destroy_fnp      fnp,            // pointer to callback function
    void                *argp=NULL)     // arbitrary argument for fn


void OI_d_tech::set_destroy(
    OI_callback         *objp,          // memfnp's object
    OI_destroy_memfnp   memfnp,         // pointer to callback member function
    void                *argp=NULL)     // arbitrary argument for memfnp
```

The **set_destroy** functions register a callback function to be invoked whenever the object is about to be destroyed. For example, you may wish to save the state of an application before it is terminated by a window manager. This callback is identified within OI as a **cbDestroy** callback function (see Section 6.18, "Determining and Adding Callbacks; Multiple Callbacks," on page 6-117). *memfnp* points to a member function for the object pointed to by *objp*. If your destroy callback function is a member function, when it is invoked it will be called as if you had written *objp->memfnp*. See Section 2.5, "Callbacks and Event-Driven Programming," on page 2-16 for more explanation.

argp is optional, and may be any valid expression that can be cast to a pointer. You can use it to pass additional information to the function *fn* or *memfnp*.

Writing the Destroy Callback Function

If the **cbDestroy** callback function is not a member function, write it in this form:

```
void fn(
        OI_d_tech  *oi_objp,          // pointer to OI object
        void        *argp)            // arbitrary argument
```

and if the **cbDestroy** callback function is a member function, write it in this form:

```
void obj_class::memfn(
        OI_d_tech  *oi_objp,          // pointer to OI object
        void        *argp)            // arbitrary argument
```

where *obj_class* is the class of the object whose member function is *memfn*. When your callback function is invoked, *argp* will be the argument specified in the **set_destroy** call, and *oi_objp* will be a pointer to the OI object which is about to be destroyed.

6.3.8   Root Window and Orphanage

Sometimes you need to find the root and/or the orphanage—the ultimate ancestors of all objects. These are the routines to use.

abs_root   (Member function)

```
OI_d_tech *OI_d_tech::abs_root( )
```

abs_root returns a pointer to an object corresponding to the absolute root window. Some window managers support a "virtual" root by interposing a window between the real root and the "virtual" root. (**swm** or **tvtwm**, for example, do this; **olvwm**, **vtwm** and **mvwm** do not.) If the user is running a window manager which supports a virtual root, and this object is part of a tree which has been reparented to a virtual root, the object returned represents the actual root, not the virtual root. You should normally use **abs_root** only to find the physical size of the display; for most other purposes, use **root**.

root   (Member function)

```
OI_d_tech *OI_d_tech::root( )
```

root returns a pointer to the logical root window for the object. If the user is running a window manager which supports a virtual root, and this object is part of a tree which has been reparented to a virtual root, the object returned represents the virtual root, not the actual root.

If the user is running a window manager which does not support a virtual root, **abs_root** and **root** return the same thing.

orphanage   (Member function)

```
OI_d_tech *OI_d_tech::orphanage( )
```

orphanage returns a pointer to the orphanage attached to the current object's connection.

is_orphanage (Member function)

```
OI_bool OI_d_tech::is_orphanage( )
```

is_orphanage returns OI_yes if the object is the orphanage; otherwise it returns OI_no.

is_root (Member function)

```
OI_bool OI_d_tech::is_root( )
```

is_root returns OI_yes if the object is the root or virtual root; otherwise it returns OI_no.

is_root_or_orphanage (Member function)

```
OI_bool OI_d_tech::is_root_or_orphanage( )
```

is_root_or_orphanage returns OI_yes if the object is the root, the virtual root or the orphanage; otherwise it returns OI_no.

6.4 Inquiring and Changing an Object's State

An object's *state* controls the visibility of the object and whether it can accept input. An object can have the following states:

OI_active
OI_inactive
OI_not_displayed
OI_active_not_displayed

See layout_associated_object or set_associated_object for a description of these values. The functions described here allow you to query the current state of an object and to change an object's state. You can also change an object's state when you associate it with its parent using layout_associated_object or set_associated_object.

is_visible (Member function)

```
OI_bool OI_d_tech::is_visible( )
```

is_visible returns OI_yes if the object and all ancestors are in either the OI_active or OI_inactive states; otherwise it returns OI_no. Note that even if is_visible returns OI_yes, the object may not be physically visible. It may be obscured by another object, it may be in a scroll box and not positioned in the viewport, or the entire application may be off the visible portion of the display.

set_state (Member function)

```
OI_stat OI_d_tech::set_state(
   OI_state            state)          // new state
```

set_state sets the state of the object to *state*. If *state* has the same value as the current state of the object, set_state has no effect.

wait_state_change   (Member function)

```
void OI_d_tech::wait_state_change(
   OI_state              state,            // new state
   OI_bool               restrict=OI_no)   // restrict interaction to this object?
```

wait_state_change sets the state of the object to *state* then processes events until the object state is no longer *state*. If *restrict* is **OI_yes**, user interaction is restricted to this object and all of its descendants, as long as this application has the input focus.

state   (Member function)

```
OI_state OI_d_tech::state( )
```

state returns the current state of the object.

6.5   Inquiring an Object's "Value"

Some objects, but not all, have a "value", represented by an ASCII string. The value of some text objects is the text in the object; the value of one dimensional display objects (gauges, sliders, scroll bars) is the current value of the display object converted to a string.

alpha_value   (Member function)

```
char *OI_d_tech::alpha_value( )
```

The value of an **OI_static_text** object is the value returned by **OI_static_text::text( )**; the value of an **OI_entry_field** object is the value returned by **OI_entry_field::part_text( )**. The value of any object derived from **OI_ctlr_1d** is the results of **OI_ctlr_1d::value( )**, converted to a string. The value of a menu object is a concatenation of the names of all its cells currently in the selected state, separated by spaces. Unnamed cells are ignored.

Important: in all cases the returned value is **malloc**'d memory and you must **free** this memory yourself.

6.6   Cloning Objects

If you have painstakingly built an object tree and discover you need another one just like it, you can clone it rather than build another one. An example of cloning that comes with every OI application is the hypertext help facility. Once the help window is popped up, the user can clone a copy by choosing the "clone" menu cell, and find new help text to read while still viewing the old one.

clone   (Member function)

```
OI_d_tech *OI_d_tech::clone( )
```

clone creates a copy of the object and all its descendants and returns a pointer to the new object. The parent of a cloned object is the orphanage, just as for all other newly created objects; after calling **clone** you will need to associate the new object somewhere in your object tree. **clone** returns NULL if it fails.

clone_subobjects   (Member function)

```
OI_stat OI_d_tech::clone_subobjects(
    OI_d_tech            *dtp)              // pointer to new parent object
```

clone_subobjects makes clones of all children of the object and their descendants and parents them to *dtp*. **clone_subobjects** returns NULL if it fails. **clone_subobjects** parents the cloned children using **set_associated_object** with the same position and state as they have in the original object. This may not be the desired behavior if some of the children are laid out.

6.7   Repositioning and Resizing Objects

The *position* or *location* of an object relative to its parent is the x and y offset, in pixels, of the object's outer upper-left hand corner from the parent's inside upper left-hand corner. By *outside* we mean the outermost part of the object, including its X window border. By *inside* we mean the area inside any X window border or frame area.

6.7.1   Determining Object Location

These functions allow you to find the location of an object relative to the parent object's upper left corner.

loc   (Member function)

```
void OI_d_tech::loc(
    long                     *xp,          // pointer to x coordinate returned
    long                     *yp)          // pointer to y coordinate returned
```

loc backfills *xp* and *yp* with the location in pixels of the upper-left outside corner of the object. The location is the offset from the parent object's upper-left inside corner.

loc_x   (Member function)

```
long OI_d_tech::loc_x( )
```

loc_x returns the x coordinate of the upper-left outside corner of the object relative to the upper-left inside corner of its parent.

loc_y   (Member function)

```
long OI_d_tech::loc_y( )
```

loc_y returns the y coordinate of the upper-left outside corner of the object relative to the upper-left inside corner of its parent.

ancestor_loc (Member function)

```
void OI_d_tech::ancestor_loc(
    OI_d_tech              *ancstrp,      // pointer to ancestor
    long                   *xp,           // pointer to returned x coordinate
    long                   *yp)           // pointer to returned y coordinate
```

ancestor_loc backfills *xp* and *yp* with the location in pixels of the upper-left outside corner of the object relative to the upper-left inside corner of an ancestor specified by *ancstrp*. If *ancstrp* is not an ancestor of the object, *xp* and *yp* are set to OI_def_loc.

ancestor_loc_x (Member function)

```
long OI_d_tech::ancestor_loc_x(
    OI_d_tech              *ancstrp)       // pointer to ancestor
```

ancestor_loc_x returns the x coordinate of the upper-left outside corner of the object relative to the upper-left inside corner of an ancestor specified by *ancstrp*. If *ancstrp* is not an ancestor of the object, ancestor_loc_x returns OI_def_loc.

ancestor_loc_y (Member function)

```
long OI_d_tech::ancestor_loc_y(
    OI_d_tech              *ancstrp)       // pointer to ancestor
```

ancestor_loc_y returns the y coordinate of the upper-left outside corner of the object relative to the upper-left inside corner of an ancestor specified by *ancstrp*. If *ancstrp* is not an ancestor of the object, ancestor_loc_y returns OI_def_loc.

decoration_offset (Member function)

```
void OI_d_tech::decoration_offset(
    OI_number              *xp,           // pointer to x component
    OI_number              *yp)           // pointer to y component
```

decoration_offset backfills *xp* and *yp* with the horizontal and vertical offsets of the object from its window decoration's upper-left corner (from the window decoration supplied by the window manager). You should only call this function for a top-level or unclipped object, such as an OI_app_window object, because other objects have no window decoration supplied by the window manager. If your application is running under a reparenting window manager (that is, your top-level object is reparented to a window manager's window that contains your object and which may be larger than your object), this offset may be larger than zero. If the window manager does not reparent client objects, the offset is zero. (olwm, mwm, twm, and swm are all window managers which reparent client objects.) If you call this function for an object that is not a top-level or unclipped object, the offset is zero regardless of the window manager. In order for this function to return meaningful information, the top-level object must be known to the window manager at the time the function is invoked, and it must be in state OI_active or OI_inactive.

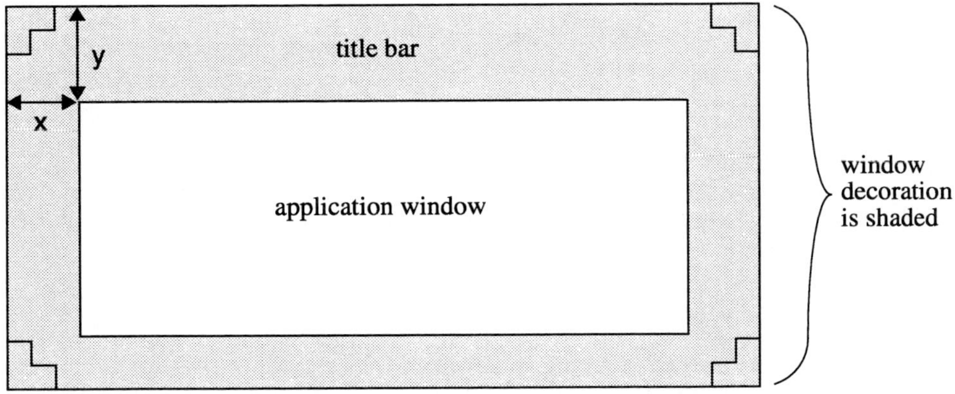

Figure 6-11   x and y Values Backfilled by decoration_offset

decoration_offset_x   (Member function)

```
OI_number OI_d_tech::decoration_offset_x( )
```

decoration_offset_x returns the horizontal component of the offset of a top-level object from
its window manager's outside window origin. See **decoration_offset** for more explanation.

decoration_offset_y   (Member function)

```
OI_number OI_d_tech::decoration_offset_y( )
```

decoration_offset_y returns the vertical component of the offset of a top-level object from its
window manager's outside window origin. See **decoration_offset** for more explanation.

in_obj   (Member function)

```
OI_bool OI_d_tech::in_obj(
    long              x,           // x coordinate relative to object origin
    long              y)           // x coordinate relative to object origin


OI_bool OI_d_tech::in_obj(
    long              x,           // x coordinate relative to object origin
    long              y,           // x coordinate relative to object origin
    int               wid,         // width of region to be considered
    int               ht)          // height of region to be considered
```

The first form of **in_obj** returns **OI_yes** if the coordinates (x,y), relative to the object origin, lie
within the object; otherwise it returns **OI_no**. If the coordinates lie within the decoration for the
object (that is, within the window border), they are considered to be inside the object.

The second form of **in_obj** returns **OI_yes** if any of the region with upper-left corner at (x,y)
and size *wid* x *ht* is within the object; otherwise it returns **OI_no**.

is_within_abs_root   (Member function)

```
OI_bool OI_d_tech::is_within_abs_root(
    long               x,              // x coordinate to be tested
    long               y,              // y coordinate to be tested
    OI_d_tech          *prnt_obj=NULL) // pointer to pseudo parent object
```

is_within_abs_root returns **OI_yes** if placing the object at (x,y) relative to *prnt_obj*'s upper-left corner will leave the entire object visible on the display; otherwise it returns **OI_no**. *prnt_obj* is a pointer to another object which is this object's logical parent for this operation. If *prnt_obj* is NULL, the object's actual parent is used.

6.7.2   Sizing Objects

Many OI objects can be resized. Top-level objects or objects whose visibility is not constrained by its parent's borders (see **allow_clip** and **disallow_clip**) can be resized using the window manager's resizing capabilities. Other objects can be resized from within the program, but cannot normally be resized directly by the user. Some objects can be resized in only one direction. For example, you cannot change the width of a vertical scroll bar, slider or gauge. You can inquire as to whether an object can be resized and change its resize permissions to either allow or prevent resizing.

is_horz_resize   (Member function)

```
OI_bool OI_d_tech::is_horz_resize( )
```

is_horz_resize( ) returns **OI_yes** if the object is allowed to be resized horizontally; otherwise it returns **OI_no**.

allow_horz_resize   (Member function)

```
void OI_d_tech::allow_horz_resize( )
```

allow_horz_resize configures the object so that it can be resized horizontally.

disallow_horz_resize   (Member function)

```
void OI_d_tech::disallow_horz_resize( )
```

disallow_horz_resize configures the object so that it cannot be resized horizontally.

is_vert_resize   (Member function)

```
OI_bool OI_d_tech::is_vert_resize( )
```

is_vert_resize returns **OI_yes** if the object is allowed to be resized vertically; otherwise it returns **OI_no**.

allow_vert_resize   (Member function)

```
void OI_d_tech::allow_vert_resize( )
```

allow_vert_resize configures the object so that it can be resized vertically.

disallow_vert_resize   (Member function)

```
void OI_d_tech::disallow_vert_resize( )
```

disallow_vert_resize configures the object so that it cannot be resized vertically.

is_resize   (Member function)

```
OI_bool OI_d_tech::is_resize( )
```

is_resize returns **OI_yes** if the object is allowed to be resized in at least one direction; otherwise it returns **OI_no**.

allow_resize   (Member function)

```
void OI_d_tech::allow_resize( )
```

allow_resize configures the object so that it can be resized in both directions.

disallow_resize   (Member function)

```
void OI_d_tech::disallow_resize( )
```

disallow_resize configures the object so that it cannot be resized in any direction. Note that this function has no effect if the object is a top-level or unclipped object. **disallow_resize** automatically calls **disallow_wm_decoration(OI_wm_resize)**.

set_resize   (Member function)

```
void OI_d_tech::set_resize(
    OI_resize_fnp       fnp,            // pointer to callback function
    void                *argp=NULL)     // arbitrary argument for fn


void OI_d_tech::set_resize(
    OI_callback         *objp,          // memfnp's object
    OI_resize_memfnp    memfnp,         // pointer to callback member function
    void                *argp=NULL)     // arbitrary argument for memfnp
```

The **set_resize** functions register a callback function to be invoked immediately after the object has been resized. This callback is identified within OI as a **cbResize** callback function (see Section 6.18, "Determining and Adding Callbacks; Multiple Callbacks," on page 6-117). *memfnp* points to a member function for the object pointed to by *objp*. If your resize function is a member function, when it is invoked it will be called as if you had written *objp->memfnp*. See Section 2.5, "Callbacks and Event-Driven Programming," on page 2-16 for more explanation.

argp is optional, and may be any valid expression that can be cast to a pointer. You can use it to pass additional information to the function *fn* or *memfnp*.

Writing the Resize Callback Function

If the **cbResize** callback function is not a member function, write it in this form:

```
void fn(
        OI_d_tech  *oi_objp,        // pointer to resized OI object
        void       *argp)           // arbitrary argument
```

and if the **cbResize** callback function is a member function, write it in this form:

```
void obj_class::memfn(
        OI_d_tech  *oi_objp,        // pointer to resized OI object
        void       *argp)           // arbitrary argument
```

where *obj_class* is the class of the object whose member function is *memfn*. When your callback function is invoked, *argp* will be the argument specified in the **set_resize** call, and *oi_objp* will be a pointer to the OI object which has been resized.

When the callback function is invoked, the object will have already been resized. If you call the **size** or **space** functions for it, the new values will be returned.

size   (Member function)

```
void OI_d_tech::size(
    OI_number          *widthp,        // pointer to returned width
    OI_number          *heightp)       // pointer to returned height
```

size backfills *widthp* and *heightp* with the inside dimensions, in pixels, of the object. This is its size exclusive of any X Window border or frame.

size_x   (Member function)

```
OI_number OI_d_tech::size_x( )
```

size_x returns the inside width of the object, in pixels. This is its size exclusive of any X Window border or frame.

size_y   (Member function)

```
OI_number OI_d_tech::size_y( )
```

size_y returns the inside height of the object, in pixels. This is its size exclusive of any X Window border or frame.

set_size   (Member function)

```
OI_stat OI_d_tech::set_size(
    OI_number          width,          // width of new size
    OI_number          height)         // height of new size
```

set_size changes the object's size if the object allows resizing. If the object requires sizes in some increments other than 1, **set_size** may truncate down to the next increment. **set_size** specifies the "logical size" of an object. For example, it is the size of the interior usable space of an **OI_app_window** object—not the total size of the object.

space (Member function)

```
void OI_d_tech::space(
    OI_number          *widthp,         // pointer to returned outside width
    OI_number          *heightp)        // pointer to returned outside height
```

space backfills *widthp* and *heightp* with the outside dimensions, in pixels, of the object. This is the total space occupied by the object, including any X Window borders. For a top-level object or an object whose visibility is not constrained by its parent's borders (see **allow_clip** and **disallow_clip**), it also includes the window manager decoration.

space_x (Member function)

```
OI_number OI_d_tech::space_x( )
```

space_x returns the outside width of the object, in pixels. This is the total width occupied by the object, including any X Window borders. For a top-level object or an object whose visibility is not constrained by its parent's borders (see **allow_clip** and **disallow_clip**), it also includes the window manager decoration.

space_y (Member function)

```
OI_number OI_d_tech::space_y( )
```

space_y returns the outside height of the object, in pixels. This is the total height occupied by the object, including any X Window borders. For a top-level object or an object whose visibility is not constrained by its parent's borders (see **allow_clip** and **disallow_clip**), it also includes the window manager decoration.

6.7.3   Stacking Objects

Objects that appear to overlap or obscure one another on the screen are *stacked*. The functions discussed here give you some control over the stacking order for objects. Stacking order is normally relative to sibling objects, but is also influenced by whether objects can be clipped or not. OI considers all top-level objects and objects whose visibility is not constrained by its parent's borders (see **allow_clip** and **disallow_clip**) when determining stacking order.

is_map_raised (Member function)

```
OI_bool OI_d_tech::is_map_raised( )
```

is_map_raised returns **OI_yes** if the object will be raised to the top of the stack (it will not be obscured by its siblings) when it is made visible; otherwise it returns **OI_no**.

allow_map_raised (Member function)

```
void OI_d_tech::allow_map_raised( )
```

allow_map_raised forces the object to be raised to the top of the stack (it will be in front of any sibling objects) when it is made visible. For a top-level object or an object whose visibility is not constrained by its parent's borders (see **allow_clip** and **disallow_clip**), this forces the object to be in front of all other objects in the application, not just siblings.

disallow_map_raised   (Member function)

```
void OI_d_tech::disallow_map_raised( )
```

disallow_map_raised prevents the object from being raised when it is made visible. Consequently, it maintains its position in the stacking order. This is the default.

6.7.4   Scrolled Object Tracking

When an object follows a scroll object when it is scrolled, it is said to be *tracking* the scroll object. By default an object does not track its parent. For example, if you have an OI_scroll_text with a child which is an OI_glyph, you may want the glyph to be "attached" at a certain place in the text. In this case the glyph tracks the text as it moves up and down (or left and right). If you mark a place in the text with a glyph (as you might with break points in code for a debugger, or with paragraph marks in a word processor), you would want the glyph to track the text. By default, objects do not track, and unless you specifically allow tracking, the glyph remains stationary on the screen while the text moves. OI only supports the member functions discussed below for objects which are parented to an OI_base_text object or to an object of one of OI_base_text's subclasses.

allow_track   (Member function)

```
void OI_d_tech::allow_track(
    OI_orient            dir
             =(OI_orient)OI_horizontal|OI_vertical)   // tracking direction
```

allow_track( ) forces the object to track its parent. *dir* specifies the directions in which this object should track its **base_text** parent. *dir* must be one of

OI_horizontal	tracks horizontally
OI_vertical	tracks vertically
(OI_orient)OI_horizontal|OI_vertical.	tracks both vertically and horizontally

dir = OI_vertical means this object moves with the text if the text moves vertically, but does not move with the text if the text moves horizontally.

You should call **allow_track** for the object before parenting it using **set_associated_object**. You should not parent a tracking object using **layout_associated_object**, since its position is determined by the text, not the size and position of other objects.

disallow_track   (Member function)

```
void OI_d_tech::disallow_track(
    OT_orient            dir
             =(OI_orient)OI_vertical|OI_horizontal)   // tracking direction
```

disallow_track prevents this object from tracking in the directions specified by *dir*. If the object tracks in a direction not specified by *dir*, the object will still track in that direction. The default is for an object not to track its parent in any direction.

is_track (Member function)

```
OI_bool OI_d_tech::is_track(
    OI_orient            dir=(OI_orient)0)  // tracking direction
```

is_track returns **OI_yes** if the object is marked to track its parent in direction *dir*. *dir* must be one of the values shown for **allow_track** above. If you omit *dir*, **is_track** returns **OI_yes** if the object tracks its parent in any direction. If the object does not track its parent in direction *dir*, **is_track** returns **OI_no**.

track_type (Member function)

```
OI_orient OI_d_tech::track_type( )
```

track_type returns the directions in which the object can track its parent. This will be one of

(OI_orient)0	does not track
OI_horizontal	tracks horizontally
OI_vertical	tracks vertically
(OI_orient)OI_horizontal|OI_vertical.	tracks both vertically and horizontally

6.8 Drag-and-Drop

Drag-and-drop refers to a mechanism by which users can transfer data, with visual feedback, between objects within a single application or between applications. A *drag-source* object is one that can respond to drag initiation. A *drop-site* is an object that can accept dropped data. Data to be transferred can be any type, ranging from characters selected in a text object to pixmap data or labels, or any other data you desire to transfer in a drag-and-drop operation. A *drag-and-drop operation* refers to a single complete mechanism which starts with the drag initiation by the user and ends with the data transfer from the drag-source object to the drop-site object.

A drag-and-drop operation can either move or copy data. To *move* the data means to transfer the data to the drop-site then delete the data from the drag-source. To *copy* the data means to transfer the data to the drop-site without deleting it from the drag-source.

OI's drag-and-drop protocols, which facilitate all aspects of the drag-and-drop operation, sit on top of the generic X11 selection mechanism. OI understands and implements the two separate and incompatible drag-and-drop protocols specified by the Open Software Foundation for OSF/Motif and by Sun Microsystems for XView and OLIT toolkits. The OI drag-and-drop model is independent of any particular interaction model under which an OI client application is run. This means that an OI application running either the Motif or OPEN LOOK model can drop data on or accept dragged data from itself, another OI application, a Motif-based application, or an OPEN LOOK-based application.

Default drag-and-drop user interaction is as follows: The user selects a drag-source object by pressing the DRAG (Motif) or SELECT (OPEN LOOK) mouse button while the pointer is over the object. While holding the mouse button down, the user moves the mouse pointer to a drop-site, then drops the object on the drop-site by releasing the mouse button.

An OI_static_text, OI_entry_field or OI_multi_text object by default allows the PRIMARY selection to be dragged and dropped. A typical user interaction scenario for these objects is as follows: The user marks some text by pressing, dragging, and releasing the SELECT mouse button across the desired text. Then the user presses the DRAG mouse button (Motif) or SELECT mouse button (OPEN LOOK) on the selected text. The user moves the mouse pointer, with the mouse button still pressed, over a drop-site. and releases the mouse button. If the drop-site knows to request the appropriate type of data from the dropped drag-source, the text will be transferred to the drop-site and deleted from the text drag-source object—the text will be moved, not copied.

In order for your application to participate in drag-and-drop operations, you must do the following: If you want to have an object which can be dragged, you must enable an object to be a drag-source object. If you want to have an object which can receive a dragged object, you must enable an object to be a drop-site object. If you only enable drag-source objects, they can be dropped on other applications which provide drop-sites, and conversely, if you only enable drop-site objects, they can receive drag-source objects from other applications. You can, obviously, also enable both drag-source and drop-site objects in the same application, in which case the user can perform drag-and-drop operations within the application itself. You set up the drag-source object so that it "knows" what data it can transfer if and when requested to do so. You set up the drop-site object so that it will request data from the drag-source object when the drop-site is the recipient of a drag-and-drop operation. Once you have set up the drag-source object as described below in Section 6.8.1, "Creating a Drag-source Object," or set up a drop-site as described below in Section 6.8.2, "Creating a Drop-Site Object," you have no more responsibilities in handling either the drag-source object or the drop-site object. OI handles all data transfers at the time the object is dropped.

OI text object (OI_static_text, OI_entry_field, and OI_base_text) are automatically configured to be drag-sources. OI_entry_field and OI_base_text objects are automatically configured to be drop-sites as well.

6.8.1   Creating a Drag-source Object

To enable an object to be a drag-source object, you must do at least the first three of the following things:

- Mark the drag-source object as an object that can be dragged.
- Provide a translation to get the drag started.
- Provide a way to define the data the drag-source object will transfer when dropped on a drop-site.
- Optionally, you can provide a *drag preview* callback, which is called when a drag operation begins, as well as throughout the drag process until a drop occurs or the drag-and-drop operation otherwise terminates. Typically, you write this callback to provide visual feedback to the user to indicate that a drag operation is in process. For example, you could animate the pointer, change its color, or allow the object itself to be dragged.

The next four sections describe these operations in more detail.

6.8.1.1 Marking an Object as a Drag-source Object

Call **allow_drag** for the object. You do not need to do this for an OI_entry_field, OI_static_text or OI_multi_text object, as these objects are by default drag-source objects. You can specify two different cursors, one to display when the pointer is over a drop-site and one to display when the pointer is not over a drop-site, in the call to **allow_drag**. See Section 6.8.1.4, "Providing Visual Feedback During the Drag," below, for more details on these cursors.

To disable a drop-site, call **disallow_drag** for the object.

6.8.1.2 Providing a Translation to Start the Drag

You must provide a translation in order for the object to be dragged. You must at a minimum provide one translation using **drag_move_start** or **drag_copy_start** (see Table 6-11, "OI_d_tech Translation Functions" on page 6-138), although you may provide several mouse events that start the drag. The following code fragment is an example of a simple translation that causes pressing mouse button one on the static text object to start a move drag operation:

```
static  char            *dragTrans = "#override \n\
                                     <Btn1Down>: drag_move_start( )\n";

        OI_static_text    *stp;
stp->allow_drag( );
stp->override_translations(dragTrans);
```

6.8.1.3 Defining Data the Drag-source Object will Transfer to a Drop-site

You must specify what data the drag-source object is to transfer to the drop-site. After the drag-source object is dropped at the drop-site, the drop-site will request data by sending a **SelectionRequest** event to the drag-source object. There are several ways to specify data for the drag-source object.

- The text objects OI_entry_field, OI_static_text and OI_multi_text by default allow the PRIMARY selection to be dragged.
- You can specify static data for the object, using the member function **set_selection_data**. You name the data in the first argument to **set_selection_data**. If you have more than one piece of data that the drag-source object should be able to transfer, you call **set_selection_data** once for each piece of data, giving each piece of data a unique name in the first argument. It is then the responsibility of the drop-site object to request all the pieces of data, by name, in which it is interested.
- You can register a callback function to dynamically determine data via the member function **set_selection_convert**. You can register only one callback using **set_selection_convert**, but it can be instead of, or in addition to, static data specified by **set_selection_data**. OI executes the callback for the drag-source object whenever it receives a **SelectionRequest** event. You write the callback to provide whatever data is appropriate for your application or execute any other actions.
- If the drag-source object may be dropped on an OSF/Motif application drop-site, you must use the member function **set_selection_targets** to register the list of selection data names that the drag-source object can transfer. This list must include all the static data you specified

via calls to **set_selection_data** as well as all the names of data that can be processed by the callback registered via **set_selection_convert**.

Figure 6-12 shows the order of processing when a drag-source object receives a **SelectionRequest** event. See Program 6-1, "Allow Drag from Drag-Source Objects (Sender.C)," on pages 6-69 through 6-75 for an example of multiple **set_selection_data** calls for the static text object "DRAG ME", and both multiple **set_selection_data** calls and a **set_selection_convert** call for the static text object "WILL DELETE."

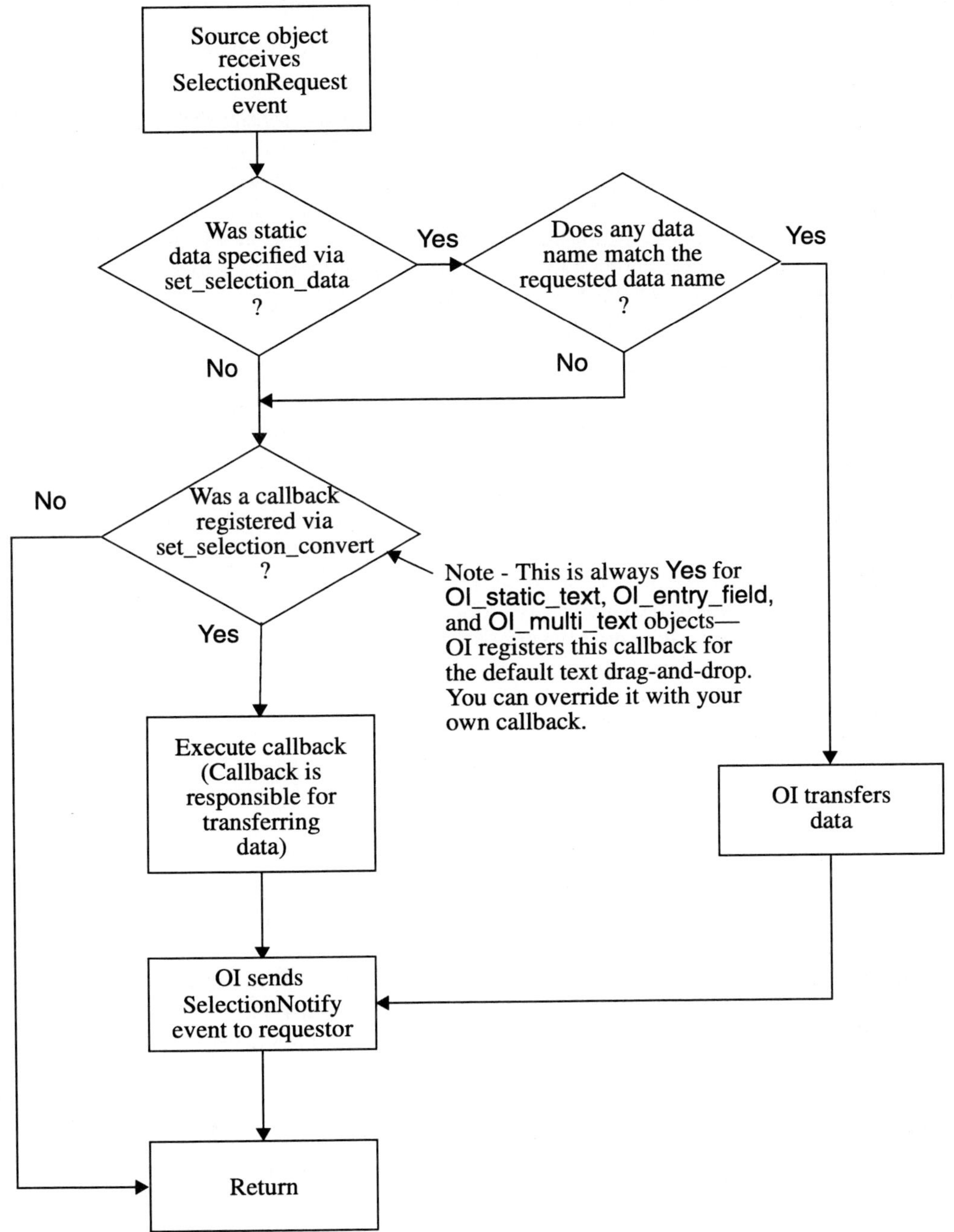

Figure 6-12   Drag-source Object SelectionRequest Event Processing

6.8.1.4   Providing Visual Feedback During the Drag

The user often finds it helpful if you supply visual feedback during the drag which indicates that a drag is in process.

When you call **allow_drag** for the drag-source object, you can specify two different cursors, one to display when the pointer is over a drop-site and one to display when the pointer is not over a drop-site. This lets the user know when it is "safe" to release the mouse button. See the function **make_cursors** in Program 6-1, "Allow Drag from Drag-Source Objects (Sender.C)," on pages 6-69 through 6-75 for an example of creating cursors to use in **allow_drag**. If you do specify cursors in this manner, you must supply a hot-spot for the cursor in the X bitmap files for the cursors (the files specified by ***.xbm** in Program 6-1). You must also specify the x and y pixel coordinates of the hot-spot in the third and fourth arguments to **make_cursor**.

You can also register a drag preview callback function, using the member function **set_drag_preview**. The callback is executed when the drag operation begins (when the user presses the mouse button while the pointer is over the drag-source object), as well as during the drag process. You can write the drag preview callback function to perform any operation you deem necessary, although typically the drag preview callback is used to provide visual feedback to the user during the drag. Both Program 6-1, "Allow Drag from Drag-Source Objects (Sender.C)," on pages 6-69 through 6-75 and Program 6-3, "Drag the Drag-Source Object Itself (DragLive.C)," on pages 6-80 through 6-82 show examples of the use of drag preview callbacks. Program 6-1 uses the drag preview to change the color of the cursor to that of the drag-source object's color. The drag preview function in Program 6-3 actually moves the drag-source object about, so that the user sees the object attached to the mouse pointer at all times.

6.8.1.5   Drag Member Functions

allow_drag   (Member function)

```
void OI_d_tech::allow_drag(
    Cursor              drag_crsr=None,      // drag cursor
    Cursor              drop_crsr=None)      // drop-site cursor
```

allow_drag conditions this object to be draggable. *drag_crsr* is the shape of the mouse pointer displayed while the object is being dragged. *drop_crsr* is the shape of the mouse pointer displayed while the object is over a valid drop-site. These cursors must have hot-spots. By default, **OI_entry_field**, **OI_static_text** and **OI_multi_text** objects are enabled to be drag-source objects. For these objects in Motif mode, OI uses the standard Motif copy and move cursors; there is no special cursor for drop-site feedback. For these objects in OPEN LOOK mode, OI uses the standard OPEN LOOK copy and move cursors, including modified cursors for drop-site feedback.

disallow_drag   (Member function)

```
void OI_d_tech::disallow_drag( )
```

disallow_drag prevents this object from being a drag-source object.

is_drag   (Member function)

```
OI_bool OI_d_tech::is_drag( )
```

is_drag returns **OI_yes** if this is a drag-source object; otherwise it returns **OI_no**.

initiate_dragdrop   (Member function)

```
OI_bool OI_d_tech::initiate_dragdrop(
    OI_dnd_operation      op,            // OI_dnd_move or OI_dnd_copy
    int                   x_loc,         // x coordinate of mouse press in object
    int                   y_loc,         // y coordinate of mouse press in object
    Cursor                drag_crsr=None, // drag cursor
    Cursor                drop_crsr=None, // drop-site cursor
    OI_number             threshold=0)    // number pixels move to start drag-and-drop
```

OI calls **initiate_dragdrop** from the translation action functions **drag_move_start** and **drag_copy_start** (see Table 6-11, "OI_d_tech Translation Functions" on page 6-138), so normally you do not need to use this function. However, if you override either of these functions, you must call **initiate_dragdrop** yourself from your **drag_move_start** or **drag_copy_start**. Set *op* to **OI_dnd_move** if the drag will be a move operation (the original data will be deleted when the drop completes) or to **OI_dnd_copy** if it will be a copy (the original data will not be deleted). *x_loc* and *y_loc* are the x and y coordinates in pixels of the mouse pointer relative to the upper left corner of the drag-source object. *drag_crsr* and *drop_crsr* are the same as for **allow_drag**. *threshold* is the number of pixels the pointer must move after the mouse press before the drag-and-drop operation starts. **initiate_dragdrop** returns **OI_yes** if the drag-and-drop operation actually started; it returns **OI_no** if it failed to start.

set_selection_data   (Member function)

```
void OI_d_tech::set_selection_data(
    Atom                  sel_nam,       // selection data name
    Atom                  typ,           // data type
    void                  *data,         // pointer to data to be set
    unsigned int          count,         // number of elements in data
    unsigned int          siz)           // data element size in bits
```

set_selection_data saves static data to be used in response to a **SelectionRequest** event. *sel_nam* is the data name; this can be any arbitrary atom to identify the data. *typ* is the type of data, for example: **STRING** or **INTEGER**. You may set *sel_nam* and *typ* to any values; however, any object which issues a **SelectionRequest** to this object must understand the data name and type you set here. *data* is a pointer to the data to send to the requestor. *count* is the number of elements included in *data*. *siz* is the size, in bits, of each *data* element. (*count* * (*siz* / 8)) must yield the number of bytes pointed to by *data*. You can convert a string to an atom using the **OI_connection** member function **atom**. For example:

```
            OI_connectio    *conp;
            OI_static_text *stp;
    static char             my_string[] = "abcdef";
    stp->set_selection_data(conp->atom("MY_NAME"), conp->atom("STRING"),
                                    my_string, strlen(my_string), 8);
```

If the drag-and-drop operation is a move (**OI_dnd_move**) rather than a copy (**OI_dnd_copy**), and if the drop callback calls **delete_drop_data**, a message is sent to the drag-source object requesting that it delete the data.

set_selection_targets   (Member function)

```
void OI_d_tech::set_selection_targets(
    Atom                    *sel_nams,      // vector of selection data names
    OI_bool                 allocate=OI_yes)  // allocate new memory?
```

set_selection_targets stores a list of Atoms that are valid data names for selection conversion. Include in this list the names of any data you specify for the object with calls to **set_selection_data**, as well as all data names any selection conversion callback you register with **set_selection_convert** can convert. The object will respond with this list when requested to convert the TARGETS selection. If the object is dragged over an OSF/Motif application drop-site, the drop-site requests the TARGETS selection. (The OSF/Motif drop-site checks TARGETS to ascertain whether the drag-source object has data in which it is interested.) *sel_nams* is an array of Atoms of selection data names. Set the final element of the array to **None**. If *allocate* is **OI_yes**, OI allocates new memory to store the list; if it is **OI_no**, OI uses the array passed in. If you have a large number of objects for which you want to call **set_selection_targets** with the same target list, to be more efficient you should cache the Atoms, call **set_selection_targets** with allocate equal to **OI_no**, and let the objects share a pointer to the array.

get_selection_data   (Member function)

```
void *OI_d_tech::get_selection_data(
    const char          *sel_nam_str,    // selection data name
    const char          *targ_typ_str,   // selection conversion type
    Atom                *actual_typ,     // actual type of the converted value
    int                 *actual_fmt,     // length of a unit of data
    unsigned long       *how_many)       // number of units of data of length actual_fmt

void *OI_d_tech::get_selection_data(
    Atom                sel_nam_atm,     // selection data name
    Atom                targ_typ_atm,    // selection conversion type
    Atom                *actual_typ,     // actual type of the converted value
    int                 *actual_fmt,     // length of a unit of data
    unsigned long       *how_many)       // number of units of data of length actual_fmt
```

```
void *OI_d_tech::get_selection_data(
    const char          *targ_typ_str,     // selection conversion type
    Atom                *actual_typ,        // actual type of the converted value
    int                 *actual_fmt,        // length of a unit of data
    unsigned long       *how_many)          // number of units of data of length actual_fmt


void *OI_d_tech::get_selection_data(
    Atom                *targ_typ_atm,      // selection conversion type
    Atom                *actual_typ,        // actual type of the converted value
    int                 *actual_fmt,        // length of a unit of data
    unsigned long       *how_many)          // number of units of data of length actual_fmt
```

get_selection_data returns a pointer to the selection data for this object. The selection data is retrieved via the selection convert callback you have registered using **set_selection_convert** or from data you have registered using **set_selection_data**. *sel_nam_str* or *sel_nam_atm* is the selection name or Atom to fetch. *targ_typ_str* or *targ_typ_atm* defines how you want the selection converted (typically LENGTH, STRING, etc.). *actual_typ* is backfilled with the actual type of the converted value. *actual_fmt* is backfilled with the number of bits in each unit of data returned (8, 16, 32), and *how_many* is backfilled with the number of units of data contained in the return value. You must examine *actual_typ* and cast the return pointer appropriately.

There may be times when you want to retrieve data but you do not know the selection name; for example, the drag-and-drop code uses a transient selection that is not available until a drag-and-drop operation is performed. In this case, use the form of the member function that does not have the selection name parameter.

set_selection_convert   (Member function)

```
void OI_d_tech::set_selection_convert(
    OI_sel_cvt_fnp          fnp,             // pointer to callback function
    void                    *argp=NULL)      // arbitrary argument for fn


void OI_d_tech::set_selection_convert(
    OI_callback             *objp,           // memfnp's object
    OI_sel_cvt_memfnp       memfnp,          // pointer to callback member function
    void                    *argp=NULL)      // arbitrary argument for memfnp
```

The **set_selection_convert** functions register a callback function to be invoked whenever a **SelectionRequest** event is sent to the object. This callback is identified within OI as a **cbSelectionConvert** callback function (see Section 6.18, "Determining and Adding Callbacks; Multiple Callbacks," on page 6-117). *memfnp* points to a member function for the object pointed to by *objp*. If your selection convert callback function is a member function, when it is invoked it will be called as if you had written *objp->memfnp*. See Section 2.5, "Callbacks and Event-Driven Programming," on page 2-16 for more explanation.

argp is optional, and may be any valid expression that can be cast to a pointer. You can use it to pass additional information to the function *fn* or *memfnp*.

Writing the Selection Convert Callback Function

If the **cbSelectionConvert** callback function is not a member function, write it in this form:

```
OI_bool fn(
        OI_d_tech            *oi_objp,   // pointer to OI object
        void                 *argp,      // arbitrary argument
        const XEvent         *eventp)    // pointer to X event
```

and if the **cbSelectionConvert** callback function is a member function, write it in this form:

```
OI_bool obj_class::memfn(
        OI_d_tech            *oi_objp,   // pointer to OI object
        void                 *argp,      // arbitrary argument
        const XEvent         *eventp)    // pointer to X event
```

where *obj_class* is the class of the object whose member function is *memfn*. When your callback function is invoked, *argp* will be the argument specified in the **set_selection_convert** call, and *oi_objp* will be a pointer to the OI object which received the **SelectionRequest**. *eventp* will be a pointer to the **XEvent** structure that triggered the callback. Your callback function should examine the **xselectionrequest** member of the **XEvent** structure and attempt to complete the selection transfer. You will need to fill in the appropriate properties on the **XEvent** structure and call **XChangeProperty** for the structure. OI handles sending the **SelectionNotify** to the requestor. If the drag-and-drop operation may be a move (**OI_dnd_move**) rather than a copy (**OI_dnd_copy**), you need to provide a way to delete the data after the drop in this callback. Typically, you should respond to the DELETE target. See Program 6-1, "Allow Drag from Drag-Source Objects (Sender.C)," on pages 6-69 through 6-75 for an example, and read the ICCCM for more details.

If successful the function should return **OI_yes**, otherwise it should return **OI_no**.

set_drag_preview   (Member function)

```
void OI_d_tech::set_drag_preview(
    OI_drag_preview_fnp        fnp,            // pointer to callback function
    void                       *argp=NULL)    // arbitrary argument for fn


void OI_d_tech::set_drag_preview(
    OI_callback                *objp,          // memfnp's object
    OI_drag_preview_memfnp     memfnp,         // pointer to callback member function
    void                       *argp=NULL)    // arbitrary argument for memfnp
```

The **set_drag_preview** functions register a callback function to be invoked whenever the mouse pointer is over this object and the user presses the appropriate mouse button, starting a drag-and-drop operation. It is also called during the drag. This allows you to change the object's appearance at that time, change the cursor, or perform any other actions. You can also change cursors by calling **allow_drag** with two different cursors, in which case OI takes care of changing the cursors for you; the second cursor displays when the pointer is over a valid drop-site. This callback is identified within OI as a **cbDragPreview** callback function (see Section 6.18, "Determining and Adding Callbacks; Multiple Callbacks," on page 6-117). *memfnp* points to a member function for the object pointed to by *objp*. If your drag preview callback function is a member function, when it is invoked it will be called as if you had written *objp->memfnp*. See Section 2.5, "Callbacks and Event-Driven Programming," on page 2-16 for more explanation.

argp is optional, and may be any valid expression that can be cast to a pointer. You can use it to pass additional information to the function *fn* or *memfnp*.

Writing the Drag Preview Callback Function

If the **cbDragPreview** callback function is not a member function, write it in this form:

```
void fn(
    OI_d_tech          *oi_objp,    // pointer to OI object
    void               *argp,       // arbitrary argument
    OI_dnd_operation op,            // operation occurring
    long               x,           // x location of mouse pointer
    long               y)           // y location of mouse pointer
```

and if the **cbDragPreview** callback function is a member function, write it in this form:

```
void obj_class::memfn(
    OI_d_tech          *oi_objp,    // pointer to OI object
    void               *argp,       // arbitrary argument
    OI_dnd_operation op,            // operation occurring
    long               x,           // x location of mouse pointer
    long               y)           // y location of mouse pointer
```

where *obj_class* is the class of the object whose member function is *memfn*. When your callback function is invoked, *argp* will be the argument specified in the **set_drag_preview** call, and *oi_objp* will be a pointer to the dragged OI object. *op* will be one of the following:

OI_dnd_start	The drag-and-drop operation is starting.
OI_dnd_done	The dragged object has been dropped on the drop-site.
OI_dnd_enter	The pointer has entered a drop-site.
OI_dnd_leave	The pointer has left a drop-site.
OI_dnd_motion	The pointer has moved.

x and *y* will indicate the root position—the x and y pixel coordinates of the pointer on screen relative to the root window—of the pointer where the drop event is happening.

6.8.2   Creating a Drop-Site Object

To enable an object to be a drop-site object, you do the following things:

- Mark the drop-site object as a drop-site. OI_entry_field and OI_multi_text objects are drop-sites by default.
- Register a drop callback, which is called each time a drag-source object is dropped on the drop-site. This drop callback must request the data from the drag-source object—this is how the data is actually transferred.
- Optionally, you can provide more visual feedback by using a *drop preview* callback, which is executed when the mouse pointer moves over the drop-site during a drag operation. Typically you write the callback to do such things as change the color of the drop-site to indicate that the object is a valid drop-site.

The next three sections describe these operations in more detail.

6.8.2.1   Marking an Object as a Drop-site

Call allow_drop for the object. You do not need to do this for an OI_entry_field or OI_multi_text object, as these objects are by default drop-site objects. If you omit the arguments to allow_drop, the entire rectangular area of the object is registered as the drop-site. Alternatively you can specify the union of a number of rectangular areas as the drop-site when you call allow_drop.

To disable a drop-site, call disallow_drop for the object.

6.8.2.2   Registering a Drop Callback

You must register a drop callback using the member function set_drop. You write the drop callback to request the data from the drag-source object that was dropped on the drop-site. You must know the name(s) of the data the drag-source object can provide. These names are registered when set_selection_data and set_selection_targets is called for the drag-source object. You will need to call get_drop_data in this callback to obtain the data to be transferred from the drag-source object. You also need to query if the drag-and-drop operation was a move (OI_dnd_move) or a copy (OI_dnd_copy); if it was a move, you should call delete_drop_data after getting the data.

6.8.2.3   Providing Visual Feedback at the Drop-site During the Drag

You can provide visual feedback to the user, such as changing the drop-site object's shape or color, or outlining it, when the mouse pointer moves over the drop-site. You do this by registering a drop preview callback using the member function set_drop_preview. You can write the drop preview callback function to perform any operation you deem necessary, although typically the drop preview callback is used to provide visual feedback to the user.

6.8.2.4   Drop Member Functions

allow_drop   (Member function)

```
void OI_d_tech::allow_drop(
    OI_dnd_clip_rectangle  *rects=NULL,        // list of rectangles
    OI_number              num_rects=0)        // number of rectangles in rects
```

allow_drop conditions this object to be a drop-site; that is, you can drop other objects "into" this object. *rects* is a list of rectangles describing the drop-site, and *num_rects* is the number of these rectangles. You can use a list of rectangles to specify a non-rectangular drop-site—the drop-site will be the union of all the rectangles in *rects*. If you specify no arguments, the drop-site is defined by the boundaries of the object.

An **OI_dnd_clip_rectangle** is a structure of the form

```
struct OI_dnd_clip_rectangle {
                int       x;        // x co-ordinate of upper-left corner
                int       y;        // y co-ordinate of upper-left corner
    unsigned  long    width;    // width in pixels
    unsigned  long    height;   // height in pixels
};
```

x and *y* are the coordinates, in pixels, of the upper-left corner of the rectangle with respect to the upper-left corner of the object.

disallow_drop   (Member function)

```
void OI_d_tech::disallow_drop( )
```

disallow_drop restricts this object from being a drop-site.

is_drop   (Member function)

```
OI_bool OI_d_tech::is_drop( )
```

is_drop returns **OI_yes** if this is a drop-site object; otherwise it returns **OI_no**.

set_drop   (Member function)

```
void OI_d_tech::set_drop(
    OI_drop_fnp            fnp,            // pointer to callback function
    void                  *argp=NULL)     // arbitrary argument for fn
```

```
void OI_d_tech::set_drop(
    OI_callback           *objp,          // memfnp's object
    OI_drop_memfnp        memfnp,         // pointer to callback member function
    void                  *argp=NULL)     // arbitrary argument for memfnp
```

The **set_drop** functions register a callback function to be invoked whenever the mouse button is released over this drop-site object during a drag-and-drop operation (that is, the drag-source object is dropped on the drop-site). You must call **allow_drop** for the object as well as **set_drop** to ensure that the drop callback actually occurs. This callback is identified within OI as a

cbDrop callback function (see Section 6.18, "Determining and Adding Callbacks; Multiple Callbacks," on page 6-117). *memfnp* points to a member function for the object pointed to by *objp*. If your drop callback function is a member function, when it is invoked it will be called as if you had written *objp->memfnp*. See Section 2.5, "Callbacks and Event-Driven Programming," on page 2-16, for more explanation.

argp is optional, and may be any valid expression that can be cast to a pointer. You can use it to pass additional information to the function *fn* or *memfnp*.

Writing the Drop Callback Function

If the **cbDrop** callback function is not a member function, write it in this form:

```
void fn(
        OI_d_tech            *oi_objp,    // pointer to OI object
        void                 *argp,       // arbitrary argument
        OI_dnd_operation op,              // operation occurring
        long                 x,           // x location of mouse pointer
        long                 y)           // y location of mouse pointer
```

and if the **cbDrop** callback function is a member function, write it in this form:

```
void obj_class::memfn(
        OI_d_tech            *oi_objp,    // pointer to OI object
        void                 *argp,       // arbitrary argument
        OI_dnd_operation op,              // operation occurring
        long                 x,           // x location of mouse pointer
        long                 y)           //y location of mouse pointer
```

where *obj_class* is the class of the object whose member function is *memfn*. When your callback function is invoked, *argp* will be the argument specified in the **set_drop** call, and *oi_objp* will be a pointer to the OI object on which the data was dropped. *op* will be one of the following:

> **OI_dnd_move**   This is a data move operation
> **OI_dnd_copy**   This is a data copy operation

If *op* is **OI_dnd_move**, you should call **delete_drop_data** after successfully transferring the data.

x and *y* will indicate the root position—the x and y pixel coordinates of the pointer on screen relative to the root window—of the pointer where the drop event is happening.

You should call **get_drop_data** in this callback to obtain the data from the drag-source object. See Program 6-2, "Receive Drop to Drop-Site Objects (Receiver.C)" on pages 6-75 through 6-80 for an example.

get_drop_data   (Member function)

```
void *OI_d_tech::get_drop_data(
    const char          *sel_name)          // data name
```

In the drop callback registered by **set_drop** you should call **get_drop_data** for the drop-site object, in order to retrieve the data from the drag-source object. The data the drag-source has to transfer may be in various forms; it may be a filename, string, number, or any other data set for the drag-source. Since you do not necessarily know what type of data was dropped on the drop-site, you may have to initiate multiple calls to **get_drop_data** to determine the data type. *sel_name* specifies the name of the data requested. If the drag-source object is an OI object, *sel_name* should be one of the names used to specify static data for the drag-source object in **set_selection_data** or one of the names the selection convert callback (registered via **set_selection_convert**) can handle. The following list shows the selections that are always available in every drag-and-drop operation (although they may be NULL if they have not been set for the drag-source object). If you want to retrieve one of them it is more efficient to use one of these pre-defined variables for *sel_name* rather than the character string:

OI_dnd_file_name	"FILE_NAME"
OI_dnd_string	"STRING"
OI_dnd_file_host_name	"FILE_HOST_NAME"
OI_dnd_host_name	"HOST_NAME"
OI_dnd_length	"LENGTH"

You should call **XFree** for data returned from this call when you are done with it.

delete_drop_data   (Member function)

```
void OI_d_tech::delete_drop_data( )
```

In your drop callback you should query if the operation was **OI_dnd_move**. If so, you should call **delete_drop_data** after transferring the data. This informs the drag-source object that the transfer is complete, and the data it was dragging can be deleted. See **set_selection_data** and **set_selection_convert** for more information from the source-object's point of view.

set_drop_preview   (Member function)

```
void OI_d_tech::set_drop_preview(
    OI_drop_preview_fnp          fnp,          // pointer to callback function
    void                         *argp=NULL)   // arbitrary argument for fn


void OI_d_tech::set_drop_preview(
    OI_callback               *objp,           // memfnp's object
    OI_drop_preview_memfnp    memfnp,          // pointer to callback member function
    void                      *argp=NULL)      // arbitrary argument for memfnp
```

The **set_drop_preview** functions register a callback function to be invoked whenever a drag-and-drop operation is in process and the mouse pointer is over this object's drop-site. This allows you to preview a drop, which means you can change the object's appearance or perform any other actions. If you want to change the cursor's shape, you should instead call **allow_drag** for the drag-source object with two different cursors; the second cursor displays when the pointer is over a valid drop-site. This callback is identified within OI as a **cbDropPreview** callback function (see Section 6.18, "Determining and Adding Callbacks; Multiple Callbacks," on page 6-117). *memfnp* points to a member function for the object pointed to by *objp*. If your drop preview callback function is a member function, when it is invoked it will be called as if you had written *objp->memfnp*. See Section 2.5, "Callbacks and Event-Driven Programming," on page 2-16 for more explanation.

argp is optional, and may be any valid expression that can be cast to a pointer. You can use it to pass additional information to the function *fn* or *memfnp*.

Writing the Drop Preview Callback Function

If the **cbDropPreview** callback function is not a member function, write it in this form:

```
void fn(
        OI_d_tech             *oi_objp,    // pointer to OI object
        void                  *argp,       // arbitrary argument
        OI_dnd_operation op,               // operation occurring
        long                  x,           // x location of mouse pointer
        long                  y)           // y location of mouse pointer
```

and if the **cbDropPreview** callback function is a member function, write it in this form:

```
void obj_class::memfn(
        OI_d_tech             *oi_objp,    // pointer to OI object
        void                  *argp,       // arbitrary argument
        OI_dnd_operation op,               // operation occurring
        long                  x,           // x location of mouse pointer
        long                  y)           //y location of mouse pointer
```

where *obj_class* is the class of the object whose member function is *memfn*. When your callback function is invoked, *argp* will be the argument specified in the **set_drop_preview** call, and *oi_objp* will be a pointer to the OI object for which the drop preview is to be done. *op* will be one of the following:

OI_dnd_enter	The pointer has entered the drop-site.
OI_dnd_leave	The pointer has left the drop-site.
OI_dnd_motion	The pointer has moved.

x and *y* will indicate the root position—the x and y pixel coordinates of the pointer on screen relative to the root window—of the pointer where the drop event is happening.

Program 6-1, "Allow Drag from Drag-Source Objects (Sender.C)," on pages 6-69 through 6-75 is a program that allows the user to drag data from its drag-source objects and drop it on other clients. Dragging the "DRAG ME" object demonstrates compatibility with OpenWindows 3.x clients. You can use it in conjunction with the **dest** example program that ships with OpenWindows. Dragging any of the three color boxes demonstrates compatibility with OSF/Motif 1.2 clients. Use it in conjunction with the **DNDDemo** client that ships with Motif 1.2. The OSF/Motif **DNDDemo** only understands colors, so you will not be able to drop either of the text objects onto it.

Program 6-2, "Receive Drop to Drop-Site Objects (Receiver.C)," on pages 6-75 through 6-80 is a program that can handle drops from some other client. This application sets up two drop sites: a green drop-site box and a non-rectangular drop-site, a cross, that is initially painted red. To demonstrate compatibility with OpenWindows 3.x clients, you can use the **source1** client shipped with OpenWindows and perform the drop on the green box drop-site. To demonstrate compatibility with OSF/Motif 1.2 clients, drag colors from the **DNDDemo** client and drop them on the red cross drop-site.

Figure 6-13 shows **Sender** and **Receiver** on the screen, and Table 6-3 shows the actions and the effects of dragging and dropping objects from **Sender** to **Receiver**.

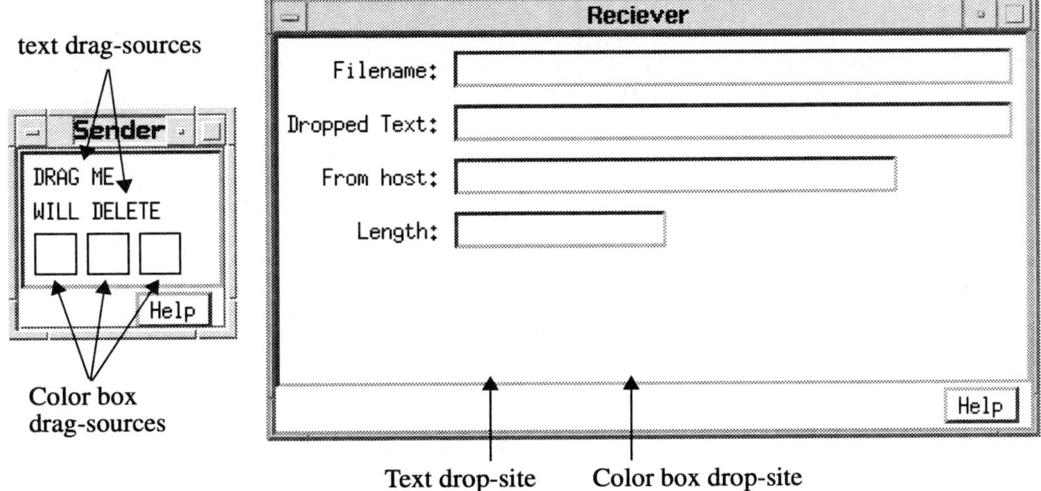

Figure 6-13 Sender and Receiver

Table 6-3 Drag-and-drop between Sender and Receiver

	Action	Effect
Text objects	Press the left mouse button on the DRAG ME or WILL DELETE static drag-source object in **Sender**. Move it.	The pointer changes to the **target** cursor.
	Move the mouse pointer over the green drop-site box or the cross-shaped drop-site object in **Receiver**.	The drop-site shows a black border. The cursor changes to the **targetok** cursor.

Table 6-3 Drag-and-drop between Sender and Receiver

	Action	Effect
	Release the mouse button while the pointer is over the green drop-site box in Receiver.	The pointer changes back to the original cursor. The green box loses its black border. All data set for the drag-source object (DRAG ME or WILL DELETE) shows in the entry fields. If you were dragging WILL DELETE, it disappears from the Sender application window.
	Release the mouse button while the pointer is over the cross-shaped drop-site in Receiver.	The pointer changes back to the original cursor. The cross loses its black border. No data is transferred because the cross does not ask the drag-source for data which the drag-source can transfer.
Color boxes	Press left mouse button on one of the drag-source colored boxes in Sender.	The pointer changes to the nopaint cursor, in the color of the colored box.
	Move the mouse pointer over the green drop-site box or the cross-shaped drop-site object in Receiver.	The drop-site shows a black rectangular border. The cursor changes to the paint cursor, still in the color of the drag-source box.
	Release the mouse button while the pointer is over the cross drop-site object in Receiver.	The cross loses its black border. The cross changes to the color of the dragged box. The pointer changes back to the original cursor.
	Release the mouse button while the pointer is over the green box drop-site in Receiver.	The pointer changes back to the original cursor. The box loses its black border. No data is transferred because the box does not ask the drag-source for data which the drag-source can transfer.

Program 6-3, "Drag the Drag-Source Object Itself (DragLive.C)," on pages 6-80 through 6-82 consists of two application windows and a static text drag-source object. DragLive demonstrates how to use the drag-and-drop interface to drag a live object around on the screen. This means that the actual drag-source object, "DRAG ME," follows the pointer during the drag, even when the pointer leaves the application; whereas in Sender, the appearance of the mouse pointer changes but the drag-source object itself remains firmly in place. In DragLive, when the user releases the mouse button and if the pointer is over a valid drop-site, the dragged object is placed in the application window at the site of the mouse pointer. If the pointer is not over a valid drop-site, the drag-source object is re-placed at the location where the drag began. In **DragLive**, any portion of either of the two application windows is a valid drop-site. Figure 6-14 shows **DragLive** on the screen.

Figure 6-14 DragLive

```c
#include    <stdio.h>                       /* Sender.C */
#include    <stdlib.h>
#include    <sysent.h>
#include    <OI/oi.H>

#include    "paint.xbm"
#include    "nopaint.xbm"
#include    "paintmask.xbm"
#include    "nopaintmask.xbm"

#include    "target.xbm"
#include    "targetmask.xbm"
#include    "targetok.xbm"
#include    "targetokmask.xbm"

// various cursors we'll use
Cursor      nopaint_cursor;
Cursor      paint_cursor;
Cursor      target_cursor;
Cursor      targetok_cursor;

// translations we'll put on objects to get things started
static char *dragTrans =        "#override \n\
                                <Btn1Down>:  drag_move_start( )\n";

// text and file name that we'll drag via the "DRAG ME" object
#define TEXT                    "This is text to drag and drop."
#define FNAME                   "dragdrop.txt"
```

```cpp
// **************************************************************************
// color_drag_preview is the drag preview callback for the color boxes
// It changes the color of the pointer to be the same as the box being dragged

void color_drag_preview(
    OI_d_tech                   *dtp,           // the object being dragged
    void*,                                      // argp
    OI_dnd_operation            op,             // the operation being previewed
    long,                                       // the X root coordinate of the pointer
    long)                                       // the Y root coordinate of the pointer
{
    XColor  other;
    XColor  color;

    switch (op) {
        case OI_dnd_start: // we started the drag,recolor the cursor
            color.pixel = dtp->bkg_pixel( );
            color.flags = DoRed|DoGreen|DoBlue;
            XQueryColor(dtp->display( ),dtp->connection( )->colormap( ),&color);
            other.red = ~0;
            other.green = ~0;
            other.blue = ~0;
            other.flags = DoRed|DoGreen|DoBlue;
            XRecolorCursor(dtp->display( ),paint_cursor,&color,&other);
            XRecolorCursor(dtp->display( ),nopaint_cursor,&color,&other);
            break;
        case OI_dnd_done: // the drag operation is finished
            break;
        case OI_dnd_motion: // the pointer moved during the drag
            break;
        case OI_dnd_enter: // the pointer entered a drop site
            // we specified two different cursors when we did the allow_drag( ) so
            // we don't need to do anything when we see enter and leave operations
            break;
        case OI_dnd_leave: // the pointer left a drop site
            break;
    }
}

// **************************************************************************
// Make a drag-source box with a unique background color

OI_box *make_color_box(
        OI_connection       *conp,          // our connection to the server
    const   char            *name,          // the name of the box
    const   char            *background)    // the background color of the box
{
        OI_box              *box;
        PIXEL               color;
        Atom                atoms[2];

    box = oi_create_box(name,20,20);            // create the box
```

```cpp
    box->allow_drag(nopaint_cursor,paint_cursor); // make the box a draggable object

    // setup the drag_preview callback so we can change the color of
    // the cursor when the drag starts
    box->set_drag_preview(color_drag_preview);

    // put some translations on to get the drag started
    box->override_translations(dragTrans);

    box->set_bkg_color(background); // color the box

    // setup the selection_name atoms that the box can convert
    atoms[0] = conp->atom("BACKGROUND");
    atoms[1] = None;
    box->set_selection_targets(atoms);

    // setup the selection data that will be used when the drop happens
    color = box->bkg_pixel( );
    box->set_selection_data(conp->atom("BACKGROUND"),conp->atom("PIXEL"),
                                        &color,1,32);

    return (box);
}

// *********************************************************************
// Create the drag and drop cursors

void make_cursors(
    OI_connection              *conp)          // our connection to the server
{
    Pixmap  targetok,targetokmask;
    Pixmap  target,targetmask;
    Pixmap  paint,paintmask;
    Pixmap  nopaint,nopaintmask;


    // First create the cursor for the "DRAG ME" object
    // Create the following pixmaps
    //   targetok - the cursor image when over a drop site
    //   targetokmask - the mask for the above cursor
    //   target - the cursor image when not over a drop site
    //   targetmask - the mask for the above cursor
    targetok = XCreateBitmapFromData(conp->display( ),conp->root( )->X_window( ),
                            targetok_bits,targetok_width,targetok_height);
    targetokmask =
XCreateBitmapFromData(conp->display( ),conp->root( )->X_window( ),
                            targetokmask_bits,targetok_width,targetok_height);
    target = XCreateBitmapFromData(conp->display( ),conp->root( )->X_window( ),
                            target_bits,target_width,target_height);
    targetmask = XCreateBitmapFromData(conp->display( ),conp->root( )->X_window( ),
                            targetmask_bits,target_width,target_height);

    // Now create the cursors using OI_connection::make_cursor( )
    targetok_cursor = conp->make_cursor(targetok,targetokmask,
```

```
                              targetok_x_hot,targetok_y_hot);
      target_cursor = conp->make_cursor(target,targetmask,target_x_hot,target_y_hot);

      // After making the cursors, we can free the pixmaps
      XFreePixmap(conp->display( ),targetok);
      XFreePixmap(conp->display( ),targetokmask);
      XFreePixmap(conp->display( ),target);
      XFreePixmap(conp->display( ),targetmask);

      // Now create the "paintbrush" cursors for the color boxes
      // Create the following pixmaps
      //      paint - the cursor image when over a drop site
      //      paintmask - the mask for the above cursor
      //      nopaint - the cursor image when not over a drop site
      //      nopaintmask - the mask for the above cursor
      paint = XCreateBitmapFromData(conp->display( ),conp->root( )->X_window( ),
                        paint_bits,paint_width,paint_height);
      paintmask = XCreateBitmapFromData(conp->display( ),conp->root( )->X_window( ),
                        paintmask_bits,paint_width,paint_height);
      nopaint = XCreateBitmapFromData(conp->display( ),conp->root( )->X_window( ),
                        nopaint_bits,paint_width,paint_height);
      nopaintmask =
XCreateBitmapFromData(conp->display( ),conp->root( )->X_window( ),
                        nopaintmask_bits,paint_width,paint_height);

      // Now create the cursors using OI_connection::make_cursor( )
      paint_cursor = conp->make_cursor(paint,paintmask,paint_x_hot,paint_y_hot);
      nopaint_cursor = conp->make_cursor(nopaint,nopaintmask,
                        paint_x_hot,paint_y_hot);

      // After making the cursors,we can free the pixmaps
      XFreePixmap(conp->display( ),paint);
      XFreePixmap(conp->display( ),paintmask);
      XFreePixmap(conp->display( ),nopaint);
      XFreePixmap(conp->display( ),nopaintmask);
}
```

```
// *****************************************************************************
// This callback actually deletes the "WILL DELETE" object after it is dropped

OI_bool selection_convert(
        OI_d_tech               *objp,
        void*,
    const   XEvent              *ep)
{
        OI_bool                 ret;

    ret = OI_no;
    if (ep->xselectionrequest.target == objp->connection( )->atom("DELETE")) {
        XChangeProperty(objp->display( ),ep->xselectionrequest.requestor,
            ep->xselectionrequest.property,objp->connection( )->atom("INTEGER"),
            32,PropModeReplace,NULL,0);
        ret = OI_yes;
        objp->delete_all_delayed( );
    }
    return(ret) ;
}

// *****************************************************************************

main (int argc,char **argv)
{
    OI_connection               *conp;
    OI_app_window               *app;
    OI_box                      *box;
    OI_static_text              *st;
    int                         row;
    char                        buff[20];
    int                         siz_txt,siz_fnam;
    char                        hname[256];
    Atom                        atoms[10];
    int                         i;

    if ((conp = OI_init(&argc,argv,"Sender","Sender")) == NULL) {
        fprintf(stderr,"%s: OI_init failed\n",argv[0]);
        exit(1);
    }

    row = 0;
    app = oi_create_app_window("app_window",200,200,"Sender");
    app->set_layout(OI_layout_row);

    // create the cursors we'll use during drag and drop operations
    make_cursors(conp);
    // create the "DRAG ME" static text object
    st = oi_create_static_text("st","DRAG ME");
    // get the size of the text and the hostname
    siz_txt = strlen(TEXT);
    siz_fnam = strlen(FNAME);
    gethostname((char*)hname,255);
```

```
// set the selection data that this object can send through a drop
st->set_selection_data(conp->atom("FILE_NAME"),conp->atom("STRING"),
                                    FNAME,siz_fnam,8);
st->set_selection_data(conp->atom("STRING"),conp->atom("STRING"),
                                    TEXT,siz_txt,8);
st->set_selection_data(conp->atom("LENGTH"),conp->atom("INTEGER"),
                                    &siz_txt,1,32);
st->set_selection_data(conp->atom("HOST_NAME"),conp->atom("STRING"),
                                    hname,strlen(hname),8);

// setup the selection_name that it can convert
i = 0;
atoms[i++] = conp->atom("FILE_NAME");
atoms[i++] = conp->atom("STRING");
atoms[i++] = conp->atom("LENGTH");
atoms[i++] = conp->atom("HOST_NAME");
atoms[i] = None;
st->set_selection_targets(atoms);

// disallow_cut_paste so it doesn't grab our mouse button press
st->disallow_cut_paste( );
// make the object draggable
st->allow_drag(target_cursor,targetok_cursor);
// put some drag translations on the object
st->override_translations(dragTrans);
// associate the object to the app_window
st->layout_associated_object(app,0,row++,OI_active);

// create the "WILL DELETE" static text object
st = oi_create_static_text("st","WILL DELETE");

// set the selection data that this object can send through a drop
st->set_selection_data(conp->atom("FILE_NAME"),conp->atom("STRING"),
                                    FNAME,siz_fnam,8);
st->set_selection_data(conp->atom("STRING"),conp->atom("STRING"),
                                    TEXT,siz_txt,8);
st->set_selection_data(conp->atom("LENGTH"),conp->atom("INTEGER"),
                                    &siz_txt,1,32);
st->set_selection_data(conp->atom("HOST_NAME"),conp->atom("STRING"),
                                    hname,strlen(hname),8);
st->set_selection_convert(selection_convert);

// setup the selection_name it can convert (these are the same is for "DRAG ME")
// note that "DELETE" is done in selection_convert
i = 0;
atoms[i++] = conp->atom("FILE_NAME");
atoms[i++] = conp->atom("STRING");
atoms[i++] = conp->atom("LENGTH");
atoms[i++] = conp->atom("HOST_NAME");
atoms[i++] = conp->atom("DELETE");
atoms[i] = None;
st->set_selection_targets(atoms);
```

```
// disallow_cut_paste so it doesn't grab out mouse button press
st->disallow_cut_paste( );
// make the object draggable
st->allow_drag(target_cursor,targetok_cursor);
// put some drag translations on the object
st->override_translations(dragTrans);
// associate the object to the app_window
st->layout_associated_object(app,0,row++,OI_active);

// Now make three boxes with colors of red,green,and blue and
// associate them to the app_window

box = make_color_box(conp,"redBox","red");
box->layout_associated_object(app,0,row,OI_active);
box = make_color_box(conp,"greenBox","green");
box->layout_associated_object(app,2,row,OI_active);
box = make_color_box(conp,"blueBox","blue");
box->layout_associated_object(app,2,row,OI_active);

// put the app_window on the display
app->set_associated_object(conp->root( ),OI_def_loc,OI_def_loc,OI_active);

OI_begin_interaction( );
OI_fini( );
}
```

Program 6-1   Allow Drag from Drag-Source Objects (Sender.C)

```
#include <stdio.h>                              /* Receiver.C */
#include <stdlib.h>
#include <OI/oi.H>


// the shape of our non-rectangular drop site
static OI_dnd_clip_rectangle  rect[] = {
    { 15, 0, 20, 50 },
    { 0, 15, 50, 20 }
};
#define NUM_RECTS(sizeof(rect)/sizeof(OI_dnd_clip_rectangle))

// ********************************************************************
// Repaint the non-rectangular drop site

void paint_rects(
            OI_d_tech               *boxp,
            void*,
    const   XEvent*)
{
    OI_connection               *conp;
    XRectangle                  *xrects;
    int                         i;

    xrects = (XRectangle *)malloc(NUM_RECTS * sizeof(XRectangle));
    for (i = 0; i < NUM_RECTS; i++) {
        xrects[i].x = rect[i].x;
        xrects[i].y = rect[i].y;
        xrects[i].width = (unsigned short)rect[i].width;
        xrects[i].height = (unsigned short)rect[i].height;
    }
    conp = boxp->connection( );
    boxp->set_gc( );

XFillRectangles(conp->display( ),boxp->X_window( ),conp->gc( ),xrects,NUM_RECTS);
    free((char*)xrects);
}


// ********************************************************************
// The drop preview callback. When we see an enter operation,
// change the color of the border of the object to highlight it.
// When we see a leave, change the border to the background color
// so the border will seem to disappear

void drop_preview(
    OI_d_tech                   *dtp,       // the object of interest
    void*,                                  // argp
    OI_dnd_operation            op,         // the drag and drop operation
    long,                                   // the X root coordinate of the pointer
    long)                                   // the Y root coordinate of the pointer
{
    switch (op) {
        case OI_dnd_enter:
```

```
            dtp->set_bdr_color("black");
            break;
        case OI_dnd_leave:
            dtp->set_bdr_pixel(dtp->bkg_pixel( ));
            break;
    }
}


// ***********************************************************************
// Something was dropped on the "green" box. Look for the
// following data and place the results in the various
// entry_fields we created.
//   OI_dnd_file_name
//   OI_dnd_string
//   OI_dnd_length

void handle_drop(
    OI_d_tech               *dtp,        // the object that caught the drop
    void*,                               // argp
    OI_dnd_operation        op,          // the drag and drop operation
    long,                                // the X root coordinate of the pointer
    long)                                // the Y root coordinate of the pointer
{
    OI_app_window           *app;        // a pointer to the app_window
    char                    *str;        // a temporary string variable
    int                     *len;        // another temp variable
    char                    buff[20];

    // find the enclosing app_window
    app = dtp->app_window( );

    // try to get the OI_dnd_file_name data
    if ((str = (char*)dtp->get_drop_data(OI_dnd_file_name))) {
        // set the text to the appropriate entry_field
        ((OI_entry_field*)app->subobject("filename"))->set_text(str);
        XFree(str);
    }

    // try to get the OI_dnd_string data
    if ((str = (char*)dtp->get_drop_data(OI_dnd_string))) {
        // set the text to the appropriate entry_field
        ((OI_entry_field*)app->subobject("text"))->set_text(str);
        XFree(str);
    }

    // get either OI_dnd_host_name or OI_dnd_file_host_name
    if ((str = (char*)dtp->get_drop_data(OI_dnd_host_name)) == NULL)
        str = (char*)dtp->get_drop_data(OI_dnd_file_host_name);
    if (str) {
        // set the text to the appropriate entry_field
        ((OI_entry_field*)app->subobject("host"))->set_text(str);
        XFree(str);
    }
```

```cpp
        // now get the OI_dnd_length data
        if ((len = (int *)dtp->get_drop_data(OI_dnd_length))) {
            sprintf(buff,"%d",*len);
            XFree((char*)len);
            // set the text to the appropriate entry_field
            ((OI_entry_field*)app->subobject("length"))->set_text(buff);
        }

        // signal the source object to delete its data if the operation was a move
        if (op == OI_dnd_move)
            dtp->delete_drop_data( );
}

// ********************************************************************
// Something was dropped on the "cross" box.
// In this case, we're looking for a piece of data that
// OI doesn't automatically fetch, "BACKGROUND"

void handle_color_drop(
    OI_d_tech                   *dtp,           // the object that handled the drop
    void*,                                      // argp
    OI_dnd_operation,                           // the drag and drop operation
    long,                                       // the X root coordinate of the drop
    long)                                       // the Y root coordinate of the drop
{
    PIXEL                       *color;

    color = (PIXEL *)dtp->get_drop_data("BACKGROUND");
    if (color) {
        dtp->set_fg_color(*color);
        XFree((char*)color);
        paint_rects(dtp,NULL,NULL);
    }
}

// ********************************************************************

main (int argc,char **argv)
{
    OI_connection               *conp;
    OI_app_window               *app;
    OI_entry_field              *ef;
    OI_box                      *box;
    int                         row;

    if ((conp = OI_init(&argc,argv,"Reciever","Reciever")) == NULL) {
        fprintf(stderr,"%s: OI_init failed\n",argv[0]);
        exit(1);
    }

    // create the top-level app_window
    app = oi_create_app_window("app_window",200,200,"Reciever");
```

```
app->set_layout(OI_layout_row_aligned);
row = 0;

// create some entry fields we'll fill in when we handle a drop
ef = oi_create_entry_field("filename",40,"Filename:"," ",200);
ef->layout_associated_object(app,0,row++,OI_active);
ef = oi_create_entry_field("text",40,"Dropped Text:"," ",200);
ef->layout_associated_object(app,0,row++,OI_active);
ef = oi_create_entry_field("host",30,"From host:"," ",200);
ef->layout_associated_object(app,0,row++,OI_active);
ef = oi_create_entry_field("length",10,"Length:"," ",200);
ef->layout_associated_object(app,0,row++,OI_active);

// create a green box to catch drops
box = oi_create_box("box",50,50);
box->set_bkg_color("green");
// turn it into a drop site
box->allow_drop( );
// setup the drop callback
box->set_drop(handle_drop);
// setup a drop preview callback
// in the drop preview callback,we're simply going to change to color
// of the border. Here we'll give the box some border width and set the
// initial color to the background so it won't show
box->set_drop_preview(drop_preview);
box->set_bvl_width(0);
box->set_bdr_width(4);
box->set_bdr_pixel(box->bkg_pixel( ));
// put the box in the app_window
box->layout_associated_object(app,0,row,OI_active);

// Now we'll create a non-rectangular drop site
box = oi_create_box("rectbox",50,50);
// paint the cross in red
box->set_fg_color("red");
// setup an expose callback so we can repaint the cross
box->set_expose(paint_rects);
// setup the drop site with the rectangles to include
box->allow_drop(rect,NUM_RECTS);
// setup the drop handler callback
box->set_drop(handle_color_drop);
// setup a drop preview callback
// in the drop preview callback,we're simply going to change to color
// of the border. Here we'll give the box some border width and set the
// initial color to the background so it won't show
box->set_drop_preview(drop_preview);
box->set_bvl_width(0);
box->set_bdr_width(4);
box->set_bdr_pixel(box->bkg_pixel( ));
// put the box in the app_window
box->layout_associated_object(app,1,row++,OI_active);

// put the app_window on the root
```

```
    app->set_associated_object(conp->root( ),OI_def_loc,OI_def_loc,OI_active);

    OI_begin_interaction( );
    OI_fini( );
}
```

Program 6-2   Receive Drop to Drop-Site Objects (Receiver.C)

```
#include <stdio.h>                                /* DragLive.C */
#include <stdio.h>
#include <stdlib.h>
#include <sysent.h>
#include <OI/oi.H>

// translations we'll put on objects to get things started
static char *dragTrans =        "#override \n\
                        <Btn1Down>:   drag_move_start( )\n";

// ********************************************************************
//      Move the "DRAG ME" object around the screen

void drag_preview(
    OI_d_tech               *dtp,          // the object being dragged
    void*,                                 // argp
    OI_dnd_operation        op,            // the operation being previewed
    long                    x,             // the X root coordinate of the pointer
    long                    y)             // the Y root coordinate of the pointer
{
    static OI_d_tech        *orig_parent;
    static OI_number        orig_x;
    static OI_number        orig_y;
            OI_d_tech       *under_pointer;
    XEvent                  fake;
    int                     locx, locy;
    Window                  child;

    switch (op) {
        case OI_dnd_start:      // the drag operation starts
            orig_parent = dtp->parent( );
            orig_x = (OI_number)dtp->loc_x( );
            orig_y = (OI_number)dtp->loc_y( );
            dtp->allow_override_redirect( );
            dtp->set_associated_object(dtp->root( ),x,y,OI_active);
            break;
        case OI_dnd_done:
            // the drag operation is finished
```

```cpp
        // move it someplace off screen so find_obj doesn't return the drag object
        dtp->set_loc(-100,-100);
        fake.xbutton.type = ButtonRelease;
        fake.xbutton.window = dtp->root( )->X_window( );
        fake.xbutton.subwindow = dtp->root( )->X_window( );
        fake.xbutton.root = dtp->root( )->X_window( );
        fake.xbutton.x = (int)x;
        fake.xbutton.y = (int)y;
        fake.xbutton.x_root = (int)x;
        fake.xbutton.y_root = (int)y;
        if ((under_pointer = dtp->connection( )->find_obj(&fake))) {
            XTranslateCoordinates(dtp->display( ),dtp->root( )->X_window( ),
                under_pointer->X_window( ),(int)x,(int)y,&locx,&locy,&child);
            dtp->set_associated_object(under_pointer,locx,locy,OI_active);
        }
        else {                  // move it back to where it started
            dtp->set_associated_object(orig_parent,orig_x,orig_y,OI_active);
        }
        break;
    case OI_dnd_motion:     // the pointer moved during the drag
        dtp->set_loc(x,y);
        break;
    }
}

// ****************************************************************

main (int argc,char **argv)
{
    OI_connection*conp;
    OI_app_window*app;
    OI_static_text*st;

    if ((conp = OI_init(&argc,argv,"DragLive","DragLive")) == NULL) {
        fprintf(stderr,"%s: OI_init failed\n",argv[0]);
        exit(1);
    }

    // create the enclosing app_window
    app = oi_create_app_window("app1",200,200,"DragLive 1");

    // create the "DRAG ME" static text object
    st = oi_create_static_text("st","DRAG ME");

    // disallow_cut_paste so it doesn't grab our mouse button press
    st->disallow_cut_paste( );

    // make the object draggable
    st->allow_drag( );

    // put some drag translations on the object
    st->override_translations(dragTrans);
```

```
     // setup the drag preview callback
     st->set_drag_preview(drag_preview);

     // associate the object to the app_window
     st->set_associated_object(app,20,20,OI_active);

     // put the app_window on the display
     app->set_associated_object(conp->root( ),50,50,OI_active);

     app = oi_create_app_window("app2",200,200,"DragLive 2");
     app->set_associated_object(conp->root( ),300,50,OI_active);

     OI_begin_interaction( );
     OI_fini( );
}
```

Program 6-3   Drag the Drag-Source Object Itself (DragLive.C)

6.9   Windowless Objects

The class hierarchy for displayable OI objects is implemented in two different ways. In one case, a window is allocated from the window system for the exclusive use of the object. Such an object is known as a *windowed* object, and is derived from OI_w_d_tech. In the other case, the object shares the window of an ancestor, normally its immediate parent. These objects are known as *windowless* objects, and are derived from OI_wl_d_tech. OI_menu_cell and OI_separator are the two OI windowless objects available for use in your application.

Normally you will not need to use the functions in this section. If you write your own OI subclasses, however, and you make your subclass windowless, you may need them. Windowless objects are sometimes more difficult to design and implement, but are more efficient if you use large numbers of them in your application. The OI event dispatching and translation mechanism is sophisticated enough to deliver events to windowless objects as well as windowed objects. You may need to modify the event coordinates before processing an event; usc window_loc for this.

window_loc   (Member function)

```
     void OI_d_tech::window_loc(
         long                    *x_locp,        // pointer to x location in pixels
         long                    *y_locp)        // pointer to y location in pixels
```

window_loc determines the position of the object in relation to the closest ancestor which is a windowed object. *x_locp* is backfilled with the distance in the x direction, in pixels, of this object's upper left corner to the windowed object's upper left corner. *y_locp* is similarly backfilled with the distance in the y direction.

window_size   (Member function)

```
void OI_d_tech::window_size(
    long                    *x_sizp,        // pointer to x size in pixels
    long                    *y_sizp)        // pointer to y size in pixels
```

window_size backfills *x_sizp* and *y_sizp* with the length and height, in pixels, of the object's closest ancestor which is a windowed object.

6.10   Click Functions

Many objects support mouse button clicking. The click operation as discussed here is in addition to the "normal" function of the object. For example, sliders, scroll bars and menu cells automatically "do something" when the user clicks on them in the proper manner.

If you want an object to respond to clicking, you must register a callback function for the object. When the user clicks on the object, the callback function is executed. Since click functions behave slightly differently depending on the type of object, the exact descriptions are detailed in the individual object chapters. Click functions are supported for the following object classes:

OI_box (and its derived classes)
OI_connection
OI_entry_field (and its derived classes)
OI_glyph
OI_multi_text
OI_scroll_box
OI_scroll_text
OI_static_text

6.11   Appearance

You can inquire and change the appearance attributes of OI objects. Some attributes can also be changed globally (for all objects) using command-line arguments at start-up time (See Chapter 3, "Compiling, Linking, and Executing an OI Program"). You or the user can modify any of the attributes discussed in this section using the X resource manager (See Chapter 39, "The OI Resource Mechanism").

Functions discussed in this section which change attribute values (ones named **set_***) have the side effect of marking that attribute as having been specifically set by the program. This prevents the user from modifying the attribute via the resource manager. You should use these functions sparingly. They should normally be used for very specific purposes, such as highlighting and unhighlighting a static text by reversing the foreground/background colors. If you want to specify default attributes such as fonts and colors for various parts of an application, you should do this through an application-specific default resources file, or by specifying default resources in your program as discussed in Chapter 39. The exception to this rule is **set_working**, which you can use with impunity.

6.11.1   Refreshing the Appearance

You can use the functions listed here to redraw an object.

repaint   (Member function)

```
void OI_d_tech::repaint(
    OI_bool              clr=OI_yes)          // clear object
```

repaint causes OI to redraw the object. If *clr* is **OI_yes** (or you omit it), OI clears the object before redrawing it. If you know the object is already clear, or the redraw operation (paint) member function always completely redraws the object, setting *clr* to **OI_no** improves performance. *Clear*, in this case, means there is nothing drawn in the object.

refresh   (Member function)

```
void OI_d_tech::refresh( )
```

refresh causes OI to redraw the object and all of its clipped descendants.

6.11.2   Frame Size

The frame is the border or bevel around the outside of an object. All OI objects have a frame, although some, such as **OI_entry_field**, normally have a frame width of zero (so you don't see it). The type of frame is determined by the interaction and appearance model. In 2D OPEN LOOK, the frame of an object is a solid line of the border pixel color (normally the same as the foreground color). In 3D OPEN LOOK, the frame is composed of two colors, a top pixel and a bottom pixel, used to give a shading effect, designed to look like a chiseled groove. In Motif, the frame is also composed of two similar colors, but is designed to look like a bevel on a picture frame so the object appears raised or lowered in relation to its surroundings. You can use the functions below to customize the frame of a particular object.

frame_width   (Member function)

```
OI_number OI_d_tech::frame_width( )
```

frame_width returns the frame width, in pixels, for the object. You should use this function rather than **bvl_width** or **bdr_width** to ensure proper operation with any interaction model.

set_frame_width   (Member function)

```
void OI_d_tech::set_frame_width(
    OI_number            wid)                 // frame width in pixels
```

set_frame_width sets the width of the outside frame for the object to *wid*. Exactly what is set depends on the interaction model for the object. It may affect the border width, bevel width, or both. You should use this function rather than **set_bdr_width** or **set_bvl_width** to ensure proper operation with any interaction model.

bdr_width   (Member function)

```
OI_number OI_d_tech::bdr_width( )
```

bdr_width returns the border width, in pixels, for the object. You should normally use the function **frame_width** instead, to allow for proper operation with all interaction models.

set_bdr_width   (Member function)

```
void OI_d_tech::set_bdr_width(
    OI_number            wid)              // border width in pixels
```

set_bdr_width sets the X Window border width for the object to *wid* pixels. You should normally use the function **set_frame_width** instead, to allow for proper operation with all interaction models.

bvl_width   (Member function)

```
OI_number OI_d_tech::bvl_width( )
```

bvl_width returns the bevel width, in pixels, for the object. You should normally use the function **frame_width** instead, to allow for proper operation with all interaction models.

set_bvl_width   (Member function)

```
void OI_d_tech::set_bvl_width(
    OI_number            wid)              // bevel width in pixels
```

set_bvl_width sets the bevel width for the object to *wid* pixels if it is painted with a 3-D appearance. You should normally use the function **set_frame_width** instead, to allow for proper operation with all interaction models.

bvl_style   (Member function)

```
OI_bevel_style OI_d_tech::bvl_style( )
```

bvl_style returns the bevel style for the object. See **set_bvl_style** for the possible values.

set_bvl_style   (Member function)

```
void OI_d_tech::set_bvl_style(
    OI_bevel_style       bv_styl)          // bevel style
```

set_bvl_style sets the bevel style for the object to *bv_styl*. This can be one of:

OI_bevel_none	No bevel
OI_bevel_in	Bevel appears indented into the screen.
OI_bevel_out	Bevel appears raised.
OI_chisel_in	Bevel appears level; a groove appears chiseled into the bevel.
OI_chisel_out	Bevel appears level; a raised groove appears in the bevel.

6.11.3 Window Decoration

OI automatically configures an object for the proper default window manager decoration. The member functions described below allow you to customize the window manager decoration around an object. These functions have no effect on objects which are clipped (the default condition).

allow_wm_decoration   (Member function)

```
void OI_d_tech::allow_wm_decoration(
   OI_wm_decoration  decor)                    // window decoration style
```

allow_wm_decoration enables components of window decoration that either an OPEN LOOK window manager or a Motif window manager place around top-level windows. You can set *decor* to a bitwise inclusive **or** of one or more of the following values:

OI_wm_title	Allow title bar.
OI_wm_resize	Allow resizing through the window manager.
OI_wm_menu_button	Allow a button with a pulldown menu of window manager options in the title bar.
OI_wm_maximize	Allow a button in the title bar whose function is to expand the window to maximum size.
OI_wm_minimize	Allow a button in the title bar whose function is to iconify the window.
OI_wm_pushpin	Allow a pushpin.
OI_wm_pushpin_in	If a pushpin is allowed, it is initially in.
OI_wm_pushpin_out	If a pushpin is allowed, it is initially out.

By default some objects allow certain decorations, and others do not. The values you specify in *decor* are added to whatever decoration is currently allowed for the object.

disallow_wm_decoration   (Member function)

```
void OI_d_tech::disallow_wm_decoration(
   OI_wm_decoration  decor)                    // window decoration style
```

disallow_wm_decoration disables components of window decoration that either an OPEN LOOK window manager or a Motif window manager place around top-level windows. You can set *decor* to a bitwise inclusive **or** of one or more of the values shown for **allow_wm_decoration** above. The values you specify in *decor* are removed from whatever decoration is currently allowed for the object. The **OI_d_tech** member function **disallow_resize** automatically calls **disallow_wm_decoration(OI_wm_resize)**.

6.11.4 Colors

A minimum of two colors is used to paint all OI objects—a foreground color and a background color. In addition, objects may have a border color (the color of an X window border). Objects painted in a 3D model have three additional color attributes—a top, bottom, and down color.

The *top* and *bottom* colors are normally shades of the background color. The top color is usually lighter, and the bottom color is darker. The top and bottom colors are used to simulate the effects of light shining on the object. The light source is considered to be located to the upper-left of the screen. The top and left edges of raised portions of objects are painted using the top color; lowered (shaded) parts of objects are painted using the bottom color.

Another color, usually darker than the background color, is known as the *down* color. It is used to accentuate the impression that the object is recessed. The down color is used to paint depressed button menu cells, depressed rectangle menu cells, the depressed part of a Motif check box in a menu, the background for a gauge, slider, or scroll bar, and can be used to highlight a glyph. If you specify the resource **downIsBackground**, the background of all objects that use the down color is painted using the background color.

You do not normally need to be concerned with the top, bottom, and down colors. They are recomputed automatically whenever you set the background color, unless you have specifically set them otherwise.

You can specify colors in two ways: as a string ("red", "blue", etc.), or as a PIXEL value. When you specify a color as a string, OI converts the string to a PIXEL value before using it. Strings are converted to PIXEL values according to the **rgb** database (/usr/lib/X11/rgb.*) used by your X server. If you are setting many attributes to the same color, it is faster to get the PIXEL color value yourself and use the version of the **set_*_color** functions which take PIXEL arguments instead of char* arguments. You can obtain the PIXEL value for a color using the OI_connection member function **str_color** or the convenience function **OI_str_color**.

For example, to set the foreground color to blue in a scroll menu using the pixel color value:

```
OI_scroll_menu          *smp;
PIXEL                   my_color;
smp = oi_create_scroll_menu(...);
my_color = OI_str_color("blue")
smp->set_fg_color(my_color);
```

set_colors   (Member function)

```
OI_stat OI_d_tech::set_colors(
    const char          *bkg_color,      // background pixel color value
    const char          *fg_color,       // foreground pixel color value
    const char          *bdr_color)      // border pixel color value


void OI_d_tech::set_colors(
    PIXEL               bkg_pxl,         // background pixel color value
    PIXEL               fg_pxl,          // foreground pixel color value
    PIXEL               bdr_pxl)         // border pixel color value
```

set_colors sets the background, foreground, and border pixel color values for the object. The first form returns OI_ok if the colors were successfully found and allocated, otherwise it returns OI_no_color. You should not use this function unless you need it for dynamic behavior. Instead, you should use the resource mechanism. To reverse the colors of an object, do this:

```
objp->set_colors(objp->fg_pixel( ),objp->bkg_pixel( ),objp->bdr_pixel( ));
```

---

is_bdr_set

(Member function)

```
OI_bool OI_d_tech::is_bdr_set( )
```

is_bdr_set returns OI_yes if the border pixel color has been explicitly set for the object using set_colors or set_bdr_color. If the border pixel color was inherited from the defaults, set using a command-line argument or through the resource manager, or if the border pixel color was not explicitly set, is_bdr_set returns OI_no.

set_bdr_color

(Member function)

```
OI_stat OI_d_tech::set_bdr_color(
   const char            *color)          // color name as a string


void OI_d_tech::set_bdr_color(
   PIXEL                 pxl)             // pixel color value
```

set_bdr_color sets the border color for the object to *color* or *pxl*, depending on the form used. The first form returns OI_ok if the color was successfully found and allocated, otherwise it returns OI_no_color. You should not use this function unless you need it for dynamic behavior. Instead, you should use the resource mechanism. Note that this color applies to borders specifically; bevels are painted using the top and bottom colors.

bdr_pixel

(Member function)

```
PIXEL OI_d_tech::bdr_pixel( )
```

bdr_pixel returns the border pixel color value for the object.

is_fg_set

(Member function)

```
OI_bool OI_d_tech::is_fg_set( )
```

is_fg_set returns OI_yes if the foreground pixel color has been explicitly set for the object using set_colors or set_fg_color. If the foreground pixel color was inherited from the defaults, set using a command-line argument or through the resource manager, or if the foreground pixel color was not explicitly set, is_fg_set returns OI_no.

set_fg_color

(Member function)

```
OI_stat OI_d_tech::set_fg_color(
   const char            *color)          // color name as a string


void OI_d_tech::set_fg_color(
   PIXEL                 pxl)             // pixel color value
```

set_fg_color sets the foreground color for the object to *color* or *pxl*, depending on the form used. The first form returns OI_ok if the color was successfully found and allocated, otherwise it returns OI_no_color. You should not use this function unless you need it for dynamic behavior. Instead, you should use the resource mechanism.

---

fg_pixel   (Member function)

```
PIXEL OI_d_tech::fg_pixel( )
```

fg_pixel returns the foreground pixel color value for the object.

is_bkg_set   (Member function)

```
OI_bool OI_d_tech::is_bkg_set( )
```

is_bkg_set returns OI_yes if the background pixel color has been explicitly set for the object using set_colors or set_bkg_color. If the background pixel color was inherited from the defaults, set using a command-line argument or through the resource manager, or if the background pixel color was not explicitly set, is_bkg_set returns OI_no.

set_bkg_color   (Member function)

```
OI_stat OI_d_tech::set_bkg_color(
    const char          *color)          // color name as a string


void OI_d_tech::set_bkg_color(
    PIXEL               pxl)             // pixel color value
```

set_bkg_color sets the background color for the object to *color* or *pxl*, depending on the form used. The first form returns OI_ok if the color was successfully found and allocated, otherwise it returns OI_no_color. You should not use this function unless you need it for dynamic behavior. Instead, you should use the resource mechanism. Unless they have been specifically set otherwise, the top, bottom, and down pixel values are recomputed based on the new background color.

bkg_pixel   (Member function)

```
PIXEL OI_d_tech::bkg_pixel( )
```

bkg_pixel returns the background pixel color value for the object.

set_bkg_pixmap   (Member function)

```
void OI_d_tech::set_bkg_pixmap(
    Pixmap              pixmap)          // pixmap id


void OI_d_tech::set_bkg_pixmap(
    const char          *filename)       // name of pixmap file as a string


void OI_d_tech::set_bkg_pixmap(
    XrmQuark            name_qrk)        // name of pixmap file as an XrmQuark
```

set_bkg_pixmap sets the background pixmap for the object. *pixmap* is an X Pixmap id; *filename* is the name, in string form, of a file containing the definition of the pixmap, and *name_qrk* is an XrmQuark representation of a file name. The file format must conform to that used by Xpm (portable X pixmaps) or the X bitmap program. If you are going to call set_bkg_pixmap several times with the same file name, it is more efficient to convert the file name string to an **XrmQuark** and use the third form of **set_bkg_pixmap**. You can convert a string to an **XrmQuark** using the Xlib function **XrmStringToQuark**.

is_top_set (Member function)

```
OI_bool OI_d_tech::is_top_set( )
```

is_top_set returns **OI_yes** if the top pixel color has been explicitly set for the object using **set_colors** or **set_top_color**. If the top pixel color was inherited from the defaults, set using a command-line argument or through the resource manager, or if the top pixel color was not explicitly set, **is_top_set** returns **OI_no**.

set_top_color (Member function)

```
OI_stat OI_d_tech::set_top_color(
    const char          *color)          // color name as a string
```

```
void OI_d_tech::set_top_color(
    PIXEL               pxl)             // pixel color value
```

set_top_color sets the top color for the object to *color* or *pxl*, depending on the form used. The first form returns **OI_ok** if the color was successfully found and allocated, otherwise it returns **OI_no_color**. You should normally not use this function; instead, you should let OI set the top color based on the background color.

top_pixel (Member function)

```
PIXEL OI_d_tech::top_pixel( )
```

top_pixel returns the top pixel color value for the object.

is_bottom_set (Member function)

```
OI_bool OI_d_tech::is_bottom_set( )
```

is_bottom_set returns **OI_yes** if the bottom pixel color has been explicitly set for the object using **set_colors** or **set_bottom_color**. If the bottom pixel color was inherited from the defaults, set using a command-line argument or through the resource manager, or if the bottom pixel color was not explicitly set, **is_bottom_set** returns **OI_no**.

set_bottom_color (Member function)

```
OI_stat OI_d_tech::set_bottom_color(
    const char          *color)          // color name as a string
```

```
void OI_d_tech::set_bottom_color(
    PIXEL               pxl               // pixel color value
```

set_bottom_color sets the bottom color for the object to *color* or *pxl*, depending on the form used. The first form returns **OI_ok** if the color was successfully found and allocated, otherwise it returns **OI_no_color**. You should normally not use this function; instead, you should let OI set the bottom color based on the background color.

bottom_pixel   (Member function)

```
PIXEL OI_d_tech::bottom_pixel( )
```

bottom_pixel returns the bottom pixel color value for the object.

is_down_set   (Member function)

```
OI_bool OI_d_tech::is_down_set( )
```

is_down_set returns OI_yes if the down pixel color has been explicitly set for the object using set_colors or set_down_color. If the down pixel color was inherited from the defaults, set using a command-line argument or through the resource manager, or if the down pixel color was not explicitly set, is_down_set returns OI_no.

set_down_color   (Member function)

```
OI_stat OI_d_tech::set_down_color(
    const char          *color)          // color name as a string


void OI_d_tech::set_down_color(
    PIXEL               pxl              // pixel color value
```

set_down_color sets the down color for the object to *color* or *pxl*, depending on the form used. The first form returns OI_ok if the color was successfully found and allocated, otherwise it returns OI_no_color. You should normally not use this function; instead, you should let OI set the down color based on the background color.

down_pixel   (Member function)

```
PIXEL OI_d_tech::down_pixel( )
```

down_pixel returns the down pixel color value for the object.

6.11.5   Cursors

You can change the shape of the mouse pointer when it is in an OI object. In the context of these functions, the mouse pointer is called a *cursor*. The graphic shapes that can be used are normally enumerated in the file **/usr/include/X11/cursorfont.h**, or you can create your own. The actual font used for displaying these cursors is named "cursor"; the various cursors can be displayed using a program such as **sfontpick** using **cursor** as its command-line argument. See Section 38.5, "Managing the Mouse Pointer," on page 38-4, for functions which change the cursor for the entire connection.

You can also change the shape of the cursor when your application is busy performing a function during which you do not want the user to be able to interact with any object in the application (for example, while you are reading the contents of a file). The *_working functions not only change the shape of the cursor, they also restrict or restore user interaction capabilities.

See Program 34-1 on page 34-16 for an example which uses **set_cursor**.

is_cursor_set (Member function)

```
OI_bool OI_d_tech::is_cursor_set( )
```

is_cursor_set returns **OI_yes** if you have explicitly set the cursor shape for the object using **set_cursor**; otherwise, it returns **OI_no**.

set_cursor (Member function)

```
void OI_d_tech::set_cursor(
    Cursor              cur)            // X Cursor

void OI_d_tech::set_cursor(
    int                 index)          // cursor index

void OI_d_tech::set_cursor(
    const char          *image,         // bitmap file name
    const char          *mask)          // bitmap file name

void OI_d_tech::set_cursor(
    Pixmap              image,          // PIXMAP
    Pixmap              mask,           // PIXMAP
    unsigned int        x_hot,          // hotspot location
    unsigned int        y_hot)          // hotspot location
```

set_cursor sets the cursor shape for the object. *cur* is an X Cursor (to make an X Cursor, see **make_cursor** on page 38-4). *index* should be one of the constants defined in the file /usr/include/X11/cursorfont.h. These constants are indices to the characters defined in the cursor font, which is normally /usr/lib/X11/fonts/misc/cursor.*. For example, both lines of code shown here set the cursor to be a gumby representation:

```
objp->set_cursor(XC_gumby);
objp->set_cursor(56);
```

image and *mask* are the bitmaps used to create a custom cursor. They are the arguments passed to **XCreatePixmapCursor**. *x_hot* and *y_hot* specify the distance, in pixels, of the cursor's hot-spot from the upper left corner of the bitmap.

abs_cursor (Member function)

```
Cursor OI_d_tech::abs_cursor( )
```

abs_cursor returns the X Window identifier for the cursor shape for the object. This is not one of the constants defined in the file /usr/include/X11/cursorfont.h; see **cursor_index**.

cursor (Member function)

```
Cursor OI_d_tech::cursor( )
```

cursor returns the X Window identifier for the cursor shape for the object only if it has been set to a cursor other than the default; otherwise it returns **None**. This is not one of the constants defined in the file /usr/include/X11/cursorfont.h; see **cursor_index**.

cursor_index   (Member function)

```
int OI_d_tech::cursor_index( )
```

cursor_index returns the index to the cursor shape for the cursor for the object. This is one of the constants defined in the file /usr/include/X11/cursorfont.h; it is the index used in the set_cursor function. If the cursor is not a font cursor, cursor_index returns -1.

is_working   (Member function)

```
OI_bool OI_d_tech::is_working( )
```

is_working returns OI_yes if the object is busy, that is, if the application is displaying a model-dependent busy cursor, and the application is currently ignoring all mouse button presses and keyboard activity. Otherwise is_working returns OI_no.

set_working   (Member function)

```
void OI_d_tech::set_working( )


void OI_d_tech::set_working(
    Cursor              cur)            // X Cursor


void OI_d_tech::set_working(
    int                 index)          // cursor index


void OI_d_tech::set_working(
    const char          *image,         // bitmap file name
    const char          *mask)          // bitmap file name


void OI_d_tech::set_working(
    Pixmap              image,          // PIXMAP
    Pixmap              mask,           // PIXMAP
    unsigned int        x_hot,          // hotspot location
    unsigned int        y_hot)          // hotspot location
```

set_working sets the working/busy cursor and makes the application *busy*, that is, makes the application ignore mouse button presses and keyboard activity. If you use the first form, OI sets the cursor in a model-dependent fashion. The Motif busy cursor is an hourglass; OPEN LOOK's is a watch. The other four forms use the working/busy cursor defined by the arguments. The arguments are identical in usage to those for the four similar forms of set_cursor.

You may also want to use the member functions **freeze** and **unfreeze** to constrain the display from changing while the application is *busy*.

clear_working   (Member function)

```
void OI_d_tech::clear_working( )
```

clear_working clears the working/busy cursor in a model-dependent fashion. This makes the application sensitive to mouse button presses and keyboard activity.

6.11.6   Fonts

You can inquire and change the text fonts used in an object. In addition, you can inquire various attributes of a particular font. Many applications function well using the default fonts. If this is true for your application, you should not set any font explicitly. This allows the user to select any font via the -font command line option or through the X resource manager. All objects support both variable and fixed-width fonts, as well as 16-bit fonts.

The initial default fonts used depend on the model being run. Table 6-4 and Table 6-5 specify these fonts.

Table 6-4   Default Fonts, OPEN LOOK

If lucida fonts are available:	
normal (menu cell)	-*-lucida-medium-r-normal-sans-*-120-*-*-*-*-*-*
bold (labels on entry field, slider, gauge, menu)	-*-lucida-bold-r-normal-sans-*-120-*-*-*-*-*-*
fixed width (entry field, multi text)	-*-lucidatypewriter-medium-r-normal-sans-*-120-*-*-*-*-*-*
If lucida fonts are not available:	
normal (menu cell)	-*-helvetica-medium-r-normal--*-120-*-*-*-*-*-*
bold (labels on entry field, slider, gauge, menu)	-*-helvetica-bold-r-normal--*-120-*-*-*-*-*-*
fixed width (entry field, multi text)	-*-courier-medium-r-normal--*-120-*-*-*-*-*-*

Table 6-5   Default Fonts, Motif

all objects	fixed

Figure 6-15 shows an application run with the default fonts in OPEN LOOK, and Figure 6-16 shows the same application run with a font specified for all objects of

-adobe-courier-medium-r-normal--12-120-75-75-m-70-iso8859-

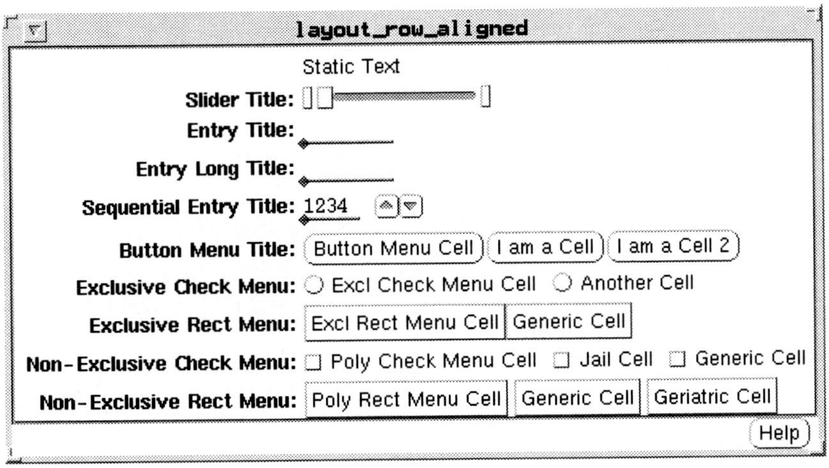

Figure 6-15   OPEN LOOK Application Run With Default Fonts

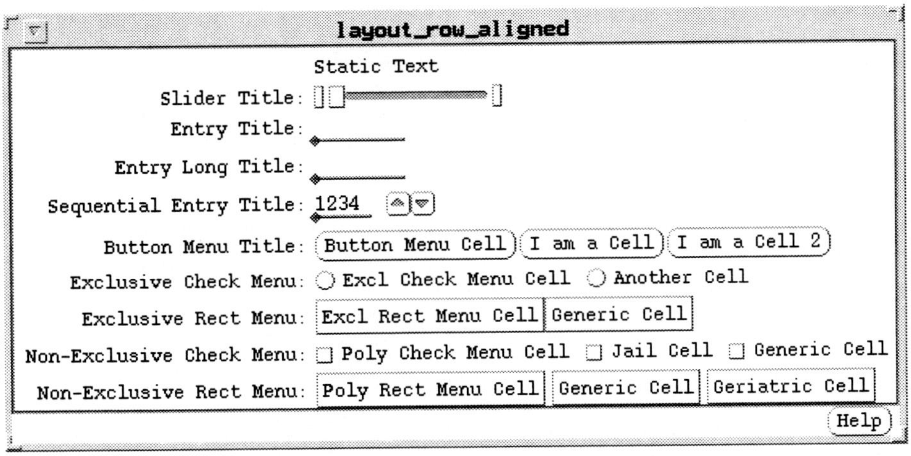

Figure 6-16   OPEN LOOK Application Run With Courier Font

font   (Member function)

```
XFontStruct *OI_d_tech::font( )
```

font returns a pointer to the X font structure for the font used by the object.

font_name (Member function)

```
char *OI_d_tech::font_name( )
```

font_name returns the name of the font used for drawing text in the object; it returns NULL if the name is unknown.

set_font (Member function)

```
void OI_d_tech::set_font(
    const char          *font_namp)         // pointer to font name
```

set_font sets the text font to use for the object. To find out what fonts are available on any particular X server, run a program such as xlsfonts or sfontpick. The values displayed by these programs are the values to use for *font_namp*.

font_ascent (Member function)

```
OI_number OI_d_tech::font_ascent( )
```

font_ascent returns the number of pixels in the logical extent of the object's current font that are above the baseline. The baseline is considered to be the first row of pixels in the descent.

font_descent (Member function)

```
OI_number OI_d_tech::font_descent( )
```

font_descent returns the number of pixels in the logical extent of the object's current font at or below the baseline. The baseline is considered to be the first row of pixels in the descent.

font_y_base (Member function)

```
OI_number OI_d_tech::font_y_base( )
```

font_y_base returns the number of pixels from the upper-left corner of the origin for the object's current font to its baseline. The baseline is considered to be the first row of pixels in the descent. This function returns the same value as does font_ascent.

font_height (Member function)

```
OI_number OI_d_tech::font_height( )
```

font_height returns the number of pixels in the character height of the object's current font with no interline spacing. This is equivalent to font_ascent( ) + font_descent( ).

font_width (Member function)

```
OI_number OI_d_tech::font_width( )
```

font_width returns the number of pixels in the widest character of the object's current font.

font_line_space (Member function)

```
OI_number OI_d_tech::font_line_space( )
```

font_line_space returns the number of pixels of spacing between lines of a multiple-line object. This spacing is always zero.

font_line_height   (Member function)

```
OI_number OI_d_tech::font_line_height( )
```

font_line_height returns the number of pixels in the height of a line of characters in the object's current font, including any inter-line spacing. This is the baseline-to-baseline distance. font_line_space is always zero, so the number returned from font_line_height is the same as that returned by font_height.

6.12   Interfaces to the Help Mechanism

There are two types of help facility available in OI.

The first is the hypertext help window that pops up when the user activates the help button in an OI_app_window or presses the help key. The hypertext help is documented in Chapter 8, "OI_app_window." The only function described here which relates to the hypertext help is hyper_help.

The second is a single line of help text, which the functions described here implement—except hyper_help. This line of text displays in the help line of the most closely related OI_app_window ancestor of the object (or of the object itself, if it is an OI_app_window). The help line is in the left portion of the window footer.

There is a help-text stack onto which you can push help lines as they are displayed in the OI_app_window, and out of which you can pop and display help lines that were previously pushed onto the stack. This help mechanism is usually driven by your program, and sometimes also used by OI objects when they need to post error messages. When OI objects use this help mechanism, they always push and pop the text to preserve anything your application has posted.

For example, if you have an OI_entry_field into which the user is to type an existing file name, and the user types characters that do not represent an existing file, you could display "File not found" in the help line of the OI_app_window ancestor of the entry field.

If you want to ring the bell when your message is displayed, use XBell. For example:

```
objp->push_help_str("File not found",OI_yes);
XBell(obj->display( ),0);
```

hyper_help   (Member function)

```
OI_help *OI_d_tech::hyper_help( )
```

hyper_help returns a pointer to the hypertext help object attached to the nearest ancestor of this object which is an OI_app_window.

push_help_str   (Member function)

```
OI_stat OI_d_tech::push_help_str(
    const char         *strp,              // help text string
    OI_bool            temp=OI_no)         // permanent/temporary flag
```

push_help_str pushes any previously displayed help text onto the help stack and displays the new text *strp* in the nearest ancestor of type OI_app_window. The new text is on top of the help stack. If *temp* is OI_no, the message is *permanent*, meaning the message remains displayed until another help message is displayed, or until you call **pop_help_str**. If *temp* is OI_yes, the message is *temporary*, meaning the message is displayed, but is removed when the next user-input event occurs—the next key press or button press.

pop_help_str   (Member function)

```
void OI_d_tech::pop_help_str(
    OI_number          n=1,            // number of levels to pop
    OI_bool            temp=OI_no)     // discard temporary status items
```

pop_help_str pops *n* levels of help from the help stack for the nearest ancestor of type OI_app_window and displays the string from the new top of the stack. If you omit *n*, it defaults to 1. If *temp* is OI_no, *n* permanent entries are popped, along with all intervening temporary entries. If *temp* is OI_yes, only lines that were pushed onto the help stack with temporary status are popped. When *temp* is OI_yes, popping stops when the first permanent entry is encountered, even if the count is not yet exhausted. **pop_help_str(0,OI_yes)** pops all temporary entries and leaves the latest permanent entry displayed.

set_help_str   (Member function)

```
OI_stat OI_d_tech::set_help_str(
    const char         *strp)          // help text string
```

set_help_str displays a string in the help line of the nearest ancestor of type OI_app_window. Any previously displayed help text is lost. This call effectively changes the value of the top line of the help stack.

help_str_posted   (Member function)

```
OI_number OI_d_tech::help_str_posted( )
```

help_str_posted returns non-zero if you have pushed any help text for this object using **push_help_str** and have not popped it. Note that this is not a reflection of the total number of items pushed onto the help stack; it only reflects those pushed for the current object. To determine the total help stack size, see **help_stack_size**.

help_str   (Member function)

```
char *OI_d_tech::help_str( )
```

help_str returns a pointer to the current help text for the most closely related OI_app_window ancestor object. **help_str** returns NULL if no OI_app_window ancestor object exists, no help line object exists for the OI_app_window, or the help line has not been set.

help_stack_size   (Member function)

```
OI_number OI_d_tech::help_stack_size( )
```

help_stack_size returns the number of items on the help stack for the most closely related OI_app_window ancestor object.

6.13   Attaching Data to an Object

All OI objects carry around an auxiliary data pointer. This is an arbitrary pointer, which you can set in your application, and is not used by OI in any manner. It provides a convenient means of associating application data structures with OI objects.

You are more likely to need to use this facility if you are used to programming in C rather than C++. If you attach some data items to an OI object, you can reference this data when you have a pointer to that object. This is useful for avoiding global data definitions. For example, you might create a slider that the user will move to control an external device such as a water valve. You can use **set_data** to associate the valve data structure with the slider. Subsequently, whenever you have a pointer to the slider, you also have access to the valve data.

If you are used to programming in C++, you will have less need for these functions, because you can derive your own class from OI classes and store the data in the object itself. Continuing with the slider example, you would create a separate class from **OI_slider** and incorporate the valve data in the object of the derived class.

set_data   (Member function)

```
void OI_d_tech::set_data(
    void                    *datp)                        // user data pointer
```

    set_data sets the auxiliary data pointer associated with the object to *datp*.

data   (Member function)

```
void *OI_d_tech::data( )
```

    data returns the auxiliary data pointer set with **set_data**.

Program 6-4 shows an example of attaching data to an object. This program creates an **OI_entry_field** into which the user is to type a color. We attach a list of valid colors to the **OI_entry_field** using the member function **set_data**. In the data entry validation callback, we retrieve the list of colors using the member function **data**. Then we compare the entry with the list of colors, and if there is a match, we set the background color for the **OI_entry_field** to that color, otherwise we return with an error status.

```c
#include <strings.h>                          /* DataExample.C */
#include <OI/oi.H>

int main(int argc, char** argv)
{
        OI_ef_entry_chk_status chk_my_entry(OI_entry_field*, void*,
                                       OI_ef_entry_chk_status);
        OI_connection           *conp;
        OI_app_window           *wp;
        OI_entry_field          *efp;
    static  char                *color_vec[] =
            {"red","blue","white","green","gray","plum","violet",NULL};

    if (conp = OI_init(&argc,argv,"DataExample")) {
        wp = oi_create_app_window("main",1,1,"set_data demo");
        wp->set_layout(OI_layout_column);

        efp = oi_create_entry_field("color_entry",20,"Color: ");
        efp->layout_associated_object(wp,1,1,OI_active);
        efp->set_entry_check(chk_my_entry);
        efp->set_data(color_vec);

        wp->set_associated_object(wp->root( ),OI_def_loc,OI_def_loc,OI_active);
        OI_begin_interaction( );
    }
}


OI_ef_entry_chk_status chk_my_entry(OI_entry_field *efp, void*,
                                       OI_ef_entry_chk_status stat)
{
        char                    **color_vec;
        char                    *prtxtp;
        OI_ef_entry_chk_status ret_val;

    ret_val = OI_ef_entry_chk_bad;
    if (stat == OI_ef_entry_chk_ok) {
        prtxtp = efp->part_text( );
        if (prtxtp) {
            color_vec = (char**)efp->data( );
            while (*color_vec) {
                if (!strcmp(*color_vec,prtxtp)) {
                    efp->set_bkg_color(prtxtp);
                    ret_val = OI_ef_entry_chk_ok;
                    break;
                }
                color_vec++;
            }
        }
    }
    return (ret_val);
}
```

Program 6-4   Attaching Data to an Object (DataExample.C)

6.14   Input Focus Management

In order to type into an OI object such as an OI_entry_field object, the object must have the input-focus. If the focus policy is OI_focus_follows_pointer, the user must normally position the mouse pointer over the object into which he/she wishes to type. The act of moving the pointer into the object delivers the *input focus* to the object. If the focus policy is OI_click_to_type, the user must position the mouse over an object and click the SELECT mouse button to set the focus to the object. Note that you can set the focus policy to either OI_focus_follows_pointer or OI_click_to_type using the OI_connection resource focusPolicy. The default is OI_click_to_type.

In any case, the input focus is given to an object only if the object can actually accept keyboard events. An object can accept keyboard events if it is an object which can inherently accept keyboard events, and if disallow_kb_input has not been called for the object. By default, the following objects accept keyboard input:

> OI_entry_field
> OI_seq_entry_field
> OI_slider
> OI_multi_text
> OI_pane_grip
> OI_scroll_text
> OI_scroll_bar
> All menus

However, you can add keyboard translations for any other types of objects; if you do, these objects will accept keyboard input. Once an object has the input focus, the object retains it until it is taken away as a consequence of the mouse pointer moving to another object which can accept input (OI_focus_follows_pointer), clicking on another object (OI_click_to_type), or as a result of focus group keyboard traversal, discussed next.

6.14.1   Focus Groups

OI implements a mechanism called *focus groups*. A focus group is a group of objects with a defined order of keyboard-activated input-focus traversal. Using the appropriate keystrokes, the user can traverse among objects in a given focus group with or without actually entering data, and, using a different set of keystrokes, the user can traverse from one focus group to another. OI sets up a default keyboard traversal ordering for objects that can accept keyboard input. You can also establish your own traversal ordering.

Runtime interaction keyboard traversal works as follows: When the user completes the data entry operation in one object in a focus group, the input focus automatically moves to the next object in the group, ready to start entering data there. The Up (or Right) Arrow key (and sometimes the Return key) moves the input focus from one object to the next within the current focus group. The Down (or Left) Arrow key moves the input focus to the previous object within the current focus group. Striking Tab or Ctrl/Tab moves the focus from the current focus group to the next, and striking Shift/Tab or Ctrl/Shift/Tab moves the focus from the current focus group to the previous focus group.

(Since multi text objects accept Tab as an input character, Ctrl/Tab must be used in these objects to move to the next group, and similarly, Ctrl/Shift/Tab must be used to move to the previous group.)

6.14.1.1 Default Keyboard Traversal

The default keyboard traversal algorithm makes each object that can accept keyboard input a focus group, so that using the Tab key (in conjunction with Ctrl and Shift as necessary) moves the focus from one object to the next or previous. If you have used the automatic layout facility, the default traversal order follows the layout sequence. This sequence is by rows if the layout method is

    OI_layout_row
    OI_layout_row_aligned
    OI_layout_row_column
    OI_layout_titled_row_column
    OI_layout_row_column_aligned
    OI_layout_wrapped_row.

The sequence is by columns if the layout method is

    OI_layout_column
    OI_layout_wrapped_column.

If the layout is OI_layout_vert_tree, the default traversal order is from top to bottom, traversing the left-most nodes first, then the next to left-most, recursively, until finally the right-most nodes are visited. If the layout is OI_layout_horz_tree, the same method of traversal is used, except the order is from left to right, traversing the top-most nodes first.

If you have used manual layout, the default traversal order corresponds to the order in which you associated the objects to the top-level parent object.

6.14.1.2 Establishing Keyboard Traversal Groups

Using the member functions set_first_focus, set_next, and set_next_group, you can establish your own focus groups and traversal order, both among groups and within each group. To establish a focus group, use set_next to set up a chain from one object to another. The user can move among the objects for which you have called set_next using the Up and Down Arrow (Left and Right Arrow) keys and the Return key. All the objects you have chained together using set_next comprise a single focus group. If you chain a completely different set of objects together using set_next, they comprise a different focus group. You can connect the focus groups using the member function set_next_group, pointing to the first object of the new group that you wish to receive the input focus. The user is then able to change the focus from any object in one group to the first object in the next group by striking Tab or Ctrl/Tab. To change the focus to the last object in the previous focus group, the user can strike Shift/Tab or Shift/Ctrl/Tab.

If you call set_first_focus for an object (usually a container with other objects as children), you can specify which of the object's children should get the input focus when the container object receives the focus.

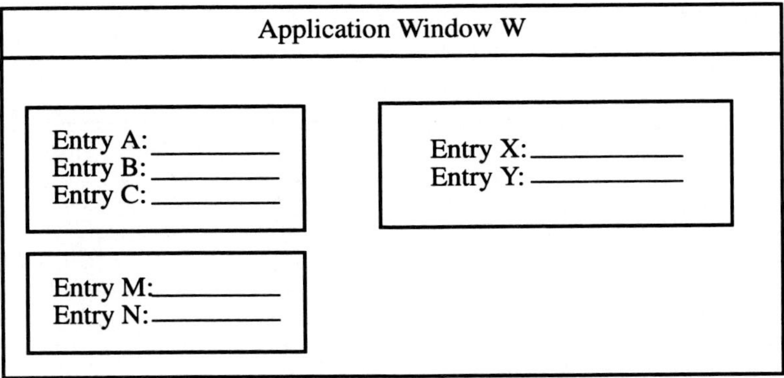

Figure 6-17   Focus Groups

For example, using Figure 6-17 as a diagram of OI objects, suppose you set up the traversal order in this fashion:

```
A->set_next_group(M)
A->set_next(B)
B->set_next(C)
M->set_next_group(X)
M->set_next(N)
X->set_next(Y)
W->set_first_focus(A)
```

This arrangement establishes three focus groups; each group is depicted in Figure 6-17 surrounded by a small rectangle. When the user moves the mouse pointer into the application window W (or clicks in W, depending on the focus policy), then A receives the input focus. The user can then move among the objects without moving the mouse as shown in Table 6-6.

Table 6-6 Focus Movements for Focus Groups in Figure 6-15

If Focus is on	Tab	Shift/Tab	Down Arrow	Up Arrow
A	Moves focus to M.	Moves focus to Y.	Moves focus to B.	Does nothing.
B	Moves focus to M.	Moves focus to Y.	Moves focus to C.	Moves focus to A.
C	Moves focus to M.	Moves focus to Y.	Does nothing.	Moves focus to B.
M	Moves focus to X.	Moves focus to C.	Moves focus to N.	Does nothing.
N	Moves focus to X.	Moves focus to C.	Does nothing.	Moves focus to M.
X	Moves focus to A.	Moves focus to N.	Moves focus to Y.	Does nothing.
Y	Moves focus to A.	Moves focus to N.	Does nothing.	Moves focus to X.

All menus respond to keyboard traversal. Each menu is considered to be a focus group, and its menu cells are the elements in the group.

Notice that any focus group is a doubly-linked list—it has pointers pointing backwards as well as forwards. For this reason you should not create a focus group which is an inverted tree, with more than one object funneling into a single object.

6.14.1.3 Traversing Focus Groups Programmatically

Whether you are using the default keyboard traversal established by OI or you have set up your own focus groups, you can move among the objects in a group from within your program. You do this using the member functions set_focus_next, set_focus_prev, next_entry, and set_focus_next_tab.

set_next   (Member function)

```
void OI_d_tech::set_next(
    OI_d_tech            *nxtp)          // pointer to next object
```

set_next establishes the object *nxtp* as the next object after this one within the focus group.

next   (Member function)

```
OI_d_tech *OI_d_tech::next( )
```

next returns a pointer to the next object in the focus group. It returns NULL if **set_next** has not been called for this object.

prev   (Member function)

```
OI_d_tech *OI_d_tech::prev( )
```

prev returns a pointer to the previous object in the focus group. It returns NULL if there is no
such object.

next_entry   (Member function)

```
void OI_d_tech::next_entry(
    OI_number          which)              // direction control
```

next_entry sets the input focus to an object in the focus group depending on the value of *which*.
next_entry activates the next object if *which* > 0, the previous object if *which* < 0, or the current
object if *which* = 0.

set_focus_next   (Member function)

```
void OI_d_tech::set_focus_next(
    OI_d_tech*,                            // unused
    const XEvent*,                         // unused
    const char *const*,                    // unused
    unsigned int*)                         // unused
```

set_focus_next exists so that you can use it in translations (see Chapter 40, "The OI
Translation Mechanism"). Therefore, its argument sequence looks like the standard translation
routine arguments. However, all arguments are ignored. To activate the next object in the focus
group, call **set_focus_next**, using NULL for all arguments. Doing this is equivalent to calling
next_entry(1).

set_next_group   (Member function)

```
void OI_d_tech::set_next_group(
    OI_d_tech          *nxtp)              // pointer to first object in next group
```

set_next_group establishes the object *nxtp* as the first object to obtain input focus in the next
focus group.

set_focus_next_tab   (Member function)

```
void OI_d_tech::set_focus_next_tab(
    OI_d_tech*,                            // unused
    const XEvent*,                         // unused
    const char *const*,                    // unused
    unsigned int*)                         // unused
```

set_focus_next_tab exists so that you can use it in translations (see Chapter 40, "The OI
Translation Mechanism"). Therefore, its argument sequence looks like the standard translation
routine arguments. However, all arguments are ignored. To activate the first object in the next
focus group, call **set_focus_next_tab**, using NULL for all arguments.

set_focus_next_window (Member function)

```
void OI_d_tech::set_focus_next_window(
    OI_d_tech*,                     // unused
    const XEvent*,                  // unused
    const char *const*,             // unused
    unsigned int*)                  // unused
```

set_focus_next_window exists so that you can use it in translations (see Chapter 40, "The OI Translation Mechanism"). Therefore, its argument sequence looks like the standard translation routine arguments. However, all arguments are ignored. To activate the first object in the next top level object, call **set_focus_next_window**, using NULL for all arguments.

set_focus_prev (Member function)

```
void OI_d_tech::set_focus_prev(
    OI_d_tech*,                     // unused
    const XEvent*,                  // unused
    const char *const*,             // unused
    unsigned int*)                  // unused
```

set_focus_prev exists so that you can use it in translations (see Chapter 40, "The OI Translation Mechanism"). Therefore, its argument sequence looks like the standard translation routine arguments. However, all arguments are ignored. To activate the previous object in the focus group, call **set_focus_prev**, using NULL for all arguments. Doing this is equivalent to calling **next_entry**(-1).

set_focus_prev_tab (Member function)

```
void OI_d_tech::set_focus_prev_tab(
    OI_d_tech*,                     // unused
    const XEvent*,                  // unused
    const char *const*,             // unused
    unsigned int*)                  // unused
```

set_focus_prev_tab exists so that you can use it in translations (see Chapter 40, "The OI Translation Mechanism"). Therefore, its argument sequence looks like the standard translation routine arguments. However, all arguments are ignored. To activate the first object in the previous focus group, call **set_focus_prev_tab**, using NULL for all arguments.

set_focus_prev_window (Member function)

```
void OI_d_tech::set_focus_prev_window(
    OI_d_tech*,                     // unused
    const XEvent*,                  // unused
    const char *const*,             // unused
    unsigned int*)                  // unused
```

set_focus_prev_window exists so that you can use it in translations (see Chapter 40, "The OI Translation Mechanism"). Therefore, its argument sequence looks like the standard translation routine arguments. However, all arguments are ignored. To activate the first object in the previous top level object, call **set_focus_prev_window**, using NULL for all arguments.

set_first_focus   (Member function)

```
void OI_d_tech::set_first_focus(
    OI_d_tech              *frstp)          // pointer to first focus object
```

set_first_focus establishes the object *frstp* as the first object to obtain input focus when this object receives the input focus.

first_focus   (Member function)

```
OI_d_tech *OI_d_tech::first_focus( )
```

first_focus returns a pointer to the object set in **set_first_focus**. It returns NULL if you have not called **set_first_focus** for this object.

set_focus   (Member function)

```
void OI_d_tech::set_focus(
    Time                  tm=CurrentTime,   // time stamp from X event
    OI_bool               force=OI_no)      // force use of tm?
```

set_focus sets the input focus to the object, but only if some other object has not received the input focus with a time stamp later than the time stamp of this **set_focus**. If an X event structure is available with a time stamp in it (for example, if you are in a callback routine registered via **OI_dispatch_insert**), you should call **set_focus** with *tm* set to this time stamp. If you omit *tm*, OI uses **CurrentTime**. If *force* is **OI_no**, OI uses the most recent of *tm* and the last known time. The "last known time" is the time stamp from the last X event for the connection for this object that had a time stamp. If *force* is **OI_yes**, OI uses *tm* as the time stamp for this call to **set_focus**.

set_focus_in   (Member function)

```
void OI_d_tech::set_focus_in(
    OI_focus_fnp          fnp,              // pointer to callback function
    void                  *argp=NULL)       // arbitrary argument for fn
```

```
void OI_d_tech::set_focus_in(
    OI_callback           *objp,            // memfnp's object
    OI_focus_memfnp       memfnp,           // pointer to callback member function
    void                  *argp=NULL)       // arbitrary argument for memfnp
```

The **set_focus_in** functions register a callback function to be invoked whenever the object gains input focus. This callback is identified within OI as a **cbFocusin** callback function (see Section 6.18, "Determining and Adding Callbacks; Multiple Callbacks," on page 6-117). *memfnp* points to a member function for the object pointed to by *objp*. If your gain-focus function is a member function, when it is invoked it will be called as if you had written *objp->memfnp*. See Section 2.5, "Callbacks and Event-Driven Programming," on page 2-16 for more explanation.

argp is optional, and may be any valid expression that can be cast to a pointer. You can use it to pass additional information to the function *fn* or *memfnp*.

Writing the Gain-Focus Callback Function

If the **cbFocusin** callback function is not a member function, write it in this form:

```
void fn(
        OI_d_tech  *oi_objp,             // pointer to OI object
        void       *argp)                // arbitrary argument
```

and if the **cbFocusin** callback function is a member function, write it in this form:

```
void obj_class::memfn(
        OI_d_tech  *oi_objp,             // pointer to OI object
        void       *argp)                // arbitrary argument
```

where *obj_class* is the class of the object whose member function is *memfn*. When your callback function is invoked, *argp* will be the argument specified in the **set_focus_in** call, and *oi_objp* will be a pointer to the OI object which has received focus.

set_focus_out   (Member function)

```
void OI_d_tech::set_focus_out(
    OI_focus_fnp      fnp,               // pointer to callback function
    void              *argp=NULL)        // arbitrary argument for fn


void OI_d_tech::set_focus_out(
    OI_callback       *objp,             // memfnp's object
    OI_focus_memfnp   memfnp,            // pointer to callback member function
    void              *argp=NULL)        // arbitrary argument for memfnp
```

The **set_focus_out** functions register a callback function to be invoked whenever the object loses input focus. This callback is identified within OI as a **cbFocusout** callback function (see Section 6.18, "Determining and Adding Callbacks; Multiple Callbacks," on page 6-117). *memfnp* points to a member function for the object pointed to by *objp*. If your lost-focus function is a member function, when it is invoked it will be called as if you had written *objp->memfnp*. See Section 2.5, "Callbacks and Event-Driven Programming," on page 2-16 for more explanation.

argp is optional, and may be any valid expression that can be cast to a pointer. You can use it to pass additional information to the function *fn* or *memfnp*.

Writing the Lost-Focus Callback Function

If the **cbFocusout** callback function is not a member function, write it in this form:

```
void fn(
        OI_d_tech   *oi_objp,        // pointer to OI object
        void        *argp)           // arbitrary argument
```

and if the **cbFocusout** callback function is a member function, write it in this form:

```
void obj_class::memfn(
        OI_d_tech   *oi_objp,        // pointer to OI object
        void        *argp)           // arbitrary argument
```

where *obj_class* is the class of the object whose member function is *memfn*. When your callback function is invoked, *argp* will be the argument specified in the **set_focus_out** call, and *oi_objp* will be a pointer to the OI object which has lost the focus.

6.15   Classifying an Object

There may be times when you have a pointer to an object (usually a pointer to an OI_d_tech) and you need to find out more specifically what type it is. For example, if you are clearing all OI_entry_field objects that are descendants of some object, (clearing a data entry screen), you need to know which descendants are entry fields in order to call **set_text** for them. See Example 6-4, "Clearing All Entry Field Descendants of an Object," on page 6-32 for an example of this.

is_derived_from   (Member function)

```
OI_bool OI_d_tech::is_derived_from(
    const char          *name)        // class name as string


OI_bool OI_d_tech::is_derived_from(
    XrmQuark            qrk)           // class name converted to XrmQuark


OI_bool OI_d_tech::is_derived_from(
    OI_class            *cls_obj)      // class
```

is_derived_from returns **OI_yes** if the object is derived from the specified type of object. For the purposes of this function, an object is considered to be derived from its own class as well as all its base classes. *name* is the OI class of the object, delimited by quotes (for example, "OI_app_window" or "OI_menu_cell"). *qrk* is an **XrmQuark** representation of the OI class name. You can convert a string to an **XrmQuark** using the Xlib function **XrmStringToQuark**.

If you are going to call **is_derived_from** many times, it is most efficient to use the third form. *cls_obj* is a pointer to the desired class object. Use *class_type*::clsp for this pointer. For example, to find out if an object is derived from an **OI_poly_menu**, set *cls_obj* to **OI_poly_menu::clsp**.

model (Member function)

```
OI_model_type OI_d_tech::model( )
```

model returns the user interface model for the object. This will be one of:

> OI_openlook
> OI_motif
> OI_openlook_3d

You should normally not need to use this function, since all model dependencies are automatically handled by the objects themselves.

6.16   X Interface Routines

There are many types of applications which can be written using the OI toolkit without any direct interfacing to the X window system on your part. However, for some types of applications you will have occasion to call functions from the X Library (Xlib) yourself. The functions below give you access to some useful X window system structures.

X_window (Member function)

```
Window OI_d_tech::X_window( )
```

X_window returns the X window System identifier for the "most useful" X window of the object. If the object's X window has not yet been created, **X_window** causes one to be created for it. Some OI objects are made up of more than one X window. For example, an **OI_app_window** has one X window for the outside and another for the interior box. The outside window contains the main menu, help line, state string, and the interior box. When you associate objects with an **OI_app_window**, you are actually putting them in the interior box. **X_window** returns the "window of interest" (the interior box of an **OI_app_window**, the scrolled box for an **OI_scroll_box**). You can usually think of it as the window into which you put other objects, or the window in which the text appears.

outside_X_window (Member function)

```
Window OI_d_tech::outside_X_window( )
```

outside_X_window returns the X window system identifier for the outermost X window used to enclose the object. This is the same as the value returned by **X_window** for most simple OI objects such as **OI_static_text**, **OI_gauge**, and **OI_slider**.

connection (Member function)

```
OI_connection *OI_d_tech::connection( )
```

connection returns a pointer to the connection object on which the current object is located. You can use it to find out other information about the X server such as the host name and screen number (by calling **OI_connection** member functions such as **screen_num**, etc.).

display   (Member function)

```
Display *OI_d_tech::display( )
```

display returns a pointer to the X window system Display structure for the X connection on which the object is located.

attach_X_window   (Member function)

```
void OI_d_tech::attach_X_window(
    Window              win)                    // window id
```

attach_X_window attaches *win* to be used as the object's own window; that is, *win* is treated as belonging to this object. When the object is parented, *win* will be reparented into the object tree hierarchy, effectively becoming part of this application. For example, if you start an **xclock**, find its X window id, and call **attach_X_window** for an **OI_box** object using the **xclock**'s window id, the **xclock** ceases to appear as a separate application on the display; it becomes "wrapped" in the **OI_box**'s application. The **xclock** application can still draw into the window, but the positioning, ancestry and size of the window are now controlled by the OI application as well as the **xclock** application. You would normally call **attach_X_window** immediately after the object is created and before it is parented.

Your use of **attach_x_window** will most likely be as follows (be sure to set the frame width to zero before calling **attach_X_window**):

```
    Window              xw;
    OI_box              bp;
xw = XCreateWindow(...);                     // Some special requirements
bp = oi_create_box("display_box", 1, 1);
bp->set_frame_width(0);
bp->attach_X_window(xw);                     // Force object to use a specific window
```

allow_override_redirect   (Member function)

```
void OI_d_tech::allow_override_redirect( )
```

allow_override_redirect marks the object's X window as an **override_redirect** window in the X Window sense. Calling **allow_override_redirect** prevents the window manager from reparenting the window or modifying the window's attributes. You should not normally need to use this member function, since OI automatically marks appropriate windows as **override_redirect** in most cases. This member function is only relevant for an object that has its own private X window. All displayable OI objects have private X windows except those listed in Section 6.9, "Windowless Objects," page 6-82.

If you have a need for an application window or dialog box which has absolutely no decoration provided by the window manager, do the following things:

- Create the object.
- Call the member function **X_window** to force the X window for the object to be created.
- Call **allow_override_redirect** for the object.

- Parent the object.

Override-redirect windows are basically invisible to the window manager—this means that you'll get no decoration, but you'll also be unable to move, resize, or restack the window using the window manager. For this reason, the ICCCM recommends against doing this.

disallow_override_redirect (Member function)

```
void OI_d_tech::disallow_override_redirect( )
```

disallow_override_redirect negates the effects of **allow_override_redirect**.

allow_transient (Member function)

```
void OI_d_tech::allow_transient(
    Window              win)                    // X window id
```

allow_transient marks the object's X window as a **transient_for** window in the X Windows sense. *win* specifies another X window for which this window is a transient. It is typically the window id of a main window for an application, usually obtainable with

```
    OI_app_window          *wp;
wp->outside_X_window( );
```

You should not normally need to use this member function, since OI automatically marks appropriate windows as transients in most cases. This member function is only relevant for an object that has its own private X window. All displayable OI objects have private X windows except those listed in Section 6.9, "Windowless Objects," page 6-82.

disallow_transient (Member function)

```
void OI_d_tech::disallow_transient( )
```

disallow_transient negates the effect of **allow_transient**.

6.17   Forming a UNIX Command

You can form a UNIX command or other string from values extracted from OI objects.

One way to do this is to use the **OI_base_text** member function **exec_cmd**. See Chapter 31, "OI_base_text and OI_multi_text," for a description of this function.

Another way to do this is the following: first mark objects as being *substitution arguments*, using the member function **allow_user_arg**. You call **allow_user_arg** for each object from which you desire to extract text to form the command. You then call **form_cmd** for the object at the head of the subtree within which your substitution argument objects reside. You call **form_cmd** with one argument—a template string. This template looks like the final form of the command you want to build, but with markers, or placeholders, where OI substitutes the values from the argument objects. **form_cmd** traverses the subtree starting at the object for which you called it, and replaces placeholders in the template string with text extracted from the argument objects. The text extracted for an object will be the text returned by the **alpha_value** member function.

You can also mark an object as being a *required argument* using **allow_user_arg_rqd**. This means that the user must enter text (if it is an **OI_entry_field** or **OI_seq_entry_field**) or make a choice (if it is a menu) before **form_cmd** is executed, or else **form_cmd** returns with an error. In this way you can be assured that required values have been entered or chosen before forking the command or using the constructed string in any capacity.

Program 6-5 shows an example using these facilities. This program allows the user to choose options for a UNIX **ls** command, then builds the command from a template using menu argument substitution, and finally forks the result as a separate process. Figure 6-18 shows this program running.

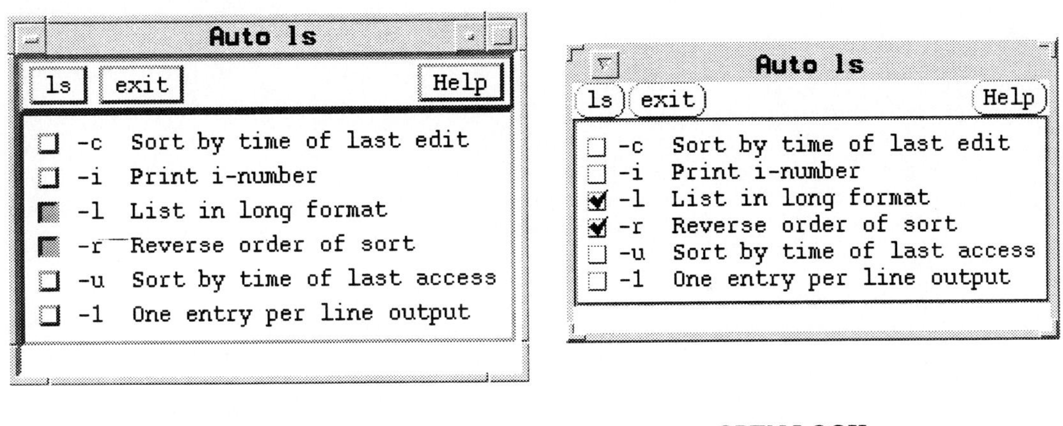

Motif   OPEN LOOK

Figure 6-18   Building and Forking a UNIX Command

```c
#include <OI/oi.H>                               /* AutoLS.C */
int main(int argc, char** argv)
{
        void                    build_n_fork(OI_menu_cell*,void*,OI_number);
        OI_connection           *conp;
        OI_app_window           *wp;
        OI_button_menu          *bmp;
        OI_poly_check_menu      *pcmp;
        OI_menu_cell            *cellp;
    static  OI_cell_spec        ls_exit[] = {
        {"dir","ls",build_n_fork},
        {"exit","exit",(OI_action_fnp)OI_end_interaction},
        };
    static  OI_cell_spec        optns[] = {
        {"-c","-c Sort by time of last edit"},
        {"-i","-i Print i-number"},
        {"-l","-l List in long format"},
        {"-r","-r Reverse order of sort"},
        {"-u","-u Sort by time of last access"},
        {"-1","-1 One entry per line output"},
        };
    if (conp = OI_init(&argc,argv,"AutoLS")) {
        wp = oi_create_app_window("main",1,1,"Auto ls");
        wp->set_layout(OI_layout_row);
        bmp = oi_create_button_menu("ls",
                            OI_count(ls_exit),&ls_exit[0],OI_horizontal);
        wp->set_main_menu(bmp);
        pcmp = oi_create_poly_check_menu("ls_options",
                            OI_count(optns),&optns[0],OI_vertical);
        pcmp->layout_associated_object(wp,1,2,OI_active);
        pcmp->allow_user_arg( );                 // mark menu for form_cmd arguments
        cellp = ((OI_menu_cell*)(bmp->subobject("dir")));
        cellp->change_arg(pcmp);                 // send ptr to "ls_options" to callback
        wp->set_associated_object(wp->root( ),OI_def_loc,OI_def_loc,OI_active);
        OI_begin_interaction( );
        OI_fini( );
    }
}
void build_n_fork(OI_menu_cell*,void *argp, OI_number)
{
        OI_d_tech               *dtp;
    dtp = (OI_d_tech*)argp;
    OI_fork(dtp->form_cmd("ls $1"));              // build ls command from menu cell names
    return;                                       // and fork it
}
```

Program 6-5 Building and Forking a UNIX Command (AutoLS.C)

In this program the user chooses the options for the **ls** command by clicking on cells in the poly check menu. When the user clicks on the button labeled "ls", the action callback function build_n_fork is executed. build_n_fork builds the **ls** command with options taken from the poly check menu cells, and forks the **ls** command. The results of the **ls** command appear in the window from which the example was run.

We register the action callback function build_n_fork by specifying it in the OI_cell_spec structure for the button with name "dir". pcmp is the argument passed to the action callback function build_n_fork for the argument *argp*. pcmp cannot be specified in the OI_cell_spec structure for the "dir" menu cell because it is a local variable and its value is not specified until run-time, so instead, we call the member function change_arg for the menu cell "dir".

Because allow_user_arg is called for the poly check menu as a whole, the argument substitution in the template is done by concatenating the names of all cells of the poly check menu which are in the selected state, blank separated. Thus if the cells named "-c" and "-r" are selected, the UNIX command forked will be:

```
ls -c -r
```

It is possible to call **allow_user_arg** for each cell of a menu instead of the menu itself, but this requires the template to be as long as the menu. For Program 6-5, this would mean the template would have to be:

```
"ls $1 $2 $3 $4 $5 $6"
```

form_cmd   (Member function)

```
char *OI_d_tech::form_cmd(
    const char          *tptp)         // pointer to command template
```

form_cmd returns a string formed by substituting values from OI objects into a template string *tptp*. You can use form_cmd to make UNIX commands that you subsequently fork (see OI_fork in Chapter 5, "Initialization, Termination, and Other Independent Functions"); you can use it for other purposes as well. For example, you could use it to build a record to add to a database.

tptp is a null-terminated template string containing argument placeholders of the form "*$n*" where *n* is an integer. *tptp* may also contain other arbitrary text. You can use the backslash character (\) to escape characters in the template string. To include a "$" character in the string, use "\$". An example of a template string might be

```
"find . -name $1 -exec $2 {} \;"
```

where $1 is to be replaced with the file name search criteria, and $2 is to be replaced with the program to execute for each file found.

form_cmd uses the object for which you called it as the head of an object (sub)tree to be searched for substitution arguments. form_cmd recursively descends the object tree starting at (and including) this object, searching for objects that are marked as *substitution arguments* (that is, for which you have called allow_user_arg). The order of search is the order in which you inserted objects into the tree using set_associated_object or layout_associated_object; each substitution argument is substituted for a placeholder *$n* in the template *tptp*, where *n* corresponds to the argument number of the object. When a substitution argument is found, the search does not continue below that object. The search continues with the next sibling of the object, until all object substitution arguments are found.

Argument numbers start at 1 for the first argument found in the tree, and increase sequentially. Note that the value for each object found replaces all occurrences of the corresponding $n in the template string. Also note that the value for a menu is the concatenated string of ALL of the values of its cells that have been selected by the user (blank separated), so that the values for all the selected menu cells together replace one occurrence of $n. See Program 6-5 for an example of menu argument substitution.

An object is only used as a substitution argument if you mark it properly. Call **allow_user_arg** for an object you wish to mark for use as a substitution argument. If you wish the substitution argument to be a *required argument* (meaning that the user must make an entry or a choice to supply **form_cmd** with an argument), call **allow_user_arg_rqd** for the object as well.

If, during OI's search of the object tree for substitution arguments, an object is found which is marked as a substitution argument and which has no value, and you have not called **allow_user_arg_rqd** for the object, OI removes (does not use) the corresponding $n from the template string. If the argument object has no value and you have flagged the object as a *required argument*, then **form_cmd** fails and returns a NULL pointer.

See Program 6-5 on page 6-114 and Figure 6-18 on page 6-113 for an example of building a UNIX command using menu argument substitution and forking the command as a separate process.

is_user_arg   (Member function)

```
OI_bool OI_d_tech::is_user_arg( )
```

is_user_arg returns **OI_yes** if you have marked the object as supplying substitution arguments; otherwise it returns **OI_no**.

allow_user_arg   (Member function)

```
void OI_d_tech::allow_user_arg( )
```

allow_user_arg marks the object as one that supplies substitution arguments for the function **form_cmd**.

disallow_user_arg   (Member function)

```
void OI_d_tech::disallow_user_arg( )
```

disallow_user_arg marks the object as one that does not supply substitution arguments. This is the default.

is_user_arg_rqd   (Member function)

```
OI_bool OI_d_tech::is_user_arg_rqd( )
```

is_user_arg_rqd returns **OI_yes** if you have marked the object as a *required argument*; otherwise it returns **OI_no**.

allow_user_arg_rqd   (Member function)

```
void OI_d_tech::allow_user_arg_rqd( )
```

allow_user_arg_rqd marks the object as a *required argument*. (See *required argument* definition above.) If you have so marked an object, and the user has not made an entry or choice, **form_cmd** returns with an error (a NULL) when called. Note that you must also call **allow_user_arg** for any object for which you call **allow_user_arg_rqd**, or it will not be marked as supplying substitution arguments for **form_cmd**.

disallow_user_arg_rqd   (Member function)

```
void OI_d_tech::disallow_user_arg_rqd( )
```

disallow_user_arg_rqd marks the object as not being a *required argument*.

6.18   Determining and Adding Callbacks; Multiple Callbacks

It is usually more convenient to register callbacks for OI objects using the various member functions for the object which register callbacks of the various types for that object. For example, you would use the member function **set_entry_check** to register a validation callback function (a callback of type **cbEntryFieldEntryCheck**; see Table 6-7) for an **OI_entry_field** object. However, you can use the member functions described here for the same purpose. In addition, you will need the functions in this section in order to:

- Get a pointer to a callback which has been registered for an object (**callback_get**). You specify the callback type as the argument. This is either a character string or the character string expressed as an XrmQuark. Valid callback types are shown in Table 6-7. For example, if you have a pointer **sbp** to an **OI_scroll_bar** object, you could get a pointer to the default handle-motion callback member function in either of these ways:
  ```
  sbp->callback_get(q_cbCtlr1d);
  ```
  or
  ```
  sbp->callback_get(OI_n_cbCtlr1d);
  ```
- Register multiple callbacks of the same type for an object. For example, you may want to have more than one validation callback function for an **OI_entry_field** object. You do this using **callback_add**. When OI executes multiple callbacks of the same type for an object, they are executed in the order in which they were registered.
- Remove a callback for an object. You can remove a single callback or all callbacks of a given type for an object (**callback_delete**).
- Delete all callbacks of a given type for an object and replace them with a new callback. (**callback_set**).
- Execute a callback in your own code. In preparation for this, you will need to lock the callback using **callbacks_lock** so that no portion of the application can try to execute it at the same time. When done, you unlock the callback using **callbacks_unlock**. Ordinarily you only do this if you are subclassing.

These functions make use of objects of class **OI_cb_inf**. An **OI_cb_inf** object contains information about the callback which you do not ordinarily deal with directly. However, if you are making your own OI subclass, and want to be able to register callbacks for it that are of different type than those

OI automatically supplies, you will need to use **OI_cb_inf** objects. The **OI_cb_inf** object contains all the information necessary to call the callback and specify the parameters to the callback. See Chapter 41, "Deriving Your Own Classes," for more information.

The callback type used as the first argument to these functions should be one of those in Table 6-7 or one you have created yourself for your own subclass. Not all callback types are available for all objects. Check the table at the back of each chapter for the class you are using.

Table 6-7 Automatically Supplied Callback Types

Callback Type	Value	String	Quark
OI_animate_fnp / memfnp	OI_n_cbAnimate	"cbAnimate"	q_cbAnimate
OI_action_fnp / memfnp	OI_n_cbCellAction	"cbCellAction"	q_cbCellAction
OI_click_fnp / memfnp	OI_n_cbClick	"cbClick"	q_cbClick
OI_ctlr_1d_fnp / memfnp	OI_n_cbCtlr1d	"cbCtlr1d"	q_cbCtlr1d
OI_scroll_2d_fnp / memfnp	OI_n_cbCtlr2d	"cbCtlr2d"	q_cbCtlr2d
OI_app_window_fnp / memfnp	OI_n_cbDeiconify	"cbDeiconify"	q_cbDeiconify
OI_destory_fnp / memfnp	OI_n_cbDestroy	"cbDestroy"	q_cbDestroy
OI_drag_preview_fnp / memfnp	OI_n_cbDragPreview	"cbDragPreview"	q_cbDragPreview
OI_drop_fnp / memfnp	OI_n_cbDrop	"cbDrop"	q_cbDrop
OI_drop_preview_fnp / memfnp	OI_n_cbDropPreview	"cbDropPreview"	q_cbDropPreview
OI_ef_char_chg_fnp / memfnp	OI_n_cbEfCharChg	"cbEntryFieldCharChg"	q_cbEfCharChg
OI_ef_char_check_fnp / memfnp	OI_n_cbEfCharCheck	"cbEntryFieldCharCheck"	q_cbEfCharCheck
OI_ef_entry_check_fnp / memfnp	OI_n_cbEfEntryCheck	"cbEntryFieldEntryCheck"	q_cbEfEntryCheck

Table 6-7 Automatically Supplied Callback Types

Callback Type	Value	String	Quark
OI_obj_event_fnp / memfnp	OI_n_cbExpose	"cbExpose"	q_cbExpose
OI_focus_fnp / memfnp	OI_n_cbFocusin	"cbFocusin"	q_cbFocusin
OI_focus_fnp / memfnp	OI_n_cbFocusout	"cbFocusout"	q_cbFocusout
OI_grip_moved_fnp / memfnp	OI_n_cbGripMoved	"cbGripMoved"	q_cbGripMoved
OI_grip_start_stop_fnp / memfnp	OI_n_cbGripStart	"cbGripStart"	q_cbGripStart
OI_grip_start_stop_fnp / memfnp	OI_n_cbGripStop	"cbGripStop"	q_cbGripStop
OI_app_window_fnp / memfnp	OI_n_cbIconify	"cbIconify"	q_cbIconify
OI_help_fnp / memfnp	OI_n_cbKeyHelp	"cbKeyHelp"	q_cbKeyHelp
OI_menu_end_fnp / memfnp	OI_n_cbMenuEnd	"cbMenuEnd"	q_cbMenuEnd
OI_mt_char_chg_fnp / memfnp	OI_n_cbMtCharChg	"cbMultiTextCharChg"	q_cbMtCharChg
OI_mt_char_check_fnp/ memfnp	OI_n_cbMtCharCheck	"cbMultiTextCharCheck"	q_cbMtCharCheck
OI_mt_entry_check_fnp / memfnp	OI_n_cbMtEntryCheck	"cbMultiTextEntryCheck"	q_cbMtEntryCheck
OI_pan_paint_fnp / memfnp	OI_n_cbPanPaint	"cbPanPaint"	q_cbPanPaint
OI_pin_fnp / memfnp	OI_n_cbPin	"cbPin"	q_cbPin
OI_pre_popup_fnp / memfnp	OI_n_cbPrePopup	"cbPrePopup"	q_cbPrePopup
OI_destroy_fnp / memfnp	OI_n_cbProtocolDelete	"cbProtocolDelete"	q_cbProtocolDelete

Table 6-7 Automatically Supplied Callback Types

Callback Type	Value	String	Quark
OI_sequence_fnp / memfnp	OI_n_cbSeqDecCheck	"cbSeqDecCheck"	q_cbSeqDecCheck
OI_sequence_fnp / memfnp	OI_n_cbSeqIncCheck	"cbSeqIncCheck"	q_cbSeqIncCheck
OI_resize_fnp / memfnp	OI_n_cbResize	"cbResize"	q_cbResize
OI_app_window_fnp / memfnp	OI_n_cbSaveYourself	"cbSaveYourself"	q_cbSaveYourself
OI_sel_cvt_fnp / memfnp	OI_n_cbSelection-Convert	"cbSelectionConvert"	q_cbSelection-Convert
OI_wait_fnp / memfnp	OI_n_cbTermAction	"cbTermAction"	q_cbTermAction
OI_pin_fnp / memfnp	OI_n_cbUnpin	"cbUnpin"	q_cbUnpin

callback_set   (Member function)

```
OI_cb_inf *OI_d_tech::callback_set(
    const char          *typ_str,       // callback type
    OI_fnp              fnp,            // pointer to callback function
    void                *argp=NULL)     // arbitrary argument for fn

OI_cb_inf *OI_d_tech::callback_set(
    const char          *typ_str,       // callback type
    OI_callback         *objp,          // memfnp's object
    OI_memfnp           memfnp,         // pointer to callback member function
    void                *argp=NULL)     // arbitrary argument for memfnp

OI_cb_inf *OI_d_tech::callback_set(
    XrmQuark            typ_qrk,        // callback type
    OI_fnp              fnp,            // pointer to callback function
    void                *argp=NULL)     // arbitrary argument for fn

OI_cb_inf *OI_d_tech::callback_set(
    XrmQuark            typ_qrk,        // callback type
    OI_callback         *objp,          // memfnp's object
    OI_memfnp           memfnp,         // pointer to callback member function
    void                *argp=NULL)     // arbitrary argument for memfnp
```

callback_set removes any callback(s) of type *typ_str* or *typ_qrk* already registered for the object, then registers the callback function *fnp* or *memfnp* of the specified type for the object. *memfnp* points to a member function for the object pointed to by *objp*. If your callback is a member function, when it is invoked it will be called as if you had written *objp->memfnp*. See Section 2.5, "Callbacks and Event-Driven Programming," on page 2-16 for more explanation. *argp* is optional, and may be any valid expression that can be cast to a pointer. You can use it to pass additional information to the function *fn* or *memfnp*.

callback_add   (Member function)

```
OI_cb_inf *OI_d_tech::callback_add(
    const char          *typ_str,        // callback type
    OI_fnp              fnp,             // pointer to callback function
    void                *argp=NULL)      // arbitrary argument for fn


OI_cb_inf *OI_d_tech::callback_add(
    const char          *typ_str,        // callback type
    OI_callback         *objp,           // memfnp's object
    OI_memfnp           memfnp,          // pointer to callback member function
    void                *argp=NULL)      // arbitrary argument for memfnp


OI_cb_inf *OI_d_tech::callback_add(
    XrmQuark            typ_qrk,         // callback type
    OI_fnp              fnp,             // pointer to callback function
    void                *argp=NULL)      // arbitrary argument for fn


OI_cb_inf *OI_d_tech::callback_add(
    XrmQuark            typ_qrk,         // callback type
    OI_callback         *objp,           // memfnp's object
    OI_memfnp           memfnp,          // pointer to callback member function
    void                *argp=NULL)      // arbitrary argument for memfnp
```

The **callback_add** functions register a callback function of type *typ_str* or *typ_qrk* for the object. No callbacks of the specified type for the object are deleted—instead, the callback is added to the list of callbacks for the object of the specified type. This may result in multiple callbacks of this type for the object. The arguments are the same as for **callback_set**.

callback_delete   (Member function)

```
void OI_d_tech::callback_delete(
    const char          *typ_str)          // callback type


void OI_d_tech::callback_delete(
    XrmQuark            typ_qrk)           // callback type


void OI_d_tech::callback_delete(
    const char          *typ_str,          // callback type
    OI_fnp              fnp,               // pointer to callback function
    void                *argp=NULL)        // arbitrary argument for fn


void OI_d_tech::callback_delete(
    const char          *typ_str,          // callback type
    OI_callback         *objp,             // memfnp's object
    OI_memfnp           memfnp,            // pointer to callback member function
    void                *argp=NULL)        // arbitrary argument for memfnp


void OI_d_tech::callback_delete(
    XrmQuark            typ_qrk,           // callback type
    OI_fnp              fnp,               // pointer to callback function
    void                *argp=NULL)        // arbitrary argument for fn


void OI_d_tech::callback_delete(
    XrmQuark            typ_qrk,           // callback type
    OI_callback         *objp,             // memfnp's object
    OI_memfnp           memfnp,            // pointer to callback member function
    void                *argp=NULL)        // arbitrary argument for memfnp
```

The single-parameter form of **callback_delete** removes all callbacks of type *typ_str* or *typ_qrk* for the object. The other forms of **callback_delete** remove only the callback *fnp* or *memfnp* from the list of callbacks for the object; all arguments in the call must match the arguments used when the callback was registered for the object.

callback_get   (Member function)

```
OI_cb_inf *OI_d_tech::callback_get(
    const char          *typ_str,          // callback type
    OI_cb_inf           *cbp=NULL)         // pointer to previous callback found


OI_cb_inf *OI_d_tech::callback_get(
    XrmQuark            typ_qrk,           // callback type
    OI_cb_inf           *cbp=NULL)         // pointer to previous callback found
```

callback_get returns a pointer to a callback for the object of type *typ_str* or *typ_qrk*. If you set *cbp* to NULL or omit it, **callback_get** returns a pointer to the first callback of the given type for the object. If you set *cbp* to point to a callback for the object, **callback_get** returns the callback following *cbp* in the list of multiple callbacks for the object. If *cbp* is the last callback in the list, **callback_get** returns NULL. The result is undefined if *cbp* does not belong to the object. If there are multiple callbacks for the object of type *typ_str* or *typ_qrk*, you can use a loop to retrieve them all (this example also executes each callback):

```
OI_cb_inf *cbp;

if (callbacks_lock(type_quark)) {
    for (cbp=NULL ; cbp=callback_get(type_quark,cbp) ; )
        cbp->callback( );                // execute the callback
    callbacks_unlock(type_quark);
}
```

callbacks_lock   (Member function)

```
OI_bool OI_d_tech::callbacks_lock(
    const char          *typ_str)        // callback type


OI_bool OI_d_tech::callbacks_lock(
    XrmQuark            typ_qrk)          // callback type
```

You will only need **callbacks_lock** if you are implementing your own subclass with its own callbacks (see Chapter 41, "Deriving Your Own Classes"). **callbacks_lock** locks all the callbacks of type *typ_str* or *typ_qrk* for the object in preparation for executing the callbacks. **callbacks_lock** returns **OI_yes** if any callbacks of the given type exist and are not already locked; otherwise it returns **OI_no** and leaves the callback unlocked.

callbacks_unlock   (Member function)

```
void OI_d_tech::callbacks_unlock(
    const char          *typ_str)        // callback type


void OI_d_tech::callbacks_unlock(
    XrmQuark            typ_qrk)          // callback type
```

You will only need **callbacks_unlock** if you are implementing your own subclass with its own callbacks (see Chapter 41, "Deriving Your Own Classes"). **callbacks_unlock** unlocks all callbacks of type *typ_str* or *typ_qrk* for the object so that they are available again for execution.

6.19 Error Status Inquiry

You only need to use this function when you are writing the constructor for your own subclass. This is because all OI functions that provide an error status return that status. For more on error handling, see Section 5.4, "Error Message Routines," on page 5-8.

error_status   (Member function)

```
OI_stat OI_d_tech::error_status( )
```

error_status returns the error status of the last operation. A returned value of **OI_ok** implies everything is normal, a value greater than zero implies a non-fatal error, and a value less than zero implies a fatal error. For possible return values, see Table 5-1 and Table 5-2 on page 5-14.

6.20 Resource Management

Because OI is a dynamic toolkit, it does not fetch resources at the time an object is first created. Since the path to the object in the object tree is not known when an object is created, and since resource specifications include this path, resource fetching must be delayed until the complete path to the object is known. Resource fetching occurs for any object:

- Whenever the object is parented to another object, and the top ancestor of the new parent is parented to a root object (in other words, the object will not be in the **orphanage** when parenting is complete).
- Whenever any ancestor is reparented, and the top ancestor of the new parent is a root object, excluding the **orphanage**.

The standard resources for an object are fetched automatically. *Standard resources* include all resources for the object's final class and for all of its base classes. You can also fetch additional resources for any object, and you can re-fetch resources at any point in your program.

In addition, you can prevent resources from being fetched for any object.

allow_object_resources   (Member function)

```
void OI_d_tech::allow_object_resources( )
```

allow_object_resources allows OI to fetch resources for this object. This is the default behavior.

disallow_object_resources   (Member function)

```
void OI_d_tech::disallow_object_resources( )
```

disallow_object_resources prevents OI from fetching resources for this object. If you use this function, you should call it before you associate the object with another object.

resource_value   (Member function)

```
char *OI_d_tech::resource_value(
    const char          *res)           // resource name


char *OI_d_tech::resource_value(
    XrmQuark            res_qrk)         // resource name as quark
```

resource_value queries the object and returns the value of the resource *res* or *res_qrk* for the object, expressed as a string. The value returned is stored in a statically allocated buffer. You should copy it if you will need it for future use.

set_resource_value   (Member function)

```
void OI_d_tech::set_resource_value(
    const char          *res,               // resource name
    const char          *val_str,           // value as string
    OI_bool             rec_file=OI_yes)    // record as from file


void OI_d_tech::set_resource_value(
    XrmQuark            res_qrk,            // resource name as quark
    const char          *val_str,           // value as string
    OI_bool             rec_file=OI_yes)    // record as from file
```

set_resource_value sets the resource *res* or *res_qrk* for the object to *val_str*. The OI resource database is not affected. If *rec_file* is **OI_yes**, OI records the resource as being from a resource file.

get_resources   (Member function)

```
void OI_d_tech::get_resources(
    OI_resource         *resources,         // array of OI_resource structures
    unsigned int        count,              // number of resources to fetch
    void                *base,              // base address
    XrmQuark            *no_ftch=NULL)      // resources not to fetch
```

get_resources causes OI to fetch a set of resources on behalf of the object from the OI resource database. This allows you to fetch additional resources other than the standard resources for an object. *resources* is an array of **OI_resource** structures, *count* is the number of resources to fetch, and *base* is the base address in memory where OI should place the results of the resource fetching. The offset into *base* for each resource is specified in the **OI_resource** structure.

no_ftch is an array of resource names as **XrmQuark**s of resources not to fetch.

The **OI_resource** structure is described in Chapter 39, "The OI Resource Mechanism."

get_sub_resources   (Member function)

```
void OI_d_tech::get_sub_resources(
    const char          *nam,         // instance name for resource subcategory
    const char          *cls,         // class name for resource subcategory
    OI_resource         *resources,   // array of OI_resource structures
    unsigned int        count,        // number of resources to fetch
    void                *base,        // base address
    XrmQuark            *no_ftch=NULL) // resources not to fetch

void OI_d_tech::get_sub_resources(
    XrmQuark            nam_qrk,      // instance name for resource subcategory
                                      // represented as an XrmQuark
    XrmQuark            cls_qrk,      // class name for resource subcategory
                                      // represented as an XrmQuark
    OI_resource         *resources,   // array of OI_resource structures
    unsigned int        count,        // number of resources to fetch
    void                *base,        // base address
    XrmQuark            *no_ftch=NULL) // resources not to fetch
```

get_sub_resources pushes *nam* and *cls* onto the resource manager stack, to the right of all object hierarchy elements, then fetches resources on behalf of the object. The other parameters are the same as those for **get_resources**. *nam_qrk* is an XrmQuark representation of the name, and *cls_qrk* is an XrmQuark representation of the class. If you are going to call **get_sub_resources** several times, it is more efficient to convert the name and class strings to XrmQuarks and use the second form of **get_sub_resources**. You can convert a string to an XrmQuark using the Xlib function XrmStringToQuark.

Normally, the last item for the resource stack is the current object name and the current object class name. This results in resources being fetched using specifications of the form:

```
... .object_name.resource
... .class_name.resource_class
```

Using **get_sub_resources**, you can append a sub-category between the object name and the resource name:

```
... .object_name.sub_name.resource
... .class_name.sub_class.resource_class
```

For example, suppose you had an **OI_entry_field** in which you were displaying different kinds of employees, and those employees were not represented by OI objects but were instead represented by your own C++ classes. You might have different employee types: salaried and hourly. If you wanted to modify the color of an object named **curr_emps** based on whether the employee was salaried or hourly, you could look for resources on the basis of the type:

```
... .curr_emps.salaried.foreground
... .OI_entry_field.EmployeeType.Foreground
```

and similarly for background and any other attributes of interest.

update_resources   (Member function)

```
void OI_d_tech::update_resources(
    OI_bool              updt_chld=OI_no)    // update descendants?
```

update_resources re-fetches the standard resources for the object. For example, if you have a program which dynamically modifies the OI resource database, you could use this function to see your changes take effect immediately. Note that just modifying the .Xdefaults file or other resource file during application execution time does not allow the resources to be updated. *updt_chld* determines whether resources are re-fetched for descendants of this object or not; a value of OI_yes indicates they should be.

update_specific_resources   (Member function)

```
void OI_d_tech::update_specific_resources(
    const char *const *rsrcs,               // names of resources to fetch
    unsigned int      count,                // number of resources to fetch
    OI_bool           updt_chld=OI_no)      // update descendants?
```

update_specific_resources re-fetches *count* resources specified by strings in the array *rsrcs*. *updt_chld* determines whether resources are re-fetched for descendants of this object or not; a value of OI_yes indicates they should be.

6.21   Interfacing to the Translations Mechanism

OI supports a translation mechanism which allows the user to modify program behavior by changing translations specified via an X resource. The translations specify a mapping of X event sequences to procedures to be called when the sequence of events occurs. For a more detailed description of the translation mechanism and some examples, see Chapter 40, "The OI Translation Mechanism."

The functions discussed in this section (except push_actions) take a string as a specification for one or more translations. Each translation in the string should be followed by the sequence "\n" as a separator. For readability, you may want to write each translation on a separate line; in this case use the "\" character for string continuation. Following is an example of the argument; it tells OI to translate the key press event Ctrl P into a call to the function print and the event Ctrl Q into a call to the function quit:

```
char my_trans[] = "\
    Ctrl<Key>P:print( )\n\
    Ctrl<Key>Q:quit( )\n"
```

The member functions augment_translations, override_translations substitute_translations, and set_translations provide the means of specifying translations for your objects. However, since the information is provided in string form, additional information is necessary to allow OI to bind a string to the actual address of a procedure to call. This capability is provided by the push_actions member function.

In the chapter for each OI object, we list the translation names for standard translation callable functions provided with the toolkit. If you specify translations which use only these functions, you need not call push_actions. However, if you write any of your own translation action routines, you must use push_actions to inform the toolkit of the mappings.

augment_translations   (Member function)

```
void OI_d_tech::augment_translations(
    const char        *trns)              // translations string
```

augment_translations modifies the translations for the object. If *trns* defines translations for events which do not have previously defined translations for this object, the new translations are added at the bottom of the translation table. If *trns* defines translations for events which already have translations for this object, the new translations are ignored. Each translation is considered separately for addition, not the group as a whole.

override_translations   (Member function)

```
void OI_d_tech::override_translations(
    const char        *trns)              // translations string
```

override_translations modifies the translations for the object. All translations defined by *trns* are added at the top of the translation table.

substitute_translations   (Member function)

```
void OI_d_tech::substitute_translations(
    const char        *trns)              // translations string
```

substitute_translations modifies the translations for the object. If *trns* defines translations for events which do not have previously defined translations for this object, the new translations are added at the bottom of the translation table. If *trns* defines translations for events which already have translations for this object, the new translations override the existing ones. Each translation is considered separately for addition, not the group as a whole.

set_translations   (Member function)

```
void OI_d_tech::set_translations(
    const char        *trns)              // translations string
```

set_translations sets the translations for the object to *trns*. The existing translations for the object are discarded and are replaced with *trns*. You should seldom use this function, since it discards all of the normal translations for the object (these translations implement much of the standard look and feel of OPEN LOOK and Motif). If you want to remove all translations without adding new ones, set *trns* to NULL.

push_actions   (Member function)

```
void OI_d_tech::push_actions(
    OI_actions_rec      *actions,        // pointer to OI_actions_rec structure
    OI_number           count)           // number of entries in actions
```

push_actions pushes a list of **OI_actions_rec** structures onto the object's action list.

An **OI_actions_rec** is a structure which defines a mapping from a character string name for an action, such as "forward_character", to an actual function address. The function address can be either a free-standing function or a member function. If it is a member function and you set the object pointer in the **OI_actions_rec** structure to NULL, the member function is called on behalf of the OI object for which it is registered.

OI_actions_rec looks like this:

```
struct OI_actions_rec{
    char                    *fn_nam;  // function name
    OI_translation_fnp      fnp;      // function to execute
    OI_callback             *objp;    // pointer to object if memfnp is not NULL
    OI_translation_memfnpmemfnp;      // member function to execute
};
```

push_actions gives OI information about how to map a named function to a real function address. *fn_nam* is the name of the action function. *fnp* is a pointer to a free-standing function; *memfnp* is a pointer to a member function. You should set only one of *fnp* or *memfnp* to a function address; set the other to NULL. No functions are called until you install translations for these functions, and the user actually generates the X events needed to trigger an action function for the object.

push_compiled_actions   (Member function)

```
void OI_d_tech::push_compiled_actions(
    OI_compiled_action_table    cmp_act)    // compiled action table
```

push_compiled_actions pushes a compiled action table onto the object's action list. To create a compiled action table, call the free-standing function **OI_compile_action_table** with the same arguments with which you would call **push_actions**. Using this function rather than **push_actions** speeds processing if you call it many times with the same table. **OI_compile_action_table** is discussed more fully in Chapter 5, "Initialization, Termination, and Other Independent Functions."

call_action_proc   (Member function)

```
OI_bool OI_d_tech::call_action_proc(
   const char        *fn_nam,       // name of the action routine
   const XEvent       *event,       // contents of event argument passed to fn_nam
   const char *const *params,       // contents of the params argument passed to fn_nam
   unsigned int       num_params)   // number of entries in params

OI_bool OI_d_tech::call_action_proc(
   XrmQuark           fn_nam,        // name of the action routine
   const XEvent       *event,        // contents of event argument to pass to fn_nam
   const char *const *params,        // contents of the params argument passed to fn_nam
   unsigned int       num_params)    // number of entries in params
```

call_action_proc searches for the action routine name *fn_nam* in the translation tables for object. If it does not find it there, it then searches the action tables for the connection for the object. If found, the function is invoked with the specified *event* and *params* parameters. call_action_proc returns OI_yes if the function was found and invoked; otherwise it returns OI_no.

6.21.1   Accelerators and Mnemonics

An accelerator is a translation which is valid for an object regardless of whether the object is visible or has the input focus. A mnemonic is an accelerator which is in effect only when the object is visible. Accelerators and mnemonics are described in Chapter 40, "The OI Translation Mechanism;" you should look there for descriptions of how to use the functions shown below. These functions allow you to install accelerators for any object. Note that menu cells show accelerator and mnemonic labels; no other objects have visual hints to the user that accelerators or mnemonics are installed.

set_accelerators   (Member function)

```
void OI_d_tech::set_accelerators(
   const char        *acl)           // accelerator translations string
```

set_accelerators sets the accelerators for the object to *acl*. The existing accelerators for the object are discarded and are replaced with *acl*. Any accelerators installed via the X resource manager are lost.

set_mnemonics   (Member function)

```
void OI_d_tech::set_mnemonics(
   const char        *mnem)          // mnemonics translations string
```

set_mnemonics sets the mnemonics for the object to *mnem*. The existing mnemonics for the object are discarded and are replaced with *mnem*. Any mnemonics installed via the X resource manager are lost.

6.22 Resources

OI fetches the resources shown in Table 6-8 for an OI_d_tech object. For more information on resource management, see Chapter 39, "The OI Resource Mechanism."

All OI objects respond to the following X resources:

Table 6-8 OI_d_tech Resources

Resource	Description	Possible Values
accelerators	Specifies a translation table that is bound with its actions in the context of a particular object.	See Chapter 40, "The OI Translation Mechanism"
background	Specifies the background color for the object.	Color string
backgroundPixmap	Specifies a pixmap for tiling the background of the object. You specify a file name; OI uses the OI_connection resource bitmapFilePath as the path to use if you do not specify a complete pathname.	File name of Xpm or Bitmap format file
bevelStyle	Specifies the bevel style.	Bevel_in Bevel_out Chisel_in Chisel_out Bevel_none
bevelWidth	Specifies the bevel width in pixels. Note—you should normally use FrameWidth instead.	Non-negative integer
borderColor	Specifies the border color for the object.	Color string
borderWidth	Specifies the border width in pixels. Note—you should normally use FrameWidth instead.	Non-negative integer
bottomBevelColor	Specifies the color to use when painting the bottom bevel of a 3D object.	Color string

Table 6-8 OI_d_tech Resources

Resource	Description	Possible Values
bottomSpace	Specifies the number of pixels of space to insert below the object when it is laid out in its parent.	Non-negative integer
children	For hypertext help and user-interface builder generated files only. This resource is a comma separated list of children.	child-object-name.class-type
clip	If on, specifies the object should be clipped to its parent.	Boolean
cursor	Specifies the cursor to display when the pointer is within the object. You can find valid cursors in /usr/inclu-de/X11/cursorfont.h. When you specify a cursor using this resource, remove the XC_ prefix from the cursor name.	Cursor name
defaultHorizontalSpace	Specifies the number of pixels of space to insert to the left and right of a child object which does not have its horizontal space specifically set, when it is laid out in the current object.	Non-negative integer
defaultVerticalSpace	Specifies the number of pixels of space to insert to the top and bottom of a child object which does not have its vertical space specifically set, when it is laid out in the current object.	Non-negative integer
downColor	Specifies the background color of a depressed 3D object.	Color string
downIsBackground	If on, specifies that the down color should be the same as the background color.	Boolean

Table 6-8 OI_d_tech Resources

Resource	Description	Possible Values
focusFrameColor	Specifies the color to use to paint the focus frame.	Color string
focusFramePixmap	Specifies the pixmap to use when drawing the focus frame.	Xpm or Bitmap format file name
focusFrameWidth	Specifies the width of the focus frame.	Non-negative integer
foreground	Specifies the foreground color for the object.	Color string
frameWidth	Specifies the frame width in pixels.	Non-negative integer
gravity	Specifies the gravity of the object.	grav_north grav_south grav_east grav_west grav_northwest grav_northeast grav_southwest grav_southeast grav_center
helpFile	Specifies the name of the help file to be used when keyboard help is activated for the object.	File name
helpTopic	Specifies the topic name in the help file to use when keyboard help is activated for the object.	Help topic name
horzMove	If on, specifies that the object can be moved in the horizontal direction.	Boolean
horzResize	If on, specifies that the object can be resized in the horizontal direction.	Boolean
independentLoc	If on, and the object is not clipped, specifies that the object will not change its position to maintain its position relative to its parent when its parent is moved.	Boolean

Table 6-8 OI_d_tech Resources

Resource	Description	Possible Values
language	Specifies the language for the object. The language resource is fetched before all other resources so that you can define other attributes, such as font and text, depending on the language used.	Any string
layout	Specifies the layout method.	OI_layout_none OI_layout_row OI_layout_row_aligned OI_layout_column OI_layout_row_column OI_layout_titled_row_column OI_layout_row_column_aligned OI_layout_wrapped_row OI_layout_wrapped_column OI_layout_horz_tree OI_layout_vert_tree
leftSpace	Specifies the number of pixels of space to insert to the left of the object.	Non-negative integer
mapRaised	If on, specifies that the object must always be raised above its siblings when its state is changed to make it visible.	Boolean
mnemonics	Specifies additional mnemonic actions (translations) to be used for the object when it is visible.	Valid key translation
move	If on, specifies that the object can be moved.	Boolean
objectResources	If off, specifies that resources will not be fetched for the object.	Boolean
placement	Specifies the size of an object (width x height) and its location.	*See note below table.

Table 6-8 OI_d_tech Resources

Resource	Description	Possible Values
resize	If on, specifies that the object can be resized	Boolean
rightSpace	Specifies the number of pixels of space to insert to the right of the object when it is laid out in its parent.	Non-negative integer
state	Specifies the state of the object.	active inactive not_displayed active_not_displayed
sizeTrack	Forces the object to track its parent's size.	size_track_none size_track_horizontal size_track_vertical size_track_full
topBevelColor	Specifies the color to use when painting the top bevel of a 3D object.	Color string
topSpace	Specifies the number of pixels of space to insert above the object when it is laid out in its parent.	Non-negative integer
track	If on, causes the object to scroll when the parent is scrolled. Meaningful only if the parent is an OI_base_text object.	Boolean
translations	Specifies a translation list. A translation list is a list of events and actions that are to be performed when the events occur.	See Chapter 40, "The OI Translation Mechanism"
translations.augment	Specifies a translation list.	See Chapter 40, "The OI Translation Mechanism"
translations.override	Specifies a translation list.	See Chapter 40, "The OI Translation Mechanism"
translations.substitute	Specifies a translation list.	See Chapter 40, "The OI Translation Mechanism"

Table 6-8 OI_d_tech Resources

Resource	Description	Possible Values
userArg	If on, specifies that the object can be used to supply an argument value for a call to form_cmd.	Boolean
userArgRqd	If on, specifies that the object must have a value when used as an argument value for a call to form_cmd.	Boolean
vertMove	If on, specifies that the object can be moved in the vertical direction.	Boolean
vertResize	If on, specifies that the object can be resized in the vertical direction.	Boolean

*Note: possible values for **placement** resource:

If the object is laid out, use

> wxh lxxx

where w and h are the width and height of the object. If the object does not respond to width and height parameters (such as OI_entry_field), omit wxh. "l" indicates a layout specification. For row, column or grid layout methods, xxx is of the form

> cNrM

where N is the column number and M is the row number. For tree layout methods, xxx is of the form

> lp:P,s:S

where P is the name of the parent node and S is the name of the sibling node.

If the object is not laid out, use

> wxh +x+y

where w and h are the width and height of the object and x and y are its pixel location within its parent. x and y may be OI_def_loc, indicating default location. You can use either + or - in front of the x and/or y;+ indicates the object's location is relative to the upper left corner of the parent and - indicates the location is relative to the lower right corner of the parent. If the object does not respond to width and height parameters (such as OI_entry_field), omit wxh.

Examples of **placement** resources:

```
*my_box.placement:  100x200  +10+200
*my_box.placement:  100x200  lc5r10
*my_box.placement:  100x200  lp:box_parent_node,s:<null>
```

6.23 Translations

Any OI object can have default translations installed for it. The default translations differ depending on the type of object and which model the application is using. The translations shown in Table 6-9 and Table 6-9 are installed for all objects which can accept keyboard input focus.

Table 6-9 Default OI_d_tech Translations, Motif

			Event Sequence	Action Functions Called
			<FocusIn>:	paint_focus_frame( )
			<FocusOut>:	clear_focus_frame( )
			<Key>Up:	set_focus_prev( )
			<Key>Prior:	set_focus_prev_tab( )
	Shift		<Key>Tab:	set_focus_prev_tab( )
	Shift	Ctrl	<Key>Tab:	set_focus_prev_tab( )
Alt			<Key>Tab:	set_focus_next_window( )
			<Key>Down:	set_focus_next( )
			<Key>Next:	set_focus_next_tab( )
			<Key>Tab:	set_focus_next_tab( )
		Ctrl	<Key>Tab:	set_focus_next_tab( )
Alt	Shift		<Key>Tab:	set_focus_prev_window( )
			<Key>F10:	activate_main_menu( )
			<Key>F4:	activate_popup( )

Table 6-10 Default OI_d_tech Translations, OPEN LOOK

		Event Sequence	Action Functions Called
		<Key>Up:	set_focus_prev( )
		<Key>Prior:	set_focus_prev_tab( )
Shift		<Key>Tab:	set_focus_prev_tab( )
Shift	Ctrl	<Key>Tab:	set_focus_prev_tab( )
		<Key>Down:	set_focus_next( )
		<Key>Next:	set_focus_next_tab( )
		<Key>Tab:	set_focus_next_tab( )

Table 6-10   Default OI_d_tech Translations, OPEN LOOK

Event Sequence	Action Functions Called
Ctrl <Key>Tab:	set_focus_next_tab( )

The next table, Table 6-11, describes the actions taken by the OI_d_tech action functions.

Table 6-11   OI_d_tech Translation Functions

Function Name	Description
activate_main_menu( )	Activates / deactivates main menu.
activate_popup( )	Activates / deactivates immediate popup child menu or nearest popup menu on ancestor(s).
clear_focus_frame( )	Removes the focus enhancement from the object.
drag_end( )	Cleans up following the drag. drag_end is a virtual function that is overridden in OI_multi_text, OI_entry_field, and OI_static_text so that they can provide text drag-and-drop cursors.
drag_copy_start( )	Initiates a drag operation allowing the user to drag data from one application and drop it on another. The operation is OI_dnd_copy, which means the data is not deleted from the drag-source object when the drop-site receives the data. drag_copy_start is a virtual function that is overridden in OI_multi_text, OI_entry_field, and OI_static_text so that they can provide text drag-and-drop cursors.
drag_move_start( )	Initiates a drag operation allowing the user to drag data from one application and drop it on another. The operation is OI_dnd_move, which means the data is deleted from the drag-source object when the drop-site receives the data. drag_move_start is a virtual function that is overridden in OI_multi_text, OI_entry_field, and OI_static_text so that they can provide text drag-and-drop cursors.
focus_in( )	Draws changes to the object when the object gains focus.
focus_out( )	Draws changes to the object when the object loses focus.
paint_focus_frame( )	Draws the focus enhancement around the object.

Table 6-11 OI_d_tech Translation Functions

Function Name	Description
set_focus_next( )	Moves the focus to the next object in the focus group.
set_focus_next_tab( )	Moves the focus to the first object in the next focus group.
set_focus_next_window( )	Moves the focus to the first object in the next top level object.
set_focus_prev( )	Moves the focus to the previous object in the focus group.
set_focus_prev_tab( )	Moves the focus to the last object in the previous focus group.
set_focus_prev_window( )	Moves the focus to the first object in the previous top level object.

6.24 Callback Functions

Table 6-12 lists the callbacks available for an OI_d_tech object and the page number of the corresponding explanatory material.

Table 6-12 OI_d_tech Callbacks

Callback Type	Callback Typedef	Description	Page Number
cbDestroy	OI_destroy_fnp/memfnp	Destroy callback function	6-39
cbDragPreview	OI_drag_preview_fnp/memfnp	Drag preview callback function	6-60
cbDrop	OI_drop_fnp/memfnp	Drop callback function	6-63
cbDropPreview	OI_drop_preview_fnp/memfnp	Drop preview callback function	6-65
cbFocusin	OI_focus_fnp/memfnp	Gain-focus callback function	6-107
cbFocusout	OI_focus_fnp/memfnp	Lost-focus callback function	6-108
cbResize	OI_resize_fnp/memfnp	Resize callback function	6-47
cbSelectionConvert	OI_sel_cvt_fnp/memfnp	Selection convert callback function	6-59

Chapter 7

OI_box

OI_box Functions

OI_box Member Functions

The following functions are available to an **OI_box** object, but are described in their own chapter.

OI_d_tech Member Functions

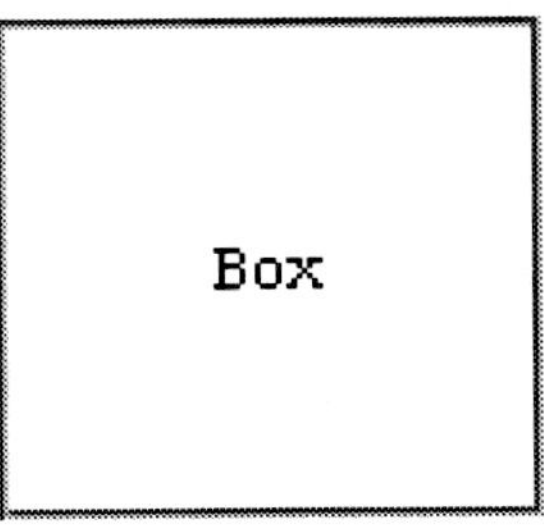

OI_box

7.1   Description

An OI_box is a rectangular region in which you can place OI objects or other graphics. The rectangle is surrounded by a frame; the box size specifications are for the interior region excluding the frame. OI_dialog_box is a subclass of OI_box; the interior of an OI_app_window is also an OI_box. Thus an OI_app_window and an OI_dialog_box each have all the functionality of an OI_box.

Before using an OI_box, be sure that you don't really need an OI_app_window or an OI_dialog_box instead. Some possible uses of an OI_box are as a container to group other objects so they may be treated as a unit, or as a region in which to draw graphics. If you do not wish the box's frame to be visible, you can set the frame width to zero using set_frame_width.

7.2   Class Tree

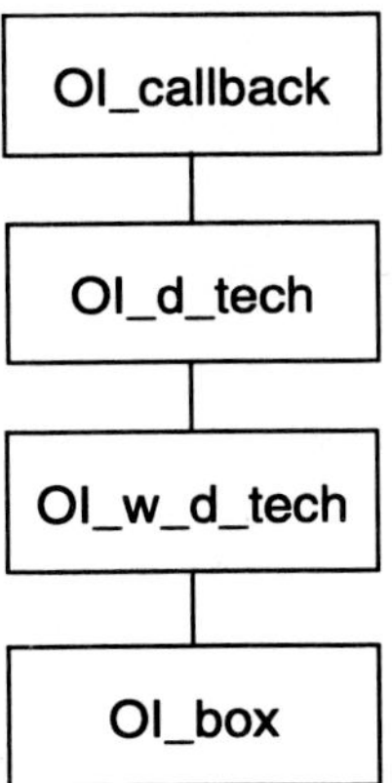

7.3   Runtime Interaction

Since **OI_box** is basically a container, OI provides very little in the way of user interaction mechanisms for it. The user can click the mouse on the interior of an **OI_box**, and the program can recognize the click and its position.

7.4   OI_box Creation

oi_create_box   (Free-standing function)

```
OI_box *oi_create_box(
    const char          *namp,          // name for object
    OI_number           width,          // horizontal size of box in pixels
    OI_number           height)         // vertical size of box in pixels
```

oi_create_box creates an **OI_box** object with name *namp*. The box is *width* pixels wide and *height* pixels tall. **oi_create_box** returns a pointer to the object. If the dimensions of the box are invalid (that is, 0 or less), or if the create failed for other reasons, **oi_create_box** returns NULL.

If you use the automatic layout facility and will be laying out objects inside the **OI_box** (that is, you will call **set_layout** for the **OI_box**), you can set *width* and *height* to 1, and OI will make the box grow to contain any objects you place within it.

7.5   Base Class Member Functions

You can use all of the member functions of **OI_d_tech** for an **OI_box**. **OI_d_tech** member functions which need further explanation when applied to **OI_box** objects are discussed below.

7.5.1   Click Functions

An **OI_box** object can respond to mouse button clicks if the mouse pointer is over the **OI_box**. If you want an **OI_box** object to respond to mouse clicks, you must register a click callback function for the box object. When the user clicks on the object, your callback function will be executed.

set_click   (Member function)

```
void OI_box::set_click(
    OI_click_fnp        fnp,            // pointer to callback function
    void                *argp=NULL)     // arbitrary argument for fnp

void OI_box::set_click(
    OI_callback         *objp,          // memfnp's object
    OI_click_memfnp     memfnp,         // pointer to callback member function
    void                *argp=NULL)     // arbitrary argument for memfnp
```

The **set_click** functions register a callback function to be invoked whenever the user clicks a mouse button one or more times on an **OI_box** object. This callback is identified within OI as a **cbClick** callback function (see Section 6.18, "Determining and Adding Callbacks; Multiple

Callbacks," on page 6-117). *memfnp* points to a member function for the object pointed to by *objp*. If your click function is a member function, when it is invoked it will be called as if you had written *objp->memfnp*. See Section 2.5, "Callbacks and Event-Driven Programming," on page 2-16 for more explanation.

argp is optional, and may be any valid expression that can be cast to a pointer. You can use it to pass additional information to the function *fnp* or *memfnp*.

The button press and release must be separated by no more than clickDelta milliseconds for a press/release sequence to be considered a click. For multiple clicks, a release and subsequent press must also be separated by no more than clickDelta milliseconds. clickDelta is an OI_connection resource, which defaults to 500.

If you want to establish more than one click callback for the same object, you must use the OI_d_tech member function callback_add.

Writing the Click Callback Function

If the cbClick callback function is not a member function, write it in this form:

```
void fn(
        OI_d_tech   *oi_objp,      // pointer to OI object clicked on
        void        *argp,         // arbitrary argument
        OI_number   n_clicks,      // number of clicks
        OI_number   btn,           // mouse button number clicked
        OI_number   mod,           // modifier bits on at click time
        OI_number   x,             // x position where click occurred
        OI_number   y)             // y position where click occurred
```

and if the cbClick callback function is a member function, write it in this form:

```
void obj_class::memfn(
        OI_d_tech   *oi_objp,      // pointer to OI object clicked on
        void        *argp,         // arbitrary argument
        OI_number   n_clicks,      // number of clicks
        OI_number   btn,           // mouse button number clicked
        OI_number   mod,           // modifier bits on at click time
        OI_number   x,             // x position where click occurred
        OI_number   y)             // y position where click occurred
```

where *obj_class* is the class of the object whose member function is *memfn*.

When your callback function is invoked, *argp* will be the argument specified in the set_click call. *oi_objp* will be a pointer to the OI object where the click occurred. *mod* will contain the modifier bits on when the button was released. These will be zero unless the user holds down one of the modifier keys on the keyboard at the time of the mouse click. *mod* may have any combination (0 or more) of the following values, combined with a bitwise inclusive or.

OI_mod_shift	Shift key down during click.
OI_mod_lock	Lock key down during click.
OI_mod_control	Control key down during click.
OI_mod_meta	Mod1 key down during click.

When more than one click occurs, the callback function will be invoked once for each click. For example, a double click will cause the function to be called first with *n_clicks*=1, then with *n_clicks*=2. If your application is performing a different operation depending on the number of clicks, the operations for a greater number of clicks should be compatible with those for fewer clicks.

x and *y* will be the position in pixels where the click occurred, relative to the upper-left corner of the box.

Program 7-1 shows an example in which the location of the mouse pointer at the time of the click, relative to the upper-left corner of the box, is printed on the terminal emulator from which the application was started.

```
#include <OI/oi.H>                              /* ClickBox.C */

int main(int argc, char** argv)
{
        void                    where_am_i(OI_d_tech*,void*,
                                OI_number,OI_number,OI_number,OI_number,OI_number);

        OI_connection           *conp;
        OI_app_window           *wp;
        OI_box                  *bp;

    if (conp = OI_init(&argc,argv,"ClickBox")) {
        wp = oi_create_app_window("main",1,1,"Click");
        wp->set_layout(OI_layout_row);

        bp = oi_create_box("my_box",100,100);
        bp->set_click(where_am_i);
        bp->layout_associated_object(wp,1,1,OI_active);

        wp->set_associated_object(wp->root( ),OI_def_loc,OI_def_loc,OI_active);
        OI_begin_interaction( );
        OI_fini( );
    }
}


void where_am_i(OI_d_tech *oi_objp,void*,
        OI_number,OI_number,OI_number,OI_number xloc,OI_number yloc)
{
    printf("Click on %s at location %d, %d\n",oi_objp->name( ),xloc,yloc);
    return;
}
```

Program 7-1   Print Location of Mouse Click (ClickBox.C)

7.5.2   X Interface Routines

X_window   (Member function)

```
Window OI_box::X_window( )
```

outside_X_window   (Member function)

```
Window OI_box::outside_X_window( )
```

In 3-D models, two X windows are used to implement an **OI_box**. **X_window** returns the window id of the interior X window, which you should use for all drawing operations. **outside_X_window** returns the window id of the exterior window, which OI uses to draw the 3-D bevel. If you set the frame width to zero or if the application is run using a 2D model, only one X window is allocated, and both functions return the same value.

7.6   OI_box Member Functions

7.6.1   Setting Minimal Size

set_minimum_size   (Member function)

```
void OI_box::set_minimum_size(
    OI_number          x,           // horizontal size in pixels
    OI_number          y)           // vertical size in pixels
```

If you are using automatic layout and the box is a size-tracker, the size set by **set_minimum_size** is the minimum size the box can be.

7.6.2   Positioning an OI_box Using Aligned Layout

If you use a layout method of **OI_layout_row_aligned** or **OI_layout_row_column_aligned** for the parent of an **OI_box** object, you can specify whether the **OI_box** object should line up with the labels of other aligned objects or the value portion of other aligned objects. OI establishes an *alignment point* for these layout methods; this point is the reference for the vertical alignment of all objects in a visual column. Each object is then positioned so its own alignment point lies at the overall alignment point for that column space. For entry fields, the alignment point is just after the label.

For an **OI_box** object, **OI_alignment_left** means the alignment point will be placed at the box's left edge, causing the box to appear to the right of the alignment point, or in the value region of any **OI_entry_field** objects which are aligned with it. **OI_alignment_default** is the same as **OI_alignment_left**.

OI_alignment_right means the alignment point will be placed at the box's right edge, causing the box to appear to the left of the alignment point, with its right edge at the alignment point—it will be right justified in the "label" area.

set_alignment   (Member function)

```
void OI_box::set_alignment(
    OI_alignment        aln)                    // alignment to use
```

set_alignment causes the OI_box object to be aligned as specified by *aln*, whenever the box is laid out in a parent which is using OI_layout_row_aligned or OI_layout_row_column_aligned. *aln* may be one of:

OI_alignment_left	Use the left edge of the box as the alignment point.
OI_alignment_right	Use the right edge of the box as the alignment point.
OI_alignment_default	OI_alignment_left

alignment   (Member function)

```
OI_alignment OI_box::alignment( )
```

alignment returns the alignment type in use for the OI_box object. This will be one of OI_alignment_left, OI_alignment_right, or OI_alignment_default

7.6.3   Positioning Objects Within an OI_box

You will only need to use the functions described in this section if you are not using OI's automatic layout facility. The following discussion assumes you are manually laying out your application.

An OI_box keeps track of the last (farthest from the upper-left corner) position occupied by the insertion of other objects. For example, inserting an object whose total space requirements are 100x200 pixels at location 10,20 in the box sets the box's last-used position to 109,219 and its next-available location to 110,220. No constraints are enforced as far as object placement is concerned; child objects may obscure each other, and the state of a child object (that is, whether it is visible or not) does not affect the computation of the next available location.

If you are placing objects in the box without using the automatic layout facility, you can place them at the avail_loc position plus a few pixels and be assured that they will not overlap each other. Note, however, that clipping to the parent's boundaries (only the portion of the child that exists within the parent's boundaries is visible) will occur unless you specify otherwise using the OI_d_tech member function disallow_clip. You may want to resize the box to match the space occupied by its children when all parenting is complete, using the OI_d_tech member function set_size as shown in Program 7-2 below.

OI fetches X resources for all children when a top-level object is parented to the root, or when an object is reparented to another object which has a top-level ancestor parented to the root (that is, not in the orphanage). Therefore, you should be sure to parent the top-level ancestor to the root before using these functions for any object. Otherwise, the resource fetching that occurs when you parent the ancestor to the root may alter object size, font or other attributes, causing space requirements to change.

Program 7-2 is an example of manually positioning objects in a vertical column in a box using the avail_loc_y function, and resizing the box after it has all its children. Notice that the OI_app_window object uses the automatic layout facility, but the OI_box object is manually laid out. Notice also the order in which parenting is done to avoid the re-spacing problems discussed above.

```c
#include <OI/oi.H>                              /* AvailLoc.C */
int main(int argc, char** argv)
{
          OI_connection        *conp;
          OI_app_window        *wp;
          OI_box               *bp;
          OI_static_text       *tp;
          OI_slider            *sp;
    const int                  SPACING=10;

    if (conp = OI_init(&argc,argv,"AvailLoc")) {
        wp = oi_create_app_window("main",1,1,"Main");
        wp->set_layout(OI_layout_row);
        wp->set_associated_object(wp->root( ),// do not display the app window yet
            OI_def_loc,OI_def_loc,OI_not_displayed);

        bp = oi_create_box("my_box",1,1);
        bp->layout_associated_object(wp,1,1,OI_active); // ancestor parented to root

        tp = oi_create_static_text("my_text","Some Text");
        tp->set_associated_object(bp,SPACING,SPACING,OI_active);

        sp = oi_create_slider("my_slider",100,OI_horizontal);
        sp->set_associated_object(bp,SPACING,bp->avail_loc_y( )+SPACING,OI_active);

        tp = oi_create_static_text("my_text","Some More Text");
        tp->set_associated_object(bp,SPACING,bp->avail_loc_y( )+SPACING,OI_active);

        bp->set_size(bp->avail_loc_x( )+SPACING,bp->avail_loc_y( )+SPACING);
        wp->set_state(OI_active);                // now let the app window display

        OI_begin_interaction( );
        OI_fini( );
    }
}
```

Program 7-2 Manually Positioning Objects in an OI_box (AvailLoc.C)

Program 7-2 produces the applications shown in Figure 7-1.

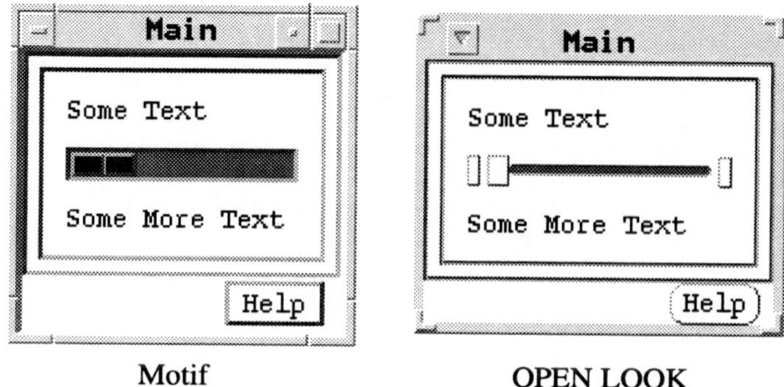

Motif   OPEN LOOK

Figure 7-1 Manually Positioning Objects in an OI_box

avail_loc   (Member function)

```
void OI_box::avail_loc(
    OI_number          *lxp,              // x coordinate in pixels
    OI_number          *lyp)              // y coordinate in pixels
```

Upon return from avail_loc, *lxp* and *lyp* are set to the pixel coordinates of the last position used + 1. The coordinates are relative to the upper left corner of the box.

avail_loc_x   (Member function)

```
OI_number OI_box::avail_loc_x( )
```

avail_loc_x returns the x coordinate in pixels of the last x position used + 1.

avail_loc_y   (Member function)

```
OI_number OI_box::avail_loc_y( )
```

avail_loc_y returns the y coordinate in pixels of the last y position used + 1.

set_avail_loc   (Member function)

```
void OI_box::set_avail_loc(
    OI_number          lx,                // x coordinate in pixels
    OI_number          ly)                // y coordinate in pixels
```

set_avail_loc sets the pixel coordinates of the next-available location to *lx* and *ly*. The coordinates are relative to the upper-left corner of the box.

set_avail_loc_x   (Member function)

```
void OI_box::set_avail_loc_x(
    OI_number          lx)                // x coordinate in pixels
```

set_avail_loc_x sets the x coordinate in pixels of the next-available location to *lx*.

set_avail_loc_y   (Member function)

```
void OI_box::set_avail_loc_y(
    OI_number            ly)                     // y coordinate in pixels
```

set_avail_loc_y sets the y coordinate in pixels of the next-available location to *ly*.

7.6.4   Expose Events

You may need to know if an *X expose event* occurs on an OI_box object. An X expose event occurs if some window obscures any part of the box and that window is moved or deleted, or if the OI_box object moves from a not-visible to a visible state. For example, if you have drawn your own non-OI graphics in the box, and an X expose event occurs, you need to redraw the graphics. OI automatically redraws its own objects in the box.

set_expose   (Member function)

```
void OI_box::set_expose(
    OI_obj_event_fnp        fnp,               // pointer to callback function
    void                    *argp=NULL)        // arbitrary argument for fnp


void OI_box::set_expose(
    OI_callback             *objp,             // memfnp's object
    OI_obj_event_memfnp     memfnp,            // pointer to callback member function
    void                    *argp=NULL)        // arbitrary argument for memfnp
```

The **set_expose** functions register a callback function to be invoked whenever X expose events occur on the box. This callback is identified within OI as a **cbExpose** callback function (see Section 6.18, "Determining and Adding Callbacks; Multiple Callbacks," on page 6-117). *memfnp* points to a member function for the object pointed to by *objp*. If your expose function is a member function, when it is invoked it will be called as if you had written *objp->memfnp*. See Section 2.5, "Callbacks and Event-Driven Programming," on page 2-16 for more explanation.

argp is optional, and may be any valid expression that can be cast to a pointer. You can use it to pass additional information to the function *fnp* or *memfnp*.

If you want to establish more than one expose callback function for the same object, use the OI_d_tech member function **callback_add**

Writing the Expose Callback Function

If the **cbExpose** callback function is not a member function, write it in this form:

```
void fn(
        OI_d_tech        *objp,          // pointer to object where event occurred
        void             *argp,          // arbitrary argument
        const XEvent     *ep)            // pointer to X expose event
```

and if the **cbExpose** callback function is a member function, write it in this form:

```
void obj_class::memfn(
        OI_d_tech        *objp,          // pointer to object where event occurred
        void             *argp,          // arbitrary argument
        const XEvent     *ep)            // pointer to X expose event
```

where *obj_class* is the class of the object whose member function is *memfn*. When your callback function is invoked, *argp* will be the argument specified in the **set_expose** call.

7.7   Resources

All resources from an **OI_box** object's base classes are available to it; in addition, OI fetches the resources shown in Table 7-1. For more information on resource management, see Chapter 39, "The OI Resource Mechanism."

Table 7-1   OI_box Resources

Resource	Description	Possible Values	Default Value
alignment	Specifies the alignment of the box with respect to the alignment point of the parent. (See page 7-5.)	OI_alignment_default OI_alignment_left OI_alignment_right	OI_alignment_left

7.8   Translations

All translations from an **OI_box** object's base classes are available to it; it has no additional translations. For more information on translations, see Chapter 40, "The OI Translation Mechanism."

7.9   Callback Functions

Table 7-2 lists the callbacks available for an **OI_box** object and the page number where the callback is documented. In addition, all of the callbacks from an **OI_box** object's base classes are available to it. See Section 6.18, "Determining and Adding Callbacks; Multiple Callbacks," on page 6-117 for additional information about manipulating callbacks.

Table 7-2 OI_box Callbacks

Callback Type	Callback Typedef	Description	Page Number
cbClick	OI_click_fnp/memfnp	Click callback function	7-2
cbExpose	OI_obj_event_fnp/memfnp	Expose callback function	7-9

Chapter 8

OI_app_window

OI_app_window Functions

OI_app_window Member Functions

The following functions are available to an **OI_app_window** object, but are described in their own chapters.

OI_box Member Functions

OI_d_tech Member Functions

OI Programmer's Guide

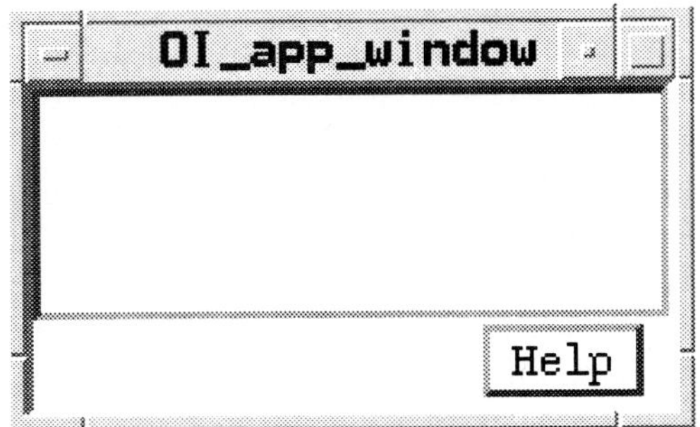

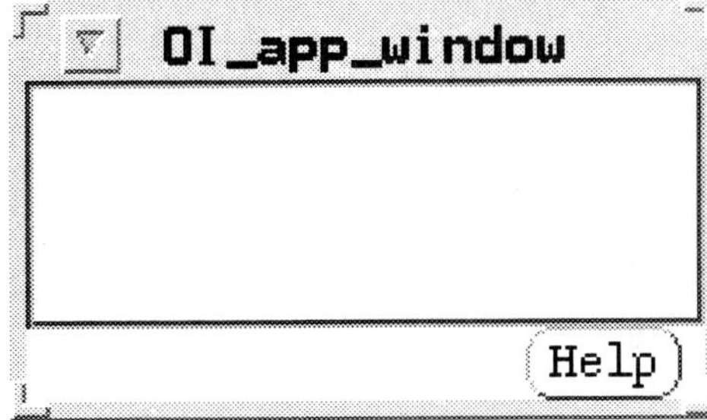

OI_app_window

8.1   Description

An OI_app_window is the outside wrapping for an application. The *window decoration*, the outside appearance of the OI_app_window object, is supplied by the window manager. The window decoration includes the title bar, the narrow border along both sides and the bottom, and the four re-size handles at the corners.

8.1.1   Window Decoration

The *title bar* is usually located at the top of the OI_app_window object, although technically it could appear anywhere. In the images above, the title bar stretches across the full width of the OI_app_window, and contains a pull-down menu button on the left and some text ("OI_app_window"). The title bar of the Motif (left) image also contains an iconify button and a full-size button. The contents and appearance of the title bar are controlled by the window manager. Most window managers allow you to modify the text portion using OI_app_window member functions. The text displayed as the title by the window manager is logically two parts: a "permanent" part (the *title*) and a changeable message part (the *longterm message*). The title is initially set by the fourth argument (*titlep*) to the oi_create_app_window function, but the user may override this via command-line arguments or the X resource manager. The longterm message is initially NULL. OI sends the window manager text for the title bar which is the concatenation of the two parts, with " -- " inserted between them; it is up to the window manager to determine what text, if any, it displays in the title bar. If the longterm message is NULL, the " -- " is omitted. Figure 8-1 and Figure 8-2 on page 8-3 show application windows whose title bars have both the title and the longterm message set. While you may change the permanent part (title) via the set_title member function, we recommend against doing so, since this title is the text the user will use to identify the application on the screen.

8.1.2 Footer

The bottom portion of an OI_app_window object consists of a *footer* region containing a left-justified **help text** line and a right-justified **state** string. The help text line is typically used to display one-line error messages when the user has made an entry error. The state message area is usually used to display things such as the current mode of the application (Add, Modify, Delete, etc.). The OI_app_window objects shown in the chapter header above have no text in these regions, but those shown in Figure 8-1 and Figure 8-2 do; the help text line contains "'Invalid' message", and the state string is "Modify". In the application windows shown in the chapter header above, there is a *help* button in the footer. Pressing this button causes the *hypertext help* object to appear; it is generally used to display more complex help information about the application, although it can be used to display any information desired. The windows shown in Figure 8-1 and Figure 8-2 do not have a **help** button in the footer; the reason for this is explained below.

8.1.3 Main Menu

Just below the title bar is the *main menu* for the application. The "bare-bones" OI_app_window objects shown in the chapter header above do not have main menus, but those shown in Figure 8-1 and Figure 8-2 do have main menus. Most applications need some form of top-level, or main, menu. You call the member function set_main_menu to parent a menu (which must be a horizontal button menu) as a main menu to an OI_app_window object. Designating a menu as a main menu does not change the functionality of the menu; it merely affects the menu's appearance on the screen.

The Motif Style Guide specifies that the main menu should appear at the top of the main window, and help, if provided, should be available via a help pull-down menu on the far right of the main menu. It further specifies that all buttons in the main menu should have pull-down menus attached to them. The set_main_menu function allows you to inform the OI_app_window which menu you wish to use as a main menu. If you designate a main menu in this fashion, OI automatically removes the **help** button from the footer and places it to the right of the main menu. To be Motif compliant, you should attach pull-down menus to all main menu cells. You may attach a pull-down menu to the help button programmatically, or you may specify topics to be included in a pull-down menu in a custom hypertext help file (see Section 8.6.3, "Hypertext Help Mechanism," on page 8-18).

Applications are not required to have a main menu, and for some applications it doesn't make sense. If you do not set a main menu, the **help** button remains in the lower-right corner of the footer.

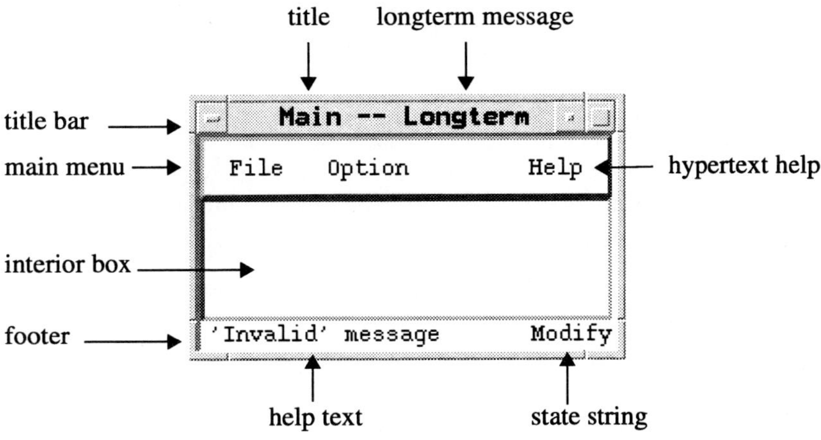

Figure 8-1   Parts of an OI_app_window, Motif

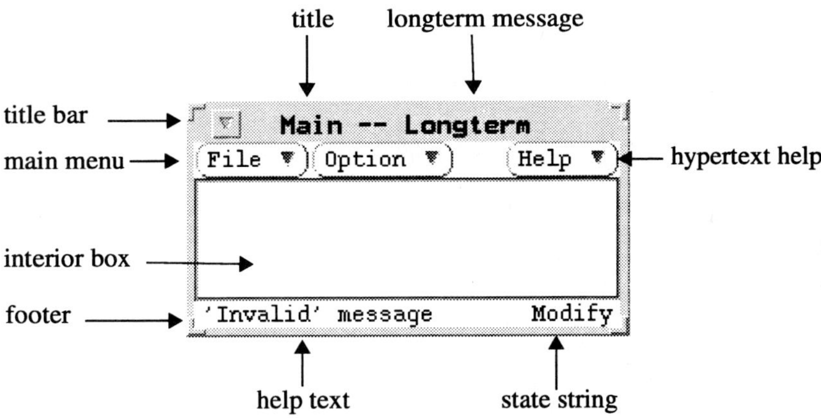

Figure 8-2   Parts of an OI_app_window, OPEN LOOK

8.1.4   Two Kinds of Help

As you may have noticed, there are two types of help available from an **OI_app_window** object. One is the **hypertext help** object which is attached to the **help** button in the window. OI automatically provides generic help for OI objects in this help object; you can also provide your own application-specific help text via external files. The interface to the hypertext help facility and the associated **OI_app_window** member functions are described in Section 8.6.3, "Hypertext Help Mechanism," on page 8-18.

The other type of help is a single line of text that appears in the help text line in the left portion of the **OI_app_window** footer (the text "'Invalid' message" in Figure 8-1 and Figure 8-2). OI puts error messages here; you can also put messages here using the **OI_d_tech** member functions **set_help_str** and **push_help_str**. There is a *help-text stack* onto which you can push help lines as you display them in the **OI_app_window** footer, and out of which you can pop and display lines that were previously pushed on the help stack. Do not confuse this stack with the stack used in the **hypertext help** object. Functions with which to manipulate the single help text line are in Chapter 6, "OI_d_tech" (Section 6.12, "Interfaces to the Help Mechanism," on page 6-97).

Figure 8-3 points out the two different types of help, and Table 8-1 lists the functions to use for each type of help.

Table 8-1   Help Functions for Use With the Two Types of Help

Type of Help	Functions	Where Documented
Help Text Line	OI_d_tech::push_help_str OI_d_tech::pop_help_str OI_d_tech::set_help_str OI_d_tech::help_str_posted OI_d_tech::help_str OI_d_tech::help_stack_size	Section 6.12 on page 6-97
Hypertext Help	OI_app_window::help_menu OI_app_window::help_menu_cell OI_app_window::hyper_help OI_app_window::push_help OI_app_window::pop_help OI_app_window::set_help OI_app_window::help_file OI_app_window::help_topic OI_app_window::set_key_help OI_app_window::help OI_app_window::help_dismiss	Section 8.6.3 on page 8-18

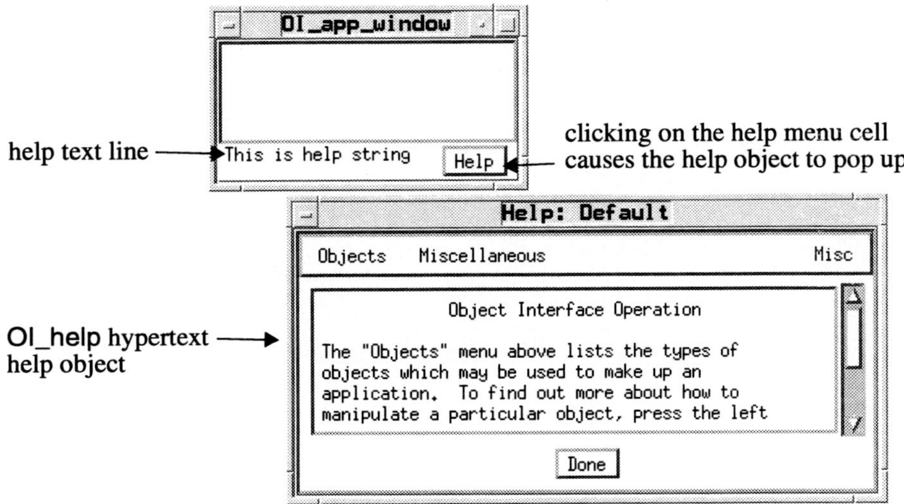

Figure 8-3   OI_app_window With Help Activated

8.1.5   Interior Region

The remainder of the OI_app_window object image is the interior region, where application objects other than the main menu are placed.

Note that if you call the OI_d_tech member function **size** for an OI_app_window object, the numbers returned are the dimensions of the interior region of the OI_app_window object. If you call **space** for an OI_app_window object, the numbers returned are the dimensions of the outside edges of the object, including the window manager decoration.

Program 8-1 shows the code that generated the windows shown in Figure 8-1 and Figure 8-2.

```
#include <OI/oi.H>                               /* AugAppWindow.C */

int main(int argc, char** argv)
{

          OI_connection         *conp;
          OI_app_window         *wp;
          OI_menu               *mp;
   static OI_cell_spec          file_cells[] = {
          {"open_file","View"},
          {"copy_file","Copy"},
          {"exit","Exit",(OI_action_fnp)OI_end_interaction},
   };
   static OI_menu_spec          file_menu =
          {"file_menu",OI_count(file_cells),file_cells,OI_vertical};

   static OI_menu_spec          opt_menu = {"opt_menu",0,NULL,OI_vertical};

   static OI_cell_spec          main_cells[] = {
          {"do_file","File",NULL,NULL,NULL_PMF,NULL,OI_text_cell,&file_menu},
          {"do_option","Option",NULL,NULL,NULL_PMF,NULL,OI_text_cell,&opt_menu},
   };

   if (conp = OI_init(&argc,argv,"AugAppWindow")) {
      wp = oi_create_app_window("main",170,60,"Main");
      mp = oi_create_button_menu("main_menu",OI_count(main_cells),
                                        main_cells,OI_horizontal);
      wp->set_main_menu(mp);

      wp->set_longterm("Longterm");
      wp->set_state_str("Modify");
      wp->push_help_str("'Invalid' message ",OI_yes);

      wp->set_associated_object(wp->root( ),OI_def_loc,OI_def_loc,OI_active);
      OI_begin_interaction( );
      OI_fini( );
   }
}
```

Program 8-1   Fully Loaded OI_app_window (AugAppWindow.C)

8.1.6   Parenting an OI_app_window

Ordinarily, an **OI_app_window** object is the top-level object upon which you will build your object tree and in which you display other objects. You may have more than one **OI_app_window** object in a given application. While you may use other types of OI objects as top-level objects, this is not normally done, since the **OI_app_window** object provides the mechanism for most window manager interaction.

Since an **OI_app_window** object is usually a top-level object, you need to associate (parent) it to the root object before calling **OI_begin_interaction**. You may do this any time after creating the **OI_app_window** object, making sure to use **set_associated_object**, not layout_associated_object. The root object is an object over which you have little control, and using layout_associated_object for it makes little sense. If the arguments you specify for position are OI_def_loc, the user will be allowed to place the application window using the window manager's default placement policy. If, on the other hand, you specify particular x and y coordinates for placement, OI places the window at those coordinates without user interaction. In any case, the user may override your positioning specifications via the -geometry command-line argument or by specifying a geometry resource through the X resource manager. Finally, you should usually make at least one OI_app_window object visible before calling OI_begin_interaction, since otherwise the user will never see your application. One reason you might want your entire application to be invisible would be if you had an application which monitors some condition and only becomes visible when a certain set of conditions is met.

If you use the automatic layout facility for the main window, and if you make your main window visible before all child objects have been placed in it, the user will see the window change size as you add objects. Since this is somewhat disconcerting to the user, we recommend that you not make your main window visible until all child objects have been placed in it. For best results, use one of the following sequences:

```
wp = oi_create_app_window(...);
wp->set_associated_object(wp->root( ),OI_def_loc,OI_def_loc,OI_not_displayed);
... add objects to wp
wp->set_state(OI_active);
OI_begin_interaction( );
```

or

```
wp = oi_create_app_window(...);
... add objects to wp
wp->set_associated_object(wp->root( ),OI_def_loc,OI_def_loc,OI_active);
OI_begin_interaction( );
```

If you are manually placing objects inside the OI_app_window object (that is, if you are not using the automatic layout facility), you should use the first method. The reason for this is that OI does not fetch resources, which may affect object sizes, until the top-level object is parented to the root. If you are using the automatic layout facility, either method works, since the automatic layout mechanism automatically resizes the object within which other objects are laid out so that fetching resources after the objects are parented to the OI_app_window object is not a problem.

8.2   Class Tree

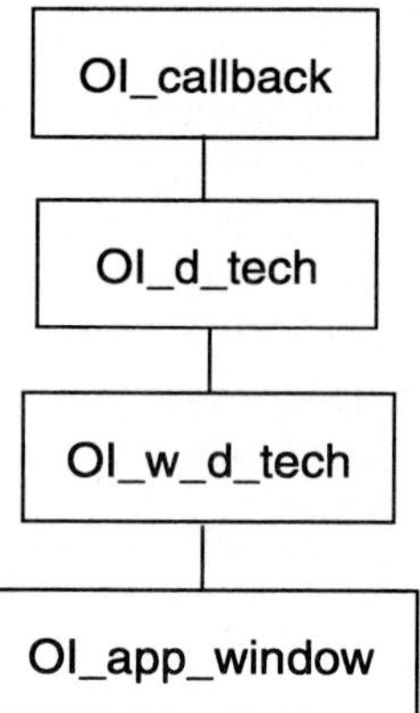

8.3   Runtime Interaction

Clicking the SELECT mouse button on the help button displays the hypertext help dialog box, as does pressing the HELP key while the mouse pointer is over any object in the application. The difference is that when you press the HELP key, OI displays in the help dialog box a magnified image of the portion of the object the mouse pointer points to. In OPEN LOOK, this image is a magnifying glass containing the magnified portion of the object, and in Motif, this image is a rectangle containing the magnified portion. In addition, the help context is set to the text for the object under the pointer. Figure 8-5 on page 8-18, shows this type of help in action.

The default keys used for the HELP key are defined in Table 8-2. You can modify the set of keys searched for the HELP key via the OI_connection resource helpTranslations. See Chapter 40, "The OI Translation Mechanism," for a description of "Mod1". The entry "Mod1 /" means hold the Mod1 key down while striking the "/" key.

Table 8-2   OI_app_window HELP Key

Keyboard	HELP key
If keyboard has help key	Help key
If window manager does not have F1 grabbed	F1
If window manager has F1 grabbed	Mod1 /

8.4   OI_app_window Creation

oi_create_app_window   (Free-standing function)

```
OI_app_window *oi_create_app_window(
    const char  *namp,                              // pointer to name for object
    OI_number   width,                              // width of interior box in pixels
    OI_number   height,                             // height of interior box in pixels
    const char  *titlep,                            // text for title bar
    OI_glyph    *glyphp=OI_app_window_def_icon,     // pointer to glyph for window icon
    OI_bool     iconic=OI_no)                       // initial iconic state
```

oi_create_app_window creates an OI_app_window object with name *namp* and returns a pointer to the created object.

width and *height* specify the size of the window. This is the interior box size; the title bar and other decoration are drawn exterior to this box. If you are using the OI layout facility, you should size the OI_app_window object at 1x1 pixels. It will grow to encompass any other objects you place inside it.

titlep specifies the initial title for the OI_app_window object. This is normally displayed by the window manager in the title bar. However, a user may override this title by specifying -name or -title as a command-line argument when invoking the application, or through the X resource manager. You may subsequently change the title while your application is running via the member functions set_title and set_longterm.

glyphp and *iconic* are optional. *glyphp* points to an OI_glyph object to use when the window is made into an icon; if you omit *glyphp*, the standard OI icon is used. If you supply a glyph, OI changes the glyph's name to a standard internal OI name when it makes the glyph into an icon, and you can no longer access the glyph by the name you originally gave it. If you have specified a label for the glyph, the window manager uses this label as the icon label (if the window manager displays labels for icons). *iconic* is OI_yes if the initial state of the window is to be iconic (the window manager displays the icon instead of the application window); if you omit it or it is OI_no, the initial state is normal (the window manager displays the application window, not the icon). For example, to use your own customized icon from the file "mail_icon.bm" with label "Mail":

```
OI_app_window      *wp;
OI_glyph           *iconp;
iconp = oi_create_glyph("mail_icon","mail_icon.bm","Mail");
wp = oi_create_app_window("mail",1,1,"Mail Reader",iconp);
```

Note that since OI changes the name of the glyph used for an icon, if you now try this line:

```
gp = wp->subobject("mail_icon");
```

gp will be NULL, meaning the subobject was not found. If you need a pointer to the icon, use the following call:

```
gp = wp->icon( );
```

8.5   Base Class Member Functions

Since an OI_app_window is a derived class of OI_d_tech, and since the interior region is an OI_box, you can use all of the member functions of OI_box and OI_d_tech for an OI_app_window object.

You can use the OI_box click functions (set_click) for an OI_app_window. The functions apply to the interior region of the OI_app_window object.

You can use the OI_box next-available location functions (avail_loc and related functions) for an OI_app_window object. The functions apply to the interior region of the OI_app_window object.

You can use the OI_box set_expose member functions for an OI_app_window object. The functions apply to the interior region of the OI_app_window object.

8.6   OI_app_window Member Functions

8.6.1   Accessing and Changing Component Parts

You may access the individual components of an OI_app_window object. Most of these are *internal* OI objects—objects that OI creates itself and parents to the OI_app_window. The items you can access are:

- main menu
- title
- longterm message
- static text help object
- state message
- icon
- help menu
- hypertext help object
- interior box

You can use the functions discussed below to manipulate the components. You can delete an OI_app_window component part by calling the del function on its behalf or using the C++ delete operator. However, we don't recommend this, since these components provide your application with useful capabilities and functionality.

If you need to replace or completely delete the default help object, you can obtain a pointer to the object using the functions documented in Section 8.6.3.4 on page 8-30.

main_menu   (Member function)

```
OI_menu *OI_app_window::main_menu( )
```

main_menu returns a pointer to the main menu for the OI_app_window if one is present; otherwise it returns NULL. A menu is only a main menu if it has been parented to the OI_app_window using the member function set_main_menu.

set_main_menu   (Member function)

```
void OI_app_window::set_main_menu(
    OI_menu                 *mp)            // pointer to menu
```

set_main_menu attaches *mp* to the **OI_app_window** as the main menu. *mp* should be a horizontal button menu; if it is vertical or not a button menu, the menu is not parented to the application window at all. OI moves the help menu button from the window footer to appear to be the last cell in the main menu, although it remains a separate object. OI gives the help menu button an **OI_grav_east** gravity and makes the main menu into a horizontal size-tracker. If you want to be strictly Motif Style Guide compliant, you should attach a pull-down menu to each cell in the main menu. OI changes the name of the menu, so that you can no longer access the menu with the name you originally gave it. You should access the menu using

```
mp = wp->main_menu( );
```

title   (Member function)

```
char *OI_app_window::title( )
```

title returns the current title text for the **OI_app_window**. This does not include the longterm message portion.

set_title   (Member function)

```
OI_stat OI_app_window::set_title(
    const char              *titlep)        // title text
```

set_title changes the "permanent" part of the **OI_app_window** title text to *titlep*.

longterm   (Member function)

```
char *OI_app_window::longterm( )
```

longterm returns the current longterm message text of the **OI_app_window** title text; it returns NULL if none is set.

set_longterm   (Member function)

```
OI_stat OI_app_window::set_longterm(
    const char              *lngp)          // text for longterm message
```

set_longterm changes the longterm message portion of the window title text to *lngp*.

state_str   (Member function)

```
char *OI_app_window::state_str( )
```

state_str returns the current text for the state (right) portion of the **OI_app_window** footer.

set_state_str (Member function)

```
OI_stat OI_app_window::set_state_str(
    const char        *txtp)              // state text
```

set_state_str changes the text in the state (right) portion of the **OI_app_window** footer to *txtp*. This region is usually used to display things such as the current mode of the application (Add, Modify, Delete, etc.).

icon (Member function)

```
OI_glyph *OI_app_window::icon( )
```

icon returns a pointer to the icon for the **OI_app_window**. This is the icon that will be used if the application is iconified by the window manager.

state_obj (Member function)

```
OI_static_text *OI_app_window::state_obj( )
```

state_obj returns a pointer to the **OI_app_window**'s state string static text object (the right portion of the window footer).

help_obj (Member function)

```
OI_static_text *OI_app_window::help_obj( )
```

help_obj returns a pointer to the static text **help** object for the **OI_app_window**. Ordinarily, you will not need to use this function, as you can manipulate the text in this area using the **OI_d_tech** functions for this purpose. (See Section 6.12, "Interfaces to the Help Mechanism," on page 6-97.)

help_menu (Member function)

help_menu is documented under 8.6.3, "Hypertext Help Mechanism," on page 8-18.

hyper_help (Member function)

```
OI_help *OI_app_window::hyper_help( )
```

hyper_help is documented under 8.6.3, "Hypertext Help Mechanism," on page 8-18.

interior (Member function)

```
OI_box *OI_app_window::interior( )
```

interior returns a pointer to the **OI_box** object which is the interior box of the **OI_app_window**.

8.6.2   Window Manager Communication

The user, via the window manager, is allowed to change certain aspects of your application in a manner outside your control. Your application may be iconified, de-iconified, resized, or terminated. You can do nothing to prevent any of these from occurring. However, your application can be notified of and react to the event. The functions discussed below allow you to manage iconify and de-iconify cases, as well as save the state of your application, if necessary, when it is about to be terminated.

You can set a top-level **OI_app_window** object (one parented to the root) so that it can be exited without causing the program to exit. This state is set on a per-application-window basis. By default, if an application window is "quit" via a window manager function, the application exits. Use **set_protocol_delete** if you have multiple **OI_app_window** objects and you do not want your entire application to terminate when the user exits one of them.

iconify   (Member function)

```
void OI_app_window::iconify( )
```

This function forces your application to return to an iconic state, just as if the user had instructed the window manager to iconify it.

set_iconify   (Member function)

```
void OI_app_window::set_iconify(
    OI_app_window_fnp       fnp,            // pointer to callback function
    void                    *argp=NULL)     // arbitrary argument for fnp

void OI_app_window::set_iconify(
    OI_callback             *objp,          // memfnp's object
    OI_app_window_memfnp    memfnp,         // pointer to callback member function
    void                    *argp=NULL)     // arbitrary argument for memfnp
```

The **set_iconify** functions register a callback function to be invoked whenever the application window changes to iconic state. The callback will be invoked immediately after the window becomes iconified. This callback is identified within OI as a **cblconify** callback function (see Section 6.18, "Determining and Adding Callbacks; Multiple Callbacks," on page 6-117). If your iconify function is a member function, when it is invoked it will be called as if you had written *objp->memfnp*. See Section 2.5, "Callbacks and Event-Driven Programming," on page 2-16 for more explanation.

argp is optional, and may be any valid expression that can be cast to a pointer. You can use it to pass additional information to the function *fnp* or *memfnp*.

Note that you will get an iconify callback when you change the state of the object to **OI_not_displayed** or unparent it. This is because these actions cause the same X event to be generated as the act of iconifying the window.

Writing the Iconify Callback Function

If the **cbIconify** callback function is not a member function, write it in this form:

```
void fn(
        OI_app_window   *awp,          // pointer to iconified window
        void            *argp)         // arbitrary argument
```

and if the **cbIconify** callback function is a member function, write it in this form:

```
void obj_class::memfn(
        OI_app_window   *awp,          // pointer to iconified window
        void            *argp)         // arbitrary argument
```

where *obj_class* is the class of the object whose member function is *memfn*. When your callback function is invoked, *awp* will point to the **OI_app_window** which was iconified, and *argp* will be the argument specified in the **set_iconify** call.

deiconify   (Member function)

```
void OI_app_window::deiconify( )
```

This function forces your application to return to its full operational state, just as if the user had instructed the window manager to de-iconify it.

set_deiconify   (Member function)

```
void OI_app_window::set_deiconify(
    OI_app_window_fnp       fnp,          // pointer to function to call
    void                    *argp=NULL)   // arbitrary argument for fnp


void OI_app_window::set_deiconify(
    OI_callback             *objp,        // memfnp's object
    OI_app_window_memfnp    memfnp,       // pointer to member function to call
    void                    *argp=NULL)   // arbitrary argument for memfnp
```

The **set_deiconify** functions are used to register a callback function to be invoked the first time the window is mapped and whenever the application window changes from iconic state to normal state. If you need to take different actions for a start-up mapping and a deiconify mapping, use a variable in your program to keep track of application initialization and test it each time the callback is executed. You may want to test your application with the -iconic command-line parameter. This callback is identified within OI as a **cbDeiconify** callback function (see Section 6.18, "Determining and Adding Callbacks; Multiple Callbacks," on page 6-117). The arguments are the same as for **set_iconify**, and the callback function has the same form.

set_save_yourself   (Member function)

```
void OI_app_window::set_save_yourself(
    OI_app_window_fnp      fnp,            // pointer to function to call
    void                   *argp=NULL)     // arbitrary argument for fnp

void OI_app_window::set_save_yourself(
    OI_callback            *objp,          // memfnp's object
    OI_app_window_memfnp   memfnp,         // pointer to member function to call
    void                   *argp=NULL)     // arbitrary argument for memfnp
```

The **set_save_yourself** functions are used to register a callback function to be invoked whenever the window manager sends a **WM_SAVE_YOURSELF** message to the application window. The arguments are the same as for **set_iconify**, and the callback function has the same form. This callback is identified within OI as a **cbSaveYourself** callback function (see Section 6.18, "Determining and Adding Callbacks; Multiple Callbacks," on page 6-117).

A window manager will send a **WM_SAVE_YOURSELF** message to the application when some occurrence causes the window manager to unexpectedly kill the application. The message will be sent first, then at some unspecified later time, but usually a very short time later, the application will be killed. You should use this function if it is possible and desirable to save the state of the application for a later restart. The callback function specified in **set_save_yourself** should save any data necessary to restart the application. You should not try to display any information for the user in the callback function, since you may only have a limited amount of time in which to save your state. You do not have any assurance that the application will not die while in the save-yourself callback.

wm_state   (Member function)

```
OI_wm_state OI_app_window::wm_state( )
```

wm_state returns the state relative to the window manager. This will be one of:

     OI_WM_WithdrawnState   Neither the icon nor the top level window is displayed.
     OI_WM_IconicState   The **OI_app_window** is in iconic state.
     OI_WM_NormalState   The **OI_app_window** is in displayed state.

is_protocol_delete   (Member function)

```
OI_bool OI_app_window::is_protocol_delete( )
```

is_protocol_delete returns **OI_yes** if **set_protocol_delete** has been called for the **OI_app_window**, and **OI_no** if it has not.

---

set_protocol_delete (Member function)

```
void OI_app_window::set_protocol_delete(
    OI_destroy_fnp      fnp,                // pointer to callback function
    void                *argp=NULL)         // arbitrary argument for fnp

void OI_app_window::set_protocol_delete(
    OI_callback         *objp,              // memfnp's object
    OI_destroy_memfnp   memfnp,             // pointer to callback member function
    void                *argp=NULL)         // arbitrary argument for memfnp
```

The **set_protocol_delete** functions register a callback to be invoked whenever the application window receives a window manager "delete window" message. OI does not delete the window in response to the window manager "delete window" message if a protocol delete callback has been registered, but instead calls the callback set by this function. This callback is identified within OI as a **cbProtocolDelete** callback function (see Section 6.18, "Determining and Adding Callbacks; Multiple Callbacks," on page 6-117). *memfnp* points to a member function for the object pointed to by *objp*. If your callback function is a member function, when it is invoked it will be called as if you had written *objp->memfnp*. See Section 2.5, "Callbacks and Event-Driven Programming," on page 2-16 for more explanation.

argp is optional, and may be any valid expression that can be cast to a pointer. You can use it to pass additional information to the function *fnp* or *memfnp*.

Writing the Protocol Delete Callback Function

If the **cbProtocolDelete** callback function is not a member function, write it in this form:

```
void fn(
        OI_d_tech   *oi_objp,       // pointer to OI object
        void        *argp)          // arbitrary argument
```

and if the **cbProtocolDelete** callback function is a member function, write it in this form:

```
void obj_class::memfn(
        OI_d_tech   *oi_objp,       // pointer to OI object
        void        *argp)          // arbitrary argument
```

where *obj_class* is the class of the object whose member function is *memfn*. When your callback function is invoked, *argp* will be the argument specified in the **set_protocol_delete** call, and *oi_objp* will be a pointer to the OI object which is about to be destroyed.

Program 8-2 is an example of using **set_protocol_delete**. It creates an **OI_app_window** object as the main application window; it creates two additional **OI_app_window** objects with protocol delete enabled. The additional **OI_app_window** objects are made visible by activating the button menu in the main **OI_app_window**.

```c
#include <OI/oi.H>              /* ProtocolDelete.C */
#include <string.h>
void win_killed(OI_d_tech *p, void*)
{
    p->set_state(OI_not_displayed);
    p->set_loc(p->loc_x( ),p->loc_y( ));// prevent user positioning after 1st time
    return;
}
void activate(OI_menu_cell *, void *argp, OI_number)
{
            OI_app_window       *wp;
    wp = (OI_app_window*) argp;
    wp->set_state(OI_active);
    return;
}
int main(int argc, char**argv)
{
            OI_connection       *conp;
            OI_app_window       *wp;                        // ptr to main app_window
            OI_app_window       *aux_wp;                    // ptr to auxiliary app window
            OI_menu             *mp;
    static  OI_cell_spec        win_cells[] = {
        {"options","Options",&activate},
        {"prps","Properties",&activate},
        };
    static  OI_menu_spec        win_mnu =
        {"win_pd",OI_count(win_cells),&win_cells[0],OI_vertical};
    static  OI_cell_spec        cells[] = {
        {"windows","Windows",NULL,NULL,NULL_PMF,NULL,OI_text_cell,&win_mnu},
        };
    if (conp = OI_init(&argc,argv,"ProtocolDelete")) {
        wp = oi_create_app_window("main",100,50,"ProtocolDelete");
        mp = oi_create_button_menu("mn_menu",OI_count(cells),cells,OI_horizontal);
        wp->set_main_menu(mp);
        wp->set_associated_object(wp->root( ),OI_def_loc,OI_def_loc,OI_active);
        aux_wp = oi_create_app_window("options",300,200,"Option Window");
        aux_wp->disallow_clip( );
        ((OI_menu_cell*)(mp->descendant("options")))->change_arg(aux_wp);
        aux_wp->set_protocol_delete(win_killed);
        aux_wp->set_associated_object(wp,OI_def_loc,OI_def_loc,OI_not_displayed);
        aux_wp = oi_create_app_window("prps",300,200,"Property Window");
        aux_wp->disallow_clip( );
        ((OI_menu_cell*)(mp->descendant("prps")))->change_arg(aux_wp);
        aux_wp->set_protocol_delete(win_killed);
        aux_wp->set_associated_object(wp,OI_def_loc,OI_def_loc,OI_not_displayed);
        OI_begin_interaction( );
        OI_fini( );
    }
}
```

Program 8-2   Protocol Delete (ProtocolDelete.C)

8.6.3   Hypertext Help Mechanism

8.6.3.1   Description

There are two forms of help available in an OI_app_window: (1) a *hypertext help* pop-up dialog box, which is described in this section, and (2) a single *help text line* displayed in the OI_app_window footer, which is described in Section 8.1.4, on page 8-3, and in Chapter 6, "OI_d_tech." (Section 6.12, "Interfaces to the Help Mechanism," on page 6-97)

OI automatically attaches a hypertext help object to each OI_app_window object. The object is of class OI_help, which is derived from OI_dialog_box, and contains the help reference material.

Hypertext help refers to the method used in the OI_help object, whereby the user can traverse and read information on different topics by traversing a set of cascading menus to find the topic of interest or by clicking the SELECT mouse button when the pointer is over highlighted help text. The reference material to be displayed exists in one or more *hypertext help files,* each of which may contain information on one or more topics.

Figure 8-4 shows the parts of an OI_help object.

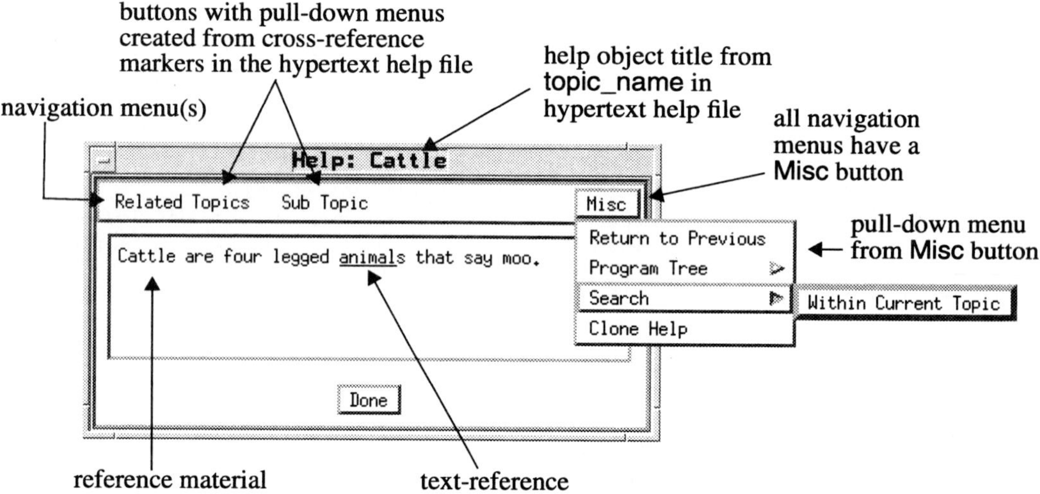

Figure 8-4   Parts of a Hypertext Help Object

As you can see from this figure, an OI_help object is a dialog box with a menu at the top. The title of the dialog box, if window decoration is supplied by the window manager, is taken from the current topic as specified in the hypertext help file. The menu, and the set of cascading menus associated with it, is called the *navigation menu,* and is one of the means by which the user changes the displayed reference material (traverses topics of interest). The labels on all the cells of the navigation menu except the last are taken from the hypertext help file(s) as described in Section 8.6.3.3 on page 8-22. When the user chooses a new topic from the menu, OI changes the text displayed to the new topic, and the title of the dialog box to the new topic label.

The navigation menu also includes a **Misc** menu cell at the far right. Attached to it is a pull-down menu with four buttons. The buttons and their functions are:

Return to Previous	Allows the user to return to the previous topic.
Program Tree	Allows the user to see the *program tree*, which is the path, or list of topic names, which has been taken through the reference material. The user can return to any previously traversed topic using this set of cascading menus.
Search	Used to search for text within the current topic.
Clone Help	Allows the user to clone a copy of the **help** object, that is, to create another, identical **OI_help** object. If the **help** object is cloned, the user can view different portions of the reference material in each of the cloned objects.

The highlighted (underlined) text is a *text-reference,* which means that there is a link from the highlighted text to an appropriate context. When the user clicks on highlighted text, the context switches to the linked text.

Both the application and the user have control over the context, or topic, of the information displayed in the **help** object(s). If you do not provide your own help file(s), OI displays generic help for the OI objects when the **OI_help** object is activated. If you create your own hypertext help file, you may include a combination of text, bitmaps (glyph objects), and OI objects, as well as specifying related topics. In this case, the OI generic help is still also available.

The **OI_help** object maintains a stack onto which you can push a new help topic and file name, and from which you can pop entries (and display the corresponding reference material) that were previously pushed onto the stack. In this manner, you can cause the **help** object always to display information relative to the particular part of the application being used. The user traversal of the hypertext help through the navigation menu does not modify the stack; only calls to **push_help** and **pop_help** do that. Do not confuse this stack with the **OI_app_window** help stack for the help line in the **OI_app_window** object footer.

8.6.3.2 Activating and Manipulating Hypertext Help

The **OI_help** dialog box can be activated in one of three ways.

- The application activates help by calling the member function **help**.
- The user clicks on the **help** menu button in the **OI_app_window** object.
- The user moves the mouse pointer to some portion of the application and presses the HELP key. The HELP key is one of the keys defined in Table 8-2 on page 8-8. When help is activated this way, a magnified image of the area under the pointer is displayed to emphasize the object to which the help applies. Figure 8-5 and Figure 8-6 show the result of placing the mouse pointer over the "Sta" in "This is Static Text" and pressing the HELP key.

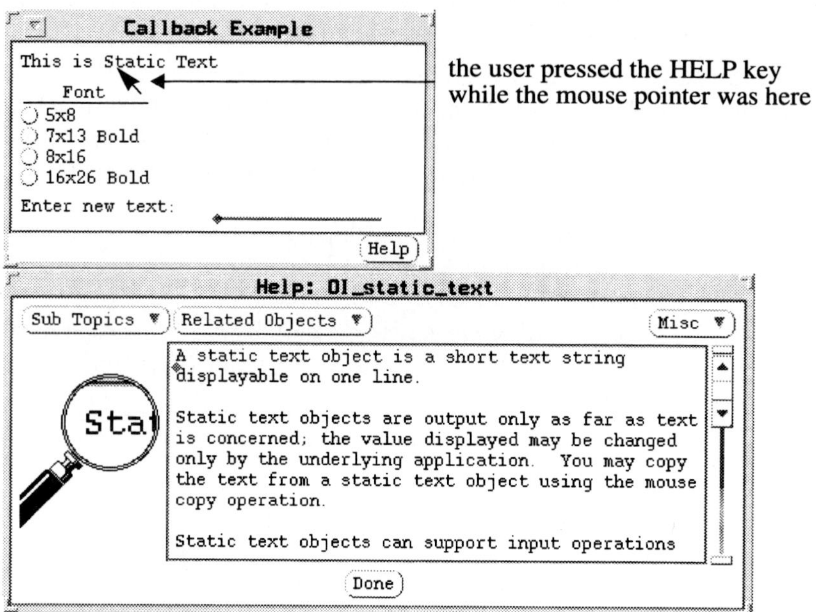

the user pressed the HELP key
while the mouse pointer was here

Figure 8-5   Hypertext Help With Magnified Image, OPEN LOOK

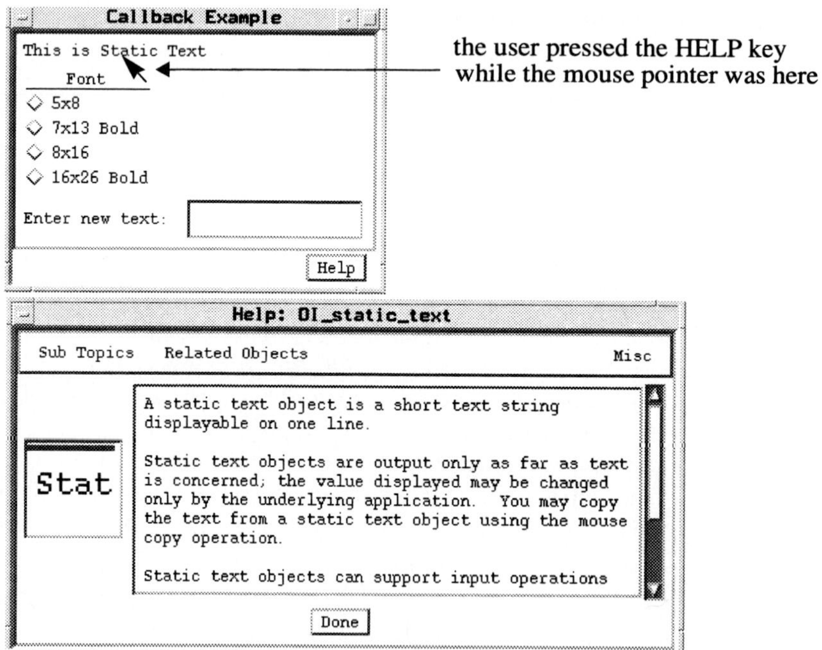

the user pressed the HELP key
while the mouse pointer was here

Figure 8-6   Hypertext Help With Magnified Image, Motif

The context (and consequently the help information displayed if the OI_help object is visible) can be changed in the following ways:

- The application may change the context by calling one of the OI_app_window member functions set_help, push_help, or pop_help. If the user has cloned the help object in order to view two or more items at once, this method of changing the context affects only the original help object. If you call set_help, it sets the help context immediately but does not affect the help stack. If you call push_help, it sets the help context immediately and also pushes the help context onto the help stack. Whenever an item is popped off the stack, the previous context from the stack appears.
- The user may select one of the menu buttons in the navigation menu at the top of the OI_help dialog box. This method affects the context of the help object containing the menu.
- The user can click on any highlighted text (reverse video or underline) displayed in the help object, and the context will switch to the one specified for the highlighted text.
- The user may press the HELP key with the mouse pointer over some portion of the application. If the user has cloned the help object in order to view two or more items at once, this method of changing the context affects only the original help object.
- In the Motif model, the user can select "On Context" from the pull-down menu attached to the help button. The mouse pointer changes to a question mark. The user may then position the question mark over some portion of the application and click again. This selects help in the same way as positioning the pointer and pressing the HELP key.

Initiating help by clicking on the help menu button and initiating help from the keyboard usually produce different results. By default, activating the help button brings up the help object with default OI help on generic object interface operation, whereas activating help from the keyboard produces a magnified image of the area under the mouse pointer and the text in the help object describes that particular object.

You can change the behavior by registering a key-help callback, by calling set_help or push_help, or by supplying the resources appHelpFile, appHelpTopic, helpFile and helpTopic. Table 8-3 shows how the help context is set when help is activated from the keyboard.

Table 8-3 Help Context for Keyboard-Activated Help

Is key-help callback registered?	Are helpFile and/or helpTopic resources set?	Then help context is set to:
No	No	Default help context for object based on class derivation.
No	Yes	Help context from helpFile and helpTopic.
Yes, but fails	No	Default help context for object based on class derivation.
Yes, but fails	Yes	Help context from helpFile and helpTopic.

Table 8-3 Help Context for Keyboard-Activated Help

Is key-help callback registered?	Are helpFile and/or helpTopic resources set?	Then help context is set to:
Yes, and succeeds	Irrelevant	Help context from key-help callback.

The initial help context when the application starts is by default the OI generic help; it is also the first item in the help stack. If the resources **appHelpFile** and **appHelpTopic** are available from the resource database, they become the second item in the help stack at the time **OI_init** is executed. Each time you call **push_help**, that file and topic are added to the stack; each time you call **pop_help**, that file and topic are popped from the stack and the current context returns to the previous stack item. Whenever the user presses the HELP key, context is set as shown in Table 8-3.

8.6.3.3 Making a Hypertext Help File

A *hypertext help file* is an ASCII text file located in an arbitrary directory. The general form of the hypertext help file is

OI_default lines (if any)
Text-reference lines that pertain to the entire file
Topic 1
Any number of lines pertaining to topic 1, including cross-references and text-references
Topic 2
Any number of lines pertaining to topic 2, including cross-references and text-references
. . .
Topic n
Any number of lines pertaining to topic n, including cross-references and text-references

Comment lines may appear anywhere in the file.

You may disperse your help information among several different help files; they can cross-reference each other as shown below.

In more detail, the hypertext help file contains:

- Comment lines. Any line that begins with "!" is a comment line. Comment lines are not displayed in the hypertext help window.

- Any number of lines at the top of the file in the form

  @OI_default@ *topic_label* **@** *topic_namc* **@** *topic_file*

  These are used to create a pull-down menu for the **help** button. *topic_label* is used as the cell label in the pull-down. *topic_name* and *topic_file* are identical in nature to the items of the same name for **@Topic@** (see below). These lines must be the first lines in the file, with the exception that comment lines may precede them.

- Any number of lines at the top of the file in the form

  @OI_text_ref@ *ref_label* **@** *topic_name* **@** *topic_file*

These are text-references which are global to this help file. Every string displayed in the body of the help text which matches *ref_label* is highlighted with reverse video or underlining. If the user clicks on the highlighted text, the context switches to *topic_name* in *topic_file*. *topic_name* and *topic_file* are identical in nature to the items of the same name for @Topic@ (see below).

- Any number of topics and information relating to the topics in the following form:

  - A line of the form

    @Topic@ *topic_label* @ *topic_name*

    Topic is a keyword indicating that this is the topic title line. *topic_label* is used as the title in the help display. *topic_name* is optional and if you omit it, it defaults to *topic_label*. *topic_name* is the name by which you refer to this topic when you cross-reference it from a different topic. *topic_label* and *topic_name* apply to all following text until the next @Topic@ line. The text between @Topic@ lines can contain any number of the following items in any order (except where specified otherwise):

- Text lines to be displayed. Text must be no longer than 50 characters between newlines, but you may include any number of lines.

- Bitmaps to be displayed. A line beginning with @OI_Bitmap@ specifies a reference to a bitmap or Xpm format file. This file is used to generate a glyph object which is inserted in place of the @OI_Bitmap@ line when the text is displayed.

- Actual OI objects to be displayed. Lines beginning with @OI_Compound_Object@ specify references to object configuration files. The object is constructed from the configuration file and is inserted in place of the @OI_Compound_Object@ line when the text is displayed. The configuration file can be generated by the OI companion product ObjectBuilder, or you can create a configuration file using any editor. The format is identical to X resource specification format, but the format details are beyond the scope of this book. topLevel is the resource which specifies the name and class of the top-most object in the object tree. Other specifications in the configuration file are resources for the object(s). This is a sample configuration file:

```
! This file will display a single-celled button menu in a box
! It is referenced from a line in a help file as follows:
!                    @OI_Compound_Object@this_file_name
!
*topLevel:                                    my_box.OI_box
*my_box.layout:                               OI_layout_row
*my_box.children:                             my_button_menu.OI_button_menu
*my_box.my_button_menu.state:                 ACTIVE
*my_box.my_button_menu.placement:             1c1r1
*my_box.my_button_menu.children:              my_menu_cell.OI_menu_cell
*my_box.my_button_menu.orientation:           VERTICAL
*my_box.my_button_menu.my_menu_cell.state:            ACTIVE
*my_box.my_button_menu.my_menu_cell.placement:        1c1r1
*my_box.my_button_menu.my_menu_cell.label:            "Button Menu"
```

Example 8-1   Object Configuration File Referenced in Hypertext Help File

- Cross-reference markers. These markers form one of the connections in the hypertext and provide the navigation menu with cell labels. Any lines starting with @ which are not @Topic@, @OI_default@, @OI_Bitmap@ or @OI_Compound_Object@ indicate cross references. These lines have the format

  `@`*ref_typ*`@`*topic_label*`@`*topic_name*`@`*topic_file*

  where *ref_typ* is an arbitrary string indicating the type of reference. Each different *ref_type* is used to create a menu cell in the navigation menu with cell label *ref_typ*. All references of the same *ref_typ* within a given topic are used to create a pull-down menu for that *ref_typ*; the cell labels in the pull-down menu come from the *topic_label* fields. When the user chooses an item from the navigation menu, the help context is changed to the topic *topic_name* (that is, the reference material following a line which begins @Topic@*@*topic_name*) in the file *topic_file*. If you omit the file name, the current file is assumed. If you omit *topic_name*, it is assumed to be the same as *topic_label*. If you want to reference topics in any of the default OI help files, use the file name OI_default. If you want to refer to default help for an OI object, specify the class of the object as *topic_name*; for example:

  `@`*ref_type*`@`Static Text`@`OI_static_text`@`OI_default
- Text-references. These text-references are local to the given topic. The text-reference is identical in form to the global text-reference described on page 8-22.

Table 8-4 shows all the hypertext help file keywords.

Table 8-4   Hypertext Help File Keywords

Keyword	Type of Line
!	Comment
OI_default	Cell label and topic for help pull-down menu
Topic	Topic title
OI_Bitmap	Bitmap file name
OI_Compound_Object	Object configuration file name
OI_text_ref	Text reference within the help text

Program 8-3, next, shows an application using a custom hypertext help file. The hypertext help file itself is shown in Example 8-3 on page 8-29, and the resulting application is shown in Figure 8-7 on page 8-29. OI moves the help button next to the main menu so that it appears to be part of the main menu. Program 8-3 provides the help button with a pull-down menu using an @OI_default line at the start of the help file.

Program 8-3 uses several different types of objects and techniques which are discussed in other chapters in this book. In this respect, this program should be considered an "advanced" program; if you are just beginning your journey through the OI labyrinth, you may want to skip this one until later. We have used all these techniques here because we are trying to mimic a real application.

```c
#include <OI/oi.H>                                  /* AppWithHelp.C */

int main(int argc, char** argv)
{
                void            process_horses(OI_menu_cell*,void*,OI_number);
                void            process_cattle(OI_menu_cell*,void*,OI_number);
                void            process_sheep(OI_menu_cell*,void*,OI_number);
                void            do_help(OI_menu_cell*,void*,OI_number);

                OI_connection   *conp;
                OI_app_window   *wp;
                OI_menu         *mp,*pull_mp;
                OI_menu_cell    *mcp;
                OI_dialog_box   *dbp;

        static  OI_cell_spec    main_cells[] = {
                {"animals","Farm Animals"},
            };
        static  OI_cell_spec    animal_cells[] = {
                {"horses","Horses",&process_horses},
                {"cattle","Cattle",&process_cattle},
                {"sheep","Sheep",&process_sheep},
            };

    if (conp = OI_init(&argc,argv,"AppWithHelp")) {
        wp = oi_create_app_window("main",170,60,"OI_app_window");
        wp->push_help("farm_animals","help.hp");
        mp = oi_create_button_menu("menu",OI_count(main_cells),&main_cells[0],
                                        OI_horizontal);

        wp->set_main_menu(mp);

        // Make pull-down menu to attach to main menu "animals" button
        pull_mp = oi_create_button_menu("farm",OI_count(animal_cells),
                                        &animal_cells[0],OI_vertical);
        mcp = (OI_menu_cell*)mp->subobject("animals");
        pull_mp->set_associated_object(mcp,OI_def_loc,OI_def_loc,
                                        OI_active_not_displayed);

        // Make dialog box to process horses, attach to "horses" menu cell
        dbp = oi_message_dialog_box("horse_box","Process horses in this box");
        dbp->set_associated_object(pull_mp->subobject("horses"),OI_def_loc,
                                        OI_def_loc,OI_not_displayed);
        mcp = (OI_menu_cell*)pull_mp->subobject("horses");
        // use allow_subbox on menu cell since we use wait_button on dialog box
        mcp->allow_subbox( );
```

```cpp
        // Make dialog box to process cattle, attach to "cattle" menu cell
        dbp = oi_message_dialog_box("cattle_box","Process cattle in this box");
        dbp->set_associated_object(pull_mp->subobject("cattle"),OI_def_loc,
                                        OI_def_loc,OI_not_displayed);
        mcp = (OI_menu_cell*)pull_mp->subobject("cattle");
        mcp->allow_subbox( );

        // Make dialog box to process sheep, attach to "sheep" menu cell
        dbp = oi_message_dialog_box("sheep_box","Process sheep in this box");
        dbp->set_associated_object(pull_mp->subobject("sheep"),OI_def_loc,
                                        OI_def_loc,OI_not_displayed);
        mcp = (OI_menu_cell*)pull_mp->subobject("sheep");
        mcp->allow_subbox( );

        wp->set_associated_object(wp->root( ),OI_def_loc,OI_def_loc,OI_active);
        OI_begin_interaction( );
        OI_fini( );
    }
}

void process_horses(OI_menu_cell *cellp, void*, OI_number)
{
        static OI_dialog_box  *dbp;

    cellp->app_window( )->push_help(cellp->name( ),"help.hp");
    dbp = (OI_dialog_box*)cellp->subobject("horse_box");
    dbp->wait_button( );
    cellp->app_window( )->pop_help( );
    return;
}

void process_cattle(OI_menu_cell *cellp, void*, OI_number)
{
        static OI_dialog_box  *dbp;

    cellp->app_window( )->push_help(cellp->name( ),"help.hp");
    dbp = (OI_dialog_box*)cellp->subobject("cattle_box");
    dbp->wait_button( );
    cellp->app_window( )->pop_help( );
    return;
}

void process_sheep(OI_menu_cell *cellp, void*, OI_number)
{
        static OI_dialog_box  *dbp;

    cellp->app_window( )->push_help(cellp->name( ),"help.hp");
    dbp = (OI_dialog_box*)cellp->subobject("sheep_box");
    dbp->wait_button( );
    cellp->app_window( )->pop_help( );
    return;
}
```

```
void do_help(OI_menu_cell *cellp, void*, OI_number)
{
    cellp->app_window( )->set_help(cellp->name( ),"help.hp");
    cellp->app_window( )->help( );
    return;
}
```

Program 8-3   Hypertext Help Usage (AppWithHelp.C)

The three functions, **process_horses**, **process_cattle**, and **process_sheep**, could be condensed into one function if each of the dialog boxes were named with the same name as the menu cell to which it is attached, or if the name was passed as the **void*** argument in the callback. We did not do this, in order to make the example easier to follow. If the dialog boxes were named the same as the cells to which they were parented, the three functions could be consolidated into this one:

```
void process_animals(OI_menu_cell *cellp, void*, OI_number)
{
    static  OI_dialog_box       *dbp;

    cellp->app_window( )->push_help(cellp->name( ),"help.hp");
    dbp = (OI_dialog_box*)cellp->subobject(cellp->name( ));
    dbp->wait_button( );
    cellp->app_window( )->pop_help( );
    return;
}
```

Example 8-2   Hypertext Help Usage, Consolidated Menu Cell Callback

The hypertext **help** file named "help.hp" which is used in Program 8-3 is shown below in Example 8-3. Notice that we have used labels and topic names which are identical except for the capitalization of the first letter. You might wonder why we don't just use the capitalized word for both the label and the name. This would be fine, but if there is a chance that you would want to use a different language (French, for example) for your application, you could change all the labels and text to the other language, leaving the names alone. In this way, you would not have to change any of your code (the cell names of the menu in the main application are used to find the appropriate topic); you would change only the help text file. Note that lines in this file that begin "@Sub Topic" and "@Related Topics" are cross-reference markers (See @*ref_typ* on page 8-24).

```
!
!   help.hp
!
!   Lines that start with "!" are comment lines
!
@OI_default@General@farm_animals
@OI_text_ref@animal@animals
@OI_text_ref@Animal@animals
@Topic@Farm Animals@farm_animals
@Sub Topic@Horses@horses
@Sub Topic@Cattle@cattle
@Sub Topic@Sheep@sheep
Many different kinds of animals can be found on
a farm. Here we define three kinds.
```

```
@Topic@Animals@animals
@Related Topics@Horses@horses
@Related Topics@Cattle@cattle
@Related Topics@Sheep@sheep
An animal is any of a kingdom (Animalia) of living beings
typically differing from plants in capacity for spontaneous
movement and rapid motor response to stimultaion.

@Topic@Horses@horses
@Related Topics@Cattle@cattle
@Related Topics@Sheep@sheep
@Sub Topic@Mares@mares
@Sub Topic@Stallions@stallions
A horse is a four legged animal that people ride.
@Topic@Mares@mares
@Related Topics@Horses@horses
@Related Topics@Cows@cows
@Related Topics@Ewes@ewes
A mare is a female horse.
@Topic@Stallions@stallions
@Related Topics@Horses@horses
@Related Topics@Bulls@bulls
@Related Topics@Rams@rams
A stallion is a male horse.
@Topic@Cattle@cattle
@Related Topics@Horses@horses
@Related Topics@Sheep@sheep
@Sub Topic@Cows@cows
@Sub Topic@Bulls@bulls
Cattle are four legged animals that say moo.
@Topic@Cows@cows
@Related Topics@Cattle@cattle
@Related Topics@Mares@mares
@Related Topics@Ewes@ewes
Cows are female cattle.
@Topic@Bulls@bulls
@Related Topics@Cattle@cattle
@Related Topics@Stallions@stallions
@Related Topics@Rams@rams
Bulls are male cattle.
@Topic@Sheep@sheep
@Related Topics@Horses@horses
@Related Topics@Sheep@sheep
@Sub Topic@Ewes@ewes
@Sub Topic@Rams@rams
Sheep are four legged animals that are really,
really, really dumb. They are one of the few
animals that make cattle look intelligent.
@Topic@Ewes@ewes
@Related Topics@Sheep@sheep
@Related Topics@Cows@cows
@Related Topics@Mares@mares
A ewe is a female sheep.
```

```
@Topic@Rams@rams
@Related Topics@Sheep@sheep
@Related Topics@Bulls@bulls
@Related Topics@Stallions@stallions
A ram is a male sheep.
@Topic@Options@options
Your options are few.
```

Example 8-3   Hypertext Help File

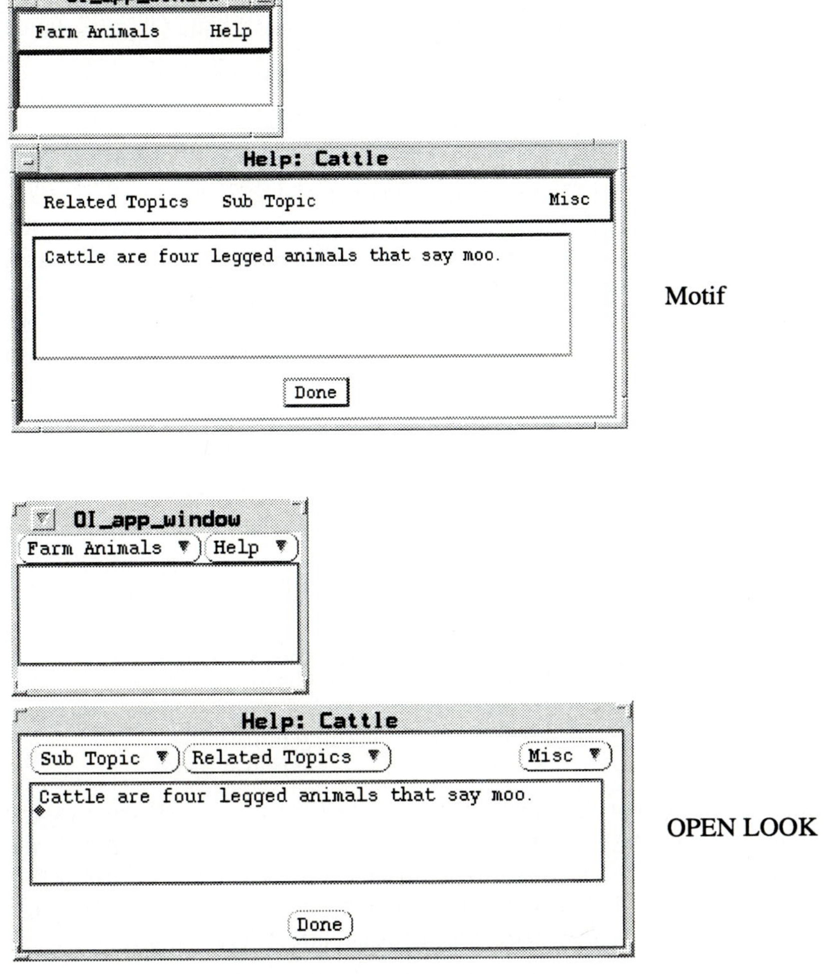

Figure 8-7   Hypertext Help Usage

8.6.3.4   Member Functions

help_menu   (Member function)

```
OI_menu *OI_app_window::help_menu( )
```

help_menu returns a pointer to the top-level help menu used to activate the hypertext help facility for the OI_app_window. Generally, the only reason you would use this function is to delete the help menu object.

hyper_help   (Member function)

```
OI_help *OI_app_window::hyper_help( )
```

hyper_help returns a pointer to the hypertext help object for the OI_app_window.

help_menu_cell   (Member function)

```
OI_menu_cell *OI_app_window::help_menu_cell( )
```

help_menu_cell returns a pointer to the help cell in the OI_app_window's help menu. When you designate a main menu, OI automatically moves the help button adjacent to it. According to the Motif Style Guide, a main menu should only contain pull-down menus—that is, you can't have a plain button. If you want to be strictly Motif Style Guide compliant, you should attach a pull-down menu to the help button since the help button appears to be part of the main menu. You may do this programmatically or by providing @OI_default lines at the start of your help file. You could set it up for the major topics your application has for help, and have each button do something like:

```
main_window->set_help(new_topic, new_file);
main_window->help( );
```

help   (Member function)

```
void OI_app_window::help( )
```

help activates the hypertext help mechanism. This is equivalent to the user clicking on the help menu button.

set_help   (Member function)

```
OI_stat OI_app_window::set_help(
    const char        *topic,              // help topic
    const char        *file=NULL)          // help file name
```

set_help sets the current help context to topic *topic* in file *file*. OI passes the file name *file* through the function OI_translate_filename, which processes environment variables or '~' characters and attempts to produce an equivalent full pathname. (OI_translate_filename is described in Chapter 5, "Initialization, Termination, and Other Independent Functions.") If you omit *file*, OI uses the current file. set_help does not affect the help stack. As a general rule, you should only use set_help in a case where the user has requested help, such as in a key-help callback function. In the case when you are merely changing the help context to match what your application is currently doing, you should use push_help.

push_help   (Member function)

```
OI_stat OI_app_window::push_help(
   const char          *topic,          // help topic
   const char          *file=NULL)      // help file name
```

push_help pushes the current help topic name and file name onto the help stack and sets the new help context to topic *topic* in file *file*. If you omit *file*, the current file is used.

pop_help   (Member function)

```
OI_stat OI_app_window::pop_help(
   const char          *topic=NULL,     // help topic
   const char          *file=NULL)      // help file name
```

pop_help pops the help stack until *topic* and *file* are at the top of the stack; they become the current context. If *topic* and/or *file* is NULL, one entry is popped from the stack.

void_help_context   (Member function)

```
void OI_app_window::void_help_context( )
```

void_help_context forces a re-read of the help file the next time the **OI_help** object becomes visible. If you dynamically change the contents of the help file, you should call this function each time you change the help file.

help_file   (Member function)

```
char *OI_app_window::help_file( )
```

help_file returns the current help file name.

help_topic   (Member function)

```
char *OI_app_window::help_topic( )
```

help_topic returns the current help topic name.

help_dismiss   (Member function)

```
void OI_app_window::help_dismiss( )
```

help_dismiss dismisses the **OI_help** object, as though the user had clicked on the "Done" button at the bottom of the help dialog box.

set_key_help   (Member function)

```
void OI_app_window::set_key_help(
    OI_help_fnp        fnp,              // pointer to callback function
    void               *argp=NULL)       // arbitrary argument for fnp


void OI_app_window::set_key_help(
    OI_callback        objp,             // memfnp's object
    OI_help_memfnp     *memfnp,          // pointer to callback member function
    void               *argp=NULL)       // arbitrary argument for memfnp
```

You can use a key-help callback function if you need to determine dynamically what help to use when the user requests help from the keyboard. The set_key_help functions register a callback function to be invoked whenever the hypertext help facility is initiated from the keyboard. The user initiates help by positioning the pointer over an object and pressing the HELP key or in Motif by selecting "On Context" from the help pull-down menu and then clicking on an application object. This callback is identified within OI as a cbKeyHelp callback function (see Section 6.18, "Determining and Adding Callbacks; Multiple Callbacks," on page 6-117). When the member function is invoked, it will be called as if you had written *objp->memfnp*. See Section 2.5, "Callbacks and Event-Driven Programming," on page 2-16 for more explanation.

argp is optional, and may be any valid expression that can be cast to a pointer. You can use it to pass additional information to the function *fnp* or *memfnp*.

Writing the Key-Help Callback Function

If the cbKeyHelp callback function is not a member function, write it in this form:

```
int fn(
    OI_d_tech   *oi_objp,       // pointer to OI object
    void        *argp)          // arbitrary argument
```

and if the cbKeyHelp callback function is a member function, write it in this form:

```
int obj_class::memfn(
    OI_d_tech   *oi_objp,       // pointer to OI object
    void        *argp)          // arbitrary argument
```

where *obj_class* is the class of the object whose member function is *memfn*. When your callback function is invoked, *argp* will be the argument specified in the set_key_help call, and *oi_objp* will be a pointer to the OI object under the mouse pointer at the time the user pressed the HELP key.

OI uses the value returned from this function to determine whether the help context has been set for the object or not. If your callback sets the help context, return 1. If you want OI to set the default context for the object, return 0.

If you have named your objects appropriately, or provided other information for your objects via the set_data function, you should be able to determine the help topic and file needed by the user. You should then use set_help in the callback to set the help text appropriately. Do not use push_help or pop_help in this callback, as their use will in all likelihood destroy the logical correspondence of the help stack with the application context.

To add a set_key_help call to Program 8-3 on page 8-27 (assuming the names of the dialog boxes have been changed to match the cell labels), add this line to the main program:

```
wp->set_key_help(do_key_help);
```

And add this function:

```
int do_key_help(OI_d_tech *dtp, void*)
{
    int                 ret;                   // 1 => topic set, 0 => not set

    if (dtp->app_window( )->set_help(dtp->name( ),"help.hp") == OI_ok)
        ret = 1;
    else
        ret = 0;
    return(ret);
}
```

Example 8-4   Key-Help Callback Function

The return value for do_key_help in Example 8-4 allows OI to properly set the default help when the mouse pointer is over an object for which you do not have help.

8.6.3.5   Help Object Resources

The OI_help class has some resources of its own, shown in Table 8-5. For example, to set the text-reference enhancement to underline for all OI_help objects, you could put the following line in your .Xdefaults file:

```
*OI*OI_help.InlineEnhance:          underline
```

Table 8-5   OI_help Resources

Resource	Description	Possible Values	Default Value
inlineEnhance	Specifies the type of enhancement to use on text which is text-reference.	underline reverse	reverse
viewportFitsText	If true, the OI_help dialog box will expand to fit the text if necessary. If false, it remains at the default 50-character width.	boolean	false

8.6.3.6   Using Resources to Establish Hypertext Help

You can use resources in the X resource database so that you don't need to use push_help at the start of the program and set_key_help in many situations. Use the OI_d_tech resources helpFile and helpTopic for this purpose. Suppose you include in your application default resources (for example, the /usr/lib/X11/app-defaults/*app_class* file) a helpFile and helpTopic specification for each object for which you would like a help topic to be specified. Then if you do not register a key-help callback, OI automatically uses the topic and file specified by these resources. You can also use the OI_app_window resources appHelpFile and appHelpTopic to set the default help context for the entire application. The benefit of using resources rather than set_key_help is that you can change the help files, including topic names, without changing the code, and everything still works.

8.7　Resources

All resources from an OI_app_window object's base classes are available to it; in addition, OI fetches the resources shown in Table 8-6. If you are planning to use resources to set help, see the OI_d_tech resources helpFile and helpTopic. For more information on resource management, see Chapter 39, "The OI Resource Mechanism."

Table 8-6　OI_app_window Resources

Resource	Description	Possible Values	Default Value
appHelpFile	Specifies the hypertext help file to use to establish the initial help context.	Valid file path name	NULL
appHelpTopic	Specifies the topic in the help file to use to establish the initial help context.	Topic name in help file	NULL
geometry	Specifies the initial size and location for the application window, in pixels, in logical root window coordinates.	wid x ht + $xloc$ + $yloc$	(No default)
iconFilename	Specifies the name of a bitmap file to use for the icon image.	Valid file path name	NULL
iconGeometry	Specifies the initial application icon location, in pixels, in logical root window coordinates.	wid x ht + $xloc$ + $yloc$	(No default)
iconic	If on, specifies that the initial state of the application window will be iconic.	Boolean	False
iconX	Specifies the x location, in pixels, of the initial application icon location.	Non-negative integer	(No default)
iconY	Specifies the y location, in pixels, of the initial application icon location.	Non-negative integer	(No default)

Table 8-6 OI_app_window Resources

Resource	Description	Possible Values	Default Value
longterm	Specifies the longterm message.	Any printable string	NULL
title	Specifies the title.	Any printable string	NULL

8.8 Translations

All translations from an OI_app_window object's base classes are available to it; it has no additional translations.

8.9 Callback Functions

Table 8-7 lists the callbacks available for an OI_app_window object and the page number of the corresponding explanatory material. In addition, all of the callbacks from an OI_app_window object's base classes are available to it. See Section 6.18, "Determining and Adding Callbacks; Multiple Callbacks," on page 6-117 for additional information about manipulating callbacks.

Table 8-7 OI_app_window Callbacks

Callback Type	Callback Typedef	Description	Page Number
cbIconify	OI_app_window_fnp/memfnp	Iconify callback function	8-13
cbDeiconify	OI_app_window_fnp/memfnp	Deiconify callback function	8-14
cbKeyHelp	OI_help_fnp/memfnp	Key-help callback function	8-32
cbProtocolDelete	OI_destroy_fnp/memfnp	Protocol delete callback function	8-16
cbSaveYourself	OI_app_window_fnp/memfnp	Save yourself callback function	8-15

Chapter 9

OI_static_text

OI_static_text Functions

OI_static_text Member Functions

The following functions are available to an **OI_static_text** object, but are described in their own chapter.

OI_d_tech Member Functions

OI_static_text

9.1 Description

An **OI_static_text** is an object that displays a text string on a single line. The text string cannot contain any control characters except tab. The size of an **OI_static_text** object is just large enough to accommodate the string. Changing the font causes the object to be resized to accommodate the new font. You can change the text in an **OI_static_text** object at any time. An **OI_static_text** object can be used any time you need to display text items on a single line. Typical uses are labels or headers for groups of objects or graphics.

9.2 Class Tree

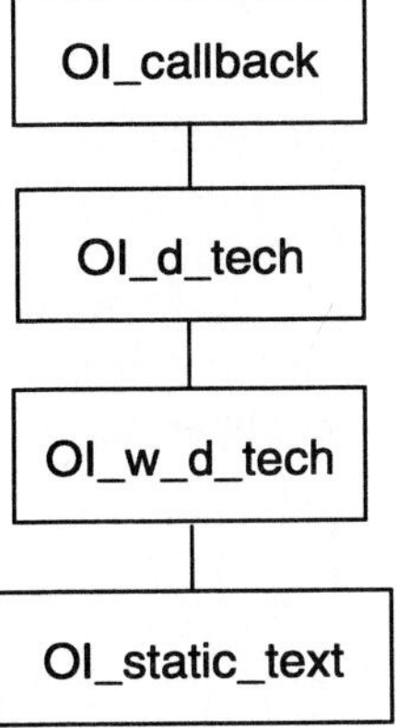

9.3 Runtime Interaction

The default translations for an **OI_static_text** object provide the following runtime interaction. See Section 9.9, "Translations," on page 9-12 if you need to change these.

By default, **OI_static_text** objects support text selecting and copying using the mouse. You can select text one of two ways. You may position the cursor over the first character to be copied, press the SELECT mouse button, drag the cursor across the characters to be copied, and release the button. The selected characters become highlighted. Or you may click the SELECT mouse button twice in the **OI_static_text** object to select a word, or three times to select the entire line. To paste the text into another object (an entry field, for example), use the paste mechanism for that object.

9.4 OI_static_text Creation

oi_create_static_text   (Free-standing function)

```
OI_static_text *oi_create_static_text(
    const char        *namp,          // pointer to name for object
    const char        *text)          // text string to display
```

oi_create_static_text creates an **OI_static_text** object with name *namp* and text string *text* and returns a pointer to the created object.

9.5 Base Class Member Functions

You can use all of the member functions of **OI_d_tech** for an **OI_static_text** object. **OI_d_tech** member functions which need further explanation when applied to **OI_static_text** objects are discussed below.

9.5.1 Click Functions

An **OI_static_text** object can respond to mouse button clicks in ways other than the default selection discussed earlier. If you want an **OI_static_text** object to respond to mouse clicks, you must register your click callback function for the static text object. When the user clicks on the object, your callback function will be executed.

Because **OI_static_text** objects respond to mouse events for select operations by default, a mouse button click on the **OI_static_text** object will not fall through to its parent object, even if the **OI_static_text** object does not have a click function registered for it. In order to allow mouse clicks to fall through to the parent object, you must disable the cut and paste operation for the **OI_static_text** object (see **disallow_cut_paste** on page 9-6 or **cutPaste** on page 9-11), and you must not register a click callback for the **OI_static_text** object.

set_click   (Member function)

```
void OI_static_text::set_click(
    OI_click_fnp        fnp,           // pointer to callback function
    void                *argp=NULL)    // arbitrary argument for fnp


void OI_static_text::set_click(
    OI_callback         *objp,         // memfnp's object
    OI_click_memfnp     *memfnp,       // pointer to callback member function
    void                *argp=NULL)    // arbitrary argument for memfnp
```

The **set_click** functions register a callback function to be invoked whenever the user clicks a mouse button one or more times on an **OI_static_text** object. This callback is identified within OI as a **cbClick** callback function (see Section 6.18, "Determining and Adding Callbacks; Multiple Callbacks," on page 6-117). If your click function is a member function, when it is invoked it will be called as if you had written *objp->memfnp*. See Section 2.5, "Callbacks and Event-Driven Programming," on page 2-16 for more explanation.

argp is optional, and may be any valid expression that can be cast to a pointer. You can use it to pass additional information to the function *fnp* or *memfnp*.

The button press and release must be separated by no more than clickDelta milliseconds for a press/release sequence to be considered a click. For multiple clicks, a release and subsequent press must also be separated by no more than clickDelta milliseconds. clickDelta is an OI_connection resource, which defaults to 500.

Writing the Click Callback Function

If the cbClick callback function is not a member function, write it in this form:

```
void fn(
    OI_d_tech   *oi_objp,       // pointer to OI object clicked on
    void        *argp,          // arbitrary argument
    OI_number   n_clicks,       // number of clicks
    OI_number   btn,            // mouse button number clicked
    OI_number   mod,            // modifier bits on at click time
    OI_number   char_psn,       // character # where click occurred
    OI_number   zro)            // always 0
```

and if the cbClick callback function is a member function, write it in this form:

```
void obj_class::memfn(
    OI_d_tech   *oi_objp,       // pointer to OI object clicked on
    void        *argp,          // arbitrary argument
    OI_number   n_clicks,       // number of clicks
    OI_number   btn,            // mouse button number clicked
    OI_number   mod,            // modifier bits on at click time
    OI_number   char_psn,       // character # where click occurred
    OI_number   zro)            // always 0
```

where *obj_class* is the class of the object whose member function is *memfn*.

When your callback function is invoked, *argp* will be the argument specified in the set_click call. *oi_objp* will be a pointer to the OI object where the click occurred. *mod* will contain the modifier bits on at click time. These will be zero unless the user holds down one or more of the modifier keys on the keyboard at the time of the mouse button release. *mod* may have any combination (0 or more) of the following values, ored together.

OI_mod_shift	Shift key down during click.
OI_mod_lock	Lock key down during click.
OI_mod_control	Control key down during click.
OI_mod_meta	Mod1 key down during click.

char_psn will be the character number on which the click occurred; the first position is 0. When more than one click occurs, the callback function will be invoked once for each click. For example, a double click will cause the function to be called first with *n_clicks*=1, then with *n_clicks*=2. If your application is performing a different operation depending on the number of clicks, the operations for a greater number of clicks should be compatible with those for fewer clicks. For example, a single click could mean select a word, and two clicks could mean select the entire text.

9.6　OI_static_text Member Functions

9.6.1　Changing Text

The text in an **OI_static_text** object is set at the time the static text is created. At any point in your program, however, you can inquire and change all or part of the text. The first character position in the text is character number 0, and **length( )** -1 is that last character in the text.

length (Member function)

```
OI_number OI_static_text::length( )
```

length returns the number of characters in the text. This does not include the terminating null. This function is equivalent to the C or C++ library call **strlen**.

text (Member function)

```
char *OI_static_text::text( )
```

text returns the text string, null terminated.

set_text (Member function)

```
OI_stat OI_static_text::set_text(
    const char          *new_text)          // new text
```

set_text changes the text string to *new_text*. This causes the object to be resized to accommodate the new string. To "clear out" the text, you may call **set_text** with *new_text* set to NULL. Changing the text may change the width of the **OI_static_text** object. If you parented it using **layout_associated_object**, this may cause other objects in the layout to shift positions.

change_char (Member function)

```
OI_stat OI_static_text::change_char(
    OI_number           psn,                // character position
    char                c)                  // new character
```

change_char changes the character at position *psn* in the text to *c*. It returns **OI_ok** if successful, and **OI_bad_value** if *psn* or *c* is invalid.

change_chars (Member function)

```
OI_stat OI_static_text::change_chars(
    OI_number           psn,                // starting change character position
    OI_number           len,                // number characters to replace
    const char          *textp)             // replacement text
```

change_chars deletes *len* characters starting at position *psn* (0 <= *psn* < length( ))in the text and inserts the characters in *textp*. *textp* must be null-terminated, and can be of any length,

---

although at most *len* characters will be inserted at position *psn*. It returns OI_ok if successful, and OI_bad_value if *psn* or *len* is invalid.

is_modified   (Member function)

```
OI_bool OI_static_text::is_modified( )
```

is_modified returns OI_yes if the static text characters have been changed since the last clear_modified call; otherwise it returns OI_no.

clear_modified   (Member function)

```
void OI_static_text::clear_modified( )
```

clear_modified clears the condition that the static text characters were changed. An immediate subsequent call to the function is_modified will return OI_no.

9.6.2   Text Selection

As mentioned above, the user can select any or all of the text from an OI_static_text object and paste it into another object. *Select* means to mark out text and copy it into an internal buffer. If this capability is enabled (which it is by default), a mouse button click on the OI_static_text object does not fall through to its parent object, even if the OI_static_text object does not have a click callback function registered for it. In order to allow mouse clicks to fall through to the parent object, you must disable the cut and paste operation for the OI_static_text object, and you must not register a click callback for the OI_static_text object. Table 9-1 shows the operations possible depending on the settings of cutPaste and clickSelect. These values are controlled by the member functions allow/disallow_cut_paste and allow/disallow_click_select discussed below, or the resources cutPaste and clickSelect.

Table 9-1 OI_static_text Options Controlling Mouse Text Selection

cutPaste	clickSelect	Operations possible
on	on	Select text either by mouse press-drag-release operation or by multiple clicks. Clicks do not fall through to the parent object.
on	off	Select text by mouse press-drag-release operation only. Clicks do not fall through to the parent object.
off	any	No text selection is possible. Clicks fall through to the parent.

is_click_select   (Member function)

```
OI_bool OI_static_text::is_click_select( )
```

is_click_select returns OI_yes if the object allows the user to select the text from the object using multiple mouse clicks; otherwise, it returns OI_no.

allow_click_select   (Member function)

```
void OI_static_text::allow_click_select( )
```

allow_click_select configures the object to allow the user to select the text using multiple mouse clicks (this is the default).

disallow_click_select   (Member function)

```
void OI_static_text::disallow_click_select( )
```

disallow_click_select configures the object to prevent the user from selecting the text using multiple mouse clicks.

is_cut_paste   (Member function)

```
OI_bool OI_static_text::is_cut_paste( )
```

is_cut_paste returns **OI_yes** if the object allows the user to select the text from the object using the mouse; otherwise, it returns **OI_no**.

allow_cut_paste   (Member function)

```
void OI_static_text::allow_cut_paste( )
```

allow_cut_paste configures the object to allow the user to select the text using the mouse (this is the default).

disallow_cut_paste   (Member function)

```
void OI_static_text::disallow_cut_paste( )
```

disallow_cut_paste configures the object to prevent the user from selecting the text using the mouse. You can use this function to allow click events to fall through to ancestor objects.

selection_coords   (Member function)

```
OI_bool OI_static_text::selection_coords(
    OI_number          *start,          // starting character position
    OI_number          *end)            // ending character position
```

selection_coords backfills *start* and *end* with the starting and ending character numbers of the currently selected text in the static text. It returns **OI_no** if the static text has no currently selected text; otherwise it returns **OI_yes**.

selection_data   (Member function)

```
char *OI_static_text::selection_data(
    const char         *sel_name)       // name of selection
```

```
char *OI_static_text::selection_data(
    Atom               sel_name_atm)     // name of selection converted to Atom
```

selection_data returns a pointer to a character string containing the current selection named *sel_name* or *sel_name_atm*. Specify *sel_name* to be "PRIMARY", "SECONDARY" or "CLIPBOARD", or specify *sel_name_atm* to be PRIMARY, SECONDARY, or CLIPBOARD.

The named selection is often text that the user has marked using the mouse. selection_data returns NULL if the object does not own the selection or if there is no current selection. Do not confuse this selection with that set using the OI_d_tech member function set_selection_data or the data returned from the callback registered via the OI_d_tech member function set_selection_convert (see page 6-59).

9.6.3   Controlling Text Appearance

You can enhance portions of the text using several different enhancements. You can "layer" enhancements of different portions of the text; repeated calls to set_enhance cause the enhancement attributes to be combined with older ones, using a bitwise boolean or. For example, if you call set_enhance to underline characters 10 through 40, then call set_enhance again to reverse characters 20 through 25, then the text appears underlined for characters 10 through 19 and 26 through 40, and appears in underlined reverse video for characters 20 through 25. If you do not remove the reverse enhancement, but remove the underline enhancement, all characters in the text appear with no enhancement except characters 20 through 25, which appear in reverse video.

By default, any tabs in the text are ignored. However, you can specify tab stops for this text, in which case the tabs are displayed. If you are using a variable-width text font, the tab spacing units used are the width of the widest character in the font, usually "W". In other words, a tab width of 4 is equivalent to the space taken up by the characters "WWWW".

get_enhance   (Member function)

```
OI_enhance OI_static_text::get_enhance(
    OI_number          charno)          // char number
```

get_enhance returns the type of enhancement in effect on character *charno*. The value returned is a bitwise inclusive or of one or more of the attributes listed under set_enhance below.

set_enhance   (Member function)

```
void OI_static_text::set_enhance(
    OI_number       charno,             // starting char number
    OI_number       len,                // length of enhancement
    OI_enhance      enhance,            // type of enhancement
    const char      *fg_color,          // foreground color
    const char      *bg_color,          // background color
    const char      *fontname=NULL)     // new font name
```

```
void OI_static_text::set_enhance(
    OI_number      charno,                        // starting char number
    OI_number      len,                           // length of enhancement
    OI_enhance     enhance,                        // type of enhancement
    PIXEL          fg_pxl=OI_unknown_pixel,        // foreground color
    PIXEL          bg_pxl=OI_unknown_pixel,        // background color
    const char     *fontname=NULL)                 // new font name
```

set_enhance enhances the specified text. *len* is the number of characters to enhance. *enhance* is a bitwise inclusive **or** of one or more of the following attributes:

OI_enhance_none	No enhancement
OI_enhance_reverse	Enhance using reverse video
OI_enhance_underline	Enhance using underline
OI_enhance_centerline	Enhance using a horizontal line through the text center
OI_enhance_overline	Enhance using a line over the text
OI_enhance_bold	Enhance using boldface
OI_enhance_italic	Enhance using italics
OI_enhance_font_change	Enhance using the font specified by *fontname*
OI_enhance_foreground	Enhance the foreground using the color specified by *fg_color* or *fg_pxl*
OI_enhance_background	Enhance the background using the color specified by *bg_color* or *bg_pxl*

fg_color or *fg_pxl* is used only if you specify **OI_enhance_foreground**. Similarly, *bg_color* or *bg_pxl* is used only if you specify **OI_enhance_background**. *fontname* is used only if you specify **OI_enhance_font_change**.

Note that if you use the default font in Motif (fixed), you cannot enhance using bold or italics, because there is no equivalent bold or italic font for fixed font.

Subsequent calls to **set_enhance** cause the enhancement attributes specified to be combined with any that are currently present using a bitwise inclusive **or**. The enhancement attribute remains in effect until you call **remove_enhance** specifying all or part of the enhancement or until you call **clear_enhance**.

clear_enhance   (Member function)

```
void OI_static_text::clear_enhance( )
```

clear_enhance removes all text enhancements.

remove_enhance   (Member function)

```
void OI_static_text::remove_enhance(
    OI_number           charno,         // starting char number
    OI_number           len,            // length of enhancement
    OI_enhance          enhance)        // type of enhancement
```

remove_enhance removes a specific text enhancement. The parameters are the same as those in **set_enhance**. Note: If you add or delete characters, the starting character number in the call to **remove_enhance** must match the new character number of the enhancement.

set_tab_width   (Member function)

```
void OI_static_text::set_tab_width(
    OI_number           tab_width)      // tab width in characters
```

set_tab_width creates a tab table with a tab stop every *tab_width* characters, to be used both in the menu title and the menu cell labels. The table defaults to a size large enough to support tabbing of up to 80 columns of text. The table is dynamically resized if any associated text has tabs past 80 columns. If you set *tab_width* to zero, tabs are effectively ignored; this is the default.

set_tabs_custom   (Member function)

```
void OI_static_text::set_tabs_custom(
    OI_number           *tab_tbl,       // pointer to tab stop table
    OI_number           n_tabs,         // number of tabs in tab_tbl
    OI_number           def_wid=8)      // default tab width
```

set_tabs_custom sets the first *n_tabs* tab stops in the menu title and cell labels to those specified in *tab_tbl*. Each element of *tab_tbl* specifies the column number where the next tab stop is to be placed. If there are more than *n_tabs* tabs in text, their spacing is set to *def_wid* characters. If you set *tab_tbl* to NULL or *n_tabs* to zero, the display of tabs is disabled; this is the default.

For example, if you want tabs at columns 4, 12, 20, and 36, then every 4 after that if needed, you would use these lines:

```
OI_menu             *mp;
OI_number           my_tabs[] = {4, 12, 20, 36};
OI_number           n_tabs = OI_count(my_tabs);
mp->set_tabs_custom(my_tabs, n_tabs, 4);
```

9.6.4   Positioning an OI_static_text Using Aligned Layout

If you use a layout method of OI_layout_row_aligned or OI_layout_row_column_aligned for the parent of an OI_static_text object, you can specify whether the static text should line up with the labels of other aligned objects or the value portions of other aligned objects. OI establishes an *alignment point* for these layout methods; this point is the reference for the vertical alignment of all objects in a visual column. Each object is then positioned so its own alignment point lies at the overall alignment point for that column space. For entry fields, the alignment point is just after the label.

For static text, OI_alignment_left means the alignment point will be placed at the static text's left edge, causing the text to appear to the right of the alignment point, or in the value region of any OI_entry_field objects which are aligned with it. OI_alignment_default is the same as OI_alignment_left.

OI_alignment_right means the alignment point will be placed at the text's right edge, causing the static text to appear to the left of the alignment point with its right edge at the alignment point; it will be in the "label" area, right justified.

set_alignment (Member function)

```
void OI_static_text::set_alignment(
   OI_alignment      aln)              // alignment to use
```

set_alignment causes the OI_static_text object to be aligned in the method specified by *aln*, whenever the box is laid out in a parent which is using OI_layout_row_aligned or OI_layout_row_column_aligned. *aln* may be one of:

OI_alignment_left	Align the left edge of the box with the right end of the labels of siblings in the same visual column.
OI_alignment_right	Align the left edge of the box with the left end of the text or value portion of siblings in the same visual column.
OI_alignment_default	OI_alignment_left

alignment (Member function)

```
OI_alignment OI_static_text::alignment( )
```

alignment returns the alignment method in use for the OI_static_text object. This will be one of OI_alignment_left, OI_alignment_right, or OI_alignment_default

9.7   An OI_static_text Programming Example

Program 9-1 shows an example of a click function for an OI_static_text object. When the user clicks on the OI_static_text object, the static text string is printed on the xterm from which the program was started.

```c
#include <OI/oi.H>                          /* ClickStatTxt.C */

int main(int argc, char** argv)
{
        void                    print_text(OI_d_tech*,void*,
                                OI_number,OI_number,OI_number,OI_number,OI_number);

        OI_connection           *conp;
        OI_app_window           *wp;
        OI_static_text          *stp;

    if (conp = OI_init(&argc,argv,"ClickStatTxt")) {
        wp = oi_create_app_window("main",1,1,"Click");
        wp->set_layout(OI_layout_row);

        stp = oi_create_static_text("my_text","This is a static text object");
        stp->set_click(print_text);
        stp->layout_associated_object(wp,1,1,OI_active);

        wp->set_associated_object(wp->root( ),OI_def_loc,OI_def_loc,OI_active);
        OI_begin_interaction( );
        OI_fini( );
    }
}

void print_text(OI_d_tech *dtp,void*,
            OI_number,OI_number,OI_number,OI_number,OI_number)
{
    printf("%s\n",((OI_static_text*)dtp)->text( ));
    return;
}
```

Program 9-1 Print Text Under Mouse Click (ClickStatTxt.C)

9.8   Resources

All resources from an **OI_static_text** object's base classes are available to it; in addition, OI fetches the resources shown in Table 9-2 for an **OI_static_text** object. For more information on resource management, see Chapter 39, "The OI Resource Mechanism."

Table 9-2 OI_static_text Resources

Resource	Description	Possible Values	Default Value
alignment	Specifies the alignment of the text with respect to the alignment point of the parent. (See page 9-9)	OI_alignment_default OI_alignment_left OI_alignment_right	OI_alignment_left

Table 9-2 OI_static_text Resources

Resource	Description	Possible Values	Default Value
clickSelect	If on, selection by multiple click will be allowed (This is the default). If off, multiple click selection will be disabled. See Table 9-1 on page 9-5.	Boolean	true
cutPaste	If on, mouse select operations will be allowed (this is the default). If off, all mouse select operations will be disabled. See Table 9-1 on page 9-5.	Boolean	true
font	Specifies the font to use.	Valid font name	Default font
text	Specifies the actual text string.	Text string	(No default)

9.9   Translations

An OI_static_text object has default translations installed for it. The default translations differ depending on which model the application is using. In addition to the translations listed in the table below, the default translations for an OI_static_text object also includes the default translations for all of its base classes.

Table 9-4 and Table 9-4 show the default OI_static_text translations. Table 9-5 describes what action each action function performs.

See Chapter 40, "The OI Translation Mechanism" for a description of the Event Sequence entries in Table 9-4.

Table 9-3 Default OI_static_text Translations, Motif

	Event Sequence	Action Functions Called
	<Btn1Down>:	select_start( )
!Shift	<Btn1Down>:	extend_start( )
	<Btn1Motion>:	select_adjust( )
	<Btn1Up>:	select_end( )
~Shift ~Mod1	<Btn2Down>:	drag_copy_start( ) secondary_start(SECONDARY)
~Shift	<Btn2Motion>:	secondary_adjust(SECONDARY)
~Shift	<Btn2Up>:	secondary_end(SECONDARY)

Table 9-3 Default OI_static_text Translations, Motif

Event Sequence	Action Functions Called
<Btn3Down>:	click_down( )
<Btn3Up>:	click_up( )
<Key>Escape:	cancel_select( )

Table 9-4 Default OI_static_text Translations, OPEN LOOK

Event Sequence	Action Functions Called
<Btn1Down>:	select_start( )
<Btn1Motion>:	select_adjust( )
<Btn1Up>:	select_end( )
<Btn2Down>:	extend_start( )
<Btn2Motion>:	select_adjust( )
<Btn2Up>:	select_end( )
<Btn3Down>:	click_down( )
<Btn3Up>:	click_up( )

In Table 9-5, *selection* means characters that have been highlighted and are in the X window selection property, and *start-of-selection* means the character position in the OI_static_text object in which the selection starts. *PRIMARY* and *SECONDARY* selections are the selections stored in the X properties of the same names.

Table 9-5 OI_static_text Translation Functions

Function Name	Description
cancel_select( )	If a selection is in progress using the mouse, deselects all the currently selected characters and terminates the selection process.
click_down( )	Starts timing for a mouse button click.
click_up( )	Ends mouse button click timing and makes click callback.
drag_copy_start( )	Changes the cursor to be an image of text being dragged. Begins a drag-and-drop operation using OI_dnd_copy (the dragged characters will not be deleted once the drop is complete).

Table 9-5 OI_static_text Translation Functions

Function Name	Description
drag_move_start( )	Changes the cursor to be an image of text being dragged. Begins a drag-and-drop operation using OI_dnd_move (the dragged characters will be deleted once the drop is complete).
extend_start( )	Moves start-of-selection to character under the mouse pointer.
secondary_adjust( )	Extends the selection to the new mouse pointer position. Underlines the selection.
secondary_end( )	Completes the selection process and saves the selection in the SECONDARY selection.
secondary_start( )	Begins selecting text for inclusion in the SECONDARY selection.
select_adjust( )	Extends the selection to the mouse pointer location.
select_end( )	Completes the selection process and saves the selection as the PRIMARY selection. If the time between press and release is less than ClickDelta milliseconds, calls click callback if one is registered.
select_start( )	Begins selecting text for inclusion in the PRIMARY selection at the mouse pointer location. Saves the time to determine if button click occurred.

9.10 Callback Functions

Table 9-6 lists the callbacks available for an OI_static_text object and the page number where the callback is documented. In addition, all of the callbacks from an OI_static_text object's base classes are available to it. See Section 6.18, "Determining and Adding Callbacks; Multiple Callbacks," on page 6-117 for additional information about manipulating callbacks.

Table 9-6 OI_static_text Callbacks

Callback Type	Callback Typedef	Description	Page Number
cbClick	OI_click_fnp/memfnp	Click callback function	9-2

Chapter 10
OI_entry_field

OI_entry_field Functions

OI_entry_field Member Functions

The following functions are available to an **OI_entry_field** object, but are described in their own chapter.

OI_d_tech Member Functions

OI_entry_field

10.1 Description

An OI_entry_field object is a region for entering or displaying a single line of text. Visually it consists of an optional label followed by the text entry area. OI keeps an internal representation of the text, which may or may not contain the same characters as the viewed text entry area. For example, the visual text entry area may contain a mask (for password entry), but the internal representation would contain the actual letters typed by the user. The text entry area may be shorter than the internal representation, in which case the user can scroll the text entry area. When it is created, the size of an OI_entry_field object accommodates the number of characters in the label plus the number of displayed characters in the text entry area plus a small amount of surrounding white space. If you change the font, the object resizes itself accordingly. You can specify different fonts for the label and the text entry area. If any default text string is specified in the call to oi_create_entry_field, the default text becomes the initial value for the entry field.

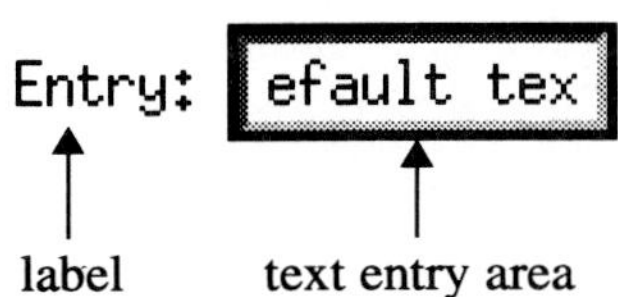

Figure 10-1   Parts of an OI_entry_field object, Motif

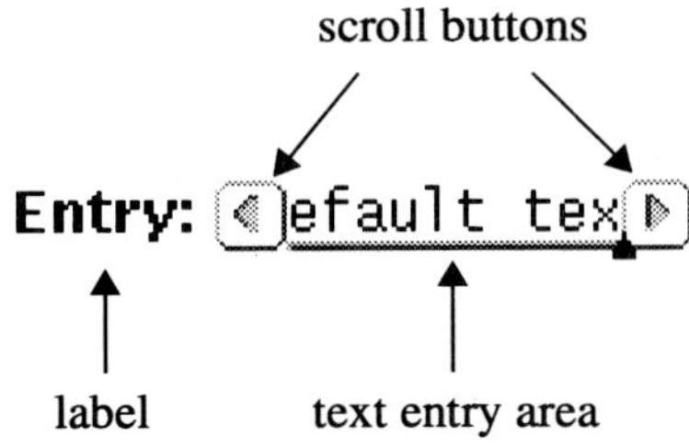

Figure 10-2   Parts of an OI_entry_field object, OPEN LOOK

By default, each input character is validated by an OI default character validation callback function before the character is inserted. The default validation check requires that characters be printable ISO Latin-1 characters. (Note that the set of printable ASCII characters is a subset of the set of printable ISO Latin-1 characters.) Invalid characters are not inserted; instead, the bell sounds, and a message is sent to the help line of the nearest ancestor which is an OI_app_window object. If you require different validation, you can write a per-character validation callback function and register it using set_char_check. If you register your own per-character validation callback function, it may be a complete replacement for the default character check callback, or a further refinement of it. The check callback is made immediately after the user types the character in the field, but before the new character is inserted; you may also register a function to be called after insertion is complete, using set_char_chg.

By default, no end-of-entry validation is done. If you require validation of the entire entry, or need to perform additional tasks upon the completion of the entry, you can write an end-of-entry validation callback function and register it using set_entry_check.

You can mark an OI_entry_field object as output-only; in this mode you can use it as a labelled area with a value displayed by the application, but which the user cannot change.

You can change the text echoed in the entry by specifying a mask. For example, if you specify the mask to be all "X"s or all blanks for a password entry field, this mask appears in the text entry area regardless of characters typed by the user. In addition, you can register a click callback function for an OI_entry_field object so that it can respond to mouse clicks. You can also define a default keyboard focus traversal ordering for several OI_entry_field objects by using the focus group facility (see Section 6.14.1, "Focus Groups," on page 6-101).

Since OI_entry_field is derived from OI_lang_server_input, whenever you create an OI_entry_field, you automatically get the functionality of an OI_lang_server_input object. The purpose of the OI_lang_server_input object is to provide the interface to a language server so that your application can use languages such as Japanese which require an input server.

10.2   Class Tree

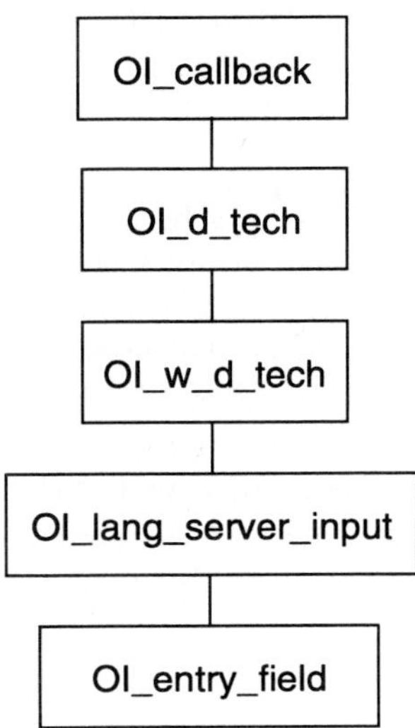

10.3   Runtime Interaction

The following discussion describes the default behavior of an OI_entry_field object. Most of this behavior is defined through default translations. If you need to change these, see Section 10.8, "Translations," on page 10-31, and Chapter 40, "The OI Translation Mechanism."

Text input to an OI_entry_field object is possible only when the entry field has the input focus If you are using the OI_focus_follows_pointer input focus policy. When you move the mouse pointer over the OI_entry_field object, it gets the focus. If you then move the pointer out of the object, but do not move it to another object that can have the input focus, the focus remains on the OI_entry_field object. However, as soon as the pointer moves to another object which can take the input focus, the entry field loses the focus. If the focus policy is OI_click_to_type, you must click the mouse over the entry field to give it the focus. The default focus policy for is OI_click_to_type. You can change the focus policy using the OI_connection resource focusPolicy. An entry field can also obtain the input focus via keyboard focus traversal. OI uses default algorithms for keyboard focus traversal, discussed in Section 6.14, "Input Focus Management," on page 6-101. Alternatively, you may set up an explicit traversal ordering using one of the OI_d_tech focus group member functions such as set_next. If the entry field obtains the focus in this manner, the location of the mouse pointer is irrelevant.

During text entry, a *cursor* appears, showing the point of entry in the text. This cursor is separate and different from the mouse pointer. In Motif, the cursor is an I-beam. In OPEN LOOK the *active cursor* (the cursor appearing when the entry field has the input focus) is a solid triangle, whereas the *inactive cursor* (the cursor appearing when the entry field does not have the input focus) is a stippled diamond.

If you position the mouse pointer over the text entry area and click, the cursor is positioned at the character under the pointer. In addition, any click callback function that has been registered for the OI_entry_field object is executed.

10.3.1   Scrolled Entry Field

If the maximum number of characters that can be entered exceeds the number of characters displayed in the text entry area, the text can be scrolled. During entry, if the cursor reaches the right side of the text entry area, as you enter new characters the characters scroll to the left. When this occurs, if you are running in OPEN LOOK mode, a button glyph for scrolling the text appears at the end of the display area where characters are hidden. Clicking the SELECT mouse button on this glyph scrolls the characters back on the display, one character at a time. Motif does not provide scrolling buttons or any indication that there is more text. Both the Motif and OPEN LOOK models allow you to press the right or left arrow key repeatedly until the cursor reaches the right or left side of the text entry area to scroll the characters right or left, allowing you to view in succession each character in the field.

10.3.2   Entering Text

As you type characters, first they are validated, then they appear in the text entry area. If the cursor is not at the end of the current entry but is on an existing character (that is, in the middle of the entry somewhere), and if the entry field is in *insert* mode (OI_ef_mode_insert), any newly typed character appears at the cursor location, and existing characters move to the right to accommodate the new character. If the entry field is in *replace* mode (OI_ef_mode_replace), any newly typed character replaces the existing character following the cursor location. Any characters input at the end of the line are appended to the line. The initial character entry mode is OI_ef_mode_insert.

OI installs default translations for an OI_entry_field object which cause certain key presses to perform specific actions. The default translations differ depending on which model you are running. See Table 10-2 and Table 10-3 on page 10-31 for default translations. You can remap these keys to suit individual preferences.

10.3.3   Cut and Paste

An OI_entry_field supports text selection, copy and paste using the mouse pointer. Text can be selected and copied in several different manners. You can move the mouse pointer to the first character desired, press the SELECT mouse button, and move the pointer across the text. The selected characters become highlighted. Release the mouse button when the desired characters are highlighted; the selected text is now marked for a subsequent paste operation. You can also click twice to select a single word and click three times to select the entire text. In addition, keyboard translations allow selecting text from the keyboard.

To paste previously selected text into an entry field, if you are running in the OPEN LOOK mode, move the mouse pointer to the desired text insertion location and strike the COPY key, then strike the PASTE key (special keys are defined in Chapter 3, "Compiling, Linking, and Executing an OI Program"). In the Motif model, click the DRAG (middle) mouse button. The text is inserted at the current entry field cursor position just as if it had been typed by the user.

You can also drag text and drop it in a valid drop-site such as another entry field. First you mark out text using the SELECT mouse button in the manner just described, completing the mouse press button press, move and release. Then, if you are using the Motif model, press the DRAG mouse button over the selected text, and the cursor changes to the drag-text cursor. Holding the mouse button down, move the mouse pointer to the desired drop-site, then release the button. The selected text is removed from the original entry field and placed in the drop-site—a *move* of the text is performed. If you hold the Control key down as you drag the text using the DRAG mouse button, the text is placed in the drop-site but not removed from the original entry field—a *copy* of the text is performed. If you are using the OPEN LOOK model, the same behavior is evidenced with the exception that you must use the SELECT mouse button to drag selected text, and the cursor shows the first few characters of the text being dragged.

10.4 OI_entry_field Creation

oi_create_entry_field   (Free-standing function)

```
OI_entry_field *oi_create_entry_field(
    const char          *namp,          // pointer to name for object
    OI_number           dsp_len,        // number of chars in text entry area
    const char          *lbl=NULL,      // string for label
    const char          *dflt_ent=NULL, // string for default entry
    OI_number           max_len=0)      // max number of chars in field
```

If *lbl* is not NULL, it is used as a label for the entry field and is placed to the left of the text entry area. If you omit *lbl*, it defaults to NULL. If *dflt_ent* is not NULL, it is used as the default entry and the initial text value. If you omit *dflt_ent*, it defaults to NULL.

dsp_len is the number of character positions to be displayed in the text entry area, and *max_len* is the maximum number of characters to be stored in the internal representation. You must specify *dsp_len*, but you may omit *max_len*, in which case it defaults to the same length as *dsp_len*. If not omitted, *max_len* must be greater than or equal to *dsp_len*. If *max_len* > *dsp_len*, the user can scroll the characters displayed in the text entry area so that *max_len* characters can be entered.

10.5 Base Class Member Functions

You can use all of the member functions of OI_d_tech for an OI_entry_field object.

10.5.1 Click Functions

An OI_entry_field object can respond to mouse button clicks if the mouse pointer is over the OI_entry_field. If you want an OI_entry_field object to respond to mouse clicks, you must register a click callback function for the entry field object. When the user clicks on the object, the callback function (which you write yourself) will be executed.

set_click   (Member function)

```
void OI_entry_field::set_click(
    OI_click_fnp          fnp,              // pointer to callback function
    void                  *argp=NULL)       // arbitrary argument for fnp

void OI_entry_field::set_click(
    OI_callback           *objp,            // memfnp's object
    OI_click_memfnp       memfnp,           // pointer to callback member function
    void                  *argp=NULL)       // arbitrary argument for memfnp
```

The **set_click** functions register a callback function to be invoked whenever the user clicks a mouse button one or more times on an **OI_entry_field** object. This callback is identified within OI as a **cbClick** callback function (see Section 6.18, "Determining and Adding Callbacks; Multiple Callbacks," on page 6-117). *memfnp* points to a member function for the object pointed to by *objp*. If your click function is a member function, when it is invoked it will be called as if you had written *objp->memfnp*. See Section 2.5, "Callbacks and Event-Driven Programming," on page 2-16 for more explanation.

argp is optional, and may be any valid expression that can be cast to a pointer. You can use it to pass additional information to the function *fnp* or *memfnp*.

The button press and release must be separated by no more than **clickDelta** milliseconds for a press/release sequence to be considered a click. For multiple clicks, a release and subsequent press must also be separated by no more than **clickDelta** milliseconds. **clickDelta** is an **OI_connection** resource, which defaults to 500.

Writing the Click Callback Function

If the **cbClick** callback function is not a member function, write it in this form:

```
void fn(
    OI_d_tech   *oi_objp,       // pointer to OI object clicked on
    void        *argp,          // arbitrary argument
    OI_number   n_clicks,       // number of clicks
    OI_number   btn,            // mouse button number clicked
    OI_number   mod,            // modifier bits on at click time
    OI_number   char_psn,       // character number where click occurred
    OI_number   zro)            // always 0
```

and if the cbClick callback function is a member function, write it in this form:

```
void obj_class::memfn(
        OI_d_tech  *oi_objp,        // pointer to OI object clicked on
        void       *argp,          // arbitrary argument
        OI_number  n_clicks,       // number of clicks
        OI_number  btn,            // mouse button number clicked
        OI_number  mod,            // modifier bits on at click time
        OI_number  char_psn,       // character number where click occurred
        OI_number  zro)            // always 0
```

where *obj_class* is the class of the object whose member function is *memfn*.

When your callback function is invoked, *argp* will be the argument specified in the set_click call. *oi_objp* will be a pointer to the OI object where the click occurred. *mod* will contain the modifier bits on at click time. These will be zero unless the user holds down one or more of the modifier keys on the keyboard at the time of the mouse click. *mod* may have any combination (0 or more) of the following values, combined with a bitwise inclusive or.

OI_mod_shift	Shift key down during click.
OI_mod_lock	Lock key down during click.
OI_mod_control	Control key down during click.
OI_mod_meta	Mod1 key down during click.

char_psn will be the character number on which the click occurred; the first position is 0. This is the character number relative to the entire text string, not just the visible portion. If the click occurred above, below or on the label or above the text (but still within the boundaries of the entry field object), *char_psn* will be 0. If the click occurred below the text, *char_psn* will be n_chars.

When more than one click occurs, the callback function will be invoked once for each click. For example, a double click will cause the function to be called first with *n_clicks*=1, then with *n_clicks*=2. If your application is performing a different operation depending on the number of clicks, the operations for a greater number of clicks should be compatible with those for fewer clicks. For example, a single click could mean select a word, and two clicks could mean select the entire text.

10.6   OI_entry_field Member Functions

10.6.1   Controlling Appearance

You can change the label and the length of the text entry area. If the application is run using OPEN LOOK, you can control whether or not the text entry area is underlined. Note that the underline is a useful user-feedback mechanism if you are using the callback function registered by set_entry_check; the underline is dashed when an incomplete entry is present, but solid when a valid entry is present. Because of this feature, you should not normally disallow (turn off) the underline. You can mask entered characters; this is useful if your application needs some security similar to entering passwords (this is an example of the displayed characters in the text entry area not being the same as the characters in the internal representation).

You can enhance portions of the text using several different enhancements. You can "layer" enhancements of different portions of text; repeated calls to set_enhance cause the enhancement attributes to be combined with older ones, using a bitwise boolean or. For example, if you call set_enhance to underline characters 10 through 40, then call set_enhance again to reverse characters 20 through 25, then the text appears underlined for characters 10 through 19 and 26 through 40, and appears in underlined reverse video for characters 20 through 25. If you do not remove the reverse enhancement, but remove the underline enhancement, all characters appear with no enhancement except characters 20 through 25, which appear in reverse video.

label   (Member function)

```
char *OI_entry_field::label( )
```

label returns the label for the entry field, null terminated.

set_label   (Member function)

```
void OI_entry_field::set_label(
    const char          *lbl)                    // new label string
```

set_label sets the label to *lbl*.

set_label_font   (Member function)

```
void OI_entry_field::set_label_font(
    const char          *font)                   // font for label
```

set_label_font sets the font for the label only to *font*.

set_label_char   (Member function)

```
void OI_entry_field::set_label_char(
    OI_number           psn,         // character position
    char                c)           // new character
```

set_label_char changes the character in position *psn* of the label (the first character is in position 0) to character *c*. *psn* must be less than the number of characters in the label.

set_label_chars   (Member function)

```
OI_stat OI_entry_field::set_label_chars(
    OI_number           psn,             // starting change character position
    OI_number           len,             // number characters to replace
    const char          *textp)          // replacement text
```

set_label_chars deletes *len* characters from the label starting at position *psn* (0 <= *psn* < length( )) and inserts the characters in *textp*. *textp* must be null-terminated, and can be of any length, although at most *len* characters will be inserted at position *psn*. It returns OI_ok if successful, and OI_bad_value if *psn* or *len* is invalid.

label_right_space   (Member function)

```
OI_number OI_entry_field::label_right_space( )
```

label_right_space returns the number of pixels between the label and the entry area.

set_label_right_space   (Member function)

```
void OI_entry_field::set_label_right_space(
    OI_number          pxls)              // space in pixels
```

set_label_right_space sets the number of pixels between the label and the entry area to *pxls*.

entry_loc   (Member function)

```
OI_number OI_entry_field::entry_loc( )
```

entry_loc returns the offset, in pixels, from the left edge of the OI_entry_field object to the left edge of the first character in the text entry area. The value returned does not include any window borders, if present. If you are using manual layout rather than the automatic layout mechanism, you may find this function useful in setting up vertical alignment of multiple OI_entry_field objects at the separation point between labels and text entry areas.

dsp_length   (Member function)

```
OI_number OI_entry_field::dsp_length( )
```

dsp_length returns the number of character positions displayed in the text entry area. This is the argument *dsp_len* from the call to **oi_create_entry_field** or the last call to **set_dsp_length**.

set_dsp_length   (Member function)

```
OI_stat OI_entry_field::set_dsp_length(
    OI_number          dsp_len)          // number of chars to display
```

set_dsp_length sets the number of character positions to display in the text entry area. If dsp_len is greater than the maximum number of characters allowed in the entry field (*max_len*), then *max_len* is set to *dsp_len*.

is_underline   (Member function)

```
OI_bool OI_entry_field::is_underline( )
```

is_underline returns OI_yes if the line under the text entry area is displayed and the current model is OPEN LOOK; otherwise it returns OI_no.

allow_underline   (Member function)

```
void OI_entry_field::allow_underline( )
```

allow_underline turns on displaying of the line under the text entry area in the OPEN LOOK model. This is the default. This function has no effect if the application is run in Motif mode.

disallow_underline   (Member function)

```
void OI_entry_field::disallow_underline( )
```

disallow_underline turns off displaying of the line under the text entry area in the OPEN LOOK model. This function has no effect if the application is run in Motif mode.

is_inactive_cursor   (Member function)

```
OI_bool OI_entry_field::is_inactive_cursor( )
```

is_inactive_cursor returns OI_yes (the default) if the "inactive" cursor will appear when the entry field does not have the input focus; otherwise it returns OI_no. The "inactive" cursor only appears in the OPEN LOOK model and is a gray diamond. The "active" cursor in OPEN LOOK is a black triangle and always appears when the entry field has the input focus.

allow_inactive_cursor   (Member function)

```
void OI_entry_field::allow_inactive_cursor( )
```

allow_inactive_cursor configures the entry field so that the "inactive" cursor will appear when the entry field does not have the input focus. The "inactive" cursor only appears in the OPEN LOOK model. This function has no effect if the application is run in Motif mode.

disallow_inactive_cursor   (Member function)

```
void OI_entry_field::disallow_inactive_cursor( )
```

disallow_inactive_cursor configures the entry field so that the "inactive" cursor will not appear when the entry field does not have the input focus. This function has no effect if the application is run in Motif mode.

get_enhance   (Member function)

```
OI_enhance OI_entry_field::get_enhance(
    OI_number          charno)              // char number
```

get_enhance returns the type of enhancement in effect on character charno. The value returned is a bitwise inclusive or of one or more of the attributes listed under set_enhance below.

set_enhance   (Member function)

```
void OI_entry_field::set_enhance(
    OI_number       charno,                 // starting char number
    OI_number       len,                    // length of enhancement
    OI_enhance      enhance,                 // type of enhancement
    const char      *fg_color,               // foreground color
    const char      *bg_color,               // background color
    const char      *fontname=NULL)          // new font name
```

```
void OI_entry_field::set_enhance(
    OI_number       charno,                      // starting char number
    OI_number       len,                         // length of enhancement
    OI_enhance      enhance,                      // type of enhancement
    PIXEL           fg_pxl=OI_unknown_pixel,      // foreground color
    PIXEL           bg_pxl=OI_unknown_pixel,      // background color
    const char      *fontname=NULL)               // new font name
```

set_enhance enhances *len* characters starting with *charno*. *enhance* is a bitwise inclusive **or** of one or more of the following attributes:

OI_enhance_none	No enhancement
OI_enhance_reverse	Enhance using reverse video
OI_enhance_underline	Enhance using underline
OI_enhance_centerline	Enhance using a horizontal line through the text center
OI_enhance_overline	Enhance using a line over the text
OI_enhance_bold	Enhance using boldface
OI_enhance_italic	Enhance using italics
OI_enhance_font_change	Enhance using the font specified by *fontname*
OI_enhance_foreground	Enhance the foreground using the color specified by *fg_color* or *fg_pxl*
OI_enhance_background	Enhance the background using the color specified by *bg_color* or *bg_pxl*

fg_color or *fg_pxl* is used only if you specify OI_enhance_foreground. Similarly, *bg_color* or *bg_pxl* is used only if you specify OI_enhance_background. *fontname* is used only if you specify OI_enhance_font_change.

Note that if you use the default font in Motif (fixed), you cannot enhance using bold or italics, because there is no equivalent bold or italic font for fixed font.

Subsequent calls to **set_enhance** cause the enhancement attributes specified to be combined with any that are currently present using a bitwise inclusive **or**. The enhancement attribute remains in effect until you call **remove_enhance** specifying all or part of the enhancement or until you call **clear_enhance**.

clear_enhance   (Member function)

```
void OI_entry_field::clear_enhance( )
```

clear_enhance removes all text enhancements.

remove_enhance   (Member function)

```
void OI_entry_field::remove_enhance(
    OI_number          charno,          // starting char number
    OI_number          len,             // length of enhancement
    OI_enhance         enhance)         // type of enhancement
```

remove_enhance removes a specific text enhancement. The parameters are the same as those in **set_enhance**. Note: If you add or delete characters, the starting character number in the call to **remove_enhance** must match the new character number of the enhancement.

set_mask   (Member function)

```
void OI_entry_field::set_mask(
    const char          *mask_strp)      // mask character
```

set_mask sets a display mask which OI uses when echoing the characters input by the user. This should always be a single-character string. This character is echoed in place of any characters the user types. For example:

```
OI_entry_field          *tp ;
tp->set_mask("X") ;
```

If the user types "John Doe" in the entry area, the string "XXXXXXXX" appears on the screen, and the internal representation contains "John Doe".

Note that if the user copies text that has been masked from an **OI_entry_field** object using cut and paste with the mouse, the visual display characters will be the characters pasted in the new location.

mask   (Member function)

```
char *OI_entry_field::mask( )
```

mask returns a pointer to the string of output mask characters. NULL is returned if no mask is set.

10.6.2   Controlling Input Mode and Length

When an entry field is initially created, it is writable; that is, the user is allowed to enter characters into the text area. If the entry field is to be output-only, you must turn off the input capability. In addition, you may modify the maximum allowable text length at any time.

max_length   (Member function)

```
OI_number OI_entry_field::max_length( )
```

max_length returns the maximum number of characters allowed in the internal representation. This is the argument *max_len* in the call to **oi_create_entry_field** or the last call to **set_max_length**.

set_max_length   (Member function)

```
OI_stat OI_entry_field::set_max_length(
    OI_number          max_len)              // max number of chars in field
```

set_max_length sets the maximum allowable length of the entered string. If *max_len* is less than the number of displayable character positions (*dsp_len*), *dsp_len* is set to *max_len*. If *max_len > dsp_len*, the characters displayed in the text entry area can be scrolled.

mode   (Member function)

```
OI_ef_mode OI_entry_field::mode( )
```

mode returns the current character entry mode, either **OI_ef_mode_insert** or **OI_ef_mode_replace**.

set_mode   (Member function)

```
void OI_entry_field::set_mode(
    OI_ef_mode          ent_mod)             // entry mode
```

set_mode sets the character entry mode to *ent_mod*, which may be either **OI_ef_mode_insert** (a newly inserted character is entered between existing characters at the cursor position) or **OI_ef_mode_replace** (a newly inserted character replaces the existing character following the cursor position).

is_kb_input   (Member function)

```
OI_bool OI_entry_field::is_kb_input( )
```

is_kb_input returns **OI_yes** if the entry field may be modified by the user; otherwise it returns **OI_no**.

allow_kb_input   (Member function)

```
void OI_entry_field::allow_kb_input( )
```

allow_kb_input configures the entry field to allow modification by the user. This is the default.

disallow_kb_input   (Member function)

```
void OI_entry_field::disallow_kb_input( )
```

disallow_kb_input makes the entry field read only.

10.6.3   User Text Selection

As mentioned above, the user can select any or all of the text from an **OI_entry_field** object and paste it elsewhere using the mouse. These functions allow you to modify the user text selection capabilities.

is_click_select   (Member function)

```
OI_bool OI_entry_field::is_click_select( )
```

is_click_select returns **OI_yes** if the object allows the user to select the text from the object using multiple mouse clicks (default); otherwise, it returns **OI_no**.

allow_click_select   (Member function)

```
void OI_entry_field::allow_click_select( )
```

allow_click_select configures the entry field to allow the user to select text using multiple mouse clicks (default).

disallow_click_select   (Member function)

```
void OI_entry_field::disallow_click_select( )
```

disallow_click_select configures the entry field to prevent the user from selecting text using multiple mouse clicks.

selection_coords   (Member function)

```
OI_bool OI_entry_field::selection_coords(
    OI_number           *start,          // starting character position
    OI_number           *end)            // ending character position
```

selection_coords backfills *start* and *end* with the starting and ending character numbers of the currently selected text in the entry field. It returns **OI_no** if the entry field has no currently selected text; otherwise it returns **OI_yes**.

selection_data   (Member function)

```
char *OI_entry_field::selection_data(
    const char          *sel_name)       // name of selection
```

```
char *OI_entry_field::selection_data(
    Atom                sel_name_atm)     // name of selection converted to Atom
```

selection_data returns a pointer to a character string containing the current selection named *sel_name* or *sel_name_atm*. Specify *sel_name* to be "PRIMARY", "SECONDARY" or "CLIPBOARD", or specify *sel_name_atm* to be PRIMARY, SECONDARY, or CLIPBOARD. The named selection is often text that the user has marked using the mouse. **selection_data** returns NULL if the object does not own the selection or if there is no current selection. Do not confuse this selection with that set using the **OI_d_tech** member function **set_selection_data** or the data returned from the callback registered via the **OI_d_tech** member function **set_selection_convert** (see page 6-59).

10.6.4   Retrieving and Manipulating the Text

You can use the functions described below to determine the current value and default value of the text in an **OI_entry_field** object, and to change those values. In all cases, the first character position in the entry area is position 0.

length (Member function)

```
OI_number OI_entry_field::length( )
```

length returns the number of characters entered so far into the entry field.

default_text (Member function)

```
char *OI_entry_field::default_text( )
```

default_text returns the text for the default entry. If none has been set, default_text returns NULL.

set_default_text (Member function)

```
OI_stat OI_entry_field::set_default_text(
    const char          *dflt_ent,       // default entry string
    OI_bool             chk=OI_yes,       // whether to execute validation function
    OI_bool             rpt_errs=OI_yes)  // report errors?
```

set_default_text sets the text for both the default entry and the current entry to *dflt_ent*, as if the user had deleted the current entry and typed *dflt_ent* followed by a Return key. If *chk* is OI_yes, the callback function registered by set_entry_check is called, if *chk* is OI_no, it is not called. If you omit *chk*, the default is OI_yes. If *rpt_errs* is OI_yes, and if the validation function was executed for *dflt_ent*, and if *dflt_ent* is invalid, an error message is posted to stderr. If *rpt_errs* is OI_no, no error message is posted regardless of the validity of *dflt_ent*.

part_text (Member function)

```
char *OI_entry_field::part_text( )
```

part_text returns the current entry, regardless of whether it is valid or not or whether it has been terminated or not. If the current entry is the empty string, part_text returns NULL. The string returned is null-terminated, and is not padded to the maximum length permitted by *max_len*. Trailing blanks are considered valid characters and are not stripped.

text (Member function)

```
char *OI_entry_field::text( )
```

If the internal representation contains a validated entry, text returns it; otherwise, text returns NULL. In order for an entry to be considered validated, if an end-of-entry validation function is defined (if a callback has been registered by set_entry_check), it must have returned OI_ef_entry_chk_ok. The validation function is called whenever the user presses the Return key. Also, if the resource validateText is true (the default), whenever you call text the validation function (if any) is called before returning a value, but only if the validation function has not already been called for the current set of characters in the entry field.

The string text returns is null-terminated, and is not padded to the maximum length permitted by *max_len*. Trailing blanks are considered valid characters and are not stripped.

Note that if you are writing a validation callback function (See Section 10.6.5, "Data Entry Callbacks," on page 10-18) and need to look at the entry, you should call part_text, not text, to avoid an infinite loop of recursive function calls. If you are writing a character-change callback (a callback registered by **set_char_chg**), you should also use **part_text** unless it is possible for all partial entries a user can type to also be valid.

set_text   (Member function)

```
OI_stat OI_entry_field::set_text(
    const char          *entry,            // new entry text
    OI_bool             chk=OI_yes)        // whether to execute validation function
```

set_text sets the entry text to *entry*, as if the user had deleted the current entry and typed *entry* followed by a Return key. If *chk* is **OI_yes**, the callback function registered by **set_entry_check** is called; if *chk* is **OI_no**, it is not called. If you omit *chk*, the default is **OI_yes**. You must set *chk* to **OI_no** if you are calling set_text from within an entry or character check validation routine to prevent infinite recursion.

insert_char   (Member function)

```
OI_bool OI_entry_field::insert_char(
    OI_number           psn,               // position to insert character
    char                chr)               // character to insert
```

insert_char inserts the character *chr* at the specified position *psn*. *psn* must be in the range $0 <= psn <= $ length( ). **insert_char** returns **OI_yes** if the insert is successful; otherwise it returns **OI_no**.

replace_char   (Member function)

```
OI_bool OI_entry_field::replace_char(
    OI_number           psn,               // position to replace character
    char                chr)               // character to replace
```

replace_char replaces the character at position *psn* with character *chr*. *psn* must be in the range $0 <= psn < $ length( ). **replace_char** returns **OI_yes** if the replace is successful; otherwise it returns **OI_no**.

delete_char   (Member function)

```
OI_bool OI_entry_field::delete_char(
    OI_number           psn)               // position to delete character
```

delete_char deletes the character at position *psn*. *psn* must be in the range $0 <= psn < $ length( ). **delete_char** returns **OI_yes** if the delete is successful; otherwise it returns **OI_no**.

insert_chars   (Member function)

```
OI_bool OI_entry_field::insert_chars(
    OI_number              psn,              // position to insert characters
    OI_number              n_chars,          // number of characters to insert
    const char             *text)            // characters to insert
```

insert_chars inserts the first *n_chars* characters from the string *text* at the specified position *psn* in the entry field. *psn* must be in the range 0 <= *psn* <= length( ). insert_chars returns OI_yes if the insert is successful; otherwise it returns OI_no.

replace_chars   (Member function)

```
OI_bool OI_entry_field::replace_chars(
    OI_number              psn,              // starting position to replace characters
    OI_number              n_chars,          // number of characters to replace
    const char             *text)            // characters to replace
```

replace_chars replaces *n_chars* characters starting at position *psn* with *n_chars* characters from the string *text*. *psn* must be in the range 0 <= *psn* < length( ). replace_chars returns OI_yes if the replace is successful; otherwise it returns OI_no. If *psn* + *n_chars* is greater than the field length, the text is extended to include the extra characters.

delete_chars   (Member function)

```
OI_bool OI_entry_field::delete_chars(
    OI_number              psn,              // starting position for delete
    OI_number              n_chars)          // number of characters to delete
```

delete_chars deletes *n_chars* characters starting at position *psn*. *psn* must be in the range 0 <= *psn* < length( ). delete_chars returns OI_yes if the delete is successful; otherwise it returns OI_no.

position   (Member function)

```
OI_number OI_entry_field::position( )
```

position returns the current position of the cursor (entry point).

set_position   (Member function)

```
OI_bool OI_entry_field::set_position(
    OI_number              psn)              // position to set entry point cursor
```

set_position sets the position of the cursor (entry point) between characters *psn* - 1 and *psn*. *psn* must be in the range 0 <= *psn* <= length( ). If *psn* = 0, the cursor is set to the beginning of the entry. set_position returns OI_yes if it is successful; otherwise it returns OI_no.

is_modified   (Member function)

```
OI_bool OI_entry_field::is_modified( )
```

is_modified returns OI_yes if the entry field text characters have been changed, either programmatically or by the user, since the last clear_modified call; otherwise it returns OI_no.

clear_modified   (Member function)

```
void OI_entry_field::clear_modified( )
```

clear_modified clears the condition that the entry field text characters were changed, either programmatically or by the user. An immediate subsequent call to any of the functions is_modified, is_user_modified or is_prog_modified will return OI_no.

is_user_modified   (Member function)

```
OI_bool OI_entry_field::is_user_modified( )
```

is_user_modified returns OI_yes if the entry field text characters have been changed by the user since the last clear_user_modified or clear_modified call; otherwise it returns OI_no.

clear_user_modified   (Member function)

```
void OI_entry_field::clear_user_modified( )
```

clear_user_modified clears the condition that the entry field text characters were changed by the user, so that an immediate subsequent call to is_user_modified will return OI_no.

is_prog_modified   (Member function)

```
OI_bool OI_entry_field::is_prog_modified( )
```

is_prog_modified returns OI_yes if the entry field text characters have been changed programmatically since the last clear_prog_modified or clear_modified call; otherwise it returns OI_no.

clear_prog_modified   (Member function)

```
void OI_entry_field::clear_prog_modified( )
```

clear_prog_modified clears the condition that the entry field text characters were changed programmatically, so that an immediate subsequent call to is_prog_modified will return OI_no.

10.6.5   Data Entry Callbacks

You may need to inspect, validate, or change an entry, either character-by-character as the user types, or after the entry has been terminated by a Return key. The functions in this section allow you to register a callback function (which you write yourself) to perform any of these tasks.

In order for an entry to be considered *validated*, it must have been terminated by a Return or Tab key and, if an end-of-entry validation function is defined (if a callback has been registered by set_entry_check), the callback function must have returned OI_ef_entry_chk_ok. Note that one of the parameters to the text member function can force the validation callback to be executed.

As already noted, if you are writing a validation or entry-modification callback function and need to look at the entry, you should use part_text, not text.

It is possible to register multiple validation or change callbacks for an entry field using the OI_d_tech member function callback_add. If you do this, when the event occurs that triggers the callback (a character is entered, or the return key is pressed), OI executes the multiple callbacks in the order in which they were registered.

For example, suppose you wanted to allow entering a Tab character into the entry field, which the default character entry function does not allow. You could leave the default character validation function in place, and add your own using **callback_add**. In your callback, if the *prv_stat* value were OI_ef_char_chk_insert, you would merely return, since you would know that the character entered was a printable character. If the *prv_stat* value were OI_ef_char_chk_bad, you would return OI_ef_char_chk_insert if the character were a Tab, otherwise you would return OI_ef_char_chk_bad. Since the default translations map Tab to do keyboard focus traversal, you would also need to modify the translations.

See Program 10-1 on page 10-21 for an example of a simple validation function for hexadecimal characters.

set_char_check   (Member function)

```
void OI_entry_field::set_char_check(
    OI_ef_char_check_fnp       fnp,        // pointer to callback function
    void                       *argp=NULL) // arbitrary argument for fnp


void OI_entry_field::set_char_check(
    OI_callback                *objp,      // memfnp's object
    OI_ef_char_check_memfnp    memfnp,     // pointer to callback member function
    void                       *argp=NULL) // arbitrary argument for memfnp
```

The **set_char_check** functions register a callback function to be invoked each time the user attempts to enter a character into the text entry area. *fnp* or *memfnp* replaces the existing character validation callback function(s), if any. This callback is identified within OI as a **cbEntryFieldCharCheck** callback function (see Section 6.18, "Determining and Adding Callbacks; Multiple Callbacks," on page 6-117). In general, the callback function registered here is meant to be a character validation function, to be used if you need to check each character as it is entered rather than waiting until the entire entry has been made. OI calls the character validation callback function only for characters which have no "special" meaning—it does not call it for characters for which control translations are defined (such as left and right arrow; see Section 10.8, "Translations," on page 10-31). *memfnp* points to a member function for the object pointed to by *objp*. If your character validation function is a member function, when it is invoked it will be called as if you had written *objp->memfnp*. See Section 2.5, "Callbacks and Event-Driven Programming," on page 2-16 for more explanation.

argp is optional, and may be any valid expression that can be cast to a pointer. You can use it to pass additional information to the function *fnp* or *memfnp*.

Writing the Character Validation Callback Function

If the cbEntryFieldCharCheck callback function is not a member function, write it in this form:

```
OI_ef_char_chk_status fn(
    OI_entry_field          *efp,        // entry field where char was entered
    void                    *argp,       // arbitrary argument
    OI_ef_char_chk_status   prv_stat,    // status from previous char check
    OI_number               psn,         // position of character in entry
    char                    c)           // character entered
```

and if the cbEntryFieldCharCheck callback function is a member function, write it in this form:

```
OI_ef_char_chk_status obj_class::memfn(
    OI_entry_field          *efp,        // entry field where char was entered
    void                    *argp,       // arbitrary argument
    OI_ef_char_chk_status   prv_stat,    // status from previous char check
    OI_number               psn,         // position of character in entry
    char                    c)           // character entered
```

where *obj_class* is the class of the object whose member function is *memfn*.

When your callback function is invoked, *efp* will be a pointer to the entry field where the character was entered. *argp* will be the argument specified in the set_char_check call.

prv_stat will be the return value of the cbEntryFieldCharCheck function, if any, called before this one for this entry validation. If this is the only cbEntryFieldCharCheck callback function registered for the entry field, *prv_stat* will be OI_ef_char_chk_insert. If there are multiple cbEntryFieldCharCheck callbacks for the entry field—that is, if you have registered other cbEntryFieldCharCheck callbacks for this entry field using the OI_d_tech member function callback_add (or you have registered this one using callback_add)—and if the order of registration dictates that another callback is called before this one, then *prv_stat* will be the return value from the previous callback.

psn will be the position of the character in the entry (the first character is in position 0), and *c* will be the character entered.

Write this function to return an OI_ef_char_chk_status with one of the following values:

OI_ef_char_chk_bad	Character is invalid
OI_ef_char_chk_insert	Character is ok, insert it
OI_ef_char_chk_ignore	Character is ok, discard it

If the function returns OI_ef_char_chk_bad, OI sounds the bell. You may write the function to post error messages via push_help_str, to activate dialog boxes, or to perform other actions. If you do not post an error message using push_help_str when the function will return OI_ef_char_chk_bad, then OI will display a generic error message. You must use push_help_str rather than set_help_str because otherwise OI will overwrite the message you display with the generic message.

If you call **part_text** from within the callback function, the new character *c* will not be in the string returned by **part_text**; it is not added to either the display in the text entry area or the internal representation until after the character validation callback function returns.

Program 10-1 shows a simple validation function for hexadecimal characters.

```
#include <OI/oi.H>                              /* ValidHex.C */

int main(int argc, char** argv)
{
        OI_ef_char_chk_status validate_hex(OI_entry_field*, void*,
                                        OI_ef_char_chk_status, OI_number,char);

        OI_connection           *conp;
        OI_app_window           *wp;
        OI_entry_field          *efp;

    if (conp = OI_init(&argc,argv,"ValidHex")) {
        wp = oi_create_app_window("main",1,1,"Hex");
        wp->set_layout(OI_layout_row);

        efp = oi_create_entry_field("hex_entry",10,"Enter hex number: ");
        efp->set_char_check(validate_hex);
        efp->layout_associated_object(wp,1,1,OI_active);

        wp->set_associated_object(wp->root( ),OI_def_loc,OI_def_loc,OI_active);
        OI_begin_interaction( );
        OI_fini( );
    }
}

OI_ef_char_chk_status validate_hex(OI_entry_field*, void*, OI_ef_char_chk_status,
                                        OI_number psn,char c)
{
        OI_ef_char_chk_status ret_val;

    if (psn >= 0) {
        if (isxdigit(c))
            ret_val = OI_ef_char_chk_insert;
        else
            ret_val = OI_ef_char_chk_bad;
    }
    else
        ret_val = OI_ef_char_chk_insert;

    return (ret_val);
}
```

Program 10-1   Validate Hexadecimal Entry (ValidHex.C)

def_c_check   (Member function)

```
OI_ef_char_chk_status OI_entry_field::def_c_check(
    OI_entry_field          *efp,         // entry field where char was entered
    void                    *argp,        // arbitrary argument
    OI_ef_char_chk_status   prv_stat,     // previous char check return value, if any
    OI_number               psn,          // position of character in entry
    char                    c)            // character entered
```

def_c_check is the default character check function. You should use this function as the first
argument to set_char_check if you want to restore the default character check callback.
def_c_check allows the entry of any printable character except Tab.

set_entry_check   (Member function)

```
void OI_entry_field::set_entry_check(
    OI_ef_entry_check_fnp   fnp,          // pointer to callback function
    void                    *argp=NULL)   // arbitrary argument for fnp
```

```
void OI_entry_field::set_entry_check(
    OI_callback              *objp,        // memfnp's object
    OI_ef_entry_check_memfnp memfnp,       // pointer to callback member function
    void                     *argp=NULL)   // arbitrary argument for memfnp
```

The set_entry_check functions register a callback function to be invoked when the entry is
completed (when the user presses the Tab or Return key). *fnp* or *memfnp* replaces the existing
entry validation callback function(s), if any. This callback is identified within OI as a
cbEntryFieldEntryCheck callback function (see Section 6.18, "Determining and Adding
Callbacks; Multiple Callbacks," on page 6-117). In general, the callback function registered
here is meant to be an entry validation function, to be used if you need to perform validation
checking on the entry, although you may perform other actions to be triggered by the completed
entry. Since the Up and Down arrow keys also signal end of entry, OI will call this function
when the user presses either of these keys as well. *memfnp* points to a member function for the
object pointed to by *objp*. If your entry check function is a member function, when it is invoked
it will be called as if you had written *objp->memfnp*. See Section 2.5, "Callbacks and
Event-Driven Programming," on page 2-16 for more explanation.

argp is optional, and may be any valid expression that can be cast to a pointer. You can use it to
pass additional information to the function *fnp* or *memfnp*.

Writing the Entry Validation Callback Function

If the cbEntryFieldEntryCheck callback function is not a member function, write it in this
form:

```
OI_ef_entry_chk_status fn(
    OI_entry_field            *efp,        // entry field where char was entered
    void                      *argp,       // arbitrary argument
    OI_ef_entry_chk_status    prv_stat)    // status from previous entry check
```

and if the **cbEntryFieldEntryCheck** callback function is a member function, write it in this form:

```
OI_ef_entry_chk_status obj_class::memfn(
    OI_entry_field          *efp,       // entry field where char was entered
    void                    *argp,      // arbitrary argument
    OI_ef_entry_chk_status  prv_stat)   // status from previous entry check
```

where *obj_class* is the class of the object whose member function is *memfn*. When your callback function is invoked, *argp* will be the argument specified in the **set_entry_check** call, and *efp* will be a pointer to the entry field where the Return key was pressed.

prv_stat will be the return value of the **cbEntryFieldEntryCheck** function, if any, called before this one for this entry validation. If this is the only **cbEntryFieldEntryCheck** callback function registered for the entry field, *prv_stat* will be **OI_ef_entry_chk_ok**. If there are multiple **cbEntryFieldEntryCheck** callbacks for the entry field—that is, if you have registered other **cbEntryFieldEntryCheck** callbacks for this entry field using the **OI_d_tech** member function **callback_add** (or you have registered this one using **callback_add**)—and if the order of registration dictates that another callback is called before this one, then *prv_stat* will be the return value from the previous callback.

Write the entry validation callback function *fn* or *memfn* to return an **OI_ef_entry_chk_status** which may be one of the values:

OI_ef_entry_chk_bad	Entry is invalid
OI_ef_entry_chk_ok	Entry is ok

If the function returns **OI_ef_entry_chk_bad**, OI sounds the bell. You may write the function to post error messages via **push_help_str**, to activate dialog boxes, or to perform other actions. If you do not post an error message using **push_help_str** when the function will return **OI_ef_entry_chk_bad**, then OI will display a generic error message. You must use **push_help_str** rather than **set_help_str** because otherwise OI will overwrite the message you display with the generic message. If you use **push_help_str**, you must call it on behalf of the entry field object whose callback this is.

If the application is run using the OPEN LOOK model and if the underline facility is enabled (**allow_underline**, the default), the line under the text in the data entry area is dotted until the entry validation callback function returns **OI_ef_entry_chk_ok**, at which point the underline becomes a solid line. If no validation callback is registered, the line remains solid.

Program 10-2 validates the user's color-name entry by comparing the entry with color names stored in an array. If there is a match, the validation routine returns signaling success. If not, the validation routine displays a help message and returns signaling failure. In this example, a pointer to the color array is passed to the callback routine via the arbitrary argument in the callback registration function **set_entry_check**. See Program 10-3 on page 10-27 for another way to pass the color array to the callback routine.

```c
#include <OI/oi.H>                          /* ValidColor.C */
#include <strings.h>

int main(int argc, char **argv)
{
        OI_ef_entry_chk_status   val_entry(OI_entry_field*, void*,
                                        OI_ef_entry_chk_status);

        OI_connection            *conp;
        OI_app_window            *wp;
        OI_entry_field           *efp;

    static char                  *colors[] =
            {"red","blue","black","green","gray","plum","purple",NULL};

    if (conp = OI_init(&argc,argv,"ValidColor")) {
        wp = oi_create_app_window("main",1,1,"Do Colors");
        wp->set_layout(OI_layout_row);

        efp = oi_create_entry_field("color_entry",20,"Color: ");
        efp->layout_associated_object(wp,1,1,OI_active);
        efp->set_entry_check(val_entry,colors);

        wp->set_associated_object(wp->root( ),OI_def_loc,OI_def_loc,OI_active);
        OI_begin_interaction( );
        OI_fini( );
    }
}


OI_ef_entry_chk_status val_entry(OI_entry_field *efp, void* argp,
                                        OI_ef_entry_chk_status)
{
        OI_ef_entry_chk_status ret_val;
        char                   *prtxtp;
        char                   **colorp;

    ret_val = OI_ef_entry_chk_bad;
    if (prtxtp = efp->part_text( )) {
        colorp = (char**)argp;
        while(*colorp) {
            if (!strcmp(*colorp++,prtxtp)) {
                ret_val = OI_ef_entry_chk_ok;
                break;
                }
        }
    }
    if (ret_val == OI_ef_entry_chk_bad)
        efp->push_help_str("Not in color table",OI_yes);

    return(ret_val);
}
```

Program 10-2   Validate Color After Entry is Complete (ValidColor.C)

set_char_chg (Member function)

```
void OI_entry_field::set_char_chg(
    OI_ef_char_chg_fnp        fnp,          // pointer to callback function
    void                      *argp=NULL)   // arbitrary argument for fnp


void OI_entry_field::set_char_chg(
    OI_callback               *objp,        // memfnp's object
    OI_ef_char_chg_memfnp     memfnp,       // pointer to callback member function
    void                      *argp=NULL)   // arbitrary argument for memfnp
```

The **set_char_chg** functions register a callback function to be invoked each time a valid character has been entered into the data entry area. This callback is identified within OI as a **cbEntryFieldCharChg** callback function (see Section 6.18, "Determining and Adding Callbacks; Multiple Callbacks," on page 6-117). *memfnp* points to a member function for the object pointed to by *objp*. If your change-character function is a member function, when it is invoked it will be called as if you had written *objp->memfnp*. See Section 2.5, "Callbacks and Event-Driven Programming," on page 2-16 for more explanation.

argp is optional, and may be any valid expression that can be cast to a pointer. You can use it to pass additional information to the function *fnp* or *memfnp*.

In contrast to the **set_char_check** callback procedure, the **set_char_chg** callback procedure *fnp* or *memfnp* is called after the character has been entered and all character validation has been performed (the callback routine specified in **set_char_check**, if any, has returned a "success" value). If you call **part_text** from the callback function, the new character will be in the string returned; it has already been added to the entry field.

Writing the Change-Character Callback Function

If the **cbEntryFieldCharChg** callback function is not a member function, write it in this form:

```
void fn(
        OI_entry_field    *efp,     // entry field where char was entered
        void              *argp)    // arbitrary argument
```

and if the **cbEntryFieldCharChg** callback function is a member function, write it in this form:

```
void obj_class::memfn(
        OI_entry_field    *efp,     // entry field where char was entered
        void              *argp)    // arbitrary argument
```

where *obj_class* is the class of the object whose member function is *memfn*. When your callback function is invoked, *argp* will be the argument specified in the **set_char_chg** call, and *efp* will be a pointer to the entry field where the character was entered.

Program 10-3 compares the user's partial entry after each character is typed with the colors in a color array. If there is a unique match, the entry field is completed with the color. Note that we use **set_data** and **data** to associate the color array with the entry field, rather than passing it in the callback argument, as was done in Program 10-2. Of course, in this small example, we could have put the color array in the callback routine, but in general, several routines may need to know about the colors, so we used this opportunity to show how it is done. In a real application, you would probably get the color information from a file.

```c
#include <OI/oi.H>                    /* AutoTerm.C */
#include <strings.h>
int main(int argc, char **argv)
{
                void              chk_n_cmplt(OI_entry_field*,void*);
                OI_connection     *conp;
                OI_app_window     *wp;
                OI_entry_field    *efp;
        static  char              *colors[] =
                {"red","blue","black","green","gray","plum","purple",NULL};

    if (conp = OI_init(&argc,argv,"AutoTerm")) {
        wp = oi_create_app_window("main",1,1,"Auto Complete");
        wp->set_layout(OI_layout_column);
        efp = oi_create_entry_field("color_entry",20,"Color: ");
        efp->layout_associated_object(wp,1,1,OI_active);
        efp->set_char_chg(chk_n_cmplt);
        efp->set_data(colors);
        wp->set_associated_object(wp->root( ),OI_def_loc,OI_def_loc,OI_active);
        OI_begin_interaction( );
    }
}
```

```
void chk_n_cmplt(OI_entry_field *efp, void*)
{
                char            *prtxtp;        // ptr to text in entry field
                char            **colorp;       // ptr to vector of color strings
                char            *strp;          // ptr to text to display
    while (prtxtp = efp->part_text( )) {
        strp = NULL;
        for (colorp=(char**)efp->data( );*colorp;colorp++) {// loop through colors
            if (!strncmp(*colorp,prtxtp,strlen(prtxtp))) {
                if (!strp)                      // no match has yet been found
                    strp = *colorp;
                else                            // match already found, not unique
                    goto done;
            }
        }

        if (strp) {                             // display unique match
            efp->set_text(strp,OI_no);
            break;
        }
        else                                    // remove char - doesn't match any color
            efp->delete_char(strlen(prtxtp)-1);
    }
done:
    return;
}
```

Program 10-3   Auto Complete Color Entry (AutoTerm.C)

10.6.6   Program Control

It is sometimes necessary to force the user to fill in a particular entry field before continuing with any other processing. An example would be password validation at the start of a program with restricted access. You can use the function below for such situations.

wait_done   (Member function)

```
void OI_entry_field::wait_done( )
```

wait_done activates the entry field, then processes events until the user presses the Return key (or equivalent). Input on all other objects is temporarily suspended until the entry field processing is completed.

Program 10-4 shows an example of using **wait_done** to get the user's ID before continuing with the application. A completion callback is registered for the user ID entry field to validate the ID.

```c
#include <OI/oi.H>                              /* GetId.C */
#include <strings.h>
int main(int argc, char** argv)
{
        OI_ef_entry_chk_status validate_id(OI_entry_field*, void*,
                                        OI_ef_entry_chk_status);
        OI_connection           *conp;
        OI_app_window           *wp;
        OI_entry_field          *efp;
    if (conp = OI_init(&argc,argv,"GetId")) {
        wp = oi_create_app_window("main",1,1,"ID Check");
        wp->set_layout(OI_layout_row);
        efp = oi_create_entry_field("id_entry",10,"Enter ID: ");
        efp->layout_associated_object(wp,1,1,OI_not_displayed);
        efp->set_entry_check(validate_id);
        wp->set_associated_object(wp->root( ),OI_def_loc,OI_def_loc,OI_active);
        efp->wait_done( );
        // for a real application, build the rest of object tree for application here
        OI_begin_interaction( );
        OI_fini( );
    }
}
OI_ef_entry_chk_status validate_id(OI_entry_field *efp,void*,
                                        OI_ef_entry_chk_status)
{
        OI_ef_entry_chk_status ret_val;
        char                    **namp;
    static  char                *names[] = {"bob","carol","ted","alice",NULL};
    ret_val = OI_ef_entry_chk_bad;
    if (efp->part_text( )) {
        for (namp = names;*namp;namp++) {
            if (!strcmp(efp->part_text( ),*namp)) {
                ret_val = OI_ef_entry_chk_ok;
                break;
            }
        }
    }
    return(ret_val);
}
```

Program 10-4   Get and Validate User ID (GetId.C)

10.7 Resources

All resources from an **OI_entry_field** object's base classes are available to it; in addition, OI fetches the resources shown in Table 10-1. For more information on resource management, see Chapter 39, "The OI Resource Mechanism."

Table 10-1 OI_entry_field Resources

Resource	Description	Possible Values	Default Value
clickSelect	If on, selection by multiple click will be allowed. If off, clicking the mouse does not select any text.	Boolean	true
defaultText	Specifies the default text for the object.	Any printable string	NULL
displayLength	Specifies the length of the entry area (*dsp_len*).	Positive integer	(No default)
font	Specifies the font to use for the entry area.	Valid font name	Default font
inactiveCursor	If on, the "inactive" cursor will appear when the entry field does not have the input focus. If off, no cursor appears in this case. (Applies to OPEN LOOK only.)	Boolean	true
keyboardInput	If on, specifies that the user is allowed to modify the text in the text entry area.	Boolean	true
label	Specifies the entry field label.	Any printable string	NULL
label.font	Specifies the font for the label.	Valid font name	Default font
label.rightSpace	Specifies the space to the right of the label, in pixels.	Non-negative integer	5

Table 10-1 OI_entry_field Resources

Resource	Description	Possible Values	Default Value
Margin	Specifies the space, in pixels, between the entry field text and the surrounding bevel (Motif only). The number specified is applied to either side and to the top and the bottom of the text. This resource is available for the class only, not the instance (you must always use the initial capital "M").	Non-negative integer	1
marginHeight / Margin	Specifies the space, in pixels, between the entry field text and the surrounding bevel (Motif only). The number specified is applied to the top and the bottom of the text. The instance name is marginHeight; the class name is Margin.	Non-negative integer	1
marginWidth / Margin	Specifies the space, in pixels, between the entry field text and the surrounding bevel (Motif only). The number specified is applied to either side of the text. The instance name is marginWidth; the class name is Margin.	Non-negative integer	1
mask	Specifies a single character to be displayed in place of any actual characters in the text entry area.	Single printable character	(No default)
maximumLength	Specifies the maximum length of the text (*max_len*).	Positive integer	(No default)
pasteAtPointer	If true, paste is at mouse pointer position. If false, paste is at input cursor position.	Boolean	true
text	Specifies the initial text.	Any printable string	NULL
underline	If on, specifies that a line should be drawn under the text entry area. (Applies to OPEN LOOK only.)	Boolean	true

Table 10-1 OI_entry_field Resources

Resource	Description	Possible Values	Default Value
validateText	If on, specifies that the entry validation callback should be called whenever you call the text function and the entry has not already been validated.	Boolean	true

10.8 Translations

An OI_entry_field object has default translations installed for it. Most of these translations cause certain keys to perform specific actions. The default translations differ depending on which model the application is using. In addition to the translations listed in the tables below, the default translations for an OI_entry_field object include the default translations for all of its base classes.

There are three tables in this section. Table 10-2 and Table 10-2 show the default OI_entry_field translations. Table 10-4 describes what action each action function performs.

See Chapter 40, "The OI Translation Mechanism" for a description of the Event Sequence entries in Table 10-2 and Table 10-3.

Table 10-2 Default OI_entry_field Translations, Motif

			Event Sequence	Action Functions Called
			<Key>:	input_character( )
		Mod1	<Key>asciitilde:	toggle_mode( )
	Ctrl		<Key>backslash:	unselect_all( )
	Ctrl		<Key>BackSpace:	delete_to_beginning_of_line( )
			<Key>BackSpace:	delete_previous_character( )
Shift		Mod1	<Key>Delete:	cut_primary( )
Shift		~Mod1	<Key>Delete:	cut_clipboard( )
Ctrl			<Key>Delete:	delete_to_end_of_line( )
			<Key>Delete:	delete_next_character( )
			<Key>Down:	next_object( )
			<Key>Escape:	cancel_select( )
		Mod1	<Key>I:	insert_mode( )
Ctrl		Mod1	<Key>Insert:	copy_primary( )
	Ctrl		<Key>Insert:	copy_clipboard( )
Shift			<Key>Insert:	paste_clipboard( )
	Ctrl	Mod1	<Key>KP_0:	copy_primary( )

Table 10-2   Default OI_entry_field Translations, Motif

Event Sequence				Action Functions Called
	Ctrl		<Key>KP_0:	copy_clipboard( )
Shift			<Key>KP_0:	paste_clipboard( )
Shift	Ctrl		<Key>Left:	backward_word(extend)
Shift			<Key>Left:	backward_character(extend)
	Ctrl		<Key>Left:	backward_word( )
			<Key>Left:	backward_character( )
			<Key>Linefeed:	replace_with_default( )
		Mod1	<Key>L6:	copy_primary( )
			<Key>L6:	copy_clipboard( )
			<Key>L8:	paste_clipboard( )
		Mod1	<Key>L10:	cut_primary( )
			<Key>L10:	cut_clipboard( )
		Mod1	<Key>R:	replace_mode( )
			<Key>Return:	newline( )
Shift	Ctrl		<Key>Right:	forward_word(extend)
Shift			<Key>Right:	forward_character(extend)
	Ctrl		<Key>Right:	forward_word( )
			<Key>Right:	forward_character( )
Shift			<Key>R7:	beginning_of_line(extend)
			<Key>R7:	beginning_of_line( )
	Ctrl		<Key>R9:	backward_view( )
Shift			<Key>R13:	end_of_line(extend)
			<Key>R13:	end_of_line( )
	Ctrl		<Key>R15:	forward_view( )
	Ctrl		<Key>slash:	select_all( )
	!Ctrl		<Key>space:	set_anchor( )
!Shift			<Key>space:	key_select( )
Shift	Ctrl		<Key>Tab:	previous_tab_group( )
Shift			<Key>Tab:	previous_tab_group( )
	Ctrl		<Key>Tab:	next_tab_group( )
			<Key>Tab:	next_tab_group( )
			<Key>Up:	previous_object( )
~Shift	~Ctrl	~Mod1	<Btn1Down>:	take_focus( ) select_start( )
	!Ctrl		<Btn1Down>:	move_insertion( )
!Shift			<Btn1Down>:	extend_start( )

Table 10-2 Default OI_entry_field Translations, Motif

			Event Sequence	Action Functions Called
	~Ctrl		<Btn1Motion>:	select_adjust( )
			<Btn1Up>:	select_end( )
~Shift	~Ctrl	~Mod1	<Btn2Down>:	drag_move_start( ) secondary_start(SECONDARY)
~Shift	Ctrl	~Mod1	<Btn2Down>:	drag_copy_start( ) secondary_start(SECONDARY)
~Shift	~Ctrl	Mod1	<Btn2Motion>:	secondary_adjust(SECONDARY)
~Shift			<Btn2Motion>:	secondary_adjust(SECONDARY)
~Shift	~Ctrl	Mod1	<Btn2Up>:	move_selection( )
~Shift			<Btn2Up>:	secondary_end(SECONDARY)
			<Btn3Down>:	click_down( )
			<Btn3Up>:	click_up( )
			<FocusIn>:	paint_focus_frame( ) focus_in( )
			<FocusOut>:	clear_focus_frame( ) focus_out( )

Table 10-3 Default OI_entry_field Translations, OPEN LOOK

			Event Sequence	Action Functions Called
			<Key>:	input_character( )
	Ctrl	~Mod1	<Key>A:	beginning_of_line( )
		Mod1	<Key>asciitilde:	toggle_mode( )
	Ctrl	~Mod1	<Key>B:	backward_character( )
	~Ctrl	Mod1	<Key>B:	backward_word( )
Shift	Ctrl	~Mod1	<Key>BackSpace:	delete_previous_word( )
	Ctrl	~Mod1	<Key>BackSpace:	delete_to_beginning_of_line( )
Shift		~Mod1	<Key>BackSpace:	delete_next_character( )
		~Mod1	<Key>BackSpace:	delete_previous_character( )
	Ctrl	~Mod1	<Key>D:	delete_next_character( )
	~Ctrl	Mod1	<Key>D:	delete_next_word( )
Shift		Mod1	<Key>Delete:	delete_all_characters( )
Shift	Ctrl	~Mod1	<Key>Delete:	delete_next_word( )
	Ctrl	~Mod1	<Key>Delete:	delete_to_end_of_line( )
Shift		~Mod1	<Key>Delete:	delete_next_character( )
		~Mod1	<Key>Delete:	delete_previous_character( )
			<Key>Down:	next_object( )
	~Ctrl		<Key>Down:	next_object( )

Table 10-3   Default OI_entry_field Translations, OPEN LOOK

			Event Sequence	Action Functions Called
	Ctrl	~Mod1	<Key>E:	end_of_line( )
	Ctrl	~Mod1	<Key>F:	forward_character( )
	~Ctrl	Mod1	<Key>F:	forward_word( )
	Ctrl	~Mod1	<Key>H:	delete_previous_character( )
	~Ctrl	Mod1	<Key>H:	delete_previous_word( )
		Mod1	<Key>I:	insert_mode( )
	Ctrl		<Key>Insert:	copy_clipboard( )
Shift			<Key>Insert:	paste_clipboard( )
	Ctrl	~Mod1	<Key>K:	delete_to_end_of_line( )
	~Ctrl	Mod1	<Key>K:	delete_to_beginning_of_line( )
	Ctrl		<Key>KP_0:	copy_clipboard( )
Shift			<Key>KP_0:	paste_clipboard( )
	Ctrl	Mod1	<Key>Left:	select_all( )
Shift	Ctrl		<Key>Left:	backward_word(extend)
Shift			<Key>Left:	backward_character(extend)
	Ctrl		<Key>Left:	backward_word( )
		Mod1	<Key>Left:	backward_word( )
			<Key>Left:	backward_character( )
			<Key>Linefeed:	replace_with_default( )
			<Key>L6:	copy_clipboard( )
			<Key>L8:	paste_clipboard( )
			<Key>L10:	cut_clipboard( )
		Mod1	<Key>R:	replace_mode( )
			<Key>Return:	newline( )
Shift	Ctrl		<Key>Right:	forward_word(extend)
Shift			<Key>Right:	forward_character(extend)
	Ctrl		<Key>Right:	forward_word( )
		Mod1	<Key>Right:	forward_word( )
			<Key>Right:	forward_character( )
Shift			<Key>R7:	beginning_of_line(extend)
			<Key>R7:	beginning_of_line( )
Shift			<Key>R13:	end_of_line(extend)
			<Key>R13:	end_of_line( )
Shift	Ctrl		<Key>Tab:	previous_tab_group( )
Shift			<Key>Tab:	previous_tab_group( )

Table 10-3 Default OI_entry_field Translations, OPEN LOOK

			Event Sequence	Action Functions Called
	Ctrl		<Key>Tab:	next_tab_group( )
			<Key>Tab:	next_tab_group( )
Shift	Ctrl	~Mod1	<Key>U:	delete_to_end_of_line( )
~	Ctrl	~Mod1	<Key>U:	delete_to_beginning_of_line( )
			<Key>Up:	previous_object( )
	~Ctrl		<Key>Up:	previous_object( )
Shift		Mod1	<Key>{:	scroll_left_edge( )
		Mod1	<Key>[:	scroll_left( )
Shift		Mod1	<Key>}:	scroll_right_edge( )
		Mod1	<Key>]:	scroll_right( )
~Shift	~Ctrl	~Mod1	<Btn1Down>:	take_focus( ) drag_move_start( ) select_start( )
~Shift	Ctrl	~Mod1	<Btn1Down>:	drag_copy_start( )
	~Ctrl		<Btn1Motion>:	select_adjust( )
			<Btn1Up>:	select_end( )
			<Btn2Down>:	extend_start( )
			<Btn2Motion>:	select_adjust( )
			<Btn2Up>:	select_end( )
			<Btn3Down>:	click_down( )
			<Btn3Up>:	click_up( )
			<FocusIn>:	focus_in( )
			<FocusOut>:	focus_out( )

Table 10-4 describes the actions taken by the action functions. In Table 10-4, *selection* means characters that have been highlighted and are in the X window selection property, and *start-of-selection* means the character position in the OI_entry_field object in which the selection starts. *PRIMARY, SECONDARY* and *CLIPBOARD* selections are the selections stored in the X properties of the same names.

Table 10-4 OI_entry_field Translation Functions

Function Name	Description
backward_character( )	Moves the cursor left one character.
backward_view( )	Moves the cursor one viewport to the left (if the field is scrolled).

Table 10-4 OI_entry_field Translation Functions

Function Name	Description
backward_word( )	Moves the cursor left one word. A word is delineated by white space.
beginning_of_line( )	Moves the cursor to the beginning of the entry.
cancel_select( )	If a selection is in progress using the mouse, deselects all the currently selected characters and terminates the selection process.
clear_focus_frame	Removes highlighting to indicate the object no longer has the keyboard input focus.
click_down( )	Processes button down event in case click callback is set. Does not do any selection processing (see select_start).
click_up( )	Processes button up event and dispatches to click callback if one is set. Does not do any text selection (see select_end).
copy_clipboard( )	Copies the currently selected text to the CLIPBOARD selection.
copy_primary( )	Inserts the PRIMARY selection at the current insertion point.
cut_clipboard( )	Copies the currently selected text to the CLIPBOARD selection and deletes the PRIMARY selection from its original source, if possible.
cut_primary( )	Inserts the PRIMARY selection at the current insertion point and deletes the PRIMARY selection from its original source, if possible.
delete_all_characters( )	Deletes all characters in the entry.
delete_next_character( )	Deletes the character to the right of the cursor.
delete_next_word( )	Deletes from the current insertion point through the whitespace at the end of the text containing the insertion point.
delete_previous_character( )	Deletes the character to the left of the cursor.
delete_previous_word( )	Deletes from the current insertion point up to, but not including, the whitespace at the beginning of the text containing the insertion point.
delete_to_beginning_of_line( )	Deletes all the characters to the left of the cursor.

Table 10-4 OI_entry_field Translation Functions

Function Name	Description
delete_to_end_of_line( )	Deletes all the characters to right of the cursor.
drag_copy_start( )	Changes the cursor to be an image of text being dragged. Begins a drag-and-drop operation using OI_dnd_copy (the dragged characters will not be deleted once the drop is complete).
drag_move_start( )	Changes the cursor to be an image of text being dragged. Begins a drag-and-drop operation using OI_dnd_move (the dragged characters will be deleted once the drop is complete).
end_of_line( )	Moves the cursor to the end of the entry.
extend_start( )	Moves start-of-selection to character under the mouse pointer.
focus_in( )	Sets input-focus to the object.
focus_out( )	Gives up input-focus.
forward_character( )	Moves the cursor right one character.
forward_view( )	Moves the cursor one viewport to the right (if the field can be scrolled).
forward_word( )	Moves the cursor right one word. A word is delineated by whitespace.
input_character( )	Inserts character at the cursor position.
insert_mode( )	Sets the character entry mode to OI_ef_mode_insert.
insert_selection( )	Pastes text from the PRIMARY selection at the cursor position.
key_select( )	Marks the text from the anchor point to the cursor as the PRIMARY selection.
move_insertion( )	Sets the insertion point to the mouse pointer position; does not clear the current selection if it is in the same object.
move_selection( )	If the SECONDARY selection is active for this object then copies the SECONDARY selection text to the cursor location and deletes the original selected text. Otherwise, if the PRIMARY selection is active for this object and was set using the mouse, copies the PRIMARY selection text to the cursor location and deletes the original selected text.

Table 10-4 OI_entry_field Translation Functions

Function Name	Description
newline( )	End of entry. This causes the end-of-entry validation function to be called. If it returns OI_ef_cntry_ohk_ok, and an object has been registered via the set_next function, the new object obtains input focus. Otherwise, the OI_entry_field object retains the input focus.
next_object( )	Same as newline( ).
next_tab_group( )	Transfers the input focus to the next tab group.
paint_focus_frame	Highlights the object to indicate it has the keyboard input focus.
paste_clipboard( )	Deletes any currently selected text. The contents of the CLIP-BOARD are then inserted in its place. If no text is currently selected, the contents of the CLIPBOARD are inserted at the insertion point.
previous_object( )	Completes the entry as if the Return key had been pressed and goes to the previous object, if one exists.
previous_tab_group( )	Transfers the input focus to the previous tab group.
replace_mode( )	Sets the character entry mode to OI_ef_mode_replace.
replace_with_default( )	Replaces the current entry with the default entry.
scroll_left( )	Scrolls the text one full viewport to the left.
scroll_left_edge( )	Scrolls the text so the extreme left edge is visible.
scroll_right( )	Scrolls the text one full viewport to the right.
scroll_right_edge( )	Scrolls the text so the extreme right edge is visible.
secondary_adjust( )	Extends the selection to the new mouse pointer position. If Motif is being used, underline the selection.
secondary_end( )	Completes the selection process and saves the selection in the SECONDARY selection.
secondary_start( )	Begins selecting text for inclusion in the SECONDARY selection.
select_adjust( )	Extends the selection to the mouse pointer location.

Table 10-4 OI_entry_field Translation Functions

Function Name	Description
select_all( )	Marks the entire text as the PRIMARY selection.
select_end( )	Completes the selection process and saves the selection as the PRIMARY selection. Also, if the time between press and release is less than clickDelta milliseconds, calls click callback if one is registered.
select_start( )	Begins selecting text for inclusion in the PRIMARY selection at the mouse pointer location. Moves cursor to the pointer position. Saves the time to determine if button click occurred.
set_anchor( )	Set the anchor for selection at the current insertion point.
take_focus( )	Sets the keyboard input focus to the OI_entry_field object.
toggle_mode( )	Toggles the character entry mode between OI_ef_mode_insert and OI_ef_mode_replace. The initial character entry mode is OI_ef_mode_insert.
unselect_all( )	Deselects any currently selected text. Clears the PRIMARY selection if it is owned by the process.

10.9 Callback Functions

Table 10-5 lists the callbacks available for an OI_entry_field object and the page number where the callback is documented. In addition, all of the callbacks from an OI_entry_field object's base classes are available to it. See Section 6.18, "Determining and Adding Callbacks; Multiple Callbacks," on page 6-117 for additional information about manipulating callbacks.

Table 10-5 OI_entry_field Callbacks

Callback Type	Callback Typedef	Description	Page Number
cbClick	OI_click_fnp/memfnp	Click callback function	10-6
cbEntryFieldCharChg	OI_ef_char_chg_fnp / memfnp	Character change callback function	10-25
cbEntryFieldCharCheck	OI_ef_char_check_fnp / memfnp	Character validation callback function	10-19
cbEntryFieldEntryCheck	OI_ef_entry_check_fnp / memfnp	Entry validation callback function	10-22

Chapter 11
OI_seq_entry_field

OI_seq_entry_field Functions

OI_seq_entry_field Member Functions

The following functions are available to an **OI_seq_entry_field** object, but are described in their own chapter.

OI_entry_field Member Functions

OI_d_tech Member Functions

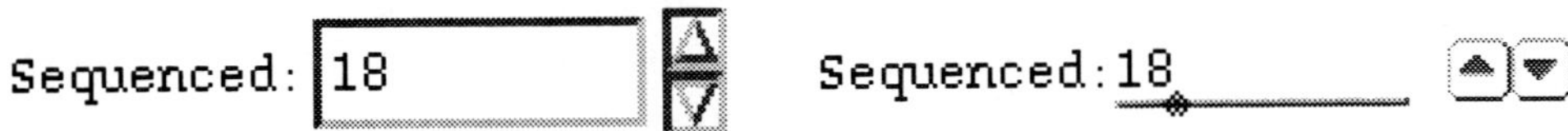

OI_seq_entry_field

11.1   Description

An OI_seq_entry_field is an OI_entry_field with special capabilities to handle sequenced entries. There are two buttons that appear on the screen to the right of the data entry area; the button labeled with an up arrow is used to increment the entry, and the button labeled with the down arrow is used to decrement it.

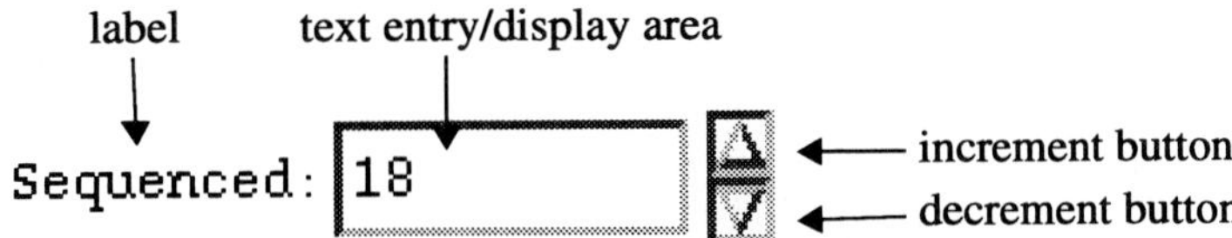

Figure 11-1   Parts of an OI_seq_entry_field, Motif

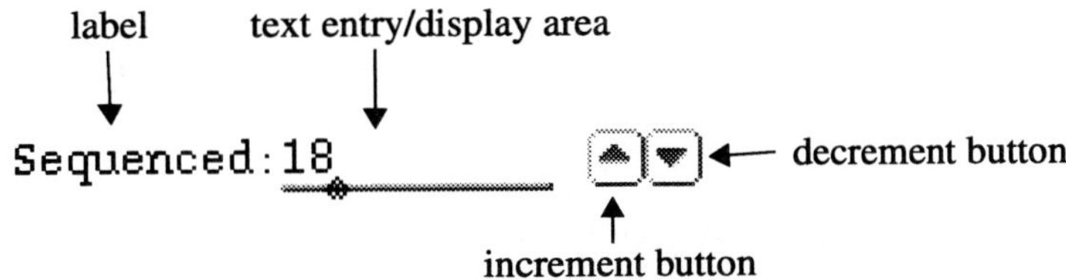

Figure 11-2   Parts of an OI_seq_entry_field, OPEN LOOK

The default OI_seq_entry_field object handles base 10 integers. Each time the user activates the increment button, the default OI increment function is executed that reads the value in the data entry area, increments it, and displays the new value in the data entry area. Similarly, if the user activates the decrement button, the default OI decrement function is executed to decrement the displayed value. Any character entered into the data entry area is validated by the default OI character validation function before the character is inserted into the field; only digits and the characters "+" and "-" are considered valid. There is no default end-of-entry validation performed.

You can supply different increment and decrement functions (see **set_increment** and **set_decrement** below) to tailor an **OI_seq_entry_field** object to handle any form of sequence, non-numeric as well as numeric. If you register your own increment or decrement callbacks, the default increment and decrement callbacks are not executed. In this case, you are responsible for displaying the new incremented or decremented value in your callback by calling the **OI_entry_field** member function **set_text**. Similarly, you can register per-character validation callbacks or end-of-entry validation callbacks using the **OI_entry_field** member functions.

You might use an **OI_seq_entry_field** object to allow the user to enter hexadecimal numbers, such as a memory address; this example is shown in Program 11-1 on page 11-9.

11.2   Class Tree

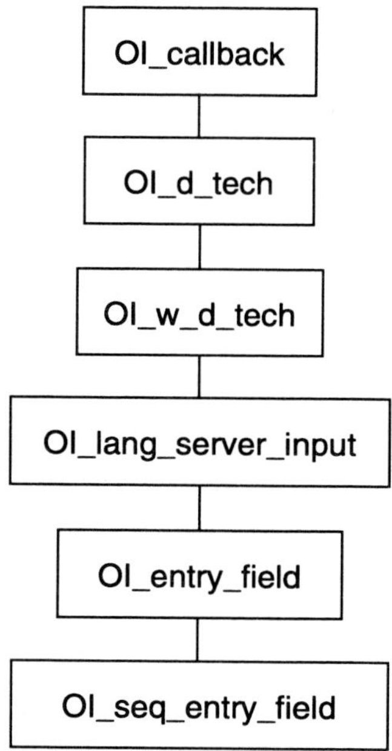

11.3   Runtime Interaction

To increment the entry by one unit click the SELECT mouse button on the increment button to the right of the data entry area. Click on the decrement button to decrement the entry by one unit. Depress and hold the SELECT mouse button over the increment button to repeatedly increment the entry, one unit at a time, until you release the mouse button. Similarly, depress and hold the SELECT mouse button over the decrement button to repeatedly decrement the entry. To enter an entirely new value, type into the data entry area in the same fashion as you would into an **OI_entry_field** data entry area.

The default translations installed for an **OI_seq_entry_field** object allow you to increment the value by striking the Up Arrow Key on the keyboard while the input focus is on the object and decrement it by striking the Down Arrow Key. All default key translations for an OI_entry_field also work for an OI_seq_entry_field object.

11.4   OI_seq_entry_field Creation

oi_create_seq_entry_field   (Free-standing function)

```
OI_seq_entry_field *oi_create_seq_entry_field(
    const char          *namp,          // pointer to name for object
    OI_number           dsp_len,        // number chars in text entry area
    const char          *lbl=NULL,      // string for label
    const char          *dflt_ent=NULL, // string for default entry
    OI_number           max_len=0)      // max number of chars in field
```

The arguments for oi_create_seq_entry_field are identical to those for oi_create_entry_field. If *lbl* is not NULL, it is used as a label for the entry field and is placed to the left of the text entry area. If you omit *lbl*, it defaults to NULL. If *dflt_ent* is not NULL, it is used as the default entry and the initial text value. If you omit *dflt_ent*, it defaults to NULL.

dsp_len is the number of character positions to be displayed in the text entry area, and *max_len* is the number of characters to be stored in the internal representation. You must specify *dsp_len*, but you may omit *max_len*, in which case it defaults to the same length as *dsp_len*. If not omitted, *max_len* must be greater than or equal to *dsp_len*. If *max_len* > *dsp_len*, the user can scroll the characters displayed in the text entry area so that *max_len* characters can be entered.

11.5   Base Class Member Functions

You can use all of the member functions of OI_d_tech and OI_entry_field for an OI_seq_entry_field object. Note that set_click is defined specifically for an OI_entry_field; this definition applies to an OI_seq_entry_field as well.

11.6   OI_seq_entry_field Member Functions

11.6.1   Increment/Decrement Rate Interval

set_interval   (Member function)

```
void OI_seq_entry_field::set_interval(
    OI_number                   rate)       // increment or decrement rate
```

set_interval sets the rate, in milliseconds, at which the sequential entry field's value changes when the increment or decrement button is held down. The default is 250 milliseconds.

interval   (Member function)

```
OI_number OI_seq_entry_field::interval( )
```

interval returns the current rate, in milliseconds, at which the sequential entry field's value changes when the increment or decrement button is held down.

11.6.2   End-of-entry Validation

Normally, if you register an end-of-entry validation callback function, OI invokes it only upon completion of an entry in the data entry area (that is, when the user strikes the Return key), not when the entry is incremented or decremented using the increment and decrement display buttons. In other words, the default increment and decrement callback functions do not call the end-of-entry validation procedure. You can change this arrangement using the following functions.

is_inc_dec_chk   (Member function)

```
OI_bool OI_seq_entry_field::is_inc_dec_chk( )
```

is_inc_dec_chk returns **OI_yes** if the end-of-entry validation procedure (if any) will be called by the default increment and decrement functions; otherwise **is_inc_dec_chk** returns **OI_no**.

allow_inc_dec_chk   (Member function)

```
void OI_seq_entry_field::allow_inc_dec_chk( )
```

allow_inc_dec_chk causes the end-of-entry validation callback function (if any) to be called from the default increment and decrement functions.

disallow_inc_dec_chk   (Member function)

```
void OI_seq_entry_field::disallow_inc_dec_chk( )
```

disallow_inc_dec_chk restores the default state, where the increment and decrement functions do not call the end-of-entry validation procedure.

def_c_check   (Member function)

```
OI_ef_char_chk_status OI_seq_entry_field::def_c_check(
    OI_entry_field          *efp,        // object where char was entered
    void                    *argp,       // arbitrary argument
    OI_ef_char_chk_status   prv_stat,    // previous char check return value, if any
    OI_number               psn,         // position of character in entry
    char                    c)           // character entered
```

def_c_check is the default character check function. You should not call this function yourself; you should use this function as the first argument to **set_char_check** if you want to restore the default character check callback. **def_c_check** allows the entry of any digit, and the "+" and "-" characters.

11.6.3   Increment-Decrement Callback Functions

If you supply your own increment and decrement functions, you can tailor **OI_seq_entry_field** to handle any form of sequence, non-numeric as well as numeric. If you register your own increment or decrement callbacks, the default increment and decrement callbacks are not executed; you are responsible for displaying the new incremented or decremented value from within your callback. Also, if you have registered an end-of-entry validation callback function and wish it to be called when the entry is incremented or decremented using the increment or decrement display buttons, you must call it yourself from within your increment and decrement callback procedures. You can call is_inc_dec_chk from the increment and decrement procedures to determine whether or not to call the end-of-entry callback.

set_increment   (Member function)

```
void OI_seq_entry_field::set_increment(
     OI_ef_sequence_fnp      fnp,              // pointer to callback function
     void                    *argp=NULL)       // arbitrary argument for fnp


void OI_seq_entry_field::set_increment(
     OI_callback             *objp,            // memfnp's object
     OI_ef_sequence_memfnp memfnp,             // pointer to callback member function
     void                    *argp=NULL)       // arbitrary argument for memfnp
```

The **set_increment** functions register a callback function to be invoked whenever the user activates the increment button in the **OI_seq_entry_field** object. This callback is identified within OI as a **cbSeqIncCheck** callback function (see Section 6.18, "Determining and Adding Callbacks; Multiple Callbacks," on page 6-117). If your increment function is a member function, when it is invoked it will be called as if you had written *objp->memfnp*. See Section 2.5, "Callbacks and Event-Driven Programming," on page 2-16 for more explanation.

argp is optional, and can be any valid expression that can be cast to a pointer. You can use it to pass additional information to the function *fnp* or *memfnp*.

Writing the Increment Callback Function

If the **cbSeqIncCheck** callback function is not a member function, write it in this form:

```
OI_ef_sequence_status  fn(
     OI_seq_entry_field        *sefp,       // OI_seq_entry_field to be
                                            //   incremented
     void                      *argp,       // arbitrary argument
     OI_ef_sequence_status     prv_stat)    // status from previous increment
                                            //   callback, if any
```

and if the **cbSeqIncCheck** callback function is a member function, write it in this form:

```
OI_ef_sequence_status  obj_class::memfn(
     OI_seq_entry_field        *sefp,       // OI_seq_entry_field to be
                                            //   incremented
     void                      *argp,       // arbitrary argument
     OI_ef_sequence_status     prv_stat)    // status from previous increment
                                            //   callback, if any
```

where *obj_class* is the class of the object whose member function is *memfn*.

When your callback function is invoked, *argp* will be the argument specified in the **set_increment** call.

prv_stat will be the return value of the **cbSeqIncCheck** function, if any, called before this one for this increment. If this is the only **cbSeqIncCheck** callback function registered for the entry field, *prv_stat* will be OI_ef_sequence_ok. If there are multiple cbSeqIncCheck callbacks for the sequential entry field—that is, if you have registered other cbSeqIncCheck callbacks for this sequential entry field using the OI_d_tech member function callback_add (or you have registered this one using callback_add)—and if the order of registration dictates that another callback is called before this one, then *prv_stat* will be the return value from the previous callback.

The increment function should operate as follows:
- Retrieve the existing string value using *sefp*->part_text.
- Increment it in whatever manner is necessary.
- Reset the text to the new string value using *sefp*->set_text. The second argument to set_text determines whether or not OI executes the end-of-entry validation routine.
- Return OI_ef_sequence_ok if successful and OI_ef_sequence_bad otherwise.

def_increment   (Member function)

```
OI_ef_sequence_status OI_seq_entry_field::def_increment(
    OI_seq_entry_field      *efp,        // pointer to OI_seq_entry_field
    void                    *argp,       // arbitrary argument
    OI_ef_sequence_status   prv_stat)    // previous increment return value, if any
```

def_increment is the default increment function for an OI_seq_entry_field object. To restore the default increment function, you should call set_increment with def_increment as its *memfnp* argument.

set_decrement   (Member function)

```
void OI_seq_entry_field::set_decrement(
    OI_ef_sequence_fnp      fnp,          // pointer to callback function
    void                    *argp=NULL)   // arbitrary argument for fnp
```

```
void OI_seq_entry_field::set_decrement(
    OI_callback             *objp,              // memfnp's object
    OI_ef_sequence_memfnp memfnp,              // pointer to callback member function
    void                    *argp=NULL)   // arbitrary argument for memfnp
```

The routine registered by set_decrement should be identical to that of set_increment except that it performs a decrement instead of an increment. This callback is identified within OI as a cbSeqDecCheck callback function (see Section 6.18, "Determining and Adding Callbacks; Multiple Callbacks," on page 6-117).

def_decrement   (Member function)

```
OI_ef_sequence_status OI_seq_entry_field::def_decrement(
    OI_seq_entry_field      *efp,        // pointer to OI_seq_entry_field
    void                    *argp,       // arbitrary argument
    OI_ef_sequence_status   prv_stat)    // previous increment return value, if any
```

def_decrement is the default decrement function for an **OI_seq_entry_field** object. To restore the default decrement function, you should call **set_decrement** with **def_decrement** as its *memfnp* argument.

11.7   An OI_seq_entry_field Programming Example

Program 11-1 shows a program to enter, increment, or decrement positive hexadecimal integers. It illustrates how you can use an **OI_seq_entry_field** object with non-numeric characters. Note that in order to allow the user to enter alphanumeric characters, we register a character validation routine, **validate_hex**. This validation routine only allows entry of characters used to represent hexadecimal numbers. The routines **inc_hex** and **dec_hex** perform the increment and decrement of the hexadecimal number, respectively.

For brevity, we have not checked for integers larger than 0xffffffff.

```c
#include <OI/oi.H>                              /* SeqHex.C */
#include <stdlib.h>

int main(int argc, char** argv)
{
        OI_ef_sequence_status  inc_hex(OI_seq_entry_field*,void*,
                                        OI_ef_sequence_status);
        OI_ef_sequence_status  dec_hex(OI_seq_entry_field*,void*,
                                        OI_ef_sequence_status);
        OI_ef_char_chk_status  validate_hex(OI_entry_field*, void*,
                                        OI_ef_char_chk_status, OI_number,char);

        OI_connection          *conp;
        OI_app_window          *wp;
        OI_seq_entry_field     *sep;

    if (conp = OI_init(&argc,argv,"SeqHex")) {
        wp = oi_create_app_window("main_window",1,1,"Hex Demo");
        wp->set_layout(OI_layout_row);

        sep = oi_create_seq_entry_field("hex",7,"Hex Integer: ","0");
        sep->layout_associated_object(wp,1,1,OI_active);
        sep->set_char_check(validate_hex);
        sep->set_increment(inc_hex);
        sep->set_decrement(dec_hex);

        wp->set_associated_object(wp->root( ),OI_def_loc,OI_def_loc,OI_active);
        OI_begin_interaction( );
        OI_fini( );
    }
}


OI_ef_char_chk_status validate_hex(OI_entry_field*, void*,
                                OI_ef_char_chk_status stat, OI_number psn, char c)
{
        OI_ef_char_chk_status  ret_val;

    ret_val = OI_ef_char_chk_bad;
    if (stat == OI_ef_char_chk_insert) {
        if (psn >= 0) {
            if (isxdigit(c))
                                ret_val = OI_ef_char_chk_insert;
        }
        else
            ret_val = OI_ef_char_chk_insert;
    }
    return (ret_val);
}
```

```c
OI_ef_sequence_status inc_hex(OI_seq_entry_field *sep, void*,
                                        OI_ef_sequence_status stat)
{
        long                    nbr;
        char                    string[10];

    if (stat == OI_ef_sequence_ok) {
        if (sep->part_text( ) == NULL)
            sep->set_text("0",OI_no);
        nbr = strtol(sep->part_text( ),NULL,16);
        nbr++;
        sprintf(string,"%x",nbr);
        sep->set_text(string,OI_no);
    }
    return(stat);
}

OI_ef_sequence_status dec_hex(OI_seq_entry_field *sep, void*,
                                        OI_ef_sequence_status stat)
{
        long                    nbr;
        char                    string[10];

    if (stat == OI_ef_sequence_ok) {
        if (sep->part_text( ) == NULL)
            sep->set_text("0",OI_no);
        nbr = strtol(sep->part_text( ),NULL,16);
        if (nbr)
            nbr--;
        sprintf(string,"%x",nbr);
        sep->set_text(string,OI_no);
    }
    return(stat);
}
```

Program 11-1   Hexadecimal Integer Entry (SeqHex.C)

11.8   Resources

All resources from an OI_seq_entry_field object's base classes are available to it; in addition, OI fetches the resources shown in Table 11-1. For more information on resource management, see Chapter 39, "The OI Resource Mechanism."

Table 11-1   OI_seq_entry_field Resources

Resource	Description	Possible Values	Default Value
incDecChk	If on, an increment or decrement operation will cause the end of entry callback to be executed.	Boolean	false
interval	Specifies the rate, in milliseconds, at which the sequential entry field's value changes when the increment or decrement button is held down.	Positive integer	250

11.9   Translations

All translations from an OI_seq_entry_field object's base classes are available to it; in addition the translations shown in Table 11-2 are available to it. See Chapter 40, "The OI Translation Mechanism" for a description of the Event Sequence entries in these tables as well as additional information on how to read these tables.

Table 11-2   OI_seq_entry_field Default Translations

Event Sequence	Action Functions Called
<Key>Up:	paint_increment(down) increment( ) paint_increment(up)
<Key>Down:	paint_decrement(down) decrement( ) paint_decrement(up)

Table 11-3 describes the actions taken by the action functions.

Table 11-3   OI_seq_entry_field Translation Functions

Function	Action
decrement(n)	Calls the decrement function n times. If n is omitted, n=1.
increment(n)	Calls the increment function n times. If n is omitted, n=1.

Table 11-3 OI_seq_entry_field Translation Functions

Function	Action
paint_decrement(updn)	Paints the decrement button. If updn="DOWN" the button is painted pressed down; if updn="UP" it is painted normal.
paint_increment(updn)	Paints the increment button. If updn="DOWN" the button is painted pressed down; if updn="UP" it is painted normal.

11.10 Callback Functions

Table 11-4 lists the callbacks available for an OI_seq_entry_field object and the page number where the callback is documented. In addition, all of the callbacks from an OI_seq_entry_field object's base classes are available to it. See Section 6.18, "Determining and Adding Callbacks; Multiple Callbacks," on page 6-117 for additional information about manipulating callbacks.

Table 11-4 OI_seq_entry_field Callbacks

Callback Type	Callback Typedef	Description	Page Number
cbSeqIncCheck	OI_ef_sequence_fnp / memfnp	Increment callback function	11-5
cbSeqDecCheck	OI_ef_sequence_fnp / memfnp	Decrement callback function	11-6

Chapter 12

OI_menu

OI_menu Member Functions

The following functions are available to an **OI_menu** object, but are described in their own chapter.

OI_d_tech Member Functions

OI Programmer's Guide

OI_menu

12.1 Description

A menu provides a way to make one or more selections from a list of items. Menu items appear on the screen as a row, column or rectangular array of *menu cells*—objects which are children of the menu object.

OI_menu is the base class for all menu types. OI supports several different types of menus, but since all types are derived from OI_menu, you can use all OI_menu member functions for any type of menu. The logical relationships among the menu classes are shown in Figure 12-1. OI_menu has four subclasses, OI_basic_menu, OI_abbr_menu, OI_menu_box, and OI_scroll_menu. The subclasses of OI_basic_menu are, as you might expect, all the basic menu types. OI_abbr_menu (an abbreviated menu), OI_menu_box (a menu-box), and OI_scroll_menu (a scroll menu) are "wrappings" for the three basic menu types.

OI_basic_menu has three subclasses which define the selection characteristics and capabilities of a menu. These are OI_trans_menu, OI_excl_menu, and OI_poly_menu. OI_trans_menu (transient menu) is a menu consisting of *momentary-selection* items. OI_excl_menu (exclusive menu) is a menu consisting of *longterm-selection* items which allows at most one cell to be in the selected state at any time. OI_poly_menu (non-exclusive menu) is a menu consisting of longterm-selection items which allows any number of cells to be in the selected state at any time.

Momentary-selection cells trigger a callback function when selected by the user. They then return to the deselected state immediately after returning from the callback function. *longterm-selection* cells also trigger a callback function (if one is registered) when selected by the user. However, they then stay in the selected state until deselected by the user. Upon deselection, the callback function again is triggered and the cell remains in the deselected state. You can query the state of a menu at any time to determine which cells are in the selected state.

You will never create a menu of type OI_menu, OI_basic_menu, or OI_trans_menu. These classes exist only to provide properties and functions common to their derived classes. You may create menus of any other menu subclass.

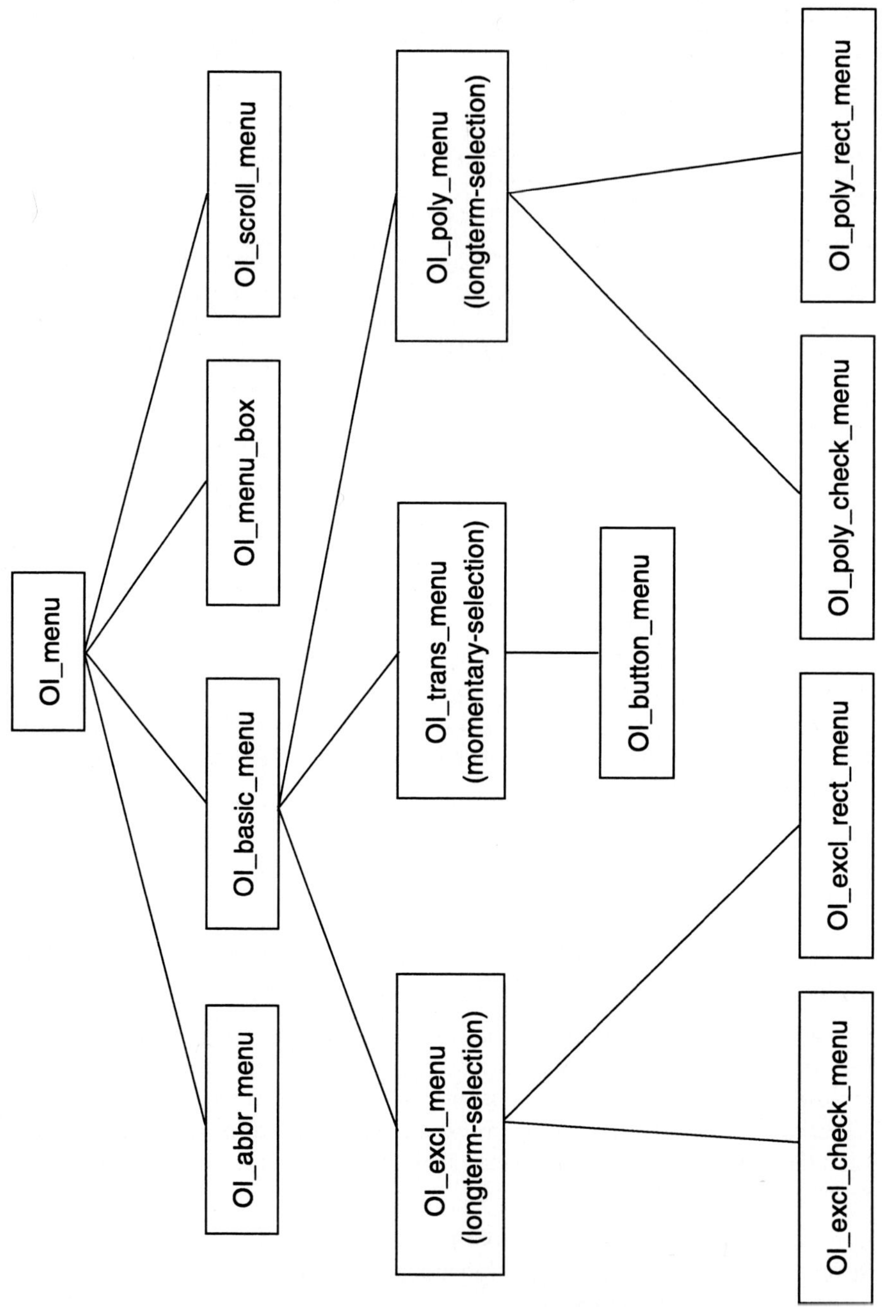

Figure 12-1   OI_Menu Class Tree

OI_abbr_menu, OI_menu_box, and OI_scroll_menu are essentially "containers" for any of the menu classes on the bottom two rows of Figure 12-1. An OI_abbr_menu is an abbreviated menu; it is a shortened version of an OI_trans_menu or an OI_excl_menu, and is described in Chapter 17, "OI_abbr_menu." An OI_menu_box is a box into which you can place menus of different types and have them behave as a single menu; it is discussed in Chapter 35, "OI_menu_box." A scroll menu, OI_scroll_menu, contains viewport onto a menu object, surrounded by scroll bars that the user may use to scroll the menu items—in general, there are more items in the menu than can be seen in the viewport at one time. Scroll menus are discussed in Chapter 34, "OI_scroll_menu."

The cells in a menu are independent OI objects of type OI_menu_cell which are children of the menu. Any OI_menu_cell object may be used in any type of menu, and can be created independently of the menu itself. The behavior and appearance of a menu cell is determined by the type of menu it is associated with. A menu cell may be moved from one menu to another, causing its appearance and behavior to change to correspond to that required by its new parent. Figure 12-2 through Figure 12-6 show menus and menu cells for each of the five types of menus (those on the bottom two rows of Figure 12-1) which are available in OI (still excluding the "containers," OI_abbr_menu, OI_menu_box, and OI_scroll_menu). In these figures, the Motif version is on the left; OPEN LOOK is on the right.

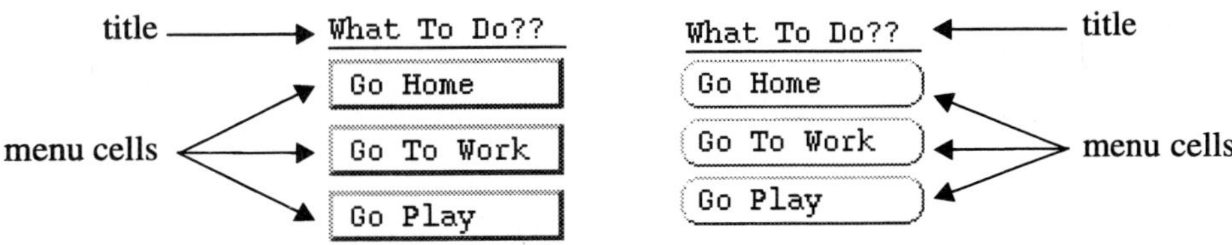

Figure 12-2   Parts of an OI_button_menu

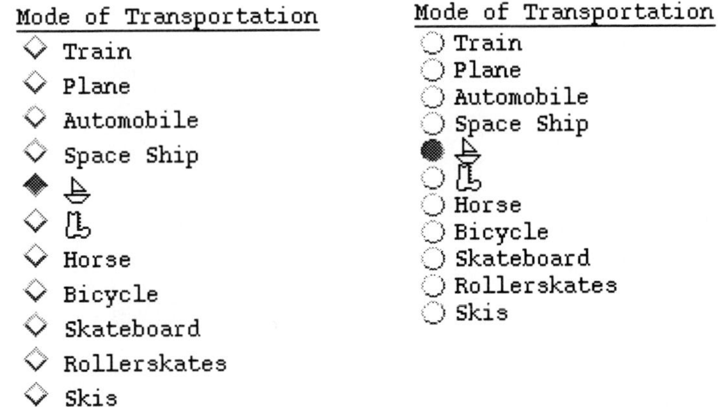

Figure 12-3   OI_excl_check_menu

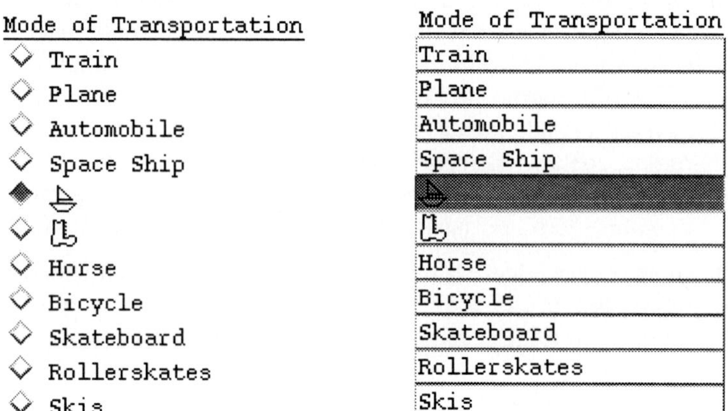

Figure 12-4   OI_excl_rect_menu

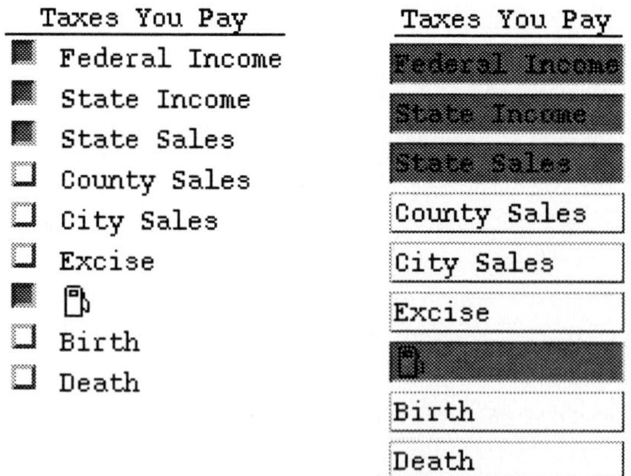

Figure 12-5   OI_poly_check_menu

Figure 12-6   OI_poly_rect_menu

Note that if you create an OI_excl_rect_menu or an OI_poly_rect_menu object and your application is run using the Motif model, you get a check menu, not a rectangle menu. This is because Motif does not support a free-standing rectangle menu. However, if you use OI_scroll_menu as a wrapping for an OI_excl_rect_menu or an OI_poly_rect_menu, and your application is run using the Motif model, you in fact get a rectangle menu. This is because Motif supports scrolled rectangle menus for these menu uses.

When you have a list of items which should cause immediate actions, use a *button menu* (a transient menu). An example would be a menu which is used to initiate some action—send mail, write a file, delete a record, etc.

If you have items which are mutually exclusive and where information must be retained for later inspection, use an *exclusive menu*. For example, an exclusive menu could be used to indicate the current insertion mode in a word processor—replace mode or insert mode. Another example would be the display format for a number—decimal, octal, or hexadecimal. In both of these cases, the information carried by the menu is retained after the selection is made, so the program can query it at a later point in time, and so the user can see what the current selection is.

Use a *poly menu* in situations similar to the ones for which you would use an exclusive menu, but where more than one item can be selected simultaneously. A poly menu allows any number, 0 through total number of cells, to be in the selected state. An example would be a menu containing a list of diagnostics, where the user could select which diagnostics should be run.

A menu may have a default cell. If you set a default cell for a menu, the user can activate it using some shortcuts, but otherwise it is no different from any other menu cell. The default cell has an extra outline if the application is running using the OPEN LOOK model. In the Motif model, an extra bevel appears. Figure 12-7 shows a menu with the cell labeled "Go Play" as the default cell.

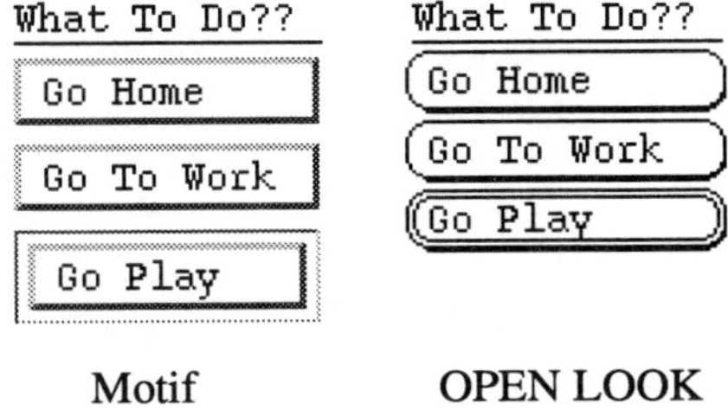

Figure 12-7   Button Menu with Default Cell

The cells in a menu are numbered in a monotonically increasing sequence. The top (or left) cell is number 0; moving down the menu (or to the right) the cell numbers increase by one for each cell. If a menu is created using an OI_cell_spec structure (see below), the cells are numbered and positioned in the menu in the order in which they are declared in the structure. If a menu is created using a vector of pointers to cells, the cell numbers are undefined until the cells are added to a menu. When they are added to a menu, the cells are numbered and positioned in the menu in the order they appear in the vector of cell pointers. If a cell is unparented from a menu, the cell numbers of all cells which follow it are decreased by one. If a new cell is added to a menu, the cell numbers of all cells which follow it are increased by one.

12.1.1   Creating Menus and Menu Cells

When you create a menu, the pointer you use should be as high up the class tree as possible. For example:

```
OI_menu *mp;
mp = oi_create_button_menu(...);
```

The main reason for this is to make things easier for yourself during code development and maintenance. Suppose you create a button menu using a pointer which is declared to be of type OI_button_menu*. You then write several separate functions using the menu, and each time you declare the pointer to be of type OI_button_menu*. Two months down the road you decide that since the screen has become so crowded, what you really need instead is an abbreviated menu; now you have to go through all your routines and change the pointers from type OI_button_menu* to type OI_abbr_menu*. If you had declared the button menu originally to be of type OI_menu*, then you would only need to change one line of code: the create menu call.

There are two forms of the create function for each menu, one for each of the two situations you may encounter when you create a menu. If you know the menu cell contents in advance, you use the menu create function (for example, oi_create_button_menu) with an OI_cell_spec* as the third argument. In this case, you declare a static OI_cell_spec structure (see Chapter 13, "OI_menu_cell") with the information for each menu cell. The menu creation mechanism automatically generates the individual cell objects and parents them to the menu object. Thus, the menu cells are created *implicitly*.

If you do not know the cell contents in advance, you create the menu cells *explicitly* (before creating the menu) by calling the function oi_create_menu_cell once for each cell, and store the pointers to the cells in a vector. You can either allocate space for the pointers to the cells using an array, or, if you cannot put an upper bound on the number of cells before execution time, you can use malloc or new to get space for the array of pointers. You then create the menu using the menu creation function with an OI_menu_cell** as the third argument, passing it the pointer to the array of cell pointers.

Regardless of the way you create a menu, its cells are still OI_menu_cell objects, and you can use any of the member functions for an OI_menu_cell for these cells.

Once a menu is created, you can add new cells to it using the member function add_cell, or remove existing cells from it using the OI_d_tech member functions unparent or del or the C++ delete operator.

Program 12-1 and Program 12-2 show examples of both ways to create a menu. They each create the same menu; it is the button menu shown at the head of this chapter. The same mechanism can be used for any type of menu.

```
#include <OI/oi.H>                              /* BtnMnuImplicit.C */

int main(int argc, char **argv)
{
          OI_connection      *conp;
          OI_app_window      *wp;
          OI_menu            *mp;

       static  OI_cell_spec   cells[] = {
           {"Home","Go Home"},
           {"Work","Go To Work"},
           {"Play","Go Play"},
           };

    if (conp = OI_init(&argc,argv,"BtnMnuImplicit")) {
        wp = oi_create_app_window("main",1,1,"Buttons");
        wp->set_layout(OI_layout_row);
        mp = oi_create_button_menu("button_menu",OI_count(cells),&cells[0],
                                    OI_vertical,"What To Do?? ");
        mp->layout_associated_object(wp,2,10,OI_active);
        wp->set_associated_object(wp->root( ),OI_def_loc,OI_def_loc,OI_active);
        OI_begin_interaction( );
        OI_fini( );
    }
}
```

Program 12-1   Menu Creation: Implicitly Created Menu Cells (BtnMnuImplicit.C)

Note the use of the macro **OI_count** in Program 12-1. It returns the number of elements in the array supplied as the argument.

```
#include<OI/oi.H>                              /* BtnMnuExplicit.C */

int main(int argc,char **argv)
{
            OI_connection        *conp;
            OI_app_window        *wp;
            OI_menu              *mp;
            OI_menu_cell         *cellp[3];    // pointers to cells for menu

     if(conp=OI_init(&argc,argv,"BtnMnuExplicit")){
         wp=oi_create_app_window("main",1,1,"Buttons");
         wp->set_layout(OI_layout_row);

         cellp[0]=oi_create_menu_cell("Home","Go Home");
         cellp[1]=oi_create_menu_cell("Work","Go To Work");
         cellp[2]=oi_create_menu_cell("Play","Go Play");

         mp=oi_create_button_menu("button_menu",
                          OI_count(cellp),&cellp[0],OI_vertical,"WhatToDo??");
         mp->layout_associated_object(wp,2,10,OI_active);
         wp->set_associated_object(wp->root( ),OI_def_loc,OI_def_loc,OI_active);
         OI_begin_interaction( );
         OI_fini( );
     }
}
```

Program 12-2   Menu Creation: Explicitly Created Menu Cells (BtnMnuExplicit.C)

When you create a menu using a vector of pointers to explicitly-created OI_menu_cell objects (not a vector of OI_cell_specs), the actual OI_menu_cell objects you created are used in the menu; they are not copied or cloned. Consequently, you should not reuse the same OI_menu_cell objects in creating another menu. If you attempt it, they will be unparented from the old menu when they are inserted in a new menu.

On the other hand, you can reuse OI_cell_spec definitions in more than one menu, since the create functions create new OI_menu_cell objects from the OI_cell_specs each time.

12.1.2   Defining Menu-Selection Actions

If you wish some specific action to occur when the user clicks on a menu cell, you must write an action callback routine for that cell and then register the routine in the call to oi_create_menu_cell, in the static OI_cell_spec structure, or using the OI_menu_cell member function change_action. You will usually register callbacks for cells in a button menu, since a button menu does not remember its state, and the action callback function is the only way to perform any action for a button menu. For an exclusive menu or a non-exclusive (poly) menu, you may wish not to register any callbacks for the cells. In this case, no action is taken when the user changes a cell from the deselected to the selected state or from the selected state to the deselected state. Instead, at some later point in time you query the menu as to which cells are selected, if any, and perform the specific actions for cells in the selected state.

If you do register action callbacks for the cells in a menu, they function as follows: whenever the user clicks on a menu cell, the action callback routine for that cell is executed, regardless of whether the click causes the cell to go from the deselected state to the selected state, or from the selected state to the deselected state. Note that the actions performed for the three different types of menus when a cell is clicked on are slightly different:

In a *transient (button) menu*, clicking on a cell causes the cell to change to the selected state. The cell fires (the action callback function is executed), and then the cell returns to the deselected state.

In a *non-exclusive (poly) menu*, clicking on a cell may change the cell from the deselected state to the selected state or from the selected state to the deselected state, and in either case, the cell "fires" (the action callback function is executed). You may determine which transition is occurring using the OI_menu_cell member function **selected**.

When the user clicks on a cell in an *exclusive menu*, more than one cell may be affected. If the cell which is clicked on is in the deselected state, the cell (if any) that was previously in the selected state changes to the deselected state, and the current cell changes to the selected state. In this case, two callbacks are made: first the function registered for the cell that was previously in the selected state is called, then the function for the cell being selected.

Because for both exclusive and non-exclusive menus OI invokes the cell's action callback both when the cell is selected and when it is deselected, you need to make your action callbacks for these menu types have a structure similar to this:

```
void cell_callback (OI_menu_cell *cellp, void*, OI_number)
{
    if (cellp->selected( )) {
        // do stuff here; the cell has just been selected
    }
    else
        // do stuff here; the cell has just been deselected
    }
    return;
}
```

Example 12-1   Callback Structure for a Cell in a Poly Menu

Program 12-3 shows a button menu with action callback functions registered for each button. In this case, when any menu button is activated, the menu cell's name and label are displayed in the window from which the program was started. Figure 12-8 shows this program in action.

```
#include <OI/oi.H>                           /* MenuAction.C */

int main(int argc, char **argv)
{
                void            fire_cell(OI_menu_cell*,void*,OI_number);

                OI_connection  *conp;
                OI_app_window  *wp;
                OI_menu        *mp;

        static  OI_cell_spec   cells[] = {
                {"world","Hello, world!",&fire_cell},
                {"universe","Hello,universe!",&fire_cell},
                };

    if (conp = OI_init(&argc,argv,"MenuAction")) {
        wp = oi_create_app_window("main",100,50,"Cell Fire Demo");
        mp = oi_create_button_menu("popup",
                            OI_count(cells),&cells[0],OI_horizontal);
        wp->set_main_menu(mp);
        wp->set_associated_object(wp->root( ),OI_def_loc,OI_def_loc,OI_active);
        OI_begin_interaction( );
        OI_fini( );
    }
}

void fire_cell (OI_menu_cell *cellp, void *, OI_number)
{
    printf("name:\"%s\" label:\"%s\"\n",cellp->name( ),cellp->label( ));
    return;
}
```

Program 12-3 Menu With Action Callbacks (MenuAction.C)

Motif   OPEN LOOK

Figure 12-8 Menu With Action Callbacks

Program 12-4 shows an **OI_poly_check_menu** with choices for ice cream toppings. The user can change these selections at will, then when the user clicks on the "Make Sundae" button, the button callback is activated. This callback queries the poly menu and prints out a list of toppings to put on the sundae. Figure 12-9 shows this program in action.

```c
#include <OI/oi.H>                            /* SelectedQuery.C */
int main(int argc, char **argv)
{
                void            make_sundae(OI_menu_cell*,void*,OI_number);

            OI_connection   *conp;
            OI_app_window   *wp;
            OI_menu         *mp;
            OI_menu_cell    *cellp;

        static  OI_cell_spec   topping_cells[] = {
                {"nuts","Nuts"},
                {"chips","Chocolate Chips"},
                {"mm","M&M's"},
                {"cherry","Cherry"},
                {"cream","Whipped Cream"},
                {"fudge","Chocolate Fudge"},
                {"sprinkles","Sprinkles"},
                };

    if (conp = OI_init(&argc,argv,"SelectedQuery")) {
        wp = oi_create_app_window("main",100,50,"Sundae Shop");
        wp->set_layout(OI_layout_row);

        mp = oi_create_poly_check_menu("toppings",OI_count(topping_cells),
                            &topping_cells[0],OI_vertical,"Toppings");
        mp->layout_associated_object(wp,10,10,OI_active);
        cellp = oi_create_menu_cell("make_sundae","Make Sundae",&make_sundae,mp);
        mp = oi_create_button_menu("main_menu",1,&cellp,OI_horizontal);

        wp->set_main_menu(mp);
        wp->set_associated_object(wp->root( ),OI_def_loc,OI_def_loc,OI_active);
        OI_begin_interaction( );
        OI_fini( );
    }
}
void make_sundae (OI_menu_cell *, void *argp, OI_number)
{
            OI_menu             *mp;        // pointer to topping menu
            OI_menu_cell        *cellp;     // pointer to selected cell in topping menu

    mp = (OI_menu*) argp;
    printf("Make a sundae with the following toppings:\n");
    for (cellp=mp->next_selection(NULL) ; cellp ; cellp=mp->next_selection(cellp))
        printf(" %s\n",cellp->label( ));
    return;
}
```

Program 12-4   Non-exclusive Menu with Later Query (SelectedQuery.C)

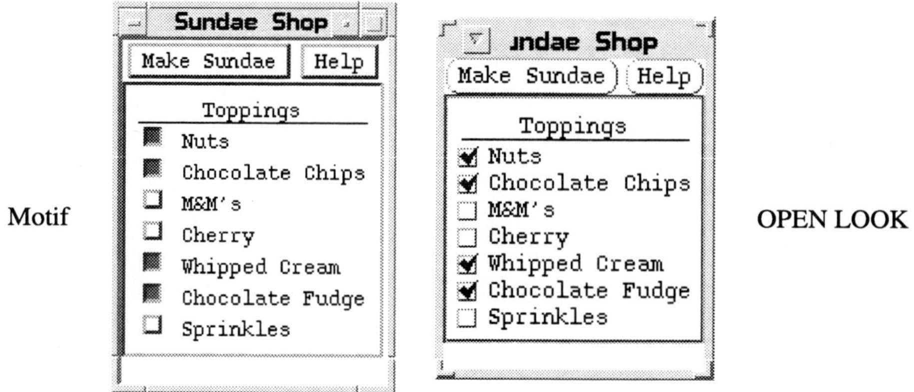

Figure 12-9   Non-exclusive Menu with Later Query

12.1.3   Pop-up Menus

A *pop-up* menu is one that is ordinarily not visible, but becomes visible when the user depresses the MENU mouse button while the pointer is on the menu's parent object (or in the case of a window manager, on the root window). To make a pop-up menu, create a normal menu, then associate it, using **set_associated_object**, with the object (or root) from which the pop-up is to be activated. (Never use **layout_associated_object** for a menu which is to be a pop-up—it doesn't make sense, and confuses the layout mechanism.) In the call to **set_associated_object** set both the x and y locations to **OI_def_loc**, and set the state of the menu to **OI_active_not_displayed**. OI takes care of the rest; when the user presses the mouse button on the parent object, the menu pops up, the user can move the pointer to the desired selection, and release the button. The action callback function for the selected cell is executed, and then the pop-up menu is removed from the screen. You may use **OI_scroll_menu** or **OI_menu_box** objects as pop-up menus, as well as any of the basic menus.

Note that if the pop-up menu is a non-exclusive (poly) menu, the user can make only one choice, then the menu disappears. For this reason, you may decide never to use a poly menu as a pop-up. If you do wish to use one, however, you can make it possible for the user to make more than one selection without having to re-pop-up the menu several times by making the menu a *tearoff* menu (Motif) or supplying the menu with a *pushpin* (OPEN LOOK) by using the member functions **allow_tearoff** or **allow_pushpin**, or the resource **pushpin**. A tearoff menu and a pushpin menu behave the same—the user "tears off" or "pins up" the pop-up menu, making it permanently visible. The user makes desired selections, keeps the menu around as long as desired, and then can dismiss the menu using the window manager or unpin the menu if the window manager has supplied a pushpin.

Program 12-5 shows a program which brings up an empty application window. Clicking or depressing the MENU mouse button in the window pops up the menu.

```
#include <OI/oi.H>                              /* PopUp.C */

int main(int argc, char **argv)
{
                OI_connection  *conp;
                OI_app_window  *wp;
                OI_menu        *mp;

        static  OI_cell_spec   cells[] = {
                {"step","Step"},
                {"next","Next"},
                {"cont","Continue"},
                };

    if (conp = OI_init(&argc,argv,"PopUp")) {
        wp = oi_create_app_window("main",200,100,"Popup Demo");

        mp = oi_create_button_menu("popup",OI_count(cells),
                                        &cells[0],OI_vertical,"Action");
        mp->set_associated_object(wp,OI_def_loc,OI_def_loc,
                                        OI_active_not_displayed);

        wp->set_associated_object(wp->root( ),OI_def_loc,OI_def_loc,OI_active);
        OI_begin_interaction( );
        OI_fini( );
    }
}
```

Program 12-5   Pop-up Menu (PopUp.C)

Figure 12-10 shows the results of running the pop-up menu example and depressing the MENU mouse button in the empty application window.

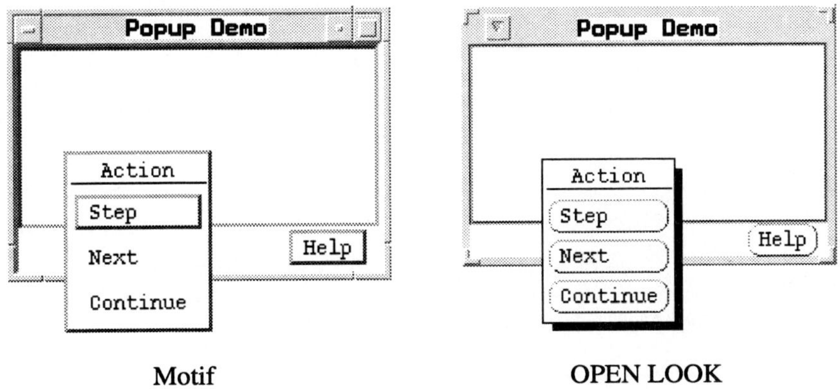

Motif   OPEN LOOK

Figure 12-10   Pop-up Menus

Figure 12-11 shows the same program with the following resource in the .Xdefaults file:

```
PopUp*popup*pushpin:            True
```

This figure shows on the left a menu popped up but not torn off or pinned and on the right a menu that has been torn off or pinned

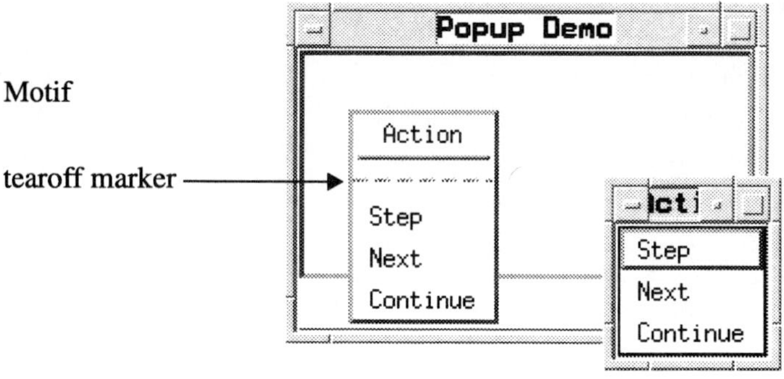

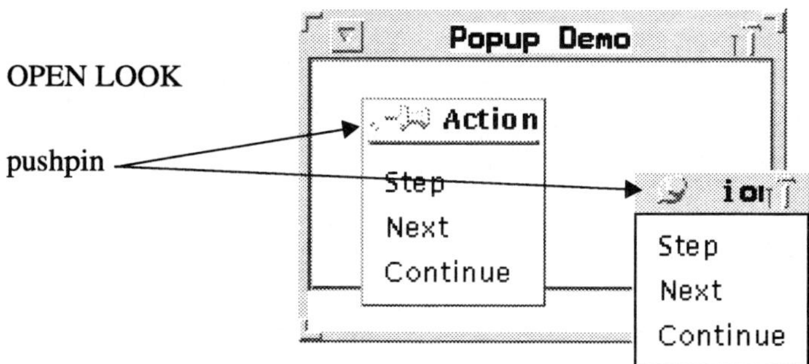

Figure 12-11 Tearoff and Pushpin Menus

12.1.4   Pull-down, Pull-right Menus (Submenus)

A pull-down or pull-right menu is one that is ordinarily not visible and which is parented to a cell in another menu; thus it is a *submenu* of the first menu. When the user depresses the mouse button with the pointer on its parent cell, the menu appears on the screen. (The particular interaction needed to get a submenu to appear varies slightly depending on the interaction model being used. See "Runtime Interaction," below.) If you create the parent menu with **OI_vertical** orientation, the submenu will be a pull-right menu—that is, the submenu will appear to the right of the parent cell. If you create the parent menu with OI_horizontal orientation, the submenu will be a pull-down menu—the submenu will appear below the parent cell. You can give the submenu either horizontal or vertical orientation, regardless of whether it is a pull-down or pull-right submenu. Submenus can be created either explicitly or implicitly, and nested to any level.

To *explicitly* create a submenu: use one of the menu create functions oi_create_*menutype* (for example, oi_create_button_menu) to create the submenu. Then proceed as you would for a pop-up menu, associating the submenu to the parent cell using set_associated_object (not layout_associated_object) with the menu cell from which the submenu is to be activated. In the call to set_associated_object, use OI_def_loc, OI_def_loc as the location, and set the state of the submenu to OI_active_not_displayed. As for pop-up menus, you may use any basic menu or an object of type OI_scroll_menu or OI_menu_box for a pull-down or pull-right submenu.

To *implicitly* create a submenu: specify the submenu and its cells using the OI_menu_spec and OI_cell_spec structures. In the parent cell's OI_cell_spec specification, set the OI_menu_spec* parameter to point to the OI_menu_spec for the submenu.

See Chapter 13, "OI_menu_cell," for complete specifications on creating submenus using OI_menu_spec.

Program 12-6 produces two implicitly created pull-down menus. Figure 12-12 shows the program in Program 12-6 running using both the OPEN LOOK and Motif models.

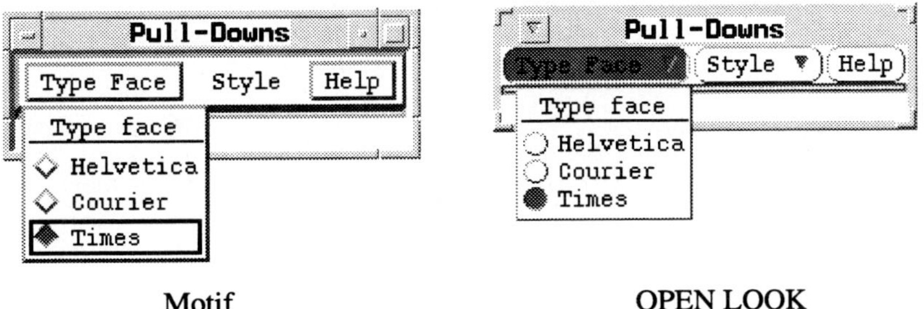

Figure 12-12   Pull-down Menus

```
#include <OI/oi.H>                        /* PullDownImp.C */

int main(int argc, char **argv)
{
                OI_connection  *conp;
                OI_app_window  *wp;
                OI_menu        *mp;

        static  OI_cell_spec   type_cells[] = {
                {"helvetica","Helvetica"},
                {"times","Times"},
                {"courier","Courier"},
                };
        static  OI_cell_spec   style_cells[] = {
                {"roman","Roman"},
                {"italic","Italic"},
                };
        static  OI_menu_spec   style_mnu =
                {"style_mnu",OI_count(style_cells),&style_cells[0],OI_vertical,
                                "Styles",0,&OI_excl_menu::clsp};
        static  OI_menu_spec   type_mnu =
                {"type_mnu",OI_count(type_cells),&type_cells[0],OI_vertical,
                                "Type Face",0,&OI_excl_menu::clsp};
        static  OI_cell_spec   text_cells[] = {
                {"tp_fac","Type Face",NULL,NULL,NULL_PMF,NULL,
                                OI_text_cell,&type_mnu},
                {"style","Style",NULL,NULL,NULL_PMF,NULL,
                                OI_text_cell,&style_mnu},
            };

    if (conp = OI_init(&argc,argv,"PullDownImp")) {
        wp = oi_create_app_window("main",1,1,"Pull-Downs");
        wp->set_layout(OI_layout_row);

        mp = oi_create_button_menu("text_spec_menu",OI_count(text_cells),
                                &text_cells[0],OI_horizontal);
        wp->set_main_menu(mp);
        wp->set_associated_object(wp->root( ),OI_def_loc,OI_def_loc,OI_active);

        OI_begin_interaction( );
        OI_fini( );
    }
}
```

Program 12-6   Implicitly Created Pull-down Menus (PullDownImp.C)

Program 12-7 shows two explicitly created pull-down menus.

```
#include <OI/oi.H>                               /* PullDownExp.C */

int main(int argc, char **argv)
{
                OI_connection  *conp;
                OI_app_window  *wp;
                OI_menu        *bmp;
                OI_menu        *mp;

        static  OI_cell_spec   type_cells[] = {
                {"helvetica","Helvetica"},
                {"courier","Courier"},
                {"times","Times"},
                };
        static  OI_cell_spec   style_cells[] = {
                {"plain","Plain"},
                {"italic","Italic"},
                };
        static  OI_cell_spec   text_cells[] = {
                {"tp_fac","Type Face"},
                {"style","Style"},
                };

    if (conp = OI_init(&argc,argv,"PullDownExp")) {
        wp = oi_create_app_window("main",1,1,"Pull-Downs");
        wp->set_layout(OI_layout_row);

        bmp = oi_create_button_menu("text_spec_menu",OI_count(text_cells),
                                    &text_cells[0],OI_horizontal);
        wp->set_main_menu(bmp);

        mp = oi_create_excl_check_menu("style_mnu",OI_count(style_cells),
                                    &style_cells[0],OI_vertical,"Styles");
        mp->set_associated_object(bmp->subobject("style"),OI_def_loc,OI_def_loc,
                                    OI_active_not_displayed);
        mp = oi_create_excl_check_menu("type_mnu",OI_count(type_cells),
                            &type_cells[0],OI_vertical,"Type face");
        mp->set_associated_object(bmp->subobject("tp_fac"),OI_def_loc,OI_def_loc,
                                    OI_active_not_displayed);
        wp->set_associated_object(wp->root( ),OI_def_loc,OI_def_loc,OI_active);
        OI_begin_interaction( );
        OI_fini( );
    }
}
```

Program 12-7   Explicitly Created Pull-down Menus (PullDownExp.C)

Figure 12-12 on page 12-15 shows the program in Program 12-7 running using both the OPEN LOOK and Motif models. (The applications created by Program 12-6 and Program 12-7 have identical appearance.)

When the application is run using an OPEN LOOK model, a menu cell which has an attached submenu shows a *submenu-marker* on its face—a triangular arrow indicating that a pull-down or pull-right menu will appear if the user properly activates the parent cell.

When the application is run using the Motif model, a cell which has an attached submenu appears *flat*—it does not have a button outline—if it is in a horizontal menu. If the menu is vertical, the cell with the attached submenu has an arrow marker similar to OPEN LOOK's submenu-marker.

12.2   Class Tree

See also Figure 12-1, "OI_Menu Class Tree," on page 12-2.

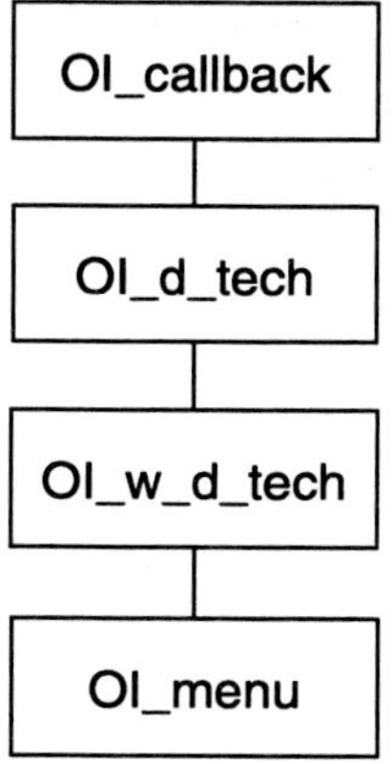

12.3   Runtime Interaction

12.3.1   Keyboard Traversal

A menu can have the keyboard input focus. Because of this, menus are part of the focus group keyboard traversal mechanism. All the rules regarding focus group traversal apply; see Section 6.14.1, "Focus Groups," on page 6-101 for a discussion of these. A menu's cells constitute a focus group. The translations which set up the keyboard traversal functionality are described in Chapter 13, "OI_menu_cell." The keyboard traversal functionality is discussed in Section 13.3, "Runtime Interaction," on page 13-5 and the translations which produce the keyboard traversals are shown in Section 13.8, "Translations," on page 13-36.

Runtime interaction for abbreviated menus is described in Chapter 17, "OI_abbr_menu," and runtime interaction for scroll menus is described in Chapter 34, "OI_scroll_menu."

12.3.2   OPEN LOOK Runtime Interaction

To select a cell in a menu, position the mouse pointer over the cell and click the SELECT mouse button. The selected cell will be highlighted in different fashions, depending on the type of menu. (See Figure 12-3 through Figure 12-6 for examples of selected cell highlighting.) Clicking on a menu cell causes the action callback routine (if any) for the cell to be called. If a menu cell has a submenu, and the submenu has a default cell, the submenu's default cell will be selected and its callback executed (unless that default cell has a submenu with its own default cell—OI keeps "walking" down the menus until it finds the lowest default cell and then fires that one).

To activate a pop-up menu, position the mouse pointer over the object where the pop-up can appear (the parent object), and press the MENU mouse button; the pop-up menu will become visible. Hold the button down while you move the pointer to your desired selection on the pop-up menu. When the pointer is over the desired cell, release the mouse button. To dismiss the menu without making a selection, release the mouse button when the pointer is not over a cell.

An alternate way to activate a pop-up menu is to click the MENU mouse button on the parent object, which makes the menu appear. Position the mouse pointer over the desired selection and click the MENU button again. To dismiss the menu without making a selection, click the mouse button when the pointer is not over a cell.

To activate a pull-down or pull-right menu (a submenu), position the mouse pointer over the parent cell (marked by a submenu-marker on its face—a triangular arrow) and press the MENU mouse button. The submenu becomes visible. Hold the button down while you move the pointer to your desired selection on the submenu. When the pointer is over the desired cell, release the mouse button. The selection is made, and the submenu disappears from the screen. Submenus may also be activated by clicking the MENU mouse button over the parent cell. The next MENU click, if the mouse pointer is over a cell, selects a cell and dismisses the menu as for a pop-up. If the MENU mouse pointer is not over the cell, the next click dismisses the menu.

If there is a pushpin in the upper left hand corner of the pop-up, pull-down or pull-right menu, you can "pin" the menu on the screen, so that it does not disappear when you release the MENU mouse button. To do so, move the mouse pointer (while still holding the MENU mouse button down) to the pushpin, then release the mouse button. You can then view the menu, make your selection (or selections, if the menu is a non-exclusive (poly) menu) by clicking on the menu cells. To cause the menu to disappear—to "unpin" it—you proceed in one of two ways: 1) Move the mouse pointer over the pushpin, press the SELECT mouse button, drag the pointer to the right until the pushpin changes to the "unpinned" image, then release the mouse button, or 2) Move the mouse pointer over the pushpin and click the SELECT mouse button.

12.3.3 Motif Runtime Interaction

Interaction with ordinary menus (not submenus) and with pop-up menus in Motif is identical to interaction with the same objects in OPEN LOOK.

To activate a pull-down or pull-right menu (a submenu) in Motif, position the mouse pointer over the parent cell (indicating there is a submenu attached by appearing as a flat menu cell) and press the SELECT mouse button; the submenu becomes visible. Hold the button down while you move the pointer to your desired selection on the submenu. When the pointer is over the desired cell, release the mouse button. The selection is made, and the submenu disappears from the screen. Submenus may also be activated by clicking the SELECT mouse button over the parent cell. The next SELECT click, if the mouse pointer is over a cell, selects a cell and dismisses the menu as for a pop-up. If the mouse pointer is not over the cell, the next SELECT click dismisses the menu.

If there is a tearoff marker (dashed line) under the title and above the cells (vertical menu) or under the cells (horizontal menu) in a pop-up, pull-down or pull-right menu, you can "tear off" the menu, so that it does not disappear when you release the MENU mouse button. To do so, move the mouse pointer (while still holding the MENU mouse button down) to the tearoff marker, then release the mouse button. You can then view the menu, make your selection (or selections, if the menu is a non-exclusive (poly) menu) by clicking on the menu cells. Use the window manager to dismiss the menu.

12.4 OI_menu Creation

Since OI_menu, OI_trans_menu, OI_excl_menu, and OI_poly_menu are base classes for the actual menus you use in applications, you cannot directly create objects of these types. Instead, you create a more specific object such as an OI_button_menu. For example, even if you use the function oi_create_excl_menu, the actual object created is either of type OI_excl_check_menu or OI_excl_rect_menu. The exact calls to create a menu of a particular type are detailed in the appropriate chapter for the various menu types (Chapters 14 through 17 and Chapter 34).

12.5 Base Class Member Functions Usable with Any Menu

You can use all of the member functions of OI_d_tech for any type of menu. In addition, the member functions below may be used with any menu.

12.6 OI_menu Member Functions

12.6.1 Selecting a Cell

You may find it necessary for your program, rather than the user, to select and deselect the cells in a menu. This normally occurs for OI_excl_menu and OI_poly_menu objects, when your program has read some startup conditions and you need to set up an appropriate initial configuration. Use the member functions described below for this purpose.

select   (Member function)

```
OI_stat OI_menu::select(
    OI_bool              on_off,          // select or deselect
    const char           *cell_name,      // name of cell
    OI_bool              do_cb=OI_yes)     // execute the cell's callback?
```

select selects or deselects the cell with name *cell_name*. Selecting a cell is the equivalent of positioning the pointer over a cell in the deselected state and clicking the SELECT mouse button.

The following table shows the effect of calling **select**:

Table 33-1

Conditions					Results	
on_off	menu cell's state previous to select call	menu cell's parent	do_cb	callback registered for menu cell	menu cell's callback called	menu cell's state following select call
OI_yes	deselected	n/a	OI_yes	yes	yes	selected
OI_yes	deselected	n/a	OI_yes	no	no	selected
OI_yes	deselected	n/a	OI_no	n/a	no	selected
OI_yes	selected	n/a	n/a	n/a	no	selected
OI_no	deselected	n/a	n/a	n/a	no	deselected
OI_no	selected	See note*	OI_yes	yes	yes	deselected
OI_no	selected	n/a	OI_no	n/a	no	deselected

*Note: The menu cell is a child of an OI_poly_menu, or it is a child of an OI_excl_menu for which you have called the OI_excl_menu member function **allow_unsel** or for which the resource **unselect** is **true**.

Note that there is also a **select** member function for the OI_menu_cell class. Use the above function if you have a pointer to a menu and wish to turn a named cell on or off. Use the OI_menu_cell member function if you have a pointer to a menu cell and wish to turn that particular cell on or off.

If you have a cell with a name containing the character '/', you will not be able to use **select** because the slash character is used to represent an object tree path; in this case you will have to use **num_select** (see below). For example, OI would interpret the name "fed/state/local" as the name of an object named "local" which is the child of an object named "state", which is the child of an object name "fed". The best solution is never to put the character '/' in any object name.

num_select   (Member function)

```
OI_stat OI_menu::num_select(
    OI_bool             on_off,          // select or deselect
    OI_number           cell_num,        // number of cell
    OI_bool             do_cb=OI_yes)    // execute cell's callback?
```

num_select selects or deselects the cell whose number is *cell_num*. Cells are numbered starting at zero for the left-most or topmost cell in the menu. If *on_off* is OI_yes, the cell is selected as for select. If *on_off* is OI_no, the cell is deselected. If *do_cb* is OI_yes, and a callback has been registered for the cell, it is executed; otherwise no cell callback is executed.

Be careful how you use this function. If you change the order of menu cells, code which uses num_select will usually malfunction, since the selected cell will no longer be the desired one. The primary purpose of num_select is to allow selection of cells that have been generated dynamically from information available only at execution time, such as file names or mail message headers.

12.6.2   Identifying Cells

The functions described below allow you to find out how many cells a menu has, obtain a pointer to a particular cell in a menu, or obtain a pointer to each cell which is in the selected state.

num_cells   (Member function)

```
OI_number OI_menu::num_cells( )
```

num_cells returns the number of cells in the menu. This function is similar to the OI_d_tech function num_props but counts only children of the menu which are OI_menu_cell objects.

cell_number   (Member function)

```
OI_number OI_menu::cell_number(
    const char          *cell_name)          // name of cell
```

cell_number returns the number of the cell whose name is *cell_name*. It returns -1 if no cell with the specified name exists.

multi_selected   (Member function)

```
OI_menu_cell **OI_menu::multi_selected(
    OI_number          *n_cell=NULL)          // number of cells in selected state
```

multi_selected returns a pointer to a null-terminated vector of cell pointers, each of which points to a cell that is currently in the selected state. multi_selected returns NULL if no cells are currently in the selected state. If *n_cell* is not NULL, multi_selected backfills *n_cell* with the number of cells in the selected state. The returned vector is allocated from dynamic memory, and when you no longer need it, you should release it using free.

For example, to print out the names of all selected cells in a poly menu, do this (see next_selection for an alternate way that does not allocate a vector of cell pointers):

```
        OI_menu             *mp;         // ptr to menu
        OI_menu_cell        **sel_vecp;  // ptr to vector of ptrs to cells
        OI_menu_cell        **pp;        // ptr to specific selected cell ptr

    if (sel_vecp = mp->multi_selected( )) {
        for (pp = sel_vecp ; *pp ; pp++)
            printf("name:%s\n",(*pp)->name( ));
        free((char*)sel_vecp);
    }
```

num_multi_selected   (Member function)

```
OI_number *OI_menu::num_multi_selected(
    OI_number          *n_cell)          // number of cells in selected state
```

num_multi_selected returns a pointer to a vector of cell numbers of the cells that are currently in the selected state. **num_multi_selected** returns NULL if no cells are currently in the selected state. If *n_cell* is not NULL, **num_multi_selected** backfills *n_cell* with the number of cells in the selected state. The returned vector is allocated from dynamic memory, and when you no longer need it, you should release it using **free**.

next_selection   (Member function)

```
OI_menu_cell *OI_menu::next_selection(
    OI_menu_cell       *cellp)          // pointer to cell
```

next_selection is used to traverse all cells currently in the selected state. If *cellp* is NULL, **next_selection** returns a pointer to the first cell in the selected state (if any). On subsequent calls, it returns a pointer to the next cell after *cellp* that is in the selected state. It returns NULL when there are no more cells in the selected state.

The example below is an alternate way to print out the names of all selected cells in a poly menu (see **multi_selected** for a different way to do this).

```
OI_menu            *mp;          // ptr to menu
OI_menu_cell       *cellp;       // ptr to selected cells

for (cellp=mp->next_selection(NULL);cellp;cellp=mp->next_selection(cellp))
    printf(" %s\n",cellp->name( ));
```

selected   (Member function)

```
OI_menu_cell *OI_menu::selected( )
```

selected returns a pointer to the cell that is currently in the selected state. **selected** returns NULL if no cell is currently in the selected state. If you call **selected** for a menu type that supports simultaneous selection of more than one cell, it returns a pointer to the first cell which is in the selected state.

Note that the **OI_menu_cell** class also has a member function named **selected**. Use the **OI_menu** member function if you have a pointer to a menu and wish to know which cell, if any, is selected. Use the **OI_menu_cell** member function if you have a pointer to a menu cell and wish to know if that particular cell is selected or not.

num_selected   (Member function)

```
OI_number OI_menu::num_selected( )
```

num_selected returns the number of the cell that is currently in the selected state, $0 <= n <$ total number of cells. **num_selected** returns -1 if no cell is currently in the selected state. If you call **num_selected** for a menu type that supports simultaneous selection of more than one cell, it returns the number of the first cell which is in the selected state.

numbered_cell   (Member function)

```
OI_menu_cell *OI_menu::numbered_cell(
    OI_number            n)                          // number of cell to find
```

numbered_cell returns a pointer to the *n*th cell in the menu, $0 <= n <$ total number of cells in the menu. Cell numbers are determined by the ordering of the OI_cell_spec or OI_menu_cell arrays used when the menu was constructed. Cells should normally be referred to and extracted by name rather than by number, to allow rearranging their order in a menu. Note also that adding or deleting cells may cause the numbers of the remaining cells in the menu to change. If *n* is invalid, **numbered_cell** returns NULL.

12.6.3   Adding a Cell

Use this function if you need to add a cell to a menu after it has been created. To remove cells, use the OI_d_tech member functions **unparent**, **del**, **delete_all**, **delete_delayed**, or **delete_all_delayed**, or the C++ **delete** operator.

add_cell   (Member function)

```
void OI_menu::add_cell(
    OI_menu_cell         *cellp,                     // pointer to cell
    OI_number            n,                          // new cell's number
    OI_bool              do_cb=OI_yes)               // execute the cell's callback?
```

add_cell adds a new cell to the menu at position *n*. That is, the new cell becomes cell number *n*, and all other cells that are displaced (from *n* to the total number of cells) are renumbered upwards by 1. If *do_cb* is OI_yes, and a callback has been registered for the cell, it is executed; otherwise no cell callback is executed.

12.6.4   Default Cell Management

A menu may have a default cell, which is generally marked on the screen with a double outline (OPEN LOOK) or extra bevel (Motif) on the cell or check-mark glyph. You establish a default cell by using the member functions **set_default_cell** or **num_set_default_cell**. You may want to establish default cells in abbreviated menus and in pull-down and pull-right menus, to allow the user to select the default cell without having to pop up the menu. You may also want to establish a default cell in button or exclusive menus to indicate the "normal" choice.

default_cell   (Member function)

```
OI_menu_cell *OI_menu::default_cell( )
```

default_cell returns a pointer to the default cell in a menu; it returns NULL if there is no default cell set.

set_default_cell   (Member function)

```
OI_stat OI_menu::set_default_cell(
    const char          *cell_name)          // new default cell name
```

set_default_cell establishes the cell whose name is *cell_name* as the default cell for the menu. If you set *cell_name* to NULL, the default cell is cleared—the menu has no default cell.

num_default_cell   (Member function)

```
OI_number OI_menu::num_default_cell( )
```

num_default_cell returns the number of the current default cell, if there is one, $0 <= n <$ total number of cells. num_default_cell returns -1 if no cell is currently a default.

num_set_default_cell   (Member function)

```
OI_stat OI_menu::num_set_default_cell(
    OI_number           n)                   // new default cell number
```

num_set_default_cell establishes the *n*th cell as the default cell for the menu. Cells are numbered starting at zero; *n* should be greater than or equal to 0 and less than the total number of cells.

12.6.5   Finding Pop-up Menu Locations

As a general rule, OI locates the upper-left corner of a pop-up menu at the mouse pointer location at the time of the mouse button press. However, if this location is so close to the edge of the screen that not all of the pop-up menu would be on the screen, OI relocates the pop-up so that it is entirely visible. You can use the following functions to determine the pointer location at the time of the mouse button press, before the menu is relocated.

popup_loc   (Member function)

```
void OI_menu::popup_loc(
    long                *xp,                 // pointer to backfilled x location
    long                *yp)                 // pointer to backfilled y location
```

popup_loc returns the coordinates of the location of the button press which brought up this pop-up menu. *xp* and *yp* are backfilled with the x and y coordinates in pixels of the location with respect to the upper left corner of this menu's parent. This location will normally be the coordinates of this menu's upper left corner, unless OI has repositioned the menu to make it fully visible.

popup_loc_x   (Member function)

```
long OI_menu::popup_loc_x( )
```

popup_loc_x returns the x coordinate of the button press which brought up this popup menu. See popup_loc.

popup_loc_y   (Member function)

```
long OI_menu::popup_loc_y( )
```

popup_loc_y returns the y coordinate of the button press which brought up this popup menu. See popup_loc.

12.6.6   Modifying Behavior

There are several aspects of menu behavior that you can modify.

You can make a very long menu *wrap*—that is, you can specify the maximum number of menu cells to appear in a row (horizontal menus) or a column (vertical menus). If there are more cells than this wrap-limit, the cells appear next to the original portion of the menu (in the next row or column) and so on, with no row or column having more than the wrap-limit number of cells. By default, menus do not wrap; you must use the function set_wrap_limit, or set the resource wrapLimit, to make a menu wrap. Note that you could also consider using an abbreviated menu or a scroll menu instead.

If you wish a menu to be a tearoff menu or have a pushpin, you should use either the member function allow_tearoff or allow_pushpin. The functions allow/disallow/is_tearoff and is_torn_off are interchangeable with allow/disallow/is_pushpin and is_pinned—both sets of functions work for both Motif and OPEN LOOK, and the appearance of the application will be appropriate for the model with which it is run. You can register callbacks to be executed when the menu becomes torn-off (pinned) or taken down (unpinned).

You can register a callback to be invoked before a pop-up or pull-down/right menu is brought up using set_pre_popup. You can also register a pre-popup callback function for the cell to which the submenu is attached; see Chapter 13, "OI_menu_cell." The pre-popup callback allows you to customize a pop-up or pull-down/pull-right menu immediately before it becomes visible. For example, you could create an empty menu, and add cells to it just before it becomes visible, or you could create a normal menu and change some of the cell labels or states before it becomes visible.

You need to use set_menu_end to register a callback for a menu (as opposed to a menu cell) if you need to modify the menu after a cell in the menu has been selected and as a result of that cell being selected. You should not modify the menu from a cell callback, since the menu is still busy. OI needs to finish manipulating the cell currently activated before it can begin the activation sequence on another cell (See Figure 2-11, "Callback Event Processing Sequence," on page 2-28). When a cell of the menu is activated, this is the order of events:

> Paint the cell busy.
> Execute any callback for the cell.
> Paint the cell normal.
> Execute any callback for the menu set via set_menu_end.

For example, you would use set_menu_end if you need to select a different cell or add or delete a cell as a result of the first cell's being selected.

By default, pop-up, pull-down and pull-right menus are persistent. This means that when a cell in one of these types of menus is selected, the menu stays visible until the selected cell completes firing—that is, until the callback function for the cell has been called and returns. You can change this behavior so that the menu disappears as soon as the mouse button is released, using **disallow_persistent**.

You may also change the mouse button assignments used to activate a menu. This is strongly discouraged, however, since your application will not behave in a standard (OPEN LOOK or Motif) way if you do this.

wrap_limit   (Member function)

```
OI_number OI_menu::wrap_limit( )
```

wrap_limit returns the maximum number of menu cells that will appear in the menu before wrapping occurs. By default, no wrapping occurs.

set_wrap_limit   (Member function)

```
void OI_menu::set_wrap_limit(
    OI_number              wrp_lmt)          // wrap limit
```

set_wrap_limit sets the maximum number of cells that appear in a column for vertical menus or in a row for horizontal menus to *wrp_lmt*. A value of 0 implies no limit—no wrapping occurs.

set_pre_popup   (Member function)

```
void OI_menu::set_pre_popup(
    OI_pre_popup_fnp       fnp,              // pointer to callback function
    void                   *argp=NULL)       // arbitrary argument for fnp


void OI_menu::set_pre_popup(
    OI_callback            objp,             // memfnp's object
    OI_pre_popup_memfnp    memfnp,           // pointer to callback member function
    void                   *argp=NULL)       // arbitrary argument for memfnp
```

The **set_pre_popup** functions register a callback function to be invoked before the menu becomes visible as a pop-up or pull-down/right menu. This callback is identified within OI as a **cbPrePopup** callback function (see Section 6.18, "Determining and Adding Callbacks; Multiple Callbacks," on page 6-117). If your action callback function is a member function, when it is invoked it will be called as if you had written *objp->memfnp*. See Section 2.5, "Callbacks and Event-Driven Programming," on page 2-16 for more explanation.

argp is optional, and may be any valid expression that can be cast to a pointer. You can use it to pass additional information to the function *fnp* or *memfnp*.

Writing the Pre-Popup Callback Function

If the **cbPrePopup** callback function is not a member function, write it in this form:

```
void fn(
        OI_d_tech          *objp,        // pointer to menu whose callback this is
        void               *argp)        // arbitrary argument
```

and if the **cbPrePopup** callback function is a member function, write it in this form:

```
void obj_class::memfn(
        OI_d_tech          *objp,        // pointer to menu whose callback this is
        void               *argp)        // arbitrary argument
```

where *obj_class* is the class of the object whose member function is *memfn*.

When your callback function is invoked, *argp* will be the argument specified in the **set_pre_popup** call.

set_menu_end   (Member function)

```
void OI_menu::set_menu_end(
    OI_menu_end_fnp        fnp,          // pointer to callback function
    void                   *argp=NULL)   // arbitrary argument for fnp


void OI_menu::set_menu_end(
    OI_callback            objp,         // memfnp's object
    OI_menu_end_memfnp     memfnp,       // pointer to callback member function
    void                   *argp=NULL)   // arbitrary argument for memfnp
```

The **set_menu_end** functions register a callback function to be invoked whenever the menu completes a cell activation. This callback is identified within OI as a **cbMenuEnd** callback function (see Section 6.18, "Determining and Adding Callbacks; Multiple Callbacks," on page 6-117). If your action callback function is a member function, when it is invoked it will be called as if you had written *objp->memfnp*. See Section 2.5, "Callbacks and Event-Driven Programming," on page 2-16 for more explanation.

argp is optional, and may be any valid expression that can be cast to a pointer. You can use it to pass additional information to the function *fnp* or *memfnp*.

Do not use **set_menu_end** to register a callback for the button menu in a dialog box, as OI registers its own callback for this menu. Use the **OI_dialog_box** member function **set_term_action** instead.

Writing the Menu-End Callback Function

If the cbMenuEnd callback function is not a member function, write it in this form:

```
void fn(
        OI_menu              *mnup,      // pointer to menu whose callback this is
        OI_menu_cell         *cellp,     // pointer to cell which was activated
        void                 *argp,      // arbitrary argument
        OI_number            btn)        // mouse button # which activated cell
```

and if the cbMenuEnd callback function is a member function, write it in this form:

```
void obj_class::memfn(
        OI_menu              *mnup,      // pointer to menu whose callback this is
        OI_menu_cell         *cellp,     // pointer to cell which was activated
        void                 *argp,      // arbitrary argument
        OI_number            btn)        // mouse button # which activated cell
```

where *obj_class* is the class of the object whose member function is *memfn*.

When your callback function is invoked, *argp* is the argument specified in the set_menu_end call. *cellp* points to the cell which was activated; *cellp* is NULL if the menu was dismissed without a cell selection. *btn* is the mouse button number which activated the cell.

is_persistent   (Member function)

```
OI_bool OI_menu::is_persistent( )
```

is_persistent returns OI_yes if the menu stays visible the entire time a cell callback is being executed. It returns OI_no if it disappears immediately after the mouse button is released.

allow_persistent   (Member function)

```
void OI_menu::allow_persistent( )
```

allow_persistent prevents a pop-up menu from disappearing until all callback routines have been executed. This is the default.

disallow_persistent   (Member function)

```
void OI_menu::disallow_persistent( )
```

disallow_persistent causes a pop-up or pull-down/pull-right menu to disappear as soon as the mouse button is released.

is_tearoff   (Member function)

```
OI_bool OI_menu::is_tearoff( )
```

is_tearoff returns OI_yes if the menu is configured to be tearoff menu, otherwise it returns OI_no. is_tearoff is synonymous with is_pushpin.

allow_tearoff   (Member function)

```
void OI_menu::allow_tearoff( )
```

allow_tearoff indicates that the menu should be a tearoff menu. You should normally only use allow_tearoff for pop-up, pull-down or pull-right menus. allow_tearoff is synonymous with allow_pushpin.

disallow_tearoff   (Member function)

```
void OI_menu::disallow_tearoff( )
```

disallow_tearoff causes the menu not to be a tearoff menu. This is the default. disallow_tearoff is synonymous with disallow_pushpin.

is_torn_off   (Member function)

```
OI_bool OI_menu::is_torn_off( )
```

is_torn_off returns OI_yes if the menu is torn off; otherwise it returns OI_no. is_torn_off is synonymous with is_pinned.

is_pushpin   (Member function)

```
OI_bool OI_menu::is_pushpin( )
```

is_pushpin returns OI_yes if the menu is configured to have a pushpin, otherwise it returns OI_no. is_pushpin is synonymous with is_tearoff.

allow_pushpin   (Member function)

```
void OI_menu::allow_pushpin( )
```

allow_pushpin indicates that the menu should have a pushpin if possible. You should normally only use allow_pushpin for pop-up, pull-down or pull-right menus. allow_pushpin is synonymous with allow_tearoff.

disallow_pushpin   (Member function)

```
void OI_menu::disallow_pushpin( )
```

disallow_pushpin removes the pushpin (if any) from the menu. This is the default. disallow_pushpin is synonymous with disallow_tearoff.

is_pinned   (Member function)

```
OI_bool OI_menu::is_pinned( )
```

is_pinned returns OI_yes if the menu is pinned; otherwise it returns OI_no. is_pinned is synonymous with is_torn_off.

set_pin   (Member function)

```
void OI_menu::set_pin(
    OI_pin_fnp          fnp,              // pointer to callback function
    void                *argp=NULL)       // arbitrary argument for fnp


void OI_menu::set_pin(
    OI_callback         *objp,            // memfnp's object
    OI_pin_memfnp       memfnp,           // pointer to callback member function
    void                *argp=NULL)       // arbitrary argument for memfnp
```

The set_pin functions register a callback function to be invoked whenever the menu is pinned. OI executes the callback before making the pinned copy of the menu visible. This callback is identified within OI as a cbPin callback function (see Section 6.18, "Determining and Adding Callbacks; Multiple Callbacks," on page 6-117). *memfnp* points to a member function for the object pointed to by *objp*. If your function is a member function, when it is invoked it will be called as if you had written *objp->memfnp*. See Section 2.5, "Callbacks and Event-Driven Programming," on page 2-16 for more explanation.

argp is optional, and can be any valid expression that can be cast to a pointer. You can use it to pass additional information to the function *fnp* or *memfnp*.

Writing the Pin Callback Function

If the cbPin callback function is not a member function, write it in this form:

```
void fn(
    OI_d_tech           *objp,            // pointer to menu which was pinned
    void                *argp)            // arbitrary argument
```

and if the cbPin callback function is a member function, write it in this form:

```
void obj_class::memfn(
    OI_d_tech           *objp,            // pointer to menu which was pinned
    void                *argp)            // arbitrary argument
```

where *obj_class* is the class of the object whose member function is *memfn*.

When your callback function is invoked, *argp* will be the argument specified in the set_pin call.

set_unpin
(Member function)

```
void OI_menu::set_unpin(
    OI_pin_fnp          fnp,          // pointer to callback function
    void                *argp=NULL)   // arbitrary argument for fnp

void OI_menu::set_unpin(
    OI_callback         *objp,        // memfnp's object
    OI_pin_memfnp       memfnp,       // pointer to callback member function
    void                *argp=NULL)   // arbitrary argument for memfnp
```

The set_unpin functions register a callback function to be invoked whenever the menu is unpinned. OI executes the callback after the menu is removed from the screen. This callback is identified within OI as a cbUnpin callback function (see Section 6.18, "Determining and Adding Callbacks; Multiple Callbacks," on page 6-117). All arguments and the form of the unpin callback function are identical to those for set_pin.

trigger
(Member function)

```
OI_number OI_menu::trigger( )
```

trigger returns the mouse button number that will activate a menu cell. The default trigger is the SELECT mouse button for all models (mouse button 1).

trigger_mods
(Member function)

```
OI_number OI_menu::trigger_mods( )
```

trigger_mods returns the modifier key bits required for a menu cell to activate. See set_trigger for possible values.

set_trigger
(Member function)

```
OI_stat OI_menu::set_trigger(
    OI_number           btn,          // button number
    OI_number           mod=0)        // modifier key bits
```

set_trigger sets the mouse button number *btn* and modifier key bits *mod* required for a menu cell to activate. *mod* may be a combination of zero or more of the following, ored together. The default is zero (no modifiers).

OI_mod_shift	Shift key down during click.
OI_mod_lock	Lock key down during click.
OI_mod_control	Control key down during click.
OI_mod_meta	Mod1 key down during click.

You should use set_trigger only if you are writing a special application, such as a window manager, that needs to conform to an external specification that defines which mouse button activates menu cells. Do not use this function if you are interested in writing an application that conforms to the standard look-and-feel.

menu_trigger   (Member function)

```
OI_number OI_menu::menu_trigger( )
```

menu_trigger returns the mouse button number that causes the menu to activate as a pop-up.
The default menu trigger is the MENU mouse button (button 3) for all models.

menu_trigger_mods   (Member function)

```
OI_number OI_menu::menu_trigger_mods( )
```

menu_trigger_mods returns the modifier keys required for the menu to activate as a pop-up.
See set_trigger for possible values.

set_menu_trigger   (Member function)

```
OI_stat OI_menu::set_menu_trigger(
     OI_number           btn,          // button number
     OI_number           mod=0)        // modifier key bits
```

set_menu_trigger sets the mouse button number *btn* and modifier key bits *mod* required for a
pop-up menu to activate. See set_trigger for possible values.

You should use set_menu_trigger only if you are writing a special application, such as a
window manager, that needs to conform to an external specification that defines which mouse
button activates pop-up menus.

12.6.7   Controlling Appearance

Depending on the appearance model used and other circumstances, such as whether the menu is a
pop-up or not, menu cells which are in the deselected state may or may not have an outline. You can
prevent menu cells in the deselected state from being outlined; you can also force them to be
outlined. However, it is probably best to allow the user to specify this aspect of cell appearance via
the OI_menu resource cellOutline.

You can use the functions below to modify menu appearance and retrieve information about the
menu such as its title and orientation.

By default, any tabs in the text for the menu title and the menu cell labels are not displayed. However,
you can specify tab stops for this text, in which case the tabs are displayed. If you are using a
variable-width font, the tab spacing units used are the width of the widest character in the font,
usually "W". In other words, a tab width of 4 is equivalent to the space taken up by the characters
"WWWW".

is_cell_outline   (Member function)

```
OI_bool OI_menu::is_cell_outline( )
```

is_cell_outline returns OI_yes if the menu paints a cell outline for each cell that is in a
deselected state, otherwise it returns OI_no.

allow_cell_outline   (Member function)

```
void OI_menu::allow_cell_outline( )
```

allow_cell_outline conditions the menu to paint outlines for each cell that is in a deselected state.

disallow_cell_outline   (Member function)

```
void OI_menu::disallow_cell_outline( )
```

disallow_cell_outline prevents a menu from painting a cell outline for each cell that is in a deselected state.

orientation   (Member function)

```
OI_orient OI_menu::orientation( )
```

orientation returns the orientation of the menu, either OI_horizontal or OI_vertical.

title   (Member function)

```
char *OI_menu::title( )
```

title returns the title of the menu. The title is set when the menu is created, and may be NULL.

set_title   (Member function)

```
void OI_menu::set_title(
const char                    *titlep)          // pointer to new title
```

set_title sets the menu title to be *titlep*. If *titlep* is NULL, the title is removed.

label_right_space   (Member function)

```
OI_number OI_menu::label_right_space( )
```

label_right_space returns the number of pixels between the label and the first menu cell for a horizontal menu. This has no significance for a vertical menu.

set_label_right_space   (Member function)

```
void OI_menu::set_label_right_space(
    OI_number               pxls)          // space in pixels
```

set_label_right_space sets the number of pixels between the label and the first menu cell to *pxls* for a horizontal menu. This has no significance for a vertical menu.

set_tab_width   (Member function)

```
void OI_menu::set_tab_width(
    OI_number              tab_width)          // tab width in characters
```

set_tab_width creates a tab table with a tab stop every *tab_width* characters, to be used both in the menu title and the menu cell labels. The table defaults to a size large enough to support tabbing of up to 80 columns of text. The table is dynamically resized if any associated text has tabs past 80 columns. If you set *tab_width* to zero, tabs are not displayed; this is the default.

set_tabs_custom   (Member function)

```
void OI_menu::set_tabs_custom(
    OI_number          *tab_tbl,        // pointer to tab stop table
    OI_number          n_tabs,          // number of tabs in tab_tbl
    OI_number          def_wid=8)       // default tab width
```

set_tabs_custom sets the first *n_tabs* tab stops in the menu title and cell labels to those specified in *tab_tbl*. Each element of *tab_tbl* specifies the column number where the next tab stop is to be placed. If there are more than *n_tabs* tabs in any line of the **OI_menu** text, their spacing is set to *def_wid* characters. If you set *tab_tbl* to NULL or *n_tabs* to zero, the display of tabs is disabled; this is the default.

For example, if you want tabs at columns 4, 12, 20, and 36, then every 4 after that if needed, you would use these lines:

```
        OI_menu               *mp;
        OI_number             my_tabs[] = {4, 12, 20, 36};
        OI_number             n_tabs = OI_count(my_tabs);
    mp->set_tabs_custom(my_tabs, n_tabs, 4);
```

12.7 Resources

All resources from an **OI_menu** object's base classes are available to it; in addition, OI fetches the resources shown in Table 12-2. For more information on resource management, see Chapter 39, "The OI Resource Mechanism." For more information on the individual resources in the table, see the **OI_menu** member function with a similar name.

Table 12-2 OI_menu Resources

Resource	Description	Possible Values	Default Value
cellOutline	If on, cell outline is painted in pop-up menus.	Boolean	true
label.font	Specifies font for menu title.	Valid font	Default font
label.rightSpace	For horizontal menus only. Specifies the amount of space, in pixels, between the label (title) on the menu and the start of the rest of the menu.	Non-negative integer	5
orientation	Specifies menu orientation.	horizontal vertical	vertical

Table 12-2　OI_menu Resources

Resource	Description	Possible Values	Default Value
persistent	Applies only to pop-up and pull-down menus. If on, specifies that the menu remains displayed until all menu and menu cell callback routines have been executed. If off, OI takes the menu down as soon as a cell in the menu fires.	Boolean	true
pushpin	If on, adds a pushpin to the menu.	Boolean	false
title	Specifies the title of the menu.	Text string	NULL
wrapAround	If on, specifies that keyboard menu traversal should wrap around.	Boolean	false
wrapLimit	Specifies the maximum number of menu cells that will appear in the menu before wrapping will occur. A value of 0 implies no limit.	Non-negative integer	0

12.8　Translations

An OI_menu object has default translations installed for it. In addition to the translations listed in the table below, the default translations for an OI_menu object also includes the default translations for all of its base classes. Most of the translations which implement the keyboard traversal of menus are translations for the OI_menu_cell children objects; see Chapter 13, "OI_menu_cell," page 13-22.

Table 12-3 shows the default OI_menu translations. Table 12-4 describes the action functions available. See Chapter 40, "The OI Translation Mechanism" for a description of the Event Sequence entries in Table 12-3.

Table 12-3　Default OI_menu Translations

Event Sequence	Action Functions Called
<ButtonRelease>:	deactivate_all( )
<ClientMessage>:	deactivate_all( )

Table 12-4 OI_menu Translation Functions

Function Name	Description
unpin( )	If the menu has been pinned up, unpins it. This is particularly useful when running an application in OPEN LOOK mode with a non-OPEN LOOK window manager (one which does not understand pushpins).
deactivate( )	If this is a pop-up, pull-right or pull-down menu, take it and any submenus down.
deactivate_all( )	If this is a pop-up, pull-right or pull-down menu, take it and any submenus down, and any parent pop-up, pull-right or pull-down menus, to the top of the chain.

12.9   Callback Functions

Table 12-5 lists the callbacks available for an OI_menu object and the page number where the callback is documented. In addition, all of the callbacks from an OI_menu object's base classes are available to it. See Section 6.18, "Determining and Adding Callbacks; Multiple Callbacks," on page 6-117 for additional information about manipulating callbacks.

Table 12-5 OI_menu Callbacks

Callback Type	Callback Typedef	Description	Page Number
cbMenuEnd	OI_menu_end_fnp/memfnp	Menu-end callback function	12-28
cbPin	OI_pin_fnp/memfnp	Pin callback function	12-31
cbPrePopup	OI_pre_popup_fnp/memfnp	Pre-popup callback function	12-27
cbUnpin	OI_pin_fnp/memfnp	Unpin callback function	12-32

Chapter 13
OI_menu_cell

OI_menu_cell Functions

OI_menu_cell Member Functions

The following functions are available to an **OI_menu_cell** object, but are described in their own chapter.

OI_d_tech Member Functions

OI_menu_cell

13.1 Description

An OI_menu_cell is an individual cell in a menu. Regardless of the type of menu you are using, the items in the menu are always OI_menu_cell objects. These cells are children of the menu. The appearance of the cell and its behavior are determined by the menu in which the cell resides. You can use any OI_menu_cell member function for the cells of any menu.

A menu cell is always in one of two conditions—selected or deselected. A cell in the *selected* state is one which is "turned on"; if the cell is visible in a menu, it is highlighted in some manner. A cell in the *deselected* state is one which is "turned off"; it is not highlighted. A cell in a transient menu (OI_button_menu) is only in the selected state during the period when its action callback function is being executed. A cell in an exclusive (OI_excl_*_menu) or a non-exclusive (OI_poly_*_menu) menu maintains its state until it is explicitly turned on (or off), at which point it is in the selected (or deselected) state.

If a menu cell has a callback registered for it, the callback is executed on specified occasions as shown in Table 13-1. The selected member function can be used from within the callback function to determine if the cell is in the selected or deselected state at the time of the callback.

Table 13-1 When a Menu Cell Callback is Executed

If the cell belongs to	The callback is executed
Any type of menu	When the cell is activated (when it goes from the deselected state to the selected state).
Not a button menu	When the cell is deselected.

The only types of objects that you should associate as children of a menu cell are objects derived either from OI_menu or from OI_dialog_box.

Figure 13-1 shows the visual attributes of menu cells belonging to the different types of menus.

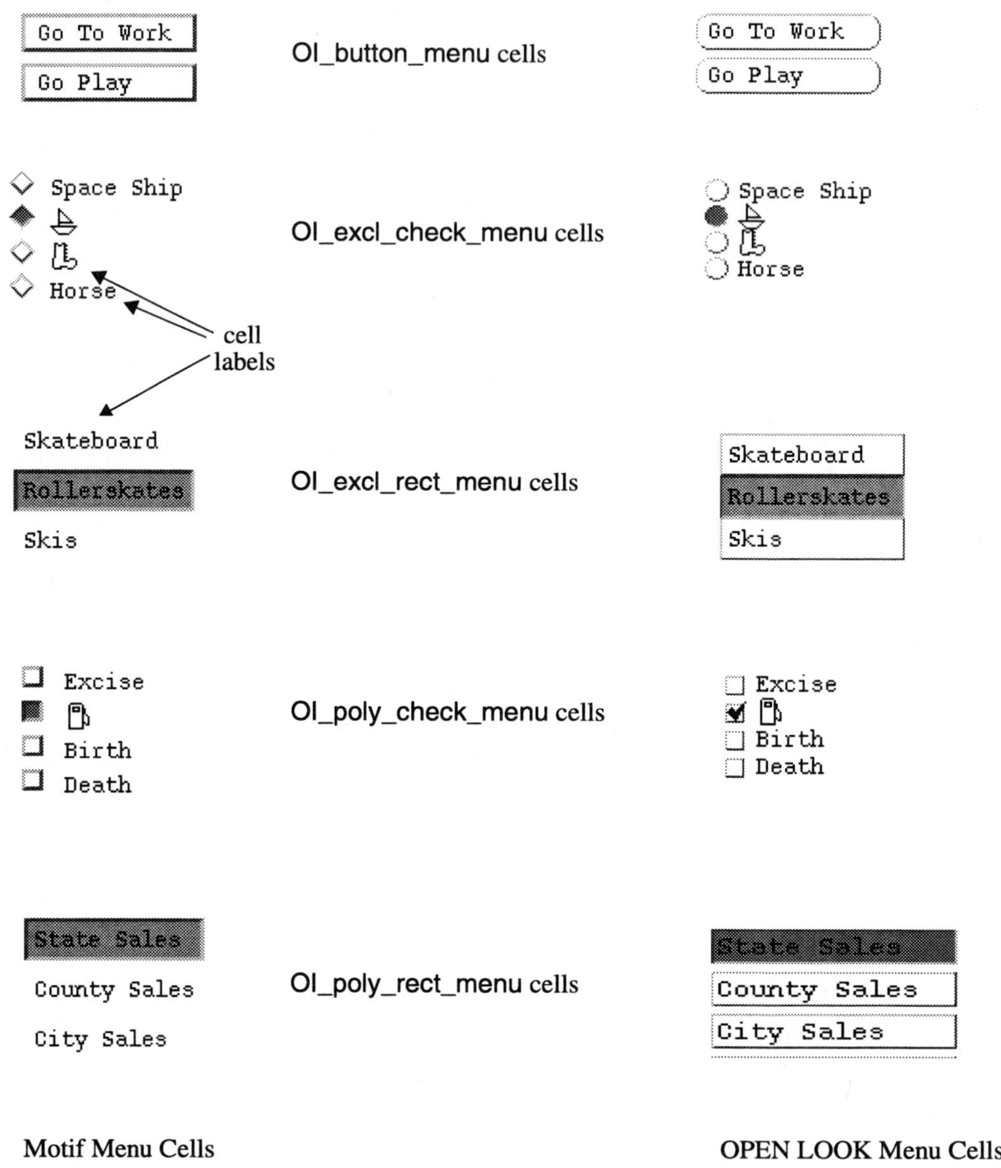

Figure 13-1   Menu Cell Appearance

13.1.1   Submenus Associated with a Menu Cell

You can attach a submenu to a menu cell. When you do this, the submenu behaves as a pull-down menu if the parent cell is in a horizontal menu, or as a pull-right menu if the parent cell is in a vertical menu. To make a submenu which behaves as a pull-down or pull-right menu, you create the submenu and then associate it to the parent cell with state OI_active_not_displayed. In the OPEN LOOK model, the parent cell will contain a *submenu-marker*, a triangular arrow on the face of the menu cell, which indicates that a submenu is the child of the menu cell. In the Motif model, if the cell with a submenu child is in a horizontal menu, the cell will have a flat face—that is, it will not be beveled. If the submenu is on a cell in a vertical menu, the Motif cell will have a similar submenu-marker as the OPEN LOOK cell—a triangular arrow. When the cell is activated using the MENU mouse button, the submenu will appear. Examples of cells with submenus are shown in Figure 13-2.

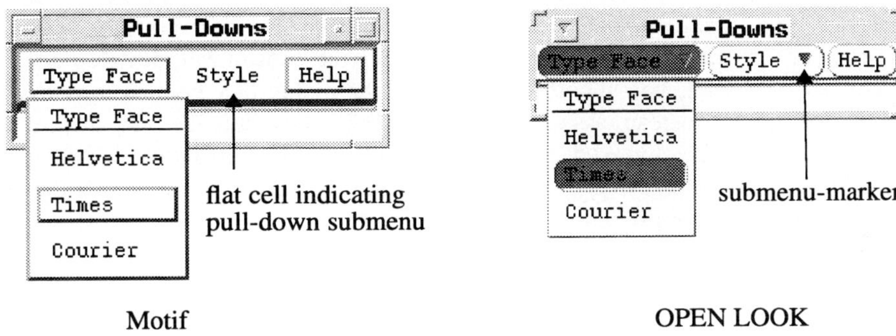

Motif   OPEN LOOK

Figure 13-2   Menu Cells with Submenus Attached

You can create a submenu explicitly (dynamically) by calling oi_create_*menutype* and parenting the submenu to the parent menu cell using set_associated_object, or you can create one implicitly (statically), by filling in an OI_menu_spec structure and referencing it when you create the menu cell (see Section 13.4.3 on page 13-10.)

13.1.2   Dialog Boxes Associated with a Menu Cell

You can cause a dialog box to automatically appear when a menu cell is activated by associating the dialog box with the menu cell with state OI_active_not_displayed. The face of the OI_menu_cell will contain a *dialog-box-marker*—three dots—which indicates that a dialog box will pop up when the menu cell is activated. See Figure 13-3.

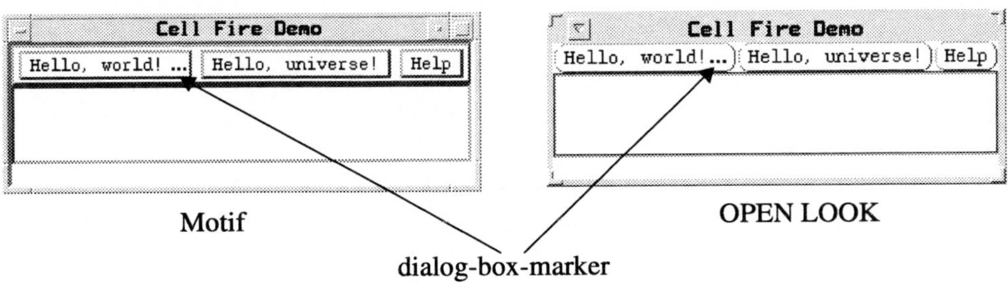

Motif   OPEN LOOK

dialog-box-marker

Figure 13-3   Menu Cell with Dialog-box-marker

Unlike a submenu, the dialog box cannot be created implicitly; it must be explicitly created using the oi_create_dialog_box function, and then associated with the menu cell.

If you have associated a dialog box with state OI_active_not_displayed with a menu cell, the following occurs when the cell is activated: first the action callback function for the cell (if any) is called. When the action callback is finished and if the dialog box is still parented to the menu cell, OI activates the dialog box and issues a wait_button member function call for the dialog box. If the call to set_associated_object for the dialog box was made with location OI_def_loc, the dialog box is placed at the default location (determined by the interaction model being used), relative to the parent cell. Otherwise the dialog box is placed at the location you specify relative to the cell origin. If you desire to have the callback function called *after* the wait_button call, or if you need both a before and after callback call, you should not associate the dialog box with the cell using state OI_active_not_displayed. Instead, associate the dialog box using state OI_not_displayed, and activate the dialog box and execute wait_button in the callback function for the cell. This implies that if you associate a dialog box in a menu cell callback, then it will pop up when the callback returns—this is a good way to build dialog boxes dynamically.

See Program 18-1, "Dialog Box with OK Button Callback (OKCallback.C)" on page 18-19 for an example.

13.1.3   Accelerators and Mnemonics

Even though all OI objects support accelerators and mnemonics (see Chapter 40, "The OI Translation Mechanism," for descriptions of accelerators and mnemonics), the only visual reminder that they exist appears on menu cells. The accelerator label appears to the right of the original cell label; the mnemonic label appears by default as an underline in the cell label.

13.2   Class Tree

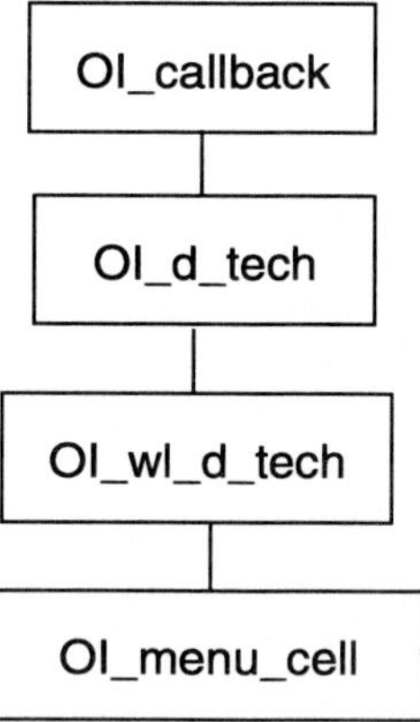

13.3 Runtime Interaction

To select a menu cell, move the mouse pointer to the cell and click the SELECT mouse button. In a similar manner, if the menu cell belongs to a menu that allows the user to deselect cells (an OI_poly_menu or an OI_excl_menu for which you have called the OI_excl_menu member function allow_unsel or for which the resource unselect is true), clicking on a cell that is in the selected state deselects the cell.

If an action callback function has been registered for a cell, clicking on the cell causes the callback function to be executed, regardless of the selection state of the cell. In other words, the callback function is executed if the click changes the state of the cell to deselected as well as if the click changes the state to selected. The exception to this is that when you click on a cell in a button menu, a single call to the action callback is made.

When you click on a cell in an exclusive menu (OI_excl_rect_menu or OI_excl_check_menu), a call is made to the previously selected cell's action callback (if any) to notify that the cell is turning off, followed by a call to the selected cell's action callback (if any) to notify that the new cell is turning on.

When you click on a cell in an exclusive menu (OI_excl_rect_menu or OI_excl_check_menu) which is already in the selected state (and you have not called allow_unsel and unselect is false), by default, the cell's callback is called again. You can turn this off by calling the OI_excl_menu member function disallow_resel for the menu.

The default translations for OI_menu_cell objects set up the keyboard traversal functionality shown in Table 13-2. See Section 13.8, "Translations," on page 13-22 for the actual translations.

Table 13-2 OI_menu-cell Keyboard Traversals

Conditions	Key Sequence	Action
Motif model; focus in some object	F10	Toggles input focus between the main menu and the current object.
Motif mode; focus on cell in main menu after F10	Escape	Move focus back to object in the window.
Horizontal menu	Right arrow	Moves to the next cell in the menu, or, if the focus is on the last cell, moves to the first cell.
Horizontal menu	Left arrow	Moves to the previous cell in the menu, or, if the focus is on the first cell, moves to the last cell.
Horizontal menu, cell has submenu	Down arrow	Brings up the submenu.

Table 13-2 OI_menu-cell Keyboard Traversals

Conditions	Key Sequence	Action
Vertical menu	Down arrow	Moves to the next cell in the menu, or, if the focus is on the last cell, moves to the first cell.
Vertical menu	Up arrow	Moves to the previous cell in the menu, or, if the focus is on the first cell, moves to the last cell.
Vertical menu, cell has submenu	Right arrow	Brings up the submenu.
Vertical submenu	Left arrow	Dismisses this menu.
Not a submenu or popup menu	Tab	Moves focus to next object which is in the focus chain. (If the default focus chain does not meet your needs, you can customize your own via the OI_d_tech member function set_next*.)
Not a submenu or popup menu	Shift Tab	Moves focus to previous object which is in the focus chain.
Cell has no submenu	Return	Fires the current cell.
Button menu cell, has submenu	Return	Brings up the submenu.
Cell has no submenu	Spacebar	Fires the current cell.
Button menu cell, has submenu	Spacebar	Brings up the submenu.
Vertical submenu is visible	Escape	Dismisses the current vertical submenu, but only if the submenu is not on a main menu cell.
Motif model	F4	Activates the pop-up menu (if one exists on object) at location 0,0 relative to the upper-left corner of the parent.

13.4 OI_menu_cell Creation

A menu cell can be created one of two ways: explicitly, using a call to oi_create_menu_cell, or implicitly, from a cell specification (OI_cell_spec) passed to a menu creation function. If you need to create and add a cell to an existing menu during execution time, use the oi_create_menu_cell call to create it, then parent it to a menu using the OI_menu member function add_cell. This method is useful if you do not know ahead of time what image or text should appear on the face of the cell or how many cells you will need in the menu. However, if the menu is well-defined, you can make a static structure, OI_cell_spec, containing all the necessary information for each cell in the menu, then simply point to the structure in the menu create call.

13.4.1   Explicit Menu Cell Creation

oi_create_menu_cell   (Free-standing function)

```
OI_menu_cell *oi_create_menu_cell(
    const char          *namp,              // pointer to object name
    const char          *labelp,            // pointer to cell label info
    OI_action_fnp       fnp=NULL,           // pointer to cell action callback function
    void                *argp=NULL,         // arbitrary argument for fnp
    OI_menu_cell_type   type=OI_text_cell,  // type of menu cell
    OI_menu_spec        *menu_ptr=NULL,     // pointer to submenu specification
    OI_number           wid=0,              // width of label pixmap
    OI_number           ht=0,               // height of label pixmap
    OI_number           dpth=0,             // depth of label pixmap
    unsigned long       ctl_bits=0,         // control bits
    OI_gravity          grvty               // gravity of cell
                        =OI_grav_unknown)


OI_menu_cell *oi_create_menu_cell(
    const char          *namp,              // pointer to object name
    const char          *labelp,            // pointer to cell label info
    OI_callback         *objp,              // memfnp's object
    OI_action_memfnp    memfnp,             // pointer to callback member function
    void                *argp=NULL,         // arbitrary argument for memfnp
    OI_menu_cell_type   type=OI_text_cell,  // type of menu cell
    OI_menu_spec        *menu_ptr=NULL,     // pointer to submenu specification
    OI_number           wid=0,              // width of label pixmap
    OI_number           ht=0,               // height of label pixmap
    OI_number           dpth=0,             // depth of label pixmap
    unsigned long       ctl_bits=0,         // control bits
    OI_gravity          grvty               // gravity of cell
                        =OI_grav_unknown)
```

The oi_create_menu_cell functions create a menu cell and register an action callback function. The action callback function (if any) is invoked whenever the cell is activated (fires). For an OI_excl_menu or OI_poly_menu cell, this occurs twice: when the cell is selected, and when it is deselected. For an OI_button_menu cell, this occurs once: when the cell is selected. When the member function is invoked, it will be called as if you had written *objp->memfnp*.

See Section 2.5, "Callbacks and Event-Driven Programming," on page 2-16 for more explanation.

namp points to the name of the cell. If you set *namp* to NULL, the cell's name is the same as its label, but only if the cell's *type* is OI_text_cell. If *type* is anything else and *namp* is NULL, OI will give the cell a name.

You can set *fnp* or *memfnp* to NULL, indicating that there is no action callback function for the menu cell. You will often want to set *fnp* or *memfnp* to NULL for an OI_excl_menu or an OI_poly_menu cell, because the user typically uses these menus to select and deselect menu cells, and your application will subsequently query the menu to discover which cells are in the selected state and then perform the necessary tasks for those cells.

argp is optional, and can be any valid expression that can be cast to a pointer. You can use it to pass additional information to the function *fnp* or *memfnp*.

See Section 13.4.4, "Action Callback Functions," on page 13-11 for a description of how to write the action callback function.

type specifies the type of image label to be displayed on the face of the cell. Depending on the value of *type*, *labelp* is expected to contain image information of different types; *wid*, *ht*, and *dpth* are also dependent upon the value of *type*. *type* can have the following values:

OI_text_cell	The cell label is plain text. *labelp* must point to the text, and *wid*, *ht*, and *dpth* are ignored. This is the default.
OI_icon_cell	The label image is a glyph created from a bitmap or XPM file. *labelp* must point to a string specifying the bitmap or XPM file (the file name) to use to create the glyph for the cell label image. *wid*, *ht*, and *dpth* are ignored.
OI_icon_data_cell	The label image is a glyph created from character data. *labelp* must point to a character array containing the pixmap data itself. The format of the character array is the same as the output of the bitmap program. *wid*, *ht*, and *dpth* are the width, height, and depth (in pixels) of the pixmap represented by the data. Currently, only single-bit pixmaps are supported (that is, those with depth of 1). In order for these bitmaps to function on a color display, you should set *dpth* to zero; the create function creates a pixmap of depth 1 and the cell is painted using the pixmap as a mask.
OI_icon_pixmap_cell	The label image is a glyph created from a user-created pixmap. The pixmap can be created using XCreatePixmap, XCreatePixmapFromBitmapData, or XCreateBitmapFromData or similar Xlib library function, or any of the XPM functions for the same purpose. *labelp* must be an X pixmap and must be cast to

a char*; *wid*, *ht*, and *dpth* are as specified for OI_icon_data_cell.

OI_separator_cell   The cell is a do-nothing cell which merely spaces the cells in the menu for visual effect. It has a line or bevel drawn in place of a label.

menu_ptr points to a complete menu specification for a pull-down or pull-right submenu for the cell. If the cell will not have a submenu attached to it, specify *menu_ptr* to be NULL. If you will be creating a submenu separately using a call to oi_create_*menutype* and then associating it with this cell, you should also set *menu_ptr* to be NULL. Otherwise, see Section 13.4.3, "Submenu Specification—OI_menu_spec," on page 13-10 for a description of the value for *menu_ptr*.

ctl_bits can be 0, or any boolean combination of the following values, ored together:

OI_cell_select   The cell is in the selected state.
OI_cell_default   The cell is the default cell.
OI_cell_subbox   The cell should have a dialog box marker.
OI_cell_submenu   The cell should have a submenu marker.

The OI_cell_subbox and OI_cell_submenu bits should only be set if the menu is not actually going to have a submenu or dialog box attached to it, but you wish to give the impression that it does. Set only zero or one of OI_cell_subbox or OI_cell_submenu—never both. For example, you may have a dialog box parented someplace else, or parented in state OI_not_displayed, and you will pop it up in your callback routine.

grvty specifies in which direction the cell tries to migrate if the user enlarges the menu so that it contains extra space not used by the cells.

See Program 12-2, "Menu Creation: Explicitly Created Menu Cells (BtnMnuExplicit.C)" on page 12-8 for an example.

13.4.2   Implicit Menu Cell Creation—OI_cell_spec

To implicitly create the menu cells for a menu you are creating, define an array of OI_cell_spec structures with data for each menu cell of the menu, then pass the address of the array of OI_cell_spec structures to the oi_create_*menutype* call.

```
struct OI_cell_spec {
    const char          *namp;          // pointer to cell name
    const char          *labelp;        // pointer to cell label info
    OI_action_fnp       fnp;            // pointer to action callback function
    OI_callback         *objp;          // memfnp's object
    OI_action_memfnp    memfnp;         // pointer to action callback member function
    void                *argp;          // arbitrary argument for *fnp or *memfnp
    OI_menu_cell_type   type;           // type of menu cell
    struct OI_menu_spec *menu_ptr;      // pointer to submenu specification
    OI_number           wid;            // width of pixmap data
    OI_number           ht;             // height of pixmap data
    OI_number           dpth;           // depth of pixmap data
    unsigned long       ctl_bits;       // control bits
    OI_gravity          grvty;          // gravity for cell
};
```

The values that each of these variables should have are the same as the parameters for the oi_create_menu_cell functions in the previous section. If you specify a non-NULL value for *fnp*, then you must specify NULL for *objp* and NULL (or NULL_PMF) for *memfnp*; if you specify a non-NULL value for *objp* and *memfnp*, then you must specify NULL for *fnp*. (NULL_PMF is a special form of NULL pointer which you must use instead of NULL for a member function pointer if you are using AT&T's cfront 2.00.04 compiler or a compiler based on this version.)

See Program 12-1, "Menu Creation: Implicitly Created Menu Cells (BtnMnuImplicit.C)" on page 12-7 for an example.

13.4.3   Submenu Specification—OI_menu_spec

If you choose to specify an entire submenu specification at compile time, you must specify an OI_cell_spec structure with the submenu's cell information, then specify an OI_menu_spec structure with the submenu's menu information, pointing to the submenu's OI_cell_spec specifications. This submenu specification is what you pass as the parameter *menu_ptr* in the parent cell's call to oi_create_menu_cell if the parent cell is created explicitly or in the parent cell's OI_cell_spec specification if the parent cell is created implicitly.

```
struct OI_menu_spec {
    char            *namp;          // menu object name
    OI_number       n_cell;         // number of cells in the submenu
    OI_cell_spec    *cell_specp;    // pointer to menu cell specification
    OI_orient       orient;         // menu orientation
    char            *titlep;        // pointer to menu title
    long            ctl_bits;       // control bits
    OI_class        **mnu_typ;      // type of menu desired
};
```

namp is the name of the menu. *n_cell* is the number of cells in the submenu. *cell_specp* is a pointer to the OI_cell_spec structure for the submenu. *orient* is the menu orientation, either OI_horizontal or OI_vertical. *titlep* is the submenu title; if NULL, the submenu will have no title.

ctl_bits can be 0 or any boolean combination of the following values, ored together:

OI_menu_pushpin	The menu has a pushpin.
OI_menu_no_persistent	The menu is not a persistent menu.
OI_menu_no_outline_cell	Do not outline the cells of the menu.
OI_menu_unsel	Allow all cells of the menu to be in the deselected state.

mnu_typ is the class of menu to create. Use *&menu_type*::clsp to create a menu of type *menu_type*. For example, to create a menu of type OI_poly_check_menu, set *mnu_typ* to &OI_poly_check_menu::clsp. If you omit *mnu_typ* or set it to 0, an OI_button_menu object is created.

The following line is an example of an OI_menu_spec submenu specification:

```
static  OI_menu_spec        type_mnu =
    {"type_mnu",OI_count(type_cells),&type_cells[0],OI_vertical,
                    "Type Face",0,&OI_excl_check_menu::clsp};
```

See Program 12-6, "Implicitly Created Pull-down Menus (PullDownImp.C)," on page 12-16 for an example.

13.4.4   Action Callback Functions

A cell's action routine is invoked when the cell activation state changes. For longterm-selection menus (OI_excl_menu and OI_poly_menu), this implies that the function is called when a cell goes from the deselected state to the selected state, as well as when it goes from the selected state to the deselected state. This callback is identified within OI as a cbCellAction callback function (see Section 6.18, "Determining and Adding Callbacks; Multiple Callbacks," on page 6-117).

If the **cbCellAction** callback function specified in the **oi_create_menu_cell** call or in the **OI_cell_spec** structure is not a member function, write it in this form:

```
void fn(
    OI_menu_cell        *cellp,          // cell that was activated
    void                *argp,           // arbitrary argument
    OI_number           mse_btn)         // mouse button number
```

and if the **cbCellAction** callback function is a member function, write it in this form:

```
void obj_class::memfn(
    OI_menu_cell        *cellp,          // cell that was activated
    void                *argp,           // arbitrary argument
    OI_number           mse_btn)         // mouse button number
```

where *obj_class* is the class of the object whose member function is *memfn*.

When your callback function is invoked, *argp* will be the argument specified in the oi_create_menu_cell call or in the **OI_cell_spec** specification. *mse_btn* will be the mouse button number used to select (or deselect) the cell.

There are several examples in Chapter 12, "OI_menu," of cells with action callbacks.

13.5   Base Class Member Functions

You can use all of the member functions of OI_d_tech for an OI_menu_cell object. If you call the OI_d_tech member function set_bkg_pixmap for an OI_menu_cell object, OI converts the cell to type OI_icon_pixmap_cell.

13.6   OI_menu_cell Member Functions

13.6.1   Selection

The functions **select** and **selected** have the same names and purposes as member functions for OI_menu. Use the OI_menu_cell functions if you have a pointer to a menu cell; use the OI_menu member functions if you have a pointer to a menu.

selected   (Member function)

```
OI_bool OI_menu_cell::selected( )
```

selected returns OI_yes if the cell is currently in the selected state, otherwise it returns OI_no.

select   (Member function)

```
void OI_menu_cell::select(
    OI_bool              on_off,           // select-deselect flag
    OI_bool              do_cb=OI_yes)     // execute cell's callback?
```

The following table shows the effect of calling **select**:

Conditions					Results	
on_off	menu cell's state previous to select call	menu cell's parent	do_cb	callback registered for menu cell	menu cell's callback called	menu cell's state following select call
OI_yes	deselected	n/a	OI_yes	yes	yes	selected
OI_yes	deselected	n/a	OI_yes	no	no	selected
OI_yes	deselected	n/a	OI_no	n/a	no	selected
OI_yes	selected	n/a	n/a	n/a	no	selected
OI_yes	n/a	orphanage	n/a	n/a	no	selected
OI_no	deselected	n/a	n/a	n/a	no	deselected
OI_no	selected	See note*	OI_yes	yes	yes	deselected
OI_no	selected	n/a	OI_no	n/a	no	deselected
OI_no	n/a	orphanage	n/a	n/a	no	deselected

*Note: The menu cell is a child of an **OI_poly_menu**, or it is a child of an **OI_excl_menu** for which you have called the **OI_excl_menu** member function **allow_unsel** or for which the resource **unselect** is true.

13.6.2   Attaching Objects at Runtime

Using **add_subtree**, you can attach an object tree to a menu cell at runtime, using a configuration file which describes the objects. For example, you might want to create a dialog box with objects in it and attach the dialog box to a menu cell during execution of your application. Usually you create a configuration file using a builder such as ObjectBuilder or by editing a configuration file originally created by a builder.

add_subtree   (Member function)

```
void OI_menu_cell::add_subtree(
    OI_menu_cell          *cellp,              // pointer to menu cell
    void                  *filnamp,            // configuration file name
    OI_number             )                    // not used
```

add_subtree builds the objects from the configuration file *filnamp* and attaches them to the menu cell pointed to by *cellp*. The third argument is not used; it exists so that you can use **add_subtree** as a menu cell callback function. OI assumes that the file *filnamp* contains only one top level object. The object is associated in state OI_active_not_displayed at (OI_def_loc, OI_def_loc).

13.6.3   Pre-Submenu Activation Callbacks

You may want to change part of your application after the user activates a cell but before the cell's submenu becomes visible. For example, you may want to dynamically build the submenu that will be popped up, or you may want to modify an existing submenu before it becomes visible depending upon current information. To do this, use set_pre_popup to register a callback function to be invoked before any submenu is activated. Your callback function can then build or change the submenu. If you use the pre-popup function to build a submenu and attach it to the cell, be sure to call allow_submenu for the cell after it is first created (or set the OI_cell_submenu bit in the OI_cell_spec for the cell) so that the cell will display a submenu-marker even if no pull-down is yet present.

You can also register a pre-popup callback function for the submenu itself; see Chapter 12, "OI_menu."

set_pre_popup   (Member function)

```
void OI_menu_cell::set_pre_popup(
    OI_pre_popup_fnp           fnp,            // pointer to callback function
    void                       *argp=NULL)     // arbitrary argument for fnp


void OI_menu_cell::set_pre_popup(
    OI_callback                objp,           // memfnp's object
    OI_pre_popup_memfnp        memfnp,         // pointer to callback member function
    void                       *argp=NULL)     // arbitrary argument for memfnp
```

The set_pre_popup functions register a callback function to be invoked before any submenu on the cell becomes visible as a pop-up or pull-down/right menu. This callback is identified within OI as a cbPrePopup callback function (see Section 6.18, "Determining and Adding Callbacks; Multiple Callbacks," on page 6-117). If your action callback function is a member function, when it is invoked it will be called as if you had written *objp->memfnp*. See Section 2.5, "Callbacks and Event-Driven Programming," on page 2-16 for more explanation.

argp is optional, and can be any valid expression that can be cast to a pointer. You can use it to pass additional information to the function *fnp* or *memfnp*.

Writing the Pre-Popup Callback Function

If the **cbPrePopup** callback function is not a member function, write it in this form:

```
void fn(
    OI_d_tech        *objp,        // pointer to menu cell whose callback this is
    void             *argp)        // arbitrary argument
```

and if the **cbPrePopup** callback function is a member function, write it in this form:

```
void obj_class::memfn(
    OI_d_tech        *objp,        // pointer to menu cell whose callback this is
    void             *argp)        // arbitrary argument
```

where *obj_class* is the class of the object whose member function is *memfn*.

When your callback function is invoked, *argp* will be the argument specified in the set_pre_popup call.

13.6.4   Submenu Mapping Delay

OI maps (makes visible) most submenus immediately upon the user pressing the mouse button on the parent menu cell (or when the cell is selected through keyboard translations, accelerators, mnemonics, or programmatically). However, in the Motif model, if the menu cell is in a vertical menu, there is a *mapping delay*—a period of time which must elapse before the submenu appears. When the user rapidly traverses a pull-down menu, the mapping delay prevents pull-right menus from popping up until the pointer pauses on a particular cell.

If the user presses and releases the mouse button on a cell in less time than the mapping delay ("clicks" on the cell), the menu cell's action callback <u>is</u> executed and the submenu does <u>not</u> appear. If the user presses the mouse button for a period of time greater than the mapping delay, the action callback is <u>not</u> executed and the submenu <u>does</u> appear.

You can inquire and change this value using these functions, or the resource **mappingDelay**.

set_mapping_delay   (Member function)

```
void OI_menu_cell::set_mapping_delay(
    OI_number        dly)          // submenu mapping delay
```

set_mapping_delay sets the time, in milliseconds, after a Motif menu cell in a vertical menu becomes active that its sub-menu is mapped (becomes visible) to *dly*.

mapping_delay   (Member function)

```
OI_number OI_menu_cell::mapping_delay( )
```

mapping_delay returns the current mapping delay value. The default is 180 milliseconds.

13.6.5   Modifying Action Callbacks

These functions affect the callback to be executed when the menu cell is activated (fires). A menu cell in an **OI_button_menu** fires when the user clicks on it; a cell in other types of menus fires whenever the cell changes from the deselected state to the selected state or visa versa. A cell can also fire if you call a member function such as **select** for it.

OI supports multiple callbacks of the same type for a single object. The functions described here apply to the first **cbCellAction** callback if you have registered more than one.

get_action   (Member function)

```
OI_action_fnp OI_menu_cell::get_action( )
```

get_action returns a pointer to the free-standing callback function that is to be executed when the cell is activated. **get_action** returns NULL if the callback function registered is a member function instead of a free-standing function or if no callback function is registered for the cell.

get_action_memfn   (Member function)

```
OI_action_memfnp OI_menu_cell::get_action_memfn( )
```

get_action_memfn returns a pointer to the callback member function that is to be executed when the cell is activated. **get_action_memfn** returns NULL if the callback function registered is a free-standing function instead of a member function or if no callback function is registered for the cell.

get_obj   (Member function)

```
OI_callback *OI_menu_cell::get_obj( )
```

get_obj returns a pointer to the object that will be used to invoke the member function to be executed when the cell is activated. **get_obj** returns NULL if the callback function registered is a free-standing function instead of a member function or if no callback function is registered for the cell.

change_action   (Member function)

```
void OI_menu_cell::change_action(
    OI_action_fnp        fnp,            // pointer to callback function
    void                 *argp=NULL)     // arbitrary argument for fnp


void OI_menu_cell::change_action(
    OI_callback          *objp,          // memfnp's object
    OI_action_memfnp     memfnp,         // pointer to callback member function
    void                 *argp=NULL)     // arbitrary argument for memfnp
```

The **change_action** functions register a callback function to be invoked whenever the cell fires. A menu cell can have at most one action callback. If the cell already has a callback function, **change_action** replaces it with the new one. This callback is identified within OI as a **cbCellAction** callback function (see Section 6.18, "Determining and Adding Callbacks; Multiple Callbacks," on page 6-117). When the member function is invoked, it will be called as if you had written *objp->memfnp*. See Section 2.5, "Callbacks and Event-Driven Programming," on page 2-16 for more explanation.

argp is optional, and can be any valid expression that can be cast to a pointer. You can use it to pass additional information to the function *fnp* or *memfnp*.

See Section 13.4.4, "Action Callback Functions," on page 13-11 for information on writing the action callback function.

get_arg (Member function)

```
void *OI_menu_cell::get_arg( )
```

get_arg returns the argument pointer that will be passed to the callback action function.

change_arg (Member function)

```
void OI_menu_cell::change_arg(
    void              *argp)          // arbitrary argument
```

change_arg changes the argument pointer that is passed to the callback action routine when it is executed. The callback function itself is unchanged.

13.6.6 Position in Parent Menu

Sometimes you may find it necessary to find the position of a cell in its parent menu. You should avoid this if possible, since reordering cells in a menu may cause code based on cell position to malfunction. However, if you wish to add a new cell next to an existing cell, you must determine the existing cell's position. This is because you must specify the new cell's position when you use the member function **add_cell**.

number (Member function)

```
OI_number OI_menu_cell::number( )
```

number returns the relative position of the cell in its parent menu, $0 <= n <$ number of cells in the menu. number returns -1 if the cell is not associated with a menu.

13.6.7 Default Cell Management

set_default (Member function)

```
OI_stat OI_menu_cell::set_default( )
```

set_default establishes this cell as a default cell in its menu.

13.6.8 Controlling Appearance

These functions allow you to manipulate the appearance of the face of the menu cell. You can change the label, add a dialog-box-marker or submenu-marker to a cell that does not actually have a dialog box or submenu as a child, or add an accelerator or mnemonic label.

is_subbox (Member function)

```
OI_bool OI_menu_cell::is_subbox( )
```

is_subbox returns OI_yes if the cell will display a dialog-box-marker, either because it has a dialog box as a child, or because allow_subbox is in effect. Otherwise is_subbox returns OI_no.

allow_subbox (Member function)

```
void OI_menu_cell::allow_subbox( )
```

allow_subbox forces a cell to display a dialog-box-marker when the cell has no children. You may wish to use allow_subbox for a menu cell if you do not parent a dialog box to the cell; instead, your action callback routine for the cell will pop up the dialog box. See Program 18-6, "Use of allow_subbox (Subbox.C)" on page 18-39 for an example.

disallow_subbox (Member function)

```
void OI_menu_cell::disallow_subbox( )
```

disallow_subbox removes the dialog-box-marker displayed on a cell with allow_subbox. Do not call disallow_subbox for a cell which actually has a dialog box as a child, as this will cause unpredictable behavior.

is_submenu (Member function)

```
OI_bool OI_menu_cell::is_submenu( )
```

is_submenu returns OI_yes if the cell will display a submenu-marker, either because it has a submenu as a child, or because allow_submenu is in effect. Otherwise is_submenu returns OI_no.

allow_submenu (Member function)

```
void OI_menu_cell::allow_submenu( )
```

allow_submenu forces a cell to display a submenu-marker, even when the cell has no children. If the application is run using OPEN LOOK, the submenu-marker is an arrow. If the application is run using Motif, if the menu is horizontal, the cell has a flat cell face, and if the menu is vertical, the submenu-marker is an arrow. You may wish to use allow_submenu for a menu cell if you do not parent a submenu to the cell; instead your action callback routine for the cell will pop up the submenu.

disallow_submenu (Member function)

```
void OI_menu_cell::disallow_submenu( )
```

disallow_submenu removes the submenu-marker displayed on a cell with allow_submenu. Do not call disallow_submenu for a cell which actually has a submenu as a child, as this will cause unpredictable behavior.

label   (Member function)

```
char *OI_menu_cell::label( )
```

label returns a pointer to the text string for the cell label. If, when the menu cell was created, *labelp* pointed to text, then a pointer to the text is returned. The pointer is not to the original string, but to an OI private copy. You should consider this string read-only; you should copy it if you need to change it. If *labelp* pointed to a file name or static data, then label returns NULL.

length   (Member function)

```
OI_number OI_menu_cell::length( )
```

length returns the length of the cell label, in pixels, if the label is text. Otherwise length returns zero.

set_label   (Member function)

```
OI_stat OI_menu_cell::set_label(
    const char          *labelp)              // new label
```

set_label changes the label on the menu cell to *labelp*. If the cell is of type OI_icon_cell, OI_icon_data_cell, or OI_icon_pixmap_cell, it is converted to type OI_text_cell. If the cell is of type OI_separator_cell, it is unaffected.

set_label_char   (Member function)

```
OI_stat OI_menu_cell::set_label_char(
    OI_number           psn,                  // character position to change
    char                c)                    // new character
```

set_label_char changes the character at position *psn* (first character is in position 0) of the cell label to *c*. This call only makes sense if the cell is of type OI_text_cell; if the cell is of another type, the behavior of set_label_char is undefined.

set_label_chars   (Member function)

```
OI_stat OI_menu_cell::set_label_chars(
    OI_number           psn,                  // starting change character position
    OI_number           len,                  // number characters to replace
    const char          *textp)               // replacement text
```

set_label_chars replaces characters starting at position *psn* (0 <= *psn* < length( ))in the cell label with characters in *textp*. The number of characters replaced is whichever is smallest of *len*, length(*textp*), length(label( )). *textp* must be null-terminated. set_label_chars returns OI_ok if successful, and OI_no_char if *psn* is invalid.This call only makes sense if the cell is of type OI_text_cell; if the cell is of another type set_label_chars does nothing.

13.6.9   Setting Accelerator and Mnemonic Labels

When you specify an accelerator or mnemonic through the OI_d_tech member functions set_accelerators or set_mnemonics, or the user sets them using the OI_d_tech resources accelerators or mnemonics, OI modifies the labels of the cells to which the accelerator or mnemonic applies. If the cell cannot respond to a mnemonic, OI does not supply a default mnemonic label.

All accelerator and mnemonic labels can be overridden either through the OI_menu_cell member functions set_accelerator_label and set_mnemonic_label or through the OI_menu_cell resources acceleratorLabel and mnemonicLabel.

You can change the style of the label using the OI_connection resource mnemonicStyle.

For example, suppose you insert the following line into your .Xdefaults file:

```
HelloExit*exit.mnemonics: Ctrl <Key>x:fire( )
```

When you run the HelloExit program, you can quit the application by striking Control-x when the input focus is anywhere in the top level object (the OI_app_window object). Figure 13-4 shows the visual effect of this resource.

Figure 13-4   HelloExit with Mnemonic

If you decide that you want the mnemonic label to be other than the default created from the Mnemonics resource, you could add the following line to your .Xdefaults file:

```
HelloExit*exit.mnemonics: Ctrl <Key>x:fire( )
HelloExit*exit.mnemonicLabel: ^x
```

The application would now appear as in Figure 13-5.

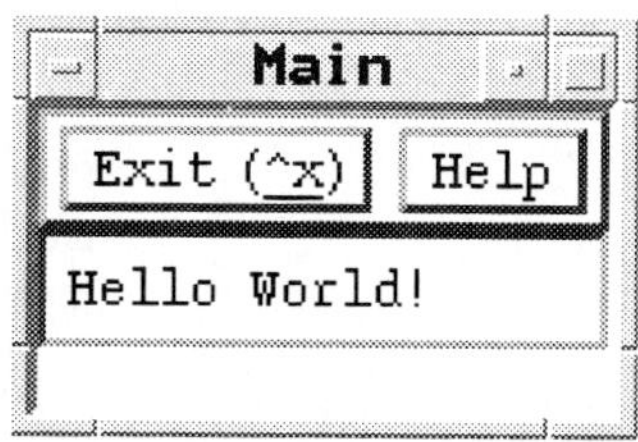

Figure 13-5   HelloExit with Mnemonic Label Explicitly Set

set_accelerator_label   (Member function)

```
OI_stat OI_menu_cell::set_accelerator_label(
    const char          *acc_lblp)              // new label
```

set_accelerator_label sets the accelerator label on the menu cell to *acc_lblp*.

set_mnemonic_label   (Member function)

```
OI_stat OI_menu_cell::set_mnemonic_label(
    const char          *mnem_lblp)           // new label
```

set_mnemonic_label sets the mnemonic label on the menu cell to *mnem_lblp*.

13.7 Resources

All resources from an **OI_menu_cell** object's base classes are available to it; in addition, OI fetches the resources shown in Table 13-3. For more information on resource management, see Chapter 39, "The OI Resource Mechanism."

Table 13-3 OI_menu_cell Resources

Resource	Description	Possible Values	
acceleratorLabel	Specifies the accelerator label to add to the cell label.	Any printable text	NULL
defaultCell	If on, marks the cell as the default cell in the menu.	Boolean	false
font	Specifies the font of the menu cell label.	Font name	Default font
label	Specifies the label of the menu cell.	Text string	(No default)
mappingDelay	Specifies the time, in milliseconds, after a Motif menu cell in a vertical menu becomes active that its sub-menu is mapped (becomes visible).	Non-negative integer	180
mnemonicLabel	Specifies the mnemonic label to add to the cell label.	Any printable text	NULL
selected	If on, the cell will initially be in the selected state. This resource should only be used for menu cells in exclusive or nonexclusive menus (not button menus).	Boolean	false
separator	Makes the cell a separator cell.	Boolean	false
subbox	If on, the cell will appear as if it has a dialog box attached.	Boolean	false
submenu	If on, the cell will appear as if it has a pull-down or pull-right submenu attached.	Boolean	false

13.8 Translations

All translations from an OI_menu_cell object's base classes are available to it; in addition the translations shown in Table 13-4 are available to it. See Chapter 40, "The OI Translation Mechanism" for a description of the Event Sequence entries in these tables as well as additional information on how to read these tables.

Table 13-4 OI_menu_cell Default Translations

Event Sequence	Action Functions Called
<BtnMotion>:	button_motion( )
<ButtonPress>:	button_press( )
<ButtonRelease>:	button_release( )
<EnterNotify>:	enter( )
<FocusIn>:	focus_in( )
<FocusOut>:	focus_out( )
<Key>:	menu_key( )
<Key>Control_L:	control( )
<Key>Control_R:	control( )
<Key>Down:	down( )
<Key>Escape:	cancel( )
<Key>Left:	left( )
<Key>Return:	display_submenu( ) select( )
<Key>Right:	right( )
<Key>Up:	up( )
<Key>space:	display_submenu( ) select( )
<KeyRelease>Control_L:	control( )
<KeyRelease>Control_R:	control( )
<LeaveNotify>:	leave( )
Alt <Key>space:	display_submenu( )

Table 13-5 OI_menu_cell Translation Functions

Function Name	Description
button_motion( )	In the OPEN LOOK model, examines amount of movement since cell was first entered and potentially causes submenu activation. May only be used with mouse motion events.
button_press( )	Brings down submenu if one is active from another cell. Temporarily selects the cell and highlights it. May only be used with mouse button events.
button_release( )	Causes cell to fire if no pulldown attached. Depending on the model, may fire the default cell in a submenu or bring up a submenu in click to stay up mode. May only be used with mouse button events.
cancel( )	Cancels the entire menu interaction associated, bringing down all sub-menus.
control( )	In the OPEN LOOK model, switches control between default selection setting and normal menu interaction, depending on whether key is being pressed or released.
display_submenu( )	Causes a submenu attached to the menu cell to be displayed as if it were activated using the mouse.
down( )	Traverses to the cell below the current one. If the first argument is "select", toggles the cell selection state and fires the cell.
enter( )	Temporarily toggles the cell selection state.
fire( )	Activates the menu cell as if the user had clicked a mouse button on it. This translation is usually used when you want to bind a keyboard accelerator or mnemonic to a particular function which is normally activated by a menu button.
leave( )	Returns the cell selection state to its condition before the menu interaction sequence started.
left( )	Traverses to the cell to the left of the current one. If the first argument is "select", toggles the cell selection state and fires the cell.
menu_key( )	Revectors unknown key events to the parent menu.
right( )	Traverses to the cell to the right of the current one. If the first argument is "select", toggles the cell selection state and fires the cell.

Table 13-5 OI_menu_cell Translation Functions

Function Name	Description
select( )	Toggles the state of the cell and fires the cell.
up( )	Traverses to the cell above the current one. If the first argument is "select", toggles the cell selection state and fires the cell.

13.9 Callback Functions

Table 13-6 lists the callbacks available for an OI_menu_cell object and the page number where the callback is documented. In addition, all of the callbacks from an OI_menu_cell object's base classes are available to it. See Section 6.18, "Determining and Adding Callbacks; Multiple Callbacks," on page 6-117 for additional information about manipulating callbacks.

Table 13-6 OI_menu_cell Callbacks

Callback Type	Callback Typedef	Description	Page Number
cbCellAction	OI_action_fnp/memfnp	Cell action callback function	13-11, 13-16
cbPrePopup	OI_pre_popup_fnp/memfnp	Pre-popup callback function	13-14

Chapter 14
OI_button_menu and OI_trans_menu

OI_button_menu and OI_trans_menu Functions

The following functions are available to **OI_button_menu** and **OI_trans_menu objects**, but are described in their own chapters.

OI_menu Member Functions

OI_d_tech Member Functions

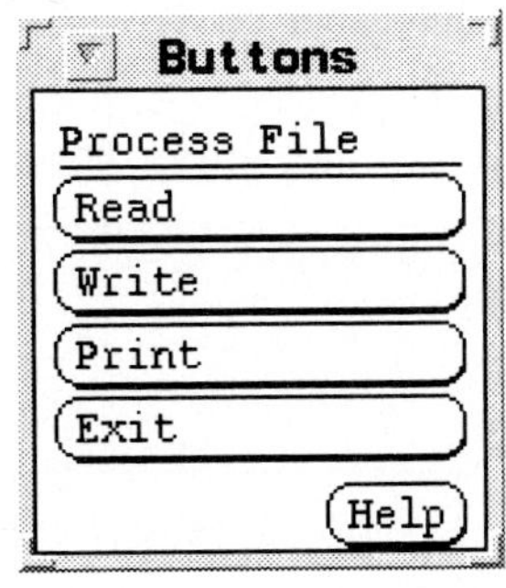

OI_button_menu and OI_trans_menu

14.1   Description

OI_trans_menu is the interaction method for menus whose cells have a momentary-selection characteristic. An OI_button_menu object is an OI_trans_menu in which the cells appear as ovals (OPEN LOOK model) or beveled rectangles (Motif model) with text or a glyph as the label. Currently, OI_button_menu is the only subclass of OI_trans_menu. You never directly create an OI_trans_menu object, only an OI_button_menu object. A menu cell in a button menu is activated (it triggers a call to its callback function) when the user clicks on the cell. The cell is in the selected state only during the period when the callback function is executing. After returning from the callback function, the cell returns to the deselected state. Since the cells in an OI_button_menu object do not preserve their selection condition, you probably will want to register an action callback function for each cell in the menu.

Use a transient menu (OI_button_menu) any time you are presenting items where choosing an item causes something to happen immediately. As an example, a menu containing the items "Read", "Write", "Print" and "Exit" should be an OI_button_menu.

14.2   Class Tree

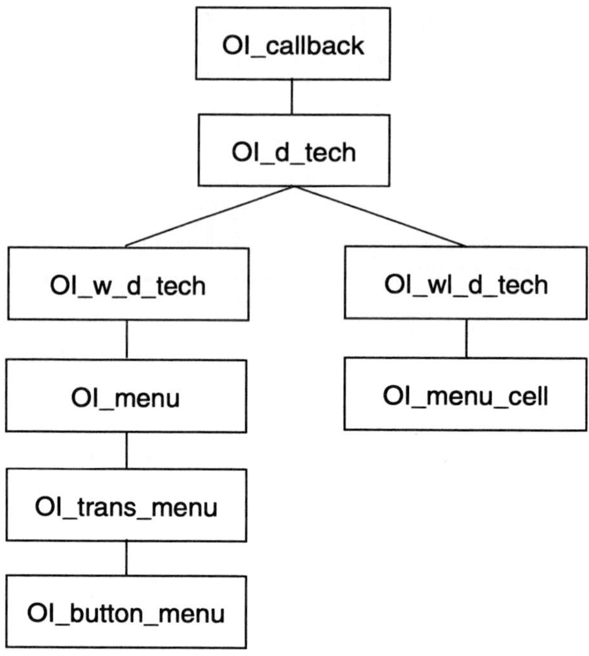

14.3   Runtime Interaction

Runtime interaction and functionality for OI_button_menu objects are similar, with a few differences, for the two interaction models. Motif ignores default cells, whereas OPEN LOOK uses default cells as menu selection accelerators. Both models respond to accelerators and mnemonics (see Chapter 40, "The OI Translation Mechanism")as well as keyboard traversal (see Chapter 13, "OI_menu_cell," page 13-22).

We first discuss Motif interaction and functionality in the subsections below, then that for OPEN LOOK.

14.3.1   Motif Runtime Interaction

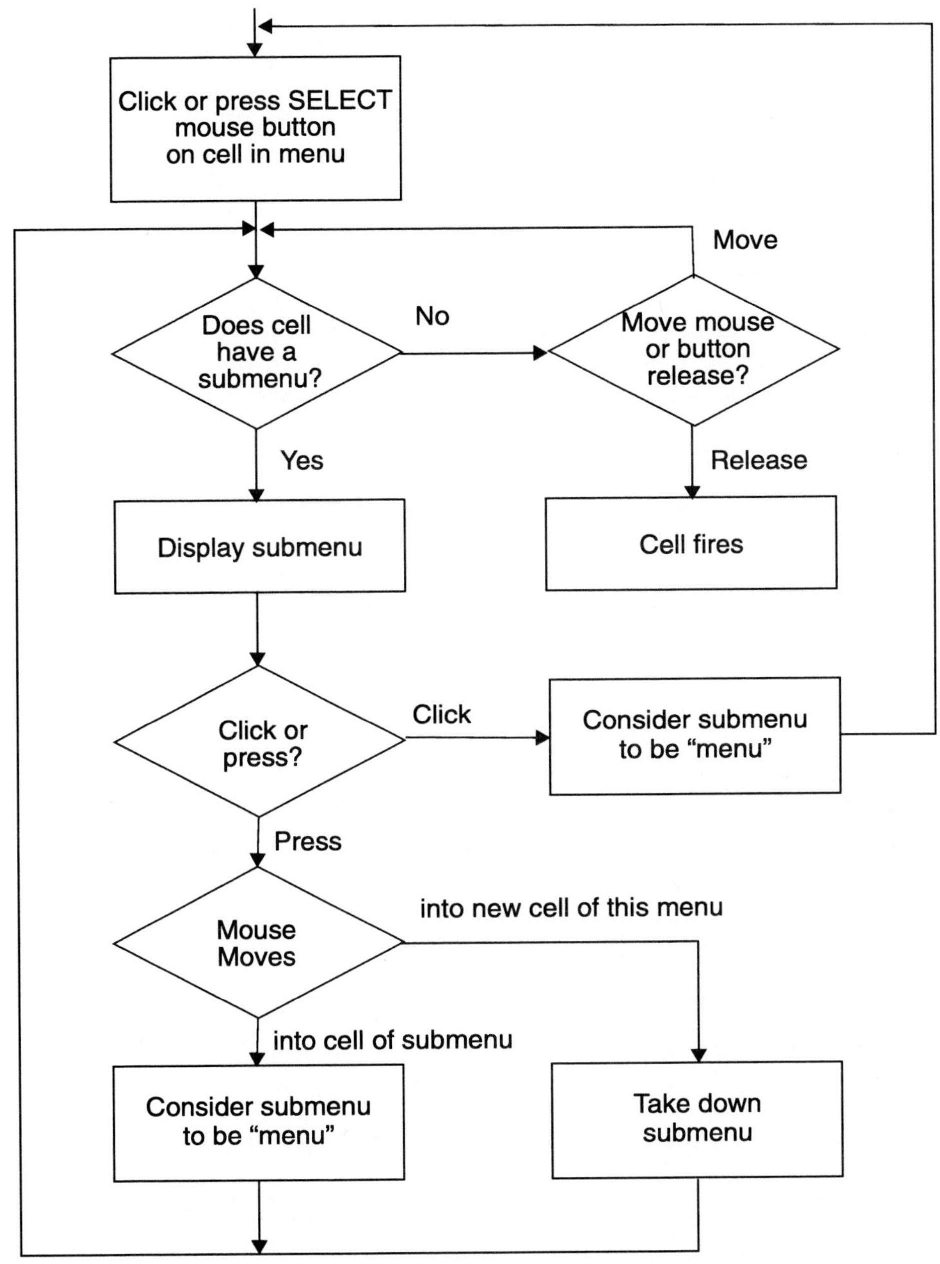

Figure 14-1   Motif OI_button_menu Action Callback Execution

14.3.1.1 Motif Cell Selection

To select a cell in an OI_button_menu object, move the mouse pointer over the desired cell, then click the SELECT mouse button. The selected cell becomes highlighted. If you press and hold the SELECT mouse button and move the pointer across the menu, only the cell directly under the pointer is highlighted. As you leave one cell and enter another, the old cell becomes un-highlighted and the new one becomes highlighted. When you release the mouse button, the cell under the pointer at that time is the one selected. When you select a cell that has no submenu associated with it, a call is made to the cell's action callback function. You can select a cell using the keyboard traversal mechanism, as well.

14.3.1.2 Motif Pop-up Menu Activation

If a menu is associated with an object other than a menu cell in state OI_active_not_displayed, it is a pop-up menu. Press the MENU mouse button over the parent object to cause the menu to become visible, then select a cell by releasing the button when the pointer is over the desired cell.

14.3.1.3 Motif Pull-down and Pull-right Menu Activation

If a submenu (a pull-down or pull-right menu) is associated with the cell you select, the action callback routine for the cell is <u>not</u> called. If you click to select the cell, its submenu appears and remains on the screen until you click the SELECT button again. If you move the mouse pointer over one of the submenu cells when you click the second time, that cell fires and its action callback function is executed (unless that cell also has a submenu attached to it, in which case its submenu appears).

If, instead of clicking, you press and hold the mouse button on the parent cell, its submenu becomes visible and remains on the screen until you release the SELECT button. The cell which is under the mouse pointer (if any) when you release the mouse button is the one that fires, and its action callback function is executed (unless that cell also has a submenu attached to it). This interaction is shown in Figure 14-1.

You can also use the keyboard traversal mechanism to traverse pull-down and pull-right menus.

14.3.2   OPEN LOOK Runtime Interaction

14.3.2.1 OPEN LOOK Cell Selection

Selecting a cell in a button menu the OPEN LOOK model is identical to that for Motif, except that you may use either the SELECT or MENU mouse button to select the cell.

14.3.2.2 OPEN LOOK Pull-down and Pull-right Menu Activation

If the cell under the pointer has a submenu (a pull-down or pull-right menu) associated with it, and if you press the MENU mouse button, the submenu becomes visible. You can then traverse the submenu and select a cell from it by releasing the mouse button while the pointer is over the desired cell. If you move the pointer off the submenu—to the left for a vertical submenu or to the top for a horizontal submenu—while the MENU mouse button is still depressed, the submenu disappears.

If you click the MENU mouse button (rather than pressing it) on a cell with a submenu attached, the submenu pops up. You can then select a cell from the submenu by clicking on it.

Default cells perform as menu accelerators. If a menu cell has a submenu attached, and if the submenu has a default cell (and no further submenu attached to the default cell), clicking on the original cell causes the default cell of the submenu to fire without bringing up the submenu. The cell which actually fires (its action callback is executed) is determined according to this algorithm:

```
fire_cell = cell selected from visible menu.
while fire_cell has a submenu and submenu has a default cell set:
     fire_cell = default cell in submenu.
execute callback for fire_cell.
```

Figure 14-2 shows a more complete version of this algorithm.

You can tell which cell will fire by pressing the SELECT mouse button and holding it down over a cell in the visible menu. If a cell from a submenu will fire upon button release, the label in the visible cell changes to the label for the default cell which would fire. Moving the mouse pointer out of the menu and releasing the button dismisses the action without causing any cell to fire.

You can also use the keyboard traversal mechanism to traverse pull-down and pull-right menus.

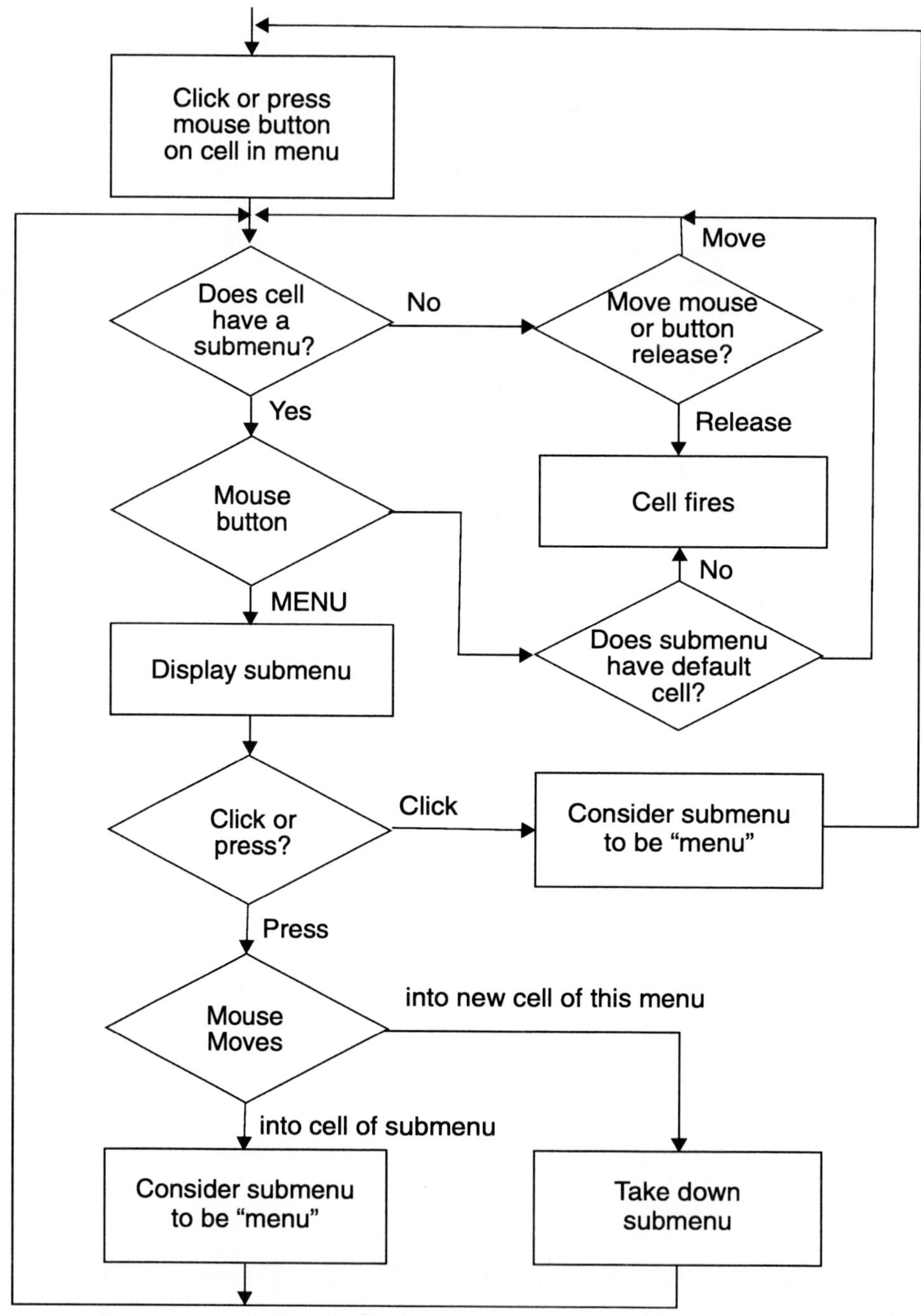

Figure 14-2   OPEN LOOK OI_button_menu Action Callback Execution

14.3.2.3 Changing the Default Cell

If the application is run using Motif, default cells are ignored. However, if the application is run using OPEN LOOK, the default cell can serve as a selection accelerator; that is, you can activate the default cell on a submenu without having to pull up (display) the submenu, as described above.

If the menu has a default cell set, it is displayed with an extra border. Unless the menu is a pull-down or pull-right menu or an abbreviated menu, there is no need to change the default cell; it has no effect. To change the default cell, press the MENU mouse button to bring up the menu, move the mouse pointer to the desired cell, then release the MENU mouse button while simultaneously pressing the MENUDEFAULT key on the keyboard (normally the Control key). The default selection for the menu changes to the cell under the pointer when you release the button; no cell is actually activated.

Figure 14-3 shows a submenu with a default cell, "Courier".

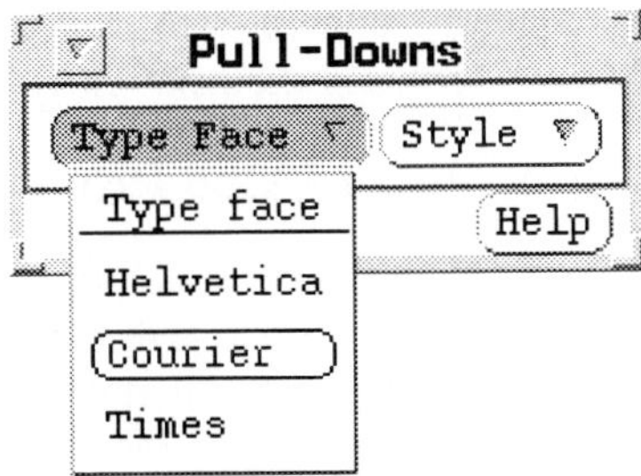

Figure 14-3   Default Cell in Submenu, OPEN LOOK

14.3.3   OPEN LOOK Pop-up Menu Activation

OPEN LOOK pop-up menus are activated in the same manner as are Motif pop-up menus.

14.4   OI_button_menu Creation

There are two forms of create function for an OI_button_menu object, one for each of the two situations you will encounter when you create a menu. In the first case, you know the menu cell contents in advance, and you can create static structures describing the menu cells. You can let the OI menu creation code create the individual menu cells for you. In the second case you do not know the cell specifications in advance. In this case you must create the menu cells yourself (using oi_create_menu_cell) and then create the menu using these cells.

14.4.1   Creating an OI_button_menu From Menu Cell Specifications

When you use this method, you declare an OI_cell_spec structure (see Chapter 13, "OI_menu_cell"), in which you define all the information about each menu cell. One of the arguments to the first form of oi_create_button_menu is a pointer to this structure; the menu creation mechanism automatically generates the individual OI_menu_cell objects from the OI_cell_spec and parent them to the OI_button_menu object. Since the cell specifications are not kept as part of the final menu (they are only used to create the menu cells, which are then kept as part of the final menu), you may reuse the same cell specifications to create more than one menu.

oi_create_button_menu   (Free-standing function)

```
OI_button_menu *oi_create_button_menu(
    const char        *namp,                // pointer to object name
    OI_number         n_cell,               // number of cells in menu
    OI_cell_spec      *cell_specp,          // pointer to cell info
    OI_orient         orient=OI_vertical,   // orientation of menu
    const char        *titlep=NULL)         // title for menu
```

cell_specp points to the **OI_cell_spec** structure. If you omit *orient*, **OI_vertical** is assumed. If you omit *titlep* or if it is NULL, the menu will have no title.

The macro **OI_count** is the easiest way to specify *n_cell*. It takes a single argument, the name of the **OI_cell_spec** structure which is pointed to by *cell_specp*. See Program 12-1, "Menu Creation: Implicitly Created Menu Cells (BtnMnuImplicit.C)" on page 12-7 for an example.

14.4.2 Creating an OI_button_menu Using Previously Created Menu Cells

To create a menu from menu cells, rather than cell specifications, you must first create the individual menu cells. The function for creating menus from menu cells expects a vector of pointers to cells as one of its arguments. The vector itself is not retained in the final menu, so you may use a local array on the stack or allocated from the heap. To create the menu cells, you call the function oi_create_menu_cell once for each cell (See Chapter 13, "OI_menu_cell"), storing the result in the vector of cell pointers. Then you create the menu using the second form of oi_create_button_menu, passing it a pointer to the array of cell pointers. The menu creation mechanism automatically parents the cells to the **OI_button_menu** object. Since the actual cells are kept as part of the final menu, you cannot reuse the same cells to create more than one menu. To copy cells to use in a new menu, use the **OI_d_tech** member function **clone**.

oi_create_button_menu   (Free-standing function)

```
OI_button_menu *oi_create_button_menu(
    const char        *namp,                // pointer to object name
    OI_number         n_cell,               // number of cells in menu
    OI_menu_cell      **cellp,              // pointer to cells
    OI_orient         orient=OI_vertical,   // orientation of menu
    const char        *titlep=NULL)         // title for menu
```

cellp points to the menu cells that you create dynamically using calls to oi_create_menu_cell. If you omit *orient*, **OI_vertical** is assumed. If you omit *titlep* or it is NULL, the menu will have no title. See Program 12-2, "Menu Creation: Explicitly Created Menu Cells (BtnMnuExplicit.C)" on page 12-8 for an example.

14.5 Base Class Member Functions

You can use all of the member functions of OI_d_tech and OI_menu for an OI_button_menu object. You can use the member functions of OI_menu_cell for the cells of an OI_button_menu object.

14.5.1 Selection Inquiry Functions

Since a button menu deselects a cell as soon as its action callback function has returned, the **selected** function returns NULL and the **num_selected** function returns -1 except when called from within the cell action callback function. If you call **selected** from within the cell action callback function, it returns a pointer to the cell that activated the action callback. You should write all of your cell action callback functions to test whether the cell is in the selected or deselected state regardless of the type of menu to which the cell belongs. This ensures that the cell action function will always be correct even if someone changes the menu type at some later date.

14.6 Resources

All resources from OI_d_tech are available to an OI_button_menu object; in addition, OI fetches the resources shown in Table 14-1. For more information on resource management, see Chapter 39, "The OI Resource Mechanism."

Table 14-1   OI_button_menu Resources

Resource	Description	Possible Values	Default Value
mainMenu	If on, specifies that the menu should be used as the main menu for the enclosing OI_app_window.	Boolean	false

14.7 Translations

All translations from an OI_button_menu object's base classes are available to it; it has no additional translations.

14.8 Callback Functions

There are no callbacks specifically for an OI_button_menu object. All of the callbacks from an OI_button_menu object's base classes are available to it.

Chapter 15
OI_excl_menu, OI_excl_check_menu, OI_excl_rect_menu

OI_excl_menu, OI_excl_check_menu, OI_excl_rect_menu Functions

OI_excl_menu Member Functions

The following functions are available to an **OI_excl_menu** object, but are described in their own chapter.

OI_menu Member Functions

OI_d_tech Member Functions

OI_excl_menu,
OI_excl_check_menu,
OI_excl_rect_menu

15.1 Description

An OI_excl_menu (exclusive menu) is a menu which has a longterm-selection characteristic where at most one cell can be in the selected state at any time. There are two forms of exclusive menus, both derived from OI_excl_menu: OI_excl_check_menu and OI_excl_rect_menu. They are identical in function; only the appearance differs. A cell in an exclusive menu has *longterm-selection* characteristics. This means that when selected by the user, the cell triggers a callback function if one is registered, then stays in the selected state until it is deselected by the user (typically by the user selecting another cell), at which point it triggers the callback function again, then stays in the deselected state. At any time, you can query the state of a longterm-selection menu to determine which cell, if any, is in the selected state. You will seldom register any action callback functions for the cells of an exclusive menu; instead, you will query the menu after the user makes selections, and then perform the necessary tasks depending on which cell (if any) is in the selected state.

The cells in an OI_excl_check_menu object appear as *bullets* (diamonds in the Motif model, circles in the OPEN LOOK model) displayed next to labels or glyphs. The bullets are either filled, indicating that the cell is in the selected state, or empty, indicating that the cell is in the deselected state. OI_excl_check_menu objects in both the Motif and OPEN LOOK models are pictured at the top of this chapter.

The cells in an OI_excl_rect_menu object appear as labels or glyphs enclosed in rectangles. The rectangle enclosing a selected cell is enhanced with a heavier outline (OPEN LOOK 2D) or a different shading (Motif and OPEN LOOK 3D). However, Motif limits the use of an OI_excl_rect_menu to a scrolling menu. For this reason, when your program is run using Motif, calls to create an OI_excl_rect_menu are automatically converted to the corresponding calls to create an OI_excl_check_menu object unless the menu is being used in an OI_scroll_menu (See Chapter 34, "OI_scroll_menu."). OI_excl_rect_menu objects in both the Motif and OPEN LOOK models are pictured in Figure 15-1.

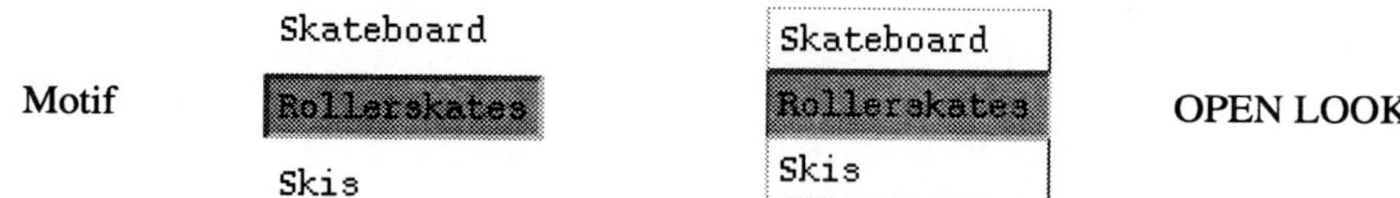

Figure 15-1 OI_excl_rect_menus

By default, it is not possible to turn off all the cells in an exclusive menu. However, you can condition the menu so that all cells can be turned off using the member function allow_unsel.

You should use an exclusive menu for those situations where the user can select at most a single item, and where the selection must stay in evidence until it is changed to something else. For example, an interface for choosing a custom automobile might use an exclusive menu to allow the user to select which kind of radio, if any, is desired. Since the automobile can have at most one radio in it, and since the user should be able to see which options have been chosen long after the choice has been made, an exclusive menu is the right object to use for this function. The menu cells would not have any action callbacks set for them. At the time the user finally instructs the program to order the car, the program would check which cell, if any, is selected.

An example of an exclusive menu where action callback functions would be registered for the menu cells is the following: A travel agent might have a package where a button labeled "Make Reservation" pops up a dialog box containing information for each leg of a trip. The dialog box might have an exclusive menu for the type of transportation desired—air, rail, steamship, and automobile. Selecting a mode of transportation might display a list of schedules for the chosen mode of travel. The callback registered for each cell would do the work necessary to present the schedule of possible departures.

15.2 Class Tree

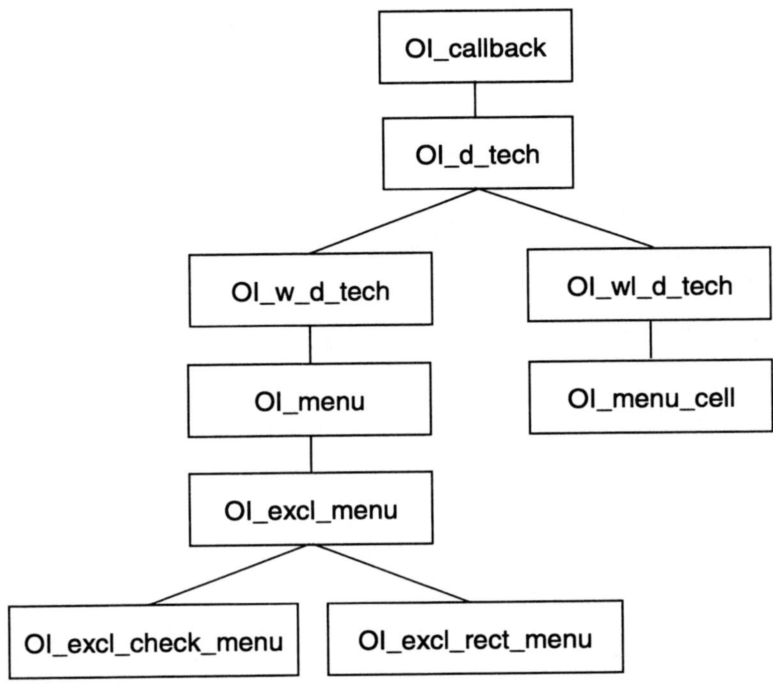

15.3 Runtime Interaction

To select a cell in an exclusive menu, move the mouse pointer over the desired cell and click the SELECT mouse button. The selected cell will be highlighted. If you press and hold the SELECT mouse button and move the pointer across the menu, only the cell directly under the pointer will become highlighted; when you release the mouse button, the cell under the pointer at that time will be the one selected. By default, an OI_excl_menu always has exactly one cell in the selected state. When you click on a cell that is in the deselected state, the previously selected cell becomes deselected, and the new cell becomes selected. The action callback functions (if any) for both cells are executed, first the function for the cell becoming deselected, then the function for the cell becoming selected. Within the callback function, you can use the OI_menu_cell member function selected to determine if the cell is being turned on or off. If you click on a cell in the selected state, the cell's state will not change, but the action callback function will be executed.

If allow_unsel has been called for the menu, the menu can have either zero or one cell in the selected state. In this case, the above discussion holds true except that clicking on a cell in the selected state will cause it to become deselected (and the action callback function will be executed).

Pull-down, pull-right and pop-up menu activations behave in the same fashion as OI_button_menu. Changing the default cell is also the same.

Exclusive menus respond to accelerators and mnemonics (see Chapter 40, "The OI Translation Mechanism"), as well as keyboard traversal (see Chapter 13, "OI_menu_cell," page 13-page 22).

15.4   Exclusive Menu Creation

There are two forms of create function for each of the exclusive menu types, one for each of the two situations you will encounter when you create a menu. In the first case, you know the menu cell contents in advance, and you can create static structures describing the menu cells. You can let the OI menu creation code create the individual menu cells for you. In the second case you do not know the cell specifications in advance. In this case you must create the menu cells yourself (using oi_create_menu_cell) and then create the menu using these cells.

15.4.1   Creating an OI_excl_menu From Menu Cell Specifications

If you know the contents of the menu in advance, declare an OI_cell_spec structure (see Chapter 13, "OI_menu_cell"), in which you define all the information for each cell. One of the arguments of the three forms of oi_create_excl_*_menu shown here is a pointer to this structure; the menu creation mechanism automatically generates the individual OI_menu_cell objects from the OI_cell_spec and parent them to the menu. Since the cell specifications are not kept as part of the final menu (they are only used to create the menu cells, which are then kept as part of the final menu), you may reuse the same cell specifications to create more than one menu.

You can use any of the three functions below to create an exclusive menu from static cell specifications. The first form, oi_create_excl_menu, creates a default exclusive menu for the model being used. This is an OI_excl_check_menu object for all models. The second form, oi_create_excl_check_menu, creates an OI_excl_check_menu object. The third form, oi_create_excl_rect_menu, creates an OI_excl_rect_menu object, unless the model is Motif. In Motif, oi_create_excl_rect_menu creates an OI_excl_check_menu object, since Motif does not support free-standing rectangle exclusive menus. (As noted above, you can make a exclusive rectangle Motif menu in an OI_scroll_menu object. See Chapter 34.)

oi_create_excl_menu   (Free-standing function)

```
    OI_excl_menu *oi_create_excl_menu(
        const char          *namp,              // pointer to object name
        OI_number           n_cell,             // number of cells in menu
        OI_cell_spec        *cell_specp,         // pointer to cell info
        OI_orient           orient=OI_vertical,  // orientation of menu
        const char          *titlep=NULL)        // title for menu
```

oi_create_excl_check_menu   (Free-standing function)

```
    OI_excl_check_menu *oi_create_excl_check_menu(
        const char          *namp,              // pointer to object name
        OI_number           n_cell,             // number of cells in menu
        OI_cell_spec        *cell_specp,         // pointer to cell info
        OI_orient           orient=OI_vertical,  // orientation of menu
        const char          *titlep=NULL)        // title for menu
```

oi_create_excl_rect_menu   (Free-standing function)

```
OI_excl_rect_menu *oi_create_excl_rect_menu(
    const char          *namp,            // pointer to object name
    OI_number           n_cell,           // number of cells in menu
    OI_cell_spec        *cell_specp,       // pointer to cell info
    OI_orient           orient=OI_vertical, // orientation of menu
    const char          *titlep=NULL)      // title for menu
```

cell_specp points to the OI_cell_spec structure. If you omit *orient*, OI_vertical is assumed. If you omit *titlep* or it is NULL, the menu will have no title.

15.4.2   Creating an OI_excl_menu Using Previously Created Menu Cells

To create a menu from menu cells, rather than cell specifications, you must first create the individual menu cells. The function for creating menus from menu cells expects a vector of pointers to cells as one of its arguments. The vector itself is not retained in the final menu; you can use a local array on the stack, a permanently allocated global array, or space allocated from the heap using malloc. To create the menu cells, you call the function oi_create_menu_cell once for each cell (see Chapter 13, "OI_menu_cell"), storing the result in the vector of cell pointers. You then create the menu using one of the forms of oi_create_excl_*_menu shown below, passing it a pointer to the array of cell pointers. The menu creation mechanism automatically parents the cells to the menu. Since the actual cells are kept as part of the final menu, you cannot reuse the same cells to create more than one menu. If you do attempt to reuse them, they will be unparented from the original menu and reparented to the new menu.

You can use any of the three functions below to create an exclusive menu from a vector of menu cell pointers.

oi_create_excl_menu   (Free-standing function)

```
OI_excl_menu *oi_create_excl_menu(
    const char          *namp,            // pointer to object name
    OI_number           n_cell,           // number of cells in menu
    OI_menu_cell        **cellp,           // pointer to cells
    OI_orient           orient=OI_vertical, // orientation of menu
    const char          *titlep=NULL)      // title for menu
```

oi_create_excl_check_menu   (Free-standing function)

```
OI_excl_check_menu *oi_create_excl_check_menu(
    const char          *namp,            // pointer to object name
    OI_number           n_cell,           // number of cells in menu
    OI_menu_cell        **cellp,           // pointer to cells
    OI_orient           orient=OI_vertical, // orientation of menu
    const char          *titlep=NULL)      // title for menu
```

oi_create_excl_rect_menu   (Free-standing function)

```
OI_excl_rect_menu *oi_create_excl_rect_menu(
    const char          *namp,              // pointer to object name
    OI_number           n_cell,             // number of cells in menu
    OI_menu_cell        **cellp,            // pointer to cells
    OI_orient           orient=OI_vertical, // orientation of menu
    const char          *titlep=NULL)       // title for menu
```

cellp points to the menu cells that you create dynamically using calls to oi_create_menu_cell.
If you omit *orient*, OI_vertical is assumed. If you omit *titlep* or it is NULL, the menu will have
no title.

15.5   Base Class Member Functions

You can use all of the member functions of OI_d_tech and OI_menu for an OI_excl_menu,
OI_excl_check_menu, or OI_excl_rect_menu object. You can use the member functions of
OI_menu_cell for the cells of any exclusive menu.

15.6   OI_excl_menu Member Functions

The functions described below apply to all forms of exclusive menus, whether an
OI_excl_check_menu or an OI_excl_rect_menu.

15.6.1   Controlling Click Cell Deselection and Callback Execution

By default, an exclusive menu always has exactly one cell in the selected state. Using the functions
described below, you can change the menu to be able to have either zero or one cell in the selected
state. If you have called allow_unsel for an exclusive menu, and the user clicks on the cell which is
in the selected state, the cell will change to the deselected state and the action callback function
registered for the cell will be executed. The menu will then have zero cells in the selected state.

By default, if a cell is in the selected state, and the user clicks on it, its action callback (if any) is
executed. This is called *re-selecting* a cell. If you do not want your cell callback to be executed if the
cell is already in the selected state, that is, if you do not want the menu to allow re-selecting, you can
call disallow_resel for the menu.

is_unsel   (Member function)

```
OI_bool OI_excl_menu::is_unsel( )
```

is_unsel returns OI_yes if the menu allows deselecting all cells, otherwise is_unsel returns
OI_no.

allow_unsel   (Member function)

```
void OI_excl_menu::allow_unsel( )
```

allow_unsel conditions the menu to allow deselecting all cells.

disallow_unsel   (Member function)

```
void OI_excl_menu::disallow_unsel( )
```

disallow_unsel conditions the menu to prevent deselecting all cells. This is the default.

is_resel   (Member function)

```
OI_bool OI_excl_menu::is_resel( )
```

is_resel returns OI_yes if the menu allows re-selection; that is, allows an already-selected cell to execute its callback if it is clicked on. Otherwise is_resel returns OI_no.

allow_resel   (Member function)

```
void OI_excl_menu::allow_resel( )
```

allow_resel conditions the menu to allow cell re-selection. This is the default.

disallow_resel   (Member function)

```
void OI_excl_menu::disallow_resel( )
```

disallow_resel conditions the menu to not allow cell re-selection.

15.7 An OI_excl_menu Programming Example

Program 15-1 shows the code that generated the exclusive menus pictured at the top of this chapter.

```
#include <OI/oi.H>                              /* ExclMenu.C */

int main(int argc, char **argv)
{
                OI_connection   *conp;
                OI_app_window   *wp;
                OI_menu         *mp;

        static OI_cell_spec   mode_cells[] = {
                {"add","Add"},
                {"change","Change"},
                {"delete","Delete"},
                };

    if (conp = OI_init(&argc,argv,"ExclMenu")) {
        wp = oi_create_app_window("main",1,1,"ExclMenu");
        wp->set_layout(OI_layout_row);

        mp = oi_create_excl_check_menu("access_mode",OI_count(mode_cells),
                        &mode_cells[0],OI_vertical,"Data Access Mode");
        mp->layout_associated_object(wp,10,10,OI_active);
        wp->set_associated_object(wp->root( ),OI_def_loc,OI_def_loc,OI_active);
        OI_begin_interaction( );
        OI_fini( );
    }
}
```

Program 15-1   OI_excl_check_menu for Data Access Mode (ExclMenu.C)

15.8   Resources

All resources from an **OI_excl_menu** object's base classes are available to it; in addition, OI fetches the resources shown in Table 15-1. For more information on resource management, see Chapter 39, "The OI Resource Mechanism."

Table 15-1   OI_excl_menu Resources

Resource	Description	Possible Values	Default Value
unselect	If on, specifies that all cells in the menu may be in the deselected state at one time.	Boolean	false

15.9   Translations

All translations from an **OI_excl_menu** object's base classes are available to it; it has no additional translations.

15.10 Callback Functions

All of the callbacks from an OI_excl_menu object's base classes are available to it; it has no additional callbacks.

Chapter 16
OI_poly_menu, OI_poly_check_menu, OI_poly_rect_menu

The following functions are available to an **OI_poly_menu** object, but are described in their own chapter.

OI_menu Member Functions

OI_d_tech Member Functions

OI Programmer's Guide

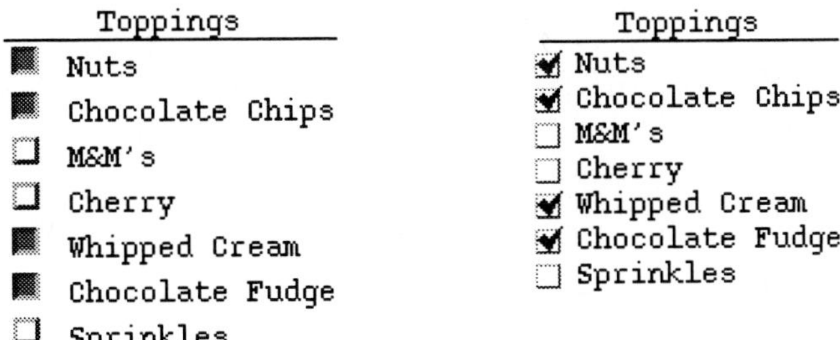

OI_poly_menu,
OI_poly_check_menu,
OI_poly_rect_menu

16.1 Description

An **OI_poly_menu** (non-exclusive menu) is a menu which has a longterm-selection characteristic which allows more than one cell to be in the selected state at any time. There are two forms of non-exclusive menu, both derived from **OI_poly_menu**: **OI_poly_check_menu** and **OI_poly_rect_menu**. They are identical in function; only the appearance differs. A cell in a non-exclusive menu has a *longterm-selection* characteristic. This means that when selected by the user, the cell triggers a callback function if one is registered, then stays in the selected state until it is deselected by the user, at which point it triggers the callback function again, then stays in the deselected state. At any time, you can query the state of a longterm-selection menu to determine which cells, if any, are in the selected state. Typically, you will not register any action callback functions for the cells of a non-exclusive menu; instead, you will query the menu after the user makes selections, and then perform the necessary tasks depending on which cells (if any) are in the selected state.

The cells in an **OI_poly_check_menu** object appear as check-boxes (squares in both the **OPEN LOOK** and Motif models), displayed next to labels or glyphs. The check-boxes are checked in the **OPEN LOOK** model and filled in the Motif model to indicate that the cell is in the selected state. The check-boxes are empty in both models to indicate that the cell is in the deselected state. **OI_poly_check_menu** objects in both the Motif and OPEN LOOK models are pictured at the top of this chapter.

The cells in an **OI_poly_rect_menu** object appear as labels or glyphs enclosed in rectangles. The rectangle enclosing a selected cell is enhanced with a heavier outline or interior shading. However, Motif limits the use of an **OI_poly_rect_menu** to a scrolling menu (see Chapter 34, "OI_scroll_menu"). For this reason, when your program is run using Motif, calls to create an **OI_poly_rect_menu** will automatically be converted to the corresponding calls to create an **OI_poly_check_menu** unless the menu is being used in an **OI_scroll_menu**.

OI_poly_rect_menu objects in both the Motif and OPEN LOOK models are pictured in Figure 16-1.

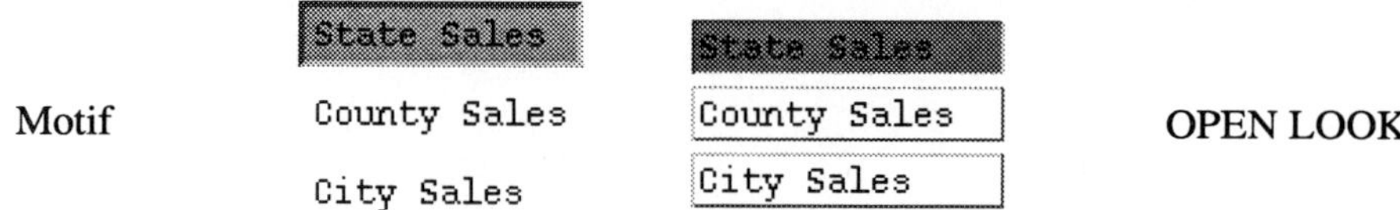

Motif   OPEN LOOK

Figure 16-1   OI_poly_rect_menus

A non-exclusive menu does not have a default cell.

You should use a non-exclusive menu for those situations where the user may select zero or more items from a group. For example, a non-exclusive menu is the best object to use when presenting any quantity which represents a bit field, such as file protections in most operating systems. Another example would be a system for entering the toppings desired on an ice cream sundae. This example is pictured at the beginning of this chapter.

16.2   Class Tree

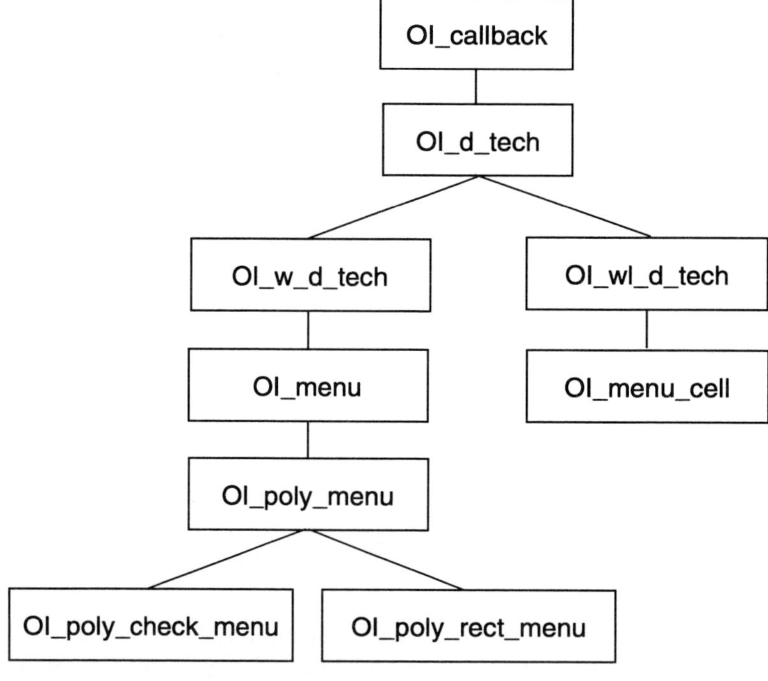

16.3   Runtime Interaction

To select a cell, move the mouse pointer over the desired cell and click the SELECT mouse button. The same actions deselect a cell that is in the selected state. Cells in the selected state are highlighted.

If you press and hold the SELECT mouse button and move the pointer across the menu, each cell changes its selection state as the pointer moves into it; when the pointer leaves the cell, the cell reverts to the selection state it previously had. When you release the mouse button, the menu remains in the selection state you see as you release the button. When you click on a cell that is in the deselected state, changing it to selected, the action callback function for the cell (if any) is invoked. Note that the action callback function is also invoked when you click on a cell that is in the selected state, changing it to deselected. Within the callback function, you can use the OI_menu_cell member function **selected** to determine if the cell is being turned on or off.

Pull-down, pull-right and pop-up menu activation behave in the same fashion as OI_button_menu.

Motif menus respond to the keyboard translation mechanism and mnemonics; these are described in earlier chapters.

16.4   Non-exclusive Menu Creation

There are two forms of create function for each of the non-exclusive menu types, one for each of the two situations you will encounter when you create a menu. In the first case, you know the menu cell contents in advance, and you can create static structures describing the menu cells. You can let the OI menu creation code create the individual menu cells for you. In the second case you do not know the cell specifications in advance. In this case you must create the menu cells yourself (using oi_create_menu_cell) and then create the menu using these cells.

16.4.1   Creating an OI_poly_menu From Menu Cell Specifications

When you use this method, you declare an OI_cell_spec structure (see Chapter 13, "OI_menu_cell"), in which you define all the information about each menu cell. One of the arguments to the oi_create_poly_*_menu functions described in this section is a pointer to the OI_cell_spec structure; the menu creation mechanism automatically generates the individual OI_menu_cell objects from the OI_cell_spec and parents them to the menu. Since the cell specifications are not kept as part of the final menu (they are only used to create the menu cells, which are then kept as part of the final menu), you may reuse the same cell specifications to create more than one menu.

You can use any of the three functions below to create a non-exclusive menu from static cell specifications. The first form, oi_create_poly_menu, creates a default non-exclusive menu for the model being used. This is an OI_poly_check_menu object for all models. The second form, oi_create_poly_check_menu, creates an OI_poly_check_menu object. The third form, oi_create_poly_rect_menu, creates an OI_poly_rect_menu object, unless the model is Motif. In Motif, oi_create_poly_rect_menu creates an OI_poly_check_menu object, since Motif does not support free-standing rectangle non-exclusive menus. (As noted above, you can make a rectangle non-exclusive Motif menu in an OI_scroll_menu object. See Chapter 34.)

See Program 12-4, "Non-exclusive Menu with Later Query (SelectedQuery.C)," on page 12-11 for an example of non-exclusive menu creation.

oi_create_poly_menu   (Free-standing function)

```
OI_poly_menu *oi_create_poly_menu(
    const char          *namp,              // pointer to object name
    OI_number           n_cell,             // number of cells in menu
    OI_cell_spec        *cell_specp,        // pointer to cell info
    OI_orient           orient=OI_vertical, // orientation of menu
    const char          *titlep=NULL)       // title for menu
```

oi_create_poly_check_menu   (Free-standing function)

```
OI_poly_check_menu *oi_create_poly_check_menu(
    const char          *namp,              // pointer to object name
    OI_number           n_cell,             // number of cells in menu
    OI_cell_spec        *cell_specp,        // pointer to cell info
    OI_orient           orient=OI_vertical, // orientation of menu
    const char          *titlep=NULL)       // title for menu
```

oi_create_poly_rect_menu   (Free-standing function)

```
OI_poly_rect_menu *oi_create_poly_rect_menu(
    const char          *namp,              // pointer to object name
    OI_number           n_cell,             // number of cells in menu
    OI_cell_spec        *cell_specp,        // pointer to cell info
    OI_orient           orient=OI_vertical, // orientation of menu
    const char          *titlep=NULL)       // title for menu
```

cell_specp points to the OI_cell_spec structure. If you omit *orient*, OI_vertical is assumed. If you omit *titlep* or set it to NULL, the menu will have no title.

16.4.2 Creating an OI_poly_menu Using Previously Created Menu Cells

To create a menu from menu cells, rather than cell specifications, you must first create the individual menu cells using oi_create_menu_cell. The form of oi_create_poly_*_menu function for creating menus from menu cells expects a vector of pointers to cells as one of its arguments. The vector itself is not retained in the final menu; you may use a local array on the stack, a permanently allocated global array, or space allocated from the heap using malloc. To create the menu cells, you call the function oi_create_menu_cell once for each cell (see Chapter 13, "OI_menu_cell"), storing the result in the vector of cell pointers. Then you create the menu using one of the forms of oi_create_poly_*_menu shown in this section, passing it a pointer to the array of cell pointers. The menu creation mechanism will automatically parent the cells to the menu. Since the actual cells are kept as part of the final menu, you cannot reuse the same cells to create more than one menu.If you do reuse this array, you will find that the menu cells are reparented to the new menu.

You can use any of the three functions below to create a non-exclusive menu from a vector of menu cell pointers.

oi_create_poly_menu   (Free-standing function)

```
OI_poly_menu *oi_create_poly_menu(
    const char        *namp,               // pointer to object name
    OI_number         n_cell,              // number of cells in menu
    OI_menu_cell      **cellp,             // pointer to cells
    OI_orient         orient=OI_vertical,  // orientation of menu
    const char        *titlep=NULL)        // title for menu
```

oi_create_poly_check_menu   (Free-standing function)

```
OI_poly_check_menu *oi_create_poly_check_menu(
    const char        *namp,               // pointer to object name
    OI_number         n_cell,              // number of cells in menu
    OI_menu_cell      **cellp,             // pointer to cells
    OI_orient         orient=OI_vertical,  // orientation of menu
    const char        *titlep=NULL)        // title for menu
```

oi_create_poly_rect_menu   (Free-standing function)

```
OI_poly_rect_menu *oi_create_poly_rect_menu(
    const char        *namp,               // pointer to object name
    OI_number         n_cell,              // number of cells in menu
    OI_menu_cell      **cellp,             // pointer to cells
    OI_orient         orient=OI_vertical,  // orientation of menu
    const char        *titlep=NULL)        // title for menu
```

cellp points to the menu cells that you create dynamically using calls to **oi_create_menu_cell**. If you omit *orient*, **OI_vertical** is assumed. If you omit *titlep* or set it to NULL, the menu will have no title.

16.5   Base Class Member Functions

You can use all of the member functions of **OI_d_tech** and **OI_menu** for an **OI_poly_menu**, **OI_poly_check_menu**, or **OI_poly_rect_menu** object. You can use the member functions of **OI_menu_cell** for the cells of any menu.

16.6   Resources

All resources from an **OI_poly_menu** object's base classes are available to it; it has no additional resources. For more information on resource management, see Chapter 39, "The OI Resource Mechanism."

16.7   Translations

All translations from an **OI_poly_menu** object's base classes are available to it; it has no additional translations.

16.8   Callback Functions

All of the callbacks from an OI_poly_menu object's base classes are available to it; it has no additional callbacks.

Chapter 17

OI_abbr_menu

OI_abbr_menu Functions

OI_abbr_menu Functions

The following functions are available to an **OI_abbr_menu** object, but are described in their own chapters.

OI_menu Member Functions

OI_excl_menu Member Functions

OI_d_tech Member Functions

Mode of Transportation `Rollerskates▱`

Mode of Transportation `▼Rollerskates`

OI_abbr_menu

17.1 Description

An OI_abbr_menu is an abbreviated menu—a compound OI object which includes an OI_basic_menu object as one of its components and possibly an OI_scroll_menu object. The OI_basic_menu can be either an OI_button_menu or an OI_excl_menu. An OI_abbr_menu object appears as a title followed by the label of the default cell (OI_button_menu) or the currently selected cell (OI_excl_menu). In the OPEN LOOK model, a button glyph appears between the title and the cell label. The full menu is available as a pop-up. This pop-up menu is referred to as the *underlying* menu. If there is no default or currently selected cell in the menu, the first cell of the menu becomes the default cell if the underlying menu is an OI_button_menu, or the selected cell if the underlying menu is an OI_excl_menu.

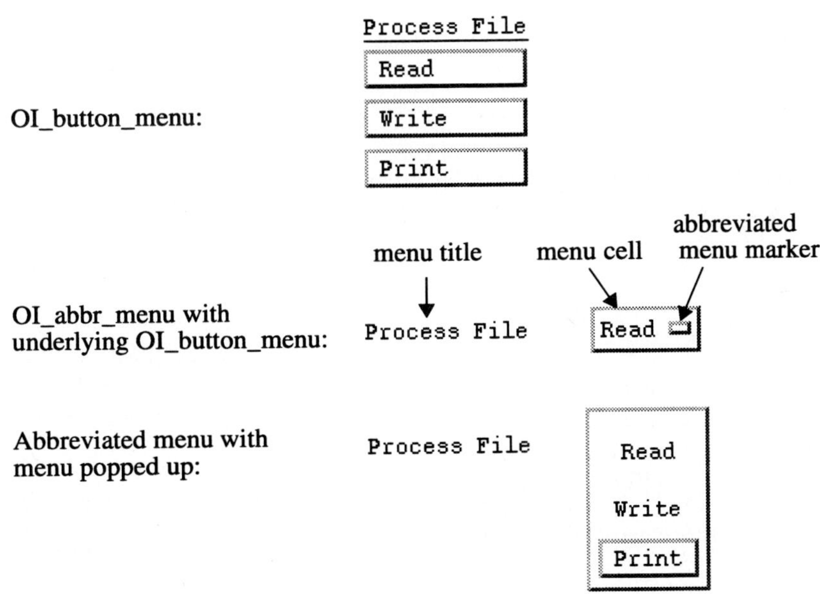

Figure 17-1 Parts of an OI_abbr_menu with underlying OI_button_menu, Motif

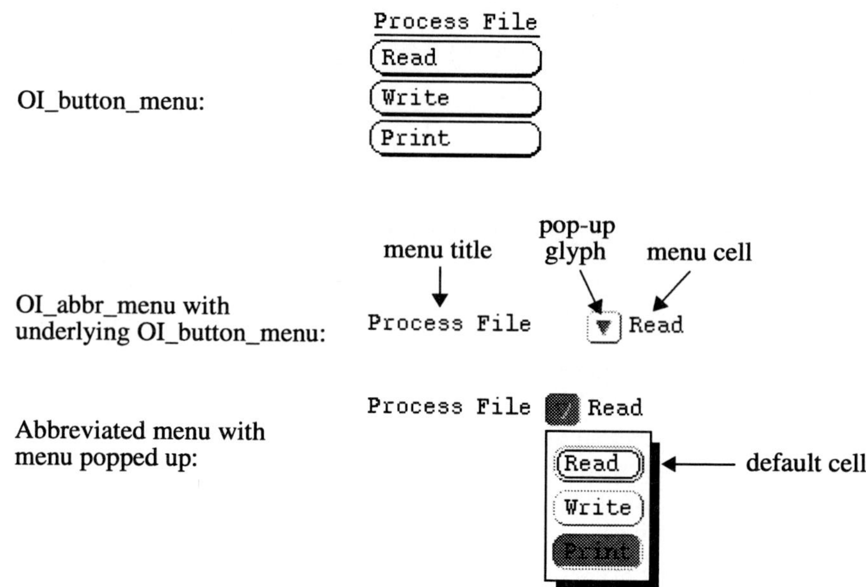

**Figure 17-2   Parts of an OI_abbr_menu with underlying OI_button_menu,
OPEN LOOK**

Figure 17-1 shows an OI_abbr_menu with an underlying OI_button_menu using Motif; Figure 17-2 shows the same menu in OPEN LOOK.

You can create the abbreviated menu with an OI_scroll_menu object as the underlying menu; something you might want to do if the menu contains many cells. In this case, when the menu is popped up, only the menu cells in the viewport become visible. You can control the number of cells in the viewport. Figure 17-3 shows an OI_abbr_menu object with an underlying OI_excl_menu contained in an OI_scroll_menu object.

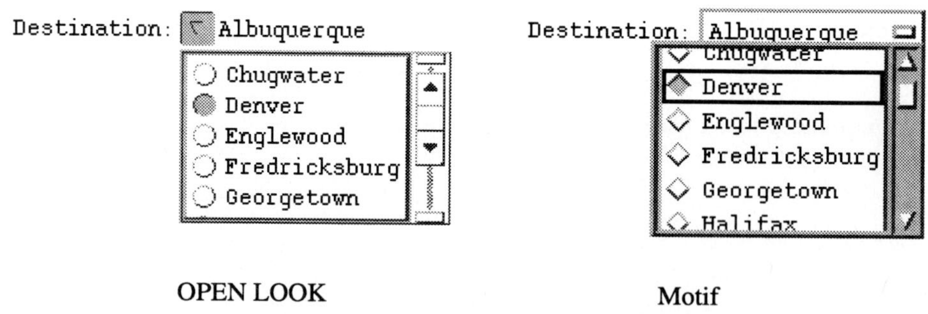

OPEN LOOK   Motif

**Figure 17-3   OI_abbr_menu Showing Popped-up OI_scroll_menu with an
OI_excl_menu**

Use an abbreviated menu when you are short of space on the screen or when the selections in the menu will not change for long periods of time. For example, an abbreviated menu might be used to denote the current record modification mode in a database (Add/Change/Delete), since one often selects a mode and then processes numerous records.

17.2   Class Tree

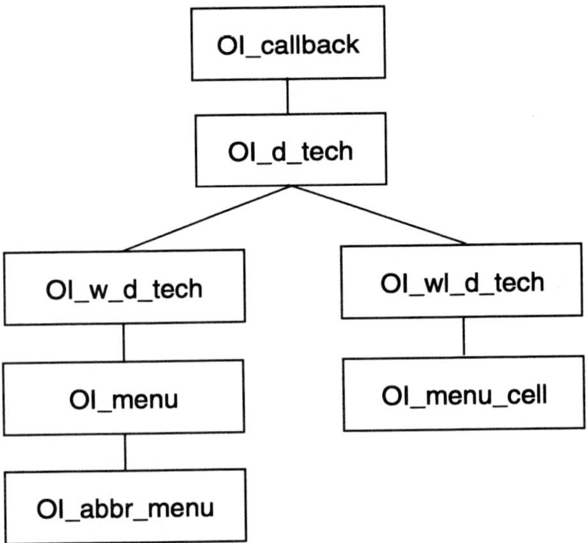

17.3   Runtime Interaction

17.3.1   Motif Runtime Interaction

The following sections describe the mouse interaction with a Motif abbreviated menu. In addition, a Motif abbreviated menus responds, through translations, to keyboard interaction. If the abbreviated menu has the focus, press the Return key to bring up the underlying menu. Use the arrow keys to move up or down the menu (or left or right for a horizontal menu), changing the focus to a new menu cell. Press the Return key again to choose the cell with the current focus.

17.3.1.1 Motif Runtime Interaction, Underlying OI_button_menu

Clicking or pressing and releasing the SELECT mouse button on the displayed menu cell causes the underlying menu to pop up. The menu will appear and behave as a normal pop-up menu; you can select any item from the menu by moving the mouse pointer to the desired cell and releasing the mouse button. The cell selected from the pop-up menu will fire (its callback will be executed), and it will also become the cell whose label is displayed when the pop-up menu is dismissed.

17.3.1.2 Motif Runtime Interaction, Underlying OI_excl_menu

Clicking the SELECT mouse button on the displayed menu cell causes the cell whose label is displayed to fire (its callback is executed). To pop up the underlying menu, press the SELECT mouse button on the cell. The underlying menu will appear and behave as a normal pop-up menu; you can select any item from the menu by moving the mouse pointer to the desired cell and releasing the mouse button. If the cell you select is the same as the one previously selected (the one displayed in the OI_abbr_menu object), its action callback function will be executed for the cell in the selected state. If the cell you select is different from the one previously selected, the callback for the previously selected cell will be activated for the cell in the deselected state, then the callback for the newly selected cell will be activated for the cell in the selected state. In any case, the newly-selected cell will be displayed in the OI_abbr_menu object when the pop-up menu is dismissed. This means that the cell which appears in the abbreviated menu is always the same as the currently selected cell in the underlying menu.

17.3.1.3 Motif Runtime Interaction, Underlying OI_scroll_menu

Press the SELECT mouse button to bring up the pop up scroll menu. If the desired cell appears in the scroll menu, you can move the mouse pointer over that cell and release the mouse button to select the cell. If you want to move the scroll bar you can move the pointer to the arrow at either end of the scroll bar and move the bar incrementally until the desired cell appears, move the pointer to the cell, and release the mouse button. Alternatively, to pin the scroll menu on the screen, move the pointer over the scroll bar and release the mouse button. Then move the scroll bar and choose the desired cell in the same manner as you would for a normal OI_scroll_menu object. Once a selection is made, the popped-up scroll menu disappears and the selected cell appears in the abbreviated menu.

17.3.2   OPEN LOOK Runtime Interaction

17.3.2.1 OPEN LOOK Runtime Interaction, Underlying OI_button_menu

Clicking or pressing and releasing the SELECT mouse button on the pop-up glyph causes the default cell (the one whose label is displayed) to fire (its callback is executed). To pop up the underlying menu, press the MENU mouse button on the pop-up glyph. The underlying menu will appear and behave as a normal pop-up menu; you can select any item from the menu by moving the mouse pointer to the desired cell and releasing the mouse button. The cell selected from the pop-up menu will fire, but the cell displayed in the OI_abbr_menu object (the default cell) will remain unchanged when the button menu is dismissed. To change the default cell, see Section 14.3.2.3, "Changing the Default Cell," on page 14-7.

17.3.2.2 OPEN LOOK Runtime Interaction, Underlying OI_excl_menu

Clicking or pressing and releasing the SELECT mouse button on the pop-up glyph causes the cell whose label is displayed to fire (its callback is executed). To pop up the underlying menu, press the MENU mouse button on the pop-up glyph. All other runtime interaction for an OPEN LOOK abbreviated menu with an underlying OI_excl_menu is the same as for Motif (see above).

17.3.2.3 OPEN LOOK Runtime Interaction, Underlying OI_scroll_menu

Click the SELECT mouse button to choose the default cell. Click the MENU mouse button on the pop-up glyph to bring up the pop-up scroll menu and pin it to the screen. Then move the scroll bar and choose the desired cell in the same manner as you would for a normal OI_scroll_menu object.

17.4 OI_abbr_menu Creation

If you already have a menu in your application, and you decide that for space-saving purposes (or other considerations) you want to change it to an abbreviated menu, you need only change the oi_create_*menutype* call to be a call to oi_create_abbr_menu and add the second argument specifying the type of abbreviated menu you desire. If you have declared the menu pointer variable to be of type OI_menu* rather than OI_*menutype*, then you need change no other code. On the other hand, if you have declared the pointer to be of the particular menu type (say, OI_button_menu*), then you must change it either to OI_menu* or to OI_abbr_menu*.

There are four forms of the create function for an OI_abbr_menu. You can read about creating menus from menu cell specifications and from previously created menu cells in the chapter describing the particular type of menu you are abbreviating (see Chapter 14, "OI_button_menu and OI_trans_menu," and Chapter 15, "OI_excl_menu, OI_excl_check_menu, OI_excl_rect_menu"). To make your abbreviated menu be a scroll menu when it is popped up, you specify a viewport size.

If the underlying menu is an OI_excl_menu, the first cell in the menu is put in the selected state at the time you create the abbreviated menu. If you call the OI_excl_menu member function allow_unsel or set the resource unselect to OI_yes for the abbreviated menu with an exclusive underlying menu, the callback for the first cell in the menu (if any) is executed with state unselected, and no cell label appears in the abbreviated menu.

oi_create_abbr_menu   (Free-standing function)

```
OI_abbr_menu *oi_create_abbr_menu(
    const char          *namp,               // pointer to object name
    OI_class            *menu_typ,           // type of menu
    OI_number           n_cell=0,            // number of cells in menu
    OI_cell_spec        *cell_specp=NULL,    // pointer to cell info
    OI_orient           orient=OI_vertical,  // orientation of menu
    const char          *titlep=NULL,        // title for menu
    OI_number           vps=0)               // viewport size—number of menu cells
```

oi_create_abbr_menu

(Free-standing function)

```
OI_abbr_menu *oi_create_abbr_menu(
    const char          *namp,                      // pointer to object name
    OI_class            *menu_typ,                  // type of menu
    OI_number           n_cell,                     // number of cells in menu
    OI_menu_cell        **cellp,                    // pointer to cells
    OI_orient           orient=OI_vertical,         // orientation of menu
    const char          *titlep=NULL,               // title for menu
    OI_number           vps=0)                      // viewport size—number of menu cells
```

oi_create_abbr_menu

(Free-standing function)

```
OI_abbr_menu *oi_create_abbr_menu(
    const char          *namp,                      // pointer to object name
    const char          *menu_typ_nam,              // type of menu
    OI_number           n_cell=0,                   // number of cells in menu
    OI_cell_spec        *cell_specp=NULL,           // pointer to cell info
    OI_orient           orient=OI_vertical,         // orientation of menu
    const char          *titlep=NULL,               // title for menu
    OI_number           vps=0)                      // viewport size—number of menu cells
```

oi_create_abbr_menu

(Free-standing function)

```
OI_abbr_menu *oi_create_abbr_menu(
    const char          *namp,                      // pointer to object name
    const char          *menu_typ_nam,              // type of menu
    OI_number           n_cell,                     // number of cells in menu
    OI_menu_cell        **cellp,                    // pointer to cells
    OI_orient           orient=OI_vertical,         // orientation of menu
    const char          *titlep=NULL,               // title for menu
    OI_number           vps=0)                      // viewport size—number of menu cells
```

These functions create an **OI_abbr_menu** object; the functions are identical except for the pointer to the cells. In the first form, *cell_specp* points to the **OI_cell_spec** structure that you declare and fill with data describing the cells to create for the menu. Use the second form when you already have the menu cells created; *cellp* points to a vector of menu cells to use for the menu.

menu_typ determines the type of menu which is being abbreviated. It must be one of the standard basic menu types; possible values are (see the paragraph on *vps*, below, to enclose one of these types in an OI_scroll_menu for the abbreviated menu):

OI_button_menu::clsp
OI_excl_menu::clsp
OI_excl_check_menu::clsp
OI_excl_rect_menu::clsp

You can use *menu_typ_nam* instead of *menu_typ* to determine the type of menu which is being abbreviated. It must be one of the standard basic menu types as a text string; possible values are:

"OI_button_menu"
"OI_excl_menu"
"OI_excl_check_menu"
"OI_excl_rect_menu"

If you omit *orient*, OI_vertical is assumed. If you omit *titlep* or set it to NULL, the menu will have no title.

vps specifies the viewport size. If you specify a value for *vps* greater than zero, the underlying menu will become an OI_scroll_menu object, containing the menu type you specify in *menu_typ* or *menu_typ_nam*, and showing *vps* cells in the viewport.

Program 17-1 creates an abbreviated menu with an underlying OI_excl_menu. The callback for each cell is designed to show when a callback is executed, and whether the cell is being turned on or off. Figure 17-4 and Figure 17-5 show the program in operation.

```c
#include <OI/oi.H>                /* AbbrExclMenu.C */

int main(int argc, char **argv)
{
                void            do_fn(OI_menu_cell*,void*,OI_number);

                OI_connection   *conp;
                OI_app_window   *wp;
                OI_menu         *mp;

        static OI_cell_spec   cells[] = {
                {"add","Add",do_fn},
                {"change","Change",do_fn},
                {"delete","Delete",do_fn},
                };

    if (conp = OI_init(&argc,argv,"AbbrMenu")) {
        wp = oi_create_app_window("main",1,1,"AbbrMenu");
        wp->set_layout(OI_layout_row);

        mp = oi_create_abbr_menu("menu",OI_EXCL_MENU,OI_count(cells),
                                      &cells[0],OI_vertical,"Process File");
        mp->layout_associated_object(wp,2,10,OI_active);

        wp->set_associated_object(wp->root( ),OI_def_loc,OI_def_loc,OI_active);
        OI_begin_interaction( );
        OI_fini( );
    }
}

void do_fn(OI_menu_cell *mcp, void*, OI_number)
{
    if (mcp->selected( ))
        printf("Action function for %s was called on selection\n",mcp->name( ));
    else
        printf("Action function for %s was called on de-selection\n",mcp->name( ));
    return;
}
```

Program 17-1   OI_abbr_menu with Underlying OI_excl_menu (AbbrExclMenu.C)

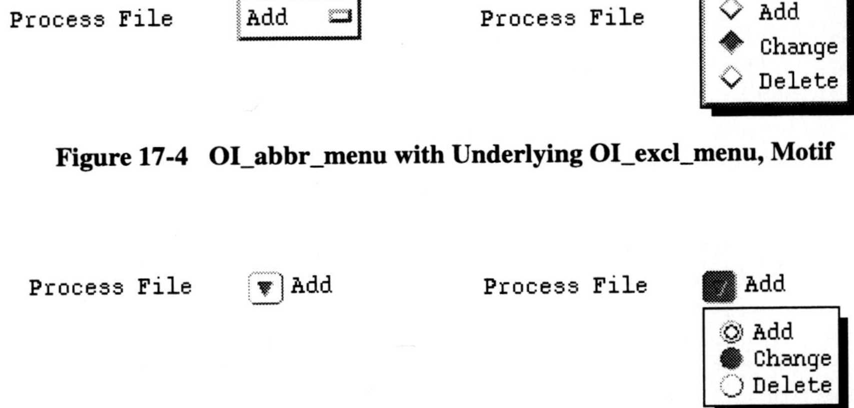

Figure 17-4   OI_abbr_menu with Underlying OI_excl_menu, Motif

Figure 17-5   OI_abbr_menu with Underlying OI_excl_menu, OPEN LOOK

17.5   Base Class Member Functions

You can use all of the member functions of OI_d_tech and OI_menu for an OI_abbr_menu object. If you are abbreviating an OI_excl_menu, you can use the member functions for those classes for the OI_abbr_menu object. You can use the member functions of OI_menu_cell for the cells of an OI_abbr_menu.

17.6   OI_abbr_menu Member Functions

17.6.1   Setting the Viewport Size

If you specify a viewport size in the call to oi_create_abbr_menu, the underlying menu is an OI_scroll_menu object. You can query the current viewport size or change the viewport size by using these functions.

view_size   (Member function)

```
OI_number OI_abbr_menu::view_size( )
```

view_size returns the current size of the viewport in the underlying scroll menu. If the underlying menu is not a scroll menu, view_size returns 0.

set_view_size   (Member function)

```
void OI_abbr_menu::set_view_size(
    OI_number          vps)                    // viewport size in menu cells
```

set_view_size sets the viewport size to *vps*. If the underlying menu is currently a scroll menu and you set *vps* to 0, the menu is changed to the basic menu type. If the underlying menu is currently not a scroll menu and you set *vps* to a positive number, the menu is changed to a scroll menu.

17.7 Resources

All resources from an **OI_abbr_menu** object's base classes are available to it; in addition, OI fetches the resources shown in Table 17-1. For more information on resource management, see Chapter 39, "The OI Resource Mechanism."

Table 17-1 OI_abbr_menu Resources

Resource	Description	Possible Values	Default Value
orientation	Specifies the orientation of the underlying menu	vertical horizontal	(No default)
subMenuType	Specifies the type of underlying menu.	OI_button_menu OI_excl_menu OI_excl_check_menu OI_excl_rect_menu	(No default)
viewSize	Specifies the size, in menu cells, of the underlying menu. If **viewSize** is 0, the underlying menu will not be a scroll menu. If **viewSize** > 0, the underlying menu will be a scroll menu.	Non-negative integer	(No default)

17.8 Translations

An **OI_abbr_menu** object has default translations installed for it. In addition to the translations listed in the table below, the default translations for an **OI_abbr_menu** object also include the default translations for all of its base classes.

Table 17-2 shows the default **OI_menu** translations. Table 17-3 describes the action functions available. See Chapter 40, "The OI Translation Mechanism" for a description of the Event Sequence entries in Table 17-2.

Table 17-2 Default OI_abbr_menu Translations

Event Sequence	Action Functions Called
<FocusIn>:	focus_in( )
<FocusOut>:	focus_out( )

Table 17-3 OI_abbr_menu Translation Functions

Function Name	Description
focus_in( )	Gives the focus to the menu. In Motif, paints the focus border.
focus_out( )	Gives up the focus. In Motif, removes the focus border.

17.9 Callback Functions

All of the callbacks from an **OI_abbr_menu** object's base classes are available to it; it has no additional callbacks.

Chapter 18
OI_dialog_box

OI_dialog_box Functions

OI_dialog_box Member Functions

OI_box Member Functions

The following functions are available to an **OI_dialog_box** object, but are described in their own chapter.

OI_d_tech Member Functions

OI Programmer's Guide

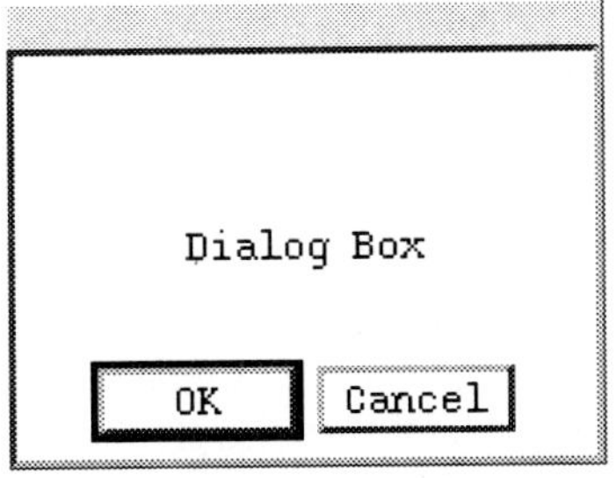
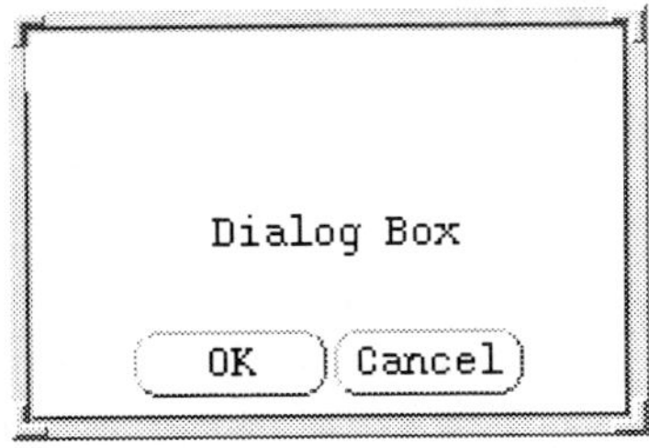

OI_dialog_box

18.1   Description

An OI_dialog_box is a composite object; it is an OI_box with a child OI_button_menu centered at the bottom. The button menu is a horizontal menu that by default contains two buttons labeled "OK" and "Cancel". By default, these buttons are "do-nothing" buttons—they do not have callback functions registered for them and merely dismiss the dialog box. You can customize the menu by registering callbacks for the default menu cells, or by specifying the entire menu at the time the dialog box is created. (You do not always need to register callbacks for the menu cells if you use the wait_button function—see Section 18.6.1 on page 18-20.) When necessary, you can restrict user input from occurring anywhere on the screen except in the dialog box by using the member functions wait_button or set_term_action.

You will generally use a dialog box as a container for other objects (children objects) to collect specific information from the user. Your dialog box will usually not be initially visible; instead, the dialog box will be *activated* (become visible and ready to accept input) by some user action such as clicking on a menu cell. A dialog box used in this manner is referred to as a *pop-up* dialog box. You expect the user to interact with the children objects, then click on a button at the bottom of the box when done.

A dialog box can be one of two types—modal or modeless. A *modal* pop-up dialog box is one that pops up and waits for user interaction, restricting user interaction to itself (although only within its application), then disappears when one of the buttons at the bottom of the box is pressed. When you parent a modal dialog box to a menu cell the following happens when the menu cell fires: the dialog box pops up, and the menu cell remains painted pressed down. No other cell of that menu can be activated until the modal dialog box is taken down. A *modeless* dialog box is one that appears on the screen when the parent menu cell fires, but this time the parent menu cell immediately returns, so that the cells of the menu are available again for user interaction. The dialog box remains on the screen, and the user can interact with the objects in the dialog box or with other objects in the application. The dialog box disappears when the user presses one of the buttons at the bottom of the box.

Some examples of dialog box usage are: You may wish to pop up an error or informational dialog box to inform the user of problems encountered during application execution. You could use a dialog box containing several OI_entry_field and OI_menu objects which pops up when the user clicks on a menu cell labeled "Send Mail". Another example is the help object that pops up when the user clicks on the help button in an OI_app_window. The help object is a dialog box with a customized button menu; the dialog box contains several other OI objects used to display help information.

Most window managers supply a title bar for a dialog box. The title bar contains the title and longterm message if you have set them; you use the title and longterm message for a dialog box in the same manner as for an OI_app_window object. If you do not specifically set these items (using the member functions described below), they do not appear in the title bar. If the window manager is an OPEN LOOK window manager, and your application is run using one of the OPEN LOOK models, and you have asked for a pushpin on the dialog box, the pushpin also appears in the title bar. The pushpin enables the user to keep a pop-up dialog box visible, even after it is dismissed, by "pinning" it up. The user can then make additional entries by changing the dialog box information and clicking on the buttons at the bottom without having to pop up the dialog box each time. A Motif dialog box can be pinned as well, but the conditions are more complex; this is discussed later in this chapter. A Motif pushpin appears next to the button menu at the bottom of the box and not in the title bar.

If a dialog box has a title, a longterm message, or a pushpin, OI makes the dialog box unclipped (its X window becomes a top-level window), so that the window manager can display these items in the title bar.

Figure 18-1 and Figure 18-2 show dialog boxes with title bar items.

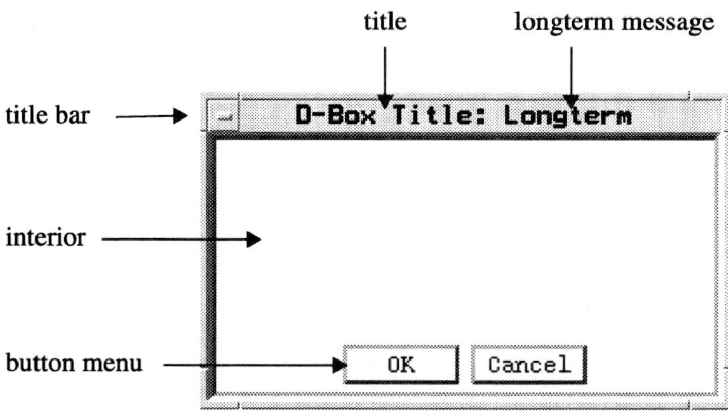

Figure 18-1   Dialog Box with Title Bar Items, Motif

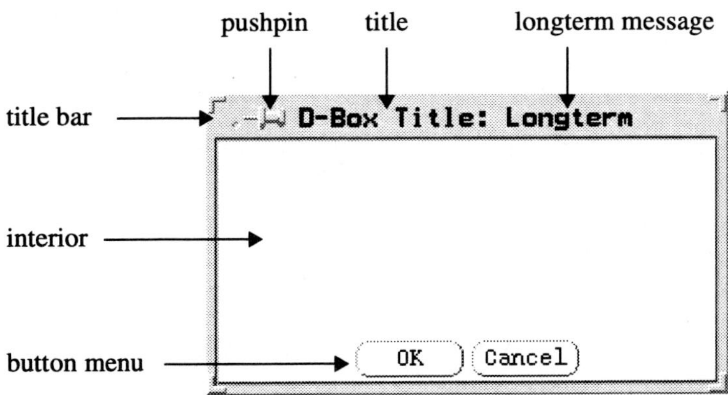

Figure 18-2   Dialog Box with Title Bar Items, OPEN LOOK

OI supplies several specialized forms of dialog boxes. Called convenience dialog boxes, they are listed in Table 18-1 and Table 18-2 and displayed in Figure 18-3 through Figure 18-7. One of these may fit your needs exactly. If not, you can create your own custom dialog box from the plain dialog box (OI_dialog_box) or by adding to one of the convenience dialog boxes. The convenience dialog boxes are discussed in Chapters 19 through 23.

Note that when your application is run using OPEN LOOK, the six dialog boxes listed in Table 18-1 are the same; they are an OPEN LOOK "Notice". Also, the dialog boxes listed in Table 18-2 are OPEN LOOK "Command" dialogs with additional objects added to give them their functionality.

Some of the Motif dialog boxes have a help button added to their menus. When activated, this button automatically invokes the help object for the nearest ancestor OI_app_window (the behavior of this help button is identical that of the help button in an OI_app_window object). If you have customized the help context prior to popping up the dialog box, it is displayed; otherwise, the default help appears. Customizing the help context is described in Chapter 8, "OI_app_window."

Table 18-1   Convenience Dialog Boxes Derived from OI_ms_dialog_box

OI Name	Motif Name	Usage
OI_error_dialog_box	XmErrorDialog	Displays an error message.
OI_info_dialog_box	XmInformationDialog	Displays information.
OI_message_dialog_box	XmMessageDialog	Displays any message.
OI_question_dialog_box	XmQuestionDialog	Displays a question and waits for an answer.
OI_warn_dialog_box	XmWarningDialog	Displays a warning message.
OI_work_dialog_box	XmWorkingDialog	Informs user that a potentially time-consuming operation is in progress.

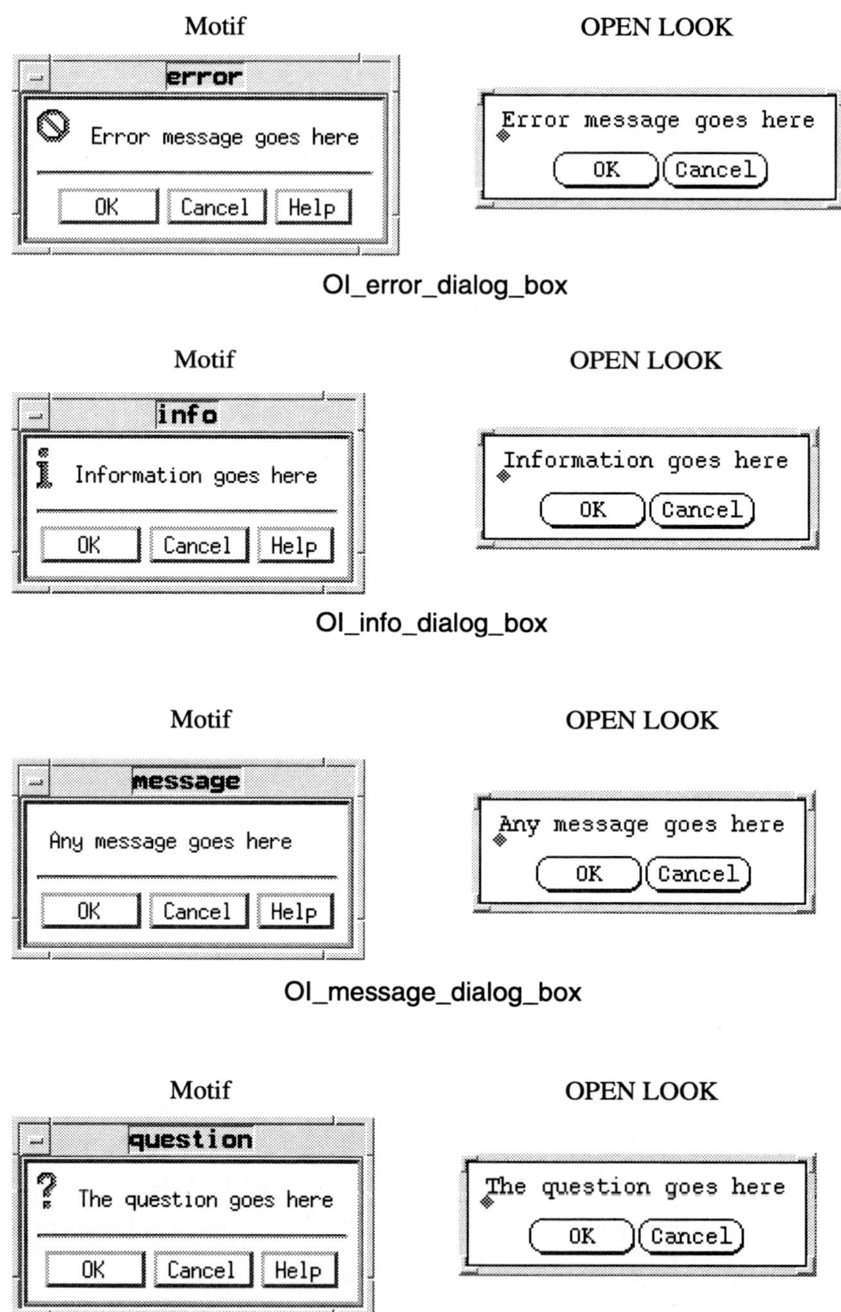

OI_error_dialog_box

OI_info_dialog_box

OI_message_dialog_box

OI_question_dialog_box

Motif   OPEN LOOK

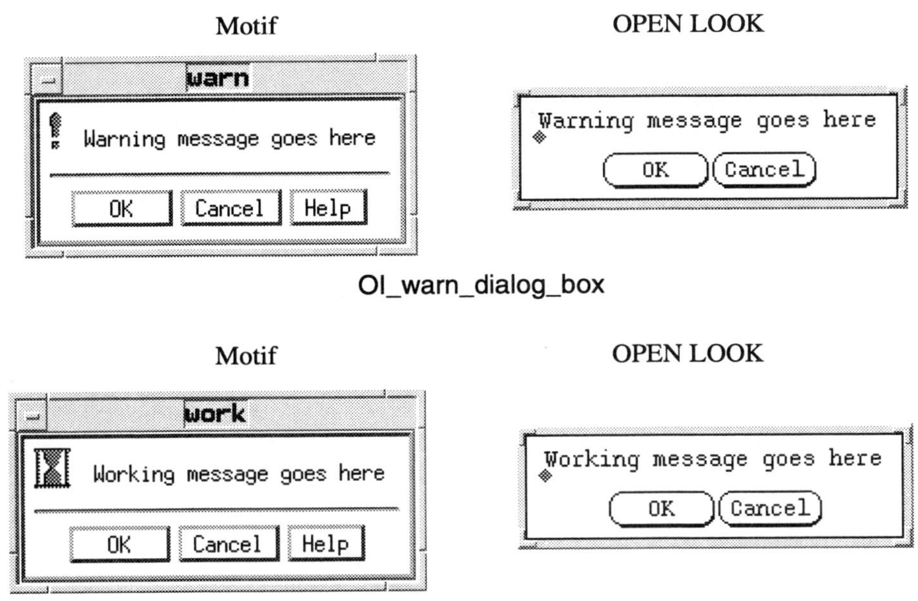

OI_warn_dialog_box

OI_work_dialog_box

Figure 18-3   Convenience Dialog Boxes Derived from OI_ms_dialog_box

Table 18-2   Other Convenience Dialog Boxes

OI Name	Motif Name	Usage
OI_command_dialog_box	XmCommand	Allows selection from a menu of commands. Allows entry of new commands. Previously entered commands are maintained as a history in the menu.
OI_file_dialog_box	XmFileSelectionDialog	Allows user to traverse directories, view the names of files in a directory, and choose a single file.
OI_prompt_dialog_box	XmPromptDialog	Prompts the user for input in a single field.
OI_select_dialog_box	XmSelectionDialog	Allows choice of selections from a menu of selections or a value entered in an entry field.

Motif   OPEN LOOK

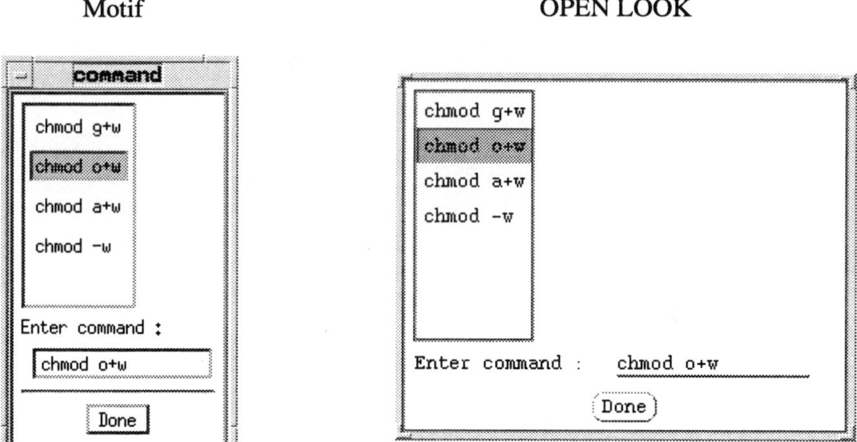

Figure 18-4   OI_command_dialog_box

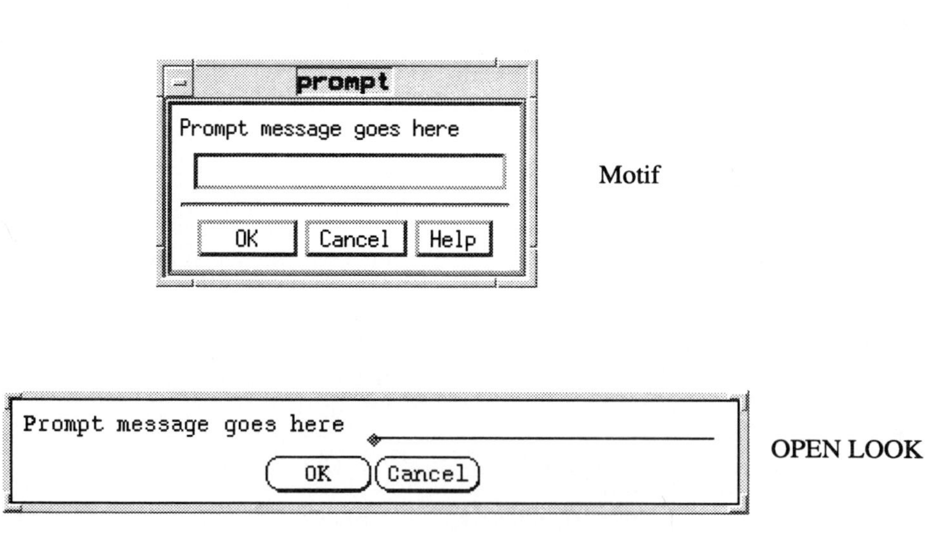

Figure 18-5   OI_prompt_dialog_box

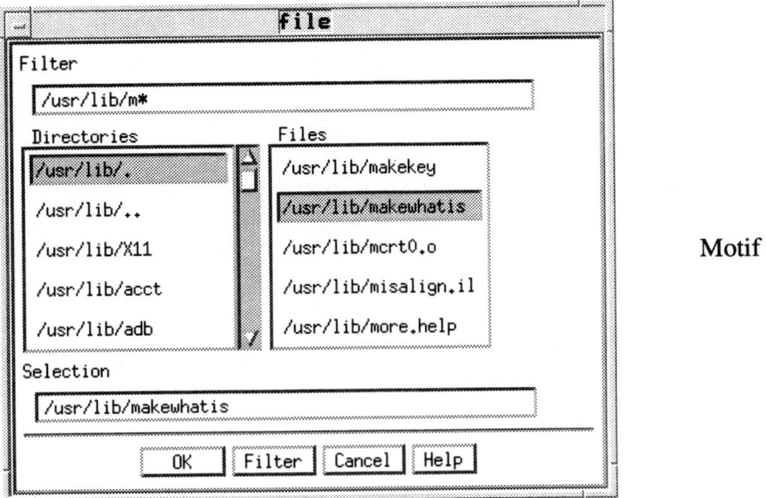

Motif

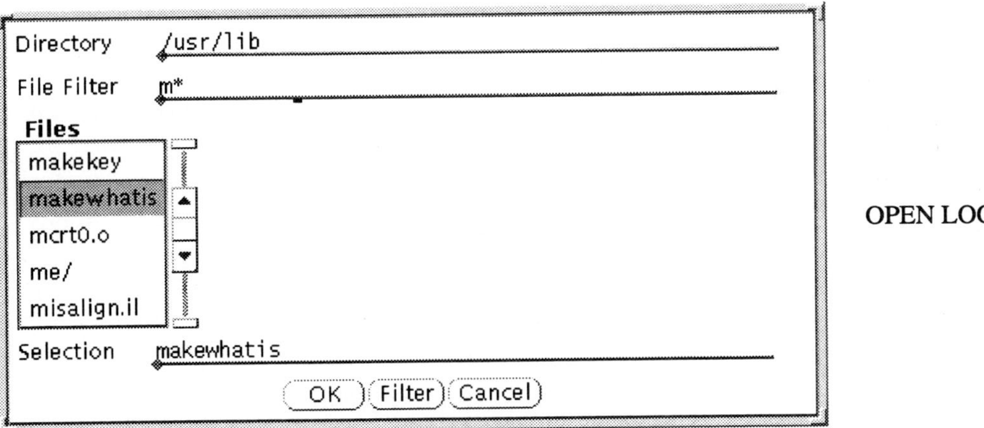

OPEN LOOK

Figure 18-6   OI_file_dialog_box

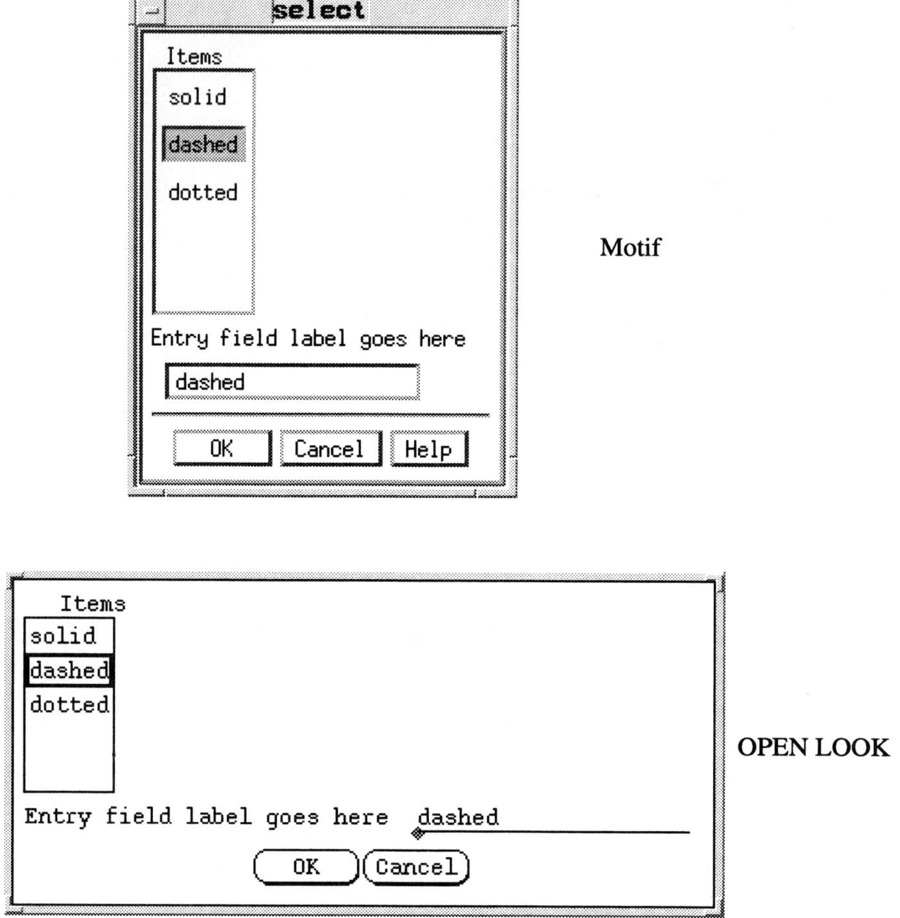

Figure 18-7   OI_select_dialog_box

18.1.1   Using a Dialog Box as an Ordinary Object

You can associate a dialog box with its parent in the OI_active state, in which case it will immediately be visible (assuming its ancestors are all visible). If you do this, there is no distinction between a modal and modeless dialog box. Usually, however, an OI_app_window or an OI_box is a better object to choose for this situation.

18.1.2   Using a Dialog Box as a Pop-Up Object

As mentioned previously, a dialog box is normally used as a *pop-up* object; it is normally not visible when the program first starts up. Instead, it pops up as a result of some action initiated by the user or some other input or condition encountered while processing. The dialog box then stays visible until the user dismisses it by clicking on one of the buttons in the button menu at the bottom of the dialog box.

OI provides three related mechanisms for making this pop-up process easy to program. You can make a dialog box be a pop-up using any of the methods shown in Table 18-3.

Table 18-3   Creating a Pop-up Dialog Box

How popped up	Mode	Description
Automatically	Modal	Create the dialog box and associate it with a menu cell in state OI_active_not_displayed. (This causes a *dialog-box-marker*—an ellipses, or three dots—to appear on the face of the menu cell.) Whenever the user clicks on the menu cell, OI calls wait_button to automatically activate the dialog box—it becomes visible and ready to accept input. By default, the dialog box is modal. If you need to validate the contents of the dialog box before allowing the box to be cleared from the screen, use the member function set_term_action to set up the validation routine that will be invoked when one of the buttons in the dialog box menu is activated. An example of this might be a menu, one of whose cells is labeled "Print," which would activate a dialog box. The dialog box would contain entry fields in which the user could specify items such as printer name, whether to print last page first, etc.
Automatically	Modeless	Create the dialog box in the same manner as an automatic modal dialog box, except call the member function allow_modeless or set the resource modeless to true. Using the "Print" dialog box example, you would make the dialog box modeless if the user might need to choose another cell in the menu with the "Print" cell before finishing with the Print dialog box.

Table 18-3 Creating a Pop-up Dialog Box

How popped up	Mode	Description
Programmatically	Modal	Create the dialog box and associate it with its parent in state OI_not_displayed. When you want the dialog box to pop up, call the member function wait_button. This function sets the state of the dialog box to OI_active (making it visible), and does not return until the user clicks on one of the buttons at the bottom of the dialog box (or when you fire one of these cells programmatically, or call the member function take_down). For example, if you need to display error information and want the user to read it before continuing with any other action, you can use wait_button to activate a dialog box containing error information with the *restrict* parameter set. The user then cannot interact with any other object in this application until the dialog box is completed and must click on one of the menu cells in the dialog box before continuing.
Programmatically	Modeless	Create the dialog box and associate it with its parent in state OI_not_displayed. When you want the dialog box to pop up, call the member function popup. This function sets the state of the dialog box to OI_active (making it visible), then immediately returns. The user is free to interact with the dialog box or to interact with other objects in the application. The dialog box disappears when the user clicks on a menu cell at the bottom of the dialog box (or when you fire one of these cells programmatically, or call the member function take_down).

You can allow the user to *pin up* a dialog box—so that it is always visible—by using the member function allow_pushpin or setting the resource pushpin to true. Since this makes it possible for the user to manipulate the objects in the dialog box at any point in time, it should only be used for those dialog boxes where it makes sense; that is, your program must be prepared to process interactions from the dialog box at any time. For your dialog box to have a pushpin when run under Motif, you or the user must specify the OI_connection resource motifPushpin for your application, as well as calling allow_pushpin for the dialog box. This extra step is necessary because if you need to be strictly Motif compliant, you may not want pushpins—it is not "normal" Motif. A Motif pushpin appears next to the button menu at the bottom of the box and not in the title bar.

If you are using a dialog box as a pop-up object, you will most likely want to make it be *unclipped*; that is, to make it not be constrained to lie within its parent's boundaries. You can do this by using the OI_d_tech member function disallow_clip or setting the resource clip to false. Note that OI automatically forces any dialog box that is parented to a menu cell to be unclipped. In addition, since the title bar which contains the title and longterm message is owned by the window manager (not the program which created the dialog box), if you set a title or longterm message for a dialog box, OI forces the dialog box to be unclipped. Also, if you give the dialog box a pushpin, the dialog box automatically becomes unclipped.

18.1.3   Dialog Box Control Flow

There are two basic ways to trigger processing of the information in a dialog box. One is to set an action callback function for one or more of the cells in the button menu at the bottom of the dialog box. The other is to call wait_button, and upon return check to see which cell (if any) the user clicked on to terminate the call. If you use wait_button in this manner, you should not put a pushpin on the dialog box unless you have registered action callbacks for any menu cells whose function requires additional processing. This is because the wait_button call returns as soon as the dialog box is pinned, and subsequent clicks on the cells of the button menu have no effect unless the cells have action callbacks.

The order of execution of control functions and callback functions in activating a dialog box via a menu cell or a wait_button or popup call is as follows:

1. If the dialog box is associated in state OI_active_not_displayed with a menu cell, and the menu cell is activated, the callback action function for the menu cell (if any) is activated first. Nothing further happens until the menu cell callback returns. This allows you to modify the dialog box contents in the menu cell callback, if you need to, before the dialog box is made visible.
2. The dialog box is made visible and is activated. (OI does this automatically if the dialog box is associated with a menu cell; otherwise this happens when you call wait_button or popup.) If you called popup to activate the dialog box, popup returns immediately.
3. The user interacts with any descendant objects in the dialog box.
4. The user clicks on a cell in the button menu at the bottom of the dialog box; the callback action function registered for the cell (if any) is invoked.
5. If you have registered a validation callback function for the dialog box, it is called. You register the validation function either in the call to wait_button (if you activated the dialog box yourself), or by calling set_term_action some time prior to activating the dialog box.
6. If the original state of the dialog box was OI_active_not_displayed and if the validation callback (if any) returned successfully, the dialog box is cleared from the screen. If the dialog box is cleared from the screen and you called wait_button to activate it, the wait_button call returns. If the dialog box is not cleared from the screen, interaction continues again at step 3.
7. If, instead of clicking on a menu cell, the user pins the dialog box, and you activated the dialog box with a call to wait_button, the wait_button call returns NULL immediately.

The flow of control for a pop-up dialog box is diagrammed in Figure 18-8 through Figure 18-10.

The usefulness of the validation callback routine can now be explained. If the dialog box is to be cleared from the screen, it is done after the callback for whichever button menu cell the user activated is completed. Whether you have used the default button menu or have created your own customized button menu, it would be a waste to make each cell's action callback check for valid contents of the dialog box. Not only that, but if the contents were not valid, the dialog box would be cleared from the screen anyway. If you register a validation callback, the dialog box is retained on the screen if the validation callback returns a "not-valid" value. If a "not-valid" value is returned, you can display an error message, and the user can correct the entries in the dialog box and choose a button menu cell again. In this way, the dialog box remains on the screen until its contents are valid.

(Be sure to allow the user to choose the "Cancel" cell without having to have "valid" dialog box contents.)

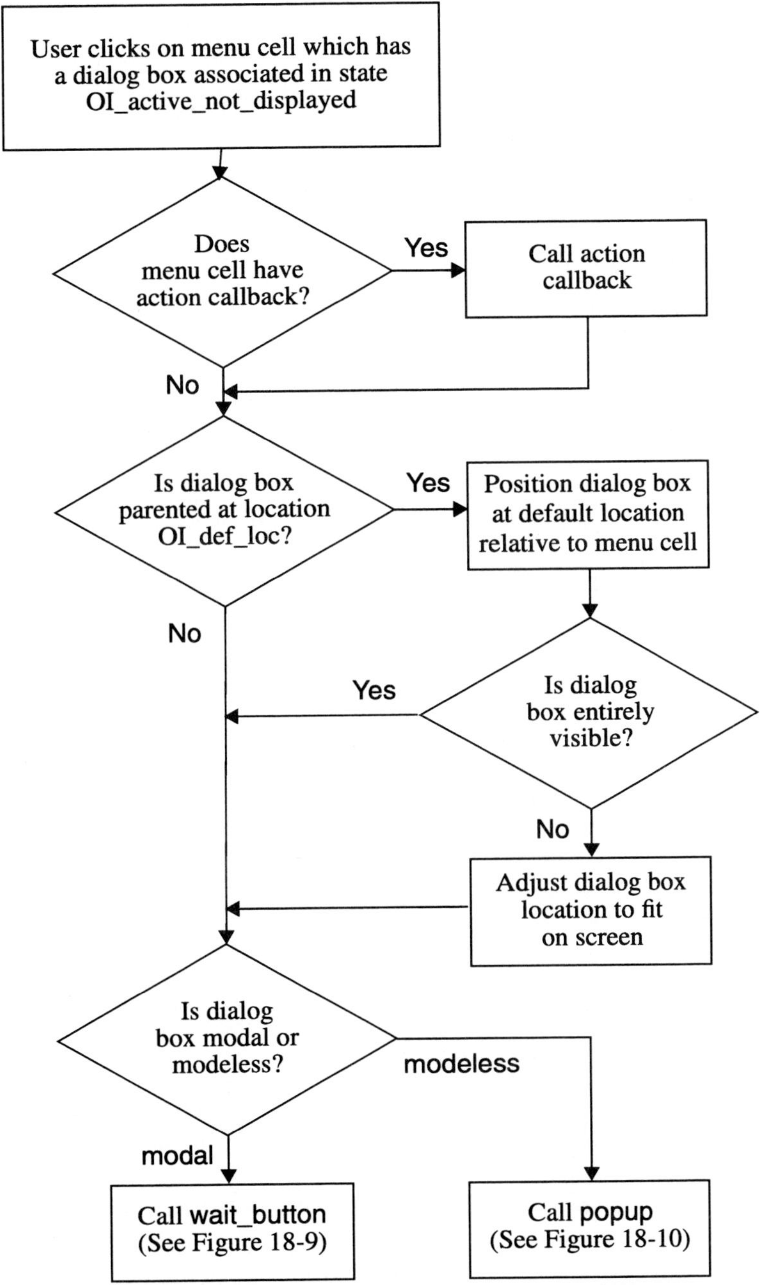

Figure 18-8   OI's Actions on Popping up a Dialog Box

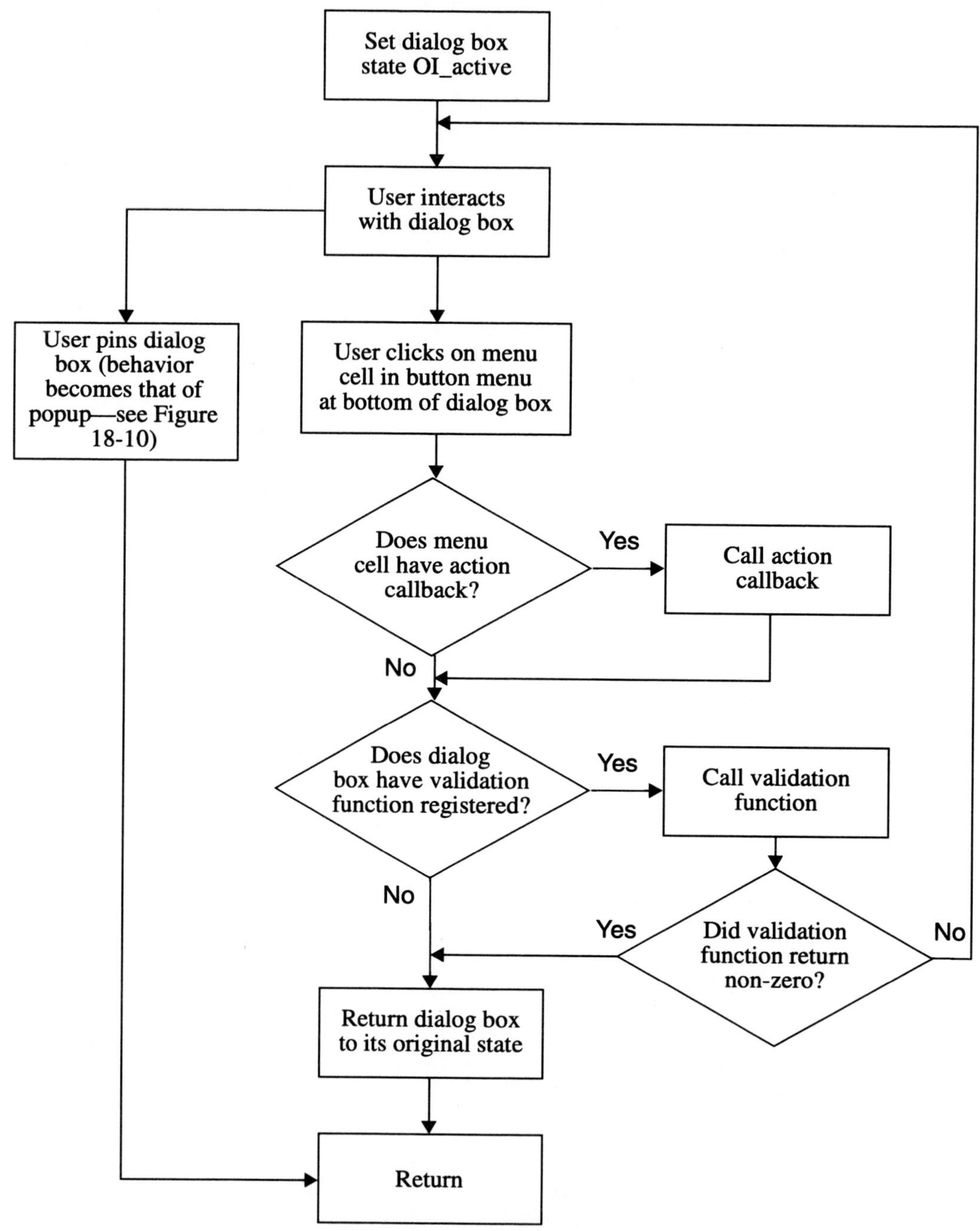

Figure 18-9   wait_button Flow of Control

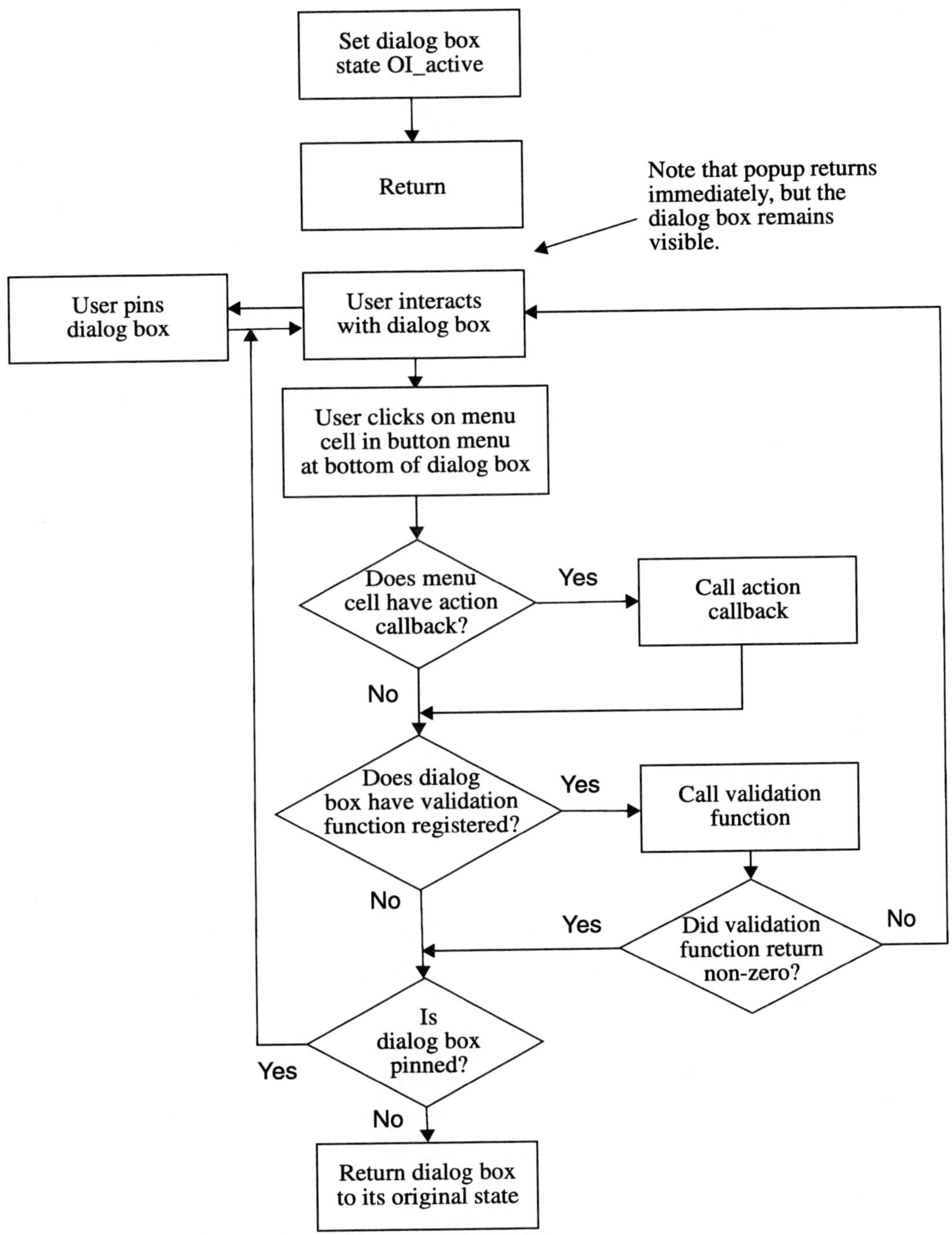

Figure 18-10   popup Flow of Control

18.2   Class Tree

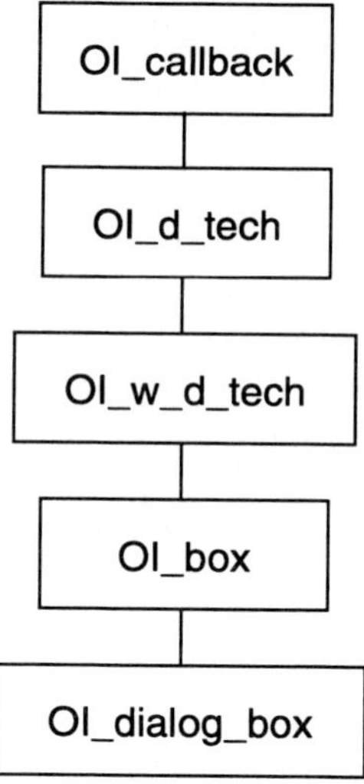

18.3   Runtime Interaction

A dialog box has no special interactions from the user's perspective. The button menu at the bottom behaves like a normal button menu, and any other objects placed in the box behave normally. The only unique feature is that a dialog box is often used as a pop-up object, and clicking on one of the buttons results in the dialog box disappearing after the processing is complete. As the programmer, you can control three aspects of this behavior. First, you can disable the rest of the application when a dialog box pops up, so that the user can only interact with objects in the dialog box. Second, you can validate the information in the dialog box and prevent it from being dismissed if the contents are invalid. Third, you can make the dialog box be either modal or modeless. These behavioral aspects are discussed further under the member functions below.

18.3.1   OPEN LOOK Runtime Interaction

As mentioned previously, an OPEN LOOK dialog box can have an additional item in its title bar—a pushpin. To pin a dialog box, click on the pushpin. To unpin it, click again on the pushpin. When a dialog box is unpinned, it disappears, even if no button menu cell has been fired. The ramifications of pushpin behavior are discussed from the programmer's point of view under allow_pushpin and wait_button. Also note that you must be running an OPEN LOOK window manager—such as olwm or swm—for the pushpin to appear if the application is run in OPEN LOOK mode. This is because in OPEN LOOK, the pushpin is in the title bar for the dialog box, which is maintained by the window manager. Non-OPEN LOOK window managers—such as twm and mwm—do not know about pushpins. Figure 18-11 shows an OPEN LOOK dialog box with a pushpin.

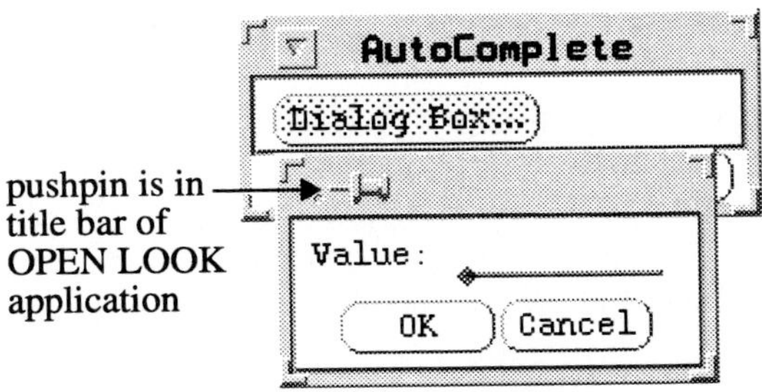

Figure 18-11   OPEN LOOK Dialog Box with Pushpin

18.3.2   Motif Runtime Interaction

A dialog box under Motif has no additional functionality over the general functionality discussed above.

If the programmer used the member function allow_pushpin for the dialog box or the resource pushPin is true for the dialog box, and the OI_connection resource motifPushpin is true, it will have a pushpin when run under Motif. The pushpin appears next to the button menu at the bottom of the dialog box. To pin the dialog box, click the SELECT mouse button on the pushpin; to unpin it click the SELECT mouse button on it again. Figure 18-12 shows a Motif dialog box with a pushpin.

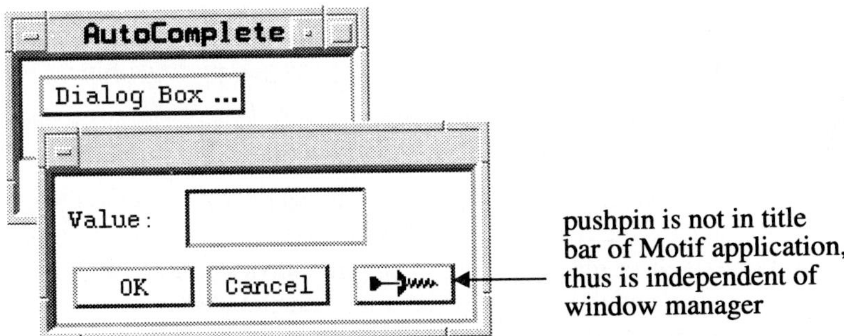

Figure 18-12   Motif Dialog Box with Pushpin

18.4   OI_dialog_box Creation

There are two forms of create function for OI_dialog_box, one for each of two situations you will encounter when you create a dialog box. In the first case, you know the button menu cell contents in advance, and you can define the menu cells *statically*, using a vector of OI_cell_spec structures to describe the cells. In the second case you do not know ahead of time what image or text should appear on the face of the cells, or you know you may need to change the menu cell contents during execution, or you do not even know how many cells the menu will contain until execution time. In these cases, you must create the menu *dynamically*, using a vector of menu cells.

18.4.1   Creating a Dialog Box with Statically-defined Button Menu Cells

You can statically define the menu cells for the button menu at the bottom of the dialog box by using the OI_cell_spec structure (see Chapter 13, "OI_menu_cell"). One of the arguments in the first form of oi_create_dialog_box is a pointer to this structure; the menu creation mechanism automatically generates the individual OI_menu_cell objects from the OI_cell_spec structures and parent them to the button menu at the bottom of the dialog box.

If you intend to use the default button menu in your dialog box, you do not need to declare any OI_cell_spec structures; simply omit the parameters *n_cell* and *cell_specp*.

oi_create_dialog_box   (Free-standing function)

```
OI_dialog_box *oi_create_dialog_box(
    const char        *namp,            // pointer to object name
    OI_number         width,            // width of interior in pixels
    OI_number         height,           // height of interior in pixels
    OI_number         n_cell=-1,        // number of cells in menu
    OI_cell_spec      *cell_specp=NULL) // pointer to cell specs for menu
```

width and *height* are the dimensions of the interior of the dialog box; *height* does not include the height of the button menu or the title bar at the top of the dialog box (if any). When the dialog box is created, it will have exterior dimensions sufficient to contain the interior of the box and the button menu. If you will be using the OI layout facility to position children in the dialog box (you use set_layout and layout_associated_object rather than set_associated_object to parent children to the dialog box), you can specify *width* and *height* of 1, and the layout code will make the dialog box grow to encompass any objects you place within it.

cell_specp points to the OI_cell_spec structure that you declare and fill with data describing the menu cells for the button menu at the bottom of the dialog box.

If you omit *n_cell* and *cell_specp*, or if *n_cell* is less than zero, the dialog box is created with the default button menu. The names of the default cells are "OK" and "Cancel". The default labels are the same as the names. The initial action callback routine and argument for these default cells are NULL. If you are using the default menu and wish to register an action callback function for a cell, use the OI_menu_cell member function change_action. If you wish to set only the argument to be passed to the action callback function, use change_arg.

Program 18-1 produces a dialog box with the default button menu at the bottom of the dialog box; a callback is registered for the "OK" menu cell using the OI_menu_cell member function change_action. The dialog box is parented to a cell in a menu in the main application window.

```
#include <OI/oi.H>                 /* OKCallback.C */

int main(int argc, char **argv)
{
                void            ok_action(OI_menu_cell*,void*,OI_number);

                OI_connection   *conp;
                OI_app_window   *wp;
                OI_dialog_box   *dbp;
                OI_menu_cell    *cellp;
                OI_menu         *mp;

        static  OI_cell_spec    cells[] = {
                {"box_button","Box Here"},
                {"no_box","None Here"},
                {"no_box_2","None Here Either"},
                };

    if (conp = OI_init(&argc,argv,"OKCallback")) {
        wp = oi_create_app_window("main",1,1,"OKCallback");
        wp->set_layout(OI_layout_row);

        mp = oi_create_button_menu("menu",OI_count(cells),&cells[0],
                                    OI_vertical,"Dialog Boxes");
        mp->layout_associated_object(wp,2,10,OI_active);

        dbp = oi_create_dialog_box("my_db",200,100);
        cellp = (OI_menu_cell*)dbp->buttons( )->subobject("OK");
        cellp->change_action(&ok_action);
        dbp->set_associated_object(mp->subobject("box_button"),OI_def_loc,
                                    OI_def_loc,OI_active_not_displayed);

        wp->set_associated_object(wp->root( ),OI_def_loc,OI_def_loc,OI_active);
        OI_begin_interaction( );
        OI_fini( );
    }
}

void ok_action (OI_menu_cell *mcp,void*,OI_number)
{
    printf("Button %s activated\n",mcp->name( ));
    return;
}
```

Program 18-1   Dialog Box with OK Button Callback (OKCallback.C)

18.4.2   Creating a Dialog Box with Dynamically-created Button Menu Cells

You can also create the menu cells for the button menu at the bottom of a dialog box at execution
time. You can either allocate space for the pointers to the cells using an array, or, if you do not know
the maximum number of cells before execution time, you can use malloc or new to obtain space for
the array of pointers. You call the function oi_create_menu_cell once for each cell (see Chapter

13, "OI_menu_cell"). In this case you create the dialog box using the following form of oi_create_dialog_box, passing it a pointer to the array of cell pointers. The menu creation mechanism parents the cells to the button menu at the bottom of the dialog box.

oi_create_dialog_box   (Free-standing function)

```
OI_dialog_box *oi_create_dialog_box(
     const char          *namp,            // pointer to object name
     OI_number           width,            // width of interior in pixels
     OI_number           height,           // height of interior in pixels
     OI_number           n_cell,           // number of cells in menu
     OI_menu_cell        **cellp)          // pointer to cells for menu
```

All arguments for this form of **oi_create_dialog_box** are the same as for the previous form except *cellp*. *cellp* points to a vector of pointers to menu cells you have already created dynamically using calls to **oi_create_menu_cell**.

18.5   Base Class Member Functions

You can use all of the member functions of **OI_d_tech** and **OI_box** for an **OI_dialog_box** object.

You can use all of the member functions available to **OI_button_menu** for the button menu subobject of an **OI_dialog_box** object. These include the member functions of **OI_menu** and the member functions of **OI_menu_cell** for the cells of the menu.

size_y   (Member function)

```
OI_number OI_dialog_box::size_y( )
```

size_y returns the usable size in the vertical direction for the dialog box. This is the *height* parameter in the original creation call for the dialog box if it has not been resized. In any case, it is the total vertical size disregarding the space taken up by the title bar at the top (if any) and the button menu at the bottom.

18.6   OI_dialog_box Member Functions

18.6.1   Activating the Dialog Box

You should only use the **wait_button** or **popup** functions described here if you associate the dialog box with its parent in an **OI_not_displayed** state. If the parent is a menu cell, you may associate the dialog box in state **OI_active_not_displayed**; if you do, you should not activate the dialog box in your program—OI activates it automatically when the user clicks on the parent menu cell.

If you want a modal dialog box—one which is taken down when the user clicks on a button at the bottom of the box—and you do not want to parent the dialog box to a menu cell, use **wait_button**. If you want a modeless dialog box—one which stays on the screen while the user interacts with other objects, potentially for a long period of time—and you do not want to parent the dialog box to a menu cell, use **popup** and **take_down**.

wait_button   (Member function)

```
OI_menu_cell *OI_dialog_box::wait_button(
    OI_bool              restrict=OI_no,      // restrict input to dialog box
    OI_wait_fnp          fnp=NULL,            // pointer to validation callback function
    void                 *argp=NULL)          // arbitrary argument for fnp

OI_menu_cell *OI_dialog_box::wait_button(
    OI_bool              restrict=OI_no,      // restrict input to dialog box
    OI_callback          *objp,               // memfnp's object
    OI_wait_memfnp       memfnp,              // pointer to validation callback member function
    void                 *argp=NULL)          // arbitrary argument for memfnp
```

The **wait_button** functions activate the dialog box, then allow events to be processed until one of the buttons in the button menu is activated. After the user activates one of the buttons, the dialog box is returned to its original state (usually **OI_not_displayed**, in which case the dialog box is cleared from the screen). In other words, wait_button causes the dialog box to be modal. **wait_button** usually returns a pointer to the menu cell which the user clicked on to dismiss the dialog box. You can check the cell's name to see which cell was used. It is possible for **wait_button** to return a NULL pointer. This indicates that the dialog box was brought down and no button was clicked by the user. This can occur when the user pins a dialog box using the pushpin.

In the call to **wait_button** you can also register a validation function to be called before returning. The validation callback is executed only *after* the action callback function registered for the activated menu cell (if any) executes and returns. This callback is identified within OI as a **cbTermAction** callback function (see Section 6.18, "Determining and Adding Callbacks; Multiple Callbacks," on page 6-117). If your validation function is a member function, when it is invoked it will be called as if you had written *objp->memfnp*. See Section 2.5, "Callbacks and Event-Driven Programming," on page 2-16 for more explanation.

If you have registered a validation callback using **set_term_action**, and you set *fnp* or *memfnp* to NULL in the call to **wait_button**, the callback registered by **set_term_action** will be used. If you specify a function in *fnp* or *memfnp* in your call to **wait_button**, it will be used instead of any callback registered by **set_term_action**. In addition, it will override any previous call to **set_term_action**, that is, the new function is now the registered validation callback function.

If *restrict* is **OI_yes**, input on all other objects in this application except descendants of the dialog box is temporarily suspended until the dialog box processing is completed and **wait_button** returns. If you omit *restrict*, the default value of **OI_no** is used, and input is not restricted to the dialog box.

argp is optional, and can be any valid expression that can be cast to a pointer. You can use it to pass additional information to the function *fnp* or *memfnp*.

You should write the validation function in the manner described under "Writing the Validation Callback Function" in Section 18.6.2 on page 18-27.

It is permissible to call **wait_button** before you call **OI_begin_interaction**. Program 18-2 shows a main application window and a user-validation dialog box which pops up centered in the application window immediately before starting the rest of the program. Note the way the validation function locates the entry field. The results of running Program 18-2 are shown in Figure 18-13. See Program 18-4 on page 18-29 for an alternate way to locate the entry field.

```c
#include <OI/oi.H>                              /* ValidUser.C */
#include <strings.h>

int main(int argc, char **argv)
{
        int                   valid_user(OI_menu_cell*,void*,OI_number);

        OI_connection         *conp;
        OI_app_window         *wp;
        OI_dialog_box         *dbp;
        OI_menu_cell          *cellp;
        OI_entry_field        *efp;

    if (conp = OI_init(&argc,argv,"ValidUser")) {
        wp = oi_create_app_window("main",1,1,"ValidUser");
        wp->set_layout(OI_layout_row);

        dbp = oi_create_dialog_box("validate_db",1,1) ;
        dbp->set_layout(OI_layout_row);
        efp = oi_create_entry_field("validate_ef",10,"User id: ");
        efp->layout_associated_object(dbp,10,10,OI_active);
        dbp->layout_associated_object(wp,1,1,OI_not_displayed);
        wp->set_associated_object(wp->root( ),OI_def_loc,OI_def_loc,OI_active);
        if (cellp = dbp->wait_button(OI_yes,&valid_user)) {
            if (!strcmp(cellp->name( ),"OK")) {

                // build the rest of the application here

                OI_begin_interaction( );
            }
        }
        OI_fini( );
    }
}

int valid_user(OI_menu_cell *cellp, void*, OI_number)
{
        OI_entry_field        *efp;
        int                   ok;
    ok = 1;
    if (!strcmp(cellp->name( ),"OK")) {
        efp = (OI_entry_field*)cellp->ancestor_derived_from("OI_dialog_box")->
                                subobject("validate_ef");

        // Check for valid user here
        // If user is not valid, then set
        //   ok = 0;
    }
    return(ok);
}
```

Program 18-2   Dialog Box for User ID Validation (ValidUser.C)

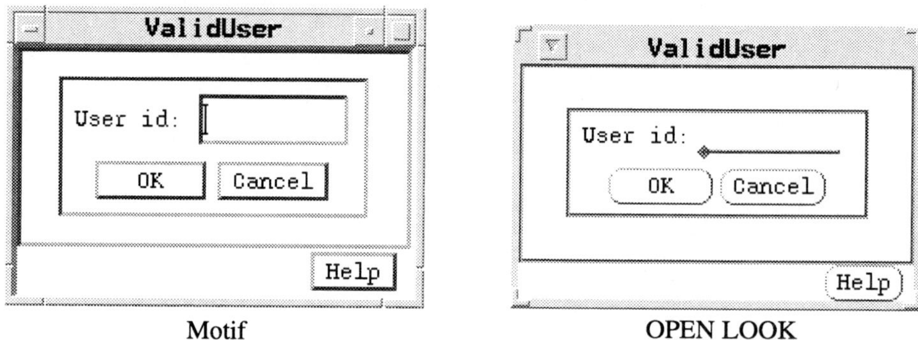

Motif   OPEN LOOK

Figure 18-13   Dialog Box for User ID Validation

popup   (Member function)

```
void OI_dialog_box::popup(
    OI_wait_fnp          fnp=NULL,          // pointer to validation callback function
    void                 *argp=NULL)        // arbitrary argument for fnp


void OI_dialog_box::popup(
    OI_callback          *objp,             // memfnp's object
    OI_wait_memfnp       memfnp,            // pointer to validation callback member function
    void                 *argp=NULL)        // arbitrary argument for memfnp
```

The **popup** functions activate the dialog box then return immediately. The dialog box's parent menu cell returns to its original state, and the user can interact with the dialog box or other objects in the application. In other words, **popup** causes the dialog box to be modeless.

In the call to **popup** you can also register a validation function to be called before returning. This callback is identified within OI as a **cbTermAction** callback function (see Section 6.18, "Determining and Adding Callbacks; Multiple Callbacks," on page 6-117). The validation callback is executed only *after* the action callback function registered for the activated menu cell (if any) executes and returns. If your validation function is a member function, when it is invoked it will be called as if you had written *objp->memfnp*. See Section 2.5, "Callbacks and Event-Driven Programming," on page 2-16 for more explanation.

If you have registered a validation callback using **set_term_action**, and you set *fnp* or *memfnp* to NULL in the call to **popup**, the callback registered by **set_term_action** will be used. If you specify a function in *fnp* or *memfnp* in your call to **popup**, it will be used instead of any callback registered by **set_term_action**. In addition, it will override any previous call to **set_term_action**, that is, the new function is now the registered validation callback function.

argp is optional, and can be any valid expression that can be cast to a pointer. You can use it to pass additional information to the function *fnp* or *memfnp*.

You should write the validation function in the manner described under "Writing the Validation Callback Function" in Section 18.6.2 on page 18-27.

take_down   (Member function)

```
void OI_dialog_box::take_down(
    OI_menu            *mnup=NULL,        // pointer to dialog box menu
    OI_menu_cell       *cellp=NULL,       // pointer to menu cell which fired
    void               *argp=NULL,        // arbitrary argument
    OI_number          btn=0)             // mouse button number
```

You can call **take_down** to cause the normal dialog box interaction to complete. No callback for any cell in the button menu is executed when you call **take_down**. The validation callback function (if any) is executed, using the *cellp* and *btn* arguments. If you have no validation function registered for the dialog box, you should call **take_down** with no arguments (let it use the defaults). If you need to call it with some arguments, *mnup* should point to the button menu at the bottom of the dialog box, *cellp* should point to the cell which supposedly fired, argp should be NULL, and *btn* is the mouse button number which supposedly was used to fire *cellp*. Because the mouse button functions can be changed through translations, you should express *btn* as:

```
btn = dialog_box_pointer->buttons( )->trigger( );
```

Program 18-3 illustrates a method to automatically complete the dialog box interaction when the user strikes the Return key in an entry field in the dialog box. The entry field validation routine is called when the Return key is pressed, and if the entry field is not empty, the dialog box is dismissed.

```c
#include <OI/oi.H>                                    /* AutoComplete.C */
#include <strings.h>

int main(int argc, char **argv)
{
               OI_ef_entry_chk_status      finish_up(OI_entry_field*,void*,
                                                      OI_ef_entry_chk_status);

               OI_connection               *conp;
               OI_app_window               *wp;
               OI_dialog_box               *dbp;
               OI_entry_field              *efp;
               OI_menu                     *mp;
       static  OI_cell_spec                cells[] = {
                                           {"popup","Dialog Box"},
                                           };

    if (conp = OI_init(&argc,argv,"AutoComplete")) {
        wp = oi_create_app_window("main",1,1,"AutoComplete");
        wp->set_layout(OI_layout_row);
        mp = oi_create_button_menu("menu",OI_count(cells),&cells[0],OI_horizontal);
        mp->layout_associated_object(wp,10,10,OI_active);
        dbp = oi_create_dialog_box("pop_up_db",1,1) ;
        dbp->set_layout(OI_layout_row);
        efp = oi_create_entry_field("val_ef",10,"Value: ");
        efp->set_entry_check(&finish_up);
        efp->layout_associated_object(dbp,10,10,OI_active);
        dbp->set_associated_object(mp->subobject("popup"),OI_def_loc,OI_def_loc,
                                   OI_active_not_displayed);
        wp->set_associated_object(wp->root( ),OI_def_loc,OI_def_loc,OI_active);
        OI_begin_interaction( );
        OI_fini( );
    }
}


OI_ef_entry_chk_status  finish_up(OI_entry_field *efp, void*,
                                          OI_ef_entry_chk_status stat)
{
           OI_ef_entry_chk_status       ret;
           OI_dialog_box                *dbp;
           OI_menu_cell                 *cellp;

    ret = OI_ef_entry_chk_bad;
    if (stat == OI_ef_entry_chk_ok && efp->part_text( )) {
        ret = OI_ef_entry_chk_ok;
        dbp = (OI_dialog_box*)efp->ancestor_derived_from("OI_dialog_box");
        cellp = (OI_menu_cell*)dbp->buttons( )->subobject("OK");
        dbp->take_down( );
    }
    return(ret);
}
```

Program 18-3   Dialog Box with Automatic Completion (AutoComplete.C)

is_modeless (Member function)

```
OI_bool OI_dialog_box::is_modeless( )
```

is_modeless returns **OI_yes** if the dialog box is modeless and **OI_no** if it is modal.

allow_modeless (Member function)

```
void OI_dialog_box::allow_modeless( )
```

allow_modeless conditions the dialog box to be modeless. This means that if the dialog box is parented to a menu cell in state **OI_active_not_displayed**, when the menu cell fires, the dialog box will be put in state **OI_active**, and then the menu cell will return.

disallow_modeless (Member function)

```
void OI_dialog_box::disallow_modeless( )
```

disallow_modeless conditions the dialog box to be modal. This means that if the dialog box is parented to a menu cell in state **OI_active_not_displayed**, when the menu cell fires, the dialog box will be put in state **OI_active**, and the menu cell will return only when the dialog box comes down. This is the default condition.

18.6.2 Validating the Dialog Box Contents

If you activate the dialog box yourself using **wait_button** (see above section), you can register a validation function in that call, and you do not need to call **set_term_action**. If, however, you parent the dialog box to a menu cell so that OI can activate the dialog box automatically when the cell is activated, you need to call **set_term_action** if you want to register a validation function. See the discussion under Section 18.1.3, "Dialog Box Control Flow" on page 18-11 on the uses of validation callback functions.

set_term_action (Member function)

```
void OI_dialog_box::set_term_action(
    OI_bool          restrict=OI_no,    // restrict input to dialog box
    OI_wait_fnp      fnp=NULL,          // pointer to callback function
    void             *argp=NULL)        // arbitrary argument for fnp


void OI_dialog_box::set_term_action(
    OI_bool          restrict=OI_no,    // restrict input to dialog box
    OI_callback      *objp,             // memfnp's object
    OI_wait_memfnp   memfnp,            // pointer to callback member function
    void             *argp=NULL)        // arbitrary argument for memfnp
```

The **set_term_action** functions register a validation function to be invoked whenever any one of the cells in the dialog box's button menu is activated. The validation callback is executed only *after* the action callback function registered for the activated menu cell (if any) executes and returns. This callback is identified within OI as a **cbTermAction** callback function (see Section 6.18, "Determining and Adding Callbacks; Multiple Callbacks," on page 6-117). *memfnp* points to a member function for the object pointed to by *objp*. If your validation function is a member function, when it is invoked it will be called as if you had written *objp->memfnp*. See Section 2.5, "Callbacks and Event-Driven Programming," on page 2-16 for more explanation.

If *restrict* is OI_yes, input on all other objects in this application except descendants of the dialog box is temporarily suspended until the dialog box processing is completed. If you omit *restrict*, the default value of OI_no is used, and input is not restricted to the dialog box.

argp is optional, and can be any valid expression that can be cast to a pointer. You can use it to pass additional information to the function *fnp* or *memfnp*.

Writing the Validation Callback Function

If the cbTermAction callback function is not a member function, write it in this form:

```
int  fn(
        OI_menu_cell  *cellp,        // pointer to button menu cell which fired
        void          *argp,         // arbitrary argument
        OI_number     btn)           // mouse button number used to fire cell
```

and if the cbTermAction callback function is a member function, write it in this form:

```
int  obj_class::memfn(
        OI_menu_cell  *cellp,        // pointer to button menu cell which fired
        void          *argp,         // arbitrary argument
        OI_number     btn)           // mouse button number used to fire cell
```

where *obj_class* is the class of the object whose member function is *memfn*.

When your callback function is invoked, *cellp* will be a pointer to the menu cell which the user activated. *argp* will be the argument specified in the wait_button or set_term_action call. *btn* will be the mouse button number that was used to activate the menu cell (and should normally be ignored).

Program 18-4 creates a main application window with a one-celled button menu; when the button is activated, a dialog box automatically pops up. The dialog box has an entry field in it. Note that the main application window and the dialog box use the automatic layout facility to size themselves and position their children. The dialog box uses the default "OK" and "Cancel" buttons, and has a validation function which only allows the dialog box to be taken down when the entry field is not empty. The void* pointer *argp* is used to pass the entry field pointer to the validation routine. The results of running Program 18-4 are shown in Figure 18-14. See Program 18-2 on page 18-23 for a different method of locating the entry field.

```
#include <OI/oi.H>                          /* GetAValue.C */
#include <strings.h>

int main(int argc, char **argv)
{
                int             valid_stuff(OI_menu_cell*,void*,OI_number);

                OI_connection   *conp;
                OI_app_window   *wp;
                OI_dialog_box   *dbp;
                OI_menu         *mp;
                OI_entry_field  *efp;
        static  OI_cell_spec    cells[] = {
                {"popup","Dialog Box"},
                };

    if (conp = OI_init(&argc,argv,"GetAValue")) {
        wp = oi_create_app_window("main",1,1,"GetAValue");
        wp->set_layout(OI_layout_row);

        mp = oi_create_button_menu("menu",OI_count(cells),&cells[0],OI_horizontal);
        mp->layout_associated_object(wp,10,10,OI_active);

        dbp = oi_create_dialog_box("pop_up_db",1,1) ;
        dbp->set_layout(OI_layout_row);
        efp = oi_create_entry_field("val_ef",10,"Value: ");
        efp->layout_associated_object(dbp,10,10,OI_active);

        dbp->set_term_action(OI_yes,&valid_stuff,efp);
        dbp->set_associated_object(mp->subobject("popup"),OI_def_loc,OI_def_loc,
                                                OI_active_not_displayed);

        wp->set_associated_object(wp->root( ),OI_def_loc,OI_def_loc,OI_active);
        OI_begin_interaction( );
        OI_fini( );
    }
}

int valid_stuff(OI_menu_cell *cellp, void *argp, OI_number)
{
    OI_entry_field              *efp;
    int                         ok;

    ok = 1;
    if (!strcmp(cellp->name( ),"OK")) {
        efp = (OI_entry_field*)argp;
        if (!efp->part_text( ))
            ok = 0;
    }
    return(ok);
}
```

Program 18-4   Validate Pop-up Dialog Box Value (GetAValue.C)

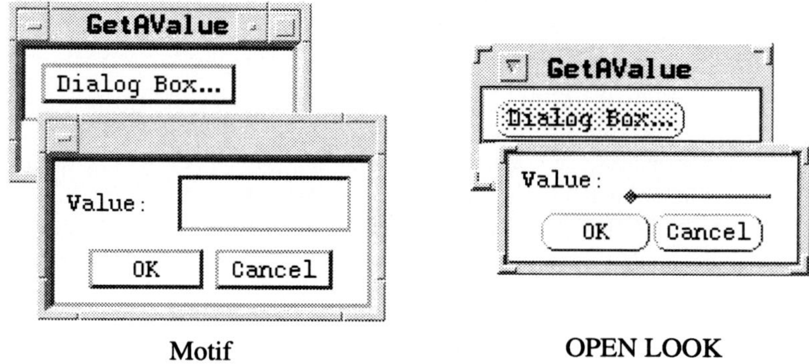

Motif   OPEN LOOK

Figure 18-14   Validate Pop-up Dialog Box Value

18.6.3   Accessing the Button Menu

When OI creates a dialog box, it creates the button menu itself and places it at the bottom of the dialog box. As such it is an *internal* object, and you don't normally have or need access to it. However, there are situations when you may need to locate it. For example, if you use the default "OK" and "Cancel" buttons, but you want to set a callback for the "OK" button, you need access to the button menu so you can find the "OK" menu cell.

Similarly, you may wish to simulate firing one of the buttons. For example, if you have a dialog box with a single entry field in it, you might like the user action of striking the Return key to be the same as clicking on the "OK" button.

The function below gives you access to the button menu.

buttons   (Member function)

```
OI_button_menu *OI_dialog_box::buttons( )
```

buttons returns a pointer to the button menu at the bottom of the dialog box. It is possible, but usually not a good idea, to make an **OI_dialog_box** object with no buttons in its menu, in which case **buttons** returns a pointer to a menu which has no cells in it. You can dynamically add cells to the menu if you wish. Once you have a pointer to this menu, you can use all the **OI_menu** and **OI_menu_cell** member functions.

The code fragment below shows how to set a callback function for the "OK" button.

```
OI_dialog_box      *dbp;
OI_menu_cell       *cellp;
cellp = (OI_menu_cell*)dbp->buttons( )->subobject("OK");
cellp->change_action(&callback_function,(void*)arg);
```

18.6.4　Forking a New Process From the Dialog Box

fork and fork_nowait are designed to be used only as the action routine for a cell in the button menu at the bottom of a dialog box. OI uses the template string *tptp* to form a command using the OI_d_tech member function form_cmd, using only objects in the dialog box containing the cell. The resulting command is then executed as for OI_fork or OI_fork_nowait. For example, if fork is specified as the action routine for the "OK" button in a dialog box, clicking on the "OK" button causes the values of all objects in the dialog box for which you have called allow_user_arg to be substituted in the template string. The resulting string is then used as a command line and is forked as a separate process, using the command /bin/sh -c followed by the string. See Section 6.17, "Forming a UNIX Command" on page 6-112 for more explanation.

fork   (Member function)

```
void OI_dialog_box::fork(
    OI_menu_cell        *cellp,      // pointer to activated menu cell
    void                *tptp,       // template string
    OI_number           btn)         // mouse button number used to activate menu cell
```

fork_nowait   (Member function)

```
int OI_dialog_box::fork_nowait(
    OI_menu_cell        *cellp,      // pointer to activated menu cell
    void                *tptp,       // template string
    OI_number           btn)         // mouse button number used to activate menu cell
```

fork_nowait and fork are identical except that fork waits until the forked process terminates before returning and fork_nowait returns without waiting.

Program 18-5 shows a dialog box which appears when the button "ls" is activated. fork_nowait is specified to be the action routine for the "OK" button. The user can choose among "ls" options in a menu in the dialog box; clicking on the "OK" button causes the ls command to be forked, and a directory listing appears on the xterm from which the program was run. Compare this program with Program 6-5, on page 6-114, which performs the identical function without a dialog box.

```c
#include <OI/oi.H>                              /* DialogLS.C */
int main (int argc, char** argv)
{
            OI_connection       *conp;
            OI_app_window       *wp;
            OI_button_menu      *bmp;
            OI_poly_check_menu*pcmp;
            OI_menu_cell        *cellp;
            OI_dialog_box       *dbp;
    static  OI_cell_spec        ls_exit[] = {
            {"dir","ls"},
            {"exit","exit",(OI_action_fnp)OI_end_interaction},
            };
    static  OI_cell_spec        optns[] = {
            {"-c","-c Sort by time of last edit"},
            {"-i","-i Print i-number"},
            {"-l","-l List in long format"},
            {"-r","-r Reverse order of sort"},
            {"-u","-u Sort by time of last access"},
            {"-1","-1 One entry per line output"},
            };

    if (conp = OI_init(&argc,argv,"AutoLS")) {
        wp = oi_create_app_window("main",1,1,"Auto ls");
        wp->set_layout(OI_layout_column);
        bmp = oi_create_button_menu("ls",OI_count(ls_exit),&ls_exit[0],
                                    OI_horizontal);
        wp->set_main_menu(bmp);
        dbp = oi_create_dialog_box("fork_ls",1,1);
        dbp->set_layout(OI_layout_column);
        dbp->set_associated_object(bmp->subobject("dir"),OI_def_loc,OI_def_loc,
                                    OI_active_not_displayed);
        pcmp = oi_create_poly_check_menu("ls_options",OI_count(optns),&optns[0],
                                    OI_vertical);
        pcmp->layout_associated_object(dbp,1,2,OI_active);
        pcmp->allow_user_arg( );
        cellp = (OI_menu_cell*)dbp->buttons( )->subobject("OK");
        cellp->change_action(dbp, (OI_action_memfnp)&(OI_dialog_box::fork_nowait),
                                    "ls $1");
        wp->set_associated_object(wp->root( ),OI_def_loc,OI_def_loc,OI_active);
        OI_begin_interaction( );
        OI_fini( );
    }
}
```

Program 18-5   Building and Forking a UNIX Command (DialogLS.C)

18.6.5   Using Pushpins

In simple dialog box interactions, the dialog box appears on the screen; the user fills it out and then dismisses it by clicking on one of the cells in the button menu at the bottom of the dialog box. However, if many of these sequences must be performed, it is annoying to have the dialog box pop up each time. The user would like to be able to keep the dialog box visible until all the entries are finished.

You can simply set the state of the dialog box to OI_active, which circumvents all automatic management of the dialog box, or you can use a pushpin to allow this. To allow the dialog box to have a pushpin so that the user can pin the dialog box on the screen when your application is run under OPEN LOOK, these things must happen:

- You must tell OI that you want a pushpin on the dialog box by using allow_pushpin or setting the resource pushpin to true.
- Your program must be prepared to accept input from the dialog box at any time, since once it is pinned up, the user has access to it until it is unpinned.
- The user must be running a window manager which understands OPEN LOOK, since the pushpin is part of the title bar decoration which is provided by the window manager.

To allow the dialog box to have a pushpin when your application is run under Motif, these things must happen:

- You must tell OI that you want a pushpin on the dialog box by using allow_pushpin or setting the resource pushpin to true.
- You must set the OI_connection resource motifPushpin for your application.
- Your program must be prepared to accept input from the dialog box at any time, since once it is pinned up, the user has access to it until it is unpinned.

If you tell OI you want a pushpin, but the user is not running an OPEN LOOK window manager, or the user is using the Motif interaction model, everything is still ok. Your program will still function correctly; the pushpin just won't be available to the user.

is_pushpin   (Member function)

```
OI_bool OI_dialog_box::is_pushpin( )
```

is_pushpin returns OI_yes if you have called allow_pushpin for the dialog box, otherwise it returns OI_no. Note that it is possible for is_pushpin to return OI_yes even if no pushpin appears on the dialog box.

allow_pushpin   (Member function)

```
void OI_dialog_box::allow_pushpin( )
```

allow_pushpin informs the window manager that the dialog box should have a pushpin. This function has no effect if the user is running under the Motif interaction model, unless the OI_connection resource motifPushpin is also set to true. If the OPEN LOOK model is being used, but a non-OPEN LOOK window manager such as twm or mwm is being used, no pushpin actually appears.

disallow_pushpin   (Member function)

```
void OI_dialog_box::disallow_pushpin( )
```

disallow_pushpin informs the window manager that the dialog box should not have a pushpin.

is_pinned   (Member function)

```
OI_bool OI_dialog_box::is_pinned( )
```

is_pinned returns OI_yes if the dialog box is pinned, otherwise it returns OI_no. If you have called pin for the dialog box, and the application is run under conditions that do not allow a pushpin—so that the dialog box is not actually pinned—is_pinned returns OI_no.

pin   (Member function)

```
void OI_dialog_box::pin( )
```

pin pins the dialog box if it has a pushpin and is unpinned, otherwise it does nothing. Ordinarily you should call this before the dialog box is made visible.

unpin   (Member function)

```
void OI_dialog_box::unpin( )
```

unpin unpins the dialog box if it is pinned, otherwise it does nothing.

set_pin   (Member function)

```
void OI_dialog_box::set_pin(
    OI_pin_fnp          fnp,              // pointer to callback function
    void                *argp=NULL)       // arbitrary argument for fnp


void OI_dialog_box::set_pin(
    OI_callback         *objp,            // memfnp's object
    OI_pin_memfnp       memfnp,           // pointer to callback member function
    void                *argp=NULL)       // arbitrary argument for memfnp
```

The set_pin functions register a callback function to be invoked whenever the dialog box is pinned. This callback is identified within OI as a cbPin callback function (see Section 6.18, "Determining and Adding Callbacks; Multiple Callbacks," on page 6-117). *memfnp* points to a member function for the object pointed to by *objp*. If your function is a member function, when it is invoked it will be called as if you had written *objp->memfnp*. See Section 2.5, "Callbacks and Event-Driven Programming," on page 2-16 for more explanation.

argp is optional, and can be any valid expression that can be cast to a pointer. You can use it to pass additional information to the function *fnp* or *memfnp*.

Writing the Pin Callback Function

If the cbPin callback function is not a member function, write it in this form:

```
void fn(
        OI_d_tech        *objp,        // pointer to dialog box which was pinned
        void             *argp)        // arbitrary argument
```

and if the cbPin callback function is a member function, write it in this form:

```
void obj_class::memfn(
        OI_d_tech        *objp,        // pointer to dialog box which was pinned
        void             *argp)        // arbitrary argument
```

where *obj_class* is the class of the object whose member function is *memfn*.

When your callback function is invoked, *argp* will be the argument specified in the set_pin call.

set_unpin   (Member function)

```
void OI_dialog_box::set_unpin(
    OI_pin_fnp           fnp,          // pointer to callback function
    void                 *argp=NULL)   // arbitrary argument for fnp


void OI_dialog_box::set_unpin(
    OI_callback          *objp,        // memfnp's object
    OI_pin_memfnp        memfnp,       // pointer to callback member function
    void                 *argp=NULL)   // arbitrary argument for memfnp
```

The set_unpin functions register a callback function to be invoked whenever the dialog box is unpinned. This callback is identified within OI as a cbUnpin callback function (see Section 6.18, "Determining and Adding Callbacks; Multiple Callbacks," on page 6-117). All arguments and the form of the unpin callback function are identical to those for set_pin.

18.6.6   Controlling Appearance

Dialog boxes can have a title bar if the window manager being used at the time the program runs supports title bars. The title bar, if it exists, is initially empty. A dialog box, like other OI objects, is initially clipped by its parent. That is, if any portion of the dialog box would extend outside the boundaries of its immediate parent, that portion does not display. If you set a title, a longterm message, or a pushpin on a dialog box, OI forces the dialog box to be unclipped. This means that it will be known to the window manager, which will give it a title bar if it is able to do so. Also, the user will normally have some means of changing its location relative to its parent. However, the dialog box still "tracks" its parent, just as it would if it were clipped. That is, when you move the parent, the dialog box moves to maintain the same location relative to its parent. This behavior can be disabled using the OI_d_tech member function allow_independent_loc( ) or setting the resource independentLoc to true.

longterm   (Member function)

```
char *OI_dialog_box::longterm( )
```

longterm returns the current longterm message text of the title bar.

set_longterm   (Member function)

```
OI_stat OI_dialog_box::set_longterm(
    const char           *lngp)              // text for longterm message
```

set_longterm changes the longterm message portion of the title bar to *lngp*. It also forces the dialog box to be unclipped.

title   (Member function)

```
char *OI_dialog_box::title( )
```

title returns the current title text for the dialog box.

set_title   (Member function)

```
OI_stat OI_dialog_box::set_title(
    const char           *titlep)            // title text
```

set_title changes the title text to *titlep*. It also forces the dialog box to be unclipped.

18.6.7   Using the Automatic Layout Facility with Dialog Boxes

When adding children to a dialog box, you will usually find it convenient to use the OI automatic layout facility. For a layout method of **OI_layout_row**, no special precautions need be observed. However, if you want to use any other layout method, you must do some minor extra work. You should create an extra box with frame width zero, set its layout method to the desired layout method, and lay out the box in the dialog box. You then lay out the children objects in the box. This ensures that the dialog buttons are properly positioned with respect to your other objects. The code fragment below illustrates this technique for **OI_layout_column** layout method.

```
OI_dialog_box           *dbp;
OI_box                  *bp;

dbp = oi_create_dialog_box("db",1,1);
dbp->set_layout(OI_layout_row);
bp = oi_create_box("layout_box",1,1);
bp->set_frame_width(0);
bp->set_layout(OI_layout_column);
bp->layout_associated_object(dbp,0,0,OI_active);
//   create children
//   parent children to bp using layout_associated_object
```

18.7 Resources

All resources from an **OI_dialog_box** object's base classes are available to it; in addition, OI fetches the resources shown in Table 18-4. For more information on resource management, see Chapter 39, "The OI Resource Mechanism."

Table 18-4 OI_dialog_box Resources

Resource	Description	Possible Values	Default Value
longterm	Specifies the longterm message.	Printable string	NULL
modeless	Specifies whether an automatically popped-up dialog box should be treated as a modeless dialog box.	Boolean	false
pinned	If yes, specifies that the dialog box should be pinned when the application starts, if it has a pushpin.	Boolean	false
pushpin	If yes, specifies the dialog box should have a pushpin. This has no effect on the dialog box if it is run under the Motif model, unless you have also specified the OI_connection resource motifPushpin. If you use this resource and the application was not written with the understanding that a pushpin might be available, you can cause the application to crash, as the dialog box callbacks may not be written appropriately.	Boolean	false
restrictTerm	If true, input will be restricted to the dialog box when it is popped up in wait_button; otherwise, input will not be restricted.	Boolean	false
title	Specifies the title.	Printable string	NULL

18.8   Translations

All translations from an OI_dialog_box object's base classes are available to it; it has no additional translations.

18.9   Callback Functions

Table 18-5 lists the callbacks available for an OI_dialog_box object and the page number of the corresponding explanatory material. In addition, all of the callbacks from an OI_dialog_box object's base classes are available to it.

Table 18-5   OI_dialog_box Callbacks

Callback Type	Callback Typedef	Description	Page Number
cbTermAction	OI_wait_fnp/memfnp	Validation callback function	18-21, 18-24, 18-27
cbPin	OI_pin_fnp/memfnp	Pin callback function	18-34
cbUnpin	OI_pin_fnp/memfnp	Unpin callback function	18-35

18.10 Final Example

Program 18-6 shows the use of the OI_menu_cell member function allow_subbox, which puts a dialog box marker on a menu cell even if the menu cell has no dialog box attached. In this program, the dialog box is not created until the user clicks on the menu cell (you might want to do this if the objects you will place in the dialog box depend upon some runtime events). The callback for the menu cell creates the dialog box, parents it to the menu cell, and removes the creation callback from the menu cell. This arrangement still allows OI to do the automatic popup (both the first time, after the dialog box is created, and subsequent times as well), but allows you to defer creation of the object until needed. You could also keep the menu cell callback registration, instead of removing it, and in the second and subsequent calls, you could modify the dialog box if necessary before OI pops it up.

```c
#include <OI/oi.H>                              /* Subbox.C */

int main(int argc, char **argv)
{
                void            make_db(OI_menu_cell*,void*,OI_number);

                OI_connection   *conp;
                OI_app_window   *wp;
                OI_menu_cell    *cellp;
                OI_menu         *mp;

        static OI_cell_spec  cells[] = {
                {"box_button","Box Here",&make_db},
                {"no_box","None Here"},
                };

    if (conp = OI_init(&argc,argv,"Subbox")) {
        wp = oi_create_app_window("main",1,1,"Subbox");
        wp->set_layout(OI_layout_row);
        mp = oi_create_button_menu("menu",OI_count(cells),&cells[0],
                                        OI_vertical,"Dialog Boxes");
        mp->layout_associated_object(wp,2,10,OI_active);

        cellp = (OI_menu_cell*)mp->subobject("box_button");
        cellp->allow_subbox( );

        wp->set_associated_object(wp->root( ),OI_def_loc,OI_def_loc,OI_active);
        OI_begin_interaction( );
        OI_fini( );
    }
}

void make_db (OI_menu_cell *mcp, void* ,OI_number)
{
            OI_dialog_box       *dbp;

    dbp = oi_create_dialog_box("my_db",200,100) ;
    // put any special objects in my_db here
    dbp->set_associated_object(mcp,OI_def_loc,OI_def_loc,OI_active_not_displayed);

    mcp->change_action(NULL);
    return;
}
```

Program 18-6   Use of allow_subbox (Subbox.C)

Chapter 19
Convenience Dialog Boxes Derived from OI_ms_dialog_box

The following functions are available to an **OI_ms_dialog_box** object, but are described in their own chapter.

OI_dialog_box Member Functions

OI_box Member Functions

OI_d_tech Member Functions

Convenience Dialog Boxes Derived from OI_ms_dialog_box

19.1 Description

There are six convenience dialog boxes which are derived from OI_ms_dialog_box; they are listed in Table 19-1 and displayed in Figure 19-1 through Figure 19-6. You never explicitly create an OI_ms_dialog_box object; it is the base class for the six dialog boxes described in this chapter. These six convenience dialog boxes are quite similar. In the Motif model, they are identical except for the glyph displayed in the box and the title in the title bar. In the OPEN LOOK model, these dialog boxes are identical; they are the equivalent of an OPEN LOOK "Notice". The OPEN LOOK "Notice" is a dialog box with no title, no longterm message, and no pushpin (which means that, if the user is running an OPEN LOOK window manager, the dialog box will have no title bar). Each convenience dialog box derived from OI_ms_dialog_box contains an OI_multi_text object and possibly an OI_glyph object. You can supply your own glyph for these dialog boxes; if you do, both the OPEN LOOK and the Motif dialog box will contain the glyph.

Table 19-1   Convenience Dialog Boxes Derived from OI_ms_dialog_box

OI Name	Motif Name	Usage
OI_error_dialog_box	XmErrorDialog	Displays an error message.
OI_info_dialog_box	XmInformationDialog	Displays information.
OI_message_dialog_box	XmMessageDialog	Displays any message.
OI_question_dialog_box	XmQuestionDialog	Displays a question and request an answer.
OI_warn_dialog_box	XmWarningDialog	Displays a warning message.
OI_work_dialog_box	XmWorkingDialog	Informs user that a potentially time-consuming operation is in progress.

19.2   Class Tree

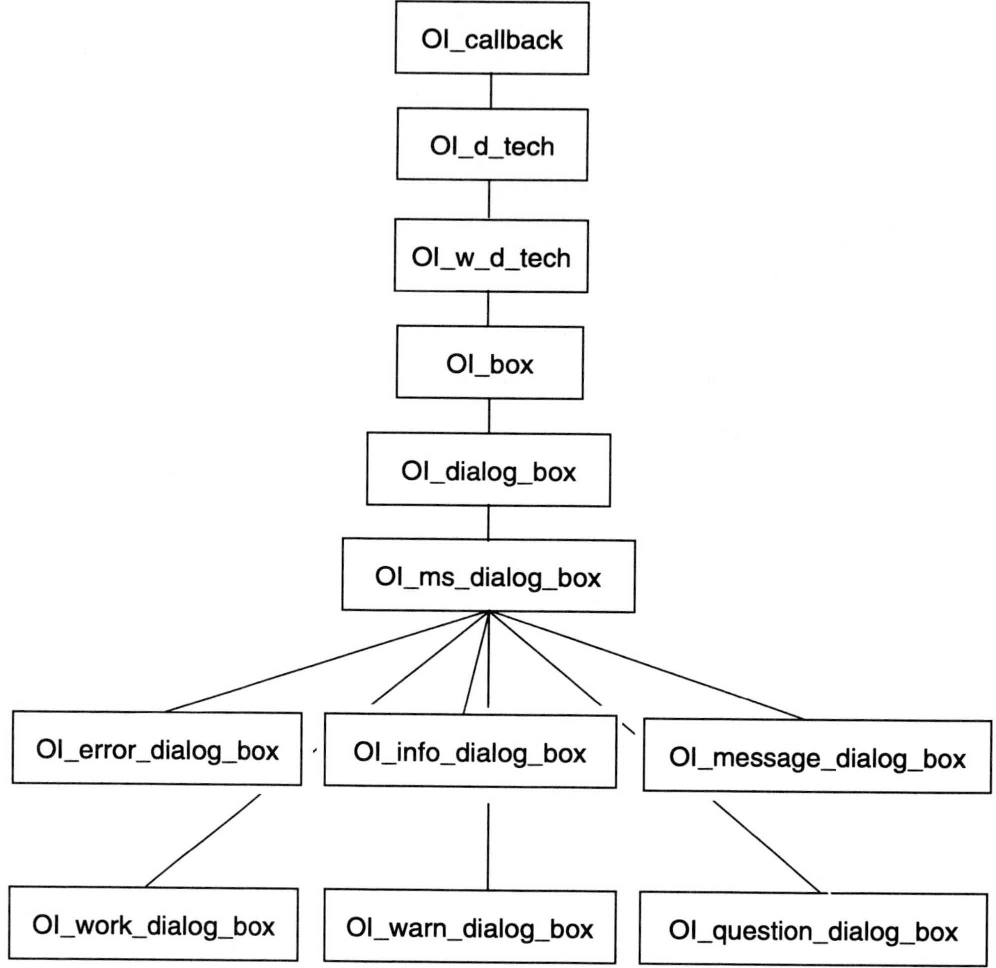

19.3   Runtime Interaction

The runtime interaction for these dialog boxes is identical to that for the general OI_dialog_box object.

19.4   Creating an OI_ms_dialog_box Convenience Dialog Box

As with OI_dialog_box, there are two forms of create function for each of these convenience dialog boxes, one to create the button menu at the bottom of the dialog box using a vector of OI_cell_spec structures to describe the cells, and one to create it using a vector of previously created

OI_menu_cell objects. Each of the six, except OI_message_dialog_box, has an identical set of arguments for each of their two forms. If you are using OI_cell_spec structures, the arguments are:

`const char`	`*namp`	pointer to object name
`const char`	`*txtp=NULL`	text to display
`OI_number`	`num=-1`	number of cells in button menu
`OI_cell_spec`	`*cell_specp=NULL`	pointer to cell information
`OI_glyph`	`*glyphp=NULL`	glyph pointer

If you are using previously created OI_menu_cell objects, the arguments are:

`const char`	`*namp`	pointer to object name
`const char`	`*txtp`	text to display
`OI_number`	`num`	number of cells in button menu
`OI_menu_cell`	`**mcellp`	pointer to cells
`OI_glyph`	`*glyphp=NULL`	glyph pointer

namp is the object name for the dialog box.

txtp is the text to be displayed in the dialog box. Because the text in these dialog boxes is placed in an internal OI_multi_text object, the text can be of any length, with a few restrictions, with lines separated by '\n' characters. See Chapter 31, "OI_base_text and OI_multi_text" for more information.

num is the number of cells in the button menu at the bottom of the dialog box. *cell_specp* is a pointer to the OI_cell_spec structure containing the cell information for the button menu at the bottom of the dialog box. *glyphp* is a pointer to a bitmap to use as the glyph in the dialog box. *mcellp* is a pointer to a vector of pointers to menu cells to use for the button menu at the bottom of the dialog box. The create functions for OI_message_dialog_box have the same arguments except that there is no glyph pointer.

Notice that OI controls the size of the dialog box; the size depends on the size of the glyph, text and menu specified.

num and *cell_specp* or *mcellp* specify the button menu at the bottom of the dialog box. If you omit *num*, it defaults to -1, in which case OI uses the default cells. Under the OPEN LOOK model the default button menu contains two cells ("OK" and "Cancel"). Under the Motif model the default button menu contains three cells ("OK", "Cancel" and "Help"). OI supplies a default callback for the "Help" button which activates the normal OI help mechanism.

You can omit or default all of the arguments except *namp*. If you do not specify *glyphp*, OI uses a default glyph under the Motif model and none under the OPEN LOOK model. If you do specify *glyphp*, then it is used irrespective of the model. The glyph is always placed to the left of the text specified by *txtp*. If you do not specify *txtp*, OI creates a convenience dialog box with no text.

Figure 19-1 through Figure 19-6 show the default appearance of the convenience dialog boxes derived from OI_ms_dialog_box; that is, the create function for each of these figures specified only *namp* and *txtp*.

oi_create_error_dialog_box   (Free-standing function)

```
OI_error_dialog_box *oi_create_error_dialog_box(
    const char          *namp,              // pointer to object name
    const char          *txtp=NULL,         // text to display
    OI_number           num=-1,             // number of cells in button menu
    OI_cell_spec        *cell_specp=NULL,   // pointer to cell information
    OI_glyph            *glyphp=NULL)       // glyph pointer

OI_error_dialog_box *oi_create_error_dialog_box(
    const char          *namp,              // pointer to object name
    const char          *txtp,              // text to display
    OI_number           num,                // number of cells in button menu
    OI_menu_cell        **mcellp,           // pointer to cells
    OI_glyph            *glyphp=NULL)        // glyph pointer
```

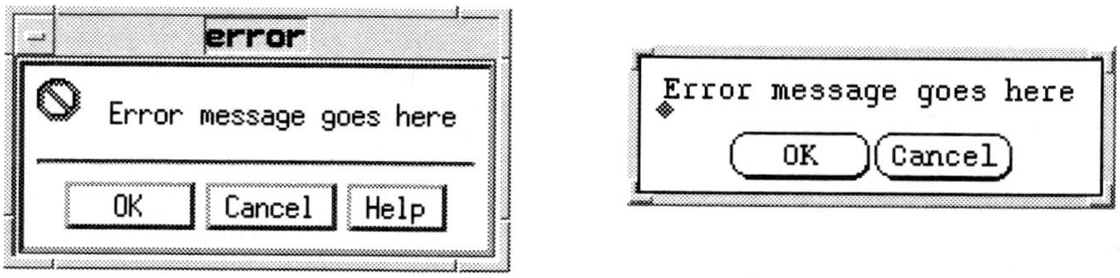

Motif   OPEN LOOK

Figure 19-1   OI_error_dialog_box

oi_create_info_dialog_box   (Free-standing function)

```
OI_info_dialog_box *oi_create_info_dialog_box(
    const char          *namp,              // pointer to object name
    const char          *txtp=NULL,         // text to display
    OI_number           num=-1,             // number of cells in button menu
    OI_cell_spec        *cell_specp=NULL,   // pointer to cell information
    OI_glyph            *glyphp=NULL)       // glyph pointer

OI_info_dialog_box *oi_create_info_dialog_box(
    const char          *namp,              // pointer to object name
    const char          *txtp,              // text to display
    OI_number           num,                // number of cells in button menu
    OI_menu_cell        **mcellp,           // pointer to cells
    OI_glyph            *glyphp=NULL)        // glyph pointer
```

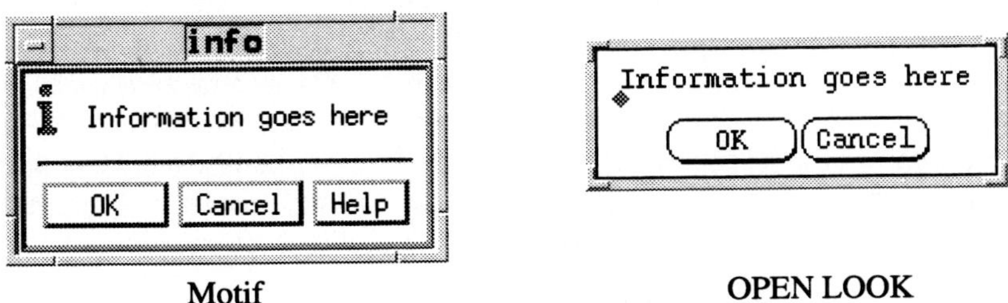

Motif   OPEN LOOK

Figure 19-2 OI_info_dialog_box

oi_create_message_dialog_box   (Free-standing function)

```
OI_message_dialog_box *oi_create_message_dialog_box(
     const char          *namp,             // pointer to object name
     const char          *txtp=NULL,        // text to display
     OI_number           num=-1,            // number of cells in button menu
     OI_cell_spec        *cell_specp=NULL)  // pointer to cell information

OI_message_dialog_box *oi_create_message_dialog_box(
     const char          *namp,             // pointer to object name
     const char          *txtp,             // text to display
     OI_number           num,               // number of cells in button menu
     OI_menu_cell        **mcellp)          // pointer to cells
```

Motif   OPEN LOOK

Figure 19-3 OI_message_dialog_box

oi_create_question_dialog_box   (Free-standing function)

```
OI_question_dialog_box *oi_create_question_dialog_box(
    const char          *namp,              // pointer to object name
    const char          *txtp=NULL,         // text to display
    OI_number           num=-1,             // number of cells in button menu
    OI_cell_spec        *cell_specp=NULL,   // pointer to cell information
    OI_glyph            *glyphp=NULL)       // glyph pointer

OI_question_dialog_box *oi_create_question_dialog_box(
    const char          *namp,              // pointer to object name
    const char          *txtp,              // text to display
    OI_number           num,                // number of cells in button menu
    OI_menu_cell        **mcellp,           // pointer to cells
    OI_glyph            *glyphp=NULL)        // glyph pointer
```

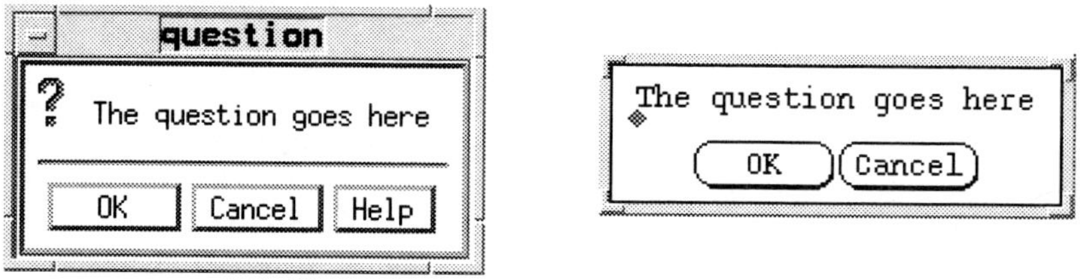

Motif   OPEN LOOK

Figure 19-4   OI_question_dialog_box

oi_create_warn_dialog_box   (Free-standing function)

```
OI_warn_dialog_box *oi_create_warn_dialog_box(
    const char          *namp,              // pointer to object name
    const char          *txtp=NULL,         // text to display
    OI_number           num=-1,             // number of cells in button menu
    OI_cell_spec        *cell_specp=NULL,   // pointer to cell information
    OI_glyph            *glyphp=NULL)        // glyph pointer

OI_warn_dialog_box *oi_create_warn_dialog_box(
    const char          *namp,              // pointer to object name
    const char          *txtp,              // text to display
    OI_number           num,                // number of cells in button menu
    OI_menu_cell        **mcellp,           // pointer to cells
    OI_glyph            *glyphp=NULL)        // glyph pointer
```

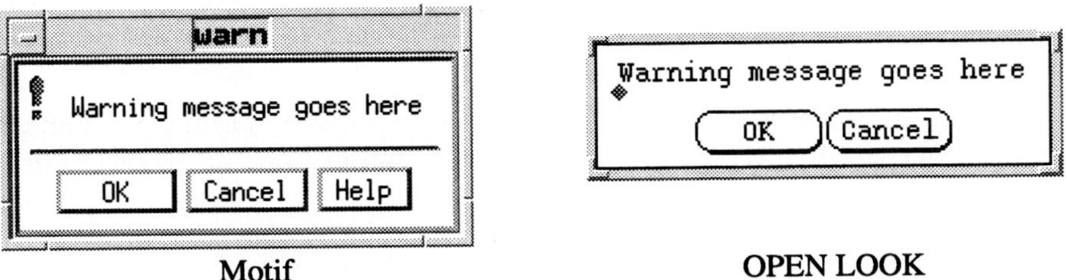

Motif   OPEN LOOK

Figure 19-5 OI_warn_dialog_box

oi_create_work_dialog_box   (Free-standing function)

```
OI_work_dialog_box *oi_create_work_dialog_box(
    const char          *namp,              // pointer to object name
    const char          *txtp=NULL,         // text to display
    OI_number           num=-1,             // number of cells in button menu
    OI_cell_spec        *cell_specp=NULL,   // pointer to cell information
    OI_glyph            *glyphp=NULL)       // glyph pointer

OI_work_dialog_box *oi_create_work_dialog_box(
    const char          *namp,              // pointer to object name
    const char          *txtp=NULL,         // text to display
    OI_number           num,                // number of cells in button menu
    OI_menu_cell        **mcellp,           // pointer to cells
    OI_glyph            *glyphp=NULL)        // glyph pointer
```


Motif   OPEN LOOK

Figure 19-6 OI_work_dialog_box

19.5   Base Class Member Functions

You can use all of the member functions of OI_d_tech, OI_box, and OI_dialog_box for an OI_ms_dialog_box convenience dialog box.

You can use all of the member functions available to OI_button_menu for the button menu subobject. These include the member functions of OI_menu and the member functions of OI_menu_cell for the cells of the menu.

19.6   OI_ms_dialog_box Member Functions

You can change the text that appears in the convenience dialog box's internal OI_multi_text object at any time using these functions. OI adjusts the convenience dialog box size to accommodate the change in the size of the text displayed. OI limits the number of lines that can be viewed to 20 and the number of characters per line to 80.

set_text_to_file   (Member function)

```
OI_stat OI_ms_dialog_box::set_text_to_file(
    const char            *namp)                    // file name
```

```
OI_stat OI_ms_dialog_box::set_text_to_file(
    FILE                  *fp)                      // file
```

set_text_to_file clears the current text from the OI_multi_text object in the convenience dialog box and sets it to the contents of the file *namp* or *fp*.

append_file   (Member function)

```
OI_stat OI_ms_dialog_box::append_file(
    const char            *namp,                    // file name
    OI_bool               scrl=OI_no)               // discard scrolled lines?
```

```
OI_stat OI_ms_dialog_box::append_file(
    FILE                  *fp)                      // file
    OI_bool               scrl=OI_no)               // discard scrolled lines?
```

append_file appends the contents of the file *namp* or *fp* to the end of the current text in the OI_multi_text object in the convenience dialog box. If the total number of lines exceeds the maximum number of lines specified when the object was created, and if *scrl* = OI_yes, OI discards those lines scrolled off the top. If *scrl* = OI_no, OI makes the OI_multi_text object contain more lines, up to a maximum of 20.

set_text_to_string   (Member function)

```
OI_stat OI_ms_dialog_box::set_text_to_string(
    const char            *txt)                     // string
```

set_text_to_string clears the current text from the OI_multi_text object in the convenience dialog box and sets it to *txt*.

append_string   (Member function)

```
OI_stat OI_ms_dialog_box::append_string(
    const char          *txt,           // string
    OI_bool             scrl=OI_no)     // keep scrolled lines?
```

append_string appends *txt* to the end of the current text in the **OI_multi_text** object in the convenience dialog box. *scrl* is used in the same manner as for **append_file**.

set_text   (Member function)

```
OI_stat OI_ms_dialog_box::set_text(
    OI_text_fnp         fnp)            // pointer to callback function
```

```
OI_stat OI_ms_dialog_box::set_text(
    OI_callback         *objp,          // memfnp's object
    OI_text_memfnp      memfnp)         // pointer to callback member function
```

The **set_text** functions register a function to supply text lines to initialize the **OI_multi_text** object in the convenience dialog box. When the member function is invoked, it will be called as if you had written *objp->memfnp*. See Section 2.5, "Callbacks and Event-Driven Programming," on page 2-16 for more explanation.

set_text clears the **OI_multi_text** object, then repeatedly calls *fnp* or *memfnp* to get successive lines of text to fill the **OI_multi_text** object.

Writing the Text Function

If the function is not a member function, write it in this form:

```
char *fn( )
```

and if the function is a member function, write it in this form:

```
char *obj_class::memfn( )
```

where *obj_class* is the class of the object whose member function is *memfn*.

Write the function to return a single line of text, null terminated and not containing any newline characters. When no more lines are available, return NULL.

19.7 Resources

All resources from an **OI_ms_dialog_box** object's base classes are available to it; it has no additional resources.

If you want to set the initial text of an **OI_ms_dialog_box** object via resources, you must specify the internal object **@text**. For example, if your application **MyApp** has an **OI_ms_dialog_box** object named **MyDialog**, and the text is in **my_file**, you would insert the following line into the resource file:

```
MyApp*MyDialog.@text.textFile:          my_file
```

19.8 Translations

All translations from an OI_ms_dialog_box object's base classes are available to it; it has no additional translations.

19.9 Callbacks

All callbacks from an OI_ms_dialog_box object's base classes are available to it; it has no additional callbacks.

Chapter 20
OI_prompt_dialog_box

OI_prompt_dialog_box Functions

OI_prompt_dialog_box Member Functions

The following functions are available to an **OI_prompt_dialog_box** object, but are described in their own chapter.

OI_dialog_box Member Functions

OI_box Member Functions

OI_d_tech Member Functions

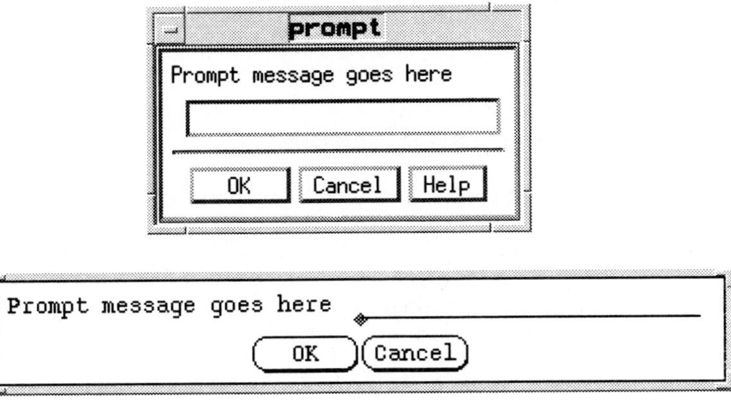

OI_prompt_dialog_box

20.1 Description

An OI_prompt_dialog_box is a dialog box containing an entry field. This dialog box is used to prompt the user for a single line of text.

20.2 Class Tree

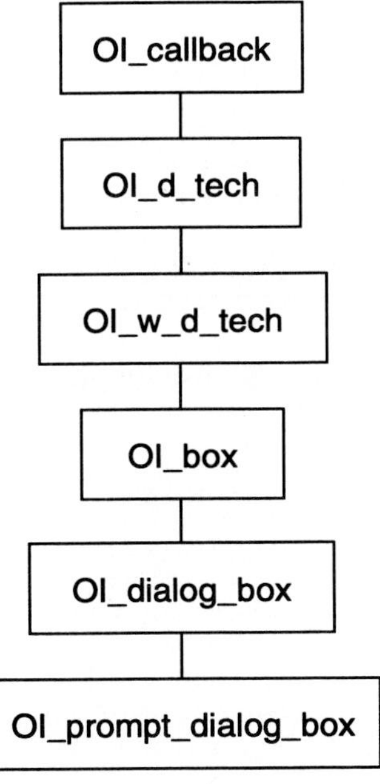

20.3   Runtime Interaction

The runtime interaction for an OI_prompt_dialog_box object is identical to that for the general OI_dialog_box object.

20.4   OI_prompt_dialog_box Creation

As with OI_dialog_box, there are two forms of create function for OI_prompt_dialog_box, one to create the button menu at the bottom of the dialog box using a vector of OI_cell_spec structures to describe the cells, and one to create it using a vector of OI_menu_cell objects.

Figure 20-1 and Figure 20-2 show an OI_prompt_dialog_box for which only *namp, dsplen* and *labelp* were specified.

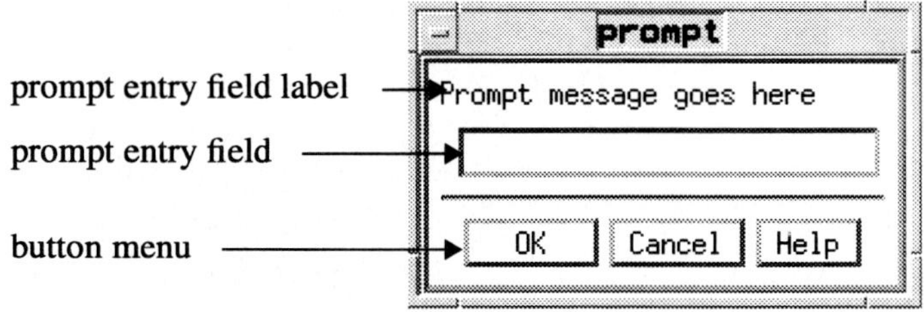

Figure 20-1   Parts of an OI_prompt_dialog_box, Motif

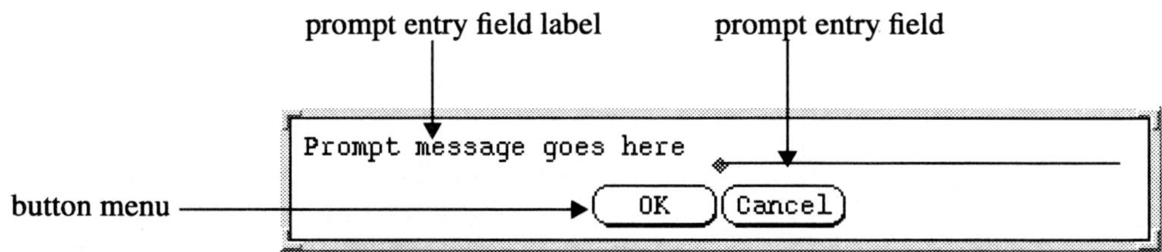

Figure 20-2   Parts of an OI_prompt_dialog_box, OPEN LOOK

oi_create_prompt_dialog_box   (Free-standing function)

```
OI_prompt_dialog_box *oi_create_prompt_dialog_box(
    const char    *namp,                        // pointer to object name
    OI_number      dsplen
                   =OI_prompt_db_def_ef_width,   // number of characters to display
                                                 // in prompt entry field
    const char    *labelp="Selection ",          // label for prompt entry field
    const char    *defstr=NULL,                   // default prompt entry field text
    OI_number      maxlen=-1,                     // max number chars in entry field
    OI_number      num=-1,                        // number of cells in button menu
    OI_cell_spec  *cell_specp=NULL)               // pointer to cell information


OI_prompt_dialog_box *oi_create_prompt_dialog_box(
    const char    *namp,                          // pointer to object name
    OI_number      dsplen,                         // number of characters to display
                                                   // in prompt entry field
    const char    *labelp,                         // label for prompt entry field
    const char    *defstr,                         // default prompt entry field text
    OI_number      maxlen,                          // max number chars in entry field
    OI_number      num,                             // number of cells in button menu
    OI_menu_cell  **mcellp)                          // pointer to cells
```

namp is the object name for the dialog box. *dsplen* specifies the displayed length of the text entry area for the prompt entry field and defaults to 50 characters. *labelp* is the label for the prompt entry field and defaults to "Selection ". *defstr* is the default text value of the prompt entry field. *maxlen* is the maximum number of characters for the prompt entry field and defaults to *dsplen*. *num* is the number of cells in the button menu at the bottom of the dialog box. *cell_specp* is a pointer to the **OI_cell_spec** structure containing the cell information for the button menu at the bottom of the dialog box. *mcellp* is a pointer to a vector of pointers to menu cells to use for the button menu at the bottom of the dialog box.

OI controls the size of the dialog box; the size depends on the label length, the menu specified, and *dsplen*.

num and *cell_specp* or *mcellp* specify the button menu at the bottom of the dialog box. If you omit *num*, it defaults to -1, in which case OI uses the default cells. Under the OPEN LOOK model the default button menu contains two cells ("OK" and "Cancel"). Under the Motif model the default button menu contains three cells ("OK", "Cancel" and "Help"). OI supplies a default callback for the "Help" button which activates the normal OI help mechanism.

You can omit or default all of the arguments except *namp*.

20.5   Base Class Member Functions

You can use all of the member functions of **OI_d_tech**, **OI_box**, and **OI_dialog_box** for an **OI_prompt_dialog_box** object.

You can use all of the member functions available to **OI_button_menu** for the button menu subobject. These include the member functions of **OI_menu** and the member functions of **OI_menu_cell** for the cells of the menu.

20.6   OI_prompt_dialog_box Member Functions

The member functions described below are all convenience functions for manipulating the entry field. With the exception of **entry_field** (which returns a pointer to the entry field itself), they all map directly to a corresponding **OI_entry_field** member function. (The corresponding **OI_entry_field** member functions have the same names with "selection_" omitted.)

entry_field   (Member function)

```
OI_entry_field *OI_prompt_dialog_box::entry_field( )
```

entry_field returns a pointer to the underlying prompt **OI_entry_field**.

selection_part_text   (Member function)

```
char *OI_prompt_dialog_box::selection_part_text( )
```

selection_part_text returns a pointer to the current text string of the entry field.

selection_text   (Member function)

```
char *OI_prompt_dialog_box::selection_text( )
```

selection_text returns a pointer to the current text of the entry field if it is a valid entry (that is, if the user has pressed the Return key, and the entry validation routine (if any) has returned a valid-entry status), otherwise it returns NULL.

set_selection_default_text   (Member function)

```
void OI_prompt_dialog_box::set_selection_default_text(
    const char        *defstr,           // default entry field text
    OI_bool           chk=OI_yes)        // call entry validation callback?
```

set_selection_default_text sets the default text for the prompt entry field to *defstr*. If *chk* is **OI_yes**, the entry field validation function is called.

set_selection_text   (Member function)

```
void OI_prompt_dialog_box::set_selection_text(
    const char        *str,              // entry field text
    OI_bool           chk=OI_yes)        // call entry validation callback?
```

set_selection_text sets the text for the prompt entry field to *str*. If *chk* is **OI_yes**, the entry field validation function is called.

selection_label   (Member function)

```
char *OI_prompt_dialog_box::selection_label( )
```

selection_label returns a pointer to the prompt entry field label string.

---

set_selection_label   (Member function)

```
void OI_prompt_dialog_box::set_selection_label(
    const char          *labelp)                    // prompt entry field label
```

set_selection_label sets the label of the prompt entry field to *labelp*.

20.7   Resources

All resources from an **OI_prompt_dialog_box** object's base classes are available to it; it has no additional resources.

20.8   Translations

All translations from an **OI_prompt_dialog_box** object's base classes are available to it; it has no additional translations.

20.9   Callbacks

All callbacks from an **OI_prompt_dialog_box** object's base classes are available to it; it has no additional callbacks.

Chapter 21
OI_select_dialog_box

OI_select_dialog_box Functions

OI_select_dialog_box Member Functions

The following functions are available to an **OI_select_dialog_box** object, but are described in their own chapter.

OI_prompt_dialog_box Member Functions

OI_dialog_box Member Functions

OI_box Member Functions

OI_d_tech Member Functions

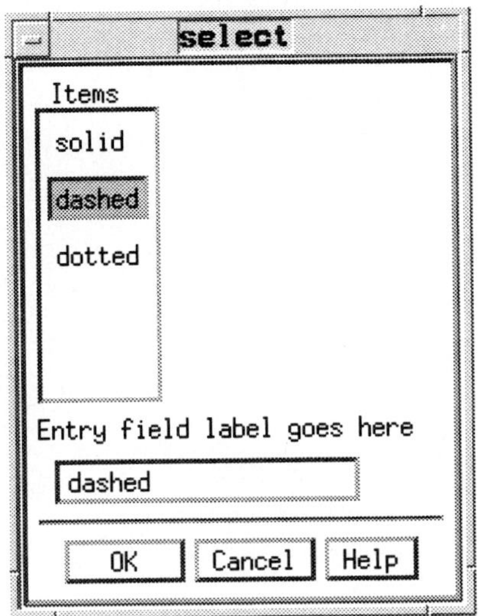

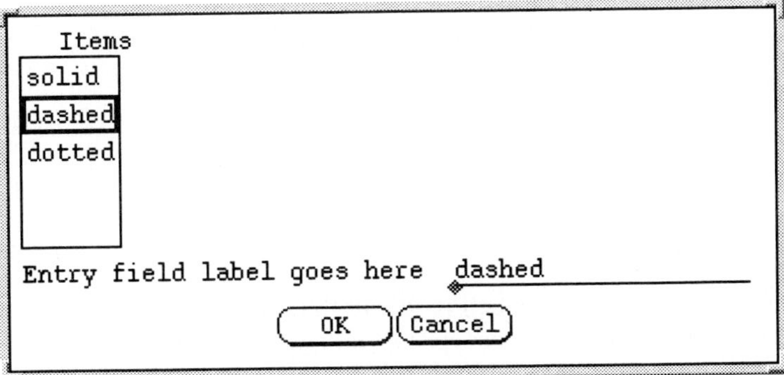

OI_select_dialog_box

21.1 Description

An OI_select_dialog_box is a prompt dialog box with the addition of a scroll menu. Its purpose is to allow the user to choose a selection from the menu or to enter a selection in the entry field through the keyboard. For example, you might use an OI_select_dialog_box object to present printer choices to the user. You would fill the scroll menu with printer choices, and the user could type in a file name in the entry field if a print-to-disk is desired. This example is shown in Program 21-1 on page 21-6.

21.2 Class Tree

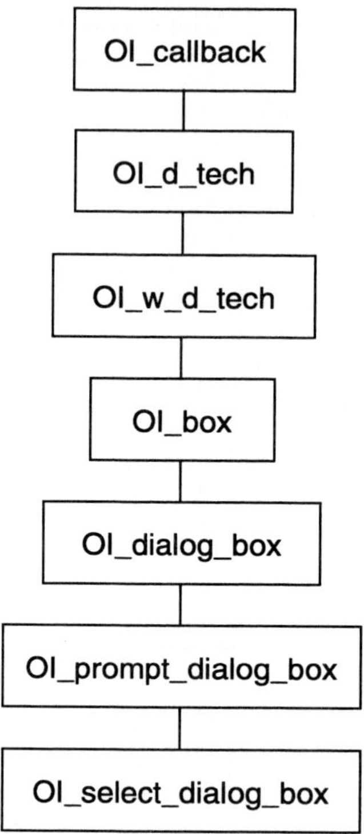

21.3 Runtime Interaction

To activate a selection, click on a menu cell in the scroll menu; the cell label will be entered into the entry field—but only if the menu cell is of type OI_text_cell. If you wish to enter an item that is not on the menu, type the text in the entry field. Click on the "OK" or "Cancel" button when you are done.

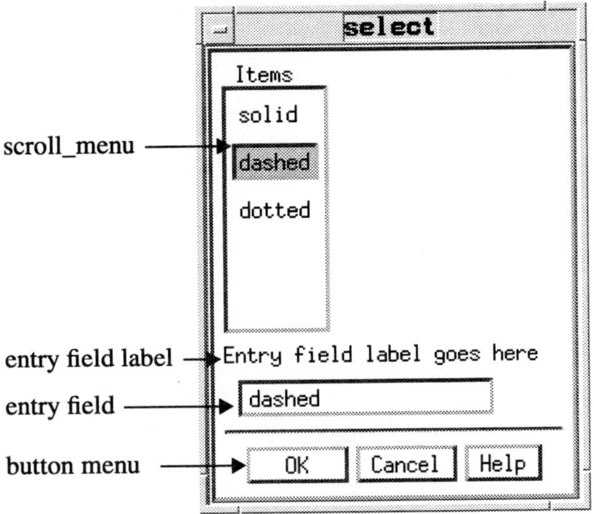

Figure 21-1   Parts of an OI_select_dialog_box, Motif

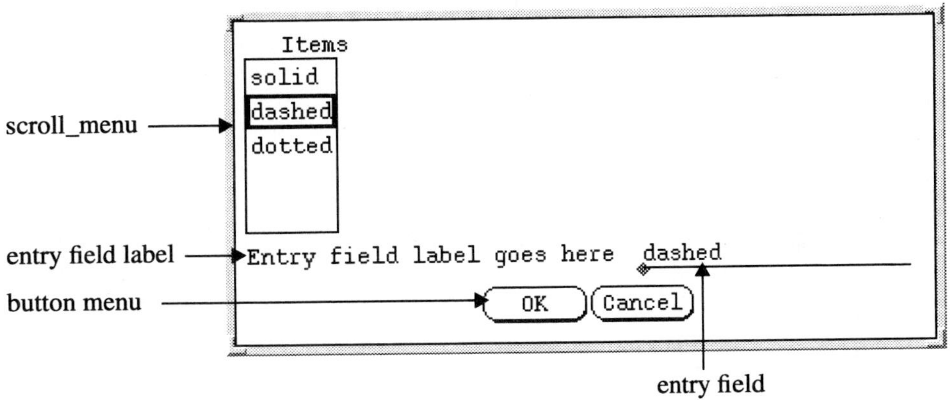

Figure 21-2   Parts of an OI_select_dialog_box, OPEN LOOK

21.4   OI_select_dialog_box Creation

As with OI_dialog_box, there are two forms of create function for OI_select_dialog_box: one to create the button menu at the bottom of the dialog box using a vector of OI_cell_spec structures to describe the cells, and one to create it using a vector of OI_menu_cell objects.

oi_create_select_dialog_box   (Free-standing function)

```
OI_select_dialog_box *oi_create_select_dialog_box(
    const char    *namp,                              // pointer to object name
    OI_number     dsplen
                  =OI_prompt_db_def_ef_width,         // number of characters to display
                                                      // in select entry field
    const char    *labelp="Selection ",              // label for select entry field
    const char    *defstr=NULL,                       // default select entry field text
    OI_number     maxlen=-1,                           // max number chars in entry field
    OI_number     smnu_num=-1,                         // number of cells in scroll menu
    OI_cell_spec  *smnu_cspecp=NULL,                   // pointer to cell information for
                                                       // scroll menu
    const char    *smnu_titlp="Items",                // title for scroll menu
    OI_number     num=-1,                              // number of cells in button menu
    OI_cell_spec  *cell_specp=NULL)                    // pointer to cell information for
                                                       // button menu


OI_select_dialog_box *oi_create_select_dialog_box(
    const char    *namp,                              // pointer to object name
    OI_number     dsplen,                              // number of characters to display
                                                       // in select entry field
    const char    *labelp,                            // label for select entry field
    const char    *defstr,                            // default select entry field text
    OI_number     maxlen,                              // max number chars in entry field
    OI_number     smnu_num,                            // number of cells in scroll menu
    OI_menu_cell  **smnu_mcellp,                       // pointer to cell information for
                                                       // scroll menu
    const char    *smnu_titlp="Items",                // title for scroll menu
    OI_number     num=-1,                              // number of cells in button menu
    OI_menu_cell  **mcellp=NULL)                       // pointer to cells for button menu
```

namp is the object name for the dialog box. *dsplen* specifies the displayed length of the select
entry field. *labelp* is the label for the select entry field. *defstr* is the initial text value of the select
entry field. *maxlen* is the maximum number of characters for the select entry field and defaults
to *dsplen*. *smnu_num* specifies the number of cells for the scroll menu. *smnu_cspecp* is a pointer
to the OI_cell_spec structure which contains the cell information for the scroll menu.
smnu_mcellp is a vector of pointers to menu cells to use for the scroll menu. *num* is the number
of cells in the button menu at the bottom of the dialog box. *cell_specp* is a pointer to the
OI_cell_spec structure containing the cell information for the button menu at the bottom of the
dialog box. *mcellp* is a pointer to a vector of menu cells to use for the button menu at the bottom
of the dialog box.

Notice that OI controls the size of the dialog box; the size depends on the entry field label length,
the menus specified, and *dsplen*.

You may omit or default all of the arguments except *namp*. If you omit *dsplen*, it defaults to 50 characters. *labelp* defaults to "Selection ". *smnu_num* defaults to -1, in which case a scroll menu without any cells is created. The initial size of the scroll menu viewport is 5 menu cells. *smnu_titlp* defaults to "Items". *num* and *cell_specp* or *mcellp* specify the button menu at the bottom of the dialog box. If you omit *num*, it defaults to -1, in which case OI uses the default cells. Under the OPEN LOOK model the default button menu contains two cells ("OK" and "Cancel"). Under the Motif model the default button menu contains three cells ("OK", "Cancel" and "Help"). OI supplies a default callback for the "Help" button which activates the normal OI help mechanism.

21.5 Base Class Member Functions

You can use all of the member functions of OI_d_tech, OI_box, OI_dialog_box, and OI_prompt_dialog_box for an OI_select_dialog_box object.

You can use all of the member functions available to OI_button_menu for the button menu subobject. These include the member functions of OI_menu and the member functions of OI_menu_cell for the cells of the menu.

21.6 OI_select_dialog_box Member Functions

You can manipulate the scroll menu separately if necessary.

change_menu   (Member function)

```
OI_stat OI_select_dialog_box::change_menu(
    OI_number          smnu_num,            // number of cells in new scroll menu
    OI_cell_spec        *smnu_cspecp,       // cell structures for new menu
    const char          *smnu_titlp=NULL)   // title for new scroll menu


OI_stat OI_select_dialog_box::change_menu(
    OI_number          smnu_num,            // number of cells in new scroll menu
    OI_menu_cell        **smnu_mcellp,      // cells for new scroll menu
    const char          *smnu_titlp=NULL)   // title for new scroll menu
```

change_menu changes the underlying OI_scroll_menu object to the one specified by the parameters. change_menu's parameters are identical to the ones of the same names in oi_create_select_dialog_box.

21.7 An OI_select_dialog_box Programming Example

Program 21-1 shows a program which allows the user to select a printer or a file Figure 21-3 and Figure 21-4 show this program in action; the user has typed characters in the entry field.

```c
#include <OI/oi.H>                         /* SelectPrinter.C */
int main(int argc, char **argv)
{
            void                        printit(OI_menu_cell*,void*,OI_number);

            OI_connection               *conp;
            OI_app_window               *wp;
            OI_select_dialog_box        *sdbp;
            OI_menu                     *mp;
            OI_menu_cell                *cellp;

        static  OI_cell_spec            cells[] = {
            {"print","Print"},
            };
        static  OI_cell_spec            printers[] = {
            {"lwo","lwo"},
            {"lwe","lwe"},
            {"lws","lws"},
            {"lpmis","lpmis"},
            {"lpeng","lpeng"},
            {"lpmfg","lpmfg"},
        };

    if (conp = OI_init(&argc,argv,"SelectPrinter")) {
        wp = oi_create_app_window("main",1,1,"SelectPrinter");
        wp->set_layout(OI_layout_row);

        mp = oi_create_button_menu("menu",OI_count(cells),&cells[0],OI_vertical);
        mp->layout_associated_object(wp,2,10,OI_active);

        sdbp = oi_create_select_dialog_box("print_db",30,"Printer or File: ",NULL,
                            100,OI_count(printers),&printers[0],"Printers") ;
        sdbp->set_associated_object(mp->subobject("print"),OI_def_loc,OI_def_loc,
                            OI_active_not_displayed);
        cellp = (OI_menu_cell*)sdbp->buttons( )->subobject("OK");
        cellp->change_action(&printit,sdbp->entry_field( ));

        wp->set_associated_object(wp->root( ),OI_def_loc,OI_def_loc,OI_active);
        OI_begin_interaction( );
        OI_fini( );
    }
}


void printit(OI_menu_cell*,void *argp,OI_number)
{
        OI_entry_field                  *efp;

    efp = (OI_entry_field*)argp;
    printf("Printer selected was %s\n",efp->part_text( ));
    return;
}
```

Program 21-1   Allow User to Select Printer (SelectPrinter.C)

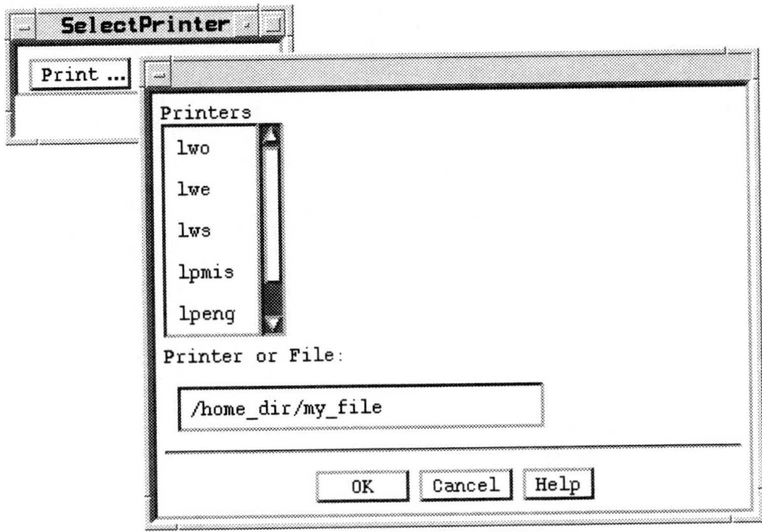

Figure 21-3   Printer Select, Motif

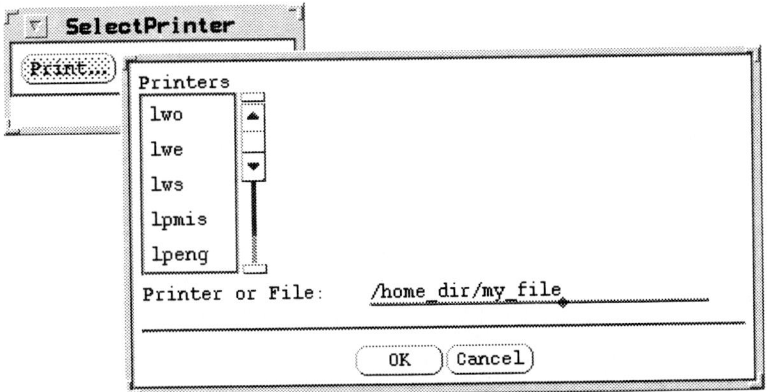

Figure 21-4   Printer Select, OPEN LOOK

21.8   Resources

All resources from an OI_select_dialog_box object's base classes are available to it; it has no additional resources.

21.9 Translations

All translations from an OI_select_dialog_box object's base classes are available to it; it has no additional translations.

21.10 Callbacks

All callbacks from an OI_select_dialog_box object's base classes are available to it; it has no additional callbacks.

Chapter 22
OI_file_dialog_box

OI_file_dialog_box Functions

OI_file_dialog_box Member Functions

The following functions are available to an **OI_file_dialog_box** object, but are described in their own chapter.

OI_select_dialog_box Member Functions

OI_prompt_dialog_box Member Functions

OI_dialog_box Member Functions

OI_box Member Functions

OI_d_tech Member Functions

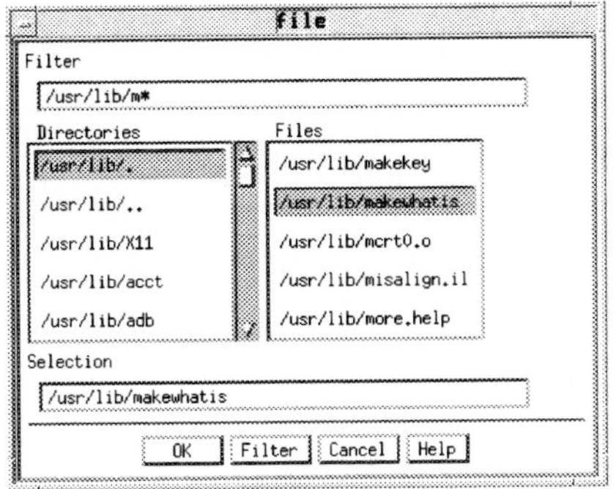

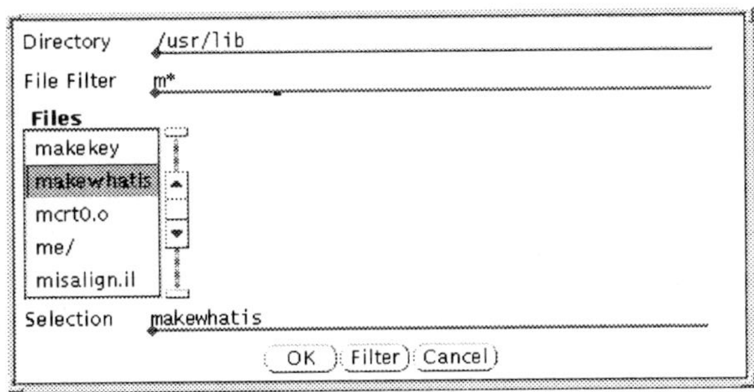

OI_file_dialog_box

22.1 Description

An OI_file_dialog_box allows the user to view directories and choose a file. The dialog box contains different objects depending on which interaction model is being used. The Motif OI_file_dialog_box object contains a Filter entry field, a scroll menu of directories, and a scroll menu showing the non-directory files in the current directory. Beneath these is an entry field that shows the current file selection, followed by a four-button dialog box button menu. The OPEN LOOK OI_file_dialog_box object contains an entry field showing the current directory, a Filter entry field, and a scroll menu showing the files in the current directory. Beneath these is an entry field that shows the current file selection, followed by a three-button dialog box button menu.

Files in the current directory which are not themselves directories must match the filter expression in order to be eligible for display. In the OPEN LOOK model, both directory files and filtered regular files appear in the "Files" display. In the Motif model, directory files show in the "Directories" display and filtered regular files show in the "Files" display.

22.2   Class Tree

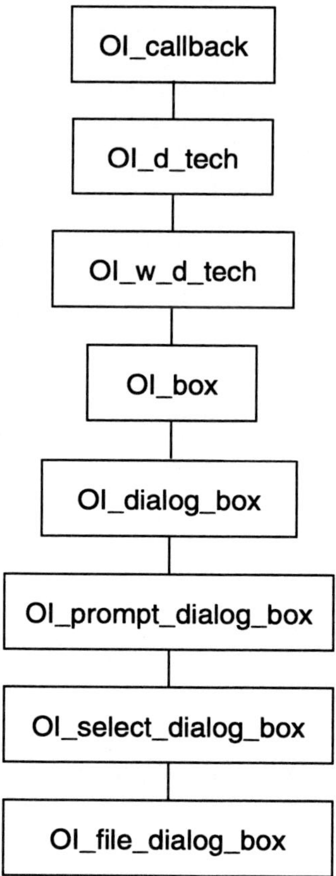

22.3   Runtime Interaction, Motif

When the file dialog box is activated, OI displays the filter string initialized in the create function to *dir/filtr* in the Filter entry field. OI then searches the directory specified in the create function as *dir*. All files in *dir* which are themselves directories are placed in the Directory scroll menu—they are not subject to filter processing. All files in *dir* which meet the criteria specified by the filter *filtr* are displayed in the Files scroll menu. In the Motif version, *dir* is also displayed in the Selection entry field.

You can change the filter to any file specification using a C Shell type pattern-matching expression. If you strike the Return key in the Filter entry field or click on the "Filter" button, OI applies the file filter; the Files scroll menu and the Selection entry field change to reflect the files which match the filter. For example, in Figure 22-1, the filter has been changed to search for any file beginning with "m*" in the directory /usr/lib. If you strike the Up (or Down) Arrow key while the Filter entry field has the focus, the selection in the Directory scroll menu moves up (or down) and updates the Filter entry field with the selected directory.

You can change directories by clicking twice on the directory of choice in the Directory scroll menu, or by typing the directory as part of the filter. The Files scroll menu shows the names of all the files in the current directory which are not themselves directories and which match the filter. Clicking once on one of these file names causes the file name to appear in the Selection entry field. Clicking twice on one of these file names causes the file to appear in the Selection entry field and the dialog box to be dismissed as though you had clicked on the "OK" button. If you strike the Up (or Down) Arrow key while the Directory scroll menu has the focus, the selection in this menu moves up (or down) and updates the Filter entry field with the selected directory.

The Up (or Down) Arrow key works in a similar manner for the Selection entry field and the Files scroll menu.

Note that the entire path name of all files and directories appears in all entry fields and scroll menus when using Motif.

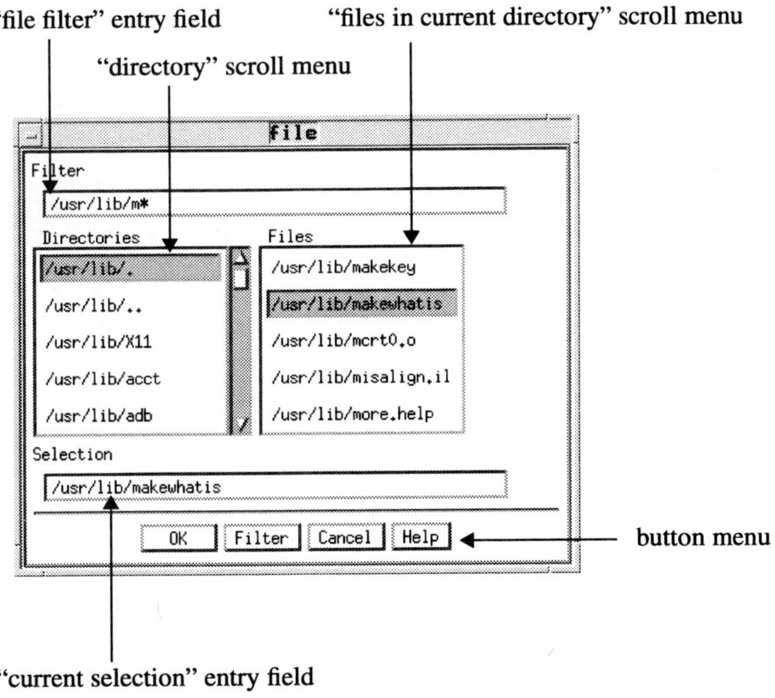

Figure 22-1   Parts of an OI_file_dialog_box, Motif

22.4   Runtime Interaction, OPEN LOOK

A file dialog box behaves in nearly the same way under OPEN LOOK as it does under Motif. The main difference is that there is no Directory scroll menu; instead the current directory appears in the Directory entry field. The names of files in the current directory appear in the Files scroll menu, whether they are directories themselves or regular files. However, entries which are directories have a trailing "/". Files in the current directory which are themselves directories are not subject to filter processing; other files must pass through the filter to be eligible for display.

To change the current directory, click twice on a directory in the scroll menu, enter the directory as part of the filter, or enter the directory into the Directory entry field.

You can either use a **C Shell** type pattern matching expression or an **ed** regular expression for the filter. By default the filter is a **C Shell** expression. To change the expression type, press the MENU mouse button when the pointer is over the Filter entry field and select the desired filter type from the menu which pops up.

In OPEN LOOK, the Filter entry field, the Files scroll menu and the Selection entry field all show file names relative to the directory displayed in the Directory entry field. This is in contrast to the full path name that is used in the Motif model. See Figure 22-2.

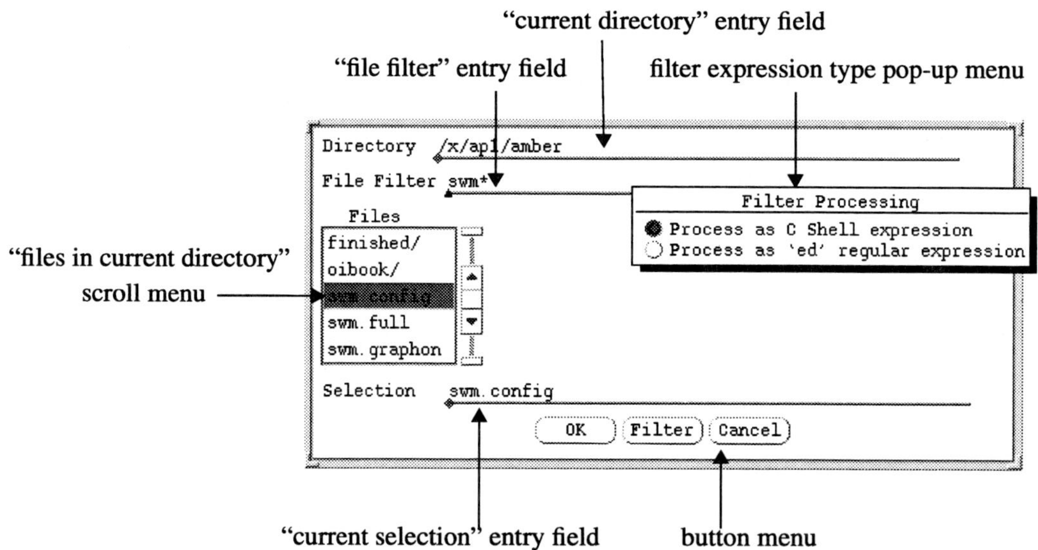

Figure 22-2   Parts of an OI_file_dialog_box, OPEN LOOK

22.5   OI_file_dialog_box Creation

As with OI_dialog_box, there are two forms of create function for OI_file_dialog_box, one to create the button menu at the bottom of the dialog box from a vector of OI_cell_spec structures, and one to create it from a vector of OI_menu_cell objects.

oi_create_file_dialog_box   (Free-standing function)

```
OI_file_dialog_box *oi_create_file_dialog_box(
    const char    *namp,                // pointer to object name
    const char    *dir=".",             // directory in which to search for files
    const char    *filtr="*",           // filter to apply when searching
    OI_number      num=-1,              // number of cells in button menu
    OI_cell_spec *cell_specp=NULL)      // pointer to cell information for button menu


OI_file_dialog_box *oi_create_file_dialog_box(
    const char    *namp,                // pointer to object name
    const char    *dir,                 // directory name to search for files
    const char    *filtr,               // filter to apply when searching
    OI_number      num,                 // number of cells in button menu
    OI_menu_cell **mcellp)              // pointer to cells for button menu
```

namp is the object name for the dialog box. *dir* specifies the starting directory in which to search for files, and defaults to the current directory. *filtr* specifies the csh expression to use to filter non-directory files when searching and defaults to "*", in which case OI displays all the files in the directory *dir*. *num* is the number of cells in the button menu at the bottom of the dialog box. *cell_specp* is a pointer to the OI_cell_spec structure containing the cell information for the button menu at the bottom of the dialog box. *mcellp* is a pointer to a vector of pointers to menu cells to use for the button menu at the bottom of the dialog box. If you omit *num*, it defaults to -1, in which case OI uses the default cells. Under the OPEN LOOK model the default button menu contains three cells ("OK", "Filter" and "Cancel"). Under the Motif model the default button menu contains four cells ("OK", "Filter", "Cancel" and "Help"). OI supplies a default callback for the "Help" button which activates the normal OI help mechanism.

OI controls the size of the dialog box; the size depends on the objects in the dialog box.

22.6   Base Class Member Functions

You can use all of the member functions of OI_d_tech, OI_box, OI_dialog_box, OI_prompt_dialog_box, and OI_select_dialog_box for an OI_file_dialog_box object.

You can use all of the member functions available to OI_button_menu for the button menu subobject. These include the member functions of OI_menu and the member functions of OI_menu_cell for the cells of the menu.

22.7 OI_file_dialog_box Member Functions

The functions below allow you to query the current values of the various parts of the file selection dialog box, and to programmatically change the current context.

pathname   (Member function)

```
char *OI_file_dialog_box::pathname( )
```

pathname returns a pointer to the full path of the file in the Selection entry field. This includes all directories from the root ("/") through the actual file. **pathname** returns NULL if no valid file has been selected.

directory   (Member function)

```
char *OI_file_dialog_box::directory( )
```

directory returns a pointer to the current directory. Note that **directory** can be different from **pathname** with the final file name removed, because the user can type a file name from a different directory into the Selection entry field.

filter   (Member function)

```
char *OI_file_dialog_box::filter( )
```

filter returns a pointer to the filter string.

set_files   (Member function)

```
int OI_file_dialog_box::set_files(
   const char          *dir=NULL,          // new directory
   const char          *filtr=NULL)        // new filter
```

set_files sets the current directory to *dir* and the filter to *filtr*. If *dir* is NULL, the directory remains unchanged. Similarly, if *filtr* is NULL, the filter remains unchanged. After setting the new values for the directory and the filter, OI searches the directory for the files, using the new filter. The scroll menu(s) are updated with the new file names and the entry field(s) are set to the new directory.

filter_label   (Member function)

```
char *OI_file_dialog_box::filter_label( )
```

filter_label returns a pointer to the Filter entry field label.

set_filter_label   (Member function)

```
void OI_file_dialog_box::set_filter_label(
   const char          *lbl)               // filter label
```

set_filter_label sets the label for the Filter entry field to *lbl*.

update   (Member function)

```
int OI_file_dialog_box::update( )
```

update uses the current values for directory and filter to update the contents of the scroll menu(s). Under the Motif model, **update** enters the current directory in the Selection entry field; under the OPEN LOOK model, **update** leaves the Selection entry field blank. Calling **update** is functionally equivalent to clicking on the "Filter" button.

select_file   (Member function)

```
void OI_file_dialog_box::select_file(
    const char          *path)          // file name including full path
```

select_file selects the scroll menu cell which matches *path*, if one exists, then fires the 0th button (by default this is the "OK" button) on the dialog box to dismiss it as if the user had activated the indicated cell.

22.8 An OI_file_dialog_box Programming Example

Program 22-1 shows an OI_file_dialog_box object used to get a file name from the user. The contents of the file are then displayed in an OI_multi_text object.

```c
#include <OI/oi.H>                          /* FileToMulti.C */

int main(int argc, char **argv)
{
                void                    file_to_multi(OI_menu_cell*,void*,OI_number);

                OI_connection           *conp;
                OI_app_window           *wp;
                OI_file_dialog_box      *fdbp;
                OI_menu                 *mp;
                OI_menu_cell            *cellp;
                OI_multi_text           *mtp;

        static  OI_cell_spec            cells[] = {
                                        {"file","Select File"}
                                        };

    if (conp = OI_init(&argc,argv,"FileToMulti")) {
        wp = oi_create_app_window("main",1,1,"FileToMulti");
        wp->set_layout(OI_layout_row);
        mp = oi_create_button_menu("menu",OI_count(cells),&cells[0],OI_horizontal);
        wp->set_main_menu(mp);

        fdbp = oi_create_file_dialog_box("file_db") ;
        fdbp->set_associated_object(mp->subobject("file"),OI_def_loc,OI_def_loc,
                                    OI_active_not_displayed);
        mtp = oi_create_multi_text("lines",5,50);
        mtp->layout_associated_object(wp,1,1,OI_active);

        cellp = (OI_menu_cell*)fdbp->buttons( )->subobject("OK");
        cellp->change_action(&file_to_multi);
        cellp->change_arg(mtp);

        wp->set_associated_object(wp->root( ),OI_def_loc,OI_def_loc,OI_active);
        OI_begin_interaction( );
        OI_fini( );
    }
}

void file_to_multi(OI_menu_cell *mcp, void *argp, OI_number)
{
        OI_file_dialog_box      *fdbp;
        OI_multi_text           *mtp;

    fdbp = (OI_file_dialog_box*)mcp->ancestor("file_db");
    mtp = (OI_multi_text*)argp;
    mtp->set_text_to_file(fdbp->pathname( ));
    return;
}
```

Program 22-1 Select File, Display Contents (FileToMulti.C)

22.9 Resources

All resources from an OI_file_dialog_box object's base classes are available to it; in addition, OI fetches the resources shown in Table 22-1. For more information on resource management, see Chapter 39, "The OI Resource Mechanism."

Table 22-1 OI_file_dialog_box Resources

Resource	Description	Possible Values	Default Value
filter	Expression for initial filter limiting files to display.	File selection expression in the form accepted by C shell	"*"
filterLabel	Text for label of Filter entry field in dialog box.	Any printable string	NULL

22.10 Translations

All translations from an OI_file_dialog_box object's base classes are available to it; it has no additional translations.

22.11 Callback Functions

All callbacks from an OI_file_dialog_box object's base classes are available to it; it has no additional callbacks.

Chapter 23
OI_command_dialog_box

OI_command_dialog_box Functions

The following functions are available to an **OI_command_dialog_box** object, but are described in their own chapter.

OI_select_dialog_box Member Functions

OI_prompt_dialog_box Member Functions

OI_dialog_box Member Functions

OI_box Member Functions

OI_d_tech Member Functions

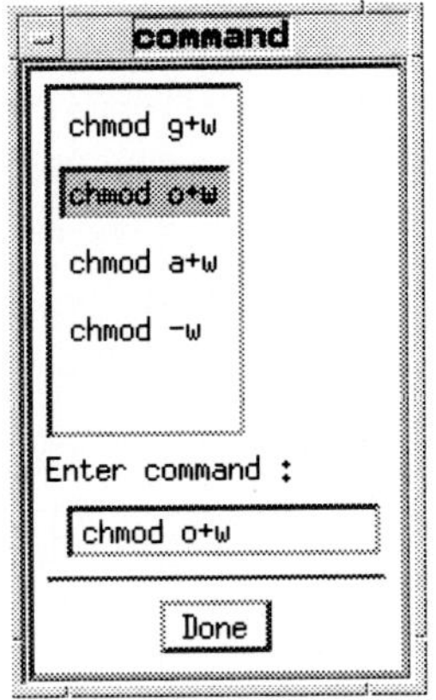
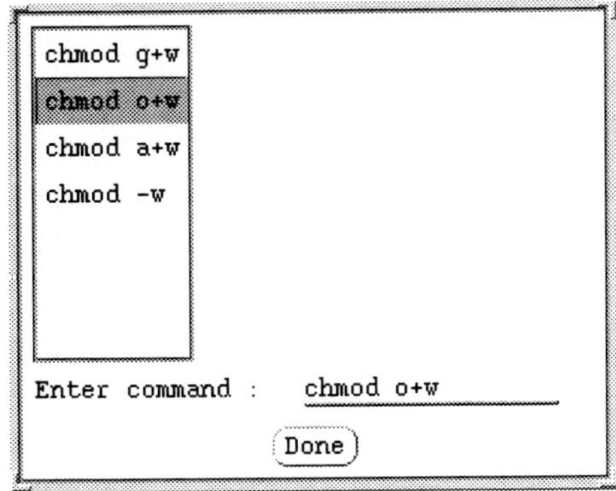

OI_command_dialog_box

23.1 Description

An OI_command_dialog_box is a dialog box containing a scroll menu and an entry field. Its purpose is to allow the user to enter a command in the entry field, and to provide a history of commands in the scroll menu. The button menu at the bottom of the dialog box contains a single "Done" button.

If the user clicks on a menu cell in the scroll menu (causing its label to appear in the OI_entry_field object), OI calls the entry validation callback for the OI_entry_field object automatically.

23.2 Class Tree

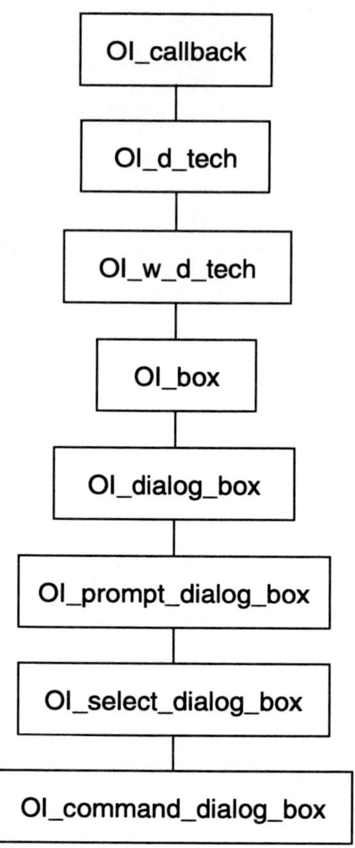

23.3 Runtime Interaction

To enter a new command, type the text in the entry field and press the Return key. The command appears in the scroll menu as the last entry, adding to the command history. If you wish to activate a command in the scroll menu, click on the appropriate menu cell; the cell label is entered into the entry field. To dismiss the dialog box, click on the "Done" button.

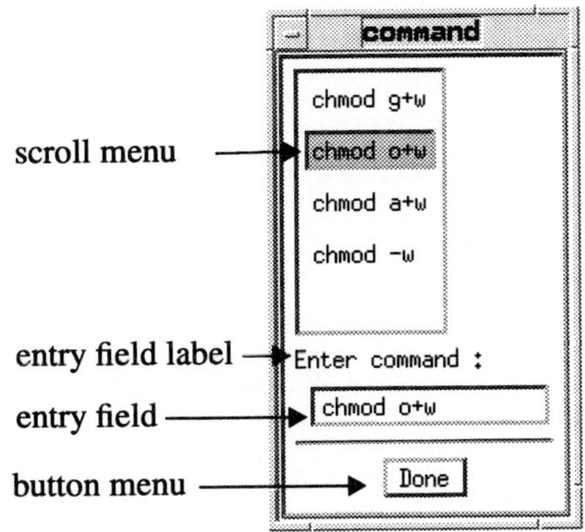

Figure 23-1   Parts of an OI_command_dialog_box, Motif

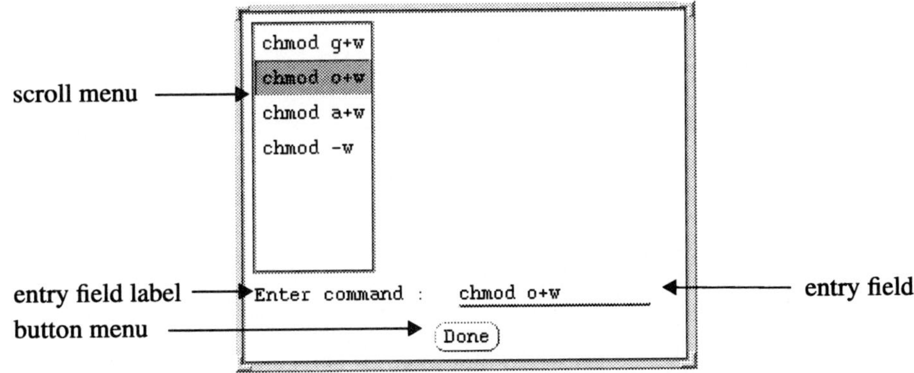

Figure 23-2   Parts of an OI_command_dialog_box, OPEN LOOK

23.4   OI_command_dialog_box Creation

As with OI_dialog_box, there are two forms of create function for OI_command_dialog_box, one to create the button menu at the bottom of the dialog box using a vector of OI_cell_spec structures to describe the cells, and one to create it using a vector of OI_menu_cell objects.

oi_create_command_dialog_box   (Free-standing function)

```
OI_command_dialog_box *oi_create_command_dialog_box(
    const char      *namp,                                   // pointer to object name
    OI_number       dsplen
                    =OI_prompt_db_def_ef_width,              // # of characters to
                                                             // display in entry field
    const char      *labelp="Command Line",                  // label for entry field
    const char      *defstr=NULL,                            // default entry field text
    OI_number       maxlen
                    =OI_command_db_def_ef_max_width,         // max # chars in entry field
    OI_number       smnu_num=-1,                             // initial # of cells in
                                                             // scroll menu
    OI_cell_spec    *smnu_cspecp=NULL,                       // pointer to initial cell
                                                             // info for scroll menu
    const char      *smnu_titlp=NULL,                        // title for scroll menu
    OI_number       num=-1,                                  // # of cells in button menu
    OI_cell_spec    *cell_specp=NULL)                        // pointer to cell info
                                                             // for button menu


OI_command_dialog_box *oi_create_command_dialog_box(
    const char      *namp,                                   // pointer to object name
    OI_number       dsplen,                                  // # of characters to
                                                             // display in entry field
    const char      *labelp,                                 // label for entry field
    const char      *defstr,                                 // default entry field text
    OI_number       maxlen,                                  // max # chars in entry field
    OI_number       smnu_num,                                // initial # of cells in
                                                             // scroll menu
    OI_menu_cell    **smnu_mcellp,                           // pointer to initial cell
                                                             // info for scroll menu
    const char      *smnu_titlp=NULL,                        // title for scroll menu
    OI_number       num=-1,                                  // # of cells in button menu
    OI_menu_cell    **mcellp=NULL)                           // pointer to cells for
                                                             // button menu
```

namp is the object name for the dialog box. *dsplen* specifies the displayed length of the entry field. *labelp* is the label for the entry field. *defstr* is the default text value for the entry field. *maxlen* is the maximum number of characters for the entry field and defaults to *dsplen*. *smnu_num* specifies the number of cells being passed in *smnu_cspecp* or *smnu_mcellp*. *smnu_cspecp* is a pointer to the OI_cell_spec structure which contains the cell information for the scroll menu. *smnu_mcellp* is a vector of menu cells to use for the scroll menu. *num* is the number of cells in the button menu at the bottom of the dialog box. *cell_specp* is a pointer to the OI_cell_spec structure containing the cell information for the button menu at the bottom of the dialog box. *mcellp* is a pointer to a vector of pointers to menu cells to use for the button menu at the bottom of the dialog box.

OI controls the size of the dialog box; the size depends on the entry field label length, the menus specified, and *dsplen*.

You can omit or default all of the arguments except *namp*. If you omit *dsplen*, it defaults to 50 characters. *labelp* defaults to "Command Line". *maxlen* defaults to *dsplen*. *smnu_num* defaults to -1, in which case a scroll menu without any cells is created. The initial size of the scroll menu viewport is 5 menu cells. *smnu_titlp* defaults to NULL. *num* and *cell_specp* or *mcellp* specify the button menu at the bottom of the dialog box. If you omit *num*, it defaults to -1, in which case OI creates a button menu with a single cell labeled "Done".

23.5   Base Class Member Functions

You can use all of the member functions of OI_d_tech, OI_box, OI_dialog_box, OI_prompt_dialog_box, and OI_select_dialog_box for an OI_command_dialog_box object.

You can use all of the member functions available to OI_button_menu for the button menu subobject. These include the member functions of OI_menu and the member functions of OI_menu_cell for the cells of the menu.

23.6   Resources

All resources from an OI_command_dialog_box object's base classes are available to it; it has no additional resources.

23.7   Translations

All translations from an OI_command_dialog_box object's base classes are available to it; it has no additional translations.

23.8   Callback Functions

All of the callbacks from an OI_command_dialog_box object's base classes are available to it; it has no additional callbacks.

Chapter 24
OI_paned_box

OI_paned_box, OI_pane Functions

OI_paned_box, OI_pane, OI_pane_grip, OI_grip Member Functions

The following functions are available to an **OI_paned_box** object, but are described in their own chapter.

OI_box Member Functions

OI_d_tech Member Functions

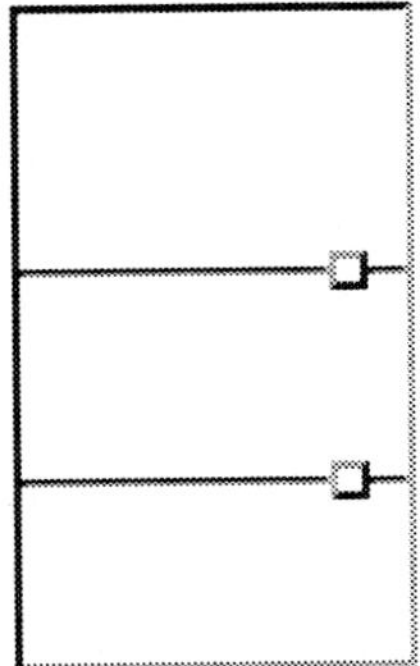

OI_paned_box

24.1 Description

An OI_paned_box object is a horizontal or vertical stack of boxes, called *panes* (OI_pane objects), whose sizes within the paned-box the user can change using the *pane-grip* (OI_pane_grip object) which sits between each adjacent pair of panes. The grip consists of a *handle* (OI_grip object) and two OI_separator objects, one on either side of the handle. Figure 24-1 shows the parts of an OI_paned_box object. Optionally, the separators can be hidden, leaving only the handle displayed There are member functions and resources with which you can control the behavior and appearance of an OI_paned_box object as a whole, and the OI_pane and OI_pane_grip components.

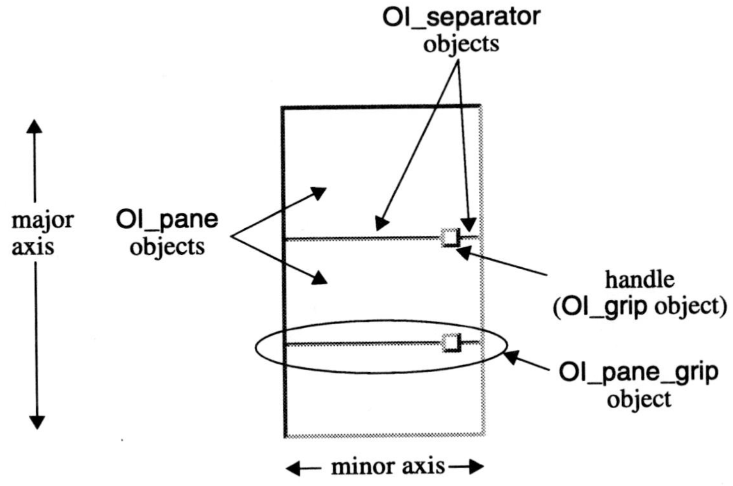

Figure 24-1   Parts of an OI_paned_box

Typically you use a paned-box to display two or more objects or sets of objects which the user will want to see more of or less of on a regular basis. For example, if you were writing a debugger or a file browser, you could display the contents of a different file in each pane. The user could then control how much of each file is displayed within the confines of the paned-box.

If a paned-box is vertical, its major axis is the y axis, and its minor axis is the x axis. Conversely, if it is horizontal, its major axis is the x axis, and its minor axis is the y axis. The major and minor axes of OI_pane and OI_pane_grip objects are parallel to those of the enclosing OI_paned_box object. The dimension of a paned-box along its minor axis is always the greatest of all its panes' minor axis sizes or the size with which it was created or set.

You can create panes independently of creating a paned-box. At the time of creation they are parented to the orphanage; you can associated them with a paned-box at a later time. You can also create a pane and add it to a paned-box in one step using the member function add_pane. You can remove panes from a paned-box using the OI_d_tech member function unparent or one of the OI_d_tech object deletion member functions, or the C++ delete operator.

You cannot create a pane-grip independently of creating a pane or paned-box. Whenever a pane is created, an associated pane-grip is created. The grip appears below the pane in a vertical paned-box and to the right of the pane in a horizontal paned-box. If the minimum and maximum size restrictions for a pane are equal, or if the OI_d_tech resource allowResize is turned off, OI does not place a pane-grip below or to the right of the pane, although it creates a pane-grip and stores it for later use.

You must associate any objects you wish to put in the paned-box to the individual pane within the paned-box. Do not associate objects to the OI_paned_box object itself.

A pane may never become smaller than 1 pixel along its major axis. You can change the frame-width of the pane to 0 for a less-busy look.

24.2 Class Tree

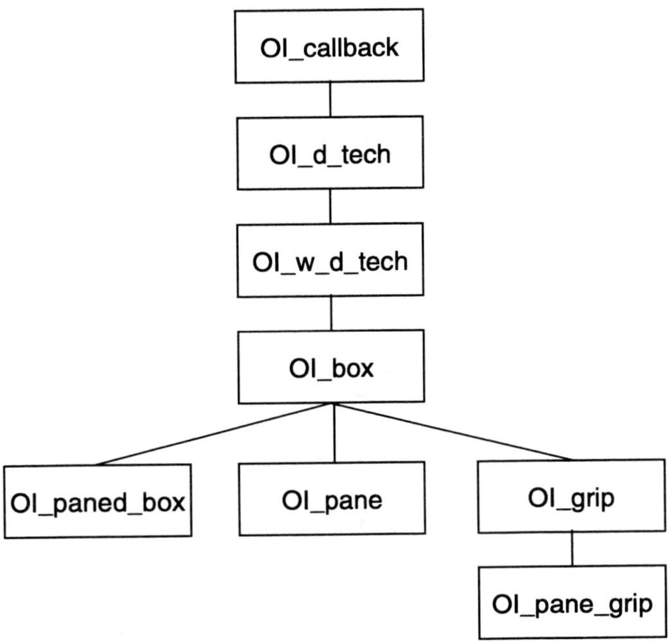

24.3 Runtime Interaction

When the mouse pointer moves over the grip, the cursor changes to a cross hair. To move the grip, press the SELECT mouse button while the mouse pointer is on the grip. As you move the mouse, the grip handle also moves. If real-time-drag is in effect (see page 24-6), the panes' sizes change as you drag the grip. If real-time-drag is not in effect (the default), a line appears next to the grip handle, to show where the grip will be when you release the mouse button, but the sizes of the panes do not change until you release the mouse button.

If there are more than two panes in the paned-box, dragging a grip to a point past the minimum size of its adjacent pane causes other panes to shrink—that is, if you move a grip as far in one direction as it can go, adjacent grips move, if possible, to allow further changing of the size of the pane.

You can move a grip via the keyboard as well as with the mouse, using the default translations (see Section 24.12, "Translations," on page 24-14). Transfer the input focus to a grip by pressing Tab (the grip is part of the default input focus chain). Once the grip has focus, you move it using the up, down, left or right arrow keys. Modify the arrow keys with the Shift key to cause the grip to move in larger increments.

24.4 OI_paned_box Creation

oi_create_paned_box   (Free-standing function)

```
OI_paned_box *oi_create_paned_box(
    const char        *namp,          // name for object
    OI_number         width,          // horizontal size of paned-box in pixels
    OI_number         height,         // vertical size of paned-box in pixels
    OI_orient         orient,         // orientation
    OI_number         n_panes)        // number of panes in paned-box
```

oi_create_paned_box creates an **OI_paned_box** object with name *namp*, *width* pixels wide and *height* pixels tall. *orient* should be either **OI_horizontal** or **OI_vertical**. *n_panes* is the number of panes to be placed in the paned-box initially. The available space in the paned-box is divided evenly among the *n_panes* panes.

24.5 OI_pane Creation

oi_create_pane   (Free-standing function)

```
OI_pane *oi_create_pane(
    const char *namp,                                // name for object
    OI_number  width,                                // horizontal size of box in pixels
    OI_number  height,                               // vertical size of box in pixels
    OI_number  min=OI_def_pane_min,                  // minimum pane size
    OI_number  max=OI_number_max,                    // maximum pane size
    OI_number  grip_wid=OI_pane_grip_def_width,      // grip handle width
    OI_number  grip_ht=OI_pane_grip_def_height,      // grip handle height
    OI_number  indent=OI_pane_grip_def_indent,       // indentation of handle from edge
    OI_bool    shw_sp=OI_pane_grip_def_show_sep)     // should separators show?
```

oi_create_pane creates an **OI_pane** object with name *namp*, *width* pixels wide and *height* pixels tall. *min* and *max* are the minimum and maximum sizes to which the pane will be allowed to shrink or grow. *min* must not be less than 1. *max* must not be greater than the largest **OI_number**, which is **OI_number_max**, nor less than *min*. If *min* and *max* are equal, no pane-grip is placed below (if the parent is a vertical paned-box) or to the right (if the parent is a horizontal paned-box) of the pane, although a pane-grip is created and stored for later use.

grip_wid and *grip_ht* specify the size of the grip handle; they default to **OI_pane_grip_def_width** (6 pixels) and **OI_pane_grip_def_height** (6 pixels). *indent* is the distance from the edge of the pane to place the grip handle. For a vertical paned-box, a positive value indicates the distance of the left edge of the handle to the left edge of the pane. For a horizontal paned-box, a positive value indicates the distance of the top edge of the handle to the top of the pane. Similarly, a negative value indicates the distance from the right or bottom edges. The default is **OI_pane_grip_def_indent** (-10 pixels). If *show_sp* is **OI_yes**, the separators in the grip will be visible; the default is **OI_pane_grip_def_show_sep** (**OI_yes**).

If you use the automatic layout facility and will be laying out objects inside the OI_pane object (that is, you will call set_layout for the pane), you can set *width* and *height* to 1, and OI will make the pane grow to contain any objects you place within it.

You can use an OI_pane object in the same way as an OI_box object, with the advantage that you can add it to an OI_paned_box object.

24.6   Base Class Member Functions

You can use all of the member functions of OI_d_tech and OI_box for an OI_paned_box, OI_pane, or OI_pane_grip object.

24.7   OI_paned_box Member Functions

24.7.1   Finding, Adding and Deleting Panes

The panes in an OI_paned_box object are numbered in monotonically increasing order starting with zero, top to bottom (vertical paned-box) or left to right (horizontal paned-box). To add a new pane to the paned-box, you can create and add it in one step using add_pane, or you can create a pane first using oi_create_pane and then add it using the second form of add_pane. To remove a pane from the paned-box, use the OI_d_tech member function unparent, the C++ delete operator, or one of the OI_d_tech delete functions.

add_pane   (Member function)

```
void OI_paned_box::add_pane(
    const char  *namp,                                    // object name
    OI_number   pos,                                      // position of pane
    OI_number   width,                                    // horizontal size of box in pixels
    OI_number   height,                                   // vertical size of box in pixels
    OI_number   min=OI_def_pane_min,                      // minimum pane size
    OI_number   max=OI_number_max,                        // maximum pane size
    OI_number   grip_wid=OI_pane_grip_def_width,          // grip handle width
    OI_number   grip_ht=OI_pane_grip_def_height,          // grip handle height
    OI_number   indent=OI_pane_grip_def_indent,           // indentation of grip from edge
    OI_bool     shw_sp=OI_pane_grip_def_show_sep)         // should separators show?

void OI_paned_box::add_pane(
    OI_pane                 *panep,                       // pointer to pane object
    OI_number               pos)                          // position of pane
```

add_pane adds a pane to the OI_paned_box object at position *pos*. The first form creates a pane before adding it; the arguments after *pos* are the same as those for oi_create_pane. The second form adds an already existing pane to the paned-box. If there is already a pane at position *pos*, then OI increments the positions of the existing panes with positions greater than *pos* to make room for the new pane.

num_panes   (Member function)

```
OI_number OI_paned_box::num_panes( )
```

num_panes returns the number of panes in the paned-box.

numbered_pane   (Member function)

```
OI_pane *OI_paned_box::numbered_pane(
    OI_number              pos)              // position of pane to find
```

numbered_pane returns a pointer to the OI_pane object in position *pos* in the paned-box.

next_pane   (Member function)

```
OI_pane *OI_paned_box::next_pane(
    OI_pane                *pnp)             // pointer to pane
```

next_pane returns a pointer to the pane following *pnp*. If *pnp* is NULL, **next_pane** returns a pointer to the first pane. If *pnp* points to the last pane or *pnp* is not in a paned-box, **next_pane** returns NULL.

prev_pane   (Member function)

```
OI_pane *OI_paned_box::prev_pane(
    OI_pane                *pnp)             // pointer to pane
```

prev_pane returns a pointer to the pane previous in order to *pnp*. If *pnp* is NULL, **prev_pane** returns a pointer to the last pane. If *pnp* points to the first pane or *pnp* is not in a paned-box, **prev_pane** returns NULL.

24.7.2   Changing an OI_paned_box Object's Behavior

You can condition the paned-box to react in different ways when the user moves a grip.

If *real-time-drag* is in effect, it means that a pane's size changes while its controlling grip moves. In this case the separator between panes moves with the grip, and any objects inside the pane become obscured as the pane shrinks or become visible as the pane grows. If real-time-drag is not in effect (the default), the appearance of the panes and separator do not change while the grip is moving; instead a line appears showing where the separator will be placed once the user releases the mouse button. When the mouse button is released, the panes are repainted with their new sizes. You set real-time-drag via the member functions **allow/disallow_real_time_drag** or the resource **realTimeDrag**.

If *resize-by-grip* is in effect, and if the user moves the grip beyond the end of the paned-box, the paned-box grows to accommodate the new larger size of the pane. If resize-by-grip is not in effect (the default), the pane is constrained to grow no larger than the current size of the paned-box allows. You set resize-by-grip via the member functions **allow/disallow_resize_by_grip** or the resource **resizeByGrip**.

allow_real_time_drag   (Member function)

```
void OI_paned_box::allow_real_time_drag( )
```

allow_real_time_drag conditions the paned-box so that when the user drags the grip, the corresponding pane changes size in real time with the drag.

disallow_real_time_drag   (Member function)

```
void OI_paned_box::disallow_real_time_drag( )
```

disallow_real_time_drag conditions the paned-box so that when the user drags the grip, the corresponding pane remains its original size until the drag is complete. A line appears and moves with the grip. This is the default.

is_real_time_drag   (Member function)

```
OI_bool OI_paned_box::is_real_time_drag( )
```

is_real_time_drag returns OI_yes if real-time-drag is in effect; otherwise it returns OI_no.

allow_resize_by_grip   (Member function)

```
void OI_paned_box::allow_resize_by_grip( )
```

allow_resize_by_grip conditions the paned-box so that moving a grip can enlarge the paned-box if that is the only way the grip's movement can be realized.

disallow_resize_by_grip   (Member function)

```
void OI_paned_box::disallow_resize_by_grip( )
```

disallow_resize_by_grip conditions the paned-box so that the grip only resizes the panes within the OI_paned_box object's boundaries. This is the default.

is_resize_by_grip   (Member function)

```
OI_bool OI_paned_box::is_resize_by_grip( )
```

is_resize_by_grip returns OI_yes if resize-by-grip is in effect; otherwise it returns OI_no.

orientation   (Member function)

```
OI_orient OI_paned_box::orientation( )
```

orientation returns the orientation of the paned-box. This will be either OI_horizontal or OI_vertical.

set_orientation   (Member function)

```
void OI_paned_box::set_orientation(
    OI_orient            orient)          // Orientation
```

set_orientation sets the orientation to *orient*, which must be one of OI_horizontal or OI_vertical.

24.8   OI_pane Member Functions

Use these member functions to inquire and control an individual pane in a paned-box.

number   (Member function)

```
OI_number OI_pane::number( )
```

number returns the position of this pane in its **OI_paned_box** parent object, relative to the other panes in the paned-box. The returned value will be in the range 0 <= number < number of panes in the paned-box, or -1 if the pane is not associated with a paned-box.

grip   (Member function)

```
OI_pane_grip *OI_pane::grip( )
```

grip returns a pointer to this pane's corresponding grip. This is the grip below the pane for a vertical paned-box and the grip to the right of the pane for a horizontal paned-box.

maximum   (Member function)

```
OI_number OI_pane::maximum( )
```

maximum returns the maximum allowable size of the pane in pixels in the direction of the major axis. The default size is the maximum value for an **OI_number**, defined to be **OI_number_max**.

set_max_size   (Member function)

```
void OI_pane::set_max_size(
   OI_number          mx)              // maximum allowable size, in pixels
```

set_max_size sets the maximum allowable size for the pane in the direction of the major axis to *mx*.

minimum   (Member function)

```
OI_number OI_pane::minimum( )
```

minimum returns the minimum allowable size of the pane in pixels in the direction of the major axis. The default is **OI_def_pane_min**.

set_min_size   (Member function)

```
void OI_pane::set_min_size(
   OI_number          mn)              // minimum allowable size, in pixels
```

set_min_size sets the minimum allowable size for the pane in the direction of the major axis to *mn*.

24.9   OI_pane_grip Member Functions

The OI_pane_grip grip consists of an OI_grip handle and two OI_separator objects, one on either side of the handle. The OI_grip handle is itself derived from OI_box.

pane   (Member function)

```
OI_pane *OI_pane_grip::pane( )
```

pane returns a pointer to the pane controlled by this grip. This is the pane above the grip for a vertical paned-box and the pane to the left of the grip for a horizontal paned-box.

set_handle_indent   (Member function)

```
void OI_pane_grip::set_handle_indent(
    OI_number              indnt)        // minimum allowable size, in pixels
```

set_handle_indent sets the handle indentation for the grip to *indnt*. The handle indentation is the distance, in pixels, the handle appears along the grip from the edge of the pane. For a vertical paned-box, a positive value indicates the distance of the left edge of the handle to the left edge of the pane. For a horizontal paned-box, a positive value indicates the distance of the top edge of the handle to the top of the pane Similarly, a negative value indicates the distance from the right or bottom edges.

handle_indent   (Member function)

```
OI_number OI_pane_grip::handle_indent( )
```

handle_indent returns the handle indentation.

allow_show_sep   (Member function)

```
void OI_pane_grip::allow_show_sep( )
```

allow_show_sep causes the grip's separators to be displayed. This is the default.

disallow_show_sep   (Member function)

```
void OI_pane_grip::disallow_show_sep( )
```

disallow_show_sep causes the grip's separators to be hidden.

is_show_sep   (Member function)

```
OI_bool OI_pane_grip::is_show_sep( )
```

is_show_sep returns OI_yes if the grip's separators are visible; otherwise it returns OI_no.

24.10 OI_grip Member Functions

Ordinarily, you will not need these functions since OI manages all the grip movement for you. If, however, you need to do extra work when the grip moves, you can register callbacks using these functions.

set_start   (Member function)

```
void OI_grip::set_start(
    OI_grip_fnp            fnp,           // pointer to callback function
    void                   *argp=NULL)    // arbitrary argument for fnp

void OI_grip::set_start(
    OI_callback            *objp,         // memfnp's object
    OI_grip_memfnp         memfnp,        // pointer to callback member function
    void                   *argp=NULL)    // arbitrary argument for memfnp
```

The **set_start** functions register a callback function to be invoked whenever the user initiates interaction with the grip—that is, whenever the user presses the SELECT mouse button on the grip handle or moves the grip using keyboard translations. This callback is identified within OI as a **cbGripStart** callback function (see Section 6.18, "Determining and Adding Callbacks; Multiple Callbacks," on page 6-117). If your start-motion function is a member function, when it is invoked it will be called as if you had written *objp->memfnp*. See Section 2.5, "Callbacks and Event-Driven Programming," on page 2-16 for more explanation.

argp is optional, and may be any valid expression that can be cast to a pointer. You can use it to pass additional information to the function *fnp* or *memfnp*.

Writing the Grip Start-motion Callback Function

If the **cbGripStart** callback function is not a member function, write it in this form:

```
void fn(
        OI_grip            *grp,          // pointer to grip being moved
        void               *argp,         // arbitrary argument
        long               loc_x,         // pointer x location
        long               loc_y)         // pointer y location
```

and if the **cbGripStart** callback function is a member function, write it in this form:

```
void obj_class::memfn(
        OI_grip            *grp,          // pointer to grip being moved
        void               *argp,         // arbitrary argument
        long               loc_x,         // pointer x location
        long               loc_y)         // pointer y location
```

where *obj_class* is the class of the object whose member function is *memfn*. When your callback function is invoked, *argp* will be the argument specified in the **set_start** call. If the grip is being moved via the mouse, *loc_x* and *loc_y* will be the location of the mouse pointer relative to the upper left corner of the grip handle. If the grip is being moved via keyboard translations, *loc_x* and *loc_y* will be 0. If you intend to call **OI_pane_grip** member functions for *grp*, you must cast it to **OI_pane_grip***.

set_moved   (Member function)

```
void OI_grip::set_moved(
    OI_grip_fnp              fnp,              // pointer to callback function
    void                     *argp=NULL)       // arbitrary argument for fnp


void OI_grip::set_moved(
    OI_callback              *objp,            // memfnp's object
    OI_grip_memfnp           memfnp,           // pointer to callback member function
    void                     *argp=NULL)       // arbitrary argument for memfnp
```

The **set_moved** functions register a callback function to be invoked whenever the grip moves. The callback is called repeatedly as the grip is dragged; it will be called at least once regardless of whether the grip motion is via the mouse or via keyboard translations. This callback is identified within OI as a **cbGripMoved** callback function (see Section 6.18, "Determining and Adding Callbacks; Multiple Callbacks," on page 6-117). If your motion function is a member function, when it is invoked it will be called as if you had written *objp->memfnp*. See Section 2.5, "Callbacks and Event-Driven Programming," on page 2-16 for more explanation.

argp is optional, and may be any valid expression that can be cast to a pointer. You can use it to pass additional information to the function *fnp* or *memfnp*.

Writing the Grip Motion Callback Function

If the **cbGripMoved** callback function is not a member function, write it in this form:

```
void fn(
        OI_grip              *grp,             // pointer to grip being moved
        void                 *argp,            // arbitrary argument
        long                 delta_x,          // distance grip moved in x direction
        long                 delta_y)          // distance grip moved in y direction
```

and if the **cbGripMoved** callback function is a member function, write it in this form:

```
void obj_class::memfn(
        OI_grip              *grp,             // pointer to grip being moved
        void                 *argp,            // arbitrary argument
        long                 delta_x,          // distance grip moved in x direction
        long                 delta_y)          // distance grip moved in y direction
```

where *obj_class* is the class of the object whose member function is *memfn*. When your callback function is invoked, *argp* will be the argument specified in the **set_moved** call. *delta_x* and *delta_y* will be the distance the grip has moved from the location it had when grip interaction was initiated. One of these values is always 0 because a grip can only move in one direction—in the direction of the major axis. This allows you to add the delta values to determine the delta in the major axis direction without needing to determine if the associated paned-box has a vertical or horizontal orientation. If you intend to call OI_pane_grip member functions for *grp*, you must cast it to OI_pane_grip*.

set_stop   (Member function)

```
void OI_grip::set_stop(
    OI_grip_fnp              fnp,            // pointer to callback function
    void                     *argp=NULL)     // arbitrary argument for fnp

void OI_grip::set_stop(
    OI_callback              *objp,          // memfnp's object
    OI_grip_memfnp           memfnp,         // pointer to callback member function
    void                     *argp=NULL)     // arbitrary argument for memfnp
```

The **set_stop** functions register a callback function to be invoked whenever interaction with the grip ends—that is, whenever the user releases the SELECT mouse button after dragging the grip, or when the grip has been moved using keyboard translations. This callback is identified within OI as a **cbGripStop** callback function (see Section 6.18, "Determining and Adding Callbacks; Multiple Callbacks," on page 6-117). If your stop-motion function is a member function, when it is invoked it will be called as if you had written *objp->memfnp*. See Section 2.5, "Callbacks and Event-Driven Programming," on page 2-16 for more explanation.

argp is optional, and may be any valid expression that can be cast to a pointer. You can use it to pass additional information to the function *fnp* or *memfnp*.

Writing the Grip Stop-motion Callback Function

If the **cbGripStop** callback function is not a member function, write it in this form:

```
void fn(
        OI_grip              *grp,           // pointer to grip being moved
        void                 *argp,          // arbitrary argument
        long                 loc_x,          // pointer x location
        long                 loc_y)          // pointer y location
```

and if the **cbGripStop** callback function is a member function, write it in this form:

```
void obj_class::memfn(
        OI_grip              *grp,           // pointer to grip being moved
        void                 *argp,          // arbitrary argument
        long                 loc_x,          // pointer x location
        long                 loc_y)          // pointer y location
```

where *obj_class* is the class of the object whose member function is *memfn*. When your callback function is invoked, *argp* will be the argument specified in the **set_stop** call. If the grip was moved via the mouse, *loc_x* and *loc_y* will be the location of the mouse pointer relative to the upper left corner of the grip handle. If the grip was moved via keyboard translations, *loc_x* and *loc_y* will be 0. If you intend to call OI_pane_grip member functions for *grp*, you must cast it to OI_pane_grip*.

24.11 Resources

All resources from an **OI_paned_box** object's base classes are available to it; in addition, OI fetches the resources shown in Table 24-1 through Table 24-1. For more information on resource management, see Chapter 39, "The OI Resource Mechanism."

Table 24-1   OI_paned_box Resources

Resource	Description	Possible Values	Default Value
orientation	Specifies the orientation of the stack of **OI_pane** objects.	horizontal vertical	vertical
realTimeDrag	**True** specifies that panes change size as a grip is dragged. **False** specifies the size changes only after the mouse button release.	Boolean	false
resizeByGrip	**True** specifies that moving a grip can resize the **OI_paned_box** object. **False** specifies that the grip only resizes the panes within the **OI_paned_box** object.	Boolean	false

Table 24-2   OI_pane Resources

Resource	Description	Possible Values	Default Value
maxSize	Specifies the maximum allowable size, in pixels, for the pane in the direction of the **OI_paned_box** object's major axis.	Integer > 0	OI_number_max
minSize	Specifies the minimum allowable size, in pixels, for the pane in the direction of the **OI_paned_box** object's major axis.	Integer > 0	1

Table 24-3 OI_pane_grip Resources

Resource	Description	Possible Values	Default Value
handleIndent	Specifies the distance, in pixels, the handle is indented on the grip.	integer	-10
showSep	Specifies whether the OI_separator object in the grip should be visible.	Boolean	true

24.12 Translations

The translations shown in Figure 24-1 are installed for an OI_pane_grip object. In addition, the translations for the base classes for an OI_paned_box, OI_pane, and OI_pane_grip are available to them. For more information on translations, see Chapter 40, "The OI Translation Mechanism."

Table 24-4 Default OI_pane_grip Translations

Event Sequence		Action Functions Called
	<Btn1Down>:	press( )
	<Btn1Motion>:	drag( )
	<Btn1Up>:	release( )
	<FocusIn>:	focus_in( )
	<FocusOut>:	focus_out( )
	<Key>Down:	move(1)
	<Key>Left:	move(-1)
	<Key>Right:	move(1)
	<Key>Up:	move(-1)
Ctrl	<Key>Down:	move(4)
Ctrl	<Key>Left:	move(-4)
Ctrl	<Key>Right:	move(4)
Ctrl	<Key>Up:	move(-4)

The next table, Table 24-5, describes the actions taken by the **OI_paned_box** action functions.

Table 24-5 OI_pane_grip Translation Functions

Function Name	Description
drag( )	Gets new pointer location, draws line (if real-time-drag is not in effect) or resizes panes (if real-time-drag is in effect), calls the registered cbGripMoved callback, if any.
focus_in( )	Draws changes to the object when the object gains focus.
focus_out( )	Draws changes to the object when the object loses focus.
move( )	Moves the grip the distance specified, in pixels, in the argument. This function is approximately the equivalent of press( ) drag( ) release( ).
press( )	Grabs the pointer, sets the start position, and calls the registered cbGripStart callback, if any.
release( )	Calls the registered cbGripStop callback, if any, and releases the pointer.

24.13 Callback Functions

Table 24-6 lists the callbacks available for an **OI_grip** object and the page number where the callback is documented. There are no extra callbacks for **OI_paned_box**, **OI_pane** or **OI_pane_grip** objects. All of the callbacks for these object's base classes are available to them. See Section 6.18, "Determining and Adding Callbacks; Multiple Callbacks," on page 6-117 for additional information about manipulating callbacks.

Table 24-6 OI_paned_box Callbacks

Callback Type	Callback Typedef	Description	Page Number
cbGripStart	OI_grip_fnp/memfnp	Grip start-motion callback function	24-10
cbGripMoved	OI_grip_fnp/memfnp	Grip motion callback function	24-11
cbGripStop	OI_grip_fnp/memfnp	Grip stop-motion callback function	24-12

Chapter 25
OI_glyph

OI_glyph Functions

OI_glyph Member Functions

The following functions are available to an **OI_glyph** object, but are described in their own chapter.

OI_d_tech Member Functions

OI_glyph

25.1 Description

An OI_glyph is a rectangular object containing an X Window System Pixmap image. There are no restrictions on the image size other than those imposed by the X server.

When you create a glyph, you can either specify one image or two different images to be used. If you specify one image, it will be the one used for the glyph. If you specify two, one will be the "normal" image, which is displayed by default, and the other will be the "active" image, which is displayed when a mouse button is pressed when the pointer is on the glyph. Using two images for a glyph allows the glyph appearance to change when the user clicks on it.

You can use one of three different forms of image for an OI_glyph object. They are:

- A single bitmap mask. The mask bits are displayed using the foreground color, and the unmasked bits are displayed using the background color. With this type of glyph, you need not specify two images to get the appearance to change when the user clicks on the glyph. OI can do it automatically by reversing the foreground and background pixels.
- A full Pixmap. This Pixmap may be in full color. Because each pixel in a Pixmap specifies a particular color, you must specify two complete Pixmaps if you want the glyph to be able to change when the user clicks on it.
- A series of bitmap masks to overlay each other. Each mask is used to paint a particular color, usually one of foreground, background, top, bottom, and down pixels. This produces a three-dimensional looking shaded image, which can also be made to "depress" when the user clicks on it.

You can generate the Pixmap images for an OI_glyph object in any of several ways. You can generate the Pixmap yourself, you can specify an array of character data describing the Pixmap, or you can specify the name of a file or files containing the Pixmap data. You can use either bitmap or XPM format files.

An OI_glyph object can be used as an icon for an OI_app_window. One of the parameters in the create call for an OI_app_window object is a pointer to a glyph to be used as an icon by the window manager if the application is iconified. The label you supply when you create the OI_glyph object is passed to the window manager as well; if the window manager labels its icons, it uses this label. Note that if the glyph is to be used as an icon for an OI_app_window, OI renames it with its own internal name. This is done when you call oi_create_app_window with a pointer to the glyph as one of the arguments. For this reason, you should use the OI_app_window member function icon to get a pointer to the **OI_app_window**'s icon glyph, rather than functions such as **descendant** or **subobject**, which require the object's name as a parameter.

You can *animate* an **OI_glyph** object. Animation is simulated by changing the Pixmap image in the glyph at short time intervals and is discussed in Section 25.6.1 on page 25-16.

A glyph may be *shaped*—it need not occupy a rectangular area of the display. You can supply a shape mask so that, for example, they glyph actually occupies only those pixels painted with the image foreground. This allows any clear area to be transparent, so the object beneath the glyph is visible.

25.2   Class Tree

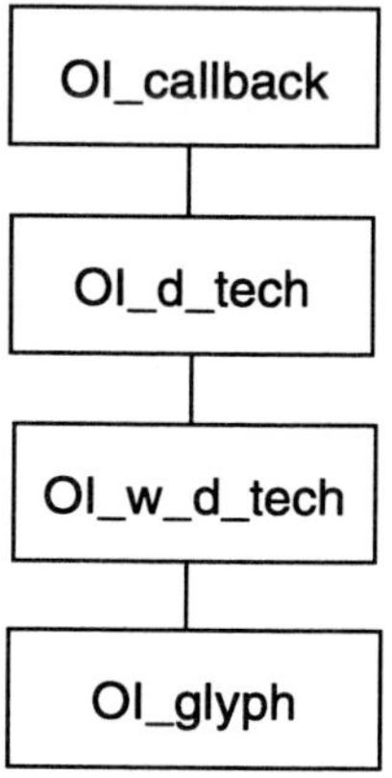

25.3   Runtime Interaction

An **OI_glyph** object is often used for display purposes only. However, if you register a click function for the glyph, it is called when you click on the glyph.

25.4   OI_glyph Creation

There are several different ways to create an **OI_glyph** object; these different forms of the create function are described in the following sections. Which one you use depends on the source of the image data and the type of glyph you are creating. The first few arguments to each of the create functions are specific to that form of create. However, four of the arguments to each of the glyph create functions are identical; these arguments are described in the next section.

25.4.1   Arguments Common to all oi_create_glyph Functions

All oi_create_glyph functions contain these four arguments:

```
const char          *lbl                    // pointer to glyph label
```

lbl, if not NULL, points to a label text string. The only time the label is used is when the glyph is being used as an icon for an **OI_app_window** object; the label is passed to the window manager along with the glyph. Future OI releases may display the label above or below the glyph image in all cases, so you may want to specify NULL for *lbl* except when the glyph is to be used as the icon for an OI_app_window.

```
OI_pic_type        typ                    // glyph type
```

typ can be either of these values:

OI_pic_mask   Image is a 1- bit deep mask used to define foreground/background areas.
OI_pic_full   Image is a full pixmap.

When you create an OI_glyph object, you specify either one or two images. Specifying a single image is identical to specifying two images which are the same. The second image is used when the glyph is being painted in an *active* state, that is, when a mouse button is pressed while the pointer is on the glyph, and you have registered a click callback for the glyph.

```
OI_bool            hilite=OI_no        // highlight Pixmap when glyph is active?
```

hilite indicates whether the glyph should be highlighted when a mouse button is pressed while the pointer is on the glyph. It defaults to OI_no. In order for the highlighting to take place, you must register a click function for the glyph. If you specify two images for the glyph ("normal" and "active" images) the active image is the one used for the highlighting. In addition, if the image is a mask and not a full depth Pixmap (*typ* is OI_pic_mask), the colors used to paint the active image are altered depending on the screen color characteristics and the interaction model. On a monochrome screen, and on all screens using the 2-D OPEN LOOK model, the foreground and background colors are reversed for the active image. On color screens using the Motif or the 3-D OPEN LOOK model, the background color is changed to the "down" color.

```
OI_bool            delpm=OI_yes        // Pixmap disposition flag
```

If at some time you destroy the OI_glyph object or change the image(s) for the glyph, OI must know what to do with the glyph's current Pixmap. You specify the disposition of the Pixmap with *delpm*. If *delpm* is OI_yes (the default), the Pixmap is destroyed when the glyph is destroyed or its image is changed.

Important:

> You should set *delpm* to OI_no when you are using Pixmaps you have created independently and you are assuming responsibility for freeing the Pixmaps after objects are destroyed. If you plan to clone a glyph, you must set *delpm* to OI_no; otherwise, deleting one of the cloned glyphs (or the original) invalidates the Pixmap used for the image in the remaining glyphs (probably causing a core dump).

25.4.2   Creating an OI_glyph Object from a File in Bitmap Format

oi_create_glyph   (Free-standing function)

```
OI_glyph *oi_create_glyph(
    const char        *namp,               // object name
    const char        *filep,              // bitmap file name
    const char        *lbl=NULL,           // glyph label
    OI_pic_type       typ=OI_pic_mask,     // glyph type
    OI_bool           hilite=OI_no,        // highlight the glyph upon button press?
    OI_bool           delpm=OI_yes)        // destroy the Pixmap?


OI_glyph *oi_create_glyph(
    const char        *namp,               // object name
    const char        *normal_filep,       // "normal" image file name
    const char        *active_filep,       // "active" image file name
    const char        *lbl,                // glyph label
    OI_pic_type       typ=OI_pic_mask,     // glyph type
    OI_bool           hilite=OI_no,        // highlight the glyph upon button press?
    OI_bool           delpm=OI_yes)        // destroy the Pixmap?
```

In these two create functions, you specify the name of a file (*filep*, or *normal_filep* and *active_filep*) containing the data describing the glyph image. The file must be in a format identical to that created by the **XPM** utilities or the X program **bitmap**. Use the first of these two functions if you are specifying only a single image for the glyph; use the second if you are specifying a "normal" and an "active" image.

Program 25-1 shows a glyph created from a bitmap-format file; Figure 25-1 shows the application running.

```
#include <OI/oi.H>                              /* FileGlyph.C */

int main (int argc, char** argv)
{

        OI_connection           *conp;
        OI_app_window           *wp;
        OI_glyph                *gp;

    if (conp = OI_init(&argc,argv,"FileGlyph")) {
        wp = oi_create_app_window("main",1,1,"FileGlyph");
        wp->set_layout(OI_layout_column);

        gp = oi_create_glyph("file_glyph","../bitmaps/thinker.bm");
        gp->layout_associated_object(wp,1,1,OI_active);

        wp->set_associated_object(wp->root( ),OI_def_loc,OI_def_loc,OI_active);
        OI_begin_interaction( );
        OI_fini( );
    }
}
```

Program 25-1   Create an OI_glyph Object from a Bitmap-format File (FileGlyph.C)

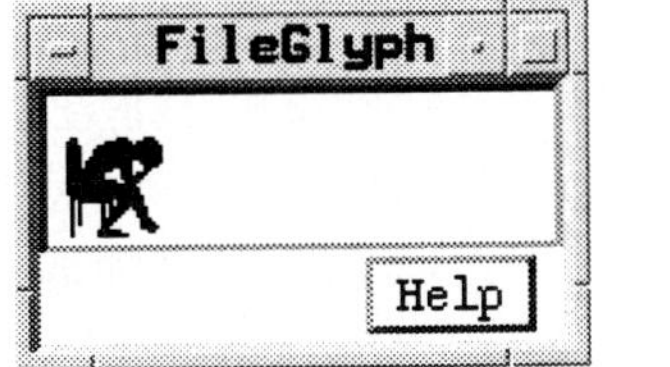

Figure 25-1   OI_glyph With thinker.bm Image

25.4.3   Creating an OI_glyph Object from Character Data

The functions discussed here create an OI_glyph object from static data instead of a file. You may want to use one of these two forms of the create function if you don't want to worry about whether the file describing the image is present or not—you can include the file in your program when it is compiled, and create the image from the static data.

oi_create_glyph   (Free-standing function)

```
OI_glyph *oi_create_glyph(
    const char          *namp,        // object name
    const char          *datp,        // image character array
    const char          *lbl,         // glyph label
    OI_pic_type         typ,          // glyph type
    OI_number           wid,          // width of image in pixels
    OI_number           ht,           // height of image in pixels
    OI_number           dpth=0,       // depth of image in pixels
    OI_bool             hilite=OI_no,  // highlight the glyph upon button press?
    OI_bool             delpm=OI_yes)  // destroy the Pixmap?


OI_glyph *oi_create_glyph(
    const char          *namp,        // object name
    const char          *normal_datp, // "normal" image character array
    const char          *active_datp, // "active" image character array
    const char          *lbl,         // glyph label
    OI_pic_type         typ,          // glyph type
    OI_number           wid,          // width of image in pixels
    OI_number           ht,           // height of image in pixels
    OI_number           dpth=0,       // depth of image in pixels
    OI_bool             hilite=OI_no,  // highlight the glyph upon button press?
    OI_bool             delpm-OI_yes)  // destroy the Pixmap?
```

In these two create functions, you specify a character array (*datp* or *normal_datp* and *active_datp*) containing the data describing the image. The data must be stored in the same format as that generated by the X bitmap program or **XPM** version 3 files. Use the first of these two functions if you are specifying only a single image for the glyph; use the second if you are specifying a "normal" and an "active" image.

wid, *ht* and *dpth* specify the width, height, and depth in pixels of the image to be created. When *typ* is **OI_pic_mask**, *dpth* is ignored. *wid* and *ht* are required.

Program 25-2 shows a glyph created from character data taken from the same bitmap file thinker.bm as was used in Program 25-1. The contents of thinker.bm, which was created by the X program bitmap, is shown in Example 25-1.

```
#define thinker_width 32
#define thinker_height 32
static char thinker_bits[] = {
 0x00, 0x00, 0x00, 0x00, 0x00, 0x00, 0x00, 0x00, 0x00, 0x00, 0x00, 0x00,
 0x00, 0x00, 0x00, 0x00, 0x00, 0x00, 0x00, 0x00, 0x00, 0x00, 0x00, 0x00,
 0x06, 0xe0, 0x70, 0x00, 0x07, 0xfc, 0xfd, 0x00, 0x0f, 0xff, 0xff, 0x01,
 0x8f, 0xff, 0xff, 0x01, 0x8f, 0xff, 0xff, 0x01, 0xcf, 0xff, 0xff, 0x01,
 0xef, 0xff, 0xf9, 0x01, 0xef, 0xff, 0xf1, 0x00, 0xff, 0xcf, 0x31, 0x00,
 0xff, 0xc3, 0x1d, 0x00, 0xff, 0xc3, 0x0f, 0x00, 0xff, 0x9f, 0x07, 0x00,
 0xff, 0xff, 0x03, 0x00, 0xff, 0xff, 0x07, 0x00, 0xff, 0xff, 0x07, 0x00,
 0xfe, 0xff, 0x0f, 0x00, 0xfa, 0xef, 0x0f, 0x00, 0x0a, 0xea, 0x0f, 0x00,
 0x0a, 0xfa, 0x1e, 0x00, 0x0a, 0x7a, 0x1c, 0x00, 0x0a, 0x3a, 0x1c, 0x00,
 0x0a, 0x1e, 0x38, 0x00, 0x0a, 0x0e, 0x78, 0x00, 0x02, 0x06, 0xf8, 0x00,
 0x02, 0x3f, 0x60, 0x00, 0x02, 0xff, 0x00, 0x00};
```

Example 25-1   Contents of "thinker.bm"


```
#include <OI/oi.H>                         /* DataGlyph.C */

int main (int argc, char** argv)
{

           OI_connection         *conp;
           OI_app_window         *wp;
           OI_glyph              *gp;

#include "../bitmaps/thinker.bm"

    if (conp = OI_init(&argc,argv,"DataGlyph")) {
        wp = oi_create_app_window("main",1,1,"DataGlyph");
        wp->set_layout(OI_layout_column);

        gp = oi_create_glyph("data_glyph",&thinker_bits[0],NULL,OI_pic_mask,
                                     thinker_width,thinker_height);
        gp->layout_associated_object(wp,1,1,OI_active);

        wp->set_associated_object(wp->root( ),OI_def_loc,OI_def_loc,OI_active);
        OI_begin_interaction( );
        OI_fini( );
    }
}
```

Program 25-2   Create an OI_glyph Object from Character Data (DataGlyph.C)

25.4.4   Creating an OI_glyph Object from a Pixmap

You may want to use one of these two forms of the create function if you want to optimize your program when the same image is to appear in many glyphs. Using these forms saves the time needed to create the image Pixmap for all but the first image. You can make a Pixmap from a bitmap file by calling **XCreateBitmapFromData** with the character data created by the **bitmap** program or by using one of the **XPM** functions with an **XPM** format file. Since your program creates the image Pixmap, you should normally assume responsibility for destroying it, and you should usually set *delpm* to OI_no.

oi_create_glyph   (Free-standing function)

```
OI_glyph *oi_create_glyph(
    const char      *namp,              // object name
    Pixmap          pm,                 // Pixmap
    const char      *lbl,               // glyph label
    OI_pic_type     typ,                // glyph type
    OI_number       wid,                // width of image in pixels
    OI_number       ht,                 // height of image in pixels
    OI_number       dpth=0,             // depth of image in pixels
    OI_bool         hilite=OI_no,       // highlight the glyph upon button press?
    OI_bool         delpm=OI_yes)       // destroy the Pixmap?


OI_glyph *oi_create_glyph(
    const char      *namp,              // object name
    Pixmap          *normal_pm,         // "normal" Pixmap
    Pixmap          *active_pm,         // "active" Pixmap
    const char      *lbl,               // glyph label
    OI_pic_type     typ,                // glyph type
    OI_number       wid,                // width of image in pixels
    OI_number       ht,                 // height of image in pixels
    OI_number       dpth=0,             // depth of image in pixels
    OI_bool         hilite=OI_no,       // highlight the glyph upon button press?
    OI_bool         delpm=OI_yes)       // destroy the Pixmap?
```

In these two create functions, you specify a Pixmap (*pm* or *normal_pm* and *active_pm*) for the image. Use the first of these two functions if you are specifying only a single image for the glyph; use the second if you are specifying a "normal" and an "active" image.

wid, ht and *dpth* specify the width, height, and depth in pixels of the image to be created. When *typ* is **OI_pic_mask**, *dpth* is ignored.

Program 25-3 shows a glyph created from a Pixmap. The Pixmap is created from data from the same bitmap file, thinker.bm, as the previous two programs used.

```c
#include <OI/oi.H>                              /* PixGlyph.C */

int main (int argc, char** argv)
{

        OI_connection           *conp;
        OI_app_window           *wp;
        OI_glyph                *gp;
        Pixmap                  pm;

#include "../bitmaps/thinker.bm"

    if (conp = OI_init(&argc,argv,"PixGlyph")) {
        wp = oi_create_app_window("main",1,1,"PixGlyph");
        wp->set_layout(OI_layout_column);

        pm = XCreateBitmapFromData(conp->display( ),conp->root( )->X_window( ),
                        &thinker_bits[0],thinker_width,thinker_height);

        gp = oi_create_glyph("pix_glyph",pm,NULL,OI_pic_mask,thinker_width,
                        thinker_height,0,OI_no,OI_no);
        gp->layout_associated_object(wp,1,1,OI_active);

        wp->set_associated_object(wp->root( ),OI_def_loc,OI_def_loc,OI_active);
        OI_begin_interaction( );

        XFreePixmap(conp->display( ),pm);
        OI_fini( );
    }
}
```

Program 25-3   Create an OI_glyph Object from a Pixmap (PixGlyph.C)

25.4.5   Creating a 3-D OI_glyph Object by Layering Masked Images

You can create a glyph with a "3-D" look by using masks to control painting more than one color in
the image.

25.4.5.1 Colors Used in a Layered-Mask 3-D OI_glyph Object

Typically, the colors used are the foreground color, the background color, and three shades of the
background color known as the top, bottom, and down colors. OI automatically computes these three
colors from the background color. The colors are named according to the part of a 3-D color OI
object (such as a menu cell) which they are used to render; OI's rendering assumes a light source in
the upper-left corner of the display, and the object is raised above the background. You specify the

colors for your masks using values of type OI_pic_pixel. The possible values for an OI_pic_pixel are shown in Table 25-1.

Table 25-1 OI_pic_pixel values

Value	Description	Color
OI_pic_fg	foreground color	
OI_pic_bg	background color	
OI_pic_top	color of top/left bevel	lighter shade of background color
OI_pic_bottom	color of bottom/right bevel	darker shade of background color
OI_pic_down	"highlighted" background color	darker shade intermediate between background and bottom colors
OI_pic_none	custom color	value specified elsewhere (see oi_create_pic_file_mask below)

If you specify your own foreground, background, top, bottom, or down colors using OI_d_tech member functions or through resources, these colors will be the ones used in rendering your image.

On a monochrome screen, OI_pic_top and OI_pic_bottom translate to the foreground color, and OI_pic_down translates to the background color. This allows the "active" image to appear in reverse video using normal 3-D glyph painting on a monochrome screen.

25.4.5.2 Specifying the Masks for a Layered-Mask 3-D OI_glyph Object

You specify the masks for a layered-mask 3-D glyph in an OI_pic_spec_mask object, which you then pass to the glyph create function. You create the OI_pic_spec_mask object in one of three ways, depending on whether the data for the masks is stored in a file, a character array, or a previously created Pixmap. The three functions to do this are:

---

oi_create_pic_file_mask   (Free-standing function)

```
OI_pic_spec_mask *oi_create_pic_file_mask(
    const char       *filep,                     // mask bitmap file name
    OI_pic_pixel      normal_px,                 // "normal" OI-defined pixel value
    OI_pic_pixel      active_px,                 // "active" OI-defined pixel value
    PIXEL             nml_pxl=OI_unknown_pixel,  // "normal" pixel value if
                                                 // normal_px is OI_pic_none
    PIXEL             act_pxl=OI_unknown_pixel)  // "active" pixel value if active_px
                                                 // is OI_pic_none
```

oi_create_pic_data_mask   (Free-standing function)

```
OI_pic_spec_mask *oi_create_pic_data_mask(
    const char       *datp,                      // mask bitmap character array
    OI_pic_pixel      normal_px,                 // "normal" OI-defined pixel value
    OI_pic_pixel      active_px,                 // "active" OI-defined pixel value
    PIXEL             nml_pxl=OI_unknown_pixel,  // "normal" pixel value if
                                                 // normal_px is OI_pic_none
    PIXEL             act_pxl=OI_unknown_pixel)  // "active" pixel value if active_px
                                                 // is OI_pic_none
```

oi_create_pic_pixmap_mask   (Free-standing function)

```
OI_pic_spec_mask *oi_create_pic_pixmap_mask(
    Pixmap            pm,                        // one-bit deep pixmap for mask
    OI_pic_pixel      normal_px,                 // "normal" OI-defined pixel value
    OI_pic_pixel      active_px,                 // "active" OI-defined pixel value
    PIXEL             nml_pxl=OI_unknown_pixel,  // "normal" pixel value if
                                                 // normal_px is OI_pic_none
    PIXEL             act_pxl=OI_unknown_pixel)  // "active" pixel value if active_px
                                                 // is OI_pic_none
```

filep points to a file containing the image data. The file must be in a format identical to that created by the X bitmap program. *datp* is a character array containing the image data. The data must be stored in the same format as that generated by the X bitmap program. *pm* is a Pixmap for the image.

normal_px and *active_px* are OI_pic_pixel values from Table 25-1 and indicate the color to use when painting this portion of the image in "normal" or "active" state. If *normal_px* or *active_px* is OI_pic_none, then *nml_pxl* and *act_pxl* specify an actual pixel value to be used; otherwise *nml_pxl* and *act_pxl* are ignored, and you can omit them.

25.4.5.3 Creating a Layered-Mask 3-D OI_glyph Object

oi_create_glyph   (Free-standing function)

```
OI_glyph *oi_create_glyph(
    const char        *namp,           // object name
    OI_number         n_mask,          // number of masks to make image
    OI_pic_spec_mask  **pics,          // vector of image masks
    const char        *lbl=NULL,       // glyph label
    OI_number         wid=0,           // width of image in pixels
    OI_number         ht=0,            // height of image in pixels
    OI_bool           hilite=OI_no,    // highlight the glyph upon button press?
    OI_bool           delpm=OI_yes)    // destroy the Pixmap?
```

n_mask specifies the number of masks used to create the image, and the entries in the array of OI_pic_spec_mask objects describe the masks as discussed above. The masks must all be of the same size, *wid* by *ht*.

Program 25-4 shows a glyph image using layered masks. Because all shading (using top, bottom and down colors) is done in relationship to the background color, and because the cube represented by the 3-D glyph is meant to be seen in shades of the foreground color, the program reverses foreground and background colors for the glyph. Explicitly setting the foreground and background colors in this manner overrides any foreground and background colors set via resources for the glyph. If you wanted the colors to be set via resources, you could invert the bitmaps and not set the foreground and background colors programmatically. If you are writing an application where the glyphs are displayed using the background colors, you will not need to reverse the foreground and background colors.

Figure 25-2 shows the bitmaps used to create the 3-D image, and Figure 25-3 shows the final result.

```c
#include <OI/oi.H>                              /* 3DGlyph.C */

int main (int argc, char** argv)
{

        OI_connection           *conp;
        OI_app_window           *wp;
        OI_glyph                *gp;
        OI_pic_spec_mask        **pics;
        int                     num_pix;

    if (conp = OI_init(&argc,argv,"3DGlyph")) {
        wp = oi_create_app_window("main",1,1,"3DGlyph");
        wp->set_layout(OI_layout_column);

        num_pix = 4;
        pics = (OI_pic_spec_mask **)malloc(sizeof(OI_pic_spec_mask *) * num_pix);
        pics[0] = oi_create_pic_file_mask("../bitmaps/cube.1.bm",
                                    OI_pic_top,OI_pic_bottom);
        pics[1] = oi_create_pic_file_mask("../bitmaps/cube.2.bm",
                                    OI_pic_bg,OI_pic_down);
        pics[2] = oi_create_pic_file_mask("../bitmaps/cube.3.bm",
                                    OI_pic_bottom,OI_pic_top);
        pics[3] = oi_create_pic_file_mask("../bitmaps/cube.4.bm",
                                    OI_pic_fg,OI_pic_fg);

        gp = oi_create_glyph("3D_glyph",num_pix,pics,NULL,32,32);
        free((char*)pics);
                // reverse foreground and background colors
        gp->set_pixels(gp->fg_pixel( ),gp->bkg_pixel( ),gp->bdr_pixel( ));
        gp->layout_associated_object(wp,1,1,OI_active);

        wp->set_associated_object(wp->root( ),OI_def_loc,OI_def_loc,OI_active);
        OI_begin_interaction( );
        OI_fini( );
    }
}
```

Program 25-4   Create a Layered-Mask 3-D OI_glyph Object (3DGlyph.C)

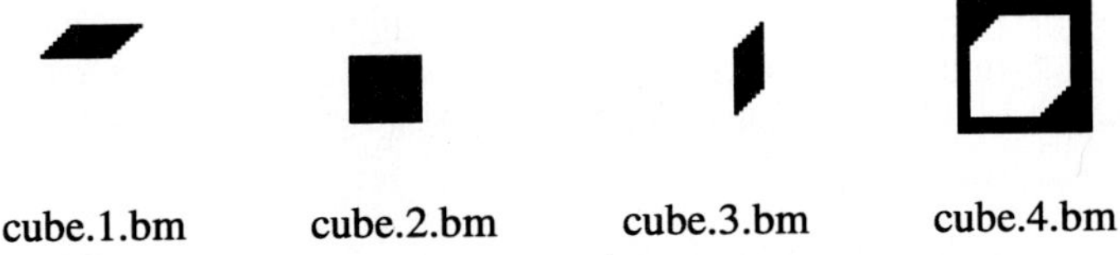

cube.1.bm   cube.2.bm   cube.3.bm   cube.4.bm

Figure 25-2   Bitmap File Images Used in 3DGlyph

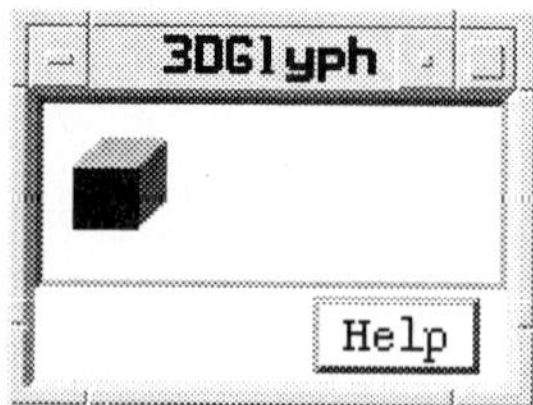

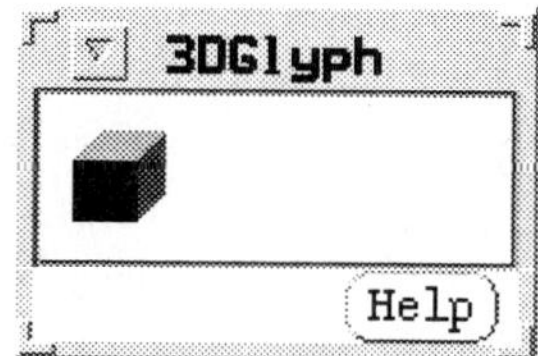

Figure 25-3   Layered-Mask 3-D OI_glyph Object

25.5   Base Class Member Functions

You can use all of the member functions of OI_d_tech for an OI_glyph object.

25.5.1   Click Functions

An OI_glyph object can respond to mouse button clicks if the mouse pointer is over the glyph. If you want an OI_glyph object to respond to mouse clicks, you must register a click callback function for the glyph object. When the user clicks on the object, your callback function is executed. Also, if you want your glyph to be highlighted or the "active" pixmap to be displayed, you must register a click function for the glyph.

set_click   (Member function)

```
void OI_glyph::set_click(
    OI_click_fnp        fnp,              // pointer to callback function
    void                *argp=NULL)       // arbitrary argument for fnp


void OI_glyph::set_click(
    OI_callback         *objp,            // memfnp's object
    OI_click_memfnp     memfnp,           // pointer to callback member function
    void                *argp=NULL)       // arbitrary argument for memfnp
```

The set_click functions register a callback function to be invoked whenever the user clicks a mouse button one or more times on an OI_glyph object. This callback is identified within OI as a cbClick callback function (see Section 6.18, "Determining and Adding Callbacks; Multiple Callbacks," on page 6-117). *memfnp* points to a member function for the object pointed to by *objp*. If your click function is a member function, when it is invoked it will be called as if you had written *objp->memfnp*. See Section 2.5, "Callbacks and Event-Driven Programming," on page 2-16 for more explanation.

argp is optional, and can be any valid expression that can be cast to a pointer. You can use it to pass additional information to the function *fnp* or *memfnp*.

The button press and release must be separated by no more than clickDelta milliseconds for a press/release sequence to be considered a click. For multiple clicks, a release and subsequent press must also be separated by no more than clickDelta milliseconds. clickDelta is an OI_connection resource, which defaults to 500.

OI supports multiple callbacks of the same type for a single object. The functions described here apply to the first cbCellAction callback if you have registered more than one.

Writing the Click Callback Function

If the cbClick callback function is not a member function, write it in this form:

```
void fn(
        OI_d_tech      *oi_objp,        // pointer to object clicked on
        void           *argp,           // arbitrary argument
        OI_number      n_clicks,        // number of clicks
        OI_number      btn,             // mouse button number clicked
        OI_number      mod,             // modifier bits on at click time
        OI_number      x,               // x position where click occurred
        OI_number      y)               // y position where click occurred
```

and if the cbClick callback function is a member function, write it in this form:

```
void obj_class::memfn(
        OI_d_tech      *oi_objp,        // pointer to object clicked on
        void           *argp,           // arbitrary argument
        OI_number      n_clicks,        // number of clicks
        OI_number      btn,             // mouse button number clicked
        OI_number      mod,             // modifier bits on at click time
        OI_number      x,               // x position where click occurred
        OI_number      y)               // y position where click occurred
```

where *obj_class* is the class of the object whose member function is *memfn*.

When your callback function is invoked, *argp* will be the argument specified in the set_click call. *x* and *y* will be the pixel position of the pointer at the time of the click, relative to the upper left-hand corner of the glyph. *mod* will contain the modifier bits on at click time. These will be zero unless the user holds down one or more of the modifier keys on the keyboard at the time the mouse button is released. *mod* can be any combination (0 or more) of the following values, ored together.

OI_mod_shift	Shift key down during click.
OI_mod_lock	Lock key down during click.
OI_mod_control	Control key down during click.
OI_mod_meta	Mod1 key down during click.

When more than one click occurs, the callback function will be invoked once for each click. For example, a double click will cause the function to be called first with *n_clicks*=1, then with *n_clicks*=2. If your application is performing a different operation depending on the number of clicks, the operations for a greater number of clicks should be compatible with those for fewer clicks. For example, a single click could mean animate the glyph once, and two clicks could mean animate the glyph continuously.

25.6 OI_glyph Member Functions

25.6.1 Animation

You can animate a glyph via two different member functions. Use the simplest form, **animate**, when the size, position and time interval between frames for the animation are constant. This form essentially animates the image in place. Use the other form, **animate_custom**, when you intend to change the size of the image, change its position on the screen, or vary the interval between frames.

Animation is accomplished by rapidly changing the Pixmap used to render the glyph image. You can animate a glyph through its sequence of Pixmaps once, or continuously.

is_animate   (Member function)

```
OI_bool OI_glyph::is_animate( )
```

is_animate returns **OI_yes** if animation is currently in progress for the glyph; otherwise **is_animate** returns **OI_no**.

animate   (Member function)

```
void OI_glyph::animate(
    long            ms,                              // time between frames
    long            n_pm,                            // number of Pixmaps in the series
    Pixmap          *pmp,                            // pointer to Pixmaps
    unsigned int    cont=OI_animate_single,          // continuous or not
    unsigned int    term=OI_animate_term_stable)     // ending Pixmap
```

animate specifies a series of uniform size Pixmaps to be displayed at fixed intervals, and starts the animation. *ms* is the time between frames, in milliseconds.

pmp is a pointer to the Pixmaps. You can use the **OI_connection** member function **uniform_pixmap_series** to generate a Pixmap series from a sequence of bitmap files.

cont can have one of two values:

OI_animate_single	(default) specifies that the **OI_glyph** should be animated once only (run through the animation Pixmap series once).
OI_animate_term_continuous	specifies that the **OI_glyph** should be animated continuously (running through the animation Pixmap series repeatedly) until you call **animate_off**.

term specifies the pixmap to be used when animation is terminated. *term* can be one of:

OI_animate_term_stable	(default) specifies that the **OI_glyph** is to revert to the original Pixmap after the animation terminates.
OI_animate_term_last	specifies that the **OI_glyph** should retain the image of the last Pixmap after the animation terminates.

animate_custom   (Member function)

```
void OI_glyph::animate_custom(
    OI_animate_fnp      fnp,            // pointer to callback function
    void                *argp=NULL)     // arbitrary argument for fnp


void OI_glyph::animate_custom(
    OI_callback         *objp,          // memfnp's object
    OI_animate_memfnp   memfnp,         // pointer to callback member function
    void                *argp=NULL)     // arbitrary argument for memfnp
```

This is a more sophisticated animation sequence than animate. The animate_custom functions register a callback function to be invoked to determine the next frame to be painted. OI calls the callback function immediately to determine the first frame to use; OI subsequently calls it for all further frames until you terminate animation using a call to animate_off, or until the callback function returns a NULL. This callback is identified within OI as a cbAnimate callback function (see Section 6.18, "Determining and Adding Callbacks; Multiple Callbacks," on page 6-117). If your animation function is a member function, when it is invoked it will be called as if you had written *objp->memfnp*. See Section 2.5, "Callbacks and Event-Driven Programming," on page 2-16 for more explanation.

argp is optional, and can be any valid expression that can be cast to a pointer. You can use it to pass additional information to the function *fnp* or *memfnp*.

Writing the Animation Callback Function

If the cbAnimate callback function is not a member function, write it in this form:

```
OI_animate_item *fn(
        OI_glyph    *oi_objp,       // pointer to animated glyph
        void        *argp)          // arbitrary argument
```

and if the cbAnimate callback function is a member function, write it in this form:

```
OI_animate_item *obj_class::memfn(
        OI_glyph    *oi_objp,       // pointer to animated glyph
        void        *argp)          // arbitrary argument
```

where *obj_class* is the class of the object whose member function is *memfn*. When your callback function is invoked, *argp* will be the argument specified in the animate_custom call.

You must write this function to return a pointer to an OI_animate_item describing the next frame, or NULL, indicating that the sequence should be terminated. An OI_animate_item is defined as:

```
struct OI_animate_item {
    Pixmap              pm;                 // Pixmap
    long                ms;                 // interval to next frame
    OI_origin           psn;                // new position for glyph
    OI_xy               siz;                // size of pm
    OI_bool             pm_chg;             // set if pm has changed
    void                *usr_datp;          // arbitrary data
}
```

ms is the time interval in milliseconds to wait before painting the next frame. *psn* and *siz* are defined in structures below. Set *pm_chg* to **OI_yes** if *pm* specifies a Pixmap ID different from the last one used, or if the Pixmap ID is the same but its contents have changed (that is, you have modified it using Xlib drawing function calls). Set it to **OI_no** otherwise (that is, the image is the same and it is only being moved).

You can use the **OI_connection** member function **pixmap_series** to generate the **OI_animate_item** structures for you for your specified bitmaps and default values for the other elements of the structures before the animation starts. If you do this, each call to your animation callback function should return a pointer to the next **OI_animate_item** in the series, after you have changed any of its elements as necessary.

The **OI_origin** structure is defined as:

```
struct OI_origin {
    long                x;                  // x position in pixels
    long                y;                  // y position in pixels
}
```

The **OI_xy** structure is defined as:

```
struct OI_xy {
    OI_number           x;                  // width in pixels
    OI_number           y;                  // height in pixels
}
```

animate_off   (Member function)

```
void OI_glyph::animate_off(
    unsigned int        final=OI_animate_term_stable) // final bitmap specification
```

animate_off terminates any animation sequence currently in progress for the **OI_glyph**. *final* specifies which bitmap should remain after the animation terminates. If *final* is **OI_animate_term_stable**, the glyph returns to the bitmap specified before the animation began. If *final* is **OI_animate_term_last**, the glyph keeps the last bitmap displaying when the animation terminated.

Program 25-5 shows an application window containing a single-button menu and an OI_glyph. The glyph can be animated by clicking on the menu cell. Figure 25-4 shows the bitmap images used in the animation sequence, and Figure 25-5 shows the application running.

This program creates an OI_glyph subclass, AnimGlyph. An object of class AnimGlyph is comprised of an OI_glyph, a pointer to the pixmaps to use in the animation, and the number of pixmaps in the animation sequence. It also has two member functions: AnimGlyph, which is the constructor, and btn_animate, which performs the actual animation. The program also shows how to use the OI_connection member function uniform_pixmap_series to generate a Pixmap series from a sequence of bitmap files.

```c
#include <OI/oi.H>              /* AnimGlyph.C */

    class   AnimGlyph : public OI_glyph {    // class AnimGlyph definition
            long              numpix;        // number of pixmaps
            Pixmap            *pmp;          // ptr to pixmaps
          public:
                              AnimGlyph(char*, char*, char* ) ;
            void              btn_animate(OI_menu_cell*, void*, OI_number) ;
          } ;

AnimGlyph::AnimGlyph(                          // constructor for AnimGlyph
          char              *usr_namp,
          char              *perm_filp,
          char              *animate_filp)
          : OI_glyph(usr_namp,perm_filp,perm_filp,NULL,OI_pic_mask,OI_no)
{
    numpix = conp->uniform_pixmap_series(&pmp,animate_filp);
}
void AnimGlyph::btn_animate(OI_menu_cell*, void*, OI_number)// member function
{
    animate(100,numpix,pmp,OI_animate_single) ;
    return ;
}

int main (int argc, char **argv)
{
            OI_connection       *conp;
            OI_app_window       *wp;
            OI_menu             *mp;
            OI_menu_cell        *mcp;
            AnimGlyph           *aniglyp;

    static  OI_cell_spec       cells[] = {
            {"animate","Animate"},
            };

    if (conp = OI_init(&argc,argv,"AnimGlyph")) {
        wp = oi_create_app_window("main",1,1,"AnimGlyph");
        wp->set_layout(OI_layout_row,20,20);
        mp = oi_create_button_menu("menu",OI_n_cells(cells),&cells[0],OI_vertical);
        mp->layout_associated_object(wp,10,10,OI_active);
        aniglyp = new AnimGlyph("glyph","../bitmaps/bird1.bm",
                                        "../bitmaps/bird@.bm");
        aniglyp->set_gravity(OI_grav_center);
        aniglyp->layout_associated_object(wp,1,1,OI_active);
        mcp = (OI_menu_cell*)mp->subobject("animate");
        mcp->change_action(aniglyp,(OI_action_memfnp)&AnimGlyph::btn_animate);
        wp->set_associated_object(wp->root( ),OI_def_loc,OI_def_loc,OI_active);
        OI_begin_interaction( );
    }
}
```

Program 25-5   Animated Glyph (AnimGlyph.C)

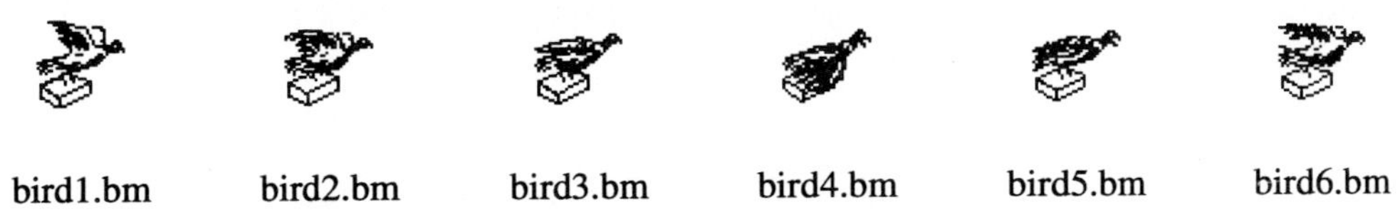

bird1.bm bird2.bm bird3.bm bird4.bm bird5.bm bird6.bm

Figure 25-4 Images Used in Animated Glyph

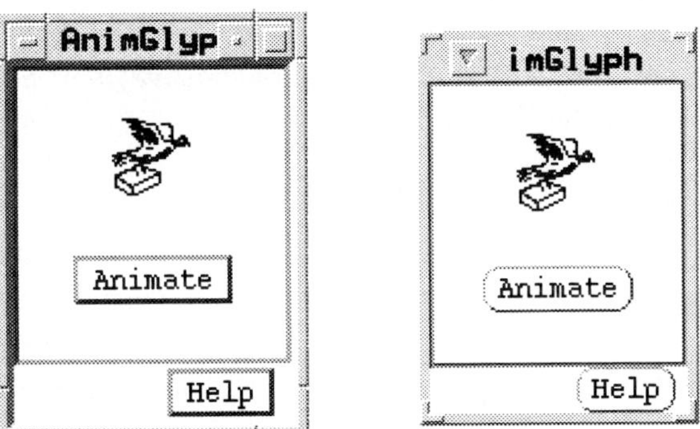

Figure 25-5 Animated Glyph

25.6.2 Changing the OI_glyph Appearance

An OI_glyph is a frame within which a Pixmap is displayed. The image contents of the glyph can be changed using set_file, set_active_file_name, set_pixel_data and set_pixmap. Use set_file or set_active_file_name if your new images are in bitmap files, set_pixel_data if they are stored as character data, and set_pixmap if you are using Pixmaps. You can also set these attributes via the resources file and activeFile.

You can cause the glyph to paint (or not to paint) using its "active" image when the mouse is pressed on the glyph by using the member function set_highlight or the resource highlight.

file_name   (Member function)

```
char *OI_glyph::file_name(
    OI_number        file_num=0)        // bitmap file name
```

file_name returns a pointer to the name of the *file_num*th bitmap file. If you created the glyph with a single bitmap file, file_name returns the name of this file. If you created the glyph with a "normal" and an "active" bitmap file, file_name returns the normal file name if *file_num* is 0 and the active file name if *file_num* is 1. If you created the glyph as a layered-mask 3-D glyph, file_name returns the name of the *file_num*th bitmap file in the OI_pic_spec_mask object. If you created the OI_glyph with something other than file names (or changed the OI_glyph using some function other than set_file), the value returned by file_name is undefined.

set_file   (Member function)

```
OI_stat OI_glyph::set_file(
    const char              *normal_filep,          // "normal" image file name
    const char              *active_filep=NULL,     // "active" image file name
    OI_pic_type             typ=OI_pic_mask,        // glyph type
    OI_bool                 hilite=OI_no,           // highlight the glyph upon button press?
    OI_bool                 delpm=OI_yes)           // destroy the Pixmap?
```

This form of set_file sets the glyph image to *normal_filep* when it is in the "normal" state and *active_filep* when it is in the "active" state. If you omit *active_filep*, *normal_filep* is used for the "active" state as well as for the "normal" state. All other arguments are used in the same manner as the oi_create_glyph arguments.

```
OI_stat OI_glyph::set_file(
    OI_number               n_mask,                 // number of masks to make image
    OI_pic_spec_mask        **pics,                 // vector of image masks
    OI_bool                 hilite=OI_no,           // highlight the glyph upon button press?
    OI_bool                 delpm=OI_yes)           // destroy the Pixmap?
```

In this form of set_file, all arguments are used in the same manner as the oi_create_glyph arguments for a layered-mask 3-D glyph. The image in the glyph is changed immediately to the new image. You must create the elements of *pics* using oi_create_pic_file_mask.

set_active_file_name   (Member function)

```
OI_stat OI_glyph::set_active_file_name(
    const char              *filep)                 // "active" image file name
```

set_active_file_name sets the glyph image to *filep* when it is in the "active" state.

set_pixel_data   (Member function)

```
OI_stat OI_glyph::set_pixel_data(
    const char              *datp,                  // pointer to bitmap data
    OI_number               wid,                    // width of bitmap data
    OI_number               ht,                     // height of bitmap data
    OI_number               dpth=0,                 // depth of bitmap data
    OI_bool                 hilite=OI_no,           // highlight the glyph upon button press?
    OI_bool                 delpm=OI_yes)           // Pixmap disposition flag
```

```
OI_stat OI_glyph::set_pixel_data(
    const char          *normal_datp,      // pointer to bitmap data
    const char          *active_datp,      // pointer to bitmap data
    OI_number           wid,               // width of bitmap data
    OI_number           ht,                // height of bitmap data
    OI_number           dpth=0,            // depth of bitmap data
    OI_bool             hilite=OI_no,      // highlight the glyph upon button press?
    OI_bool             delpm=OI_yes)      // Pixmap disposition flag


OI_stat OI_glyph::set_pixel_data(
    OI_number           n_mask,            // number of masks to make image
    OI_pic_spec_mask    **pics,            // vector of image masks
    OI_number           wid,               // width of bitmap data
    OI_number           ht,                // height of bitmap data
    OI_bool             hilite=OI_no,      // highlight the glyph upon button press?
    OI_bool             delpm=OI_yes)      // Pixmap disposition flag
```

set_pixel_data sets the glyph image to the specified bitmap data. All arguments are used in the same manner as the **oi_create_glyph** arguments. If you use the third form, you must create the elements of *pics* using **oi_create_pic_data_mask**.

---

set_pixmap   (Member function)

```
OI_stat OI_glyph::set_pixmap(
    Pixmap              pm,                 // Pixmap
    OI_number           wid,                // width of bitmap data
    OI_number           ht,                 // height of bitmap data
    OI_number           dpth=0,             // depth of bitmap data
    OI_bool             hilite=OI_no,       // highlight the glyph upon button press?
    OI_bool             delpm=OI_yes)       // Pixmap disposition flag


OI_stat OI_glyph::set_pixmap(
    Pixmap              normal_pm,          // "normal" Pixmap
    Pixmap              active_pm,          // "active" Pixmap
    OI_number           wid,                // width of bitmap data
    OI_number           ht,                 // height of bitmap data
    OI_number           dpth=0,             // depth of bitmap data
    OI_bool             hilite=OI_no,       // highlight the glyph upon button press?
    OI_bool             delpm=OI_yes)       // Pixmap disposition flag


OI_stat OI_glyph::set_pixmap(
    OI_number           n_mask,             // number of masks to make image
    OI_pic_spec_mask    **pics,             // vector of image masks
    OI_number           wid,                // width of bitmap data
    OI_number           ht,                 // height of bitmap data
    OI_bool             hilite=OI_no,       // highlight the glyph upon button press?
    OI_bool             delpm=OI_yes)       // Pixmap disposition flag
```

set_pixmap sets the glyph image to the specified Pixmap. All arguments are used in the same manner as the **oi_create_glyph** arguments. If you use the third form, you must create the elements of *pics* using **oi_create_pixmap_mask**.

active_bkg   (Member function)

```
OI_pic_pixel OI_glyph::active_bkg(
    PIXEL               *px=NULL)           // PIXEL value to be backfilled
```

active_bkg returns the type for the active background color of the **OI_glyph**. This is the color used to paint the background of the glyph whenever the glyph is active. The value returned will be one of the values shown in Table 25-1, "OI_pic_pixel values" on page 25-10. If *px* is not null, it will be backfilled with the actual PIXEL value of the background color.

---

set_active_bkg (Member function)

```
void OI_glyph::set_active_bkg(
    OI_pic_pixel        picval,                  // pixel color value
    PIXEL               px=OI_unknown_pixel)     // color if picval is OI_pic_none
```

set_active_bkg sets the type for the background color of the "active" image for the glyph to *picval*. See Table 25-1, "OI_pic_pixel values," on page 25-10 for possible values for *picval*. If you specify OI_pic_none for *picval*, you must supply a color PIXEL value for *px*. If you specify any other value for picval, *px* is ignored. Subsequently, whenever the glyph is active, its background is painted with the color corresponding to type *picval*. This has no effect when the image type (*typ*) is OI_pic_full.

is_highlight (Member function)

```
OI_bool OI_glyph::is_highlight( )
```

is_highlight returns OI_yes if the glyph will be highlighted when the user presses a mouse button when the mouse pointer is over the glyph; otherwise it returns OI_no.

set_highlight (Member function)

```
void OI_glyph::set_highlight(
    OI_bool             hi_lt=OI_yes)     // highlight glyph?
```

If *hi_lt* is OI_yes or omitted, set_highlight conditions the glyph to be highlighted—that is, to use its "active" image and color—when the user presses a mouse button when the mouse pointer is over the glyph. If *hi_lt* is OI_no, the glyph is conditioned not to be highlighted.

label (Member function)

```
char *OI_glyph::label( )
```

label returns the label of the OI_glyph.

set_label (Member function)

```
OI_stat OI_glyph::set_label(
    const char          *lbl)     // label for glyph
```

set_label sets the glyph label to *lbl*. The only time the label is used is when the glyph is being used as an icon for an OI_app_window object; the label is passed to the window manager along with the glyph.

25.6.3   Using Shape Masks

An OI_glyph object has its own X window, and by default, the X Window system only allows rectangular windows. Therefore, by default a glyph must be rectangular. However, if your system has the X shape extension installed, you can make a glyph be another shape.

Your site may or may not have the shape extension installed. To find out, run xdpyinfo. To set the window to an arbitrary shape, use the member function set_shape or the resource shapeFile and specify a bitmap whose on (or 1) bits define the shape of the window you want. Each bit in the bitmap that is on becomes part of the glyph window; each bit that is off is not a part of the window, and at these points whatever underlies the glyph shows through. The bitmap that specifies the shape of the window is called a *shape mask*, or a *bounding mask*.

Note: the use of the X shape extension is much slower than using a rectangular window, because the server must perform a large amount of extra work.

It is common to create a glyph, then specify the same bitmap for the shape mask, although it does not have to be done this way. An example of this is shown next.

Using the same program that produced Figure 25-1, "OI_glyph With thinker.bm Image," first we specify (using the command line parameter -xrm), that the application window have a background Pixmap of **dots.bm**, which is simply a set of dots that tile the **OI_app_window** object. We use dots in this example to differentiate the background of the **OI_app_window** object from the glyph:

```
FileGlyph -xrm "*OI_app_window*backgroundPixmap: dots.bm"
```

Next we specify the resource **shapeFile** to be the same bitmap that the glyph is using; the dotted bitmap tiling the application window now "shows through" the glyph:

```
FileGlyph -xrm "*OI_app_window*backgroundPixmap: dots.bm"
        -xrm "*shapeFile: thinker.bm"
```

is_shaped   (Member function)

```
OI_bool OI_glyph::is_shaped( )
```

is_shaped returns **OI_yes** if the glyph is using a shape mask; it returns **OI_no** if the glyph is using a rectangular window.

set_shape   (Member function)

```
void OI_glyph::set_shape(
    Pixmap              pm)              // shape Pixmap
void OI_glyph::set_shape(
    const char          *filep,          // shape bitmap file name
void OI_glyph::set_shape(
    const char          *datp,           // image character array
    OI_number           wid,             // width of image in pixels
    OI_number           ht,              // height of image in pixels
```

set_shape sets the shape (or bounding) mask. The first form sets it to the Pixmap *pm*. The second form sets it to the bitmap in the file *filep*. The third form sets it to the character data specified in *datp*, with width *wid* and height *ht*. The data must be stored in the same format as that generated by the X bitmap program.

shape_bound_mask   (Member function)

```
Pixmap OI_glyph::shape_bound_mask( )
```

shape_bound_mask returns the shape mask Pixmap, if there is one.

shape_file_name   (Member function)

```
char *OI_glyph::shape_file_name( )
```

shape_file_name returns the name of the shape mask file for the glyph, if there is one.

25.7 Resources

All resources from an **OI_glyph** object's base classes are available to it; in addition, OI fetches the resources shown in Table 25-2. For more information on resource management, see Chapter 39, "The OI Resource Mechanism."

Table 25-2 OI_glyph Resources

Resource	Description	Possible Values	Default Value
activeFile	Specifies the name of the file containing the bitmap to use when the user presses a mouse button with the pointer on the glyph.	Bitmap or XPM format file name	NULL
file	Specifies the bitmap file to use as the default image.	Bitmap or XPM format file name	NULL
highlight	Specifies whether to highlight the glyph with the "active" image and color when the user presses a mouse button with the pointer on the glyph.	Boolean	false
label	Specifies the label for the glyph.	Any printable string	NULL
shapeFile	Specifies the bitmap file to use as the shape bounding mask.	Bitmap file name	(No default)

25.8 Translations

All translations from an **OI_glyph** object's base classes are available to it; it has no additional translations.

25.9 Callback Functions

Table 25-3 lists the callbacks available for an OI_glyph object and the page number where the callback is documented. In addition, all of the callbacks from an OI_glyph object's base classes are available to it. See Section 6.18, "Determining and Adding Callbacks; Multiple Callbacks," on page 6-117 for additional information about manipulating callbacks.

Table 25-3 OI_glyph Callbacks

Callback Type	Callback Typedef	Description	Page Number
cbClick	OI_click_fnp/memfnp	Click callback function	25-14
cbAnimate	OI_animate_fnp/memfnp	Animate callback function	25-17

Chapter 26
OI_display_1d

OI_display_1d Member Functions

The following functions are available to an **OI_display_1d** object, but are described in their own chapter.

OI_d_tech Member Functions

OI_display_1d

26.1 Description

An OI_display_1d is an object used to display the value of a one-dimensional quantity. It has no visual attributes or user interaction attributes; it is merely the mathematical model for representing display values. The OI_display_1d object has values for resources such as number of tick marks and tick labels, but it has no concept of where these items are placed on the screen, or even if the derived object supports these items. Thus, though OI_display_1d contains the mathematical model for displaying a one-dimensional quantity, it has no concept of its appearance. If you need to create a new one-dimensional display object, you can derive the new class from OI_display_1d.

You never directly create an OI_display_1d object; you get one whenever you create an object whose class is derived from OI_display_1d. You may need to use OI_display_1d member functions for classes derived from OI_display_1d, which are OI_ctlr_1d, OI_gauge, OI_scroll_bar and OI_slider.

26.2 Class Tree

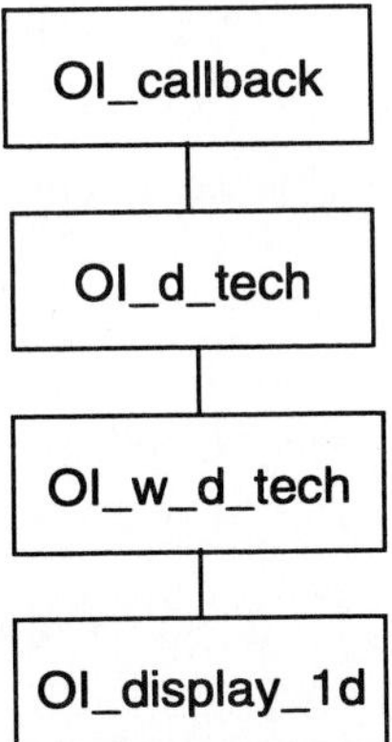

26.3 Base Class Member Functions

You can use all of the member functions of OI_d_tech for an OI_display_1d object.

26.4 OI_display_1d Member Functions

Many OI_display_1d member functions control the appearance of objects created which are instances of a subclass of OI_display_1d. These functions belong to OI_display_1d instead of the subclass because the attributes controlled by OI_display_1d are common to all the subclasses. These attributes are such things as whether and where tick marks show and what type of labeling should appear.

For any **OI_display_1d** object, *user-units* are defined to be the units which the span of the object represents. They are arbitrary units, which can represent any units of measure you please. The important point is that they can differ from pixels. For example, a display object may be 100 pixels long, but it may represent a span of 300 user-units, with a minimum of 100 and a maximum of 399. Furthermore, the display object need not be linear or rectangular with the units spread in one direction only. It is possible to derive a class from **OI_display_1d** with visual attributes appropriate for a semi-circular meter or a logarithmic gauge.

An **OI_display_1d** object controls the ability to show the current value as numeric characters. You can control whether the value appears numerically, and whether the user can control the value by typing into the value field, by using the member function **set_current_value_type** or the resource **showValue**.

26.4.1 Getting and Changing the Value

maximum   (Member function)

```
long OI_display_1d::maximum( )
```

maximum returns the maximum allowable value for the **OI_display_1d** object, in user-units.

minimum   (Member function)

```
long OI_display_1d::minimum( )
```

minimum returns the minimum allowable value for the **OI_display_1d** object, in user-units.

span   (Member function)

```
long OI_display_1d::span( )
```

span returns the span of the **OI_display_1d** object in user-units. This is equivalent to:

maximum( ) - minimum( ) + 1

set_span   (Member function)

```
OI_stat OI_display_1d::set_span(
    long                    max_val,        // maximum allowable value, in user-units
    long                    min_val)        // minimum allowable value, in user-units


OI_stat OI_display_1d::set_span(
    long                    span)           // span, in user-units
```

set_span changes the maximum and minimum user-units that the **OI_display_1d** object represents to *max_val* and *min_val*. Negative values are allowed. *min_val* must be less than *max_val*.

The single parameter **set_span** is equivalent to a call to the two-parameter **set_span** with these parameters:

```
set_span(minimum( ) + span - 1,minimum( )).
```

If you have not specified a minimum for the display object, it is assumed to be zero, and the single parameter **set_span** is equivalent to a call to the two-parameter **set_span** with these parameters:

```
set_span(span - 1,0).
```

value   (Member function)

```
long OI_display_1d::value( )
```

value returns the current value of the **OI_display_1d** object. The value returned is in the range

minimum( ) <= value <= maximum( )

set_value   (Member function)

```
OI_stat OI_display_1d::set_value(
    long                  new_val)          // new value, in user-units
```

set_value sets the current value for the **OI_display_1d** object to *new_val*. *new_val* should be in the range min_val <= *new_val* <= max_val, where min_val and max_val are the values passed to the create function for the object, or to the latest call to **set_span** (if any).

current_value_type   (Member function)

```
OI_display_1d_current OI_display_1d::current_value_type( )
```

current_value_type returns the current value type for the object. It will be one of the values shown for **set_current_value_type**, below.

set_current_value_type   (Member function)

```
void OI_display_1d::set_current_value_type(
    OI_display_1d_current    ctyp)          // new type of value
```

set_current_value_type sets the type for the value for the **OI_display_1d** object to *ctyp*. *ctyp* must be one of the following:

OI_display_1d_current_none	Do not show the value as numeric characters.
OI_display_1d_current_ro	Show the value as numeric characters in a read-only fashion.
OI_display_1d_current_rw	Show the value as numeric characters in a read-write fashion—that is, the user can change the current value by typing into the value field.

decimal_position   (Member function)

```
OI_number OI_display_1d::decimal_position( )
```

decimal_position returns the position of the decimal in the numerical display and labels, in number of characters from the right. If no decimal position has been set via **set_decimal_position** or the resource **decimalPosition**, **decimal_position** returns 0.

set_decimal_position   (Member function)

```
OI_stat OI_display_1d::set_decimal_position(
    OI_number              d_pos)                 // decimal position
```

set_decimal_position sets the display value for the decimal point to be *d_pos* characters from the right. Note that the values used internally (for **span**, etc.) are still long integers; setting the decimal point merely causes the point to appear *d_pos* characters from the right on any displayed numerical values. If *d_pos* is 0, no decimal point appears. If *d_pos* is negative, no decimal point appears and the corresponding number of zeros appear to the right of the value. The following table shows the effects of positive, zero or negative values for *d_pos*:

d_pos	internal value	value displayed
1	5	0.5
0	5	5
-1	5	50

set_decimal_position returns OI_ok if the decimal point was successfully set; otherwise it returns OI_bad_value.

26.4.2 Setting Labels and Tick Marks

label   (Member function)

```
char *OI_display_1d::label( )
```

label returns a pointer to the label.

set_label   (Member function)

```
void OI_display_1d::set_label(
    const char            *lbl)                   // new label
```

set_label sets the label to *lbl*.

label_right_space   (Member function)

```
OI_number OI_display_1d::label_right_space( )
```

label_right_space returns the amount of space, in pixels, that appears between the label and the beginning of the display portion of the object. This applies only to horizontal objects.

set_label_right_space   (Member function)

```
void OI_display_1d::set_label_right_space(
    OI_number          rt_sp)              // space in pixels
```

set_label_right_space sets the amount of space, in pixels, that appears between the label and the beginning of the display portion of the object to be *rt_sp*. This applies only to horizontal objects.

end_label_type   (Member function)

```
OI_display_1d_ends OI_display_1d::end_label_type( )
```

end_label_type returns the type of end labels for the object. It will be one of the values shown for **set_end_type**, below.

set_end_type   (Member function)

```
void OI_display_1d::set_end_type(
    OI_display_1d_ends    ends)            // end label type
```

set_end_type sets the end label type to *ends*. *ends* can be one of

OI_display_1d_ends_none	Do not display labels at end points.
OI_display_1d_ends_numeric	OI supplies numeric end labels.
OI_display_1d_ends_strings	You supply end labels as text using the member functions **set_max_label** and **set_min_label** or the resources **maxLabel** and **minLabel**.

max_label   (Member function)

```
char *OI_display_1d::max_label( )
```

max_label returns a pointer to the label for the maximum end if there is one, otherwise it returns NULL.

set_max_label   (Member function)

```
void OI_display_1d::set_max_label(
    const char          *mx_lbl)           // new maximum label
```

set_max_label sets the label at the maximum end (the right or top) to *mx_lbl*. **set_max_label** has no effect unless the end type is **OI_display_1d_ends_strings** (see **set_end_type** above or the resource **endType**).

min_label   (Member function)

```
char *OI_display_1d::min_label( )
```

min_label returns a pointer to the label for the minimum end if there is one, otherwise it returns NULL.

set_min_label   (Member function)

```
void OI_display_1d::set_min_label(
    const char            *mn_lbl)              // new minimum label
```

set_min_label sets the label at the minimum end (the left or bottom) to *mn_lbl*. set_min_label has no effect unless the end type is OI_display_1d_ends_strings (see set_end_type above or the resource endType).

set_label_font   (Member function)

```
void OI_display_1d::set_label_font(
    const char            *font)                // font for labels
```

set_label_font sets the font for the object's labels to be *font*. This applies to the label for the entire object as well as any maximum or minimum labels and tick labels.

num_ticks   (Member function)

```
OI_number OI_display_1d::num_ticks( )
```

num_ticks returns the number of ticks.

set_num_tick   (Member function)

```
void OI_display_1d::set_num_tick(
    OI_number             num_tk)               // number of ticks
```

set_num_tick sets the number of ticks for the object to *num_tk*. If the tick type is OI_display_1d_ticks_ends_custom or OI_display_1d_ticks_all_custom and if the number of custom labels are less than *num_tk* then the remaining ticks are painted without any label.

tick_position   (Member function)

```
OI_position OI_display_1d::tick_position( )
```

tick_position returns the positioning of the tick marks. This will be one of the values listed under set_tick_position.

set_tick_position   (Member function)

```
void OI_display_1d::set_tick_position(
    OI_position           tk_psn)               // tick position
```

set_tick_position sets the tick positioning to *tk_psn*. *tk_psn* can be one of

OI_right	Display the ticks to the right of a vertical display object.
OI_left	Display the ticks to the left of a vertical display object.
OI_top	Display the ticks on the top of a horizontal display object.
OI_bottom	Display the ticks on the bottom of a horizontal display object.
OI_default_position	If the object is horizontal, this is OI_bottom; if it is vertical this is OI_right.

tick_type   (Member function)

```
OI_display_1d_ticks OI_display_1d::tick_type( )
```

tick_position returns the type of tick marks. This will be one of:

OI_right
OI_left
OI_top
OI_bottom

set_tick_type   (Member function)

```
void OI_display_1d::set_tick_type(
    OI_display_1d_ticks     tk_typ)          // tick type
```

set_tick_type sets the type of tick mark labels for the object to *tk_typ*. *tk_typ* may be one of

OI_display_1d_ticks_none	Display no tick mark labels.
OI_display_1d_ticks_ends	OI supplies beginning and ending tick mark labels as numeric values.
OI_display_1d_ticks_all	OI supplies numeric value labels for all tick marks.
OI_display_1d_ticks_ends_custom	You supply beginning and ending tick mark labels as strings using the member function set_tick_labels or the resource tickLabels.
OI_display_1d_ticks_all_custom	You supply labels for all tick marks using the member function set_tick_labels or the resource tickLabels.

If *tk_typ* is OI_display_1d_ticks_ends_custom or OI_display_1d_ticks_all_custom, then the custom tick label array is used to set the values of the tick labels. If the number of custom labels is less than the number of ticks, then the remaining ticks are painted without any label.

tick_labels   (Member function)

```
char **OI_display_1d::tick_labels( )
```

tick_labels returns a pointer to a NULL-terminated vector of strings which are the labels for the ticks, if there are any.

set_tick_labels   (Member function)

```
void OI_display_1d::set_tick_labels(
    const char * const *lbls)                // label vector
```

set_tick_labels sets the tick labels to *lbls*. set_tick_labels has no effect unless the tick type is OI_display_1d_ticks_ends_custom   or   OI_display_1d_ticks_all_custom   (see set_tick_type above or the resource tickType). *lbls* must be a NULL-terminated vector of strings. You are responsible for assuring that there are the correct number of labels in the array of strings *lbls*. If the number of new custom labels is less than current number of ticks, then the remaining ticks are painted without any labels.

26.4.3   Member Functions Needed When Subclassing

You use the member functions described in this section only when you are subclassing from
OI_display_1d. They are virtual functions which you override to implement functionality specific
to your new class. (See Chapter 41, "Deriving Your Own Classes," for more information.)

paint_current   (Member function)

```
void OI_display_1d::paint_current( )
```

Write paint_current to draw a representation of the current value. paint_current is typically
used to draw an exact numeric representation which corresponds to the visual approximation
the object normally provides. For example, in a slider it draws the current value in the current
value field (OPEN LOOK) or next to the handle (Motif).

paint_value   (Member function)

```
void OI_display_1d::paint_value(
    long                    val)         // current value
```

Write paint_value to update the visual approximation of the current value to *val*. For example,
in a gauge it updates the mercury.

re_layout   (Member function)

```
void OI_display_1d::re_layout( )
```

OI calls re_layout when some aspect of the object has changed which affects it geometry. Write
re_layout to recompute any geometry related parameters you class stores internally.

26.5 Resources

All resources from an OI_display_1d object's base classes are available to it; in addition, OI fetches
the resources shown in Table 26-1. For more information on resource management, see Chapter 39,
"The OI Resource Mechanism."

For more information on the interrelations of the resources specified in Table 26-1, see the create
function in the chapters on the classes derived from OI_display_1d.

Table 26-1 OI_display_1d Resources

Resource	Description	Possible Values
decimalPosition	Specifies the placement of a decimal point in numerical labels, from the right.	Integer
endType	Specifies whether minimum and maximum value labels are to be displayed at the ends of the object	none, numeric, strings

Table 26-1 OI_display_1d Resources

Resource	Description	Possible Values
font	Specifies the font to use for all text in the object	Valid font
label	Specifies the text to use for the label on the object	Any printable text
label.font	Specifies a font for the label only. This resource overrides the Font resource.	Valid font
label.rightSpace	Specifies the space, in pixels, between the end of the label and the rest of the object.	Non-negative number
maximum	Specifies the maximum value in user-units.	Long
maxLabel	Specifies a label to use for the maximum end of the controller	Any printable text
minimum	Specifies minimum value in user-units.	Long
minLabel	Specifies a label to use for the minimum end of the controller	Any printable text
numTick	Specifies the number of tick marks to appear	Non-negative integer
showValue	Specifies whether the current value is to be displayed as a numeric field (if derived class supports it).	none, read_only, read_write
tickLabels	Specifies a list of custom tick mark labels. Required if tickType is ends_custom or all_custom.	Comma separated list of quoted strings
position	Specifies where the ticks are to appear.	right, left, top, bottom, default_position
tickType	Specifies which tick labels are to appear	none, ends, all, ends_custom, all_custom

Table 26-1 OI_display_1d Resources

Resource	Description	Possible Values
value	Specifies the current value for the object. You can use this to set an initial value for the object. You can also use it to dynamically control the object.	Long

26.6 Translations

All translations from an OI_display_1d object's base classes are available to it; it has no additional translations.

26.7 Callback Functions

There are no callbacks specifically for an OI_display_1d object. All of the callbacks from an OI_display_1d object's base classes are available to it.

Chapter 27
OI_gauge

OI_gauge Functions

OI_gauge Member Functions

The following functions are available to an **OI_gauge** object, but are described in their own chapter.

OI_display_1d Member Functions

OI_d_tech Member Functions

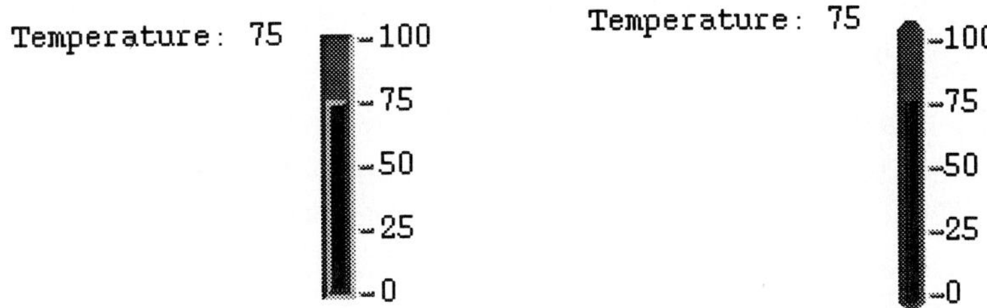

OI_gauge

27.1 Description

An OI_gauge is an object used to represent the value of a one-dimensional quantity. It consists of a long bar with optional attributes which include a gauge label, current value text, a minimum and maximum label, tick marks, and tick labels. A portion of the bar is filled in, or shaded (the "mercury"), representing the current value for the quantity.

An example of an application where gauges could be used would be to represent the water height in different reservoirs and holding tanks for a real-time water flow control system. Another example would be in a debugger; while it loads symbols, it could display the number of currently loaded symbols in a gauge.

27.2 Class Tree

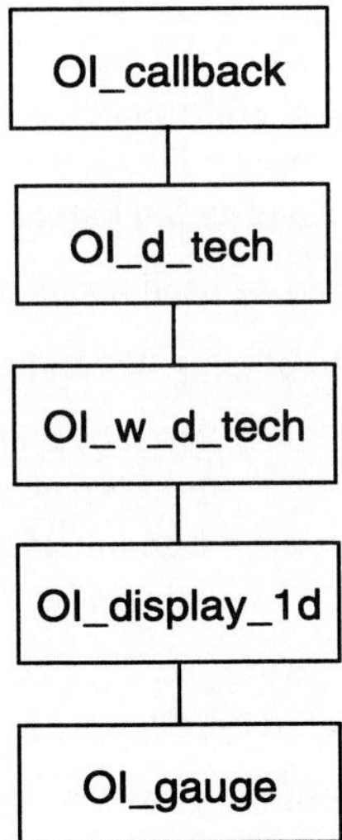

27.3 Runtime Interaction

A gauge is for display purposes only.

27.4 OI_gauge Creation

oi_create_gauge   (Free-standing function)

```
OI_gauge *oi_create_gauge(
    const char      *namp,                    // pointer to name for object
    OI_number       len,                      // length in pixels along major axis
    OI_orient       orient,                   // orientation of gauge
    long            max_value,                // maximum allowable value
    long            min_value=0,              // minimum allowable value
    const char      *lbl=NULL,                // gauge label
    OI_gauge_ends   end_typ
                    =OI_gauge_ends_none,      // gauge end labels type
    const char      *min_lbl=NULL,            // label for minimum end
    const char      *max_lbl=NULL,            // label for maximum end
    OI_bool         show_val=OI_no,           // display current value as text?
    OI_number       n_ticks=0,                // number of ticks to display
    OI_gauge_ticks  tick_typ
                    =OI_gauge_ticks_none,     // tick type
    const char * const *tick_lbls=NULL)       // pointer to vector of tick labels
```

orient is the orientation of the gauge and can be either **OI_horizontal** or **OI_vertical**.

len is the number of pixels to be used for the dynamic portion of the gauge bar along the major axis. That is, the values from *min_value* through *max_value* are distributed over a bar of length *len*. The total size of the gauge is larger than this, since the ends of the bar are not included in this dynamic region, and the decoration options may add additional space. *max_value* and *min_value* specify the range of values which the gauge is to represent. These are referred to as *user-units*. Negative values are allowed. *max_value - min_value* is scaled to *len* pixels. If you omit *min_value*, it defaults to 0.

lbl points to a null-terminated text string to be used as a label for the gauge; it defaults to NULL.

end_typ specifies the type of end labels to display. It can have one of the following values:

OI_gauge_ends_none	No labels are displayed at end points.
OI_gauge_ends_numeric	End labels are numeric values supplied by OI.
OI_gauge_ends_strings	End labels are labeled with text which you supply in *min_lbl* and *max_lbl*.

If you specify *end_typ* to be **OI_gauge_ends_strings**, *min_lbl* and *max_lbl* must contain the text for the labels. Otherwise *min_lbl* and *max_lbl* are ignored.

If *show_val* is **OI_yes**, the current value of the gauge is displayed as a character string. By default, no current value is displayed.

n_ticks is the number of tick marks to place along the bar. *tick_typ* is the type of tick mark labels to display. It can have one of the following values:

OI_gauge_ticks_none	No tick mark labels are displayed.
OI_gauge_ticks_ends	Beginning and ending tick marks are labeled with numeric values supplied by OI.
OI_gauge_ticks_all	All tick marks are labeled with numeric values supplied by OI.
OI_gauge_ticks_ends_custom	Beginning and ending tick marks are labeled with strings which you provide in *tick_lbls*.
OI_gauge_ticks_all_custom	All tick marks are labeled with strings which you provide in *tick_lbls*.

tick_typ defaults to OI_gauge_ticks_none.

If you use either OI_gauge_ticks_ends or OI_gauge_ticks_all, OI labels the tick marks with integers. In order to assure that the tick marks occur along the bar at integral intervals, *max_val - min_val* must be evenly divisible by *n_ticks* - 1. If you do not follow this rule, the integer labels will be attached to tick marks that are not at integral values, and as a result the mercury in the bar will not look as though it matches the correct value for a gauge with a small span. See Program 27-1 on page 27-8.

For OI_gauge_ticks_ends_custom, there must be two strings in the array *tick_lbls*, and for OI_gauge_ticks_all_custom, there must be *n_ticks* strings in the array *tick_lbls*.

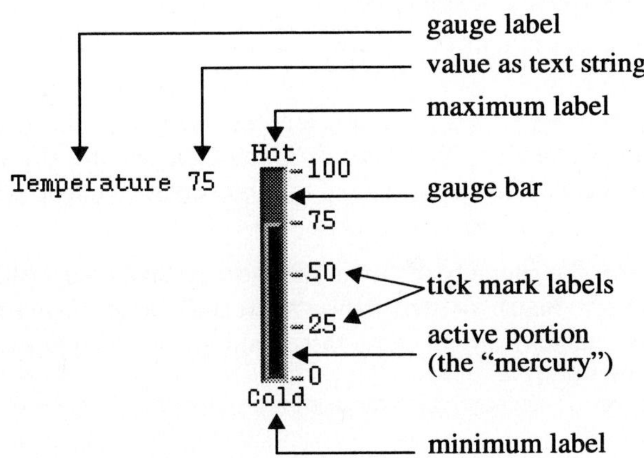

Figure 27-1   Parts of an OI_gauge, Motif

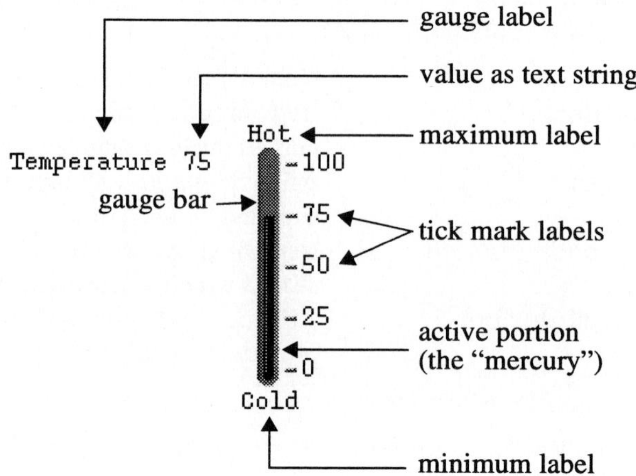

Figure 27-2   Parts of an OI_gauge, OPEN LOOK

27.5   Base Class Member Functions

You can use all of the member functions of OI_d_tech and OI_display_1d for an OI_gauge object.

27.6   OI_gauge Member Functions

27.6.1   Controlling Appearance and Size

The *major axis* of a gauge is along its length. If it is a horizontal gauge, this is the x direction; if it is a vertical gauge, this is the y direction. The *minor axis* is along its width—the direction orthogonal to the major axis. You can set and change the size of a gauge along its major axis, but not along its minor axis.

You can set the major size of the gauge based on either the total size (using set_major_size), the total bar size (using set_bar_size), or the active "mercury" range (using set_pixel_range), depending on your needs. Changing any of these three values also changes the value of the other two. See Figure 27-3 and Figure 27-4.

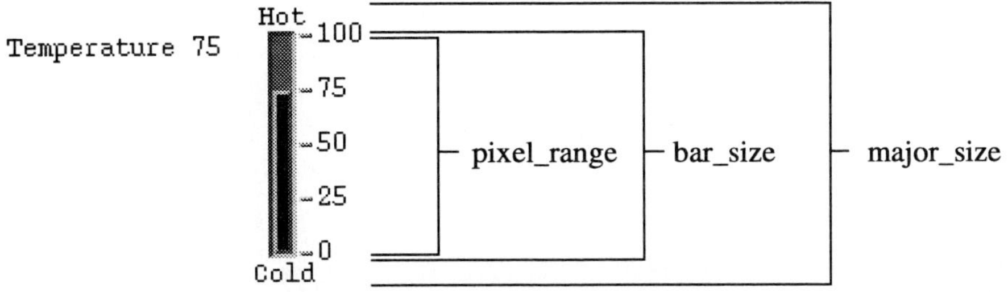

Figure 27-3   Gauge Sizes, Motif

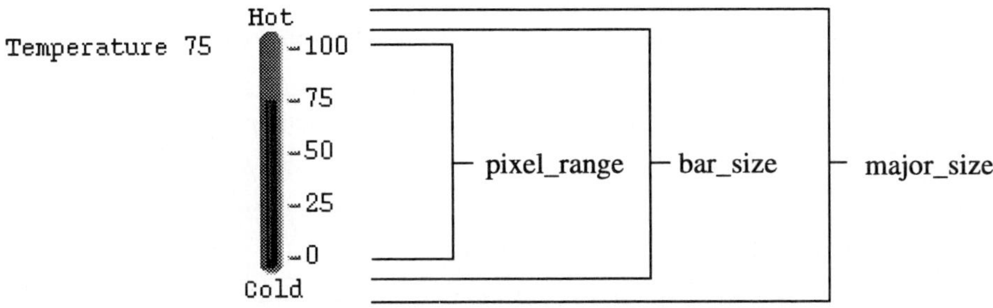

Figure 27-4   Gauge Sizes, OPEN LOOK

Calling the OI_d_tech member function set_size has the same effect as calling set_major_size for the major axis direction; the value in the other direction (for the minor axis) is ignored.

orientation   (Member function)

```
OI_orient OI_gauge::orientation( )
```

orientation returns the orientation of the gauge, either OI_horizontal or OI_vertical.

major_size   (Member function)

```
OI_number OI_gauge::major_size( )
```

major_size returns the length in pixels of the gauge along its major axis, including all decoration. This is a short form for:

```
if (orientation( ) == OI_horizontal)
    siz = size_x( );
else
    siz = size_y( );
return(siz);
```

set_major_size (Member function)

```
OI_stat OI_gauge::set_major_size(
    OI_number        size)                    // length in pixels
```

set_major_size changes the length in pixels of the gauge along its major axis. This is the total length of the gauge, including all decoration.

bar_size (Member function)

```
OI_number OI_gauge::bar_size( )
```

bar_size returns the length in pixels of the gauge bar along its major axis, not including the gauge labels and other decoration, but including the ends of the bar itself.

set_bar_size (Member function)

```
OI_stat OI_gauge::set_bar_size(
    OI_number        size)                    // length in pixels
```

set_bar_size changes the size of the gauge bar along its major axis. *size* is the number of pixels in the gauge bar, not including labels, tick marks, or any surrounding white space, but including the ends of the bar itself.

pixel_range (Member function)

```
OI_number OI_gauge::pixel_range( )
```

pixel_range returns the length of the gauge bar in pixels; this length includes only the portion of the bar which can show the value (the "mercury").

set_pixel_range (Member function)

```
OI_stat OI_gauge::set_pixel_range(
    OI_number        size)                    // bar size in pixels
```

set_pixel_range changes the length of the gauge bar along its major axis to *size* pixels; this length includes only the portion of the bar which can show the value (the "mercury").

active_pixel (Member function)

```
PIXEL OI_gauge::active_pixel( )
```

active_pixel returns the pixel value for the color used to paint the active portion (the "mercury") of the gauge.

set_active_color   (Member function)

```
OI_stat OI_gauge::set_active_color(
    const char          *clr)              // color name

void OI_gauge::set_active_color(
    PIXEL               pxl)               // pixel color
```

set_active_color sets the color value for the color used to paint the active portion (the "mercury") of the gauge. By default, the foreground color is used. You can obtain a pixel value for a named color such as "red" by using the OI_connection member function str_color.

27.7   An OI_gauge Programming Example

Program 27-1 uses a gauge to show the number of children in an application window. The user can add more children by clicking on the "Add New Object" menu button. Since in a real application, you may not be in control of the quantity you are measuring with a gauge, Program 27-1 uses a time-out function to trigger the gauge update, not the actual addition of the child object, to simulate updating a gauge with outside information. The results of running this program, and clicking on the "Add New Object" button three times are shown in Figure 27-5. There are five children shown, which include the main menu, the gauge, and three boxes of different sizes.

```c
#include <OI/oi.H>                              /* Gauge.C */
int main(int argc, char** argv)
{
                void            set_the_gauge(void*);
                void            add_obj(OI_menu_cell*,void*,OI_number);
                OI_connection   *conp;
                OI_app_window   *wp;
                OI_gauge        *gp;
                OI_menu         *mp;
                OI_menu_cell    *cellp;
        static  OI_cell_spec    cells[] = {
                {"add","Add New Object",add_obj},
                {"exit","Exit",(OI_action_fnp)OI_end_interaction},
                };
    if (conp = OI_init(&argc,argv,"Gauge")) {
        wp = oi_create_app_window("main",1,1,"Gauge");
        wp->set_layout(OI_layout_column);
        mp = oi_create_button_menu("main_menu",OI_count(cells),&cells[0],
                        OI_horizontal);
        wp->set_main_menu(mp);
        cellp = (OI_menu_cell*)(mp->subobject("add"));
        cellp->change_arg(wp);
        gp = oi_create_gauge("gauge",100,OI_vertical,10,0,"Number of Children: ",
            OI_gauge_ends_none,NULL,NULL,OI_yes,6,OI_gauge_ticks_all);
        gp->layout_associated_object(wp,(OI_number)0,(OI_number)0,OI_active);
        OI_add_timeout(200,set_the_gauge,gp);
        wp->set_associated_object(wp->root( ),OI_def_loc,OI_def_loc,OI_active);
        OI_begin_interaction( );
        OI_fini( );
    }
}
void add_obj(OI_menu_cell*, void *argp, OI_number)
{
                OI_box          *bp;
        static  int             siz = 10;
        static  int             column = 0;
    siz++;
    bp = oi_create_box("new_box",siz,siz);
    if (++column > 10)
        column = 1;
    bp->layout_associated_object((OI_d_tech*)argp,column,siz,OI_active);
}
void set_the_gauge(void *argp)
{
                OI_gauge        *gp;
    gp = (OI_gauge*)argp;
    if (gp->app_window( )->num_props( ) > gp->maximum( ))
        gp->set_span(gp->maximum( ) + 11);
    gp->set_value(gp->app_window( )->num_props( ));
}
```

Program 27-1   Show Number of Children (Gauge.C)

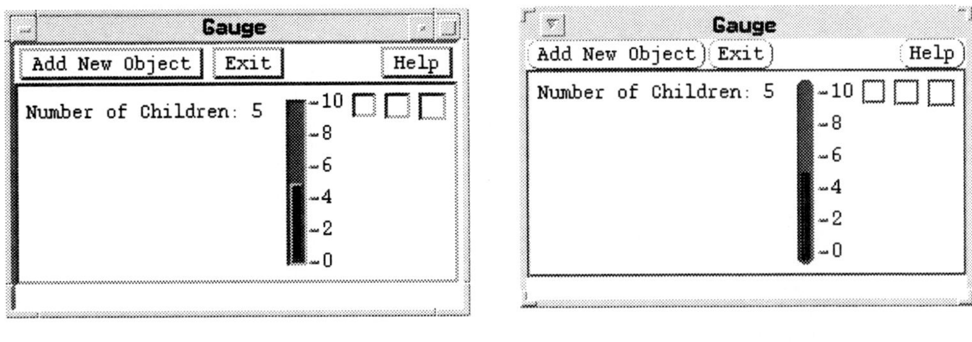

| Motif | OPEN LOOK |

Figure 27-5   Show Number of Children

27.8 Resources

All resources from an **OI_gauge** object's base classes are available to it; in addition, OI fetches the resources shown in Table 27-1. For more information on resource management, see Chapter 39, "The OI Resource Mechanism."

Table 27-1   OI_gauge Resources

Resource	Description	Possible Values	Default Value
barActiveColor	Specifies the color to use for the active portion of the bar (the "mercury").	Valid color	Foreground color
orientation	Specifies the orientation of the gauge.	horizontal, vertical	(No default)
pixelRange	Specifies the length of the gauge bar.	Positive integer	(No default)

27.9 Translations

All translations from an **OI_gauge** object's base classes are available to it; it has no additional translations.

27.10 Callbacks

All callbacks from an **OI_gauge** object's base classes are available to it; it has no additional callbacks.

Chapter 28
OI_ctlr_1d

OI_ctlr_1d Member Functions

The following functions are available to an **OI_ctlr_1d** object, but are described in their own chapter.

OI_display_1d Member Functions

OI_d_tech Member Functions

OI_ctlr_1d

28.1 Description

OI_ctlr_1d is the base class for all OI one-dimensional controllers which 1) represent the current value and 2) allow the user to change the value. OI supports different types of one-dimensional controllers, but since all types are derived from OI_ctlr_1d, you can use all OI_ctlr_1d member functions for any type of one-dimensional controller. OI provides two classes derived from OI_ctlr_1d: OI_slider and OI_scroll_bar. You never directly create an OI_ctlr_1d object; this class exists only to provide properties and functions common to its derived classes.

An OI_ctlr_1d object has no concept of its appearance. It is a mathematical model of a measurable quantity consisting of a maximum and minimum value, and a handle representing the current value.

The *span* of a controller is the number of user-units covered by the controller, from the minimum value through the maximum value, inclusive. *user-units* are defined when you create the controller and are redefined if you call the OI_display_1d member function set_span; they are arbitrary units.

You can write a callback function to change the item being controlled when the user changes the controller handle position. When the handle moves, OI executes the callback function.

28.2 Class Tree

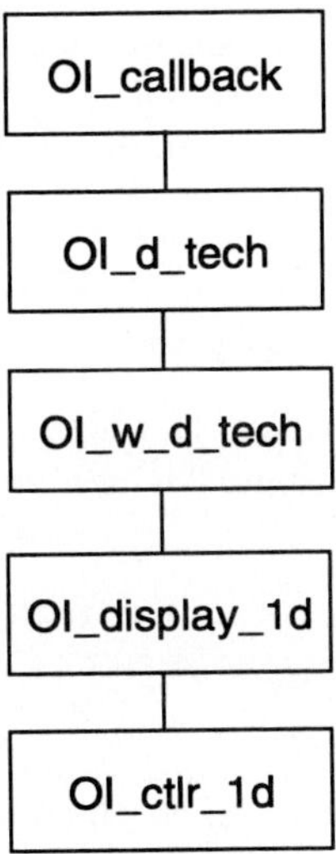

28.3 Base Class Member Functions

You can use all of the member functions of OI_d_tech and OI_display_1d for an OI_ctlr_1d object.

28.4   OI_ctlr_1d Member Functions

28.4.1   Controller Handle Action

You can query the location of the handle and set the handle location with these functions.

handle_loc   (Member function)

```
long OI_ctlr_1d::handle_loc( )
```

handle_loc returns the current position of the handle, in user-units. The value returned is in the range minimum( ) <= value <= maximum( ). handle_loc returns the same value as the OI_display_1d member function value.

prev_handle_loc   (Member function)

```
long OI_ctlr_1d::prev_handle_loc( )
```

prev_handle_loc returns the previous position of the handle, in user-units. The value returned is in the range minimum( ) <= value <= maximum( ). The previous position is defined as the position the handle had on the previous call to the handle motion callback function.

set_handle_loc   (Member function)

```
OI_stat OI_ctlr_1d::set_handle_loc(
   long                    loc,              // new value in user-units
   OI_bool                 mov_obj=OI_yes)   // call handle motion callback?
```

set_handle_loc positions the handle at location *loc*, in user-units. *loc* should be in the range minimum( ) <= *loc* <= maximum( ). *mov_obj* specifies whether the handle motion callback function is to be called. If you omit *mov_obj*, the default is OI_yes. Do not call this function from within the handle motion callback.

interval   (Member function)

```
OI_number OI_ctlr_1d::interval( )
```

interval returns the rate, in milliseconds, at which the controller's handle moves and value changes when the SELECT mouse button is held down on the handle. The default is 100 milliseconds.

set_interval   (Member function)

```
void OI_ctlr_1d::set_interval(
   OI_number               intrvl)           // timing interval
```

set_interval sets the rate, in milliseconds, at which the controller's handle moves and value changes when the SELECT mouse button is held down on the handle to *intrvl*.

is_motion_callback   (Member function)

```
OI_bool OI_ctlr_1d::is_motion_callback( )
```

is_motion_callback returns OI_yes if allow_motion_callback( ) is in effect; otherwise it returns OI_no. Unless you have called disallow_motion_callback or have set the resource motionCallback to false, this returns OI_yes.

allow_motion_callback   (Member function)

```
void OI_ctlr_1d::allow_motion_callback( )
```

allow_motion_callback causes the handle motion callback to be called for each new handle position when the handle is dragged. The callback may not be called for all possible handle values. For example, if the user moves the handle from value 1 to value 100, the callback might be called when the handle is at value 7, 32, 83, and 100 only, depending on how rapidly the user moves the handle and quickly the system and network respond. allow_motion_callback is the default condition.

disallow_motion_callback   (Member function)

```
void OI_ctlr_1d::disallow_motion_callback( )
```

disallow_motion_callback prohibits continuous calls to the handle motion callback when the controller handle is moved by dragging the handle. The callback function will be executed once, only when the mouse button is released at the final position. Consequently, the controlled object will be updated only when the mouse button is released. You may want to use this function if you encounter performance degradation due to the time necessary to update the controlled item's display.

28.4.2   Changing the Handle Motion Callback

You register the handle motion function when you create an object derived from OI_ctlr_1d (an OI_slider or OI_scroll_bar). You can use the functions described in this section to change that function.

OI supports multiple callbacks, meaning you can have more than one callback of a given type for an object. For an OI_ctlr_1d object, this means that you can have more than one handle motion callback. The functions described in this section apply to the first cbCtlr1d callback if more than one is registered. If you have multiple callbacks registered and need to change them, use the OI_d_tech callback_* member functions (see 6.18, "Determining and Adding Callbacks; Multiple Callbacks," on page 6-117).

change_action   (Member function)

```
void OI_ctlr_1d::change_action(
    OI_ctlr_1d_fnp      fnp,              // pointer to function to call
    void                *argp=NULL)       // arbitrary argument for fnp


void OI_ctlr_1d::change_action(
    OI_callback         *objp,            // memfnp's object
    OI_ctlr_1d_memfnp   memfnp,           // pointer to member function to call
    void                *argp=NULL)       // arbitrary argument for memfnp
```

The change_action functions register a callback function to be invoked whenever the controller handle location changes. This callback is identified within OI as a cbCtlr1d callback function (see Section 6.18, "Determining and Adding Callbacks; Multiple Callbacks," on page 6-117). Use change_action only if you wish to change the callback function that was registered initially when you created the controller, or if you did not register any callback function when you created the controller. If your handle motion function is a member function, when it is invoked it will be called as if you had written *objp->memfnp*. See Section 2.5, "Callbacks and Event-Driven Programming," on page 2-16 for more explanation.

argp is optional, and can be any valid expression that can be cast to a pointer. You can use it to pass additional information to the function *fnp* or *memfnp*.

Writing the Handle Motion Callback Function

If the cbCtlr1d callback function is not a member function, write it in this form:

```
void fn(
        OI_ctlr_1d        *oi_objp,    // pointer to controller
        void              *argp,       // arbitrary argument
        OI_scroll_event   typ,         // type of handle movement
        long              n)           // direction of handle movement
```

and if the cbCtlr1d callback function is a member function, write it in this form:

```
void obj_class::memfn(
        OI_ctlr_1d        *oi_objp,    // pointer to controller
        void              *argp,       // arbitrary argument
        OI_scroll_event   typ,         // type of handle movement
        long              n)           // direction of handle movement
```

where *obj_class* is the class of the object whose member function is *memfn*.

When your callback function is invoked, *oi_objp* will be a pointer to the controller to which the callback applies.

typ, in conjunction with *n*, will specify the type of operation to be performed, and will be one of the following:

OI_scroll_unit	Move *n* user-units relative to the current location.
OI_scroll_viewport	Move *n* viewports relative to the current location.
OI_scroll_extreme	Move as far as possible.
OI_scroll_position	Move to absolute position *n*.

In the first three types, $n > 0$ implies movement toward the end of the controller, and $n < 0$ implies movement toward the beginning. If *typ* is OI_scroll_position, the handle has been positioned to the absolute position *n*, in user-units, from the start of the controller; n will be in the range minimum( ) <= n <= maximum( ) - view_span( ). For example, suppose you have a horizontal scroll bar with a span of 1000 user-units, a viewport of 100 user-units, and the minimum value is zero. If the handle is positioned to the far right so that *typ* is OI_scroll_extreme, *n* will be 900.

get_arg   (Member function)

```
void *OI_ctlr_1d::get_arg( )
```

get_arg returns the argument pointer that will be passed to the controller handle motion callback function. This is the argument passed in the create function for the object, or the argument set in the last call to change_action or change_arg.

change_arg   (Member function)

```
void OI_ctlr_1d::change_arg(
    void                    *argp)          // arbitrary user argument
```

change_arg changes the argument pointer that will be passed to the controller handle motion callback function.

28.4.3   Controlling Appearance and Size

Each time a change occurs in the range of the item the controller controls, you need to call the OI_display_1d member function set_span to reflect the change. The appearance of the controller may change each time you call set_span. For example, suppose the handle is at the half-way point on the controller, and the controlled item increases in length once each minute, and you call set_span each time it changes. As the span increases, the handle moves toward the beginning of the controller, since the user-units it represents becomes a smaller and smaller fraction of the total range represented, and the handle's relative position becomes closer and closer to the beginning. If the controlled object changes size rapidly, this handle movement repainting may cause performance problems. In this case, you may want to call disallow_span_update for the controller, then call allow_span_update at some later time.

view_span   (Member function)

```
long OI_ctlr_1d::view_span( )
```

If the controller corresponds to a view of the controlled object (as in the case of OI_scroll_bar), in general only a portion of the controlled object is visible in the viewport. view_span returns the number of user-units spanned by the view of the controlled object. (To set the view span, use a member function for the object such as set_view for an OI_scroll_bar.)

is_span_update (Member function)

```
OI_bool OI_ctlr_1d::is_span_update( )
```

is_span_update returns **OI_yes** if the controller is conditioned to reposition and resize, if necessary, whenever the span changes (the default condition); otherwise it returns **OI_no**.

allow_span_update (Member function)

```
void OI_ctlr_1d::allow_span_update( )
```

allow_span_update configures the controller to allow its appearance to be updated each time a change is made in the range of the item being controlled by the controller (each time you call the **OI_display_1d** member function **set_span**). The update may change the position of the handle. This is the default condition. If you have previously called **disallow_span_update**, calling **allow_span_update** causes the controller to be updated immediately.

disallow_span_update (Member function)

```
void OI_ctlr_1d::disallow_span_update( )
```

disallow_span_update configures the controller so that its appearance is not updated each time a change is made in the span of the item being controlled by the controller (each time you call the **OI_display_1d** member function **set_span**). You should only set this condition temporarily—for example, if the controlled item is increasing in size rapidly for a short period of time. When the controlled item is stable again, you should set the controller back to **allow_span_update** to force the controller appearance to be updated properly.

28.5 Resources

All resources from an **OI_ctlr_1d** object's base classes are available to it; in addition, OI fetches the resources shown in Table 28-1. For more information on resource management, see Chapter 39, "The OI Resource Mechanism."

Table 28-1 OI_ctlr_1d Resources

Resource	Description	Possible Values	Default Value
interval	Specifies the rate, in milliseconds, at which the controller's handle moves and value changes when the SELECT mouse button is held down on the handle.	Positive integer	100
motionCallback	If on, specifies that the handle action callback should be made each time the handle moves.	Boolean	true

28.6 Translations

All translations from an OI_ctlr_1d object's base classes are available to it; it has no additional translations.

28.7 Callback Functions

Table 28-2 lists the callbacks available for an OI_ctlr_1d object and the page number of the corresponding explanatory material. In addition, all of the callbacks from an OI_ctlr_1d object's base classes are available to it. See Section 6.18, "Determining and Adding Callbacks; Multiple Callbacks," on page 6-117 for additional information about manipulating callbacks.

Table 28-2 OI_ctlr_1d Callbacks

Callback Type	Callback Typedef	Description	Page Number
cbCtlr1d	OI_ctlr_1d_fnp/memfnp	Handle motion callback function	28-4

Chapter 29
OI_slider

OI_slider Functions

OI_slider Member Functions

The following functions are available to **OI_slider** objects, but are described in their own chapter.

OI_ctlr_1d Member Functions

OI_display_1d Member Functions

OI_d_tech Member Functions

OI Programmer's Guide

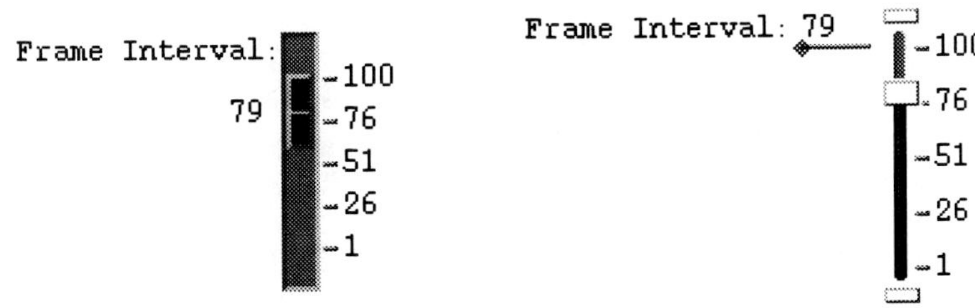

OI_slider

29.1 Description

An OI_slider is a controller for a one-dimensional quantity. It displays a graphical representation of the current value and allows the user to change the value. It consists of a long bar with a handle which can slide from one end of the bar to the other. The bottom of a vertical slider, or the left end of a horizontal slider, represents the minimum possible value, while the other end represents the maximum. The position of the slider handle along the bar represents the current value.

The *span* of a slider is the number of user-units represented by the entire length of the slider. *user-units* are defined when you create the slider and redefined if you call the member function set_span.

A slider has several optional attributes: a label, maximum and minimum value labels (either numeric or customized text), tick marks, and tick mark labels of various sorts. You can also control whether the current value displays as text, and whether, in the OPEN LOOK model, this text can be changed by the user (thus changing the current value of the slider).

An OI_slider object is in many respects similar to an OI_scroll_bar object. The difference in usage is that an OI_scroll_bar object is meant to control the positioning of an item (text, graphics, etc.) within a viewport, whereas an OI_slider object should be used to control some other one-dimensional quantity. A slider might be used to represent a valve with continuous settings that would control the rate of flow of a liquid. The user could open and close the valve to whatever degree is necessary by moving the slider handle. A slider could also be used to control the magnification of a graphic image. The slider on the OI Periodic Chart on page 1-10 controls the interval between frames of the glyph animation.

You can write a callback function to manipulate the item being controlled when the user changes the slider handle position. When the handle moves, OI executes the callback function.

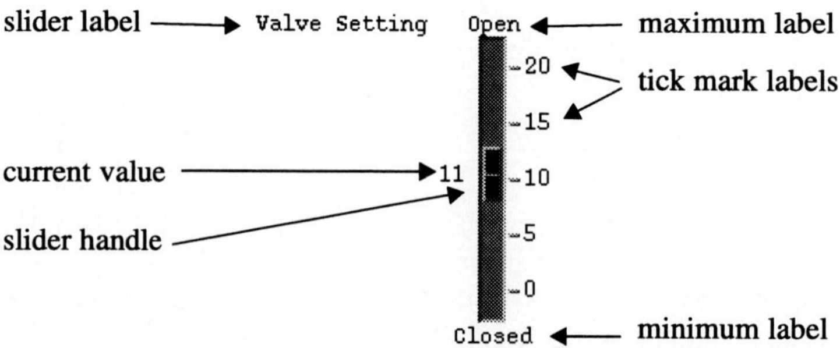

Figure 29-1   Parts of an OI_slider Object, Motif

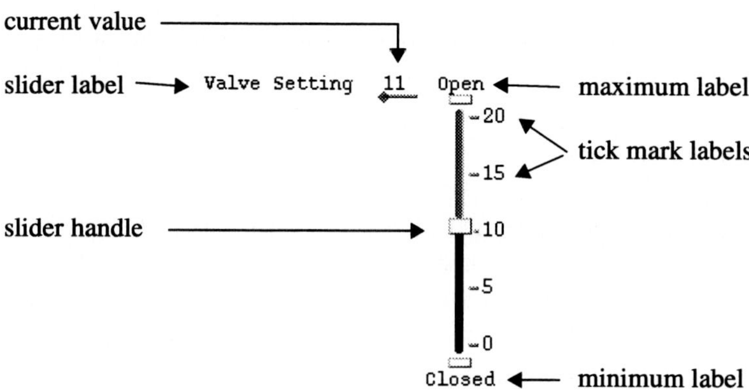

Figure 29-2   Parts of an OI_slider Object, OPEN LOOK

29.2 Class Tree

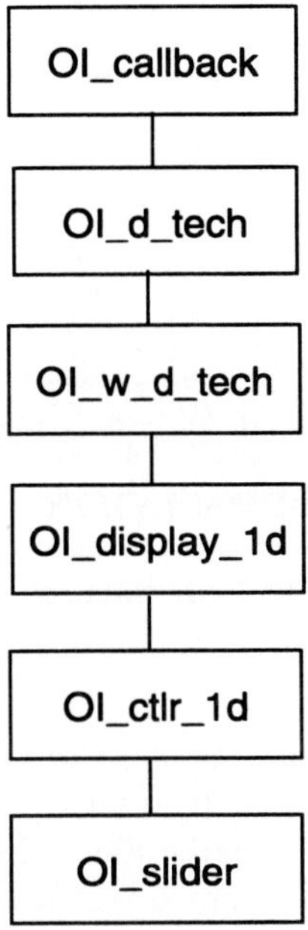

29.3 Runtime Interaction

The default translations for an **OI_slider** object provide the following runtime interaction. See Section 29.9, "Translations," on page 29-15, if you need to change these.

To move a slider handle, position the mouse pointer over the slider handle and press the SELECT mouse button. With the mouse button still pressed, the handle moves correspondingly if you move the mouse pointer along the slider's major axis.

Instead of positioning the pointer over the handle, you can position it above or below the handle for a vertical slider, or to the left or right of the handle for a horizontal slider. In this case, clicking the SELECT mouse button moves the slider handle one user-unit in the direction of the pointer. The handle may or may not move with each click, depending on the range represented by the slider and the slider bar length.

You can press and hold the SELECT mouse button (instead of clicking) when the pointer is positioned on the slider bar above or below the handle (or to the left or right). You do not need to move the pointer; the handle moves one user-unit at timed intervals until either you release the mouse button or the handle reaches the end of the slider.

You can also press the DRAG (Motif) or ADJUST (OPEN LOOK) mouse button (usually the middle mouse button), which causes the slider handle to jump to the mouse pointer, then drag the handle as for the SELECT button.

You can control a slider through keyboard interaction, if the keyboard input focus is on the slider. Pressing the up (down) arrow in a vertical slider moves the slider handle up (down) one user-unit. Pressing the left (right) arrow in a horizontal slider moves the slider handle left (right) one user-unit.

29.3.1   Runtime Interaction, Motif

In addition to the general interaction described above, if you are running Motif, you can move the handle to either end of the slider by clicking the SELECT mouse button on the slider bar while pressing the Ctrl key.

If the mouse pointer is within the slider, you can press the Up, Down, Left or Right Arrow key in conjunction with the Ctrl key, to move the slider handle in the expected direction four user-units.

29.3.2   Runtime Interaction, OPEN LOOK

In addition to the general interaction described above, if you are running OPEN LOOK, you can click on the small box at either end of the slider; this causes the handle to move to that end of the slider.

If the call to oi_create_slider specified a value of OI_slider_current_rw for *cur_typ*, you can change the position of the handle on the slider by entering a new value in user-units into the current-value entry field which is located to the left of the slider. If you use this method, you must terminate the newly-entered value by pressing the Return key, at which point the slider handle moves to that value.

29.4 OI_slider Creation

oi_create_slider   (Free-standing function)

```
OI_slider *oi_create_slider(
    const char          *namp,                   // object name
    OI_number           len,                     // major axis length in pixels
    OI_orient           orient,                  // orientation of slider
    long                max_val=-1,              // maximum value in user-units
    long                min_val=0,               // minimum value in user-units
    OI_ctlr_1d_fnp      fnp=NULL,                // function for slider movement
    void                *argp=OI_def_arg,        // arbitrary argument for fnp
    const char          *lbl=NULL,               // string for slider's label
    OI_slider_ends      end_typ                  // whether min & max labels
                        =OI_slider_ends_none,    // appear
    const char          *min_lab=NULL,           // minimum value label
    const char          *max_lab=NULL,           // maximum value label
    OI_slider_current   cur_typ                  // whether current value is
                        =OI_slider_current_none, // displayed
    int                 n_ticks=0,               // number of ticks to appear
    OI_slider_ticks     tick_typ
                        =OI_slider_ticks_none,   // which tick mark labels appear
    const char * const *tick_labels=NULL)        // custom tick mark labels
```

```
OI_slider *oi_create_slider(
    const char          *namp,                           // object name
    OI_number           len,                             // major axis length in pixels
    OI_orient           orient,                          // orientation of slider
    long                max_val,                         // maximum value in user-units
    long                min_val,                         // minimum value in user-units
    OI_callback         *objp,                           // memfnp's object
    OI_ctlr_1d_memfnp    memfnp,                         // member function for slider
                                                         // movement
    void                *argp=OI_def_arg,                // arbitrary argument for memfnp
    const char          *lbl=NULL,                       // string for slider's label
    OI_slider_ends       end_typ                         // whether min & max labels
                        =OI_slider_ends_none,            // appear
    const char          *min_lab=NULL,                   // minimum value label
    const char          *max_lab=NULL,                   // maximum value label
    OI_slider_current    cur_typ                         // whether current value is
                        =OI_slider_current_none,         // displayed
    int                  n_ticks=0,                      // number of ticks to appear
    OI_slider_ticks      tick_typ
                        =OI_slider_ticks_none,           // which tick mark labels appear
    const char * const  *tick_labels=NULL)               // custom tick mark labels
```

The **oi_create_slider** functions create an **OI_slider** object and also register a callback function
to be invoked whenever the slider handle is moved. If your handle motion function is a member
function, when it is invoked it will be called as if you had written *objp->memfnp*. See Section
2.5, "Callbacks and Event-Driven Programming," on page 2-16 for more explanation.

len is the length in pixels of the slider bar. *len* specifies only the portion of the bar along which
the handle can move; that is, the values from *min_val* through *max_val* are distributed over a
bar of length *len*. The total size of the slider object in the major-axis direction includes the end
bar decoration plus space taken by labels, and is longer than *len*. See Figure 29-3 and Figure 29-
4 on page 29-9.

orient indicates the orientation of the major axis of the slider and can have one of two values:
OI_vertical or **OI_horizontal**.

max_val and *min_val* specify the range over which the slider is to operate, in user-units. If you
omit them, the range is taken to be from zero to *len* - 1.

If the slider handle-movement callback function is a free-standing function, specify the function
as *fnp*; use *memfnp* if it is a member function. This callback is identified within OI as a **cbCtlr1d**
callback function (see Section 6.18, "Determining and Adding Callbacks; Multiple Callbacks,"
on page 6-117).

argp is optional, and can be any valid expression that can be cast to a pointer. You can use it to
pass additional information to the function *fnp* or *memfnp*.

lbl points to a null-terminated string to be used as a label for the slider; it defaults to NULL.

end_typ specifies whether minimum and maximum value labels are displayed at the top and bottom (for a vertical slider) or left and right (for a horizontal slider). The possible values are:

OI_slider_ends_none	No end labels. This is the default.
OI_slider_ends_numeric	Numeric end labels.
OI_slider_ends_strings	End labels are text supplied by the programmer.

min_lab and *max_lab* are not used unless *end_typ* is OI_slider_ends_strings.

cur_typ specifies whether the current value is to be displayed as an integer. If the current value is to be displayed, and if the slider is vertical, the current value is located to the left of the upper left corner of the slider in OPEN LOOK model, and to the left of the slider handle in the Motif model. For a horizontal slider, the current value is placed to the left of the slider. The possible values are:

OI_slider_current_none	The current value is not displayed. This is the default.
OI_slider_current_ro	The current value is displayed, but can only be changed by moving the slider handle.
OI_slider_current_rw	The current value is displayed and can be changed by typing a new value into the displayed current-value field. The new current value must be terminated by pressing the Return key, which causes the slider handle to be moved to that value. The value can also be changed by moving the slider handle. In the Motif model OI_slider_current_rw does not allow the user to enter a new value from the keyboard; in Motif it is synonymous with OI_slider_current_ro.

n_ticks is the number of tick marks to appear along the slider bar; the default is 0.

tick_typ specifies which tick labels, if any, are to appear. Possible values are:

OI_slider_ticks_none	There are no labels on tick marks. This is the default.
OI_slider_ticks_ends	The beginning and end tick marks are labeled with their numeric values.
OI_slider_ticks_all	All tick marks are labeled with their numeric values.
OI_slider_ticks_ends_custom	Only the beginning and end tick marks are labeled. The labels must be null-terminated strings which you provide in *tick_labels*. There must be two strings in *tick_labels*, one for the beginning label and one for the end label.
OI_slider_all_custom	All tick marks are labeled. The labels must be null-terminated strings which you provide in *tick_labels*. There must be *n_ticks* strings in *tick_labels*.

OI uses the callback function *fnp*—or the user object *objp* and the member callback function *memfnp*—and the argument *argp* to inform your program of changes in the slider handle position. If the user changes the handle position to a given position by entering a number into the value display or by clicking on a position on the bar, the callback function is executed once. If the user moves the handle in a "continuous" manner by dragging the handle along the bar, the callback function may be called numerous times. When the slider detects a SELECT mouse button press (but not a click), it effectively loops until the mouse button is released. The loop is analogous to:

```
while (mouse button depressed) {
    if (handle has moved)
        execute callback.
}
```

The number of times the callback is executed in this case depends on how fast the user moves the handle and how long it takes the callback function to execute and return.

The form of the **cbCtlr1d** callback is as explained in Chapter 28, "OI_ctlr_1d," page 28-4.

Here is an example of both a minimum and a more complex slider creation:

```
    OI_slider               *sp ;
sp = oi_create_slider("my_slider",300,OI_vertical);
sp = oi_create_slider("frosting_dispenser",300,OI_horizontal,100,1,
    &change_frosting,NULL,"Frosting",OI_slider_ends_numeric,NULL,NULL,
    OI_slider_current_ro,3,OI_slider_ticks_all);
```

Example 29-1   Slider Creation Examples

29.5   Base Class Member Functions

You can use all of the member functions of OI_d_tech, OI_display_1d, and OI_ctlr_1d for an OI_slider object. In particular, to access and manipulate handle position, you use OI_ctlr_1d member functions.

29.6   OI_slider Member Functions

29.6.1   Controlling Size

Each time a change occurs in the range of the item the slider controls, you will need to call set_span to reflect the change. The appearance of the slider may change each time you call set_span. For example, suppose the handle is at the half-way point on the slider, the controlled item increases in length once each minute (and you call set_span each time), and the user never moves the handle. As the span increases, the handle moves toward the beginning of the slider, since the user-units it represents become a smaller and smaller fraction of the total range represented.

The *major axis* of a slider is along its length. If it is a horizontal slider, this is the x direction; if it is a vertical slider, this is the y direction. The *minor axis* is along the slider width—the direction orthogonal to the major axis. You can change the length of a slider along its major axis, but not along its minor axis.

The *bar end decoration* of the slider bar is the portion of the bar which extends beyond the tick marks at either end. This does not include the end labels, if any.

You can set the major size of the slider based on either the total size (using the OI_d_tech member function set_size), the total bar size (using set_bar_size), or the active handle range (using set_pixel_range), depending on your needs. Changing any of these three values also changes the value of the other two.

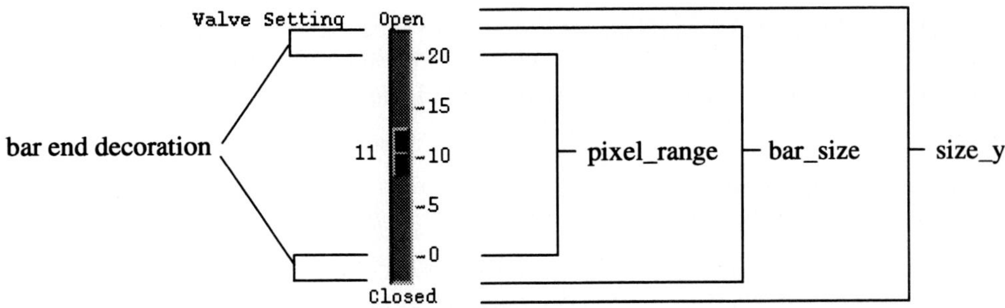

Figure 29-3   Slider Sizes, Motif

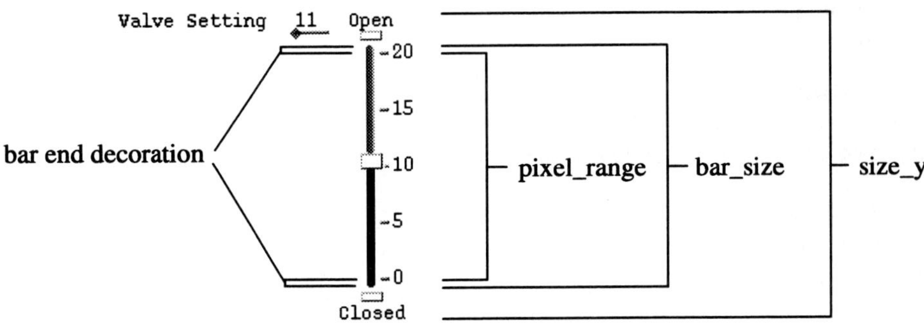

Figure 29-4   Slider Sizes, OPEN LOOK

bar_size   (Member function)

```
OI_number OI_slider::bar_size( )
```

bar_size returns the length, in pixels, of the bar of the slider along its major axis, including the bar end decoration and the handle.

set_bar_size   (Member function)

```
OI_stat OI_slider::set_bar_size(
    OI_number          size)              // bar size in pixels
```

set_bar_size changes the length of the bar of the slider along its major axis to *size* pixels.

pixel_range   (Member function)

```
OI_number OI_slider::pixel_range( )
```

pixel_range returns the length of the portion of the slider bar along which the handle can move, in pixels. This length does not include any bar end decoration. This is the *len* argument in the oi_create_slider function. See Figure 29-3 and Figure 29-4 above.

set_pixel_range   (Member function)

```
OI_stat OI_slider::set_pixel_range(
    OI_number          size)                 // bar size in pixels
```

set_pixel_range changes the length of the slider bar along its major axis. The portion of the bar along which the handle can register values is set to *size* pixels. This is the *len* argument in the oi_create_slider function.

major_space   (Member function)

```
OI_number OI_slider::major_space( )
```

major_space returns the space occupied by the slider along its major axis. This is a short form for:

```
if (orientation( )==OI_horizontal)
    siz = space_x( );
else
    siz = space_y( );
return(siz);
```

minor_space   (Member function)

```
OI_number OI_slider::minor_space( )
```

minor_space returns the space occupied by the slider along its minor axis. This is a short form for:

```
if (orientation( )==OI_horizontal)
    siz = space_y( );
else
    siz = space_x( );
return(siz);
```

set_major_size   (Member function)

```
OI_stat OI_slider::set_major_size(
    OI_number          size)                 // length in pixels
```

set_major_size changes the length in pixels of the slider along its major axis. This is the total length of the slider, including all decoration.

minimum_bar_size (Member function)

```
OI_number OI_slider::minimum_bar_size( )
```

A slider must have enough space for the buttons at either end and for the handle; minimum_bar_size returns the minimum allowable size in pixels along the major axis of the slider.

minimum_size_x (Member function)

```
OI_number OI_slider::minimum_size_x( )
```

minimum_size_x returns the minimum allowable size along the horizontal axis of the slider.

minimum_size_y (Member function)

```
OI_number OI_slider::minimum_size_y( )
```

minimum_size_y returns the minimum allowable size along the vertical axis of the slider.

orientation (Member function)

```
OI_orient OI_slider::orientation( )
```

orientation returns the orientation of the slider, either OI_horizontal or OI_vertical.

29.6.2 Controlling Color

The *active portion* of the slider is the portion of the slider bar from the beginning to the current value—the "mercury" in the bar. The *inactive portion* of the slider is the portion of the slider bar that has no "mercury" in it.

active_pixel (Member function)

```
PIXEL OI_slider::active_pixel( )
```

active_pixel returns the pixel value for the color used to paint the active portion of the slider bar.

set_active_color (Member function)

```
OI_stat OI_slider::set_active_color(
    const char        *color)          // color name

void OI_slider::set_active_color(
    PIXEL             px)              // color pixel
```

set_active_color sets the color to use for the active portion of the slider bar to *color* or *px*, depending on which form is used. You can use the OI_connection member function str_color to convert a string representation of a color to a pixel value.

inactive_pixel   (Member function)

```
PIXEL OI_slider::inactive_pixel( )
```

inactive_pixel returns the pixel value for the color used to paint the inactive portion of the slider bar.

set_inactive_color   (Member function)

```
OI_stat OI_slider::set_inactive_color(
    const char          *color)              // color name

void OI_slider::set_inactive_color(
    PIXEL               px)                  // pixel color
```

set_inactive_color sets the color to use for the inactive portion of the slider bar to *color* or *px*, depending on which form is used. You can use the **OI_connection** member function **str_color** to convert a string representation of a color to a pixel value.

29.7   An OI_slider Programming Example

Program 29-1 shows a slider with which the user can change the size of a box named **siz_box**. **siz_box** is placed within a large box with frame width zero to prevent the laid-out application window from resizing when **siz_box** is resized. This application is shown in Figure 29-5 and Figure 29-6.

```c
#include <OI/oi.H>                              /* Slider.C */
int main (int argc, char** argv)
{
        void handle(OI_ctlr_1d*,void*,OI_scroll_event,long);

        OI_connection           *conp;
        OI_app_window           *wp;
        OI_slider               *sp;
        OI_box                  *bp;
        OI_box                  *siz_bp;

    if (conp = OI_init(&argc,argv,"Slider")) {
        wp = oi_create_app_window(NULL,1,1,"Slider");
        wp->set_layout(OI_layout_column);

        bp = oi_create_box("stationary_box",160,160);
        bp->set_frame_width(0);
        bp->layout_associated_object(wp,20,10,OI_active);

        siz_bp = oi_create_box("siz_box",10,10);
        siz_bp->set_associated_object(bp,1,1,OI_active);
        sp = oi_create_slider("slider",150,OI_vertical,150,10,&handle,siz_bp,
                        "Box Size",OI_slider_ends_strings,"Small","Large",
                        OI_slider_current_rw,8,OI_slider_ticks_all);
        sp->layout_associated_object(wp,10,10,OI_active);

        wp->set_associated_object(wp->root( ),OI_def_loc,OI_def_loc,OI_active);
        OI_begin_interaction( );
        OI_fini( );
    }
}

void handle(OI_ctlr_1d *sp, void *argp, OI_scroll_event, long)
{
        OI_box                  *bp;
        int                     siz;

    bp = (OI_box*)argp;
    siz = (int)sp->handle_loc( );
    bp->set_size(siz,siz);
    return;
}
```

Program 29-1 Controlling an Object with a Slider (Slider.C)

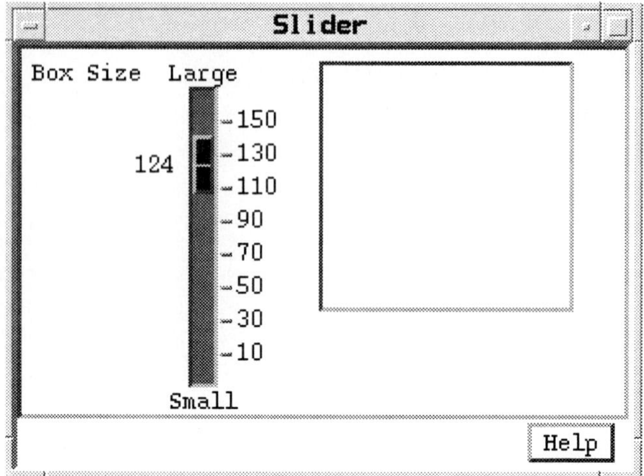

Figure 29-5   Controlling an Object with a Slider, Motif

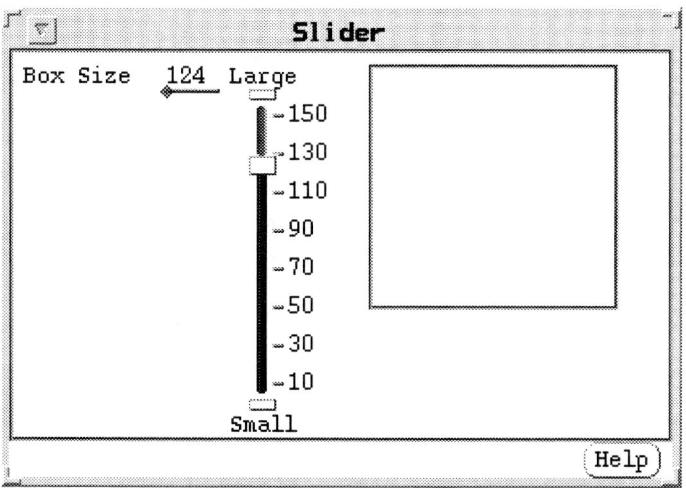

Figure 29-6   Controlling an Object with a Slider, OPEN LOOK

29.8   Resources

All resources from an **OI_slider** object's base classes are available to it. In addition, OI fetches the resources shown in Table 29-1. For more information on resource management, see Chapter 39, "The OI Resource Mechanism."

Table 29-1 OI_slider Resources

Resource	Description	Possible Values	Default Value
barActiveColor	Specifies the color for the active portion of the slider bar.	Valid color	Foreground color
barInactiveColor	Specifies the color for the inactive portion of the slider bar.	Valid color	(No default)
barSize	Specifies the length of the bar including the bar end decoration, in pixels. If you specify barSize, do not specify pixelRange.	Positive integer	(No default)
orientation	Specifies the slider orientation.	horizontal, vertical	(No default)
pixelRange	Specifies the length of the bar along which the handle can move. If you specify pixelRange, do not specify barSize.	Positive integer	(No default)

29.9 Translations

All translations from an OI_slider object's base classes are available to it; in addition, the translations shown in Table 29-2 and Table 29-3 are available to it. See Chapter 40, "The OI Translation Mechanism" for a description of the Event Sequence entries in these tables as well as additional information on how to read these tables.

Table 29-2 OI_slider Default Translations, Motif

Event Sequence				Action Functions Called
~Shift	~Ctrl	~Mod1	<Btn1Down>:	select( )
~Shift	~Ctrl	~Mod1	<Btn1Up>:	release( )
~Shift	Ctrl	~Mod1	<Btn1Down>:	top_or_bottom( )
~Shift	Ctrl	~Mod1	<Btn1Up>:	release( )
~Shift	~Ctrl	~Mod1	<Btn1Motion>:	moved( )
~Shift	~Ctrl	~Mod1	<Btn2Down>:	select( )
~Shift	~Ctrl	~Mod1	<Btn2Up>:	release( )
~Shift	~Ctrl	~Mod1	<Btn2Motion>:	moved( )
~Shift	~Ctrl	~Mod1	<Key>Up:	increment_up( )
~Shift	~Ctrl	~Mod1	<Key>Down:	increment_down( )

Table 29-2 OI_slider Default Translations, Motif

Event Sequence				Action Functions Called
~Shift	~Ctrl	~Mod1	<Key>Left:	increment_left( )
~Shift	~Ctrl	~Mod1	<Key>Right:	increment_right( )
~Shift	Ctrl	~Mod1	<Key>Up:	increment_up(4)
~Shift	Ctrl	~Mod1	<Key>Down:	increment_down(4)
~Shift	Ctrl	~Mod1	<Key>Left:	increment_left(4)
~Shift	Ctrl	~Mod1	<Key>Right:	increment_right(4)
~Shift	~Ctrl	~Mod1	<Key>R7:	top_or_bottom(LEFT)
~Shift	Ctrl	~Mod1	<Key>R7:	top_or_bottom(LEFT)
~Shift	~Ctrl	~Mod1	<Key>Home:	top_or_bottom(LEFT)
~Shift	Ctrl	~Mod1	<Key>Home:	top_or_bottom(LEFT)
~Shift	~Ctrl	~Mod1	<Key>R13:	top_or_bottom(RIGHT)
~Shift	Ctrl	~Mod1	<Key>R13:	top_or_bottom(RIGHT)
~Shift	~Ctrl	~Mod1	<Key>End:	top_or_bottom(RIGHT)
~Shift	Ctrl	~Mod1	<Key>End:	top_or_bottom(RIGHT)
			<FocusIn>:	focus_in( )
			<FocusOut>:	focus_out( )

As you would expect, the "increment_right(4)" in Table 29-2 means "call the function increment_right with an argument of 4." See Table 29-4 for a description of this argument.

Table 29-3 OI_slider Default Translations, OPEN LOOK

Event Sequence				Action Functions Called
~Shift	~Ctrl	~Mod1	<Btn1Down>:	select( )
~Shift	~Ctrl	~Mod1	<Btn1Up>:	release( )
~Shift	~Ctrl	~Mod1	<Btn1Motion>:	moved( )
~Shift	~Ctrl	~Mod1	<Btn2Down>:	select( )
~Shift	~Ctrl	~Mod1	<Btn2Up>:	release( )
~Shift	~Ctrl	~Mod1	<Btn2Motion>:	moved( )
~Shift	~Ctrl	~Mod1	<Key>Up:	increment_up( )
~Shift	~Ctrl	~Mod1	<Key>Down:	increment_down( )
~Shift	~Ctrl	~Mod1	<Key>Left:	increment_left( )
~Shift	~Ctrl	~Mod1	<Key>Right:	increment_right( )
			<Key>Prior:	set_focus_prev_tab( )
Shift	Ctrl		<Key>Tab:	set_focus_prev_tab( )

Table 29-3 OI_slider Default Translations, OPEN LOOK

	Event Sequence	Action Functions Called
Shift	<Key>Tab:	set_focus_prev_tab( )
	<Key>Next:	set_focus_next_tab( )
Ctrl	<Key>Tab:	set_focus_next_tab( )
	<Key>Tab:	set_focus_next_tab( )
	<Key>:	other_key( )

Table 29-4 describes the actions taken by the action functions. Those which are not described in table 28-4 are member functions of one of OI_slider's base classes.

Table 29-4 OI_slider Translation Functions

Function	Action
increment_down(arg)	Moves handle down *arg* user-units. If *arg* is omitted, default to 1. Calls handle motion callback.
increment_left(arg)	Moves handle left *arg* user-units. If *arg* is omitted, default to 1. Calls handle motion callback.
increment_right(arg)	Moves handle right *arg* user-units. If *arg* is omitted, default to 1. Calls handle motion callback.
increment_up(arg)	Moves handle up *arg* user-units. If *arg* is omitted, default to 1. Calls handle motion callback.
focus_in( )	Checks the detail of a FocusIn event and paints the focus frame if appropriate.
focus_out( )	Checks the detail of a FocusOut event and clears the focus frame if appropriate.
moved( )	Processes button motion events. This includes changing the location of the handle on the bar and updating the current value display if the slider has one. Calls handle motion callback if allow_motion_callback is in effect.
other_key( )	Passes the event on to the OI_entry_field child object which is displaying the current value.

Table 29-4 OI_slider Translation Functions

Function	Action
release( )	Ends button event sequence processing. In the OPEN LOOK model, this includes changing the appearance of the handle. Updates the current value display if the slider has one. Calls handle motion callback.
select( )	Starts button event sequence processing. In the OPEN LOOK model, this includes changing the appearance of the handle.
top_or_bottom(arg)	Moves handle to start/end. *arg* may be TOP or BOTTOM or LEFT or RIGHT. If *arg* is omitted, and the event is a button press, the handle moves to the end in the direction of the button press. Calls handle motion callback.

29.10 Callback Functions

Table 29-5 lists the callbacks available for an OI_slider object and the page number of the corresponding explanatory material. In addition, all of the callbacks from an OI_slider object's base classes are available to it.

Table 29-5 OI_slider Callbacks

Callback Type	Callback Typedef	Description	Page Number
cbCtlr1d	OI_ctlr_1d_fnp/memfnp	Handle motion callback function	29-5

Chapter 30
OI_scroll_bar

OI_scroll_bar Functions

OI_scroll_bar Member Functions

The following functions are available to **OI_scroll_bar** objects, but are described in their own chapter.

OI_ctlr_1d Member Functions

OI_display_1d Member Functions

OI_d_tech Member Functions

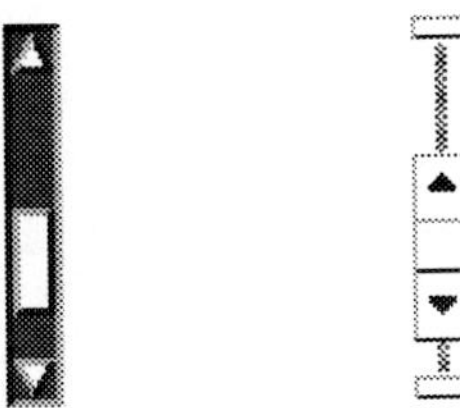

OI_scroll_bar

30.1   Description

An OI_scroll_bar object is used to control the value of a one-dimensional quantity and to represent its current value. Other OI objects, such as OI_scroll_text, OI_scroll_menu, and OI_scroll_box, make use of scroll bars. When you use these other OI objects, you will not need the member functions described here; each of these other objects takes care of programming its own scroll bar. Therefore, unless you are building your own specially-controlled object, you don't need to know how to program an OI_scroll_bar. You may want to read the first three sections of this chapter, however, to become familiar with scroll bar usage.

Functionally, there is very little difference between OI_scroll_bar and OI_slider. However, convention dictates that an OI_scroll_bar object be used when the purpose of the control is to position some other quantity, such as text, in a viewport. An OI_slider object is used for situations not related to positioning within a viewport.

A scroll bar consists of a long bar with a button at each end, and a handle which can slide from one end of the bar to the other. The OPEN LOOK handle has a button at both ends; each button contains an arrow pointing toward the beginning or end of the OI_scroll_bar object. Ordinarily, the scroll bar is displayed next to the object it controls. Figure 30-1 and Figure 30-2 show an example of a scroll bar (which is actually part of an OI_scroll_text), next to the object it controls (the text). In this example, the text is 100 lines long, and only a portion of the text can be seen at one time in the viewport.

The *span* of the scroll bar is the number of arbitrary units represented by the entire length of the scroll bar. The arbitrary units are *user-units*. In Figure 30-1 and Figure 30-2, for the vertical scroll bar, one user-unit is one line of text, and the span of the scroll bar is the number of lines of text in the entire text file, in this case 100. The handle location represents which relative portion of the controlled object is currently in view.

Figure 30-1 and Figure 30-2 each show two scroll bars controlling the viewed text in an OI_scroll_text.

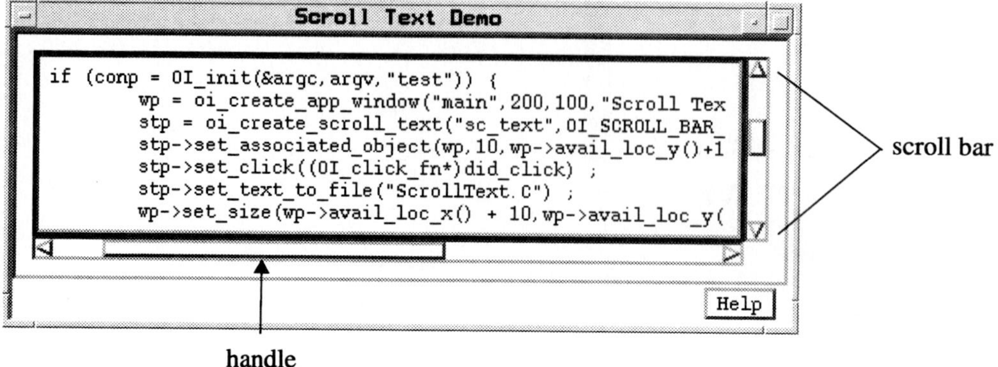

Figure 30-1   Parts of an OI_scroll_bar, Motif

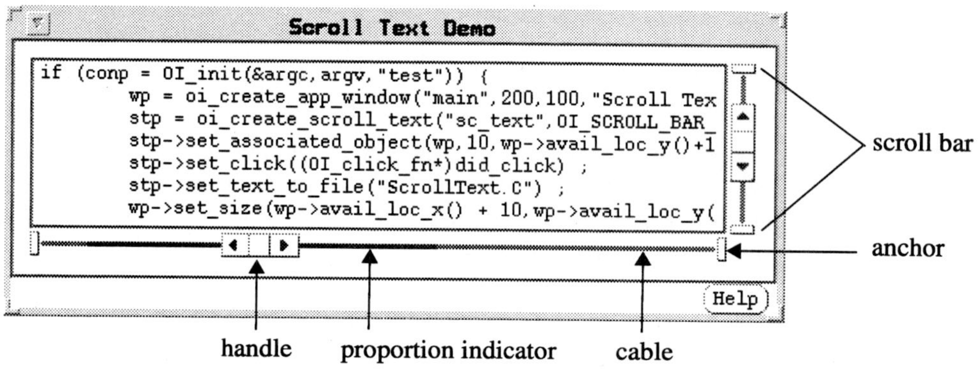

Figure 30-2   Parts of an OI_scroll_bar, OPEN LOOK

In Figure 30-1, the Motif example, the length of the handle represents the portion of the controlled object appearing in the viewport. The handle itself grows and shrinks depending on the relative size of the viewport compared to the total object spanned by the scroll bar. The length of the rest of the scroll bar up to the triangular buttons at either end represents the remainder of the controlled object.

In Figure 30-2, the OPEN LOOK example, there is a *cable* (a line 3 pixels wide) extending from the handle to either end of the scroll bar. The *proportion indicator* is the solid-colored (in this case black) part of the cable closest to the handle. The proportion indicator, along with the handle itself, represents the portion of the controlled object appearing in the viewport. The length of the proportion indicator grows and shrinks depending on the relative size of the viewport compared to the total object spanned by the scroll bar. The stippled portion of the cable represents the remainder of the controlled object. The box at either end of the cable is called the *anchor*.

There is a minimum size for the handle; if the portion of the controlled object appearing in the viewport is so small that the handle size would be less than the minimum, the handle is made the minimum size. In this situation, the entire OPEN LOOK cable is stippled.

You must inform the OI_scroll_bar object of the length of the controlled object that the bar represents by calling the OI_ctlr_1d member function **set_span**, and of the viewport size by calling **set_view**. If the length of the controlled object changes (text is added, for example), you must call **set_span** again to keep the scroll bar current. Similarly, if you change the size of the viewport, you must call **set_view** again to update the scroll bar. Again, these are only concerns when you are controlling the scroll bar directly, not when you are using one supplied by OI as part of an OI_scroll_box, OI_scroll_text, or OI_scroll_menu object.

30.2 Class Tree

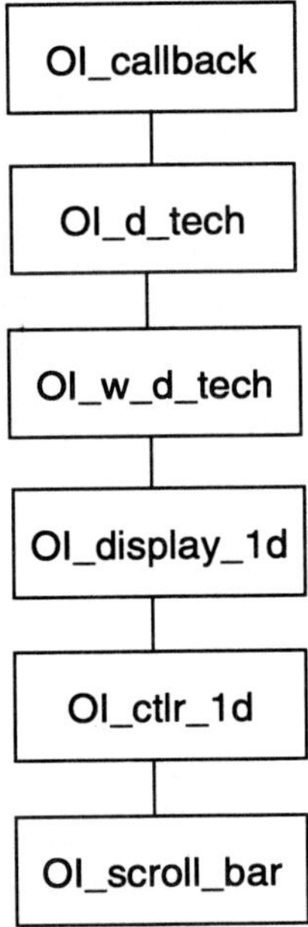

30.3 Runtime Interaction

The default translations for an OI_scroll_bar object provide the following runtime interaction. See Section 30.9, "Translations," on page 30-13, if you need to change these.

Note that if the scroll bar is combined with another type of object to form a new composite object, such as OI_scroll_text, some translations for the composite object may override the default OI_scroll_bar translations.

All the runtime interaction for a scroll bar relates to controlling the object to which the scroll bar is connected. This is the *controlled object*. You may want to envision a particular object, such as the display of text from a file (in which case one *user-unit* could be one line of text), in the following discussions.

If you move the pointer over the middle of the handle, then press the SELECT mouse button, you can drag the handle along the major axis of the scroll bar; the portion of the controlled object appearing in the viewport changes accordingly.

If you click the SELECT mouse button with the pointer on the bar to either side of the handle, the viewed portion of the controlled object moves one complete viewport toward that end. For example, if the scroll bar is controlling a viewport containing lines of text, and the viewport is eight lines tall, this action causes the next (or previous) eight text lines to be displayed in the viewport.

If you position the pointer over one of the arrow buttons at either end of the handle (OPEN LOOK) or the triangular buttons at either end of the scroll bar (Motif), then click the SELECT mouse button, the view of the controlled object moves in the direction indicated by the arrow on the handle-button one user-unit. If instead of clicking, you press the SELECT mouse button here, the view moves in a regularly-timed manner, one user-unit at a time (the view *scrolls*), until you release the mouse button or the handle reaches the end of the scroll bar. The default interval between movements is 200 milliseconds (five times per second).

You can make the handle jump to any portion of the bar by pressing the DRAG (Motif) or ADJUST (OPEN LOOK) mouse button (usually the middle mouse button) while the mouse pointer points to the location on the bar to which you would like the handle to move. Once the handle has jumped to the new position, you can, while still depressing the mouse button, drag the handle along the bar.

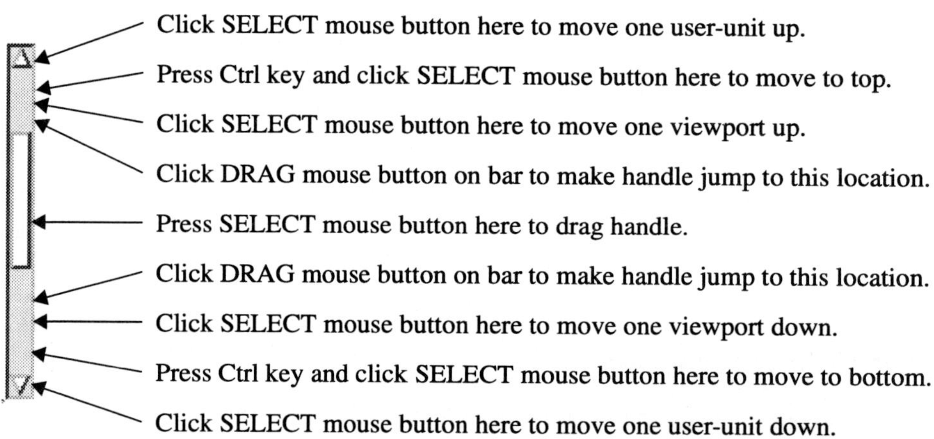

Figure 30-3   OI_scroll_bar Mouse Button User Interaction, Motif

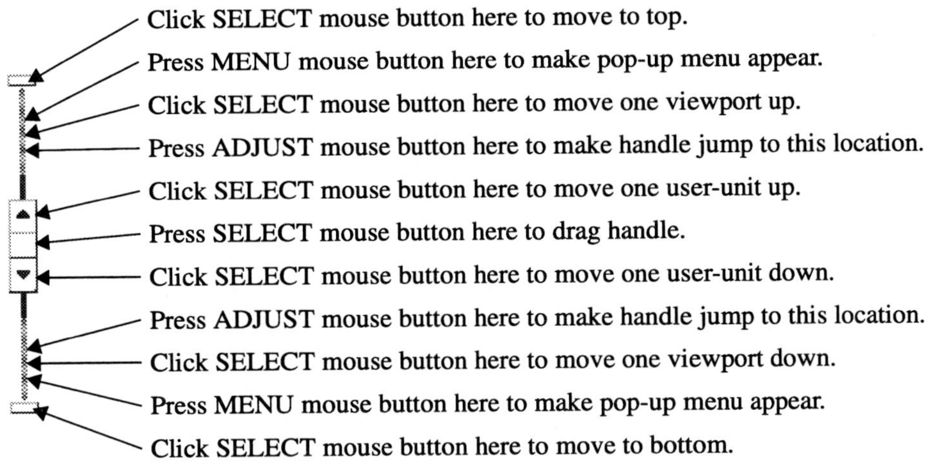

Figure 30-4   OI_scroll_bar Mouse Button User Interaction, OPEN LOOK

You can also control a scroll bar through keyboard interaction if the mouse pointer is within the scroll bar. Striking the Up (Down) Arrow key in a vertical scroll bar moves the scroll bar handle up (down) one user-unit. The Left and Right Arrow keys work in a similar fashion for a horizontal scroll bar.

30.3.1   Runtime Interaction, Motif

In addition to the above user interactions, you can move to either end of the controlled object by positioning the pointer on the button at either end of the scroll bar or in any portion of the bar outside the handle, pressing the Ctrl key, and clicking the SELECT mouse button. Striking an Arrow key in a scroll bar while depressing the Ctrl key moves the scroll bar handle one viewport in the appropriate direction.

30.3.2   Runtime Interaction, OPEN LOOK

In addition to the above user interactions, you can move to either end of the controlled object by clicking the SELECT mouse button on the anchor box at either end of the scroll bar.

If you press or click the MENU mouse button on an OPEN LOOK scroll bar, a menu pops up, as shown in Figure 30-5. In this menu, "Here" means the location of the mouse pointer when you pressed the button. Thus, "Here to Left" means move the contents of the controlled object (in this case, the box with the sine wave) to the left until the portion of the box which intersects a vertical line drawn from the mouse pointer coincides with the left edge of the box. "Left to Here" means move the contents of the controlled object to the right until the portion currently appearing on the left edge is directly above the mouse pointer. "Here to Right" and "Right to Here" perform analogous functions. (If you are using a vertical scroll bar, the menu appears with "Here to Top", "Top to Here",

"Here to Bottom", and "Bottom to Here".) "Previous" means move the contents of the controlled object to whatever position it had previous to the last handle movement.

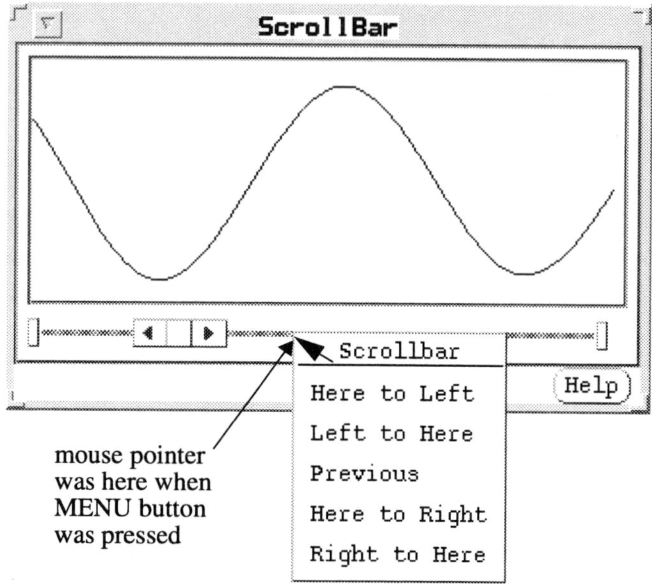

Figure 30-5   Pop-up Menu on OPEN LOOK Scroll Bar

30.4   OI_scroll_bar Creation

oi_create_scroll_bar   (Free-standing function)

```
OI_scroll_bar *oi_create_scroll_bar(
    const char          *namp,          // pointer to object name
    OI_number           len,            // major axis length in pixels
    OI_orient           orient,         // orientation
    OI_ctlr_1d_fnp      fnp=NULL,       // pointer to callback function
    void                *argp=NULL)     // arbitrary argument for fnp

OI_scroll_bar *oi_create_scroll_bar(
    const char          *namp,          // pointer to object name
    OI_number           len,            // major axis length in pixels
    OI_orient           orient,         // orientation
    OI_callback         *objp,          // memfnp's object
    OI_ctlr_1d_memfnp   memfnp,         // pointer to callback member function
    void                *argp=NULL)     // arbitrary argument for memfnp
```

As well as creating an OI_scroll_bar object, the oi_create_scroll_bar functions register a callback function to be invoked whenever the handle of the scroll bar moves. This callback is identified within OI as a cbCtlr1d callback function (see Section 6.18, "Determining and Adding Callbacks; Multiple Callbacks," on page 6-117). If your handle motion function is a member function, when it is invoked it will be called as if you had written *objp->memfnp*. See Section 2.5, "Callbacks and Event-Driven Programming," on page 2-16, for more explanation.

argp is optional, and can be any valid expression that can be cast to a pointer. You can use it to pass additional information to the function *fnp* or *memfnp*.

OI uses the callback function *fnp*—or the user object *objp* and the member callback function *memfnp*—and the argument *argp* to inform your program of changes in the scroll bar handle position. If the user changes the handle to a new position through any of the mouse actions or keyboard actions that result in the scroll bar handle being changed to a specified new position, the callback function is executed once. If the user moves the handle in a "continuous" manner by dragging the handle along the bar, the callback function may be called numerous times. The number of times the callback is executed in this case depends on how fast the user moves the handle and how long it takes the callback function to execute and return.

The form of the callback is as explained in Chapter 28, "OI_ctlr_1d," page 28-4.

30.5   Base Class Member Functions

You can use all of the member functions of OI_d_tech, OI_display_1d and OI_ctlr_1d for an OI_scroll_bar object. In particular, to access and manipulate the handle position, use OI_ctlr_1d member functions, and to change the span, use OI_display_1d member functions.

30.6   OI_scroll_bar Member Functions

30.6.1   Modifying Representation of the Controlled Object

set_view   (Member function)

```
OI_stat OI_scroll_bar::set_view(
    long                    view_span,        // user-units in viewport
    OI_number               pix=0)            // pixels in one user-unit
```

set_view informs the scroll bar of the characteristics of the quantity being controlled with relation to any viewport where it appears. *view_span* is the number of units of the object that fit in the viewport. *pix* is the number of pixels occupied by one unit of the quantity being controlled. *view_span* must use the same user-units as *span* in the OI_ctlr_1d member function **set_span**. For a text object, for example, the units of span could be lines, in which case *pix* would be the number of pixels required for one line. *pix* is important only in cases where the length of the scroll bar matches the length of the viewport (the normal situation). If the scroll bar length does not match the viewport size, *pix* should usually be 1. If you use the default value of 0, OI uses the current value for pixels per user-unit. This is so you can call **set_view** to change the view size without changing or even knowing the unit size.

30.6.2   Controlling Appearance

The *major axis* of a scroll bar is its length. If it is a horizontal scroll bar, this is its size in the x direction; if it is a vertical scroll bar, this is its size in the y direction. The *minor axis* is the scroll bar width—the size in the direction orthogonal to the major axis. You can set and change the major axis size of the scroll bar, but not the minor axis, which is set by OI.

major_space   (Member function)

```
OI_number OI_scroll_bar::major_space( )
```

major_space returns the space occupied by the scroll bar along its major axis. This is a short form for:

```
if (orientation( ) == OI_horizontal)
    siz = space_x( );
else
    siz = space_y( );
return(siz);
```

minor_space   (Member function)

```
OI_number OI_scroll_bar::minor_space( )
```

minor_space returns the space occupied by the scroll bar along its minor axis. This is a short form for:

```
if (orientation( ) == OI_horizontal)
    siz = space_y( );
else
    siz = space_x( );
return(siz);
```

major_size   (Member function)

```
OI_number OI_scroll_bar::major_size( )
```

major_size returns the length of the scroll bar along its major axis. This is a short form for:

```
if (orientation( ) == OI_horizontal)
    siz = size_x( );
else
    siz = size_y( );
return(siz);
```

set_major_size   (Member function)

```
OI_stat OI_scroll_bar::set_major_size(
    OI_number           size)              // length in pixels
```

set_major_size sets the size of the scroll bar along its major axis (its length). The minor axis size cannot be changed.

orientation   (Member function)

```
OI_orient OI_scroll_bar::orientation( )
```

orientation returns the orientation of the scroll bar, either OI_horizontal or OI_vertical.

set_orientation   (Member function)

```
void OI_scroll_bar::set_orientation(
    OI_orient           ornt)            // scroll bar orientation
```

set_orientation sets the orientation of the scroll bar. *ornt* can be either OI_horizontal or OI_vertical.

30.7   An OI_scroll_bar Programming Example

Program 30-1 shows a program which allows the user to control the display of a signal using a scroll bar. The "signal" in this case is a damped sine wave. The results of running the program are shown in Figure 30-6 on page 30-13.

The functions in Program 30-1 perform the following tasks:

- The main program creates a viewport box in which to display the signal and creates a scroll bar to control the display of the signal. The signal curve is set to be 1000 user-units long, and the viewport is 100 user-units long, to fit in a box 300 pixels long. Note that the user-units are completely arbitrary, and could be any units from centimeters to miles. In the call to oi_create_scroll_bar, the function **mov_crv** is registered as the handle motion callback. The main program also registers the function **expose** to be called whenever an Expose or a GraphicsExpose event occurs on the viewport box.

- **disp_curve** displays the curve from horizontal value *start_unit* to value *end_unit*. On the first call to **disp_curve**, the graphics context (GC) is created which will be used on this and all subsequent calls to **disp_curve**. The GC is needed in order to use Xlib functions to draw the signal curve.

- **disp_full_curve** calls **disp_curve** with the appropriate parameters to display the entire portion of the signal that should currently show in the viewport box.

- **disp_partial_curve** is called when only a portion of the curve needs to be redrawn. It moves the portion that need not be redrawn to its new location and calls **disp_curve** with the appropriate parameters to display the portion of the curve that does need to be redrawn.

- **expose** is a callback function which is executed whenever an Expose or a GraphicsExpose event occurs on the viewport box. It redraws the entire portion of the signal that currently appears in the viewport box. Performance of this routine could be improved if it were written to only redraw that portion covered by the Expose event.

  An Expose event occurs when a region is freshly exposed on the screen (for example, if another window partially covers this one, and the other window is moved away). A GraphicsExpose occurs when a graphics operation occurs on the window and part of the region being manipulated (copied or drawn) is not visible (usually because of another window obscuring this one). If another window is covering part of this window and the user moves the scroll bar, part of the curve that must be redrawn will be behind the other window, and a GraphicsExpose event will be generated.

The check for count == 0 in expose assures that the curve is only repainted once. When Expose events are generated, they are generated as rectangular regions, with as many regions as are necessary to get the exposed space covered. Since expose redraws the entire curve regardless of the number of regions, we only want to paint once. count equal to 0 indicates that this is the last Expose event.

- mov_crv is a callback function which is executed whenever the handle on the scroll bar is moved. Depending on the type of handle motion, mov_crv calls disp_partial_curve or disp_full_curve to draw the needed portion of the signal curve.

```
#include <math.h>
#include <OI/oi.H>                              /* ScrollBar.C */
    static GC draw_gc = 0;

int main (int argc, char **argv)
{
            void                   mov_crv(OI_ctlr_1d*,void*,OI_scroll_event,long);
            void                   expose(OI_d_tech*,void*,const XEvent*);
            OI_connection          *conp;
            OI_app_window          *wp;
            OI_scroll_bar          *sbp;
            OI_box                 *bp;

    if (conp = OI_init(&argc,argv,"ScrollBar")) {
        wp = oi_create_app_window("main",1,1,"ScrollBar");
        wp->set_layout(OI_layout_column);
        bp = oi_create_box("curve_box",300,120);
        bp->layout_associated_object(wp,1,1,OI_active);
        sbp = oi_create_scroll_bar("sc_bar",300,OI_horizontal,&mov_crv,(void*)bp);
        sbp->set_span(1000);
        sbp->set_view(100,3);
        sbp->layout_associated_object(wp,1,2,OI_active);
        bp->set_expose(expose,sbp);
        wp->set_associated_object(wp->root( ),OI_def_loc,OI_def_loc,OI_active);
        OI_begin_interaction( );
    }
}
```

```
void disp_curve(OI_ctlr_1d *sbp, long start_unit, long end_unit)
{
        long                    i;
        int                     x1,y1,x2,y2;
        OI_box                  *bp;
        XGCValues               gcv;
        double                  damping;

    bp = (OI_box*)sbp->app_window( )->subobject("curve_box");

    if (!draw_gc) {
        gcv.foreground = bp->fg_pixel( );
        gcv.background = bp->bkg_pixel( );
        draw_gc = XCreateGC(bp->display( ),bp->X_window( ),
                        GCForeground|GCBackground,&gcv);
    }

    x1 = (int)(bp->size_x( )/sbp->view_span( )*(start_unit - sbp->handle_loc( )));
    damping = (sbp->span( ) - 0.1*(9*start_unit+1))/(sbp->span( ) - 1);
    y1 = (int)(damping*sin(double(start_unit)/10.0)*bp->size_y( )/2.0 +
                                        bp->size_y( )/2.0);

    for (i = start_unit + 1 ; i <= end_unit ; i++) {
        x2 = (int)(bp->size_x( )/sbp->view_span( )*(i - sbp->handle_loc( )));
        damping = (sbp->span( ) - 0.1*(9*i+1))/(sbp->span( ) - 1);
        y2 = (int)(damping*sin(double(i)/10.0)*bp->size_y( )/2.0 +
                                        bp->size_y( )/2.0);
        XDrawLine(bp->display( ),bp->X_window( ),draw_gc,x1,y1,x2,y2);
        x1 = x2;
        y1 = y2;
    }
    return;
}

void disp_full_curve(OI_ctlr_1d *sbp)
{
        OI_box                  *bp;

    if (sbp->app_window( )) {
        bp = (OI_box*)sbp->app_window( )->subobject("curve_box");
        XClearWindow(bp->display( ),bp->X_window( ));
        disp_curve(sbp,sbp->handle_loc( ),sbp->handle_loc( )+sbp->view_span( ));
    }
    return;
}
```

```c
void disp_partial_curve(OI_ctlr_1d *sbp, long num_u)
{
        int     num_pix;
        OI_box *bp;

    bp = (OI_box*)sbp->app_window( )->subobject("curve_box");
    if (num_u > 0) {
        num_pix = (int)(bp->size_x( )/sbp->view_span( )*num_u);
        XCopyArea(bp->display( ),bp->X_window( ),bp->X_window( ),draw_gc,
                            num_pix,0,bp->size_x( )-num_pix,bp->size_y( ),0,0);
        XClearArea(bp->display( ),bp->X_window( ),(int)(bp->size_x( ) - num_pix),
                            0,num_pix,bp->size_y( ),False);
        disp_curve(sbp,sbp->handle_loc( ) + sbp->view_span( ) - num_u,
                            sbp->handle_loc( ) + sbp->view_span( ));
    }
    else {
        num_pix = (int)(bp->size_x( )/sbp->view_span( )*(-num_u));
        XCopyArea(bp->display( ),bp->X_window( ),bp->X_window( ),draw_gc,
                            0,0,bp->size_x( )-num_pix,bp->size_y( ),num_pix,0);
        XClearArea(bp->display( ),bp->X_window( ),0,0,
                            num_pix,bp->size_y( ),False);
        disp_curve(sbp,sbp->handle_loc( ),sbp->handle_loc( ) - num_u);
    }
    return;
}

void expose(OI_d_tech*, void *argp, const XEvent *ep)
{
        OI_scroll_bar *sbp;

    sbp = (OI_scroll_bar*)argp;
    if ((ep->type == Expose) && (ep->xexpose.count==0))
        disp_full_curve(sbp);
    else if ((ep->type == GraphicsExpose) && (ep->xgraphicsexpose.count==0))
        disp_full_curve(sbp);
}

void mov_crv(OI_ctlr_1d *sbp, void*, OI_scroll_event typ, long n)
{
    switch (typ) {
     case OI_scroll_unit:
        disp_partial_curve(sbp,n);
        break;
     case OI_scroll_viewport:
     case OI_scroll_extreme:
     case OI_scroll_position:
        disp_full_curve(sbp);
        break;
    }
    return;
}
```

Program 30-1   Using an OI_scroll_bar to Control a Signal Display (ScrollBar.C)

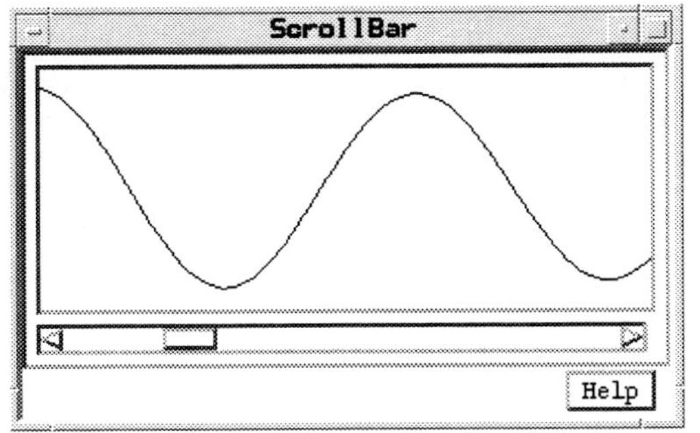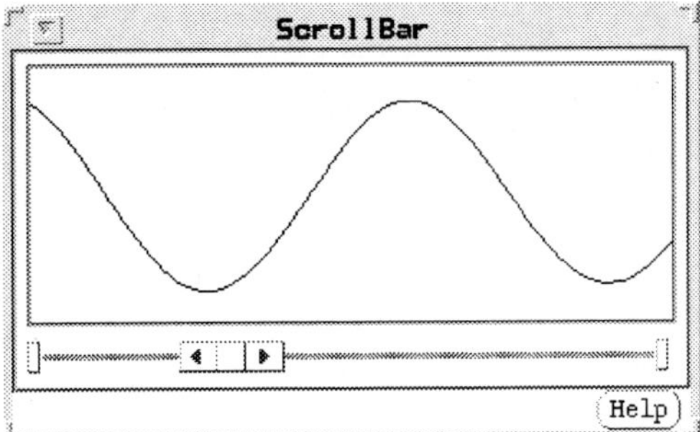

Figure 30-6   Using an OI_scroll_bar to Control a Signal Display

30.8   Resources

All resources from an OI_scroll_bar object's base classes are available to it. In addition, OI fetches the resources shown in Table 30-1. For more information on resource management, see Chapter 39, "The OI Resource Mechanism."

Table 30-1   OI_scroll_bar Resources

Resource	Description	Possible Values	Default Value
orientation	Specifies the scroll bar orientation.	horizontal, vertical	(No default)
pixelRange	Specifies the length of the bar along which the handle can move.	Positive integer	(No default)

30.9   Translations

All translations from an OI_scroll_bar object's base classes are available to it; in addition the translations shown in Table 30-2 and Table 30-3 are available to it. See Chapter 40, "The OI Translation Mechanism" for a description of the Event Sequence entries in these tables as well as additional information on how to read these tables.

Table 30-2   OI_scroll_bar Default Translations, Motif

Event Sequence				Action Functions Called
~Shift	~Ctrl	~Mod1	<Btn1Down>:	select( )

Table 30-2   OI_scroll_bar Default Translations, Motif

	Event Sequence			Action Functions Called
~Shift	Ctrl	~Mod1	<Btn1Down>:	top_or_bottom( )
~Shift	~Ctrl	~Mod1	<Btn2Down>:	select( )
~Shift	~Ctrl	~Mod1	<BtnUp>:	release( )
~Shift	~Ctrl	~Mod1	<BtnMotion>:	moved( )
~Shift	~Ctrl	~Mod1	<Key>Up:	increment_up( )
~Shift	~Ctrl	~Mod1	<Key>Down:	increment_down( )
~Shift	~Ctrl	~Mod1	<Key>Left:	increment_left( )
~Shift	~Ctrl	~Mod1	<Key>Right:	increment_right( )
~Shift	Ctrl	~Mod1	<Key>Up:	page_up( )
~Shift	Ctrl	~Mod1	<Key>Down:	page_down( )
~Shift	Ctrl	~Mod1	<Key>Left:	page_left( )
~Shift	Ctrl	~Mod1	<Key>Right:	page_right( )
~Shift	~Ctrl	~Mod1	<Key>R9:	page_up( )
~Shift	Ctrl	~Mod1	<Key>R9:	page_left( )
~Shift	~Ctrl	~Mod1	<Key>R15:	page_down( )
~Shift	Ctrl	~Mod1	<Key>R15:	page_right( )
~Shift	~Ctrl	~Mod1	<Key>R7:	top_or_bottom(LEFT)
~Shift	Ctrl	~Mod1	<Key>R7:	top_or_bottom(LEFT)
~Shift	~Ctrl	~Mod1	<Key>Home:	top_or_bottom(LEFT)
~Shift	Ctrl	~Mod1	<Key>Home:	top_or_bottom(LEFT)
~Shift	~Ctrl	~Mod1	<Key>R13:	top_or_bottom(RIGHT)
~Shift	Ctrl	~Mod1	<Key>R13:	top_or_bottom(RIGHT)
~Shift	~Ctrl	~Mod1	<Key>End:	top_or_bottom(RIGHT)
~Shift	Ctrl	~Mod1	<Key>End:	top_or_bottom(RIGHT)
			<EnterNotify>	enter( )
			<LeaveNotify>	leave( )

Table 30-3   OI_scroll_bar Default Translations, OPEN LOOK

	Event Sequence			Action Functions Called
~Shift	~Ctrl	~Mod1	<Btn1Down>:	select( )
~Shift	~Ctrl	~Mod1	<Btn2Down>:	select( )
~Shift	~Ctrl	~Mod1	<Btn3Down>:	popup( )
~Shift	~Ctrl	~Mod1	<BtnUp>:	release( )

Table 30-3 OI_scroll_bar Default Translations, OPEN LOOK

Event Sequence				Action Functions Called
~Shift	~Ctrl	~Mod1	<BtnMotion>:	moved( )
~Shift	~Ctrl	~Mod1	<Key>Up:	increment_up( )
~Shift	~Ctrl	~Mod1	<Key>Down:	increment_down( )
~Shift	~Ctrl	~Mod1	<Key>Left:	increment_left( )
~Shift	~Ctrl	~Mod1	<Key>Right:	increment_right( )
~Shift	Ctrl	~Mod1	<Key>Up:	page_up( )
~Shift	Ctrl	~Mod1	<Key>Down:	page_down( )
~Shift	~Ctrl	~Mod1	<Key>F35:	page_down( )
~Shift	Ctrl	~Mod1	<Key>Right:	page_right( )
~Shift	Ctrl	~Mod1	<Key>Left:	page_left( )
~Shift	~Ctrl	~Mod1	<Key>F29:	page_up( )
			<EnterNotify>	enter( )
			<LeaveNotify>	leave( )

Table 30-4 describes the actions taken by the action functions. Each action function is an OI_scroll_bar member function and has the same argument list:

Table 30-4 OI_scroll_bar Translation Functions

Function	Action
enter( )	Activates the scroll bar when it is used to control a pop-up or pull-down scroll menu. If the pointer moves into the beginning-of-file or end-of-file region, the scroll bar begins scrolling in that direction.
increment_down(arg)	Moves handle down *arg* user-units. If *arg* is omitted, uses 1. Calls handle motion callback.
increment_left(arg)	Moves handle left *arg* user-units. If *arg* is omitted, uses 1. Calls handle motion callback.
increment_right(arg)	Moves handle right *arg* user-units. If *arg* is omitted, uses 1. Calls handle motion callback.
increment_up(arg)	Moves handle up *arg* user-units. If *arg* is omitted, uses 1. Calls handle motion callback.
leave( )	Deactivates the scroll bar.

Table 30-4 OI_scroll_bar Translation Functions

Function	Action
moved( )	Processes button motion events. This includes changing the location of the handle on the bar. Calls handle motion callback if allow_motion_-callback is in effect.
page_down( )	Moves handle down one viewport. Calls handle motion callback.
page_left( )	Moves handle left one viewport. Calls handle motion callback.
page_right( )	Moves handle right one viewport. Calls handle motion callback.
page_up( )	Moves handle up one viewport. Calls handle motion callback.
release( )	Ends button event sequence processing. In the OPEN LOOK model, this includes changing the appearance of the handle. Calls handle motion callback.
select( )	Starts button event sequence processing. In the OPEN LOOK model, this includes changing the appearance of the handle.
top_or_bottom(arg)	Moves handle to start/end. *arg* can be TOP or BOTTOM or LEFT or RIGHT. If *arg* is omitted, and the event is a button press, the handle moves to the end in the direction of the button press. Calls handle motion callback.

30.10 Callback Functions

Table 30-5 lists the callbacks available for an OI_scroll_bar object and the page number where the callback is documented. In addition, all of the callbacks from an OI_scroll_bar object's base classes are available to it. See Section 6.18, "Determining and Adding Callbacks; Multiple Callbacks," on page 6-117 for additional information about manipulating callbacks.

Table 30-5 OI_scroll_bar Callbacks

Callback Type	Callback Typedef		Page Number
cbCtlr1d	OI_ctlr_1d_fnp/memfnp	Scroll callback function	30-6

Chapter 31
OI_base_text and OI_multi_text

OI_multi_text Functions

OI_base_text Member Functions

The following functions are available to an **OI_base_text** object, but are described in their own chapter.

OI_d_tech Member Functions

```
This is a sample of an OI_multi_text object.

The text may be read only, or read-write.

You can move the insertion cursor with the arrow k
on your keyboard. You can scroll text up or down,
or right, to view text that is not currently withi
viewport.

You can cut and paste text using the mouse and the
```

OI_base_text and OI_multi_text

31.1 Description

The classes OI_base_text and OI_multi_text are very closely related. The sole purpose of the OI_base_text class is to insulate you from needing to know whether you are dealing with an OI_multi_text object or an OI_scroll_text object—both are derived from OI_base_text, and both have much functionality in common. OI_base_text defines the interface which is identical for both OI_multi_text and OI_scroll_text. This arrangement allows you to write procedures which manipulate an object either of type OI_multi_text or of type OI_scroll_text without having to determine which of the two types you have.

Almost every discussion in this chapter can refer equally well to OI_multi_text or OI_base_text.

An OI_multi_text object is a viewport onto a an underlying text structure consisting of zero or more lines. You can control the size of the viewport and manipulate the text displayed in the text object. If the text in the underlying child text structure is longer in either direction than the viewport, the user can control the portion of text appearing in the viewport. If you set the OI_multi_text object to be read only, the user can not enter and modify text.

When you or the user enters text into an OI_multi_text object, if the entered text is longer than the viewport—either vertically or horizontally—then part of it does not appear on the screen. The user can position the text to view the desired portion. An OI_multi_text object has default translations for various keys to provide convenient manipulation features. In addition, an OI_multi_text object supports text copy and paste using the mouse and keyboard.

By default, each input character is validated by an OI default character validation callback function before the character is inserted into the line. The default validation check requires that characters be printable ISO Latin-1 characters. (Note that the set of printable ASCII characters is a subset of the set of printable ISO Latin-1 characters.) Invalid characters are not inserted, the bell sounds, and a message is sent to the help line of the nearest OI_app_window ancestor. If you require different validation, you can write a per-character validation callback function and register it using set_char_check. If you register your own per-character validation callback function, it may either totally replace, or be in addition to, the default character check callback function.

By default, no end-of-line validation is done when the user strikes the Return key. If you require validation of the entire line, or need to perform additional tasks upon the completion of the entry, you can write an end-of-line validation callback function and register it using set_entry_check.

You can register a callback routine to be executed when the user clicks a mouse button anywhere inside the OI_multi_text object's viewport.

If you create another object as a child of an OI_multi_text object (for example, an OI_glyph to illustrate the text), and you want this subobject to maintain its position relative to the text when the text is moved by the user, you must call the OI_d_tech member function allow_track for the subobject before you parent it to the OI_multi_text object. If you do not call allow_track for the subobject, it maintains its position in the viewport, regardless of the motion of the text.

If the text that will appear in an object is likely to be of such a size that it will all fit within the viewport, you probably should put it in an OI_multi_text object. If, however, the text has the potential to be large enough that it will not all be visible, consider using an OI_scroll_text instead.

31.2 Class Tree

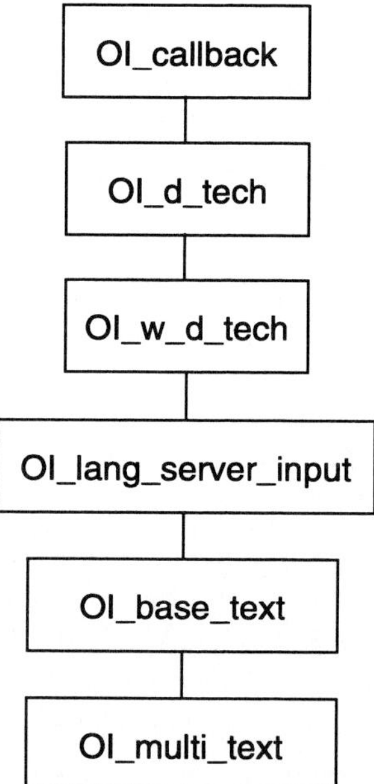

31.3 Runtime Interaction

The default translations for an OI_multi_text object provide the following runtime interaction. See Section 31.9, "Translations," on page 31-37, if you need to change these.

During text entry, a *cursor* appears, showing the point of entry in the text. This cursor is separate and different from the mouse pointer.

If you position the mouse pointer over the text area and click the SELECT mouse button, the cursor is positioned at the character under the pointer. In addition, any click callback function that has been registered for the OI_multi_text object is executed.

31.3.1   Scrolled Text Entry

When the number of characters on a line exceeds the number of characters displayed in the text entry area, the text entry area can be scrolled. During text entry, if the cursor reaches the right side of the text entry area, and wordwrap is not set, or the right margin is beyond the right side of the text entry are, the characters scroll to the left as you enter new characters. If you press the Right or Left Arrow key repeatedly until the cursor reaches the left or right side of the text area, the characters also scroll left or right, allowing you to view in succession each character in the text. Similarly, using the Up or Down Arrow keys scrolls the text vertically.

31.3.2   Entering Text

When you type a character, it is first validated, then it appears in the text area. If the cursor is not at the end of the text but is on an existing character (that is, in the middle of the text somewhere), and if the OI_base_text object is in *insert* mode, any newly-typed character appears at the cursor location, and existing characters move to the right to accommodate the new character. If the OI_base_text object is in *replace* mode, any newly-typed character replaces the existing character at the cursor location. Any character input at the end of the line is appended to the line. The initial character entry mode is *insert*.

An OI_base_text object normally has some default translations installed for it which cause certain key presses to perform specific actions. The default translations differ depending on which model you are running. See Table 31-3 and Table 31-4 on page 31-38 and 31-40. You can remap these keys to suit individual preferences.

31.3.3   Text Selection; Cut and Paste

An OI_base_text object supports text copy and paste using the mouse and keyboard. To select text, that is, copy it to the PRIMARY selection buffer, move the mouse pointer to the first character desired, press the SELECT button, and drag the mouse pointer across the text. The selected characters become highlighted. Release the mouse button when the desired characters are highlighted. You can also select text by clicking the SELECT mouse button if the mouse pointer is over the OI_base_text object. A double click selects the word under the pointer (a word is delimited by blanks, tabs, or end-of-line). A triple click selects the entire line under the pointer. Four clicks selects a paragraph (paragraph delimiters are beginning/end of file, an empty line, or a line with only whitespace). Five clicks selects the entire text.

Each click of the mouse button must be separated by less than clickDelta milliseconds to be considered a multiple click. clickDelta is an OI_connection resource, which defaults to 500.

To paste previously selected text into an **OI_base_text** object, position the pointer at the desired position. If you are running in Motif mode, click the DRAG (usually the middle) mouse button. The text is inserted at the current **OI_base_text** cursor position. If you are running in OPEN LOOK mode, strike COPY key (usually L6) followed by the PASTE key (usually L8). The COPY key copies the previously selected text to the clipboard, and the PASTE key inserts the clipboard text at the current cursor position.

31.3.4   Wordwrap

If you set wordwrap on, when you reach the right margin as you are entering text, the text automatically breaks at any white space and begins again at the next line. If wordwrap is off (the default), you must strike the Return key to cause the text to start on the next line. Unless specifically set, the right margin defaults to the width of the text entry area.

31.4   OI_multi_text Creation

oi_create_multi_text   (Free-standing function)

```
OI_multi_text *oi_create_multi_text(
    const char          *namp,          // pointer to object name
    OI_number           view_lines,     // number of lines possible in viewport
    OI_number           view_chars,     // number of characters possible in viewport
    OI_number           max_lines=0,    // initial max number of lines
    OI_number           max_chars=0)    // initial max number of characters per line
```

The **OI_multi_text** object's viewport is sized to accommodate *view_lines* lines of text in height and *view_chars* characters of text in width. If you change the font (using **OI_d_tech** member functions), the text object and the viewport are resized accordingly.

The object is initially capable of holding a total of *max_lines* and *max_chars* characters per line. If you omit these parameters or set them to zero, they default to the corresponding *view_lines* and *view_chars* values. If you insert new lines using **insert_scroll_line**, only a total of *max_lines* lines are kept. However if you insert new lines using **insert_line**, **set_text**, or **set_text_to_file**, *max_lines* grows as needed so the entire text is always available. In contrast, *max_chars* never changes (unless you call the function **set_cols**)—it is merely a "hint" to OI as to what buffer size to make for a line. If more than *max_chars* characters are entered in a line, they are always retained (as long as the line is retained), but this does not affect the value of *max_chars*—that is, it is possible that at some point the actual number of characters in the line may be greater than *max_chars*.

31.5   Base Class Member Functions

You can use all of the member functions of **OI_d_tech** for an **OI_base_text** object, and all the member functions of **OI_d_tech** and **OI_base_text** for an **OI_multi_text** object.

31.5.1   Click Functions

As mentioned above, an **OI_multi_text** object can respond to clicks of the SELECT mouse button if the mouse pointer is over the **OI_multi_text** object. By default, clicking on the text causes specified portions of the text to be copied to the PRIMARY buffer. You can also register a click callback function for the object; when the user clicks on the object (using any mouse button), the callback function (which you write yourself) is executed, after the default selection is performed.

set_click   (Member function)

```
void OI_base_text::set_click(
    OI_click_fnp        fnp,              // pointer to callback function
    void               *argp=NULL)        // arbitrary argument for fnp


void OI_mbase_text::set_click(
    OI_callback        *objp,             // memfnp's object
    OI_click_memfnp     memfnp,           // pointer to callback member function
    void               *argp=NULL)        // arbitrary argument for memfnp
```

The **set_click** functions register a callback function to be invoked whenever the user clicks a mouse button one or more times on an **OI_multi_text** object. This callback is identified within OI as a **cbClick** callback function (see Section 6.18, "Determining and Adding Callbacks; Multiple Callbacks," on page 6-117). If your click function is a member function, when it is invoked it will be called as if you had written *objp->memfnp*. See Section 2.5, "Callbacks and Event-Driven Programming," on page 2-16, for more explanation.

argp is optional, and can be any valid expression that can be cast to a pointer. You can use it to pass additional information to the function *fnp* or *memfnp*.

The button press and release must be separated by no more than **clickDelta** milliseconds for a press/release sequence to be considered a click. For multiple clicks, a release and subsequent press must also be separated by no more than **clickDelta** milliseconds. **clickDelta** is an **OI_connection** resource, which defaults to 500.

Writing the Click Callback Function

If the **cbClick** callback function is not a member function, write it in this form:

```
void fn(
        OI_d_tech   *oi_objp,       // pointer to object clicked on
        void        *argp,          // arbitrary argument
        OI_number   n_clicks,       // number of clicks
        OI_number   btn,            // mouse button number clicked
        OI_number   mod,            // modifier bits on at click time
        OI_number   lin,            // line number where click occurred
        OI_number   chr)            // character number where click occurred
```

and if the **cbClick** callback function is a member function, write it in this form:

```
void obj_class::memfn(
    OI_d_tech    *oi_objp,      // pointer to object clicked on
    void         *argp,         // arbitrary argument
    OI_number    n_clicks,      // number of clicks
    OI_number    btn,           // mouse button number clicked
    OI_number    mod,           // modifier bits on at click time
    OI_number    lin,           // line number where click occurred
    OI_number    chr)           // character number where click occurred
```

where *obj_class* is the class of the object whose member function is *memfn*.

When your callback function is invoked, *argp* will be the argument specified in the **set_click** call.

lin and *chr* will be the line number and character number where the click occurred. The line number returned is relative to the first line in the OI_multi_text object, not relative to the viewport. Lines are numbered starting with 0 at the top of the text, and characters are numbered starting with 0 at the beginning of each line. If the click occurred to the right of the last character in a line, *chr* will be the number of the last character plus 1. If the click occurred below any line in the text, *lin* will be the number of the last line plus 1 and *chr* will be 0.

mod will contain the modifier bits on at click time. These will be zero unless the user holds down one of the modifier keys on the keyboard at the time of the mouse click. *mod* may have any combination (0 or more) of the following values, combined with a bitwise inclusive **or**.

OI_mod_shift	Shift key down during click.
OI_mod_lock	Lock key down during click.
OI_mod_control	Control key down during click.
OI_mod_meta	Mod1 key down during click.

When more than one click occurs, the callback function will be invoked once for each click. For example, a double click will cause the function to be called first with *n_clicks*=1, then with *n_clicks*=2. If your application is performing a different operation depending on the number of clicks, the operations for a greater number of clicks should be compatible with those for fewer clicks. For example, two clicks normally means select a word, and three clicks means select the entire line.

31.6 OI_base_text Member Functions

All the functions defined here are OI_base_text member functions; OI_multi_text has no additional member functions.

In all of the OI_base_text member functions referencing line or character numbers, the lines are numbered starting at zero at the top of the text, and the characters in each line are numbered starting at zero at the left edge of the text. Unless otherwise specified, these numbers are relative to the entire text object, not relative to what can be seen on the screen in the viewport.

31.6.1 Loading the OI_base_text with Text

You can use the functions below to load an **OI_base_text** object with text. Except for the append_* functions, they remove all existing text (if any exists) before adding any new text.

In each of the functions that add text to the object, if the number of characters in the line after the insertion will be greater than *max_chars*, the text is inserted, but *max_chars* does not change. Instead, the actual number of characters in the line is greater than *max_chars*. In other words, max_chars is used by OI internally as a hint and does not actually reflect the maximum number of characters in any one line.

When specifying a file name, you may use either an absolute file path and name or a relative one.

current_file   (Member function)

```
char *OI_base_text::current_file( )
```

current_file returns the file name parameter of the last **set_text_to_file** call made with a char* parameter. It returns NULL if you have not made such a call to **set_text_to_file**, or if you have made an intervening call to any of the following functions:

  set_text_to_file with a FILE* parameter
  set_text_to_string
  set_text
  clear_text

set_text_to_file   (Member function)

```
OI_stat OI_base_text::set_text_to_file(
    const char          *namp)          // file name

OI_stat OI_base_text::set_text_to_file(
    FILE                *filp)          // file descriptor
```

set_text_to_file clears the contents of the **OI_base_text** object and fills it with the contents of the file with name *namp* or the file with descriptor *filp*. If you use the second form, OI assumes you have opened *filp*, and **set_text_to_file** does not close it. If wordwrap is on (you have called **allow_wrap** or the resource **wrap** is **true**), **set_text_to_file** wraps the text after reading it in, and before displaying it.

set_text_to_file returns **OI_ok** if the text was loaded correctly, **OI_no_file** if the program could not find a file with name *namp*, and **OI_no_mem** if there was not enough memory to load the file.

set_text_to_string   (Member function)

```
OI_stat OI_base_text::set_text_to_string(
    const char          *strp)                  // text string
```

set_text_to_string clears the contents of the **OI_base_text** object and fills it with the text in *strp*. If wordwrap is on (you have called **allow_wrap** or the resource **wrap** is true), **set_text_to_string** wraps the text after reading it in, and before displaying it.

set_text_to_string returns **OI_ok** if the string was loaded correctly, and **OI_no_mem** if there was not enough memory to load the string.

set_text   (Member function)

```
OI_stat OI_base_text::set_text(
    OI_text_fnp          fnp)                    // pointer to text function


OI_stat OI_base_text::set_text(
    OI_callback          *objp,                  // memfnp's object
    OI_text_memfnp       memfnp)                 // pointer to text member function
```

The **set_text** functions call the text function (*fnp* or *memfnp*) to supply text for the **OI_base_text** object. At the time you call **set_text**, it clears the **OI_base_text** object, then calls the text function repeatedly to get successive lines of text to fill the object, until the text function returns a NULL.

memfnp points to a member function for the object pointed to by *objp*. If your text function is a member function, when it is invoked it will be called as if you had written *objp->memfnp*. See Section 2.5, "Callbacks and Event-Driven Programming," on page 2-16, for more explanation.

Writing the Text Function

If the text function is not a member function, write it in this form:

```
char  fn( )
```

and if the text function is a member function, write it in this form:

```
char  obj_class::memfn( )
```

where *obj_class* is the class of the object whose member function is *memfn*.

Write this function to return a pointer to the next line of text you want added to the **OI_base_text** object. OI copies this string into the object. The text returned should not contain any control characters other than tabs, although any newline characters are considered to be string terminators, and they are treated the same way as '\0' characters. Any carriage returns are regarded as invalid characters and produce a warning message, but they do not affect the displayed text.

When there are no more lines to add to the object, your function should return NULL.

append_file   (Member function)

```
OI_stat OI_base_text::append_file(
    const char          *namp,          // file name
    OI_bool             scrl=OI_no)     // text object sizing flag


OI_stat OI_base_text::append_file(
    FILE*               filp,           // file descriptor
    OI_bool             scrl=OI_no)     // text object sizing flag
```

append_file appends lines of text from either the file named *namp*, or the FILE descriptor *filp*, after the last line in the object. If you use the second form, OI assumes you have opened *filp*, and **append_file** does not close it. If you set *scrl* to **OI_no**, (the default), if there will be more than *max_lines* lines of text after appending the text, **max_lines** grows a sufficient amount to encompass all the lines of text. If you set *scrl* to **OI_yes**, if the total number of lines after the insertion is greater than *max_lines*, the first line(s) from the text object are discarded, and *max_lines* does not change.

append_string   (Member function)

```
OI_stat OI_base_text::append_string(
    const char          *str,           // text to append
    OI_bool             scrl=OI_no)     // text object sizing flag
```

append_string appends lines of text from the string *str* after the last line in the object. *scrl* is identical in function to the *scrl* parameter for **append_file**.

31.6.2   Writing Text to a File

output_text   (Member function)

```
OI_stat OI_base_text::output_text(
    const char          *namp,          // file name
    OI_bool             apnd=OI_no)     // append to file?


OI_stat OI_base_text::output_text(
    FILE                *filp,          // file descriptor
    OI_bool             apnd=OI_no)     // append to file?
```

output_text writes all lines of text from the base text object to the file named *namp* or the file descriptor *filp*.

If you use the first form, and if you set *apnd* to **OI_yes**, *namp* is opened for append, and lines are appended to the current contents of the file; if you omit *apnd* or set it to **OI_no**, *namp* is opened for write, and lines are written to the file.

If you use the second form, OI assumes you have opened *filp*, and **output_text** does not close it. Setting *apnd* to **OI_yes** causes lines to be written to the end of *filp*, and omitting *apnd* or setting it to **OI_no** causes lines to be written at the current location in *filp*.

31.6.3   Finding Text

The functions below allow you to search for a string in an **OI_base_text** object, or get a pointer to
the actual text for any line.

find_string   (Member function)

```
OI_bool OI_base_text::find_string(
    OI_number              *linp,              // pointer to line number
    OI_number              *chrp,              // pointer to character number
    const char             *stringp,           // pointer to search string
    OI_bool                wrap=OI_no,         // wrap-around search flag
    OI_bool                reverse=OI_no)      // enable backward searching?
```

find_string searches for the string *stringp* starting at line *linp* and character *chrp*. If the string
is found, *linp* and *chrp* are backfilled with its line number and the character position of the first
character in *stringp*. The first line is numbered 0; the first character (in every line) is numbered
0. If *wrap* is **OI_yes**, the search wraps around from the last line to the first, forcing a search of
all lines. Otherwise, the search terminates at the end of the text in the object. If you omit *wrap*,
it defaults to **OI_no**. If *reverse* is **OI_yes**, **find_string** starts at *linep* and character *chrp* and
searches toward the beginning. If *reverse* is **OI_no** (the default), the search is in the forward
direction.

find_string returns **OI_yes** if successful, otherwise it returns **OI_no**. Note that if *stringp* exists
in the text, but not all on one line, **find_string** fails.

text   (Member function)

```
char *OI_base_text::text(
    OI_number              lineno)             // line number
```

text returns a pointer to the text string for the line at line number *lineno*. The string is
null-terminated. The returned value is a pointer to an internal static buffer which is overwritten
with each call to text. You should copy the returned value (using strdup) if you are planning to
save it for later use.

31.6.4   Modifying Text

Use these functions to modify a portion of the text in the **OI_base_text** object or check to see if the
text has been modified. Remember that the top-most line in the object is line number 0, and the
left-most character in any line is character number 0.

In each of the functions that add text to the object or replace characters in the object, if the number
of characters in the line after the insertion will be greater than *max_chars*, the character is inserted,
but *max_chars* does not change. Instead, the actual number of characters in the line is greater than
max_chars.

Unless noted otherwise, if there are more than *max_lines* lines of text in any text to be added,
max_lines grows an arbitrary amount, but always a sufficient amount to encompass all the lines of
text. In other words, *max_lines* is never less than the actual number of lines in the object.

clear_text   (Member function)

```
void OI_base_text::clear_text( )
```

clear_text clears all the text from the object.

delete_char   (Member function)

```
OI_stat OI_base_text::delete_char(
    OI_number          lineno,            // line number
    OI_number          charno)            // character number
```

delete_char deletes the single character in character position *charno* in line *lineno*. If wrap is on, and the deletion allows text compression onto the preceding line or from the following line, the text will be re-wrapped.

delete_chars   (Member function)

```
OI_stat OI_base_text::delete_chars(
    OI_number          lineno,            // line number
    OI_number          startno,           // starting character number
    OI_number          n_chars)           // number of characters to delete
```

delete_chars deletes *n_chars* characters from line number *lineno* starting with character number *startno*. If *n_chars* is greater than the number of characters in the line past *startno*, all the characters in line *lineno* from *startno* to the end of the line are deleted. If wrap is on, and the deletion allows text compression onto the preceding line or from the following line, the text will be re-wrapped.

delete_line   (Member function)

```
OI_stat OI_base_text::delete_line(
    OI_number          lineno)            // line number
```

delete_line deletes the line at line number *lineno*. If wrap is on, and the deletion allows text compression onto the preceding line or from the following line, the text will be re-wrapped.

delete_lines   (Member function)

```
OI_stat OI_base_text::delete_lines(
    OI_number          lineno,            // line number
    OI_number          n_lines)           // number of lines to delete
```

delete_lines deletes *n_lines* lines starting with the line at line number *lineno*. If wrap is on, and the deletion allows text compression onto the preceding line or from the following line, the text will be re-wrapped.

insert_char   (Member function)

```
OI_stat OI_base_text::insert_char(
    OI_number              lineno,              // line number
    OI_number              charno,              // character number
    char                   c,                   // character to insert
    OI_number              *newlinno=NULL,      // pointer to new line number
    OI_number              *newchrno=NULL)      // pointer to new character number
```

insert_char inserts the character *c* before the character in position *charno*, in line number *lineno*. If *charno* is -1, insert_char inserts *c* after the last character in line number *lineno*. If wrap is on, and the insertion allows text compression onto the preceding line (such as an insertion of a blank in the middle of a word, thus making two shorter words), or causes the line to exceed the right margin, the text will be re-wrapped. If *newlinno* and *newchrno* are not NULL, *newlinno* and *newchrno* are backfilled with the new line and character position of the character following *c* after *c* has been inserted. *newlinno* is always the same number as *lineno*, unless *c* is a newline character or the line was wrapped.

insert_chars   (Member function)

```
OI_stat OI_base_text::insert_chars(
    OI_number              lineno,              // line number
    OI_number              charno,              // character number
    OI_number              n_chars,             // number of characters to insert
    const char             *textp,              // pointer to text to insert
    OI_number              *newlinno=NULL,      // pointer to new line number
    OI_number              *newchrno=NULL)      // pointer to new character number
```

insert_chars inserts *n_chars* characters of text *textp* before the character in position *charno*, in line number *lineno*. If *charno* is -1, insert_chars inserts *textp* after the last character in line number *lineno*. *textp* need not be null-terminated. A newline character in the text causes a new line to be generated as for insert_line. Include no other control characters in the text except tab. If wrap is on, and the insertion allows text compression onto the preceding line (such as an insertion of a blank in the middle of a word, thus making two shorter words), or causes the line to exceed the right margin, the text will be re-wrapped. If *newlinno* and *newchrno* are not NULL, *newlinno* and *newchrno* are backfilled with the new line and character position of the character following the inserted text, after the text is inserted.

insert_scroll_chars   (Member function)

```
OI_stat OI_base_text::insert_scroll_chars(
    OI_number           lineno,              // line number
    OI_number           charno,              // character number
    OI_number           n_chars,             // number of characters to insert
    const char          *textp,              // pointer to text to insert
    OI_number           *newlinno=NULL,      // pointer to new line number
    OI_number           *newchrno=NULL)      // pointer to new character number
```

insert_scroll_chars inserts *n_chars* characters of text *textp* before the character in position *charno*, in line number *lineno*. If *charno* is -1, insert_scroll_chars inserts *textp* after the last character in line number *lineno*. *textp* need not be null-terminated. A newline character in the text causes a new line to be generated as for insert_scroll_line. If the total number of lines after the insertion is greater than *max_lines*, insert_scroll_chars discards the first line(s) from the text object, and *max_lines* does not change. The number of characters in any line, however, is not affected. If you do not set *newlinno* and *newchrno* to NULL, *newlinno* and *newchrno* are backfilled with the new line and character position of the character following the inserted text, after the text is inserted.

insert_line   (Member function)

```
OI_stat OI_base_text::insert_line(
    OI_number           lineno,              // line number
    const char          *textp)              // pointer to text to insert
```

insert_line inserts a new line of text *textp* before line number *lineno*. If *lineno* is -1, insert_line inserts *textp* after the last line in the object. *textp* must be null-terminated, and it may not contain imbedded newline characters. Do not include any other control characters in the text except tab. If wrap is on, and the insertion allows text compression onto the preceding line (such as an insertion of a blank in the middle of a word, thus making two shorter words), or causes the line to exceed the right margin, the text will be re-wrapped.

insert_scroll_line   (Member function)

```
OI_stat OI_base_text::insert_scroll_line(
    OI_number           lineno,              // line number
    const char          *textp)              // pointer to text to insert
```

insert_scroll_line inserts a new line of text *textp* before line number *lineno*. If *lineno* is -1, insert_scroll_line inserts *textp* after the last line in the object. *textp* must be null-terminated, and it may not contain imbedded newline characters. If wrap is on, and the insertion allows text compression onto the preceding line (such as an insertion of a blank in the middle of a word, thus making two shorter words), or causes the line to exceed the right margin, the text will be re-wrapped. insert_scroll_line is different than insert_line in that if the total number of lines after the insertion is greater than *max_lines*, insert_scroll_line discards the first line(s) from the text object, and *max_lines* does not change.

replace_char   (Member function)

```
OI_stat OI_base_text::replace_char(
    OI_number           lineno,          // line number
    OI_number           charno,          // character number
    char                c)               // character to insert
```

replace_char replaces the character in line number *lineno*, in position *charno*, with the character *c*. *c* may not be a control character other than tab.

replace_chars   (Member function)

```
OI_stat OI_base_text::replace_chars(
    OI_number           lineno,          // line number
    OI_number           charno,          // character number
    OI_number           n_chars,         // number of characters to replace
    const char          *textp)          // pointer to text to insert
```

replace_chars replaces *n_chars* characters of text with the string in *textp*, starting at the character in position *charno*, in line number *lineno*. *textp* must be *n_chars* long; it need not be null-terminated, and may not contain any control characters other than tab. In particular, do not include any newline characters. If *charno* + *n_chars* is greater than the number of characters in the line, the line is extended to accommodate all the characters.

replace_line   (Member function)

```
OI_stat OI_base_text::replace_line(
    OI_number           lineno,          // line number
    const char          *textp)          // pointer to text to insert
```

replace_line replaces the text in line number *lineno* with the string *textp*. *textp* must be null-terminated, and may not contain any newline characters. If wrap is on, and the insertion allows text compression onto the preceding line (such as an insertion of a blank in the middle of a word, thus making two shorter words), or causes the line to exceed the right margin, the text will be re-wrapped.

is_modified   (Member function)

```
OI_bool OI_base_text::is_modified( )
```

is_modified returns OI_yes if any text characters have been changed, either programmatically or by the user, since the last clear_modified call; otherwise it returns OI_no.

clear_modified   (Member function)

```
void OI_base_text::clear_modified( )
```

clear_modified clears the condition that text characters were changed, either programmatically or by the user. An immediate subsequent call to any of the functions is_modified, is_user_-modified or is_prog_modified will return OI_no.

is_user_modified (Member function)

```
OI_bool OI_base_text::is_user_modified( )
```

is_user_modified returns OI_yes if any text characters have been changed by the user since the last clear_user_modified or clear_modified call; otherwise it returns OI_no.

clear_user_modified (Member function)

```
void OI_base_text::clear_user_modified( )
```

clear_user_modified clears the condition that text characters were changed by the user, so that an immediate subsequent call to is_user_modified will return OI_no.

is_prog_modified (Member function)

```
OI_bool OI_base_text::is_prog_modified( )
```

is_prog_modified returns OI_yes if any text characters have been changed programmatically since the last clear_prog_modified or clear_modified call; otherwise it returns OI_no.

clear_prog_modified (Member function)

```
void OI_base_text::clear_prog_modified( )
```

clear_prog_modified clears the condition that text characters were changed programmatically, so that an immediate subsequent call to is_prog_modified will return OI_no.

31.6.5 Validating Input Text

If you need to validate user entry, use these functions to register a callback validation function to be called when the user enters characters in the OI_base_text object.

set_char_check (Member function)

```
void OI_base_text::set_char_check(
    OI_mt_char_check_fnp      fnp=NULL,        // pointer to callback function
    void                      *argp=NULL)      // arbitrary argument for fnp

void OI_base_text::set_char_check(
    OI_callback               *objp,           // memfnp's object
    OI_mt_char_check_memfnp    memfnp=NULL,     // pointer to callback member function
    void                      *argp=NULL)      // arbitrary argument for memfnp
```

The set_char_check functions register a callback function to be invoked each time the user enters a character. This callback is identified within OI as a cbMultiTextCharCheck callback function (see Section 6.18, "Determining and Adding Callbacks; Multiple Callbacks," on page 6-117). If your validation function is a member function, when it is invoked it will be called as if you had written *objp->memfnp*. See Section 2.5, "Callbacks and Event-Driven Programming," on page 2-16, for more explanation.

argp is optional, and can be any valid expression that can be cast to a pointer. You can use it to pass additional information to the function *fnp* or *memfnp*.

Writing the Character Validation Callback Function

If the **cbMultiTextCharCheck** callback function is not a member function, write it in this form:

```
OI_mt_char_chk_status fn(
    OI_base_text              *oi_objp,     // OI_base_text where char was
                                            //   entered
    void                      *argp,        // arbitrary argument
    OI_mt_char_chk_status     prev_stat,    // status from preceding check if multiple
                                            //   callbacks
    OI_number                 lineno,       // line number in which to insert char
    OI_number                 nc,           // char number in line
    char                      c)            // entered character
```

and if the **cbMultiTextCharCheck** callback function is a member function, write it in this form:

```
OI_mt_char_chk_status obj_class::memfn(
    OI_base_text              *oi_objp,     // OI_base_text where char was
                                            //   entered
    void                      *argp,        // arbitrary argument
    OI_mt_char_chk_status     prev_stat,    // status from preceding check if multiple
                                            //   callbacks
    OI_number                 lineno,       // line number in which to insert char
    OI_number                 charno,       // char number in line
    char                      c)            // entered character
```

where *obj_class* is the class of the object whose member function is *memfn*.

When your callback function is invoked, *argp* will be the argument specified in the **set_char_check** call. *lineno* will be the line number for the entered character (starting with 0 at the top of the text object), *charno* will be the character number in the line for the entered character (starting with 0 at the left of the text object), and *c* will be the entered character.

prv_stat will be the return value of the **cbMultiTextCharCheck** function, if any, called before this one for this entry validation. If this is the only **cbMultiTextCharCheck** callback function registered for the object, *prv_stat* will be **OI_mt_char_chk_ok**. If there are multiple **cbMultiTextCharCheck** callbacks for the object—that is, if you have registered other **cbMultiTextCharCheck** callbacks for this object using the **OI_d_tech** member function **callback_add** (or you have registered this one using **callback_add**)—and if the order of registration dictates that another callback is called before this one, then *prv_stat* will be the return value from the previous callback.

Write this function to return an **OI_mt_char_chk_status** with one of the following values:

OI_mt_char_chk_insert	The character is valid and should be inserted.
OI_mt_char_chk_bad	The character is invalid.
OI_mt_char_chk_ignore	The character is valid but do not insert it.

If the function returns **OI_mt_char_chk_bad**, OI sounds the bell. Your callback function may post error messages via **push_help_str**, activate dialog boxes, or perform other actions. If you do not post an error message using push_help_str when the function returns OI_mt_char_chk_bad, then OI displays a generic message. You must use push_help_str rather than set_help_str because otherwise the message you display will be superseded by the generic message OI displays. You should specify the second argument to push_help_str to be OI_yes, indicating that this is a temporary message, so that the message will be removed when the next user-input event occurs—the next key press or button press.

def_c_check   (Member function)

```
OI_mt_char_chk_status OI_multi_text::def_c_check(
    OI_d_tech                *efp,        // entry field where char was entered
    void                     *argp,       // arbitrary argument
    OI_mt_char_chk_status    prev_stat,   // status from preceding check if multiple callbacks
    OI_number                lineno,      // line number of entry
    OI_number                charno,      // character position of entry
    char                     c)           // character entered
```

def_c_check is the default character check function. You should use this function as the first argument to set_char_check if you want to restore the default character check callback. def_c_check allows the entry of any printable character plus tab and newline.

set_entry_check   (Member function)

```
void OI_base_text::set_entry_check(
    OI_mt_entry_check_fnp       fnp=NULL,        // pointer to callback function
    void                        *argp=NULL)      // arbitrary argument for fnp
```

```
void OI_base_text::set_entry_check(
    OI_callback                 *objp,           // memfnp's object
    OI_mt_entry_check_memfnp    memfnp=NULL,     // pointer to callback member function
    void                        *argp=NULL)      // arbitrary argument for memfnp
```

The set_entry_check functions register a callback function to be invoked whenever a line is completed (that is, when the user strikes the Return key). This callback is identified within OI as a cbMultiTextEntryCheck callback function (see Section 6.18, "Determining and Adding Callbacks; Multiple Callbacks," on page 6-117). If your validation function is a member function, when it is invoked it will be called as if you had written *objp->memfnp*. See Section 2.5, "Callbacks and Event-Driven Programming," on page 2-16, for more explanation.

prv_stat will be the return value of the cbMultiTextEntryCheck function, if any, called before this one for this entry validation. If this is the only cbMultiTextEntryCheck callback function registered for the object, *prv_stat* will be OI_mt_entry_chk_ok. If there are multiple cbMultiTextEntryCheck callbacks for the object—that is, if you have registered other cbMultiTextEntryCheck callbacks for this object using the OI_d_tech member function callback_add (or you have registered this one using callback_add)—and if the order of registration dictates that another callback is called before this one, then *prv_stat* will be the return value from the previous callback.

argp is optional, and can be any valid expression that can be cast to a pointer. You can use it to pass additional information to the function *fnp* or *memfnp*.

Writing the Line Entry Validation Callback Function

If the cbMultiTextEntryCheck callback function is not a member function, write it in this form:

```
OI_mt_entry_chk_status fn(
    OI_base_text              *oi_objp,  // OI_base_text where line was
                                         //   entered
    void                      *argp,     // arbitrary argument
    OI_mt_entry_chk_status prev_stat, // status from preceding check if multiple
                                         //   callbacks
    OI_number                 lineno)    // line number
```

and if the cbMultiTextEntryCheck callback function is a member function, write it in this form:

```
OI_mt_entry_chk_status obj_class::memfn(
    OI_base_text              *oi_objp,  // OI_base_text where line was
                                         //   entered
    void                      *argp,     // arbitrary argument
    OI_mt_entry_chk_status prev_stat, // status from preceding check if multiple
                                         //   callbacks
    OI_number                 lineno)    // line number
```

where *obj_class* is the class of the object whose member function is *memfn*.

When your callback function is invoked, *argp* will be the argument specified in the set_entry_check call, and *lineno* will be the number of the line being validated (starting at 0).

Write this function to return an OI_mt_entry_chk_status with one of the following values:

OI_mt_entry_chk_ok	The entry is valid.
OI_mt_entry_chk_bad	The entry is invalid.
OI_mt_entry_chk_ignore	The entry is valid, but do not open a new line.

If the function returns OI_mt_entry_chk_ok, OI opens a new line and moves the cursor to the beginning of the new line. If the return status is OI_mt_entry_chk_ignore, no new line is opened and the cursor is not repositioned.

If the function returns OI_mt_entry_chk_bad, OI sounds the bell. Your callback function may post error messages via push_help_str, activate dialog boxes, or perform other actions. If you do not post an error message using push_help_str when the function returns OI_mt_entry_chk_bad, then OI displays a generic message. You must use push_help_str rather than set_help_str because otherwise the message you display will be superseded by the generic message OI displays. You should specify the second argument to push_help_str to be OI_yes, indicating that this is a temporary message, so that the message will be removed when the next user-input event occurs—the next key press or button press.

set_char_chg   (Member function)

```
void OI_base_text::set_char_chg(
    OI_mt_char_chg_fnp        fnp,          // pointer to callback function
    void                      *argp=NULL)   // arbitrary argument for fnp


void OI_base_text::set_char_chg(
    OI_callback               *objp,        // memfnp's object
    OI_mt_char_chg_memfnp      memfnp,      // pointer to callback member function
    void                      *argp=NULL)   // arbitrary argument for memfnp
```

The **set_char_chg** functions register a callback function to be invoked each time a valid character has been entered into the base text object. *memfnp* points to a member function for the object pointed to by *objp*. This callback is identified within OI as a **cbMultiTextCharChg** callback function (see Section 6.18, "Determining and Adding Callbacks; Multiple Callbacks," on page 6-117). If your change-character function is a member function, when it is invoked it will be called as if you had written *objp->memfnp*. See Section 2.5, "Callbacks and Event-Driven Programming," on page 2-16, for more explanation.

argp is optional, and may be any valid expression that can be cast to a pointer. You can use it to pass additional information to the function *fnp* or *memfnp*.

In contrast to the **set_char_check** callback procedure, the **set_char_chg** callback procedure *fnp* or *memfnp* is called after the character has been entered and all character validation has been performed (the callback routine specified in **set_char_check**, if any, has returned a "success" value). In other words, this callback is called after the character is already inserted.

Writing the Change-Character Callback Function

If the **cbMultiTextCharChg** callback function is not a member function, write it in this form:

```
void fn(
    OI_base_text        *btp,      // base text where char was entered
    void                *argp)     // arbitrary argument
```

and if the **cbMultiTextCharChg** callback function is a member function, write it in this form:

```
void obj_class::memfn(
    OI_base_text        *btp,      // entry field where char was entered
    void                *argp)     // arbitrary argument
```

where *obj_class* is the class of the object whose member function is *memfn*. When your callback function is invoked, *argp* will be the argument specified in the **set_char_chg** call, and *btp* will be a pointer to the base text object where the character was entered.

31.6.6   Scrolling the Text Object

scroll   (Member function)

```
void OI_base_text::scroll(
    OI_ctlr_1d         *ctlr,        // controller to scroll
    void               *ornt,        // orientation, in case there is no controller
    OI_scroll_event    typ,          // type of scrolling to do
    long               n_scrl)       // units to scroll
```

scroll positions the viewport over the object-box as if the user had moved the handle on a single controller. *ctlr* points to the controller to scroll, if there is one (for example, if the OI_multi_text object is part of a more complex object such as OI_scroll_text). If there is no controller or if the controller may disappear, you should set *ornt* to "OI_vertical" or "OI_horizontal", depending upon which way you want the text to scroll. *typ* specifies the type scrolling to do. Depending on the value of *typ*, *n_scrl* has different meanings. *typ* can be one of these values:

OI_scroll_unit   Scroll *n_scrl* characters (lines).
OI_scroll_viewport   Scroll *n_scrl* full viewports.
OI_scroll_extreme   Scroll to the extreme end.
OI_scroll_position   Scroll to the absolute position *n_scrl*, in characters (lines).

If *typ* is OI_scroll_unit, OI_scroll_viewport or OI_scroll_extreme, a positive value for *n_scrl* implies move down or right, and a negative value implies move up or left.

scroll_2d   (Member function)

```
void OI_base_text::scroll_2d(
    OI_panner*,                      // unused
    void*,                           // unused
    OI_scroll_event    typ,          // type of scrolling to do
    long               x,            // characters to scroll horizontally
    long               y)            // lines to scroll vertically
```

scroll_2d positions the viewport over the object-box as if it were scrolled in two dimensions at once. *typ* specifies the type scrolling to do, as specified for **scroll**, above. *x* and *y* are the equivalent of *n_scrl* for **scroll**, one for each of the two directions.

31.6.7   Controlling Keyboard Input

If the OI_base_text is to be a display-only object, you should disable keyboard input using disallow_kb_input. You can also control whether text insertion overwrites existing text (OI_mt_mode_replace) or inserts new text (OI_mt_mode_insert).

mode   (Member function)

```
OI_mt_mode OI_base_text::mode( )
```

mode returns the current text input mode of the OI_base_text object. This will be either OI_mt_mode_insert or OI_mt_mode_replace.

set_mode (Member function)

```
void OI_base_text::set_mode(
    OI_mt_mode        md)                    // input mode
```

set_mode sets the insert mode to *md*. *md* can be either OI_mt_mode_insert or OI_mt_mode_replace.

is_kb_input (Member function)

```
OI_bool OI_base_text::is_kb_input( )
```

is_kb_input returns OI_yes if the OI_base_text object can be modified through keyboard input; otherwise it returns OI_no.

allow_kb_input (Member function)

```
void OI_base_text::allow_kb_input( )
```

allow_kb_input configures the OI_base_text object so that it can be modified through keyboard input. This is the default.

disallow_kb_input (Member function)

```
void OI_base_text::disallow_kb_input( )
```

disallow_kb_input makes the OI_base_text object read only.

31.6.8   User Text Selection

As mentioned above, the user can select any or all of the text from an OI_base_text object and paste it elsewhere using the mouse or keyboard. These functions allow you to modify the user text selection capabilities.

is_click_select (Member function)

```
OI_bool OI_base_text::is_click_select( )
```

is_click_select returns OI_yes if the object allows the user to select the text from the object using multiple mouse clicks (default); otherwise, it returns OI_no.

allow_click_select (Member function)

```
void OI_base_text::allow_click_select( )
```

allow_click_select configures the base text object to allow the user to select text using multiple mouse clicks (default).

disallow_click_select (Member function)

```
void OI_base_text::disallow_click_select( )
```

disallow_click_select configures the base text object to prevent the user from selecting text using multiple mouse clicks.

selection_coords   (Member function)

```
OI_bool OI_base_text::selection_coords(
    OI_number         *strt_lin,      // starting line number
    OI_number         *strt_chr,      // starting character position
    OI_number         *end_lin,       // ending line number
    OI_number         *end_chr)       // ending character position
```

selection_coords backfills *strt_lin, strt_chr, end_lin,* and *end_chr* with the starting and ending line and character numbers of the currently selected text in the object. It returns OI_no if the object has no currently selected text; otherwise it returns OI_yes.

selection_data   (Member function)

```
char *OI_base_text::selection_data(
    const char        *sel_name)      // name of selection
```

```
char *OI_base_text::selection_data(
    Atom              sel_name_atm)   // name of selection converted to Atom
```

selection_data returns a pointer to a character string containing the current selection named *sel_name* or *sel_name_atm*. Specify *sel_name* to be "PRIMARY", "SECONDARY" or "CLIPBOARD", or specify *sel_name_atm* to be PRIMARY, SECONDARY, or CLIPBOARD. The named selection is often text that the user has marked using the mouse. selection_data returns NULL if the object does not own the selection or if there is no current selection. Do not confuse this selection with that set using the OI_d_tech member function set_selection_data or the data returned from the callback registered via the OI_d_tech member function set_selection_convert (see page 6-59).

31.6.9   Positioning the Input Cursor

Some applications, such as debuggers, need to automatically position text to indicate the current context. The functions below allow you to determine the current location of the text input cursor and change its position. Changing the input cursor location may move the text in the object to keep the cursor visible.

cursor_char   (Member function)

```
OI_number OI_base_text::cursor_char( )
```

cursor_char returns the character number of the current cursor location.

cursor_line   (Member function)

```
OI_number OI_base_text::cursor_line( )
```

cursor_line returns the line number of the current cursor location.

cursor_column   (Member function)

```
OI_number OI_base_text::cursor_column( )
```

cursor_column returns the column number of the current cursor location. cursor_column considers each tab to be expanded to the equivalent number of displayed characters.

set_position   (Member function)

```
OI_stat OI_base_text::set_position(
    OI_number          lineno,                         // line number
    OI_number          charno,                         // character number
    OI_psn_type        psn_type=OI_psn_default)        // position type
```

set_position sets the cursor position to character number *charno* in line number *lineno*. The OI_base_text object moves the text within the viewport if necessary to keep the cursor visible. *psn_type* determines how the text will be repositioned within the viewport when the cursor is positioned. You can omit *psn_type* or set it to a combination (bitwise inclusive or) of the position types shown in Table 31-1. In specifying *psn_type*, you should include exactly one selection from each of the Vertical positioning and Horizontal positioning categories in Table 31-1; you may optionally include OI_psn_vert_keep and/or OI_psn_horz_keep.

Table 31-1   OI_base_text Position Types

Category	OI_psn_type	Description
Vertical positioning	OI_psn_vert_top	Position *charno, lineno* at top of viewport
	OI_psn_vert_bottom	Position *charno, lineno* at bottom of viewport
	OI_psn_vert_center	Position *charno, lineno* at center of viewport
	OI_psn_vert_default	If *charno, lineno* is visible, do nothing, else move to nearest viewport edge (top or bottom)
Vertical Repositioning Criteria	OI_psn_vert_keep	If visible, do nothing
Horizontal positioning	OI_psn_horz_left	Position *charno, lineno* at left of viewport
	OI_psn_horz_right	Position *charno, lineno* at right of viewport
	OI_psn_horz_center	Position *charno, lineno* at center of viewport

Table 31-1   OI_base_text Position Types

Category	OI_psn_type	Description
	OI_psn_horz_default	If *charno, lineno* is visible, do nothing, else move to nearest viewport edge (left or right)
Horizontal Repositioning Criteria	OI_psn_horz_keep	If visible, do nothing

psn_type defaults to OI_psn_default which is OI_psn_horz_default | OI_psn_horz_keep | OI_psn_vert_default | OI_psn_vert_keep, which means that if the cursor is visible after it is repositioned, leave the text positioning alone, and if the cursor is not visible, position the text so that the cursor is on the nearest viewport border.

The position algorithm is as follows:

> If *psn_type* contains OI_psn_vert_keep and line *lineno* is in the viewport:
>> Leave as is.
> Else:
>> If *psn_type* contains OI_psn_vert_top:
>>> Force line *lineno* to be top-most line in the viewport.
>> Else if *psn_type* contains OI_psn_vert_bottom:
>>> Force line *lineno* to be bottom-most line in the viewport.
>> Else if *psn_type* contains OI_psn_vert_center:
>>> Force line *lineno* to be at middle of the viewport.
>> Else vertical positioning is default:
>>> If line *lineno* is off the viewport at bottom:
>>>> Force line *lineno* to be bottom-most line.
>>> If line *lineno* is off the viewport at top:
>>>> Force line *lineno* to be top-most line.
> If *psn_type* contains OI_psn_horz_keep and character *charno* is in the viewport:
>> Leave as is.
> Else:
>> If *psn_type* contains OI_psn_horz_left:
>>> Force character *charno* to be left-most character in the viewport.
>> Else if *psn_type* contains OI_psn_horz_right:
>>> Force character *charno* to be right-most character in the viewport.
>> Else if *psn_type* contains OI_psn_horz_center:
>>> Force character *charno* to be at middle of the viewport.
>> Else horizontal positioning is default:
>>> If character *charno* is off the viewport at right:
>>>> Force character *charno* to be right-most character.
>>> If character *charno* is off the viewport at left:
>>>> Force character *charno* to be left-most character.

31.6.10 Controlling Text Appearance

The functions described below allow you to control the text appearance in several ways:

You can specify whether or not *wordwrap* is on. If wordwrap is *off* (the default), the text is displayed exactly as specified from the input. Wordwrap *on* means that OI does not allow the text to go beyond the right margin, but breaks it at any white space (blank or newline) and wraps the ensuing text to the next line. By default, the right margin is at the edge of the viewport.

You can specify tab stops in an **OI_base_text** object. If you are using a variable-width font, the tab spacing units used are the width of the widest character in the font, usually "W". In other words, a tab width of 4 is equivalent to the space taken up by the characters "WWWW".

You can specify whether the object is to have different cursors depending upon whether the object has the input focus or not.

You can enhance portions of the text using several different enhancements, including underline, reverse video, foreground and background color, and font. You can "layer" enhancements of different portions of a line of text; repeated calls to **set_enhance** cause the enhancement attributes to be combined with older ones, using a bitwise boolean **or**. For example, if you call **set_enhance** to underline characters 10 through 40 of line 3, then call **set_enhance** again to reverse characters 20 through 25 of line 3, then line 3 appears underlined for characters 10 through 19 and 26 through 40, and appears in underlined reverse video for characters 20 through 25. If you do not remove the reverse enhancement, but remove the underline enhancement, all characters in line 3 appear with no enhancement except characters 20 through 25, which appear in reverse video.

is_wrap   (Member function)

```
OI_bool OI_base_text::is_wrap( )
```

is_wrap returns **OI_yes** if the **OI_base_text** object allows wordwrap; otherwise it returns **OI_no**.

allow_wrap   (Member function)

```
void OI_base_text::allow_wrap( )
```

allow_wrap sets wordwrap on, causing the text to break at white space at the right margin and wrap to the next line. A tab in the text causes wordwrap to be turned off until the next newline. The right margin (set by **set_right_margin** or the resource **rightMargin**) is used as the wrapping boundary. The right margin defaults to zero, which means use the width of the viewport for the wrapping boundary.

disallow_wrap   (Member function)

```
void OI_base_text::disallow_wrap( )
```

disallow_wrap sets wordwrap off. This is the default.

wrap   (Member function)

```
void OI_base_text::wrap(
    OI_number          strt=0,            // starting line number
    OI_number          end=0)             // ending line number
```

wrap performs wordwrap on lines *strt* through *end*. *end*=0 implies the end of the text.

right_margin   (Member function)

```
OI_number OI_base_text::right_margin( )
```

right_margin returns the position of the right margin for word wrap.

set_right_margin   (Member function)

```
OI_bool OI_base_text::set_right_margin(
    OI_number          rt_mrgn)           // right margin
```

set_right_margin sets the right margin to *rt_mrgn*, in characters from the left edge of the viewport. If *rt_mrgn* = 0, use the viewport width as the right margin. Calling **set_right_margin** does NOT automatically force the text to be re-wrapped to the new margin. **set_right_margin** returns **OI_yes** if successful, otherwise it returns **OI_no**.

tab_width   (Member function)

```
OI_number OI_base_text::tab_width( )
```

tab_width returns the number of characters in a single tab width.

set_tab_width   (Member function)

```
OI_stat OI_base_text::set_tab_width(
    OI_number          tab_width)         // tab width in characters
```

set_tab_width creates a tab table with a tab stop every *tab_width* characters. The table defaults to a size large enough to support tabbing of up to 80 columns of text. The table is dynamically resized if any associated text has tabs past 80 columns. The default tab stop setting is 8.

set_tabs_custom   (Member function)

```
OI_stat OI_base_text::set_tabs_custom(
    OI_number          *tab_tbl,          // pointer to tab stop table
    OI_number          n_tabs,            // number of tabs in tab_tbl
    OI_number          def_wid=8)         // default tab width
```

set_tabs_custom sets the first *n_tabs* tab stops in the **OI_base_text** object to those specified in *tab_tbl*. Each element of *tab_tbl* specifies the column number where the next tab stop is to be placed. You cannot set *tab_tbl* to NULL, and *n_tabs* must be greater than 0. If there are more than *n_tabs* tabs in any line of the **OI_base_text** text, their spacing is set to *def_wid* characters.

For example, if you want tabs at columns 4, 12, 20, and 36, then every 4 after that if needed, you would use these lines:

```
        OI_base_text    *btp;
    static  OI_number        my_tabs[] = {4, 12, 20, 36};
  btp->set_tabs_custom(my_tabs, OI_count(my_tabs), 4);
```

is_inactive_cursor   (Member function)

```
OI_bool OI_base_text::is_inactive_cursor( )
```

is_inactive_cursor returns OI_yes (the default) if the "inactive" cursor will appear when the base text object does not have the input focus; otherwise it returns OI_no. The "inactive" cursor only appears in the OPEN LOOK model and is a stippled diamond. The "active" cursor in OPEN LOOK is a solid triangle and always appears when the base text object has the input focus.

allow_inactive_cursor   (Member function)

```
void OI_base_text::allow_inactive_cursor( )
```

allow_inactive_cursor configures the base text object so that the "inactive" cursor will appear when the base text object does not have the input focus. The "inactive" cursor only appears in the OPEN LOOK model. This function has no effect if the application is run in Motif mode.

disallow_inactive_cursor   (Member function)

```
void OI_base_text::disallow_inactive_cursor( )
```

disallow_inactive_cursor configures the base text object so that the "inactive" cursor will not appear when the base text object does not have the input focus. This function has no effect if the application is run in Motif mode.

get_enhance   (Member function)

```
OI_enhance OI_base_text::get_enhance(
    OI_number          lineno,          // line number
    OI_number          charno)          // char number
```

get_enhance returns the type of enhancement in effect on character *charno* in line *lineno*. The value returned is a bitwise inclusive or of one or more of the attributes listed under set_enhance below.

set_enhance   (Member function)

```
void OI_base_text::set_enhance(
    OI_number    lineno,                                  // line number
    OI_number    charno,                                  // starting char number
    OI_number    len,                                     // length of enhancement
    OI_enhance   enhance,                                 // type of enhancement
    const char   *fg_clr,                                 // foreground color
    const char   *bg_clr,                                 // background color
    const char   *font_name=NULL)                         // font name


void OI_base_text::set_enhance(
    OI_number    lineno,                                  // line number
    OI_number    charno,                                  // starting char number
    OI_number    len,                                     // length of enhancement
    OI_enhance   enhance,                                 // type of enhancement
    PIXEL        fg_pxl=OI_UNKNOWN_PIXEL,                 // foreground pixel
    PIXEL        bg_pxl=OI_UNKNOWN_PIXEL,                 // background pixel
    const char   *font_name=NULL)                         // font name
```

set_enhance enhances *len* characters starting with *charno*. *enhance* is a bitwise inclusive **or** of one or more of the following attributes:

OI_enhance_none	No enhancement
OI_enhance_reverse	Enhance using reverse video
OI_enhance_underline	Enhance using underline
OI_enhance_centerline	Enhance using a line through the center of the character(s)
OI_enhance_overline	Enhance using a line over the character(s)
OI_enhance_bold	Enhance using boldface
OI_enhance_italic	Enhance using italics
OI_enhance_font_change	Enhance using the font specified by *font_name*
OI_enhance_foreground	Enhance the foreground using the color specified by *fg_clr* or *fg_pxl*
OI_enhance_background	Enhance the background using the color specified by *bg_clr* or *bg_pxl*

fg_color or *fg_pxl* is used only if you specify OI_enhance_foreground. Similarly, *bg_color* or *bg_pxl* is used only if you specify OI_enhance_background. *fontname* is used only if you specify OI_enhance_font_change.

Subsequent calls to **set_enhance** cause the enhancement attributes specified to be combined with any that are currently present using a bitwise inclusive **or**. The enhancement attribute remains in effect until you call **remove_enhance** specifying all or part of the enhancement or until you call **clear_enhance** for the line.

clear_enhance   (Member function)

```
void OI_base_text::clear_enhance(
    OI_number          lineno)              // line number
```

clear_enhance removes all text enhancements on the specified line.

remove_enhance   (Member function)

```
void OI_base_text::remove_enhance(
    OI_number          lineno,             // line number
    OI_number          charno,             // starting char number
    OI_number          len,                // length of enhancement
    OI_enhance         enhance)            // type of enhancement
```

remove_enhance removes a specific text enhancement. The parameters are the same as those in **set_enhance**. Note: Suppose you call **set_enhance** to enhance some characters on a given line, say line 4, and then either delete or add lines so that the enhanced line is no longer line 4. If you want to remove the enhancement, you must call **remove_enhance** with the new line number. Similarly, if you add or delete characters in the line, the starting character number in the call to **remove_enhance** must match the new character number of the enhancement.

31.6.11   Determining Character and Line Positions and Characteristics

There are situations where you may need to know some of the metrics for the text. For example, if you are dynamically building a customized glyph, you may want to know something about the character size. The functions below give you most of the useful metrics for the text in an **OI_base_text** object.

char_width   (Member function)

```
OI_number OI_base_text::char_width( )
```

char_width returns the width of a single character. The value is in pixels, and includes inter-character white space. For a font with proportional spacing, **char_width** returns the width of the widest character in the font.

line_height   (Member function)

```
OI_number OI_base_text::line_height( )
```

line_height returns the height of a single line. The value is in pixels, and includes inter-line white space.

line_width   (Member function)

```
OI_number OI_base_text::line_width(
    OI_number          lineno)            // line number
```

line_width returns the number of characters in line number *lineno*. This is the actual number of characters in the text, not necessarily the number of characters visible in the viewport.

ulcwf   (Member function)

```
void OI_base_text::ulcwf(
    OI_number          *lineno,          // line number
    OI_number          *charno)          // character number
```

ulcwf backfills *lineno* with the line number of the line that is at the top edge of the viewport and *charno* with the character number of the character that is at the left edge of the viewport. See **ulcwf_line** and **ulcwf_char** for more explanation. (**ulcwf** stands for <u>u</u>pper <u>l</u>eft <u>c</u>orner of the <u>w</u>indow <u>f</u>rame.)

ulcwf_char   (Member function)

```
OI_number OI_base_text::ulcwf_char( )
```

ulcwf_char returns the character number of the character that is at the left edge of the viewport. If the entire text fits between the left and right edges of the viewport, or if the user has not moved the viewport, this number is zero. If some text is wider than the viewport, and the user has moved the viewport in order to see the right portion of the text, this number is greater than zero.

ulcwf_pixel   (Member function)

```
OI_number OI_base_text::ulcwf_pixel( )
```

ulcwf_pixel returns the pixel number of the upper left corner of the character that is at the left edge of the viewport. See discussion under **ulcwf_char** for possible return values.

ulcwf_line   (Member function)

```
OI_number OI_base_text::ulcwf_line( )
```

ulcwf_line returns the line number of the line that is at the top edge of the viewport. If the entire text fits between the top and bottom edges of the viewport, or if the user has not moved the viewport, this number is zero. If the text is longer than the viewport, and the user has moved the viewport in order to see the bottom portion of the text, this number is greater than zero.

max_chars   (Member function)

```
OI_number OI_base_text::max_chars( )
```

max_chars returns the value set for *max_chars* when the **OI_base_text** object was created, or the value sent to the function **set_cols** if you have called it. This value is independent of the number of characters existing in any line of text.

max_lines   (Member function)

```
OI_number OI_base_text::max_lines( )
```

max_lines returns the current value for *max_lines*. This is the value set at the time the **OI_base_text** object was created, unless you have called **set_lines** for the **OI_base_text**, or unless the number of lines added to the **OI_base_text** surpassed the old value of *max_lines* and caused OI to increase it. In any case, the value returned is always greater than or equal to the actual number of lines of text in the **OI_base_text** object.

max_n_chars   (Member function)

```
OI_number OI_base_text::max_n_chars( )
```

max_n_chars returns the maximum number of characters in the longest line of text. This value may be larger than the viewport width if the text is wider than the viewport; it may also be larger than the initial value of *max_chars* if long lines were inserted at some time.

max_n_pixels   (Member function)

```
OI_number OI_base_text::max_n_pixels( )
```

max_n_pixels returns the number of pixels in the longest line of text. This value may be larger than the viewport width if the text is wider than the viewport. Note that if a variable width font is in use, the line(s) which contain *max_n_chars* characters are not necessarily the same as the line(s) which are *max_n_pixels* long.

n_lines   (Member function)

```
OI_number OI_base_text::n_lines( )
```

n_lines returns the total number of lines of text in the **OI_base_text** object. This may be larger than the length of the viewport if there is a large amount of text. n_lines is always less than *max_lines*.

set_lines   (Member function)

```
OI_stat OI_base_text::set_lines(
    OI_number          max_lines)          // max number of lines
```

set_lines sets the maximum number of lines in the object to *max_lines*. This does not change the viewport size. If the object contains more than *max_lines* lines when this function is called, OI discards all lines past *max_lines*-1.

set_cols   (Member function)

```
void OI_base_text::set_cols(
    OI_number          max_chars)          // max number of characters
```

set_cols sets the default maximum number of characters per line. This does not change the viewport size. In contrast to *max_lines*, *max_chars* never changes (unless you call the function set_cols again)—it is merely a "hint" to OI as to what buffer size to make for a line. If more than *max_chars* characters are entered in a line, they are in fact entered, but this does not affect the value of *max_chars*.

The only good reason to call set_cols is if you are using an **OI_base_text** object to hold text from several different files, and you know that their record lengths are drastically different. In this case, you may want to call set_cols before filling the **OI_base_text** object with the next file's text. The benefit here is some speed, efficiency, and memory savings—the code all works without resetting the value of *max_chars*.

31.6.12 Translating Between Pixel Coordinates and Character Positions

If you are writing an application which needs to position other objects precisely in relation to particular lines or characters, you will need the functions below. An example would be a debugger which positions an OI_glyph object to the left of a line where a breakpoint is set.

char_xy_position   (Member function)

```
OI_stat OI_base_text::char_xy_position(
    OI_number        lineno,        // line number
    OI_number        charno,        // character number
    long             *x,            // pointer to x pixel coordinate
    long             *y)            // pointer to y pixel coordinate
```

char_xy_position backfills x and y to the pixel coordinates of the upper-left corner of the character at line number *lineno* and character number *charno*, with relationship to the top-left corner of the text window (ignoring the viewport). The top line (in the text, not necessarily the viewport) is line number zero and the left-most character (again, in the text, not necessarily the viewport) is character number zero. The coordinates of the top left character are not pixel location (0,0) as you might expect, however, because of the white space and, in 3-D models, the bevel, surrounding the text. The pixel coordinates of the upper-left character are very small numbers; the pixel x coordinate increases for characters to the right of this one, and the pixel y coordinate increases for lines below this one.

char_xy_position returns OI_ok if *lineno* and *charno* correspond to an actual character in the text, and OI_out_of_bounds if they do not.

xy_char_position   (Member function)

```
OI_stat OI_base_text::xy_char_position(
    long             x,             // x pixel coordinate
    long             y,             // y pixel coordinate
    OI_number        *lineno,       // pointer to line number
    OI_number        *charno)       // pointer to character number
```

xy_char_position backfills *lineno* and *charno* with the line and character numbers in which the pixel at (x,y) is located. The character so represented need not be within the viewport—see the description of char_xy_position above.

xy_char_position returns OI_ok if the x,y coordinates correspond to an actual character in the text, and OI_out_of_bounds if they do not.

view_char_position   (Member function)

```
OI_stat OI_base_text::view_char_position(
    long            x,              // x pixel coordinate
    long            y,              // y pixel coordinate
    OI_number       *lineno,        // pointer to line number
    OI_number       *charno)        // pointer to character number
```

view_char_position backfills *lineno* and *charno* with the line and character numbers in which the pixel at (x,y) is located. **view_char_position** is identical to **xy_char_position**, except the x,y coordinates are with respect to the top-left corner of the viewport, not the underlying text. The values backfilled in *lineno* and *charno* are with respect to the underlying text, however, just as in **xy_char_position**.

view_char_position returns **OI_ok** if the x,y coordinates correspond to an actual character in the text, and **OI_out_of_bounds** if they do not.

31.6.13 Manipulating Viewport Size

The functions below allow you to retrieve and change the viewport size. You should usually not need these functions, since in general you should allow the user to control the viewport size via the resource manager; you may also want to use the automatic layout facility and make the **OI_base_text** object a size-tracker to allow OI to resize the object as necessary. However, in some situations you may need to use these functions; for example, you might have a custom configuration which does not easily fit the layout code.

view_size   (Member function)

```
void OI_base_text::view_size(
    OI_number       *view_lines,    // number of lines possible in viewport
    OI_number       *view_chars)    // number of characters possible in viewport
```

view_size backfills *view_lines* and *view_chars* with the current viewport size in lines and characters.

set_view_size   (Member function)

```
OI_stat OI_base_text::set_view_size(
    OI_number       view_lines,     // number of lines possible in viewport
    OI_number       view_chars)     // number of characters possible in viewport
```

set_view_size sets the viewport size to *view_lines* lines of text in height and *view_chars* characters of text in width. If you change the font (using **OI_d_tech** member functions), the text object and the viewport are resized accordingly. Calling **set_view_size** does NOT automatically force a re-wrap of the text.

view_n_chars   (Member function)

```
OI_number OI_base_text::view_n_chars( )
```

view_n_chars returns the width of the viewport in characters. This may differ from the original value if the **OI_base_text** object has been resized.

view_n_lines   (Member function)

```
OI_number OI_base_text::view_n_lines( )
```

view_n_lines returns the length of the viewport in lines. This may differ from the original value if the **OI_base_text** object has been resized.

31.6.14 Communicating with the Outside World

exec_cmd   (Member function)

```
OI_bool OI_base_text::exec_cmd(
    const char          *cmd_str,          // command string
    OI_base_text        *outp=NULL,        // stdout text goes here
    OI_base_text        *errp=NULL,        // stderr text goes here
    OI_bool             apnd=OI_no)        // append output?
```

exec_cmd opens a pipe to the command specified in *cmd_str*. The text in the **OI_base_text** object is given to the command on **stdin**. Any output from the command on **stdout** is inserted into *outp*, and any output from the command on **stderr** is inserted into *errp*. If you set *apnd* to **OI_yes**, the **stdout** output is appended to *outp* and **stderr** output is appended to *errp*; otherwise, both *outp* and *errp* are cleared before the output lines are inserted.

If you set *cmd_str* to NULL, **/bin/sh** is used as the command. This has the effect of executing the text in the object as a shell script using **/bin/sh** as the shell.

exec_cmd does not return until command execution is complete. **exec_cmd** returns **OI_yes** if the pipe to the command was opened successfully; otherwise it returns **OI_no**.

31.7 An OI_multi_text Programming Example

Program 31-1 shows an **OI_multi_text** object with text from a file. When the user clicks on a line in the text, the click callback creates a stop-sign glyph and places it at the beginning of that line. The glyph is made to track its parent; that is, it moves with the text if the user scrolls the text in any direction. The results are shown in Figure 31-1 on page 31-36.

Note that we call **allow_track** for the glyph before parenting it to the multi-text; otherwise it might not initially be placed correctly. Also note that the background for the glyph is forced to be the same as the background for the text object using the function **set_bkg_pixel**. If this had not been done, and if the application were run using a color other than the default for the whole application for the background for the multi-text, the glyph background would be different than the multi-text's background. Alternatively, we could have used the shape capability of the glyph to only display the foreground bits; however, forcing the background gives better performance.

If the text had any characters in the first column, they would be overwritten by the glyph when the user clicked on that line.

```c
#include <OI/oi.H>                            /* MultiText.C */

int main (int argc, char **argv)
{
        void                    glyph_here(OI_d_tech*,void*,OI_number,OI_number,
                                        OI_number,OI_number,OI_number);

        OI_connection           *conp;
        OI_app_window           *wp;
        OI_multi_text           *mtp;

    if (conp = OI_init(&argc,argv,"MultiText")) {
        wp = oi_create_app_window("main",1,1,"Multi_text Demo");
        wp->set_layout(OI_layout_column);

        mtp = oi_create_multi_text("text",7,60);
        mtp->layout_associated_object(wp,1,1,OI_active);
        mtp->set_text_to_file("mlttxt.txt");
        mtp->set_click(glyph_here);

        wp->set_associated_object(wp->root( ),OI_def_loc,OI_def_loc,OI_active);
        OI_begin_interaction( );
    }
}

void glyph_here(OI_d_tech *objp, void*, OI_number, OI_number,
                                        OI_number, OI_number lin, OI_number)
{
        OI_base_text            *btp;
        OI_glyph                *gp;
        long                    x_pos,y_pos;

    btp = (OI_base_text*)objp;

    if (btp->char_xy_position(lin,0,&x_pos,&y_pos) == OI_ok) {
        gp = oi_create_glyph("stop","../bitmaps/stop.bm");
        gp->set_bkg_pixel(btp->bkg_paint_pixel( ));
        gp->allow_track( );
        gp->set_associated_object(btp,x_pos,y_pos,OI_active);
    }

    return;
}
```

Program 31-1   OI_multi_text with OI_glyph at Click Line(MultiText.C)

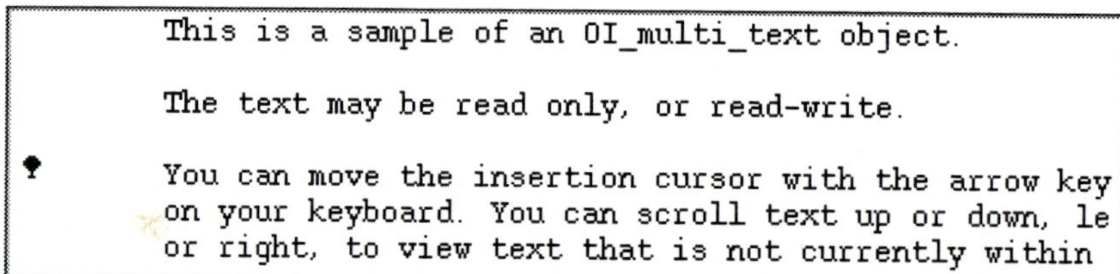

Figure 31-1   OI_multi_text With OI_glyph at Click Line

31.8   Resources

All resources from an **OI_base_text** object's base classes are available to it; in addition, OI fetches the resources shown in Table 31-2. For more information on resource management, see Chapter 39, "The OI Resource Mechanism."

Table 31-2   OI_base_text Resources

Resource	Description	Possible Values	Default Value
clickSelect	If **true**, specifies that clicking with the mouse in the text entry area should select the word, the entire line, the paragraph, or the entire text (depending on the number of clicks). If **false**, clicking the mouse will not select any text.	Boolean	true
font	Specifies the font to use for text in the viewport.	Any valid font	Default font
inactiveCursor	If **true**, the "inactive" cursor should appear when the multi text does not have the input focus. If **false**, no cursor appears in this case. (Applies to OPEN LOOK only.)	Boolean	true
keyboardInput	If **true**, input from user is accepted.	Boolean	true
maxChars	Specifies the initial maximum number of characters per line.	Non-negative integer	(No default)

Table 31-2 OI_base_text Resources

Resource	Description	Possible Values	Default Value
maxLines	Specifies the initial maximum number of lines.	Non-negative integer	(No default)
pasteAtPointer	If true, paste is at mouse pointer position. If false, paste is at input cursor position.	Boolean	true
rightMargin	Specifies the right margin for the wrapping boundary for wordwrap. 0 implies use the width of the viewport.	Non-negative integer	0
tabWidth	Specifies the size of a tab, in characters.	Non-negative integer	8
text	Specifies the initial text to be displayed.	Text string	NULL
textFile	Specifies the name of the text file from which to initially fill the object.	Absolute or relative file name	NULL
viewChars	Specifies the number of characters the viewport will initially accommodate.	Non-negative Integer	(No default)
viewLines	Specifies the number of lines of text the viewport will initially accommodate.	Non-negative Integer	(No default)
wrap	If true, set wordwrap on.	Boolean	false

31.9 Translations

All translations from an OI_multi_text object's base classes are available to it; in addition the translations shown in Table 31-3 and Table 31-4 are available to it. See Chapter 40, "The OI Translation Mechanism" for a description of the Event Sequence entries in these tables as well as additional information on how to read these tables.

Table 31-3   OI_multi_text Default Translations, Motif

			Event Sequence	Action Functions Called
			<Key>:	input_character( )
		Mod1	<Key>asciitilde:	toggle_mode( )
	Ctrl		<Key>backslash:	unselect_all( )
	Ctrl	~Mod1	<Key>BackSpace:	delete_to_beginning_of_line( )
		~Mod1	<Key>BackSpace:	delete_previous_character( )
		Mod1	<Key>D:	delete_this_line( )
Shift		Mod1	<Key>Delete:	cut_primary( )
Shift		~Mod1	<Key>Delete:	cut_clipboard( )
	Ctrl	~Mod1	<Key>Delete:	delete_to_end_of_line( )
		~Mod1	<Key>Delete:	delete_next_character( )
Shift	Ctrl		<Key>Down:	forward_paragraph(extend)
	Ctrl		<Key>Down:	forward_paragraph( )
Shift			<Key>Down:	next_line(extend)
			<Key>Down:	next_line( )
			<Key>Escape:	cancel_select( )
			<Key>F4:	activate_popup( )
			<Key>F10:	activate_main_menu( )
		Mod1	<Key>I:	insert_mode( )
	Ctrl	Mod1	<Key>Insert:	copy_primary( )
	Ctrl		<Key>Insert:	copy_clipboard( )
Shift			<Key>Insert:	paste_clipboard( )
	Ctrl	Mod1	<Key>KP_0:	copy_primary( )
	Ctrl		<Key>KP_0:	copy_clipboard( )
Shift			<Key>KP_0:	paste_clipboard( )
Shift	Ctrl		<Key>Left:	backward_word(extend)
	Ctrl		<Key>Left:	backward_word( )
Shift			<Key>Left:	backward_character(extend)
			<Key>Left:	backward_character( )
			<Key>Linefeed:	newline( )
		Mod1	<Key>L6:	copy_primary( )
			<Key>L6:	copy_clipboard( )
			<Key>L8:	paste_clipboard( )
		Mod1	<Key>L10:	cut_primary( )
			<Key>L10:	cut_clipboard( )

Table 31-3   OI_multi_text Default Translations, Motif

Event Sequence				Action Functions Called
Shift		Mod1	<Key>O:	open_previous_line( )
		Mod1	<Key>O:	open_next_line( )
		Mod1	<Key>R:	replace_mode( )
			<Key>Return:	newline( )
Shift	Ctrl		<Key>Right:	forward_word(extend)
	Ctrl		<Key>Right:	forward_word( )
Shift			<Key>Right:	forward_character(extend)
			<Key>Right:	forward_character( )
Shift	Ctrl		<Key>R7:	beginning_of_file(extend)
	Ctrl		<Key>R7:	beginning_of_file( )
	Ctrl	Mod1	<Key>R7:	delete_to_beginning_of_file( )
Shift			<Key>R7:	beginning_of_line(extend)
			<Key>R7:	beginning_of_line( )
	Ctrl		<Key>R9:	scroll_left( )
Shift			<Key>R9:	scroll_up(extend)
			<Key>R9:	scroll_up( )
Shift	Ctrl		<Key>R13:	end_of_file(extend)
	Ctrl		<Key>R13:	end_of_file( )
	Ctrl	Mod1	<Key>R13:	delete_to_end_of_file( )
Shift			<Key>R13:	end_of_line(extend)
			<Key>R13:	end_of_line( )
	Ctrl		<Key>R15:	scroll_right( )
Shift			<Key>R15:	scroll_down(extend)
			<Key>R15:	scroll_down( )
	Ctrl		<Key>slash:	select_all( )
	!Ctrl		<Key>space:	set_anchor( )
!Shift			<Key>space:	key_select( )
Shift	Ctrl		<Key>Tab:	previous_tab_group( )
Shift			<Key>Tab:	previous_tab_group( )
	Ctrl		<Key>Tab:	next_tab_group( )
			<Key>Tab:	input_character( )
Shift	Ctrl		<Key>Up:	backward_paragraph(extend)
	Ctrl		<Key>Up:	backward_paragraph( )
Shift			<Key>Up:	previous_line(extend)
			<Key>Up:	previous_line( )

Table 31-3   OI_multi_text Default Translations, Motif

Event Sequence				Action Functions Called
~Shift	~Ctrl	~Mod1	<Btn1Down>:	take_focus( ) select_start( )
			<Btn1Motion>:	select_adjust( )
			<Btn1Up>:	select_end( )
	!Ctrl		<Btn1Down>:	move_insertion( )
!Shift			<Btn1Down>:	extend_start( )
~Shift	Ctrl	~Mod1	<Btn2Down>:	drag_copy_start( ) secondary_start(SECONDARY)
~Shift	~Ctrl	~Mod1	<Btn2Down>:	drag_move_start( ) secondary_start(SECONDARY)
~Shift	~Ctrl	Mod1	<Btn2Motion>:	secondary_adjust(SECONDARY)
~Shift			<Btn2Motion>:	secondary_adjust(SECONDARY)
~Shift	~Ctrl	Mod1	<Btn2Up>:	move_selection( )
~Shift			<Btn2Up>:	secondary_end(SECONDARY)
			<Btn3Down>:	click_down( )
			<Btn3Up>:	click_up( )
			<FocusIn>:	focus_in( ) paint_focus_frame( )
			<FocusOut>:	focus_out( ) clear_focus_frame( )

Table 31-4   OI_multi_text Default Translations, OPEN LOOK

Event Sequence				Action Functions Called
			<Key>:	input_character( )
	Ctrl	~Mod1	<Key>A:	beginning_of_line( )
		Mod1	<Key>asciitilde:	toggle_mode( )
	Ctrl	~Mod1	<Key>B:	backward_character( )
	~Ctrl	Mod1	<Key>B:	backward_word( )
Shift	Ctrl	~Mod1	<Key>BackSpace:	delete_previous_word( )
	Ctrl	~Mod1	<Key>BackSpace:	delete_to_beginning_of_line( )
	Shift	~Mod1	<Key>BackSpace:	delete_next_character( )
		~Mod1	<Key>BackSpace:	delete_previous_character( )
	Ctrl	~Mod1	<Key>D:	delete_next_character( )
	~Ctrl	Mod1	<Key>D:	delete_next_word( )
		Mod1	<Key>D:	delete_this_line( )
	Shift	Mod1	<Key>Delete:	delete_all_characters( )
Shift	Ctrl	~Mod1	<Key>Delete:	delete_next_word( )

Table 31-4 OI_multi_text Default Translations, OPEN LOOK

Event Sequence				Action Functions Called
	Ctrl	~Mod1	<Key>Delete:	delete_to_end_of_line( )
Shift		~Mod1	<Key>Delete:	delete_next_character( )
		~Mod1	<Key>Delete:	delete_previous_character( )
		Mod1	<Key>Down:	end_of_file( )
		~Mod1	<Key>Down:	next_line( )
	Ctrl	Mod1	<Key>Down:	delete_to_end_of_file( )
	Ctrl	~Mod1	<Key>E:	end_of_line( )
	Ctrl	~Mod1	<Key>F:	forward_character( )
	~Ctrl	Mod1	<Key>F:	forward_word( )
	Ctrl	~Mod1	<Key>H:	delete_previous_character( )
	~Ctrl	Mod1	<Key>H:	delete_previous_word( )
		Mod1	<Key>I:	insert_mode( )
Shift			<Key>Insert:	paste_clipboard( )
	Ctrl		<Key>Insert:	copy_clipboard( )
	Ctrl	~Mod1	<Key>K:	delete_to_end_of_line( )
	~Ctrl	Mod1	<Key>K:	delete_to_beginning_of_line( )
Shift			<Key>KP_0:	paste_clipboard( )
	Ctrl		<Key>KP_0:	copy_clipboard( )
	Ctrl	Mod1	<Key>Left:	select_line( )
Shift	Ctrl		<Key>Left:	backward_word(extend)
	Ctrl		<Key>Left:	backward_word( )
Shift			<Key>Left:	backward_character(extend)
		Mod1	<Key>Left:	backward_word( )
			<Key>Left:	backward_character( )
			<Key>Linefeed:	newline( )
			<Key>L6:	copy_clipboard( )
			<Key>L8:	paste_clipboard( )
			<Key>L10:	cut_clipboard( )
	Ctrl	~Mod1	<Key>N:	next_line( )
Shift		Mod1	<Key>O:	open_previous_line( )
		Mod1	<Key>O:	open_next_line( )
	Ctrl	~Mod1	<Key>P:	previous_line( )
		Mod1	<Key>R:	replace_mode( )
			<Key>Return:	newline( )
Shift	Ctrl		<Key>Right:	forward_word(extend)

Table 31-4 OI_multi_text Default Translations, OPEN LOOK

Event Sequence				Action Functions Called
	Ctrl		<Key>Right:	forward_word( )
Shift			<Key>Right:	forward_character(extend)
		Mod1	<Key>Right:	forward_word( )
			<Key>Right:	forward_character( )
Shift	Ctrl		<Key>R7:	beginning_of_pane( )
	Ctrl		<Key>R7:	beginning_of_file( )
Shift			<Key>R7:	beginning_of_line(extend)
	Ctrl	Mod1	<Key>R7:	delete_to_beginning_of_file( )
			<Key>R7:	beginning_of_line( )
Shift	Ctrl		<Key>R13:	end_of_pane( )
	Ctrl		<Key>R13:	end_of_file( )
Shift			<Key>R13:	end_of_line(extend)
	Ctrl	Mod1	<Key>R13:	delete_to_end_of_file( )
			<Key>R13:	end_of_line( )
		Mod1	<Key>R9:	scroll_top( )
			<Key>R9:	scroll_up( )
		Mod1	<Key>R15:	scroll_bottom( )
			<Key>R15:	scroll_down( )
Shift	Ctrl		<Key>Tab:	previous_tab_group( )
Shift			<Key>Tab:	previous_tab_group( )
	Ctrl		<Key>Tab:	next_tab_group( )
			<Key>Tab:	input_character( )
Shift	Ctrl	~Mod1	<Key>U:	delete_to_end_of_line( )
	Ctrl	~Mod1	<Key>U:	delete_to_beginning_of_line( )
		Mod1	<Key>Up:	beginning_of_file( )
		~Mod1	<Key>Up:	previous_line( )
	Ctrl	Mod1	<Key>Up:	delete_to_beginning_of_file( )
Shift		Mod1	<Key>{:	scroll_left_edge( )
		Mod1	<Key>[:	scroll_left( )
Shift		Mod1	<Key>}:	scroll_right_edge( )
		Mod1	<Key>]:	scroll_right( )
~Shift	~Ctrl	~Mod1	<Btn1Down>:	take_focus( ) drag_move_start( ) select_start( )
~Shift	Ctrl	~Mod1	<Btn1Down>:	drag_copy_start( )
~Shift	~Ctrl	~Mod1	<Btn1Down>:	take_focus( ) select_start( )

Table 31-4 OI_multi_text Default Translations, OPEN LOOK

Event Sequence	Action Functions Called
<Btn1Motion>:	select_adjust( )
<Btn1Up>:	select_end( )
<Btn2Down>:	extend_start( )
<Btn2Motion>:	select_adjust( )
<Btn2Up>:	select_end( )
<Btn3Down>:	click_down( )
<Btn3Up>:	click_up( )
<FocusIn>:	focus_in( )
<FocusOut>:	focus_out( )

Table 31-5 describes the actions taken by the action functions.

Table 31-5 OI_multi_text Translation Functions

Function Name	Description
backward_character( )	Moves the cursor backwards one character. Wraps to the previous line if necessary. Repositions the text in the viewport if necessary.
backward_paragraph( )	Moves the cursor backwards one paragraph. Positions the cursor at the beginning of the paragraph. Repositions the text in the viewport if necessary.
backward_word( )	Moves the cursor backwards one word. Positions the cursor at the beginning of the word. Repositions the text in the viewport if necessary.
backward_view( )	Moves the cursor to the left edge of the viewport. If the cursor is already at the left edge of the viewport, shifts the text to display the next view to the left and positions the cursor at the left edge of the viewport.
beginning_of_file( )	Moves the cursor to the beginning of the text. Repositions the text in the viewport if necessary.
beginning_of_line( )	Moves the cursor to the beginning of the current line. Repositions the text in the viewport if necessary.
beginning_of_pane( )	Moves the cursor to the position in front of the first visible character in the first line currently visible in the viewport.

Table 31-5 OI_multi_text Translation Functions

Function Name	Description
cancel_select( )	Cancels any selection which is in progress. Applies only while mouse button is down.
click_down( )	Starts timing for a mouse button click.
click_up( )	Ends mouse button click timing and makes click callback.
copy_clipboard( )	Copies the PRIMARY selection (the currently selected text) to the CLIPBOARD selection.
copy_primary( )	Inserts contents of the PRIMARY selection at the cursor location.
copy_start( )	Begin a drag and drop operation without deleting the selected text from the OI_multi_text object. copy_start is similar to the OI_d_tech translation drag_start except that the operation used is OI_dnd_copy.
cut_clipboard( )	Copies the PRIMARY selection to the CLIPBOARD selection, then deletes the PRIMARY selection.
cut_primary( )	Inserts the contents of the PRIMARY selection at the cursor location, then deletes the PRIMARY selection.
delete_all_characters( )	Deletes all the characters on the current line (the one the cursor is in), but leaves an empty line. Positions the cursor at the beginning of the line.
delete_next_character( )	If the cursor is at the end of the line, joins the following line with the current line, otherwise deletes the character to the right of the cursor and closes up the space.
delete_next_word( )	If the cursor is at the end of the line, joins the following line with the current line, otherwise deletes the word to the right of the cursor and closes up the space.
delete_previous_character( )	If the cursor is at the beginning of the line, joins the current line with the previous line, otherwise deletes the character to the left of the cursor and closes up the space.
delete_previous_word( )	If the cursor is at the beginning of the line, joins the current line with the previous line, otherwise deletes the word to the left of the cursor and closes up the space.
delete_this_line( )	Deletes the line the cursor is in and closes up the space.

Table 31-5 OI_multi_text Translation Functions

Function Name	Description
delete_to_beginning_of_line( )	Deletes from the beginning of the current line to the cursor position and closes up the space.
delete_to_end_of_line( )	Deletes from the cursor position to the end of the current line and closes up the space.
end_of_file( )	Moves the cursor to the end of the text. Repositions the text in the viewport if necessary.
end_of_line( )	Moves the cursor to the end of the current line. Repositions the text in the viewport if necessary.
end_of_pane( )	Moves the cursor to the position after the last character on the last line currently visible.
extend_start( )	Begins a **PRIMARY** selection as for **select_start**, but initially includes all text from the mouse pointer to the cursor.
focus_in( )	Paints focus indicators to indicate that the object has the input focus.
focus_out( )	Paints focus indicators to indicate that the object does not have the input focus.
forward_character( )	Moves the cursor forward one character. Wraps to the next line if necessary. Repositions the text in the viewport if necessary.
forward_paragraph( )	Moves the cursor forward one paragraph. Positions the cursor at the beginning of the paragraph. Repositions the text in the viewport if necessary.
forward_word( )	Moves the cursor forward one word. Positions the cursor at the beginning of the word. Repositions the text in the viewport if necessary.
forward_view( )	Moves the cursor to the right edge of the viewport. If the cursor is already at the right edge of the viewport, shifts the text to display the next view to the right and position the cursor at the right edge of the viewport.
input_character( )	Inserts the character at the current cursor position. Works only for key events.

Table 31-5 OI_multi_text Translation Functions

Function Name	Description
input_convert( )	Works only for key events. Passes key event to language server for conversion. When the server is done converting (this may take several key events), inserts the result at the cursor position.
insert_mode( )	Puts the object in insert mode. This means that any characters inserted are placed at the current cursor location and are inserted between the two adjacent characters.
insert_selection(*arg*)	Inserts text from an X selection at the cursor position. If no arguments are present, the PRIMARY selection is used. Otherwise, *arg* is used as the name of the selection to use.
insert_string(*arg*)	Inserts the string *arg* at the cursor location. Use "\n" to indicate newlines and the Tab key (not "\t") to indicate tabs when specifying the string *arg*.
key_select( )	Puts all the text between the point marked by set_anchor to the current cursor location in the PRIMARY selection.
move_insertion( )	Moves the cursor to the location under the mouse pointer without clearing the PRIMARY selection.
move_selection( )	If the SECONDARY selection is active for this object then copies the SECONDARY selection text to the cursor location and deletes the original selected text. Otherwise, if the PRIMARY selection is active for this object and was set using the mouse, copies the PRIMARY selection text to the cursor location and deletes the original selected text.
newline( )	If an end-of-line callback is registered, calls it. If no end-of-line callback exists or if the end-of-line callback returned OI_mt_entry_chk_ok, then inserts a new line after the line the cursor is in, and positions the cursor at the beginning of the new line.
next_line( )	Moves the cursor to the next line. Repositions the text in the viewport if necessary.
next_object( )	Sets the input focus to the next object in the focus chain (if any).
next_page( )	Scrolls the text so that the next page towards the end of the text becomes visible.

Table 31-5 OI_multi_text Translation Functions

Function Name	Description
next_tab_group( )	Sets the input focus to the focus object in the next tab group (if any).
open_next_line( )	Inserts a blank line following the line containing the cursor. Rearranges the text accordingly.
open_previous_line( )	Inserts a blank line previous to the line containing the cursor. Rearranges the text accordingly.
paste_clipboard( )	Inserts the text from the CLIPBOARD selection at the cursor location.
previous_line( )	Moves the cursor to the previous line. Repositions the text in the viewport if necessary.
previous_object( )	Sets the input focus to the previous object in the focus chain.
previous_tab_group( )	Sets the input focus to the focus object in the previous tab group, if any.
previous_page( )	Scrolls the text so that the previous page towards the beginning of the text becomes visible.
process_return( )	If an end-of-line callback is registered, calls it. If no end-of-line callback exists or if the end-of-line callback returned OI_mt_entry_chk_ok, then positions the cursor at the beginning of the next line. If there is no next line (that is, the cursor is in the last line of text), inserts a new line at the end of the text and position the cursor there.
replace_mode( )	Puts the object in replace mode. This means that any characters input replace the character to the right of the current cursor location. Any characters input at the end of the line are appended to the line.
scroll_bottom( )	Scrolls to the last line of the text.
scroll_down( )	Scrolls one full viewport towards the end of the text.
scroll_left( )	Scrolls one full viewport towards the left of the text.
scroll_left_edge( )	Scrolls to the first character in the line.
scroll_right( )	Scrolls one full viewport towards the right of the text.

Table 31-5 OI_multi_text Translation Functions

Function Name	Description
scroll_right_edge( )	Scrolls to the last character position in the object. This may be well past the last character in the current line.
scroll_top( )	Scrolls to the first line of the text.
scroll_up( )	Scrolls one full viewport towards the beginning of the text.
secondary_adjust( )	Adjusts the SECONDARY selection to include all text from the secondary_start position to the position under the mouse pointer.
secondary_end( )	Completes the selection process and saves the selection as the SECONDARY selection. Also processes button-up event and calls click callback if one is registered.
secondary_start( )	Begins selecting text at the current location under the pointer for the SECONDARY selection. Underlines the selected text.
select_adjust( )	Adjusts the PRIMARY selection to include all text from the select_start position to the position under the pointer.
select_all( )	Puts the entire text in the PRIMARY selection. Highlights the selection.
select_end( )	Completes the selection process and saves the selection as the PRIMARY selection. Also processes button-up event and calls click callback if one is registered.
select_line( )	Selects the entire current line as the PRIMARY selection.
select_start( )	Begins selecting text at the mouse pointer location for the PRIMARY selection. Highlights the selection. Also processes button-down event in case click callbacks are registered.
set_anchor( )	Marks the current cursor location as the start for a keyboard-defined selection.
start_input_conversion( )	Sends all subsequent characters to the input server for conversion.
stop_input_conversion( )	Treats subsequent characters normally (quits sending characters to the input server).
toggle_mode( )	If the current mode is insert mode, changes it to replace mode. If the current mode is replace mode, changes it to insert mode.
take_focus( )	Sets the focus to the OI_multi_text object.

Table 31-5   OI_multi_text Translation Functions

Function Name	Description
unselect_all( )	Unselects any currently selected text.

31.10 Callback Functions

Table 31-6 lists the callbacks available for an **OI_base_text** object and the page number where the callback is documented. In addition, all of the callbacks from an **OI_base_text** object's base classes are available to it. See Section 6.18, "Determining and Adding Callbacks; Multiple Callbacks," on page 6-117 for additional information about manipulating callbacks.

Table 31-6   OI_base_text Callbacks

Callback Type	Callback Typedef	Description	Page Number
cbClick	OI_click_fnp / memfnp	Click callback function	31-5
cbMultiTextCharCheck	OI_mt_char_check_fnp / memfnp	Character Validation Callback Function	31-15
cbMultiTextEntryCheck	OI_mt_entry_check_fnp / memfnp	Line Entry Validation Callback Function	31-17
cbMultiTextCharChg	OI_mt_char_chg_fnp / memfnp	Change-Character Callback Function	31-19

Chapter 32
OI_scroll_text

OI_scroll_text Functions

OI_scroll_text Member Functions

The following functions are available to an **OI_scroll_text** object, but are described in their own chapter.

OI_base_text Member Functions

OI_d_tech Member Functions

```
#include <OI/oi.H>                        /* ScrBarScrollText.
int main (int argc, char **argv)
{
                void                      did_click (OI_scroll
                OI_connection             *conp ;
                OI_app_window             *wp ;
                OI_scroll_text            *stp ;
```

```
#include <OI/oi.H>                        /* ScrBarScrollText.
int main (int argc, char **argv)
{
                void                      did_click (OI_scroll
                OI_connection             *conp ;
                OI_app_window             *wp ;
                OI_scroll_text            *stp ;
```

OI_scroll_text

32.1 Description

An **OI_scroll_text** is a multi-text object surrounded by controllers (scroll bars or a panner) that can
be used to reposition the text in the multi-text's viewport. The OI_scroll_text object is actually a
composite of several OI objects: an *outside-box*, the *controllers* (one or two OI_scroll_bars or an
OI_panner), and the *text* (an OI_multi_text). These objects are diagrammed in Figure 32-1.

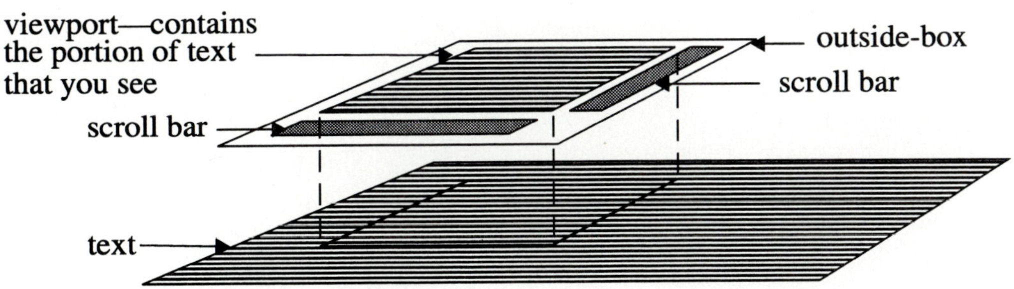

Figure 32-1   Parts of an OI_scroll_text Object with Scroll Bars

In practice you will never notice the *outside-box* in Figure 32-1, because it has a frame-width of zero.
The outside-box exists merely to contain all the parts of the OI_scroll_text object that are visible,
so that moving the entire OI_scroll_text object from one part of the screen to another, or other

---

operations that need to be performed on the entire object, can be done with ease. There is no separate viewport in a scroll-text as there is in a scroll-box or scroll-menu, because the multi-text already implements all the viewport functionality.

Figure 32-2 shows the object tree that OI builds internally to make an OI_scroll_text object.

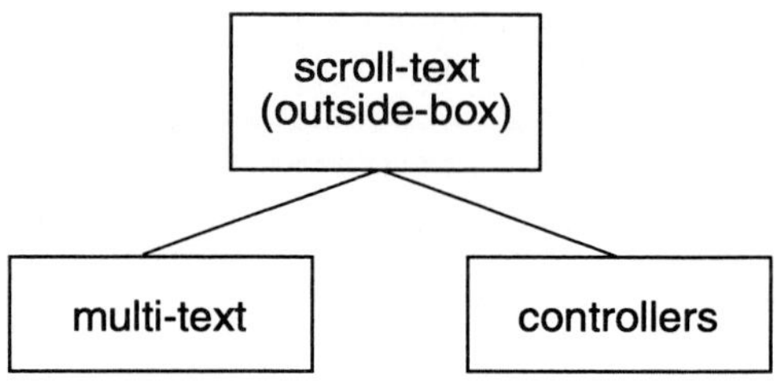

Figure 32-2 OI_scroll_text Internal Object Tree

If you use the OI_d_tech function **parent** or **child** to find your way around the object tree, remember that OI does not return pointers to intermediate internal objects.

User-units are the units in which locations, sizes, and scrolled movements are specified. For an OI_scroll_text object, they are defined to be one line per user-unit in the vertical direction, and one character per user-unit in the horizontal direction. For variable width fonts, this is the width of the widest character in the font, usually "W".

Use an OI_scroll_text object whenever the amount of text to be displayed and/or entered is substantially larger than the amount of screen space available for text display. An OI_scroll_text object allows the user to move great distances within the text with ease.

32.2 Class Tree

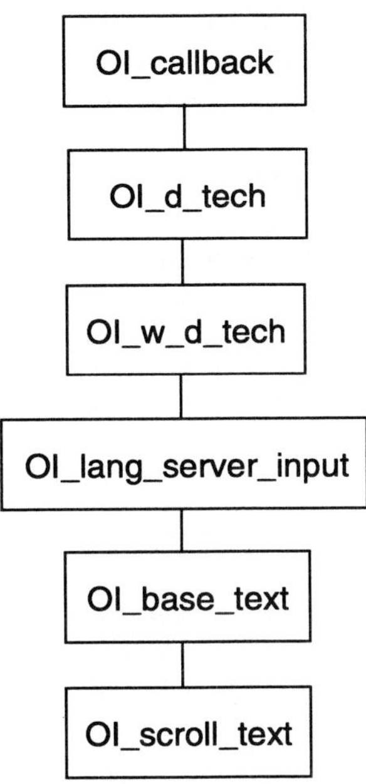

32.3 Runtime Interaction

To view different portions of the underlying text, use the controllers surrounding the multi-text. Additional information about scroll bars can be found in Chapter 30, "OI_scroll_bar," and about panners in Chapter 36, "OI_panner." For example, if you grab the handle of a vertical scroll bar with the mouse pointer and move it up, the text in the underlying viewport moves up a corresponding amount. If you move the handle 1/3 of the distance from the beginning of the scroll bar to its end, the text moves 1/3 of the distance from the beginning of the underlying text to its end. Figure 32-3 and Figure 32-4 show the effect of moving a scroll bar handle a short distance. Figure 32-5 shows the effect of moving a panner a short distance.

You can use all the navigational capabilities of OI_multi_text for the underlying OI_multi_text object; that is, you can use all the default translations OI installs for an OI_multi_text object. See Chapter 31, "OI_base_text and OI_multi_text" for more information.

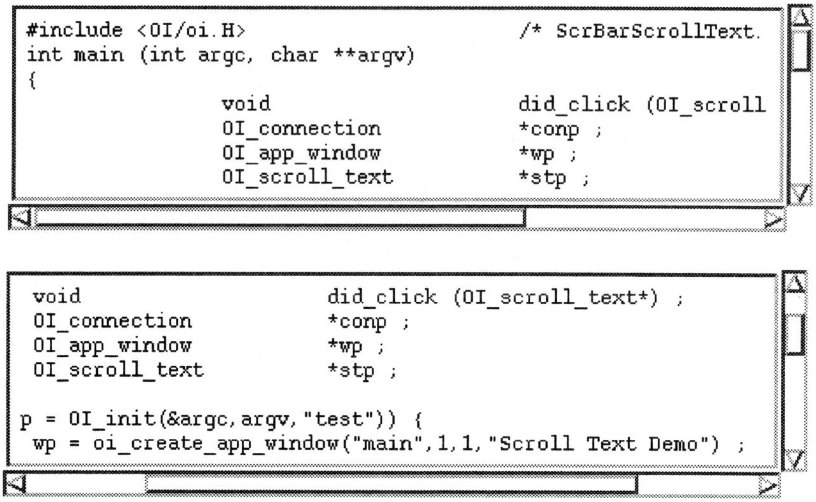

```
#include <OI/oi.H>                        /* ScrBarScrollText.
int main (int argc, char **argv)
{
                void                      did_click (OI_scroll
                OI_connection             *conp ;
                OI_app_window             *wp ;
                OI_scroll_text            *stp ;
```

```
  void                      did_click (OI_scroll_text*) ;
  OI_connection             *conp ;
  OI_app_window             *wp ;
  OI_scroll_text            *stp ;

p = OI_init(&argc, argv, "test")) {
  wp = oi_create_app_window("main", 1, 1, "Scroll Text Demo") ;
```

Figure 32-3   Scroll-Text with Handle Moved, Motif

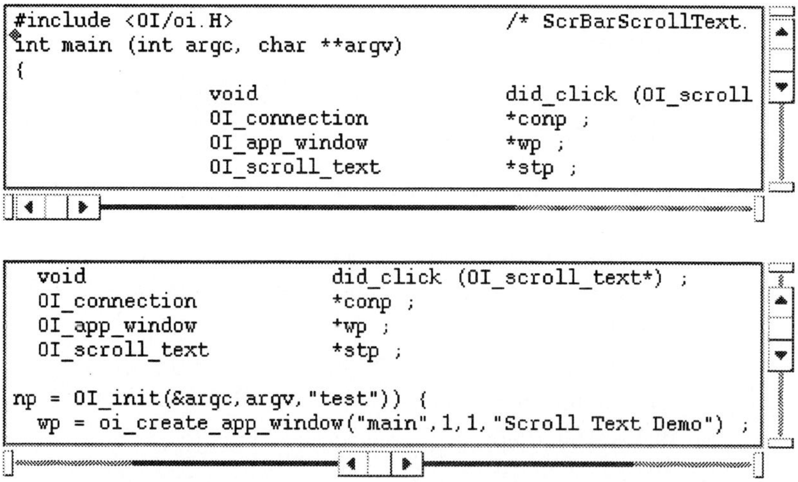

```
#include <OI/oi.H>                        /* ScrBarScrollText.
int main (int argc, char **argv)
{
                void                      did_click (OI_scroll
                OI_connection             *conp ;
                OI_app_window             *wp ;
                OI_scroll_text            *stp ;
```

```
  void                      did_click (OI_scroll_text*) ;
  OI_connection             *conp ;
  OI_app_window             *wp ;
  OI_scroll_text            *stp ;

np = OI_init(&argc, argv, "test")) {
  wp = oi_create_app_window("main", 1, 1, "Scroll Text Demo") ;
```

Figure 32-4   Scroll-Text with Handle Moved, OPEN LOOK

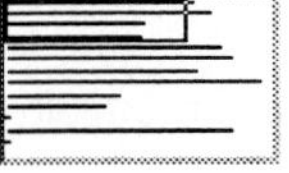

```
#include <OI/oi.H>                        /* PannerScrollText.
int main (int argc, char **argv)
{
            void                did_click (OI_scroll
            OI_connection       *conp ;
            OI_app_window       *wp ;
            OI_scroll_text      *stp ;
```

```
    void                did_click (OI_scroll_text*) ;
    OI_connection       *conp ;
    OI_app_window       *wp ;
    OI_scroll_text      *stp ;

np = OI_init(&argc, argv, "test")) {
```

Figure 32-5   Scroll-Text with Panner Moved

To enter text in a scroll-text, position the viewport over the area in which you wish to enter text, then enter text as you would for an **OI_multi_text** object. You can use all of **OI_base_text** and **OI_multi_text**'s text manipulation facilities, including all resources and translations, for an **OI_scroll_text** object (see Chapter 31, "OI_base_text and OI_multi_text").

32.4   OI_scroll_text Creation

oi_create_scroll_text   (Free-standing function)

```
OI_scroll_text *oi_create_scroll_text(
    const char      *namp,          // object name
    OI_number       controllers,    // type of controllers
    OI_number       view_lines,     // number of lines in viewport
    OI_number       view_chars,     // number of chars in width of viewport
    OI_number       max_lines=0,    // number of lines in text object
    OI_number       max_chars=0)    // number of characters in width of text object
```

controllers specifies the type of controllers the OI_scroll_text object should have. Possible controllers are:

OI_scroll_bar_both	Both vertical and horizontal OI_scroll_bar.
OI_scroll_bar_vertical	Vertical OI_scroll_bar.
OI_scroll_bar_horizontal	Horizontal OI_scroll_bar.
OI_scroll_bar_left	Vertical OI_scroll_bar at the left.
OI_scroll_bar_right	Vertical OI_scroll_bar at the right.
OI_scroll_bar_top	Horizontal OI_scroll_bar at the top.
OI_scroll_bar_bottom	Horizontal OI_scroll_bar at the bottom.
OI_scroll_panner	OI_panner above the object-box.

You can combine these controller types using a bitwise inclusive or to produce the set of controllers you desire, with the following constraints:

- You cannot combine a panner with any other controller.
- Left, right, and vertical scroll bars cannot be combined with each other in any way.
- Top, bottom, and horizontal scroll bars cannot be combined with each other in any way.

If you want vertical and/or horizontal scroll bars, you should use OI_scroll_bar_both, OI_scroll_bar_vertical or OI_scroll_bar_horizontal, and let OI place the scroll bars in the default position (left or right, top or bottom) for the particular interaction model being run, unless you have a good reason for placing the scroll bars in a particular location.

view_lines, view_chars, max_lines and *max_chars* are identical to the parameters with the same names for oi_create_multi_text. They are repeated here for convenience.

The viewport is sized to accommodate *view_lines* lines of text in height and *view_chars* characters of text in width. If you change the font (using OI_d_tech member functions), the text object and the viewport are resized accordingly.

The object is initially capable of holding a total of *max_lines* and *max_chars* characters per line. If you omit these values or set them to zero, they default to the corresponding *view_lines* and *view_chars* values. If you insert new lines using the OI_base_text member function insert_scroll_line, only a total of *max_lines* lines are kept. However if you insert new lines using one of the OI_base_text member functions insert_line, set_text, or set_text_to_file, *max_lines* grows as needed so the entire text is always available. In contrast, *max_chars* never changes (unless you call the function set_cols)—it is merely a "hint" to OI as to what buffer size to make for a line. If more than *max_chars* characters are entered in a line, they are always retained (as long as the line is retained), but this does not affect the value of *max_chars*—that is, the number of characters in a line may be longer than *max_chars*.

32.5 Base Class Member Functions

You can use all of the member functions of OI_d_tech and OI_base_text for an OI_scroll_text object.

32.5.1 Click Functions

An OI_scroll_text object can respond to mouse button clicks. See Chapter 31, "OI_base_text and OI_multi_text" for default click behavior. If you want an OI_scroll_text object to respond to mouse clicks, you must register a click callback function for the scroll-text object. When the user clicks on the object, the callback function (which you write yourself) will be executed. Note that whether you register a click function or not, every time the user clicks on the interior of the viewport, the input cursor moves to the nearest legal entry point to the location of the click. This point will be either the character under the mouse pointer, or if there is no character under the mouse pointer, the last character in the line containing the mouse pointer. If there are no characters in the line, the cursor moves to the start of that line.

set_click   (Member function)

```
void OI_scroll_text::set_click(
    OI_click_fnp        fnp,              // pointer to callback function
    void                *argp=NULL)       // arbitrary argument for fnp


void OI_scroll_text::set_click(
    OI_callback         *objp,            // memfnp's object
    OI_click_memfnp     memfnp,           // pointer to callback member function
    void                *argp=NULL)       // arbitrary argument for memfnp
```

The **set_click** functions register a callback function to be invoked whenever the user clicks a mouse button one or more times on an OI_scroll_text object. This callback is identified within OI as a cbClick callback function (see Section 6.18, "Determining and Adding Callbacks; Multiple Callbacks," on page 6-117). If your click function is a member function, when it is invoked it will be called as if you had written *objp->memfnp*. See Section 2.5, "Callbacks and Event-Driven Programming," on page 2-16 for more explanation.

argp is optional, and can be any valid expression that can be cast to a pointer. You can use it to pass additional information to the function *fnp* or member function *memfnp*.

The button press and release must be separated by no more than clickDelta milliseconds for a press/release sequence to be considered a click. For multiple clicks, a release and subsequent press must also be separated by no more than clickDelta milliseconds. clickDelta is an OI_connection resource, which defaults to 500.

Writing the Click Callback Function

If the cbClick callback function is not a member function, write it in this form:

```
void fn(
        OI_d_tech  *oi_objp,      // pointer to object clicked on
        void        *argp,        // arbitrary argument
        OI_number  n_clicks,      // number of clicks
        OI_number  btn,           // mouse button number clicked
        OI_number  mod,           // modifier bits on at click time
        OI_number  lin,           // line number where click occurred
        OI_number  chr)           // character position where click occurred
```

and if the cbClick callback function is a member function, write it in this form:

```
void obj_class::memfn(
        OI_d_tech  *oi_objp,      // pointer to object clicked on
        void        *argp,        // arbitrary argument
        OI_number  n_clicks,      // number of clicks
        OI_number  btn,           // mouse button number clicked
        OI_number  mod,           // modifier bits on at click time
        OI_number  lin,           // line number where click occurred
        OI_number  chr)           // character position where click occurred
```

where *obj_class* is the class of the object whose member function is *memfn*.

When your callback function is invoked, *argp* will be the argument specified in the set_click call. *oi_objp* will be a pointer to the object where the click occurred. *mod* will contain the modifier bits on at click time. These will be zero unless the user holds down one of the modifier keys on the keyboard at the time of the mouse click. *mod* can have any combination (0 or more) of the following values, combined with a bitwise inclusive or.

OI_mod_shift	Shift key down during click.
OI_mod_lock	Lock key down during click.
OI_mod_control	Control key down during click.
OI_mod_meta	Mod1 key down during click.

When more than one click occurs, the callback function will be invoked once for each click. For example, a double click will cause the function to be called first with *n_clicks*=1, then with *n_clicks*=2. If your application is performing a different operation depending on the number of clicks, the operations for a greater number of clicks should be compatible with those for fewer clicks. For example, by default, a double click means select a word, and three clicks mean select a line.

lin and *chr* will be the line number and character number where the click occurred. Lines are numbered starting with 0 at the top of the text, and characters are numbered starting with 0 at the beginning of each line. If the click occurred to the right of the last character in a line, *chr* will be the number of the last character plus 1. If the click occurred below any line in the text, *lin* will be the number of the last line plus 1 and *chr* will be 0.

32.6 OI_scroll_text Member Functions

32.6.1 Positioning the Viewport

Use the functions discussed in this section to query the viewport position or set the viewport position. To fully understand the x and y values used to position the viewport, consider Figure 32-6.

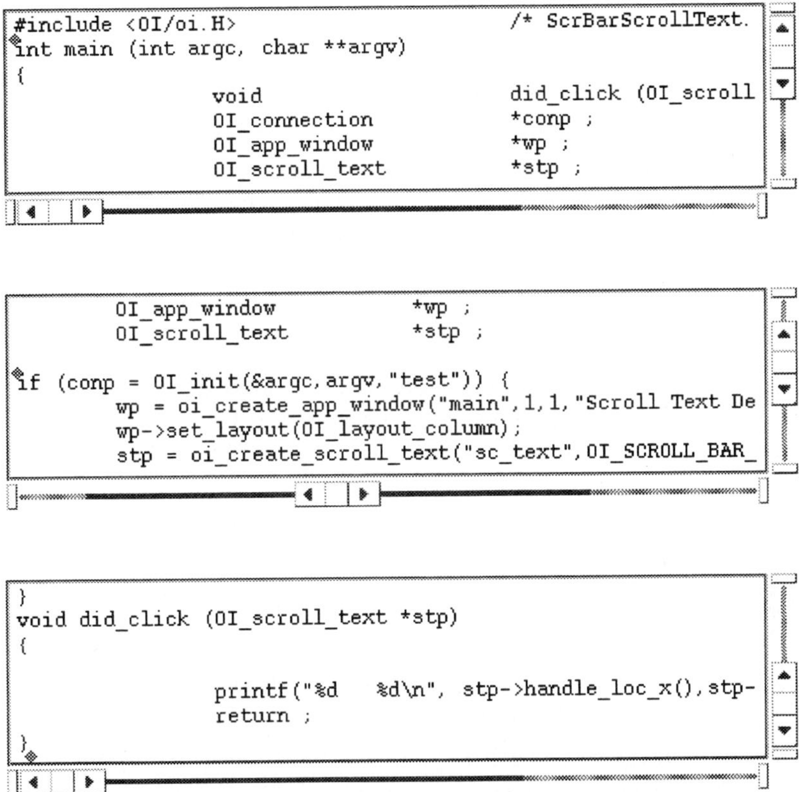

Figure 32-6 Scroll-Text Handle Locations

Figure 32-6 shows an OI_scroll_text object whose underlying multi-text contains 25 lines and whose viewport shows seven lines. In the top scroll-text, the handles are in the starting position, and the handle locations are x=0,y=0. In the middle scroll-text, the handles have been moved to location x=8,y=5. The bottom scroll-text shows the vertical scroll bar is as far down as it can go; the handles are in location x=0,y=18. Considering the first line as line 0, lines 18 through 24 are visible in the bottom scroll-text.

The viewport shows seven user-units (lines) vertically and the multi-text contains 25 user-units vertically; these values determine which portions of the multi-text are visible when the handle is at any position. For the example in Figure 32-6, the possible vertical handle locations and which lines of text are visible are shown in the table below.

Vertical Handle Location	Lines Visible
0	0 through 6
1	1 through 7
2	2 through 8
.	
.	
.	
17	17 through 23
18	18 through 24

Notice that if you wish to have line 23 visible, you do not set the vertical handle location to 23. If you want line 8 visible, you can set the vertical handle location to 2, 3, 4, 5, 6, 7, or 8. The general algorithm for determining which lines and characters will be visible in the viewport is:

> If the vertical handle is at location n, then lines n through n + *view_lines* - 1 will be in the viewport. Similarly, if the horizontal handle is at location n, then characters n through n + *view_chars* - 1 will be in the viewport.

A valid vertical handle location can be any integer in the range 0 to multi-text size (in lines) minus viewport size (in lines), and similarly for horizontal handle locations. If you attempt to set a location outside the possible range of handle locations, the location of the viewport will not change, and OI will display an error message.

These rules and algorithms for handle locations hold true regardless of whether you are using scroll bars or a panner for your scroll-text.

handle_loc   (Member function)

```
void OI_scroll_text::handle_loc(
   long              *loc_x,        // location in x direction
   long              *loc_y)        // location in y direction
```

handle_loc backfills *loc_x* and *loc_y* with the current x and y position of the viewport in user-units. *loc_x* will be in the range

$$0 <= loc\_x <= \text{max\_n\_chars( )} - \text{view\_n\_chars( )}$$

Similarly, *loc_y* will be in the range

$$0 <= loc\_y <= \text{n\_lines( )} - \text{view\_n\_lines( )}$$

handle_loc_x   (Member function)

```
long OI_scroll_text::handle_loc_x( )
```

handle_loc_x returns the current horizontal position of the viewport in characters (user-units). The value returned will be in the range

$$0 <= \text{handle\_loc\_x( )} <= \text{max\_n\_chars( )} - \text{view\_n\_chars( )}$$

handle_loc_y   (Member function)

```
long OI_scroll_text::handle_loc_y( )
```

handle_loc_y returns the current vertical position of the viewport in lines (user-units). The value returned will be in the range

$$0 <= \text{handle\_loc\_y}(\ ) <= \text{n\_lines}(\ ) - \text{view\_n\_lines}(\ )$$

set_handle_loc   (Member function)

```
OI_stat OI_scroll_text::set_handle_loc(
   long                    loc_x,          // x location
   long                    loc_y)          // y location
```

set_handle_loc positions the viewport over the underlying multi-text object as if the user had moved the handle on a horizontal controller to location *loc_x* and a vertical controller to location *loc_y*. *loc_x* and *loc_y* are in user-units (ordinarily characters and lines, respectively). They must be in the range

$$0 <= loc\_x <= \text{max\_n\_chars}(\ ) - \text{view\_n\_chars}(\ )$$

and

$$0 <= loc\_y <= \text{n\_lines}(\ ) - \text{view\_n\_lines}(\ )$$

set_handle_loc_x   (Member function)

```
OI_stat OI_scroll_text::set_handle_loc_x(
   long                    loc_x)          // x location
```

set_handle_loc_x positions the viewport over the underlying multi-text object as if the user had moved the handle on a horizontal controller to location *loc_x*. *loc_x* is in user-units (characters). *loc_x* must be in the range

$$0 <= loc\_x <= \text{max\_n\_chars}(\ ) - \text{view\_n\_chars}(\ )$$

set_handle_loc_y   (Member function)

```
OI_stat OI_scroll_text::set_handle_loc_y(
   long                    loc_y)          // y location
```

set_handle_loc_y positions the viewport over the underlying multi-text object as if the user had moved the handle on a horizontal controller to location *loc_y*. *loc_y* is in user-units (lines). *loc_y* must be in the range

$$0 <= loc\_y <= \text{n\_lines}(\ ) - \text{view\_n\_lines}(\ )$$

32.6.2   Accessing Subobjects

You can use the functions below to access the individual components of an OI_scroll_text object. You will seldom need to access these components, as most OI_scroll_text manipulation can be done through other functions without retrieving the separate parts of the OI_scroll_text object.

multi_text (Member function)

```
OI_multi_text *OI_scroll_text::multi_text( )
```

multi_text returns a pointer to the underlying multi-text object. You should not normally need to use this function, as you can use all of the **OI_base_text** member functions directly for an **OI_scroll_text** object.

horz_scroll_bar (Member function)

```
OI_scroll_bar *OI_scroll_text::horz_scroll_bar( )
```

horz_scroll_bar returns a pointer to the horizontal scroll bar, if one exists; otherwise it returns NULL.

vert_scroll_bar (Member function)

```
OI_scroll_bar *OI_scroll_text::vert_scroll_bar( )
```

vert_scroll_bar returns a pointer to the vertical scroll bar, if one exists; otherwise it returns NULL.

left_scroll_bar (Member function)

```
OI_scroll_bar *OI_scroll_text::left_scroll_bar( )
```

left_scroll_bar returns a pointer to the left scroll bar, if one exists; otherwise it returns NULL.

right_scroll_bar (Member function)

```
OI_scroll_bar *OI_scroll_text::right_scroll_bar( )
```

right_scroll_bar returns a pointer to the right scroll bar, if one exists; otherwise it returns NULL.

top_scroll_bar (Member function)

```
OI_scroll_bar *OI_scroll_text::top_scroll_bar( )
```

top_scroll_bar returns a pointer to the top scroll bar, if one exists; otherwise it returns NULL.

bottom_scroll_bar (Member function)

```
OI_scroll_bar *OI_scroll_text::bottom_scroll_bar( )
```

bottom_scroll_bar returns a pointer to the bottom scroll bar, if one exists; otherwise it returns NULL.

panner (Member function)

```
OI_panner *OI_scroll_text::panner( )
```

panner returns a pointer to the panner, if one exists; otherwise it returns NULL.

32.6.3 Controlling Behavior

The functions below are used to control behavior as described in the next paragraphs. Note that many of these items can also be controlled via resources, and it is usually better to allow the user to control these via the resource mechanism. The only good reason to set these in your program is to prevent the user from setting them through the resource mechanism.

The relationship between the number of lines and characters in the text and the multi-text view size determines whether or not a controller is actually needed. For example, if the multi-text is as wide as the longest line, no horizontal scroll bar is needed. As the text is modified, this relationship will probably change. It may also change due to the user resizing the object via the window manager. You can control whether or not the controllers disappear if they are not needed, and what happens to the space they formerly occupied.

An OI_scroll_text object normally provides "instant" feedback when the user drags the controller to reposition the text. By this we mean that the text constantly updates as the controller is dragged. On some hardware, this dynamic update may cause performance to deteriorate; if necessary you can disable this type of update.

Another aspect of performance involves modifications to the controller span update. Whenever you add or delete a line of text, the controllers are notified of this change so they can keep their span consistent. A span update may force a controller to repaint. (For example, a scroll bar handle or cable may get longer or shorter.) If you are adding or deleting many lines all at once, this frequent update may cause performance to deteriorate. You can turn span updates on or off to alleviate this problem.

The gravity set for the scroll-text affects its behavior when its controllers appear and disappear. By default an OI_scroll_text object has **OI_grav_northwest** gravity; you can change it by using the **OI_d_tech** member function **set_gravity**. For example, if gravity is **OI_grav_northwest** and a right scroll bar is present, nothing shifts when the right scroll bar appears and disappears, because the upper-left corner is the anchor point. If gravity is **OI_grav_northeast**, the viewport and any other controller (horizontal scroll bar) shift right when the right scroll bar disappears, then shift back left when it reappears.

is_motion_callback   (Member function)

```
OI_bool OI_scroll_text::is_motion_callback( )
```

is_motion_callback returns **OI_yes** if the controllers are configured to provide continual updating of the text while the handle is being dragged; otherwise it returns **OI_no**.

allow_motion_callback   (Member function)

```
void OI_scroll_text::allow_motion_callback( )
```

allow_motion_callback conditions the controllers so that the underlying multi-text is updated continually while the handle is being dragged. This is the normal (default) condition.

disallow_motion_callback   (Member function)

```
void OI_scroll_text::disallow_motion_callback( )
```

disallow_motion_callback conditions the object so that the underlying multi-text will not be repositioned for each movement of the handle while the handle is being dragged. The multi-text will be updated only when the button is released at the final position.

is_span_update   (Member function)

```
OI_bool OI_scroll_text::is_span_update( )
```

is_span_update returns OI_yes if the controllers are configured to resize and repaint, if necessary, whenever their span changes (lines and/or characters are added or deleted). Otherwise is_span_update returns OI_no.

allow_span_update   (Member function)

```
void OI_scroll_text::allow_span_update( )
```

allow_span_update conditions the controller(s) so that their appearance will be updated each time a change is made in the size of the underlying multi-text. The appearance update may change the position or the length of the handle on a scroll bar controller or the size of the viewport rectangle in a panner. This is the default condition.

disallow_span_update   (Member function)

```
void OI_scroll_text::disallow_span_update( )
```

disallow_span_update conditions the controller(s) so that their appearance will not be updated each time a change is made in the size of the underlying multi-text. You should only set this condition temporarily—for example, when you are filling the multi-text object with many lines all at once. When you are done adding text, you should set the controllers back to allow_span_update to force the controller appearance to be updated properly.

controller_visibility   (Member function)

```
OI_controller_visibility OI_scroll_text::controller_visibility( )
```

controller_visibility returns one of the values listed under set_controller_visibility.

set_controller_visibility   (Member function)

```
void OI_scroll_text::set_controller_visibility(
    OI_controller_visibility ctlr)        // controller and space disposition
```

set_controller_visibility configures the object's controllers to automatically appear and disappear, depending on the size relationship between the underlying multi-text object and the viewport, and what to do with the extra space remaining if the controllers disappear. *ctlr* can be one of the following:

OI_controller_visibility_no_change	Controllers are always visible. This is the default.
OI_controller_visibility_disappear	Controllers disappear, leaving a hole.
OI_controller_visibility_expand	Expand the rest of the object to use up extra space.
OI_controller_visibility_collapse	Collapse the object to use up extra space.

If *ctlr* is OI_controller_visibility_no_change, the controllers are always visible. If *ctlr* is any of the other values, and the viewport completely spans the multi-text in a given direction, the controller for that direction is made invisible. If *ctlr* is OI_controller_visibility_disappear, the spacing is unchanged, leaving a hole. If *ctlr* is OI_controller_visibility_expand, the viewport expands to fill the space vacated by the controller. If *ctlr* is OI_controller_visibility_collapse, the scroll-text object shrinks.

32.7 Using Derived Classes as Components of an OI_scroll_text

If you create a subclass of OI_multi_text, OI_panner or OI_scroll_bar that you wish to use instead of the standard OI classes for the components of an OI_scroll_text object, you must call one of the functions below to tell OI to use your class instead. For example, you might want the OI_scroll_text object to control an object of class my_text_n_glyphs instead of class OI_multi_text. To do this, you must call one of the set_*_class functions described below before you create an OI_scroll_text object for which you wish to use your class. Also, your class must be a full-fledged OI class as discussed in Chapter 41, "Deriving Your Own Classes."

The set_*_class functions are static member functions since they must be called before creating any OI_scroll_text object using these sub-components. For example, to use my_text_n_glyphs, your code would contain the following lines:

```
    OI_scroll_text          *stp;
  OI_scroll_text::set_multi_text_class(my_text_n_glyphs::clsp);
  stp = oi_create_scroll_text("fancy_text",OI_scroll_bar_both,20,80);
```

To reset to the default:

```
  OI_scroll_text::set_multi_text_class(OI_muli_text::clsp);
```

set_multi_text_class   (Member function)

```
static void OI_scroll_text::set_multi_text_class(
    OI_class              *cls)          // class pointer
```

```
static void OI_scroll_text::set_multi_text_class(
    const char            *cls_nam)      // class name
```

set_multi_text_class instructs OI to use *cls* or *cls_nam* as the class for the OI_multi_text component of any OI_scroll_text object you subsequently create.

data_changed   (Member function)

```
void OI_scroll_text::data_changed( )
```

You will only need to use **data_changed** if you are using a panner as a controller for the OI_scroll_text object, and you have used an object of your own class as the OI_multi_text component of the OI_scroll_text object—that is, you have called **set_multi_text_class**. If these conditions are true, you should also have your own panner paint callback function to draw the miniaturized version of the scrolled object in the panner. You should call **data_changed** whenever the data in the controlled text object has changed but the view and span have not changed (for example, the user has typed a letter, but its line is still shorter than the width of the viewport). You must do this to cause OI to call your panner paint function so that the miniature drawing in the panner will be redrawn.

set_panner_class   (Member function)

```
static void OI_scroll_text::set_panner_class(
    OI_class            *cls)                    // class pointer
```

```
static void OI_scroll_text::set_panner_class(
    const char          *cls_nam)               // class name
```

set_panner_class instructs OI to use *cls* or *cls_nam* as the class for the OI_panner component of any OI_scroll_text object you subsequently create.

set_scroll_bar_class   (Member function)

```
static void OI_scroll_text::set_scroll_bar_class(
    OI_class            *cls)                    // class pointer
```

```
static void OI_scroll_text::set_scroll_bar_class(
    const char          *cls_nam)               // class name
```

set_scroll_bar_class instructs OI to use *cls* or *cls_nam* as the class for the OI_scroll_bar component of any OI_scroll_text object you subsequently create.

32.8   An OI_scroll_text Programming Example

Program 32-1, below, shows the code for a primitive directory browser. The resulting application is shown in Figure 32-7 on page 32-19. The name of the directory shows in the entry field at the top, and all the files in the directory appear in the scroll-text. The application starts with the user's home directory in the entry field. The user can click on a directory name in the scroll-text; that directory name is appended to the directory name in the entry field, and the new directory is shown in the scroll-text. Alternatively, the user can type a directory name in the entry field, and that name is used as the new directory. If the name in the entry field is not a directory, the application displays an error message in the help string area of the application window. This browser is primitive partly because, in order to keep it short, not all cases are properly handled. For example, if the user clicks on ". ." in the scroll-text, the directory changes appropriately, but the ". ." is merely appended to the path in the entry field.

This program shows the use of the independent function OI_translate_filename. Because each file name in the entry field is put through OI_translate_filename, the user can enter environment variables such as $HOME or use such notation as ~mylogin, and these will be translated to the appropriate path and file name.

```c
#include <OI/oi.H>                        /* BrowseDir.C */
#include "dirent.h"
#include "strings.h"

        void                    fill_text_with_dir(OI_base_text*,char*);

int main (int argc, char **argv)
{
        OI_ef_entry_chk_status use_entry(OI_entry_field*,void*,
                                        OI_ef_entry_chk_status);
        void                    did_click (OI_d_tech*,void*,OI_number,OI_number,
                                        OI_number,OI_number,OI_number);
        OI_connection           *conp;
        OI_app_window           *wp;
        OI_entry_field          *efp;
        OI_scroll_text          *stp;
        char                    *filenamp;

    if (conp = OI_init(&argc,argv,"BrowseDir")) {
        wp = oi_create_app_window("main",1,1,"Directory Browser");
        wp->set_layout(OI_layout_column);

        efp = oi_create_entry_field("file_field",50,"Directory:",NULL,1000);
        efp->layout_associated_object(wp,1,0,OI_active);
        filenamp = OI_translate_filename("$HOME");
        efp->set_text(filenamp);

        stp = oi_create_scroll_text("sc_text",OI_scroll_bar_both,7,60);
        stp->layout_associated_object(wp,1,1,OI_active);
        stp->set_click(did_click,efp);

        efp->set_entry_check(use_entry,stp);
        fill_text_with_dir(stp,efp->part_text( ));
        wp->set_associated_object(wp->root( ),OI_def_loc,OI_def_loc,OI_active);
        OI_begin_interaction( );
    }
}

OI_ef_entry_chk_status use_entry(OI_entry_field *efp, void *argp,
                                        OI_ef_entry_chk_status stat)
{
        char                    *filenamp;
    if (stat == OI_ef_entry_chk_ok) {
        filenamp = OI_translate_filename(efp->part_text( ));
        efp->set_text(filenamp,OI_no);
        fill_text_with_dir((OI_base_text*)argp,filenamp);
    }
    return(stat);
}
```

```
void fill_text_with_dir(OI_base_text *btp, char *dirnamp)
{
        DIR                     *dirp;
        dirent                  *direntp;

    btp->clear_text( );
    if (dirp = opendir(dirnamp)) {
        while(direntp = readdir(dirp))
            btp->insert_line(-1,direntp->d_name);
        closedir(dirp);
    }
    else
        btp->push_help_str("Not a directory",OI_yes);
    return;
}


void did_click(OI_d_tech *objp, void *argp, OI_number,
                            OI_number, OI_number, OI_number lin, OI_number)
{
        OI_base_text            *btp;
        OI_entry_field          *efp;
        char                    buffer[1000];

    btp = (OI_base_text*)objp;
    efp = (OI_entry_field*)argp;
    strcpy(buffer,efp->part_text( ));
    strcat(buffer,"/");
    strcat(buffer,btp->text(lin));
    efp->set_text(buffer,OI_yes);
    return;
}
```

Program 32-1 Directory Browser Using an OI_scroll_text (BrowseDir.C)

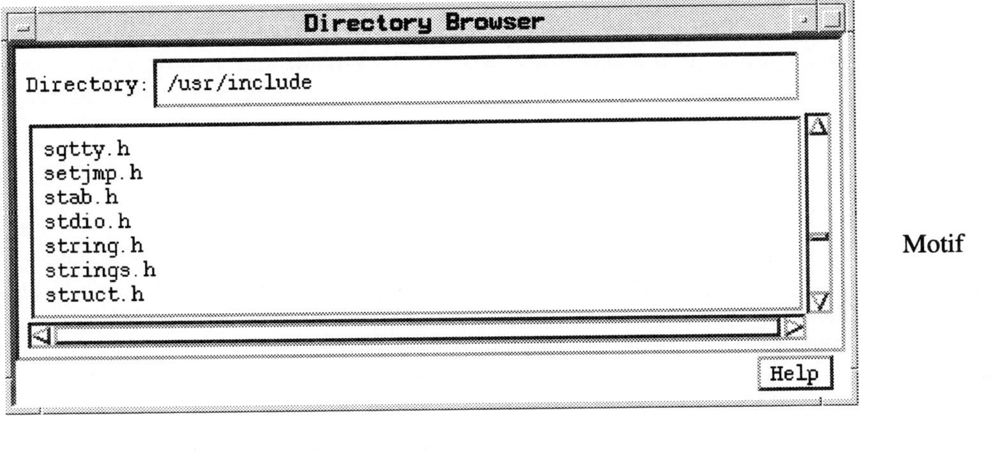

Motif

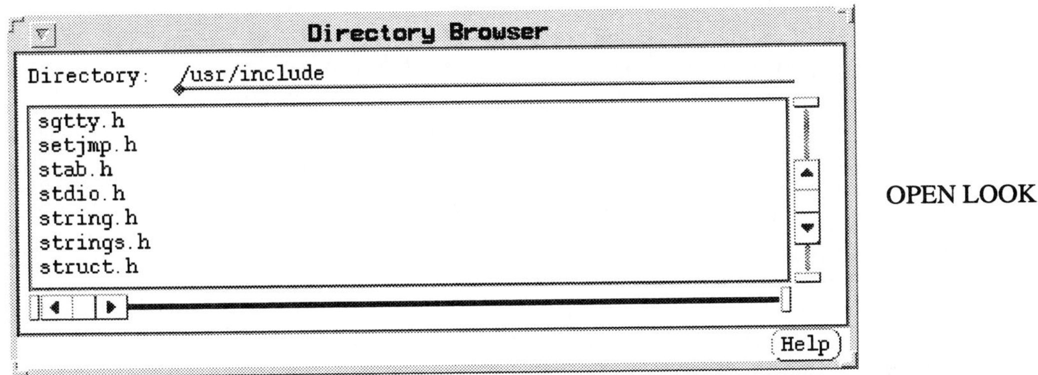

OPEN LOOK

Figure 32-7   Directory Browser Using an OI_scroll_text

32.9 Resources

All resources from an **OI_scroll_text** object's base classes are available to it; in addition, OI fetches the resources shown in Table 32-1. For more information on resource management, see Chapter 39, "The OI Resource Mechanism."

Table 32-1 OI_scroll_text Resources

Resource	Description	Possible Values	Default Value
controllerVisibility	See **set_controller_visibility** on page 32-14.	no_change disappear collapse expand	no_change
controllers	Specifies controllers to use. Can be combined using "+".	scroll_bar_both scroll_bar_vertical scroll_bar_horizontal scroll_bar_left scroll_bar_right scroll_bar_top scroll_bar_bottom panner	scroll_bar_both
motionCallback	If **on**, a call to the handle action callback will be made each time the handle moves. If **off**, the call is made only when the button is released.	Boolean	true
spanUpdate	If **on**, specifies that the appearance of the controller(s) will be updated each time a change is made in the size of the underlying multi-text.	Boolean	true

32.10 Translations

All translations from an **OI_scroll_text** object's base classes are available to it; it has no additional translations.

32.11 Callback Functions

Table 32-2 lists the callbacks available for an OI_scroll_text object and the page number where the callback is documented. In addition, all of the callbacks from an OI_scroll_text object's base classes are available to it. See Section 6.18, "Determining and Adding Callbacks; Multiple Callbacks," on page 6-117 for additional information about manipulating callbacks.

Table 32-2   OI_scroll_text Callbacks

Callback Type	Callback Typedef	Description	Page Number
cbClick	OI_click_fnp/memfnp	Click callback function	32-7

Chapter 33
OI_scroll_box

OI_scroll_box Functions

OI_scroll_box Member Functions

The following functions are available to an **OI_scroll_box** object, but are described in their own chapter.

OI_box Member Functions

OI_d_tech Member Functions

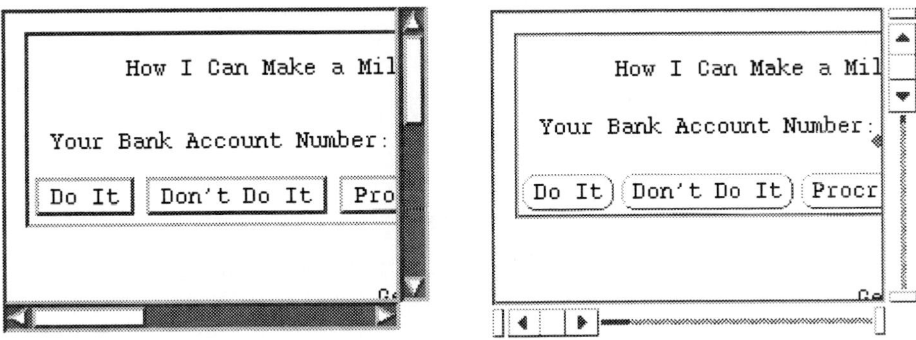

OI_scroll_box

33.1 Description

An **OI_scroll_box** is a viewport surrounded by controllers (either scroll bars or a panner) that can be used to re-position objects in the viewport. The **OI_scroll_box** object is actually a composite of several OI objects: an *outside-box* (an **OI_box**), the *controllers* (**OI_scroll_bar** or **OI_panner**), the *viewport* (an interior **OI_box**), and the *object-box* (yet another **OI_box**). Optionally, *headings* can be placed at the top, bottom, left or right of the viewport. These objects are diagrammed in Figure 33-1 and Figure 33-2.

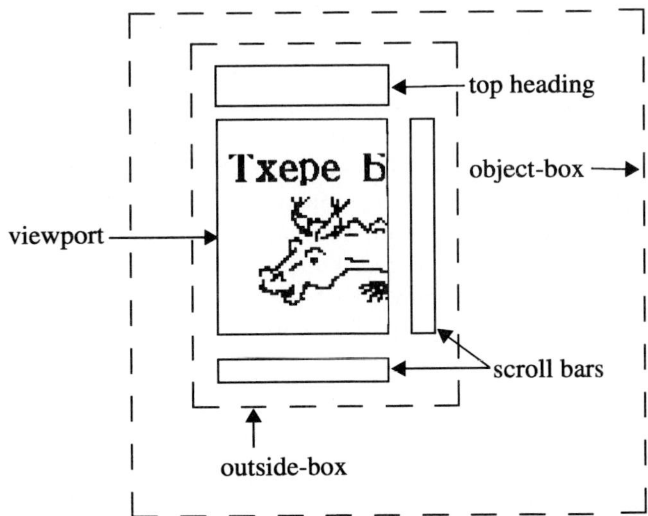

Figure 33-1   Parts of an OI_scroll_box object with Scroll Bars

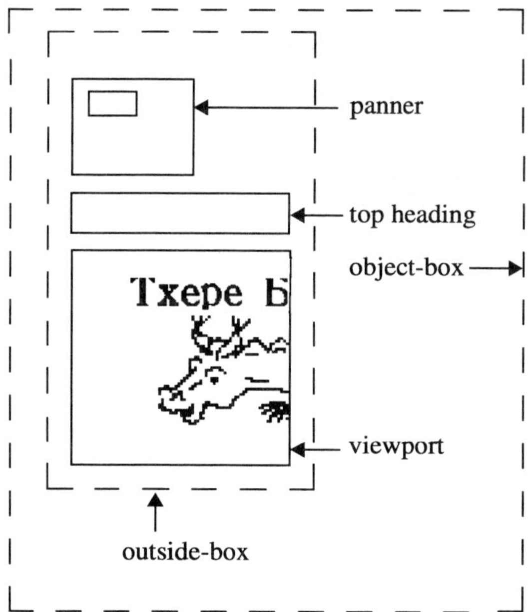

Figure 33-2   Parts of an OI_scroll_box Object with Panner

In Figure 33-1 and Figure 33-2, the *outside-box* is represented by dotted lines, although in practice you usually do not see it (it has a default frame width of 0). The outside-box exists merely to contain all the parts of the OI_scroll_box object that are visible, so that moving the entire OI_scroll_box object from one part of the display to another, or other operations that need to be performed on an entire object, can be done with ease. The *object-box* is the box which is scrolled, and is the box into which you put the objects you wish to be seen through the *viewport*. The only portion of the object-box that appears in an OI_scroll_box object is that portion which is directly under the viewport. In Figure 33-1 and Figure 33-2, an entire dragon is in the object-box, but only her head and one front foot are visible in the viewport. You can think of the viewport as remaining fixed on the screen, and the object-box as sliding around underneath the viewport when the controllers are manipulated. The portion of the object-box that moves out from under the viewport becomes invisible, and the portion of the object-box that moves so as to be under the viewport becomes visible.

You can optionally place one or more *heading(s)* in the scroll box object. Figure 33-1 and Figure 33-2 each show a top heading; you can place a heading at top, bottom, left or right. Top and bottom headings do not scroll up or down, but they do scroll left and right. Similarly, left and right headings do not scroll left or right, but they do scroll up and down. Thus the heading is always visible. The heading is actually an OI_box object with frame-width of zero; you can set layout on it and put other OI objects in it. You could use a heading, for example, if you were making a spread sheet. The top heading could contain column heading information, and the left heading could contain row heading information.

Figure 33-3 shows the object tree that OI builds to make an OI_scroll_box object. Note that the object-box is a child of the viewport box, not of the outside-box.

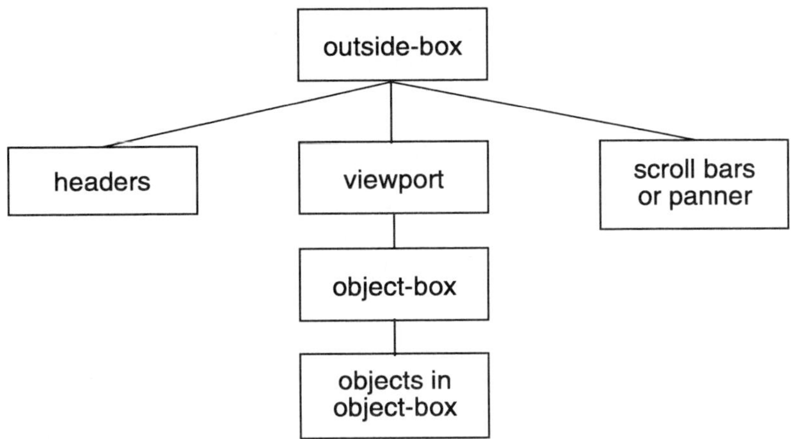

Figure 33-3 Scroll Box Internal Object Tree

When you parent another object to an OI_scroll_box object, the object is actually associated with the underlying object-box. You can obtain a pointer to this object-box by using the object_box member function (see below). If you use the OI_d_tech member functions parent or child to move around the object tree, remember that OI does not return pointers to intermediate internal objects. For example, if you have a pointer *gp* to an object (say, a glyph) that you have associated with the scroll box, the glyph is physically located in the object-box. The expression

```
gp->parent( )
```

returns a pointer to the scroll box (the outside-box), not the object-box, because both the object-box and the viewport are internal OI objects.

User-units are the units in which locations, sizes, and scrolled movements are specified. For an OI_scroll_box object, they are defined to be a certain number of pixels per user-unit; you establish these user-units in the create call, but you can change them at any time by calling the set_units member function.

For example, Figure 33-4 shows a grid of rectangular objects placed in an OI_scroll_box object running in Motif mode. There is a top heading with T-* labels and a left heading with L-* labels.

Each rectangle is 25 pixels wide by 15 pixels high. The layouts in the scroll box and the headings specify 4 pixels of spacing between objects in each direction. Each small rectangle within the scroll box has its column and row number displayed in its interior. The goal in this example is to specify the user-units to be one unit per small rectangle, so that moving the scroll bar one unit will move the display of rectangles by exactly one rectangle.

In this example, the boxes are laid out using a default spacing of four pixels. The amount of space from the left edge of one rectangle to the left edge of the next in the Motif and 3-D OPEN LOOK models is 33 pixels, because the frame of each small rectangle takes up 2 pixels (25 + 4 + 2 + 2 = 33). Similarly, the vertical space is 23 pixels (15 + 4 + 2 + 2 = 23). In the 2-D OPEN LOOK model, the corresponding horizontal space is 31 pixels, because the frame of each small rectangle takes up 1 pixel (25 + 4 + 1 + 1 = 31). Similarly, the vertical space in 2-D OPEN LOOK is 21 pixels (15 + 4 + 1 + 1 = 21). Because of the differences in the models, you may find it difficult to deal with the number of pixels directly. The code that produced this figure sets the user-units to be space_x( )+4 in the horizontal direction and space_y( )+4 in the vertical direction, thus letting OI resolve the issue of number of pixels per user-unit.

The viewport was specified to be 5 user-units wide and 4 user-units high, resulting in 20 individual rectangular graphics in the viewport at any time. The code that produced this example is in Program 33-1 on page 33-20.

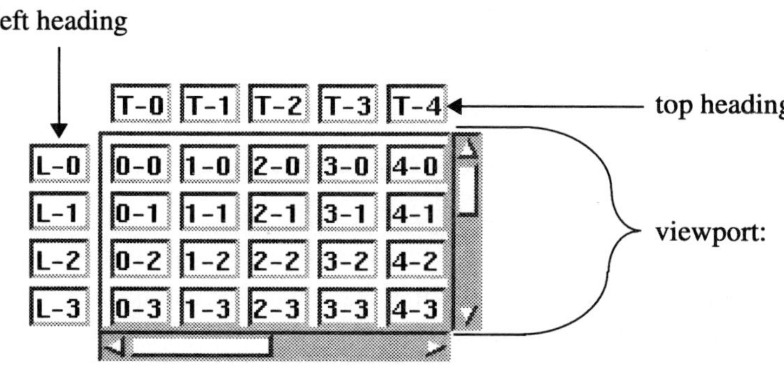

Figure 33-4   Scroll Box Viewport, Headings, and User-Units Example

A scroll box supports mouse click functions. If you register a click callback function for a scroll box, the only clicks that trigger the callback are those that occur within the viewport, on a portion of the object-box where no child object appears. If the user clicks on an object that is a child of the object-box, the child object normally intercepts the click. For example, in the scroll box pictured in Figure 33-4, if you click on the interior of one of the small boxes, the click does not fall through to the scroll box. You must click on the space between the small boxes for the scroll box to receive the click.

Before using an OI_scroll_box object, check to be sure that one of the more specialized scrolling objects (OI_scroll_text or OI_scroll_menu) is not more appropriate for your intended task, as those objects have more functionality than a scroll-box. The scroll box example in the OI periodic table on page 1-10 shows an OI_scroll_box object with an OI_dialog_box object and an OI_excl_check_menu as children of the object-box.

33.2 Class Tree

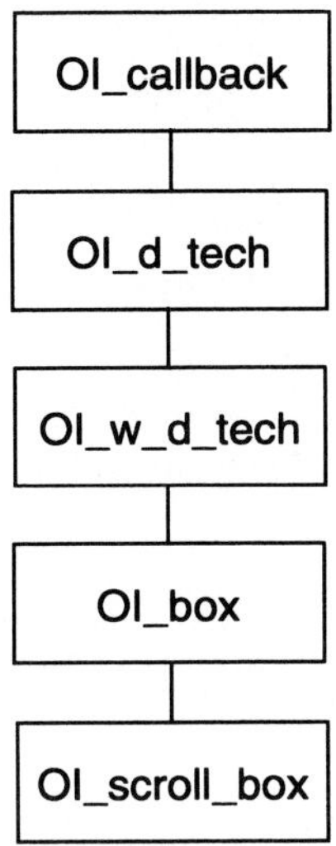

33.3 Runtime Interaction

To view different portions of the underlying object-box, use the controllers surrounding the viewport. For more information about scroll bars, see Chapter 30, "OI_scroll_bar," and for panners, see Chapter 36, "OI_panner." For example, if you grab the handle of a vertical scroll bar with the mouse and move it up, the viewport onto the underlying object-box moves up a corresponding amount—that is, the contents of the object-box appears to move down in the viewport. If you move the handle 1/3 of the distance from the beginning of the scroll bar to its end, the viewport moves 1/3 of the distance from the beginning of the underlying object-box to its end. Figure 33-5 shows the effect of moving the panner on a scroll box with a panner, and Figure 33-6 shows the effect of moving the scroll bar handle on a scroll box with scroll bars.

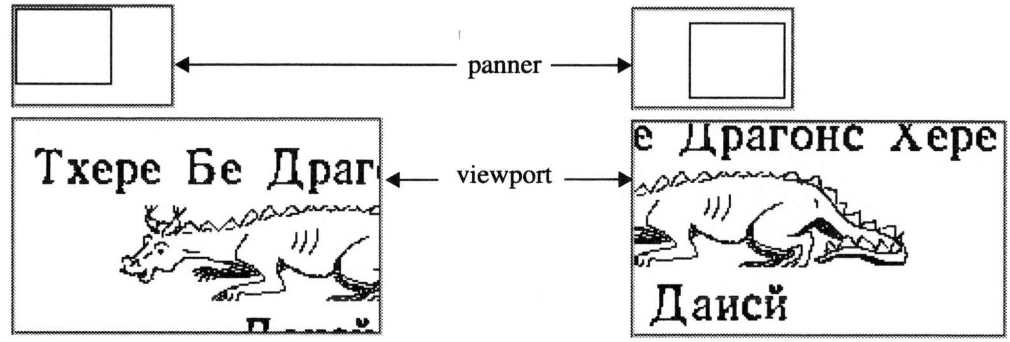

Figure 33-5   Scroll Box with Panner Moved

Figure 33-6   Scroll Box with Scroll Bar Handles Moved

33.4   OI_scroll_box Creation

oi_create_scroll_box   (Free-standing function)

```
OI_scroll_box *oi_create_scroll_box(
    const char        *namp,              // object name
    OI_number         controllers,        // types of controllers
    OI_number         view_size_x,        // viewport x size in user-units
    OI_number         view_size_y,        // viewport y size in user-units
    OI_number         object_size_x,      // object x size in user-units
    OI_number         object_size_y,      // object y size in user-units
    OI_number         pix_x=1,            // number of pixels/user-unit in x direction
    OI_number         pix_y=1)            // number of pixels/user-unit in y direction
```

controllers specifies the type of controllers the OI_scroll_box is to have. Possible controllers are:

OI_scroll_bar_both	Both vertical and horizontal OI_scroll_bars.
OI_scroll_bar_horizontal	Horizontal OI_scroll_bar.
OI_scroll_bar_vertical	Vertical OI_scroll_bar.
OI_scroll_bar_left	Vertical OI_scroll_bar at the left.
OI_scroll_bar_right	Vertical OI_scroll_bar at the right.
OI_scroll_bar_top	Horizontal OI_scroll_bar at the top.
OI_scroll_bar_bottom	Horizontal OI_scroll_bar at the bottom.
OI_scroll_panner	OI_panner above the object-box.

You may combine these controller types with a bitwise inclusive or to produce the set of controllers for the OI_scroll_box object you desire, with the following constraints:

- You cannot combine a panner with any other controller.
- Left, right, and vertical scroll bars cannot be combined with each other in any way.
- Top, bottom, and horizontal scroll bars cannot be combined with each other in any way.

If you want vertical and/or horizontal scroll bars, you should use OI_scroll_bar_vertical and/or OI_scroll_bar_horizontal, and let OI place the scroll bars in the default position (left or right, top or bottom) for the particular interaction model being run, unless you have a good reason for placing the scroll bars in a particular location.

pix_x and *pix_y* specify the number of pixels per user-unit in the x and y directions respectively. If you omit them, they default to 1. When the box is scrolled, it moves in user-units.

view_size_x and *view_size_y* specify the size of the viewport box in the units defined by *pix_x* and *pix_y*. The viewport size is specified in user-units, not in pixels.

object_size_x and *object_size_y* specify the size of the underlying object-box that is to be viewed through the viewport. The object-box size is specified in user-units, not in pixels.

If you are using scroll bars for controllers, and you specify *pix_x* and *view_size_x* (or *pix_y* and *view_size_y*) so small that there is not enough length for the scroll bars, OI adjusts the view size upward to accommodate the minimum scroll bar length.

33.5   Base Class Member Functions

You can use all of the member functions of OI_d_tech and OI_box for an OI_scroll_box object.

33.5.1   Click Functions

An OI_scroll_box object can respond to mouse button clicks if the mouse pointer is over the OI_scroll_box. If you want an OI_scroll_box object to respond to mouse clicks, you must register a click callback function for the scroll box object. When the user clicks on the object, the callback function (which you write yourself) will be executed. Notice that the click will be on the object-box which underlies the viewport.

set_click   (Member function)

```
void OI_scroll_box::set_click(
    OI_click_fnp        fnp,              // pointer to callback function
    void                *argp=NULL)       // arbitrary argument for fnp


void OI_scroll_box::set_click(
    OI_callback         *objp,            // memfnp's object
    OI_click_memfnp     memfnp,           // pointer to callback member function
    void                *argp=NULL)       // arbitrary argument for memfnp
```

The **set_click** functions register a callback function to be invoked whenever the user clicks a mouse button one or more times on an **OI_scroll_box** object. *memfnp* points to a member function for the object pointed to by *objp*. This callback is identified within OI as a **cbClick** callback function (see Section 6.18, "Determining and Adding Callbacks; Multiple Callbacks," on page 6-117). If your click function is a member function, when it is invoked it will be called as if you had written *objp->memfnp*. See Section 2.5, "Callbacks and Event-Driven Programming," on page 2-16 for more explanation.

argp is optional, and can be any valid expression that can be cast to a pointer. You can use it to pass additional information to the function *fnp* or the member function *memfnp*.

The button press and release must be separated by no more than **clickDelta** milliseconds for a press/release sequence to be considered a click. For multiple clicks, a release and subsequent press must also be separated by no more than **clickDelta** milliseconds. **clickDelta** is an **OI_connection** resource, which defaults to 500.

Writing the Click Callback Function

If the **cbClick** callback function is not a member function, write it in this form:

```
void fn(
        OI_d_tech  *oi_objp,        // pointer to object clicked on
        void       *argp,           // arbitrary argument
        OI_number  n_clicks,        // number of clicks
        OI_number  btn,             // mouse button number clicked
        OI_number  mod,             // modifier bits on at click time
        OI_number  x,               // x position where click occurred
        OI_number  y)               // y position where click occurred
```

and if the **cbClick** callback function is a member function, write it in this form:

```
void obj_class::memfn(
        OI_d_tech  *oi_objp,        // pointer to object clicked on
        void       *argp,          // arbitrary argument
        OI_number  n_clicks,       // number of clicks
        OI_number  btn,            // mouse button number clicked
        OI_number  mod,            // modifier bits on at click time
        OI_number  x,              // x position where click occurred
        OI_number  y)              // y position where click occurred
```

where *obj_class* is the class of the object whose member function is *memfn*.

When your callback function is invoked, *argp* will be the argument specified in the **set_click** call. *oi_objp* will be a pointer to the object where the click occurred, in this case the **OI_scroll_box** object. *x* and *y* will be the coordinates where the click occurred. These coordinates will be in pixels, relative to the origin of the object-box underlying the viewport. *mod* will contain the modifier bits on at click time. These will be zero unless the user holds down one of the modifier keys on the keyboard at the time of the mouse click. *mod* can have any combination (0 or more) of the following values, combined with a bitwise inclusive **or**.

OI_mod_shift	Shift key down during click.
OI_mod_lock	Lock key down during click.
OI_mod_control	Control key down during click.
OI_mod_meta	Mod1 key down during click.

When more than one click occurs, the callback function will be invoked once for each click. For example, a double click will cause the function to be called first with *n_clicks*=1, then with *n_clicks*=2. If your application is performing a different operation depending on the number of clicks, the operations for a greater number of clicks should be compatible with those for fewer clicks.

33.5.2   X Window IDs

Since an **OI_scroll_box** object is composed of many OI objects, you may be interested in the X Window ID's available through these functions.

X_window   (Member function)

```
Window OI_scroll_box::X_window( )
```

X_window returns the X Window ID for the object-box, not the **OI_scroll_box** object as a whole. This is the X window ID you would use to draw the representation of the scrolled object if you are using Xlib calls to draw rather than placing other OI objects in the scroll box.

outside_X_window   (Member function)

```
Window OI_scroll_box::outside_X_window( )
```

outside_X_window returns the X Window ID for the outside container box.

33.6 OI_scroll_box Member Functions

33.6.1   Positioning the Viewport

Use these functions to query the viewport position or set the viewport position. To fully understand the x and y values used to position the viewport, consider Figure 33-7.

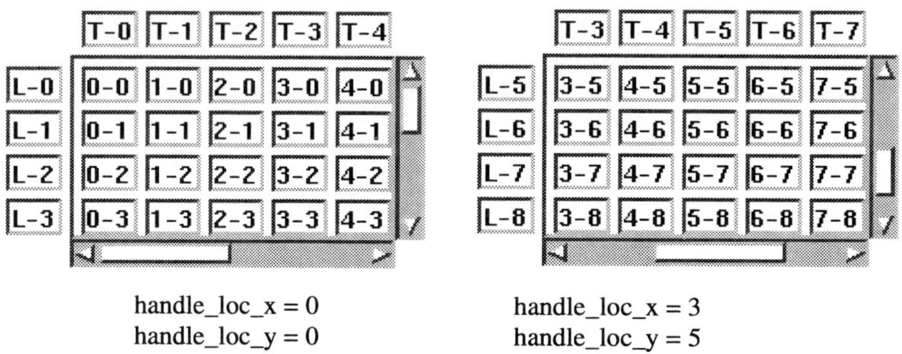

Figure 33-7   Scroll Box Handle Locations

This example shows the same OI_scroll_box object with a grid of small rectangles that we saw in Figure 33-4 on page 33-4. There are nine small rectangles across and nine down, each with its column-row number displayed on its face. (Row is vertical numbering and corresponds to y values; column is horizontal numbering and corresponds to x values.) One user-unit equals the size of one small rectangle in each direction. In the scroll box on the left, the handles are in the starting position, and the handle locations are x=0, y=0. In the box on the right, the handles have been moved, and are in location x=3, y=5.

The viewport shows four user-units vertically and the object-box contains nine user-units vertically; these values determine which portions of the object-box are visible when the handle is at any position. The possible handle locations and which rows of rectangles are visible are shown in the table below:

OI_scroll_box Handle Locations; Objects Visible in Viewport

Vertical Handle Location	Rows of Rectangles Visible
0	0 through 3
1	1 through 4
2	2 through 5
3	3 through 6
4	4 through 7
5	5 through 8

Notice that if you wish to have row number 7 visible, you do not set the handle location to 7; you can set it to 4 or 5. If you want row 4 visible, you can set the handle location to 1, 2, 3, or 4. The general algorithm for determining which user-units will be visible in the viewport is:

If the horizontal handle is at location n, then items will be in the viewport which correspond to user-units n through $n + view\_size\_x$ - 1. Similarly, if the vertical handle is at location n, then items will be in the viewport which correspond to user-units n through $n + view\_size\_y$ - 1.

A valid handle location can be any integer in the range 0 to object-box size (in user-units) minus viewport size (in user-units). If you attempt to set a location outside the possible range of handle locations, the location of the viewport does not change, and OI sends a message to the error handler.

handle_loc   (Member function)

```
void OI_scroll_box::handle_loc(
    long                    *loc_x,          // location in x direction, in user-units
    long                    *loc_y)          // location in y direction, in user-units
```

handle_loc backfills *loc_x* and *loc_y* with the current x and y position of the viewport in user-units. *loc_x* will be in the range 0 < *loc_x* <= object_size_x ( ) - view_size_x( ). Similarly, *loc_y* will be in the range 0 < *loc_y* <= object_size_y( ) - view_size_y( ).

handle_loc_x   (Member function)

```
long OI_scroll_box::handle_loc_x( )
```

handle_loc_x returns the current horizontal position of the viewport in user-units, with the same range restrictions as handle_loc.

handle_loc_y   (Member function)

```
long OI_scroll_box::handle_loc_y( )
```

handle_loc_y returns the current vertical position of the viewport in user-units, with the same range restrictions as handle_loc.

set_handle_loc   (Member function)

```
OI_stat OI_scroll_box::set_handle_loc(
    long                    loc_x,           // x location, in user-units
    long                    loc_y)           // y location, in user-units
```

set_handle_loc positions the viewport over the object-box as if the user had moved the handle on a horizontal controller to location *loc_x* and a vertical controller to location *loc_y*.

set_handle_loc_x   (Member function)

```
OI_stat OI_scroll_box::set_handle_loc_x(
    long                    loc_x)           // x location, in user-units
```

set_handle_loc_x positions the viewport over the object-box as if the user had moved the handle on a horizontal controller to location *loc_x*.

set_handle_loc_y   (Member function)

```
OI_stat OI_scroll_box::set_handle_loc_y(
    long                    loc_y)              // y location, in user-units
```

set_handle_loc_y positions the viewport over the object-box as if the user had moved the handle on a horizontal controller to location *loc_y*.

scroll   (Member function)

```
void OI_scroll_box::scroll(
    OI_ctlr_1d              *ctlr,              // controller to scroll
    void                    *ornt,              // orientation, in case there is no controller
    OI_scroll_event         typ,               // type of scrolling to do
    long                    n_scrl)             // units to scroll
```

scroll positions the viewport over the object-box as if the user had moved the handle on a single controller. *ctlr* points to the controller to scroll. Because of the possibility that there might be no controller, you should set *ornt* to "OI_vertical" or "OI_horizontal", depending upon which way you want the scroll box to scroll. *typ* specifies the type scrolling to do. Depending on the value of *typ*, *n_scrl* has different meanings. *typ* can be one of these values:

OI_scroll_unit	Scroll *n_scrl* user-units.
OI_scroll_viewport	Scroll *n_scrl* full viewports.
OI_scroll_extreme	Scroll to the extreme end.
OI_scroll_position	Scroll to the absolute position *n_scrl*, in user-units.

If *typ* is OI_scroll_unit, OI_scroll_viewport or OI_scroll_extreme, a positive value for *n_scrl* implies move down or right, and a negative value implies move up or left.

scroll_2d   (Member function)

```
void OI_scroll_box::scroll_2d(
    OI_panner               *pnr,               // panner to scroll
    void*,                                      // unused
    OI_scroll_event         typ,               // type of scrolling to do
    long                    x,                 // units to scroll in x direction
    long                    y)                 // units to scroll in y direction
```

scroll_2d positions the viewport over the object-box as if the user had moved the panner. *pnr* points to the panner to scroll. *typ* specifies the type scrolling to do, as specified for **scroll**, above. *x* and *y* are the equivalent of *n_scrl* for **scroll**, one for each of the two directions.

33.6.2   Changing Sizes

The functions below allow you to query and change the sizes of the viewport and object-box, and to modify the user-units.

view_size   (Member function)

```
void OI_scroll_box::view_size(
    OI_number            *size_x,        // horizontal viewport size, in user-units
    OI_number            *size_y)        // vertical viewport size, in user-units
```

view_size backfills *size_x* and *size_y* with the size of the viewport, in user-units, in the x and y directions, respectively.

view_size_x   (Member function)

```
OI_number OI_scroll_box::view_size_x( )
```

view_size_x returns the size of the viewport in the x direction, in user-units.

view_size_y   (Member function)

```
OI_number OI_scroll_box::view_size_y( )
```

view_size_y returns the size of the viewport in the y direction, in user-units.

set_view_size   (Member function)

```
OI_stat OI_scroll_box::set_view_size(
    OI_number            size_x,         // horizontal viewport size, in user-units
    OI_number            size_y)         // vertical viewport size, in user-units
```

set_view_size sets the size of the viewport to *size_x* by *size_y* user-units.

object_size   (Member function)

```
void OI_scroll_box::object_size(
    OI_number            *size_x,        // horizontal object-box size, in user-units
    OI_number            *size_y)        // vertical object-box size, in user-units
```

object_size backfills *size_x* and *size_y* with the size in user-units of the object-box (which is behind the viewport) in the x and y directions respectively.

object_size_x   (Member function)

```
OI_number OI_scroll_box::object_size_x( )
```

object_size_x returns the size in user-units of the object-box (which is behind the viewport) in the x direction.

object_size_y   (Member function)

```
OI_number OI_scroll_box::object_size_y( )
```

object_size_y returns the size in user-units of the object-box (which is behind the viewport) in the y direction.

set_object_size   (Member function)

```
OI_stat OI_scroll_box::set_object_size(
    OI_number              size_x,              // horizontal object-box size
    OI_number              size_y)              // vertical object-box size
```

set_object_size sets the size of the object-box (the box behind the viewport) to *size_x* by *size_y*. Specify *size_x* and *size_y* in user-units. If you use the OI automatic layout facility for laying out objects within the scroll box (that is, you call **set_layout** for the scroll box), you should not call **set_object_size**, since the layout mechanism determines the size of the object-box.

units   (Member function)

```
void OI_scroll_box::units(
    OI_number              *vw_x,               // horizontal pixels per user-unit
    OI_number              *vw_y)               // vertical pixels per user-unit
```

units backfills *vw_x* and *vw_y* with the number of pixels per user-unit in the x and y directions respectively. These are the *pix_x* and *pix_y* arguments in **oi_create_scroll_box** or **set_units**.

units_x   (Member function)

```
OI_number OI_scroll_box::units_x( )
```

units_x returns the number of pixels per user-unit in the x direction. This is the *pix_x* argument in **oi_create_scroll_box** or **set_units**.

units_y   (Member function)

```
OI_number OI_scroll_box::units_y( )
```

units_y returns the number of pixels per user-unit in the y direction. This is the *pix_y* argument in **oi_create_scroll_box** or **set_units**.

set_units   (Member function)

```
OI_stat OI_scroll_box::set_units(
    OI_number              pix_x,               // number of pixels/user-unit in x direction
    OI_number              pix_y)               // number of pixels/user-unit in y direction
```

set_units sets the number of pixels for a single user-unit in each direction. The initial values are *pix_x* and *pix_y* as specified in the **oi_create_scroll_box** function, or 1 if you omit these parameters in the create call. When you call **set_units**, the viewport and object-box grows or shrinks so that the view size and object-box size retain the same number of user-units as before the call to **set_units**. For example, if the viewport is 5 user-units long, and each user-unit is 6 pixels, the viewport is 30 pixels long. If you call **set_units** with a value of *pix_x* = 20, the viewport remains 5 user-units long, but it becomes 100 pixels long.

33.6.3   Accessing Subobjects

33.6.3.1 Managing Headers

You may have zero, one or up to four headings. The headings are always visible; top and bottom headings scroll left and right with the contents of the scroll box. Similarly the left and right headings scroll up and down. You can place other objects in the headings, such as static text or glyphs.

To remove a heading, obtain a pointer to the heading object (using a *_heading function), and then delete the object.

top_heading   (Member function)

```
OI_d_tech *OI_scroll_box::top_heading( )
```

top_heading returns a pointer to the top heading subobject. If there is no top heading, one is created.

is_top_heading   (Member function)

```
OI_bool OI_scroll_box::is_top_heading( )
```

is_top_heading returns OI_yes if there is a top heading for the scroll box; otherwise it returns OI_no.

bottom_heading   (Member function)

```
OI_d_tech *OI_scroll_box::bottom_heading( )
```

bottom_heading returns a pointer to the bottom heading subobject. If there is no bottom heading, one is created.

is_bottom_heading   (Member function)

```
OI_bool OI_scroll_box::is_bottom_heading( )
```

is_bottom_heading returns OI_yes if there is a bottom heading.

left_heading   (Member function)

```
OI_d_tech *OI_scroll_box::left_heading( )
```

left_heading returns a pointer to the left heading subobject. If there is no left heading, one is created.

is_left_heading   (Member function)

```
OI_bool OI_scroll_box::is_left_heading( )
```

is_left_heading returns OI_yes if there is a left heading.

right_heading   (Member function)

```
OI_d_tech *OI_scroll_box::right_heading( )
```

right_heading returns a pointer to the right heading subobject. If there is no right heading, one is created.

is_right_heading   (Member function)

```
OI_bool OI_scroll_box::is_right_heading( )
```

is_right_heading returns OI_yes if there is a right heading.

33.6.3.2 Other Subobjects

You can use the functions described here to access the individual components of an OI_scroll_box object other than headers. You will seldom need these, as most OI_scroll_box manipulation can be done through other functions without retrieving the separate parts of the OI_scroll_box object.

viewport   (Member function)

```
OI_box *OI_scroll_box::viewport( )
```

viewport returns a pointer to the viewport object.

object_box   (Member function)

```
OI_box *OI_scroll_box::object_box( )
```

object_box returns a pointer to the object-box being scrolled.

horz_scroll_bar   (Member function)

```
OI_scroll_bar *OI_scroll_box::horz_scroll_bar( )
```

horz_scroll_bar returns a pointer to the horizontal scroll bar, if one exists; otherwise it returns NULL.

vert_scroll_bar   (Member function)

```
OI_scroll_bar *OI_scroll_box::vert_scroll_bar( )
```

vert_scroll_bar returns a pointer to the vertical scroll bar, if one exists; otherwise it returns NULL.

left_scroll_bar   (Member function)

```
OI_scroll_bar *OI_scroll_box::left_scroll_bar( )
```

left_scroll_bar returns a pointer to the left scroll bar, if one exists; otherwise it returns NULL.

right_scroll_bar   (Member function)

```
OI_scroll_bar *OI_scroll_box::right_scroll_bar( )
```

right_scroll_bar returns a pointer to the right scroll bar, if one exists; otherwise it returns NULL.

top_scroll_bar   (Member function)

```
OI_scroll_bar *OI_scroll_box::top_scroll_bar( )
```

top_scroll_bar returns a pointer to the top scroll bar, if one exists; otherwise it returns NULL.

bottom_scroll_bar   (Member function)

```
OI_scroll_bar *OI_scroll_box::bottom_scroll_bar( )
```

bottom_scroll_bar returns a pointer to the bottom scroll bar, if one exists; otherwise it returns NULL.

panner   (Member function)

```
OI_panner *OI_scroll_box::panner( )
```

panner returns a pointer to the panner, if one exists; otherwise it returns NULL.

33.6.4   Controlling Behavior

The relationship between object-box size and viewport size determines whether a controller is actually needed or not. For example, if the viewport is as wide as the object-box, but not as tall, only a vertical controller is needed. In many situations, changing data or the user resizing the scroll box via the window manager changes this relationship. You may want the controllers to disappear if they are not needed; you can use the functions below to control this behavior.

You can also control whether the outside-box of the **OI_scroll_box** object collapses or whether the viewport expands when the controllers disappear. As shown in Figure 33-1 on page 33-1 and Figure 33-2 on page 33-2, the outside-box of an **OI_scroll_box** object is large enough to contain the viewport and the scroll bar(s) or the panner. If you specify that the object should collapse when the controllers disappear, it is the outside-box that collapses to the size of the viewport. You will usually want the outside-box not to collapse, especially if it is laid out in its parent and you do not want the parent to grow and shrink each time a controller appears or disappears.

The gravity set for the scroll box affects its behavior when its controllers appear and disappear. By default an **OI_scroll_box** object has **OI_grav_northwest** gravity; you can change it by using the **OI_d_tech** member function **set_gravity**. For example, if gravity is **OI_grav_northwest** and a right scroll bar is present, nothing shifts when the right scroll bar appears and disappears, because the upper-left corner is the anchor point. If gravity is **OI_grav_northeast**, the viewport and any other controller (horizontal scroll bar) shift right when the right scroll bar disappears, then shift back left when it reappears.

controller_visibility   (Member function)

```
OI_controller_visibility OI_scroll_box::controller_visibility( )
```

controller_visibility returns one of the values listed under **set_controller_visibility**.

set_controller_visibility   (Member function)

```
void OI_scroll_box::set_controller_visibility(
    OI_controller_visibility ctlr)      // controller and space disposition
```

set_controller_visibility configures the object's controllers to automatically appear and disappear, depending on the size relationship between the underlying box object and the viewport, and what to do with the extra space remaining if the controllers disappear. *ctlr* can be one of the following:

OI_controller_visibility_no_change	Controllers are always visible. This is the default.
OI_controller_visibility_disappear	Controllers disappear, leaving a hole.
OI_controller_visibility_expand	Expand the rest of the object to use up extra space.
OI_controller_visibility_collapse	Collapse the object to use up extra space.

If *ctlr* is OI_controller_visibility_no_change, the controllers are always visible. If *ctlr* is any of the other values, and the viewport completely spans the box in a given direction, the controller for that direction is made invisible. If *ctlr* is OI_controller_visibility_disappear, the spacing is unchanged, leaving a hole. If *ctlr* is OI_controller_visibility_expand, the viewport expands to fill the space vacated by the controller. If *ctlr* is OI_controller_visibility_collapse, the scroll-box object shrinks.

is_motion_callback   (Member function)

```
OI_bool OI_scroll_box::is_motion_callback( )
```

is_motion_callback returns OI_yes if the controllers are configured to provide continual updating of the view of the underlying object while the handle is being dragged; otherwise it returns OI_no.

allow_motion_callback   (Member function)

```
void OI_scroll_box::allow_motion_callback( )
```

allow_motion_callback conditions the controllers so that the view of the underlying object is updated continuously while the handle is being dragged. This is the normal (default) condition.

disallow_motion_callback   (Member function)

```
void OI_scroll_box::disallow_motion_callback( )
```

disallow_motion_callback conditions the object so that the underlying object-box will not be repositioned for each movement of the handle while the handle is being dragged. The view of the object-box will be updated only when the button is released at the final position.

is_span_update   (Member function)

```
OI_bool OI_scroll_box::is_span_update( )
```

is_span_update returns OI_yes if the controllers are configured to resize and repaint, if necessary, whenever their span changes (lines and/or characters are added or deleted). Otherwise is_span_update returns OI_no.

allow_span_update   (Member function)

```
void OI_scroll_box::allow_span_update( )
```

allow_span_update conditions the controller(s) so that their appearance will be updated each time a change is made in the size of the underlying object-box. The appearance update may change the position or the length of the handle on a scroll bar controller or the size of the viewport rectangle in a panner. This is the default condition.

disallow_span_update   (Member function)

```
void OI_scroll_box::disallow_span_update( )
```

disallow_span_update conditions the controller(s) so that their appearance will not be updated each time a change is made in the size of the underlying object-box. You should only set this condition temporarily—for example, when you are filling the object-box object with a large amount of information. When this condition is complete, you should set the controllers back to allow_span_update to force the controller appearance to be updated properly.

33.7   An OI_scroll_box Programming Example

Program 33-1 produces the small boxes in the OI_scroll_box object used as examples throughout this chapter. If the user clicks on the scroll box in the spaces between the "text" boxes, this program displays the handle locations in the terminal emulator from which the application was initiated. Figure 33-4 on page 33-4 and Figure 33-7 on page 33-10 show the program in action.

```
#include <OI/oi.H>                             /* ScrollBox.C */
int main (int argc, char **argv)
{
            void      what_loc (OI_scroll_box*);

            OI_connection        *conp;
            OI_app_window        *wp;
            OI_scroll_box        *sbp;
            OI_box               *bp;
            OI_static_text       *stp;
            OI_d_tech            *lhedp,*thedp;
            int                  i,j;
            char                 num_name[50];
    const   int                  BOXSPACE    = 4;
    const   int                  NBOX        = 9;
```

```
    if (conp = OI_init(&argc,argv,"ScrollBox")) {
        wp = oi_create_app_window("main_window",1,1,"Scroll Box Demo");
        wp->set_layout(OI_layout_column);
        sbp = oi_create_scroll_box("scroll_box",OI_scroll_bar_both,5,4,9,9);
        thedp = sbp->top_heading( );
        thedp->set_layout(OI_layout_column,BOXSPACE,BOXSPACE);
        lhedp = sbp->left_heading( );
        lhedp->set_layout(OI_layout_column,BOXSPACE,BOXSPACE);
        sbp->set_click((OI_click_fnp)&what_loc);
        sbp->set_layout(OI_layout_column,BOXSPACE,BOXSPACE);
        for (i = 0; i<NBOX; i++) {
            bp = oi_create_box("left_hed",25,15);
            stp = oi_create_static_text("text",sprintf(num_name,"L-%i",i));
            stp->set_associated_object(bp,1,1,OI_active);
            bp->layout_associated_object(lhedp,1,i,OI_active);
            for (j = 0; j<NBOX; j++) {
                if (i == 0) {
                    bp = oi_create_box("top_hed",25,15);
                    stp = oi_create_static_text("text",sprintf(num_name,"T-%i",j));
                    stp->set_associated_object(bp,1,1,OI_active);
                    bp->layout_associated_object(thedp,j,1,OI_active);
                }
                sprintf(num_name,"%i-%i",j,i);
                bp = oi_create_box(num_name,25,15);
                stp = oi_create_static_text("text",num_name);
                stp->set_associated_object(bp,1,1,OI_active);
                bp->layout_associated_object(sbp,j,i,OI_active);
            }
        }
        sbp->set_units(bp->space_x( )+BOXSPACE,bp->space_y( )+BOXSPACE);
        sbp->set_view_size(5,4);
        sbp->layout_associated_object(wp,1,1,OI_active);
        wp->set_associated_object(wp->root( ),OI_def_loc,OI_def_loc,OI_active);
        OI_begin_interaction( );
    }
}
void what_loc (OI_scroll_box *sbp)
{
        printf("%d    %d\n", sbp->handle_loc_x( ),sbp->handle_loc_y( ));
        return;
}
```

Program 33-1   Rectangles in a Scroll Box (ScrollBox.C)

Items to note about this program:

- The prototype for an **OI_click_fnp** specifies an **OI_d_tech*** as the first argument. Since we
  know it will be an **OI_scroll_box**, we have defined the callback function **what_loc** with a
  pointer to an **OI_scroll_box**. Since this callback does not use any of the other arguments, they
  are omitted. Because of these differences, when we register the click function **what_loc** for
  the scroll box, we have to cast it to be an **OI_click_fnp**, because its parameters are not

identical to those for a default OI_click_fnp. In general, we do not recommend this practice; we show it here as an example of one programming possibility. We strongly recommend writing the function to conform to the prototype.

- When we create the scroll box, we omit the user-units specifications because we do not know the size of the user-unit we will be using. Since we want user-units to be one rectangle's distance in each direction, and since we do not know under which model the user will run the application, the user-units are specified later in a model-independent way (as discussed previously in this chapter), by calling set_units.
- We also call set_view_size after calling set_units. In the call to oi_create_scroll_box we specify a unit size of 1, and a viewport size of 5,4. This would result in a viewport of only 5 by 4 pixels—too small for the minimum scroll bar length. Therefore OI adjusts the view size upward. Once we change the size of the user-units by calling set_units, the viewport remains the same size in number of user-units, and is quite large. We must call set_view_size to restore the originally-desired viewport size.
- If you move each of the scroll bars to the end position, the result is as shown in Figure 33-8.

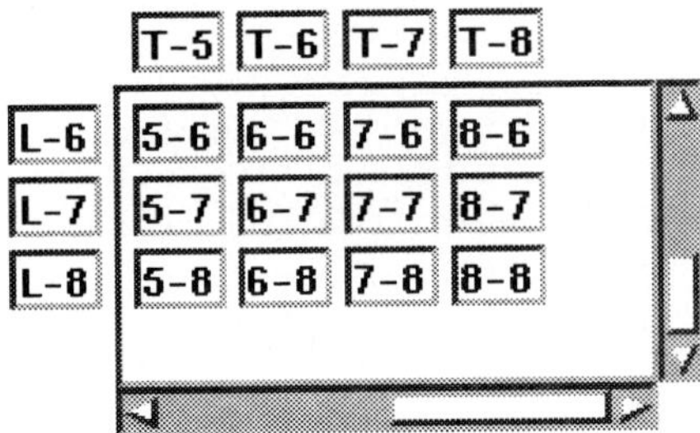

Figure 33-8   Scroll Box Example With Controllers Moved to Ends

As you can see, there is extra white space at the end of the layout in each direction. This is because we have specified the user-units to be the distance from the left edge of a small rectangle to the left edge of the next rectangle. There are four pixels of white space between each rectangle. There are also four pixels of white space between the left edge of the object-box and the first rectangle, and between the right edge of the object-box and the last rectangle, and similarly for the top and bottom. The controllers always move the object-box an integral number of user-units. Because of the extra four pixels at the end of the layout, the controllers scroll another entire user-unit, causing the extra white space to appear at the end in both directions. You can do one of several things about this problem:

1. Ignore it and live with it.
2. Make the user-units be 1, rather than the size of a small rectangle. Scrolling will then take place by increments of 1 pixel, and the underlying boxes at the edges of the viewport will be only partially visible.
3. Force the white space at the left, right, top and bottom edges of the scroll box to be two pixels instead of four pixels, thus making the number of user-units integral at the end of the layout. The code segment shown in Example 33-1 can replace the i,j loop

in Program 33-1 to do this job. With this enhancement, the program now produces the appearance shown in Figure 33-9 when the scroll bars are in position 0,0 and 4,5.

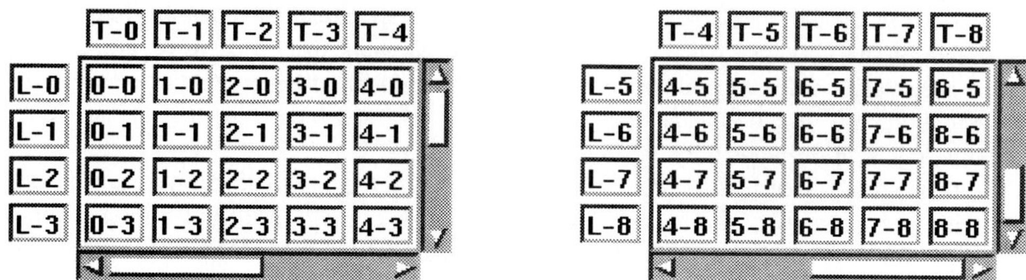

Figure 33-9   Scroll Box With Smaller Edge Spacing

```
for (i = 0; i<NBOX; i++) {
    bp = oi_create_box("left_hed",25,15);
    if (i == 0)
        bp->set_top_space(BOXSPACE/2);
    if (i == NBOX-1)
        bp->set_bottom_space(BOXSPACE/2);
    stp = oi_create_static_text("text",sprintf(num_name,"L-%i",i));
    stp->set_associated_object(bp,1,1,OI_active);
    bp->layout_associated_object(lhedp,1,i,OI_active);
    for (j = 0; j<NBOX; j++) {
        if (i == 0) {
            bp = oi_create_box("top_hed",25,15);
            if (j == 0)
                bp->set_left_space(BOXSPACE/2);
            if (j == NBOX-1)
                bp->set_right_space(BOXSPACE/2);
            stp = oi_create_static_text("text",sprintf(num_name,"T-%i",j));
            stp->set_associated_object(bp,1,1,OI_active);
            bp->layout_associated_object(thedp,j,1,OI_active);
        }
        sprintf(num_name,"%i-%i",j,i);
        bp = oi_create_box(num_name,25,15);
        if (j == 0)
            bp->set_left_space(BOXSPACE/2);
        if (j == NBOX-1)
            bp->set_right_space(BOXSPACE/2);
        if (i == 0)
            bp->set_top_space(BOXSPACE/2);
        if (i == NBOX-1)
            bp->set_bottom_space(BOXSPACE/2);
        stp = oi_create_static_text("text",num_name);
        stp->set_associated_object(bp,1,1,OI_active);
        bp->layout_associated_object(sbp,j,i,OI_active);
    }
}
```

Example 33-1   Code to Produce Smaller Edge Spacing in the Scroll Box Layout

33.8 Resources

All resources from an OI_scroll_box object's base classes are available to it; in addition, OI fetches the resources shown in Table 33-1. For more information on resource management, see Chapter 39, "The OI Resource Mechanism."

Table 33-1 OI_scroll_box Resources

Resource	Description	Possible Values	Default Value
controllers	Controllers to use for scroll box. Can be combined using "+".	scroll_bar_both scroll_bar_vertical scroll_bar_horizontal scroll_bar_left scroll_bar_right scroll_bar_top scroll_bar_bottom panner	scroll_bar_both
controllerVisibility	See set_controller_visibility on page 33-17.	no_change disappear expand collapse	no_change
objectBoxHeight	Height of object-box, in user-units.	Positive integer	(No default)
objectBoxWidth	Width of object-box, in user-units.	Positive integer	(No default)
unitX	User-units in the x direction.	Positive integer	1
unitY	User-units in the y direction.	Positive integer	1
viewHeight	Height of viewport, in user-units.	Positive integer	(No default)
viewWidth	Width of viewport, in user-units.	Positive integer	(No default)

33.9 Translations

All translations from an OI_scroll_box object's base classes are available to it; it has no additional translations.

33.10 Callback Functions

Table 33-2 lists the callbacks available for an OI_scroll_box object and the page number where the callback is documented. In addition, all of the callbacks from an OI_scroll_box object's base classes are available to it. See Section 6.18, "Determining and Adding Callbacks; Multiple Callbacks," on page 6-117 for additional information about manipulating callbacks.

Table 33-2   OI_scroll_box Callbacks

Callback Type	Callback Typedef	Description	Page Number
cbClick	OI_click_fnp/memfnp	Click callback function	33-8

Chapter 34
OI_scroll_menu

OI_scroll_menu Functions

OI_scroll_menu Member Functions

The following functions are available to an **OI_scroll_menu** object, but are described in their own chapter.

OI_menu Member Functions

OI_excl_menu Member Functions

OI_d_tech Member Functions

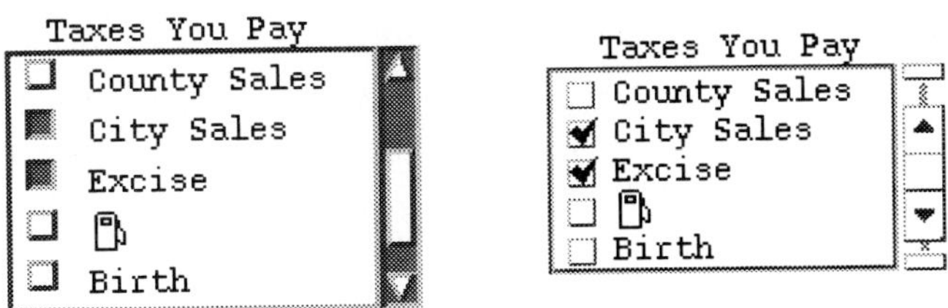

OI_scroll_menu

34.1 Description

An OI_scroll_menu is a viewport over a menu object, together with a scroll bar that can be used to reposition the menu in the viewport. Only a small number of menu cells are visible in the viewport at any one time. The OI_scroll_menu object is actually a composite of several OI objects: a *container*—a scroll box containing the *controller(s)* (OI_scroll_bar(s) or OI_panner), the *viewport* (OI_box), and an object box containing the actual *menu* and its *menu cells*. These objects are diagrammed in Figure 34-1.

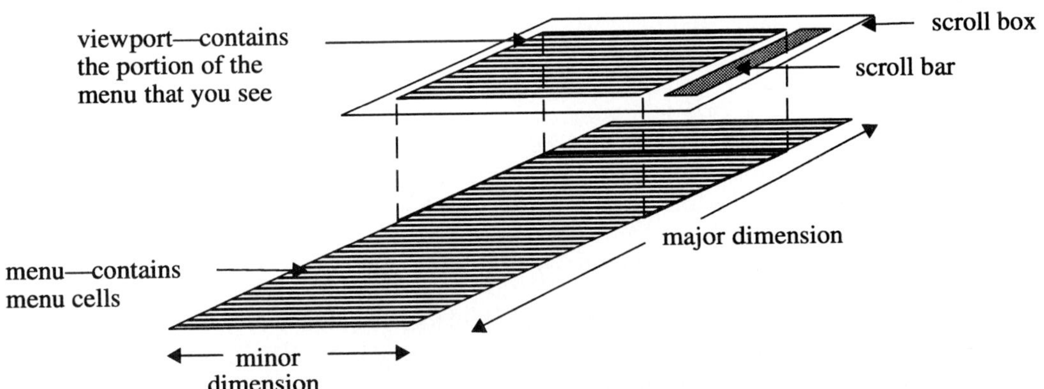

Figure 34-1 Parts of an OI_scroll_menu Object

In practice, you seldom see the container shown in Figure 34-1, because it has a default frame width of zero. The container exists merely to contain all the parts of the OI_scroll_menu object, so that moving the entire OI_scroll_menu from one part of the display to another, or other operations that need to be performed on the entire object, can be done with ease. If the scroll menu orientation is OI_vertical, you normally control the size of the viewport in the vertical direction only; the viewport is normally one menu-cell wide. Conversely, if the scroll menu orientation is OI_horizontal, you normally control the size of the viewport in the horizontal direction only. It is possible to put two scroll bars or a panner on the scroll menu and scroll it in two directions if you specify that the size in the minor dimension can be less than the size of a single cell. The menu can contain any number of cells. The only portion of the menu that is visible in an OI_scroll_menu object is that portion which is directly under the viewport. You can think of the viewport as remaining fixed on the screen, and the menu as sliding around underneath the viewport when the scroll-bar is manipulated. The portion of the menu that moves out from under the viewport becomes invisible, and the portion of the menu that moves so as to be under the viewport becomes visible. You can use an OI_scroll_menu object as a pop-up or a pull-down/ or pull-right menu.

Figure 34-2 shows the internal object tree OI builds to make an OI_scroll_menu object.

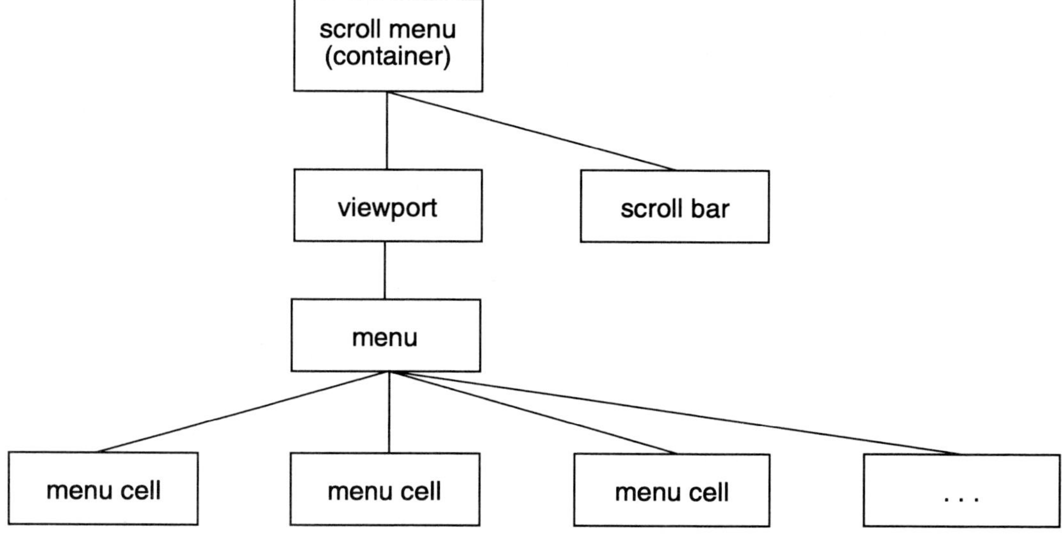

Figure 34-2   Scroll Menu Internal Object Tree

Note: If you use the OI_d_tech function **parent** or **child** to move around the object tree, remember that OI does not return pointers to intermediate internal objects. For example, if you have created a scroll menu with the underlying menu as an OI_button_menu, and you have a pointer *p* to an object that you have associated with one of the menu cells (for example, a pop-up dialog-box), the line

```
p->parent( )
```

returns a pointer to the menu cell to which the dialog box is attached, and

```
p->parent( )->parent( )
```

returns a pointer to the scroll menu. Use the OI_d_tech member function **abs_parent** to obtain a pointer to an internal intermediate object.

User-units are the units in which locations, sizes, and scrolled movements are specified. For a vertical OI_scroll_menu object, by default a vertical user-unit is one menu cell, and a horizontal unit is one pixel. For a horizontal scroll menu, a horizontal user-unit is one menu cell and a vertical unit is one pixel.

An OI_scroll_menu object is an obvious choice when the menu is too long to fit conveniently (or at all) on the screen, or if the screen is crowded and you want to reduce the space taken up by a long menu. You may want to use an OI_abbr_menu object instead, especially if the user usually uses the menu's default cell.

34.2 Class Tree

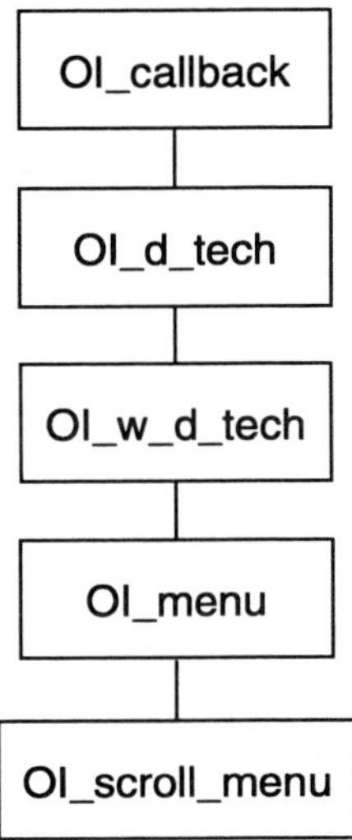

34.3 Runtime Interaction

To view different portions of the underlying menu, use the scroll bar alongside the viewport. For more information on scroll bars, see Chapter 30, "OI_scroll_bar." For example, if you grab the handle of a vertical scroll bar with the mouse and move it up, the viewport onto the underlying menu moves up a corresponding amount—that is, the menu cells appear to move down within the viewport. If you move the handle one third of the distance from the beginning of the scroll bar to its end, the viewport moves one third of the distance from the beginning of the underlying menu to its end.

Another way to cause the menu to scroll is to do the following: position the mouse pointer over a menu cell in the viewport. Press the SELECT mouse button, then drag the mouse pointer off the menu in the direction you wish the menu to scroll. The menu scrolls, causing new cells to appear. The default scrolling interval can be changed by using the resource scrollMenuTimeout (see Section 34.8, "Resources," on page 34-16).

34.4 OI_scroll_menu Creation

oi_create_scroll_menu   (Free-standing function)

```
OI_scroll_menu *oi_create_scroll_menu(
    const char      *namp,                // pointer to object name
    OI_number       controller,           // controller type
    OI_number       view_size,            // number of cells visible in viewport
    OI_class        *mnu_typ,             // menu type
    OI_number       n_cell,               // number of cells in menu
    OI_cell_spec    *cell_specp,          // pointer to cell information
    OI_orient       orient=OI_vertical,   // menu orientation
    const char      *titlep=NULL)         // pointer to menu title


OI_scroll_menu *oi_create_scroll_menu(
    const char      *namp,                // pointer to object name
    OI_number       controllers,          // controller type
    OI_number       view_size,            // number of cells visible in viewport
    OI_class        *mnu_typ,             // menu type
    OI_number       n_cell,               // number of cells in menu
    OI_menu_cell    **cellp,              // pointer to menu cells
    OI_orient       orient=OI_vertical,   // menu orientation
    const char      *titlep=NULL)         // pointer to menu title


OI_scroll_menu *oi_create_scroll_menu(
    const char      *namp,                // pointer to object name
    OI_number       controller,           // controller type
    OI_number       view_size,            // number of cells visible in viewport
    const char      *mnu_typ_nam,         // menu type
    OI_number       n_cell,               // number of cells in menu
    OI_cell_spec    *cell_specp,          // pointer to cell information
    OI_orient       orient=OI_vertical,   // menu orientation
    const char      *titlep=NULL)         // pointer to menu title


OI_scroll_menu *oi_create_scroll_menu(
    const char      *namp,                // pointer to object name
    OI_number       controllers,          // controller type
    OI_number       view_size,            // number of cells visible in viewport
    const char      *mnu_typ_nam,         // menu type
    OI_number       n_cell,               // number of cells in menu
    OI_menu_cell    **cellp,              // pointer to menu cells
    OI_orient       orient=OI_vertical,   // menu orientation
    const char      *titlep=NULL)         // pointer to menu title
```

These four forms of oi_create_scroll_menu differ only with respect to the following parameters: how the menu type is defined (either OI_class* or const char*) and how the menu cells are defined (either OI_cell_spec* or OI_menu_cell**).

The first and third forms of oi_create_scroll_menu create a scroll menu using menu cell information stored in the structure *cell_specp*. If you need to create the menu cells during execution time using calls to oi_create_menu_cell, use the second or fourth form.

All parameters to the second form oi_create_scroll_menu are identical to the parameters to the first form, with the exception of *cellp*, which is a pointer to menu cells you have previously created with calls to oi_create_menu_cell. The parameters for the third and fourth form are the same as the first and second except for the menu class parameter, *mnu_typ* or *mnu_typ_nam*.

controller specifies the type of controller desired. Possible values are:

OI_scroll_bar_vertical	Vertical OI_scroll_bar.
OI_scroll_bar_horizontal	Horizontal OI_scroll_bar.
OI_scroll_bar_both	Both vertical and horizontal OI_scroll_bar.
OI_scroll_bar_left	Vertical OI_scroll_bar at the left.
OI_scroll_bar_right	Vertical OI_scroll_bar at the right.
OI_scroll_bar_top	Horizontal OI_scroll_bar at the top.
OI_scroll_bar_bottom	Horizontal OI_scroll_bar at the bottom.
OI_scroll_panner	Panner

Unless you have a good reason for placing the scroll bar in a particular location, you should use OI_scroll_bar_vertical or OI_scroll_bar_horizontal, and let OI place the scroll bar in the default position (left or right, top or bottom) for the particular interaction model being run. If you want two scroll bars or a panner (that is, if you want the scroll menu to be scrollable in two directions), you must either call disallow_track_cells or set the resource trackCells to true, and you may want to call set_minor_units for the scroll menu.

view_size specifies the number of menu cells that should initially be visible in the viewport.

In the first two forms of oi_create_scroll_menu, *mnu_typ* specifies the class of menu to be scrolled. Use *menu_type*::clsp to create a menu of type *menu_type*. For example, to create a menu of type OI_poly_check_menu, set *mnu_typ* to OI_poly_check_menu::clsp.

In the last two forms of oi_create_scroll_menu, *mnu_typ_nam* is the type of menu to be scrolled as a string, for example, "OI_poly_check_menu".

Possible menu types are:

OI_button_menu::clsp	"OI_button_menu"
OI_excl_menu::clsp	"OI_excl_menu"
OI_excl_check_menu::clsp	"OI_excl_check_menu"
OI_excl_rect_menu::clsp	"OI_excl_rect_menu"
OI_poly_menu::clsp	"OI_poly_menu"
OI_poly_check_menu::clsp	"OI_poly_check_menu"
OI_poly_rect_menu::clsp	"OI_poly_rect_menu"

If possible, use **OI_EXCL_MENU** and **OI_POLY_MENU** for exclusive and non-exclusive menus, since they allow the interaction model to make the most appropriate choice.

All other parameters are identical to the parameters in the create call for the menu desired; read the corresponding "Creation" section in the chapter for that type of menu.

34.5 Base Class Member Functions

You can use all of the member functions of **OI_d_tech** for an **OI_scroll_menu** object; in addition, you can use all of the member functions for **OI_menu** and, if your underlying menu is an exclusive menu, the member functions for **OI_excl_menu**.

34.5.1 Selecting Menu Cells

These two functions perform identically to their **OI_menu** counterparts, with the addition of positioning the viewport appropriately.

select   (Member function)

```
OI_stat OI_scroll_menu::select(
    OI_bool           on_off,            // select or deselect cell
    const char        *cell_namep,       // cell name
    OI_bool           do_cb=OI_yes)      // execute the cell's callback?
```

select selects or deselects the cell with name *cell_name*. Selecting a cell is the equivalent of positioning the pointer over a cell in the deselected state and clicking the SELECT mouse button. In addition, the viewport is moved, if necessary, to force the named cell to be visible in the viewport. See **select** on page 12-20 for a detailed discussion of the effect of calling **select** for a menu.

num_select   (Member function)

```
OI_stat OI_scroll_menu::num_select(
    OI_bool           on_off,            // select or deselect cell
    OI_number         n,                 // cell number
    OI_bool           do_cb=OI_yes)      // execute cell's callback?
```

num_select selects or deselects the cell whose number is *cell_num*. Cells are numbered starting at zero for the left-most or topmost cell in the menu. If *on_off* is **OI_yes**, the cell is selected as for **select**. If *on_off* is **OI_no**, the cell is deselected. If *do_cb* is **OI_yes**, and a callback has been registered for the cell, it is executed; otherwise no cell callback is executed. In addition, the viewport is moved, if necessary, to force cell number *n* to be visible in the viewport.

You should use this function carefully; if you re-order the menu cells you may have to change the parameter *n* for **num_select**. In general, unless you are certain of a cell's number, you should use the **select** member function to avoid inadvertently firing the incorrect cell.

34.6 OI_scroll_menu Member Functions

34.6.1 Positioning the Viewport

Use these functions to query the viewport position or set the viewport position. To fully understand
the x and y values used to position the viewport, consider Figure 34-3.

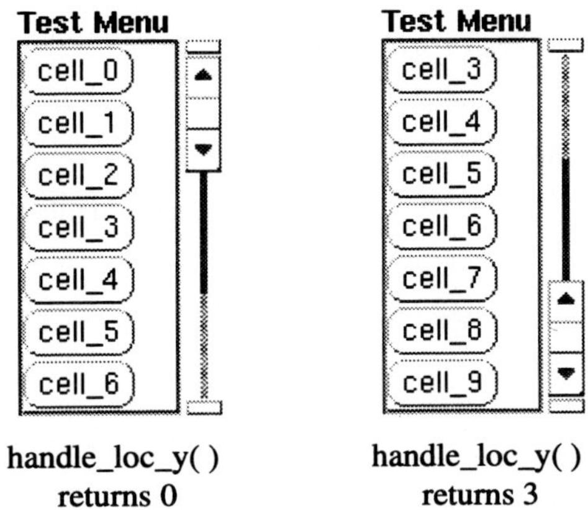

handle_loc_y( )
returns 0

handle_loc_y( )
returns 3

Figure 34-3 Scroll Menu Handle Locations

Figure 34-3 shows an OI_scroll_menu object whose underlying menu contains 10 cells and whose
viewport shows seven cells. In the scroll menu on the left, the handle of the scroll bar is in the starting
position, and the vertical handle location is 0. In the right scroll menu, the handle has been moved
to its lowest position, which is 3.

The viewport shows seven cells (user-units) vertically, and the menu contains 10 cells; these values
determine which portions of the menu are visible when the handle is at any position. The possible
handle locations and which cells are visible are shown in the table below.

Vertical Handle Location	Menu Cells Visible
0	0 through 6
1	1 through 7
2	2 through 8
3	3 through 9

Notice that if you wish to have cell number 7 visible, you do not set the handle location to 7; you
can set it to 1, 2 or 3. In general, if the handle is at location n, then menu cells n through n + *view_size*
- 1 are in the viewport.

A valid handle location can be any integer in the range 0 to menu size minus viewport size (*n_cell* -
view_size). If you attempt to set an invalid handle location, the scroll bar does not move, and OI posts
an error message.

handle_loc   (Member function)

```
void OI_scroll_menu::handle_loc(
    long                    *loc_x,         // location in x direction
    long                    *loc_y)         // location in y direction
```

handle_loc backfills *loc_x* and *loc_y* with the current position of the viewport in user-units. If the menu is horizontal, *loc_y* will be 0, and *loc_x* will be in the range

$$0 <= loc\_x <= \text{num\_cells( ) - view\_size\_x( )}$$

Similarly, if the menu is vertical, *loc_x* will be 0 and *loc_y* will be in the range

$$0 <= loc\_y <= \text{num\_cells( ) - view\_size\_y( )}$$

handle_loc_x   (Member function)

```
long OI_scroll_menu::handle_loc_x( )
```

If the menu is horizontal, handle_loc_x returns the current horizontal position of the viewport in user-units. If the menu is vertical, handle_loc_x returns 0. The number returned for a horizontal menu will be in the range

$$0 <= \text{handle\_loc\_x( )} <= \text{num\_cells( ) - view\_size\_x( )}$$

If the menu is vertical, handle_loc_x returns 0 unless the view size has been forced to be smaller using **set_view_size_minor** or due to size-tracking modifications, in which case handle_loc_x returns the current location of the handle expressed in user-units.

handle_loc_y   (Member function)

```
long OI_scroll_menu::handle_loc_y( )
```

If the menu is vertical, handle_loc_y returns the current vertical position of the viewport in user-units. If the menu is horizontal, handle_loc_y returns 0. The number returned for a vertical menu will be in the range

$$0 <= \text{handle\_loc\_y( )} <= \text{num\_cells( ) - view\_size\_y( )}$$

If the menu is horizontal, handle_loc_y returns 0 unless the view size has been forced to be smaller using **set_view_size_minor** or due to size-tracking modifications, in which case handle_loc_y returns the current location of the handle expressed in user-units.

set_handle_loc   (Member function)

```
OI_stat OI_scroll_menu::set_handle_loc(
    long                    loc_x,          // x location in user-units
    long                    loc_y)          // y location in user-units
```

set_handle_loc positions the viewport over the underlying menu as if the user had moved the handle on a horizontal scroll bar to location *loc_x* and a vertical scroll bar to location *loc_y*. *loc_x* and *loc_y* are in user-units—cells for the major dimension and normally 1 for the minor dimension. See **set_units_minor**.

set_handle_loc_x   (Member function)

```
OI_stat OI_scroll_menu::set_handle_loc_x(
    long                    loc_x)        // x location in user-units (cells)
```

set_handle_loc_x positions the viewport over the underlying menu as if the user had moved
the handle on a horizontal scroll bar to location *loc_x*. *loc_x* is in user-units—cells for the major
dimension and normally 1 for the minor dimension. See **set_units_minor**.

set_handle_loc_y   (Member function)

```
OI_stat OI_scroll_menu::set_handle_loc_y(
    long                    loc_y)        // y location in user-units (cells)
```

set_handle_loc_y positions the viewport over the underlying menu as if the user had moved
the handle on a vertical scroll bar to location *loc_y*. *loc_y* is in user-units—cells for the major
dimension and normally 1 for the minor dimension. See **set_units_minor**.

34.6.2   Changing the Underlying Menu

For some applications, the contents of a scroll menu must change dynamically. An example would
be a file browser where a scroll menu shows all of the file names in a particular directory. One way
to do this would be to delete all the old menu cells and add a new one for each new entry. However,
the function below is much more efficient. See Chapter 13, "OI_menu_cell," for a discussion of the
parameters and of menu cell creation.

change_menu   (Member function)

```
OI_stat OI_scroll_menu::change_menu(
    OI_number               n_cell,       // number of cells in menu
    OI_menu_cell            **cellp,       // pointer to menu cells
    const char              *titlep=NULL)  // menu title


OI_stat OI_scroll_menu::change_menu(
    OI_number               n_cell,       // number of cells in menu
    OI_cell_spec            *cell_specp,   // pointer to cell specification
    const char              *titlep=NULL)  // menu title
```

change_menu changes the underlying menu to a similar one constructed using the new
information. If you omit *titlep*, it defaults to NULL, and the menu title is not changed.

34.6.3   Changing Sizes

The functions below allow you to query and change the viewport size. You should usually not need
these functions, since in general you should allow the user to control the viewport size via the
resource manager. In addition, you should use the automatic layout facility; OI resizes the object as
necessary if you make the **OI_scroll_menu** object a size-tracker. However, in some situations you
may need to use these functions; for example, you might have a custom configuration which does
not easily fit the layout code, or your menu cells may be so long that you need to reduce the size of
the scroll menu in the minor direction.

view_size   (Member function)

```
void OI_scroll_menu::view_size(
    OI_number              *view_x,      // number of cells possible in viewport in x direction
    OI_number              *view_y)      // number of cells possible in viewport in y direction
```

view_size backfills *view_x* and *view_y* with the current viewport size in user-units—cells for the major dimension and normally 1 for the minor dimension. See **set_units_minor**.

view_size_x   (Member function)

```
OI_number OI_scroll_menu::view_size_x( )
```

view_size_x returns the size of the viewport in the x direction, in user-units—cells for the major dimension and normally 1 for the minor dimension. See **set_units_minor**.

view_size_y   (Member function)

```
OI_number OI_scroll_menu::view_size_y( )
```

view_size_y returns the size of the viewport in the y direction, in user-units—cells for the major dimension and normally 1 for the minor dimension. See **set_units_minor**.

set_view_size   (Member function)

```
OI_stat OI_scroll_menu::set_view_size(
    OI_number        size)              // viewport size
```

set_view_size sets the size of the viewport to *size* cells. The viewport size only changes in the direction of the orientation of the scroll menu (**OI_vertical** or **OI_horizontal**).

set_units_minor   (Member function)

```
OI_stat OI_scroll_menu::set_units_minor(
    OI_number         n)               // user-units in pixels
```

set_units_minor changes the units used to control scrolling in the minor dimension (horizontal for a vertical menu, vertical for a horizontal menu) to *n*. By default, the units in the minor dimension is 1 pixel. A scroll menu's default size is sufficient for a full cell to be visible in the minor dimension. Scrolling in the minor direction is only possible if you have reduced the default minor view size by calling **set_view_size_minor** or if you have made the scroll menu a size-tracker and the scroll menu has been forced to be smaller via a resize of the container in which it is laid out. **set_units_minor** only makes sense if the scroll menu has controllers that allow it to be scrolled in both directions.

set_view_size_minor   (Member function)

```
OI_stat OI_scroll_menu::set_view_size_minor(
    OI_number         n)               // size in minor dimension in user-units
```

set_view_size_minor changes the viewport size in the minor dimension to be *n* units. By default, the units in the minor dimension are 1 unit and the view size is sufficient for an entire cell to be visible. **set_view_size_minor** only makes sense if the scroll menu has controllers that allow it to be scrolled in both directions.

is_track_cells   (Member function)

```
void OI_scroll_menu::is_track_cells( )
```

is_track_cells returns true if you have called **allow_track_cells** for the object or the resource **trackCells** has been set to true.

allow_track_cells   (Member function)

```
void OI_scroll_menu::allow_track_cells( )
```

allow_track_cells conditions the menu to track the size of cells contained in the menu; that is, to ensure that the widest or tallest cells are fully visible. If the menu is vertical, the menu will be as wide as its widest cell, and if the menu is horizontal, the menu will be as tall as its tallest cell. This is the default.

disallow_track_cells   (Member function)

```
void OI_scroll_menu::disallow_track_cells( )
```

disallow_track_cells conditions the menu not to track the size of cells contained in the menu. If you call **disallow_track_cells** for a scroll menu (or set the resource **trackCells** to **false**) and add the appropriate controllers (two scroll bars or a panner), the scroll menu can be scrolled in both directions.

34.6.4   Accessing Subobjects

You can use the functions below to access the individual components of an OI_scroll_menu object. You will seldom need these, as most OI_scroll_menu manipulation can be done through other functions without retrieving the separate parts of the OI_scroll_menu object.

menu   (Member function)

```
OI_basic_menu *OI_scroll_menu::menu( )
```

menu returns a pointer to the underlying menu being scrolled. You should not normally use this function; instead, you should use OI_menu member functions for the OI_scroll_menu object.

horz_scroll_bar   (Member function)

```
OI_scroll_bar *OI_scroll_menu::horz_scroll_bar( )
```

horz_scroll_bar returns a pointer to the horizontal scroll bar, if one exists; otherwise it returns NULL.

vert_scroll_bar   (Member function)

```
OI_scroll_bar *OI_scroll_menu::vert_scroll_bar( )
```

vert_scroll_bar returns a pointer to the vertical scroll bar, if one exists; otherwise it returns NULL.

left_scroll_bar   (Member function)

```
OI_scroll_bar *OI_scroll_menu::left_scroll_bar( )
```

left_scroll_bar returns a pointer to the left scroll bar, if one exists; otherwise it returns NULL.

right_scroll_bar   (Member function)

```
OI_scroll_bar *OI_scroll_menu::right_scroll_bar( )
```

right_scroll_bar returns a pointer to the right scroll bar, if one exists; otherwise it returns NULL.

top_scroll_bar   (Member function)

```
OI_scroll_bar *OI_scroll_menu::top_scroll_bar( )
```

top_scroll_bar returns a pointer to the top scroll bar, if one exists; otherwise it returns NULL.

bottom_scroll_bar   (Member function)

```
OI_scroll_bar *OI_scroll_menu::bottom_scroll_bar( )
```

bottom_scroll_bar returns a pointer to the bottom scroll bar, if one exists, otherwise it returns NULL.

34.6.5   Controlling Behavior

The functions described below are used to control behavior as described in the next paragraphs. You may not want to set these items directly. Behavior can also be controlled via resources, and it is usually better to allow the user to control these through the resource mechanism. The only good reason to set these in your program is to prevent the user from setting them via the resource mechanism.

The relationship between the number of cells in the menu and the viewport size determines whether a scroll bar is actually needed or not. If you add or delete cells from the menu, this relationship may change. You may want the scroll bar to disappear when it is not needed.

controller_visibility   (Member function)

```
OI_controller_visibility OI_scroll_menu::controller_visibility( )
```

controller_visibility returns one of the values listed under **set_controller_visibility**.

set_controller_visibility   (Member function)

```
void OI_scroll_menu::set_controller_visibility(
    OI_controller_visibility ctlr)         // controller and space disposition
```

set_controller_visibility configures the object's controllers to automatically appear and disappear, depending on the size relationship between the underlying menu object and the viewport, and what to do with the extra space remaining if the controllers disappear. *ctlr* can be one of the following:

OI_controller_visibility_no_change	Controllers are always visible. This is the default.
OI_controller_visibility_disappear	Controllers disappear, leaving a hole.
OI_controller_visibility_expand	Expand the rest of the object to use up extra space.
OI_controller_visibility_collapse	Collapse the object to use up extra space.

If *ctlr* is OI_controller_visibility_no_change, the controllers are always visible. If *ctlr* is any of the other values, and the viewport completely spans the menu in a given direction, the controller for that direction is made invisible. If *ctlr* is OI_controller_visibility_disappear, the spacing is unchanged, leaving a hole. If *ctlr* is OI_controller_visibility_expand, the viewport expands to fill the space vacated by the controller. If *ctlr* is OI_controller_visibility_collapse, the scroll menu object shrinks.

34.7   An OI_scroll_menu Programming Example

Program 34-1 is an OI program that allows the user to view all the cursors in the file /usr/include/X11/cursorfont.h. In the program, we read the contents of this file and create a scroll menu with the cursor names as menu cells. When the user activates one of these menu cells, we set the cursor to be the corresponding symbol. The results of running this program are shown in Figure 34-4. Note that we created the scroll menu with no menu cells, and subsequently created and parented the cells to the menu using add_cell. Also note that we bracketed the add_cell loop with calls to suspend_layout and resume_layout so that OI would not spend a lot of time rearranging the menu layout after each add_cell.

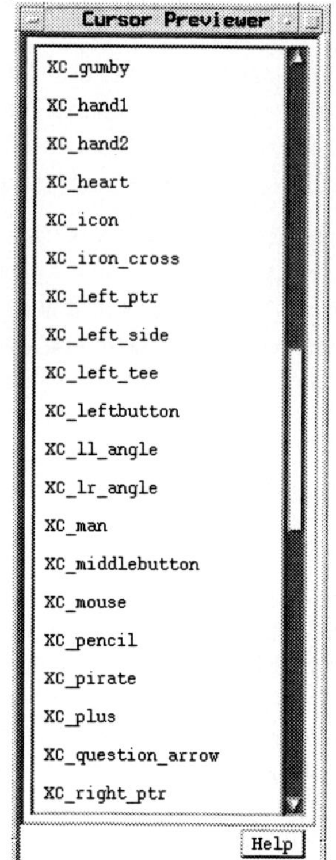

Motif

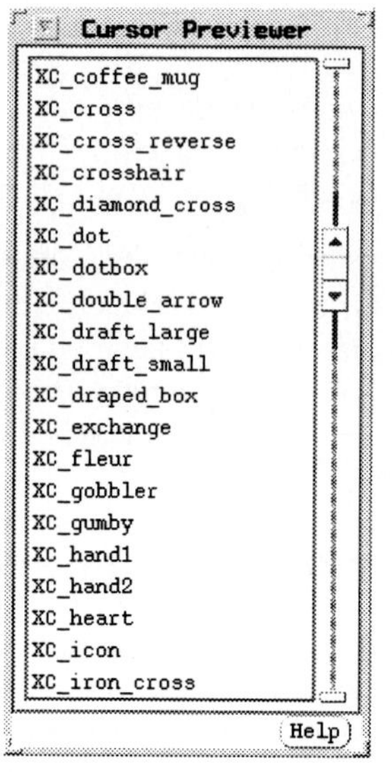

OPEN LOOK

Figure 34-4   Select Cursor

```c
#include <OI/oi.H>                              /* CursView.C */
#include <strings.h>                            /* for strncmp, strlen */
#define    CURSORS   "/usr/include/X11/cursorfont.h"
void see_cursor(OI_menu_cell* cellp,void *argp,OI_number)
{
    if(cellp->selected( )){
        if(cellp && cellp->app_window( )&& cellp->app_window( )->is_visible( ))
            cellp->app_window( )->set_cursor((int)argp);
    }
}

void populate_menu_with_cursors(OI_menu *mp)
{
        FILE                    *fi;
        int                     index;
        char                    buf[256];
        char                    cursor[256];
        OI_menu_cell            *cellp ;

    if (fi = fopen(CURSORS,"r")) {
        mp->suspend_layout( );
        while (fgets(buf,sizeof(buf),fi)) {
            if (strncmp(buf,"#define",strlen("#define")))
                continue ;
            sscanf(buf,"%*s %s %d",cursor,&index);
            if (!strcmp(cursor,"XC_num_glyphs"))
                continue;
            cellp = oi_create_menu_cell(cursor,cursor,see_cursor,(void*)index);
            mp->add_cell(cellp,mp->num_cells( ));
        }
        mp->resume_layout( );
    }
}

int main(int argc,char **argv)
{
        OI_connection           *conp;
        OI_app_window           *wp;
        OI_menu                 *mp;

    if (conp = OI_init(&argc,argv,"CursView")) {
        wp = oi_create_app_window("main",1,1," Cursor Previewer");
        wp->set_layout(OI_layout_column);

        mp = oi_create_scroll_menu("cursors",
            OI_scroll_bar_vertical,20,OI_EXCL_RECT_MENU,0,(OI_cell_spec*)NULL,
                                                OI_vertical);
        mp->layout_associated_object(wp,1,1,OI_active);
        populate_menu_with_cursors(mp);

        wp->set_associated_object(conp->root( ),OI_def_loc,OI_def_loc,OI_active);
        OI_begin_interaction( );
    }
```

```
    OI_fini( );
}
```

Program 34-1   Select Cursor (CursView.C)

34.8   Resources

All resources from an OI_scroll_menu object's base classes are available to it; in addition, OI fetches the resources shown in Table 34-1. For more information on resource management, see Chapter 39, "The OI Resource Mechanism."

Table 34-1   OI_scroll_menu Resources

Resource	Description	Possible Values	Default Value
controllers	Specifies the type of scroll bar.	scroll_bar_vertical scroll_bar_horizontal scroll_bar_left scroll_bar_right scroll_bar_top scroll_bar_bottom	(No default)
controllerVisibility	See set_controller_visibility on page 34-12.	no_change disappear expand collapse	no_change
scrollMenuTimeout	Specifies the time interval at which the menu scrolls when the mouse is dragged off the end of the menu (see Section 34.3, "Runtime Interaction" on page 34-3).	Positive integer	400
subMenuType	Specifies the type of underlying menu.	OI_button_menu OI_excl_menu OI_excl_check_menu OI_excl_rect_menu OI_poly_menu OI_poly_check_menu OI_poly_rect_menu	(No default)

Table 34-1 OI_scroll_menu Resources

Resource	Description	Possible Values	Default Value
trackCells	If true, the menu tracks the size of cells in the menu.	Boolean	true
viewSize	Specifies the number of cells in the viewport.	Positive integer	(No default)

34.9 Translations

All translations from an OI_scroll_menu object's base classes are available to it, as well as all the translations for the underlying menu. It has no additional translations.

34.10 Callback Functions

All of the callbacks from an OI_scroll_menu object's base classes are available to it; it has no callbacks of its own.

Chapter 35
OI_menu_box

OI_menu_box Functions

The following functions are available to an **OI_menu_box** object, but are described in their own chapter.

OI_menu Member Functions

OI_d_tech Member Functions

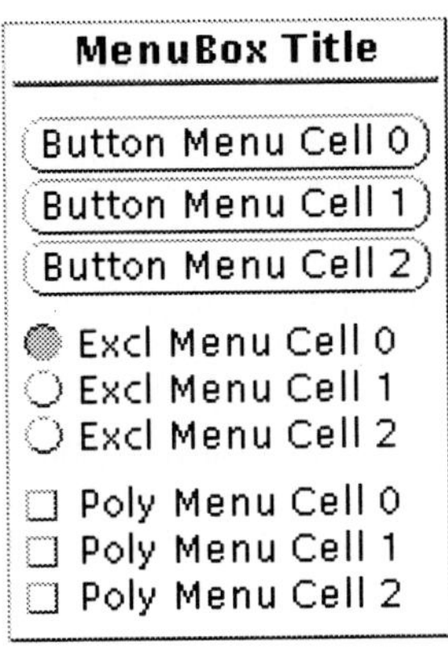

OI_menu_box

35.1   Description

An OI_menu_box object is a menu container which allows you to combine mixed menu types into a single menu. The menu-box is designed to contain basic menu types (OI_button_menu, OI_excl_menu, OI_poly_menu). You can set a layout method for the menu-box; the menus you associate to the menu-box are arranged according to the layout method. As much as is possible, the menu cells behave as though they belong to a single menu—the menu-box.

For example, you may need a pulldown menu that has both exclusive choice and multiple choice entries. You create such a menu by creating an OI_menu_box object, an OI_excl_menu object, and an OI_poly_menu object. You then associate the OI_excl_menu and the OI_poly_menu objects to the menu-box.

OI_menu_box has no member functions of its own; instead you use OI_menu member functions.

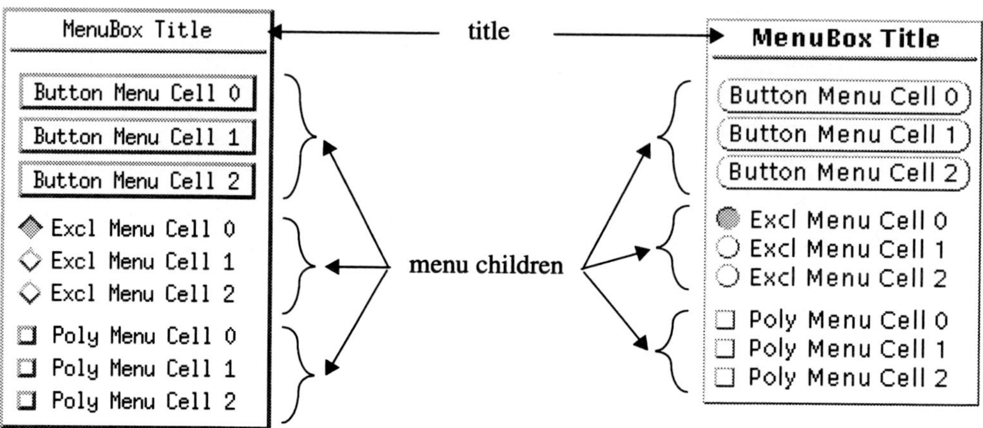

Figure 35-1   Parts of an OI_menu_box

35.2   Class Tree

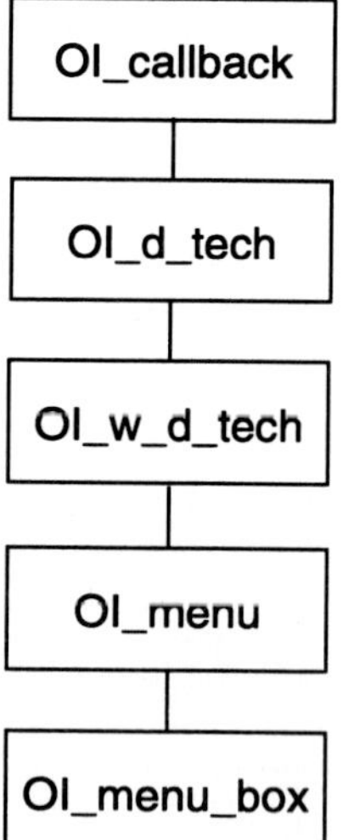

35.3   Runtime Interaction

The cells in an OI_menu_box object behave appropriately for the type of menu to which they belong. Thus different cells in a menu-box may behave differently from each other. The effect of the default translations (see Chapter 13, "OI_menu_cell," page 13-22) is as follows: the up or down arrow key (left or right for a horizontal menu) moves the focus to the next or previous cell in the menu within the menu-box. The tab or Shift-tab key moves the focus to the next or previous menu within the menu-box.

35.4   OI_menu_box Creation

oi_create_menu_box   (Free-standing function)

```
OI_menu_box *oi_create_menu_box(
    const char        *namp,              // name for object
    const char        *titlep=NULL)       // menu-box title
```

oi_create_menu_box creates an OI_menu_box object with name *namp* and title *titlep*.

35.5   Base Class Member Functions

You can use all of the member functions of OI_d_tech for an OI_menu_box.

Because OI_menu_box is simply a container for other menus, only some of the member functions defined by its base class, OI_menu, are useful for an OI_menu_box object. Several OI_menu member functions do not return meaningful results. Table 35-1 shows the OI_menu member functions which can be used with a menu-box, and Table 35-2 shows the OI_menu member functions which are not meaningful for a menu-box. If you need to use any of the functions in Table 35-2, obtain a pointer to the menu within the menu-box and use the member function directly on the menu.

Table 35-1   OI_menu Member Functions Useful for OI_menu_box

OI_menu Member Function	Additional Notes
allow_persistent	
allow_pushpin	
allow_tearoff	
disallow_persistent	
disallow_pushpin	
disallow_tearoff	
is_persistent	
is_pinned	
is_torn_off	
is_pushpin	

Table 35-1 OI_menu Member Functions Useful for OI_menu_box

OI_menu Member Function	Additional Notes
is_tearoff	
label_right_space	
menu_trigger	
menu_trigger_mods	
numbered_cell	Returns a pointer to the nth cell in the menu-box. For a menu-box, `numbered_cell` traverses its children menus in the layout order, until it finds the nth cell.
popup_loc	
popup_loc_x	
popup_loc_y	
set_label_right_space	
set_menu_end	
set_menu_trigger	
set_pin	
set_pre_popup	
set_title	
set_unpin	
set_wrap_limit	
title	
wrap_limit	

Do not use the OI_menu member functions listed in Table 35-2 for an OI_menu_box object. If you call these functions for an OI_menu_box object, they either do nothing or the returned value is meaningless.

Table 35-2 OI_menu Member Functions Meaningless for OI_menu_box

OI_menu Member Function—DO NOT USE	Return Value
add_cell	(Does nothing)
allow_cell_outline	(Does nothing)
cell_number	-1
default_cell	NULL
disallow_cell_outline	(Does nothing)
is_cell_outline	OI_yes or OI_no
multi_selected	NULL
next_selection	NULL
num_cells	0
num_default_cell	-1
num_multi_selected	NULL
num_select	OI_status
num_selected	0
num_set_default_cell	OI_status
orientation	OI_horizontal
select	OI_status
selected	NULL
set_default_cell	OI_status
set_tab_width	(Does nothing)
set_tabs_custom	(Does nothing)
set_trigger	OI_status
set_wrap_limit	(Does nothing)

Table 35-2   OI_menu Member Functions Meaningless for OI_menu_box

OI_menu Member Function—DO NOT USE	Return Value
trigger	meaningless integer
trigger_mods	meaningless integer
wrap_limit	meaningless integer

35.6   OI_menu_box Example

Program 35-1 shows a sample menu-box with three different types of menus associated to it. When you click on a menu cell, the callback prints out all the selected cells in its menu (not the menu-box). This program produces the menu-boxes shown on page 35-1.

```
#include <OI/oi.H>                              /* MenuBox.C */

void callback0(OI_menu_cell *objp, void*, OI_number)
{
        OI_menu                 *mnup;
        OI_menu_cell            **cells;
        int                     i;

    mnup = (OI_menu*)objp->parent( );
    if (cells = mnup->multi_selected( )) {
        for (i=0 ; cells[i] ; i++)
            fprintf(stderr, "%s\n",cells[i]->full_name( ));
        free(cells);
    }
    return;
}
```

```c
int main (int argc, char** argv)
{
        OI_connection        *conp;
        OI_app_window        *wp;
        OI_menu_box          *mnubox;
        OI_menu              *menu;
    static OI_cell_spec       btn_cells[] = {
        {"btn_cell0","Button Menu Cell 0", callback0},
        {"btn_cell1","Button Menu Cell 1", callback0},
        {"btn_cell2","Button Menu Cell 2", callback0},
        };
    static OI_cell_spec       excl_cells[] = {
        {"excl_cell0","Excl Menu Cell 0", callback0},
        {"excl_cell1","Excl Menu Cell 1", callback0},
        {"excl_cell2","Excl Menu Cell 2", callback0},
        };
    static OI_cell_spec       poly_cells[] = {
        {"poly_cell0","Poly Menu Cell 0", callback0},
        {"poly_cell1","Poly Menu Cell 1", callback0},
        {"poly_cell2","Poly Menu Cell 2", callback0},
        };

    if (conp = OI_init(&argc, argv, "MenuBox", "MenuBox")) {
        wp = oi_create_app_window("app_window",1,1,"MenuBox");
        wp->set_layout(OI_layout_row);
        mnubox = oi_create_menu_box("mnubox", "MenuBox Title");
        mnubox->set_layout(OI_layout_row);

        menu = oi_create_button_menu("button_menu", OI_n_cells(btn_cells),
                                     btn_cells, OI_vertical);
        menu->layout_associated_object(mnubox, (OI_number)0, 0, OI_active);

        menu = oi_create_excl_check_menu("excl_check_menu", OI_n_cells(excl_cells),
                                     excl_cells, OI_vertical);
        menu->layout_associated_object(mnubox, (OI_number)0, 1, OI_active);

        menu = oi_create_poly_check_menu("poly_check_menu", OI_n_cells(poly_cells),
                                     poly_cells, OI_vertical);
        menu->layout_associated_object(mnubox, (OI_number)0, 2, OI_active);

        mnubox->layout_associated_object(wp, 10, 10, OI_active);
        wp->set_associated_object(wp->root( ),OI_def_loc,OI_def_loc,OI_active);
        OI_begin_interaction( );
        OI_fini( );
    }
}
```

Program 35-1   Sample OI_menu_box Object (MenuBox.C)

35.7 Resources

All resources from an OI_menu_box object's base classes are available to it; it has no additional resources. However, not all of the OI_menu resources effect for a menu-box.

The OI_menu resources which are useful for an OI_menu_box object are:

    label.font
    label.rightSpace
    persistent
    pushpin
    title

The OI_menu resources which do not apply to a menu-box are:

    cellOutline
    orientation
    wrapAround
    wrapLimit

35.8 Translations

All translations from an OI_menu_box object's base classes are available to it; it has no additional translations.

35.9 Callback Functions

All the callbacks from an OI_menu_box object's base classes are available to it; it has no additional callbacks.

Chapter 36
OI_panner

OI_panner Functions

OI_panner Member Functions

The following functions are available to an **OI_panner** object, but are described in their own chapter.

OI_d_tech Member Functions

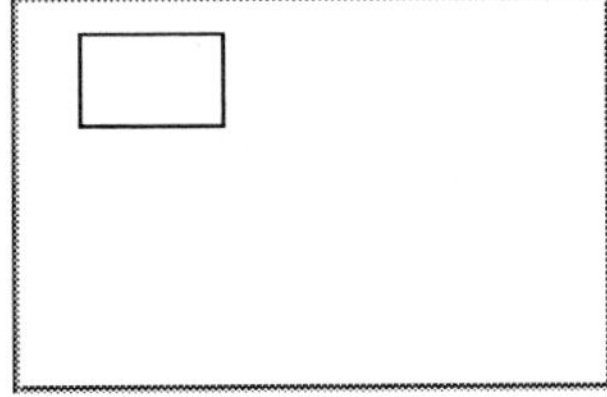

OI_panner

36.1 Description

An OI_panner object is used to control or represent the value of a two-dimensional quantity. It is typically used to control scrolling in an OI_scroll_box or an OI_scroll_text object. When you use either of these other two OI objects, you will <u>not</u> need the member functions described here; each of these other objects takes care of controlling its own panner (if used). Therefore, unless you are building your own specially-controlled object, you don't need to know how to program an OI_panner. However, you do need to know how a panner works, so reading the first three sections of this chapter is worthwhile.

An OI_panner object consists of an *outside-box* with a smaller, *viewport rectangle* within it. The controlled or represented quantity, typically another object or object tree, is located in an independent (usually separate) position on the screen; only a portion of the quantity is visible on the screen. The outside-box of the OI_panner object represents the entire extent of the quantity being controlled; the inner viewport rectangle represents the viewport showing the portion of the controlled quantity actually appearing on the screen.

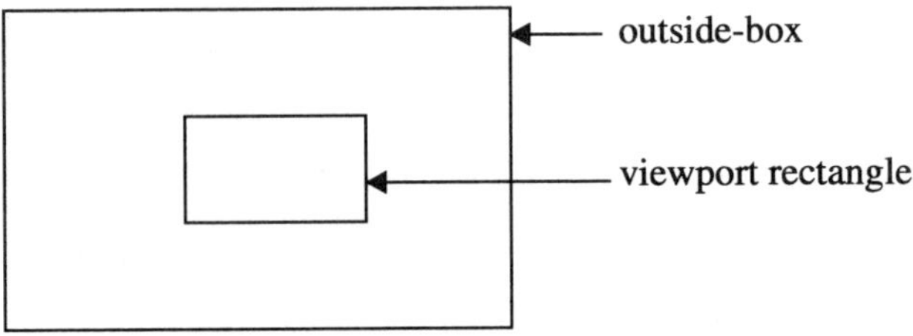

Figure 36-1   Parts of a Panner

In order for the panner to function correctly, when the user moves the viewport rectangle within the outside-box, the portion of the controlled quantity that appears on the screen should change to be that section represented by the position of the viewport rectangle within the outside-box. If you are using another OI object which uses an OI_panner object as a component (OI_scroll_text or OI_scroll_box), OI takes care of moving the controlled quantity when the user moves the panner. If you are using a panner to control your own two dimensional quantity, you must write the routine which produces the change in the viewed portion of the controlled quantity yourself. This routine is the OI_scroll_2d_fnp *fnp* or OI_scroll_2d_memfnp *memfnp*, the *panner scroll callback function* (see Section 36.4, "OI_panner Creation," on page 36-3).

You can, if you desire, paint a miniaturized version of the controlled quantity in the outside-box. You must write an OI_pan_paint_fnp *pan_fnp* or an OI_pan_paint_memfnp *pan_memfnp* to do this (see Section 36.4 on page 36-3).

User-units are the units in which locations and sizes are specified. For an OI_panner object, they are defined to be a certain number of pixels per user-unit. If you intend to use user-units other than 1 pixel/user-unit (the default), you must call the OI_panner member function set_pix to define them before calling either set_span or set_view.

To create and use an OI_panner object to control a quantity, you must, as a minimum, call the following routines:

```
oi_create_panner     // Set panner size and register callbacks
set_pix              // Define user-units (Use only if scrolling increment is in units
                     // other than single pixels)
set_span             // Define span of controlled quantity
set_view             // Define number of user-units in viewport
```

You can use an OI_panner object to control the portion of a two-dimensional object that the user sees on the screen. For example, you might use a panner to allow the user to control which portion of a geographical map is displayed on the screen. You would put a small representation of the entire map in the outside-box of the panner—the viewport rectangle would then show which portion of the actual map displays on the screen.

36.2   Class Tree

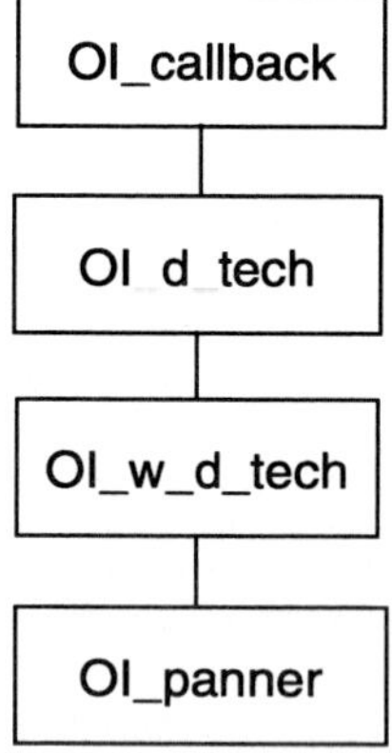

36.3   Runtime Interaction

When you move the mouse pointer into an OI_panner object and press the SELECT mouse button, the pointer warps to the middle of the viewport rectangle. Subsequent motion of the mouse moves the rectangle around in the outside-box until you release the mouse button. The viewport rectangle is constrained to stay within the outside-box.

You can also control an OI_panner object using keyboard translations; see Section 36.9, "Translations," on page 36-16.

36.4 OI_panner Creation

oi_create_panner   (Free-standing function)

```
OI_panner *oi_create_panner(
    const char          *namp,              // object name
    OI_number           size_x,             // x dimension in pixels
    OI_number           size_y,             // y dimension in pixels
    OI_scroll_2d_fnp    fnp=NULL,           // pointer to panner scroll callback function
    void                *argp=NULL,         // arbitrary argument for fnp
    OI_pan_paint_fnp    pan_fnp=NULL,       // pointer to panner paint callback function
    void                *pan_argp=NULL)     // arbitrary argument for pan_fnp


OI_panner *oi_create_panner(
    const char          *namp,              // object name
    OI_number           size_x,             // x dimension in pixels
    OI_number           size_y,             // y dimension in pixels
    OI_scroll_2d_fnp    fnp,                // pointer to panner scroll callback function
    void                *argp,              // arbitrary argument for fnp
    OI_callback         *pan_objp,          // pan_memfnp's object
    OI_pan_paint_memfnp pan_memfnp,         // pointer to panner paint callback function
    void                *pan_argp=NULL)     // arbitrary argument for pan_memfnp


OI_panner *oi_create_panner(
    const char          *namp,              // object name
    OI_number           size_x,             // x dimension in pixels
    OI_number           size_y,             // y dimension in pixels
    OI_callback         *objp,              // memfnp's object
    OI_scroll_2d_memfnp memfnp,             // pointer to panner scroll callback function
    void                *argp=NULL,         // arbitrary argument for memfnp
    OI_pan_paint_fnp    pan_fnp=NULL,       // pointer to panner paint callback function
    void                *pan_argp=NULL)     // arbitrary argument for pan_fnp
```

```
OI_panner *oi_create_panner(
    const char              *namp,              // object name
    OI_number               size_x,             // x dimension in pixels
    OI_number               size_y,             // y dimension in pixels
    OI_callback             *objp,              // memfnp's object
    OI_scroll_2d_memfnp     memfnp,             // pointer to panner scroll callback function
    void                    *argp,              // arbitrary argument for memfnp
    OI_callback             *pan_objp,          // pan_memfnp's object
    OI_pan_paint_memfnp     pan_memfnp,         // pointer to panner paint callback function
    void                    *pan_argp=NULL)     // arbitrary argument for pan_memfnp
```

The **oi_create_panner** functions create a panner and register two callback functions. There are four forms, as indicated above; they are overloaded functions (they have the same name and return value type, but a different set of arguments). The arguments are identical except for the method used to register the two callback functions. Choose the form of **oi_create_panner** that fits the combination of member functions and/or free-standing functions you wish to use for the callback functions.

size_x and *size_y* are specified in pixels, and determine the dimensions of the outside-box of the panner.

objp points to a C++ object, and *memfnp* points to a member function for that object. When the member function is invoked, it will be called as if you had written *objp->memfnp*. Similarly, *pan_objp* points to a C++ object, and *pan_memfnp* points to a member function for that object.

OI calls the panner scroll callback function *fnp* or *memfnp* whenever the panner viewport is moved (usually by the user). This callback is identified within OI as a **cbCtlr2d** callback function (see Section 6.18, "Determining and Adding Callbacks; Multiple Callbacks," on page 6-117). OI calls the panner paint callback function *pan_fnp* or *pan_memfnp* whenever an expose event occurs on the panner, and is designed to be used to paint a miniaturized version of the controlled object inside the panner. This callback is identified within OI as a **cbPanPaint** callback function.

argp is optional, and can be any valid expression that can be cast to a pointer. You can use it to pass additional information to the functions *fnp* or *memfnp*. Similarly, *pan_argp* is optional; you can use it to pass additional information to the functions *pan_fnp* or *pan_memfnp*. Notice that in two of the above forms, if you do not wish to specify *argp*, you must insert NULL as a place holder.

If you omit *pan_fnp* (or *pan_obj* and *pan_memfnp*) and *argp*, they default to NULL and no miniature version of the controlled object is painted—the interior of the panner will be the default background color.

Writing the Panner Scroll Callback Function

Each time the user (or the application) moves the panner viewport, OI invokes the panner scroll callback function. Its function is to move the controlled object to reflect the motion just completed by the panner viewport. Program 36-1 on page 36-15 shows an example of a panner scroll callback function.

If the **cbCtlr2d** panner scroll callback function is not a member function, write it in this form:

```
void fn(
        OI_panner               *oi_objp,       // pointer to panner to be scrolled
        void                    *argp,          // arbitrary argument
        OI_scroll_event         typ,            // type of scrolling done
        long                    x,              // horizontal units to scroll
        long                    y)              // vertical units to scroll
```

and if the **cbCtlr2d** panner scroll callback function is a member function, write it in this form:

```
void obj_class::memfn(
        OI_panner               *oi_objp,       // pointer to panner to be scrolled
        void                    *argp,          // arbitrary argument
        OI_scroll_event         typ,            // type of scrolling done
        long                    x,              // horizontal units to scroll
        long                    y)              // vertical units to scroll
```

where *obj_class* is the class of the object whose member function is *memfn*.

When your callback function is invoked, *argp* will be the argument specified in the oi_create_panner call (or in the **change_arg** call—see below).

typ will specify the type of operation to be performed, and for a panner will be one of the following:

OI_scroll_2d_unit	Move x user-units horizontally and y user-units vertically relative to the current location.
OI_scroll_2d_viewport	Move x viewports horizontally and y viewports vertically relative to the current location.
OI_scroll_2d_extreme	Move as far as possible horizontally and vertically.
OI_scroll_2d_position	Move to absolute position (x,y).

For the first three types of scrolling, x and y specify the number of units to scroll the controlled object. x or $y > 0$ implies a forward direction; x or $y < 0$ implies a reverse direction.

Writing the Panner Paint Callback Function

If you wish the interior of the panner to contain a miniaturized version of the controlled object, you must write a panner paint callback function to accomplish this. OI calls this function each time an expose event occurs on any portion of the panner (including when the panner is first made visible). Program 36-1 on page 36-15 shows an example of a panner paint callback function.

If the **cbPanPaint** callback function is not a member function, write it in this form:

```
void pan_fn(
        OI_panner              *oi_objp,   // pointer to panner to be repainted
        void                   *pan_argp,  // arbitrary argument
        XExposeEvent           *xeventp)   // pointer to expose event
```

and if the **cbPanPaint** callback function is a member function, write it in this form:

```
void obj_class::pan_memfn(
        OI_panner              *oi_objp,   // pointer to panner to be repainted
        void                   *pan_argp,  // arbitrary argument
        XExposeEvent           *xeventp)   // pointer to expose event
```

where *obj_class* is the class of the object whose member function is *pan_memfn*.

When your callback function is invoked, *pan_argp* will be the argument specified in the **oi_create_panner** call (or in the **change_paint_arg** call—see below).

36.5   Base Class Member Functions

You can use all of the member functions of **OI_d_tech** for an **OI_panner** object.

36.6   OI_panner Member Functions

36.6.1   Modifying Representation of the Controlled Object

Use the member functions below to configure the panner. These functions establish the relationship between the viewport size and the outside-box, and their relationship to the actual quantity being controlled.

set_pix   (Member function)

```
OI_stat OI_panner::set_pix(
   OI_number          pix_x,            // x pixels per object unit
   OI_number          pix_y)            // y pixels per object unit
```

set_pix sets the number of pixels occupied by one unit of the object being controlled in each direction. For example, if the panner controls a text object in which lines are always 14 pixels high and characters are 9 pixels wide (assuming a fixed-width character set), the line

```
panp->set_pix(9,14)
```

assures that scrolling always occurs in increments of lines and characters. In this case the user-units are 9 pixels per unit horizontally and 14 pixels per unit vertically. If you do not call **set_pix**, the default user-units are 1,1.

span_x   (Member function)

```
long OI_panner::span_x( )
```

span_x returns the horizontal size of the object being panned, in user-units.

span_y   (Member function)

```
long OI_panner::span_y( )
```

span_y returns the vertical size of the object being panned, in user-units.

set_span   (Member function)

```
OI_stat OI_panner::set_span(
    long               span_x,        // x span in user-units
    long               span_y)        // y span in user-units
```

set_span notifies the panner of the size of the controlled object, in user-units. It is equivalent to changing the scale of the panner. When you call this function, the physical size of the panner does not change. However, the size of the viewport rectangle may change if the proportion of the entire object viewed by the viewport is changed. You should call set_pix to establish the user-units (if they are not to be the default of 1,1) before calling set_span.

view_x   (Member function)

```
long OI_panner::view_x( )
```

view_x returns the number of user-units spanned horizontally by the viewport rectangle.

view_y   (Member function)

```
long OI_panner::view_y( )
```

view_y returns the number of user-units spanned vertically by the viewport rectangle.

set_view   (Member function)

```
OI_stat OI_panner::set_view(
    long               view_x,        // x user-units in viewport
    long               view_y)        // y user-units in viewport
```

set_view sets the number of units of the object (in user-units) that fit in the viewport in each direction. This function may change the size of the viewport rectangle. You should call set_pix to establish the user-units (if they are not to be the default of 1,1) before calling set_view.

pan_size_x   (Member function)

```
OI_number OI_panner::pan_size_x( )
```

pan_size_x returns the horizontal size of the panner viewport rectangle in pixels.

pan_size_y   (Member function)

```
OI_number OI_panner::pan_size_y( )
```

pan_size_y returns the vertical size of the panner viewport rectangle in pixels.

36.6.2 Controlling Appearance

The functions below allow you to paint a miniaturized representation of the controlled object in the viewport rectangle. Use the functions paint_* to get the geometry information necessary to paint the miniature. Program 36-1 on page 36-15 shows an example using these functions.

change_paint (Member function)

```
void OI_panner::change_paint(
    OI_pan_paint_fnp        pan_fnp,        // pointer to callback function
    void                    *pan_argp=NULL) // arbitrary argument for pan_fnp

void OI_panner::change_paint(
    OI_callback             *pan_objp,      // pan_memfnp's object
    OI_pan_paint_memfnp     pan_memfnp,     // pointer to callback member function
    void                    *pan_argp=NULL) // arbitrary argument for pan_memfnp
```

The change_paint functions are overloaded functions which register a callback function to be invoked whenever the panner must be repainted. This is a cbPanPaint callback function. *pan_argp* can be any valid expression that can be cast to a pointer. *pan_objp* points to a C++ object whose member function *pan_memfnp* is to be called.

pan_fnp and *pan_memfnp* are as described for the Panner Paint Callback Functions in the oi_create_panner function defined on page 36-3.

get_paint_arg (Member function)

```
void *OI_panner::get_paint_arg( )
```

get_paint_arg returns the argument pointer that will be passed to the panner paint callback function.

change_paint_arg (Member function)

```
void OI_panner::change_paint_arg(
    void                    *pan_argp)      // arbitrary argument
```

change_paint_arg sets the argument pointer that will be passed to the pan paint callback function when it is called.

data_changed (Member function)

```
void OI_panner::data_changed( )
```

If you have your own panner paint callback function to draw a miniaturized version of the scrolled object in the panner, you should call data_changed whenever the data in the controlled object has changed but the view and span have not changed. You must do this to cause OI to call your panner paint function so that the miniature drawing in the panner will be redrawn.

paint_height   (Member function)

```
OI_number OI_panner::paint_height( )
```

paint_height returns the height of the rectangle available for painting the miniature representation of the controlled object, in pixels.

paint_width   (Member function)

```
OI_number OI_panner::paint_width( )
```

paint_width returns the width of the rectangle available for painting the miniature representation of the controlled object, in pixels.

paint_org_x   (Member function)

```
OI_number OI_panner::paint_org_x( )
```

paint_org_x returns the x coordinate of the upper left corner of the rectangle available for painting the miniature representation of the controlled object, in pixels. This pixel location is relative to the panner X_window.

paint_org_y   (Member function)

```
OI_number OI_panner::paint_org_y( )
```

paint_org_y returns the y coordinate of the upper left corner of the rectangle available for painting the miniature representation of the controlled object, in pixels. This pixel location is relative to the panner X_window.

36.6.3   Positioning the Panner Viewport

The *location* of the viewport rectangle within the outside-box is defined to be an x and a y coordinate which together represent the offset of the upper left corner of the viewport rectangle from the upper left corner of the outside-box. You can determine this position from both a physical viewpoint (pixels), and a logical viewpoint (user-units).

pan_loc_x   (Member function)

```
OI_number OI_panner::pan_loc_x( )
```

pan_loc_x returns the x location of the upper left corner of the viewport rectangle within the outside-box, in pixels.

pan_loc_y   (Member function)

```
OI_number OI_panner::pan_loc_y( )
```

pan_loc_y returns the y location of the upper left corner of the viewport rectangle within the outside-box, in pixels.

view_psn_x   (Member function)

```
long OI_panner::view_psn_x( )
```

view_psn_x returns the logical x location of the upper left corner of the viewport rectangle within the controlled object, in user-units.

view_psn_y   (Member function)

```
long OI_panner::view_psn_y( )
```

view_psn_y returns the logical y location of the upper left corner of the viewport rectangle within the controlled object, in user-units.

set_pan_win_loc   (Member function)

```
OI_stat OI_panner::set_pan_win_loc(
    long                    loc_x,           // x position in user-units
    long                    loc_y)           // y position in user-units
```

set_pan_win_loc sets the location of the viewport rectangle within the outside-box. If you do this, OI calls your panner scroll callback function, effectively moving the object as if the user had pressed the mouse button and dragged the panner viewport rectangle to the new location.

36.6.4   Modifying Motion Callbacks

The functions below allow you to modify the panner scroll callback functions dynamically.

change_action   (Member function)

```
void OI_panner::change_action(
    OI_scroll_2d_fnp        fnp,             // pointer to callback function
    void                    *argp=NULL)      // arbitrary argument for fnp


void OI_panner::change_action(
    OI_callback             *objp,           // memfnp's object
    OI_scroll_2d_memfnp     memfnp,          // pointer to callback member function
    void                    *argp=NULL)      // arbitrary argument for memfnp
```

These **change_action** functions are overloaded functions which register a callback function to be invoked whenever the panner viewport location changes. *argp* can be any valid expression that can be cast to a pointer. *objp* points to a C++ object whose member function *memfnp* is to be called.

fnp and *memfnp* are as described for the Panner Scroll Callback Functions in the **oi_create_panner** function defined on page 36-3.

get_arg   (Member function)

```
void *OI_panner::get_arg( )
```

get_arg returns the argument pointer that will be passed to the panner scroll callback function when it is called.

change_arg   (Member function)

```
void OI_panner::change_arg(
    void                    *argp)          // arbitrary argument
```

change_arg sets the argument pointer that will be passed to the panner scroll callback function
when it is called.

36.7   An OI_panner Programming Example

Program 36-1, below, and Figure 36-2, on page 36-15, show an example of a program which allows
the user to control the display of a signal using a panner. The "signal" in this case is a damped sine
wave. This program is similar to Program 30-1, "Using an OI_scroll_bar to Control a Signal Display
(ScrollBar.C)," on page 30-12. The comments regarding Program 30-1 apply also to Program 36-1.
One difference is that in order to shorten the example, in Program 36-1 the curve is repainted entirely
each time the panner motion callback is executed instead of moving a portion of the curve and
repainting a portion of the curve. Also, using the panner rather than a scroll bar, we are able to paint
a miniaturized view of the entire curve in the panner. This is done in the function disp_mini_curve.

```c
#include <math.h>
#include <OI/oi.H>                          /* Panner.C */

    static GC                  draw_gc = 0;

int main (int argc, char **argv)
{
        void                   mov_curve (OI_panner*,void*,OI_scroll_event,
                                                      long,long);
        void                   disp_mini_curve(OI_panner *pp, void *bp,
                                                      XExposeEvent *ep);
        void                   expose(OI_d_tech*,void*,const XEvent*);
        OI_connection          *conp;
        OI_app_window          *wp;
        OI_panner              *pp;
        OI_box                 *bp;

    if (conp = OI_init(&argc,argv,"Panner")) {
        wp = oi_create_app_window("main",1,1,"Panner");
        wp->set_layout(OI_layout_column);

        bp = oi_create_box("curve_box",300,120);
        bp->layout_associated_object(wp,1,2,OI_active);

        pp = oi_create_panner("panner",90,60,&mov_curve,bp,&disp_mini_curve);
        pp->set_span(300,200);
        pp->set_view(100,100);
        pp->layout_associated_object(wp,1,1,OI_active);

        bp->set_expose(expose,pp);

        wp->set_associated_object(wp->root( ),OI_def_loc,OI_def_loc,OI_active);
        OI_begin_interaction( );
    }
}
```

```
void disp_curve(OI_panner *pp, OI_d_tech *objp, long start_x_unit, long end_x_unit)
{
        long            i;
        int             x1,y1,x2,y2;
        XGCValues       gcv;
        double          damping;

    if (!draw_gc) {
        gcv.foreground = objp->fg_pixel( );
        gcv.background = objp->bkg_pixel( );
        draw_gc = XCreateGC(objp->display( ),objp->X_window( ),
                                        GCForeground|GCBackground,&gcv);
    }

    x1 = (int)(objp->size_x( )/pp->view_x( )*(start_x_unit - pp->view_psn_x( )));
    damping = (pp->span_x( ) - 0.1*(9*start_x_unit+1))/(pp->span_x( ) - 1);
    y1 = (int)(damping*sin(double(start_x_unit)/10.0)*pp->span_y( )/2.0
                                        + pp->span_y( )/2.0);
    y1 = (int)(objp->size_y( )/pp->view_y( )*(y1 - pp->view_psn_y( )));

    for (i = start_x_unit + 1 ; i <= end_x_unit ; i++) {
        x2 = (int)(objp->size_x( )/pp->view_x( )*(i - pp->view_psn_x( )));
        damping = (pp->span_x( ) - 0.1*(9*i+1))/(pp->span_x( ) - 1);
        y2 = (int)(damping*sin(double(i)/10.0)*pp->span_y( )/2.0
                                        + pp->span_y( )/2.0);
        y2 = (int)(objp->size_y( )/pp->view_y( )*(y2 - pp->view_psn_y( )));
        XDrawLine(objp->display( ),objp->X_window( ),draw_gc,x1,y1,x2,y2);
        x1 = x2;
        y1 = y2;
    }

    return;
}

void mov_curve (OI_panner *pp, void *argp, OI_scroll_event, long, long)
{
        OI_box                  *bp;

    bp = (OI_box*)argp;
    if (pp->app_window( )) {
        XClearWindow(bp->display( ),bp->X_window( ));
        disp_curve(pp,bp,pp->view_psn_x( ),pp->view_psn_x( ) + pp->view_x( ));
    }
    return;
}
```

```
void disp_mini_curve(OI_panner *pp, void*, XExposeEvent*)
{

        long                    i;
        int                     x1,y1,x2,y2;
        XGCValues               gcv;
        double                  damping;
        long                    start_x_unit,end_x_unit;
        double                  ratio,y_adjust;

    if (!draw_gc) {
        gcv.foreground = pp->fg_pixel( );
        gcv.background = pp->bkg_pixel( );
        draw_gc = XCreateGC(pp->display( ),pp->X_window( ),
                                        GCForeground|GCBackground,&gcv);
    }

    start_x_unit = pp->paint_org_x( );
    end_x_unit = pp->paint_width( );
    ratio = (double)(pp->span_x( ))/(end_x_unit - start_x_unit);
    y_adjust = (pp->paint_height( ) + pp->paint_org_y( ))/2.0;
    x1 = (int)start_x_unit;
    damping = (pp->paint_width( ) - 0.1*(9*start_x_unit+1))/
                                        (pp->paint_width( ) - 1);
    y1 = (int)(damping*sin(double(ratio*0.0)/10.0)*y_adjust + y_adjust);

    for (i = start_x_unit + 1 ; i <= end_x_unit ; i++) {
        x2 = (int)i;
        damping = (pp->paint_width( ) - 0.1*(9*i+1))/(pp->paint_width( ) - 1);
        y2 = (int)(damping*sin(double(ratio*(i - start_x_unit))/10.0)*y_adjust
                                        + y_adjust);
        XDrawLine(pp->display( ),pp->X_window( ),draw_gc,x1,y1,x2,y2);
        x1 = x2;
        y1 = y2;
    }

    return;
}
```

```
void expose(OI_d_tech*, void *argp, const XEvent *ep)
{
          OI_panner                *pp;

    pp = (OI_panner*)argp;
    if ((ep->type == Expose) && (ep->xexpose.count==0))
        disp_curve(pp,pp->app_window( )->subobject("curve_box"),pp->view_psn_x( ),
                                        pp->view_psn_x( ) + pp->view_x( ));
        else if ((ep->type == GraphicsExpose) && (ep->xgraphicsexpose.count==0))
        disp_curve(pp,pp->app_window( )->subobject("curve_box"),pp->view_psn_x( ),
                                        pp->view_psn_x( ) + pp->view_x( ));

    return;
}
```

Program 36-1   Using an OI_panner to Control a Signal Display (Panner.C)

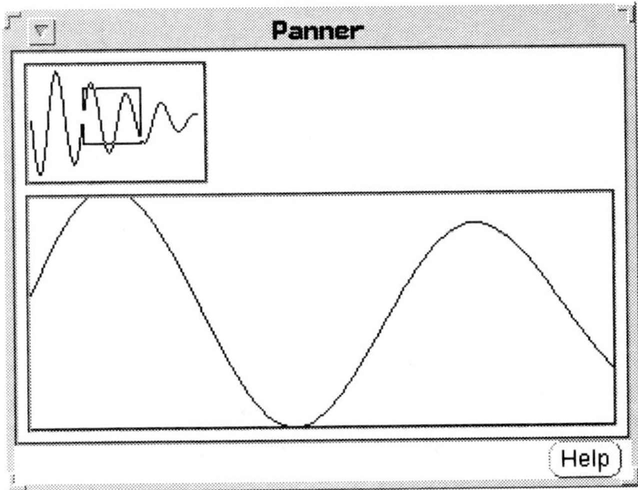

Figure 36-2   Using an OI_panner Object to Control a Signal Display

36.8   Resources

All resources from an OI_panner object's base classes are available to it; in addition, OI fetches the resources shown in Table 36-1. For more information on resource management, see Chapter 39, "The OI Resource Mechanism."

Table 36-1   OI_panner Resources

Resource	Description	Possible Values	Default Value
pixelsX	Specifies the number of pixels per user-unit in the horizontal direction.	Positive integer	1
pixelsY	Specifies the number of pixels per user-unit in the vertical direction.	Positive integer	1
spanX	Specifies the logical span of the object being controlled in the horizontal direction. This resource should be specified in user-units, not pixels. If pixelsX is 5 and the object being controlled is 350 pixels wide, spanX is 70.	Positive integer	(No default)
spanY	Specifies the logical span of the object being controlled in the vertical direction. This resource should be specified in user-units, not pixels. If pixelsY is 5 and the object being controlled is 350 pixels wide, spanY is 70.	Positive integer	(No default)
viewX	Specifies the horizontal logical size of the viewport to the object being controlled. This determines the size of the panner rectangle used for scrolling. This resource should be specified in user-units, not pixels.	Positive integer	(No default)
viewY	Specifies the vertical logical size of the viewport to the object being controlled. This determines the size of the panner rectangle used for scrolling. This resource should be specified in user-units, not pixels.	Positive integer	(No default)

36.9   Translations

An OI_panner object has default translations installed for it. In addition to the translations listed in the tables below, the default translations for an OI_panner object include the default translations for all of its base classes. Table 36-2 shows the default OI_panner translations. Table 36-3 describes what task each action function performs.

Table 36-2   Default OI_panner Translations

Event Sequence				Action Functions Called
Shift	~Ctrl	~Mod1	<Key>Down:	scroll_view_down( )
Shift	~Ctrl	~Mod1	<Key>Left:	scroll_view_left( )
Shift	~Ctrl	~Mod1	<Key>Right:	scroll_view_right( )
Shift	~Ctrl	~Mod1	<Key>Up:	scroll_view_up( )
~Shift	Ctrl	~Mod1	<Key>Down:	scroll_max_down( )
~Shift	Ctrl	~Mod1	<Key>Left:	scroll_max_left( )
~Shift	Ctrl	~Mod1	<Key>Right:	scroll_max_right( )
~Shift	Ctrl	~Mod1	<Key>Up:	scroll_max_up( )
~Shift	~Ctrl	~Mod1	<Btn1Down>:	press( )
~Shift	~Ctrl	~Mod1	<Btn1Motion>:	motion( )
			<Btn1Up>:	release( )
~Shift	~Ctrl	~Mod1	<Key>Down:	scroll_unit_down( )
~Shift	~Ctrl	~Mod1	<Key>Left:	scroll_unit_left( )
~Shift	~Ctrl	~Mod1	<Key>Right:	scroll_unit_right( )
~Shift	~Ctrl	~Mod1	<Key>Up:	scroll_unit_up( )

Table 36-3   OI_panner Translation Functions

Function Name	Description
motion( )	Assumes the event (2nd argument) is a MotionNotify event; extracts the coordinates from the event and moves the panner viewport, performing any callbacks as necessary.
press( )	Records the location of the panner at the time the mouse button is pressed; grabs the mouse pointer.
release( )	Releases the mouse pointer.
scroll_max_down( )	Moves the panner to the bottom extreme.
scroll_max_left( )	Moves the panner to the left extreme.
scroll_max_right( )	Moves the panner to the right extreme.
scroll_max_up( )	Moves the panner to the top extreme.
scroll_unit_down( )	Moves the panner one user unit down.

Table 36-3 OI_panner Translation Functions

Function Name	Description
scroll_unit_left( )	Moves the panner one user unit left.
scroll_unit_right( )	Moves the panner one user unit right.
scroll_unit_up( )	Moves the panner one user unit up.
scroll_view_down( )	Moves the panner one viewport down.
scroll_view_left( )	Moves the panner one viewport left.
scroll_view_right( )	Moves the panner one viewport right.
scroll_view_up( )	Moves the panner one viewport up.

36.10 Callback Functions

Table 36-4 lists the callbacks available for an OI_panner object and the page number where the callback is documented. In addition, all of the callbacks from an OI_panner object's base classes are available to it. See Section 6.18, "Determining and Adding Callbacks; Multiple Callbacks," on page 6-117 for additional information about manipulating callbacks.

Table 36-4 OI_panner Callbacks

Callback Type	Callback Typedef	Description	Page Number
cbCtlr2d	OI_scroll_2d_fnp/memfnp	Scroll callback function	36-3, 36-10
cbPanPaint	OI_pan_paint_fnp/memfnp	Paint callback function	36-3, 36-8

Chapter 37
OI_separator

OI_separator Functions

OI_separator Member Functions

The following functions are available to an **OI_separator** object, but are described in their own chapter.

OI_d_tech Member Functions

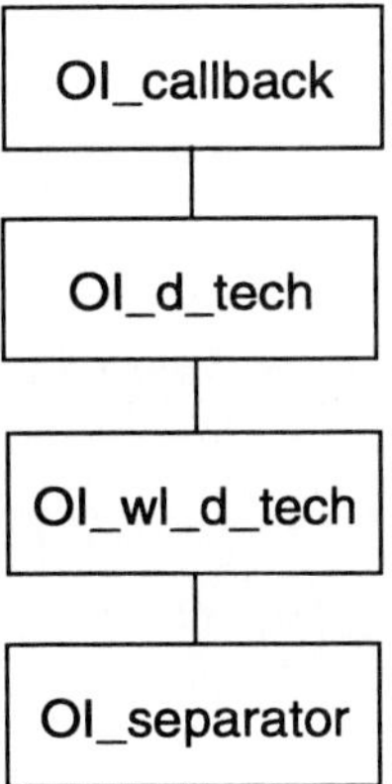

OI_separator

37.1 Description

An OI_separator is a line object which you place on the screen in strategic places to make the display more useful or pleasing to the eye by separating regions of the display. It can be either vertical or horizontal. Note that you do not use an OI_separator object to place a separator cell in a menu; instead create a menu cell of type OI_separator_cell.

37.2 Class Tree

```
OI_callback
    |
OI_d_tech
    |
OI_wl_d_tech
    |
OI_separator
```

37.3 Runtime Interaction

An OI_separator object is for display purposes only.

37.4 OI_separator Creation

oi_create_separator   (Free-standing function)

```
OI_separator *oi_create_separator(
    const char          *namp,              // name for object
    OI_number           len,                // length of separator, in pixels
    OI_orient           ornt=OI_horizontal)  // orientation of the separator
```

oi_create_separator creates an OI_separator object with name *namp* and which is *len* pixels long and has *ornt* orientation. *ornt* can be either OI_horizontal (the default) or OI_vertical.

37.5 Base Class Member Functions

You can use all of the member functions of OI_d_tech for an OI_separator.

37.6 OI_separator Member Functions

length   (Member function)

```
OI_number OI_separator::length( )
```

length returns the length of the separator in pixels.

set_length   (Member function)

```
OI_stat OI_separator::set_length(
    OI_number           len)                // length
```

set_length sets the length of the separator to *len* pixels.

orientation   (Member function)

```
OI_orient OI_separator::orientation( )
```

orientation returns the orientation of the separator. This will be either OI_horizontal or OI_vertical.

set_orientation   (Member function)

```
void OI_separator::set_orientation(
    OI_orient           ornt)               // orientation
```

set_orientation sets the orientation of the separator to *ornt*, which can be either OI_horizontal or OI_vertical.

37.7 Resources

All resources from an OI_separator object's base classes are available to it; in addition, OI fetches the resources shown in Table 37-1. For more information on resource management, see Chapter 39, "The OI Resource Mechanism."

Table 37-1   OI_separator Resources

Resource	Description	Possible Values	Default Value
length	Specifies the length in pixels.	Positive number	(No default)
orientation	Specifies the orientation.	horizontal vertical	(No default)

37.8   Translations

All translations from an OI_separator object's base classes are available to it; it has no additional translations.

37.9   Callback Functions

All callback functions from an OI_separator object's base classes are available to it; it has no additional callback functions.

OI_connection Functions

OI_connection Member Functions

OI_connection

38.1 Description

An OI_connection object represents the communication channel between an OI program and the particular X Window System display and screen upon which a group of objects is to be displayed. This communications channel is initialized when you call OI_init, which returns a pointer to the OI_connection object created. You may open more than one connection if necessary using oi_create_connection.

An OI_connection object contains information regarding:

- The X server to which it is connected
- Properties of the root window
- X resource management
- The event dispatch table
- Connection-wide mappings and translations

You can obtain information concerning all of these items, and change many of them, using the functions described in this chapter. A note on terminology—when you create a connection using OI_init, oi_create_connection or open_screen, you get a pointer to an OI_connection object. This object is referred to in this chapter as "the connection" or "this connection".

38.2 Class Tree

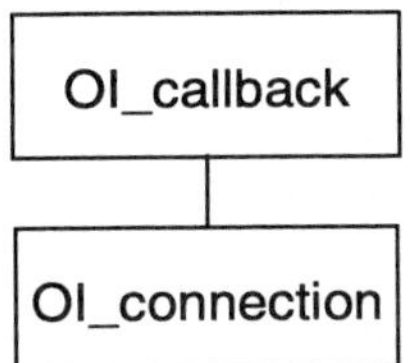

38.3 Accessing X Display Attributes

These functions allow you to query the identification of the X Window System *host*, *display* and *screen* upon which the OI objects are displayed, as well as attributes of the display and screen. *Host* is the name of the system on the network upon which this particular connection is displaying. A host system may be running more than one X server. The *display* is a number identifying the particular X server. An X server can service more than one physical or virtual screen; *screen* is the number of the screen for the X server.

hostname   (Member function)

```
char *OI_connection::hostname( )
```

hostname returns the name of the host being used for the connection. This does not include the display/screen numbers ":n.m" used to open the connection. This name is exactly what is to the

---

left of ":" in the **DISPLAY** environment variable or the -**display** command line argument. The name is not rendered into a canonical form.

display_num   (Member function)

```
int OI_connection::display_num( )
```

display_num returns the number of the display being used for the connection.

screen_num   (Member function)

```
int OI_connection::screen_num( )
```

screen_num returns the number of the screen used for the connection.

display   (Member function)

```
Display *OI_connection::display( )
```

display returns a pointer to the **Xlib Display** structure for the connection.

display_name   (Member function)

```
char *OI_connection::display_name( )
```

display_name returns the name of the X Window System display for the connection as *hostname:display.screen*.

num_screens   (Member function)

```
int OI_connection::num_screens( )
```

num_screens returns the number of screens on the display used for the connection.

has_shape   (Member function)

```
OI_bool OI_connection::has_shape( )
```

has_shape returns **OI_yes** if the X server for the connection has the shape extension installed; otherwise it returns **OI_no**.

is_color   (Member function)

```
OI_bool OI_connection::is_color( )
```

is_color returns **OI_yes** if the connection is on a color or gray-scale monitor (that is, if the number of color cells is greater than two); otherwise it returns **OI_no**. See **visual_id**, below.

visual_id   (Member function)

```
VisualID OI_connection::visual_id( )
```

visual_id returns the default X VisualID for the connection. The return value will be one of:

    StaticGray
    GrayScale
    StaticColor
    PseudoColor
    TrueColor
    DirectColor

38.4   Accessing Root Window Attributes

Root windows come in two flavors: the *absolute root window* and the *logical root window*. The absolute root window corresponds to the X Window System's root window, sized to cover the physical screen. The logical root window may be the same as the absolute root window. However, if you are running a window manager, such as **olvwm**, which supports a virtual root window, the logical root window is different from the absolute root window—it corresponds to the virtual root window used by the virtual desktop. In any case, you should normally use the logical root window for all operations except determining the size of the physical screen.

root   (Member function)

```
OI_d_tech *OI_connection::root( )
```

root returns a pointer to the logical root for the connection. This may be the same object as is returned by the function **abs_root**. However, if the window manager is placing windows on a virtual root, the object pointed to by root is different and represents the virtual root.

abs_root   (Member function)

```
OI_d_tech *OI_connection::abs_root( )
```

abs_root returns a pointer to absolute root window on the screen for the connection.

orphanage   (Member function)

```
OI_d_tech *OI_connection::orphanage( )
```

When an OI object is initially created, its parent is an object called the **orphanage**. Similarly, when an object is unparented, it is placed in the **orphanage**. This function returns a pointer to the **orphanage**. You should not normally need to use this function since OI takes care of moving objects into and out of the **orphanage** for you. You can use the **OI_d_tech** member functions **is_orphanage** and **is_root_or_orphanage** to determine if an object is the orphanage or a root object.

38.5 Managing the Mouse Pointer

You can create a cursor—the shape used for a mouse pointer—using make_cursor. The graphic shapes that can be used are normally enumerated in the file /usr/include/X11/cursorfont.h, or you can create your own. The actual font used for displaying these cursors is named "cursor".

Some common interaction scenarios involve choosing an object by placing the mouse over it and clicking. This yields an X event from which you may need to determine which object received the click. find_obj makes this a simple task.

make_cursor   (Member function)

```
Cursor OI_connection::make_cursor(
    int                 index)              // cursor index
```

```
Cursor OI_connection::make_cursor(
    const char          *image,             // bitmap file name
    const char          *mask)              // bitmap file name
```

```
Cursor OI_connection::make_cursor(
    Pixmap              image,              // PIXMAP
    Pixmap              mask,               // PIXMAP
    unsigned int        x_hot,              // hotspot location
    unsigned int        y_hot)             // hotspot location
```

make_cursor creates and returns an X Cursor which you can subsequently use to set the cursor for an object. See Section 6.11.5, "Cursors," on page 6-91, for functions which set cursors for individual objects and set "working" cursors. *index* should be one of the constants defined in the file /usr/include/X11/cursorfont.h. These constants are indices to the characters defined in the cursor font, which is normally /usr/lib/X11/fonts/misc/cursor.*. For example, both lines of code shown here return a gumby representation:

```
crs = conp->make_cursor(XC_gumby);
crs = conp->make_cursor(56);
```

image and *mask* are the bitmaps used to create a custom cursor. They are the arguments passed to XCreatePixmapCursor. *x_hot* and *y_hot* specify the distance, in pixels, of the cursor's hot spot from the upper left corner of the bitmap.

find_obj   (Member function)

```
OI_d_tech *OI_connection::find_obj(
    const XEvent        *ep,                    // pointer to X event
    OI_number           n_obj_tree=0,           // number of object trees in obj_forest.
    OI_d_tech           **obj_forest=NULL,      // forest of object trees
    OI_bool             intrnl=OI_no)           // find internal OI objects?
```

find_obj returns a pointer to the lowest level object under the mouse pointer position defined in the X event *ep*. "Lowest level object" means the object farthest down the object tree which is visible under the mouse pointer.

ep is a pointer to the X event. Typically you receive *ep* as an argument in an OI_event_fnp or OI_event_memfnp callback function that you have set up using the convenience function OI_dispatch_insert or the OI_connection member function dispatch_insert (see below).

n_obj_tree is the number of object trees in *obj_forest*.

obj_forest is an array of object trees. It is a vector of pointers to the top-level object in each of the trees in the array. The object selected by find_obj must be located in one of the object trees passed in *obj_forest*; otherwise find_obj returns NULL. If you omit *obj_forest* or set it to NULL, find_obj considers every object on the connection in its search.

intrnl specifies whether any internal OI objects should be returned. The default, OI_no, indicates that no internal objects should be returned.

38.6   Manipulating the OI Dispatch Table

OI maintains a dispatch table for each connection. Entries in this table indicate what to do when an event happens in a given window belonging to the connection. The OI library inserts and removes entries from the dispatch table for the windows for OI objects. The following functions allow you to maintain your own entries in this table. For example, you might use the dispatch table if you wanted to know if a property changed on a window. You can also use dispatch inserts for communication between programs. You will need the X Window ID for the window whose events you want dispatched; if it is a window for an OI object, you can get its ID by calling the OI_d_tech member functions X_window or outside_X_window.

Before using the dispatch table directly, check to be sure there is not an OI function which does the job for you—the OI function is more convenient if it exists. For example, see the OI_d_tech member function set_click.

dispatch_insert   (Member function)

```
void OI_connection::dispatch_insert(
    Window              win,              // X Window ID
    int                 event_type,       // event type
    unsigned long       event_mask,       // event mask
    OI_event_fnp        fnp,              // pointer to callback function
    void                *argp=NULL,       // arbitrary argument for fnp
    OI_number           psn=-1)           // position in dispatch table

void OI_connection::dispatch_insert(
    Window              win,              // X Window ID
    int                 event_type,       // event type
    unsigned long       event_mask,       // event mask
    OI_callback         *objp,            // memfnp's object
    OI_event_memfnp     memfnp,           // pointer to callback member function
    void                *argp=NULL,       // arbitrary argument for memfnp
    OI_number           psn=-1)           // position in dispatch table
```

The **dispatch_insert** functions register a callback function (*fnp* or *memfnp*) to be invoked whenever the specified event occurs. **dispatch_insert** inserts an entry into the dispatch table for the connection. *memfnp* points to a member function for the object pointed to by *objp*. If your dispatch event callback function is a member function, when it is invoked it will be called as if you had written *objp->memfnp*. See Section 2.5, "Callbacks and Event-Driven Programming," on page 2-16 for more explanation.

event_type is a constant corresponding to an X event type—for example, **EnterNotify**. These constants are listed in Table 40-2, "Event Types," on page 40-5.

event_mask comprises the same arguments that you would use in an **XSelectInput** Xlib library call. *argp* is optional, and can be any valid expression that can be cast to a pointer. You can use it to pass additional information to the function *fnp* or *memfnp*. *psn* is the position in the dispatch table in which to insert the entry. The default, -1, causes OI to insert the entry in the first available open space. If *psn* specifies a position already occupied in the table, the other entries are moved down to make room for this one.

Note that if you call **dispatch_insert** multiple times with the same arguments, multiple entries are placed in the dispatch table. This causes your callback to be executed multiple times for the single X event for which the function is registered.

Writing the Dispatch Event Callback Function

If the callback function is not a member function, write it in this form:

```
void fn(
        XEvent          *ep,            // pointer to event
        void            *argp)          // arbitrary argument
```

and if the callback function is a member function, write it in this form:

```
void obj_class::memfn(
        XEvent          *ep,            // pointer to event
        void            *argp)          // arbitrary argument
```

where *obj_class* is the class of the object whose member function is *memfn*. When your callback function is invoked, *argp* will be the argument specified in the dispatch_insert call, and *ep* will be a pointer to the event which has occurred.

dispatch_remove   (Member function)

```
void OI_connection::dispatch_remove(
        Window              win,            // X Window ID
        int                 event_type,     // event type
        unsigned long       event_mask,     // event mask
        OI_event_fnp        fnp,            // pointer to callback function
        void                *argp=NULL)     // arbitrary argument for fnp
```

```
void OI_connection::dispatch_remove(
        Window              win,            // X Window ID
        int                 event_type,     // event type
        unsigned long       event_mask,     // event mask
        OI_callback         *objp,          // memfnp's object
        OI_event_memfnp     memfnp,         // pointer to callback member function
        void                *argp=NULL)     // arbitrary argument for memfnp
```

Removes an entry from the dispatch table. The arguments are the same as for dispatch_insert. In order for an entry to be removed, all of the arguments of the call must match the arguments used to insert the event.

dispatch_discard   (Member function)

```
void OI_connection::dispatch_discard(
        Window              win)            // X Window ID
```

dispatch_discard removes all entries for window *win* from the dispatch table for this connection. You should normally use this function only for your private window and not a window corresponding to an OI object, since OI objects have their own dispatch table entries for their windows.

dispatch_group_insert   (Member function)

```
void OI_connection::dispatch_group_insert(
    Window            win,          // X Window ID
    OI_number         n,            // number of entries to insert
    OI_dispatch_entry *tp)          // pointer to table of entry items
```

dispatch_group_insert inserts a group of entries into the dispatch table. This function is a more efficient means of inserting more than one event into the dispatch table for the same window than repeated calls to **dispatch_insert**. *tp* points to a table of **OI_dispatch_entry** items; this is a structure containing data items which are analogous to the arguments to **dispatch_insert**:

```
struct OI_dispatch_entry {
    int             event;          // type of event to match, may be 0
    unsigned long   event_mask;     // event mask used to select for event, may be 0
    OI_event_fnp    fnp;            // pointer to free-standing function to call when
                                    //   event occurs
    OI_callback     *objp;          // pointer to object to call memfnp on behalf of
    OI_event_memfnp memfnp;         // pointer to member function to call when event
                                    //   occurs
    void            *argp;          // argument for fnp or memfnp
};
```

If you specify *fnp*, *objp* and *memfnp* should be NULL; similarly, if you specify *objp* and *memfnp*, *fnp* should be NULL.

dispatch_group_remove   (Member function)

```
void OI_connection::dispatch_group_remove(
    Window            win,          // X Window ID
    OI_number         n,            // number of entries to remove
    OI_dispatch_entry *tp)          // pointer to table of entry items
```

dispatch_group_remove removes a group of entries from the dispatch table. Arguments are the same as for **dispatch_group_insert**.

dispatch_ignore   (Member function)

```
void OI_connection::dispatch_ignore(
    const XEvent      *ep)          // pointer to X Event
```

dispatch_ignore causes the connection to ignore any other registered callbacks waiting for this event.

38.7 Animation Support

As discussed in Chapter 25, "OI_glyph," you can animate a glyph by displaying a series of bitmaps in sequence. The two functions described here create the necessary data structures to support animation, given a series of bitmap files. The **OI_animate_item** structures and the

Pixmap series that are generated are dependent upon the connection because they are affected by the physical characteristics of the display. Use **uniform_pixmap_series** if your bitmaps to be animated are all the same size, they are all to appear at the same location on the screen, and they will appear at equal frame intervals. Otherwise use **pixmap_series**.

uniform_pixmap_series   (Member function)

```
long OI_connection::uniform_pixmap_series(
    Pixmap              **pmp,         // Pixmaps generated
    const char          *fil_namp,     // bitmap file name template
    OI_bool             mask=OI_yes,   // single or full color bitmaps
    long                nf=0,          // number of files
    long                strt=1)        // starting bitmap-name number
```

uniform_pixmap_series generates a series of **Pixmaps** from a set of consistently-named bitmap files. OI backfills *pmp* with a pointer to a vector of generated **Pixmaps**. *fil_namp* specifies a template for bitmap file names. The file names are generated by replacing the first "@" found in *fil_namp* with a numeric string, starting at *strt*, which defaults to "1." If no "@" is found, the numeric strings are appended to the file name. *nf* specifies the number of files to read; 0 implies as many as can be found. You are responsible for freeing the *pmp* memory and pixmaps when you are through with them.

If *mask* is **OI_yes**, the Pixmaps generated are treated as 1-bit deep masks; if *mask* is **OI_no**, the Pixmaps are treated as full color bitmaps. *mask* defaults to **OI_yes**.

uniform_pixmap_series returns the number of frames actually generated.

For example, if there are four bitmaps to be included in the animation series, and they are named **cartoon1**, **cartoon2**, **cartoon3**, and **cartoon4**, and the Pixmaps are to be rendered as masks of the foreground and background colors, you could write:

```
OI_connection           *conp;
Pixmap                  *seriesp;
long                    nframe;
nframe = conp->uniform_pixmap_series(&seriesp,"cartoon");
```

If there are five bitmaps named **cartoon87.pm**, **cartoon88.pm**, **cartoon89.pm**, **cartoon90.pm**, and **cartoon91.pm**, but only the middle three are to be included in the animation series, and the Pixmaps are to be rendered as masks, the example becomes:

```
OI_connection           *conp;
Pixmap                  *seriesp;
long                    nframe;
nframe = onp->uniform_pixmap_series(&seriesp,"cartoon@.pm",OI_yes,3,88);
```

The bitmap file format can only specify whether to color a pixel or not; it cannot specify a complete color for a pixel. Because of this limitation, if you set *mask* to **OI_no** in the call to **uniform_pixmap_series** so that the Pixmaps are rendered as full Pixmaps and not as masks, they are generated in two colors, using the foreground and background colors for the root window.

pixmap_series   (Member function)

```
long OI_connection::pixmap_series(
    OI_animate_item    **frmp,              // animated series generated
    const char         *fil_namp,           // bitmap file name template
    OI_bool            mask=OI_yes,         // single or full color bitmaps
    long               nf=0,                // number of files
    long               strt=1)              // starting bitmap-name number
```

pixmap_series generates a series of OI_animate_item structures from a set of consistently-named bitmap files. OI backfills *frmp* with a pointer to a vector of generated OI_animate_item structures. *fil_namp, mask, nf,* and *strt* are the same as for uniform_pixmap_series, above.

pixmap_series returns the number of frames actually generated.

You are responsible for freeing the *frmp* memory and pixmaps in the OI_animate_item structure when you are through with them.

The OI_animate_item structure looks like this:

```
struct OI_animate_item {                    // single element of an animation sequence
    Pixmap      pm;                         // pixmap to paint
    long        ms=100;                     // time interval to next picture
    OI_origin   psn=(0,0);                  // new position for pixmap
    OI_xy       siz;                        // size of pixmap
    OI_bool     pm_chg=OI_yes;              // OI_yes => pixmap contents have changed,
                                            // even if pm unchanged
    void        *usr_datp=NULL;             // ptr to arbitrary user data structure
};
```

pixmap_series creates the OI_animate_item structures with the values of *pm* and *siz* appropriate for the bitmap files you specify in *fil_namp* and default values for the other elements. You may want to change the values of *ms, psn,* and/or *usr_datp*.

38.8   Interaction Models

By default, OI programs use the Motif interaction and appearance model. Using a command-line argument, the program can be started using the 2-D OPEN LOOK, 3-D OPEN LOOK, or Motif model (see Chapter 3, "Compiling, Linking, and Executing an OI Program"); the default start-up model for the program can also be changed via the X resource database by entering a line in the .Xdefaults file. If your program name is "xyz," then the line in .Xdefaults should be one of:

```
xyz*model:        openlook
xyz*model:        openlook2d
xyz*model:        openlook3d
xyz*model:        motif
```

"openlook" means use the 2D model on monochrome displays and the 3D model on color displays.

Each newly-created OI object is created according to a particular interaction model. An object's interaction model can be changed at any time. Also, a single application can create sets of objects using different interaction models.

model   (Member function)

```
OI_model_type OI_connection::model( )
```

model returns the current interaction model. This will be one of OI_motif, OI_openlook, or OI_openlook_3d.

set_model   (Member function)

```
void OI_connection::set_model(
    OI_model_type      mt)              // model type
```

set_model changes the model to be used for subsequent objects created on the connection. Valid values for *mt* are: OI_openlook, OI_openlook_3d, or OI_motif. You should normally not use this function; the user should be allowed to control the model via the command line or resource database.

draw_fast   (Member function)

```
OI_bool OI_connection::draw_fast( )
```

A resource, "fastdraw", indicates that when objects are rendered, appearance should be sacrificed in favor of speed. This is a useful option if the application is to be run at slow speeds (as over a modem). draw_fast returns the value of this option; normally it is off (OI_no).

38.9   Colormaps

A *Colormap* is an X resource ID used to indicate a particular color table that defines colors available on the display. The table maps pixel values to colors on the display; pixel values typically index into the table (for example, a pixel value of 3 usually refers to the fourth entry in the table). The X server uses the table entry to determine what colors to display. Refer to X documentation for an explanation of the arguments to these functions.

Unless you are writing a specialized application such as a colormap editor or a window manager, you should have little use for the colormap-related member functions. You can specify colors themselves using the OI_d_tech member functions set_*_color or set_*_pixel, although it is better form to allow the user to set colors via the X resource database. You can establish default values by putting them in an application default file or by adding entries to the default resource database using the default_resources member function.

colormap   (Member function)

```
Colormap OI_connection::colormap( )
```

colormap returns the XID of the colormap being used as the default for the connection. An XID is a number used by the X server to identify an item (for example, a Window, Colormap, Pixmap, or GC).

---

colormap_type   (Member function)

```
Atom OI_connection::colormap_type( )
```

colormap_type returns an Atom representing the type of colormap being used as the default for the connection. This will be one of the values listed under **set_standard_colormap** below. colormap_type returns **None** if a non-standard colormap is being used.

set_standard_colormap   (Member function)

```
void OI_connection::set_standard_colormap(
    Atom                    cm)                     // standard colormap
```

set_standard_colormap changes the colormap to be used by all objects on the connection to one of the standard colormaps. Acceptable values for *cm* are:

XA_RGB_DEFAULT_MAP	You can place customized colors here.
XA_RGB_BEST_MAP	A hardware-dependent even distribution of colors.
XA_RGB_GRAY_MAP	Shades of gray only.
XA_RGB_RED_MAP	Shades of red only.
XA_RGB_GREEN_MAP	Shades of green only.
XA_RGB_BLUE_MAP	Shades of blue only.

Under most circumstances, you will want to use **XA_RGB_DEFAULT_MAP**. This is the only standard colormap into which a client program can write. Consequently, it is the only standard colormap you can allocate specific colors from and have some expectation of the colors actually matching the one you requested. For example, if you ask for Navy Blue using **XA_RGB_BEST_MAP**, you get the pre-defined color closest to Navy Blue, but not necessarily an exact match. Using **XA_RGB_DEFAULT_MAP**, you should get an exact match, since the definition for Navy Blue is stored in the table when you request it; the server looks it up in the color database, normally found in /usr/lib/X11/rgb.*. Note, however, that space in the default colormap is limited. Common courtesy dictates that your program not hog all the colormap entries and cause other programs to be unable to allocate colors they need.

set_colormap   (Member function)

```
void OI_connection::set_colormap(
    Colormap                cmap,                   // X colormap identifier
    unsigned long           red_max=0,
    unsigned long           red_mult=0,
    unsigned long           green_max=0,
    unsigned long           green_mult=0,
    unsigned long           blue_max=0,
    unsigned long           blue_mult=0,
    unsigned long           base_pixel=0)
```

set_colormap sets the default colormap for the connection to a private colormap. *cmap* is the X identifier of the colormap to use as a private colormap; you obtain this identifier when you define a colormap using **XCreateColormap**. The rest of the arguments are the constants used

---

in the XStandardColormap structure. For a description of these constants, see the X documentation for the XStandardColormap structure.

38.10 Multiple Connections

If you are writing an application which needs to display on more than one X display station or screen, such as a multi-screen window manager, you will need to open more than one connection; you will need a separate connection for each screen. You can open additional connections using oi_create_connection or, if the new connection is on the same server as an existing connection, the member function open_screen.

When you create OI objects, they are created on what is known as the *default connection*. The default connection is the connection which has OI's "attention" at the moment. The default connection is the one on which any newly created-objects reside; it is the one on which the bell rings, or any other action the application performs occurs. Most applications use only one connection; if this is the case, the default connection is the one returned by the OI_init call. Whenever you create a new connection, OI automatically makes the new connection the default connection. You can also specifically set the default connection by calling the OI_connection member function make_default, although this is seldom necessary.

The default connection changes automatically in an application with multiple connections. If you have not yet called OI_begin_interaction, the default connection is the last connection you created or set using the OI_connection member function make_default. When OI_begin_interaction returns, the default connection is the same one as when OI_begin_interaction was entered.

Whenever an X event is processed, the current default connection is pushed onto a stack, and the default connection is set to be the connection corresponding to the event. The stack is popped on return from processing the event. This ensures that any objects created while a callback routine is executing are created on the same connection as the event which triggered the callback (unless, of course, you specifically change the default connection from within the callback routine).

oi_create_connection   (Free-standing function)

```
OI_connection *oi_create_connection(
    int                 *argcp,              // pointer to initialization argc
    char                **argv,              // initialization argv
    const char          *app_classp=NULL,    // application generic name
    const char          *app_namp=NULL,      // this invocation's specific name
    XrmOptionDescRec    *app_rmtblp=NULL,    // X resource option table
    int                 app_rmtbl_siz=0)     // number of entries in app_rmtblp

OI_connection *oi_create_connection(
    Display             *dpy,                // pointer to display
    int                 *argcp,              // pointer to initialization argc
    char                **argv,              // initialization argv
    const char          *app_classp=NULL,    // application generic name
    const char          *app_namp=NULL,      // this invocation's specific name
    XrmOptionDescRec    *app_rmtblp=NULL,    // X resource option table
    int                 app_rmtbl_siz=0)     // number of entries in app_rmtblp
```

oi_create_connection creates a new connection to an X server. The new connection becomes the default connection. Any new OI object that you subsequently create appears on the screen for this new default connection. Do not use this call to create the first connection for OI; use **OI_init** for that purpose, because **OI_init** performs other necessary OI initialization tasks. Remember that **OI_init** strips arguments from the command-line arguments; if you want to retrieve the original command-line argument strings for use in **oi_create_connection**, use the functions **OI_*_argc** and **OI_*_argv**. These functions can be found in Chapter 5, "Initialization, Termination, and Other Independent Functions." In general, you should only use **oi_create_connection** when you wish to open a connection to a new X server. If you wish to open an additional screen on a display for which you already have a connection, use **open_screen**.

open_screen   (Member function)

```
OI_connection *OI_connection::open_screen(
    OI_number           scn)                 // screen number
```

open_screen opens a new connection on a different screen, using the same X server as the current connection. *scn* must be in the range 0 <= *scn* < **num_screens( )**. The new connection becomes the default connection. Any new OI object that you subsequently create appears on the screen for this new default connection.

Example 38-1 shows a segment of code which creates a connection using **OI_init**, then opens all the screens on the display for that connection, using **open_screen**.

```
        OI_connection   *conp,**all_con;
        OI_number        i;

if (conp = OI_init(&argc,argv,"ScreenTest")) {
    all_con = new OI_connection *[conp->num_screens( )];
    for (i=0 ; i<conp->num_screens( ) ; i++) {
        if (i != conp->screen_num( ))
            all_con[i] = conp->open_screen(i);
        else
            all_con[conp->screen_num( )] = conp;
    }
}
```

Example 38-1   Opening More Than One Screen on a Connection

make_default   (Member function)

```
void OI_connection::make_default( )
```

make_default causes the connection on whose behalf **make_default** is called to become the default connection. Objects subsequently created are placed on this connection.

38.11 Miscellaneous Functions

make_top_level   (Member function)

```
OI_d_tech **OI_connection::make_top_level(
    const char       *nam=NULL,        // instance name to fetch
    const char       *cls=NULL,        // class name to fetch
    OI_number        *num_objs=NULL)   // number of objects in returned vector
```

make_top_level fetches the **topLevel** resource for any application currently loaded into the resource manager database. In general, **make_top_level** is used to start the construction of a configuration resource file based application.

When you build an application using an OI builder such as ObjectBuilder, the builder will generate a file containing a graphical description of your application. This configuration file describes the hierarchical structure of your application, as well as additional, non-default resources, set on an object-by-object basis.

When you compile and run the builder-generated program, the main routine fetches the configuration file and adds it to the application database. Once the resource file has been loaded into the application database, the main program calls **make_top_level** to probe the database for the **topLevel** resource. Within the configuration file, this resource would take the form of:

```
*topLevel: aaa.OI_app_window, bbb.OI_dialog_box, ccc.OI_app_window
```

This resource is a comma separated list of object_name.object_class pairs.

Since your application can have more than one top level (also known as root level) object, **make_top_level** returns a null terminated vector of the specified top level objects. When you call **make_top_level**, this routine first fetches the specified resource for your application, then carefully   walks   through   the   text   creating   **OI_minimal**   instances   (from *class_name*::make_minimal) of each specified top level object. Since your application can have more than one top level object, make_top_level allocates, using malloc, sufficient memory to create a NULL-terminated list of pointers to the objects it creates. The objects contained within the returned vector are minimal instances parented to the orphanage. No resources have yet been fetched for the objects, and no children have yet been created.

When this top level vector is parented to root (in state OI_not_displayed), resources are fetched for each object in turn ("children" is the last resource fetched for each object). It is only at this point that you will be able to access userVariables that were set on any objects in this tree of objects (including the topLevel objects).

Once all topLevel objects have been associated, you can free this vector since it was allocated for you by make_top_level.

set_data   (Member function)

```
void OI_connection::set_data(
    void                 *ud)              // user data item
```

Every connection carries around a user data pointer. This is an arbitrary pointer intended for use by the application. It provides a convenient means of associating application data structures with connections. set_data establishes the user data pointer *ud* and establishes a place *udp* to backfill with *ud* when the connection is made to be the default connection. set_data is most useful if you are working with multiple connections.

data   (Member function)

```
void *OI_connection::data( )
```

data returns a pointer to the data item for the connection which was set using set_data.

set_default_focus   (Member function)

```
void OI_connection::set_default_focus(
    OI_d_tech            *objp)            // object to have focus
```

set_default_focus establishes the object that will have the input focus when the application first receives the input focus on the connection. For more information on input focus, see Section 6.14, "Input Focus Management" on page 6-83.

default_focus   (Member function)

```
OI_d_tech *OI_connection::default_focus( )
```

default_focus returns a pointer to the object that will receive the input focus when it is first transferred to the application. default_focus returns NULL if a default focus object has not been set.

time   (Member function)

```
Time OI_connection::time( )
```

time returns the current X server time in milliseconds. Time is a long int. If an X event containing the time is already handy, it should be used instead, since this function forces a round trip to the server.

last_time   (Member function)

```
Time OI_connection::last_time( )
```

last_time returns the time of the last event received which had a time stamp from the X server.

str_color   (Member function)

```
OI_stat OI_connection::str_color(
    const char          *clr,            // color name string
    PIXEL               *pxlp,           // pointer to returned PIXEL value
    Colormap            cm=None)         // colormap used for conversion
```

str_color converts a string representation for a color value (for example, "green" or "#RRGGBB") to a PIXEL value, using the colormap *cm*. If you omit *cm*, the colormap currently in use for the connection is used. str_color returns OI_ok if it was successful, and OI_no_color if it could not find the color *clr*.

atom   (Member function)

```
Atom OI_connection::atom(
    const char          *str)            // string to convert to atom
```

OI maintains a cache of X server Atoms for each OI_connection object so that a round trip to the X server only occurs the first time the Atom is requested. atom converts *str* into an Atom, adds it to the connection's Atom cache, and returns the Atom.

build_from_configuration_file   (Member function)

```
OI_d_tech **OI_connection::build_from_configuration_file(
    const char          *fil_nam,        // configuration file name
    OI_bool             frc_ftch=OI_yes) // force fetch of resources?
```

build_from_configuration_file builds and loads a subtree from the configuration file *fil_nam*. *fil_nam* must be in X resource file format in the form created by an OI companion product, UIB, or any OI user interface builder. The definition of this file format is beyond the scope of this book. If *frc_ftch* is OI_yes, the resources for the objects built are fetched.

set_click (Member function)

```
void OI_connection::set_click(
    OI_click_fnp        fnp,            // pointer to callback function
    void                *argp=NULL)     // arbitrary argument for fnp


void OI_connection::set_click(
    OI_callback         *objp,          // memfnp's object
    OI_click_memfnp     memfnp,         // pointer to callback member function
    void                *argp=NULL)     // arbitrary argument for memfnp
```

You should only use the OI_connection member function set_click if your application will always be running without a window manager or if your application is a window manager. Otherwise, you should use the set_click member function for a particular OI object that supports click functions. The reason for this is that X only allows a single client to receive button press and release events on the root window, and these events are normally already directed to the window manager client.

The set_click functions register a callback function to be invoked whenever the user clicks a mouse button one or more times on the root window. This callback is identified within OI as a cbClick callback function (see Section 6.18, "Determining and Adding Callbacks; Multiple Callbacks," on page 6-117). *memfnp* points to a member function for the object pointed to by *objp*. If your click function is a member function, when it is invoked it will be called as if you had written *objp->memfnp*. See Section 2.5, "Callbacks and Event-Driven Programming," on page 2-16 for more explanation.

argp is optional, and can be any valid expression that can be cast to a pointer. You can use it to pass additional information to the function *fnp* or *memfnp*.

The button press and release must be separated by no more than clickDelta milliseconds for a press/release sequence to be considered a click. For multiple clicks, a release and subsequent press must also be separated by no more than clickDelta milliseconds. clickDelta is an OI_connection resource that defaults to 500.

Writing the Click Callback Function

If the cbClick callback function is not a member function, write it in this form:

```
void fn(
        OI_d_tech   *oi_objp,     // pointer to absolute root object
        void        *argp,        // arbitrary argument
        OI_number   n_clicks,     // number of clicks
        OI_number   btn,          // mouse button number clicked
        OI_number   mod,          // modifier bits on at click time
        OI_number   x,            // x location of click, root window coordinates
        OI_number   y)            // y location of click, root window coordinates
```

and if the cbClick callback function is a member function, write it in this form:

```
void obj_class::memfn(
        OI_d_tech   *oi_objp,     // pointer to absolute root object
        void        *argp,        // arbitrary argument
        OI_number   n_clicks,     // number of clicks
        OI_number   btn,          // button number which was clicked
        OI_number   mod,          // modifier bits on at click time
        OI_number   x,            // x location of click, root window coordinates
        OI_number   y)            // y location of click, root window coordinates
```

where *obj_class* is the class of the object whose member function is *memfn*.

When your callback function is invoked, *argp* will be the argument specified in the set_click call. *oi_objp* will be a pointer to the absolute root object for the connection, where the click occurred. *mod* will contain the modifier bits on at click time. These will be zero unless the user holds down one of the modifier keys on the keyboard at the time of the mouse click. *mod* can have any combination (0 or more) of the following values, combined with a bitwise inclusive or.

OI_mod_shift	Shift key down during click.
OI_mod_lock	Lock key down during click.
OI_mod_control	Control key down during click.
OI_mod_meta	Mod1 key down during click.

When more than one click occurs, the callback function will be invoked once for each click. For example, a double click will cause the function to be called first with *n_clicks*=1, then with *n_clicks*=2. If your application is performing a different operation depending on the number of clicks, the operations for a greater number of clicks should be compatible with those for fewer clicks.

38.12 Interfacing to the Resource Mechanism

These functions allow you to modify and retrieve resource values from the OI resource database, and to destroy a database. The OI resource database associates names with strings (for example, foreground and background color, button labels, interaction model). OI initializes the OI resource database and retrieves values from it as needed. OI uses several separate resource databases. By default, the following resource databases are defined:

    OI_set_database
    OI_app_database
    OI_user_database
    OI_default_database

For a description of these databases and more information on resource management, see Chapter 39, "The OI Resource Mechanism."

If you are going to call any of these functions many times, and if the function has a form with XrmQuarks as parameters, it is more efficient to convert a string to an XrmQuark and use the XrmQuark form of the function. You can convert a string to an XrmQuark using the Xlib function XrmStringToQuark.

Many of these functions refer to converters, to whether resource conversion has been performed, and to the resource prefix stack. Converter objects and the resource prefix stack are explained in Chapter 39. The converters used in these functions are those pre-registered by OI, and/or the converters you register yourself, if any.

get_resource   (Member function)

```
const char *OI_connection::get_resource(
    const char          *res_nam,        // resource name
    const char          *res_cls)        // resource class


const char *OI_connection::get_resource(
    XrmQuark            res_nam,          // resource name
    XrmQuark            res_cls)          // resource class
```

These two forms of **get_resource** fetch the value of resource *res_nam* with class *res_cls* from the OI resource database for this connection. OI prefaces *res_cls* and *res_nam* with the contents of the OI resource stack for the connection, which includes (in order):

Instance	**Class**
Application name	Application class
"oi"	"OI"
"color" or "monochrome"	"Color" or "Monochrome"
screen number (example: "screen0")	Screen number (example: "Screen0")
language (example: "defaultLanguage")	Language (example: "DefaultLanguage")
"openlook2d", "openlook3d", or "motif"	"Openlook" or "Motif"
object hierarchies (instance names)	Object hierarchies (class names)

No conversion of the resource is done; the raw resource string is returned. If no resource match is found, **get_resource** returns NULL. The value returned points directly into the resource database. <u>Do not modify or free this value!</u> Copy it if you need to modify it or save it.

```
OI_bool OI_connection::get_resource(
    const char          *res_nam,       // resource name
    char                **typp,         // pointer to type of value returned
    char                **valp,         // pointer to value returned
    OI_bool             nocase=OI_yes)   // force to lower case?
```

This form of **get_resource** fetches the value of resource *res_nam* from the OI resource database for this connection. The class used for the resource fetch is *res_nam* with the first letter capitalized.

OI backfills *typp* with a string describing the type of value returned. *typp* is always OI_r_string, although in the future it may have other values. OI backfills *valp* with the actual value for the resource, for which no conversion has been done. If *nocase* is OI_yes, then *valp* is forced to lowercase. *valp* points to static data which will be reused on the next call to **get_resource**. You should copy it if you need to modify it. **get_resource** returns OI_yes if it is successful; otherwise it returns OI_no.

get_resource_cvt   (Member function)

```
OI_bool OI_connection::get_resource_cvt(
    const char          *res_nam,       // resource name
    const char          *res_cls,       // resource class
    const char          *to_type,       // resource type to which to convert
    void                *valp)           // location for result


OI_bool OI_connection::get_resource_cvt(
    XrmQuark            res_nam,         // resource name
    XrmQuark            res_cls,         // resource class
    XrmQuark            to_type,         // resource type to which to convert
    void                *valp)           // location for result
```

get_resource_cvt fetches the value of resource *res_nam* and class *res_cls* from the OI resource database for this connection. The resource is converted from type OI_r_string to type *to_type*, and OI backfills *valp* with the result. *to_type* must be a type for which a resource converter exists. See Chapter 39 for a list of types for which predefined converters exist.

get_resource_cvt returns OI_yes if it is successful; otherwise it returns OI_no.

For example, to read in the resource "bigScreen" and convert it to a boolean value:

```
    OI_bool             bgscn;
    OI_connection       *conp;
if (conp->get_resource_cvt("bigScreen","BigScreen",OI_r_Boolean,&bgscn)) {
        // do your thing
}
```

get_resources   (Member function)

```
void OI_connection::get_resources(
    OI_resource            *list,              // resource list to fetch
    unsigned int            count,             // number of resources in the list
    void                   *base)              // base address for resource offsets
```

get_resources fetches *count* resources which are specified in *list* from the OI resource database for this connection. It converts them, and calls any callback listed in the OI_resource structures or, if no callback is defined, puts the results in *base*. *base* is the base address from which the offsets specified in the resource list are computed. The resource list structure OI_resource is described in Chapter 39. Example 38-2 shows get_resources in use.

```
struct MyRes {                               /* structure to hold my resources */
    int                 timeStart;
    int                 timeEnd;
};
MyRes MyResources;

static OI_resource resources[] = {
    {"timeStart","TimeStart",OI_r_Int,sizeof(int),
                    offsetof(MyRes,timeStart),OI_r_String,"0800"},
    {"timeEnd","TimeEnd",OI_r_Int,sizeof(int),offsetof(MyRes,timeEnd),
                    OI_r_String,"1800"},
};


    conp->get_resources(resources,OI_count(resources),&MyResources);
```

Example 38-2   Using get_resources

register_converter   (Member function)

```
void OI_connection::register_converter(
    const char             *from_type,         // type from which to convert
    const char             *to_type,           // type to which to convert
    OI_cvt                 *cvtr)              // pointer to converter object to use


void OI_connection::register_converter(
    XrmQuark                from_type,          // type from which to convert
    XrmQuark                to_type,            // type to which to convert
    OI_cvt                 *cvtr)              // pointer to converter object to use
```

register_converter registers a converter to use to convert values from one type to another for this connection. *from_type* is normally OI_r_string, since converters are usually associated with resource fetching and all resources are initially specified as strings. A converter normally has two member functions, convert and unconvert, so that it can convert in either direction.

Also, your converter should be subclassed from OI_cvt. Converters are discussed in Chapter 39, "The OI Resource Mechanism."

Example 38-3 shows how to register a converter to convert strings to hexadecimal numbers. The actual converter function **cvt_string_to_hex** is shown in Chapter 39.

```
OI_connection          *conp;
OI_cvt                 *my_converter;

my_converter = new cvt_string_to_hex( );
conp->register_converter("String","Hex",my_converter);
```

Example 38-3   Registering a Converter

is_converter   (Member function)

```
OI_bool OI_connection::is_converter(
    const char              *from_type,        // type from which to convert
    const char              *to_type)          // type to which to convert


OI_bool OI_connection::is_converter(
    XrmQuark                from_type,          // type from which to convert
    XrmQuark                to_type)            // type to which to convert
```

is_converter returns **OI_yes** if there is a converter registered to convert from *from_type* to *to_type*; otherwise it returns **OI_no**.

convert   (Member function)

```
OI_bool OI_connection::convert(
    const char              *from_type,        // type from which to convert
    XrmValue                *from_val,         // value to convert
    const char              *to_type,          // type to which to convert
    XrmValue                *to_val)           // converted value goes here


OI_bool OI_connection::convert(
    XrmQuark                from_type,          // type from which to convert
    XrmValue                *from_val,          // value to convert
    XrmQuark                to_type,            // type to which to convert
    XrmValue                *to_val)            // converted value goes here
```

convert calls a converter to convert whatever is pointed to by *from_val* from type *from_type* to a value of type *to_type*, placing the result into *to_val*. There must already be a converter registered which converts a value of *from_type* type to a value of *to_type* type. **convert** returns **OI_yes** if there is a converter registered to convert from *from_type* to *to_type* and the conversion succeeded; otherwise it returns **OI_no**. Converters are discussed in Chapter 39, "The OI Resource Mechanism."

allow_object_resources (Member function)

```
void OI_connection::allow_object_resources( )
```

allow_object_resources configures the connection so that OI fetches resources for objects on the connection. This is the default. Calling **allow_object_resources** after calling **disallow_object_resources** and parenting objects to the root will not force a resource fetch for the objects which were parented while **disallow_object_resources** was in effect.

disallow_object_resources (Member function)

```
void OI_connection::disallow_object_resources( )
```

OI normally fetches resources for an object when it is reparented and its new-top level ancestor has been placed on the root. **disallow_object_resources** configures the connection so that OI does not fetch resources for objects on the connection.

object_resources (Member function)

```
OI_bool OI_connection::object_resources( )
```

object_resources returns **OI_yes** if the connection is configured so that OI fetches resources for objects on the connection; otherwise it returns **OI_no**.

push_resource (Member function)

```
void OI_connection::push_resource(
    const char          *res_nam,      // name to push onto the resource prefix
    const char          *res_cls)      // class to push onto the resource prefix


void OI_connection::push_resource(
    XrmQuark            res_nam,        // name to push onto the resource prefix
    XrmQuark            res_cls)        // class to push onto the resource prefix
```

push_resource pushes *res_name* and *res_cls* onto the resource prefix stack on the right side of the prefix string. For more information on the resource prefix stack, see Chapter 39.

pop_resource (Member function)

```
void OI_connection::pop_resource( )
```

pop_resource pops the most recently-pushed resource name and class off the resource prefix stack. You cannot pop items which have not been pushed; that is, you cannot change OI's default prefix string settings.

default_resources (Member function)

```
void OI_connection::default_resources(
    const char * const  *res,         // pointer to vector of resource settings
    unsigned int        count)        // number of strings in *res
```

default_resources establishes default resource settings for objects on this connection. *res* is a pointer to a vector of resource settings containing *count* strings. Because these resources are inserted into the default database (**OI_default_database**), the user can override these resources by inserting strings into the .Xdefaults file. Example 38-4 shows the use of default_resources to establish default background color and font for all objects on this connection:

```
        OI_connection   *conp;
    static  char            *res_vec[] = {
        "*OI*background:pink",
        "*OI*font:-adobe-courier-medium-r-normal--12-120-75-75-m-70-iso8859-1"
        };

if (conp = OI_init(&argc,argv,"MyApp")) {
    conp->default_resources(&res_vec[0],OI_count(res_vec));
    ...
}
```

Example 38-4   Establishing Default Resources for a Connection

app_resources   (Member function)

```
void OI_connection::app_resources(
    const char * const      *res,            // pointer to vector of resource settings
    unsigned int            count)           // number of names in *res
```

app_resources establishes resource settings for objects on this connection in the OI_app_database resource database. *res* is a pointer to a vector of resource settings containing *count* strings. If you want to specify application default resources from within your program instead of in an application-defaults file, you should use default_resources instead of app_resources. This is because any resources set using app_resources can override those from a user's .Xdefaults file.

set_resources   (Member function)

```
void OI_connection::set_resources(
    const char * const      *res,            // pointer to vector of resource settings
    unsigned int            count)           // number of names in *res
```

set_resources establishes resource settings for objects on this connection in the OI_set_database resource database. *res* is a pointer to a vector of resource settings containing *count* strings. Because these resources are inserted into the OI_set_database, the user cannot override these resources. Use set_resources if you are determined that the objects on this connection will have these resources regardless of user desires.

add_resources   (Member function)

```
OI_bool OI_connection::add_resources(
    const char          *filp,              // file name
    OI_rm_db            db=OI_app_database)  // resource database to use
```

add_resources adds the resources from the file *filp* to the OI resource database for the connection specified by *db*. *filp* should be in the same format as an .Xdefaults file. *db* can have one of the following values:

OI_set_database
OI_app_database
OI_user_database
OI_default_database

See Chapter 39, "The OI Resource Mechanism," for more discussion on the four types of resource databases.

destroy_resources   (Member function)

```
OI_bool OI_connection::destroy_resources(
    OI_rm_db            db)                 // resource database to destroy
```

destroy_resources destroys the resource database for the connection specified by *db*. *db* can have one of the values shown for **add_resources**, above.

38.13 Interfacing to the Translations Mechanism

When writing an application, there are two basic situations in which you may want to reference functions to be used as translations.

One is when you are deriving a new class. In this case, you may want that class to have some member functions which are callable via a translation. This case is discussed in Chapter 41, "Deriving Your Own Classes."

The other case involves free-standing functions or member functions for non-OI objects which you want to be invoked via the OI translation mechanism.

Since translations allow the user to specify which function or functions to call via an arbitrary alpha string, there must be some mechanism for binding the translation function names in the alpha string to actual function addresses. This binding is specified in an OI_actions_rec data structure. The member function **add_actions** registers the OI_actions_rec data for use with a particular connection. This makes the function names available for use as translations. It does not, however, install any translations to make anything call the procedures specified in the OI_actions_rec; it simply makes them available for use. Once they are available, you can add translations to your .Xdefaults file to call them, or specify default translations via a resource.

There are situations where you might want your application to determine dynamically the function to call. If the result of that determination is an alpha string, the application needs a way to either bind the alpha string to a function address, or make the call indirectly. The member function call_action_proc allows you to call a translation procedure when all you know is the name of the procedure you want to call.

For more information on translations and action routines, see Chapter 40, "The OI Translation Mechanism."

add_actions   (Member function)

```
void OI_connection::add_actions(
    OI_actions_rec                 *actns,      // list of action routines
    unsigned int                   count)       // number of elements in actns


void OI_connection::add_actions(
    OI_compiled_action_table       actn_tbl)    // compiled list of action routines
```

add_actions informs OI that the *count* action functions specified in the structure pointed to by *actns* are available for use in translations for any object on the connection. The data structure **OI_actions_rec** is defined in Chapter 40, "The OI Translation Mechanism." If you plan to call **add_actions** more than once with the same set of action functions, you can do the following: "compile" the action function table using the free-standing function **OI_compile_action_table** to put the action table into OI's internal form, then use the second form of **add_actions** with the resulting "compiled" action table *actn_tbl*.

call_action_proc   (Member function)

```
OI_bool OI_connection::call_action_proc(
    OI_d_tech              *objp,       // pointer to OI object in which fn_nam is to be invoked
    const char             *fn_nam,     // name of the action routine
    const XEvent           *event,      // contents of event argument passed to fn_nam
    const char * const     *params,     // contents of the params argument passed to fn_nam
    unsigned int           num_params)  // number of entries in params


OI_bool OI_connection::call_action_proc(
    OI_d_tech              *objp,       // pointer to OI object in which fn_nam is to be invoked
    XrmQuark               fn_nam,      // name of the action routine
    const XEvent           *event,      // contents of event argument to pass to fn_nam
    const char * const     *params,     // contents of the params argument passed to fn_nam
    unsigned int           num_params)  // number of entries in params
```

call_action_proc searches for the action routine name *fn_nam* in the action function tables for object *objp*. If it does not find it there, it then searches the action tables for the connection itself. If found, the function is invoked with the specified *objp*, *event* and *params* parameters. **call_action_proc** returns **OI_yes** if the function was found and invoked; otherwise it returns **OI_no**.

38.14 Resources

OI fetches the resources shown in Table 38-1 for all objects on the connection. This fetch is done when the connection is first created. For more information on resource management, see Chapter 39, "The OI Resource Mechanism."

Table 38-1   OI_connection Resources

Resource	Description	Possible Values	Default Value
application.path	Specifies the set of pathnames to search for configuration files. This path is searched for the resource file specified when using **add_resources**.	Colon separated list of pathnames	NULL (NULL implies .:$XAPPLRESDIR/: $OI_LIB/*app_class*, where *app_class* is the argument passed to OI_init)
background	Specifies the background color for objects.	Valid color name	openlook2d: white openlook3d: #CCCCCCCCCCCC motif: #72729F9FFFFF
bevelWidth	Specifies the width of object bevels, in pixels. Note—you should normally use FrameWidth instead.	Non-negative integer	(No default)
bitmap.path	Specifies the set of pathnames to search for bitmap files.	Colon separated list of pathnames	(See Section 39.2.3, "Pixmap File Search Order," on page 39-12)
bitmapFilePath	A synonym for bitmap.Path, for compatibility with Xt-based applications.	Colon separated list of pathnames	Same as bitmap.Path, above
borderColor	Specifies the border color for objects.	Valid color name	DefaultForeground (use the foreground color)
borderWidth	Specifies the width of object borders, in pixels. Note—you should normally use FrameWidth instead.	Non-negative integer	(No default)

Table 38-1 OI_connection Resources

Resource	Description	Possible Values	Default Value
bottomBevelColor	Specifies the bottom bevel color for objects.	Valid color name	(No default, that is, compute from background color)
bottomSpace	Specifies the amount of white space to leave at the bottom of objects that are automatically laid out, in pixels.	Non-negative integer	(No default)
clickDelta	Time which must elapse between mouse button press and release for the events to be considered a "click."	Non-negative integer	500
cursor	Specifies the cursor type to use in objects.	Valid cursor name (the cursor name without the "XC_" prefix as defined in /usr/include/X11/cursorfont.h)	top_left_arrow
defaultKey	Defines the accelerator key used to activate the default cell in a menu. When a cell is found with an accelerator which matches this key, the cell is made the default, and no accelerator label is displayed for it.	Valid key	<key>Return
downColor	Specifies the down color for objects (this is the color used to depict a depressed button menu cell or other object in a "down" position).	Valid color name	(No default, that is, compute from background color)
downIsBackground	If on, specifies that the down pixel should be painted using the normal background color.	Boolean	false

Table 38-1 OI_connection Resources

Resource	Description	Possible Values	Default Value
dragRightDistance	Specifies the number of pixels the pointer must be dragged right before an OPEN LOOK pull-right menu comes up. By default it is a large number, and OPEN LOOK pull-right menus don't pop up until the pointer is moved over the arrow. This resource only affects OPEN LOOK vertical menus with pull-right submenus.	Non-negative integer	(A large number, potentially different for different hardware)
dynamicResources	If on, any change to the **RESOURCE_MANAGER** property or the **SCREEN_RESOURCES** property causes the application to dynamically update to match the changed resources.	Boolean	false
fastDraw	If on, specifies that appearance should be sacrificed for fast screen painting.	Boolean	false
focusFrameColor	The color to use to highlight the object that has the focus (only used if the application is run using the motif model).	Valid color name	DefaultForeground (use the foreground color)
focusIndicator	Specifies the type of visual feedback for the object with the input focus (only used if the application is run using an OPEN LOOK model).	none super_caret color	none
focusPolicy	Specifies the focus policy to use.	click_to_type follows_pointer	click_to_type
font	Specifies the font to use for text in objects.	Valid font	(Depends on model and object type)

OI Programmer's Guide

Table 38-1 OI_connection Resources

Resource	Description	Possible Values	Default Value
foreground	Specifies the foreground color for objects.	Valid color name	Black
helpTranslations	Specifies the set of keys eligible for use as the help key.	Valid sequence of keys and action functions	<key>Help: help( ) \n\ <key>F1: help( ) \n\ Mod1 <key>slash: help( ) \n
ignoreModifierMask	Comma or space-separated list of modifier key names. The specified modifier bits are ignored when mouse events are processed. When a mouse event is dispatched, the specified bits in the state member of the X event are cleared prior to dispatch. This is a flexible way in which your client application can ignore the "Num Lock" key. Num Lock is usually handled as one of the Mod[1-5] bits being set when active. The bit used to indicate Num Lock is highly X server dependent.	Shift Lock Control Mod1 Mod2 Mod3 Mod4 Mod5	0 (Do not ignore any modifiers)
ignoreMouseLock	If on, specifies that any mouse button events which occur while the caps lock key is down behave as though the caps lock key were up.	Boolean	true
language	Specifies the language to use.	"default", or any string	(Language imbedded in the application)
leftSpace	Specifies the amount of white space to leave at the left of objects that are automatically laid out, in pixels.	Non-negative integer	(No default)

Table 38-1 OI_connection Resources

Resource	Description	Possible Values	Default Value
mnemonicStyle	Specifies how mnemonics should be indicated for menu cells when they are present.	none underline reverse parens	underline
model	Specifies the interaction model to use.	motif openlook openlook2d openlook3d	Set the model to be compatible with the window manager in use, if it can be determined; otherwise set it to motif.
modelSpecificHints	Specifies whether objects should contain properties needed by all models (true), or only the one under which they are running (false). For example, when running in Motif mode, but using an OPEN LOOK window manager, one might want both the Motif and OPEN LOOK properties present so the window manager properties specific to the OPEN LOOK model would be present.	Boolean	true
motifPushpin	Controls whether or not pushpins are allowed in dialog boxes when running in Motif.	Boolean	false
multiClickDelta	The length of time, in milliseconds, between a mouse button release and the next press to constitute a multiple click.	Non-negative integer	500

Table 38-1 OI_connection Resources

Resource	Description	Possible Values	Default Value
resourceFile	Specifies the name of a diagnostic file to write when fetching resources. If set, all attempts to fetch resources are logged to this file. This generates a large amount of output, but is useful for debugging purposes when you are having trouble with resource specifications.	Valid file name	NULL
reverseVideo	If on, specifies that color specifications should be reversed.	Boolean	false
rightSpace	Specifies the amount of white space to leave at the right of objects that are automatically laid out, in pixels.	Non-negative integer	(No default)
standardColormap	Specifies the standard colormap to use.	rgb_default_map rgb_best_map rgb_blue_map rgb_green_map rgb_red_map rgb_gray_map	rgb_default_map
synchronous	If on, specifies that the X server should be run in synchronous mode.	Boolean	false
topBevelColor	Specifies the top bevel color for objects.	Valid color name	(No default, that is, compute from background color)
topSpace	Specifies the amount of white space to leave at the top of objects that are automatically laid out, in pixels.	Non-negative integer	(No default)

Table 38-1   OI_connection Resources

Resource	Description	Possible Values	Default Value
wmIgnoresPPosition	Notifies OI that the window manager used does not properly interpret the PPosition bit in the WM_NORMAL_HINTS property. You should set this resource to true if you are using mwm or 4Dwm as a window manager.	Boolean	false

38.15 Translations

An OI_connection has no default translations installed for it. It does have three translation functions registered, however, as shown in Table 38-2. Either the programmer or the user may use the functions nothing and noop if necessary; you might, for example, want to enforce that a certain keystroke (say, the escape key) has no effect in your application. You could then set up a line such as

```
*OI*Translations:
     <Key>Escape:      noop( )                  \n
```

The help function is defined for the connection so that OI does not have to define help key translations for each object on the connection. Through an internal mechanism, the keys defined in the OI_connection resource helpTranslations are bound to the translation function help.

See Chapter 40, "The OI Translation Mechanism" for more description of translations.

Table 38-2   OI_connection Translation Functions

Function Name	Description
nothing( )	Does nothing.
noop( )	Does nothing.
help( )	Activates the keyboard context-sensitive help mechanism.

38.16 Callback Functions

Table 38-3 lists the callbacks available for an **OI_connection** object and the page number of the corresponding explanatory material. See Section 6.18, "Determining and Adding Callbacks; Multiple Callbacks," on page 6-117 for additional information about manipulating callbacks.

Table 38-3   OI_connection Callbacks

Callback Type	Callback Typedef	Description	Page Number
(None)	OI_event_fnp/memfnp	Dispatch event callback function	38-6
cbClick	OI_click_fnp/memfnp	Click callback function	38-18

Chapter 39
The OI Resource Mechanism

The OI Resource Mechanism

39.1 Description

The OI Resource Mechanism provides a set of tools for specifying and manipulating user preferences such as geometry (including object spacing), colors, fonts, and bitmaps. You can also specify the state of an object, the language used for the object, event translations, and other attributes through resources.

The *X Resource Manager* is a term loosely applied to a collection of Xlib routines that determine a unique value for each resource of each object or application. They do this by merging a database consisting of several ASCII files, a server property, and values hardcoded by the application and applying algorithms to extract a value. Conflicts between multiple settings for the same resource are resolved according to internal precedence rules. The collection of resource settings contained in these files, properties and hardcoded values is known as the *resource database*.

Resources are <name,value> pairs used to control the attributes of a particular program or subsystem. They provide a convenient way to tailor collections of applications or collections of objects within an application with a minimum amount of work. You can set the values via the X Resource Manager, or allow OI to use default values. Each resource has a unique identifier, or name, and at runtime each object has a unique value for any named resource known to it.

The OI Resource Mechanism provides the following capabilities:

- Object attributes can be set via resources.
- Command-line arguments are merged into the resource database.
- OI automatically loads an application-specific defaults resource file.
- OI automatically loads a language-specific defaults resource file.
- The -config command-line option provides additional convenient resource file loading.
- OI provides a resource debug file.

To apply resource values to an application, the user will ordinarily look up (in this book or the man pages) which resources can be set, then do one or more of the following:

- Change the .Xdefaults file to specify resource settings for one or more objects in the application, or for the entire application.
- Run xrdb and specify resource settings for the application.
- Change the resource settings in any of several other files which OI searches when fetching resources; these files are specified in Table 39-4, on page 39-11.
- Run the application with command-line arguments to set resources.
- Change the resource values via a user interface builder such as ObjectBuilder.

OI automatically fetches resources for objects in the application. However, as the programmer, you can control resources in several ways. You can:

- Define new resource names and fetch their values for existing OI classes and objects.
- Define resource names and set their default values from a data structure within the program for any OI subclasses you create. OI automatically fetches resources at runtime for these subclasses.
- Write a member function for your subclass which OI calls when resource values are fetched for an object of that class, in which you perform actions specific to that resource.
- Cause resource values to be updated at any point in your program. You can update all resources for an object or only a few specified ones.
- Enable and disable resource fetching for any object or for all objects on a connection.
- Specify into which of the OI resource databases resource values are to be put.
- Push and pop character strings onto and off of the resource stack.

In general, the following occurs when an OI application is run (this is not an exhaustive list of all the possibilities—it is meant as an introduction to the resource mechanism operation):

- At the time the connection is made to the X server (when you call OI_init), OI *loads* the OI resource database from the .Xdefaults file, xrdb settings, or other X resource database sources. This means that OI extracts all resource names and values that exist in the X resource database, regardless of whether or not these resources are known to any portion of the application, and places them in the OI resource database.
- At any time (although ordinarily early in your application) you can add to the OI resource database from your application using the OI_connection member functions add_resources, app_resources, set_resources or default_resources.
- When an object is parented, and its most distant ancestor is associated with the root, OI fetches resources for that object from the OI resource database. To *fetch* a resource means that if a resource name is known to the object and if the name also exists in the OI resource database, the value of the resource in the OI resource database is applied to that object.
- If, during the course of the application, you know that the OI resource database has been changed, you can update resources for an object. This re-applies the new resource values from the OI resource database to the object (re-fetches resources for the object). Usually, however, resources are set up at the beginning of the program and it is not necessary to update them later.

When a resource is specified in the X resource database, it must always have three parts: the *resource name*, a *prefix* for the name which indicates to which objects, classes of objects, or applications the resource should apply, and a *value* for the resource. The resource name together with its prefix is called the *resource specification*. The resource specification together with the resource value is known as the *resource setting*.

As an example, suppose the .Xdefaults file contains the lines shown in Example 39-1:

```
*OI*background:gray95
*OI*font:-adobe-helvetica-bold-r-normal--18-180-75-75-p-103-iso8859-1
SmallExample*my_slider.orientation:horizontal
```

Example 39-1   Resource Settings

The names of these three resources, respectively, are

```
background
font
orientation
```

For a discussion on capitalization of the first letter of the resource name and its significance, see Section 39.2.7, on page 39-14.

The prefixes (prefixes are discussed in Section 39.1.2 on page 39-7), respectively, are

```
*OI*
*OI*
SmallExample*my_slider.
```

The resource values, respectively, are

```
gray95
-adobe-helvetica-bold-r-normal--18-180-75-75-p-103-iso8859-1
horizontal
```

Now let's see how these resources are applied to Program 39-1, **SmallExample**, on page 39-5. At the time OI_init is called, OI reads the three resource settings shown in Example 39-1 from the .Xdefaults file (along with any other resources specified) and places them in the OI resource database, thus *loading* the OI resource database. At this time no resource values are applied to any objects. When we call layout_associated_object for the two static text objects pointed to successively by **stp**, no resources are fetched (applied) because the application window pointed to by **wp** has not yet been parented to the root. The same is true when we call layout_associated_object for the slider pointed to by **sp**.

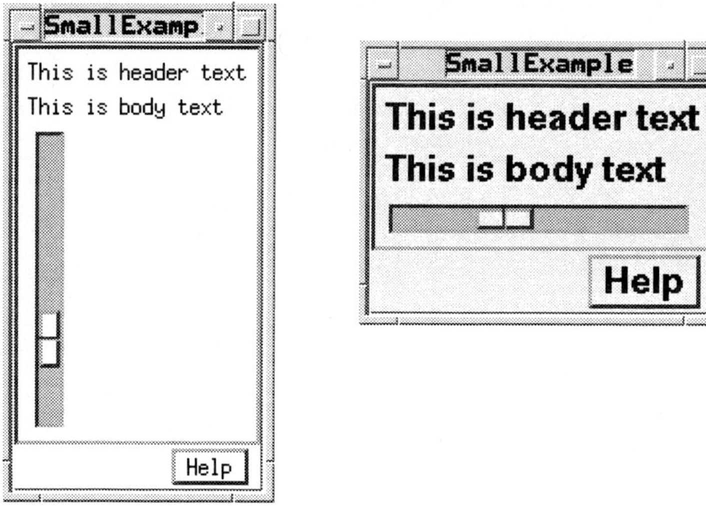

Figure 39-1   SmallExample Without and With Resources Specified

When we finally parent the application window to the root, OI automatically *fetches* resources for the application window, the static text and the slider objects from the OI resource database and applies the values to these objects. Since background is an OI_d_tech resource, and the prefix on this resource specifies any OI application, the background color for all four objects is set to have a value gray95. All four objects' font values are set to Helvetica as well, but this time the resource named font is a resource of OI_menu_cell (which applies to the "help" button in the OI_app_window), of OI_static_text, and of OI_display_1d (which is a base class of OI_slider), but not of OI_app_window. Since neither an OI_app_window nor OI_static_text object recognizes the resource named orientation, this resource is not applied to these objects. An OI_slider object does recognize orientation, however. Since the prefix is SmallExample*my_slider, which matches only the object named my_slider in this program, the slider's orientation is changed to have a value of horizontal (and thus OI paints a horizontal slider instead of the vertical one specified in the oi_create_slider statement).

Figure 39-1 shows Program 39-1, SmallExample, running. The left image shows the program running with no resources set; the right image was created using the resources listed above, inserted into the .Xdefaults file.

```c
#include <OI/oi.H>             /* SmallExample.C */

main(int argc, char** argv)
{

        OI_connection           *conp;
        OI_app_window           *wp;
        OI_static_text          *stp;
        OI_slider               *sp;

    if (conp = OI_init(&argc,argv,"SmallExample")) {

        wp = oi_create_app_window("main",1,1,"SmallExample");
        wp->set_layout(OI_layout_row);

        stp = oi_create_static_text("my_header","This is header text");
        stp->layout_associated_object(wp,1,1,OI_active);

        stp = oi_create_static_text("my_body","This is body text");
        stp->layout_associated_object(wp,1,2,OI_active);

        sp = oi_create_slider("my_slider",150,OI_vertical);
        sp->layout_associated_object(wp,1,3,OI_active);

        wp->set_associated_object(wp->root( ),OI_def_loc,OI_def_loc,OI_active);
        OI_begin_interaction( );

        OI_fini( );
    }
}
```

Program 39-1   Program Showing Resource Fetching (SmallExample.C)

39.1.1   The OI Resource Databases

The *OI resource database* consists of separate databases. They are described in Table 39-1

Table 39-1   OI Resource Database

Database Name	How Loaded	Use this OI_connection Function to Load this Database	Description
OI_set_database	programmer	set_resources add_resources	The user cannot override resources you put in OI_set_database.
OI_app_database	OI, programmer	app_resources add_resources	When OI loads its resource database during OI_init processing, it takes information from the .Xdefaults file, xrdb settings, or other X resource database sources and loads it into the OI_app_database.
OI_user_database	programmer	add_resources	The user can override any resources you put in OI_user_database.
OI_default_database	OI, programmer	default_resources add_resources	OI places defaults for the different models in OI_default_database during OI_init processing. The user can override these resources.

During OI_init processing occurs, OI loads OI_app_database and OI_default_database. By default, OI_set_database and OI_user_database are empty; they are provided for your use. You can load any of the databases at any time after calling OI_init with resources specific to your application by calling the OI_connection member functions set_resources, app_resources, default_resources, or add_resources.

When OI subsequently fetches resources for any object, it fetches resources from the databases listed in Table 39-1, in the order they are listed. If, during the fetch, OI finds a resource in one of the databases, none of the subsequent databases is searched for that resource. If you wish to load resources from a configuration file (or directly from your program), you can load them into OI_user_database if you wish the user to be able to modify them, or you can load them into OI_set_database if you wish to "lock" them (disallow user-modification). This is because OI_user_database is only queried if nothing is found in OI_app_database, and OI_app_database is only queried if nothing is found in OI_set_database.

At any time after calling OI_init, you can destroy one of these databases using the OI_connection member function **destroy_resources**. Once destroyed, it cannot be recreated during this instance of the application.

This arrangement of resource loading and fetching is shown in Figure 39-2.

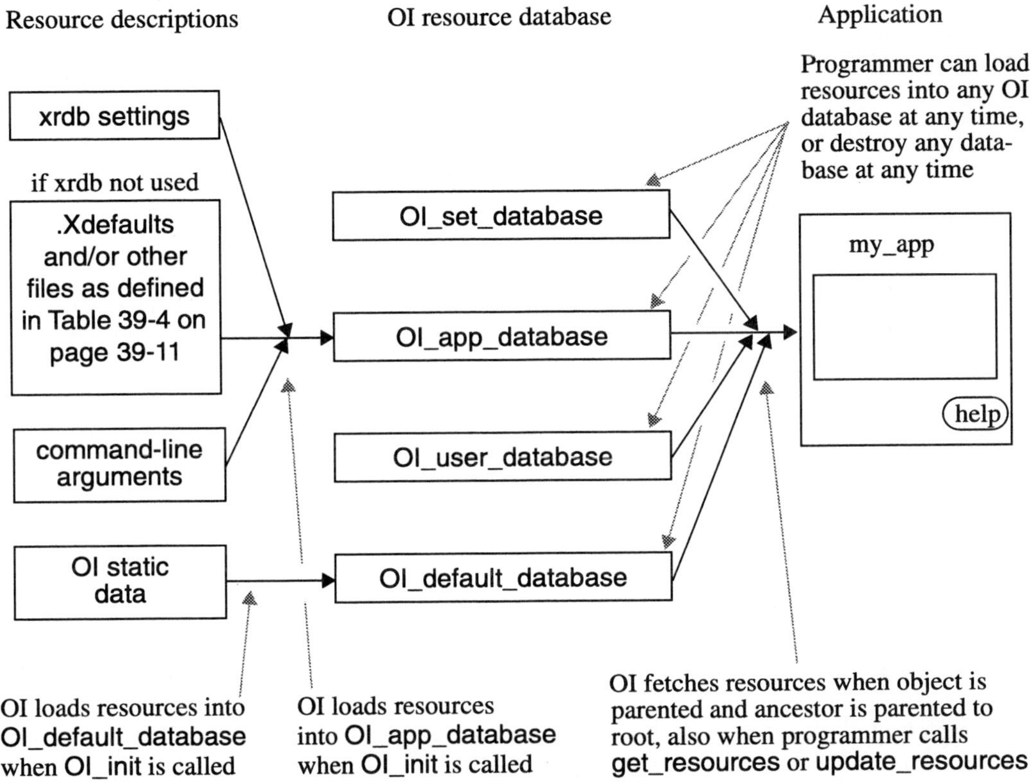

Figure 39-2 OI Resource Database Loading and Fetching

39.1.2   The Resource Stack

The OI *resource stack* is the list of prefixes that the OI resource manager attaches to the resource name when it fetches resources. This set of prefixes tells OI to which objects, classes or applications it should apply a resource. In other words, OI affixes the contents of the stack as a prefix to a resource name, and passes this string to the X resource manager. Using its precedence rules, the resource manager matches a value for the string from the resource settings the programmer or the user placed in the .Xdefaults file or other X resource database source, and passes it back to OI.

The various prefixes on the stack are called *elements* of the stack. OI establishes a default hierarchy of elements on the stack. They are shown in Table 39-2, from most general to least general, top to bottom.

Table 39-2 OI Resource Stack Elements

Instance	Instance Example	Class	Class Example
application name		Application class	
"oi"		"OI"	
screen visual	TrueColor	"Color", "Monochrome" or "Gray"	
screen number	screen0	Screen number	Screen0
language	defaultLanguage	Language	DefaultLanguage
"motif", "openlook2d", or "openlook3d"		"Motif" or "Openlook"	
object hierarchies (instance names)		Object hierarchies (class names)	

The object hierarchy (the last line in Table 39-2) is that of the objects in the application.

The possible values for *screen visual* (third line in Table 39-2) are:

    StaticGray
    GrayScale
    StaticColor
    PseudoColor
    TrueColor
    DirectColor

The "Monochrome" class string will be used if the number of color cells is less than or equal to two. "Gray" will be used if the number of color cells is greater than two and the visual is either StaticGray or GrayScale. "Color" will be used if the number of color cells is greater than two and the visual is StaticColor, PseudoColor, TrueColor, or DirectColor.

The *resource specification* for each resource for each object is made up of the entire contents of the resource stack, followed by the resource name.

Even though we refer to "the resource stack," it is actually a dual stack, as shown above. Each element on the stack has two components, a class name and an instance name. By convention, instance name components normally begin with lowercase letters and class name components normally begin with uppercase letters.

When OI asks the resource manager for resources for an object, it actually sends two strings: a class string and an instance string. Using the rules as specified in the X documentation, the actual resources are determined from these strings. For example, if we have an application whose executable name is "my_app" which specified "My_App" in the third argument to OI_init, with an OI_app_window object named "my_win" which is the parent of an OI_box object named "my_box", and if the application is running on a color screen under Motif, the two strings OI creates to fetch the background resource for the box are (assuming you have not modified the resource stack):

```
My_App.OI.Color.Screen0.DefaultLanguage.Motif.OI_app_window.OI_box.Background
my_app.oi.PseudoColor.screen0.defaultLanguage.motif.my_win.my_box.background
```

These are the resource class specification and the resource instance specification. The table below shows the correspondence between the resource stack element names as listed in Table 39-2, and the two resource strings shown above:

Resource Stack Element Name	Instance	Class
Application name	my_app	My_App
"OI"	oi	OI
screen visual	PseudoColor	Color
screen number	screen0	Screen0
language	defaultLanguage	DefaultLanguage
model	openlook3d	Openlook
object hierarchies	my_win	OI_app_window
	my_box	OI_box

You can push and pop elements to and from the resource stack; see Section 39.3.1 on page 39-21.

39.2 Using the Resource Database to Set Resources

If you do not specify any resource settings through the resource database, OI uses default values, which are usually sufficient. The user can, however, specify resource settings for the application program at runtime, if you as the programmer have not set the resources in the OI_set_database or specifically set the values programmatically. It is generally a good idea to specifically set as few resources as possible, so that the user can customize the application through resource settings. These resources can be specified in several different ways.

39.2.1   Resource Loading Sequence

The order in which OI loads its resource structure affects resource settings. OI successively loads, one on top of the other, a series of resource database sources. A *database source* is any one of several files or server properties; these sources are defined below in Table 39-4. *Loading* means that resource names and values are extracted from the files or server properties (the sources) and stored in the OI_app_database. The sources are loaded (any files needed are actually read) at the time the connection is made to the X server—that is, when you call OI_init or oi_create_connection. As each different file or source in the loading sequence is read, if there are collisions in the resource settings, the previously loaded resource is overwritten by the newly read resource.

In the following tables, if the HOME environment variable is defined, *user_home* is the value of the HOME environment variable followed by "*/*". Otherwise, *user_home* is the user default login directory followed by "*/*". Also, *application_class* is the third argument to OI_init or the name of the application if the third argument to OI_init is omitted.

When OI looks for a language override, it first checks the OI_d_tech resource language, which has precedence, then checks for the LANG environment variable. If the language resource is set, it is used "as-is" for the instance name in searching for the language resource file, as shown at the bottom of Table 39-4. The initial letter of the language resource is forced to upper case for use as the class name. If no language resource is set, the LANG environment variable is used. The first letter of the LANG variable is forced to lower case to construct the instance name and is forced to upper case to construct the class name.

The loading is done in the order shown in Table 39-3. The files or sources referred to in Table 39-3 are described in Table 39-4.

Table 39-3   OI Database Resource Loading Sequence

Load application default file
Load application user default file
Load user defaults
Load environment defaults
Load any command-line arguments.
If a language resource has been specified in any of the above places, and if it is not "default":
    Load application language defaults
    Re-merge application user defaults
    Re-merge user defaults
    Re-merge environment defaults
If the config resource has been specified in any of the above places:
    Attempt to load resources from a file with the config resource as the complete path name.
    If not found:
        Attempt to load *user_home/config*
        If not found:
            Attempt to load /usr/lib/X11/*application_class/config*

Table 39-4 Resource Database Source Definitions and Locations

Resource Database Source	**Definition**
application default file	
	$OI_LIB/app-defaults/*class* where *class* is the application class name (specified by the third argument to OI_init)
application user default file	
	If XAPPLRESDIR environment variable is defined:
	The name of the application user default file is the value of XAP-PLRESDIR environment variable followed by "/" followed by the application class name: $XAPPLRESDIR/*class*
	Else:
	Application user default file is undefined.
user defaults	
	If xrdb has been run:
	User defaults are the contents of the RESOURCE_MANAGER or the SCREEN_RESOURCES property put on the root window by xrdb.
	Else:
	User defaults are in the file *user_home*/.Xdefaults.
environment defaults	
	If XENVIRONMENT environment variable is defined:
	Environment default file name is the value of XENVIRONMENT variable: $XENVIRONMENT
	Else:
	Environment default file name is: *user_home*/.Xdefaults-*hostname* where *hostname* is the result of the gethostname( ) system call

application language defaults

Using the language resource or the LANG environment variable, as described on page 39-10, files are searched for in the following order:

Solaris:

/usr/openwin/lib/app-defaults/*class.lang-instance*
/usr/openwin/lib/app-defaults/*class.lang-class*
$OI_LIB/*class.lang-instance*
$OI_LIB/*class.lang-class*

Other operating systems:

$OI_LIB/app-defaults/*class.lang-instance*
$OI_LIB/app-defaults/*class.lang-class*
$OI_LIB/*class.lang-instance*
$OI_LIB/*class.lang-class*

where *class* is the application class name, *lang-instance* is the language instance name and *lang-class* is the language class name to be used. (For example, *class* might be Swm, *lang-instance* could be ja_JP, and *lang-class* could be Ja_JP.)

39.2.2   Application Default Resource File

The application default resource file, usually located as shown in the first line in Table 39-4, is ordinarily used to specify resource settings for an application that is run by many users on a system, so that each user does not have to modify his or her own .Xdefaults file.

For example, suppose you ship your application to a customer, and the system administrator decides that the users at the site need to use a smaller font size than your defaults dictate. The administrator can set up an application default file to specify font settings; these resources will apply only to your application. However, because the application default resource file is loaded before the user's own .Xdefaults file, the user can override them if desired.

Another reason for using this file might be that you want your application to use some different resources than the OI defaults. Another way to specify default resource settings for your application would be to add resources in your code to the OI_default_database using the OI_connection member function default_resources or add_resources. Using either of these methods, the user can still override your defaults.

39.2.3   Pixmap File Search Order

Resources of type OI_pixmap specify a file to be used to generate a pixmap. When you set a resource of type OI_pixmap, such as through the OI_d_tech resource backgroundPixmap, OI searches to find the specified *file_name*. The search is made in the following order:

1. *file_name* if the file name begins with "/" or ". /"
2. "each prefix in bitmapFilePath"/*file_name*
3. /usr/lib/X11/*application_class*/*file_name*
4. /usr/include/X11/bitmaps/*file_name*
5. *file_name* if the file name doesn't begin with "/" or ". /"

You can set the value of the resource bitmapFilePath in item 2 above using the OI_connection resource bitmapFilePath or bitmap.Path. (The resource bitmapFilePath exists for compatibility with Xt-based clients). In item 3, *application_class* is either the name of the application or the third argument to OI_init, or the name of the executable file used to invoke the application if the third parameter to OI_init was omitted or NULL.

39.2.4   Language Default Resource File

The application language default resource file, usually located as shown in the last line in Table 39-4, is ordinarily used to specify labels and text for objects in an application which are to appear in a different language from which the labels and text appear in the application code. For example, if you have written an application in English, but it is to be used at a site where the predominant language is German, this is the file you would modify to customize your application for the German environment. The settings in this file can be overridden by the user, just as the application default resource file can, by entering resource settings in the .Xdefaults file. Entries in the language default resource file should be similar in form to those shown in Example 39-4, on page 39-19.

39.2.5   When Resources are Fetched

Fetching resources means determining which resources already loaded should be applied to an object.

The OI resource mechanism is dynamic—this is different from all other X toolkits' resource mechanism. As discussed above, OI resources are loaded when you first call OI_init, and potentially fetched several times thereafter.

Object resources are automatically fetched when

- You associate an object with a parent and the parent's top-level ancestor (which may be the parent itself) is already parented to the root.
- You parent the object's top-level ancestor to the root—in other words, whenever you parent a top-level object to the root, resources are fetched for it and all of its descendants.

Object resources are automatically re-fetched when

- An object is associated with a new parent, and the object's new top-level ancestor is already parented to the root.

You can force a resource fetch (that is, a re-fetch) at any time through the OI_connection member functions get_resource, get_resource_cvt, or get_resources and the OI_d_tech member functions get_resources, get_sub_resources, or update_resources. See Figure 39-2 on page 39-7.

39.2.6   Using the -config Command-line Argument to Set Resources

If the user starts the application with the -config command-line argument, the resource settings in the specified file are loaded last. Consequently, they override any other resources set in any of the other files (unless the resources specified in the -config file are specified more specifically in one of the other files). For example, you could place your resource settings in a file named **my_resources.cf**, and then start the application by typing

```
my_app -config my_resources.cf
```

Program 39-2, on page 39-19, shows the use of a configuration resource file to start a language internationalization demo.

39.2.7   Resource Setting Format

Each resource setting must contain a resource name, a resource value, and an optional prefix. You connect these elements using the "*", "." and ":" characters, following the rules of X resource specification. The prefix should be a subset of the OI resource stack as described above.

The "*" is a "wildcard" character, and can match any number of prefix elements. The "." separates two consecutive prefix elements. The resource specification (the prefix and resource name) string is separated from the resource value by the ":" character (with optional intervening white space). You may use none, one or many elements from the resource stack as a prefix to the resource name. In other words, you do not have to fully specify resource name hierarchies. Instead of having to give a full specification for each set of objects, you can just "wildcard", or omit, the intervening components by using the "*" separator in place of the "." separator. In general, it is a good idea to use the "*" instead of "." in case you've forgotten any intervening components or in case new levels are inserted into the middle of the hierarchy, although you may want to keep the "." before the resource name itself. If the full resource specification would be

```
my_app.oi.PseudoColor.screen0.defaultLanguage.motif.my_win.my_box.background:blue
```

but you care only that the object named **my_box** in the application named **my_app** has a background of blue, independent of the other prefix elements, you can specify

```
my_app*my_box.background:blue
```

You can use either class names or instance names for each of the stack elements. If you use a class name, it applies to all instances of that class. If you use an instance name, it applies only to the instance of that element with that name.

For example, to specify that all boxes in the application **my_app** are to be blue if **my_app** is run on a color monitor, insert this line into a resource database file:

```
my_app*Color*OI_box.background:          blue
```

To specify that only the object named **my_box** is to be blue if **my_app** is run on a color monitor, use this line:

```
my_app*Color*my_box.background:          blue
```

To specify that the object named **my_box** and all of its descendants are to be blue, use this line:

```
my_app*Color*my_box*background:          blue
```

See Section 39.1.2, "The Resource Stack" for the ordering and possible values of prefix strings in a resource specification.

When you are specifying translations in a resource specification, you should use '*' instead of '.' between the object name and the translations to avoid errors in the run-time interaction with the object.

39.2.7.1 Resource Matching Precedence Rules

As mentioned above, when OI needs to set the resources for an object, it sends the resource name, prefixed by the expanded instance hierarchy and class hierarchy and all the other elements in the resource stack to the X resource manager. The resource manager determines the value for the resource by searching all the entries in the resource database. Specification precedence is as follows, using the code in Program 39-1 on page 39-5 as an example:

1. A specification that includes higher elements in the resource stack takes precedence over one that includes only lower ones.

    ```
    *Motif*background:plum            takes precedence over
    *OI_slider*background:blue
    ```

2. Instance names take precedence over class names at the same level in the hierarchy. By convention, class names are uppercase.

    ```
    *my_header.background:plum        takes precedence over
    *OI_static_text.background:blue
    ```

3. Resource stack connections made with "." take precedence over those made with "*" at the same level in the hierarchy.

    ```
    *OI_slider.background:plum         takes precedence over
    *OI_slider*background:blue
    ```

4. A resource stack element that is explicitly stated takes precedence over one that is omitted.

    ```
    SmallExample*Color*background:plum  takes precedence over
    SmallExample*background:blue
    ```

For example, if you want all text in the application **SmallExample** to have a font of:

```
-bitstream-charter-bold-i-normal--17-120-100-100-p-105-iso8859-1
```

you can insert this line into your **.Xdefaults** file:

```
SmallExample*Font:-bitstream-charter-bold-i-normal--17-120-100-100-p-105-iso8859-1
```

The result is shown in Example 39-2. This example also shows the class and instance names of each object in **SmallExample**.

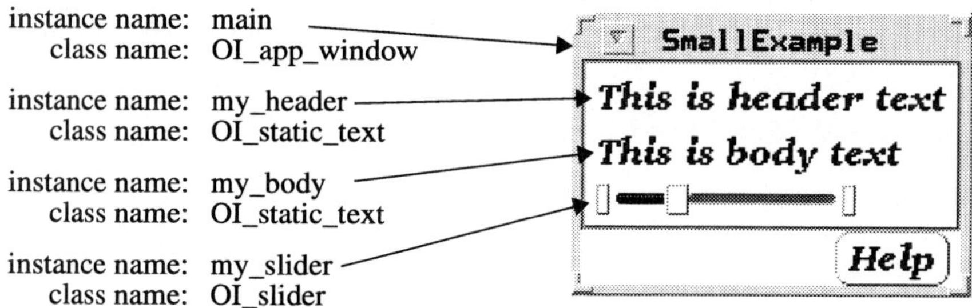

Example 39-2   Class and Instance Names for SmallExample

If, on the other hand, you only wanted the 17 point bold-face font for the header, and a smaller regular-weight font for all other objects in SmallExample, you could use:

```
SmallExample*Font:-adobe-helvetica-medium-r-normal--12-120-75-75-p-67-iso8859-1
SmallExample*my_header.Font:-bitstream-charter-bold-i-normal--17-120-100-100-p-105
-iso8859-1
```

The result would be as shown in Example 39-3.

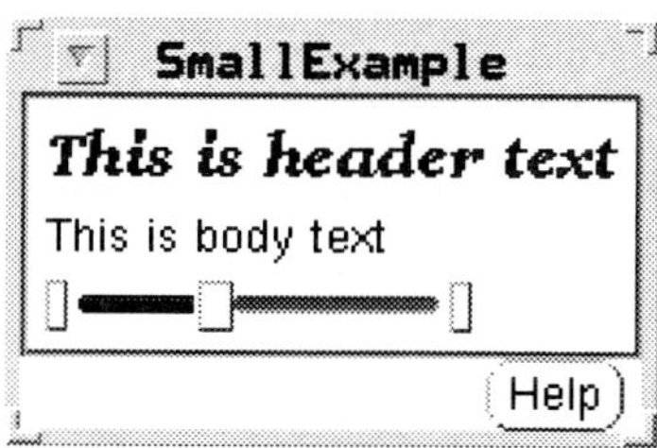

Example 39-3   SmallExample With Two Fonts

As another example, suppose you have an application window with a dialog box as a child object. If you wanted all menu cells in menus that are parented to the dialog box to be red, but all menu cells in menus that are parented to the application window to be blue, you would use:

```
*OI_app_window*OI_dialog_box*OI_menu_cell.background:red
*OI_app_window*OI_menu_cell.background:blue
```

You can place these lines in your .Xdefaults file in any order.

39.2.8   Attributes Controlled in the Resource Database

The attributes that can be controlled for each object are listed at the end of the chapter on that object in the "Resources" section. All resource names in these chapters are shown with an uppercase first letter. You can specify these resource names with either a lowercase or an uppercase first letter. Just remember that the lowercase first letter resource (the "instance" specification) always takes precedence over the capitalized version (the "class" specification). (Rule 2 on page 39-15.)

OI_connection and OI_d_tech have many of the same resources. In general, you should use OI_d_tech resources. The OI_connection resources are the application defaults, and are only used as a "first guess" for initial values when objects are created.

39.2.9   Valid Resource Values

In the resource tables at the end of each chapter, there are entries describing what values are valid for each resource. Entries such as "valid color" and "valid font" mean that the color name can be found in the default color file, usually /usr/lib/X11/rgb.*, and that the font name can be found in the default font path(s) on your system, usually /usr/lib/X11/fonts/*. Each of the subdirectories usually contain the files fonts.dir and fonts.alias, which contain the valid font names. You can usually display valid font names with a program like xlsfonts. A boolean value can be any of "true", "false", "yes", "no", 1 or 0. Some constants that you can specify in a call to a member function for an object, such as OI_horizontal, must be truncated to horizontal; that is, the constant without its leading "OI_". Check the resource tables at the end of each chapter for valid spelling of constants. In general, resource values for constants are case insensitive.

39.2.10   Internationalization Example

Program 39-2, next, shows an example of using resources to change the language that appears in objects in an application. The application comes up in the default language (English), and the user may start demos in different languages. Each demo is created by forking another copy of the original, using the file Internat.cf to provide the resources for the text in the desired language. Internat.cf contains the text for all the different languages possible in this demo. Internat.cf is shown in Example 39-4 on page 39-19. Figure 39-3, on page 39-20, shows the application running; the user has chosen to start the German demo.

You will probably need to specify a new font if you are running in Motif mode, since the default font in Motif does not have umlaut and accent characters. The bitmaps shown in Figure 39-3 were made by running the program with this command line argument:

```
Internat -font "-*-helvetica-bold-r-normal--*-120-*-*-*-*-*-*"
```

```
#include <OI/oi.H>              /* Internat.C */
#include <strings.h>

main (int argc, char **argv)
{
        OI_connection           *conp;               /* connection to the server */
        OI_app_window           *wp;                 /* enclosing app window */
        OI_button_menu          *mp;                 /* control menu */

    /*
     *  The function StartNewDemo must be defined before we define the
     *  static cell definitions, else the compiler complains.
     */
    void StartNewDemo(OI_menu_cell*, void*, OI_number);
```

```
    /*
    *    These are the cell definitions for each cell in the application.
    *    They are in English, the other langauges are specified in
    *    resource files. Each cell has a name for identification, and an
    *    English text string for the default label.
    */
    staticOI_cell_spec demo_cells[] = {
        {"en_US", "Start English Demo", StartNewDemo},
        {"de_DE", "Start German Demo", StartNewDemo},
        {"es_ES", "Start Spanish Demo", StartNewDemo},
        {"quit", "Quit", (OI_action_fnp)OI_end_interaction},
    };

    staticOI_cell_spec num_cells[] = {
        {"one", "One"},
        {"two", "Two"},
        {"three", "Three"},
    };

    if (conp = OI_init(&argc, argv, "Internat", "Internat"))
    {
        wp = oi_create_app_window("mainWin", 1, 1, "International Demo");
        wp->set_layout(OI_layout_column);

        mp = oi_create_button_menu("languageMenu", OI_count(demo_cells), demo_cells,
                                        OI_vertical, NULL);
        mp->layout_associated_object(wp, 1, 1, OI_active);
        mp = oi_create_button_menu("numMenu", OI_count(num_cells), num_cells,
                                        OI_vertical, NULL);
        mp->layout_associated_object(wp, 2, 1, OI_active);

        wp->set_associated_object(conp->root( ),OI_def_loc,OI_def_loc,OI_active);
        OI_begin_interaction( );
    }

    OI_fini( );
}

void StartNewDemo(OI_menu_cell *cell, void*, OI_number)
{

        char    command[256];  /* Character string for forked command */
        char    **common_argv;
        int     i, common_argc;

    /* Create the command string for invoked command.
     * Append OI_common_argv to the command string so that the
     * invoked process has the same attributes as the original one.
     *
     * Also, invoke command with the correct -language flag to
     * find the correct text strings file for the desired language.
     */
```

```
strcpy(command, "Internat ");

common_argc = OI_common_argc( );
common_argv = OI_common_argv( );

for (i = 0; i < common_argc; i++) {
    strcat(command, common_argv[i]);
    strcat(command, " ");
}

strcat(command, "-config Internat.cf -language ");
strcat(command, cell->name( ));
strcat(command, " &");

OI_fork(command);// Invoke the command
}
```

Program 39-2   Internationalization Demo (Internat.C)

```
Internat*de_DE*de_DE.label: Deutche Demonstration Anfangen
Internat*de_DE*es_ES.label: Spanische Demonstration Anfangen
Internat*de_DE*en_US.label: Englische Demonstration Anfangen
Internat*de_DE*quit.label: Aufh\366ren
Internat*de_DE*@help_button.label: Hilfe

Internat*de_DE*one.label: Eins
Internat*de_DE*two.label: Zwei
Internat*de_DE*three.label: Drei

Internat*es_ES*de_DE.label: Comenzar Demostraci\363n Alem\341n
Internat*es_ES*es_ES.label: Comenzar Demostraci\363n Espa\361ol
Internat*es_ES*en_US.label: Comenzar Demostraci\363n Ingles

Internat*es_ES*quit.label: Dejar
Internat*es_ES*@help_button.label: Socorro

Internat*es_ES*one.label: Uno
Internat*es_ES*two.label: Dos
Internat*es_ES*three.label: Tres
```

Example 39-4   Language-Specific Resource File (Internat.cf)

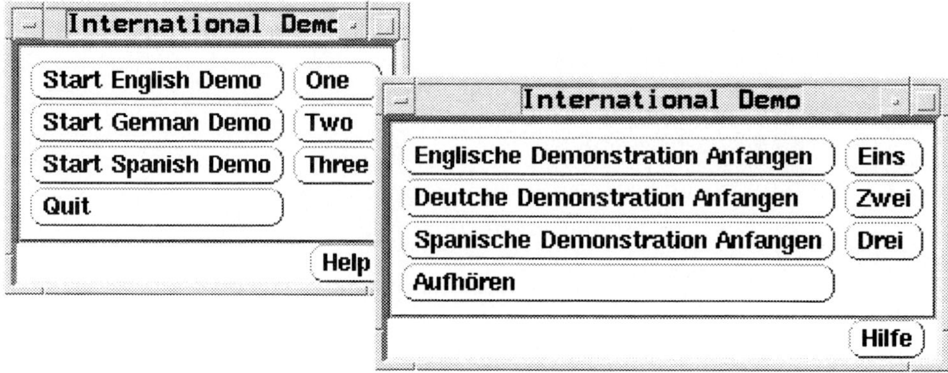

Figure 39-3   Language Demo

39.2.11   Other Resource Setting Examples

To make every background on every client application blue (this affects all clients, whether they are OI clients or not):

```
*background:        blue
```

To make every background on every OI client blue:

```
*OI*background:     blue
```

To make every background for a particular client, foo, blue:

```
foo*background:     blue
```

If you have the following two lines in your .Xdefaults file:

```
foo*background:     blue
bar*background:     red
```

and if your application is in a file my_app, but the third parameter in your call to OI_init (the class name) is foo, then if the user starts the application by typing

```
my_app
```

its background color will be blue. If the user types

```
my_app -name bar
```

the background color will be red. Notice that if the user types

```
xterm -name bar
```

the xterm's background will be red as well.

To run Motif if you are on a color monitor and OPENLOOK if on a monochrome monitor:

```
*Color*model:        Motif
*Monochrome*model:Openlook
```

To set an object named **file_info** and all of its children to pink, in any application at all:

```
*file_info*background:pink
```

To set **file_info** and all of its children to pink for application **QDB** only:

```
QDB*file_info*background:pink
```

To add a translation for Ctrl U in all entry fields in both OPEN LOOK 2-D and OPEN LOOK 3-D (the "\" character is a continuation marker):

```
*Openlook*OI_entry_field.translations.override: \
            Ctrl <Key>U: erase_line( )
```

39.3   Controlling Resources Within Your Program

39.3.1   Manipulating the Resource Stack

You may need to add to the resource stack if you want to provide different resources depending on some global condition affecting the entire application. For example, if screen size is a significant problem, you may wish to have different resources for different categories of screen size. Another example would be different modes of operation for an application, such as novice or advanced; a novice version might read in one configuration file which left out some options not normally needed by novices. An example of resources depending on screen size is shown in Program 39-3 on page 39-23.

If you need to add to the resource stack, you can do so by calling the OI_connection member functions push_resource and pop_resource, and the OI_d_tech member function get_sub_resources.

Remember that "the resource stack" is actually a dual stack—each stack element is comprised of two portions: the instance portion and the class portion. push_resource pushes the argument *res_nam* as the instance portion and *res_cls* as the class portion of a new resource stack element. The position in the stack hierarchy in which *res_nam* and *res_cls* are pushed is after the model element, but before the object hierarchies. Once you have pushed an element onto the stack using push_resource, you can fetch resources using one of the OI_connection member functions get_resource, get_resource_cvt, or get_resources, or the OI_d_tech member functions get_resources or update_resources. If you have called push_resource prior to parenting your objects to the root, your added resource prefixes will be used as part of the resource specification in the normal resource fetch which occurs when objects are parented to the root (or to an object with an ancestor which is parented to the root). Whenever you no longer need these elements on the stack, you can remove them using pop_resource, which pops the last entry on the resource stack. You cannot pop entries which you have not pushed with push_resource. Make certain your pushes and pops are symmetric.

get_sub_resources pushes the arguments *nam* and *cls* (or *nam_qrk* and *cls_qrk)* onto the resource stack as the instance portion and class portion of a new stack element. get_sub_resources pushes this new element onto the stack following all object hierarchy elements, fetches the specified resource settings, then pops *nam* and *cls* (or *nam_qrk* and *cls_qrk*) from the resource stack. The hand (☞) in the following list of resource stack elements shows where in the stack push_resource and get_sub_resources push their arguments:

- Application name/class
- "OI"
- "color" or "monochrome"
- screen number
- language
- model ("motif", "openlook", "openlook3d")

☞push_resource pushes *res_nam* and *res_cls* in this position

- object hierarchies

☞get_sub_resources temporarily pushes *nam* and *cls* (or *nam_qrk* and *cls_qrk)* in this position

As a general rule, you should use push_resource if you intend the stack element pushed to be used for every resource fetched for every object, during the element's lifetime on the stack (which is often equal to the lifetime of the application execution). In other words, use push_resource to further refine all resources for an application. get_sub_resources, on the other hand, applies only to a single object, and often is used for customized resources for that single object only. If you are changing the resource stack at different times throughout your application, use get_sub_resources so that you are spared the necessity of having to explicitly push a resource on the stack, then fetch or update the resource, and then pop the resource; get_sub_resources does all this for you with one call. On the other hand, if you use get_sub_resources you have to deal with the OI_resource structure, whereas if you use push_resource, you are spared this detail. Because of the necessity of using an OI_resource structure for get_sub_resources, the get_sub_resources example is in the next section; in this section we show two push_resource examples.

Suppose you would like your application to have different characteristics depending on the size of the screen on which it is run. Program 39-3, next, shows a program which pushes the resource with class name "ScreenSize" and instance name of either "bigScreen", "mediumScreen", or "smallScreen". Notice that we never call pop_resource; the screen size resource should be on the stack for the entire life of the application execution. If you wanted to use different fonts depending on screen size (which, if the application contained many objects on the screen at once, would make the application fit on a small screen and be easier to read on a large screen), you could put in the application-specific resource file the resource settings shown in Example 39-5. The user could override these settings by putting different fonts in the .Xdefaults file. The nice thing about using resources to set properties in this way is that any resource, not just font, could be set depending on screen size.

```
#include <OI/oi.H>              /* Screens.C */

main(int argc, char** argv)
{

          OI_connection        *conp;
          OI_app_window        *wp;
          OI_static_text       *stp;
          OI_number            wid,ht;
   static char                 big_screen[] = "bigScreen";
   static char                 med_screen[] = "mediumScreen";
   static char                 small_screen[] = "smallScreen";
          char                 *screen_size;

   if (conp = OI_init(&argc,argv,"Screens")) {

       conp->abs_root( )->size(&wid,&ht);
       if (wid > 1024)
           screen_size = big_screen;
       else if (wid > 950)
           screen_size = med_screen;
       else
           screen_size = small_screen;

       conp->push_resource(screen_size,"ScreenSize");

       wp = oi_create_app_window("main",1,1,"Screens");
       wp->set_layout(OI_layout_row);

       stp = oi_create_static_text("my_text","This is text");
       stp->layout_associated_object(wp,1,1,OI_active);

       wp->set_associated_object(wp->root( ),OI_def_loc,OI_def_loc,OI_active);
       OI_begin_interaction( );
       OI_fini( );
   }
}
```

Program 39-3   A push_resource Example (Screens.C)


```
Screens*bigScreen*font:-misc-fixed-medium-r-normal--15-140-75-75-c-90-iso8859-1
Screens*mediumScreen*font:-misc-fixed-medium-r-normal--13-120-75-75-c-70-iso8859-1
Screens*smallScreen*font:-misc-fixed-medium-r-normal--10-100-75-75-c-60-iso8859-1
```

Example 39-5   Resource Settings for Different Screen Sizes

Another push_resource example would be if you were writing a standard database application
where the user is to add, change or delete items from the database. Suppose you wanted the dialog
box in which the data entries were made to be a different color depending on whether the user were
adding, changing, or deleting data. You could make a menu with cells "add", "change", and "delete",

which the user would select depending on which function was to be performed. In the action function for the "add" menu cell, you could, at the top of the callback, insert the following code:

```
OI_connection        *conp;
OI_dialog_box        *dbp;              // points to data entry dialog box

conp->push_resource("add","EntryMode");
dbp->update_resources(OI_yes);         // OI_yes indicates apply to descendants
conp->pop_resource( );
```

The same lines would be inserted into the callbacks for the "change" and "delete" menu cells, except that the **push_resource** line would have the instance name of the current entry mode:

```
conp->push_resource("change","EntryMode");
```

and

```
conp->push_resource("delete","EntryMode");
```

Resource settings in an X Resource Database file to change the colors depending on entry mode would look like:

```
my_app*add*background:green
my_app*change*background:yellow
my_app*delete*background:red
```

39.3.2 The OI_resource Data Structure

If you create a class of your own, and desire to control resources for objects of this class, you will need to use the **OI_resource** structure in a call to the **OI_class** member function **set_resources** (see Chapter 41, "Deriving Your Own Classes" and Chapter 42, "OI_class"). If you are not creating any of your own classes, however, you will only need to use **OI_resource** if you call one of the resource-handling functions, such as the **OI_d_tech** member function **get_sub_resources** or **get_resources**, or the **OI_connection** member function **get_resources**, which use this structure as an argument. If your application has application-wide resources which are not specific to a particular subclass, the most convenient way to define them is by setting up an **OI_resource** structure in your main module and using it to fetch resources after the application is initialized via **OI_init**.

Lists of resources are defined for objects in OI through the **OI_resource** structure, which is defined in this way:

```
struct OI_resource {
    const char                  *resource_name;   // resource name
    const char                  *resource_class;  // resource class
    const char                  *resource_type;   // representation type of converted
                                                  // resource value
    unsigned int                resource_size;    // size in bytes of converted resource
                                                  // value
    unsigned int                resource_offset;  // offset from base to put res value
    const char                  *default_type;    // type of default resource value
    void                        *default_resrc;   // default resource value
    OI_resource_memfnp          put_memfnp;       // callback mem fn for resource fetch
    OI_resource_fnp             put_fnp;          // callback fn for resource fetch
    OI_resource_get_memfnp      get_memfnp;       // callback mem fn to retrieve
                                                  // current value
    OI_resource_get_fnp         get_fnp;          // callback fn to retrieve current
                                                  // value
    unsigned long               ctl_bits;         // control bits
};
```

resource_name and *resource_class* are the instance name and class name for the resource to fetch. Traditionally, these names are identical except for capitalization of the first letter for the class name (for example, "maximumValue" and MaximumValue"). *resource_type* is the data type for the resource. When OI fetches a resource, it reads it in as a string and automatically converts it to its destination type (for example, OI_r_Long).

resource_size is the size, in bytes, of the converted value. *resource_offset* is the offset, in bytes, of the storage location for the result from some base address. This base address is the object class itself if you are calling the **OI_class** member function **set_resources**. If you are using the **OI_d_tech** member functions **get_resources** or **get_sub_resources**, or the **OI_connection** member function **get_resources**, you specify the base address in an argument. When fetching resources for an object, OI uses *resource_offset* only if *put_memfnp* and *put_fnp* are empty. Similarly, when retrieving a value from the object, OI uses *resource_offset* only if *get_memfnp* and *get_fnp* are empty.

default_type is the data type for the default resource value, which is specified in *default_resrc*. If *default_type* is NULL, *default_resrc* is ignored. If *default_type* is OI_r_Immediate, *default_resrc* must be the default resource value itself (already converted to the appropriate type). Otherwise, you should set *default_type* to OI_r_String, and OI converts *default_resrc* from *default_type* to *resource_type*, using the converter registered for this conversion. If *default_type* is not NULL and the resource is not found when resources are fetched, the resource is initialized to the value from *default_resrc*. For example, to set a MaximumValue default resource for a number, if 200 is the desired default maximum, you could either set *default_type* to OI_r_Immediate and *default_resrc* to 200, or you could set *default_type* to OI_r_String and *default_resrc* to a pointer to the string "200".

If *put_memfnp* and *put_fnp* are NULL, the result of resource conversion will be placed directly in base+*resource_offset*, where base is as described above. Otherwise, either *put_memfnp* or *put_fnp* (but not both) must be non-NULL. They specify a function, (which you must write) to call to store the value. *put_memfnp* is a member function for the object; *put_fnp* is a free-standing function. These functions will be called with a single **void*** argument which points to the converted resource value. The converted value will <u>not</u> have been stored at base+*resource_offset*; it will instead be in temporary storage. You should write the put function to store the value appropriately. If a resource is found, the put function will be called. If none is found but a default type is specified, the default value will be converted to the resource type and the put function will be called with this value. Otherwise, the put function will not be called. These functions allow retrieving resources for values which are bit fields, for example, or which require manipulating the object as a result of the resource fetch. If you are dealing with strings, your put function should copy the string, since it points to internally maintained buffers that may change soon. For examples of how to write these functions, see the **VuMeter** example at the end of Chapter 41, "Deriving Your Own Classes."

get_memfnp or *get_fnp* is used to retrieve the values stored by *put_memfnp* or *put_fnp*.

Some types of applications not only read resources but also write them out. For example, a user interface builder such as ObjectBuilder may write the resources for each object into a configuration file used to reconstruct the objects when the user runs the application. Some of the control bits in the table of possible values for *ctl_bits*, below, affect the circumstances under which these programs write a particular resource.

The possible values for *ctl_bits* include any bitwise inclusive **or** combination of the following:

OI_RM_PUT_USE_DEFAULT	If the resource is not found when OI is fetching resources, OI_RM_PUT_USE_DEFAULT specifies that OI should use the default value (*default_resrc*).
OI_RM_INHIBIT_WRITE	Disable writing out this resource.
OI_RM_INHIBIT_TOP_LEVEL	Disable writing out this resource if this is a top level object.
OI_RM_INHIBIT_EDIT	This resource should not be editable when building an application using a user interface builder such as ObjectBuilder. For example, the current value of gauge should not be editable, because the value is normally set under program control.
OI_RM_PUSH	Push this resource onto the resource stack and use the next set of resources, pointed to by *default_type*. If you set OI_RM_PUSH, then you must set *default_type* to point to the first element of another table of OI_resource structures (the "next" set of resources) and set *default_resrc* to the number of entries in the other table. You must cast these two variables to be the appropriate type.

OI_RM_GET_USE_DEFAULT	If this resource value is not set from the program and the value matches the default, don't write it out.
OI_RM_MDL_ALL	(OI_RM_MDL_OL2D|OI_RM_MDL_OL3D|OI_RM_MDL_MOTIF)
OI_RM_MDL_ALL_3D	(OI_RM_MDL_OL3D | OI_RM_MDL_MOTIF)
OI_RM_MDL_ALL_2D	(OI_RM_MDL_OL2D)
OI_RM_MDL_MOTIF	This resource applies to Motif.
OI_RM_MDL_OL2D	This resource applies to 2D OPEN LOOK.
OI_RM_MDL_OL3D	This resource applies to 3D OPEN LOOK.

Following is an example for an actual resource, the OI_d_tech "background" resource. In this case, *resource_offset* is ignored because there is a callback routine specified to be activated whenever the resource is fetched for the object.

```
OI_resource resources[] = {
    {
        OI_n_background,                    // resource name
        OI_c_Background,                    // resource class
        OI_r_Pixel,                         // representation type converted resource value
        sizeof(PIXEL),                      // size in bytes of converted resource value
        0,                                  // unused because put_memfnp is specified
        0,                                  // type of specified default (none)
        0,                                  // address of default resource
        &OI_d_tech::res_bkg_pixel,          // callback mem fn for resource fetch
        NULL,                               // callback fn for resource fetch
        &OI_d_tech::bkg_pixel,              // callback mem fn to retrieve current value
        NULL                                // callback fn to retrieve current value
        OI_RM_MDL_ALL                       // control bits
    },
    ...
};
```

Program 39-4, shown next, uses an OI_resource structure in calling get_sub_resources. This program shows a gauge which displays the amount of air pressure in a tire. Because we could not connect to a real tire, we supplied a slider, with which the user can simulate leakage of air. If the amount of air remaining becomes dangerously low, the active bar ("mercury") in the gauge changes color. Bitmaps also represent the inflation of the tire. The bitmap to use at each level of severity of the air loss and the active bar color can be set using resource settings; different users may want the mercury to become red and the bitmaps to change at different pressure settings.

The resources used are shown in Example 39-6 and the running application is shown in Figure 39-4.

```c
#include <OI/oi.H>            /* Tire.C */

    const  char    n_severe0[] =     "severity0";    // severity resource name
    const  char    n_severe1[] =     "severity1";    // severity resource name
    const  char    n_severe2[] =     "severity2";    // severity resource name
    const  char    n_severe3[] =     "severity3";    // severity resource name
    const  char    n_severe4[] =     "severity4";    // severity resource name
    const  char    c_Severity[] =    "Severity";     // severity resource class
    const  char    n_tire[] =        "tire";         // tire bitmap file name
    const  char    c_Tire[] =        "Tire";         // tire bitmap file name

    struct MyRes {                                   // structure to hold my resources
        PIXEL   barActiveColor;
        char    *bitmapFile;
    };
    static MyRes MyResources = {0,0};

    static OI_resource        resources[] = {
        {OI_n_barActiveColor,OI_c_BarActiveColor,OI_r_Pixel,sizeof(PIXEL),
                        offsetof(MyRes,barActiveColor)},
        {n_tire,c_Tire,OI_r_String,sizeof(char*),offsetof(MyRes,bitmapFile)},
    };

main(int argc, char** argv)
{

        void set_air(OI_ctlr_1d*,void*,OI_scroll_event,long);

        OI_connection          *conp;
        OI_app_window          *wp;
        OI_gauge               *gp;
        OI_slider              *sp;
        OI_glyph               *picp;

    if (conp = OI_init(&argc,argv,"Tire")) {
        wp = oi_create_app_window("main",1,1,"Tire");
        wp->set_layout(OI_layout_row_aligned);

        gp = oi_create_gauge("my_gauge",200,OI_horizontal,200,0,
                        "Air Remaining:",OI_gauge_ends_none,NULL,NULL,
                        OI_no,6,OI_gauge_ticks_all);
        gp->layout_associated_object(wp,1,1,OI_active);

        picp = oi_create_glyph("tire","../bitmaps/tire0",
                        NULL,OI_pic_mask,OI_no,OI_no);
        picp->layout_associated_object(wp,2,1,OI_active);

        sp = oi_create_slider("my_slider",200,OI_horizontal,200,0,
                        &set_air,gp,"Set Air Remaining:");
        sp->set_handle_loc(sp->maximum( ));
        sp->layout_associated_object(wp,1,3,OI_active);
```

```
            wp->set_associated_object(wp->root( ),OI_def_loc,OI_def_loc,OI_active);
            OI_begin_interaction( );
            OI_fini( );
        }
}

void set_air(OI_ctlr_1d *sp, void *argp, OI_scroll_event, long)
{
        OI_gauge                *gp;
        OI_glyph                *picp;
        float                   ratio;

    gp = (OI_gauge*)argp;
    picp = (OI_glyph*)gp->parent( )->subobject("tire");
    ratio = (float)(sp->handle_loc( ))/float(sp->span( ));
    if (ratio < .2)
        gp->get_sub_resources(n_severe4,c_Severity,resources,
                              OI_count(resources),&MyResources);
    else if (ratio < .4)
        gp->get_sub_resources(n_severe3,c_Severity,resources,
                              OI_count(resources),&MyResources);
    else if (ratio < .6)
        gp->get_sub_resources(n_severe2,c_Severity,resources,
                              OI_count(resources),&MyResources);
    else if (ratio < .8)
        gp->get_sub_resources(n_severe1,c_Severity,resources,
                              OI_count(resources),&MyResources);
    else
        gp->get_sub_resources(n_severe0,c_Severity,resources,
                              OI_count(resources),&MyResources);
    gp->set_value(sp->handle_loc( ));
    gp->set_active_pixel(MyResources.barActiveColor);

    if (MyResources.bitmapFile)
        picp->set_file(MyResources.bitmapFile);
    return;
}
```

Program 39-4   A get_sub_resources Program (Tire.C)

```
Tire*severity0.tire:/user_app/bitmaps/Tire0
Tire*severity1.tire:/user_app/bitmaps/Tire1
Tire*severity2.tire:/user_app/bitmaps/Tire2
Tire*severity3.tire:/user_app/bitmaps/Tire3
Tire*severity4.tire:/user_app/bitmaps/Tire4
Tire*severity0.barActiveColor:blue
Tire*severity1.barActiveColor:green
Tire*severity2.barActiveColor:cyan
Tire*severity3.barActiveColor:magenta
Tire*severity4.barActiveColor:red
```

Example 39-6   Resource Settings in the .Xdefaults file for get_sub_resources Program

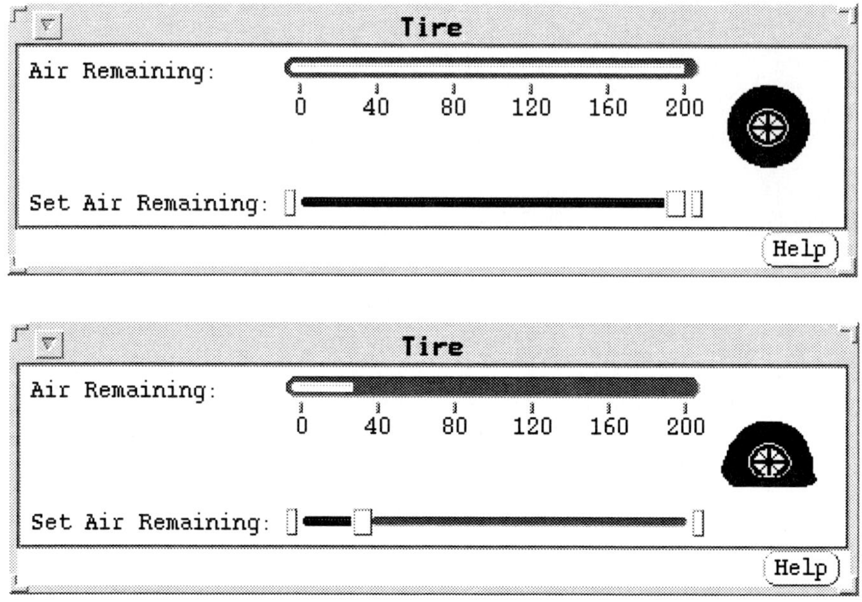

Figure 39-4   Tire Program in Two Different States

39.3.3   Defining Resources for a Class

If you have created your own OI subclass, you can register resources for it. This subject is covered in Chapter 41, "Deriving Your Own Classes."

39.3.4   Defining Command Line Options

You can use the fifth and sixth arguments to OI_init, *app_rmtblp* and *app_rmtbl_size*, to set up your own application-specific command line options.

app_rmtblp points to an X resource manager option description table containing application-specific options to be used in subsequent queries of the resource manager database. It describes the mapping between command-line arguments and resource names for resources specific to a particular application. *app_rmtbl_size* is the number of entries in the table pointed to by *app_rmtblp*.

app_rmtblp points to an **XrmOptionDescRec**, and is defined in **/usr/include/X11/Xresource.h** as

```
struct XrmOptionDescRec {
        char              *opt;              // option abbreviation in argv
        char              *spec;             // resource specifier
        XrmOptionKind     argKind;           // which option style
        caddr_t           val;               // value to provide if XrmoptionNoArg
};
```

The default table used by OI is:

```
static  XrmOptionDescRec opTable[] = {
        {"-background",    "*background",    XrmoptionSepArg, (caddr_t) NULL},
        {"-bd",            "*borderColor",   XrmoptionSepArg, (caddr_t) NULL},
        {"-bg",            "*background",    XrmoptionSepArg, (caddr_t) NULL},
        {"-bordercolor",   "*borderColor",   XrmoptionSepArg, (caddr_t) NULL},
        {"-borderwidth",   "*borderWidth",   XrmoptionSepArg, (caddr_t) NULL},
        {"-bw",            "*borderWidth",   XrmoptionSepArg, (caddr_t) NULL},
        {"-config",        "*config",        XrmoptionSepArg, (caddr_t) NULL},
        {"-debug",         "*debug",         XrmoptionNoArg,  (caddr_t) "on"},
        {"-fg",            "*foreground",    XrmoptionSepArg, (caddr_t) NULL},
        {"-fastdraw",      "*fastDraw",      XrmoptionNoArg,  (caddr_t) "on"},
        {"-fn",            "*font",          XrmoptionSepArg, (caddr_t) NULL},
        {"-font",          "*font",          XrmoptionSepArg, (caddr_t) NULL},
        {"-foreground",    "*foreground",    XrmoptionSepArg, (caddr_t) NULL},
        {"-geometry",      "*geometry",      XrmoptionSepArg, (caddr_t) NULL},
        {"-iconic",        "*iconic",        XrmoptionNoArg,  (caddr_t) "on"},
        {"-icongeometry",  "*iconGeometry",  XrmoptionSepArg, (caddr_t) NULL},
        {"-language",      "*language",      XrmoptionSepArg, (caddr_t) NULL},
        {"-motif",         "*model",         XrmoptionNoArg,  (caddr_t) "motif"},
        {"-name",          "*name",          XrmoptionSepArg, (caddr_t) NULL},
        {"-oiversion",     "*oiversion",     XrmoptionNoArg,  (caddr_t) "on"},
        {"-ol",            "*model",         XrmoptionNoArg,  (caddr_t) "openLook"},
        {"-ol2d",          "*model",         XrmoptionNoArg,  (caddr_t) "openLook2d"},
        {"-ol3d",          "*model",         XrmoptionNoArg,  (caddr_t) "openLook3d"},
        {"-openlook",      "*model",         XrmoptionNoArg,  (caddr_t) "openLook"},
        {"-openlook2d",    "*model",         XrmoptionNoArg,  (caddr_t) "openLook2d"},
        {"-openlook3d",    "*model",         XrmoptionNoArg,  (caddr_t) "openLook3d"},
        {"-reverse",       "*reverseVideo",  XrmoptionNoArg,  (caddr_t) "on"},
        {"+rv",            "*reverseVideo",  XrmoptionNoArg,  (caddr_t) "off"},
        {"-rv",            "*reverseVideo",  XrmoptionNoArg,  (caddr_t) "on"},
        {"+synchronous",   "*synchronous",   XrmoptionNoArg,  (caddr_t) "off"},
        {"-synchronous",   "*synchronous",   XrmoptionNoArg,  (caddr_t) "on"},
        {"-title",         "*OI_app_window.title",XrmoptionSepArg,(caddr_t) NULL},
        {"-xrm",           NULL,             XrmoptionResArg, (caddr_t) NULL},
} ;
```

The first element of each record, *opt*, is the command-line argument the user will type to get the desired resource. The second element, *spec*, is the resource specification; this must be the identical set of characters that would be used for the resource specification if it were to be in one of the X resource database files with the exception that the colon is missing. *argKind* describes the type of argument. As defined in **/usr/include/X11/Xresource.h**, the possible types are:

```
enum XrmOptionKind {
    XrmoptionNoArg,          // value is specified in OptionDescRec.value
    XrmoptionIsArg,          // value is the option string itself
    XrmoptionStickyArg,      // value is characters immediately following option
    XrmoptionSepArg,         // value is next argument in argv
    XrmoptionResArg,         // resource and value in next argument in argv
    XrmoptionSkipArg,        // ignore this option and the next argument in argv
    XrmoptionSkipLine,       // ignore this option and the rest of argv
    XrmoptionSkipNArgs       // ignore this option and the next OptionDescRec.value args in argv
};
```

val is the value of the resource, if applicable.

Thus, if the user types

```
my_app -title abc
```

it is equivalent to having

```
my_app*OI_app_window.title:abc
```

in a resource file.

Previously, we claimed that command-line arguments override all other X resource database resource settings. This is really only true within the context of the precedence rules of the X resource manager. If you have

```
my_app*OI_app_window.title:foo
```

in your **.Xdefaults** file, and start the application with

```
my_app -title abc
```

the application's **OI_app_window** title will be "foo", because the **.Xdefaults** setting is more specific than the command-line argument.

39.3.5   Setting Resource Values for Your Application

You can, within your program, add resource specifications for the entire connection to any of the OI resource databases. Use one of the **OI_connection** member functions below to do this. The effects of these function calls are shown in Figure 39-5.

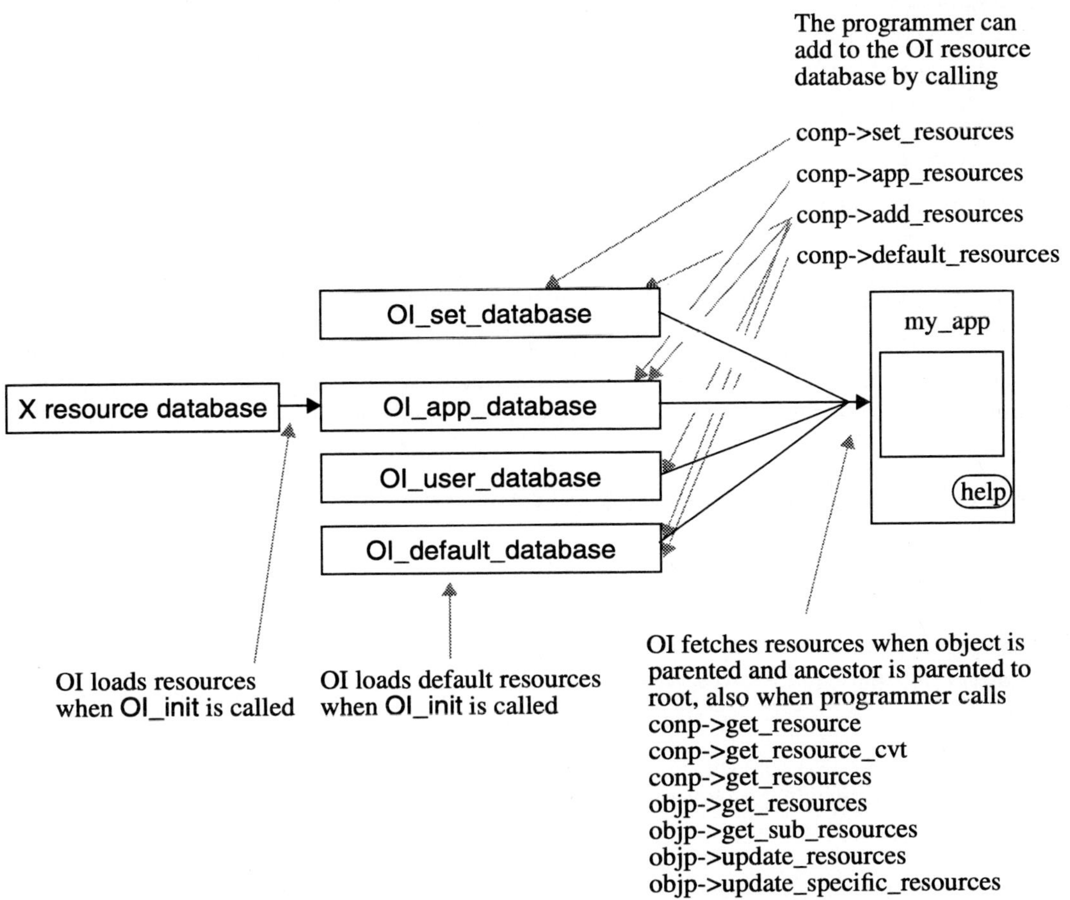

Figure 39-5   Adding and Fetching Resources

These functions are summarized here; see Chapter 38, "OI_connection" for more detail.

default_resources

default_resources establishes resource settings for objects on the connection in the resource database OI_default_database. Because they are inserted into this particular database, which is searched after the OI_app_database and only if no match is found in OI_app_database, the user can override these settings by inserting strings into his or her .Xdefaults file.

app_resources

app_resources establishes resource settings for objects on the connection in the resource database OI_app_database. Because they are inserted into OI_app_database, the user can override these settings by inserting strings into his or her .Xdefaults file. You can use app_resources to specify application default resources from within your program, instead of in an application-defaults file.

set_resources

set_resources establishes resource settings for objects on the connection in the resource database OI_set_database. Because they are inserted into the OI_set_database, which is searched before OI_app_database, the user cannot override these resources in any way.

add_resources

add_resources establishes resource settings for objects on the connection in any of the OI resource databases as specified by an argument to add_resources.

39.3.6   Fetching Resource Values for an Object

You can force OI to fetch resources from the OI Resource Database at any point in your program. The functions to do this are described in their own chapters; we merely list them here to give you a concise list of the functions available. The effects of these function calls are shown in Figure 39-5, above.

39.3.6.1 OI_connection Member Functions

These functions are summarized here; see Chapter 38, "OI_connection" for more detail.

get_resource

get_resource fetches the value of one specific resource from the OI resource database for the connection. The raw resource string is returned.

get_resource_cvt

get_resource_cvt fetches the value of one specific resource from the OI resource database for the connection. The resource value is converted from a string to the appropriate type.

get_resources

get_resources fetches the values for a list of resources from the OI resource database for the connection. The resource values are converted from a string to the appropriate type.

39.3.6.2 OI_d_tech Member Functions

These functions are summarized here; see Chapter 6, "OI_d_tech" for more detail.

get_resources

get_resources fetches the values for a list of resources from the OI resource database for the object. The resource values are converted from a string to the appropriate type. The resources are applied to the object.

get_sub_resources

get_sub_resources pushes a resource name on the resource stack, then fetches the values for a list of resources from the OI resource database for the object, then pops the name from the resource stack. The resource values are applied to the object.

set_resource_value

set_resource_value modifies an object attribute as if the resource controlling it had been set to a particular value. It does not insert into any of the resource databases for the current object.

update_resources

update_resources fetches the values for all standard resources from the OI resource database for the object and applies them to the object.

update_specific_resources

update_specific_resources fetches the values for a list of resources from the OI resource database for the object and applies them to the object.

39.3.7   Enabling/Disabling Resource Fetching

You can enable and disable resource fetching within your program. Ordinarily you would not need to do this; if you have resources that you do not want the user to change, you can set them programmatically, or you can use the OI_connection member function set_resources to put the resources into the OI_set_database where the user cannot override them. However, there are cases where this is still not sufficient. For example, a user interface builder such as ObjectBuilder may allow a user to change the resources on an object from the screen, and then need to reparent the object. If resource fetching were enabled for that object, the resources would be re-fetched for the object when it was reparented. To prevent this from happening, you can use either the OI_connection member function   disallow_object_resources,   or   the   OI_d_tech   member   function disallow_object_resources, depending upon whether you need to disable fetching for the entire connection or for a single object. To re-enable fetching, use the OI_connection member function allow_object_resources or the OI_d_tech member function allow_object_resources.

39.4   Converters

A resource value as specified in an X resource database file or in an OI_resource structure is a string of characters. In most cases, OI must convert the value to the appropriate type before it can be applied to an object. For example, a boolean value string of "true" must be converted to the value OI_yes. In addition, OI must convert values back to string form so tools such as ObjectBuilder can write out a proper configuration file.

Note that converters are not just "resource" converters. The converter mechanism is general and is not tied to resources.

39.4.1   Default OI Converters

OI has built-in converters for common resource types shown in Table 39-5. If you need conversions
to other types, you can write your own, as described in the next section.

Table 39-5   Registered OI Converters

From Type	To Type
String	Alignment
Pixel	BevelPixels
String	Boolean
String	Children
String	Class
String	ControllerVisibility
String	Controllers
CursorShape	Cursor
String	Cursor
String	CursorShape
String	Enhance
String	FocusIndicator
String	FocusPolicy
String	Geometry
String	Gravity
String	Int
String	Language
String	LanguageInputStyle
String	Layout
String	Long
String	MallocString

Table 39-5   Registered OI Converters

From Type	To Type
String	MnemonicStyle
String	Model
String	ModifierMask
String	OI_bevel_style
String	OI_char_encode_type
String	OI_display_1d_current
String	OI_display_1d_ends
String	OI_display_1d_ticks
String	OI_font
String	OI_lang_focus
String	OI_number
String	OI_pixmap
String	OI_position
String	OI_state
String	OI_track
String	Orientation
String	Path
String	Pixel
String	Quark
String	QuarkList
String	QuotedString
String	QuotedStringList
String	Short
String	SizeTrack

Table 39-5 Registered OI Converters

From Type	To Type
String	StandardColormap
String	TranslationTable

39.4.2   Creating Your Own Converters

A converter is an object of a class derived from OI_cvt. In order to create your own converter, you must

- Subclass your converter class from OI_cvt, OI's converter class.
- Write a constructor for your class.
- Write a convert function for your class.
- Write an unconvert function for your class.
- After calling OI_init, create an object of your converter class.
- Register the converter object using the OI_connection function register_converter (see page 38-22).

39.4.2.1 OI_cvt Member Functions

The constructor for your subclass will call the constructor for OI_cvt; it has no arguments.

OI_cvt has two virtual member functions, convert and unconvert, which you must override in your converter subclass. convert goes from string form to actual value, and unconvert goes from actual value back to string form. convert and unconvert use X resource manager XrmValue structures. This is a structure of the form:

```
struct   XrmValue {
         unsigned int   size;
         caddr_t        addr;
};
```

Usually, the addr member is the only member of interest; it is a pointer to the source/destination, and you will need to cast it to the appropriate type (see Example 39-7 on page 39-42). Usually the from->addr member is a pointer to the string (char*).

The size parameter is rarely of interest, since you know the variable type that you re converting to/from. If your string needs to be longer than 1024 characters, you need to malloc a static buffer and return that in the pointer the to->addr points to.

When you register your converter using the OI_connection member function register_converter, you specify the from- and to-types used by the converter.

convert

```
OI_bool OI_cvt::convert(
    OI_connection       *conp,          // pointer to the connection
    XrmValue            *fromp,         // convert from this type
    XrmValue            *top)           // convert to this type
```

✎ Write **convert** to convert a value from the *fromp* type to the *top* type.

conp is a pointer to the **OI_connection** on which the resource value will be used. *conp* is useful if, for example, your converter needs to determine if a color display is being used. *fromp* and *top* point to X resource manager structures for the source and destination of the conversion process.

Return **OI_yes** if the conversion was successful; otherwise return **OI_no**.

unconvert

```
OI_bool OI_cvt::unconvert(
    OI_connection       *conp,          // pointer to the connection
    XrmValue            *fromp,         // convert from this type
    XrmValue            *top)           // convert to this type
```

✎ Write **unconvert** to convert a value from the *fromp* type to the *top* type.

conp is a pointer to the **OI_connection** on which the resource value will be used. *fromp* and *top* point to X resource manager structures for the source and destination of the unconversion process.

Because many conversions involve enumerated types, rather than quantities which can be computed via a mathematical process, you can use the following **OI_cvt** member functions to make this process simpler.

set_values   (Member function)

```
void OI_cvt::set_values(
    void                *vp,            // vector of valid values
    int                 nv)            // number of entries in vp
```

set_values sets the *nv* valid values for the converter to *vp*. The pointer itself is saved; the values are not copied.

values   (Member function)

```
void *OI_cvt::values( )
```

values returns a pointer to the vector of valid values which was saved by **set_values**. If no vector was set, **values** returns NULL.

count (Member function)

```
int OI_cvt::count( )
```

count returns the number of values in the value table which was set by **set_values**. If no vector was set, **count** returns zero.

set_strings (Member function)

```
void OI_cvt::set_strings(
    const char* const *strp)          // list of strings
```

set_strings sets the valid strings for the converter to *strp*. *strp* must be a NULL-terminated list of strings corresponding to the values set with **set_values**.

strings (Member function)

```
const char* const *OI_cvt::strings( )
```

strings returns a pointer to the NULL-terminated vector of valid string forms which were set by **set_strings**.

39.4.2.2 Converter Examples

In the **HexEntryField** example in Program 41-2 in Chapter 41, "Deriving Your Own Classes," we added an end-of-entry callback to verify that the entry is not too large; that is, that the maximum value specified by the resource **Maximum** has not been exceeded. We specified the type of the resource as **OI_r_Long**. Therefore, the resource **Maximum** is taken to be a long of base 10. If the **Maximum** resource is set to the value "200", and if the user types "1aa" into the **HexEntryField**, the value is considered to be too large.

If we want the **Maximum** resource to be interpreted as a base 16 number, we must write a resource converter/unconverter, and then "1aa" will be less than "200". Example 39-7 shows the converter needed so that the resource **Maximum**, when specified as **Hex** in the **OI_resource** structure, will automatically assume that the resource value is a base 16 number.

```
      const    char                    *Hex = "Hex"

class cvt_string_to_hex : public OI_cvt {   // this defines the subclass
        public:
                                cvt_string_to_hex( );
        OI_bool                 convert(OI_connection *, XrmValue *, XrmValue *);
        OI_bool                 unconvert(OI_connection *, XrmValue *, XrmValue *);
};

cvt_string_to_hex::cvt_string_to_hex( )     // this is the constructor
{

    // we don't need to do anything here - more complex cases may need something here
    // such as initializing a cache.
    return;
}

OI_bool cvt_string_to_hex::convert(         // this is the conversion function
        OI_connection*,
        XrmValue                *from,       // the string to convert
        XrmValue                *to)         // where to place the result
{
        char    *str;
        long    *value;

    str = (char *)from->addr;
    value = (long *)to->addr;

    // what is missing here is any error checking!!
    *value = strtol(str,NULL,16);

    return (OI_yes);            // return value denotes success/failure
}


OI_bool cvt_string_to_hex::unconvert(
        OI_connection *,
        XrmValue                *from,       // the hex number to convert
        XrmValue                *to)         // where to place the resulting string
{
        char    **str;
        long    *value;

    value = (long *)from->addr;
    str = (char **)to->addr;

    // what is missing here is any error checking!!
    sprintf( *str, "%x", *value);

    return (OI_yes);
}
```

```
    // Put the following lines in the main program right after OI_init,
    // in OI_reg_derived_classes if you have supplied one, or in the
    // init( ) function for your derived class if the converter will
    // only be used by your class.
        OI_cvt                      *my_converter ;
        OI_connection               *conp;

    my_converter = new cvt_string_to_hex( ) ;
    conp->register_converter(OI_r_String,Hex,my_converter);
```

Example 39-7   String to Hex Converter

Note that we had to define **Hex** in Example 39-7. The strings used in the standard converters are already defined in OI; **Hex** is not among them. The strings that are defined, and for which converters already exist, are listed in the OI header file **resname.H**.

Example 39-8 shows how to use the **OI_cvt** member functions for caching string-value pairs for enumerated type converters:

```
#include <OI/defs.H>
#include <OI/cvt.H>

class OI_connection;

enum Flavor { Flavor_Chocolate, Flavor_Strawberry, Flavor_Vanilla };

class cvt_string_to_flavor : public OI_cvt {
 public:
                            cvt_string_to_flavor();
    virtual OI_bool         convert(OI_connection*, XrmValue*, XrmValue*);
    virtual OI_bool         unconvert(OI_connection*, XrmValue*, XrmValue*);
};

cvt_string_to_flavor::cvt_string_to_flavor()
{
    static char    *string_values[] = {
                "Chocolate", "Strawberry", "Vanilla", NULL };
    static Flavor  actual_values[] = {
                Flavor_Chocolate, Flavor_Strawberry, Flavor_Vanilla};

    set_strings(string_values);
    set_values(actual_values, OI_count(actual_values));
    return;
}
```

```
OI_bool cvt_string_to_flavor::convert(
      OI_connection*,
      XrmValue                 *from,        // the value to convert
      XrmValue                 *to)          // where to place the resultant string
{
          int                  i;
          char                 *str;         // pointer to string to convert
          Flavor               *valid_flavors = (Flavor*) values();
    const char*   const        *string_flavors = strings();
          OI_bool              ret;          // OI_yes => successful conversion

    ret = OI_no;
    str = (char *)from->addr;
    for (i = 0; i < count() ; i++) {
        if ((OI_CompareISOLatin1(str, string_flavors[i]) == 0)) {
            *(Flavor*)to->addr = valid_flavors[i];
            ret = OI_yes;
            break;
        }
    }
    return (ret);
}

OI_bool cvt_string_to_flavor::unconvert(
      OI_connection*,
      XrmValue                 *from,        // the value to convert
      XrmValue                 *to)          // where to place the resultant string
{
          int                  i;
          Flavor               flavor;       // converted result
          Flavor               *valid_flavors = (Flavor*) values();
    const char*const           *string_flavors = strings();
          OI_bool              ret;          // OI_yes => successful conversion

    ret = OI_no;
    flavor = *((Flavor*)from->addr);
    for (i = 0; i < count() ; i++) {
        if (flavor == valid_flavors[i]) {
            strcpy(*(char **)to->addr, string_flavors[i]);
            ret = OI_yes;
            break;
        }
    }
    return (ret);
}
```

```
// Put the following lines in the main program right after OI_init call,
// in OI_reg_derived_classes if you have supplied one, or in the
// init() function for your derived class if the converter will
// only be used by your class.

/*
        OI_connection           *conp;
        OI_cvt                  *my_converter;

my_converter = new cvt_string_to_flavor;
conp->register_converter(OI_r_string, "Flavor", my_converter);
*/
```

Example 39-8   String to enum Converter

39.5   The Resource Debug File

Debugging resource-based programs is difficult and is made no easier by the fact that the resource manager gives minimal error messages. You need answers to such questions as:

- What resources did my application try to fetch?
- What value did I get for a resource?
- What is on the resource stack?

OI provides a facility that writes a file containing information to answer these questions. If you specify

```
my_app*resourceFile: file_name
```

in your .Xdefaults file, OI writes into a file named *file_name* whenever it fetches resources for the application **my_app**. This file, which is usually quite large, will contain information reflecting the resources fetched by your program up until the time your program quit. You should specify the application name at the beginning of the resource prefix (the "my_app" in the above example line), because if you merely specify

```
*resourceFile: file_name
```

then any OI application you start will produce this large debug file.

For example, if you specify

```
Tire*resourceFile: resources.tmp
```

in your .Xdefaults file, then in the file **resources.tmp** you will see lines similar to these when you run the **Tire** program (Program 39-4, on page 39-29):

```
Fetch Tire.OI.Color.Screen0.DefaultLanguage.Openlook.Background:
    Tire.oi.PseudoColor.screen0.defaultLanguage.openlook3d.background: white
Fetch Tire.OI.Color.Screen0.DefaultLanguage.Openlook.Foreground:
    Tire.oi.PseudoColor.screen0.defaultLanguage.openlook3d.foreground: black
Fetch Tire.OI.Color.Screen0.DefaultLanguage.Openlook.BorderColor:
    Tire.oi.PseudoColor.screen0.defaultLanguage.openlook3d.borderColor:
                                        DefaultForeground
```

These are lines which OI inserts showing which resources it tried to fetch. Notice that for each resource, it sends the X resource manager both a class and an instance string. Any "@" characters in an instance string are the names of internal OI objects, as shown here:

```
Fetch Tire.OI.Color.Screen0.DefaultLanguage.Openlook.OI_app_window.OI_box.Width:
      Tire.oi.PseudoColor.screen0.defaultLanguage.openlook3d.main.@interior.width:
```

When a value appears after the ":" on a line, it indicates a value was retrieved matching the resource specifications given on that line. If no value appears, no resource was found. Remember, the values listed may come from any of the OI resource databases: OI_set_database, OI_app_database, OI_user_database, or OI_default_database.

39.6   A Programming Example: Date Book

Program 39-5 shows how to set up application-specific resources which can be set either via the .Xdefaults file (or xrdb) or overridden from command-line options. The resources are given default values in case they are not specified at all by the user.

```
#include <OI/oi.H>              /* DateBook.C */

    const   char n_timeStart[] =             "timeStart";// start time resource name
    const   char n_timeEnd[] =               "timeEnd";  // end time resource name

    const   char c_TimeStart[] =             "TimeStart";// start time resource class
    const   char c_TimeEnd[] =               "TimeEnd";  // end time resource class

    const   char DefaultTimeStart[] =        "0800";     // default start time
    const   char DefaultTimeEnd[] =          "1800";     // default end time

    const   int  DefaultTimeInterval[] = 30;             // default time interval
                                                         // (should also be a resource)

struct MyRes {                                       // structure to hold my resources
    int       timeStart;
    int       timeEnd;
};
static  MyRes MyResources;

static OI_resource resources[] = {
 { n_timeStart,c_TimeStart,OI_r_Int,sizeof(int),offsetof(MyRes,timeStart),
 OI_r_String, DefaultTimeStart },
 { n_timeEnd,c_TimeEnd,OI_r_Int,sizeof(int),offsetof(MyRes,timeEnd),
 OI_r_String, DefaultTimeEnd },
};

static  XrmOptionDescRec        opTable[] = {
    {"-start","*timeStart",XrmoptionSepArg, (caddr_t)NULL },
    {"-end","*timeEnd",XrmoptionSepArg, (caddr_t) NULL},
};
```

```
main (int argc, char **argv)
{
        char                    *convertTime(int *); // convert nmbr to a time string

        OI_connection           *conp;               // the connection to the server
        OI_app_window           *wp;                 // the enclosing app window
        OI_entry_field          *efp;                // pointer to each entry field
        int                     time;                // the current time
        int                     row;                 // put entry field in this row
        char                    *label;              // the label for each entry field

    // Open a connection to the server
    if ((conp = OI_init(&argc,argv,"DateBook",argv[0],opTable,OI_count(opTable)))){
        // go get the resources
        conp->get_resources(resources, OI_count(resources), (char *)&MyResources);
        // should make sure the fetched resources are valid

        // create main window and fill with entry fields
        wp = oi_create_app_window("myapp", 10, 10, "Date Book");
        wp->set_layout(OI_layout_row);

        for (time = MyResources.timeStart, row = 0; time <= MyResources.timeEnd;
                                        time += DefaultTimeInterval) {
            label = convertTime(&time);
            efp = oi_create_entry_field("timeSlot", 30, label, NULL);
            efp->layout_associated_object(wp, 0, row++, OI_active);
        }
        wp->set_associated_object(wp->root( ), OI_def_loc, OI_def_loc,OI_active);

        OI_begin_interaction( );
        OI_fini( );
    }
}

char *convertTime(                                   // convert *time to string form
        int                     *time)
{
    static  char                label[20];
            int                 hour;
            int                 minute;

    hour = *time/100;
    minute = *time - (hour*100);
    if (minute >= 60) {
        minute -= 60;
        hour += 1;
    }
    *time = hour*100 + minute;                        // normalize the input argument
    sprintf(label, "%02d:%02d: ", hour, minute);
    return (label);
}
```

Program 39-5   Using Resources for a Date Book (DateBook.C)

Figure 39-6 shows Program 39-5 (DateBook) run with no resource settings.

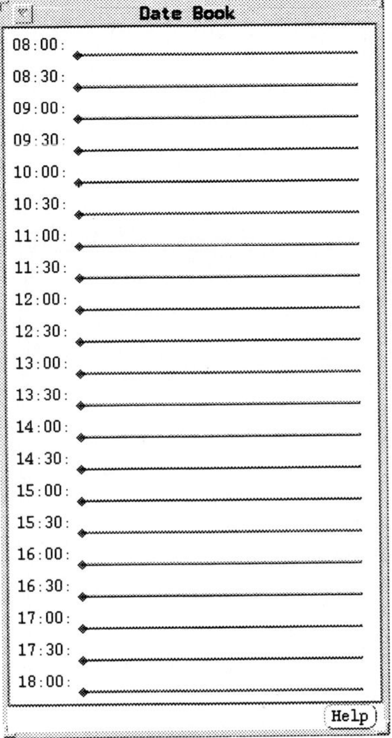

Figure 39-6 Date Book With No Resource Settings

Figure 39-7 shows Program 39-5 (DateBook) as it appears if the user inserts the following two lines in the .Xdefaults file:

```
*DateBook*timeStart:1000
*DateBook*timeEnd:1700
```

or if the DateBook is started with the following command-line arguments:

```
DateBook -start 1000 -end 1700
```

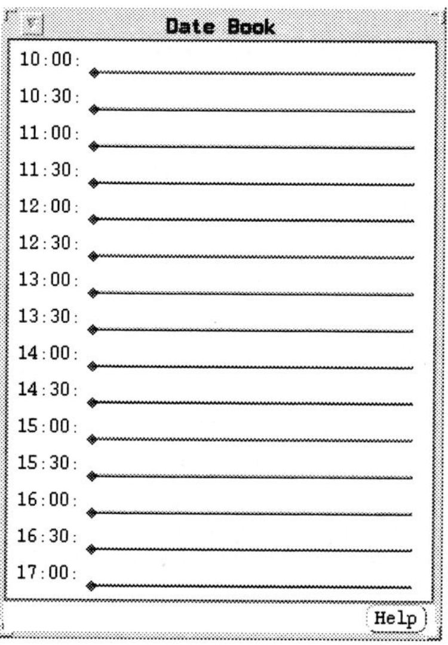

Figure 39-7   Date Book With Resource Settings

Chapter 40
The OI Translation Mechanism

The OI Translation Mechanism

40.1 Description

A *translation* is a mapping between a sequence of X events and a sequence of procedures to call when the sequence of X events occurs. A procedure specified for a translation is called an *action function*. An action function can be either a member function or a free-standing function, and is always called by the X server with a pre-determined set of parameters.

For example, in an OI_entry_field object, the default translations allow the user to strike the Left Arrow key to move the insertion point to the left one character. The translation to effect this looks like this:

```
<Key>Left:    backward_character( )
```

This translation means: if the user strikes the Left Arrow key (the event), OI executes the member function backward_character (the action function). The function backward_character moves the cursor left one character.

A more complex example is this one which is registered by default for an OI_seq_entry_field object:

```
<Key>Up:     paint_increment(down) increment( ) paint_increment(up)
```

This translation means: if the user strikes the Up Arrow key, OI executes the member function paint_increment with an argument of "down", then the member function increment, then paint_increment again with an argument of "up". paint_increment(down) paints the sequential entry increment button pressed down, increment increments the value by 1, and paint_increment(up) paints the increment button released.

Most OI objects have default translations registered for them which define their interaction with the outside world. All OI objects are driven by translations. The translations registered for each object are listed at the end of the chapter on that class of object. There are translations that are registered for an entire connection; these are documented in Chapter 38, "OI_connection." You can override any translations if necessary, or add new translations, using the techniques discussed in this chapter.

When translations are registered for an object, whether they are the default ones OI establishes or ones you register programmatically or through resources, OI inserts entries into the OI dispatch table. This table is organized by X-window ID, and defines the procedures (functions and/or member functions with corresponding objects) to be called when a given X event occurs on a given window. The X events used for translations are usually key strokes or mouse button presses or releases, although they can be any other event shown in Table 40-2 on page 40-5.

When OI receives notification of an X event on an object which has translations, OI first searches the translation table specific to that object. If the event is not found in this table, OI attempts to find the event in the translation table on the connection to which the object belongs. The first translation found that matches the X event is used—the action function(s) specified for the translation are executed.

40.1.1   Accelerator Description

An *accelerator* is a translation which is valid for an object regardless of whether the object is visible or has the input focus. In other words, an accelerator works whenever the input focus is in the top-level object which is the ancestor of the object for which the accelerator is registered. For example, you might set up Ctrl X as an accelerator that would fire the "Exit" button, causing the application to exit. Because an accelerator works top-level-object-wide, you should be sure that any accelerators you specify are unique across the application, or at least across the top-level object.

Accelerators are often used to establish functionality from the keyboard for control that would otherwise have to be accessed with the mouse. Because an accelerator works regardless of whether the object to which it applies is visible, you can specify accelerators for menu cells on pull-down or pop-up menus which are not normally visible. Typing the accelerator will then cause the cell to fire. For example, if you have a debugger written using OI, and there is a menu with cells named "continue", "next", and "step", you could specify that Ctrl C should fire the "continue" cell, Ctrl N should fire the "next" cell, and Ctrl S should fire the "step" cell. Then regardless of where the mouse pointer was in the debugger, or whether the menu was visible or not, typing one of these accelerators would cause the appropriate action to take place.

Since accelerators operate when the pointer is anywhere within the top-level object, when you specify accelerators you should consider what effect they may have on all objects. For example, if a user is likely to have emacs-like translations on OI text objects, you may wish to use Mod1 (Meta) rather than Ctrl as the modifier for your accelerators.

If you specify accelerators for a menu cell, OI modifies the label on that cell to show the accelerator as a hint to the user. You can override OI's default accelerator label with one of your own, if you desire.

40.1.2   Mnemonic Description

A *mnemonic* is an accelerator which is valid for an object only if the object is visible. Because of this, mnemonics do not have to be unique application-wide—you can specify a single keystroke to activate a menu cell in several different pull-down or pop-up menus, as long as you make sure they are menus that are never visible at the same time. For example, suppose you have an application with a main menu across the top. You would only put mnemonics on the cells of the main menu if your mnemonics were unique, because these cells are visible all the time. You could re-use a mnemonic in the submenus attached to the main menu, however, because when a given submenu is visible, no other submenu can appear (as long as the submenus don't have pushpins).

If you specify mnemonics for a menu cell, OI modifies the label on that cell to indicate the mnemonic as a hint to the user. You can override OI's default mnemonic label with one of your own, if you desire.

40.2 Syntax

The syntax uscd for the OI translation mechanism is identical to that used for the Xt translation mechanism. The syntax of a translation specification is as follows:

```
[modifier...]<event>[,<event>...][(count)][detail]: action([args])[action...]
```

where brackets ([ ]) indicate optional elements, and an ellipsis (...) indicates repetition. The colon is mandatory, as are the angle brackets, and there can be optional white space after the colon. Each translation must contain at least one event type enclosed in angle brackets, a colon, and one procedure name. The following line of code is an example of a minimal translation specification, which causes the function **input_character** to be executed whenever any key is pressed:

```
<Key>:            input_character( )
```

The next line is a translation including modifiers, detail and an argument for the specified function; it causes the function **backward_word**, with the argument "extend", to be executed whenever the Left key is pressed while the Shift and Ctrl keys are depressed:

```
Shift Ctrl  <Key>Left:      backward_word(extend)
```

The modifiers are "Shift" and "Ctrl" and indicate that the Shift and Ctrl keys must be depressed while the event specified takes place. The detail is "Left" and specifies which key must be pressed. The argument "extend" is passed as a character string to the action function **backward_word** (see Section 40.4 on page 40-15).

The next line causes the function **select_start** to be executed followed by execution of the function **select_adjust** whenever any mouse button is depressed and moved zero or more times:

```
<Btn1Down>,<Btn1Motion>(0+):select_start( )select_adjust( )
```

40.2.1 Modifiers

Event modifiers can be any of the items shown in Table 40-1. An *event modifier* is an occurrence which must coincide with the event specified in the translation specification. For many events it does not make sense to specify a modifier—modifiers usually apply to key and mouse button events only.

In these tables, the term "Mod1" refers to either of the keys labeled with a diamond on a Sun keyboard. On some keyboards, you may need to use the "Alt" or "Meta" key for the Mod1 key.

Table 40-1 Translation Event Modifiers

Modifier	Description
Shift	Shift key pressed
Ctrl	Ctrl key pressed
Mod$n$	Mod$n$ key pressed $1 <= n <= 5$
Lock	Lock key pressed

Table 40-1   Translation Event Modifiers

Modifier	Description
Meta	Meta key pressed
Hyper	Hyper key pressed
Super	Super key pressed
Alt	Alt key pressed
Button$n$	Mouse button n depressed $1 <= n <= 5$

All the X rules for specifying a modifier apply; these are the rules:

- If a "!" character is specified at the beginning of the modifiers, it means that the listed modifiers must be in exactly this state and no other modifiers can be used. For example,

```
!Shift <Btn1Down>:    extend_start( )
```

  means that the Shift key and no other modifiers must be pressed while mouse button one is pressed in order to execute the action function **extend_start**.

- If no "!" is present, it means "don't care" on all modifiers except for those expressly listed; those expressly listed must be in exactly this state. For example,

```
<Key>Escape:    escape_action( )
```

  means that pressing the Escape key either alone or in conjunction with Shift and/or Ctrl and/or Mod1 modifiers causes the action function **escape_action** to be executed. This translation:

```
Mod1    <Key>I:        insert_mode( )
```

  means that pressing the I key while the Mod1 key is depressed, and independent of whether Shift or Ctrl are pressed, causes the function **insert_mode** to be executed.

- The order in which the translations are specified determines which of two potentially conflicting translations is executed. The first match found in the translation table is used. For example, if translations are specified in this order,

```
Shift  <Key>Escape:    quit_action( )
       <Key>Escape:    escape_action( )
```

  if the user presses Shift Escape, **quit_action** is executed, but if Escape with no modifiers is pressed, **escape_action** is executed. If the two lines above were reversed in order, **escape_action** would be executed regardless of what modifier keys were pressed when the Escape key was struck.

- If a modifier is preceded by a "~" character, it means that the modifier must not be used. For example, this translation:

```
~Shift ~Ctrl ~Mod1 <Btn1Down>: select_start( )
```

  means if mouse button one is pressed, and none of Shift, Ctrl or Mod1 is pressed, then execute the action function **select_start**.

- If a ":" character appears at the beginning of the modifier list, the translation is case sensitive, otherwise case is ignored. For example, the following two lines are distinct, and match only "Q" and "q", respectively:

```
:<Key>Q:              quit( )
:<Key>q:              quit( )
```

The following two lines are equivalent and match either "Q" or "q":

```
<Key>Q:               quit( )
<Key>q:               quit( )
```

In the translation tables for individual classes of objects, you will see entries such as:

```
~Ctrl ~Shift ~Meta <Key>foo
```

This is to ensure that the translation is called only when the button or key is pressed with no modifier keys depressed. Allowing the translation to be called when modifier keys are depressed would not do any harm. However, if a new translation is added which does use the modifier keys, any users who have gotten into the habit of using a modifier key would be surprised at the new behavior.

40.2.2   Event Types

Events in a translation specification must be one of the event types or abbreviations in Table 40-2.

Table 40-2 Event Types

Event Type	Abbreviation	Description
KeyPress	Key	Key pressed
KeyPress	KeyDown	Key pressed
KeyRelease	KeyUp	Key released
ButtonPress	BtnDown	Depressed any mouse button
ButtonPress	Btn$n$Down	Depressed mouse button n, $1 <= n <= 5$
ButtonRelease	BtnUp	Released any mouse button
ButtonRelease	Btn$n$Up	Released mouse button n, $1 <= n <= 5$
MotionNotify	Motion	Mouse pointer moved
MotionNotify	PtrMoved	Mouse pointer moved
MotionNotify	MouseMoved	Mouse pointer moved
MotionNotify	BtnMotion	Mouse pointer moved with any button depressed
MotionNotify	Btn$n$Motion	Mouse pointer moved with button n depressed, $1 <= n <= 5$

Table 40-2 Event Types

Event Type	Abbreviation	Description
FocusIn		The object's X window gained the input focus
FocusOut		The object's X window lost the input focus
EnterNotify	Enter	The mouse pointer entered the object's X window
LeaveNotify	Leave	The mouse pointer left the object's X window
KeymapNotify	Keymap	Specifies which keys were depressed when EnterNotify or FocusIn event occurred
MappingNotify	Mapping	The keyboard or mouse button mapping have changed
Expose		Part of the object needs redrawing
GraphicsExpose	GrExp	During a copy, a portion of the copied object was obscured and so must be redrawn
NoExpose	NoExp	All portions of the copy were available
VisibilityNotify	Visible	There has been a change in the visibility the object's X window
CreateNotify	Create	The window for the object has been created
DestroyNotify	Destroy	The window for the object has been destroyed
UnmapNotify	Unmap	The window for the object has been unmapped
MapNotify	Map	The window for the object has been mapped
ReparentNotify	Reparent	The object's X window has been reparented, from X's point of view
ConfigureNotify	Configure	The object's X window has resized or moved
GravityNotify	Grav	The object's X window has moved due to **win-gravity** attribute
CirculateNotify	Circ	The stacking order has been modified
PropertyNotify	Prop	A property value has changed
ColormapNotify	Clrmap	The object's X window's colormap has changed
ClientMessage	Message	The object's X window has received a client message

Table 40-2 Event Types

Event Type	Abbreviation	Description
SelectionClear	SelClr	The object's X window is losing a selection
SelectionRequest	SelReq	The object's X window has received a request for a selection
SelectionNotify	Select	A requested selection has been delivered to the object's X window

The following events are only generated if you have redirected the corresponding events. Normally you only need to do this if you are writing a window manager.

ConfigureRequest	ConfigureReq	The object's X window has received a request for a move or resize
CirculateRequest	CircReq	The object's X window has received a request for a stacking order change
ResizeRequest	ResReq	The object's X window has received a request for resizing
MapRequest	MapReq	An attempt has been made to map the object's X window

40.3 Modifying Translations

You or the user can add or modify translations through the OI resource mechanism, or you can modify translations programmatically. If you do not need to add any new action functions, that is, the action functions already available will serve your purposes, you can add or modify translations using the OI resource mechanism without changing any code. If you do need to add a new action function, you must do so using the OI_d_tech member function push_actions or push_compiled_actions, the OI_connection member function add_actions, or the free-standing functions OI_add_actions as described in Section 40.4.2, "Creating and Registering Your Own Action Functions," on page 40-16. Once you have registered your new action functions, you can use them in translations as described here.

There are four ways you can add or change translations: you can

- Override translations
- Substitute translations
- Augment translations

- Replace (or Set) translations

Figure 40-1 diagrams the different effects each of these has.

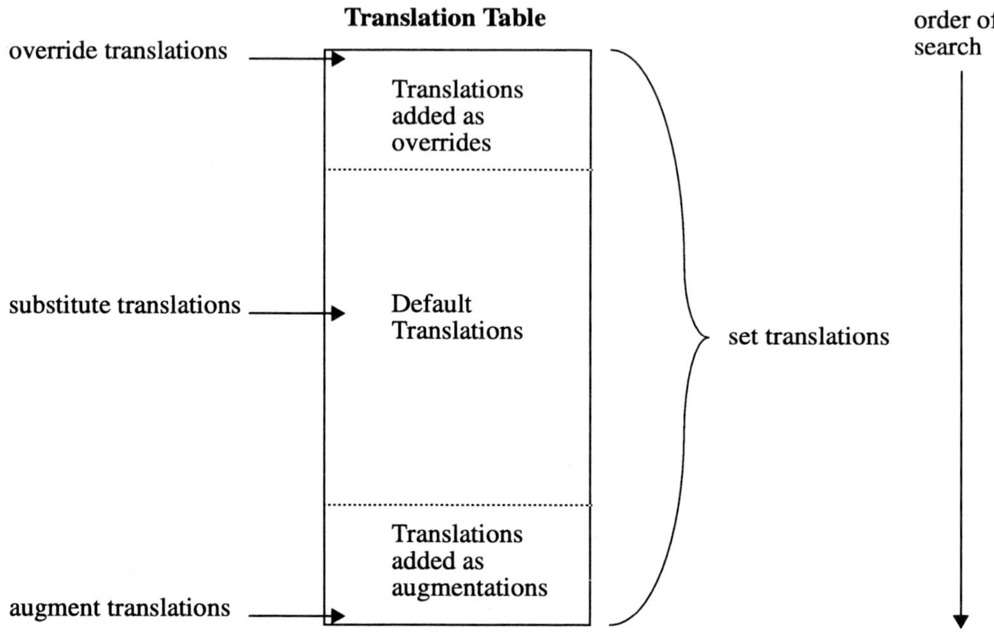

Figure 40-1   Adding and Changing Translations

There is a single translation table for each object; almost all OI objects have default translations installed. When you modify translations, you make changes in this table. The order of translations in the translation table is very important. OI searches the translation table for a translation from top to bottom, and it uses the first translation it finds that matches the event.

40.3.1   Overriding Translations

If you specify that a translation should be an *override* translation, it is merged into the translation table before any other conflicting entries, and will be found before any other translation for the same event. For example, if the translation in the table is

```
<Key>:              eat_a_peach( )
```

but you put in the override table

```
<Key>P:             eat_a_pickle( )
```

OI will find and execute the translation specifying **eat_a_pickle** if the user types a P, but any other key that is not specifically mapped will cause **eat_a_peach** to be executed. If you had specified that the same translation should be an augment translation, it would have been put at the bottom of the table, but it would never be executed, because if the user typed a P, the first translation found that would match would be <Key>: eat_a_peach( ).

Note that if there was already a translation in the table for <Key>P: eat_something( ), and you specified <Key>P: eat_a_pickle as an override translation, the result is that there is only one entry in the table for the event <Key>P—the eat_something( ) translation is superceded by the new translation.

40.3.2   Augmenting Translations

If you specify that a translation should be an *augment* translation, it is appended to the translation table, unless there is already a translation for the same event, in which case the augment translation is discarded. A good reason to augment translations is if you want to match any keyboard event that is not specifically matched in the default table. To do this you would specify something like

```
    <Key>:              eat_a_worm( )
```

as an augment translation, and all key strokes that were not previously matched would cause eat_a_worm to be executed. However, if there is already an entry in the table specifying a translation for <Key>:, yours will never be inserted into the table.

40.3.3   Substituting Translations

When you *substitute* a translation, your translation replaces the first one found in the translations table that matches your event specification. If the event does not already exist in the translation table, it is appended to the table as for an augment translation.

The following describes why you might need to substitute a translation. Suppose the existing translations contained these lines:

```
    <Key>Z:             zoom( )
    <Key>:              insert( )
```

Also suppose you wanted to intercept all keys which aren't matched explicitly. In other words, if the user presses the Z key, you want zoom to be executed (the default behavior), but for any other key you want your action function, not insert, to be executed. You would then specify a substitute translation:

```
    <Key>:              eat_a_worm( )
```

You could not use an override for this specification because the eat_a_worm( ) translation would then appear in the table above the zoom( ) translation. If this were the case, the eat_a_worm( ) translation would always be matched and executed and zoom( ) would never be executed.

You could not use an augment for this specification because there already exists a translation for <Key>: and yours would never be executed.

40.3.4   Replacing Translations

When you *set* translations, the entire translation table for the object is replaced by your translation table. Since the user interface for many objects (for example OI_entry_field) is driven entirely by translations, you should be careful when you set translations.

40.3.5   Using Resources to Modify Translations

Use the OI_d_tech resources translations, translations.override, translations.augment, or translations.substitute to change or add to the default translations registered for an object. These resources have the effect shown in Table 40-3.

Table 40-3   Translations Resources

Resource	Meaning
translations	Replace all translations in the translation table for the object with those specified by this resource.
translations.override	The translations specified by this resource are added to the translation table for the object as override translations.
translations.augment	The translations specified by this resource are added to the translation table for the object as augment translations.
translations.substitute	The translations specified by this resource are added to the translation table for the object as substitute translations.

As a convenience for those familiar with Xt-based resource specifications, you may also specify translations.override and translations.augment as translations: #override and translations: #augment respectively.

For example, one of the default translations for an OI_entry_field object is

```
~Mod1 <Key>Delete:    delete_previous_character( )
```

If you want pressing the Delete key to perform delete_next_character( ) instead, you or the user can add the following lines to the .Xdefaults file or another X resource file:

```
my_app*OI_entry_field.Translations.Substitute: \
      ~Mod1 <Key>Delete:    delete_next_character( )
```

Example 40-1   Using Resources to Change a Translation

The resource specification in Example 40-1 causes the translation specified to be substituted for the corresponding one in the default translation table. The backslash ("\") character at the end of the first line is a continuation character, indicating that the resource specification continues on the next line.

See Example 40-2 on page 40-14 for a way to register this translation programmatically.

40.3.6   Using Resources to Add Accelerators

You can add an accelerator to an object using the OI_d_tech resource **accelerators**. For example, the action function **fire**, used in an accelerator or mnemonic on a menu cell, causes the cell to be activated when the event specified in the accelerator takes place. The resource specification below puts an accelerator on the object name **exit** in the application **HelloExit** and causes the menu cell **exit** to fire whenever Ctrl x is pressed anywhere in the application window.

```
HelloExit*exit.accelerators: Ctrl <Key>x:fire( )
```

Figure 40-2 shows the default accelerator label on the menu cell **exit** when this accelerator is specified.

Figure 40-2   Default Accelerator Label

You can change the label by adding the OI_menu_cell resource **acceleratorLabel**:

```
HelloExit*exit.acceleratorLabel: ^x
```

Figure 40-3 shows the label as specified by this resource.

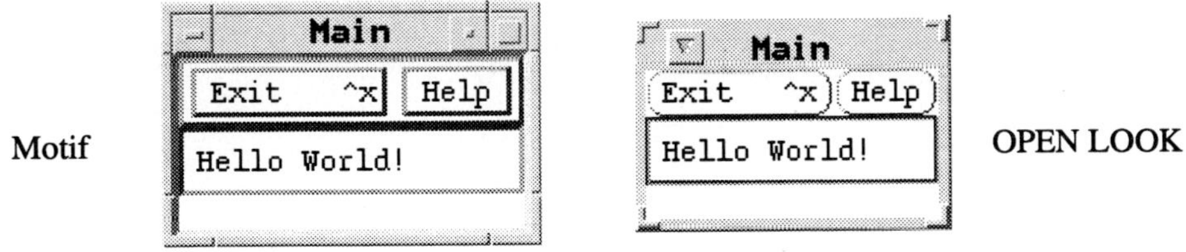

Figure 40-3   Accelerator Label Specifically Set

40.3.7   Using Resources to Add Mnemonics

The mechanism to add mnemonics to an object using resources is identical to that for adding accelerators, except you use the OI_d_tech resource mnemonics and the OI_menu_cell resource mnemonicLabel.

The following three lines put the mnemonics on the menu cells shown in Figure 40-4 and cause the labels to show the mnemonics using the default behavior of underlining.

```
PullDownImp*helvetica.mnemonics:      Ctrl <Key>H: fire( )
PullDownImp*times.mnemonics:          Ctrl <Key>T: fire( )
PullDownImp*courier.mnemonics:        Ctrl <Key>C: fire( )
```

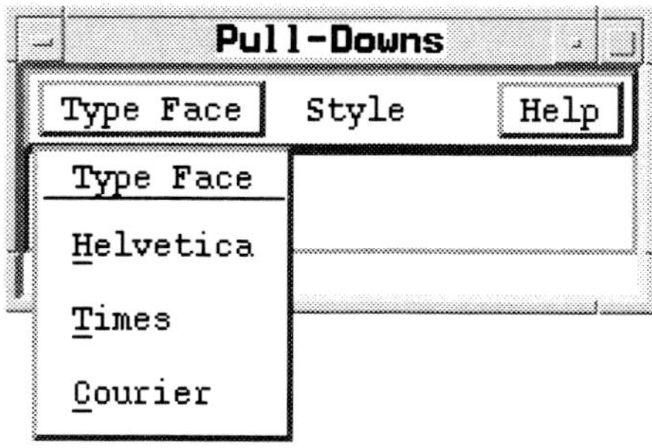

Figure 40-4   Default Mnemonic Labels

The following three lines specify the mnemonic labels shown in Figure 40-5.

```
PullDownImp*helvetica.mnemonicLabel:   Press H
PullDownImp*times.mnemonicLabel:       Press T
PullDownImp*courier.mnemonicLabel:     Press C
```

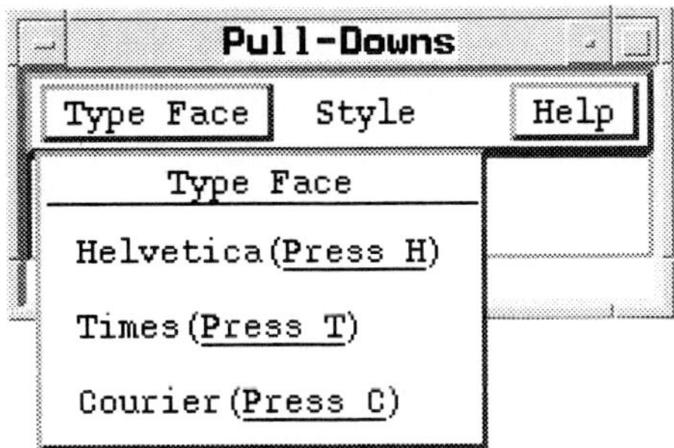

Figure 40-5 Mnemonic Label Specifically Set

You can change the style of the mnemonic label using the OI_connection resource mnemonicStyle. Possible values for this resources are:

reverse   Highlight the character with reverse video.
underline   Highlight the character with underlining.
parens   Highlight the character by surrounding with parentheses.

For example, Figure 40-5 shows the same mnemonics as in the previous examples, without the mnemonicLabel resource set, and with mnemonicStyle set as follows:

```
PullDownImp*MnemonicStyle: reverse
```

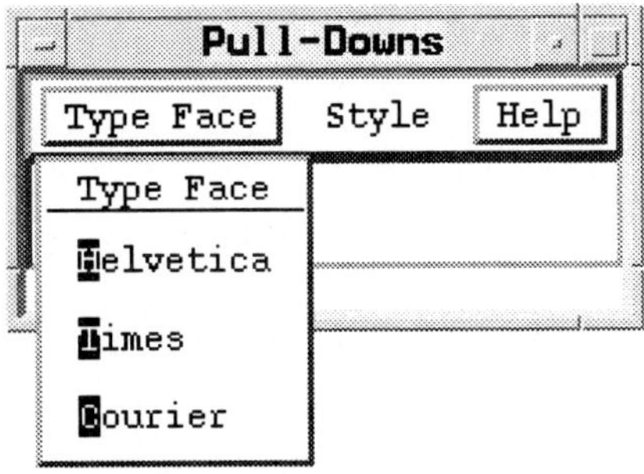

Figure 40-6 Mnemonic Style Set

40.3.8   Modifying Translations Programmatically

Use the OI_d_tech member functions override_translations, augment_translations, substitute_translations, or set_translations to add or change the default translations for an object from within your program. Each of these functions adds or modifies the translations table for an object in a manner similar to the resource with the same name. If you modify translations this way, you prevent the user from overriding them through resources.

To change the action performed when the Delete key is pressed to **delete_next_character** (this is the same translation change as shown in Example 40-1 on page 40-10), you would include these lines of code in your program:

```
static char                 my_trans[] = "\
        ~Mod1 <Key>Delete:      delete_next_character( ) \n";

        OI_entry_field          *efp;

    // create entry field or otherwise get a pointer to entry field efp first
    efp->substitute_translations(my_trans);
```

Example 40-2 Changing a Translation Programmatically

If you want to modify translations programmatically, but not prevent the user from overriding them, use the **OI_connection** member function **default_resources**, and pass in a resource specification for translations.

40.3.9   Modifying Accelerators and Mnemonics Programmatically

To modify accelerators or mnemonics in your program, use the **OI_d_tech** member functions **set_accelerators** and **set_mnemonics**. The argument for each of these functions is a translations string, identical in format to that for **set_translations**. To change the accelerator and mnemonic labels on menu cells, you can use the **OI_menu_cell** member functions **set_accelerator_label** and **set_mnemonic_label**. The following lines of code create the accelerator shown in Figure 40-2 on page 40-11:

```
static char                     my_acc[] = "\
        Ctrl <Key>x:fire( )                     \n";

        OI_menu_cell            *cellp;

    // create menu cell or otherwise get a pointer to menu cell cellp first
    cellp->set_accelerators(my_acc);
```

This line creates the accelerator label shown in Figure 40-3 on page 40-11:

```
cellp->set_accelerator_label("^x");
```

The following lines of code create the mnemonics shown in Figure 40-4 on page 40-12:

```
        OI_menu                 *mp;
        OI_menu_cell            *cellp;

    // create menu cell or otherwise get a pointer to menu cell cellp first
    cellp = (OI_menu_cell*)mp->subobject("helvetica");
    cellp->set_mnemonics("Ctrl <Key>H: fire( )\n");
    cellp = (OI_menu_cell*)mp->subobject("times");
    cellp->set_mnemonics("Ctrl <Key>T: fire( )\n");
    cellp = (OI_menu_cell*)mp->subobject("courier");
    cellp->set_mnemonics("Ctrl <Key>C: fire( )\n");
```

These lines create the mnemonic labels shown in Figure 40-5 on page 40-13:

```
cellp = (OI_menu_cell*)mp->subobject("helvetica");
cellp->set_mnemonic_label("Press H");
cellp = (OI_menu_cell*)mp->subobject("times");
cellp->set_mnemonic_label("Press T");
cellp = (OI_menu_cell*)mp->subobject("courier");
cellp->set_mnemonic_label("Press C");
```

40.4 Action Functions

A procedure to call when an X event occurs on an object is called an *action function*. An action function can be either a member function or a free-standing function. The default action functions OI registers for each object are member functions for that object.

An action function conceptually has two different sets of "arguments." The first set are arguments that you use (as the programmer or as the user) in setting up translations. The second set are the actual arguments with which OI calls the action function, and includes pointers to the first set.

The action functions listed in each chapter usually are shown with no arguments; a few of them are shown with a single argument, such as

```
paint_increment(down)
```

The argument "down" is actually sent to the action function in an *argv*, *argc* pair similar to the way command line arguments are sent to an executable.

When OI calls an action function, it calls it with these actual arguments:

```
void object_class::action_fn_name(
```

`OI_d_tech`	`*obj,`	// pointer to object where event occurred
`const XEvent`	`*ep,`	// pointer to XEvent
`const char* const`	`*argv,`	// vector of arguments
`unsigned int`	`*argc)`	// number of items in *argv*

When the action function is invoked, *obj* will be a pointer to the object in which the event(s) occurred. *ep* will be the last event in the sequence of events which triggered this action. For example, if a translation is:

```
<Key>Escape<Key>B:    my_func( )
```

then *ep* will point to the XKey event for typing B.

argv and *argc* will point to the argument values in the translation. If you have this translation:

```
<Key>A:               my_func(SECONDARY,extend)
```

then when **my_func** is called for this translation, *argc* will be 2 and *argv* will point to a vector of pointers to two strings, "SECONDARY" and "extend".

If you write your own action function, you must write it in the form shown above. You are free, however, to define the number of strings which may be used as arguments in the *argv* vector and the possible values for them.

There is no guarantee that the name of the action function you use when specifying a translation is in fact the name of the actual function executed. The *logical* action function name is the one you or the user sees in the translation function table at the end of each chapter. The *actual* action function name is the one actually called; it may be different from the logical name, and can be hidden from the user. If you create your own action functions, you can cause the logical and actual names to be the same or different. The mapping between logical and actual names is defined when you register an action function, as described in Section 40.4.2.

Program 40-1 on page 40-20 and Program 40-2 on page 40-23 show examples of action functions.

40.4.1   Activating an Action Function From within a Program

If you need to activate an action function from within your program, you should not call it directly, since you may only know the logical function name, which may be different from the actual function name. Instead, you should call the OI_d_tech member function call_action_proc or the OI_connection member function of the same name.

The first argument to the OI_d_tech member function call_action_proc is the logical name of the action function you wish to be executed—it must already be registered in the action table for the object. OI takes care of matching this character string representation of the logical name with the actual name. It looks first in the action function table for the object; if no function of that name is found there, it searches the action function table for the connection. The first occurrence of the function found is invoked.

If you call the OI_connection member function call_action_proc, the first argument is a pointer to the object for which the action function is to be called. Otherwise the function is the same as the OI_d_tech member function call_action_proc.

The following lines of code invoke the OI_entry_field action function start_secondary with an argument of "SECONDARY".

```
        OI_entry_field      *efp;
static  char                param[] = "SECONDARY";
efp->call_action_proc("start_secondary",NULL,&param,1);
```

40.4.2   Creating and Registering Your Own Action Functions

You may find that the default action functions provided by OI are sufficient for your needs, in which case you can skip this section. However, you may want to add action functions to be used as translations in situations such as these two:

- If you derive a new class, you may want that class to have some member functions which are callable via a translation. This case is discussed in Chapter 41, "Deriving Your Own Classes."
- You can write free-standing functions which you want to be invoked via the OI translation mechanism for any object.

In order to add your own action functions to your application, you must first write the action functions using the parameter list as described above. You then register the action functions in one of four ways:

- Use the OI_d_tech member function push_actions. This establishes action functions for a particular object.
- Use the free-standing function OI_compile_action_table and the OI_d_tech member function push_compiled_actions. This also establishes action functions for a particular object.
- Use the free-standing function OI_add_actions or the two-parameter form of the OI_connection member function add_actions. This establishes action functions to be available for use in translations for all objects on the current connection.
- Use the free-standing function OI_compile_action_table and the single-parameter form of the OI_connection member function add_actions. This also establishes action functions to be available for use in translations for all objects on the current connection.

Doing this makes the function names available for use as translations; it *registers* the action functions with the object or connection. Note that it does not establish any translations—you must do this using the techniques described in Sections 40.3.5 through 40.3.8.

Each of these methods uses action tables stored in an OI_actions_rec structure. As you will see below, the OI_actions_rec structure contains, among other things, the names of your action functions. This action table must be converted to OI's internal form before the action functions can be registered; part of the difference between the methods of registering action functions listed above is how the conversion of this structure takes place. Sections 40.4.2.1 through 40.4.2.3 show how this is done.

40.4.2.1 Registering Action Functions for an Object

You can use the OI_d_tech member function push_actions to convert the OI_actions_rec structure (defined in Section 40.4.2.3 below) to OI's internal form and register the action functions for an object. If you do this, your action functions will be re-converted each time you call push_actions. This can degrade performance if you place the call to push_actions within, for example, a constructor for an object of a subclass you have created. Then each time you create a new object of this class, your action functions will be re-converted.

To avoid this unnecessary computing, you can use OI_compile_action_table to convert your OI_actions_rec structure to OI's internal form. In this case, your action functions only need to be converted once, and when you actually register the functions, you use the converted versions. Note that the compiled action tables are never freed until the application terminates.

After calling OI_compile_action_table, if you want to register the functions for a particular object, you use push_compiled_actions. If you do this, for example, in the constructor for an object of your class, then each time you create an object, the already-converted action functions can be used.

40.4.2.2 Registering Action Functions for a Connection

If you register action functions for a connection, then translations using these functions can be established for any object on the connection. You can use the free-standing function OI_add_actions, or the two-parameter form of the OI_connection member function add_actions to register action functions for the current connection. If you use either of these functions, you use an unconverted OI_actions_rec structure as a parameter. If you want to convert the action table to OI's internal form before registering it, you use OI_compile_action_table to convert your action table, then use the single-parameter form of add_actions.

40.4.2.3 The OI_actions_rec Structure

Since translations allow the user to specify which function to call via an alpha string, there must be some mechanism for binding the alpha string to an actual function address. You specify this binding in a vector of OI_actions_rec structures. These structures define a mapping from a character string name for an action, such as "forward_character", to a function address, that is, a mapping from the function's logical name to its actual address. The function pointed to can be either a free-standing function or a member function. If it is a member function and you have set the object pointer to NULL for the entry, the member function is called on behalf of the OI object for which it is registered.

```
struct OI_actions_rec {
        char                    *string;      // function name
        OI_translation_fnp      proc;         // free-standing function
        OI_callback             *objp;        // pointer to object if memfnp is used
        OI_translation_memfnp   memfnp;       // member function
};
```

Using as an example the free-standing functions registered in Program 40-1 on page 40-20, the OI_actions_rec structure looks like this:

```
    static  OI_actions_rec myactions[] = {
            {"enter",enter,},
            {"leave",leave},
    };
```

With this structure, enter will be called whenever the event triggering the translation occurs on the object for which the translation is registered.

To register member functions as action functions, using as an example the action functions registered in Program 40-2 on page 40-23, the OI_actions_rec structure looks like this:

```
static  OI_actions_rec myactions[] = {
        {"enter",NULL,NULL, (OI_translation_memfnp)&MY_static_text::enter},
        {"leave",NULL,NULL, (OI_translation_memfnp)&MY_static_text::leave},
};
```

If you want one of these functions to be called for some object other than the one the translations are registered for when the event occurs, you must put a pointer to that object into objp in the

OI_actions_rec. You can then call **OI_add_actions**, **add_actions**, or **push_actions**, depending on whether the functions are to be defined for the entire connection or not. For example:

```
OI_add_actions(myactions,OI_count(myactions));
```

If you want to compile your functions first, you call **OI_compile_action_table** like this:

```
static  OI_compiled_action_table compiledActions = NULL;

compiledActions = OI_compile_action_table(myactions,OI_count(myactions));
```

You then call either **push_compiled_actions** or **add_actions**. For example:

```
objp->push_compiled_actions(compiledActions);
```

40.5   Translations Programming Examples

As a comprehensive example, three programs follow. All three implement the same behavior—a static text object which is highlighted with a black border whenever the mouse pointer moves over the object. Figure 40-7 shows the results of running any of the three programs.

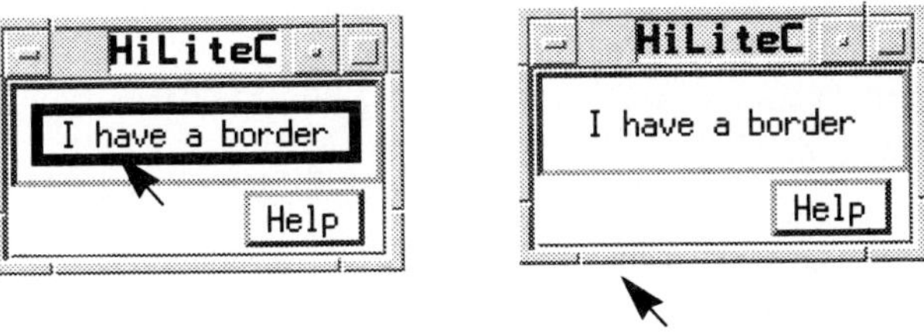

Figure 40-7   Highlighting with a Border

Program 40-1 uses free-standing action functions, while Program 40-2 uses member functions as action functions. You must have the following translations in your .**Xdefaults** or other X resource file for these two programs to work.

```
HiLiteC*my_text.translations.override: \
     <Enter>: enter( )          \n\
     <Leave>: leave( )          \n
HiLiteM*my_text.translations.override: \
     <Enter>: enter( )          \n\
     <Leave>: leave( )          \n
```

If you put this translation specification in a separate file instead of your .**Xdefaults** file (for example, **HiLite.xdefaults**), you can test it by starting your program using the -**config** command-line option:

```
myprog -config HiLite.xdefaults
```

Program 40-3 is identical to Program 40-1 except that the translations are established programmatically as default translations instead of being specified via resources. Only the main program is shown for Program 40-3 since that is the only portion that is different.

For an example of default translations established for an object subclassed from an OI class, see Chapter 41, "Deriving Your Own Classes." In this case the default translations are established in the class, not in the main program.

```
#include <OI/oi.H>                              /*** HiLiteC.C ***/

main (int argc, char **argv)
{
        OI_connection           *conp;              // the connection to the server
        OI_app_window           *wp;                // the enclosing app window
        OI_static_text          *stp;               // the text label

        void    enter(OI_d_tech*, const XEvent*, const char* const *, unsigned int*);
        void    leave(OI_d_tech*, const XEvent*, const char* const *, unsigned int*);

        static  OI_actions_rec myactions[] = {
                                {"enter",   enter },
                                {"leave",   leave }
                };

    if ((conp = OI_init(&argc, argv, "HiLiteC"))) {
        OI_add_actions(myactions, OI_count(myactions));
        wp = oi_create_app_window("main", 1, 1, "HiLiteC");
        wp->set_layout(OI_layout_row);
        stp = oi_create_static_text("my_text", " I have a border ");
        stp->set_bdr_width(4);
        stp->layout_associated_object(wp, 5, 5, OI_active);
        wp->set_associated_object(conp->root( ), OI_def_loc, OI_def_loc,
                                        OI_active);
        stp->set_bdr_pixel(stp->bkg_pixel( ));
        OI_begin_interaction( );
        OI_fini( );
    }
}

static void
enter(OI_d_tech *objp, const XEvent *, const char* const *, unsigned int *)
{
    objp->set_bdr_color("black");
    return;
}

static void
leave(OI_d_tech *objp, const XEvent *, const char* const *, unsigned int *)
{
    objp->set_bdr_pixel(objp->bkg_pixel( ));
    return;
}
```

Program 40-1   Highlight an Object when the Mouse Enters It (HiLiteC.C)

```
#include <OI/oi.H>                          /*** HiLiteM.C ***/
class MY_static_text : public OI_static_text {
    public:
                MY_static_text(const char *nam, char *txt);
        void    enter(OI_d_tech*, const XEvent*, const char * const*, unsigned int*);
        void    leave(OI_d_tech*, const XEvent*, const char * const*, unsigned int*);
};


MY_static_text::MY_static_text(const char *nam, char *txt)
                : OI_static_text(nam, txt)

{
    static OI_actions_rec myactions[] = {
        {"enter", NULL, NULL, (OI_translation_memfnp)&MY_static_text::enter},
        {"leave", NULL, NULL, (OI_translation_memfnp)&MY_static_text::leave}
    };
    push_actions(myactions, OI_count(myactions));
    disallow_cut_paste( );
}


main (int argc, char **argv)
{
        OI_connection           *conp;          // the connection to the server
        OI_app_window           *wp;            // the enclosing app window
        MY_static_text          *stp;           // the text label
    if ((conp = OI_init(&argc, argv, "HiLiteM"))) {
        wp = oi_create_app_window("main", 1, 1, "HiLiteM");
        wp->set_layout(OI_layout_row);
        stp = new MY_static_text("my_text", " I have a border ");
        stp->set_bdr_width(4);
        stp->layout_associated_object(wp, 5, 5, OI_active);
        wp->set_associated_object(conp->root( ), OI_def_loc, OI_def_loc,
                                            OI_active);
        stp->set_bdr_pixel(stp->bkg_pixel( ));
        OI_begin_interaction( );
        OI_fini( );
    }
}
void
MY_static_text::enter(OI_d_tech *, const XEvent *, const char* const *,
                                            unsigned int *)
{
    set_bdr_color("black");
    return;
}
void
MY_static_text::leave(OI_d_tech *, const XEvent *, const char* const *,
                                            unsigned int *)
{
    set_bdr_pixel(bkg_pixel( ));
    return;
}
```

Program 40-2   Highlighting Using Member Action Functions (HiLiteM.C)

Program 40-3 is identical to Program 40-1 except for the main program, so that is the only portion shown here:

```c
#include <OI/oi.H>                                  /*** HiLiteDefault.C ***/

main (int argc, char **argv)
{
        OI_connection*conp;      // the connection to the server
        OI_app_window*wp;        // the enclosing app window
        OI_static_text*stp;      // the text label

        void    enter(OI_d_tech*, const XEvent*, const char* const *, unsigned int*);
        void    leave(OI_d_tech*, const XEvent*, const char* const *, unsigned int*);

    staticOI_actions_recmyactions[] = {
                            {"enter", enter},
                            {"leave", leave}
    };
    staticOI_translation_table *defaultTranslations;
    staticchar               mytrans[] = "\
                            <Enter>: enter( ) \n\
                            <Leave>: leave( ) \n\
        ";

    if ((conp = OI_init(&argc, argv, "HiLiteDefault"))) {
     OI_add_actions(myactions, OI_count(myactions));
        wp = oi_create_app_window("main", 1, 1, "HiLiteDefault");
        wp->set_layout(OI_layout_row);
        stp = oi_create_static_text("my_text", " I have a border ");
        defaultTranslations = OI_parse_translation_table(mytrans);
        if (defaultTranslations)
            stp->override_translations(defaultTranslations);
        stp->set_bdr_width(4);
        stp->layout_associated_object(wp, 5, 5, OI_active);
        wp->set_associated_object(conp->root( ), OI_def_loc, OI_def_loc,
                                        OI_active);
        stp->set_bdr_pixel(stp->bkg_pixel( ));
        OI_begin_interaction( );
        OI_fini( ;
    }
}
```

Program 40-3   Highlighting Using Default Translations (HiLiteDefault.C)

Chapter 41

Deriving Your Own Classes

Subclassing Member Functions

Deriving Your Own Classes

41.1 Description

One of the benefits of using an object-oriented toolkit to build applications is that you can create your own classes of objects. If you subclass from an existing OI object, you get the full benefit of the OI class, plus the additional functionality you add.

The OI subclassing process uses an OI class, **OI_class**, and some of its member functions. This class is described in Chapter 42, "OI_class." You will only use this class and its functions if you are subclassing.

Throughout this chapter we differentiate among three different sets of people (or entities) and their needs: you as the author of a new subclass, the application programmer who is writing an OI application and using your subclass, and the OI library. Each of these entities has certain needs and responsibilities which are discussed along with what you need to provide in order to make the whole thing work.

You may wish to create a subclass of an OI class in several different situations. Some of these are:

1. In the most common case, you want all the functionality of a displayable OI class, but you need additional functionality as well. You do not want to change or add to any display characteristics—you allow OI to draw the object. The **HexEntryField** class shown on page 41-36 is an example of this.
2. You may need to create a *composite* object—a container object and its contained objects. For example, suppose you have a slider you use to control a valve, a glyph which depicts the purpose of the valve, and an "on/off" single-celled exclusive check menu which controls whether or not the slider is in effect. In this case, you can derive a new class from **OI_box** that contains objects of these classes and give it member functions to query and control the interior objects. You do not change or add to any display characteristics—you allow OI to draw the object. An example of composite subclassing is the **LabeledGlyphBox** class on page 41-42.
3. In the most complicated case, you create a new class derived from some base class for a displayable OI class. In this case you draw your own displayable object. An example of this is the **VuMeter** class on page 41-50.

You should include the header file <OI/subclass.H> in your subclass source file; it provides definitions for functions and classes documented in this chapter.

When deriving your own subclass, do not use "OI_" as the first characters in your class name, or "oi_" as the first characters of any function names. The OI library reserves this prefix for its exclusive use. A future release might use the same name you have chosen if you used "OI_" or "oi_" as a prefix.

When deriving a subclass from an OI object, you pick a point between two extremes, depending on your needs:

  • Make the simplest possible derivation. This gives you the functionality you need, but does not allow you to use your subclass with an interface builder such as ObjectBuilder. This involves

---

nothing more than normal C++ subclassing. The only member function absolutely necessary for the simplest possible derivation is the constructor. This implementation is discussed in Section 41.2, "Creating a Simple OI Subclass."

- Make a complete OI-compliant derivation. This gives you a fully functional OI class, usable in the ObjectBuilder interface builder, and indistinguishable from the classes supplied with the OI library. This case is more complex than the simple derivation, but provides additional capabilities for things such as object cloning and adding resources and callbacks specific to your class. This implementation is discussed in Section 41.3, "Creating a Fully OI-Compliant Subclass."

41.2   Creating a Simple OI Subclass

When you create the simplest possible subclass, you get the added functionality in your class, but with the limitations noted below. To do this, you derive a new class from a pre-existing class. The only member function absolutely necessary for the simplest possible derivation is the constructor. To create the simplest subclass, write code in the form shown in the template in Example 41-1. In this template, the new subclass is called **MyClass**, **OI_**xxx is the OI class from which the subclass is derived, *my_params* indicates the parameters for the constructor for the new subclass, and *xxx_params* indicates the parameters for the constructor for **OI_**xxx.

```
class   MyClass:public OI_xxx {
    public:
                            MyClass(my_params);
};
MyClass::MyClass(my_params)  :  OI_xxx(xxx_params) {
    // Do special things here for MyClass
}
```

Example 41-1   The Simplest Possible Subclass Template

For all OI objects, the arguments to the actual constructor for the object (*xxx_params* in Example 41-1) are identical to the arguments in the oi_create_*xxx* function call.

Before doing its work, your constructor should check the error status using the **OI_d_tech** member function **error_status**. You can see an example of this in the constructor for Program 41-1, on page 41-4.

By doing this kind of subclassing, your classes are true C++ classes.

With this kind of subclassing you will have the following restrictions:

- You cannot differentiate your class from the OI class from which it is derived. Given an arbitrary pointer to an **OI_**xxx, you cannot determine if the object is an **OI_**xxx or a **MyClass** which is derived from **OI_**xxx.
- You cannot differentiate between resources set for your class and resources set for the OI class from which it is derived—that is, the class name of the resources that are fetched will be **OI_**xxx, not **MyClass**.
- You cannot use your class with a user interface builder such as ObjectBuilder.
- You cannot clone an object of your class.

- The destroy callback will not be correct (the object will be partially destroyed at the time of the callback) if the application programmer destroys an object of your subclass using the C++ delete operator instead of the OI_d_tech member function del.

An example of actual code using this form is shown in Program 41-1. Program 41-1 does not include the header file OI/subclass.H because such a simple subclass does not need the functionality provided by this header file.

```
                                                    /* SimpleHexEF.H */
#include <OI/entfld.H>

    class HexEntryField:public OI_entry_field {
     private:
            OI_ef_char_chk_status  char_check( OI_entry_field*, void*,
                              OI_ef_char_chk_status, OI_number,char);
     public:
            HexEntryField(char*,OI_number,char* =NULL,char* =NULL);
    };
```

```
                                                    /* SimpleHexEF.C */
#include "SimpleHexEF.H"
#include <stdlib.h>

HexEntryField::HexEntryField (
            char                *namp,          // name for object
            OI_number           len,            // number characters in text entry area
            char                *labp,          // label
            char                *defp)          // default characters in entry area
            : OI_entry_field(namp,len,labp,defp,len)
{
    if (error_status( ) >= 0) {
        set_char_check(this, (OI_ef_char_check_memfnp)&HexEntryField::char_check);
    }
}
```

```
OI_ef_char_chk_status HexEntryField::char_check(
        OI_entry_field          *,
        void                    *,
        OI_ef_char_chk_status   ok,        // return value of previous char check
                                           //    fn if multiple callbacks
        OI_number               n,         // char position and first time sync flag
        char                    c)         // char typed by user
{

    if (ok == OI_ef_char_chk_insert) {
        if ((n >= 0) && !isxdigit(c))
            ok = OI_ef_char_chk_bad;
    }
    return(ok);
}




                                            /* SimpleHexEFMain.C */
#include <OI/appwin.H>
#include "SimpleHexEF.H"
main (int argc, char **argv)
{
        OI_connection           *conp;
        OI_app_window           *wp;
        HexEntryField           *hef;

    if (conp = OI_init(&argc,argv,"SimpleHexEF")) {
        wp = oi_create_app_window("main",1,1,"SimpleHexEF");
        wp->set_layout(OI_layout_column);

        hef = new HexEntryField("hex_entry",5,"Enter Hex: ");
        hef->layout_associated_object(wp, 10, 10,OI_active);

        wp->set_associated_object(wp->root( ), OI_def_loc, OI_def_loc, OI_active);
        OI_begin_interaction( );
        OI_fini( );
    }
}
```

Program 41-1   Simple Subclassing for Hex Entry Field (SimpleHexEF)

41.3   Creating a Fully OI-Compliant Subclass

The sections below describe each of the steps necessary to create a full-fledged OI subclass. You must complete all steps for a fully OI-compliant subclass; however, you may omit those steps that do not pertain to your needs. Examples of code fragments are given in some of the sections. To bring it all together, three complete examples are provided at the end of the chapter. The first, HexEntryField, is a class derived from a displayable OI class. The second, LabeledGlyphBox, is a composite class, using displayable OI classes as the building blocks. The third, VuMeter, is a class derived from a non-displayable intermediate OI class.

These are the benefits of creating a full-fledged OI subclass:

- You can differentiate your class from the OI class from which it is derived. Given an arbitrary pointer to an OI_*xxx*, you can determine if the object is an OI_*xxx* or a MyClass which is derived from OI_*xxx*.
- You can differentiate between resources set for your class and resources set for the OI class from which it is derived—that is, the class name of the resources that are fetched will be MyClass, not OI_*xxx*.
- You can use your class with the ObjectBuilder user interface builder.
- You can clone an object of your class.
- The destroy callback will be correct if the application programmer destroys an object of your subclass using the C++ delete operator instead of the OI_d_tech member function del.

The functions needed by a fully functional OI subclass are listed in Table 41-1. An application which uses a fully derived class must register the new class as described in Section 41.3.2, "Registering the Subclass," on page 41-7. You can also provide callbacks for your subclass, as described in Section 41.4, "Implementing Callbacks, on page 41-34."

Table 41-1   Member Functions Necessary for an OI-Compliant Subclass

Member Function	Purpose	When Needed	Section and Page
reg	Registers the subclass.	Always.	"Registering the Subclass" 41-7
init	Initializes the subclass, registers any new resources, translations and callbacks the subclass uses.	Always.	"Initializing the Class" 41-11
MyClass(...) MyClass(OI_class*,...) construct	Constructs an instance of the subclass. The first form of the constructor is used to create an instance of your subclass; the second form is used during the creation of an instance of a subclass derived from your subclass.	Always.	"Providing a Primary and Secondary Constructor" 41-15
create_MyClass	Calls the constructor; returns NULL if the constructor fails.	Optional convenience function, but makes your subclass look to an application programmer more like an OI class	"Providing for Failure Detection in the Constructor" 41-18

Table 41-1 Member Functions Necessary for an OI-Compliant Subclass

Member Function	Purpose	When Needed	Section and Page
~MyClass	Destroys an instance of the subclass. This destructor insures that object destruction occurs properly.	Always.	"Providing a Destructor for Proper Object Destruction" 41-19
make_minimal	Makes a minimal instance of your subclass.	Always.	"Providing a Minimal Instantiation" 41-20
clone_adjust	Makes an object of your subclass match another object of your subclass.	Needed if your subclass implements any of its own resources.	"Adjusting a Cloned Object" 41-21
set_*xxx*, new_*xxx*, *xxx*, res_*xxx*	Sets (set_*xxx*, new_*xxx*), gets (*xxx*) and resolves (res_*xxx*) a new resource *xxx*.	Needed if your subclass implements any of its own resources.	"Setting and Fetching Resources" 41-22
min_outside_size nominal_outside_size	These member functions provide OI with geometry information for automatic layout; OI needs these if your subclass is derived from an intermediate OI class.	Usually needed only if your class is derived from a non-displayable OI class.	"Managing Geometry for Automatic Layout" 41-25
paint	Draws the image.	Needed if your class renders its own screen image.	"Implementing a New Visual Appearance" 41-27
create	Adds any needed events when the X window is created.	Needed only if your class is derived from a non-displayable OI class.	"Providing for X event Selection" 41-30
disable enable	Deactivates and reactivates the object when used in the ObjectBuilder interface builder.	Needed if your subclass has additional X windows, or specifically adds dispatch entries other than those needed for painting.	"Interacting with ObjectBuilder" 41-33

41.3.1 Choosing an OI Class as Base Class

Usually you derive a subclass from a *terminal* OI class—one which can actually be instantiated and show up on the display. For example, you could derive your subclass from OI_entry_field or OI_slider. However, there are situations where you may wish to derive from some intermediate base class. You are most likely to use the intermediate base classes listed in Table 41-2. If your subclass is derived from any other OI class (such as OI_box), it is automatically derived from OI_callback, since all OI classes are ultimately derived from OI_callback.

Table 41-2 Intermediate OI Classes of Interest in Subclassing

Class	Description
OI_w_d_tech	This is the base class for any *windowed* object—an object which has its own private X window. A class derived from OI_w_d_tech is easier to implement, than one derived from OI_wl_d_tech, and more efficient in terms of compute time, since X events get delivered directly to the object. However, it consumes X resources by allocating a separate window. All displayable OI objects discussed in this book with the exception of OI_menu_cell and OI_separator are derived from OI_w_d_tech.
OI_wl_d_tech	This is the base class for any *windowless* object—an object which does not have its own private X window, but instead uses the window of its nearest ancestor, usually its immediate parent. Use it as a base class when there will be many objects of the class instantiated, and you want to minimize the X resources consumed. Implementation is slightly more complex because drawing must by normalized to the X window origin of the ancestor.
OI_display_1d	This is the base class for an output only one-dimensional quantity, such as the OI_gauge object. Use it as a base class if you want to implement a new display such as the VuMeter example at the end of this chapter.
OI_ctlr_1d	This is the base class for a one dimensional controller, such as OI_slider. Use it as a base class if you want to implement a new controller for a one-dimensional quantity.
OI_base_text	This is the base class for a text object which can contain more than one line of text. Use it as a base class if you want to implement a different multi-lined text object which may be substituted wherever an OI_multi_text or OI_scroll_text object would normally be used.

41.3.2 Registering the Subclass

You need to register your subclass with OI so that OI can fetch resources specific to your subclass, so that user interface builder applications such as ObjectBuilder can discover your subclass and use it, and so that objects of the class can be instantiated from a configuration file. A class is registered by calling **OI_register_class**, an independent OI function. You must write a public static registration member function, by convention named **reg**, which calls **OI_register_class**.

If you provide only **reg** functions for your subclasses, the application programmer must call **reg** for each subclass after calling **OI_init** but before creating any instances of your subclasses. However, OI provides a dummy **OI_reg_derived_classes** function which does nothing, but which is always called during **OI_init**. You (or the application programmer) can override this function with a new **OI_reg_derived_classes**, which calls all the registration functions for each of your subclasses. This arrangement is shown in Figure 41-1.

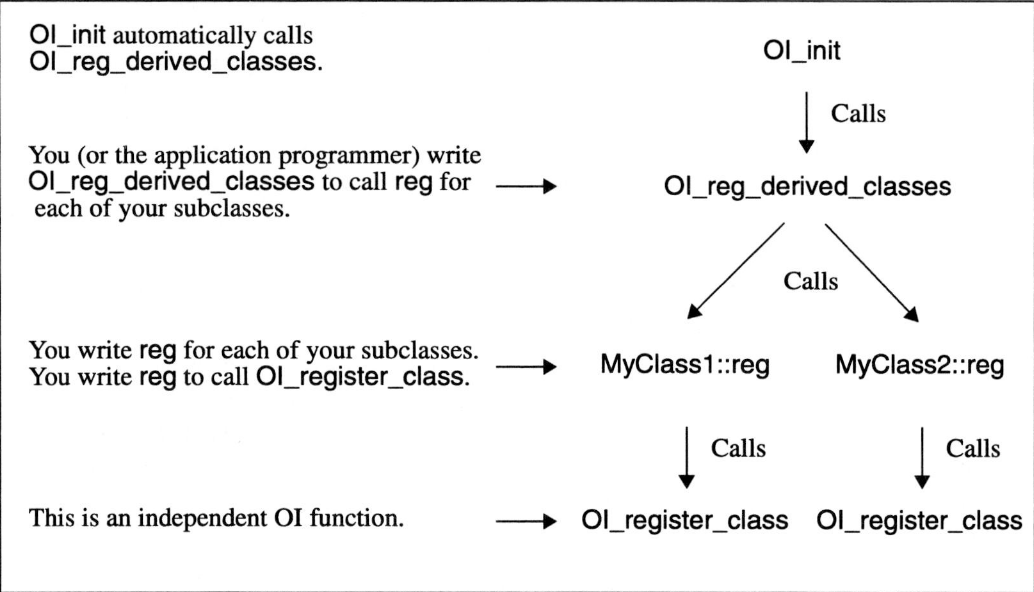

Figure 41-1 Registering a Subclass

For example, suppose you have derived two classes, **MyClass1** which is derived from **OI_box**:

```
class MyClass1 : public OI_box {
    ...
};
```

and **MyClass2** which is derived from **OI_entry_field**:

```
class MyClass2 : public OI_entry_field {
    ...
};
```

To ensure that these classes are properly registered within the hierarchy of OI objects, you write a static registration member function for **MyClass1**:

```
class MyClass1 : public OI_box {
    ...
    static void          reg( );
    ...
};
```

and

```
void MyClass1::reg( )
    OI_register_class("MyClass1","OI_box",(OI_class_init_memfnp)&MyClass1:init,
                      (OI_make_minimal_memfnp)&VuMeter::make_minimal);
    return;
};
```

and a similar declaration and code for class **MyClass2**. You or the application programmer then writes a stand-alone function **OI_reg_derived_classes** to override OI's dummy version:

```
void OI_reg_derived_classes( )
{
    MyClass1::reg( );
    MyClass2::reg( );
}
```

Note: You must register your classes only in terms of previously registered classes. That is, if in the above example you derived a class **MySubSub** from **MyClass2**, you must call **reg** for **MyClass2** before you call **reg** for **MySubSub**.

Any application that uses a fully derived class must register the additional class. If you do not provide an **OI_reg_derived_classes** to register your subclasses, you must instruct the application programmer to call **reg** once for each of your subclasses. The drawback to providing the application programmer with an **OI_reg_derived_classes** which registers all your subclasses is that then the application programmer cannot register any other OI subclasses through **OI_reg_derived_classes**. If you instruct the application programmer to write an **OI_reg_derived_classes** function, then all OI subclasses the programmer may be using can be registered in one function.

If you do provide a version of **OI_reg_derived_classes**, you can supply it to the application programmer in one of two ways. You can supply object modules to the application programmer, one of which contains your version of **OI_reg_derived_classes**. The programmer must then specifically link in your object module. Alternatively, you can provide a dynamic library which contains the new version of **OI_reg_derived_classes**. The application programmer must link this library in ahead of the normal OI library. You must make a reference to **OI_reg_derived_classes** in the dynamic library (that is take the address of **OI_reg_derived_classes**), but you must not call **OI_reg_derived_classes** in the dynamic library. The reason for this is that a reference must be made so that your version will be linked in rather than OI's version, but you must let OI call **OI_reg_derived_classes** in OI_init.

Since the procedures for dealing with dynamic libraries is system dependent, you will need to read the release notes for OI for your particular system to get the details on how to do this.

Table 41-3 shows the different options for registering a subclass.

Table 41-3 Subclass Registration Options

If the subclass author provides this	The application programmer must do this
reg function only for each subclass.	Call reg for each new class after calling OI_init but before instantiating any objects of the subclass. or Write OI_reg_derived_classes to call reg for each subclass.
reg member function for each subclass and a compiled version of OI_reg_derived_classes which calls reg for each subclass.	Link in an object module containing the new OI_reg_derived_classes.
reg member function for each subclass and OI_reg_-derived_classes plus a dynamic library containing the new version of OI_reg_derived_classes. Note: make a reference to OI_reg_derived_classes in the dynamic library to get the module linked in, but do not call OI_reg_derived_classes from the dynamic library.	Link the dynamic library in ahead of the normal OI library.

The process of registering a class creates an OI_class object for the class. This object is returned by OI_register_class, and contains information common to all objects of the class. By convention, a pointer to the class object is stored in a static, public variable named clsp, and is shared by all objects of the class. See Chapter 42, "OI_class," for more information about OI_class and its member functions.

Any function in the sections below which you write for your subclass is marked with the symbol ✎. Any function not so marked is one which you do not write; you may use it to help implement your subclass.

reg

✎ Write the reg function in this form:

```
void MyClass::reg( )
```

where *MyClass* is your class. This must be a static function. Write reg to call OI_register_class for your subclass. The first argument to OI_register_class is the class name, the second is the base class name, and the third and fourth arguments are the initialization and make_minimal functions which you write for your class and which are discussed in subsequent sections.

Example 41-2, below, shows a sample **reg** function for a subclass **VuMeter**:

```
void VuMeter::reg( )
{
    clsp = OI_register_class("VuMeter", "OI_display_1d",
        (OI_class_init_memfnp)&VuMeter::init,
        (OI_make_minimal_memfnp)&VuMeter::make_minimal);
    return;
}
```

Example 41-2   Class Registration Function

41.3.3   Initializing the Class

Early in the process of instantiating an object for a particular class, OI calls the class initialization function. OI calls the class initialization function at most once for the class for each connection. Since it is called before an object of the class exists, it must be a static member function. This initialization function is where you register the constructor arguments, and any new resources, translations, and callbacks the class implements. You can also create bitmaps or other data to be used when drawing an object of the class and store them in a cache on a per-connection basis. The class must have been properly registered in order for the class initialization function to be invoked. For this reason, you should either register your subclass via the **OI_reg_derived_classes** function or the application programmer should call the **reg** function for your subclass immediately after calling **OI_init**. Since OI invokes the class initialization function automatically, you cannot determine when or if it will be called. The only guarantee is that it will not be called until an attempt is made to instantiate an object of the class and that it will be called prior to object instantiation.

Initialization involves two general categories of operations—those which need be done only once, and those which need be done once for each connection. Examples of things which need to be done only once are registering callbacks, resources and translations for the class. Examples of things which need to be done once for each connection are creating bitmaps used for drawing the object image and creating special X cursors, GCs (graphics contexts) or other X resources used by the class.

init

✎ Write the init member function in this form:

```
OI_bool MyClass::init(
    OI_connection    *conp)                 // pointer to connection
```

where *MyClass* is your class. This must be a static function.

Write the class initialization function to perform the actions shown in Figure 41-2:

Determine whether this is the first initialization call. If so, perform the following steps:

> Register all resources implemented by the class (see Example 41-3).

> Register all callbacks implemented by the class (see Example 41-3).

> Register the constructor arguments used by the class (see Example 41-3).

> Prepare translation tables for use by the constructor. This involves the following steps:
> - Compile any action tables used by the class translations.
> - Parse any default translation tables and mark them so they will not be destroyed when the last object which uses them is destroyed. This allows them to be reused when additional objects are instantiated later.

Then do any per-connection initialization necessary.

Finally, mark the class as initialized, saving any connection-specific data.

Return OI_yes if successful and OI_no otherwise.

Figure 41-2   Steps in Initializing a Subclass

When you specify your initialization function as the third argument to OI_register_class, you must cast it to be an OI_class_init_memfnp.

A sample initialization member function is shown below in Example 41-3. The header (class definition) is incomplete, containing only those portions relevant to the example.

```
class VuMeter : public OI_display_1d {
 private:
    // Quarks for callbacks
    static  XrmQuark          q_cbPegged;    // quark for Pegged callback
    static  XrmQuark          q_cbUnpegged;  // quark for Unpegged callback
    // Quarks for resources
    static  XrmQuark          q_arc;         // quark for arc resource
    static  XrmQuark          q_bell;        // quark for bell resource
    // Translation data
    static  OI_compiled_action_table      compiledActions;
    static  OI_translation_table          *defaultTranslations;
    // Instance data
          OI_bool           bel;        // OI_yes => ring bell when pegged
 public:
    static  OI_class          *clsp;        // pointer to class record
 public:
    static  OI_bool           init(OI_connection *);
    static  VuMeter           *make_minimal(const char *, OI_minimal_type);
          void                toggle_bell(OI_d_tech *, const XEvent *,
                                      const char * const *, unsigned int *);
};

struct  VuMeter_cache {                    // unused, for example purposes only
          int             filler;
};

OI_bool VuMeter::init(
          OI_connection  *conp)            // Pointer to connection being initialized
{
    static  OI_resource     resources[] = {                    // Resource definitions
#define Offset(fld) offsetof(VuMeter,fld)
    // Resource which modifies object appearance and therefore needs a res function
            { "arc", "Arc", OI_r_Int, sizeof(int), 0, 0, 0,
                    OI_RESOURCE_MEMFN_CAST(&VuMeter::res_arc), NULL,
                    OI_RESOURCE_GET_MEMFN_CAST(&VuMeter::arc), NULL,
                    OI_RM_MDL_ALL },
    // Resource which does not need a res function
            { "bell", "Bell", OI_r_Boolean, sizeof(OI_bool), Offset(bel),
                    0, 0, NULL_PMF, NULL, NULL_PMF, NULL, OI_RM_MDL_ALL },
#undef Offset
          };
          // Binding table for member functions usable as translations
    static  OI_actions_rec stringActions[] = {
            {"toggle_bell", NULL, NULL,
                    (OI_translation_memfnp)&VuMeter::toggle_bell}
          };
          // Default translations
    static  char            *translations = "#override\n\
            Ctrl <Key>B: toggle_bell( ) \n\
            ";
          // Callback definitions
    static  OI_cb_def       cb_info[] = {
            {"cbPegged", &VuMeter::q_cbPegged, "void", "VuMeter *, void *"},
```

```
        {"cbUnpegged", &VuMeter::q_cbUnpegged, "void", "VuMeter *, void *"}
    };
    // Constructor template
static const char      *con_args[] = {
    "OI_class  *clasp                    /* final class object */",
    "const char *namp                    /* pointer to name for object */",
    "long       mx                       /* maximum value */",
    "long       mn=VuMeter_def_minimum   /* minimum value */",
    "OI_number wid=VuMeter_def_width     /* width of meter */",
    "OI_number ht=VuMeter_def_height     /* height of meter */",
    "OI_number nt=VuMeter_def_n_ticks    /* number of tick marks on scale */",
    "OI_number arc=VuMeter_def_arc       /* arc spanned, degrees */"
    };
    OI_bool               ok ;
    VuMeter_cache*cachep;             // pointer to connection-specific data

if (! clsp->class_initialized( )) {
    // Do once-only initialization here
    // Initialize quarks for resource related operations
    q_arc = XrmStringToQuark("arc");
    q_bell = XrmStringToQuark("bell");
    // register resources, callbacks, and constructor template with class
    clsp->set_resources(&resources[0], OI_count(resources));
    clsp->set_callbacks(&cb_info[0], OI_count(cb_info));
    clsp->set_constructor_args(&con_args[0], OI_count(con_args));
    // compile and save translation related data structures
    compiledActions = OI_compile_action_table(stringActions,
        OI_count(stringActions));
    defaultTranslations = OI_parse_translation_table(translations);
    defaultTranslations->set_keep( );
}
// Now do once-per-connection initialization
if (cachep = (VuMeter_cache*) malloc(sizeof(VuMeter_cache))) {
    // cachep-> = ;
    clsp->mark_initialized(conp, cachep);
    ok = OI_yes;
}
else
    ok = OI_no;
return(ok) ;
}
```

Example 41-3   Class Initialization Function

41.3.3.1 Saving the Per-Connection Cache

The OI_class object maintains a cache of per-connection data for things such as Pixmaps used for drawing. To save this data in the per-connection cache, you call the OI_class member function mark_initialized. By convention, if you are initializing a class *MyClass*, the class dependent data cache is a class of type *MyClass_cache*. *MyClass_cache* is a class which you may define to contain arbitrary information. It has no base class. For example:

```
class MyClass_cache {
    Pixmap  msk;            // Mask used to draw object
    Cursor  csr;            // Cursor used in some interaction
public:
        MyClass_cache(Pixmap p, Cursor c)           { msk=p; csr=c; }
    Pixmap  mask( )         { return(msk); }
    Cursor  cursor( )       { return(csr); }
};
```

You can retrieve the cached values later as follows:

```
MyClass_cache              *cachep;

cachep = (MyClass_cache*) clsp->class_dependent(connection( ));
```

41.3.4   Providing a Primary and Secondary Constructor

The actual constructors (as opposed to the oi_create_*xxx* form) for all OI objects have an additional, overloaded form which has an OI_class* as the first argument, ahead of all the normal arguments. Referred to as the secondary constructor(s), this form is in the protected part of the class header file. The argument is used to pass the class pointer for the final class (the actual class being created) back to the OI_d_tech constructor, for runtime efficiency. Consequently, when you write your OI subclass, you should provide two constructors. The primary constructor is the normal interface. The secondary constructor must have an OI_class* argument as the first argument; this constructor is for the case where another class is derived from your class.

Both constructors must call the constructor for the base class with a pointer to the OI_class object (*clsp* or *clasp*) as the first argument. For the primary constructor, where this class is the terminal class, this class's own clsp is passed to the base class's constructor. For the secondary constructor, where this class is being used as a base class for another class, the clasp passed in the constructor is passed to the base class's constructor. For an example of this, look at how clsp and clasp are used in Example 41-4 and Example 41-5.

constructors

✍ Write the constructors in this form:

```
MyClass::MyClass(my_args): bas_cls_cstrct(clsp, base_args)
MyClass::MyClass(clasp, my_args): bas_cls_cstrct(clasp,base_args)
```

where *MyClass* is your class, *my_args* are the arguments necessary to construct an object of your subclass, *bas_cls_cstrct* is the constructor for your subclass's base class, and *base_args* are the arguments to the constructor for the base class. *clsp* is the static OI_class pointer for this class (*MyClass*), and *clasp* is the OI_class pointer from some other class ultimately derived from this class (*MyClass*).

Note: The most common mistake when deriving a subclass is to improperly thread through the class pointers *clsp* and *clasp*.

Since two constructors are needed, and both must do basically the same thing, by convention the two constructors simply call the function construct; this is done because there is no way to force one constructor to call the other one. The construct member function may need zero or more of the original arguments. When all of the arguments are not needed by the construct function, the unused ones are generally needed by, and therefore passed to, the base class constructor.

This arrangement is shown in Example 41-4 through Example 41-6:

```
        // Constructor used when final object is of this class
VuMeter::VuMeter(
    const   char                *namp,
            long                mx,
            long                mn,
            OI_number           width,
            OI_number           height,
            OI_number           nticks,
            OI_number           arc)
        : OI_display_1d(clsp, namp, mx, mn, NULL, OI_display_1d_ends_none,
            NULL, NULL, OI_display_1d_current_none,
            nticks, OI_display_1d_ticks_all, NULL )
{
    construct(width, height, arc);
}
```

Example 41-4   Primary Constructor

```
        // Constructor used when final object is derived from this class
VuMeter::VuMeter(
            OI_class            *clasp,
    const   char                *namp,
            long                mx,
            long                mn,
            OI_number           width,
            OI_number           height,
            OI_number           nticks,
            OI_number           arc)
        : OI_display_1d(clasp, namp, mx, mn, NULL, OI_display_1d_ends_none,
            NULL, NULL, OI_display_1d_current_none,
            nticks, OI_display_1d_ticks_all, NULL )
{
    construct(width, height, arc);
}
```

Example 41-5   Secondary Constructor

```
void VuMeter::construct(
            OI_number           width,
            OI_number           height,
            OI_number           arc )
{
    if (error_status( ) >= 0) {
        // save nominal size so we can return it
        nom_x = width;
        nom_y = height;
        set_abs_size(width,height);
        n_mini_tick = VuMeter_def_n_mini_tick;
        new_arc(arc);
        set_resize(this, (OI_resize_memfnp)&VuMeter::re_layout);

        // Now put the default translations on the object
        if (compiledActions)
            push_compiled_actions(compiledActions);
        if (defaultTranslations)
            override_translations(defaultTranslations);
    }
    return;
}
```

Example 41-6   Construct Function

The documented interface for OI uses the stand-alone functions oi_create_*xxx* to instantiate an object of class OI_*xxx*. However, you need to know the arguments to the actual C++ constructor in order to derive a subclass. The arguments to the actual constructor for all OI objects are identical to the arguments in the oi_create_*xxx* function call. Remember, however, to supply the class pointer (OI_class* *clsp*) ahead of these when you call your base class constructor. You can look up the arguments in this book, or you can check the constructors in the OI header files.

Before doing its work, your construct function should check the error status using the OI_d_tech member function error_status.

If your class uses translations, your construct function should first push its table of valid actions, then install any default translations for the object. Do this using push_compiled_actions (see page 6-129) and an overloaded form of the OI_d_tech member function override_translations, defined below. Notice that in Example 41-6 the defaultTranslations have previously been created in the init function (see Example 41-3 on page 41-14). The call to override_translations adds these translations to the instance being constructed.

OI_d_tech::override_translations   (Member function)

```
    void override_translations(
        OI_translation_table *transp)        // pointer to parsed translation table
```

override_translations adds all of the translations specified in *transp* to the top of the translation table for the object. All translations defined by the already-parsed translation table *transp* are added at the top of the object's translation table. To create *transp*, use the function OI_parse_translations. When you call this form of override_translations, OI does not inhibit resource fetching for the translation table, which means that any translations set through resources will override any set using this form of **override_translations**.

41.3.4.1 Marking Internal Objects

If your subclass is a composite (it inserts other objects as children as part of its implementation), you should ordinarily mark the objects inserted to implement the class as *internal* objects. If you do not do this, the children could be removed by a user via the interface builder, and the class would no longer function properly. In addition, the children would be written to the configuration file when the interface builder saved your object, so that when your object was reinstantiated from the configuration file, duplicate children would exist. Use the **OI_d_tech** member function **allow_internal_object** to mark internal objects to prevent these unwanted side-effects.

In addition, if an application programmer might need to manipulate any of the internal objects, you should provide member functions to access them.

OI_d_tech::allow_internal_object   (Member function)

```
void allow_internal_object(
    OI_bool            mod)            // OI_yes => user modifiable
```

allow_internal_object marks the object as an internal object. This will prevent a description of the object from being saved when using the user interface builder, and will prevent a user from deleting it via the interface builder.

If *mod* is **OI_yes**, the internal object may be edited using the interface builder, although it may not be deleted.

41.3.5   Providing for Failure Detection in the Constructor

Due to the difficulty and inconvenience of reporting constructor failure in C++, you may wish to create a constructor interface function for your object similar to the **oi_create_***xxx* functions supplied by OI. The main purpose of these functions is to force the return value to NULL when the constructor fails. The application programmer can then test for a non-NULL value upon return from the constructor and take appropriate action if it has failed. At the very least, this method will ensure that when any programmer attempts to create a new object of your class and the creation fails, and if the programmer does not test the return value from the constructor, the program will fail the first time an attempt is made to use the object, as opposed to some indeterminate point in the future when the programmer accesses a corrupted or undefined portion of the failed class.

By convention, for class **MyClass**, the create function is called **create_MyClass**.

create_MyClass

✎ Write the **create_MyClass** function in this form:

> *MyClass* `*create_MyClass(`*my_args*`)`

where *MyClass* is your class and *my_args* are the arguments necessary to construct an object of
your subclass. Call the constructor for your class and return a pointer to the newly created object
or NULL if the constructor failed.

Example 41-7 below shows how this is done.

```
VuMeter *create_VuMeter(
    const   char            *np,            // object name
            long            mx,             // max value
            long            mn,             // min value
            OI_number       w,              // width
            OI_number       h,              // height
            OI_number       nticks,         // number tickmarks on scale
            OI_number       arc)            // arc for scale
{
            VuMeter         *p;

    p = new VuMeter(np, mx, mn, w, h, nticks, arc);
    if (p && (p->error_status( ) < 0)) {
        p->del( );
        p = NULL;
    }
    return(p);
}
```

Example 41-7   Constructor Interface Function for VuMeter

41.3.6   Providing a Destructor for Proper Object Destruction

OI provides for a destroy callback to be made any time an object is destroyed. When the callback is
executed, you normally want the object to still be in a usable state, so that information may be
retrieved from it if necessary. Because the C++ object destruction process destroys a class piece by
piece, you would get a pointer to an incomplete object if the callback were made from the
OI_d_tech destructor. Therefore, you should implement a destructor for your subclass, which, at
the very least, calls the **OI_d_tech** member function **pre_delete**. **pre_delete** calls the subclass's
destroy callback if it has not already been called by previous destructors, and performs cleanup
common to all OI objects.

If your subclass is a composite (a container object and its contained objects), you do not need to
delete any children which are marked as internal objects (see Section 41.3.4.1, "Marking Internal
Objects," on page 41-18). The **OI_d_tech** destructor, which is called after your class's destructor,
will take care of deleting these internal objects. If your composite's objects are not marked as
internal, you must delete them in your destructor.

destructor

✎ Write the destructor member function in this form:

```
MyClass::~MyClass( )
```

where *MyClass* is your class. You must at least call the OI_d_tech member function pre_delete.

A sample destructor appears below:

```
VuMeter::~VuMeter( )
{
    pre_delete( );
}
```

OI_d_tech::pre_delete   (Member function)

```
void pre_delete( )
```

pre_delete releases any data structures and internal interface objects associated with the current object, such as data related to selections it may currently hold. It then makes the destroy callback if one is registered for the object. It finally marks the object as invalid, so that subsequent calls will be ignored. Call pre_delete only from the destructor for an object.

41.3.7 Providing a Minimal Instantiation

You should provide OI with a way to create a minimal instance of your subclass by writing a make_minimal member function. make_minimal allows an instance of a class to be created out of context, with no knowledge of its attributes other than its name. The instance can subsequently be modified by applying attributes (resources).

make_minimal must be a static member function, since it is always used in a context where the object does not yet exist.

make_minimal is used in two contexts. In the first situation, it is used whenever OI builds an application or a portion of an application from a configuration file. In this case, OI creates a minimal object of your class when the configuration file specifies that some object should have a child object of your class. The child object is created using make_minimal, and modified by applying the appropriate attributes from the configuration file to the child.

make_minimal is also used by a user interface builder such as ObjectBuilder when it builds a palette of prototype objects for the user to drag off to create an interface. In this case, the make_minimal function is expected to create an object which is easily recognized as being of the proper type, but which takes up a small amount of space. For an example of the difference between the two situations, a truly minimal OI_entry_field would have no label and a text area only one character long; but an object more recognizable in an interface builder palette would have a label and a text area several characters wide.

make_minimal

✎ Write the **make_minimal** member function in this form:

```
MyClass *MyClass::make_minimal(
    char                *nam,          // name for minimal object
    OI_minimal_type     typ)          // type of minimal object to make
```

where *MyClass* is your class. This must be a static function. When OI calls **make_miniminal**, *nam* will be the desired object name, and *typ* will be one of

OI_minimal	Make an absolutely minimal object, to which resources will be applied when it is parented.
OI_uib_minimal	Make an object to be presented to the user as a sample representation of the object.

If *typ* is OI_minimal, you should make an absolutely minimal object because all attributes for the object will be specified via resources (for example, make a menu with no cells). If *typ* is OI_uib_minimal, you should make a minimal object with enough visual attributes to be presented recognizably on the screen.

When you specify your **make_minimal** function as the fourth argument to OI_register_class, you must cast it to be an OI_make_minimal_memfnp.

Example 41-8 shows a **make_minimal** member function.

```
VuMeter *VuMeter::make_minimal(
    const   char            *name,          // name for object
            OI_minimal_type  t)             // type of minimal object to create
{
            VuMeter         *p;

    // Check for minimal object for display in interface builder palette
    if (t == OI_uib_minimal)
        p = create_VuMeter(name, 25, 100, 1, 60, 60, 6, 90);
    else
        p = create_VuMeter(name, 10);
    return(p);
```

Example 41-8   Make Minimal Member Function

41.3.8   Adjusting a Cloned Object

OI provides the capability to duplicate an object via the **clone** member function. After cloning the object, OI calls **clone_adjust**. The purpose of **clone_adjust** is to make one object look as much like another as possible. The **clone_adjust** function will override the OI_d_tech virtual function of the same name.

clone_adjust

✎ Write the clone_adjust member function in this form:

```
void MyClass::clone_adjust(
    OI_d_tech          *dtp)          // pointer to object to match
```

where *MyClass* is your class. When OI calls clone_adjust, *dtp* will point to the object to match. Write clone_adjust to make the current object match *dtp* as closely as possible. Your clone_adjust should first call its base class's clone_adjust to force all attributes implemented in the base classes to match, then adjust the attributes specific to your subclass.

There are circumstances where OI calls clone_adjust and passes an object which is not actually an object of the current class. For this reason, you should verify the object's class derivation to be sure that the object is of your class or of a class derived from your class, before you perform the adjust operations. You cannot rely on knowledge that clone has been called to create the current object, as it is possible that clone may not have been called—OI may be simply forcing two existing objects to match as closely as possible. For example, it is perfectly legal to request a slider to match a gauge (or even two highly dissimilar objects) as closely as possible using clone_adjust. In this case, only the parts of the object with a common inheritance (up through OI_display_1d) will be adjusted.

Example 41-9 below shows the clone_adjust member function for VuMeter.

```
void VuMeter::clone_adjust (
        OI_d_tech            *dtp)         // pointer to object to match
{
        VuMeter              *objp;        // object to mimic cast to proper type

    OI_display_1d::clone_adjust(dtp) ;
    if (dtp->is_derived_from(VuMeter::clsp)) {
        objp = (VuMeter*) dtp ;
        if (is_bell( ) != objp->is_bell( ))
            toggle_bell(this,NULL,NULL,NULL);
        if (arc( ) != objp->arc( ))
            new_arc(objp->arc( ));
        if (miniTicks( ) != objp->miniTicks( ))
            new_miniTicks(objp->miniTicks( ));
    }
    return ;
}
```

Example 41-9   VuMeter clone_adjust Member Function

41.3.9   Setting and Fetching Resources

The resources which your class will implement are registered in the init function (see Example 41-3 on page 41-14). However, you must also provide member functions to actually implement the resource semantics. The internal OI convention for dealing with resources is described here; you should follow this convention:

For each resource *xxx*, supply four member functions: new_*xxx*, res_*xxx*, *xxx*, and set_*xxx*.

The member function *xxx* should return the current value of the resource and should be public. new_*xxx* should provide the mechanism for changing the resource, used in both the res_*xxx* and set_*xxx* member functions. new_*xxx* should be a protected member function to allow you to call it when you want the user to still be able to override this value via the resource mechanism. In your class's OI_resource structure, specify res_*xxx* as the member function to call to set the *xxx* resource. The res_*xxx* should be private, but some compilers refuse to allow access to this function in your init function, so you should probably make it public to ensure portability. set_*xxx* is the public interface used to set the resource value for *xxx*. Write set_*xxx* to prevent the resource from being set later via a resource fetch by marking *xxx* using set_resourceq.

If the resource is simply stored as a value in the object, and modifying the resource has no immediate effect on the appearance or internal behavior of the object, a res_*xxx* function may not be necessary. In this case, simply make the OI_resource structure specify the offset from the beginning of the object's storage to the location where the resource value is stored, and the resource converter will automatically update the value. This is the case for the bell resource in the VuMeter example. However, if the resource is one which modifies the appearance of the object, or forces a change in the internal state of the object, the res_*xxx* function is needed. This is because of the dynamic nature of OI—a resource value may change at any time, and consequently it may be necessary to reconfigure and redraw the object as a result of the resource fetch. An example of this type of change is the arc resource in the VuMeter example, which causes the display to change. It may also be desirable to use a res_*xxx* function in cases where boolean values are involved, since it allows packing many booleans into a single value instead of allocating a separate boolean variable for each resource. For example, if no res_*xxx* function is used, the smallest storage unit which may be addressed is a char; if a res_*xxx* function is used, the res_*xxx* function can "or" a one bit result into a char or unsigned value.

To make the resource implementation easy to replicate, OI_d_tech maintains a list of resource id's which have been set programmatically via set_*xxx*. You can add a resource to this list by invoking the member function set_resource or set_resourceq, and you can remove a resource from the list by invoking unset_resourceq. You should usually call set_resource or set_resourceq from your set_*xxx* function.

OI_d_tech::set_resource   (Member function)

OI_d_tech::set_resourceq   (Member function)

```
void set_resource(
    const char            *res_nam)    // resource name
void set_resourceq(
    XrmQuark              *res_namq)    // quark corresponding to resource name
```

set_resource and set_resourceq cause the object to mark the resource as having been programmatically set, which prevents subsequent alterations of the value via resource fetches. By convention, the name used for *res_nam* is the instance name for the resource, not the class name.

OI_d_tech::unset_resourceq   (Member function)

```
void unset_resourceq(
    XrmQuark                        *res_namq)    // quark corresponding to resource name
```

unset_resourceq causes the object to again respond to changes in the resource value for the resource corresponding to *res_namq*.

Example 41-10, below, shows one way to implement the resources **bell** and **arc** for the **VuMeter** example class.

```
    static  OI_resource         resources[] = {
#define Offset(fld) offsetof(VuMeter,fld)
    // Resource which modifies object appearance and therefore needs a res function
            { "arc", "Arc", OI_r_Int, sizeof(int), 0, 0, 0,
                OI_RESOURCE_MEMFN_CAST(&VuMeter::res_arc), NULL,
                OI_RESOURCE_GET_MEMFN_CAST(&VuMeter::arc), NULL,
                OI_RM_MDL_ALL },
    // Resource which does not need a res function
            { "bell", "Bell", OI_r_Boolean, sizeof(OI_bool), Offset(bel),
                0, 0, NULL_PMF, NULL, NULL_PMF, NULL, OI_RM_MDL_ALL },
#undef Offset
            };

// "arc" resource
void VuMeter::res_arc(
        void                *ptr)
{
    new_arc(*(int *)ptr);
    return;
}

void VuMeter::set_arc(
        int                 upd)
{
    set_resourceq(q_arc);
    new_arc(upd);
    return;
}

void VuMeter::new_arc(
        int                 upd)
{
    ndeg = upd;
    re_layout( );
    if (is_visible( ))
        repaint( );
    return;
}

// "bell" resource
void VuMeter::set_bell(
```

```
            OI_bool                 b)
{
    set_resourceq(q_bell);
    new_bell(b);
    return;
}

void VuMeter::new_bell(
            OI_bool                 b)
{
    bel = b;
    return;
}

void VuMeter::toggle_bell(                      // this is for a translation
            OI_d_tech           *,
    const   XEvent              *,
    const   char *const         *,
            unsigned int        *)
{
    bel = bel ? OI_no : OI_yes;
    return;
}
```

Example 41-10   Example of Functions used to Implement Resources

41.3.10 Managing Geometry for Automatic Layout

If your subclass is derived from an OI class which is an intermediate class and cannot be instantiated (for example, if it is derived from OI_display_1d), you should provide specific member functions for use in geometry negotiation for automatic layout. OI's automatic layout mechanism queries objects to discover what size they would like to be. Two virtual member functions are involved: nominal_outside_size and min_outside_size.

The purpose of nominal_outside_size is to determine the "normal" size for the object—the size the object should be if it were totally free to size itself. This can usually be computed from information contained in the object itself. For example, an OI_entry_field might compute its nominal size based on the label text, the number of characters of display text, the maximum length of a text entry, the fonts used, and border and bevel widths.

min_outside_size has two purposes. The first is to determine the absolute smallest size the object can deal with reasonably. The other is to determine what size the object will become if it is asked to use some other size. For example, a text object may actually use a size slightly smaller than the size it is asked to become, to maintain an integral number of lines in the viewport.

If an object is a composite (a container object and its contained objects) and it uses a layout method to arrange its children, these decisions are usually left to the layout method to determine.

If your subclass does not do its own painting (that is, you are adding functionality, but not changing the display attributes of an existing OI class), you probably do not need to override the nominal_outside_size and min_outside_size functions already provided by the base class.

In the **VuMeter** example at the end of the chapter, only nominal_outside_size is overridden, since the object is capable of working properly with any geometry. Note that in the example, set_size is also overridden, so that the new size can be saved as the new nominal size.

nominal_outside_size

✎ Write the nominal_outside_size member function in this form:

```
void MyClass::nominal_outside_size(
    OI_number                    *widp,        // place to backfill with nominal width
    OI_number                    *htp)         // place to backfill with nominal height
```

where *MyClass* is your class. Write nominal_outside_size to compute the nominal size of the object and backfill **widp* and **htp* with the result. Since the size is the "outside" (total) size, you must include any size taken up by the border width.

Example 41-11, below, shows the **VuMeter** nominal_outside_size function.

```
void VuMeter::nominal_outside_size (
            OI_number            *widp,        // (output) backfilled with nominal size
            OI_number            *htp)         // (output) backfilled with nominal size
{
            OI_number            fw ;          //border width offset, 2*border width
    // Since this object is not designed to have children laid out in it,
    // Just compute the absolute nominal size
    // Don't forget to include border width -- nominal *outside* size
    fw = 2 * bdr_width( ) ;
    *widp = nom_x + fw ;
    *htp = nom_y + fw ;
    return ;
}
```

Example 41-11   VuMeter nominal_outside_size Member Function

min_outside_size

✎ Write the min_outside_size member function in this form:

```
void MyClass::min_outside_size(
    OI_number                    wid,          // desired width
    OI_number                    ht,           // desired height
    OI_number                    *widp,        // place to backfill with nominal width
    OI_number                    *htp)         // place to backfill with nominal height
```

where *MyClass* is your class. Write min_outside_size to perform the following, depending upon the values passed in *wid* and *ht*:

If *wid* and *ht* are less than or equal to zero, compute the absolute minimum size which the object can tolerate and backfill **widp* and **htp* with the result.

If *wid* and *ht* are greater than zero, assume an attempt will be made to make the object the indicated size, and compute the actual size to use by sizing down if the object cannot fit the indicated size exactly. Since the size is the "outside" (total) size, include any size taken up by the border width.

Example 41-12, below, shows a template for the min_outside_size function.

```
void MyClass::min_outside_size (
    OI_number   wid,            // (input) desired size we shouldn't exceed
    OI_number   ht,             // (input) desired size we shouldn't exceed
    OI_number   *widp,          // (output) backfilled with size we will use
    OI_number   *htp)           // (output) backfilled with size we will use
{
    OI_number   bw;             // border width offset, 2 * border width

    if (abs_layout_method( ) == NULL) {
        if ((wid <= 0) || (ht <= 0)) {
            // Compute absolute minimum size here
        }
        else {
            // Compute minimum size when asked to become wid x ht
            // Adjust down, not up
        }
        // don't forget to add 2 * bdr_width( ) for outside frame...
        bw = 2 * bdr_width( );
        *widp = ... + bw;
        *htp = ... + bw;
    }
    else {
        // Object uses a layout method, let layout determine the minimum size
        abs_layout_method( )->min_outside_size(wid,ht,widp,htp);
    }
    return;
}
```

Example 41-12   min_outside_size Template

41.3.11   Implementing a New Visual Appearance

If your subclass implements a totally new object with its own visual appearance, you will need to draw its image on the display. When an object needs to be drawn, OI calls the OI_d_tech virtual function paint and passes it an Expose event. You will need to write a paint function for your subclass.

If an object is a windowless object, the coordinates for all drawing operations must be relative to the nearest ancestor window's upper-left corner. You can find these offsets using the OI_d_tech member function window_loc.

Drawing operations in X require the use of a structure known as a graphics context, or GC, which contains information (such as font and foreground and background pixel) controlling the operation being performed. A GC is a large structure, so the OI library attempts to allow objects to share a single GC for drawing purposes. The library maintains a default GC on each connection, caches the current foreground, background and font values in the default GC, and maintains its consistency across drawing operations, so that they need not be reset to "normal" after drawing. However, in order to maintain cache consistency, you must use the OI_d_tech member function set_gc, described below, when changing these values, instead of manipulating the GC directly. You should call set_gc before starting any paint operations, to insure that the GC is consistent with the object's foreground, background, and font. If you create your own GC for drawing, you do not need to call set_gc before painting. The OI_connection member function gc returns the default GC for use in drawing operations.

paint

✎ Write the paint member function in this form:

```
void MyClass::paint(
    const XEvent              *ep,        // pointer to Expose event
    void*                     )           // unused
```

where *MyClass* is your class. paint is responsible for redrawing the object whenever an expose event occurs. Expose events are generated by the X server in a series, identified by a count field which starts at the number of events in the series minus one and decrements with each event until the last one, where it is zero. OI calls paint once for each expose event.

If your subclass is derived from OI_w_d_tech (objects with their own private X window), you can treat the expose events normally; that is, for simple drawing, you can ignore all expose events in a series except the last one, and redraw the entire object when this event is fielded. Alternately, you can examine each expose event and redraw only the portion covered by the expose event.

If your subclass is derived from OI_wl_d_tech (windowless objects), painting is somewhat trickier. In this case you cannot wait until the final expose event. This is because only those events which actually cover an object are delivered to the object. The last event in a series may not cover any part of a particular windowless object, and therefore would not be delivered to it. See expose_reset, below.

expose_reset   (Member function)

✎ Write the expose_reset member function in this form:

```
void MyClass::expose_reset( )
```

To make windowless event painting more efficient, OI_wl_d_tech has a virtual function, expose_reset, which OI calls whenever the end of an expose series has been reached. You can write your own expose_reset to reset your object's notion of the beginning of an expose sequence.

Example 41-13, below, shows a template for the paint function for windowed objects; Example 41-14 shows a template for windowless objects. The VuMeter example at the end of the chapter shows an actual example for a windowed object.

```
/* Windowed object paint template */
void MyClass::paint(
    const   XEvent              *ep,            // pointer to expose event
            void                *)              // unused
{
            Display             *dpy;           // pointer to X display on which to draw
            GC                  gc;             // gc with which to draw

    // If the object only knows how to paint in its entirety,
    // only paint on the last expose event of a series
    // Otherwise, paint each individual piece according to the
    // width, height, x, and y specifications in the event
    if (ep->count == 0) {
        // Force gc consistency with object foreground and background
        set_gc( );
        // Cache display and gc (minor code optimization)
        dpy = display( );
        gc = connection( )->gc( );
        // Do our drawing here
        XDraw...(dpy,...,gc,...);
    }
    return;
}
```

Example 41-13   Windowed Object Paint Template for Simple Painting

```
/*
 *  Windowless Object Paint Template for Simple Painting
 *  Assumes the object has a private OI_bool variable named painted
 *  If the paint procedure is smart enough to paint only the exposed region,
 *  none of this is needed
 */

OI_bool MyClass::is_painted( )                  { return(painted); }
void    MyClass::set_painted( )                 { painted = OI_yes; }
```

```
void MyClass::paint(
    const   XEvent                  *ep,            // pointer to expose event
            void                    *)              // unused
{
            Display                 *dpy;           // pointer to X display on which to draw
            GC                      gc;             // gc with which to draw

    //
    if (! is_painted( )) {
        // Draw the object in its entirety here
        set_painted( );
    }
    return;
}
```

Example 41-14   Windowless Object Paint Template for Simple Painting

OI_d_tech::set_gc   (Member function)

```
void set_gc(
    PIXEL                           fg=OI_unknown_pixel,        // desired foreground
    PIXEL                           bg=OI_unknown_pixel)        // desired background
```

set_gc establishes the default GC for drawing and configures it to contain *fg*, and *bg*. After you have called **set_gc**, a call to the **OI_connection** member function **gc** will return the proper GC to use in drawing operations. When *fg* or *bg* is **OI_unknown_pixel**, they are replaced with the foreground and background pixels for the object. If you are using the default GC in the drawing operations, you must call **set_gc** before beginning any drawing. You need not restore the foreground pixel or background pixel used in the default GC when drawing is complete. However, if you modify other aspects of the GC during the paint process, you must restore them. **set_gc** automatically sets the font to the font for the object.

OI_connection::gc   (Member function)

```
void gc( )
```

gc returns the default GC for use in drawing operations if **set_gc** has been previously called.

41.3.12 Providing for X event Selection

If user interaction with your object is controlled completely by translations, the X event selection necessary for your object to function properly will occur automatically. However, if there are aspects of your object which require X event selections which are not controlled by translations, you will need to install those events by overloading the virtual **OI_d_tech** member function **create**. Your **create** function should call its base class's **create** function first, then do the additional tasks specific to itself.

Note: There may be special cases where this is not possible, such as when an object uses an X Window with a special X Visual. In this case, your **create** function must actually create the X window the object will use, and should not call its base class's **create** function.

OI calls the **create** function when it is first necessary to create the X window for an object. Its purpose is to create the actual X window which the object will use for input and display purposes, and to select any input events necessary on that window.

If your class is a subclass of a displayable OI object, you probably have little need for overriding **create**. However, if you are implementing an object derived from a non-terminal base class, you may need to provide it. In particular, if you are deriving your class from OI_w_d_tech you will need to implement it.

Your **create** function should test whether or not the X window for the object has already been created. You cannot use the normal X_window member function for this purpose, since it has the effect of causing the creation of the window if it does not yet exist. Instead use the OI_d_tech member function x_window_id, which simply returns the value of the X window, and returns 0 if none has been created.

OI_d_tech::x_window_id   (Member function)

```
Window x_window_id( )
```

x_window_id returns the Window id of the X window associated with the object. If the object is derived from OI_w_d_tech, this is the private window for the object. If the object is derived from OI_wl_d_tech, this is the window of the nearest ancestor derived from OI_w_d_tech. If the window has not yet been created, x_window_id returns zero.

create

✎ Write the **create** member function in this form:

```
OI_stat MyClass::create( )
```

where *MyClass* is your class. If the actual X window for the object already exists, do nothing. Otherwise, if your create function uses its base class create function, write **create** to perform those aspects of the create operation not already performed by the base class's **create**. If you need to create the X window, call XCreateWindow or XCreateSimpleWindow. Select any input events necessary on that window via the OI_connection member function dispatch_insert. See Example 41-15 and Example 41-16, below.

Return one of the following:

OI_win_exists	The window already exists and therefore was not created.
OI_ok	The window was created.
OI_bad_create	The create failed.

The **create** for the base class will return one of the above three values, or it may return OI_children_created, which you can treat in the same manner as OI_ok.

Example 41-15, below, shows the VuMeter **create** member function.

```
OI_stat VuMeter::create( ){
        OI_stat                 st;             // return status

    if (! x_window_id( )) {
        st = OI_display_1d::create( );
        if (st == OI_OK) {
            conp->dispatch_insert(x_window_id( ), Expose, ExposureMask,
                this, (OI_event_memfnp)&VuMeter::paint);
        }
    }
    else
        st = OI_win_exists ;
    return(st) ;
}
```

Example 41-15   Window create Function Using Base Class's create

An example of a complete **create** member function—one not using the base class's **create** function—appears below in Example 41-16. Note the use of several member functions not previously described. The **abs_*** functions return the same values as the member functions of the same name without the leading **abs_**, except the values are always for the current object, never redirected to reflect the "object of interest". **pre_create_mod** modifies the actual window used for the parent window and the origin used depending on whether the object is unclipped or not. **mod_create** adds any properties necessary for proper window manager interaction.

```
OI_stat MyClass::create( )
{
        OI_stat                 st;             // return status
        Window                  prnt;           // Window id of actual parent window
        int                     win_x,win_y;    // location of window relative to prnt
        OI_bool                 def_loc;        // OI_yes => obj is at "default" location

    if (! x_window_id( )) {
        prnt = abs_parent( )->outside_X_window( );
        win_x = loc_x( );
        win_y = loc_y( );
        def_loc = pre_create_mod(&win_x,&win_y,&prnt);
        if (X_window_id = XCreateSimpleWindow(display( ), prnt, win_x, win_y,
            OI_max((int)abs_size_x( ),1),OI_max((int)abs_size_y( ),1),bdr_width( ),
            bdr_pixel( ), bkg_paint_pixel( ))) {
            mod_create(win_x, win_y, def_loc) ;
            st = OI_ok ;
        }
        else
            st = OI_bad_create ;

    }
    else
        st = OI_win_exists;
    return(st);
}
```

Example 41-16   create Function Not Using Base Class's create

41.3.12.1 Issues of Importance for Windowless Objects

OI_wl_d_tech automatically registers an expose callback for the paint member function, so you do not normally need a create function when deriving from OI_wl_d_tech.

Not all X events contain positioning information which allows OI to determine which windowless object they belong to. If an event contains positioning information (ButtonPress, ButtonRelease, EnterNotify, Expose, FocusIn, FocusOut, GraphicsExpose, KeyPress, KeyRelease, LeaveNotify, MotionNotify), OI dispatches it only to the object(s) of interest. However, other events, such as PropertyNotify, have no positioning information and are therefore delivered to **all** windowless objects within the same windowed ancestor. As a result, if your subclass is a windowless one, you must examine events and discard them if they are not meaningful for your object.

41.3.13 Interacting with ObjectBuilder

If your subclass has additional X windows it uses in its implementation, or specifically adds dispatch entries other than those needed for proper painting, provide a disable and enable member function to deactivate and reactivate the object when used in the ObjectBuilder interface builder. The user interface builder operates in a mode different from most applications. When the user is constructing an application, the builder disables the operation of the objects so that clicking the mouse and dragging have different effects than they normally would. This capability is achieved through two OI_d_tech virtual functions, disable and enable. Normally, an object is in the enabled state; for the special builder mode the object must be in the disabled state. You need to provide a virtual override for the disable and enable functions only if your subclass has additional X windows on which it selects events, or if it is not totally driven by translations and therefore adds entries to the dispatch table. In these cases, you should provide a disable member function which removes these aspects of the object and an enable member function which reinstalls them.

disable

✎ Write the disable member function in this form:

```
void MyClass::disable( )
```

where *MyClass* is your class. Write disable to totally deactivate the object, preventing any interaction with the user but allowing normal paint processing to occur. Write disable to call its base class's disable function first, to deactivate those aspects of the object. Then deactivate any new aspects specific to your subclass. In particular, you must remove any events added to the dispatch table.

enable

✎ Write the enable member function in this form:

```
void MyClass::disable( )
```

where *MyClass* is your class. Write enable to reverse the effect of the disable function, restoring the object to normal operation.

Example 41-17, below, shows a template for the disable and enable member functions.

```
void MyClass::disable ( )
{
    if (is_enable( )) {
        BaseClass::disable( );
        if (x_window_id( )) {
            // Do special disabling here
            // Remove dispatch table entries added for user interaction
            // Do this for this object's window and any extra windows it may allocate
        }
    }
    return;
}

void MyClass::enable ( )
{
    if (! is_enable( )) {
        BaseClass::enable( );
        if (x_window_id( )) {
            // Do special re-enabling here
        }
    }
    return;
}
```

Example 41-17   enable and disable

41.4   Implementing Callbacks

As discussed in Section 41.3.3, "Initializing the Class," on page 41-11, you can implement new callback types for your subclass, which you register in the init function. The registration process makes them known in general, so they will automatically appear and be editable via the ObjectBuilder interface builder.

41.4.1   Setting, Changing, and Deleting a Callback

Once a callback is registered, the application programmer can use the OI_d_tech member functions callback_set, callback_add, callback_delete, and callback_get (in combination with OI_cb_inf class member functions) to add a new callback, delete an existing callback, or replace all callbacks of a particular type with a new callback.

If desired, you may also provide specific member functions for setting your new callbacks. If you wish to do this, the code below can serve as a template, where xxx is the type of the callback:

```
typedef void    (*OI_xxx_fnp)(OI_d_tech*, void*) ;
typedef void    (OI_callback::*OI_xxx_memfnp)(OI_d_tech*, void*) ;

void    set_xxx(OI_xxx_fnp fp, void *argp)
            { callback_set(q_cbXxx, (OI_fnp)fp, argp); }

void    set_xxx(OI_callback *objp, OI_xxx_memfnp mfp, void *argp)
            { callback_set(q_cbXxx, objp, (OI_memfnp)mfp, argp); }
```
Example 41-18   Callback Set Template

41.4.2   Performing a Callback

Remember that if you wish only to use the OI callback mechanism for your subclass—that is, you have member functions to be used as OI callback routines, and you do not wish to incorporate any other OI capabilities, you must subclass from OI_callback, the most distant base class of all displayable OI objects.

Since OI supports multiple callbacks, when it comes time to actually make a callback, OI executes a short loop. Before calling any callbacks, you must lock all callbacks of the type about to be executed, to prevent an infinite recursion situation if one of the callbacks adds a callback of the same type. When all callbacks have been executed, you must unlock them.

For each actual callback registered by the application programmer, OI creates a unique callback object. This object is of type OI_cb_inf. To execute a callback function, you must retrieve the callback object and call the member function callback, or check_callback, on its behalf.

The generic form for this process is shown in Example 41-19

```
    OI_cb_inf   *cbp;

if (callbacks_lock(q_cbMyCallbackType)) {
    for (cbp = NULL ; cbp = callback_get(q_cbMyCallbackType,cbp) ; )
        cbp->callback(this);
    callbacks_unlock(q_cbMyCallbackType);
}
```

Example 41-19   Performing a Callback

callbacks_lock and callbacks_unlock are described in Section 6.18, "Determining and Adding Callbacks; Multiple Callbacks," on page 6-117. callback and check_callback are described in section 43.3, "Performing a Callback," on page 43-3.

41.5   Preparing Your Subclass for the Application Programmer

If you are preparing your subclass for use by other programmers, you should

- provide source code, object modules or libraries to the application programmer
- provide a description of your class and its purpose
- document how to register your class
- document the resources and translations specific to your subclass
- document the callbacks specific to your subclass
- describe the user interaction for an object of your class

41.6   Complete Examples

The last two of the three examples which follow are somewhat lengthy. In particular, the VuMeter is lengthy due to the mathematics involved in doing the actual display. We decided to present all three examples because they cover the three basic types of subclassing, and are complete enough to be genuinely useful in their own right and as good models for your own subclassing efforts. As with all of the examples in this book, they are available in a normal OI distribution, so you shouldn't need to type them in by hand.

41.6.1   HexEntryField Example

The example below implements a full subclass for a hexadecimal entry field. This may be used as a guide when deriving a new subclass from a displayable OI class. The HexEntryField has a resource for setting its maximum value. The HexEntryField class fits into the OI class hierarchy as shown below.

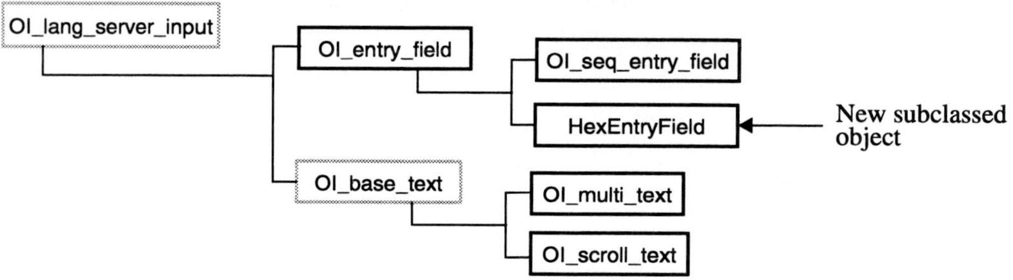

Figure 41-3   HexEntryField.H

```
                                                    /* HexEntryField.H */
#ifndef HexEntryField_H
#define HexEntryField_H

#ifndef OI_entfld_H
#include <OI/entfld.H>
#endif /* OI_entfld_H */

classHexEntryField : public OI_entry_field {
 private:
    // Quarks for resources
    static  XrmQuark            q_maximumValue;// quark for maximumValue resource
    // Instance data
            int                 mx_val;        // max value allowed
 public:
    static  OI_class            *clsp;         // pointer to class record
 private:
            OI_ef_char_chk_statuschar_check(OI_entry_field*, void*,
                                    OI_ef_char_chk_status, OI_number,
                                    char);
            void                construct(int);
            OI_ef_entry_chk_statusentry_check(OI_entry_field*, void*,
                                    OI_ef_entry_chk_status);
    static  OI_bool             init(class OI_connection*);
    static  HexEntryField       *make_minimal(const char*,OI_minimal_type);
 protected:
                                HexEntryField(OI_class*, const char*, OI_number,
                                    const char*, const char*, int);
```

```
public:
                                HexEntryField(const char*, OI_number, const char*,
                                        const char*, int);
                                ~HexEntryField( );
    virtualvoid                 clone_adjust(OI_d_tech*);
            int                 maximumValue( )                 { return(mx_val); }
    static  void                reg( );
            void                set_maximumValue(int);
} ;

/* constructor interface function */
HexEntryField  *create_HexEntryField(const char*, OI_number, const char* =NULL,
                        const char* ="0", int=0) ;


#endif /* HexEntryField_H */




                                        /* HexEntryField.C */
#include "HexEntryField.H"
#include <OI/subclass.H>
#include <stdlib.h>
#include <values.h>

/* Initializations for static variables of class */

    OI_class    *HexEntryField::clsp = NULL ;
    XrmQuark    HexEntryField::q_maximumValue = 0;

HexEntryField* create_HexEntryField(const char *unp, OI_number ln,
    const char *lbp, const char *dfp, int mx)
{
        HexEntryField*p ;

    if ((p = new HexEntryField(unp,ln,lbp,dfp,mx)) && (p->error_status( )<0)) {
        p->del( ) ;
        p = NULL ;
    }
    return (p) ;
}

void HexEntryField::reg( )
{
    clsp = OI_register_class("HexEntryField", "OI_entry_field",
        (OI_class_init_memfnp)&HexEntryField::init,
        (OI_make_minimal_memfnp)&HexEntryField::make_minimal) ;
    return ;
}
```

```
OI_bool HexEntryField::init(OI_connection *conp)
{
    static OI_resource        resources[] = {
#define Offset(fld) offsetof(HexEntryField,fld)
    // Resource which modifies object appearance and therefore needs a res function
    // Resource which does not need a res function
            { "maximumValue", "MaximumValue", OI_r_Int,
            sizeof(int), Offset(mx_val),
            0, 0, NULL_PMF, NULL, NULL_PMF, NULL, OI_RM_MDL_ALL }
    // Note! The resource is fetched as a decimal number; we should
    // probably register a converter for Hex numbers and use it
#undef Offset
        };
        // Constructor template
    static  const char      *con_args[] = {
            "OI_class      *clasp       /* final class object */",
            "const char    *namp        /* name for object */",
            "OI_number     dspln        /* number of chars in display */",
            "const char    *lblp=NULL   /* label */",
            "const char    *defstr=NULL /* default entry */",
            "int           mx=0         /* max allowed value */"
        };
        OI_bool           ok ;

    // Do initialization required once
    if (! clsp->class_initialized( )) {
        // Initialize quarks for resource related operations
        q_maximumValue = XrmStringToQuark("maximumValue");
        // register resources, callbacks, and constructor template with class
        clsp->set_resources(&resources[0], OI_count(resources));
        clsp->set_constructor_args(&con_args[0], OI_count(con_args));
    }
    // Now do initialization required for each connection
    // This object has none, so just mark object initialized on this connection
    clsp->mark_initialized(conp);
    ok = OI_yes;
    // check for initialization failure and notify user
    // if (! ok) {
    //   set_error_status(OI_bad_class_init) ;
    //   print_error("HexEntryField::init") ;
    // }
    return(ok) ;
}
```

```cpp
HexEntryField::HexEntryField (
    const   char                *namp,      // name of object
            OI_number           len,        // number of chars displayed in entry field
    const   char                *labp,      // pointer to label for field
    const   char                *defp,      // pointer to default string
            int                 mx)         // max allowed value
            : OI_entry_field(clsp,namp,len,labp,defp,len)
{
    construct(mx) ;
}


HexEntryField::HexEntryField (
            OI_class            *clasp,     // leaf class for actual object
    const   char                *namp,      // name of object
            OI_number           len,        // number of chars displayed in entry field
    const   char                *labp,      // pointer to label for field
    const   char                *defp,      // pointer to default string
            int                 mx)         // max allowed value
            : OI_entry_field(clasp,namp,len,labp,defp,len)
{
    construct(mx) ;
}


void HexEntryField::construct(
            int                 mx)         // max allowed value
{
    if (error_status( ) >= 0) {
        if (! (mx_val = mx))
            mx_val = MAXINT ;
        set_char_check(this, (OI_ef_char_check_memfnp)&HexEntryField::char_check);
        set_entry_check(this,
            (OI_ef_entry_check_memfnp)&HexEntryField::entry_check);
    }
    return ;
}


HexEntryField::~HexEntryField( )
{
    pre_delete( );
}
```

```
void HexEntryField::clone_adjust (
        OI_d_tech              *dtp)   /* pointer to object to match */
{
        HexEntryField          *objp; /* object to mimic (dtp) cast to proper type */

    OI_entry_field::clone_adjust(dtp);
    if (dtp->is_derived_from(HexEntryField::clsp)) {
        objp = (HexEntryField*) dtp;
        if (objp->maximumValue( ) != mx_val)
            mx_val = objp->maximumValue( );
    }
    return ;
}

HexEntryField *HexEntryField::make_minimal(
    const   char               *namp,       // name for object
        OI_minimal_type    typ)             // type of minimal object to create
{
        HexEntryField      *p;

    if (typ == OI_uib_minimal)
        p = create_HexEntryField(namp,8,"Hex: 0x");
    else
        p = create_HexEntryField(namp,8,NULL);

    return(p);
}

OI_ef_char_chk_status HexEntryField::char_check (
        OI_entry_field         *,
        void                   *,
        OI_ef_char_chk_status ok, // status from previous call if multiple callbacks
        OI_number              n, // char position, -1 => init
        char                   c) // character which was input
{

    if (ok == OI_ef_char_chk_insert) {
        if ((n >= 0) && !isxdigit(c))
            ok = OI_ef_char_chk_bad ;
    }
    return(ok) ;
}
```

```
OI_ef_entry_chk_status HexEntryField::entry_check (
          OI_entry_field       *,
          void                 *,
          OI_ef_entry_chk_status ok)
{
    if (ok == OI_ef_entry_chk_ok) {
        if (part_text( )) {
            if (strtol(part_text( ),NULL,16) > mx_val)
                ok = OI_ef_entry_chk_bad ;
        }
    }
    return(ok) ;
}
/****************************************************************
 * "maximumValue" resource:
 * set_maximumValue            set programatically
 ****************************************************************
*/
void    HexEntryField::set_maximumValue(int upd)
{
        set_resourceq(q_maximumValue); mx_val = upd;
}




                                        /* HexEFMain.C */
#include "HexEntryField.H"
#include <OI/appwin.H>

void OI_reg_derived_classes( )
{
    HexEntryField::reg( );
}

int main (int argc, char **argv)
{
        OI_connection*conp;
        OI_app_window*wp;
        HexEntryField*hef;

    if (conp = OI_init(&argc,argv,"HexEntryField")) {
        wp = oi_create_app_window("main",1,1,"HexEntryField");
        wp->set_layout(OI_layout_column);
        hef = create_HexEntryField("hex_entry",5,"Enter Hex: ");
        hef->layout_associated_object(wp,1,1,OI_active);
        wp->set_associated_object(wp->root( ),OI_def_loc,OI_def_loc,OI_active);
        OI_begin_interaction( );
        OI_fini( );
    }
}
```

Program 41-2   Complete Hex Entry Field (HexEntryField)

41.6.2 LabeledGlyphBox Example

The example below implements a labeled glyph. This is a simple composite subclass, consisting of a normal OI_glyph with an OI_static_text object as a label. The label may be positioned above, below, to the left, or to the right of the glyph; position may be set programmatically or via a resource. The LabeledGlyphBox class fits into the OI class hierarchy as shown below.

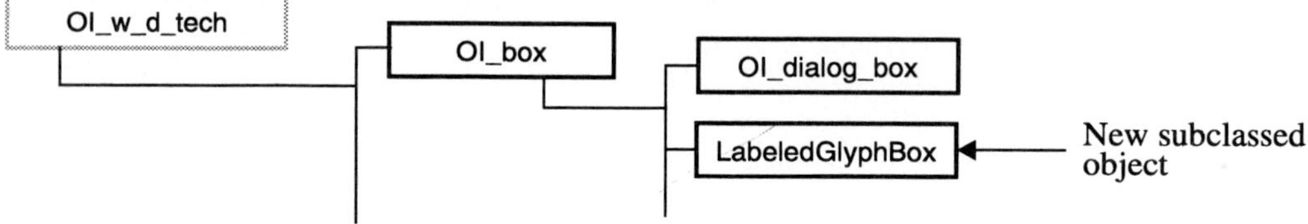

When instantiated, the object looks like this:

Figure 41-4 LabeledGlyphBox

```
                                                   /* LabeledGlyphBox.H */
#ifndef LabeledGlyphBox_H
#define LabeledGlyphBox_H

#ifndef OI_box_H
#include <OI/box.H>
#endif /* OI_box_H */

#ifndef OI_glyph_H
#include <OI/glyph.H>
#endif /* OI_glyph_H */

#ifndef OI_stattxt_H
#include <OI/stattxt.H>
#endif /* OI_stattxt_H */

#define     LabeledGlyphBox_glyph_row       100         /* row for glyph */
#define     LabeledGlyphBox_glyph_column     100         /* column for glyph */
#define     LabeledGlyphBox_label_offset     10          /* offset from glyph */

class LabeledGlyphBox : public OI_box {
 private:
    // Quarks for resources
    static XrmQuark          q_labelPosition;// quark for labelPosition resource
    // Instance data
```

```cpp
public:
    static  OI_class           *clsp;          // pointer to class record
private:
            void               construct(OI_glyph*, const char*);
    static  OI_bool            init(OI_connection *);
    static  LabeledGlyphBox    *make_minimal(const char *, OI_minimal_type);
            void               res_labelPosition(void*);
            void               new_labelPosition(OI_position);
protected:

                               LabeledGlyphBox(OI_class*, const char*, OI_glyph*,
                                       const char*);

public:

                               LabeledGlyphBox(const char*, OI_glyph*,
                                       const char*);
                               ~LabeledGlyphBox( );
    virtual void               clone_adjust(OI_d_tech*);
            OI_glyph           *glyph( );    // get pointer to glyph object
            OI_static_text     *label( );    // get pointer to label object
            OI_position        labelPosition( );
    static  void               reg( );       // register the class
            void               set_labelPosition(OI_position);
};

LabeledGlyphBox *create_LabeledGlyphBox(const char*, OI_glyph*, const char*);

#endif /* LabeledGlyphBox_H */




                                           /* LabeledGlyphBox.C */
#include "LabeledGlyphBox.H"
#include <OI/subclass.H>
#include <OI/lmrc.H>

/* Initializations for static variables of class */

    OI_class    *LabeledGlyphBox::clsp = NULL ;
    XrmQuark    LabeledGlyphBox::q_labelPosition = 0;

LabeledGlyphBox *create_LabeledGlyphBox(
    const   char               *np,          // object name
            OI_glyph           *gp,          // glyph
    const   char               *lp)          // label
{
            LabeledGlyphBox    *p;
```

```
    p = new LabeledGlyphBox(np, gp, lp);
    if (p && (p->error_status( ) < 0)) {
        p->del( );
        p = NULL;
    }
    return(p);
}

void LabeledGlyphBox::reg( )
{
    clsp = OI_register_class("LabeledGlyphBox", "OI_box",
        (OI_class_init_memfnp)&LabeledGlyphBox::init,
        (OI_make_minimal_memfnp)&LabeledGlyphBox::make_minimal);
    return;
}

OI_bool LabeledGlyphBox::init(
        OI_connection        *conp)      // pointer to connection being initialized
{
    static OI_resource        resources[] = {
#define Offset(fld) offsetof(LabeledGlyphBox,fld)
    // Resource which modifies object appearance and therefore needs a res function
        { "labelPosition", "LabelPosition",
        OI_r_OI_position, sizeof(OI_position), 0, 0, 0,
        OI_RESOURCE_MEMFN_CAST(&LabeledGlyphBox::res_labelPosition), NULL,
        OI_RESOURCE_GET_MEMFN_CAST(&LabeledGlyphBox::labelPosition), NULL,
        OI_RM_MDL_ALL },
#undef Offset
        };
        // Constructor template
    staticconstchar        *con_args[] = {
            "OI_class        *clasp        /* final class object */",
            "const char        *namp        /* name for object */",
            "OI_glyph        *gp        /* glyph to use */",
            "const char        *lbl        /* label */"
        };
        OI_bool                        ok ;

    // Do initialization required once
    if (! clsp->class_initialized( )) {
        // Initialize quarks for resource related operations
        q_labelPosition = XrmStringToQuark("labelPosition");
        // register resources, callbacks, and constructor template with class
        clsp->set_resources(&resources[0], OI_count(resources));
        clsp->set_constructor_args(&con_args[0], OI_count(con_args));
    }
    // Now do initialization required for each connection
    // Since there is none, simply mark the object initialized for this connection
    clsp->mark_initialized(conp);
    ok = OI_yes;
    return(ok) ;
}
```

```
        // Constructor used when final object is derived from this class
LabeledGlyphBox::LabeledGlyphBox(
        OI_class            *clasp,      // pointer to class record for final object
    const   char            *np,         // object name
        OI_glyph            *gp,         // pointer to glyph
    const   char            *lp)         // label
        : OI_box(clasp, np, 1, 1)
{
    construct(gp, lp);
}


        // Constructor used when final object is of this class
LabeledGlyphBox::LabeledGlyphBox(
    const   char            *np,         // object name
        OI_glyph            *gp,         // pointer to glyph
    const   char            *lp)         // label
        : OI_box(clsp, np, 1, 1)
{
    construct(gp, lp);
}


void LabeledGlyphBox::construct(
        OI_glyph            *gp,         // Glyph to use
    const   char            *lp)         // Label
{
        OI_static_text      *lblp;       // pointer to label object

    // Establish layout method
    set_layout(OI_layout_row);

    // Mark glyph as internal object which can be modified in interface builder
    gp->set_name("internal_glyph");
    gp->allow_internal_object(OI_yes);
    gp->set_gravity(OI_grav_center);
    gp->layout_associated_object(this, LabeledGlyphBox_glyph_column,
        LabeledGlyphBox_glyph_row, OI_active);
    // Now create the label, if it is not NULL
    if (lp) {
        lblp = oi_create_static_text("internal_label",lp);
        // Mark label as internal object which can be modified in interface builder
        lblp->allow_internal_object(OI_yes);
        lblp->set_gravity(OI_grav_center);
        lblp->layout_associated_object(this, LabeledGlyphBox_glyph_column,
            LabeledGlyphBox_glyph_row + LabeledGlyphBox_label_offset, OI_active);
    }
    return;
}
```

```
LabeledGlyphBox::~LabeledGlyphBox( )
{
    // Since internal glyph and label are marked as internal objects,
    // Normal OI_d_tech destructor will take care of deleting them
    pre_delete( );
}

OI_static_text*LabeledGlyphBox::label( )
             { return((OI_static_text*)subobject("internal_label")); }
OI_glyph*      LabeledGlyphBox::glyph( )
             { return((OI_glyph*)subobject("internal_glyph")); }

LabeledGlyphBox *LabeledGlyphBox::make_minimal(
    const   char            *namp,          // name for object
            OI_minimal_type  t)             // type of minimal object to create
{
            OI_glyph          *gp;           // glyph to use
            LabeledGlyphBox   *p;

    if (gp = OI_glyph::make_minimal("internal_glyph",t)) {
        // Check for minimal object for display in interface builder palette
        if (t == OI_uib_minimal)
            p = create_LabeledGlyphBox(namp, gp, "Label");
        else
            p = create_LabeledGlyphBox(namp, gp, "");
    }
    else
        p = NULL;

    return(p);
}


/*******************************************************************************
 *
 * "labelPosition" resource:
 * res_labelPositionhandle resource fetch
 * set_labelPositionset programatically
 * new_labelPositiongeneric attribute update
 *
 *******************************************************************************
 */
OI_position LabeledGlyphBox::labelPosition( )
{
        OI_position  lbl_psn;              // return value
        OI_d_tech    *lblp;               // pointer to label object
        OI_d_tech    *gp;                 // pointer to glyph object
        OI_lm_row_col*lmp;               // pointer to layout method for this object
        void         *lbl_p1,*lbl_p2;    // geometry parameters for label
        void         *g_p1,*g_p2;        // geometry parameters for glyph
        OI_bool      del_p1,del_p2;      // delete flags from geometry calls
        OI_number    diff;               // glyph row/col position relative to label
```

```
        lbl_psn = OI_default_position;
    if (lblp = label( )) {
        gp = glyph( );
        lmp = (OI_lm_row_col*) layout_method( );
        if (lmp->is_derived_from(OI_lm_row_col::clsp)) {// It better be...
            // Get the row and column position for the label and glyph
            // And determine relative position with glyph
            lmp->geometry(lblp, &lbl_p1, &del_p1, &lbl_p2, &del_p2);
            lmp->geometry(gp, &g_p1, &del_p1, &g_p2, &del_p2);
            diff = (OI_number)(int)g_p2 - (OI_number)(int)lbl_p2;
            if (diff == 0) {
                diff = (OI_number)(int)g_p1 - (OI_number)(int)lbl_p1;
                if (diff < 0)
                                lbl_psn = OT_right;// Glyph to left of label
                else
                                lbl_psn = OI_left;// Glyph to right of label
            }
            else if (diff < 0)
                lbl_psn = OI_bottom;// Glyph above label
            else
                lbl_psn = OI_top;// Glyph below label
        }
    }
    return(lbl_psn);
}


void    LabeledGlyphBox::res_labelPosition(void *ptr)
            { new_labelPosition(*(OI_position *)ptr); }
void    LabeledGlyphBox::set_labelPosition(OI_position upd)
            { set_resourceq(q_labelPosition); new_labelPosition(upd); }

void LabeledGlyphBox::new_labelPosition(
        OI_position         lbl_psn)         // desired label position
{
        OI_number           r,c;             // row and column position for label
        OI_d_tech           *lblp;           // pointer to label

    if (lblp = label( )) {
        suspend_layout( );
        lblp->remove_from_layout( );
        r = LabeledGlyphBox_glyph_row;
        c = LabeledGlyphBox_glyph_column;
        switch(lbl_psn) {
         case(OI_left):
           c -= LabeledGlyphBox_label_offset;
           break;
         case(OI_right):
           c += LabeledGlyphBox_label_offset;
           break;
         case(OI_top):
           r -= LabeledGlyphBox_label_offset;
           break;
         case(OI_bottom):
```

```
            case(OI_default_position):
                r += LabeledGlyphBox_label_offset;
                break;
            }
            lblp->add_to_layout(c,r);
            resume_layout( );
        }
        return;
}


void LabeledGlyphBox::clone_adjust (
            OI_d_tech           *dtp)            // pointer to object to match
{

            LabeledGlyphBox     *objp ;          // object to mimic cast to proper type

        OI_box::clone_adjust(dtp) ;
        if (dtp->is_derived_from(LabeledGlyphBox::clsp)) {
            objp = (LabeledGlyphBox*) dtp ;
            // Don't need to worry about labelPosition because
            // it is encoded in placement resource, already handled
            // Make the glyphs match
            glyph( )->clone_adjust(objp->glyph( ));
            // Make the labels match
            label( )->clone_adjust(objp->label( ));
        }
        return ;
}




                                        /* LabeledGlyphBoxMain.C */
#include "LabeledGlyphBox.H"
#include <OI/glyph.H>
#include <OI/appwin.H>

void OI_reg_derived_classes( )
{
    LabeledGlyphBox::reg( );
}

int main (int argc, char **argv)
{
        OI_connection*conp;
        OI_app_window*wp;
        OI_glyph*gp;
```

```
    LabeledGlyphBox*lgbp;

if (conp = OI_init(&argc,argv,"LabeledGlyphBox")) {
    wp = oi_create_app_window("main",1,1,"LabeledGlyphBox");
    wp->set_layout(OI_layout_column);
    gp = oi_create_glyph("thinker","../bitmaps/thinker.bm");
    lgbp = create_LabeledGlyphBox("my_labeled_glyph",gp,"Thinking!");
    lgbp->layout_associated_object(wp,1,1,OI_active);
    wp->set_associated_object(wp->root( ),OI_def_loc,OI_def_loc,OI_active);
    OI_begin_interaction( );
    OI_fini( );
    }
}
```

Program 41-3   Composite Subclass (LabeledGlyphBox)

41.6.3   VuMeter Example

The example below implements a full subclass for a VuMeter. This may be used as a guide when deriving a new subclass from an intermediate OI base class. The VuMeter has resources controlling the angle covered by the meter and whether or not the bell should ring when it hits its maximum value. In addition, it has new callbacks it can make when the maximum value is reached (pegged), and again when it goes below the maximum (unpegged). The bell behavior may be toggled via a translation. The VuMeter class fits into the OI class hierarchy as shown below.

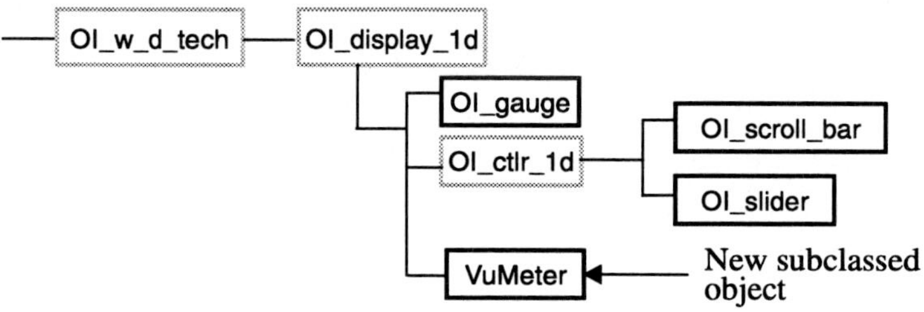

When instantiated, the object looks like this:

Figure 41-5   VuMeter

```
#ifndef VuMeter_H                               /* VuMeter.H */
#define VuMeter_H

#ifndef OI_dpy_1d_H
#include <OI/dpy_1d.H>
#endif /* OI_dpy_1d_H */

#define VuMeter_def_width        100 /* default width */
#define VuMeter_def_height       100 /* default height */
#define VuMeter_def_arc          90  /* default angle spanned by active region */
#define VuMeter_def_n_ticks      5   /* default number of main tick marks */
#define VuMeter_def_minimum      0   /* default minimum value */
#define VuMeter_def_n_mini_tick  4   /* default number of mini tick marks */

class VuMeter : public OI_display_1d {
  private:
```

```
VuMeter *create_VuMeter(
    const   char                *np,            // object name
            long                mx,             // max value
            long                mn,             // min value
            OI_number           w,              // width
            OI_number           h,              // height
            OI_number           nticks,         // number tickmarks on scale
            OI_number           arc)            // arc for scale
{
            VuMeter             *p;

    p = new VuMeter(np, mx, mn, w, h, nticks, arc);
    if (p && (p->error_status( ) < 0)) {
        p->del( );
        p = NULL;
    }
    return(p);
}


void VuMeter::reg( )
{
    clsp = OI_register_class("VuMeter", "OI_display_1d",
        (OI_class_init_memfnp)&VuMeter::init,
        (OI_make_minimal_memfnp)&VuMeter::make_minimal);
    return;
}


OI_bool VuMeter::init(
        OI_connection           *conp)          // pointer to connection being initialized
{
    static OI_resource          resources[] = {
#define Offset(fld) offsetof(VuMeter,fld)
    // Resource which modifies object appearance and therefore needs a res function
            { "arc", "Arc", OI_r_Int, sizeof(int), 0, 0, 0,
                OI_RESOURCE_MEMFN_CAST(&VuMeter::res_arc), NULL,
                OI_RESOURCE_GET_MEMFN_CAST(&VuMeter::arc), NULL,
                OI_RM_MDL_ALL },
    // Resource which does not need a res function
            { "bell", "Bell", OI_r_Boolean, sizeof(OI_bool), Offset(bel),
                0, 0, NULL_PMF, NULL, NULL_PMF, NULL, OI_RM_MDL_ALL },
#undef Offset
        };
            // Binding table for member functions usable as translations
    static OI_actions_rec       stringActions[] = {
            {"toggle_bell", NULL, NULL,
                        (OI_translation_memfnp)&VuMeter::toggle_bell}
        };
            // Default translations
    static char                 *translations = "#override\n\
                        Ctrl            <Key>B:         toggle_bell( )          \n\
            ";
            // Callback definitions
    static OI_cb_def            cb_info[] = {
```

```
                   {"cbPegged", &VuMeter::q_cbPegged, "void", "VuMeter *, void *"},
                   {"cbUnpegged", &VuMeter::q_cbUnpegged, "void", "VuMeter *, void *"}
            };
            // Constructor template
    static const char        *con_args[] = {
            "OI_class        *clasp                        /* final class object */",
            "const char       *namp                         /* name for object */",
            "long             mx                            /* maximum value */",
            "long             mn=VuMeter_def_minimum        /* minimum value */",
            "OI_number        wid=VuMeter_def_width         /* width of meter*/",
            "OI_number        ht=VuMeter_def_height         /* heightof meter*/",
            "OI_number        nt=VuMeter_def_n_ticks        /* number of tick marks */",
            "OI_number        arc=VuMeter_def_arc           /* degrees spanned */"
            };
            OI_bool          ok ;
            VuMeter_cache    *cachep;

    // Do initialization required once
    if (! clsp->class_initialized( )) {
        // Initialize quarks for resource related operations
        q_arc = XrmStringToQuark("arc");
        q_bell = XrmStringToQuark("bell");
        // register resources, callbacks, and constructor template with class
        clsp->set_resources(&resources[0], OI_count(resources));
        clsp->set_callbacks(&cb_info[0], OI_count(cb_info));
        clsp->set_constructor_args(&con_args[0], OI_count(con_args));
        // compile and save translation related data structures
        compiledActions = OI_compile_action_table(stringActions,
            OI_count(stringActions));
        defaultTranslations = OI_parse_translation_table(translations);
        defaultTranslations->set_keep( );
    }
    // Now do initialization required for each connection
    if (cachep = (VuMeter_cache*) malloc(sizeof(VuMeter_cache))) {
//      cachep-> = ;
        clsp->mark_initialized(conp, cachep);
        ok = OI_yes;
    }
    else
        ok = OI_no;
    return(ok) ;
}


        // Constructor used when final object is derived from this class
VuMeter::VuMeter(
            OI_class         *clasp,
    const   char             *namp,
            long             mx,
            long             mn,
            OI_number        width,
            OI_number        height,
            OI_number        nticks,
            OI_number        arc)
```

```
            : OI_display_1d(clasp, namp, mx, mn, NULL, OI_display_1d_ends_none,
                NULL, NULL, OI_display_1d_current_none,
                nticks, OI_display_1d_ticks_all, NULL )
{
    construct(width, height, arc);
}


        // Constructor used when final object is of this class
VuMeter::VuMeter(
    const   char                *namp,
            long                mx,
            long                mn,
            OI_number           width,
            OI_number           height,
            OI_number           nticks,
            OI_number           arc)
            : OI_display_1d(clsp, namp, mx, mn, NULL, OI_display_1d_ends_none,
                NULL, NULL, OI_display_1d_current_none,
                nticks, OI_display_1d_ticks_all, NULL )
{
    construct(width, height, arc);
}

void VuMeter::construct(
            OI_number           width,
            OI_number           height,
            OI_number           arc )
{
    if (error_status( ) >= 0) {
        // save nominal size so we can return it
        nom_x = width;
        nom_y = height;
        set_abs_size(width,height);
        n_mini_tick = VuMeter_def_n_mini_tick;
        new_arc(arc);
        set_resize(this, (OI_resize_memfnp)&VuMeter::re_layout);

        // Now put the default translations on the object
        if (compiledActions)
            push_compiled_actions(compiledActions);
        if (defaultTranslations)
            override_translations(defaultTranslations);
    }
    return;
}


VuMeter::~VuMeter( )
{
    pre_delete( );
}
```

```
VuMeter *VuMeter::make_minimal(
    const   char                *namp,          // name for object
            OI_minimal_type     t)              // type of minimal object to create
{
            VuMeter             *p;

    // Check for minimal object for display in interface builder palette
    if (t == OI_uib_minimal)
        p = create_VuMeter(namp, 10);
    else
        p = create_VuMeter(namp, 10);

    return(p);
}

/********************************************************************
 *
 * "arc" resource:
 * res_arc      handle resource fetch
 * set_arc      set programatically
 * new_arc      generic attribute update
 *
 ********************************************************************
 */
void    VuMeter::res_arc(void *ptr){ new_arc(*(int *)ptr); }
void    VuMeter::set_arc(int upd){ set_resourceq(q_arc); new_arc(upd); }

void
VuMeter::new_arc(
            int                 upd)
{
    ndeg = upd;
    re_layout( );
    if (is_visible( ))
        repaint( );
    return;
}

/********************************************************************
 *
 * "bell" resource:
 * set_bell                 set programatically
 *
 ********************************************************************
 */
void    VuMeter::set_bell(OI_bool b)
                                { set_resourceq(q_bell); bel=b; }
void    VuMeter::toggle_bell(OI_d_tech*, const XEvent*, const char *const*,
            unsigned int*)
                                { bel = bel ? OI_no : OI_yes; }
```

```
OI_stat VuMeter::create( )
{
            OI_stat               st;            // return status

    if (!x_window_id( )) {
        st = OI_display_1d::create( );
        if (st == OI_OK) {
            conp->dispatch_insert(x_window_id( ), Expose, ExposureMask,
                this, (OI_event_memfnp)&VuMeter::paint);
        }
    }
    else
        st = OI_win_exists ;
    return(st) ;
}

void VuMeter::calculate_constants( )
{
    inner_rad = diameter( ) / 3.;
    nradians = (ndeg/180.) * pi;
    start = (3.*pi - radians_spanned( )) / 2.;
    delta = radians_spanned( ) / (num_ticks( ) - 1);
    ox = oy = 0;
    return;
}

void VuMeter::re_layout( )
{
    dia = (size_x( ) < size_y( )) ? size_x( ) : size_y( );
    xo = 0;
    yo = 0;
    if (size_x( ) > diameter( ))
        xo = (size_x( ) - diameter( ))/2;
    if (size_y( ) > diameter( ))
        yo = (size_y( ) - diameter( ))/2;
    xo += diameter( )/2;
    yo += (2 * diameter( ))/3;
    calculate_constants( );
    return;
}

void VuMeter::paint(
    const   XEvent          *,        // pointer to X expose event for region to paint
            void            *)        // unused
{
    set_gc( );                // make default gc consistent with this object's fg and bg
    paint_ticks( );
    paint_tick_labels( );
    paint_value(value( ));
    return;
}

void VuMeter::paint_current( ){ }
```

```
void VuMeter::paint_value(
        long            val)
{
        int             x1, y1 ;
        double          rad ;
        double          angle ;
        GC              gc;         // Graphics Context with which to draw
        Display         *dpy;       // X display on which to draw
        OI_cb_inf       *cbp;       // pointer to callback to execute if pegged

    if (is_visible( )) {
        set_gc( );

        gc = connection( )->gc( );// optimizations and convenience
        dpy = connection( )->display( );

        // if old value was present, wipe out the needle
        // by redrawing it using the background color
        if (ox || oy) {
            set_gc(bkg_pixel( ));
            XDrawLine(dpy, x_window_id( ), gc, xo, yo, ox, oy );
        }

        // Restore foreground color for new paint
        set_gc(fg_pixel( ));

        angle = start_angle( ) + radians_spanned( ) *
            (val - minimum( )) / (maximum( ) - minimum( )) ;
        rad = (5./6.)*inner_radius( ) ;
        x1 = (int) rint(rad*cos(angle));
        y1 = (int) rint(rad*sin(angle));
        ox = x1 + xo;
        oy = y1 + yo;

        XDrawLine(dpy, x_window_id( ), gc, xo, yo, ox, oy );
    }
    // Now check to see if needle is pegged
    // If so, make pegged callback
    if (value( ) == maximum( )) {
        if (last_draw_val != maximum( )) {
            if (callbacks_lock(q_cbPegged)) {
                for (cbp = NULL ; cbp = callback_get(q_cbPegged,cbp) ; )
                        cbp->callback(this);
                callbacks_unlock(q_cbPegged);
            }
            if (is_bell( ))
                XBell(display( ),0);
        }
    }
    // or unpegged
    else if (last_draw_val == maximum( )) {
        if (value( ) != maximum( )) {
```

```
            if (callbacks_lock(q_cbUnpegged)) {
                for (cbp = NULL ; cbp = callback_get(q_cbUnpegged,cbp) ; )
                            cbp->callback(this);
                callbacks_unlock(q_cbUnpegged);
            }
        }
    }
    last_draw_val = value( );
    return;
}

void VuMeter::paint_ticks( )
{
        Display             *dpy;           // X display on which to draw
        GC                  gc;             // Graphics Context with which to draw
        int                 i,j;
        double              ticklen;        // length of tick mark
        double              cs;             // cos( start_angle( ) );
        double              sn;             // sin( start_angle( ) );
        double              angle;          // current angle being computed
        int                 x1, y1;
        int                 x2, y2;
        double              mini_angle;     // angle between mini ticks

/*
 *      num_ticks( ) returns the number of major ticks
 *      in addition to those, we need to put the miniTicks between the major ticks
 */

    gc = connection( )->gc( );
    dpy = connection( )->display( );

    angle = start_angle( );
    for (i = 0 ; i < num_ticks( ) ; i++) {
        // Compute tick length of big ticks as 1/12th the diameter
        // Only every n_mini_tick tick mark is full length
        // the rest are half length
        ticklen = diameter( )/12.;

        ticklen += inner_radius( );
        cs = cos(angle);
        sn = sin(angle);

        x1 = (int) rint( inner_radius( )*cs );
        y1 = (int) rint( inner_radius( )*sn );
        x2 = (int) rint( ticklen*cs );
        y2 = (int) rint( ticklen*sn );

        XDrawLine(dpy, x_window_id( ), gc, x1+xo, y1+yo, x2+xo, y2+yo );
        // Now paint mini ticks between labeled ticks for all but last one
        if (i < num_ticks( ) - 1) {
            for (j = 1 ; j <= VuMeter_def_n_mini_tick ; j++) {
                mini_angle = angle + j * (angle_between_ticks( ) /
```

```
                                   (VuMeter_def_n_mini_tick + 1)) ;
                ticklen = diameter( )/24.;
                ticklen += inner_radius( );
                cs = cos(mini_angle);
                sn = sin(mini_angle);
                x1 = (int) rint( inner_radius( )*cs );
                y1 = (int) rint( inner_radius( )*sn );
                x2 = (int) rint( ticklen*cs );
                y2 = (int) rint( ticklen*sn );
                XDrawLine(dpy, x_window_id( ), gc, x1+xo, y1+yo, x2+xo, y2+yo );
            }
        }
        angle += angle_between_ticks( );
    }
}


void VuMeter::paint_tick_labels( )
{
        int                     i;              // tick loop counter
        OI_number               x, y;           // position of painting
        OI_number               fh ;            // font height
        OI_number               fyb ;           // font y base
        OI_display_1d_tickslt ;                 // type of tick labeling
        OI_string               *tick_lblp ;    // label to paint on tick mark
        double                  tk ;            // where the tick ends
        double                  angle ;         // current angle being computed
        double                  cs, sn ;        // cos and sin of this angle

    lt = tick_type( ) ;
    tk = 11./24. * diameter( );
    angle = start_angle( );
    for (i = 0 ; i < num_ticks( ) ; i++) {

        if ((lt == OI_display_1d_ticks_ends) ||
            (lt == OI_display_1d_ticks_ends_custom)) {
            if (i == 0)
                tick_lblp = ply_tick_label(0) ;
            else if (i == (num_ticks( )-1))
                tick_lblp = ply_tick_label(1) ;
            else
                tick_lblp = NULL;
        }
        else
            tick_lblp = ply_tick_label(i) ;
        if (tick_lblp) {
            cs = cos( angle );
            sn = sin( angle );
            fh = tick_lblp->font_height( );
            fyb = tick_lblp->font_y_base( );
            /*
             * find x and y on the circle bounding the largest
             * tick marks. and then angularly shift the text
             * outwards so that the text sits outside.
```

```
        */
        x = ((int) rint( (tk * cs) + (tick_lblp->width( )*(cs - 1)/2) ));
        y = ((int) rint( (tk * sn) - ((fh - fyb)*sn/2) ));
        tick_lblp->draw_image_text( this, x + xo, y + yo );
    }
    angle += angle_between_ticks( );
    }
    return ;
}


void VuMeter::clone_adjust (
        OI_d_tech            *dtp)           // pointer to object to match
{
        VuMeter              *objp ;         // object to mimic cast to proper type

    OI_display_1d::clone_adjust(dtp) ;
    if (dtp->is_derived_from(VuMeter::clsp)) {
        objp = (VuMeter*) dtp ;
        if (is_bell( ) != objp->is_bell( ))
            toggle_bell(this,NULL,NULL,NULL);
        if (arc( ) != objp->arc( ))
            new_arc(objp->arc( ));
    }
    return ;
}


OI_stat VuMeter::set_size (
        OI_number            w,              // desired width
        OI_number            h)              // desired height
{
        OI_number            nx,ny;          // original nominal values
        OI_stat              st;             // return value

    // Save original nominal values in case of failure
    nx = nom_x;
    ny = nom_y;

    // Set new nominal size
    // Must be done before calling base class set_size in case
    // geometry management gets involved;
    // our nominal_outside_size and min_outside_size must work with the new values
    nom_x = w;
    nom_y = h;

    st = OI_display_1d::set_size(w,h);

    // If failure, restore original values
    if (st < 0) {
        nom_x = nx;
        nom_y = ny;
    }
    return(st);
}
```

```
void VuMeter::nominal_outside_size (
        OI_number            *widp,        // (output) backfilled with nominal size
        OI_number            *htp)         // (output) backfilled with nominal size
{
        OI_number            fw ;          // border width offset, 2 * border width

    // Since this object is not designed to have children laid out in it,
    // Just compute the absolute nominal size
    // Don't forget to include border width -- nominal *outside* size
    fw = 2 * bdr_width( ) ;
    *widp = nom_x + fw ;
    *htp = nom_y + fw ;
    return ;
}




                                            /* VuMeterMain.C */
#include <OI/appwin.H>
#include <OI/slider.H>
#include "VuMeter.H"

void
OI_reg_derived_classes( )
{
    VuMeter::reg( );
}

void
main (int argc, char **argv)
{
 /* External Procedures */
       void    chg_value(OI_ctlr_1d*,void*,OI_scroll_event,long);
       void    pegged(VuMeter*,void*);
       void    unpegged(VuMeter*,void*);
 /* Local Variables */
    const  long             mx = 500;
    const  long             mn = 100;
    const  OI_number        n_maj_ticks = 5;
    const  OI_number        wid = 100;
    const  OI_number        ht = 100;
    const  OI_number        arc = 90;

       OI_app_window        *wp;
       VuMeter              *vum;
       OI_slider            *ctlrp;

    if (OI_init(&argc,argv,"OITest")) {
        wp = oi_create_app_window("main",1,1,"VuMeter");
        wp->set_layout(OI_layout_row);
```

```
        vum = create_VuMeter("vumeter", mx, mn, wid, ht, n_maj_ticks, arc);
        vum->set_size_track( OI_size_track_full );
        vum->layout_associated_object(wp, 10, 100, OI_active);
        vum->callback_add("cbPegged",(OI_fnp)pegged);
        vum->callback_add("cbUnpegged",(OI_fnp)unpegged,(void*)vum->bkg_pixel( ));

        ctlrp = oi_create_slider("ctlr",200,OI_horizontal mx,mn,chg_value,vum,
            "Value:",OI_slider_ends_none,NULL,NULL,OI_slider_current_none,
            n_maj_ticks, OI_slider_ticks_all);
        ctlrp->layout_associated_object(wp, 10, 10, OI_active);

        wp->set_associated_object(wp->root( ), OI_def_loc, OI_def_loc, OI_active);
        OI_begin_interaction( );
        OI_fini( );
    }
}

void chg_value(OI_ctlr_1d *ctlrp, void *argp, OI_scroll_event, long)
{
        VuMeter*vump;

    vump = (VuMeter*) argp;
    vump->set_value(ctlrp->handle_loc( ));
    return;
}

void pegged(VuMeter *vump, void*)
{
    vump->set_bkg_color("red");
    return;
}

void unpegged(VuMeter *vump, void *argp)
{
    vump->set_bkg_color((PIXEL)argp);
    return;
}
```

Program 41-4 Subclass Requiring Drawing (VuMeter)

Chapter 42
OI_class

OI_class Functions

OI_class Member Functions

OI_class

42.1 Description

OI maintains a registry of classes. This registry allows one to determine all known classes and the class hierarchy. The class registry contains objects of type OI_class. An object of type OI_class stores information common to all objects of a particular class, such as resource names and types, and data used to paint the objects on a particular connection.

While the class registry is used primarily to store the class hierarchy for the displayable objects (classes derived from OI_d_tech), it may in fact be used to store information about any class hierarchy. For example, it is also used to store the hierarchy of layout methods.

42.1.1 Registering a Class

A class is registered by calling OI_register_class, which returns a pointer to the OI_class object for the class just registered.

OI_register_class   (Free-standing function)

```
OI_class *OI_register_class(
    const char            *cls_nam,    // class name to register
    const char            *bas_cls,    // base class name
    OI_class_init_memfnp   init_cls,   // member function to initialize the class
    OI_make_minimal_memfnp mk_min)     // member function to make a minimal object
```

cls_nam is the name of the class; *bas_cls* is the name of its immediate base class. If this is a root class (one with no base class), *bas_cls* may be NULL. You will never have this situation unless you are using OI_register_class to register your own hierarchy of classes which is independent of all OI hierarchies.

init_cls is a pointer to an initialization function for the class; this function is used automatically only for objects derived from OI_d_tech. The function must be a static member function. It is called once before an object of the class is instantiated on a particular connection, and allows the class object to create and cache information needed by all objects of the class on that connection. It is discussed in Chapter 41, "Deriving Your Own Classes."

mk_min is a pointer to a function which will create a "minimal" instance of the class. The function must be a static member function. If the class allows no particular customization, as do the layout methods, this function merely creates a normal member of the class. For displayable OI objects (those derived from OI_d_tech), a minimal instance is one which will be further enhanced by resources to arrive at the "final" object.

42.1.2 Class Initialization

A class may require some initialization before it is ever instantiated. This involves calling the class initialization function (the *init_cls* argument passed to OI_register_class). The member functions described below may be used to determine the initialization state and to save data specific to a particular connection. For an example of a class initialization function, see any of the examples at the end of Chapter 41, "Deriving Your Own Classes."

class_initialized (Member function)

```
OI_bool OI_class::class_initialized( )
```

class_initialized returns OI_yes if this class has ever been initialized; otherwise it returns OI_no.

The initialization function for a class (the *init_cls* argument passed to OI_register_class) is responsible for informing the object that initialization has been done using the OI_class member function mark_initialized.

mark_initialized (Member function)

```
void OI_class::mark_initialized(
    OI_connection     *conp,            // pointer to connection
    void              *cachep=NULL)     // pointer to arbitrary data
```

For each connection, you can save connection-specific class data (such as bitmaps or cursors needed specifically for that connection). This data is saved when you call mark_initialized, and can be retrieved using the OI_class member function class_dependent.

mark_initialized marks the class as initialized for connection *conp*. You can use *cachep* to point to any connection-specific data for your class.

By convention, if you are initializing a class *MyClass*, the class dependent data cache is a class of type *MyClass_cache*.

class_dependent (Member function)

```
void *OI_class::class_dependent(
    OI_connection     *conp)            // pointer to connection
```

class_dependent returns a pointer to the data you specified in *cachep* in the function mark_initialized.

42.1.3   Registering resources for a class

A class object stores a list of valid resources for the class. These are set and examined using the member functions described below. Resources are normally set as part of the class initialization process. See Section 41.3.3, "Initializing the Class," on page 41-11.

set_resources (Member function)

```
void OI_class::set_resources(
    OI_resource        *rsrc,          // vector of resources to register
    OI_number          len)            // number of resources in rsrc
```

set_resources stores definitions of resources for the class. It does not put any resources in any resource database, although the resource definitions can include a default value. The structure **OI_resource** is defined in Chapter 39, "The OI Resource Mechanism."

set_resources does not make a copy of the resource structures passed; it simply saves a pointer to them.

resources (Member function)

```
OI_resource *OI_class::resources( )
```

resources returns a pointer to the vector of resources stored by **set_resources**. These are the resources specific to the class, but do not include resource definitions for any base classes.

num_resources (Member function)

```
OI_number OI_class::num_resources( )
```

num_resources returns the number of resources set by **set_resources**. This is the number of resources specific to the class, and does not include resources for any base classes.

resource_definition (Member function)

```
OI_resource *OI_class::resource_definition(
    const char         *res)           // name of desired resource
```

```
OI_resource *OI_class::resource_definition(
    XrmQuark           *resq)          // quark corresponding to name of desired
                                       //   resource
```

These member functions return the resource definition corresponding to *res*. *res* may be either the instance name or the class name for the resource. These member functions search the class and all its ancestors to find a possible resource definition.

42.1.4   Registering Callbacks for a Class

A class object stores a list of valid callbacks for the class. These are set using the member function described below. The only callbacks set should be those for the particular class, and should not include those implemented in base classes. Callbacks are normally set as part of the class initialization process. See Section 41.3.3, "Initializing the Class," on page 41-11.

set_callbacks   (Member function)

```
void OI_class::set_callbacks(
    OI_cb_def           *cb_defp,          // vector of callback definitions
    OI_number           n_cb)             // number of callback definitions in
                                          cb_defp
```

OI_cb_def is a data structure used to define the mapping of a name to a particular callback type, and to define the interface to the callback.

```
struct OI_cb_def        {
    const char      *nam;        // callback name, traditionally of form "cbMyCallbackName"
    XrmQuark        *quarkp;     // pointer to place to store nam converted to quark; may be NULL
    const char      *ret_val;   // pointer to return value type as string
    const char      *args;      // pointer to callback argument strings, no parens, with commas:
                                "OI_d_tech*, void*,..."
};
```

If specified, *quarkp* will be backfilled with the XrmQuark corresponding to *nam*.

42.1.5   Registering the Constructor for a Class

A class object stores a synopsis of the constructor for the class. It is set using the member function described below. The constructor is normally registered during the class initialization process. See Section 41.3.3, "Initializing the Class," on page 41-11.

set_constructor_args   (Member function)

```
void OI_class::set_constructor_args(
    const char * const *argv,      // ptr to vector of character strings defining arg types
    OI_number           n_arg)     // number of arguments
```

n_arg specifies the number of arguments to the constructor, and *argv* is a vector of strings for argument declarations. The strings should contain as a minimum the argument type, but may also contain a dummy argument name and comment. If present, the comment should be bracketed by "/*" and "*/", rather than using "//", so that arguments may be inserted on the same line if an application is using the information to generate code. When OI subclasses are registered, the first argument should always be of type **OI_class***, as discussed in section 41.3.4, "Providing a Primary and Secondary Constructor," on page 41-15.

42.1.6   Determining Class Relationships

Because the class registry records the class hierarchy, it may be used to determine the relationship between classes and to enumerate all known classes. The functions and member functions described below may be used for this purpose.

The class registry is maintained as a binary tree, with each node in the tree having at most one sibling and at most one descendant. Since different types of classes may be registered, you usually start at a known node by using **OI_class_object** to find the starting node. Program 42-1 on page 42-7 shows how to walk the class tree starting at a particular node. The class tree may be visualized as follows:

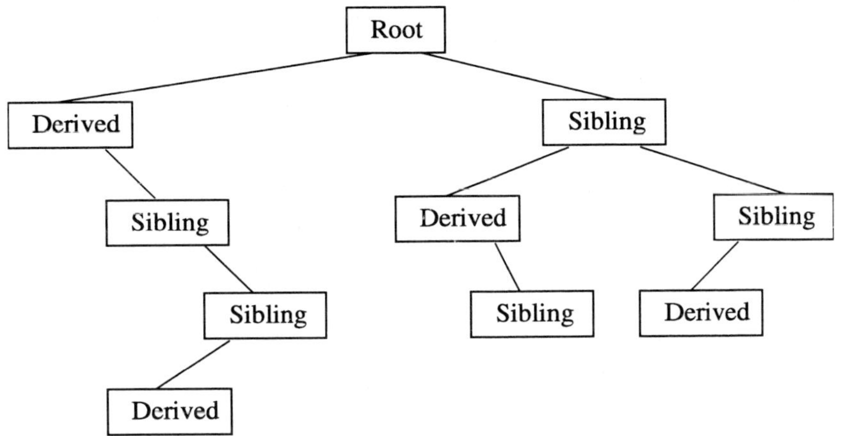

OI_class_tree   (Free-standing function)

```
OI_class *OI_class_tree( )
```

OI_class_tree returns a pointer to the first class in the class registry.

OI_class_object   (Free-standing function)

```
OI_class *OI_class_object(
    const char          *cls_nam)       // name of desired class


OI_class *OI_class_object(
    XrmQuark            *cls_namq)       // Quark corresponding to name of desired class
```

OI_class_object return a pointer to the class object for a particular class, if one exists.

next   (Member function)

```
OI_class *OI_class::next(
    OI_class            *cur_clsp)       // ptr to current class
```

next returns a pointer to the class following *cur_clsp* in the class registry. **next** will return NULL when *cur_clsp* is the last class in the registry. Since **next** traverses to the next node in the registry, regardless of whether the current node is a leaf or not, its best use is to traverse the entire tree from beginning to end.

derived   (Member function)

```
OI_class *OI_class::derived( )
```

derived returns a pointer to the class object for the first class derived from the current class. It returns NULL if no class is registered which is derived from the current class.

sibling   (Member function)

```
OI_class *OI_class::sibling( )
```

sibling returns a pointer to the immediate sibling for the current class. It returns zero if none exist.

ancestor   (Member function)

```
OI_class *OI_class::ancestor( )
```

ancestor returns a pointer to the class which is the immediate base class of the current class. It returns NULL if the current class has no base class in the class registry.

is_createable   (Member function)

```
OI_bool OI_class::is_createable( )
```

The class tree contains nodes corresponding to classes which may never be instantiated, as well as nodes for classes which may be instantiated. **is_createable** returns **OI_yes** if the class may be instantiated, and **OI_no** otherwise. The determination of whether a class may be instantiated or not is based on whether or not a make_minimal function was specified when the class was registered.

is_derived_from   (Member function)

```
OI_bool OI_class::is_derived_from(
    OI_class            *bas_clsp)          // ptr to potential base class
```

is_derived_from returns **OI_yes** if the current class is derived from class *bas_clsp*, directly or indirectly, or if *bas_clsp* is the current class. Otherwise, it returns **OI_no**.

name   (Member function)

```
const char *OI_class::name( )
```

name returns the character string corresponding to the class name, as specified when the class was registered.

```c
                                        /* WalkTree.C */
#include <OI/defs.H>
#include <OI/functs.H>
#include <OI/globals.H>
#include <OI/class.H>
#include <stdio.h>

main(
        int             argc,           // # args
        char            **argv)         // arg is class at which to start
{
 /* External Procedures: */
        void            walk_tree(OI_class*,OI_bool);
 /* Local Variables: */
        OI_class        *clsp;          // ptr to root class

    if (OI_init(&argc,argv,"WalkTree")) {
        // If no args present, walk entire tree
        if (argc <= 1)
            walk_tree(OI_class_tree( ) ,OI_no);
        // Otherwise, start at the class specified
        else {
            argv++;
            if (clsp = OI_class_object(*argv))
                walk_tree(clsp, OI_yes);
            else
                fprintf(stderr, "Class %s not registered\n", *argv);
        }
    }
}

void walk_tree(
        OI_class        *clsp,          // ptr to class at which to start
        OI_bool         is_root)        // OI_yes => don't traverse siblings
{
/* Local Variables: */
        OI_class        *p;
    static OI_number    indent = 0;     // indentation level
        OI_number       i;              // workspace

    indent++;
    for (p=clsp; p ; p=p->sibling( )) {
        for (i=0 ; i < indent ; i++)
            printf(" ");
        printf("%s\n",p->name( ));
        walk_tree(p->derived( ), OI_no);
        if (is_root)
            break;
    }
    indent--;
    return;
}
```

Program 42-1   Walk the Class Tree (WalkTree.C)

Chapter 43
OI_cb_inf

OI_cb_inf Member Functions

OI_cb_inf

43.1 Description

OI_cb_inf is the class used to store callback information. The OI_d_tech member function callback_get returns an object of this class. The member functions documented in the sections which follow may be used to retrieve information from this class, and to implement your own callbacks when subclassing.

43.2 Examining and Changing the Callback

The member functions described below allow you to examine a callback and change it.

type   (Member function)

```
XrmQuark OI_cb_inf::type( )
```

type returns the quark corresponding to the callback type. This is the quark corresponding to the callback name when it was registered during class initialization, and will be one of the values specified in Table 6-7, "Automatically Supplied Callback Types," on page 6-118 for the supplied classes.

argp   (Member function)

```
void *OI_cb_inf::argp( )
```

argp returns the user argument which will be passed as the second argument when the callback is invoked.

fnp   (Member function)

```
OI_fnp OI_cb_inf::fnp( )
```

fnp returns a pointer to the function which will be called when the callback is made. If the callback is set to call a member function on behalf of an object, this will return NULL.

objp   (Member function)

```
OI_callback *OI_cb_inf::objp( )
```

objp returns a pointer to the object on whose behalf the callback will be invoked if the callback is set to call a member function.

memfnp   (Member function)

```
OI_memfnp OI_cb_inf::memfnp( )
```

memfnp returns a pointer to the member function which will be called when the callback is made. If the callback is set to call a stand-alone function, this will return NULL.

---

set_argp (Member function)

```
void OI_cb_inf::set_argp(
   void                    *ap)          // arg to pass to callback
```

set_argp changes the argument which will be passed as the second parameter when the callback is made.

set_obj (Member function)

```
void OI_cb_inf::set_obj(
   OI_callback             *op)          // object for memfnp
```

set_obj changes the object on behalf of which the member function will be called when the callback is made.

set_fnp (Member function)

```
void OI_cb_inf::set_fnp(
   OI_fnp                  fnp)          // function to call
```

set_fnp changes the function which will be called when the callback is made. Setting *fnp* will force *objp* and *memfnp* to NULL.

set_memfnp (Member function)

```
void OI_cb_inf::set_memfnp(
   OI_memfnp               mfp)          // member function to call
```

set_memfnp changes the member function which will be called when the callback is made. Setting *mfp* will force *fnp* to NULL.

set_cb (Member function)

```
void OI_cb_inf::set_cb(
   OI_fnp                  fnp,          // function to call
   void                    *ap=NULL)     // argument to pass to fnp

void OI_cb_inf::set_cb(
   OI_callback             *op,          // object for mfp
   OI_memfnp               mfp,          // function to call
   void                    *ap=NULL)     // argument to pass to mfp
```

set_cb is a short form for calling **set_fnp** and **set_argp**, or **set_objp**, **set_memfnp**, and **set_argp**.

43.3 Performing a Callback

OI_cb_inf contains numerous overloaded forms of the member functions described in this section. You should examine the **cb_inf.H** header file to see which ones will suit your purposes. When actually making a callback from within a subclass, the callbacks must be locked and unlocked. See Section 41.4, "Implementing Callbacks," for how to do this.

callback   (Member function)

```
void OI_cb_inf::callback(
    void                    *p)          // first arg to callback
```

callback performs a callback to the function or member function contained in the OI_cb_inf object. The first parameter (*p*) is passed on to the callback as the first parameter. *argp* is inserted as the second parameter. The second through nth parameters, if present, are passed to the callback as the third through n+1st parameter.

check_callback   (Member function)

```
int OI_cb_inf::check_callback(
    void                    *p)          // first arg to callback
```

check_callback performs a callback to the function or member function contained in the OI_cb_inf object. The first parameter (*p*) is passed on to the callback as the first parameter. *argp* is inserted as the second parameter. The second through nth parameters, if present, are passed to the callback as the third through n+1st parameter.

The callback is assumed to return an int, which is returned as the value of the **check_callback** function.

Chapter 44

OI_layout_method and Its Subclasses

OI_layout_method and Its Subclasses

44.1 Description

An OI_layout_method object manages the layout of objects displayed using the OI automatic layout facility. The automatic layout facility is described in Section 6.3.2, "Using Automatic Layout," on pages 6-3 through 6-25. An OI_layout_method object is created when you call the OI_d_tech member function set_layout for the container (parent) object. The exact type of the object is determined by the first argument to set_layout, and is one of OI_layout_method's subclasses (see the class tree, below). The base class of all layout methods is OI_layout_method. For historical reasons, the class names for its subclassed layout methods differ from the name used in the set_layout call. set_layout takes an argument of type OI_layout. OI_layout is a pointer to an object of type OI_class and can be thought of as a convenience name for the class pointer. Table 44-1 shows the convenience names (used in set_layout) and the equivalent layout class pointers.

If you include the specific layout method header files in your source, you can use the class pointer as the first argument in the set_layout call instead of the convenience name. For example:

```
OI_app_window          *wp;
wp->set_layout(OI_lm_row::clsp);
```

Table 44-1 Layout Method Names

Convenience Name	Class Pointer
OI_layout_none	n/a
OI_layout_row	OI_lm_row::clsp
OI_layout_row_aligned	OI_lm_row_aligned::clsp
OI_layout_column	OI_lm_column::clsp
OI_layout_row_column	OI_lm_row_column::clsp
OI_layout_titled_row_column	OI_lm_titled_row_column::clsp
OI_layout_row_column_aligned	OI_lm_row_column_aligned::clsp
OI_layout_wrapped_row	OI_lm_wrapped_row::clsp
OI_layout_wrapped_column	OI_lm_wrapped_column::clsp
OI_layout_horz_tree	OI_lm_horz_tree::clsp
OI_layout_vert_tree	OI_lm_vert_tree::clsp

The OI layout methods have proven general enough to fill most needs. However, if they are not sufficient for your needs, you can create your own layout method by subclassing from one of the OI layout classes (see Section 44.4, "Designing Your Own Layout Method," on page 44-22).

44.2 Class Tree

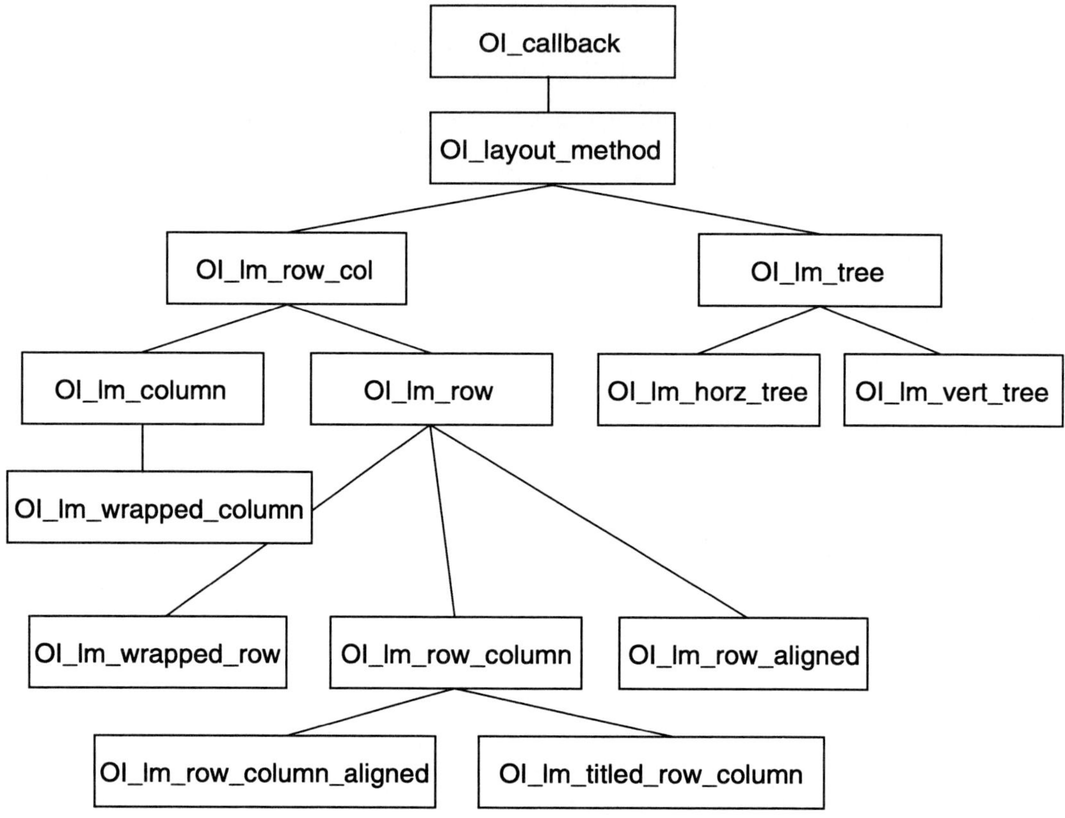

44.3 Using OI Layout Methods

See Section 6.3.2, "Using Automatic Layout," on page 6-3 for a description of the basics of using the OI automatic layout facility. In this section, we discuss in more detail layout spacing and describe the layout member functions you may need when writing your application using the OI layout methods.

44.3.1 Intricacies of Layout Spacing

Although Section 6.3.2, "Using Automatic Layout," explains the basics of the layout facility, you may need more details on the spacing and other details of the mechanism. The following sections describe these.

44.3.1.1 Row-major and Column-major Layout Spacing

See Section 6.3.2.3, "Ordering Objects Within a Row, Column, or Grid Layout," on page 6-7 for a description of the basics of ordering in these types of layouts. This section discusses the spacing in row- or column-major layouts.

The discussion below illustrates the spacing in a row-major layout. Column-major objects are laid out in a similar manner, reversing the roles of rows and columns and north/south and east/west gravity components. A row-column (or *grid)*, layout treats spacing somewhat differently; see Section 44.3.1.2, "Row-Column (Grid) Layout Spacing," on page 44-7.

Table 44-2 shows the row and column numbers for objects laid out in a row-major layout. Each object is a box containing static text; all boxes are the same height. They all have the default gravity, OI_grav_northwest. The application's layout is shown in Figure 44-1.

Table 44-2 Objects Laid Out In Two Rows in a Row-Major Layout

Object	Column Position	Row Position	Gravity
Begin	10	10	northwest
Middle	20	10	northwest
End	30	10	northwest
Dog	6	20	northwest
Mountain Lion	10	20	northwest
Bird	17	20	northwest
Horse	20	20	northwest

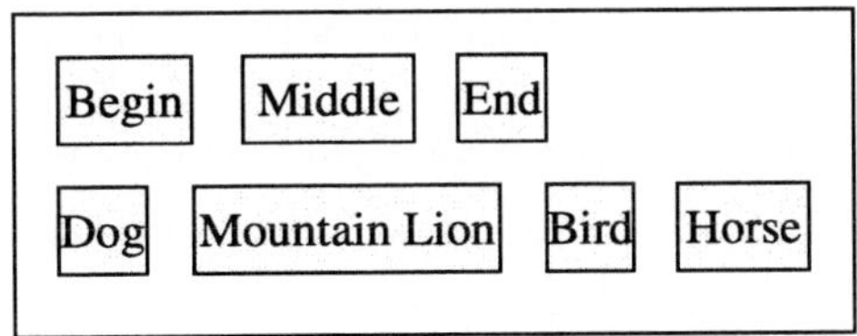

Figure 44-1 Layout for Objects in Table 44-2

Notice that in Figure 44-1 there is no vertical correspondence between the position of the object in column 20 in row 20 ("Horse") and the one in column 20 in row 10 ("Middle"). The column numbers have relevance only within their own rows. (The situation is analogous for row numbers in a column-major layout.) Also notice that there are holes in the numbering sequences, and the column numbers are not evenly spaced.

There is extra space in the first row (row 10) of the layout, since the second row is longer. Since all of the objects have default gravity, they migrate to the northwest (upper left). If the gravity for "End" were set to east (OI_grav_east), the objects would appear as shown in Figure 44-2.

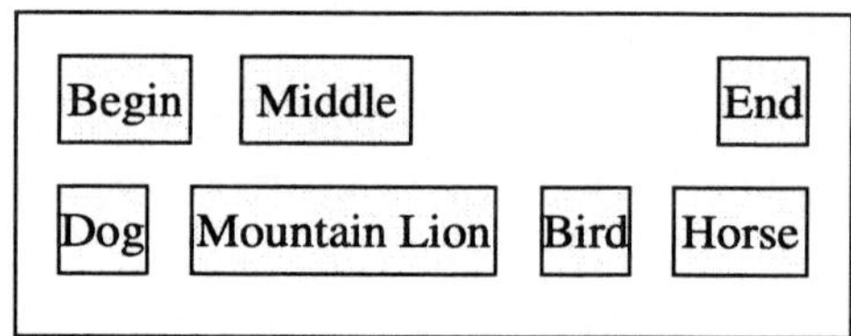

Figure 44-2   Layout for Objects in Table 44-2 if "End" Has East Gravity

The exact spacing between objects which are packed together ("Begin" and "Middle" in row 10 in Figure 44-2) is determined by the objects' total space. Laid out objects have spacing attributes that non-laid out objects do not have; these values are returned by the OI_d_tech member functions top_space, bottom_space, left_space, and right_space. The member function all_space_x returns the total horizontal space occupied by an object, which is the sum of the values returned by left_space, space_x, and right_space. Similarly, the member function all_space_y returns the vertical space, which is the sum of the values returned by top_space, space_y, and bottom_space. You normally need not deal with these attributes, since setting the default spacing using set_layout is usually more convenient. However, you can explicitly set the spacing attributes for any object before it is laid out in its parent by using the functions set_space and set_*_space.

The spacing between two objects packed together is the sum of their complementary spacing components. In the case of "Begin" and "Middle" in Figure 44-2, the space between them would be the sum of the right_space for "Begin" and the left_space for "Middle". The default spacing you specify in set_layout is the total space between two objects. The layout mechanism modifies the space attributes of objects using default spacing to achieve the desired results. The top and left space components of all objects with default spacing are set to the default values; the bottom and right space are set to zero except for objects in the last row or last column of a row. Note that an object's total space requirements are not constant if it uses the default spacing; its bottom and right space components can change as a result of other sibling objects being added or removed from the layout.

In row-major layout, the total height of a row is the largest total space for any object in the row. Within a row, objects are ordered left to right in ascending column number sequence. The minimum horizontal space required by a row is the sum of the total horizontal space in the row. Rows are ordered top to bottom by ascending row number. The final size of a row-major parent object (that is, an object for which set_layout was called with an argument of OI_layout_row or OI_layout_row_aligned) is then the size of its longest row (width) by the sum of the heights of the individual rows (height). Within each row, objects with a west gravity component (OI_grav_west, OI_grav_northwest, OI_grav_southwest) are packed to the left, and those with an east component are packed to the right. Objects with no east or west gravity component float. Objects with opposing gravity combine to form a cluster of objects which "float" as a unit. For example, an object with east gravity to the left of an object with west gravity form a cluster. Extra space is divided equally among any holes not explicitly set by the above rules. For example, consider the following objects:

Table 44-3 Objects in a Sample Row-Major Layout, All in the Same Row

Object	Column Position	Gravity	Vertical Object Size
A	10	west	10
B	20	northwest	10
C	30	southeast	10
D	40	center	10
E	60	east	10
F	70	center	30
G	80	northwest	10
H	90	northeast	10

If we assume that some other row is much longer than this row, so that there is extra space in this row, the extra space is distributed horizontally between the objects in this single row as follows:

> AB pad CD pad EFG pad H

Because of the gravity of the objects, they form *clusters*. Extra space is divided equally in the regions labeled "pad" above.

Each object in the row is positioned vertically according to its gravity also. Objects with a north gravity component (OI_grav_north, OI_grav_northwest, OI_grav_northeast) are packed to the top of the row, with only top_space whitespace above them. Objects with a south gravity component (OI_grav_south, OI_grav_southwest, OI_grav_southeast) are packed to the bottom of the row, with only bottom_space white space below them. Objects with neither a north nor a south component are vertically centered.

For the objects in Table 44-3, the final arrangement would be as shown in Figure 44-3, assuming a default spacing of 5 pixels all around:

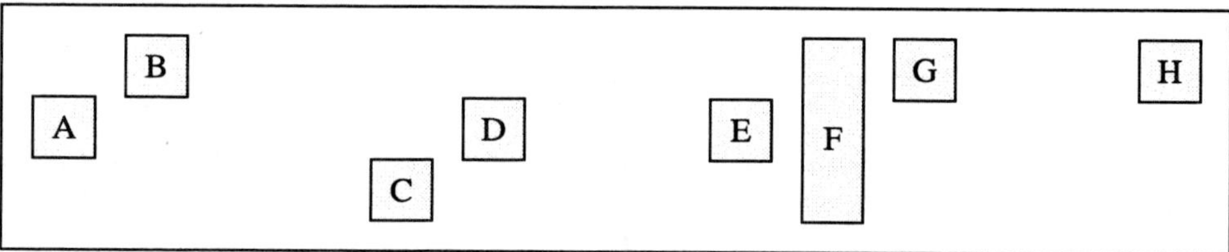

Figure 44-3   Layout for Objects in Table 44-3

Note that a single row whose elements all have an **OI_grav_south** gravity component does **not** appear at the bottom of the container if the container is taller than the row. The objects appear at the bottom of the row, but the row is packed to the top of the container, as shown in Figure 44-4:

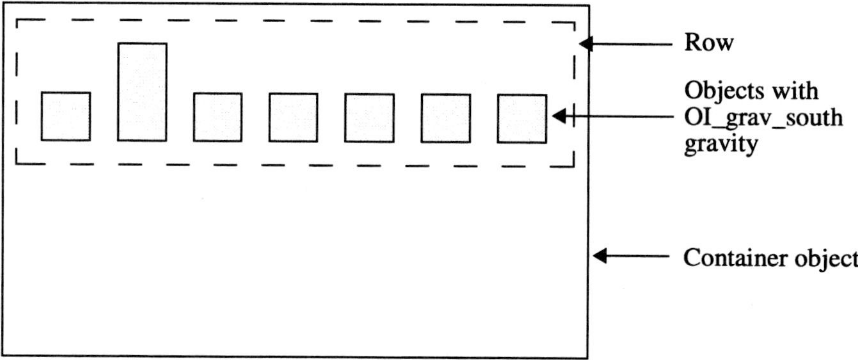

Figure 44-4   Tall Object, Single Row, Objects with OI_grav_south Gravity

To get the entire row to move to the bottom, insert an additional row above it containing a vertical size-tracking box in state **OI_not_displayed** or in state **OI_active** but with frame width of zero. The vertical size-tracking box will consume any additional space and force the following rows to the bottom of the container, as shown in Figure 44-5:

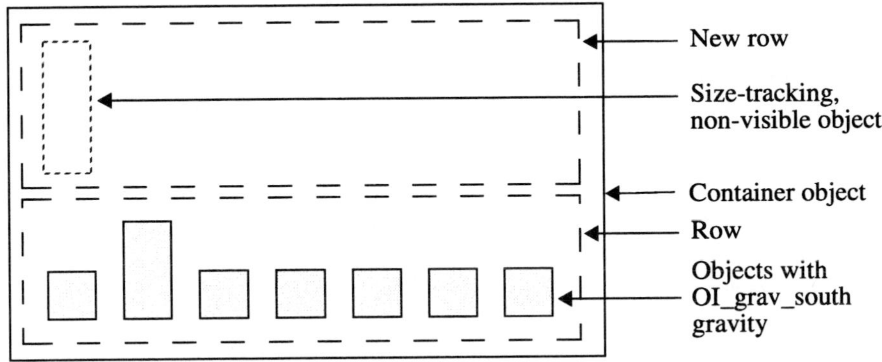

Figure 44-5   Forcing Row to Bottom

44.3.1.2 Row-Column (Grid) Layout Spacing

In a row-column layout, each column within a given row is the same height, and each row within a given column is the same width. Any particular object in the layout can be considered to be in an "invisible box" whose width is the width of the column and whose height is the height of the row. Each row is as tall as the tallest object (plus its vertical spacing) in the row, and each column is as wide as the widest object (plus its horizontal spacing) in the column. See Figure 44-6, in which all objects have OI_grav_northwest gravity.

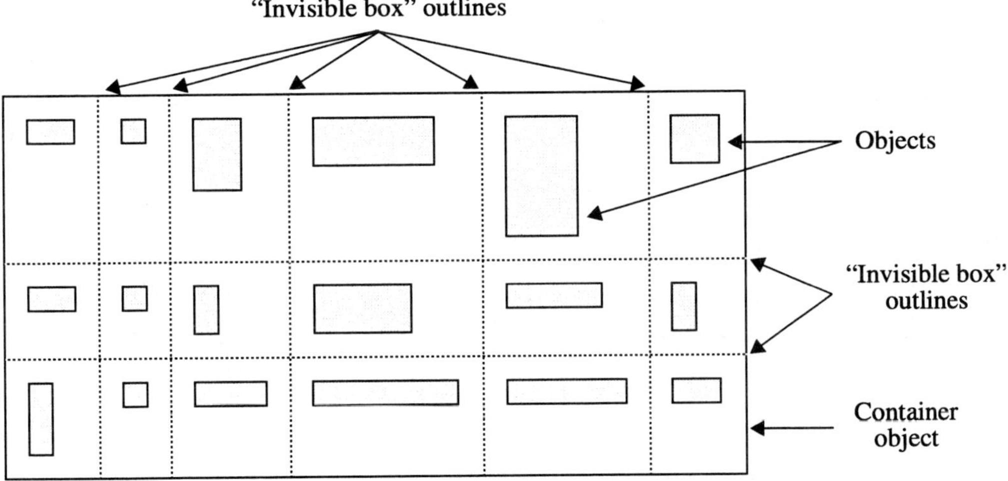

Figure 44-6   Row-Column Layout Spacing

The space attributes and gravity of an object in a row-column layout are applied in relation to the invisible box. Thus, an object with east gravity floats to the right side of the invisible box, but is never placed outside of the box itself. Similarly, a left space component specifies the space between the left edge of the object and the left edge of the invisible box.

44.3.1.3 Nesting Laid-out Objects to Achieve Different Effects

To achieve more complex layouts, you can package sub-components in a separate box with frame width zero and nest the layouts. The box can have one layout method, and the overall parent another. The box is invisible (because of zero frame-width), but allows you to generate a different visual effect than a single layout would give you. The example below shows a nested layout as well as the use of an invisible box to produce desired spacing. The overall parent has a column-major layout. All objects except "J" have default gravity; "J" has gravity OI_grav_center. The nested layout produces the display diagrammed in Figure 44-7.

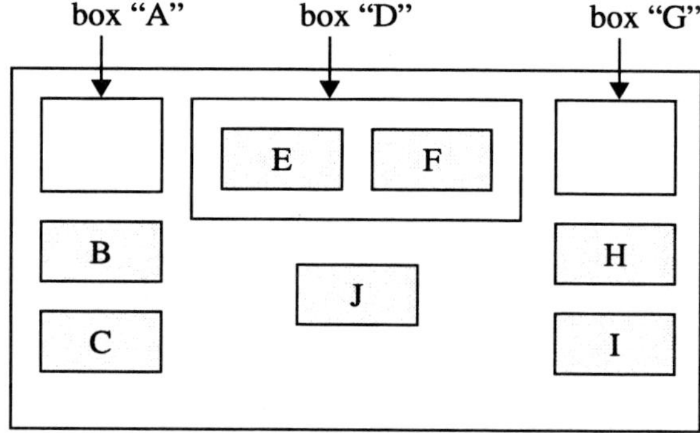

Figure 44-7   Nested Layout

If the frame widths for "A", "D" and "G" are set to zero, the layout looks like this:

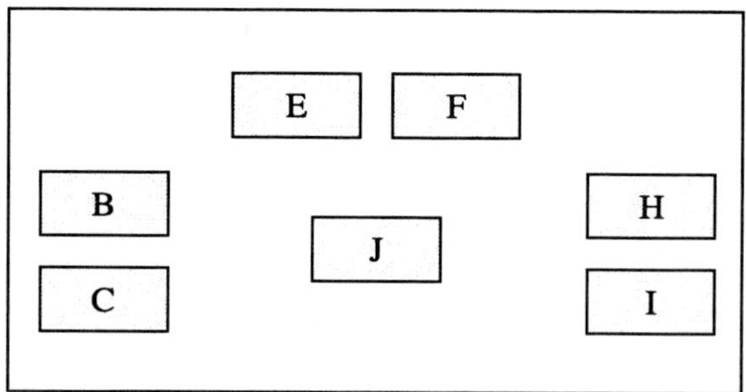

Figure 44-8   Nested Layout with Invisible Boxes

The code to produce the layout shown in Figure 44-8 is shown in Program 44-1.

Notice that when you use this technique, the space between objects inside one of the spacing boxes and a neighboring object not in a spacing box, or the space between an object inside one of the spacing boxes and the edge of the main container, is twice the normal default spacing. For example,

"E" and "F" are twice as far below the top of the main container as they would be if none of the spacing boxes were used. You can overcome this by setting the spacing components for the container box to zero.

```
#include <OI/appwin.H>                         /* NestLayouts.C */
#include <OI/box.H>
int main(int argc, char** argv)
{
        OI_connection           *conp;
        OI_app_window           *wp;
        OI_box                  *bp1;
        OI_box                  *bp2;

   if (conp = OI_init(&argc,argv,"NestLayouts")) {
        wp = oi_create_app_window("main",1,1,"NestLayouts");
        wp->set_layout(OI_layout_column);

        bp1 = oi_create_box("A",15,20);
        bp1->layout_associated_object(wp,10,10,OI_active);
        bp1->set_frame_width(0);
        bp1 = oi_create_box("B",15,10);
        bp1->layout_associated_object(wp,10,20,OI_active);
        bp1 = oi_create_box("C",15,10);
        bp1->layout_associated_object(wp,10,30,OI_active);

        bp1 = oi_create_box("D",1,1);           // D and its children
        bp1->layout_associated_object(wp,20,10,OI_active);
        bp1->set_layout(OI_layout_row);
        bp1->set_frame_width(0);
        bp2 = oi_create_box("E",15,10);
        bp2->layout_associated_object(bp1,10,10,OI_active);
        bp2 = oi_create_box("F",15,10);
        bp2->layout_associated_object(bp1,20,10,OI_active);

        bp1 = oi_create_box("G",15,20);
        bp1->layout_associated_object(wp,30,10,OI_active);
        bp1->set_frame_width(0);
        bp1 = oi_create_box("H",15,10);
        bp1->layout_associated_object(wp,30,20,OI_active);
        bp1 = oi_create_box("I",15,10);
        bp1->layout_associated_object(wp,30,30,OI_active);

        bp1 = oi_create_box("J",15,10);
        bp1->set_gravity(OI_grav_center);
        bp1->layout_associated_object(wp,20,20,OI_active);
```

```
      wp->set_associated_object(wp->root(),OI_def_loc,OI_def_loc,OI_active);
      OI_begin_interaction();
      OI_fini();
   }
}
```

Program 44-1   Nested Layout with Invisible Boxes (NestLayouts.C)

44.3.1.4 Tree Layout Example

As stated in Section 6.3.2.7, "Using Tree Layout," on page 6-11, objects are inserted into a vertical tree layout by specifying the parent-node (the node above) and the sibling-node (the node to the right) of the child object. The example below shows how a tree layout is built; the default spacing is changed using resources. In addition, the appearance of the layout is changed by making the frame width of certain objects wider, again through resources.

WalkTree, shown in Program 44-2 and Figure 44-9, displays the OI class hierarchy as static text objects in boxes laid out in a vertical tree. Note that there are two trees involved. One is the OI class tree, and the other is the layout tree. This program lays out the class tree in the natural way using a tree layout. The first argument to **WalkTree** is the class at which to start the tree. Figure 44-9 shows the results when the program is run using

```
      WalkTree OI_lang_server_input
```

and with the following resource set in the **.Xdefaults** file:

```
      WalkTree*main*layout:                          OI_layout_vert_tree
      WalkTree*defaultHorizontalSpace:               15
      WalkTree*OI_app_window.defaultVerticalSpace:   15
      WalkTree*can_create.frameWidth:                4
```

As a result of the last resource specification, Figure 44-9 shows OI classes that can be instantiated in a heavier frame than those that cannot.

```
                                    /* WalkTree.C */
#include <OI/stattxt.H>
#include <OI/appwin.H
#include <OI/box.H>
#include <stdio.h>

int main(int argc,char **argv)        // If arg present, it is class at which to start
{
        void                    walk_tree(OI_app_window*,OI_box*,OI_class*,OI_bool);
        OI_class                *clsp;         // pointer to root class
        OI_app_window           *wp;           // pointer to app window

    if (OI_init(&argc,argv,"WalkTree")) {
        wp = oi_create_app_window("main",1,1,"WalkTree");
        wp->set_layout(OI_layout_horz_tree);
        // If no args present, walk entire tree
```

```
        if (argc <= 1)
            walk_tree(wp,NULL,OI_class_tree(), OI_no) ;
        // Otherwise, start at the class specified
        else {
            argv++ ;
            if (clsp = OI_class_object(*argv))
                walk_tree(wp,NULL,clsp, OI_yes) ;
            else
                fprintf(stderr, "Class %s not registered\n", *argv) ;
        }
        wp->set_associated_object(wp->root(),OI_def_loc,OI_def_loc,OI_active);
        OI_begin_interaction();
    }
}

void walk_tree(
        OI_app_window           *wp,        // pointer to app window parent
        OI_box                  *momp,      // pointer to parent in tree
        OI_class                *clsp,      // pointer to class at which to start
        OI_bool                 is_root)    // OI_yes => this is a root node, do not
                                            //    traverse siblings
{
        OI_class                *p;
        OI_static_text          *stp;
        OI_box                  *bp,*sib;

    sib = NULL;
    for (p=clsp; p ; p=p->sibling()) {
        if (p->is_createable())
            bp = oi_create_box("can_create",1,1);
        else
            bp = oi_create_box("no_create",1,1);
        bp->set_layout(OI_layout_row);
        stp = oi_create_static_text(p->name(),p->name());
        stp->layout_associated_object(bp,1,1,OI_active);
        bp->layout_associated_object(wp,momp,sib,OI_active);
        sib = bp;
        walk_tree(wp,bp,p->derived(), OI_no) ;
        if (is_root)
            break ;
    }
    return ;
}
```

Program 44-2   Display Class Hierarchy in a Tree (WalkTree.C)

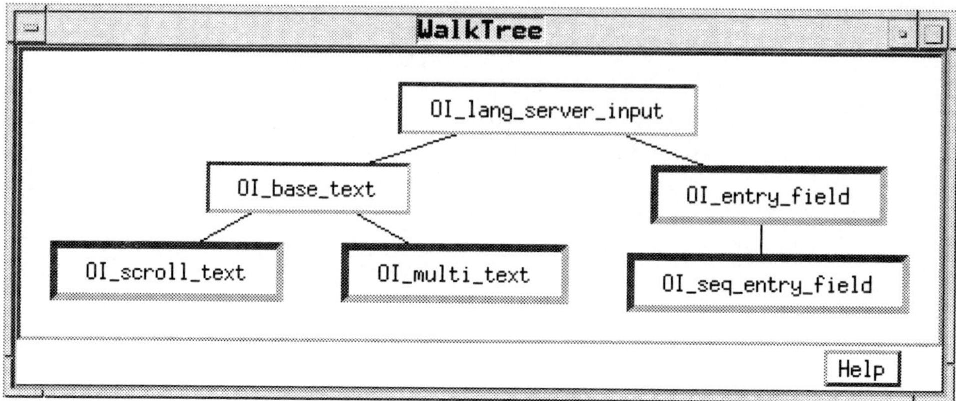

Figure 44-9 WalkTree Starting at OI_lang_server_input

44.3.2   OI_layout_method Member Functions

To use these member functions, first obtain a pointer to the layout method for an object (using the OI_d_tech member function layout_method), then call the member function on behalf of the layout object.

Subsequent sections list member functions specific to particular classes of layout methods. Consequently, you will need to cast the return value of the OI_d_tech member function layout_method to be of proper type before you call the member function. Unless you know the return value will be for an appropriate type, you should check it first using the OI_d_tech member function is_derived_from:

```
OI_d_tech                *objp;
OI_lm_row_col            *lmp;

lmp = (OI_lm_row_col*)objp->layout_method( );
if (lmp && lmp->is_derived_from(OI_lm_row_col::clsp)) {
    . . .
}
```

44.3.2.1 · Controlling Default Spacing

Every layout method has an associated horizontal and vertical offset. This is the position of the upper-left corner of the layout relative to the container object. The offsets are normally zero, but may be modified at any time using the member function set_space, in effect shifting the positioning of all the objects in the layout.

All of the OI-supplied layout methods position objects such that they all are completely visible—none of them overlap each other. However, it is possible for a layout method to deliberately arrange the objects so that some of them overlap. overlaps_children tells you if the layout method overlaps the children; for OI-supplied methods it always returns OI_no.

set_space   (Member function)

```
void OI_layout_method::set_space(
    OI_number      horz_sp,              // horizontal offset
    OI_number      vert_sp=OI_undefined) // vertical offset
```

set_space sets the horizontal and vertical space offsets for the layout. This has the effect of shifting all laid out children to the right *horz_sp* pixels and down *vert_sp* pixels. *horz_sp* and *vert_sp* may be negative.

horz_offset   (Member function)

```
OI_number OI_layout_method::horz_offset( )
```

horz_offset returns the amount, in pixels, by which the entire layout is offset from 0 horizontally.

vert_offset   (Member function)

```
OI_number OI_layout_method::vert_offset( )
```

vert_offset returns the amount, in pixels, by which the entire layout is offset from 0 vertically.

overlaps_children   (Member function)

```
OI_bool OI_layout_method::overlaps_children( )
```

overlaps_children returns **OI_yes** if children laid out in this layout method can overlap; otherwise it returns **OI_no**. Children do not overlap when laid out using any of the default OI layout methods. If you are subclassing your own layout method in which children may overlap, you should write an **overlaps_children** function which returns **OI_yes**.

44.3.2.2 Determining Layout Geometry

When dynamically adding objects to a laid-out parent, you sometimes need to know the layout geometry parameters for an existing object in order to insert a new object. For example, to insert an object between two objects in a particular row of a row layout, you need the row number and the column number of the object to the left. In addition, in order to store the geometry information in a configuration file so that the layout may be reconstructed, the ObjectBuilder user interface builder needs a way to convert geometry information to a string-based form. The functions discussed in this section perform these operations.

geometry   (Member function)

```
OI_bool OI_layout_method::geometry(
    OI_d_tech      *objp,         // pointer to object whose geometry is required
    void           **geom_1,      // first geometry value to be backfilled
    OI_bool        *del_geom_1,   // should geom_1 be deleted?
    void           **geom_2,      // second geometry value to be backfilled
    OI_bool        *del_geom_2)   // should geom_2 be deleted?
```

geometry returns **OI_yes** if *objp* is laid out using this layout method. *geom_1* and *geom_2* are backfilled with the layout geometry specifications corresponding to the object *objp*. *del_geom_1* is set to OI_yes if the corresponding value returned in *geom_1* is an object derived from OI_layout_geometry_spec which you should delete when you no longer need it. *del_geom_2* is set in like fashion for *geom_2*. geometry returns OI_no if *objp* is not laid out using this layout method, in which case all other values are undefined.

geometry_match   (Member function)

```
OI_bool OI_layout_method::geometry_match(
    OI_d_tech         *objp,        // pointer to object whose geometry is in question
    void              *geom_1,      // first geometry component
    void              *geom_2)      // second geometry component
```

geometry_match returns OI_yes if *objp* is laid out using this layout method and the layout geometry specification (*geom_1,geom_2*) corresponds to object *objp*; otherwise it returns OI_no.

44.3.2.3 Controlling Gaps in Geometry Numbering in the Layout

Some layout methods have geometry parameters which imply ordering based on some numeric sequence, for example, rows and columns are ordered in increasing numerical sequence left to right and top to bottom. In all OI-supplied layout methods, the numeric sequence is a sequence of integers, not floating point numbers. Some layout methods may allow gaps in the numerical sequence and others must be gapless. For example, the layout for menu cells does not allow gaps— the menu cells are laid out in a menu by row or column depending on the orientation of the menu. The row or column position corresponds to the cell number. Normal row or column layout allows gaps in the numbering sequence of rows and columns, but when they are used for a menu, OI disallows gaps. This means that removing a menu cell from the layout causes the row and/or column numbers of any remaining cells to be modified to remove the gap in the numbering sequence created when the cell was removed. If you call allow_gaps or disallow_gaps for a layout method, you must first be sure that the layout method understands and can handle allowing or disallowing gaps.

allow_gaps   (Member function)

```
void OI_layout_method::allow_gaps( )
```

allow_gaps conditions the layout method, if applicable, so that gaps in the numerical geometry specifications of the objects laid out using this method are allowed. For the OI-supplied layout methods, allow_gaps applies only to layout methods which use row and column numbers—that is, any layout method derived from OI_lm_row_col.

disallow_gaps   (Member function)

```
void OI_layout_method::disallow_gaps( )
```

disallow_gaps conditions the layout method, if applicable, so that there will be no gaps in numerical geometry specifications of the objects laid out using this method. For the OI-supplied layout methods, disallow_gaps applies only to layout methods which use row and column numbers—that is, any layout method derived from OI_lm_row_col.

gaps (Member function)

```
OI_bool OI_layout_method::gaps( )
```

gaps returns OI_yes if gaps are allowed in the geometry specification numbers of a layout method; otherwise it returns OI_no.

44.3.2.4 Determining Class Hierarchy

is_derived_from (Member function)

```
OI_bool OI_layout_method::is_derived_from(
    OI_class              *cp)            // pointer to layout method class
```

```
OI_bool OI_layout_method::is_derived_from(
    XrmQuark              qrk_nam)        // layout method name as quark
```

```
OI_bool OI_layout_method::is_derived_from(
    const char            *nam)           // layout method name as string
```

is_derived_from returns OI_yes if this layout method is derived from or is the same as the layout method *cp, qrk_nam* or *nam*.

44.3.2.5 Traversing Objects Controlled by the Layout Method

next_object (Member function)

```
OI_d_tech *OI_layout_method::next_object(
    OI_d_tech             *objp)          // pointer to object in layout
```

next_object returns a pointer to the next OI object after *objp* in the layout method traversal order. This order is dependent on the type of layout:

The traversal sequence is by rows if the layout method is

    OI_layout_row
    OI_layout_row_aligned
    OI_layout_row_column
    OI_layout_titled_row_column
    OI_layout_row_column_aligned
    OI_layout_wrapped_row.

The sequence is by columns if the layout method is

    OI_layout_column
    OI_layout_wrapped_column.

If the layout is OI_layout_vert_tree, the default traversal order is from top to bottom, traversing the left-most nodes first, then the next to left-most, recursively, until finally the right-most nodes are visited. If the layout is OI_layout_horz_tree, the same method of traversal is used, except the order is from left to right, traversing the top-most nodes first. Tree layout traversal order is shown in Figure 44-10.

next_object returns the first object in the layout traversal order if *objp* is NULL; it returns NULL if *objp* is the last object.

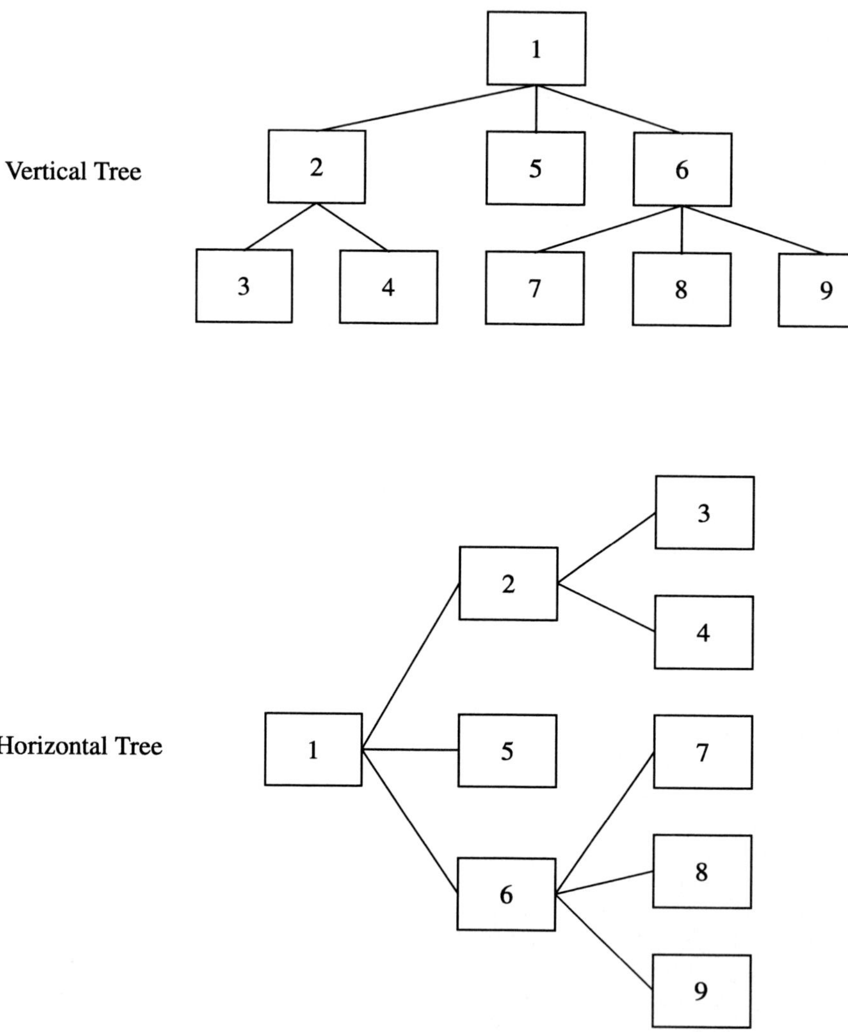

Figure 44-10   Traversal Sequence for Tree Layouts

previous_object   (Member function)

```
OI_d_tech *OI_layout_method::previous_object(
    OI_d_tech            *objp)          // pointer to object in layout
```

previous_object returns a pointer to the previous OI object before *objp* in the layout method traversal order. **previous_object** returns the last object in the layout traversal order if *objp* is NULL; it returns NULL if *objp* is the first object.

44.3.3   OI_lm_row_col Member Functions

To use these member functions, first obtain a pointer to the layout method for an object (using the OI_d_tech member function **layout_method**), then call the member function on behalf of the layout object. See the description and example of casting the return value and checking for appropriate type on page 44-12.

44.3.3.1 Inserting New Rows or Columns in the Layout

new_row   (Member function)

```
void OI_lm_row_col::new_row(
    OI_number     rowno,                  // row number
    OI_number     colno=OI_undefined)     // column number
```

new_row adjusts the row numbers in this parent object to make room for a new row. This function does not change the appearance of the layout. It re-numbers rows, if necessary, so that the next time you call **layout_associated_object** for some object, parenting it to this object, you can insert the new object between other objects that are already laid out. You do not need to call this function if you already know that there is a "hole" between the rows (the row numbers are not consecutive) where you want to insert the new object.

rowno is the row number to insert. If the layout method is derived from OI_lm_column, *colno* specifies the column number within which to insert the row, otherwise *colno* is ignored. If a row number already exists with the same number, the existing row number is incremented by one; otherwise, nothing is done. This behavior trickles forward until either a hole is found or no more rows exist to re-number.

new_column   (Member function)

```
void OI_lm_row_col::new_column(
    OI_number     colno,                  // column number
    OI_number     rowno=OI_undefined)     // row number
```

new_column adjusts the column numbers in this parent object to make room for a new column. This function performs the same operations as **new_row**, but it operates on columns instead of rows.

colno is the column number to insert. If the layout method is derived from OI_lm_row, *rowno* specifies the row number within which to insert the column, otherwise *rowno* is ignored. If a column number already exists with the same number, the existing column number is incremented by one; otherwise, nothing is done. This behavior trickles forward until either a hole is found or no more columns exist to re-number.

44.3.3.2 Determining Row and Column Numbers

row_position   (Member function)

```
OI_number OI_lm_row_col::row_position(
    OI_d_tech          *objp)         // pointer to object laid out using a row-column method
```

row_position returns the row number assigned to *objp*.

column_position   (Member function)

```
OI_number OI_lm_row_col::column_position(
    OI_d_tech          *objp)         // pointer to object laid out using a row-column method
```

column_position returns the column number assigned to *objp*.

first_row   (Member function)

```
OI_number OI_lm_row_col::first_row(
    OI_number      colno=OI_undefined)      // column number
```

first_row returns the first row number occupied for this layout. first_row returns OI_undefined if there is no first row. You can omit *colno* for layout methods derived from OI_lm_row. If the layout method is derived from OI_lm_column, *colno* is required; set it to the column whose first row number you want.

first_column   (Member function)

```
OI_number OI_lm_row_col::first_column(
    OI_number      rowno=OI_undefined)      // row number
```

first_column returns the first column number occupied for this layout. first_column returns OI_undefined if there is no first column. You can omit *rowno* for layout methods derived from OI_lm_column. If the layout method is derived from OI_lm_row, *rowno* is required; set it to the row whose first column number you want.

last_row   (Member function)

```
OI_number OI_lm_row_col::last_row(
    OI_number      colno=OI_undefined)      // column number
```

If the layout method is derived from OI_lm_row, last_row returns the number of the last row in which any of the object's children are laid out, regardless of the value of *colno*. If the layout method is derived from OI_lm_column, then *colno* is a column number, and last_row returns the number of the last row occupied in column *colno*. last_row returns OI_undefined if no rows are allocated.

last_column   (Member function)

```
OI_number OI_lm_row_col::last_column(
    OI_number    rowno=OI_undefined)        // row number
```

If the layout method is derived from OI_lm_column, last_column returns the number of the last column in which any of the object's children are laid out, regardless of the value of *rowno*. If the object's layout method is derived from OI_lm_row, then *rowno* is a row number, and last_column returns the number of the last column occupied in row *rowno*. last_column returns OI_undefined if no columns are allocated.

next_row   (Member function)

```
OI_number OI_lm_row_col::next_row(
    OI_number    rowno,                     // row number
    OI_number    colno=OI_undefined)        // column number
```

next_row returns the next occupied row number after *rowno*. If the layout method is derived from OI_lm_column, *colno* specifies the column number within which to search, otherwise *colno* is ignored. If all rows are numbered less than *row* or if row *rowno* does not exist, next_row returns OI_undefined.

next_column   (Member function)

```
OI_number OI_lm_row_col::next_column(
    OI_number    colno,                     // column number
    OI_number    rowno=OI_undefined)        // row number
```

next_column returns the next used column number after *colno*. If the layout method is derived from OI_lm_row, *rowno* specifies the row number within which to search, otherwise *rowno* is ignored. If all columns are numbered less than *colno* or if column *colno* does not exist, next_column returns OI_undefined.

prev_row   (Member function)

```
OI_number OI_lm_row_col::prev_row(
    OI_number    rowno,                     // row number
    OI_number    colno=OI_undefined)        // column number
```

prev_row returns the previous occupied row number before *rowno* in the same manner as next_row. prev_row returns OI_undefined if there are no rows previous to *rowno*, or if *rowno* does not exist.

prev_column   (Member function)

```
OI_number OI_lm_row_col::prev_column(
    OI_number    colno,                     // column number
    OI_number    rowno=OI_undefined)        // row number
```

prev_column returns the previous used column number before *colno* in the same manner as next_column. prev_column returns OI_undefined if there are no columns previous to *colno*, or if *colno* does not exist.

44.3.3.3 Determining if a Pixel Location Lies within a Row or Column

For some types of applications, you will need to determine if a pixel location falls within a particular row or column. For example, in a user interface builder, the user may drag an object and drop it over a parent. The user interface builder needs to map the drop (x,y) position to a row and column in which to insert the object. These member functions allow you to determine these values.

A row in a row-based layout is considered to extend from the top of the highest object in the row to the bottom of the lowest object in the row. Similarly, a column in a column-based layout is considered to extend from the left of the left-most object to the right of the right-most object in the column. Any other space is considered to be space between the rows/columns.

in_column   (Member function)

```
OI_number OI_lm_row_col::in_column(
    OI_number        colno,        // column number
    long             x,            // x position in pixels
    OI_number        rowno,        // row number
    OI_number        pct)          // percent of total column
```

in_column determines whether the position defined by x is located within the column *colno*. *colno* specifies the column number, and x specifies the x position to check (in pixels from the left edge of the object). If the layout method is derived from **OI_lm_row**, *rowno* specifies the row number, otherwise *rowno* is ignored. For x to be considered "in" the column, it must be located in the middle *pct* of the total column width. **in_column** returns:

> < 0 if x is to the left of the column
> 0 if x is in the middle *pct* of the column
> > 0 if x is to the right of the column

in_row   (Member function)

```
OI_number OI_lm_row_col::in_row(
    OI_number        rowno,        // row number
    long             y,            // y position in pixels
    OI_number        colno,        // column number
    OI_number        pct)          // percent of total row
```

in_row determines whether the position defined by y is located within the row *rowno*. *rowno* specifies the row number, and y specifies the y position to check (in pixels from the top edge of the object). If the layout method is derived from **OI_lm_column**, *colno* specifies the column number, otherwise *colno* is ignored. For y to be considered "in" the row, it must be located in the middle *pct* of the total row height. **in_row** returns:

> < 0 if y is above the row
> 0 if y is in the middle *pct* of the row
> > 0 if y is below the row

44.3.4   OI_lm_wrapped_row, OI_lm_wrapped_column Member Functions

To use these member functions, first obtain a pointer to the layout method for an object (using the OI_d_tech member function layout_method), then call the member function on behalf of the layout object. See the description and example of casting the return value and checking for appropriate type on page 44-12.

set_wrap   (Member function)

```
void OI_lm_wrapped_row::set_wrap(
    OI_number            max)          // maximum number of objects in the row

void OI_lm_wrapped_column::set_wrap(
    OI_number            max)          // maximum number of objects in the column
```

set_wrap sets the maximum number of objects per row (OI_lm_wrapped_row) or column (OI_lm_wrapped_column) to *max*.

wrap_num   (Member function)

```
OI_number OI_lm_wrapped_row::wrap_num( )

OI_number OI_lm_wrapped_column::wrap_num( )
```

wrap_num returns the maximum number of objects per row (OI_lm_wrapped_row) or column (OI_lm_wrapped_column). The default value is 5.

set_wrap_space   (Member function)

```
void OI_lm_wrapped_row::set_wrap_space(
    OI_number            max)          // maximum number of objects in the row

void OI_lm_wrapped_column::set_wrap_space(
    OI_number            max)          // maximum number of objects in the column
```

set_wrap_space sets the space between the mini-rows which make up a row (OI_lm_wrapped_row) or column (OI_lm_wrapped_column) when the row or column is wrapped.

wrap_space   (Member function)

```
OI_number OI_lm_wrapped_row::wrap_space( )

OI_number OI_lm_wrapped_column::wrap_space( )
```

wrap_space returns the space used between rows (OI_lm_wrapped_row) or columns (OI_lm_wrapped_column) when the row or column is wrapped. The default value is the default spacing used between rows or columns.

44.3.5   OI_lm_tree Member Functions

To use these member functions, first obtain a pointer to the layout method for an object (using the OI_d_tech member function layout_method), then call the member function on behalf of the layout object. See the description and example of casting the return value and checking for appropriate type on page 44-12.

Using these functions you can determine the parent-node, a sibling-node, or the root-node of an object laid out in a tree layout.

parent_node   (Member function)

```
OI_d_tech *OI_lm_wrapped_column::parent_node(
    OI_d_tech          *objp)              // pointer to object in layout
```

parent_node returns a pointer to the object that is the parent of *objp* in the layout tree. Note that this is different than the OI_d_tech function parent. parent returns the object that is the parent in the object tree, whereas parent_node returns the object that is the parent within the layout tree. The object returned by parent_node will be a sibling of *objp* in the object tree—that is, both *objp* and *objp*->parent_node() will be laid out in the same parent object.

sibling_node   (Member function)

```
OI_d_tech *OI_lm_wrapped_column::sibling_node(
    OI_d_tech          *objp)              // pointer to object in layout
```

sibling_node returns a pointer to the object that is the immediately following sibling of *objp* in the tree.

root_node   (Member function)

```
OI_d_tech *OI_lm_wrapped_column::root_node( )
```

root_node returns a pointer to the object that is the root of the layout tree. If a tree has multiple roots, root_node returns the first one. You can obtain subsequent roots by using the sibling_node member function.

44.4   Designing Your Own Layout Method

If necessary, you may derive your own subclass to implement a layout strategy different from those supplied with the OI library. To do so you must derive your layout method from either the base class for all layout methods, OI_layout_method, or from one of the already supplied layout methods (one of the classes shown in the class tree on page 44-2). You must also create a subclass of OI_layout_slot, as described below in Section 44.4.2, "Deriving a Slot Subclass," on page 44-25.

You must register your layout method with OI.

Your layout method must:

- Handle creation of the layout method.
- Create a slot object for each child when it is laid out to contain the layout parameters for the child and attach the slot to the child.

- Guide the layout of children when they are laid out.
- Readjust the layout when children are removed from the layout.
- Handle resize of the container object.
- Readjust the layout when a child object is resized.
- Readjust the layout when children are deleted.
- Behave correctly when the container object is deleted.
- Handle the destruction of the layout method object.

You must also implement some virtual functions for your layout method.

These subjects are covered in the following sections.

44.4.1   Deriving a Layout Method Subclass

An object of your layout method subclass is created when the application calls **set_layout** for a parent object with your layout method named as the first parameter. OI does not call the constructor directly; instead it calls **make_minimal**, which you must write, and **make_minimal** must call the constructor.

You must implement certain member functions for your layout method; these are noted in the descriptions below. Table 44-4 below lists all virtual functions of **OI_layout_method** which are usually implemented in a derived class and some static functions. You must at the very least write those functions marked in Table 44-4 as "Always Required." If you derive from **OI_layout_method** rather than one of the already supplied layout methods, you must write those functions marked in Table 44-4 as "Required when deriving from **OI_layout_method**."

Note that some of these functions are discussed in earlier sections of this chapter, while others are described in this section. Unless you are deriving from **OI_layout_method** you do not always need to override a required function. If you are deriving from an existing layout method, all of the functions have already been implemented in some form, and you need only override those functions necessary to get the modified functionality for your layout method. The functions not marked as required already have a default implementation which is satisfactory in most circumstances.

Table 44-4   Layout Member Functions

Member Function	Function Type	Always Required	Required when deriving from OI_layout_method	Page
Destructor	Virtual	Yes	Yes	41-20
bottom_space	Virtual			44-34
class_object	Virtual	Yes	Yes	44-37
conversion_specifications	Virtual		Yes	44-36
convert_xy_to_geometry	Virtual		Yes	44-36

Table 44-4 Layout Member Functions

Member Function	Function Type	Always Required	Required when deriving from OI_layout_method	Page
exact_conversion	Virtual		Yes	44-37
force_layout	Virtual		Yes	44-29
geometry	Virtual		Yes	44-13
geometry_match	Virtual		Yes	44-14
geometry_to_string	Virtual		Yes	44-35
gravity_change	Virtual			44-33
insert	Virtual		Yes	44-31
left_space	Virtual			44-34
make_minimal	Static	Yes	Yes	44-27
min_outside_size	Virtual		Yes	44-29
move	Virtual			44-32
new_default_space	Virtual			44-33
next_object	Virtual		Yes	44-15
nominal_size	Virtual		Yes	44-27
overlaps_children	Virtual			44-13
previous_object	Virtual		Yes	44-17
re_layout	Virtual		Yes	44-29
reg	Static	Yes	Yes	44-26
remove	Virtual		Yes	44-32
right_space	Virtual			44-34
size_change	Virtual			44-33
size_track_change	Virtual			44-33
slot_size_change	Virtual			44-32

Table 44-4 Layout Member Functions

Member Function	Function Type	Always Required	Required when deriving from OI_layout_method	Page
space_change	Virtual			44-32
string_to_geometry	Virtual		Yes	44-35
top_space	Virtual			44-34

You are free to impose your own notion of what the top (bottom, left, right) space for an object should mean in your layout method. For example, in the OI_lm_row layout method, left space is the space to the left of the current object, and the total space between the previous object and the current object is calculated to be the left space plus the right space for the previous object. However, in the OI_lm_row_column layout method, left space is the space between the current object and the left boundary of the "invisible box" in which the object is located. In this case, the total space between two objects may be more than the sum of the left and right space.

The space attributes are generally taken to be the minimum amount of white space which is above (below, left of, right of) the object. If an object has not been laid out, but the OI_d_tech member function set_top_space (set_bottom_space, set_left_space, set_right_space) has been called for the object, it is the minimum amount of white space which will be used when it is laid out in its parent. The application programmer can set the spacing for all objects laid out within a parent by specifying the second and third arguments in set_layout when it is called for the parent.

All of the OI-supplied layout methods position objects such that they all are completely visible—objects do not overlap. However, it is possible for your layout method to deliberately arrange the objects so that some of them overlap. This attribute is important because the OI event dispatching mechanism uses it to optimize event dispatch; non-overlapping layouts involve less work. If your layout method overlaps children, you must override the virtual function overlaps_children to return OI_yes.

44.4.2 Deriving a Slot Subclass

You must implement a subclass of OI_layout_slot for your layout method. Each time an object is laid out in its parent using your layout method, OI calls the insert member function for your layout method (see page 44-31). In insert, you must create a slot object of your OI_layout_slot subclass. You use the slot object to store geometry information specific to the laid-out object and attach it to the laid-out object using the OI_d_tech member function set_slot. You must subclass from OI_layout_slot for this object, because OI determines if an object is laid out or not by querying whether it has an OI_layout_slot object, using the OI_d_tech member function slot.

When defining the constructor for your slot subclass, you should include a pointer to the object being laid out, and in the constructor you should call the OI_d_tech member function set_slot for the object. Other than this restriction, you are free to define the parameters for the slot constructor.

OI_d_tech::set_slot   (Member function)

```
void OI_d_tech::set_slot(
    OI_layout_slot    *slt)                      // pointer to slot object
```

set_slot attaches the slot object *slt* to this laid-out object.

OI_d_tech::slot   (Member function)

```
OI_layout_slot OI_d_tech::slot( )
```

slot returns a pointer to the slot object for this laid-out object, or NULL if this object is not laid out.

44.4.3   OI_layout_method Member Functions

Any function in the sections below which you write for your layout method is marked with the symbol ✎. Any function not so marked is one which you do not write; you use it to implement your layout method.

44.4.3.1 Registering a Layout Method Subclass

reg   (Member function)

```
void OI_layout_method::reg( )
```

✎ Write reg to register your layout method for later use; make it a static member function. Before your layout method can be used, it must be registered, using the stand-alone function OI_register_layout_method (see below). OI_register_layout_method returns an OI_class pointer; this is a pointer to the class record for the layout method. You should store it in a static variable named clsp. For more description and examples on how to write this function, see Section 41.3.2, "Registering the Subclass," on page 41-7.

OI_register_layout_method   (Member function)

```
OI_class *OI_register_layout_method(
    const char                   *namp,       // name layout method will be known by
    const char                   *bas_namp,  // name base layout method is known by
    OI_make_minimal_memfnp       memfnp)     // static function to create instance
```

You do not write this function; you call OI_register_layout_method in your reg function.

namp is the name by which the layout method will be known publicly, such as "OI_layout_row". *bas_namp* is the name by which the immediate base class from which the layout method is derived is known. For historical reasons necessitated by compatibility concerns, the supplied layout methods do not use the actual class names for registration; instead, they use the convenience names for the layout method. For example, OI_lm_wrapped_row is derived from OI_lm_row, but the layout registration is done using "OI_layout_wrapped_row" and "OI_layout_row". *memfnp* is a pointer to a static member function which, when called, will generate an instance of the class; by convention, this function is named make_minimal.

OI_register_layout_method returns a pointer to the class record for the layout method.

44.4.3.2 Creating and Sizing a Layout Method Object

make_minimal   (Member function)

```
void OI_layout_method::make_minimal(
    OI_d_tech           *objp,          // parent object
    OI_minimal_type     typ)            // unused
```

✎ Write make_minimal to generate a new instance of your layout method. It must be a static function. OI calls make_minimal when it needs to create a new instance of the layout method. *objp* will point to the object where the layout method will be used (the container, or parent, object). You may ignore *typ*. You should write make_minimal to generate a new layout method by calling the constructor for your layout class.

The following code is a **make_minimal** member function template:

```
OI_layout_method* MyLayout::make_minimal(
        OI_d_tech           *dtp,           // ptr to container object
        OI_minimal_type     )
{
    return(new MyLayout(dtp));
}
```

nominal_size   (Member function)

```
void OI_layout_method::nominal_size(
    OI_number           *wid,           // nominal width
    OI_number           *ht)            // nominal height
```

✎ Write nominal_size to compute the nominal size for the layout. Backfill *wid* and *ht* with the nominal width and height for the container (parent) object. The nominal size is the size which should be used for the container in the absence of other constraints; the "natural" size needed to contain the children when laid out using this layout method.

The nominal size includes any border supplied in the container, and any offset used to position the overall layout within the container. In addition, your layout method can cache its notion of nominal size using the member function set_nominal_size_ok (see below). A template for nominal_size is shown in Example 44-1.

```
void OI_lm_horz_tree::nominal_size (
      OI_number            *widp,        // place to backfill nominal width
      OI_number            *htp)         // place to backfill nominal height
      const
{
      OI_number            nom_x, nom_y ; // computed nominal size

   if (nominal_size_ok()) {
      *widp = nom_size_x() ;
      *htp = nom_size_y() ;
   }
   else {
      // compute nom_x and nom_y nominal size here
      nom_x = ...
      nom_y = ...
      // Add in border width of container object
      if (object()) {
          bdr = 2 * object()->bdr_width() ;
          nom_x += bdr ;
          nom_y += bdr ;
      }
      // Add in offset for layout method as a whole
      nom_x += 2 * horz_offset() ;
      nom_y += 2 * vert_offset() ;
      // Cache the computed size so we don't need to recompute later
      ((OI_lm_horz_tree*)this)->set_nominal_size_ok(nom_x,nom_y) ;
      // Now backfill the result
      *widp = nom_size_x() ;
      *htp = nom_size_y() ;
   }
   return ;
}
```

Example 44-1   nominal_size

set_nominal_size_ok   (Member function)

```
void OI_layout_method::set_nominal_size_ok(
   OI_number            nom_wid,             // nominal width
   OI_number            nom_ht)              // nominal height
```

The base class for all layout methods, **OI_layout_method**, maintains a cache containing the nominal size for the layout method. **set_nominal_size_ok** records the nominal size and sets the nominal-size condition so that **nominal_size_ok** will return **OI_yes**. If you write your layout method such that it can cache the nominal size, you should call this function from the **nominal_size** function as shown in Example 44-1.

nominal_size_ok   (Member function)

```
OI_bool OI_layout_method::nominal_size_ok( )
```

You should use this bookkeeping function if your layout method saves the value of its nominal size for optimization (via **set_nominal_size_ok**). It returns **OI_yes** if the current nominal size computation is valid; otherwise it returns **OI_no**.

clear_nominal_size_ok   (Member function)

```
void OI_layout_method::clear_nominal_size_ok( )
```

clear_nominal_size_ok sets the nominal-size condition so that **is_nominal_size_ok** will return **OI_no**. You should call this function whenever a new object is inserted in or removed from the layout, or when any other condition occurs which will invalidate a previously cached nominal size.

min_outside_size   (Member function)

```
void OI_layout_method::min_outside_size(
    OI_number          w,          // desired width in pixels
    OI_number          h,          // desired height in pixels
    OI_number          *widp,      // layout width needed
    OI_number          *htp)       // layout height needed
```

✎ Write **min_outside_size** to return the size the layout method will use when asked to become a size of *w* x *h*. Backfill *widp* and *htp* with the actual width and height that will be used. If *w* and *h* are zero, return the absolute minimum size required for the layout method. Otherwise, return a size rounded down from *w* x *h* if possible.

As with **nominal_size**, the minimum size should include the object border and offset for the layout method as a whole.

44.4.3.3 Positioning Objects

re_layout   (Member function)

```
void OI_layout_method::re_layout( )
```

✎ Write **re_layout** to reposition the children in the layout according to the container (parent) object's size without changing the container object's current size. You should position the children using the **OI_d_tech** member function **set_loc**.

force_layout   (Member function)

```
void OI_layout_method::force_layout( )
```

✎ In the 4.0 version of OI, **force_layout** is a pure virtual which must be overridden in a subclass. In subsequent releases, it is virtual, but a default version exists which is adequate for most subclasses. Write **force_layout** to determine the nominal size required to contain all the children currently laid out, change the size of the object to which the layout method belongs to match this size, and reposition the children within this size. You can compute the size and resize the container object to the computed size by calling **assume_nominal_size**. Normally you reposition the children by calling **re_layout** (see below). **force_layout** should only do its work if the layout method is not already busy; therefore, you should bracket the procedure by a test of **in_layout**. Furthermore, to prevent any size changes of the container object from causing a recursive attempt to re-layout the children, you should mark the layout method as being busy by calling **set_in_layout**. Since **assume_nominal_size** adjusts the container object's size, any pending condition requiring size adjustment is cleared. A template for **force_layout** appears below:

```
if (! in_layout()) {
    set_in_layout();                      // set layout busy
    assume_nominal_size(&wid,&ht);        // compute and set containter to nominal size
    clear_needs_size_adjust();            // clear needs_size_adjust flag
    clear_in_layout();                    // set layout not busy
    re_layout();                          // re-layout the children objects
}
```

assume_nominal_size   (Member function)

```
void OI_layout_method::assume_nominal_size(
    OI_number             *widp,           // width backfilled here
    OI_number             *htp)            // height backfilled here
```

assume_nominal_size computes the default size of the container (parent) object to contain all the laid-out children. It then resizes the container object to be the computed size. The width and height of the computed nominal size are returned in *widp* and *htp*.

set_needs_size_adjust   (Member function)

```
void OI_layout_method::set_needs_size_adjust( )
```

You can call **set_needs_size_adjust** if your layout method cannot do a container size adjustment at the present time but needs to remember to do it at a later time. You may need to do this, for example, if the application programmer suspends layout (using the **OI_d_tech** member function **suspend_layout**), then resizes a child object.

clear_needs_size_adjust   (Member function)

```
void OI_layout_method::clear_needs_size_adjust( )
```

Call **clear_needs_size_adjust** after resizing the container object to fit all its children.

needs_size_adjust   (Member function)

```
OI_bool OI_layout_method::needs_size_adjust( )
```

needs_size_adjust returns **OI_yes** if the container needs to be resized because of a child object changing size; otherwise it returns **OI_no**.

set_in_layout (Member function)

```
void OI_layout_method::set_in_layout( )
```

The base class for all layout methods, **OI_layout_method**, contains a counter used to indicate whether or not the layout method is busy doing a computation. **set_in_layout** increments the in-layout counter indicating the layout method is busy doing a computation.

clear_in_layout (Member function)

```
void OI_layout_method::clear_in_layout( )
```

clear_in_layout decrements the in-layout counter maintained by OI_layout_method. You should close every call to **set_in_layout** at some point by a call to **clear_in_layout**.

in_layout (Member function)

```
OI_bool OI_layout_method::in_layout( )
```

in_layout returns **OI_yes** if any calls to **set_in_layout** have not been canceled by a corresponding call to **clear_in_layout**; otherwise it returns **OI_no**.

44.4.3.4 Inserting and Removing Objects

insert (Member function)

```
void OI_layout_method::insert(
    OI_d_tech        *objp,       // pointer to object being laid out
    void             *geom_1,     // first geometry parameter
    void             *geom_2)     // second geometry parameter
```

✎ Write **insert** to insert *objp* into the layout. OI calls **insert** when *objp* is being inserted in a layout due to an **OI_d_tech** member function **layout_associated_object** or **add_to_layout** call. *geom_1* and *geom_2* are the second and third arguments in the **layout_associated_object** call, and may be any parameters which may be cast as a **void***. They are used to define the layout geometry. Since you are defining the layout method, you are free to define the meaning and valid values for *geom_1* and *geom_2*.

If your layout method makes use of **set_nominal_size_ok** to cache the nominal size, your **insert** member function should clear the **nominal_size_ok** condition, since inserting a new object will possibly modify the nominal size. It should then do whatever work is necessary to insert *objp* into the layout. Finally, it should set the condition indicating a size-adjustment of the container is required. A template for **insert** appears below:

```
clear_nominal_size_ok();
... do actual insertion here
set_needs_size_adjust();
```

You must create a new object of your **OI_layout_slot** subclass to contain geometry information for the object being inserted. This object must be stored in the child object's slot pointer via the OI_d_tech member function **set_slot**:

```
MyLayoutSlot              *sp;              //must be derived from OI_layout_slot
sp = new MyLayoutSlot(...);
objp->set_slot(sp);
```

remove   (Member function)

```
void OI_layout_method::remove(
    OI_d_tech            *objp)                    // pointer to object in the layout
```

✎ Write **remove** to remove the object *objp* from the layout. This also involves removing any data structures your layout method maintains related to the object. Upon return from this function, OI will automatically clear the object's slot pointer to NULL. Therefore, you should delete the **OI_layout_slot** object which was stored for the object before returning.

move   (Member function)

```
void OI_layout_method::move(
    OI_d_tech            *objp,                    // pointer to object in layout
    void                 *geom_1,                  // first geometry specification
    void                 *geom_2)                  // second geometry specification
```

✎ Write **move** to move the object *objp* to a new location in the layout using *geom_1* and *geom_2* as specification for the new location. The default **move** procedure for **OI_layout_method** is adequate for most purposes. It removes the object from the layout and then re-inserts it using the new geometry specification. You may override **move** for your layout method if you wish to optimize this procedure.

44.4.3.5 Responding to Changes in Laid-out Objects

slot_size_change   (Member function)

```
void OI_layout_method::slot_size_change(
    OI_d_tech            *objp)                    // pointer to object in layout
```

✎ OI calls **slot_size_change** to notify the layout method that the object *objp* has changed size. Write **slot_size_change** to adjust the size of the container (parent) object to which it corresponds if necessary, then call **re_layout** to reposition and resize children as necessary. The default procedure supplied by the base class is suitable in most cases.

space_change   (Member function)

```
void OI_layout_method::space_change(
    OI_d_tech            *objp)                    // pointer to object in layout
```

✎ OI calls **space_change** to notify the layout method that the object *objp* has had a change in its surrounding space. Write **space_change** to rearrange the objects in the layout if necessary to account for the new spacing. The default procedure supplied by the base class is adequate in most cases; it simply clears the **nominal_size_ok** condition and then calls **force_layout**.

gravity_change   (Member function)

```
void OI_layout_method::gravity_change(
    OI_d_tech            *objp)            // pointer to object
```

✎ OI calls **gravity_change** to notify the layout method that the gravity of object *objp* has changed. Write **gravity_change** to rearrange objects in the layout if necessary taking into account *objp*'s new gravity. You can obtain *objp*'s gravity using the **OI_d_tech** member function **gravity**.

The default **gravity_change** procedure supplied by **OI_layout_method** is adequate for most purposes. It simply calls **re_layout** if the layout method is not busy. You may override this function if you wish to optimize the process, since only one object in the layout has been affected, and it may be not necessary to recompute the geometry for all objects.

size_track_change   (Member function)

```
void OI_layout_method::size_track_change(
    OI_d_tech            *objp,            // pointer to object in layout
    OI_size_track        trk)             // size tracking for objp
```

✎ OI calls **size_track_change** to notify the layout method that the object *objp*'s size-tracking has changed to *trk*. Write **size_track_change** to readjust adjust the sizes of appropriate children and re-lay them out. *trk* will be one of the values shown under the **OI_d_tech** member function **set_size_track** on page 6-24. The default procedure supplied by the base class is adequate in most cases.

44.4.3.6 Responding to Changes in the Container (Parent) Object

size_change   (Member function)

```
void OI_layout_method::size_change( )
```

✎ OI calls **size_change** to notify the layout method that the container (parent) object to which it corresponds has changed size. Write **size_change** to call **re_layout** to reposition children as necessary. The default procedure supplied by the base class is adequate in most cases.

new_default_space   (Member function)

```
void OI_layout_method::new_default_space( )
```

✎ OI calls **new_default_space** when the default spacing for the container (parent) object using the layout method has changed. Write **new_default_space** to rearrange the objects in the layout which do not have top, bottom, left, or right space specifically set to use the new default space. The default procedure supplied by the base class is adequate in most cases; it simply clears the **nominal_size_ok** condition and then calls **force_layout**.

44.4.3.7 Spacing

top_space   (Member function)

```
OI_number OI_layout_method::top_space(
   OI_d_tech            *objp)            // pointer to object
```

✎ OI calls **top_space** whenever the top space is requested for *objp* and *objp* is using default spacing for its top space. The default procedure supplied by the base class is suitable in most cases; it returns the default vertical spacing for the container object. You should override this function only if your layout method requires different default spacing depending on the position of an object in the layout. For example, the row and column layout methods use a default bottom and right space of zero for all objects except those in the last row or column.

bottom_space   (Member function)

```
OI_number OI_layout_method::bottom_space(
   OI_d_tech            *objp)            // pointer to object
```

✎ OI calls **bottom_space** whenever the bottom space is requested for *objp* and *objp* is using default spacing for its bottom space. The default procedure supplied by the base class is suitable in most cases; it returns the default vertical spacing for the container object. You should override this function only if your layout method requires different default spacing depending on the position of an object in the layout. For example, the row and column layout methods use a default bottom space of zero for all objects except those in the last row.

left_space   (Member function)

```
OI_number OI_layout_method::left_space(
   OI_d_tech            *objp)            // pointer to object
```

✎ OI calls **left_space** whenever the left space is requested for *objp* and *objp* is using default spacing for its left space. The default procedure supplied by the base class is suitable in most cases; it returns the default horizontal spacing for the container object. You should override this function only if your layout method requires different default spacing depending on the position of an object in the layout.

right_space   (Member function)

```
OI_number OI_layout_method::right_space(
   OI_d_tech            *objp)            // pointer to object
```

✎ OI calls **right_space** whenever the right space is requested for *objp* and *objp* is using default spacing for its right space. The default procedure supplied by the base class is suitable in most cases; it returns the default horizontal spacing for the container object. You should override this function only if your layout method requires different default spacing depending on the position of an object in the layout.

44.4.3.8 Geometry Conversions

The OI class OI_layout_geometry_spec is a virtual base class whose sole purpose is to provide virtual destructors for geometry specifications. When a geometry specification can fit in a cast to a void*, as is the case for all the OI-supplied layout methods, you do not need to use OI_layout_geometry_spec. However, if your layout method requires a geometry specification which will not fit in a void*, you should derive your geometry specification from OI_layout_gemetry_spec. Do this so that when you set the *del_geom_1* and *del_geom_2* parameters in the following member functions to OI_yes, the specification can be properly deleted.

geometry_to_string   (Member function)

```
char *OI_layout_method::geometry_to_string(
    OI_d_tech            *objp)      // pointer to object whose geometry is to be converted
```

✎ Write geometry_to_string to return the layout geometry for object *objp* converted into string form suitable for writing as a resource. This string is identical to that needed for the OI_d_tech resource placement. geometry_to_string should return NULL if *objp* is not laid out using this layout method.

string_to_geometry   (Member function)

```
OI_bool OI_layout_method::string_to_geometry(
    const char          *geom_str,      // layout geometry specification string
    void                **geom_1,       // first geometry component
    OI_bool             *del_geom_1,    // should geom_1 be deleted?
    void                **geom_2,       // second geometry component
    OI_bool             *del_geom_2)    // should geom_2 be deleted?
```

✎ Write string_to_geometry to convert *geom_str*, which must be a string form of a layout geometry specification for an object using this layout, into two parameters which, cast to a void*, can be used in a call to the OI_d_tech member function layout_associated_object. *geom_1* and *geom_2* should be overwritten with the geometry specifications. If the corresponding geometry specification is an object derived from OI_layout_geometry_spec, you should set *del_geom_1* and *del_geom_2* to OI_yes, meaning the application programmer should delete *geom_1* and *geom_2* after use; otherwise set them to OI_no.

string_to_geometry should return OI_yes if *geom_str* is in the appropriate format for this layout method (see the OI_d_tech resource placement) and the call is successful; otherwise it should return OI_no.

convert_xy_to_geometry   (Member function)

```
void OI_layout_method::convert_xy_to_geometry(
    OI_d_tech           *objp,          // pointer to object
    long                x,              // proposed x origin for objp
    long                y,              // proposed y origin for objp
    OI_number           pct,            // percentage of row/column valid for hit
    void                **geom_1,       // first geometry parameter
    OI_bool             *del_geom_1,    // delete geom_1?
    void                **geom_2,       // second geometry parameter
    OI_bool             *del_geom_2)    // delete geom_1?
```

✎ Write convert_xy_to_geometry to use the (x,y) coordinates for *objp* to compute a reasonable pair of geometry specifications which may be used to lay out an object at that approximate location. *geom_1* and *geom_2* must be backfilled with these geometry specifications. *pct* is a percentage factor which you should interpret to indicate inclusion in an existing part of the layout. For example, if two rows in a row or column-based layout are spaced closely together, it is difficult to specify a y coordinate which is in neither row, something which is necessary to open a new row. By specifying a *pct* of 50, only the middle part of each row is considered to be "in" the row—a y coordinate in the upper 25% or lower 25% of the row is considered to be in the empty space between rows.

Ordinarily convert_xy_to_geometry is called (for example by a user interface builder) prior to inserting a new object. If the computed location involves "opening up" a new area—such as inserting a new row between existing rows—you must write convert_xy_to_geometry to appropriately shift, according to the needs of your layout method, the geometry parameters of existing objects before returning.

If the two geometry parameters returned are objects derived from OI_layout_geometry_spec, set *del_geom_1* and *del_geom_2* to OI_yes, and the application programmer should delete *geom_1* and *geom_2* after use; otherwise, set them to OI_no.

conversion_specifications   (Member function)

```
OI_lm_convert_geometry *OI_layout_method::conversion_specifications(
    const OI_layout_method    *lmp)    // existing layout method
```

✎ Write conversion_specifications to traverse all objects contained in some other existing layout method *lmp*, and generate a list of OI_lm_convert_geometry objects which can be used to lay the same objects out using this layout method. OI will traverse the list of OI_lm_convert_geometry objects at some later time to lay out the objects using this layout method. If this layout method does not know how to do a conversion from *lmp*, you should defer to its base class to perform the operation.

An OI_lm_convert_geometry object exists solely to provide an element of the above list. To create the list, traverse all the objects in the layout and create an OI_lm_convert_geometry object for each of the objects in the layout. You must call the OI_lm_convert_geometry member function set_next to link all the OI_lm_convert_geometry objects into a list.

OI_lm_convert_geometry   (Member function)

```
OI_lm_convert_geometry(
    OI_d_tech           *objp,            // pointer to child object in layout
    void                *geom_1,          // first geometry parameter
    OI_bool             del_geom_1,       // delete geom_1?
    void                *geom_2,          // second geometry parameter
    OI_bool             del_geom_2)       // delete geom_2?


OI_lm_convert_geometry(
    OI_d_tech           *objp,            // pointer to child object in layout
    long                geom_1,           // first geometry parameter
    long                geom_2)           // second geometry parameter
```

OI_lm_convert_geometry constructs an **OI_lm_convert_geometry** object. *geom_1* and *geom_2* are the geometry parameters for the layout method. (See discussion for conversion_specifications, above.)

set_next   (Member function)

```
OI_lm_convert_geometry::set_next(
    OI_lm_convert_geometry      *cgp)     // pointer to OI_lm_convert_geometry object
```

set_next sets *cgp* to be the next **OI_lm_convert_geometry** object in a list.

exact_conversion   (Member function)

```
OI_bool OI_layout_method::exact_conversion(
    OI_class            *cls)             // pointer to layout method class


OI_bool OI_layout_method::exact_conversion(
    OI_layout_method    *lm)             // pointer to layout method
```

✎ Write **exact_conversion** to return **OI_yes** if there is an exact geometry conversion for objects laid out using class *cls* or layout method *lm* to those for this layout method. When **exact_conversion** returns **OI_yes**, the application programmer can use the parameters returned from a **geometry** member function call for a given object laid out using *cls* or *lm* to lay the same object out using this layout method.

44.4.3.9 Miscellaneous Functions

class_object   (Member function)

```
OI_class *OI_layout_method::class_object( )
```

✎ Write **class_object** to return a pointer to the class object for the layout method. This is the value returned by **OI_register_layout_method** when the layout method was registered.

Appendix A

Callbacks

Appendix B

Resources

Appendix C

List of Program Examples

Appendix D

Functions and Member Functions

OI Programmer's Guide

Index